Sociology

Readings

Tenth Edition

Sociology

Exploring the Architecture of Everyday Life

Readings

Tenth Edition

Editors

David M. Newman
DePauw University

Jodi O'Brien
Seattle University

Michelle Robertson
St. Edward's University

Los Angeles | London | New Delhi
Singapore | Washington DC

Los Angeles | London | New Delhi
Singapore | Washington DC

FOR INFORMATION:

SAGE Publications, Inc.
2455 Teller Road
Thousand Oaks, California 91320
E-mail: order@sagepub.com

SAGE Publications Ltd.
1 Oliver's Yard
55 City Road
London EC1Y 1SP
United Kingdom

SAGE Publications India Pvt. Ltd.
B 1/I 1 Mohan Cooperative Industrial Area
Mathura Road, New Delhi 110 044
India

SAGE Publications Asia-Pacific Pte. Ltd.
3 Church Street
#10-04 Samsung Hub
Singapore 049483

Printed in the United States of America

A catalog record of this book is available from the Library of Congress.

ISBN 978-1-4522-7577-2

This book is printed on acid-free paper.

Acquisitions Editor: Jeff Lasser
Editorial Assistant: Nick Pachelli
Production Editor: Bennie Clark Allen
Copy Editor: Colleen B. Brennan
Typesetter: C&M Digitals (P) Ltd.
Proofreader: Pam Suwinsky
Cover Designer: Candice Harman
Marketing Manager: Erica DeLuca

SFI label applies to text stock

14 15 16 17 18 10 9 8 7 6 5 4 3 2 1

Contents

me and Taylor

Preface

One of the greatest challenges we face as teachers of sociology is getting our students to see the relevance of the course material to their own lives and to fully appreciate its connection to the larger society. We teach our students to see that sociology is all around us. It's in our families, our careers, our media, our jobs, our classrooms, our goals, our interests, our desires, and even our minds. Sociology can be found at the neighborhood pub, in conversation with the clerk at 7-Eleven, on a date, and in the highest offices of government. It's with us when we're alone and when we're in a group of people. Sociology focuses on questions of global significance as well as private concerns. For instance, sociologists study how some countries create and maintain dominance over others and also why we find some people more attractive than others. Sociology is an invitation to understand yourself within the context of your historical and cultural circumstances.

We have compiled this collection of short articles, chapters, and excerpts with the intent of providing comprehensive examples of the power of sociology for helping us to make sense of our lives and our times. The readings are organized in a format that demonstrates

- the uniqueness of the sociological perspective
- tools of sociological analysis
- the significance of different cultures in a global world
- social factors that influence identity development and self-management
- social rules about family, relationships, and belonging
- the influence of social institutions and organizations on everyday life
- the significance of socioeconomic class, gender, and racial/ethnic backgrounds in everyday life
- the significance of social demographics, such as aging populations and migration, and
- the power of social groups and social change.

In general, our intent is to demonstrate the significance of sociology in everyday life and to show that what seems obvious is often not so obvious when subjected to rigorous sociological analysis. The metaphor of "architecture" used in the title for this reader illustrates the sociological idea that as social beings, we are constantly building and rebuilding our own social environment. The sociological promise is that if we understand these processes and how they affect us, we will be able to make more informed choices about how to live our lives and engage in our communities.

As in the first nine editions of the reader, the selections in this edition are intended to be vivid, provocative, and eye-opening examples of the practice of sociology. The readings represent a variety of styles. Some use common or everyday experiences and phenomena (such as drug use, employment, athletic performance, religious devotion, eating fast food, and the balance of work and family) to illustrate the relationship between the individual and society. Others focus on important social issues or problems (medical social control, race relations, poverty, educational inequalities, sexuality, immigration, global economics, environmental degradation, or political extremism) or on specific historical events (massacres during war, drug scares, and 9/11). Some were written quite recently; others are sociological classics. In addition to accurately representing the sociological perspective and providing rigorous coverage of the discipline, we hope the selections are thought provoking, generate lots of discussion, and are enjoyable to read.

Several of the readings in this edition are new, and all are based on research studies that were written in the past few years. Our aim is to offer more selections drawn from recent social research. We are confident that you will find them timely and relevant and will come away with a sense of being immersed in the most significant details of contemporary sociology.

To help you get the most out of these selections, we've written brief introductions that provide the sociological context for each chapter. We also have included reflection points that can be used for comparing and contrasting the readings in each chapter and across chapters. For those of you who are also reading the accompanying textbook, these introductions will furnish a quick link between the readings and information in the textbook. We have also included in these introductions brief instructions on what to look for when you read the selections in a given chapter. After each reading, you will find a set of discussion questions to ponder. Many of these questions ask you to apply a specific author's conclusions to some contemporary issue in society or to your own life experiences. It is our hope that these questions will generate a lot of classroom debate and help you see the sociological merit of the readings.

A website established for this tenth edition includes do-it-yourself reviews and tests for students, Web-based activities designed to enhance learning, and a chat room where students and teachers can post messages and debate matters of sociological significance. The site can be accessed via the SAGE website at www.sagepub.com.

Books like these are enormous projects. We would like to thank Jeff Lasser, Nick Pachelli, Bennie Clark Allen, Colleen Brennan, and the rest of the staff at SAGE for their useful advice and assistance in putting this reader together. It's always a pleasure to work with this very professional group. Enjoy!

David M. Newman
Department of Sociology/Anthropology
DePauw University
Greencastle, IN 46135
E-mail: dnewman@depauw.edu

Jodi O'Brien
Department of Sociology
Seattle University
Seattle, WA 98122
E-mail: jobrien@seattleu.edu

Michelle Robertson
Sociology Program
St. Edward's University
Austin, TX 78704-6489
E-mail: michelr@stedwards.edu

About the Editors

David M. Newman (Ph.D., University of Washington) is Professor of Sociology at DePauw University. In addition to the introductory course, he teaches courses in research methods, family, social psychology, deviance, and mental illness. He has won teaching awards at both the University of Washington and DePauw University. His other written work includes *Identities and Inequalities: Exploring the Intersections of Race, Class, Gender, and Sexuality* (2012) and *Families: A Sociological Perspective* (2008).

Jodi O'Brien (Ph.D., University of Washington) is Professor of Sociology at Seattle University. She teaches courses in social psychology, sexuality, inequality, and classical and contemporary theory. She writes and lectures on the cultural politics of transgressive identities and communities. Her other books include *Everyday Inequalities* (Basil Blackwell), *Social Prisms: Reflections on Everyday Myths and Paradoxes* (Pine Forge Press), and *The Production of Reality: Essays and Readings on Social Interaction*, Fifth Edition (Pine Forge Press).

Michelle Robertson (Ph.D., Washington State University) is Associate Professor of Sociology at St. Edward's University. In addition to the introductory course, she teaches courses in research, statistics, theory, sport, masculinities, family, and social inequality. She won a teaching award at Washington State University and does research on classroom incivility.

PART I

The Individual and Society

Taking a New Look at a Familiar World

The primary claim of sociology is that our everyday feelings, thoughts, and actions are the product of a complex interplay between massive social forces and personal characteristics. We can't understand the relationship between individuals and their societies without understanding the connection between them. As C. Wright Mills discusses in the introductory article, the "sociological imagination" is the ability to see the impact of social forces on our private lives. When we develop a sociological imagination, we gain an awareness that our lives unfold at the intersection of personal biography and social history. The sociological imagination encourages us to move beyond individualistic explanations of human experiences to an understanding of the mutual influence between individuals and society. So, rather than study what goes on within people, sociologists study what goes on between and among people, as individuals, groups, organizations, or entire societies. Sociology teaches us to look beyond individual personalities and focus instead on the influence of social phenomena in shaping our ideas of who we are and what we think we can do.

Peter Berger, another well-known sociologist, invites us to consider the uniqueness of the sociological enterprise. According to Berger, the sociologist is driven by an insatiable curiosity to understand the social conditions that shape human behavior. The sociologist is also prepared to be surprised, disturbed, and sometimes even bored by what he or she discovers. In this regard, the sociologist is driven to make sense of the seemingly "obvious" with the understanding that once explored, it may not be so obvious after all. One example of the "non-obvious" is the influence that social institutions have on our behavior. It's not always easy to see this influence. We have a tendency to see people's behavior in individualistic, sometimes even biological terms. This tendency toward "individualistic" explanations is particularly pronounced in U.S. society.

The influence of social institutions on our personal lives is often felt most forcefully when we are compelled to obey the commands of someone who is in a position of institutional authority. The social institution with the most explicit hierarchy of authority is the military. In "The My Lai Massacre: A Military Crime of Obedience," Herbert Kelman and V. Lee Hamilton describe a specific example of a crime in which the individuals involved attempted to deny responsibility for their actions by claiming that they were following the orders of a military officer who had the legitimate right to command them. This incident occurred in the midst of the Vietnam War. Arguably, people do things under such trying conditions that they wouldn't ordinarily do, even—as in this case—kill defenseless people. Kelman and Hamilton make a key sociological point by showing that these soldiers were not necessarily psychological misfits who were especially mean or violent. Instead, the researchers argue, they were ordinary people caught up in tense circumstances that made obeying the brutal commands of an authority seem like the normal and morally acceptable thing to do.

Something to Consider as You Read

As you read these selections, consider the effects of social context and situation on behavior. Even though it might appear extreme, how might the behavior of these soldiers or the university students be similar to other examples of social influence? Consider occasions in which you have done something publicly that you didn't feel right about personally. How do you explain your behavior? How might a sociologist explain your behavior? What does the sociological perspective tell you about the importance of understanding the complexity of individual outcomes in society?

The Sociological Imagination

C. Wright Mills

(1959)

"The individual can . . . know his own chances in life only by becoming aware of those of all individuals in his circumstances."

Nowadays men often feel that their private lives are a series of traps. They sense that within their everyday worlds, they cannot overcome their troubles, and in this feeling, they are often quite correct: What ordinary men are directly aware of and what they try to do are bounded by the private orbits in which they live; their visions and their powers are limited to the close-up scenes of job, family, neighborhood; in other milieux, they move vicariously and remain spectators. And the more aware they become, however vaguely, of ambitions and of threats which transcend their immediate locales, the more trapped they seem to feel.

Underlying this sense of being trapped are seemingly impersonal changes in the very structure of continent-wide societies. The facts of contemporary history are also facts about the success and the failure of individual men and women. When a society is industrialized, a peasant becomes a worker; a feudal lord is liquidated or becomes a businessman. When classes rise or fall, a man is employed or unemployed; when the rate of investment goes up or down, a man takes new heart or goes broke. When wars happen, an insurance salesman becomes a rocket launcher; a store clerk, a radar man; a wife lives alone; a child grows up without a father. Neither the life of an individual nor the history of a society can be understood without understanding both.

Yet men do not usually define the troubles they endure in terms of historical change and institutional contradiction. The well-being they enjoy, they do not usually impute to the big ups and downs of the societies in which they live. Seldom aware of the intricate connection between the patterns of their own lives and the course of world history, ordinary men do not usually know what this connection means for the kinds of men they are becoming and for the kinds of history-making in which they might take part. They do not possess the quality of mind essential to grasp the interplay of man and society, of biography and history, of self and world. They cannot cope with their personal troubles in such ways as to control the structural transformations that usually lie behind them.

Surely it is no wonder. In what period have so many men been so totally exposed at so fast a pace to such earthquakes of change? That Americans have not known such catastrophic changes as have the men and women of other societies is due to historical facts that are now quickly becoming "merely history." The history that now affects every man is world history. Within this scene and this period, in the course of a single generation, one-sixth of mankind is transformed from all that is feudal and backward into all that is modern, advanced, and fearful. Political colonies are freed, new and less visible forms of imperialism installed. Revolutions occur; men feel the intimate grip of new kinds of authority. Totalitarian societies rise, and are smashed to bits—or succeed fabulously. After two centuries of ascendancy, capitalism is shown up as only one way to make society into an industrial apparatus. After two centuries of hope, even formal democracy is restricted to a quite small portion of mankind. Everywhere in the underdeveloped world, ancient ways of life are broken up and vague expectations become urgent demands. Everywhere in the overdeveloped world, the means of authority and of violence become total in scope and bureaucratic in form. Humanity itself now lies before us, the supernation at either pole concentrating its most coordinated and massive efforts upon the preparation of World War Three.

The very shaping of history now outpaces the ability of men to orient themselves in accordance with cherished values. And which values? Even when they do not panic, men often sense that older ways of feeling and thinking have collapsed and that newer beginnings are ambiguous to the point of moral stasis. Is it any wonder that ordinary men feel they cannot cope with the larger worlds with which they are so suddenly confronted? That they cannot understand the meaning of their epoch for their own lives? That—in defense of selfhood—they become morally insensible, trying to remain altogether private men? Is it any wonder that they come to be possessed by a sense of the trap?

It is not only information that they need—in this Age of Fact, information often dominates their attention and overwhelms their capacities to assimilate it. It is not only the skills of reason that they need—although their struggles to acquire these often exhaust their limited moral energy.

What they need, and what they feel they need, is a quality of mind that will help them to use information and to develop reason in order to achieve lucid summations of what is going on in the world and of what may be happening within themselves. It is this quality, I am going to contend, that journalists and scholars, artists and publics, scientists and editors are coming to expect of what may be called the sociological imagination.

The sociological imagination enables its possessor to understand the larger historical scene in terms of its meaning for the inner life

and the external career of a variety of individuals. It enables him to take into account how individuals, in the welter of their daily experience, often become falsely conscious of their social positions. Within that welter, the framework of modern society is sought, and within that framework the psychologies of a variety of men and women are formulated. By such means the personal uneasiness of individuals is focused upon explicit troubles and the indifference of publics is transformed into involvement with public issues.

The first fruit of this imagination—and the first lesson of the social science that embodies it—is the idea that the individual can understand his own experience and gauge his own fate only by locating himself within his period, that he can know his own chances in life only by becoming aware of those of all individuals in his circumstances. In many ways it is a terrible lesson; in many ways a magnificent one. We do not know the limits of man's capacities for supreme effort or willing degradation, for agony or glee, for pleasurable brutality or the sweetness of reason. But in our time we have come to know that the limits of "human nature" are frighteningly broad. We have come to know that every individual lives, from one generation to the next, in some society; that he lives out a biography, and that he lives it out within some historical sequence. By the fact of his living he contributes, however minutely, to the shaping of this society and to the course of its history, even as he is made by society and by its historical push and shove.

The sociological imagination enables us to grasp history and biography and the relations between the two within society. That is its task and its promise. To recognize this task and this promise is the mark of the classic social analyst. It is characteristic of Herbert Spencer—turgid, polysyllabic, comprehensive; of E. A. Ross—graceful, muckraking, upright; of Auguste Comte and Emile Durkheim; of the intricate and subtle Karl Mannheim. It is the quality of all that is intellectually excellent in Karl Marx; it is the clue to Thorstein Veblen's brilliant and ironic insight, to Joseph Schumpeter's many-sided constructions of reality; it is the basis of the psychological sweep of W. E. H. Lecky no less than of the profundity and clarity of Max Weber. And it is the signal of what is best in contemporary studies of man and society.

No social study that does not come back to the problems of biography, of history, and of their intersections within a society has completed its intellectual journey. Whatever the specific problems of the classic social analysts, however limited or however broad the features of social reality they have examined, those who have been imaginatively aware of the promise of their work have consistently asked three sorts of questions:

1. What is the structure of this particular society as a whole? What are its essential components, and how are they related to one another? How does it differ from other varieties of social order? Within it, what is the meaning of any particular feature for its continuance and for its change?

2. Where does this society stand in human history? What are the mechanics by which it is changing? What is its place within and its meaning for the development of humanity as a whole? How does any particular feature we are examining affect, and how is it affected by, the historical period in which it moves? And this period—what are its essential features? How does it differ from other periods? What are its characteristic ways of history making?

3. What varieties of men and women now prevail in this society and in this period? And what varieties are coming to prevail? In what ways are they selected and formed, liberated and repressed, made sensitive and blunted? What kinds of "human nature" are revealed in the conduct and character we observe in this society in this period? And what is the meaning for "human nature" of each and every feature of the society we are examining?

Whether the point of interest is a great power state or a minor literary mood, a family, a prison, a creed—these are the kinds of questions the best social analysts have asked. They are the intellectual pivots of classic studies of man in society—and they are the questions inevitably raised by any mind possessing the sociological imagination. For that imagination is the capacity to shift from one perspective to another—from the political to the psychological; from examination of a single family to comparative assessment of the national budgets of the world; from the theological school to the military establishment; from considerations of an oil industry to studies of contemporary poetry. It is the capacity to range from the most impersonal and remote transformations to the most intimate features of the human self—and to see the relations between the two. Back of its use there is always the urge to know the social and historical meaning of the individual in the society and in the period in which he has his quality and his being.

That, in brief, is why it is by means of the sociological imagination that men now hope to grasp what is going on in the world, and to understand what is happening in themselves as minute points of the intersections of biography and history within society. In large part, contemporary man's self-conscious view of himself as at least an outsider, if not a permanent stranger, rests upon an absorbed realization of social relativity and of the transformative power of history. The sociological imagination is the most fruitful form of this self-consciousness. By its use men whose mentalities have swept only a series of limited orbits often come to feel as if suddenly awakened in a house with which they had only supposed themselves to be familiar. Correctly or incorrectly, they often come to feel that they can now provide themselves with adequate summations, cohesive assessments, comprehensive orientations. Older decisions that once appeared sound now seem to them products of a mind unaccountably dense. Their capacity for astonishment is made lively again. They acquire a new way of thinking, they experience a transvaluation of values: in a word, by their reflection and by their sensibility, they realize the cultural meaning of the social sciences.

Perhaps the most fruitful distinction with which the sociological imagination works is between "the personal troubles of milieu" and "the public issues of social structure." This distinction is an essential tool of the sociological imagination and a feature of all classic work in social science.

Troubles occur within the character of the individual and within the range of his immediate relations with others; they have to do with his self and with those limited areas of social life of which he is directly and personally aware. Accordingly, the statement and the resolution of troubles properly lie within the individual as a biographical entity and within the scope of his immediate milieu—the social setting that is directly open to his personal experience and to some extent his willful activity. A trouble is a private matter: values cherished by an individual are felt by him to be threatened.

Issues have to do with matters that transcend these local environments of the individual and the range of his inner life. They have to do with the organization of many such milieux into the institutions of an historical society as a whole, with the ways in which various milieux overlap and interpenetrate to form the larger structure of social and historical life. An issue is a public matter: some value cherished by publics is felt to be threatened. Often there is a debate about what that value really is and about what it is that really threatens it. This debate is often without focus if only because it is the very nature of an issue, unlike even widespread trouble, that it cannot very well be defined in terms of the immediate and everyday environments of ordinary men. An issue, in fact, often involves a crisis in institutional arrangements, and often too it involves what Marxists call "contradictions" or "antagonisms."

In these terms, consider unemployment. When, in a city of 100,000, only one man is unemployed, that is his personal trouble, and for its relief we properly look to the character of the man, his skills, and his immediate opportunities. But when in a nation of 50 million employees, 15 million men are unemployed, that is an issue, and we may not hope to find its solution within the range of opportunities open to any one individual. The very structure of opportunities has collapsed. Both the correct statement of the problem and the range of possible solutions require us to consider the economic and political institutions of the society, and not merely the personal situation and character of a scatter of individuals.

Consider war. The personal problem of war, when it occurs, may be how to survive it or how to die in it with honor; how to make money out of it; how to climb into the higher safety of the military apparatus; or how to contribute to the war's termination. In short, according to one's values, to find a set of milieux and within it to survive the war or make one's death in it meaningful. But the structural issues of war have to do with its causes; with what types of men it throws up into command; with its effects upon economic and political, family, and religious institutions, with the unorganized irresponsibility of a world of nation-states.

Consider marriage. Inside a marriage a man and a woman may experience personal troubles, but when the divorce rate during the first four years of marriage is 250 out of every 1,000 attempts, this is an indication of a structural issue having to do with the institutions of marriage and the family and other institutions that bear upon them.

Or consider the metropolis—the horrible, beautiful, ugly, magnificent sprawl of the great city. For many upper-class people, the personal solution to "the problem of the city" is to have an apartment with private garage under it in the heart of the city, and forty miles out, a house by Henry Hill, garden by Garrett Eckbo, on a hundred acres of private land. In these two controlled environments—with a small staff at each end and a private helicopter connection—most people could solve many of the problems of personal milieux caused by the facts of the city. But all this, however splendid, does not solve the public issues that the structural fact of the city poses. What should be done with this wonderful monstrosity? Break it all up into scattered units, combining residence and work? Refurbish it as it stands? Or, after evacuation, dynamite it and build new cities according to new plans in new places? What should those plans be? And who is to decide and to accomplish whatever choice is made? These are structural issues; to confront them and to solve them requires us to consider political and economic issues that affect innumerable milieux.

Insofar as an economy is so arranged that slumps occur, the problem of unemployment becomes incapable of personal solution. Insofar as war is inherent in the nation-state system and in the uneven industrialization of the world, the ordinary individual in his restricted milieu will be powerless—with or without psychiatric aid—to solve the troubles this system or lack of system imposes upon him. Insofar as the family as an institution turns women into darling little slaves and men into their chief providers and unweaned dependents, the problem of a satisfactory marriage remains incapable of purely private solution. Insofar as the overdeveloped megalopolis and the over-developed automobile are built-in features of the overdeveloped society, the issues of urban living will not be solved by personal ingenuity and private wealth.

What we experience in various and specific milieux, I have noted, is often caused by structural changes. Accordingly, to understand the changes of many personal milieux we are required to look beyond them. And the number and variety of such structural changes increase as the institutions within which we live become more embracing and more intricately connected with one another. To be aware of the idea of social structure and to use it with sensibility is to be capable of tracing such linkages among a great variety of milieux. To be able to do that is to possess the sociological imagination. . . .

THINKING ABOUT THE READING

Consider the political, economic, familial, and cultural circumstances into which you were born. Make a list of some of these circumstances and also some of the major historical events that have occurred in your lifetime. How do you think these historical and social circumstances may have affected your personal "biography"? Can you think of ways in which your actions have influenced the course of other people's lives? Identify some famous people and consider how the intersection of "history and biography" led them to their particular position. How might the outcome have differed if some of the circumstances in their lives were different?

Invitation to Sociology

Peter Berger

(1963)

We would say then that the sociologist (that is, the one we would really like to invite to our game) is a person intensively, endlessly, shamelessly interested in the doings of men. His natural habitat is all the human gathering places of the world, wherever men* come together. The sociologist may be interested in many other things. But his consuming interest remains in the world of men, their institutions, their history, their passions. He will naturally be interested in the events that engage men's ultimate beliefs, their moments of tragedy and grandeur and ecstasy. But he will also be fascinated by the commonplace, the everyday. He will know reverence, but this reverence will not prevent him from wanting to see and to understand. He may sometimes feel revulsion or contempt. But this also will not deter him from wanting to have his questions answered. The sociologist, in his quest for understanding, moves through the world of men without respect for the usual lines of demarcation. Nobility and degradation, power and obscurity, intelligence and folly— these are equally *interesting* to him, however unequal they may be in his personal values or tastes. Thus his questions may lead him to all possible levels of society, the best and the least known places, the most respected and the most despised. And, if he is a good sociologist, he will find himself in all these places because his own questions have so taken possession of him that he has little choice but to seek for answers.

We could say that the sociologist, but for the grace of his academic title, is the man who must listen to gossip despite himself, who is tempted to look through keyholes, to read other people's mail, to open closed cabinets. What interests us is the curiosity that grips any sociologist in front of a closed door behind which there are human voices. If he is a good sociologist, he will want to open that door, to understand these voices. Behind each closed door he will anticipate some new facet of human life not yet perceived and understood.

The sociologist will occupy himself with matters that others regard as too sacred or as too distasteful for dispassionate investigation. He will find rewarding the company of priests or of prostitutes, depending not on his personal preferences but on the questions he happens to be asking at the moment. He will also concern himself with matters that others may find much too boring. He will be interested in the human interaction that goes with warfare or with great intellectual discoveries, but also in the relations between people employed in a restaurant or between a group of little girls playing with their dolls. His main focus of attention is not the ultimate significance of what men do, but the action in itself, as another example of the infinite richness of human conduct.

In these journeys through the world of men the sociologist will inevitably encounter other professional Peeping Toms. Sometimes these will resent his presence, feeling that he is poaching on their preserves. In some places the sociologist will meet up with the economist, in others with the political scientist, in yet others with the psychologist or the ethnologist. Yet chances are that the questions that have brought him to these same places are different from the ones that propelled his fellow trespassers. The sociologist's questions always remain essentially the same: "What are people doing with each other here?" "What are their relationships to each other?" "How are these relationships organized in institutions?" "What are the collective ideas that move men and institutions?" In trying to answer these questions in specific instances, the sociologist will, of course, have to deal with economic or political matters, but he will do so in a way rather different from that of the economist or the political scientist. The scene that he contemplates is the same human scene that these other scientists concern themselves with. But the sociologist's angle of vision is different.

Much of the time the sociologist moves in sectors of experience that are familiar to him and to most people in his society. He investigates communities, institutions and activities that one can read about every day in the newspapers. Yet there is another excitement of discovery beckoning in his investigations. It is not the excitement of coming upon the totally unfamiliar, but rather the excitement of finding the familiar becoming transformed in its meaning. The fascination of sociology lies in the fact that its perspective makes us see in a new light the very world in which we have lived all our lives. This also constitutes a transformation of consciousness. Moreover, this transformation is more relevant existentially than that of many other intellectual disciplines, because it is more difficult to segregate in some special compartment of the mind. The astronomer does not live in the remote galaxies, and the nuclear physicist can, outside his laboratory, eat and laugh and marry and vote without thinking about the insides of the atom. The geologist looks at rocks only at appropriate times, and the linguist speaks English with his wife. The sociologist lives in society, on the job and off it. His own life, inevitably, is part of his subject matter. Men being what they are, sociologists

too manage to segregate their professional insights from their everyday affairs. But it is a rather difficult feat to perform in good faith.

The sociologist moves in the common world of men, close to what most of them would call real. The categories he employs in his analyses are only refinements of the categories by which other men live—power, class, status, race, ethnicity. As a result, there is a deceptive simplicity and obviousness about some sociological investigations. One reads them, nods at the familiar scene, remarks that one has heard all this before and don't people have better things to do than to waste their time on truisms—until one is suddenly brought up against an insight that radically questions everything one had previously assumed about this familiar scene. This is the point at which one begins to sense the excitement of sociology.

Let us take a specific example. Imagine a sociology class in a Southern college where almost all the students are white Southerners. Imagine a lecture on the subject of the racial system of the South. The lecturer is talking here of matters that have been familiar to his students from the time of their infancy. Indeed, it may be that they are much more familiar with the minutiae of this system than he is. They are quite bored as a result. It seems to them that he is only using more pretentious words to describe what they already know. Thus he may use the term "caste," one commonly used now by American sociologists to describe the Southern racial system. But in explaining the term he shifts to traditional Hindu society, to make it clearer. He then goes on to analyze the magical beliefs inherent in caste tabus, the social dynamics of *commensalism* and *connubium*, the economic interests concealed within the system, the way in which religious beliefs relate to the tabus, the effects of the caste system upon the industrial development of the society and vice versa—all in India. But suddenly India is not very far away at all. The lecture then goes back to its Southern theme. The familiar now seems not quite so familiar anymore. Questions are raised that are new, perhaps raised angrily, but raised all the same. And at least some of the students have begun to understand that there are functions involved in this business of race that they have not read about in the newspapers (at least not those in their hometowns) and that their parents have not told them—partly, at least, because neither the newspapers nor the parents knew about them.

It can be said that the first wisdom of sociology is this—things are not what they seem. This too is a deceptively simple statement. It ceases to be simple after a while. Social reality turns out to have many layers of meaning. The discovery of each new layer changes the perception of the whole.

Anthropologists use the term "culture shock" to describe the impact of a totally new culture upon a newcomer. In an extreme instance such shock will be experienced by the Western explorer who is told, halfway through dinner, that he is eating the nice old lady he had been chatting with the previous day—a shock with predictable physiological if not moral consequences. Most explorers no longer encounter cannibalism in their travels today. However, the first encounters with polygamy or with puberty rites or even with the way some nations drive their automobiles can be quite a shock to an American visitor. With the shock may go not only disapproval or disgust but a sense of excitement that things can *really* be that different from what they are at home. To some extent, at least, this is the excitement of any first travel abroad. The experience of sociological discovery could be described as "culture shock" minus geographical displacement. In other words, the sociologist travels at home—with shocking results. He is unlikely to find that he is eating a nice old lady for dinner. But the discovery, for instance, that his own church has considerable money invested in the missile industry or that a few blocks from his home there are people who engage in cultic orgies may not be drastically different in emotional impact. Yet we would not want to imply that sociological discoveries are always or even

usually outrageous to moral sentiment. Not at all. What they have in common with exploration in distant lands, however, is the sudden illumination of new and unsuspected facets of human existence in society. This is the excitement and . . . the humanistic justification of sociology.

People who like to avoid shocking discoveries, who prefer to believe that society is just what they were taught in Sunday School, who like the safety of the rules and the maxims of what Alfred Schuetz has called the "world-taken-for-granted," should stay away from sociology. People who feel no temptation before closed doors, who have no curiosity about human beings, who are content to admire scenery without wondering about the people who live in those houses on the other side of that river, should probably also stay away from sociology. They will find it unpleasant or, at any rate, unrewarding. People who are interested in human beings only if they can change, convert or reform them should also be warned, for they will find sociology much less useful than they hoped. And people whose interest is mainly in their own conceptual constructions will do just as well to turn to the study of little white mice. Sociology will be satisfying, in the long run, only to those who can think of nothing more entrancing than to watch men and to understand things human.

It may now be clear that we have, albeit deliberately, understated the case in the title of this chapter. To be sure, sociology is an individual pastime in the sense that it interests some men and bores others. Some like to observe human beings, others to experiment with mice. The world is big enough to hold all kinds and there is no logical priority for one interest as against another. But the word "pastime" is weak in describing what we mean. Sociology is more like a passion. The sociological perspective is more like a demon that possesses one, that drives one compellingly, again and again, to the questions that are its own. An introduction to sociology is, therefore, an invitation to a very special kind of passion.

THINKING ABOUT THE READING

Peter Berger claims that sociologists are tempted to listen to gossip, peek through keyholes, and look at other people's mail. This can be interpreted to mean that the sociologist has an insatiable curiosity about other people. What are some other behaviors and situations that might capture the attention of the sociologist? How does the sociologist differ from the psychologist or the economist or the historian? Are these fields of study likely to be in competition with sociology or to complement it?

The My Lai Massacre

A Military Crime of Obedience

Herbert Kelman and V. Lee Hamilton

(1989)

March 16, 1968, was a busy day in U.S. history. Stateside, Robert F. Kennedy announced his presidential candidacy, challenging a sitting president from his own party—in part out of opposition to an undeclared and disastrous war. In Vietnam, the war continued. In many ways, March 16 may have been a typical day in that war. We will probably never know. But we do know that on that day a typical company went on a mission—which may or may not have been typical—to a village called Son (or Song) My. Most of what is remembered from that mission occurred in the subhamlet known to Americans as My Lai 4.

The My Lai massacre was investigated and charges were brought in 1969 and 1970. Trials and disciplinary actions lasted into 1971. Entire books have been written about the army's year-long cover-up of the massacre (for example, Hersh, 1972), and the cover-up was a major focus of the army's own investigation of the incident. Our central concern here is the massacre itself—a crime of obedience—and public reactions to such crimes, rather than the lengths to which many went to deny the event. Therefore this account concentrates on one day: March 16, 1968.

Many verbal testimonials to the horrors that occurred at My Lai were available. More unusual was the fact that an army photographer, Ronald Haeberle, was assigned the task of documenting the anticipated military engagement at My Lai—and documented a massacre instead. Later, as the story of the massacre emerged, his photographs were widely distributed and seared the public conscience.

What might have been dismissed as unreal or exaggerated was depicted in photographs of demonstrable authenticity. The dominant image appeared on the cover of *Life*: piles of bodies jumbled together in a ditch along a trail—the dead all apparently unarmed. All were Oriental, and all appeared to be children, women, or old men. Clearly there had been a mass execution, one whose image would not quickly fade.

So many bodies (over twenty in the cover photo alone) are hard to imagine as the handiwork of one killer. These were not. They were the product of what we call a crime of obedience. Crimes of obedience begin with orders. But orders are often vague and rarely survive with any clarity the transition from one authority down a chain of subordinates to the ultimate actors. The operation at Son My was no exception.

"Charlie" Company, Company C, under Lt. Col. Frank Barker's command, arrived in Vietnam in December 1967. As the army's investigative unit, directed by Lt. Gen. William R. Peers, characterized the personnel, they "contained no significant deviation from the average" for the time. Seymour S. Hersh (1970) described the "average" more explicitly: "Most of the men in Charlie Company had volunteered for the draft; only a few had gone to college for even one year. Nearly half were black, with a few Mexican-Americans. Most were eighteen to twenty-two years old. The favorite reading matter of Charlie Company, like that of other line infantry units in Vietnam, was comic books" (p. 18). The action at My

Lai, like that throughout Vietnam, was fought by a cross-section of those Americans who either believed in the war or lacked the social resources to avoid participating in it. Charlie Company was indeed average for that time, that place, and that war.

Two key figures in Charlie Company were more unusual. The company's commander, Capt. Ernest Medina, was an upwardly mobile Mexican-American who wanted to make the army his career, although he feared that he might never advance beyond captain because of his lack of formal education. His eagerness had earned him a nickname among his men: "Mad Dog Medina." One of his admirers was the platoon leader Second Lt. William L. Calley, Jr., an undistinguished, five-foot-three-inch junior-college dropout who had failed four of the seven courses in which he had enrolled his first year. Many viewed him as one of those "instant officers" made possible only by the army's then-desperate need for manpower. Whatever the cause, he was an insecure leader whose frequent claim was "I'm the boss." His nickname among some of the troops was "Surfside 5½," a reference to the swashbuckling heroes of a popular television show, "Surfside 6."

The Son My operation was planned by Lieutenant Colonel Barker and his staff as a search-and-destroy mission with the objective of rooting out the Forty-eighth Viet Cong Battalion from their base area of Son My village. Apparently no written orders were ever issued. Barker's superior, Col. Oran Henderson, arrived at the staging point the day before. Among the issues he reviewed with the assembled officers were some of the weaknesses of prior operations by their units, including their failure to be appropriately aggressive in pursuit of the enemy. Later briefings by Lieutenant Colonel Barker and his staff asserted that no one except Viet Cong was expected to be in the village after 7 A.M. on the following day. The "innocent" would all be at the market. Those present at the briefings gave conflicting accounts of Barker's exact orders, but he conveyed at least a strong suggestion that the Son My area was to be obliterated. As the army's

inquiry reported: "While there is some conflict in the testimony as to whether LTC Barker ordered the destruction of houses, dwellings, livestock, and other foodstuffs in the Song My area, the preponderance of the evidence indicates that such destruction was implied, if not specifically directed, by his orders of 15 March" (Peers Report, in Goldstein et al., 1976, p. 94).

Evidence that Barker ordered the killing of civilians is even more murky. What does seem clear, however, is that—having asserted that civilians would be away at the market—he did not specify what was to be done with any who might nevertheless be found on the scene. The Peers Report therefore considered it "reasonable to conclude that LTC Barker's minimal or nonexistent instructions concerning the handling of noncombatants created the potential for grave misunderstandings as to his intentions and for interpretation of his orders as authority to fire, without restriction, on all persons found in target area" (Goldstein et al., 1976, p. 95). Since Barker was killed in action in June 1968, his own formal version of the truth was never available.

Charlie Company's Captain Medina was briefed for the operation by Barker and his staff. He then transmitted the already vague orders to his own men. Charlie Company was spoiling for a fight, having been totally frustrated during its months in Vietnam—first by waiting for battles that never came, then by incompetent forays led by inexperienced commanders, and finally by mines and booby traps. In fact, the emotion-laden funeral of a sergeant killed by a booby trap was held on March 15, the day before My Lai. Captain Medina gave the orders for the next day's action at the close of that funeral. Many were in a mood for revenge.

It is again unclear what was ordered. Although all participants were alive by the time of the trials for the massacre, they were either on trial or probably felt under threat of trial. Memories are often flawed and self-serving at such times. It is apparent that Medina relayed to the men at least some of Barker's general message—to expect Viet Cong resistance, to burn, and to kill livestock. It is not clear that he ordered the slaughter of the inhabitants, but some of the men who heard him thought he had. One of those who claimed to have heard such orders was Lt. William Calley.

As March 16 dawned, much was expected of the operation by those who had set it into motion. Therefore a full complement of "brass" was present in helicopters overhead, including Barker, Colonel Henderson, and their superior, Major General Koster (who went on to become commandant of West Point before the story of My Lai broke). On the ground, the troops were to carry with them one reporter and one photographer to immortalize the anticipated battle.

The action for Company C began at 7:30 as their first wave of helicopters touched down near the subhamlet of My Lai 4. By 7:47 all of Company C was present and set to fight. But instead of the Viet Cong Forty-eighth Battalion, My Lai was filled with the old men, women, and children who were supposed to have gone to market. By this time, in their version of the war, and with whatever orders they thought they had heard, the men from Company C were nevertheless ready to find Viet Cong everywhere. By nightfall, the official tally was 128 VC killed and three weapons captured, although later, unofficial body counts ran as high as 500. The operation at Son My was over. And by nightfall, as Hersh reported: "the Viet Cong were back in My Lai 4, helping the survivors bury the dead. It took five days. Most of the funeral speeches were made by the Communist guerrillas. Nguyen Bat was not a Communist at the time of the massacre, but the incident changed his mind. 'After the shooting,' he said, 'all the villagers became Communists'" (1970, p. 74). To this day, the memory of the massacre is kept alive by markers and plaques designating the spots where groups of villagers were killed, by a large statue, and by the My Lai Museum, established in 1975 (Williams, 1985).

But what could have happened to leave American troops reporting a victory over Viet Cong when in fact they had killed hundreds of noncombatants? It is not hard to explain the report of victory; that is the essence of a cover-up. It is harder to understand how the killings came to be committed in the first place, making a cover-up necessary.

Mass Executions and the Defense of Superior Orders

Some of the atrocities on March 16, 1968, were evidently unofficial, spontaneous acts: rapes, tortures, killings. For example, Hersh (1970) describes Charlie Company's Second Platoon as entering "My Lai 4 with guns blazing" (p. 50); more graphically, Lieutenant "Brooks and his men in the second platoon to the north had begun to systematically ransack the hamlet and slaughter the people, kill the livestock, and destroy the crops. Men poured rifle and machine-gun fire into huts without knowing—or seemingly caring—who was inside" (pp. 49–50).

Some atrocities toward the end of the action were part of an almost casual "mopping-up," much of which was the responsibility of Lieutenant LaCross's Third Platoon of Charlie Company. The Peers Report states: "The entire 3rd Platoon then began moving into the western edge of My Lai (4), for the mop-up operation. . . .The squad . . . began to burn the houses in the southwestern portion of the hamlet" (Goldstein et al., 1976, p. 133). They became mingled with other platoons during a series of rapes and killings of survivors for which it was impossible to fix responsibility. Certainly to a Vietnamese all GIs would by this point look alike: "Nineteen-year-old Nguyen Thi Ngoc Tuyet watched a baby trying to open her slain mother's blouse to nurse. A soldier shot the infant while it was struggling with the blouse, and then slashed it with his bayonet." Tuyet also said she saw another baby hacked to death by GIs wielding their bayonets. "Le Tong, a twenty-eight-year-old rice farmer, reported seeing one woman raped after GIs killed her children. Nguyen Khoa, a thirty-seven-year-old peasant, told of a thirteen-year-old girl who was raped before being killed. GIs then attacked

Khoa's wife, tearing off her clothes. Before they could rape her, however, Khoa said, their six-year-old son, riddled with bullets, fell and saturated her with blood. The GIs left her alone" (Hersh, 1970, p. 72). All of Company C was implicated in a pattern of death and destruction throughout the hamlet, much of which seemingly lacked rhyme or reason.

But a substantial amount of the killing was organized and traceable to one authority: the First Platoon's Lt. William Calley. Calley was originally charged with 109 killings, almost all of them mass executions at the trail and other locations. He stood trial for 102 of these killings, was convicted of 22 in 1971, and at first received a life sentence. Though others—both superior and subordinate to Calley—were brought to trial, he was the only one convicted for the My Lai crimes. Thus, the only actions of My Lai for which anyone was ever convicted were mass executions, ordered and committed. We suspect that there are commonsense reasons why this one type of killing was singled out. In the midst of rapidly moving events with people running about, an execution of stationary targets is literally a still life that stands out and whose participants are clearly visible. It can be proven that specific people committed specific deeds. An execution, in contrast to the shooting of someone on the run, is also more likely to meet the legal definition of an act resulting from intent—with malice aforethought. Moreover, American military law specifically forbids the killing of unarmed civilians or military prisoners, as does the Geneva Convention between nations. Thus common sense, legal standards, and explicit doctrine all made such actions the likeliest target for prosecution.

When Lieutenant Calley was charged under military law it was for violation of the Uniform Code of Military Justice (UCMJ) Article 118 (murder). This article is similar to civilian codes in that it provides for conviction if an accused:

> without justification or excuse, unlawfully kills a human being, when he—

1. has a premeditated design to kill;

2. intends to kill or inflict great bodily harm;

3. is engaged in an act which is inherently dangerous to others and evinces a wanton disregard of human life; or

4. is engaged in the perpetration or attempted perpetration of burglary, sodomy, rape, robbery, or aggravated arson. (Goldstein et al., 1976, p. 507)

For a soldier, one legal justification for killing is warfare; but warfare is subject to many legal limits and restrictions, including, of course, the inadmissibility of killing unarmed noncombatants or prisoners whom one has disarmed. The pictures of the trail victims at My Lai certainly portrayed one or the other of these. Such an action would be illegal under military law; ordering another to commit such an action would be illegal; and following such an order would be illegal.

But following an order may provide a second and pivotal justification for an act that would be murder when committed by a civilian. American military law assumes that the subordinate is inclined to follow orders, as that is the normal obligation of the role. Hence, legally, obedient subordinates are protected from unreasonable expectations regarding their capacity to evaluate those orders:

> An order requiring the performance of a military duty may be inferred to be legal. An act performed manifestly beyond the scope of authority, or pursuant to an order that a man of ordinary sense and understanding would know to be illegal, or in a wanton manner in the discharge of a lawful duty, is not excusable. (Par. 216, Subpar. *d*, Manual for Courts Martial, United States, 1969 Rev.)

Thus what *may* be excusable is the good-faith carrying out of an order, as long as that order appears to the ordinary soldier to be a legal one. In military law, invoking superior orders moves the question from one of the action's consequences—the body count—to one of evaluating the actor's motives and good sense.

In sum, if anyone is to be brought to justice for a massacre, common sense and legal codes decree that the most appropriate targets are those who make themselves executioners. This is the kind of target the government selected in prosecuting Lieutenant Calley with the greatest fervor. And in a military context, the most promising way in which one can redefine one's undeniable deeds into acceptability is to invoke superior orders. This is what Calley did in attempting to avoid conviction. Since the core legal issues involved points of mass execution—the ditches and trail where America's image of My Lai was formed—we review these events in greater detail.

The day's quiet beginning has already been noted. Troops landed and swept unopposed into the village. The three weapons eventually reported as the haul from the operation were picked up from three apparent Viet Cong who fled the village when the troops arrived and were pursued and killed by helicopter gunships. Obviously the Viet Cong did frequent the area. But it appears that by about 8:00 A.M. no one who met the troops was aggressive, and no one was armed. By the laws of war Charlie Company had no argument with such people.

As they moved into the village, the soldiers began to gather its inhabitants together. Shortly after 8:00 A.M. Lieutenant Calley told Pfc. Paul Meadlo that "you know what to do with" a group of villagers Meadlo was guarding. Estimates of the numbers in the group ranged as high as eighty women, children, and old men, and Meadlo's own estimate under oath was thirty to fifty people. As Meadlo later testified, Calley returned after ten or fifteen minutes: "He [Calley] said, 'How come they're not dead?' I said, 'I didn't know we were supposed to kill them.' He said, 'I want them dead.' He backed off twenty or thirty feet and started shooting into the people—the Viet Cong—shooting automatic. He was beside me. He burned four or five magazines. I burned off a few, about three. I helped shoot 'em"

(Hammer, 1971, p. 155). Meadlo himself and others testified that Meadlo cried as he fired; others reported him later to be sobbing and "all broke up." It would appear that to Lieutenant Calley's subordinates something was unusual, and stressful, in these orders.

At the trial, the first specification in the murder charge against Calley was for this incident; he was accused of premeditated murder of "an unknown number, not less than 30, Oriental human beings, males and females of various ages, whose names are unknown, occupants of the village of My Lai 4, by means of shooting them with a rifle" (Goldstein et al., 1976, p. 497).

Among the helicopters flying reconnaissance above Son My was that of CWO Hugh Thompson. By 9:00 or soon after, Thompson had noticed some horrifying events from his perch. As he spotted wounded civilians, he sent down smoke markers so that soldiers on the ground could treat them. They killed them instead. He reported to headquarters, trying to persuade someone to stop what was going on. Barker, hearing the message, called down to Captain Medina. Medina, in turn, later claimed to have told Calley that it was "enough for today." But it was not yet enough.

At Calley's orders, his men began gathering the remaining villagers—roughly seventy-five individuals, mostly women and children—and herding them toward a drainage ditch. Accompanied by three or four enlisted men, Lieutenant Calley executed several batches of civilians who had been gathered into ditches. Some of the details of the process were entered into testimony in such accounts as Pfc. Dennis Conti's: "A lot of them, the people, were trying to get up and mostly they was just screaming and pretty bad shot up. . . .I seen a woman tried to get up. I seen Lieutenant Calley fire. He hit the side of her head and blew it off" (Hammer, 1971, p. 125).

Testimony by other soldiers presented the shooting's aftermath. Specialist Four Charles Hall, asked by Prosecutor Aubrey Daniel how he knew the people in the ditch were dead, said: "There was blood coming from them. They were just scattered all over the ground in the ditch, some in piles and some scattered out

20, 25 meters perhaps up the ditch....They were very old people, very young children, and mothers....There was blood all over them" (Goldstein et al., 1976, pp. 501–502). And Pfc Gregory Olsen corroborated the general picture of the victims: "They were—the majority were women and children, some babies. I distinctly remember one middle-aged Vietnamese male dressed in white right at my feet as I crossed. None of the bodies were mangled in any way. There was blood. Some appeared to be dead, others followed me with their eyes as I walked across the ditch" (Goldstein et al., 1976, p. 502).

The second specification in the murder charge stated that Calley did "with premeditation, murder an unknown number of Oriental human beings, not less than seventy, males and females of various ages, whose names are unknown, occupants of the village of My Lai 4, by means of shooting them with a rifle" (Goldstein et al., 1976, p. 497). Calley was also charged with and tried for shootings of individuals (an old man and a child); these charges were clearly supplemental to the main issue at trial—the mass killings and how they came about.

It is noteworthy that during these executions more than one enlisted man avoided carrying out Calley's orders, and more than one, by sworn oath, directly refused to obey them. For example, Pfc. James Joseph Dursi testified, when asked if he fired when Lieutenant Calley ordered him to: "No I just stood there. Meadlo turned to me after a couple of minutes and said 'Shoot! Why don't you shoot! Why don't you fire!' He was crying and yelling. I said, 'I can't! I won't!' And the people were screaming and crying and yelling. They kept firing for a couple of minutes, mostly automatic and semi-automatic" (Hammer, 1971, p. 143)....

Disobedience of Lieutenant Calley's own orders to kill represented a serious legal and moral threat to a defense *based* on superior orders, such as Calley was attempting. This defense had to assert that the orders seemed reasonable enough to carry out; that they appeared to be legal orders. Even if the orders in question were not legal, the defense had to assert that an ordinary individual could not

and should not be expected to see the distinction. In short, if what happened was "business as usual," even though it might be bad business, then the defendant stood a chance of acquittal. But under direct command from "Surfside 5½," some ordinary enlisted men managed to refuse, to avoid, or at least to stop doing what they were ordered to do. As "reasonable men" of "ordinary sense and understanding," they had apparently found something awry that morning; and it would have been hard for an officer to plead successfully that he was more ordinary than his men in his capacity to evaluate the reasonableness of orders.

Even those who obeyed Calley's orders showed great stress. For example, Meadlo eventually began to argue and cry directly in front of Calley. Pfc. Herbert Carter shot himself in the foot, possibly because he could no longer take what he was doing. We were not destined to hear a sworn version of the incident, since neither side at the Calley trial called him to testify.

The most unusual instance of resistance to authority came from the skies. CWO Hugh Thompson, who had protested the apparent carnage of civilians, was Calley's inferior in rank but was not in his line of command. He was also watching the ditch from his helicopter and noticed some people moving after the first round of slaughter—chiefly children who had been shielded by their mothers' bodies. Landing to rescue the wounded, he also found some villagers hiding in a nearby bunker. Protecting the Vietnamese with his own body, Thompson ordered his men to train their guns on the Americans and to open fire if the Americans fired on the Vietnamese. He then radioed for additional rescue helicopters and stood between the Vietnamese and the Americans under Calley's command until the Vietnamese could be evacuated. He later returned to the ditch to unearth a child buried, unharmed, beneath layers of bodies. In October 1969, Thompson was awarded the Distinguished Flying Cross for heroism at My Lai, specifically (albeit inaccurately) for the rescue of children hiding in a bunker "between

Viet Cong forces and advancing friendly forces" and for the rescue of a wounded child "caught in the intense crossfire" (Hersh, 1970, p. 119). Four months earlier, at the Pentagon, Thompson had identified Calley as having been at the ditch.

By about 10:00 A.M., the massacre was winding down. The remaining actions consisted largely of isolated rapes and killings, "clean-up" shootings of the wounded, and the destruction of the village by fire. We have already seen some examples of these more indiscriminate and possibly less premeditated acts. By the 11:00 A.M. lunch break, when the exhausted men of Company C were relaxing, two young girls wandered back from a hiding place only to be invited to share lunch. This surrealist touch illustrates the extent to which the soldiers' action had become dissociated from its meaning. An hour earlier, some of these men were making sure that not even a child would escape the executioner's bullet. But now the job was done and it was time for lunch—and in this new context it seemed only natural to ask the children who had managed to escape execution to join them. The massacre had ended. It remained only for the Viet Cong to reap the political rewards among the survivors in hiding.

The army command in the area knew that something had gone wrong. Direct commanders, including Lieutenant Colonel Barker, had firsthand reports, such as Thompson's complaints. Others had such odd bits of evidence as the claim of 128 Viet Cong dead with a booty of only three weapons. But the cover-up of My Lai began at once. The operation was reported as a victory over a stronghold of the Viet Cong Forty-eighth. . . .

William Calley was not the only man tried for the event at My Lai. The actions of over thirty soldiers and civilians were scrutinized by investigators; over half of these had to face charges or disciplinary action of some sort. Targets of investigation included Captain Medina, who was tried, and various higher-ups, including General Koster. But Lieutenant Calley was the only person convicted, the only person to serve time.

The core of Lieutenant Calley's defense was superior orders. What this meant to him—in contrast to what it meant to the judge and jury—can be gleaned from his responses to a series of questions from his defense attorney, George Latimer, in which Calley sketched out his understanding of the laws of war and the actions that constitute doing one's duty within those laws:

Latimer: Did you receive any training which had to do with the obedience to orders?

Calley: Yes, sir.

Latimer: . . . what were you informed [were] the principles involved in that field?

Calley: That all orders were to be assumed legal, that the soldier's job was to carry out any order given him to the best of his ability.

Latimer: . . . what might occur if you disobeyed an order by a senior officer?

Calley: You could be court-martialed for refusing an order and refusing an order in the face of the enemy, you could be sent to death, sir.

Latimer: [I am asking] whether you were required in any way, shape or form to make a determination of the legality or illegality of an order?

Calley: No, sir. I was never told that I had the choice, sir.

Latimer: If you had a doubt about the order, what were you supposed to do?

Calley: . . . I was supposed to carry the order out and then come back and make my complaint. (Hammer, 1971, pp. 240–241)

Lieutenant Calley steadfastly maintained that his actions within My Lai had constituted, in his mind, carrying out orders from Captain Medina. Both his own actions and the orders he gave to others (such as the instruction to Meadlo to "waste 'em") were entirely in response to superior orders. He denied any intent to kill individuals and any but the most passing awareness of distinctions among the individuals: "I was ordered to go in there and destroy the enemy. That was my job on that day. That was the mission I was given. I did not sit down and think in terms of men, women, and children. They were all classified the same, and that was the classification that we dealt with, just as enemy soldiers." When Latimer asked if in his own opinion Calley had acted "rightly and according to your understanding of your directions and orders," Calley replied, "I felt then and I still do that I acted as I was directed, and I carried out the orders that I was given, and I do not feel wrong in doing so, sir" (Hammer, 1971, p. 257).

His court-martial did not accept Calley's defense of superior orders and clearly did not share his interpretation of his duty. The jury evidently reasoned that, even if there had been orders to destroy everything in sight and to "waste the Vietnamese," any reasonable person would have realized that such orders were illegal and should have refused to carry them out. The defense of superior orders under such conditions is inadmissible under international and military law. The U.S. Army's *Law of Land Warfare* (Dept. of the Army, 1956), for example, states that "the fact that the law of war has been violated pursuant to an order of a superior authority, whether military or civil, does not deprive the act in question of its character of a war crime, nor does it constitute a defense in the trial of an accused individual, unless he did not know and could not reasonably have been expected to know that the act was unlawful" and that "members of the armed forces are bound to obey only lawful orders" (in Falk et al., 1971, pp. 71–72).

The disagreement between Calley and the court-martial seems to have revolved around the definition of the responsibilities of a subordinate to obey, on the one hand, and to evaluate, on the other. This tension . . . can best be captured via the charge to the jury in the Calley court-martial, made by the trial judge, Col. Reid Kennedy. The forty-one pages of the charge include the following:

> Both combatants captured by and noncombatants detained by the opposing force . . . have

the right to be treated as prisoners. . . . Summary execution of detainees or prisoners is forbidden by law. . . . I therefore instruct you . . . that if unresisting human beings were killed at My Lai (4) while within the effective custody and control of our military forces, their deaths cannot be considered justified. . . . Thus if you find that Lieutenant Calley received an order directing him to kill unresisting Vietnamese within his control or within the control of his troops, *that order would be an illegal order.*

A determination that an order is illegal does not, of itself, assign criminal responsibility to the person following the order for acts done in compliance with it. Soldiers are taught to follow orders, and special attention is given to obedience of orders on the battlefield. Military effectiveness depends on obedience to orders. On the other hand, the obedience of a soldier is not the obedience of an automaton. A soldier is a reasoning agent, obliged to respond, not as a machine, but as a person. The law takes these factors into account in assessing criminal responsibility for acts done in compliance with illegal orders.

> The acts of a subordinate done in compliance with an unlawful order given him by his superior are excused and impose no criminal liability upon him unless the superior's order is one which a man of *ordinary sense and understanding* would, under the circumstances, know to be unlawful, or if the order in question is actually known to the accused to be unlawful. (Goldstein et al., 1976, pp. 525–526; emphasis added)

By this definition, subordinates take part in a balancing act, one tipped toward obedience but tempered by "ordinary sense and understanding."

A jury of combat veterans proceeded to convict William Calley of the premeditated murder of no less than twenty-two human beings. (The army, realizing some unfortunate connotations in referring to the victims as "Oriental human beings," eventually referred to them as "human beings.") Regarding the first specification in the murder charge, the bodies on the trail, [Calley] was convicted of premeditated murder of not less than one person. (Medical testimony had been able to pinpoint only one person whose wounds as revealed in Haeberle's photos were sure to be immediately fatal.) Regarding the second specification, the bodies in the ditch, Calley was convicted of the premeditated murder of not less than twenty human beings. Regarding additional specifications that he had killed an old man and a child, Calley was convicted of premeditated murder in the first case and of assault with intent to commit murder in the second.

Lieutenant Calley was initially sentenced to life imprisonment. That sentence was reduced: first to twenty years, eventually to ten (the latter by Secretary of Defense Callaway in 1974). Calley served three years before being released on bond. The time was spent under house arrest in his apartment, where he was able to receive visits from his girlfriend. He was granted parole on September 10, 1975.

Sanctioned Massacres

The slaughter at My Lai is an instance of a class of violent acts that can be described as sanctioned massacres (Kelman, 1973): acts of indiscriminate, ruthless, and often systematic mass violence, carried out by military or paramilitary personnel while engaged in officially sanctioned campaigns, the victims of which are defenseless and unresisting civilians, including old men, women, and children. Sanctioned massacres have occurred throughout history. Within American history, My Lai had its precursors in the Philippine war around the turn of the century (Schirmer, 1971) and in the massacres of American Indians. Elsewhere in the world, one recalls the Nazis' "final solution" for European Jews, the massacres and deportations of Armenians by Turks, the liquidation of the kulaks and the great purges in the Soviet Union, and more recently the massacres in Indonesia and Bangladesh, in Biafra and Burundi, in South Africa and Mozambique, in Cambodia and Afghanistan, in Syria and Lebanon. . . .

The occurrence of sanctioned massacres cannot be adequately explained by the existence of psychological forces—whether these be characterological dispositions to engage in murderous violence or profound hostility against the target—so powerful that they must find expression in violent acts unhampered by moral restraints. Instead, the major instigators for this class of violence derive from the policy process. The question that really calls for psychological analysis is why so many people are willing to formulate, participate in, and condone policies that call for the mass killings of defenseless civilians. Thus it is more instructive to look not at the motives for violence but at the conditions under which the usual moral inhibitions against violence become weakened. Three social processes that tend to create such conditions can be identified: authorization, routinization, and dehumanization. Through authorization, the situation becomes so defined that the individual is absolved of the responsibility to make personal moral choices. Through routinization, the action becomes so organized that there is no opportunity for raising moral questions. Through dehumanization, the actors' attitudes toward the target and toward themselves become so structured that it is neither necessary nor possible for them to view the relationship in moral terms.

Authorization

Sanctioned massacres by definition occur in the context of an authority situation, a situation in which, at least for many of the participants, the moral principles that generally govern human relationships do not apply. Thus, when acts of violence are explicitly ordered, implicitly encouraged, tacitly approved, or at least permitted by legitimate authorities, people's readiness to commit or condone them is enhanced. That such acts are authorized seems to carry automatic justification for them. Behaviorally, authorization obviates the necessity of making judgments or choices. Not only do normal moral principles become inoperative, but—particularly when the actions are explicitly ordered—a different kind of morality, linked to the duty to obey superior orders, tends to take over.

In an authority situation, individuals characteristically feel obligated to obey the orders of the authorities, whether or not these correspond with their personal preferences. They see themselves as having no choice as long as they accept the legitimacy of the orders and of the authorities who give them. Individuals differ considerably in the degree to which—and the conditions under which—they are prepared to challenge the legitimacy of an order on the grounds that the order itself is illegal, or that those giving it have overstepped their authority, or that it stems from a policy that violates fundamental societal values. Regardless of such individual differences, however, the basic structure of a situation of legitimate authority requires subordinates to respond in terms of their role obligations rather than their personal preferences; they can openly disobey only by challenging the legitimacy of the authority. Often people obey without question even though the behavior they engage in may entail great personal sacrifice or great harm to others.

An important corollary of the basic structure of the authority situation is that actors often do not see themselves as personally responsible for the consequences of their actions. Again, there are individual differences, depending on actors' capacity and readiness to evaluate the legitimacy of orders received. Insofar as they see themselves as having had no choice in their actions, however, they do not feel personally responsible for them. They were not personal agents, but merely extensions of the authority. Thus, when their actions cause harm to others, they can feel relatively free of guilt. A similar mechanism operates when a person engages in antisocial behavior that was not ordered by the authorities but was tacitly encouraged and approved by them—even if only by making it clear that such behavior will not be punished. In this situation, behavior that was formerly illegitimate is legitimized by the authorities' acquiescence.

In the My Lai massacre, it is likely that the structure of the authority situation contributed to the massive violence in both ways—that is, by conveying the message that acts of violence against Vietnamese villagers were *required,* as well as the message that such acts, even if not ordered, were *permitted* by the authorities in charge. The actions at My Lai represented, at least in some respects, responses to explicit or implicit orders. Lieutenant Calley indicated, by orders and by example, that he wanted large numbers of villagers killed. Whether Calley himself had been ordered by his superiors to "waste" the whole area, as he claimed, remains a matter of controversy. Even if we assume, however, that he was not explicitly ordered to wipe out the village, he had reason to believe that such actions were expected by his superior officers. Indeed, the very nature of the war conveyed this expectation. The principal measure of military success was the "body count"—the number of enemy soldiers killed—and any Vietnamese killed by the U.S. military was commonly defined as a "Viet Cong." Thus, it was not totally bizarre for Calley to believe that what he was doing at My Lai was to increase his body count, as any good officer was expected to do.

Even to the extent that the actions at My Lai occurred spontaneously, without reference to superior orders, those committing them had reason to assume that such actions might be tacitly approved of by the military authorities. Not only had they failed to punish such acts in most cases, but the very strategies and tactics that the authorities consistently devised were based on the proposition that the civilian population of South Vietnam—whether "hostile" or "friendly"—was expendable. Such policies as search-and-destroy missions, the establishment of free-shooting zones, the use of antipersonnel weapons, the bombing of entire villages if they were suspected of harboring guerrillas, the forced migration of masses of the rural population, and the defoliation of vast forest areas helped legitimize acts of massive violence of the kind occurring at My Lai.

Some of the actions at My Lai suggest an orientation to authority based on unquestioning obedience to superior orders, no matter how destructive the actions these orders call for. Such obedience is specifically fostered in the course of military training and reinforced by the structure of the military authority situation. It also reflects, however, an ideological orientation that may be more widespread in the general population. . . .

Routinization

Authorization processes create a situation in which people become involved in an action without considering its implications and without really making a decision. Once they have taken the initial step, they are in a new psychological and social situation in which the pressures to continue are powerful. As Lewin (1947) has pointed out, many forces that might originally have kept people out of a situation reverse direction once they have made a commitment (once they have gone through the "gate region") and now serve to keep them in the situation. For example, concern about the criminal nature of an action, which might originally have inhibited a person from becoming involved, may now lead to deeper involvement in efforts to justify the action and to avoid negative consequences.

Despite these forces, however, given the nature of the actions involved in sanctioned massacres, one might still expect moral scruples to intervene; but the likelihood of moral resistance is greatly reduced by transforming the action into routine, mechanical, highly programmed operations. Routinization fulfills two functions. First, it reduces the necessity of making decisions, thus minimizing the occasions in which moral questions may arise. Second, it makes it easier to avoid the implications of the action, since the actor focuses on the details of the job rather than on its meaning. The latter effect is more readily achieved among those who participate in sanctioned massacres from a distance—from their desks or even from the cockpits of their bombers.

Routinization operates both at the level of the individual actor and at the organizational level. Individual job performance is broken down into a series of discrete steps, most of them carried out in automatic, regularized fashion. It becomes easy to forget the nature of the product that emerges from this process. When Lieutenant Calley said of My Lai that it was "no great deal," he probably implied that it was all in a day's work. Organizationally, the task is divided among different offices, each of which has responsibility for a small portion of it. This arrangement diffuses responsibility and limits the amount and scope of decision making that is necessary. There is no expectation that the moral implications will be considered at any of these points, nor is there any opportunity to do so. The organizational processes also help further legitimize the actions of each participant. By proceeding in routine fashion—processing papers, exchanging memos, diligently carrying out their assigned tasks—the different units mutually reinforce each other in the view that what is going on must be perfectly normal, correct, and legitimate. The shared illusion that they are engaged in a legitimate enterprise helps the participants assimilate their activities to other purposes, such as the efficiency of their performance, the productivity of their unit, or the cohesiveness of their group (see Janis, 1972).

Normalization of atrocities is more difficult to the extent that there are constant reminders of the true meaning of the enterprise. Bureaucratic inventiveness in the use of language helps to cover up such meaning. For example, the SS had a set of *Sprachregelungen,* or "language rules," to govern descriptions of their extermination program. As Arendt (1964) points out, the term *language rule* in itself was "a code name; it meant what in ordinary language would be called a lie" (p. 85). The code names for killing and liquidation were "final solution," "evacuation," and "special treatment." The war in Indochina produced its own set of euphemisms, such as "protective reaction," "pacification," and "forced-draft urbanization and modernization." The use of euphemisms allows participants in sanctioned massacres to differentiate their actions from ordinary killing and destruction and thus to avoid confronting their true meaning.

Dehumanization

Authorization processes override standard moral considerations; routinization processes reduce the likelihood that such considerations will arise. Still, the inhibitions against murdering one's fellow human beings are generally so strong that the victims must also be stripped of their human status if they are to be subjected to systematic killing. Insofar as they are dehumanized, the usual principles of morality no longer apply to them.

Sanctioned massacres become possible to the extent that the victims are deprived in the perpetrators' eyes of the two qualities essential to being perceived as fully human and included in the moral compact that governs human relationships: *identity*—standing as independent, distinctive individuals, capable of making choices and entitled to live their own lives—and *community*—fellow membership in an interconnected network of individuals who care for each other and respect each other's individuality and rights (Kelman, 1973; see also Bakan, 1966, for a related distinction between "agency" and "communion"). Thus, when a group of people is defined entirely in terms of a category to which they belong, and when this category is excluded from the human family, moral restraints against killing them are more readily overcome.

Dehumanization of the enemy is a common phenomenon in any war situation. Sanctioned massacres, however, presuppose a more extreme degree of dehumanization, insofar as the killing is not in direct response to the target's threats or provocations. It is not what they have done that marks such victims for death but who they are—the category to which they happen to belong. They are the victims of policies that regard their systematic destruction as a desirable end or an acceptable means.

Such extreme dehumanization becomes possible when the target group can readily be identified as a separate category of people who have historically been stigmatized and excluded by the victimizers; often the victims belong to a distinct racial, religious, ethnic, or political group regarded as inferior or sinister. The traditions, the habits, the images, and the vocabularies for dehumanizing such groups are already well established and can be drawn upon when the groups are selected for massacre. Labels help deprive the victims of identity and community, as in the epithet "gooks" that was commonly used to refer to Vietnamese and other Indochinese peoples.

The dynamics of the massacre process itself further increase the participants' tendency to dehumanize their victims. Those who participate as part of the bureaucratic apparatus increasingly come to see their victims as bodies to be counted and entered into their reports, as faceless figures that will determine their productivity rates and promotions. Those who participate in the massacre directly—in the field, as it were—are reinforced in their perception of the victims as less than human by observing their very victimization. The only way they can justify what is being done to these people—both by others and by themselves—and the only way they can extract some degree of meaning out of the absurd events in which they find themselves participating (see Lifton, 1971, 1973) is by coming to believe that the victims are subhuman and deserve to be rooted out. And thus the process of dehumanization feeds on itself.

REFERENCES

Arendt, H. (1964). *Eichmann in Jerusalem: A report on the banality of evil.* New York: Viking Press.
Bakan, D. (1966). *The duality of human existence.* Chicago: Rand McNally.
Department of the Army. (1956). *The law of land warfare* (Field Manual, No. 27-10). Washington, DC: U.S. Government Printing Office.
Falk, R. A., Kolko, G., & Lifton, R. J. (Eds.). (1971). *Crimes of war.* New York: Vintage Books.

French, P. (Ed.). (1972). *Individual and collective responsibility: The massacre at My Lai.* Cambridge, MA: Schenkman.

Goldstein, J., Marshall, B., & Schwartz, J. (Eds.). (1976). *The My Lai massacre and its cover-up: Beyond the reach of law?* (The Peers Report with a supplement and introductory essay on the limits of law). New York: Free Press.

Hammer, R. (1971). *The court-martial of Lt. Calley.* New York: Coward, McCann, & Geoghegan.

Hersh, S. (1970). *My Lai 4: A report on the massacre and its aftermath.* New York: Vintage Books.

_____. (1972). *Cover-up.* New York: Random House.

Janis, I. L. (1972). *Victims of groupthink: A psychological study of foreign-policy decisions and fiascoes.* Boston: Houghton Mifflin.

Kelman, H. C. (1973). Violence without moral restraint: Reflections on the dehumanization of victims and victimizers. *Journal of Social Issues, 29*(4), 25–61.

Lewin, K. (1947). Group decision and social change. In T. M. Newcomb & E. L. Hartley (Eds.), *Readings in social psychology.* New York: Holt.

Lifton, R. J. (1971). Existential evil. In N. Sanford, C. Comstock, & Associates, *Sanctions for evil: Sources of social destructiveness.* San Francisco: Jossey-Bass.

_____. (1973). *Home from the war—Vietnam veterans: Neither victims nor executioners.* New York: Simon & Schuster.

Manual for courts martial, United States (Rev. ed.). (1969). Washington, DC: U.S. Government Printing Office.

Schirmer, D. B. (1971, April 24). My Lai was not the first time. *New Republic,* pp. 18–21.

Williams, B. (1985, April 14–15). "I will never forgive," says My Lai survivor. *Jordan Times* (Amman), p. 4.

THINKING ABOUT THE READING

According to Kelman and Hamilton, social processes can create conditions under which usual restraints against violence are weakened. What social processes were in evidence during the My Lai massacre? The incident they describe provides us with an uncomfortable picture of human nature. Do you think most people would have reacted the way the soldiers at My Lai did? Are we all potential massacrers? Does the phenomenon of obedience to authority go beyond the tightly structured environment of the military? Can you think of incidents in your own life when you've done something—perhaps harmed or humiliated another person—because of the powerful influence of others? How might Kelman and Hamilton explain the actions of the individuals who carried out the hijackings and attacks of September 11, 2001, or of the American soldiers who abused Iraqi prisoners in their custody?

Seeing and Thinking Sociologically

2

Where is society located? This is an intriguing question. Society shapes our behavior and beliefs through social institutions such as religion, law, education, economics, and family. At the same time, we shape society through our interactions with one another and our participation in social institutions. In this way, we can say that society exists as an objective entity that transcends us. But it is also a construction that is created, reaffirmed, and altered through everyday interactions and behavior. Humans are social beings. We constantly look to others to help define and interpret the situations in which we find ourselves. Other people can influence what we see, feel, think, and do. But it's not just other people who influence us. We also live in a *society*, which consists of socially recognizable combinations of individuals (e.g., relationships, groups, and organizations) as well as the products of human action (statuses, roles, culture, and institutions). When we behave, we do so in a social context that consists of a combination of institutional arrangements, cultural influences, and interpersonal expectations. Thus, our behavior in any given situation is our own, but the reasons we do what we do are rooted in these more complex social factors.

The social context in which we reside, whether urban, rural, suburban, exurban, or institutional, greatly influences and shapes our social interaction and individual experiences. In "The Metropolis and Mental Life," Georg Simmel uses the urban environment to investigate the social forces that affect a person's individuality and relationships. He shows how the urban environment challenges an individual's sense of independence and individuality while pushing the individual toward a very calculative and rational approach to life. Indeed, the path we take as individuals in constructing the architecture of our social environment is one shaped by these influential social forces of time and place.

This social structure provides us with a sense of order in our daily lives. But sometimes that order breaks down. In "Culture of Fear," Barry Glassner shows us how the news media function to *create* a culture that the public takes for granted. He focuses, in particular, on the emotion of fear in U.S. society. We constantly hear horror stories about such urgent social problems as deadly diseases, violent strangers, and out-of-control teens. But Glassner points out that the terrified public concern over certain issues is often inflated by the media and largely unwarranted. Ironically, when we live in a culture of fear, our most serious problems often go ignored.

In the third reading for this chapter, "The (Mis)Education of Monica and Karen," Hamilton and Armstrong explore how some institutions of higher learning are structured to serve well funded and academically accomplished out-of-state students to the detriment of modestly funded and less academically prepared in-state students. These authors identify how the social and academic structures of these types of universities negatively impact students who do not have the resources to navigate through them. This article shows that educational achievement and outcomes are not solely determined by individuals, but organizationally produced. They suggest that universities need to rethink their approaches in order to serve the needs of all students, by providing more diverse pathways to achievement, and better academic and financial resources.

Something to Consider as You Read

When reading the selections in this section, consider the kinds of rules sociologists use in deciding if something is worth studying. What rules do media journalists use in deciding whether a story is interesting? What role might politics play in decisions of both science and the media about what topics to focus on? How do such decisions shape our perception of important social problems?

The Metropolis and Mental Life

Georg Simmel

(1903)

The deepest problems of modern life flow from the attempt of the Individual to maintain the independence and individuality of his existence against the sovereign powers of society, against the weight of the historical heritage and the external culture and technique of life.

This intellectualistic quality which is thus recognized as a protection of the inner life against the domination of the metropolis, becomes ramified into numerous specific phenomena. The metropolis has always been the seat of money economy because the many-sidedness and concentration of commercial activity have given the medium of exchange an importance which it could not have acquired in the commercial aspects of rural life. But money economy and the domination of the intellect stand in the closest relationship to one another. They have in common a purely matter-of-fact attitude in the treatment of persons and things in which a formal justice is often combined with an unrelenting hardness. The purely intellectualistic person is indifferent to all things personal because, out of them, relationships and reactions develop which are not to be completely understood by purely rational methods—just as the unique element in events never enters into the principle of money. Money is concerned only with what is common to all, i.e., with the exchange value which reduces all quality and individuality to a purely quantitative level. All emotional relationships between persons rest on their individuality, whereas intellectual relationships deal with persons as with numbers, that is, as with elements which, in themselves, are indifferent, but which are of interest only insofar as they offer something objectively perceivable. It is in this very manner that the inhabitant of the metropolis reckons with his merchant, his customer, and with his servant, and frequently with the persons with whom he is thrown into obligatory association. These relationships stand in distinct contrast with the nature of the smaller circle in which the inevitable knowledge of individual characteristics produces, with an equal inevitability, an emotional tone in conduct, a sphere which is beyond the mere objective weighting of tasks performed and payments made. What is essential here as regards the economic-psychological aspect of the problem is that in less advanced cultures production was for the customer who ordered the product so that the producer and the purchaser knew one another. The modern city, however, is supplied almost exclusively by production for the market, that is, for entirely unknown purchasers who never appear in the actual field of vision of the producers themselves. Thereby, the interests of each party acquire a relentless matter-of-factness, and its rationally calculated economic egoism need not fear any divergence from its set path because of the imponderability of personal relationships. This is all the more the case in the money economy which dominates the metropolis in which the last remnants of domestic production and direct barter of goods have been eradicated and in which the amount of production on direct personal order is reduced daily. Furthermore, this psychological intellectualistic attitude and the money economy are in such close integration that no one is able to say whether it was the former that effected the latter or *vice versa*. What is certain is only that the form of life in the metropolis is the soil which nourishes this interaction most fruitfully, a point which I shall attempt to demonstrate only with the statement of the most outstanding English constitutional historian to the effect that through the entire course of English history London has never acted as the heart of England but often as its intellect and always as its money bag.

In certain apparently insignificant characters or traits of the most external aspects of life are to be found a number of characteristic mental tendencies. The modern mind has become more and more a calculating one. The calculating exactness of practical life which has resulted from a money economy corresponds to the ideal of natural science, namely that of transforming the world into an arithmetical problem and of fixing every one of its parts in a mathematical formula. It has been money economy which has thus filled the daily life of so many people with weighing, calculating, enumerating and the reduction of qualitative values to quantitative terms. Because of the character of calculability which money has there has come into the relationships of the elements of life a precision and a degree of certainty in the definition of the equalities and inequalities and an unambiguousness in agreements and arrangements, just as externally this precision has been brought about through the general diffusion of pocket watches. It is, however, the conditions of the metropolis which are cause as well as effect for this essential characteristic. The relationships and concerns of the typical metropolitan resident are so manifold and complex that, especially as a result of the agglomeration of so many persons with such differentiated interests, their relationships and activities intertwine with one another into a many-membered organism. In view of this fact, the lack of the most exact punctuality in promises and performances would cause the whole to break down into an inextricable chaos. If all the watches in Berlin suddenly went wrong in different ways even only as much as an hour, its entire economic and commercial life would be derailed for some time. Even though this may seem more superficial in its significance, it transpires that the magnitude of distances results in making all waiting and the breaking of appointments an ill-afforded waste of time. For this reason the technique of metropolitan life in general is not conceivable without all of its activities and reciprocal relationships being organized and coordinated in the most punctual way into a firmly fixed framework of time which transcends all subjective elements. But here too there emerge those conclusions which are in general the whole task of this discussion, namely, that every event, however restricted to this superficial level it may appear, comes immediately into contact with the depths of the soul, and that the most banal externalities are, in the last analysis, bound up with the final decisions concerning the meaning and the style of life. Punctuality, calculability, and exactness, which are required by the complications and extensiveness of metropolitan life are not only most intimately connected with its capitalistic and intellectualistic character but also color the content of life and are conductive to the exclusion of those irrational, instinctive, sovereign human traits and impulses which originally seek to determine the form of life from within instead of receiving it from the outside in a general, schematically precise form. Even though those lives which are autonomous and characterised by these vital impulses are not entirely impossible in the city, they are, none the less, opposed to it *in abstracto*.

The same factors which, in the exactness and the minute precision of the form of life. have coalesced into a structure of the highest impersonality, have, on the other hand, an influence in a highly personal direction. There is perhaps no psychic phenomenon which is so unconditionally reserved to the city as the blasé outlook. It is at first the consequence of those rapidly shifting stimulations of the nerves which are thrown together in all their contrasts and from which it seems to us the intensification of metropolitan intellectuality seems to be derived. On that account it is not likely that stupid persons who have been hitherto intellectually dead will be blasé. Just as an immoderately sensuous life makes one blasé because it stimulates the nerves to their utmost reactivity until they finally can no longer produce any reaction at all, so, less harmful stimuli, through the rapidity and the contradictoriness of their shifts, force the nerves to make such violent responses, tear them about so brutally that they exhaust their last reserves of strength and, remaining in the same milieu, do not have time for new reserves to form. This incapacity to react to new stimulations with the required amount of energy constitutes in fact that blase attitude which every child of a large city evinces when compared with the products of the more peaceful and more stable milieu.

Combined with this physiological source of the blasé metropolitan attitude there is another which derives from a money economy. The essence of the blasé attitude is an indifference toward the distinctions between things. Not in the sense that they are not perceived, as is the case of mental dullness, but rather that the meaning and the value of the distinctions between things, and therewith of the things themselves, are experienced as meaningless. They appear to the blasé person in a homogeneous, flat and gray color with no one of them worthy of being preferred to another. This psychic mood is the correct subjective reflection of a complete money economy to the extent that money takes the place of all the manifoldness of things and expresses all qualitative distinctions between them in the distinction of "how much." To the extent that money, with its colorlessness and its indifferent quality, can become a common denominator of all values it becomes the frightful leveler—it hollows out the core of things, their peculiarities, their specific values and their uniqueness and incomparability in a way which is beyond repair. They all float with the same specific gravity in the constantly moving stream of money. They all rest on the same level and are distinguished only by their amounts. In individual cases this coloring, or rather this de-coloring of things,

through their equation with money, may be imperceptibly small. In the relationship, however, which the wealthy person has to objects which can be bought for money, perhaps indeed in the total character which, for this reason, public opinion now recognizes in these objects, it takes on very considerable proportions. This is why the metropolis is the seat of commerce and it is in it that the purchasability of things appears in quite a different aspect than in simpler economies. It is also the peculiar seat of the blasé attitude. In it is brought to a peak, in a certain way, that achievement in the concentration of purchasable things which stimulates the individual to the highest degree of nervous energy. Through the mere quantitative intensification of the same conditions this achievement is transformed into its opposite, into this peculiar adaptive phenomenon—the blasé attitude—in which the nerves reveal their final possibility of adjusting themselves to the content and the form of metropolitan life by renouncing the response to them. We see that the self-preservation of certain types of personalities is obtained at the cost of devaluing the entire objective world, ending inevitably in dragging the personality downward into a feeling of its own valuelessness.

Cities are above all the seat of the most advanced economic division of labor. They produce such extreme phenomena as the lucrative vocation of the *quatorzieme* in Paris. These are persons who may be recognized by shields on their houses and who hold themselves ready at the dinner hour in appropriate costumes so they can be called upon on short notice in case thirteen persons find themselves at the table. Exactly in the measure of its extension the city offers to an increasing degree the determining conditions for the division of labor. It is a unit which, because of its large size, is receptive to a highly diversified plurality of achievements while at the same time the agglomeration of individuals and their struggle for the customer forces the individual to a type of specialized accomplishment in which he cannot be so easily exterminated by the other. The decisive fact here is that in the life of a city, struggle with nature for the means of life is transformed into a conflict with human beings and the gain which is fought for is granted, not by nature, but by man. For here we find not only the previously mentioned source of specialization but rather the deeper one in which the seller must seek to produce in the person to whom he wishes to sell ever new and unique needs. The necessity to specialize one's product in order to find a source of income which is not yet exhausted and also to specialize a function which cannot be easily supplanted is conducive to differentiation, refinement and enrichment of the needs of the public which obviously must lead to increasing personal variation within this public.

All this leads to the narrower type of intellectual individuation of mental qualities to which the city gives rise in proportion to its size. There is a whole series of causes for this. First of all there is the difficulty of giving one's own personality a certain status within the framework of metropolitan life. Where quantitative increase of value and energy has reached its limits, one seizes on qualitative distinctions, so that, through taking advantage of the existing sensitivity to differences, the attention of the social world can, in some way, be won for oneself. This leads ultimately to the strangest eccentricities, to specifically metropolitan extravagances of self-distanciation, of caprice, of fastidiousness, the meaning of which is no longer to be found in the content of such activity itself but rather in its being a form of "being different"—of making oneself noticeable. For many types of persons these are still the only means of saving for oneself, through the attention gained from others, some sort of self-esteem and the sense of filling a position. In the same sense there operates an apparently insignificant factor which in its effects however is perceptibly cumulative, namely, the brevity and rarity of meetings which are allotted to each individual as compared with social intercourse in a small city. For here we find the attempt to appear to-the-point, clear-cut and individual

with extraordinarily greater frequency than where frequent and long association assures to each person an unambiguous conception of the other's personality.

This appears to me to be the most profound cause of the fact that the metropolis places emphasis on striving for the most individual forms of personal existence—regardless of whether it is always correct or always successful The development of modern culture is characterised by the predominance of what one can call the objective spirit over the subjective; that is, in language as well as in law, in the technique of production as well as in art, in science as well as in the objects of domestic environment, there is embodied a sort of spirit [*Geist*], the daily growth of which is followed only imperfectly and with an even greater lag by the intellectual development of the individual. If we survey for instance the vast culture which during the last century has been embodied in things and in knowledge, in institutions and comforts, and if we compare them with the cultural progress of the individual during the same period—at least in the upper classes—we would see a frightful difference in rate of growth between the two which represents, in many points, rather a regression of the culture of the individual with reference to spirituality, delicacy and idealism. This discrepancy is in essence the result of the success of the growing division of labor. For it is this which requires from the individual an ever more one-sided type of achievement which, at its highest point, often permits his personality as a whole to fall into neglect. In any case this overgrowth of objective culture has been less and less satisfactory for the individual. Perhaps less conscious than in practical activity and in the obscure complex of feelings which flow from him, he is reduced to a negligible quantity. He becomes a single cog as over against the vast overwhelming organization of things and forces which gradually take out of his hands everything connected with progress, spirituality and value. The operation of these forces results in the transformation of the latter from a subjective form into one of purely objective existence. It need only be pointed out that the metropolis is the proper arena for this type of culture which has outgrown every personal element. Here in buildings and in educational institutions, in the wonders and comforts of space-conquering technique, in the formations of social life and in the concrete institutions of the State is to be found such a tremendous richness of crystallizing, depersonalized cultural accomplishments that the personality can, so to speak, scarcely maintain itself in the face of it. From one angle life is made infinitely more easy in the sense that stimulations, interests, and the taking up of time and attention, present themselves from all sides and carry it in a stream which scarcely requires any individual efforts for its ongoing. But from another angle, life is composed more and more of these impersonal cultural elements and existing goods and values which seek to suppress peculiar personal interests and incomparabilities. As a result, in order that this most personal element be saved, extremities and peculiarities and individualizations must be produced and they must be over-exaggerated merely to be brought into the awareness even of the individual himself. The atrophy of individual culture through the hypertrophy of objective culture lies at the root of the bitter hatred which the preachers of the most extreme individualism, in the footsteps of Nietzsche, directed against the metropolis. But it is also the explanation of why indeed they are so passionately loved in the metropolis and indeed appear to its residents as the saviors of their unsatisfied yearnings.

When both of these forms of individualism which are nourished by the quantitative relationships of the metropolis, i.e., individual independence and the elaboration of personal peculiarities, are examined with reference to their historical position, the metropolis attains an entirely new value and meaning in the world history of the spirit. The eighteenth century found the individual in the grip of powerful bonds which had become meaningless—bonds of a political, agrarian, guild and religious nature—delimitations which

imposed upon the human being at the same time an unnatural form and for a long time an unjust inequality. In this situation arose the cry for freedom and equality—the belief in the full freedom of movement of the individual in all his social and intellectual relationships which would then permit the same noble essence to emerge equally from all individuals as Nature had placed it in them and as it had been distorted by social life and historical development. Alongside of this liberalistic ideal there grew up in the nineteenth century from Goethe and the Romantics, on the one hand, and from the economic division of labor on the other, the further tendency, namely, that individuals who had been liberated from their historical bonds sought now to distinguish themselves from one another. No longer was it the "general human quality" in every individual but rather his qualitative uniqueness and irreplaceability that now became the criteria of his value. In the conflict and shifting interpretations of these two ways of defining the position of the individual within the totality is to be found the external as well as the internal history of our time. It is the function of the metropolis to make a place for the conflict and for the attempts at unification of both of these in the sense that its own peculiar conditions have been revealed to us as the occasion and the stimulus for the development of both. Thereby they attain a quite unique place, fruitful with an inexhaustible richness of meaning in the development of the mental life. They reveal themselves as one of those great historical structures in which conflicting life-embracing currents find themselves with equal legitimacy. Because of this, however, regardless of whether we are sympathetic or antipathetic with their individual expressions, they transcend the sphere in which a judge-like attitude on our part is appropriate. To the extent that such forces have been integrated, with the fleeting existence of a single cell, into the root as well as the crown of the totality of historical life to which we belong—it is our task not to complain or to condone but only to understand.

THINKING ABOUT THE READING

According to Simmel, the individual is both liberated and repressed by the social forces of modern urban life. How does the objectivism of the urban environment lead the individual to feel alienation from, or superficial relationships with, those around them? How does it make the urban individual more calculative and rational in contrast with the sentimentality of the rural individual? On the other hand, how does the metropolis allow urban dwellers more autonomy and flexibility to define themselves without the cultural pressures found in smaller communities?

Where have you lived in your lifetime—a small town or a large city? Perhaps both? Consider how the social forces of the space you live in affect your inner meaning and development of self. Have you developed a "blasé outlook" in the midst of the disorienting nature of the metropolis? Do you find more sentimentality and familiarity in your interactions within small town communities "where everyone knows your name"?

Conversely, can you give any examples of spaces within urban life that allow for the sentimentality and familiarity that Simmel associates with rural areas? Or, what social forces might impede the social intercourse and personal relationships that Simmel suggests are indicative of rural life?

Culture of Fear

Barry Glassner

(1999)

Why are so many fears in the air, and so many of them unfounded? Why, as crime rates plunged throughout the 1990s, did two-thirds of Americans believe they were soaring? How did it come about that by mid-decade 62 percent of us described ourselves as "truly desperate" about crime—almost twice as many as in the late 1980s, when crime rates were higher? Why, on a survey in 1997, when the crime rate had already fallen for a half dozen consecutive years, did more than half of us disagree with the statement "This country is finally beginning to make some progress in solving the crime problem"?[1]

In the late 1990s the number of drug users had decreased by half compared to a decade earlier; almost two-thirds of high school seniors had never used any illegal drugs, even marijuana. So why did a majority of adults rank drug abuse as the greatest danger to America's youth? Why did nine out of ten believe the drug problem is out of control, and only one in six believe the country was making progress?[2]

Give us a happy ending and we write a new disaster story. In the late 1990s the unemployment rate was below 5 percent for the first time in a quarter century. People who had been pounding the pavement for years could finally get work. Yet pundits warned of imminent economic disaster. They predicted inflation would take off, just as they had a few years earlier—also erroneously—when the unemployment rate dipped below 6 percent.[3]

We compound our worries beyond all reason. Life expectancy in the United States has doubled during the twentieth century. We are better able to cure and control diseases than any other civilization in history. Yet we hear that phenomenal numbers of us are dreadfully ill. In 1996 Bob Garfield, a magazine writer, reviewed articles about serious diseases published over the course of a year in the *Washington Post,* the *New York Times,* and *USA Today.* He learned that, in addition to 59 million Americans with heart disease, 53 million with migraines, 25 million with osteoporosis, 16 million with obesity, and 3 million with cancer, many Americans suffer from more obscure ailments such as temporomandibular joint disorders (10 million) and brain injuries (2 million). Adding up the estimates, Garfield determined that 543 million Americans are seriously sick—a shocking number in a nation of 266 million inhabitants. "Either as a society we are doomed, or someone is seriously double-dipping," he suggested.[4]

Garfield appears to have underestimated one category of patients: for psychiatric ailments his figure was 53 million. Yet when Jim Windolf, an editor of the *New York Observer,* collated estimates for maladies ranging from borderline personality disorder (10 million) and sex addiction (11 million) to less well-known conditions such as restless leg syndrome (12 million) he came up with a figure of 152 million. "But give the experts a little time," he advised. "With another new quantifiable disorder or two, everybody in the country will be officially nuts."[5]

Indeed, Windolf omitted from his estimates new-fashioned afflictions that have yet to make it into the *Diagnostic and Statistical Manual of Mental Disorders* of the American Psychiatric Association: ailments such as road rage, which afflicts more than half of Americans, according to a psychologist's testimony before a congressional hearing in 1997.[6]

The scope of our health fears seems limitless. Besides worrying disproportionately about legitimate ailments and prematurely about would-be diseases, we continue to fret over already refuted dangers. Some still worry, for instance, about "flesh-eating bacteria," a bug first rammed into our consciousness in 1994 when the U.S. news media picked up on a screamer headline in a British tabloid, "Killer Bug Ate My Face." The bacteria, depicted as more brutal than anything seen in modern times, was said to be spreading faster than the pack of photographers outside the home of its latest victim. In point of fact, however, we were not "terribly vulnerable" to these "superbugs," nor were they "medicine's worst nightmares," as voices in the media warned.

Group A strep, a cyclical strain that has been around for ages, had been dormant for half a century or more before making a comeback. The British pseudoepidemic had resulted in a total of about a dozen deaths in the previous year. Medical experts roundly rebutted the scares by noting that of 20 to 30 million strep infections each year in the United States fewer than 1 in 1,000 involve serious strep A complications, and only 500 to 1,500 people suffer the flesh-eating syndrome, whose proper name is necrotizing fasciitis. Still the fear persisted. Years after the initial scare, horrifying news stories continued to appear, complete with grotesque pictures of victims. A United Press International story in 1998 typical of the genre told of a child in Texas who died of the "deadly strain" of bacteria that the reporter warned "can spread at a rate of up to one inch per hour."[7]

Killer Kids

When we are not worrying about deadly diseases we worry about homicidal strangers. Every few months for the past several years it seems we discover a new category of people to fear: government thugs in Waco, sadistic cops on Los Angeles freeways and in Brooklyn police stations, mass-murdering youths in small towns all over the country. A single anomalous event can provide us with multiple groups of people to fear. After the 1995 explosion at the federal building in Oklahoma City first we panicked about Arabs. "Knowing that the car bomb indicates Middle Eastern terrorists at work, it's safe to assume that their goal is to promote free-floating fear and a measure of anarchy, thereby disrupting American life," a *New York Post* editorial asserted. "Whatever we are doing to destroy Mideast terrorism, the chief terrorist threat against Americans, has not been working," wrote A. M. Rosenthal in the *New York Times*.[8]

When it turned out that the bombers were young white guys from middle America, two more groups instantly became spooky: right-wing radio talk show hosts who criticize the government—depicted by President Bill Clinton as "purveyors of hatred and division"—and members of militias. No group of disgruntled men was too ragtag not to warrant big, prophetic news stories.[9]

We have managed to convince ourselves that just about every young American male is a potential mass murderer—a remarkable achievement, considering the steep downward trend in youth crime throughout the 1990s. Faced year after year with comforting statistics, we either ignore them—adult Americans estimate that people under eighteen commit about half of all violent crimes when the actual number is 13 percent—or recast them as "The Lull Before the Storm" (*Newsweek* headline). "We know we've got about six years to turn this juvenile crime thing around or our country is going to be living with chaos," Bill Clinton asserted in 1997, even while acknowledging that the youth violent crime rate had fallen 9.2 percent the previous year.[10]

The more things improve the more pessimistic we become. Violence-related deaths at the nation's schools dropped to a record low during the 1996–97 academic year (19 deaths out of 54 million children), and only one in ten public schools reported *any* serious crime. Yet *Time* and

U.S. News & World Report both ran headlines in 1996 referring to "Teenage Time Bombs." In a nation of "Children Without Souls" (another *Time* headline that year), "America's beleaguered cities are about to be victimized by a paradigm shattering wave of ultraviolent, morally vacuous young people some call 'the superpredators,'" William Bennett, the former Secretary of Education, and John DiIulio, a criminologist, forecast in a book published in 1996.[11]

Instead of the arrival of superpredators, violence by urban youths continued to decline. So we went looking elsewhere for proof that heinous behavior by young people was "becoming increasingly more commonplace in America" (CNN). After a sixteen-year-old in Pearl, Mississippi, and a fourteen-year-old in West Paducah, Kentucky, went on shooting sprees in late 1997, killing five of their classmates and wounding twelve others, these isolated incidents were taken as evidence of "an epidemic of seemingly depraved adolescent murderers" (Geraldo Rivera). Three months later in March 1998 all sense of proportion vanished after two boys ages eleven and thirteen killed four students and a teacher in Jonesboro, Arkansas. No longer, we learned in *Time,* was it "unusual for kids to get back at the world with live ammunition." When a child psychologist on NBC's "Today" show advised parents to reassure their children that shootings at schools are rare, reporter Ann Curry corrected him. "But this is the fourth case since October," she said.[12]

Over the next couple of months young people failed to accommodate the trend hawkers. None committed mass murder. Fear of killer kids remained very much in the air nonetheless. In stories on topics such as school safety and childhood trauma, reporters recapitulated the gory details of the killings. And the news media made a point of reporting every incident in which a child was caught at school with a gun or making a death threat. In May, when a fifteen-year-old in Springfield, Oregon, did open fire in a cafeteria filled with students, killing two and wounding twenty-three others, the event felt like a continuation of a "disturbing trend" (*New York Times*). The day after the shooting, on National Public Radio's "All Things Considered," the criminologist Vincent Schiraldi tried to explain that the recent string of incidents did not constitute a trend, that youth homicide rates had declined by 30 percent in recent years, and more than three times as many people were killed by lightning than by violence at schools. But the show's host, Robert Siegel, interrupted him. "You're saying these are just anomalous events?" he asked, audibly peeved. The criminologist reiterated that *anomalous* is precisely the right word to describe the events, and he called it "a grave mistake" to imagine otherwise.

Yet given what had happened in Mississippi, Kentucky, Arkansas, and Oregon, could anyone doubt that today's youths are "more likely to pull a gun than make a fist," as Katie Couric declared on the "Today" show?[13]

Roosevelt Was Wrong

We had better learn to doubt our inflated fears before they destroy us. Valid fears have their place; they cue us to danger. False and overdrawn fears only cause hardship.

Even concerns about real dangers, when blown out of proportion, do demonstrable harm. Take the fear of cancer. Many Americans overestimate the prevalence of the disease, underestimate the odds of surviving it, and put themselves at greater risk as a result. Women in their forties believe they have a 1 in 10 chance of dying from breast cancer, a Dartmouth study found. Their real lifetime odds are more like 1 in 250. Women's heightened perception of risk, rather than motivating them to get checkups or seek treatment, can have the opposite effect. A study of daughters of women with breast cancer found an inverse correlation between fear and prevention: the greater a daughter's fear of the disease the less frequent her breast self-examination. Studies of the general population—both men and women—find that large numbers of people who believe they have symptoms of cancer delay going to a doctor, often for several months. When asked why, they report they are terrified about the pain and financial ruin cancer can cause as well as poor prospects for a cure. The irony of course is that early treatment can prevent precisely those horrors they most fear.[14]

Still more ironic, if harder to measure, are the adverse consequences of public panics. Exaggerated perceptions of the risks of cancer at least produce beneficial by-products, such as bountiful funding for research and treatment of this leading cause of death. When it comes to large-scale panics, however, it is difficult to see how potential victims benefit from the frenzy. Did panics a few years ago over sexual assaults on children by preschool teachers and priests leave children better off? Or did they prompt teachers and clergy to maintain excessive distance from children in their care, as social scientists and journalists who have studied the panics suggest? How well can care givers do their jobs when regulatory agencies, teachers' unions, and archdioceses explicitly prohibit them from any physical contact with children, even kindhearted hugs?[15]

Was it a good thing for children and parents that male day care providers left the profession for fear of being falsely accused of sex crimes? In an article in the *Journal of American Culture*, sociologist Mary DeYoung has argued that day care was "refeminized" as a result of the panics. "Once again, and in the time-honored and very familiar tradition of the family, the primary responsibility for the care and socialization of young children was placed on the shoulders of low-paid women," she contends.[16]

We all pay one of the costs of panics: huge sums of money go to waste. Hysteria over the ritual abuse of children cost billions of dollars in police investigations, trials, and imprisonments. Men and women went to jail for years "on the basis of some of the most fantastic claims ever presented to an American jury," as Dorothy Rabinowitz of the *Wall Street Journal* demonstrated in a series of investigative articles for which she became a Pulitzer Prize finalist in 1996. Across the nation expensive surveillance programs were implemented to protect

children from fiends who reside primarily in the imaginations of adults.[17]

The price tag for our panic about overall crime has grown so monumental that even law-and-order zealots find it hard to defend. The criminal justice system costs Americans close to $100 billion a year, most of which goes to police and prisons. In California we spend more on jails than on higher education. Yet increases in the number of police and prison cells do not correlate consistently with reductions in the number of serious crimes committed. Criminologists who study reductions in homicide rates, for instance, find little difference between cities that substantially expand their police forces and prison capacity and others that do not.[18]

The turnabout in domestic public spending over the past quarter century, from child welfare and antipoverty programs to incarceration, did not even produce reductions in *fear* of crime. Increasing the number of cops and jails arguably has the opposite effect: it suggests that the crime problem is all the more out of control.[19]

Panic-driven public spending generates over the long term a pathology akin to one found in drug addicts. The more money and attention we fritter away on our compulsions, the less we have available for our real needs, which consequently grow larger. While fortunes are being spent to protect children from dangers that few ever encounter, approximately 11 million children lack health insurance, 12 million are malnourished, and rates of illiteracy are increasing.[20]

I do not contend, as did President Roosevelt in 1933, that "the only thing we have to fear is fear itself." My point is that we often fear the wrong things. In the 1990s middle-income and poorer Americans should have worried about unemployment insurance, which covered a smaller share of workers than twenty years earlier. Many of us have had friends or family out of work during economic downturns or as a result of corporate restructuring. Living in a nation with one of the largest income gaps of any industrialized country, where the bottom 40 percent of the population is worse off financially than their counterparts two decades earlier, we might also have worried about income inequality. Or poverty. During the mid- and late 1990s 5 million elderly Americans had no food in their homes, more than 20 million people used emergency food programs each year, and one in five children lived in poverty—more than a quarter million of them homeless. All told, a larger proportion of Americans were poor than three decades earlier.[21]

One of the paradoxes of a culture of fear is that serious problems remain widely ignored even though they give rise to precisely the dangers that the populace most abhors. Poverty, for example, correlates strongly with child abuse, crime, and drug abuse. Income inequality is also associated with adverse outcomes for society as a whole. The larger the gap between rich and poor in a society, the higher its overall death rates from heart disease, cancer, and murder. Some social scientists argue that extreme inequality also threatens political stability in a nation such as the United States, where we think of ourselves not as "haves and have nots" but as "haves and will haves." "Unlike the citizens of most other nations, Americans have always been united less by a shared past than by the shared dreams of a better future. If we lose that common future," the Brandeis University economist Robert Reich has suggested, "we lose the glue that holds our nation together."[22]. . .

Two Easy Explanations

In the following discussion I will try to answer two questions: Why are Americans so fearful lately, and why are our fears so often misplaced? To both questions the same two-word answer is commonly given. . . . [One] popular explanation blames the news media. We have so many fears, many of them off-base, the argument goes, because the media bombard us with sensationalistic stories designed to increase ratings. This explanation, sometimes called the media-effects theory . . . contains sizable kernels

of truth. When researchers from Emory University computed the levels of coverage of various health dangers in popular magazines and newspapers they discovered an inverse relationship: much less space was devoted to several of the major causes of death than to some uncommon causes. The leading cause of death, heart disease, received approximately the same amount of coverage as the eleventh-ranked cause of death, homicide. They found a similar inverse relationship in coverage of risk factors associated with serious illness and death. The lowest-ranking risk factor, drug use, received nearly as much attention as the second-ranked risk factor, diet and exercise.[23]

Disproportionate coverage in the news media plainly has effects on readers and viewers. When Esther Madriz, a professor at Hunter College, interviewed women in New York City about their fears of crime they frequently responded with the phrase "I saw it in the news." The interviewees identified the news media as both the source of their fears and the reason they believed those fears were valid. Asked in a national poll why they believe the country has a serious crime problem, 76 percent of people cited stories they had seen in the media. Only 22 percent cited personal experience.[24]

When professors Robert Blendon and John Young of Harvard analyzed forty-seven surveys about drug abuse conducted between 1978 and 1997, they too discovered that the news media, rather than personal experience, provide Americans with their predominant fears. Eight out of ten adults say that drug abuse has never caused problems in their family, and the vast majority report relatively little direct experience with problems related to drug abuse. Widespread concern about drug problems emanates, Blendon and Young determined, from scares in the news media, television in particular.[25]

Television news programs survive on scares. On local newscasts, where producers live by the dictum "if it bleeds, it leads," drug, crime, and disaster stories make up most of the news portion of the broadcasts. Evening newscasts on the major networks are somewhat less bloody, but between 1990 and 1998, when the nation's murder rate declined by 20 percent, the number of murder stories on network newscasts increased 600 percent (*not* counting stories about O.J. Simpson).[26]

After the dinnertime newscasts the networks broadcast newsmagazines, whose guiding principle seems to be that no danger is too small to magnify into a national nightmare. Some of the risks reported by such programs would be merely laughable were they not hyped with so much fanfare: "Don't miss *Dateline* tonight or YOU could be the next victim!" Competing for ratings with drama programs and movies during prime-time evening hours, newsmagazines feature story lines that would make a writer for "Homicide" or "ER" wince.[27]

"It can happen in a flash. Fire breaks out on the operating table. The patient is surrounded by flames," Barbara Walters exclaimed on ABC's "20/20" in 1998. The problem— oxygen from a face mask ignited by a surgical instrument— occurs "more often than you might think," she cautioned in her introduction, even though reporter Arnold Diaz would note later, during the actual report, that out of 27 million surgeries each year the situation arises only about a hundred times. No matter, Diaz effectively nullified the reassuring numbers as soon as they left his mouth. To those who "may say it's too small a risk to worry about" he presented distraught victims: a woman with permanent scars on her face and a man whose son had died.[28]

The gambit is common. Producers of TV newsmagazines routinely let emotional accounts trump objective information. In 1994 medical authorities attempted to cut short the brouhaha over flesh-eating bacteria by publicizing the fact that an American is fifty-five times more likely to be struck by lightning than die of the suddenly celebrated microbe. Yet TV journalists brushed this fact aside with remarks like, "whatever the statistics, it's devastating to the victims" (Catherine Crier on "20/20"), accompanied by stomach-turning videos of disfigured patients.[29]

Sheryl Stolberg, then a medical writer for the *Los Angeles Times,* put her finger on what makes the TV newsmagazines so cavalier: "Killer germs are perfect for prime time," she wrote. "They are invisible, uncontrollable, and, in the case of Group A strep, can invade the body in an unnervingly simple manner, through a cut or scrape." Whereas print journalists only described in words the actions of "billions of bacteria" spreading "like underground fires" throughout a person's body, TV newsmagazines made use of special effects to depict graphically how these "merciless killers" do their damage.[30]

In Praise of Journalists

Any analysis of the culture of fear that ignored the news media would be patently incomplete, and of the several institutions most culpable for creating and sustaining scares the news media are arguably first among equals. They are also the most promising candidates for positive change. Yet by the same token critiques such as Stolberg's presage a crucial shortcoming in arguments that blame the media. Reporters not only spread fears, they also debunk them and criticize one another for spooking the public. A wide array of groups, including businesses, advocacy organizations, religious sects, and political parties, promote and profit from scares. News organizations are distinguished from other fear-mongering groups because they sometimes bite the scare that feeds them.

A group that raises money for research into a particular disease is not likely to negate concerns about that disease. A company that sells alarm systems is not about to call attention to the fact that crime is down. News organizations, on the other hand, periodically allay the very fears they arouse to lure audiences. Some newspapers that ran stories about child murderers, rather than treat every incident as evidence of a shocking trend, affirmed the opposite. After the schoolyard shooting in Kentucky the *New York Times* ran a sidebar alongside its feature story with the headline

"Despite Recent Carnage, School Violence Is Not on Rise." Following the Jonesboro killings they ran a similar piece, this time on a recently released study showing the rarity of violent crimes in schools.[31]

Several major newspapers parted from the pack in other ways. *USA Today* and the *Washington Post,* for instance, made sure their readers knew that what should worry them is the availability of guns. *USA Today* ran news stories explaining that easy access to guns in homes accounted for increases in the number of juvenile arrests for homicide in rural areas during the 1990s. While other news outlets were respectfully quoting the mother of the thirteen-year-old Jonesboro shooter, who said she did not regret having encouraged her son to learn to fire a gun ("it's like anything else, there's some people that can drink a beer and not become an alcoholic"), *USA Today* ran an op-ed piece proposing legal parameters for gun ownership akin to those for the use of alcohol and motor vehicles. And the paper published its own editorial in support of laws that require gun owners to lock their guns or keep them in locked containers. Adopted at that time by only fifteen states, the laws had reduced the number of deaths among children in those states by 23 percent.[32]

The *Washington Post,* meanwhile, published an excellent investigative piece by reporter Sharon Walsh showing that guns increasingly were being marketed to teenagers and children. Quoting advertisements and statistics from gun manufacturers and the National Rifle Association, Walsh revealed that by 1998 the primary market for guns— white males—had been saturated and an effort to market to women had failed. Having come to see children as its future, the gun industry has taken to running ads like the one Walsh found in a Smith & Wesson catalog: "Seems like only yesterday that your father brought you here for the first time," reads the copy beside a photo of a child aiming a handgun, his father by his side. "Those sure were the good times—just you, dad and his Smith & Wesson."[33]

As a social scientist I am impressed and somewhat embarrassed to find that journalists, more often than media scholars, identify the jugglery involved in making small hazards appear huge and huge hazards disappear from sight. Take, for example, the scare several years ago over the Ebola virus. Another *Washington Post* reporter, John Schwartz, identified a key bit of hocus-pocus used to sell that scare. Schwartz called it "the Cuisinart Effect," because it involves the mashing together of images and story lines from fiction and reality. A report by *Dateline NBC* on death in Zaire, for instance, interspersed clips from *Outbreak,* a movie whose plot involves a lethal virus that threatens to kill the entire U.S. population. Alternating between Dustin Hoffman's character exclaiming, "We can't stop it!" and real-life science writer Laurie Garrett, author of *The Coming Plague,* proclaiming that "HIV is not an aberration . . . it's part of a trend," *Dateline's* report gave the impression that swarms of epidemics were on their way.[34]

Another great journalist-debunker, Malcolm Gladwell, noted that the book that had inspired *Outbreak,* Richard Preston's *The Hot Zone,* itself was written "in self-conscious imitation of a sci-fi thriller." In the real-world incident that occasioned *The Hot Zone,* monkeys infected in Zaire with a strain of Ebola virus were quarantined at a government facility in Reston, Virginia. The strain turned out not to be lethal in humans, but neither Preston in his book nor the screenwriters for *Outbreak* nor TV producers who sampled from the movie let that anticlimax interfere with the scare value of their stories. Preston speculates about an airborne strain of Ebola being carried by travelers from African airports to European, Asian, and American cities. In *Outbreak* hundreds of people die from such an airborne strain before a cure is miraculously discovered in the nick of time to save humanity. In truth, Gladwell points out in a piece in *The New Republic,* an Ebola strain that is both virulent to humans and airborne is unlikely to emerge and would mutate rapidly if it did, becoming far less potent before it had a chance to infect large numbers of people on a single continent, much less throughout the globe. "It is one of the ironies of the analysis of alarmists such as Preston that they are all too willing to point out the limitations of human beings, but they neglect to point out the limitations of microscopic life forms," Gladwell notes.[35]

Such disproofs of disease scares appear rather frequently in general-interest magazines and newspapers, including in publications where one might not expect to find them. The *Wall Street Journal,* for instance, while primarily a business publication and itself a retailer of fears about governmental regulators, labor unions, and other corporate-preferred hobgoblins, has done much to demolish medical myths. Among my personal favorites is an article published in 1996 titled "Fright by the Numbers," in which reporter Cynthia Crossen rebuts a cover story in *Time* magazine on prostate cancer. One in five men will get the disease, *Time* thundered. "That's scary. But it's also a lifetime risk—the accumulated risk over some 80 years of life," Crossen responds. A forty-year-old's chance of coming down with (not dying of) prostate cancer in the next ten years is 1 in 1,000, she goes on to report. His odds rise to 1 in 100 over twenty years. Even by the time he's seventy, he has only a 1 in 20 chance of *any* kind of cancer, including prostate.[36]

In the same article Crossen counters other alarmist claims as well, such as the much-repeated pronouncement that one in three Americans is obese. The number actually refers to how many are overweight, a less serious condition. Fewer are *obese* (a term that is less than objective itself), variously defined as 20 to 40 percent above ideal body weight as determined by current standards.[37]

Morality and Marketing

To blame the media is to oversimplify the complex role that journalists play as both proponents and doubters of popular fears. . . .Why do news organizations and their audiences find themselves drawn to one hazard rather than another?

Mary Douglas, the eminent anthropologist who devoted much of her career to studying how people interpret risk, pointed out that every society has an almost infinite quantity of potential dangers from which to choose. Societies differ both in the types of dangers they select and the number. Dangers get selected for special emphasis, Douglas showed, either because they offend the basic moral principles of the society or because they enable criticism of disliked groups and institutions. In *Risk and Culture,* a book she wrote with Aaron Wildavsky, the authors give an example from fourteenth-century Europe. Impure water had been a health danger long before that time, but only after it became convenient to accuse Jews of poisoning the wells did people become preoccupied with it.

Or take a more recent institutional example. In the first half of the 1990s U.S. cities spent at least $10 billion to purge asbestos from public schools, even though removing asbestos from buildings posed a greater health hazard than leaving it in place. At a time when about one-third of the nation's schools were in need of extensive repairs the money might have been spent to renovate dilapidated buildings. But hazards posed by seeping asbestos are morally repugnant. A product that was supposed to protect children from fires might be giving them cancer. By directing our worries and dollars at asbestos we express outrage at technology and industry run afoul.[38]

From a psychological point of view extreme fear and outrage are often projections. Consider, for example, the panic over violence against children. By failing to provide adequate education, nutrition, housing, parenting, medical services, and child care over the past couple of decades we have done the nation's children immense harm. Yet we project our guilt onto a cavalcade of bogeypeople—pedophile preschool teachers, preteen mass murderers, and homicidal au pairs, to name only a few.[39]

When Debbie Nathan, a journalist, and Michael Snedeker, an attorney, researched the evidence behind publicized reports in the 1980s and early 1990s of children being ritually raped and tortured they learned that although seven out of ten Americans believed that satanic cults were committing these atrocities, few of the incidents had actually occurred. At the outset of each ritual-abuse case the children involved claimed they had not been molested. They later changed their tunes at the urging of parents and law enforcement authorities. The ghastly tales of abuse, it turns out, typically came from the parents themselves, usually the mothers, who had convinced themselves they were true. Nathan and Snedeker suggest that some of the mothers had been abused themselves and projected those horrors, which they had trouble facing directly, onto their children. Other mothers, who had not been victimized in those ways, used the figure of ritually abused children as a medium of protest against male dominance more generally. Allegations of children being raped allowed conventional wives and mothers to speak out against men and masculinity without having to fear they would seem unfeminine. "The larger culture," Nathan and Snedeker note, "still required that women's complaints about inequality and sexual violence be communicated through the innocent, mortified voice of the child."

Diverse groups used the ritual-abuse scares to diverse ends. Well-known feminists such as Gloria Steinem and Catharine MacKinnon took up the cause, depicting ritually abused children as living proof of the ravages of patriarchy and the need for fundamental social reform.[40]

This was far from the only time feminist spokeswomen have mongered fears about sinister breeds of men who exist in nowhere near the high numbers they allege. Another example occurred a few years ago when teen pregnancy was much in the news. Feminists helped popularize the frightful but erroneous statistic that two out of three teen mothers had been seduced and abandoned by adult men. The true figure is more like one in ten, but some feminists continued to cultivate the scare well after the bogus stat had been definitively debunked.[41] . . .

Final Thoughts

The short answer to why Americans harbor so many misbegotten fears is that immense power and money await those who tap into our moral insecurities and supply us with symbolic substitutes . . . .

[Other tactics include] (1) Statements of alarm by newscasters; (2) glorification of wannabe experts are two telltale tricks of the fear mongers' trade; (3) the use of poignant anecdotes in place of scientific evidence; (4) the christening of isolated incidents as trends; and (5) depletions of entire categories of people as innately dangerous.

If journalists would curtail such practices, there would be fewer anxious and misinformed Americans. Ultimately, though, neither the ploys that narrators use nor what Cantril termed "the sheer dramatic excellence" of their presentations fully accounts for why people in 1938 swallowed a tall tale about martians taking over New Jersey or why people today buy into tales about perverts taking over cyberspace, unionizing employees taking over workplaces, heroin dealers taking over middle-class suburbs, and so forth.[42] . . .

Fear mongers have knocked the optimism out of us by stuffing us full of negative presumptions about our fellow citizens and social institutions. But the United States is a wealthy nation. We have the resources to feed, house, educate, insure, and disarm our communities if we resolve to do so.

There should be no mystery about where much of the money and labor can be found—in the culture of fear itself. We waste tens of billions of dollars and person-hours every year on largely mythical hazards like road rage, on prison cells occupied by people who pose little or no danger to others, on programs designed to protect young people from dangers that few of them ever face, on compensation for victims of metaphorical illnesses, and on technology to make airline travel—which is already safer than other means of transportation—safer still.

We can choose to redirect some of those funds to combat serious dangers that threaten large numbers of people. At election time we can choose candidates that proffer programs rather than scares.[43]

Or we can go on believing in martian invaders.

Notes

1. Crime data here and throughout are from reports of the Bureau of Justice Statistics unless otherwise noted. Fear of crime: Esther Madriz, *Nothing Bad Happens to Good Girls* (Berkeley: University of California Press, 1997), ch. 1; Richard Morin, "As Crime Rate Falls, Fears Persist," *Washington Post* National Edition, 16 June 1997, p. 35; David Whitman, "Believing the Good News," *U.S. News & World Report,* 5 January 1998, pp. 45–46.

2. Eva Bertram, Morris Blachman et al., *Drug War Politics* (Berkeley: University of California Press, 1996), p. 10; Mike Males, *Scapegoat Generation* (Monroe, ME: Common Courage Press, 1996), ch. 6; Karen Peterson, "Survey: Teen Drug Use Declines," *USA Today,* 19 June 1998, p. A6; Robert Blendon and John Young, "The Public and the War on Illicit Drugs," *Journal of the American Medical Association* 279 (18 March 1998): 827–32. In presenting these statistics and others I am aware of a seeming paradox: I criticize the abuse of statistics by fearmongering politicians, journalists, and others but hand down precise-sounding numbers myself. Yet to eschew all estimates because some are used inappropriately or do not withstand scrutiny would be as foolhardy as ignoring all medical advice because some doctors are quacks. Readers can be assured I have interrogated the statistics presented here as factual. As notes throughout the book make clear, I have tried to rely on research that appears in peer-reviewed scholarly journals. Where this was not possible or sufficient, I traced numbers back to their sources, investigated the research methodology utilized to produce them, or conducted searches of the popular and scientific literature for critical commentaries and conflicting findings.

3. Bob Herbert, "Bogeyman Economics," *New York Times,* 4 April 1997, p. A15; Doug Henwood, "Alarming Drop in Unemployment," *Extra,* September 1994, pp. 16–17; Christopher Shea, "Low Inflation and Low Unemployment Spur Economists to Debate 'Natural Rate' Theory," *Chronicle of Higher Education,* 24 October 1997, p. A13.

4. Bob Garfield, "Maladies by the Millions," *USA Today,* 16 December 1996, p. A15.

5. Jim Windolf, "A Nation of Nuts," *Wall Street Journal,* 22 October 1997, p. A22.

6. Andrew Ferguson, "Road Rage," *Time,* 12 January 1998, pp. 64–68; Joe Sharkey, "You're Not Bad, You're Sick. It's in the Book," *New York Times,* 28 September 1997, pp. Nl, 5.

7. Malcolm Dean, "Flesh-eating Bugs Scare," *Lancet* 343 (4 June 1994): 1418; "Flesh-eating Bacteria," *Science* 264 (17 June 1994): 1665; David Brown, "The Flesh-eating Bug," *Washington Post* National Edition, 19 December 1994, p. 34; Sarah Richardson, "Tabloid Strep," *Discover* (January 1995): 71; Liz Hunt, "What's Bugging Us," *The Independent,* 28 May 1994, p. 25; Lisa Seachrist, "The Once and Future Scourge," *Science News* 148 (7 October 1995): 234–35. Quotes are from Bernard Dixon, "A Rampant Non-epidemic," *British Medical Journal* 308 (11 June 1994): 1576–77; and Michael Lemonick and Leon Jaroff, "The Killers All Around," *Time,* 12 September 1994, pp. 62–69. More recent coverage: "Strep A Involved in Baby's Death," UPI, 27 February 1998; see also, e.g., Steve Carney, "Miracle Mom," *Los Angeles Times,* 4 March 1998, p. A6; KTLA, "News at Ten," 28 March 1998.

8. Jim Naureckas, "The Jihad That Wasn't," *Extra,* July 1995, pp. 6–10, 20 (contains quotes). See also Edward Said, "A Devil Theory of Islam," *Nation,* 12 August 1996, pp. 28–32.

9. Lewis Lapham, "Seen but Not Heard," *Harper's,* July 1995, pp. 29–36 (contains Clinton quote). See also Robin Wright and Ronald Ostrow, "Illusion of Immunity Is Shattered," *Los Angeles Times,* 20 April 1995, pp. Al, 18; Jack Germond and Jules Witcover, "Making the Angry White Males Angrier," column syndicated by Tribune Media Services, May 1995; and articles by James Bennet and Michael Janofsky in the *New York Times,* May 1995.

10. Tom Morganthau, "The Lull Before the Storm?" *Newsweek,* 4 December 1995, pp. 40–42; Mike Males, "Wild in Deceit," *Extra,* March 1996, pp. 7–9; *Progressive,* July 1997, p. 9 (contains Clinton quote); Robin Templeton, "First, We Kill All the 11-Year-Olds," *Salon,* 27 May 1998.

11. Statistics from "Violence and Discipline Problems in U.S. Public Schools: 1996–97," National Center on Education Statistics, U.S. Department of Education, Washington, DC, March 1998; CNN,

"Early Prime," 2 December 1997; and Tamar Lewin, "Despite Recent Carnage, School Violence Is Not on Rise," *New York Times,* 3 December 1997, p. A14. Headlines: *Time,* 15 January 1996; *U.S. News & World Report,* 25 March 1996; Margaret Carlson, "Children Without Souls," *Time,* 2 December 1996, p. 70. William J. Bennett, John J. Dilulio, and John Walters, *Body Count* (New York: Simon & Schuster, 1996).

12. CNN, "Talkback Live," 2 December 1997; CNN, "The Geraldo Rivera Show," 11 December 1997; Richard Lacayo, "Toward the Root of Evil," *Time,* 6 April 1998, pp. 38–39; NBC, "Today," 25 March 1998. See also Rick Bragg, "Forgiveness, After 3 Die in Shootings in Kentucky," *New York Times,* 3 December 1997, p. A14; Maureen Downey, "Kids and Violence," 28 March 1998, *Atlanta Journal and Constitution,* p. A12.

13. Jocelyn Stewart, "Schools Learn to Take Threats More Seriously," *Los Angeles Times,* 2 May 1998, pp. Al, 17; "Kindergarten Student Faces Gun Charges," *New York Times,* 11 May 1998, p. A11; Rick Bragg, "Jonesboro Dazed by Its Darkest Day" and "Past Victims Relive Pain as Tragedy Is Repeated," *New York Times,* 18 April 1998, p. A7, and idem, 25 May 1998, p. A8. Remaining quotes are from Tamar Lewin, "More Victims and Less Sense in Shootings," *New York Times,* 22 May 1998, p. A20; NPR, "All Things Considered," 22 May 1998; NBC, "Today," 25 March 1998. See also Mike Males, "Who's Really Killing Our Schoolkids," *Los Angeles Times,* 31 May 1998, pp. M1, 3; Michael Sniffen, "Youth Crime Fell in 1997, Reno Says," Associated Press, 20 November 1998.

14. Overestimation of breast cancer: William C. Black et al., "Perceptions of Breast Cancer Risk and Screening Effectiveness in Women Younger Than 50," *Journal of the National Cancer Institute* 87 (1995): 720–31; B. Smith et al., "Perception of Breast Cancer Risk Among Women in Breast and Family History of Breast Cancer," *Surgery* 120 (1996): 297–303. Fear and avoidance: Steven Berman and Abraham Wandersman, "Fear of Cancer and Knowledge of Cancer," *Social Science and Medicine* 31 (1990): 81–90; S. Benedict et al., "Breast Cancer Detection by Daughters of Women with Breast Cancer," *Cancer Practice* 5 (1997): 213–19; M. Muir et al., "Health Promotion and Early Detection of Cancer in Older Adults," *Cancer Oncology Nursing Journal 7* (1997): 82–89. For a conflicting finding see Kevin McCaul et al., "Breast Cancer Worry and Screening," *Health Psychology* 15 (1996): 430–33.

15. Philip Jenkins, *Pedophiles and Priests* (New York: Oxford University Press, 1996), see esp. ch. 10; Debbie Nathan and Michael Snedeker, *Satan's Silence* (New York: Basic Books, 1995), see esp. ch. 6; Jeffrey Victor, "The Danger of Moral Panics," *Skeptic* 3 (1995): 44–51. See also Noelle Oxenhandler, "The Eros of Parenthood," *Family Therapy Networker* (May 1996): 17–19.

16. Mary DeYoung, "The Devil Goes to Day Care," *Journal of American Culture* 20 (1997): 19–25.

17. Dorothy Rabinowitz, "A Darkness in Massachusetts," *Wall Street Journal,* 30 January 1995, p. A20 (contains quote); "Back in Wenatchee" (unsigned editorial), *Wall Street Journal,* 20 June 1996, p. A18; Dorothy Rabinowitz, "Justice in Massachusetts," *Wall Street Journal,* 13 May 1997, p. A19. See also Nathan and Snedeker, *Satan's Silence;* James Beaver, "The Myth of Repressed Memory," *Journal of Criminal Law and Criminology* 86 (1996): 596–607; Kathryn Lyon, *Witch Hunt* (New York: Avon, 1998); Pam Belluck, "'Memory' Therapy Leads to a Lawsuit and Big Settlement," *New York Times,* 6 November 1997, pp. A1, 10.

18. Elliott Currie, *Crime and Punishment in America* (New York: Metropolitan, 1998); Tony Pate et al., *Reducing Fear of Crime in Houston and Newark* (Washington, DC: Police Foundation, 1986); Steven Donziger, *The Real War on Crime* (New York: HarperCollins, 1996); Christina Johns, *Power, Ideology and the War on Drugs* (New York: Praeger, 1992); John Irwin et al., "Fanning the Flames of Fear," *Crime and Delinquency* 44 (1998): 32–48.

19. Steven Donziger, "Fear, Crime and Punishment in the U.S.," *Tikkun* 12 (1996): 24–27, 77.

20. Peter Budetti, "Health Insurance for Children," *New England Journal of Medicine* 338 (1998): 541–42; Eileen Smith, "Drugs Top Adult Fears for Kids' Well-being," *USA Today,* 9 December 1997, p. D1. Literacy statistic: Adult Literacy Service.

21. "The State of America's Children," report by the Children's Defense Fund, Washington, DC, March 1998; "Blocks to Their Future," report by the National Law Center on Homelessness and Poverty, Washington, DC, September 1997; reports released in 1998 from the National Center for Children in Poverty, Columbia University, New York; Douglas Massey, "The Age of Extremes," *Demography* 33 (1996): 395–412; Notes Trudy Lieberman, "Hunger in America," *Nation,* 30 March 1998, pp. 11–16; David Lynch, "Rich Poor World," *USA Today,* 20 September 1996, p. B1; Richard Wolf, "Good

Economy Hasn't Helped the Poor," *USA Today,* 10 March 1998, p. A3; Robert Reich, "Broken Faith," *Nation,* 16 February 1998, pp. 11–17.

22. Inequality and mortality studies: Bruce Kennedy et al., "Income Distribution and Mortality," *British Medical Journal* 312 (1996): 1004–7; Ichiro Kawachi and Bruce Kennedy, "The Relationship of Income Inequality to Mortality," *Social Science and Medicine* 45 (1997): 1121–27. See also Barbara Chasin, *Inequality and Violence in the United States* (Atlantic Highlands, NJ: Humanities Press, 1997). Political stability: John Sloan, "The Reagan Presidency, Growing Inequality, and the American Dream," *Policy Studies Journal* 25 (1997): 371–86 (contains Reich quotes and "will haves" phrase). On both topics see also Philippe Bourgois, *In Search of Respect: Selling Crack in El Barrio* (Cambridge: Cambridge University Press, 1996); William J. Wilson, *When Work Disappears* (New York, Knopf, 1996); Richard Gelles, "Family Violence," *Annual Review of Sociology* 11 (1985): 347–67; Sheldon Danziger and Peter Gottschalk, *America Unequal* (Cambridge, MA: Harvard University Press, 1995); Claude Fischer et al., *Inequality by Design* (Princeton, NJ: Princeton University Press, 1996).

23. Karen Frost, Erica Frank et al., "Relative Risk in the News Media," *American Journal of Public Health* 87 (1997): 842–45. Media-effects theory: Nancy Signorielli and Michael Morgan, eds., *Cultivation Analysis* (Newbury Park, CA: Sage, 1990); Jennings Bryant and Dolf Zillman, eds., *Media Effects* (Hillsdale, NJ: Erlbaum, 1994); Ronald Jacobs, "Producing the News, Producing the Crisis," *Media, Culture and Society* 18 (1996): 373–97.

24. Madriz, *Nothing Bad Happens to Good Girls,* see esp. pp. 111–14; David Whitman and Margaret Loftus, "Things Are Getting Better? Who Knew," *U.S. News & World Report,* 16 December 1996, pp. 30–32.

25. Blendon and Young, "War on Illicit Drugs." See also Ted Chiricos et al., "Crime, News and Fear of Crime," *Social Problems* 44 (1997): 342–57.

26. Steven Stark, "Local News: The Biggest Scandal on TV," *Washington Monthly* (June 1997): 38–41; Barbara Bliss Osborn, "If It Bleeds, It Leads," *Extra,* September–October 1994, p. 15; Jenkins, *Pedophiles and Priests,* pp. 68–71; "It's Murder," *USA Today,* 20 April 1998, p. D2; Lawrence Grossman, "Does Local TV News Need a National Nanny?" *Columbia Journalism Review* (May 1998): 33.

27. Regarding fearmongering by newsmagazines, see also Elizabeth Jensen et al., "Consumer Alert," *Brill's Content* (October 1998): 130–47.

28. ABC, "20/20," 16 March 1998.

29. Thomas Maugh, "Killer Bacteria a Rarity," *Los Angeles Times,* 3 December 1994, p. A29; Ed Siegel, "Roll Over, Ed Murrow," *Boston Globe,* 21 August 1994, p. 14. Crier quote from ABC's "20/20," 24 June 1994.

30. Sheryl Stolberg, "'Killer Bug' Perfect for Prime Time," *Los Angeles Times,* 15 June 1994, pp. A1, 30–31. Quotes from Brown, "Flesh-eating Bug"; and Michael Lemonick and Leon Jaroff, "The Killers All Around," *Time,* 12 September 1994, pp. 62–69.

31. Lewin, "More Victims and Less Sense"; Tamar Lewin, "Study Finds No Big Rise in Public-School Crimes," *New York Times,* 25 March 1998, p. A18.

32. "Licensing Can Protect," *USA Today, 7* April 1998, p. A11; Jonathan Kellerman, "Few Surprises When It Comes to Violence," *USA Today,* 27 March 1998, p. A13; Gary Fields, "Juvenile Homicide Arrest Rate on Rise in Rural USA," *USA Today,* 26 March 1998, p. A11; Karen Peterson and Glenn O'Neal, "Society More Violent, So Are Its Children," *USA Today, 25* March 1998, p. A3; Scott Bowles, "Armed, Alienated and Adolescent," *USA Today,* 26 March 1998, p. A9. Similar suggestions about guns appear in Jonathan Alter, "Harnessing the Hysteria," *Newsweek,* 6 April 1998, p. 27.

33. Sharon Walsh, "Gun Sellers Look to Future—Children," *Washington Post,* 28 March 1998, pp. A1, 2.

34. John Schwartz, "An Outbreak of Medical Myths," *Washington Post* National Edition, 22 May 1995, p. 38.

35. Richard Preston, *The Hot Zone* (New York: Random House, 1994); Malcolm Gladwell, "The Plague Year," *New Republic,* 17 July 1995, p. 40.

36. Erik Larson, "A False Crisis: How Workplace Violence Became a Hot Issue," *Wall Street Journal,* 13 October 1994, pp. A1, 8; Cynthia Crossen, "Fright By the Numbers," *Wall Street Journal,* 11 April 1996, pp. B1, 8. See also G. Pascal Zachary, "Junk History," *Wall Street Journal,* 19 September 1997, pp. A1, 6.

37. On variable definitions of obesity see also Werner Cahnman, "The Stigma of Obesity," *Sociological Quarterly* 9 (1968): 283–99; Susan Bordo, *Unbearable Weight* (Berkeley: University of California Press, 1993); Joan Chrisler, "Politics and Women's Weight," *Feminism and Psychology* 6 (1996): 181–84.

38. Mary Douglas and Aaron Wildavsky, *Risk and Culture* (Berkeley: University of California Press, 1982), see esp. pp. 6–9; Mary Douglas, *Risk and Blame* (London: Routledge, 1992). See also Mary Douglas, *Purity and Danger* (New York: Praeger, 1966). Asbestos and schools: Peter Cary, "The Asbestos Panic Attack," *U.S. News & World Report,* 20 February 1995, pp. 61–64; Children's Defense Fund, "State of America's Children."

39. See Marina Warner, "Peroxide Mugshot," *London Review of Books,* 1 January 1998, pp. 10–11.

40. Nathan and Snedeker, *Satan's Silence* (quote from p. 240). See also David Bromley, "Satanism: The New Cult Scare," in James Richardson et al., eds., *The Satanism Scare* (Hawthorne, NY: Aldine de Gruyter, 1991), pp. 49–71.

41. Of girls ages fifteen to seventeen who gave birth, fewer than one in ten were unmarried and had been made pregnant by men at least five years older. See Steven Holmes, "It's Awful, It's Terrible, It's . . . Never Mind," *New York Times,* 6 July 1997, p. E3.

42. CNN, "Crossfire," 27 August 1995 (contains Huffington quote); Ruth Conniff, "Warning: Feminism Is Hazardous to Your Health," *Progressive,* April 1997, pp. 33–36 (contains Sommers quote). See also Susan Faludi, *Backlash* (New York: Crown, 1991); Deborah Rhode, "Media Images, Feminist Issues," *Signs* 20 (1995): 685–710; Paula Span, "Did Feminists Forget the Most Crucial Issues?" *Los Angeles Times,* 28 November 1996, p. E8.

43. See Katha Pollitt, "Subject to Debate," *Nation,* 26 December 1994, p. 788, and idem, 20 November 1995, p. 600.

THINKING ABOUT THE READING

Glassner originally wrote this piece over a decade ago. What are some contemporary examples of cultural fears that he might include if he were writing this today? How do you determine if the fear is a cultural myth or something that should be taken seriously as a social problem? According to Glassner, how are these cultural myths created, and why are we so inclined to believe in them? Do you think a culture less organized by the medium of television would be more or less likely to support such myths?

The (Mis)education of Monica and Karen

Laura Hamilton and Elizabeth A. Armstrong

(2012)

Monica grew up in a small, struggling Midwestern community, population 3,000, that was once a booming factory town. She was from a working-class family, and paid for most of her education at Midwest U, a "moderately selective" residential university, herself. She worked two jobs, sometimes over 40 hours a week, to afford in-state tuition. Going out-of-state, or to a pricey private school, was simply out of the question without a large scholarship. Attending MU was even a stretch; one year there cost as much as four years at the regional campus near her hometown.

Karen grew up in the same small town as Monica, but in a solidly middle-class family. Her college-educated parents could afford to provide more financial assistance. But even though MU was only three hours away, her father "wasn't too thrilled" about her going so far from home. He had attended a small religious school that was only 10 minutes away.

Neither Karen nor Monica was academically well prepared for college. Both had good, but not stellar, grades and passable SAT scores, which made admission to a more selective school unlikely. Given the lower cost, ease of admission, and opportunity to commute from home, they might have started at the regional campus. However, MU offered, as Monica's mother put it, a chance to "go away and experience college life." Karen refused to look at any other school because she wanted to leave home. As she noted, "I really don't think I'm a small town girl." Monica's family was betting on MU as the best place for her to launch her dream career as a doctor.

Karen and Monica's stories offer us a glimpse into the college experiences of average, in-state students at large, mid-tier public universities.

Though they struggled to gain entrance to the flagship campus, they soon found that the structure of social and academic life there served them poorly—and had deleterious effects.

The Great Mismatch

Most four-year residential colleges and universities in the United States are designed to serve well-funded students, who have minimal (if any) caretaking responsibilities, and who attend college full-time after they graduate from high school. Yet only a minority of individuals who pursue postsecondary education in the United States fit this profile. There is a great gap between what the vast majority of Americans need and what four-year institutions offer them.

This mismatch is acutely visible at Midwest U, where Karen and Monica started their college careers. Almost half of those attending four-year colleges find themselves at schools like this one. Students from modest backgrounds who have above average, but not exceptional, academic profiles attend state flagship universities because they believe such schools offer a surefire route to economic security.

Public universities were founded to enable mobility, especially among in-state populations of students—which contributes to their legitimacy in the eyes of the public. In an era of declining state funding, schools like Midwest U have raised tuition and recruited more out-of-state students. They especially covet academically accomplished, ambitious children of affluent families.

As sociologist Mitchell Stevens describes in *Creating a Class,* elite institutions also pursue such students. While observing a small, private school, Stevens overhead an admissions officer describe an ideal applicant: "He's got great SATs [and] he's free [not requiring any financial aid] . . . . He helps us in every way that's quantifiable." Once private colleges skim off affluent, high-performing students, large, middle-tier, public universities are left to compete for the tuition dollars of less studious students from wealthy families.

How, we wondered, do in-state students fare in this context? To find out, for over five years we followed a dormitory floor of female students through their college careers and into the workforce, conducted an ethnography of the floor, and interviewed the women and their parents. What we found is that schools like MU only serve a segment of their student body well—affluent, socially-oriented, and out-of-state students—to the detriment of typical in-state students like Karen and Monica.

"I'm Supposed to Get Drunk"

Monica and Karen approached the housing application process with little information, and were unprepared for what they encountered when they were assigned to a room in a "party dorm." At MU, over a third of the freshman class is housed in such dorms. Though minimal partying took actually place in the heavily policed residence halls, many residents partied off-site, typically at fraternities, returning in the wee hours drunk and loud. Affluent students—both in and out-of-state—often requested rooms in party dorms, based on the recommendations of their similarly social siblings and friends.

Party dorms are a pipeline to the Greek system, which dominates campus life. Less than 20 percent of the student body at MU is involved in a fraternity or sorority, but these predominately white organizations enjoy a great deal of power. They own space in central campus areas, across from academic buildings and sports arenas. They monopolize the social life of first-year students, offering underage

drinkers massive, free supplies of alcohol, with virtual legal impunity. They even enjoy special ties to administrators, with officers sitting on a special advisory board to the dean of students.

Over 40 percent of Monica and Karen's floor joined sororities their first year. The pressure to rush was so intense that one roommate pair who opted out posted a disclaimer on their door, asking people to stop bugging them about it. The entire campus—including academic functions—often revolved around the schedule of Greek life. When a math test for a large, required class conflicted with women's rush, rather than excusing a group of women from a few rush events, the test itself was rescheduled.

Monica, like most economically disadvantaged students, chose not to rush a sorority, discouraged by the mandatory $60 t-shirt, as well as by the costly membership fees. Karen, who was middle class, had just enough funds to make rushing possible. However, she came to realize that Greek houses implicitly screened for social class. She pulled out her boots—practical rain boots that pegged her as a small town, in-state girl instead of an affluent, out-of-state student with money and the right taste in clothing. They were a "dead give-away," she said. She soon dropped out of rush.

Like all but a few students on the 53-person floor, Monica and Karen chose to participate in the party scene. Neither drank much in high school. Nor did they arrive armed with shot glasses or party-themed posters, as some students did. They partied because, as a woman from a similar background put it, "I'm supposed to get drunk every weekend. I'm supposed to go to parties every weekend." With little party experience, and few contacts in the Greek system, Monica and Karen were easy targets for fraternity men's sexual disrespect. Heavy alcohol consumption helped to put them at ease in otherwise uncomfortable situations. "I pretty much became an alcoholic," said Monica. "I was craving alcohol all the time."

Their forced attempts to participate in the party scene showed how poorly it suited their needs. "I tried so hard to fit in with what everybody else was doing here," Monica explained.

"I think one morning I just woke up and realized that this isn't me at all; I don't like the way I am right now." She felt it forced her to become more immature. "Growing up to me isn't going out and getting smashed and sleeping around," she lamented. Partying is particularly costly for students of lesser means, who need to grow up sooner, cannot afford to be financially irresponsible, and need the credentials and skills that college offers.

Academic Struggles and "Exotic" Majors

Partying also takes its toll on academic performance, and Monica's poor grades quickly squelched her pre-med dreams. Karen, who hoped to become a teacher, also found it hard to keep up. "I did really bad in that math class, the first elementary ed math class," one of three that were required. Rather than retake the class, Karen changed her major to one that was popular among affluent, socially oriented students on the floor: sports broadcasting.

She explained, "I'm from a really small town and it's just all I ever really knew was jobs that were around me, and most of those are teachers." A woman on her floor was majoring in sports broadcasting, which she had never considered. "I would have never thought about that. And so I saw hers, and I was like that's something that I really like. One of my interests is sports, watching them, playing them," she reasoned. "I could be a sportscaster on ESPN if I really wanted to."

Karen's experience shows the seductive appeal of certain "easy majors." These are occupational and professional programs that are often housed in their own schools and colleges. They are associated with a higher overall GPA and, as sociologists Richard Arum and Josipa Roksa report in *Academically Adrift*, lower levels of learning than majors in the more challenging sciences and humanities housed in colleges of arts and sciences.

In many easy majors, career success also depends on personal characteristics (such as appearance, personality, and aesthetic taste) that are developed outside of the classroom—often prior to entering college. Socially oriented students flock to fields like communications, fashion, tourism, recreation, fitness, and numerous "business-lite" options, which are often linked to sports or the arts, rather than the competitive business school. About a third of the student body majored in business, management, marketing, communications, journalism, and related subfields.

Karen's switch to sports broadcasting gave her more time to socialize. But education is a more practical major that translates directly into a career; hiring rests largely on the credential. In contrast, success in sports broadcasting is dependent on class-based characteristics—such as family social ties to industry insiders. Several of Karen's wealthier peers secured plum internships in big cities because their parents made phone calls for them; Karen could not even land an unpaid internship with the Triple-A baseball team located 25 minutes from her house.

No one Karen encountered on campus helped her to assess the practicality of a career in this field. Her parents were frustrated that she had been persuaded not to graduate with a recognizable marketable skill. As her mother explained, "She gets down there and you start hearing all these exotic sounding majors, which half I'm not sure quite what jobs they're going to end up with. Her mother was frustrated that Karen "went to see the advisor to make plans for her sophomore year, and they're going, 'Well, what's your passion?'" Her mother was not impressed. "How many people do their passion? To me, that's more what you do for a hobby . . . . I mean most people, that's not what their job is."

Halfway through college, when Karen realized she could not get an internship, much less a job, in sports broadcasting, her parents told her to switch back to education. The switch was costly: it was going to take her two more years to complete. As her mother complained, "When you're going through the orientation . . . they're going, 'oh, most people change their major five times.' And they make it sound like it's no big deal. But yeah, they're making big bucks by kids changing."

Leaving Midwest U Behind

Monica left MU after her first year. "I was afraid if I continued down there that I would just go crazy and either not finish school, or get myself in trouble," she explained. "And I just didn't want to do that." She immediately enrolled in a beauty school near her home. Dissatisfied with the income she earned as a hairstylist, she later entered a community college to complete an associate degree in nursing. She paid for her nursing classes as she studied, but had 10,000 dollars in student loan debt from her time at MU. Still, her debt burden was substantially smaller than if she had stayed there; some of her MU peers had amassed over 50,000 dollars in loans by graduation.

Because her GPA was too low to return to elementary education at MU, Karen transferred to a regional college during her fourth year. Since the classes she took for sports broadcasting did not fulfill any requirements, it took her six years to graduate. Karen's parents, who reported that they spent the first 10 years of their married life paying off their own loans, took out loans to cover most of the cost, and anticipated spending even longer to finance their daughter's education.

Monica and Karen were not the only ones on their dormitory floor to leave MU. Nine other in-state women, the majority of whom were from working-class backgrounds, did as well. The only out-of-state student who transferred left for a higher-ranked institution. While we were concerned that the in-state leavers, most of whom were moving down the ladder of prestige to regional campuses, would suffer, they actually did better than in-state women from less privileged families who stayed at MU. Their GPAs improved, they selected majors with a more direct payoff, and they were happier overall.

The institutions to which women moved played a large role in this transformation. As one leaver described the regional campus to which she transferred, it "doesn't have any fraternities or sororities. It only has, like, 10 buildings." But, she said, "I just really love it." One of the things she loved was that nobody cared about partying. "They're there just to graduate and get through." It prioritized the needs of a different type of student: "Kids who have lower social economic status, who work for their school."

Without the social pressures of MU, it was possible to, as Karen put it, "get away from going out all the time, and refocus on what my goal was for this part of my life." Few majors like sports broadcasting and fashion merchandising were available, reducing the possible ways to go astray academically. Those who attended regional or community colleges trained to become accountants, teachers, social workers, nurses or other health professionals. At the conclusion of our study, they had better employment prospects than those from similar backgrounds who stayed at MU.

The Importance of Institutional Context

It is tempting to assume that academic success is determined, in large part, by what students bring with them—different ability levels, resources, and orientations to college life. But Monica and Karen's stories demonstrate that what students get out of college is also organizationally produced. Students who were far more academically gifted than Monica or Karen sometimes floundered at MU, while others who were considerably less motivated breezed through college. The best predictor of success was whether there was a good fit between a given student's resources and agendas, and the structure of the university.

Monica and Karen's struggles at MU can be attributed, in part, to the dominance of a "party pathway" at that institution. These organizational arrangements—a robust, university-supported Greek system, and an array of easy majors—are designed to attract and serve affluent, socially oriented students. The party pathway is not a hard sell; the idea that college is about fun and partying is celebrated in popular culture and actively promoted by leisure and alcohol industries. The problem is that this pathway often appeals to students for whom it is ill suited.

Regardless of what they might want, students from different class backgrounds require different things. What Monica and Karen needed was a "mobility pathway." When resources are limited, mistakes—whether a semester of grades lost to partying, or courses that do not count toward a credential—can be very costly. Monica and Karen needed every course to move them toward a degree that would translate directly into a job.

They also needed more financial aid than they received—grants, not loans—and much better advising. A skilled advisor who understood Karen's background and her abilities might have helped her realize that changing majors was a bad idea. But while most public universities provide such advising support for disadvantaged students, these programs are often small, and admit only the best and brightest of the disadvantaged—not run-of-the-mill students like Monica and Karen.

Monica, Karen (and others like them) did not find a mobility pathway at MU. Since university resources are finite, catering to one population of students often comes at a cost to others, especially if their needs are at odds with one another. When a party pathway is the most accessible avenue through a university, it is easy to stumble upon, hard to avoid, and it crowds out other pathways.

As Monica and Karen's stories suggest, students are not necessarily better served by attending the most selective college they can get into. The structure of the pathways available at a given school greatly influences success. When selecting a college or university, families should consider much more than institutional selectivity. They should also assess whether the school fits the particular student's needs.

Students and parents with limited financial resources should look for schools with high retention rates among minority and first-generation students, where there are large and accessible student services for these populations. Visible Greek systems and reputations as party schools, in contrast, should be red flags.

Families should investigate what majors are available, whether they require prerequisites, and, to the extent it is possible, what additional investments are required to translate a particular major into a job. Are internships required? Will the school link the student to job opportunities, or are families expected to do so on their own? These are some questions they should ask.

Collectively, the priorities of public universities and other higher education institutions that support "party pathways" should be challenged. Reducing the number of easy majors, pulling university support from the Greek system, and expanding academic advising for less privileged students would help. At federal and state levels, greater commitment to the funding of higher education is necessary. If public universities are forced to rely on tuition and donations for funding, they will continue to appeal to those who can pay full freight. Without these changes, the mismatch between what universities offer and what most postsecondary students need is likely to continue.

THINKING ABOUT THE READING

Institutions of higher education provide opportunities to achieve social mobility. Ironically, according to Hamilton and Armstrong, universities like MU seem to do quite the opposite, in some cases. Indeed, the authors suggest that institutions like MU are structured to serve one specific population of students. What is that population? Using your sociological imagination, what organizational structures at MU shaped the decisions of students and their opportunity for academic achievement and success following graduation? What would the organizational structures look like that could have helped Monica and Karen achieve success? Furthermore, what social forces beyond the university impacted the structures of MU and the experiences of all students on campus? How, if at all, do you see some of the themes in this article reflected in your institution and campus life?

PART II

The Construction of Self and Society

Building Reality

The Social Construction of Knowledge

3

Sociologists often talk about reality as a social construction. What they mean is that truth and knowledge are discovered, communicated, reinforced, and changed by members of society. Truth doesn't just fall from the sky and hit us on the head. What is considered truth or knowledge is specific to a given culture. All cultures have specific rules for determining what counts as good and right and true. As social beings, we respond to our interpretations and definitions of situations, not to the situations themselves. We learn from our cultural environment what sorts of ideas and interpretations are reasonable and expected. Thus, we make sense of situations and events in our lives by applying culturally shared definitions and interpretations. In this way, we distinguish fact from fantasy, truth from fiction, myth from reality. This process of interpretation or "meaning making" is tied to interpersonal interaction, group membership, culture, history, power, economics, and politics.

Discovering patterns and determining useful knowledge are the goals of any academic discipline. The purpose of an academic field such as sociology is to provide the public with useful and relevant information about how society works. This task is typically accomplished through systematic social research—experiments, field research, unobtrusive observation, and surveys. But gathering trustworthy data can be difficult. People sometimes lie or have difficulty recalling past events in their lives. Sometimes the simple fact of observing people's behavior changes that behavior. Sometimes the information needed to answer questions about important, controversial issues is hard to obtain without raising ethical issues.

Moreover, sometimes the characteristics and phenomena we're interested in understanding are difficult to observe and measure. Unlike other disciplines in, say, the natural sciences, sociologists deal with concepts that can't be seen or touched. In "Concepts, Indicators, and Reality," Earl Babbie gives us a brief introduction to some of the problems researchers face when they try to transform important but abstract concepts into *indicators* (things that researchers can systematically quantify so they can generate statistical information). In so doing, he shows us that although sociologists provide us with useful empirical findings about the world in which we live, an understanding of the measurement difficulties they face will provide us with the critical eye of an informed consumer as we go about digesting research information.

In a similar vein, in "Measuring Same-Sex Relationships," Nancy Bates and Theresa J. DeMaio show us that as society changes and becomes more diverse, this has a profound impact on how accurately our government measures the population. Valid and reliable data have important implications on the resources and rights of same-sex couples. The authors' use of "think aloud" interviews in focus groups helps them to better understand how same-gender couples view their relationships, and how the U.S. Census could revise its marital status and relationship questions to more accurately capture this demographic group in the U.S. population. This article demonstrates the importance of careful and methodical social research on groups in our society in order to understand their experiences and needs.

Something to Consider as You Read

Babbie's comments remind us that even scientists must make decisions about how to interpret information. Thus, scientists, working within academic communities, define truth and knowledge in their measures and interpretations. This knowledge is often significant and useful, but we need to remember that it is the construction of a group of people following particular rules, not something that is just "out there." As you read these selections, think about the kind of information you would need or would want that might convince you to question some truth that you have always taken for granted. Also, consider the way these readings show how knowledge from official sources, such as reputable news organizations or government, can heavily influence social understanding.

Concepts, Indicators, and Reality

Earl Babbie

(1986)

Measurement is one of the fundamental aspects of social research. When we describe science as logical/empirical, we mean that scientific conclusions should (1) make sense and (2) correspond to what we can observe. It is the second of these characteristics I want to explore in this essay.

Suppose we are interested in learning whether education really reduces prejudice. To do that, we must be able to measure both prejudice and education. Once we've distinguished prejudiced people from unprejudiced people and educated people from uneducated people, we'll be in a position to find out whether the two variables are related.

Social scientific measurement operates in accordance with the following implicit model:

- Prejudice exists as a *variable*: some people are more prejudiced than others.
- There are numerous *indicators* of prejudice.
- None of the indicators provides a perfect reflection of prejudice as it "really" is, but they can point to it at least approximately.
- We should try to find better and better indicators of prejudice—indicators that come ever closer to the "real thing."

This model applies to all of the variables social scientists study. Take a minute to look through the following list of variables commonly examined in social research.

Arms race	Tolerance
Religiosity	Fascism
Urbanism	Parochialism
TV watching	Maturity
Susceptibility	Solidarity
Stereotyping	Instability
Anti-Semitism	Education
Voting	Liberalism
Dissonance	Authoritarianism
Pessimism	Race
Anxiety	Happiness
Revolution	Powerlessness
Alienation	Mobility
Social class	Consistency
Age	Delinquency
Self-esteem	Compassion
Idealism	Democracy
Prestige	Influence

Even if you've never taken a course in social science, many of these terms are at least somewhat familiar to you. Social scientists study things that are of general interest to everyone. The nuclear arms race affects us all, for example, and it is a special concern for many of us. Differences in *religiosity* (some of us are more religious than others) are also of special interest to some people. As our country has evolved from small towns to large cities, we've all thought and talked more about *urbanism*—the good and bad associated with city life. Similar interests can be identified for all of the other terms.

My point is that you've probably thought about many of the variables mentioned in the list. Those you are familiar with undoubtedly have the quality of reality for you: that is, you know they exist. Religiosity, for example, is real. Regardless of whether you're in favor of it, opposed to it, or don't care much one way or the other, you at least know that religiosity exists. Or does it?

This is a particularly interesting question for me, since my first book, *To Comfort and to Challenge* (with Charles Glock and Benjamin Ringer), was about this subject. In particular, we wanted to know why some people were more religious than others (the sources of religiosity) and what impact differences in religiosity had on other aspects of life (the consequences of religiosity). Looking for the sources and consequences of a particular variable is a conventional social scientific undertaking; the first step is to develop a measure of that variable. We had to develop methods for distinguishing religious people, nonreligious people, and those somewhere in between.

The question we faced was, if religiosity is real, how do we know that? How do we distinguish religious people from nonreligious people? For most contemporary Americans, a number of answers come readily to mind. Religious people go to church, for example. They believe in the tenets of their faith. They pray. They read religious materials, such as the Bible, and they participate in religious organizations.

Not all religious people do all of these things, of course, and a great deal depends on their particular religious affiliation, if any. Christians believe in the divinity of Jesus; Jews do not. Moslems believe Mohammed's teachings are sacred; Jews and Christians do not. Some signs of religiosity are to be found in seemingly secular realms. Orthodox Jews, for example, refrain from eating pork; Seventh-Day Adventists don't drink alcohol.

In our study, we were interested in religiosity among a very specific group: Episcopal church members in America. To simplify our present discussion, let's look at that much narrower question: How can you distinguish religious from nonreligious Episcopalians in America?

As I've indicated above, we are likely to say that religious people attend church, whereas nonreligious people do not. Thus, if we know someone who attends church every week,

we're likely to think of that person as religious; indeed, religious people joke about church members who only attend services on Easter and at Christmas. The latter are presumed to be less religious.

Of course, we are speaking rather casually here, so let's see whether church attendance would be an adequate measure of religiosity for Episcopalians and other mainstream American Christians. Would you be willing to equate religiosity with church attendance? That is, would you be willing to call religious everyone who attended church every week, let's say, and call nonreligious everyone who did not?

I suspect that you would not consider equating church attendance with religiosity a wise policy. For example, consider a political figure who attends church every Sunday, sits in the front pew, puts a large contribution in the collection plate with a flourish, and by all other evidence seems only interested in being known as a religious person for the political advantage that may entail. Let's add that the politician in question regularly lies and cheats, exhibits no Christian compassion toward others, and ridicules religion in private. You'd probably consider it inappropriate to classify that person as religious.

Now imagine someone confined to a hospital bed, who spends every waking minute reading in the Bible, leading other patients in prayer, raising money for missionary work abroad—but never going to church. Probably this would fit your image of a religious person.

These deviant cases illustrate that, while church attendance is somehow related to religiosity, it is not a sufficient indicator in and of itself. So how can we distinguish religious from nonreligious people?

Prayer is a possibility. Presumably, people who pray a lot are more religious than those who don't. But wouldn't it matter what they prayed for? Suppose they were only praying for money. How about the Moslem extremist praying daily for the extermination of the Jews? How about the athlete praying for an opponent to be hit by a truck? Like church attendance, prayer seems to have something to do with religiosity, but we can't simply equate the two.

We might consider religious beliefs. Among Christians, for example, it would seem to make sense that a person who believes in God is more religious than one who does not. However, this would require that we consider the person who says, "I'll believe anything they say just as long as I don't rot in Hell" more religious than, say, a concerned theologian who completes a lifetime of concentrated and devoted study of humbly concluding that who or what God is cannot be known with certainty. We'd probably decide that this was a misclassification.

Without attempting to exhaust all the possible indicators of religiosity, I hope it's clear that we would never find a single measure that will satisfy us as tapping the real essence of religiosity. In recognition of this, social researchers use a combination of indicators to create a *composite measure*—an index or a scale—of variables such as religiosity. Such a measure might include all of the indicators discussed so far: church attendance, prayer, and beliefs.

While composite measures are usually a good idea, they do not really solve the dilemma I've laid out. With a little thought, we could certainly imagine circumstances in which a "truly" religious person nonetheless didn't attend church, pray, or believe, and we could likewise imagine a nonreligious person who did all of those things. In either event, we would have demonstrated the imperfection of the composite measure.

Recognition of this often leads people to conclude that variables like religiosity are simply beyond empirical measurement. This conclusion is true and false and even worse.

The conclusion is false in that we can make any measurement we want. For example, we can ask people if they attend church regularly and call that a measure of religiosity just as easily as Yankee Doodle called the feather in his hat macaroni. In our case, moreover, most people would say that what we've measured is by no means irrelevant to religiosity.

The conclusion is true in that no empirical measurement—single or composite—will satisfy all of us as having captured the essence

of religiousness. Since that can never happen, we can never satisfactorily measure religiosity.

The situation is worse than either of these comments suggests in that the reason we can't measure religiosity is that it doesn't exist! Religiosity isn't real. Neither is prejudice, love, alienation, or any of those other variables. Let's see why.

There's a very old puzzle I'm sure you're familiar with: when a tree falls in the forest, does it make a sound if no one is there to hear it? High school and college students have struggled with that one for centuries. There's no doubt that the unobserved falling tree will still crash through the branches of its neighbors, snap its own limbs into pieces, and slam against the ground. But would it make a sound?

If you've given this any thought before, you've probably come to the conclusion that the puzzle rests on the ambiguity of the word *sound*. Where does sound occur? In this example, does it occur in the falling tree, in the air, or in the ear of the beholder? We can be reasonably certain that the falling tree generates turbulent waves in the air; if those waves in the air strike your ear, you will experience something we call *hearing*. We say you've heard a sound. But do the waves in the air per se qualify as sound?

The answer to this central question is necessarily arbitrary. We can have it be whichever way we want. The truth is that (1) a tree fell; (2) it created waves in the air; and (3) if the waves reached someone's ear, they would cause an experience for that person. Humans created the idea of *sound* in the context of that whole process. Whenever waves in the air cause an experience by way of our ears, we use the term *sound* to identify that experience. We're usually not too precise about where the sound happens: in the tree, in the air, or in our ears.

Our imprecise use of the term *sound* produces the apparent dilemma. So what's the truth? What's really the case? Does it make a sound or not? The truth is that (1) a tree fell; (2) it created waves in the air; and (3) if the waves reached someone's ear, they would cause an experience for that person. That's it. That's the final and ultimate truth of the matter.

I've belabored this point, because it sets the stage for understanding a critical issue in social research—one that often confuses students. To move in the direction of that issue, let's shift from sound to sight for a moment. Here's a new puzzle for you: are the tree's leaves green if no one is there to see them? Take a minute to think about that, and then continue reading.

Here's how I'd answer the question. The tree's leaves have a certain physical and chemical composition that affects the reflection of light rays off of them; specifically, they only reflect the green portion of the light spectrum. When rays from that portion of the light spectrum hit our eyes, they create an experience we call the color green.

"But are the leaves green if no one sees them?" you may ask. The answer to that is whatever we want it to be, since we haven't specified where the color green exists: in the physical/chemical composition of the leaf, in the light rays reflected from the leaf, or in our eyes.

While we are free to specify what we mean by the color green in this sense, nothing we do can change the ultimate truth, the ultimate reality of the matter. The truth is that (1) the leaves have a certain physical and chemical composition; (2) they reflect only a portion of the light spectrum; and (3) that portion of the light spectrum causes an experience if it hits our eyes. That's the ultimate truth of the universe in this matter.

By the same token, the truth about religiosity is that (1) some people to go church more than others; (2) some pray more than others; (3) some believe more than others; and so forth. This is observably the case.

At some point, our ancestors noticed that the things we're discussing were not completely independent of one another. People who went to church seemed to pray more, on the whole, than people who didn't go to church. Moreover, those who went to church and prayed seemed to believe more of the church's teachings than did those who neither went to church nor prayed. The observation of relationships such as these led them to conclude literally that "there is more here than meets the eye." The term *religiosity* was created to represent the *concept* that all the concrete observables seemed to have in common. People gradually came to believe that the concepts were real and the "indicators" only pale reflections.

We can never find a "true" measure of religiosity, prejudice, alienation, love, compassion, or any other such concepts, since none of them exists except in our minds. Concepts are "figments of our imaginations." I do not mean to suggest that concepts are useless or should be dispensed with. Life as we know it depends on the creation and use of concepts, and science would be impossible without them. Still, we should recognize that they are fictitious, then we can trade them in for more useful ones whenever appropriate.

THINKING ABOUT THE READING

Define the following terms: *poverty, happiness, academic effort, love*. Now consider what indicators you would use to determine people's levels of each of these concepts. The indicator must be something that will allow you to clearly determine whether or not someone is in a particular state (e.g., poor or not poor; happy or not happy; in love or not in love). For example, you might decide that blushing in the presence of someone is one indicator of being in love or that the number of hours a person spends studying for a test is an indicator of academic effort. What's wrong with simply asking people if they're poor, if they're in love, if they're happy, or if they work hard? Consider the connection between how a concept is defined and how it can be measured. Is it possible that sociology sometimes uses concepts that seem meaningless because they are easier to "see" and measure?

Measuring Same-Sex Relationships

Nancy Bates and Theresa J. DeMaio

(2013)

When social scientists need information about demographic trends, they immediately turn to the U.S. Census Bureau, the most highly regarded collector of data on Americans' rapidly changing lives. However, even the Census Bureau faces challenges in measuring certain trends. At the national level, Census scientists must ask their questions within the confines of federal restrictions. At the individual level, Census researchers must frame their questions in ways their respondents will comprehend, even as terms commonly ascribed to some populations are rapidly changing. The measurement of same-sex relationships challenges Census experts on all of these fronts.

Measuring Family Ties

The measurement of family relationships, living arrangements, and marital status has a long history at the U.S. Census Bureau. Over time, the census categories have changed to reflect changes in U.S. society and laws that define the institution of marriage and other legal and non-legal relationship statuses. In fact, how the census measures marital status has evolved for more than a century. In 1880, the categories consisted only of single, married and widowed/divorced. By 1890, widowed and divorced each became its own category and in 1950, the category of separated was added. For the relationship

---

United States™ Census Bureau
Measuring America

2010 American Community Survey Relationship Question

How is this person related to Person 1? Mark (X) ONE box.

☐ Husband or wife
☐ Biological son or daughter
☐ Adopted son or daughter
☐ Stepson or stepdaughter
☐ Brother or sister
☐ Father or mother
☐ Grandchild
☐ Parent-in-law

☐ Son-in-law or daughter-in-law
☐ Other relative
☐ Roomer or boarder
☐ Housemate or roommate
☐ Unmarried partner
☐ Foster child
☐ Other nonrelative

2010 American Community Survey Marital Status Question

What is this person's marital status?

☐ Now married
☐ Widowed
☐ Divorced
☐ Separated
☐ Never married

item, instructions for enumerating roommates, boarders, and lodgers go back to the nineteenth century. In 1980, the form added a combined partner/roommate category, and in the 1990 Census, the category of unmarried partner was included for the first time.

Recently, challenges in accurately measuring relationships have involved the growing recognition of same-sex couples. Unlike other countries such as Britain and Canada, U.S. laws recognizing same-sex couples vary. At the federal level, there is no legal recognition while state laws range from no legal recognition to full marriage equality. Passage of the Defense of Marriage Act (DOMA) in 1996 had ramifications for how federal statistical agencies count same-sex couples. DOMA requires the federal government to define marriage as a legal union exclusively between one man and one woman. Partly in response to DOMA, for Census 2000, an edit procedure was introduced whereby same-sex couples who checked husband or wife were automatically reallocated as unmarried partners.

When the Census Bureau announced in 2008 that the same edit procedure would be used in the 2010 Census, gay advocacy groups took notice. A coalition of many different lesbian, gay, bisexual and transgender (LGBT) groups formed a census advocacy campaign known as Our Families Count. Groups lobbied for Census to tabulate same-sex couples as they had originally reported on their Census forms. In 2009, the Census Bureau announced that, while the Census 2010 tabulations would still reflect the unmarried partner re-edit classification, the agency would produce state-by-state counts of same-sex couples who identified themselves as spouses.

Because the laws governing same-sex marriage are fragmented and constantly evolving, the federal statistical system faces an enormous challenge to accurately reflect today's increasingly complex relationship configurations. Given that approximately 42 percent of the U.S. population now resides in an area where some form of same-sex couple recognition is legal, statistical agencies must find a way to adapt their current measures.

Asking Questions about the Questions

To understand how gay and lesbian couples think about and report their relationships on official forms, the Census Bureau sponsored a two-part qualitative research project as part of a federal interagency task force. Using focus groups, we first explored the nomenclature of the current relationship and marital status questions—how do gay couples interpret them, what terms are used by this subpopulation, and under what circumstances? This enabled us to develop alternative questions that were then evaluated during one-on-one "think-aloud" interviews. This is how the Census "cognitively tests" the understanding of questions.

Between January and March 2010, investigators conducted a total of 18 focus groups across seven geographically diverse locations ranging from cities like Boston to rural areas in Georgia. Fourteen groups consisted of individuals in same-sex relationships with members recruited according to relationship status (legally married, in a domestic partnership or civil union, or had no legally recognized status). In addition, four groups consisted of persons in opposite sex relationships who were not legally married. Members of all groups were cohabiting with their partners.

We first asked participants to describe how they usually introduced their "better halves." This was followed by a request to complete a form containing the 2010 American Community Survey items of name, relationship to householder, gender, age, and date of birth followed by the marital status question (see figure on page 61). Moderators then led a discussion of how participants answered the questions and why. Moderators focused on whether answers were predicated on current legal relationship status, existing laws in their states of residence, whether participants interpreted the questions to be asking about a legal status or something else, and what alternative terms or categories they expected to see on the forms.

Listening to People Think

Following the focus groups, we crafted two new versions of the relationship and marital status items. We tested these items using "think-aloud" interview techniques where respondents read questions aloud and verbalize their thought processes as they formulate answers. Forty interviews were conducted in four different cities between March and April 2011. Locales ranged from Washington, D.C. to Charlotte, North Carolina and represented a variety of state laws regarding same-sex partner recognition. Participants were all from cohabiting couples—15 were straight and the other 25 were gay and lesbian. As in the focus groups, we recruited participants with a wide range of legal statuses ranging from married same-sex couples, same (and opposite-sex) domestic partners, and couples with no legal recognition. After completing the randomly assigned version, participants completed the alternative version followed by a debriefing that also determined which, if any, version they preferred.

We found that gay and straight participants often use the same terms upon introduction. Most often among these were: wife, husband, partner, boyfriend and girlfriend. The term partner was more often ascribed to gay and lesbian relationships (especially by opposite-sex couple groups). We also found that, particularly for gays and lesbians, participants' use of terms was not static but was conditional upon assessment of the setting. For example, a gay male from rural Georgia responded, "How would I introduce my partner? It depends on the setting. If it's this setting, I would say 'my partner [name].' If it's outside, 'my good friend [name] or 'uncle.'" So, a "wife" among friends is a "roommate" when the cable repairman comes to the house. Likewise "single" on a flex insurance health plan becomes "married" on a census form.

However, upon probing we found that most participants viewed the census questions through a legal prism believing it to be measuring state-sanctioned legally recognized relationships. Consequently, most answers aligned with legal couple statuses. Persons in same-sex couples without legal recognition residing in areas that did not recognize gay marriage indicated willingness to select "unmarried partner" because it was both legally accurate and the word "partner" was viewed as an adequate descriptor for their relationship. We also found that a legal marriage trumped local laws, at least for participants who had a legal marriage performed somewhere (inside or outside the United States). A lesbian from rural Georgia stated, "Oh, I would check off [wife], absolutely. I don't care if it would make everybody pissed off, and I really don't care if it wouldn't be recognized where I'm at. I don't care if I was in Antarctica, I would say wife, absolutely." And a gay male from Ft. Lauderdale commented, "I would still check husband or wife. As far as I'm concerned, I'm legally married, I don't care what the federal government thinks."

Encountering Resistance and Confusion

This is not to suggest that all same-sex couples were perfectly happy with the current options, particularly marital status. Participants from same-sex couples who lived in areas where marriage was not allowed and had no legal partnership status viewed the options as "marriage-centric" and without categories to describe their situations. Most marked "never married" and a few marked "divorced." Gay and lesbian participants who had been divorced from a previous heterosexual marriage felt frustrated that their marital status would be defined by a long-ago relationship unimportant compared to their current relationship.

Likewise, same-sex couples in registered domestic partnerships and civil unions expressed an undercurrent of dissatisfaction because the current options do not allow them to acknowledge the legally recognized component of their union. Overall, many did not feel any of the options adequately reflected their current lives, and felt personally discounted as expressed by comments such as this one,

"I can't answer . . . this would be blank. I couldn't answer it because 'now married' would be false in every sense . . . And 'never married' is utterly false to my heart. So I consider this unanswerable. This is one of those forms where no appropriate answer is provided." Or this one, "If you want accurate information then give me the choice to give you that information. If you're failing to get that information then the Census is not going to be correct to begin with, it's going to be skewed."

When presented with the revised questions, respondents were pleased to see the changes that attempted to accommodate their situations: moving unmarried partner to the second response category and disaggregating same-sex and opposite-sex couples. But, we had a concern as to whether there would be sensitivity issues among respondents in opposite-sex couples with the question that disaggregated response categories for same-sex and opposite-sex couples. In particular, we took notice of interviews conducted in Charlotte and North Carolina to gauge this reaction.

One straight white female expressed this view, "This [version] actually might, would offend me a little bit, because I think it's . . . I feel like we're kind of just lowering the standards . . . [as in] 'Okay we've got to conform to everyone, we want to be politically correct.' And that just really gets on my nerves, honestly . . . you know in a different part of the country, you might not be hearing this, but, that's how I feel about it." Another straight female stated, "[That version] tries too hard . . . it's making a point. [That version means] "we're gonna put it out there . . . that we're including **everybody** (emphasis added). But I get that . . . it's fine . . . we're in America." However, when pressed directly, neither indicated this opinion would lead them to discard the survey or otherwise not participate. Or, as one put it, "I wouldn't write my Congressman. I wouldn't go on Facebook about it . . . it's not that deep." Of course, this is a hypothetical judgment given in the context of a think-aloud interview, so we can only surmise their actual behavior.

The inclusion of the category "In a registered domestic partnership or civil union"

in the marital status question revealed a general lack of understanding about the concept among both gay and straight respondents and regardless of legal status. Only a few people said they were unfamiliar with either domestic partnerships or civil unions, but confusion abounded about what they were. One common misunderstanding was equating this concept to gay marriage, "In California you can do a domestic partnership, which is a same-sex marriage." Another misunderstanding equated it to common-law marriage as in this comment, "It seems like domestic partnership may be you've been living together for awhile. I think, legally after five years in North Carolina it's considered . . . I can't think of the term." Or this one, a civil union is "two people that have lived together for at least seven years." For these reasons, we recommend a separate question as a means of measuring domestic partnerships/civil unions.

Catching Up to the Future

The social and legal landscape for same-sex couples has changed dramatically since Massachusetts first recognized same-sex marriage. Since then, other states have passed similar legislation as well as civil unions and domestic partnerships for gay and lesbian couples. In this respect, federal agencies have not kept up with the times, and new measures must be constructed to reflect recognition that, in some cases, is intended to confer the same rights and responsibilities as marriage.

In reality, designing a one-size-fits-all federal form when the legal reality of same-sex partner recognition is fragmented poses a challenge for questionnaire designers. However, accurately counting gay and lesbian couples is paramount since legislative bodies, courts, and voters are making decisions that affect the day-to-day lives of this population. Will they receive partner health insurance, Social Security, or pension benefits like their straight couple counterparts? Will they be allowed to adopt children or visit their partners in the hospital?

With the qualitative testing complete, federal agencies should follow best practices and quantitatively test the new questions in an environment that closely resembles a large scale production survey. Only then can we be certain the data are valid and reliable. Ultimately, the Census Bureau and other statistical agencies must be responsive to social changes so our vital statistics accurately mirror and help support America's diverse population.

THINKING ABOUT THE READING

After studying the previous two chapters, you should have a solid understanding of the sociological perspective that demonstrates the importance of social forces and social interaction in constructing the world that we live in. You may even be excited by how much better you understand our social world! It is a very common but unwise assumption that sociology is simply "common sense." To ensure that they have an accurate understanding of the social world, sociologists rely on social research methods and ethics to scientifically study their topics. Bates and DeMaio discuss the importance and challenges of accurately measuring same-sex relationships in their work at the U.S. Census Bureau. What does this article tell you about the reality of identities, relationships, and the methodological challenges that go with them? Do you see these conflicts operating with other parts of identity and how people and groups are tracked at present or in the past?

Building Order

Culture and History

4

Culture provides members of a society with a common bond and a set of shared rules and beliefs for making sense of the world in similar ways. Shared cultural knowledge makes it possible for people to live together in a society. Sociologists refer to shared cultural expectations as social norms. Norms are the rules and standards that govern all social encounters and the mechanisms that provide order in our day-to-day lives. Shared norms make it possible to know what to expect from others and what others can expect from us. When norms are violated, we are reminded of the boundaries of social behavior. These violations lead us to notice otherwise taken-for-granted rules about what is considered right and wrong.

When we examine the social influences on our behavior, things that were once familiar and taken for granted suddenly become unfamiliar and curious. During the course of our lives, we are rarely forced to examine *why* we do the common things we do; we just do them. But, if we take a step back and examine our common customs and behaviors, they begin to look as strange as the "mystical" rituals of some far-off, exotic land. It is for this reason that Horace Miner's article "Body Ritual Among the Nacirema" has become a classic in sociology and anthropology. As you read this selection, consider the process of using the sociological imagination to understand your own life and the lives of others. When you think about other cultures, how can you be sure that your perceptions, as an outsider, are not as bizarre as Miner's perspective on the Nacirema? When done well, sociological research helps us to understand different points of view and different cultural contexts from the perspective of insiders.

Cultural clashes can be quite confusing and painful for newly arrived immigrants from countries with vastly different cultural traditions. In the article "The Melting Pot," Anne Fadiman examines the experiences of Hmong refugees in the United States. Hundreds of thousands of Hmong people have fled Laos since that country fell to communist forces in 1975. Most have settled in the United States. Virtually every element of Hmong culture and tradition stands in stark contrast to the highly modernized culture of U.S. society. The Hmong have been described in the U.S. media as simplistic, primitive, and throwbacks to the Stone Age. This article vividly portrays the everyday conflicts immigrants face as they straddle two vastly different cultures.

What happens when an industry is transported from one culture to another, especially if the cultures are very different? In the second reading for the section, James L. Watson addresses this question in the context of the transportation of the fast food industry, specifically McDonald's, to Hong Kong. McDonald's epitomizes Western cultural patterns of fast food consumption and other norms of consumer capitalism. What happens when this industry arrives in Asia? Watson observes that the result is cultural changes that reflect both globalization processes and also local resistance to those processes. Accordingly, this article demonstrates the importance of looking closely at local cultures in studying the effects of globalization.

Something to Consider as You Read

How do cultural practices provide social order? Where is this order located? In our minds? In our interactions with others? Think about what happens to your own sense of order when you become immersed in a different culture. What are some of the challenges you might face in trying to maintain your own cultural beliefs and practices while living in a completely different culture? Are some cultural practices easier to export than others? Why? As you read and compare these selections, think about why some cultures consider their ways to be better and more "real" than others. Do you think this ethnocentrism is a hallmark of all cultures or just some? How do the public display of cultural values and the environment it's done in impact the sanctions or absence of sanctions to these actions? As processes of globalization increase, what are the consequences for local cultures?

Body Ritual Among the Nacirema

Horace Miner American

(1956)

The anthropologist has become so familiar with the diversity of ways in which different peoples behave in similar situations that he is not apt to be surprised by even the most exotic customs. In fact, if all of the logically possible combinations of behavior have not been found somewhere in the world, he is apt to suspect that they must be present in some yet undescribed tribe. This point has, in fact, been expressed with respect to clan organization by Murdock (1949, p. 71). In this light, the magical beliefs and practices of the Nacirema present such unusual aspects that it seems desirable to describe them as an example of the extremes to which human behavior can go.

Professor Linton first brought the ritual of the Nacirema to the attention of anthropologists twenty years ago (1936, p. 326), but the culture of this people is still very poorly understood. They are a North American group living in the territory between the Canadian Cree, the Yaqui and Tarahumara of Mexico, and the Carib and Arawak of the Antilles. Little is known of their origin, although tradition states that they came from the east. According to Nacirema mythology, their nation was originated by a culture hero, Notgnihsaw, who is otherwise known for two great feats of strength—the throwing of a piece of wampum across the river Pa-To-Mac and the chopping down of a cherry tree in which the Spirit of Truth resided.

Nacirema culture is characterized by a highly developed market economy which has evolved in a rich natural habitat. While much of the people's time is devoted to economic pursuits, a large part of the fruits of these labors and a considerable portion of the day are spent in ritual activity. The focus of this activity is the human body, the appearance and health of which loom as a dominant concern in the ethos of the people. While such a concern is certainly not unusual, its ceremonial aspects and associated philosophy are unique.

The fundamental belief underlying the whole system appears to be that the human body is ugly and that its natural tendency is to debility and disease. Incarcerated in such a body, man's only hope is to avert these characteristics through the use of the powerful influences of ritual and ceremony. Every household has one or more shrines devoted to this purpose. The more powerful individuals in this society have several shrines in their houses and, in fact, the opulence of a house is often referred to in terms of the number of such ritual centers it possesses. Most houses are of wattle and daub construction, but the shrine rooms of the more wealthy are walled with stone. Poorer families imitate the rich by applying pottery plaques to their shrine walls.

While each family has at least one such shrine, the rituals associated with it are not family ceremonies but are private and secret. The rites are normally only discussed with children, and then only during the period when they are being initiated into these mysteries. I was able, however, to establish sufficient rapport with the natives to examine these shrines and to have the rituals described to me.

The focal point of the shrine is a box or chest which is built into the wall. In this chest are kept the many charms and magical potions without which no native believes he could live. These preparations are secured from a variety of specialized practitioners. The most powerful of these are the medicine men, whose assistance must be rewarded with substantial gifts. However, the medicine men do not provide the curative potions for their clients, but decide what the ingredients should be and then write them down in an ancient and secret language. This writing is understood only by the medicine men and by the herbalists who, for another gift, provide the required charm.

The charm is not disposed of after it has served its purpose, but is placed in the charm-box of the household shrine. As these magical materials are specific for certain ills, and the real or imagined maladies of the people are many, the charm-box is usually full to overflowing. The magical packets are so numerous that people forget what their purposes were and fear to use them again. While the natives are very vague on this point, we can only assume that the idea in retaining all the old magical materials is that their presence in the charm-box, before which the body rituals are conducted, will in some way protect the worshipper.

Beneath the charm-box is a small font. Each day every member of the family, in succession, enters the shrine room, bows his head before the charm-box, mingles different sorts of holy water in the font, and proceeds with a brief rite of ablution. The holy waters are secured from the Water Temple of the community, where the priests conduct elaborate ceremonies to make the liquid ritually pure.

In the hierarchy of magical practitioners, and below the medicine men in prestige, are specialists whose designation is best translated "holy-mouth-men." The Nacirema have an almost pathological horror of and fascination with the mouth, the condition of which is believed to have a supernatural influence on all social relationships. Were it not for the rituals of the mouth, they believe that their teeth would fall out, their gums bleed, their jaws shrink, their friends desert them, and their lovers reject them. They also believe that a strong relationship exists between oral and moral characteristics. For example, there is a ritual ablution of the mouth for children which is supposed to improve their moral fiber.

The daily body ritual performed by everyone includes a mouth-rite. Despite the fact that these people are so punctilious about care of the mouth, this rite involves a practice which strikes the uninitiated stranger as revolting. It was reported to me that the ritual consists of inserting a small bundle of hog hairs into the mouth, along with certain magical powders, and then moving the bundle in a highly formalized series of gestures.

In addition to the private mouth-rite, the people seek out a holy-mouth-man once or twice a year. These practitioners have an impressive set of paraphernalia, consisting of a variety of augers, awls, probes, and prods. The use of these objects in the exorcism of the evils of the mouth involves almost unbelievable ritual torture of the client. The holy-mouth-man opens the client's mouth and, using the above-mentioned tools, enlarges any holes which decay may have created in the teeth. Magical materials are put into these holes. If there are no naturally occurring holes in the teeth, large sections of one or more teeth are gouged out so that the supernatural substance can be applied. In the client's view, the purpose of these ministrations is to arrest decay and to draw friends. The extremely sacred and traditional character of the rite is evident in the fact that the natives return to the holy-mouth-man year after year, despite the fact that their teeth continue to decay.

It is to be hoped that, when a thorough study of the Nacirema is made, there will be careful inquiry into the personality structure of these people. One has but to watch the gleam in the eye of a holy-mouth-man, as he jabs an awl into an exposed nerve, to suspect that a certain amount of sadism is involved. If this can be established, a very interesting pattern emerges, for most of the population shows definite masochistic tendencies. It was to these that Professor Linton referred in discussing a distinctive part of the daily body ritual which is performed only by men. This part of the rite involves scraping and lacerating the surface of the face with a sharp instrument. Special women's rites are performed only four times during each lunar month, but what they lack in frequency is made up in barbarity. As part of this ceremony, women bake their heads in small ovens for about an hour. The theoretically interesting point is that what seems to be a preponderantly masochistic people have developed sadistic specialists.

The medicine men have an imposing temple, or *latipso,* in every community of any size. The more elaborate ceremonies required to treat very sick patients can only be performed at this temple. These ceremonies involve not only the thaumaturge but a permanent group of vestal maidens who move sedately about the temple chambers in distinctive costume and headdress.

The *latipso* ceremonies are so harsh that it is phenomenal that a fair proportion of the really sick natives who enter the temple ever recover. Small children whose indoctrination is still incomplete have been known to resist attempts to take them to the temple because "that is where you go to die." Despite this fact, sick adults are not only willing but eager to undergo the protracted ritual purification, if they can afford to do so. No matter how ill the supplicant or how grave the emergency, the guardians of many temples will not admit a client if he cannot give a rich gift to the custodian. Even after one has gained admission and survived the ceremonies, the guardians will not permit the neophyte to leave until he makes still another gift.

The supplicant entering the temple is first stripped of all his or her clothes. In everyday life the Nacirema avoids exposure of his body and its natural functions. Bathing and excretory acts are performed only in the secrecy of the household shrine, where they are ritualized as part of the body-rites. Psychological shock results from the fact that body secrecy is suddenly lost upon entry into the *latipso.* A man, whose own wife has never seen him in an excretory act, suddenly finds himself naked and assisted by a vestal maiden while he performs his natural functions into a sacred vessel. This sort of ceremonial treatment is necessitated by the fact that the excreta are used by a diviner to ascertain the course and nature of the client's sickness. Female clients, on the other hand, find their naked bodies are

subjected to the scrutiny, manipulation, and prodding of the medicine men.

Few supplicants in the temple are well enough to do anything but lie on their hard beds. The daily ceremonies, like the rites of the holy-mouth-men, involve discomfort and torture. With ritual precision, the vestals awaken their miserable charges each dawn and roll them about on their beds of pain while performing ablutions, in the formal movements of which the maidens are highly trained. At other times they insert magic wands in the supplicant's mouth or force him to eat substances which are supposed to be healing. From time to time the medicine men come to their clients and jab magically treated needles into their flesh. The fact that these temple ceremonies may not cure, and may even kill the neophyte, in no way decreases the people's faith in the medicine men.

There remains one other kind of practitioner, known as a "listener." This witch-doctor has the power to exorcise the devils that lodge in the heads of people who have been bewitched. The Nacirema believe that parents bewitch their own children. Mothers are particularly suspected of putting a curse on children while teaching them the secret body rituals. The counter-magic of the witch-doctor is unusual in its lack of ritual. The patient simply tells the "listener" all his troubles and fears, beginning with the earliest difficulties he can remember. The memory displayed by the Nacirema in these exorcism sessions is truly remarkable. It is not uncommon for the patient to bemoan the rejection he felt upon being weaned as a babe, and a few individuals even see their troubles going back to the traumatic effects of their own birth.

In conclusion, mention must be made of certain practices which have their base in native esthetics but which depend upon the pervasive aversion to the natural body and its functions. There are ritual fasts to make fat people thin and ceremonial feasts to make thin people fat. Still other rites are used to make women's breasts larger if they are small, and smaller if they are large. General dissatisfaction with breast shape is symbolized in the fact that the ideal form is virtually outside the range of human variation. A few women afflicted with almost inhuman hypermammary development are so idolized that they make a handsome living by simply going from village to village and permitting the natives to stare at them for a fee.

Reference has already been made to the fact that excretory functions are ritualized, routinized, and relegated to secrecy. Natural reproductive functions are similarly distorted. Intercourse is taboo as a topic and scheduled as an act. Efforts are made to avoid pregnancy by the use of magical materials or by limiting intercourse to certain phases of the moon. Conception is actually very infrequent. When pregnant, women dress so as to hide their condition. Parturition takes place in secret, without friends or relatives to assist, and the majority of women do not nurse their infants.

Our review of the ritual life of the Nacirema has certainly shown them to be a magic-ridden people. It is hard to understand how they have managed to exist so long under the burdens which they have imposed upon themselves. But even such exotic customs as these take on real meaning when they are viewed with the insight provided by Malinowski when he wrote (1948, p. 70):

> Looking from far and above, from our high places of safety in the developed civilization, it is easy to see all the crudity and irrelevance of magic. But without its power and guidance early man could not have mastered his practical difficulties as he has done, nor could man have advanced to the higher stages of civilization.

REFERENCES

Linton, R. (1936). *The study of man.* New York: Appleton-Century.

Malinowski, B. (1948). *Magic, science, and religion.* Glencoe, IL: Free Press.

Murdock, G. P. (1949). *Social structure.* New York: Macmillan.

THINKING ABOUT THE READING

What do you think of this culture? Do their ways seem very foreign, or are there some things that seem familiar? This article was written more than 50 years ago and, of course, much has changed since then. How might you update this description of the Nacirema to account for current values and rituals? Imagine you are an anthropologist from a culture completely unfamiliar with Western traditions. Using your own life as a starting point, think of common patterns of work, leisure, learning, intimacy, eating, sleeping, and so forth. Are there some customs that distinguish your group (religious, racial, ethnic, friendship, etc.) from others? See if you can find the reasons why these customs exist, which customs serve an obvious purpose (e.g., health), and which might seem arbitrary and silly to an outside observer.

The Melting Pot

Anne Fadiman

(1997)

The Lee family—Nao Kao, Foua, Chong, Zoua, Cheng, May, Yer, and True—arrived in the United States on December 18, 1980. Their luggage consisted of a few clothes, a blue blanket, and a wooden mortar and pestle that Foua had chiseled from a block of wood in Houaysouy. They flew from Bangkok to Honolulu, and then to Portland, Oregon, where they were to spend two years before moving to Merced. Other refugees told me that their airplane flights—a mode of travel that strained the limits of the familiar Hmong concept of migration—had been fraught with anxiety and shame: they got airsick, they didn't know how to use the bathroom but were afraid to soil themselves, they thought they had to pay for their food but had no money, they tried to eat the Wash'n Dris. The Lees, though perplexed, took the novelties of the trip in stride. Nao Kao remembers the airplane as being "just like a big house."

Their first week in Portland, however, was miserably disorienting. Before being placed by a local refugee agency in a small rented house, they spent a week with relatives, sleeping on the floor. "We didn't know anything so our relatives had to show us everything," Foua said. "They knew because they had lived in America for three or four months already. Our relatives told us about electricity and said the children shouldn't touch those plugs in the wall because they could get hurt. They told us that the refrigerator is a cold box where you put meat. They showed us how to open the TV so we could see it. We had never seen a toilet before and we thought maybe the water in it was to drink or cook with. Then our relatives told us what it was, but we didn't know whether we should sit or whether we should stand on it. Our relatives took us to the store but we didn't know that the cans and packages had food in them. We could tell what the meat was, but the chickens and cows and pigs were all cut up in little pieces and had plastic on them. Our relatives told us the stove is for cooking the food, but I was afraid to use it because it might explode. Our relatives said in America the food you don't eat you just throw away. In Laos we always fed it to the animals and it was strange to waste it like that. In this country there were a lot of strange things and even now I don't know a lot of things and my children have to help me, and it still seems like a strange country."

Seventeen years later, Foua and Nao Kao use American appliances, but they still speak only Hmong, celebrate only Hmong holidays, practice only the Hmong religion, cook only Hmong dishes, sing only Hmong songs, play only Hmong musical instruments, tell only Hmong stories, and know far more about current political events in Laos and Thailand than about those in the United States. When I first met them, during their eighth year in this country, only one American adult, Jeanine Hilt, had ever been invited to their home as a guest. It would be hard to imagine anything further from the vaunted American ideal of assimilation, in which immigrants are expected to submerge their cultural differences in order to embrace a shared national identity. *E pluribus unum:* from many, one.

During the late 1910s and early 1920s, immigrant workers at the Ford automotive plant in Dearborn, Michigan, were given free, compulsory "Americanization" classes. In addition to English lessons, there were lectures on work habits, personal hygiene, and table manners. The first sentence they memorized was "I am a good American." During their graduation ceremony they gathered next to a gigantic wooden pot, which their teachers stirred with ten-foot ladles. The students walked through a door into the pot, wearing traditional costumes from their countries of origin and singing songs in their native languages. A few minutes later, the door in the pot opened, and the students walked out again, wearing suits and ties, waving American flags, and singing "The Star-Spangled Banner."

The European immigrants who emerged from the Ford Motor Company melting pot came to the United States because they hoped to assimilate into mainstream American society. The Hmong came to the United States for the same reason they had left China in the nineteenth century: because they were trying to *resist* assimilation. As the anthropologist Jacques Lemoine has observed, "they did not come to our countries only to save their lives, they rather came to save their selves, that is, their Hmong ethnicity." If their Hmong ethnicity had been safe in Laos, they would have preferred to remain there, just as their ancestors—for whom migration had always been a problem-solving strategy, not a footloose impulse—would have preferred to remain in China. Unlike the Ford workers who enthusiastically, or at least uncomplainingly, belted out the "The Star-Spangled Banner" (of which Foua and Nao Kao know not a single word), the Hmong are what sociologists call "involuntary migrants." It is well known that involuntary migrants, no matter what pot they are thrown into, tend not to melt.

What the Hmong wanted here was to be left alone to be Hmong: clustered in all-Hmong enclaves, protected from government interference, self-sufficient, and agrarian. Some brought hoes in their luggage. General Vang Pao has said, "For many years, right from the start, I tell the American government that we need a little bit of land where we can grow vegetables and build homes like in Laos. . . . I tell them it does not have to be the best land, just a little land where we can live." This proposal

was never seriously considered. "It was just out of the question," said a spokesman for the State Department's refugee program. "It would cost too much, it would be impractical, but most of all it would set off wild protests from [other Americans] and from other refugees who weren't getting land for themselves." . . .

Just as newly arrived immigrants in earlier eras had been called "FOBs"—Fresh Off the Boat—some social workers nicknamed the incoming Hmong, along with the other Southeast Asian refugees who entered the United States after the Vietnamese War, "JOJs": Just Off the Jet. Unlike the first waves of Vietnamese and Cambodian refugees, most of whom received several months of vocational and language training at regional "reception centers," the Hmong JOJs, who arrived after the centers had closed, were all sent directly to their new homes. (Later on, some were given "cultural orientation" training in Thailand before flying to the United States. Their classes covered such topics as how to distinguish a one-dollar bill from a ten-dollar bill and how to use a peephole.) The logistical details of their resettlement were contracted by the federal government to private nonprofit groups known as VOLAGs, or national voluntary resettlement agencies, which found local sponsors. Within their first few weeks in this country, newly arrived families were likely to deal with VOLAG officials, immigration officials, public health officials, social service officials, employment officials, and public assistance officials. The Hmong are not known for holding bureaucrats in high esteem. As one proverb puts it, "To see a tiger is to die; to see an official is to become destitute." In a study of adaptation problems among Indochinese refugees, Hmong respondents rated "Difficulty with American Agencies" as a more serious problem than either "War Memories" or "Separation from Family." Because many of the VOLAGs had religious affiliations, the JOJs also often found themselves dealing with Christian ministers, who, not surprisingly, took a dim view of shamanistic animism. A sponsoring pastor in Minnesota told a local newspaper, "It would be wicked to just bring them over and feed and clothe them and let them go to hell. The God who made us wants them to be converted. If anyone thinks that a gospel preaching church would bring them over and not tell them about the Lord, they're out of their mind." The proselytizing backfired. According to a study of Hmong mental health problems, refugees sponsored by this pastor's religious organization were significantly more likely, when compared to other refugees, to require psychiatric treatment.

The Hmong were accustomed to living in the mountains, and most of them had never seen snow. Almost all their resettlement sites had flat topography and freezing winters. The majority were sent to cities, including Minneapolis, Chicago, Milwaukee, Detroit, Hartford, and Providence, because that was where refugee services—health care, language classes, job training, public housing—were concentrated. To encourage assimilation, and to avoid burdening any one community with more than its "fair share" of refugees, the Immigration and Naturalization Service adopted a policy of dispersal rather than clustering. Newly arrived Hmong were assigned to fifty-three cities in twenty-five different states: stirred into the melting pot in tiny, manageable portions, or, as John Finck, who worked with Hmong at the Rhode Island Office of Refugee Resettlement, put it, "spread like a thin layer of butter throughout the country so they'd disappear." In some places, clans were broken up. In others, members of only one clan were resettled, making it impossible for young people, who were forbidden by cultural taboo from marrying within their own clan, to find local marriage partners. Group solidarity, the cornerstone of Hmong social organization for more than two thousand years, was completely ignored.

Although most Hmong were resettled in cities, some nuclear families, unaccompanied by any of their extended relations, were placed in isolated rural areas. Disconnected from traditional supports, these families exhibited unusually high levels of anxiety, depression, and

paranoia. In one such case, the distraught and delusional father of the Yang family—the only Hmong family sponsored by the First Baptist Church of Fairfield, Iowa—attempted to hang himself in the basement of his wooden bungalow along with his wife and four children. His wife changed her mind at the last minute and cut the family down, but she acted too late to save their only son. An Iowa grand jury declined to indict either parent, on the grounds that the father was suffering from Post-Traumatic Stress Disorder, and the mother, cut off from all sources of information except her husband, had no way to develop an independent version of reality.

Reviewing the initial resettlement of the Hmong with a decade's hindsight, Lionel Rosenblatt, the former United States Refugee Coordinator in Thailand, conceded that it had been catastrophically mishandled. "We knew at the start their situation was different, but we just couldn't make any special provisions for them," he said. "I still feel it was no mistake to bring the Hmong here, but you look back now and say, 'How could we have done it so shoddily?'" Eugene Douglas, President Reagan's ambassador-at-large for refugee affairs, stated flatly, "It was a kind of hell they landed into. Really, it couldn't have been done much worse."

The Hmong who sought asylum in the United States were, of course, not a homogeneous lump. A small percentage, mostly the high-ranking military officers who were admitted first, were multilingual and cosmopolitan, and a larger percentage had been exposed in a desultory fashion to some aspects of American culture and technology during the war or while living in Thai refugee camps. But the experience of tens of thousands of Hmong was much like the Lees'. It is possible to get some idea of how monumental the task of adjustment was likely to be by glancing at some of the pamphlets, audiotapes, and videos that refugee agencies produced for Southeast Asian JOJs. For example, "Your New Life in the United States," a handbook published by the Language and

Orientation Resource Center in Washington, D.C., included the following tips:

Learn the meaning of "WALK"–"DON'T WALK" signs when crossing the street.

To send mail, you must use stamps.

To use the phone:

1) Pick up the receiver

2) Listen for dial tone

3) Dial each number separately

4) Wait for person to answer after it rings

5) Speak.

The door of the refrigerator must be shut.

Never put your hand in the garbage disposal.

Do not stand or squat on the toilet since it may break.

Never put rocks or other hard objects in the tub or sink since this will damage them.

Always ask before picking your neighbor's flowers, fruit, or vegetables.

In colder areas you must wear shoes, socks, and appropriate outerwear. Otherwise, you may become ill.

Always use a handkerchief or a kleenex to blow your nose in public places or inside a public building.

Never urinate in the street. This creates a smell that is offensive to Americans. They also believe that it causes disease.

Spitting in public is considered impolite and unhealthy. Use a kleenex or handkerchief.

Picking your nose or your ears in public is frowned upon in the United States.

The customs they were expected to follow seemed so peculiar, the rules and regulations so numerous, the language so hard to learn, and the emphasis on literacy and the decoding of other unfamiliar symbols so strong, that many Hmong were overwhelmed. Jonas Vangay told me, "In America, we are blind because even though we have eyes, we cannot see. We are deaf because even though we have ears, we cannot hear." Some newcomers wore pajamas as street clothes; poured water on electric stoves to extinguish them; lit charcoal fires in their living rooms; stored blankets in their refrigerators; washed rice in their toilets; washed their clothes in swimming pools; washed their hair with Lestoil; cooked with motor oil and furniture polish; drank Clorox; ate cat food; planted crops in public parks; shot and ate skunks, porcupines, woodpeckers, robins, egrets, sparrows, and a bald eagle; and hunted pigeons with crossbows in the streets of Philadelphia.

If the United States seemed incomprehensible to the Hmong, the Hmong seemed equally incomprehensible to the United States. Journalists seized excitedly on a label that is still trotted out at regular intervals: "the most primitive refugee group in America." (In an angry letter to the *New York Times*, in which that phrase had appeared in a 1990 news article, a Hmong computer specialist observed, "Evidently, we were not too primitive to fight as proxies for United States troops in the war in Laos.") Typical phrases from newspaper and magazine stories in the late seventies and eighties included "low-caste hill tribe," "Stone Age," "emerging from the mists of time," "like Alice falling down a rabbit hole." Inaccuracies were in no short supply. A 1981 article in the *Christian Science Monitor* called the Hmong language "extremely simplistic"; declared that the Hmong, who have been sewing paj ntaub [embroidered cloth] with organic motifs for centuries, make "no connection between a picture of a tree and a real tree"; and noted that "the Hmong have no oral tradition of literature. Apparently no folk tales exist." Some journalists seemed to shed all inhibition, and much of their good sense as well, when they were loosed on the Hmong. Timothy Dunnigan, a linguistic anthropologist who has taught a seminar at the University of Minnesota on the media presentation of Hmong and Native Americans, once remarked to me, "The kinds of metaphorical language that we use to describe the Hmong say far more about us, and our attachment to our own frame of reference, than they do about the Hmong."

It could not be denied that the Hmong were genuinely mysterious—far more so, for instance, than the Vietnamese and Cambodians who were streaming into the United States at the same time. Hardly anyone knew how to pronounce the word "Hmong." Hardly anyone—except the anthropology graduate students who suddenly realized they could write dissertations on patrilineal exogamous clan structures without leaving their hometowns—knew what role the Hmong had played during the war, or even what war it had been, since our government had succeeded all too well in keeping the Quiet War quiet. Hardly anyone knew they had a rich history, a complex culture, an efficient social system, and enviable family values. They were therefore an ideal blank surface on which to project xenophobic fantasies.

Not everyone who wanted to make the Hmong feel unwelcome stopped at slander. In the words of the president of a youth center in Minneapolis, his Hmong neighbors in the mid-eighties were "prime meat for predators." In Laos, Hmong houses had no locks. Sometimes they had no doors. Cultural taboos against theft and intra-community violence were poor preparation for life in the high-crime, inner-city neighborhoods in which most Hmong were placed. Some of the violence directed against them had nothing to do with their ethnicity; they were simply easy marks. But a good deal of it was motivated by resentment, particularly in urban areas, for what was perceived as preferential welfare treatment.

In Minneapolis, tires were slashed and windows smashed. A high school student getting off a bus was hit in the face and told to "go back to China." A woman was kicked in the thighs, face, and kidneys, and her purse, which contained the family's entire savings of $400, was stolen; afterwards, she forbade her children to play outdoors, and her husband, who had once commanded a fifty-man unit in the Armée Clandestine, stayed home to guard the family's belongings. In Providence, children were beaten walking home from school. In Missoula, teenagers were stoned. In Milwaukee, garden plots were vandalized

and a car was set on fire. In Eureka, California, two burning crosses were placed on a family's front lawn. In a random act of violence near Springfield, Illinois, a twelve-year-old boy was shot and killed by three men who forced his family's car off Interstate 55 and demanded money. His father told a reporter, "In a war, you know who your enemies are. Here, you don't know if the person walking up to you will hurt you."

In Philadelphia, anti-Hmong muggings, robberies, beatings, stonings, and vandalism were so commonplace during the early eighties that the city's Commission on Human Relations held public hearings to investigate the violence. One source of discord seemed to be a $100,000 federal grant for Hmong employment assistance that had incensed local residents, who were mostly unemployed themselves and believed the money should have been allocated to American citizens, not resident aliens.

One thing stands out in all these accounts: the Hmong didn't fight back.

Although on the battlefield the Hmong were known more for their fierceness than for their long livers, in the United States many were too proud to lower themselves to the level of the petty criminals they encountered, or even to admit they had been victims. An anthropologist named George M. Scott, Jr., once asked a group of Hmong in San Diego, all victims of property damage or assault, why they had not defended themselves or taken revenge. Scott wrote, "several Hmong victims of such abuse, both young and old, answered that to have done so, besides inviting further, retaliatory, abuse, would have made them feel 'embarrassed' or ashamed. In addition, the current president of Lao Family [a Hmong mutual assistance organization], when asked why his people did not 'fight back' when attacked here as they did in Laos, replied simply, 'because nothing here is worth defending to us.'"

In any case, Hmong who were persecuted by their neighbors could exercise a time-honored alternative to violence: flight. Between 1982 and 1984, three quarters of the Hmong population of Philadelphia simply left town and

joined relatives in other cities. During approximately the same period, one third of all the
Hmong in the United States moved from one
city to another. When they decided to relocate, Hmong families often lit off without
notifying their sponsors, who were invariably
offended. If they couldn't fit one of their possessions, such as a television set, in a car or
bus or U-Haul, they left it behind, seemingly
without so much as a backward glance. Some
families traveled alone, but more often they
moved in groups. When there was an exodus
from Portland, Oregon, a long caravan of over-
loaded cars motored together down Interstate
5, bound for the Central Valley of California.
With this "secondary migration," as sociologists termed it, the government's attempt to
stir the Hmong evenly into the melting pot was
definitively sabotaged.

Although local violence was often the trig-
gering factor, there were also other reasons for
migrating. In 1982, when all refugees who had
lived in the United States for more than eighteen months stopped receiving Refugee Cash
Assistance—the period of eligibility had previously been three years—many Hmong who had
no jobs and no prospects moved to states that
provided welfare benefits to two-parent families. Their original host states were often glad to
get rid of them. For a time, the Oregon Human
Resources Department, strapped by a tight
state budget, sent refugees letters that pointedly
detailed the levels of welfare benefits available
in several other states. California's were among
the highest. Thousands of Hmong also moved
to California because they had heard it was an
agricultural state where they might be able to
farm. But by far the most important reason for
relocating was reunification with other members of one's clan. Hmong clans are sometimes
at odds with each other, but within a clan, whose
thousands of members are regarded as siblings,
one can always count on support and sympathy.
A Hmong who tries to gain acceptance to a kin
group other than his own is called a *puav,* or bat.
He is rejected by the birds because he has fur and
by the mice because he has wings. Only when
a Hmong lives among his own subspecies can

he stop flitting restlessly from group to group,
haunted by the shame of not belonging.

The Hmong may have been following their
venerable proverb, "There's always another
mountain," but in the past, each new mountain
had yielded a living. Unfortunately, the most
popular areas of secondary resettlement all had
high unemployment rates, and they got higher.

By 1985, at least eighty percent of the
Hmong in Merced, Fresno, and San Joaquin
counties were on welfare.

That didn't halt the migration. Family
reunification tends to have a snowball effect.
The more Thaos or Xiongs there were in one
place, the more mutual assistance they could
provide, the more cultural traditions they
could practice together, and the more stable
their community would be. Americans, however, tended to view secondary migration as an
indication of instability and dependence.

Seeing that the Hmong were redistribut-
ing themselves as they saw fit, and that they
were becoming an economic burden on the
places to which they chose to move, the federal Office of Refugee Resettlement tried to
slow the migratory tide. The 1983 Highland
Lao Initiative, a three-million-dollar "emergency effort" to bolster employment and
community stability in Hmong communities
outside California, offered vocational training, English classes, and other enticements for
the Hmong to stay put. Though the initiative
claimed a handful of modest local successes,
the California migration was essentially
unstoppable. By this time, most Hmong JOJs
were being sponsored by relatives in America
rather than by voluntary organizations, so the
government no longer had geographic control over their placements. The influx therefore came—and, in smaller increments, is still
coming—from Thailand as well as from other
parts of America. Therefore, in addition to
trying to prevent the Hmong from moving
to high-welfare states, the Office of Refugee
Resettlement started trying to encourage
the ones who were already there to leave.
Spending an average of $7,000 per family on
moving expenses, job placement, and a month

or two of rent and food subsidies, the Planned Secondary Resettlement Program, which was phased out in 1994, relocated about 800 unemployed Hmong families from what it called "congested areas" to communities with "favorable employment opportunities"—i.e., unskilled jobs with wages too low to attract a full complement of local American workers.

Within the economic limitations of blue-collar labor, those 800 families have fared well. Ninety-five percent have become self-sufficient. They work in manufacturing plants in Dallas, on electronics assembly lines in Atlanta, in furniture and textile factories in Morganton, North Carolina. More than a quarter of them have saved enough money to buy their own houses, as have three quarters of the Hmong families who live in Lancaster County, Pennsylvania, where the men farm or work in food-processing plants, and the women work for the Amish, sewing quilts that are truthfully advertised as "locally made." Elsewhere, Hmong are employed as grocers, carpenters, poultry processors, machinists, welders, auto mechanics, tool and die makers, teachers, nurses, interpreters, and community liaisons. In a survey of Minnesota employers, the respondents were asked "What do you think of the Hmong as workers?" Eighty-six percent rated them "very good."

Some younger Hmong have become lawyers, doctors, dentists, engineers, computer programmers, accountants, and public administrators. Hmong National Development, an association that promotes Hmong self-sufficiency, encourages this small corps of professionals to serve as mentors and sponsors for other Hmong who might thereby be induced to follow suit. The cultural legacy of mutual assistance has been remarkably adaptive. Hundreds of Hmong students converse electronically, trading gossip and information—opinions on the relevance of traditional customs, advice on college admissions, personal ads—via the Hmong Channel on the Internet Relay Chat system. . . . There is also a Hmong Homepage on the World Wide Web (http://www.stolaf.edu/people/cdr/hmong/) and several burgeoning Hmong electronic mailing lists, including Hmongnet, Hmongforum, and Hmong Language Users Group.

The M.D.s and J.D.s and digital sophisticates constitute a small, though growing, minority. Although younger, English-speaking Hmong who have been educated in the United States have better employment records than their elders, they still lag behind most other Asian-Americans . . . .

For the many Hmong who live in high-unemployment areas, questions of advancement are often moot. They have no jobs at all. This is the reason the Hmong are routinely called this country's "least successful refugees." It is worth noting that the standard American tests of success that they have flunked are almost exclusively economic. If one applied social indices instead—such as rates of crime, child abuse, illegitimacy, and divorce—the Hmong would probably score better than most refugee groups (and also better than most Americans), but those are not the forms of success to which our culture assigns its highest priority. Instead, we have trained the spotlight on our best-loved index of failure, the welfare rolls. In California, Minnesota, and Wisconsin, where, not coincidentally, benefits tend to be relatively generous and eligibility requirements relatively loose, the percentages of Hmong on welfare are approximately forty-five, forty, and thirty-five (an improvement over five years ago, when they were approximately sixty-five, seventy, and sixty). The cycle of dependence that began with rice drops in Laos and reinforced with daily handouts at Thai refugee camps has been completed here in the United States. The conflicting structures of the Hmong culture and the American welfare system make it almost impossible for the average family to become independent . . . .

Few things gall the Hmong more than to be criticized for accepting public assistance. For one thing, they feel they deserve the money. Every Hmong has a different version of what is commonly called "The Promise": a written or verbal contract, made by CIA personnel in Laos, that if they fought for the Americans, the Americans would aid them if the Pathet Lao won the war. After risking their lives to rescue downed American pilots, seeing their villages flattened by incidental American bombs, and being forced to flee their country because they had supported the "American War," the Hmong expected a hero's welcome here. According to many of them, the first betrayal came when the American airlifts rescued only the officers from Long Tieng, leaving nearly everyone else behind. The second betrayal came in the Thai camps, when the Hmong who wanted to come to the United States were not all automatically admitted. The third betrayal came when they arrived here and found they were ineligible for veterans' benefits. The fourth betrayal came when Americans condemned them for what the Hmong call "eating welfare." The fifth betrayal came when the Americans announced that the welfare would stop.

Aside from some older people who consider welfare a retirement benefit, most Hmong would prefer almost any other option—if other options existed. What right-thinking Hmong would choose to be yoked to one of the most bureaucratic institutions in America? . . .

In a study of Indochinese refugees in Illinois, the Hmong exhibited the highest degree of "alienation from their environment." According to a Minnesota study, Hmong refugees who had lived in the United States for a year and a half had "very high levels of depression, anxiety, hostility, phobia, paranoid ideation, obsessive compulsiveness and feelings of inadequacy." (Over the next decade, some of these symptoms moderated, but the refugees' levels of anxiety, hostility, and paranoia showed little or no improvement.) The study that I found most disheartening was the 1987 California Southeast Asian Mental Health Needs Assessment, a statewide epidemiological survey funded by the Office of Refugee Resettlement and the National Institute of Mental Health. It was shocking to look at the bar graphs comparing the Hmong with the Vietnamese, the Chinese-Vietnamese, the Cambodians, and the Lao—all of whom, particularly the Cambodians, fared poorly compared to the general population—and see how

the Hmong stacked up: Most depressed. Most psychosocially dysfunctional. Most likely to be severely in need of mental health treatment. Least educated. Least literate. Smallest percentage in labor force. Most likely to cite "fear" as a reason for immigration and least likely to cite "a better life." . . .

"Full" of both past trauma and past longing, the Hmong have found it especially hard to deal with present threats to their old identities. I once went to a conference on Southeast Asian mental health at which a psychologist named Evelyn Lee, who was born in Macao, invited six members of the audience to come to the front of the auditorium for a role-playing exercise. She cast them as a grandfather, a father, a mother, an eighteen-year-old son, a sixteen-year-old daughter, and a twelve-year-old daughter. "Okay," she told them, "line up according to your status in your old country." Ranking themselves by traditional notions of age and gender, they queued up in the order I've just mentioned, with the grandfather standing proudly at the head of the line. "Now they come to America," said Dr. Lee. "Grandfather has no job. Father can only chop vegetables. Mother didn't work in the old country, but here she gets a job in a garment factory. Oldest daughter works there too. Son drops out of high school because he can't learn English. Youngest daughter learns the best English in the family and ends up at U.C. Berkeley. Now you line up again." As the family reshuffled, I realized that its power structure had turned completely upside down, with the twelve-year-old girl now occupying the head of the line and the grandfather standing forlornly at the tail.

Dr. Lee's exercise was an eloquent demonstration of what sociologists call "role loss." Of all the stresses in the Hmong community, role loss . . . may be the most corrosive to the ego . . . .

And in this country the real children have assumed some of the power that used to belong to their elders. The status conferred by speaking English and understanding American conventions is a phenomenon familiar to most immigrant groups, but the Hmong, whose identity has always hinged on tradition, have taken it particularly hard . . . .

Although Americanization may bring certain benefits—more job opportunities, more money, less cultural dislocation—Hmong parents are likely to view any earmarks of assimilation as an insult and a threat. "In our families, the kids eat hamburger and bread," said Dang Moua sadly, "whereas the parents prefer hot soup with vegetables, rice, and meat like tripes or liver or kidney that the young ones don't want." . . .

Sukey Waller, Merced's maverick psychologist, once recalled a Hmong community meeting she had attended. "An old man of seventy or eighty stood up in the front row," she said, "and he asked one of the most poignant questions I have ever heard: 'Why, when what we did worked so well for two hundred years, is everything breaking down?'" When Sukey told me this, I understood why the man had asked the question, but I thought he was wrong. Much has broken down, but not everything. Jacques Lemoine's analysis of the postwar hegira—that the Hmong came to the West to save not only their lives but their ethnicity—has been at least partially confirmed in the United States. I can think of no other group of immigrants whose culture, in its most essential aspects, has been so little eroded by assimilation. Virtually all Hmong still marry other Hmong, marry young, obey the taboo against marrying within their own clans, pay brideprices, and have large families. Clan and lineage structures are intact, as is the ethic of group solidarity and mutual assistance. On most weekends in Merced, it is possible to hear a death drum beating at a Hmong funeral or a *txiv neeb's* gong and rattle sounding at a healing ceremony. Babies wear strings on their wrists to protect their souls from abduction by *dabs*. People divine their fortunes by interpreting their dreams. (If you dream of opium, you will have bad luck; if you dream you are covered with excrement, you will have good luck; if you dream you have a snake on your lap, you will become pregnant.) Animal sacrifices are common, even among Christian converts, a fact I first learned when

May Ying Xiong told me that she would be unavailable to interpret one weekend because her family was sacrificing a cow to safeguard her niece during an upcoming open-heart operation. When I said, "I didn't know your family was so religious," she replied, "Oh yes, we're Mormon." . . .

I was able to see the whole cycle of adjustment to American life start all over again during one of my visits to Merced. When I arrived at the Lees' apartment, I was surprised to find it crammed with people I'd never met before. These turned out to be a cousin of Nao Kao's named Joua Chai Lee, his wife, Yeng Lor, and their nine children, who ranged in age from eight months to twenty-five years. They had arrived from Thailand two weeks earlier, carrying one piece of luggage for all eleven of them. In it were packed some clothes, a bag of rice, and, because Joua is a *txiv neeb's* assistant, a set of rattles, a drum, and a pair of divinatory water-buffalo horns. The cousins were staying with Foua and Nao Kao until they found a place of their own. The two families had not seen each other in more than a decade, and there was a festive atmosphere in the little apartment, with small children dashing around in their new American sneakers and the four barefooted adults frequently throwing back their heads and laughing. Joua said to me, via May Ying's translation, "Even though there are a lot of us, you can spend the night here too." May Ying explained to me later that Joua didn't really expect me to lie down on the floor with twenty of his relatives. It was simply his way, even though he was in a strange country where he owned almost nothing, of extending a face-saving bit of Hmong hospitality.

I asked Joua what he thought of America. "It is really nice but it is different," he said, "It is very flat. You cannot tell one place from another. There are many things I have not seen before, like that"—a light switch—"and that"—a telephone—"and that"—an air conditioner. "Yesterday our relatives took us somewhere in a car and I saw a lady and I thought she was real but she was fake." This turned out to have been a mannequin at the Merced Mall. "I couldn't stop laughing all the way home," he said. And remembering how funny his mistake had been, he started to laugh again.

Then I asked Joua what he hoped for his family's future here. "I will work if I can," he said, "but I think I probably cannot. As old as I am, I think I will not be able to learn one word of English. If my children put a heart to it, they will be able to learn English and get really smart. But as for myself, I have no hope."

THINKING ABOUT THE READING

Why has it been so difficult for Hmong refugees to adjust to life in the United States? How do the experiences of younger Hmong compare to those of their elders? Why are the Hmong such a popular target of anti-immigrant violence and persecution? Why is the U.S. government so unwilling to grant the Hmong their wish to be "left alone"? In other words, why is there such a strong desire to assimilate them into American culture? On a more general level, why is there such distaste in this society when certain ethnic groups desire to retain their traditional way of life? Consider the differences that might emerge between different generations within immigrant families. What aspects of culture are the most difficult to maintain through the generations?

McDonald's in Hong Kong

Consumerism, Dietary Change, and the Rise of a Children's Culture

James L. Watson

(1997)

Transnationalism and the Fast Food Industry*

Does the roaring success of McDonald's and its rivals in the fast food industry mean that Hong Kong's local culture is under siege? Are food chains helping to create a homogenous, "global" culture better suited to the demands of a capitalist world order? Hong Kong would seem to be an excellent place to test the globalization hypothesis, given the central role that cuisine plays in the production and maintenance of a distinctive local identity. Man Tso-chuen's great-grandchildren are today avid consumers of Big Macs, pizza, and Coca-Cola; does this somehow make them less "Chinese" than their grandfather?

The people of Hong Kong have embraced American-style fast foods, and by so doing they might appear to be in the vanguard of a worldwide culinary revolution. But they have not been stripped of their cultural traditions, nor have they become "Americanized" in any but the most superficial of ways. Hong Kong in the late 1990s constitutes one of the world's most heterogeneous cultural environments. Younger people, in particular, are fully conversant in transnational idioms, which include language, music, sports, clothing, satellite television, cyber-communications, global travel, and— of course—cuisine. It is no longer possible to distinguish what is local and what is not. In Hong Kong, the transnational *is* the local.

Eating Out: A Social History of Consumption

By the time McDonald's opened its first Hong Kong restaurant in 1975, the idea of fast food was already well established among local consumers. Office workers, shop assistants, teachers, and transport workers had enjoyed various forms of take-out cuisine for well over a century; an entire industry had emerged to deliver mid-day meals direct to workplaces. In the 1960s and 1970s thousands of street vendors produced snacks and simple meals on demand, day or night. Time has always been money in Hong Kong; hence, the dual keys to success in the catering trade were speed and convenience. Another essential characteristic was that the food, based primarily on rice or noodles, had to be hot. Even the most cosmopolitan of local consumers did not (and many still do not) consider cold foods, such as sandwiches and salads, to be acceptable meals. Older people in South China associate cold food with offerings to the dead and are understandably hesitant to eat it.

The fast food industry in Hong Kong had to deliver hot items that could compete with

---

*Seven of the world's ten busiest McDonald's restaurants are located in Hong Kong. When McDonald's first opened in 1975, few thought it would survive more than a few months. By January 1, 1997, Hong Kong had 125 outlets, which means that there was one McDonald's for every 51,200 residents, compared to one for every 30,000 people in the United States.

traditional purveyors of convenience foods (noodle shops, dumpling stalls, soup carts, portable grills).

McDonald's mid-1970s entry corresponded to an economic boom associated with Hong Kong's conversion from a low-wage, light-industrial outpost to a regional center for financial services and high-technology industries. McDonald's takeoff thus paralleled the rise of a new class of highly educated, affluent consumers who thrive in Hong Kong's ever-changing urban environment—one of the most stressful in the world. These new consumers eat out more often than their parents and have created a huge demand for fast, convenient foods of all types. In order to compete in this market, McDonald's had to offer something different. That critical difference, at least during the company's first decade of operation, was American culture packaged as all-American, middle-class food.

***

Mental Categories: Snack Versus Meal

As in other parts of East Asia, McDonald's faced a serious problem when it began operation in Hong Kong: Hamburgers, fries, and sandwiches were perceived as snacks (Cantonese *siu sihk,* literally "small eats"); in the local view these items did not constitute the elements of a proper meal. This perception is still prevalent among older, more conservative consumers who believe that hamburgers, hot dogs, and pizza can never be "filling." Many students stop at fast food outlets on their way home from school; they may share hamburgers and fries with their classmates and then eat a full meal with their families at home. This is not considered a problem by parents, who themselves are likely to have stopped for tea and snacks after work. Snacking with friends and colleagues provides a major opportunity for socializing (and transacting business) among southern Chinese. Teahouses, coffee shops, bakeries, and ice cream parlors are popular precisely because they provide a structured yet informal setting for social encounters. Furthermore, unlike Chinese restaurants and banquet halls, snack centers do not command a great deal of time or money from customers.

Contrary to corporate goals, therefore, McDonald's entered the Hong Kong market as a purveyor of snacks. Only since the late 1980s has its fare been treated as the foundation of "meals" by a generation of younger consumers who regularly eat non-Chinese food. Thanks largely to McDonald's, hamburgers and fries are now a recognized feature of Hong Kong's lunch scene. The evening hours remain, however, the weak link in McDonald's marketing plan; the real surprise was breakfast, which became a peak traffic period.

The mental universe of Hong Kong consumers is partially revealed in the everyday use of language. Hamburgers are referred to, in colloquial Cantonese, as *han bou bao*—*han* being a homophone for "ham" and *bao* the common term for stuffed buns or bread rolls. *Bao* are quintessential snacks, and however excellent or nutritious they might be, they do not constitute the basis of a satisfying (i.e., filling) meal. In South China that honor is reserved for culinary arrangements that rest, literally, on a bed of rice (*fan*). Foods that accompany rice are referred to as *sung,* probably best translated as "toppings" (including meat, fish, and vegetables). It is significant that hamburgers are rarely categorized as meat (*yuk*); Hong Kong consumers tend to perceive anything that is served between slices of bread (Big Macs, fish sandwiches, hot dogs) as *bao*. In American culture the hamburger is categorized first and foremost as a meat item (with all the attendant worries about fat and cholesterol content), whereas in Hong Kong the same item is thought of primarily as bread.

From Exotic to Ordinary: McDonald's Becomes Local

Following precedents in other international markets, the Hong Kong franchise promoted McDonald's basic menu and did not introduce items that would be more recognizable to

Chinese consumers (such as rice dishes, tropical fruit, soup noodles). Until recently the food has been indistinguishable from that served in Mobile, Alabama, or Moline, Illinois. There are, however, local preferences: the best-selling items in many outlets are fish sandwiches and plain hamburgers; Big Macs tend to be the favorites of children and teenagers. Hot tea and hot chocolate outsell coffee, but Coca-Cola remains the most popular drink.

McDonald's conservative approach also applied to the breakfast menu. When morning service was introduced in the 1980s, American-style items such as eggs, muffins, pancakes, and hash brown potatoes were not featured. Instead, the local outlets served the standard fare of hamburgers and fries for breakfast. McDonald's initial venture into the early morning food market was so successful that Mr. Ng [managing director of McDonald's Hong Kong], hesitated to introduce American-style breakfast items, fearing that an abrupt shift in menu might alienate consumers who were beginning to accept hamburgers and fries as a regular feature of their diet. The transition to eggs, muffins, and hash browns was a gradual one, and today most Hong Kong customers order breakfasts that are similar to those offered in American outlets. But once established, dietary preferences change slowly: McDonald's continues to feature plain hamburgers (but not the Big Mac) on its breakfast menu in most Hong Kong outlets.

Management decisions of the type outlined above helped establish McDonald's as an icon of popular culture in Hong Kong. From 1975 to approximately 1985, McDonald's became the "in" place for young people wishing to associate themselves with the laid-back, nonhierarchical dynamism they perceived American society to embody. The first generation of consumers patronized McDonald's precisely because it was *not* Chinese and was *not* associated with Hong Kong's past as a backward-looking colonial outpost where (in their view) nothing of consequence ever happened. Hong Kong was changing and, as noted earlier, a new consumer culture was beginning to take shape.

McDonald's caught the wave of this cultural movement and has been riding it ever since.

Today, McDonald's restaurants in Hong Kong are packed—wall-to-wall—with people of all ages, few of whom are seeking an American cultural experience. Twenty years after Mr. Ng opened his first restaurant, eating at McDonald's has become an ordinary, everyday experience for hundreds of thousands of Hong Kong residents. The chain has become a local institution in the sense that it has blended into the urban landscape; McDonald's outlets now serve as rendezvous points for young and old alike.

What's in a Smile? Friendliness and Public Service

American consumers expect to be served "with a smile" when they order fast food, but this is not true in all societies. In Hong Kong people are suspicious of anyone who displays what is perceived to be an excess of congeniality, solicitude, or familiarity. The human smile is not, therefore, a universal symbol of openness and honesty. "If you buy an apple from a hawker and he smiles at you," my Cantonese tutor once told me, "you know you're being cheated."

Given these cultural expectations, it was difficult for Hong Kong management to import a key element of the McDonald's formula—service with a smile—and make it work. Crew members were trained to treat customers in a manner that approximates the American notion of "friendliness." Prior to the 1970s, there was not even an indigenous Cantonese term to describe this form of behavior. The traditional notion of friendship is based on loyalty to close associates, which by definition cannot be extended to strangers. Today the concept of *public* friendliness is recognized—and verbalized—by younger people in Hong Kong, but the term many of them use to express this quality is "friendly," borrowed directly from English. McDonald's, through its television advertising, may be partly responsible for this innovation, but to date it has had little effect on workers in the catering industry.

During my interviews it became clear that the majority of Hong Kong consumers were uninterested in public displays of congeniality from service personnel. When shopping for fast food most people cited convenience, cleanliness, and table space as primary considerations; few even mentioned service except to note that the food should be delivered promptly. Counter staff in Hong Kong's fast food outlets (including McDonald's) rarely make great efforts to smile or to behave in a manner Americans would interpret as friendly. Instead, they project qualities that are admired in the local culture: competence, directness, and unflappability. In a North American setting the facial expression that Hong Kong employees use to convey these qualities would likely be interpreted as a deliberate attempt to be rude or indifferent. Workers who smile on the job are assumed to be enjoying themselves at the consumer's (and management's) expense: In the words of one diner I overheard while standing in a queue, "They must be playing around back there. What are they laughing about?"

Consumer Discipline?

[A] hallmark of the American fast food business is the displacement of labor costs from the corporation to the consumers. For the system to work, consumers must be educated—or "disciplined"—so that they voluntarily fulfill their side of an implicit bargain: We (the corporation) will provide cheap, fast service, if you (the customer) "earn" your own tray, seat yourself, and help clean up afterward. Time and space are also critical factors in the equation: Fast service is offered in exchange for speedy consumption and a prompt departure, thereby making room for others. This system has revolutionized the American food industry and has helped to shape consumer expectations in other sectors of the economy. How has it fared in Hong Kong? Are Chinese customers conforming to disciplinary models devised in Oak Brook, Illinois?

The answer is both yes and no. In general Hong Kong consumers have accepted the basic elements of the fast food formula, but with "localizing" adaptations. For instance, customers generally do not bus their own trays, nor do they depart immediately upon finishing. Clearing one's own table has never been an accepted part of local culinary culture, owing in part to the low esteem attaching to this type of labor. During McDonald's first decade in Hong Kong, the cost of hiring extra cleaners was offset by low wages. A pattern was thus established, and customers grew accustomed to leaving without attending to their own rubbish. Later, as wages escalated in the late 1980s and early 1990s, McDonald's tried to introduce self-busing by posting announcements in restaurants and featuring the practice in its television advertisements. As of February 1997, however, little had changed. Hong Kong consumers have ignored this aspect of consumer discipline.

What about the critical issues of time and space? Local managers with whom I spoke estimated that the average eating time for most Hong Kong customers was between 20 and 25 minutes, compared to 11 minutes in the United States fast food industry. This estimate confirms my own observations of McDonald's consumers in Hong Kong's central business districts (Victoria and Tsimshatsui). A survey conducted in the New Territories city of Yuen Long—an old market town that has grown into a modern urban center—revealed that local McDonald's consumers took just under 26 minutes to eat.

Perhaps the most striking feature of the American-inspired model of consumer discipline is the queue. Researchers in many parts of the world have reported that customers refuse, despite "education" campaigns by the chains involved, to form neat lines in front of cashiers. Instead, customers pack themselves into disorderly scrums and jostle for a chance to place their orders. Scrums of this nature were common in Hong Kong when McDonald's opened in 1975. Local managers discouraged this practice by stationing queue monitors near the registers during busy hours and, by the 1980s, orderly lines were the norm at McDonald's. The disappearance of the scrum corresponds to a general change in Hong Kong's public culture as a new generation of residents, the children of refugees, began to treat the territory as their home. Courtesy toward strangers was largely unknown in the 1960s: Boarding a bus during rush hour could be a nightmare and transacting business at a bank teller's window required brute strength. Many people credit McDonald's with being the first public institution in Hong Kong to enforce queuing, and thereby helping to create a more "civilized" social order. McDonald's did not, in fact, introduce the queue to Hong Kong, but this belief is firmly lodged in the public imagination.

Hovering and the Napkin Wars

Purchasing one's food is no longer a physical challenge in Hong Kong's McDonald's but finding a place to sit is quite another matter. The traditional practice of "hovering" is one solution: Choose a group of diners who appear to be on the verge of leaving and stake a claim to their table by hovering nearby, sometimes only inches away. Seated customers routinely ignore the intrusion; it would, in fact, entail a loss of face to notice. Hovering was the norm in Hong Kong's lower- to middle-range restaurants during the 1960s and 1970s, but the practice has disappeared in recent years. Restaurants now take names or hand out tickets at the entrance; warning signs, in Chinese and English, are posted: "Please wait to be seated." Customers are no longer allowed into the dining area until a table is ready.

Fast food outlets are the only dining establishments in Hong Kong where hovering is still tolerated, largely because it would be nearly impossible to regulate. Customer traffic in McDonald's is so heavy that the standard restaurant design has failed to reproduce American-style dining routines: Rather than ordering first and finding a place to sit afterward, Hong Kong consumers usually arrive in groups and delegate one or two people

to claim a table while someone else joins the counter queues. Children make ideal hoverers and learn to scoot through packed restaurants, zeroing in on diners who are about to finish. It is one of the wonders of comparative ethnography to witness the speed with which Hong Kong children perform this reconnaissance duty. Foreign visitors are sometimes unnerved by hovering, but residents accept it as part of everyday life in one of the world's most densely populated cities. It is not surprising, therefore, that Hong Kong's fast food chains have made few efforts to curtail the practice.

Management is less tolerant of behavior that affects profit margins. In the United States fast food companies save money by allowing (or requiring) customers to collect their own napkins, straws, plastic flatware, and condiments. Self-provisioning is an essential feature of consumer discipline, but it only works if the system is not abused. In Hong Kong napkins are dispensed, one at a time, by McDonald's crew members who work behind the counter; customers who do not ask for napkins do not receive any. This is a deviation from the corporation's standard operating procedure and adds a few seconds to each transaction, which in turn slows down the queues. Why alter a well-tested routine? The reason is simple: napkins placed in public dispensers disappear faster than they can be replaced.

***

Buffets, like fast food outlets, depend upon consumers to perform much of their own labor in return for reduced prices. Abuse of the system—wasting food or taking it home—is taken for granted and is factored into the price of buffet meals. Fast food chains, by contrast, operate at lower price thresholds where consumer abuse can seriously affect profits.

Many university students of my acquaintance reported that they had frequently observed older people pocketing wads of paper napkins, three to four inches thick, in restaurants that permit self-provisioning. Management efforts to stop this behavior are referred to, in the

Cantonese-English slang of Hong Kong youth, as the "Napkin Wars." Younger people were appalled by what they saw as the waste of natural resources by a handful of customers. As they talked about the issue, however, it became obvious that the Napkin Wars represented more—in their eyes—than a campaign to conserve paper. The sight of diners abusing public facilities reminded these young people of the bad old days of their parents and grandparents, when Hong Kong's social life was dominated by refugees who had little stake in the local community. During the 1960s and 1970s, economic insecurities were heightened by the very real prospect that Red Guards might take over the colony at any moment. The game plan was simple during those decades: Make money as quickly as possible and move on. In the 1980s a new generation of local-born youth began treating Hong Kong as home and proceeded to build a public culture better suited to their vision of life in a cosmopolitan city. In this new Hong Kong, consumers are expected to be sophisticated and financially secure, which means that it would be beneath their dignity to abuse public facilities. Still, McDonald's retains control of its napkins.

***

Children as Consumers

During the summer of 1994, while attending a business lunch in one of Hong Kong's fanciest hotels, I watched a waiter lean down to consult with a customer at an adjoining table. The object of his attention was a six-year-old child who studied the menu with practiced skill. His parents beamed as their prodigy performed; meanwhile, sitting across the table, a pair of grandparents sat bolt upright, scowling in obvious disapproval. Twenty years ago the sight of a child commanding such attention would have shocked the entire restaurant into silence. No one, save the immediate party (and this observer), even noticed in 1994.

Hong Kong children rarely ate outside their home until the late 1970s, and when they did, they were expected to eat what was put in front of them. The idea that children might actually order their own food or speak to a waiter would have outraged most adults; only foreign youngsters (notably the offspring of British and American expatriates) were permitted to make their preferences known in public. Today, Hong Kong children as young as two or three participate in the local economy as full-fledged consumers, with their own tastes and brand loyalties. Children now have money in their pockets and they spend it on personal consumption, which usually means snacks. In response, new industries and a specialized service sector has emerged to "feed" these discerning consumers. McDonald's was one of the first corporations to recognize the potential of the children's market; in effect, the company started a revolution by making it possible for even the youngest consumers to *choose* their own food.

***

Many Hong Kong children of my acquaintance are so fond of McDonald's that they refuse to eat with their parents or grandparents in Chinese-style restaurants or *dim sam* teahouses. This has caused intergenerational distress in some of Hong Kong's more conservative communities. In 1994, a nine-year-old boy, the descendant of illustrious ancestors who settled in the New Territories eight centuries ago, talked about his concerns as we consumed Big Macs, fries, and shakes at McDonald's: "A-bak [uncle], I like it here better than any place in the world. I want to come here every day." His father takes him to McDonald's at least twice a week, but his grandfather, who accompanied them a few times in the late 1980s, will no longer do so. "I prefer to eat *dim sam*," the older man told me later. "That place [McDonald's] is for kids." Many grandparents have resigned themselves to the new consumer trends and take their preschool grandchildren to McDonald's for mid-morning snacks—precisely the time of day that local teahouses were once packed with retired people. Cantonese grandparents have always played a prominent role in child minding, but until recently the children had to accommodate to the proclivities of their elders. By the 1990s grandchildren were more assertive and the mid-morning *dim sum* snack was giving way to hamburgers and Cokes.

***

Ronald McDonald and the Invention of Birthday Parties

Until recently most people in Hong Kong did not even know, let alone celebrate, their birthdates in the Western calendrical sense; dates of birth according to the lunar calendar were recorded for divinatory purposes but were not noted in annual rites. By the late 1980s, however, birthday parties, complete with cakes and candles, were the rage in Hong Kong. Any child who was anyone had to have a party, and the most popular venue was a fast food restaurant, with McDonald's ranked above all competitors. The majority of Hong Kong people live in overcrowded flats, which means that parties are rarely held in private homes.

Except for the outlets in central business districts, McDonald's restaurants are packed every Saturday and Sunday with birthday parties, cycled through at the rate of one every hour. A party hostess, provided by the restaurant, leads the children in games while the parents sit on the sidelines, talking quietly among themselves. For a small fee celebrants receive printed invitation cards, photographs, a gift box containing toys and a discount coupon for future trips to McDonald's. Parties are held in a special enclosure, called the Ronald Room, which is equipped with low tables and tiny stools—suitable only for children. Television commercials portray Ronald McDonald leading birthday celebrants on exciting safaris and expeditions. The clown's Cantonese name, Mak Dong Lou Suk-Suk ("Uncle McDonald"), plays on the intimacy of kinship and has helped transform him into one of Hong Kong's most familiar cartoon figures.

***

McDonald's as a Youth Center

Weekends may be devoted to family dining and birthday parties for younger children, but on weekday afternoons, from 3:00 to 6:00 P.M., McDonald's restaurants are packed with teenagers stopping for a snack on their way home from school. In many outlets 80 percent of the late afternoon clientele appear in school uniforms, turning the restaurants into a sea of white frocks, light blue shirts, and dark trousers. The students, aged between 10 and 17, stake out tables and buy snacks that are shared in groups. The noise level at this time of day is deafening; students shout to friends and dart from table to table. Few adults, other than restaurant staff, are in evidence. It is obvious that McDonald's is treated as an informal youth center, a recreational extension of school where students can unwind after long hours of study.

***

In contrast to their counterparts in the United States, where fast food chains have devised ways to discourage lingering, McDonald's in Hong Kong does not set a limit on table time. When I asked the managers of several Hong Kong outlets how they coped with so many young people chatting at tables that might otherwise be occupied by paying customers, they all replied that the students were "welcome." The obvious strategy is to turn a potential liability into an asset: "Students create a good atmosphere which is good for our business," said one manager as he watched an army of teenagers—dressed in identical school uniforms—surge into his restaurant. Large numbers of students also use McDonald's as a place to do homework and prepare for exams, often in groups. Study space of any kind, public or private, is hard to find in overcrowded Hong Kong.

***

Conclusions: Whose Culture Is It?

In what sense, if any, is McDonald's involved in these cultural transformations (the creation of a child-centered consumer culture, for instance)? Has the company helped to create these trends, or merely followed the market? Is this an example of American-inspired, transnational culture crowding out indigenous cultures?

The deeper I dig into the lives of consumers themselves, in Hong Kong and elsewhere, the more complex the picture becomes. Having watched the processes of culture change unfold for nearly thirty years, it is apparent to me that the ordinary people of Hong Kong have most assuredly *not* been stripped of their cultural heritage, nor have they become the uncomprehending dupes of transnational corporations. Younger people—including many of the grandchildren of my former neighbors in the New Territories—are avid consumers of transnational culture in all of its most obvious manifestations: music, fashion, television, and cuisine. At the same time, however, Hong Kong has itself become a major center for the *production* of transnational culture, not just a sinkhole for its *consumption*. Witness, for example, the expansion of Hong Kong popular culture into China, Southeast Asia, and beyond: "Cantopop" music is heard on radio stations in North China, Vietnam, and Japan; the Hong Kong fashion industry influences clothing styles in Los Angeles, Bangkok, and Kuala Lumpur; and, perhaps most significant of all, Hong Kong is emerging as a center for the production and dissemination of satellite television programs throughout East, South east, and South Asia.

A lifestyle is emerging in Hong Kong that can best be described as postmodern, postnationalist, and flamboyantly transnational. The wholesale acceptance and appropriation of Big Macs, Ronald McDonald, and birthday parties are small, but significant aspects of this redefinition of Chinese cultural identity. In closing, therefore, it seems appropriate to pose an entirely new set of questions: Where does the transnational end and the local begin? Whose culture is it, anyway? In places like Hong Kong the postcolonial periphery is fast becoming the metropolitan center, where local people are consuming and simultaneously producing new cultural systems.

***

THINKING ABOUT THE READING

According to Watson's observations, the people in Hong Kong have adopted some of the characteristics of McDonald's "fast food" culture and resisted others. How has the presence of McDonald's changed Chinese culture? How have the Chinese changed this "fast food" culture to better fit their own? What does this reading suggest about the relationship between globalization and local cultures? Consider other examples of globalized industries and the impact on local cultures.

Building Identity

Socialization

5

Sociology teaches us that humans don't develop in a social vacuum. Other people, cultural practices, historical events, and social institutions shape what we do and say, what we value, and who we become. Our self-concept, identity, and sense of self-worth are derived from our interactions with other people. We are especially tuned in to the reactions, real or imagined, of others.

Socialization is the process by which individuals learn their culture and learn to live according to the norms of their society. Through socialization, we learn how to perceive our world, gain a sense of our own identity, and discover how to interact appropriately with others. This learning process occurs within the context of several social institutions—schools, religious institutions, the media, and the family—and it extends beyond childhood. Adults must be resocialized into a new galaxy of norms, values, and expectations each time they leave or abandon current positions and enter new ones.

The conditions into which we are born shape our initial socialization in profound ways. Circumstances such as race, ethnicity, gender, and social class are particularly significant factors in socialization processes. In "Life as the Maid's Daughter," sociologist Mary Romero describes a research interview with a young Chicana regarding her recollections of growing up as the daughter of a live-in maid for a white, upper-class family living in Los Angeles. Romero describes the many ways in which this girl learns to move between different social settings, adapt to different expectations, and occupy different social positions. This girl must constantly negotiate the boundaries of inclusion and exclusion, as she struggles between the socializing influence of her own ethnic group and that of the white, upper-class employers she and her mother live with. Through this juggling, she illustrates the ways in which we manage the different, often contradictory, identities that we take on in different situations.

Similar to race and ethnicity, gender and social class play an integral role in shaping our identities. In "Tiger Girls on the Soccer Field," Hilary Levy Friedman investigates the intersection of gender and social class in the socialization process of competitive afterschool activities. She finds that the type of gender socialization employed by parents is very much dependent on their socioeconomic status and has the potential to reproduce social inequality. Despite these different versions of femininity, Friedman notes that the type of gender socialization these kids receive in afterschool activities does not necessarily always determine their future attainment.

Immigration status, racism, and globalization are also significant features in shaping this unique identity. In a popular sociological article, "The Code of the Streets," Elijah Anderson looks at the complexities of socialization among young African American men living in the inner cities. Anderson is particularly interested in the development of "manhood" and respect among these young men and the relationship between violence and survival. To survive, one must adopt the "code"—a complex system of norms, dress, rituals, and expected behavior. The third reading for this section is a contemporary study focusing on inner-city girls and their relationship to the "code." Nikki Jones suggests that these girls are no more immune to violence than boys. She provides narrative descriptions of some of the ways in which street life shapes the behavior and identity of the young women in her study.

Something to Consider as You Read

According to sociologists, we are shaped by our cultural environment and by the influences of significant people and groups in our lives. Consider some of the people or groups whose opinions matter to you. Can you imagine them as a kind of audience in your head, observing and reacting to your behavior? Think about the desire to feel included. To what extent has this desire shaped your participation in a group that has had an impact on your self-image? How important are "role models" in the socialization process? If someone is managing conflicting identities and has no role models or others in similar situations, how might this conflict affect her or his sense of self and relationships with others? What do these readings suggest about the importance of being the "right person in the right place" even if that's not all you feel yourself to be? How do power and authority affect people's sense of self and their right to be whoever they want to be in any situation? How do social conditions shape our choices and opportunities?

Life as the Maid's Daughter

Mary Romero

(1995)

Introduction

... My current research attempts to expand the sociological understanding of the dynamics of race, class, and gender in the everyday routines of family life and reproductive labor.... I am lured to the unique setting presented by domestic service ... and I turn to the realities experienced by the children of private household workers. This focus is not entirely voluntary. While presenting my research on Chicana private household workers, I was approached repeatedly by Latina/os and African Americans who wanted to share their knowledge about domestic service—knowledge they obtained as the daughters and sons of household workers. Listening to their accounts about their mothers' employment presents another reality to understanding paid and unpaid reproductive labor and the way in which persons of color are socialized into a class-based, gendered, racist social structure. The following discussion explores issues of stratification in everyday life by analyzing the life story of a maid's daughter. This life story illustrates the potential of the standpoint of the maid's daughter for generating knowledge about race, class, and gender....

Social Boundaries Presented in the Life Story

The first interview with Teresa,[1] the daughter of a live-in maid, eventually led to a life history project. I am intrigued by Teresa's experiences with her mother's white, upper-middle-class employers while maintaining close ties to her relatives in Juarez, Mexico, and Mexican friends in Los Angeles. While some may view Teresa's life as a freak accident, living a life of "rags to riches," and certainly not a common Chicana/o experience, her story represents a microcosm of power relationships in the larger society. Life as the maid's daughter in an upper-middle-class neighborhood exemplifies many aspects of the Chicano/Mexicano experience as "racial ethnics" in the United States, whereby the boundaries of inclusion and exclusion are constantly changing as we move from one social setting and one social role to another.

Teresa's narrative contains descriptive accounts of negotiating boundaries in the employers' homes and in their community. As the maid's daughter, the old adage "Just like one of the family" is a reality, and Teresa has to learn when she must act like the employer's child and when she must assume the appropriate behavior as the maid's daughter. She has to recognize all the social cues and interpret social settings correctly—when to expect the same rights and privileges as the employer's children and when to fulfill the expectations and obligations as the maid's daughter. Unlike the employers' families, Teresa and her mother rely on different ways of obtaining knowledge. The taken-for-granted reality of the employers' families do not contain conscious experiences of negotiating race and class status, particularly not in the intimate setting of the home. Teresa's status is constantly changing in response to the wide range of social settings she encounters—from employers' dinner parties with movie stars and corporate executives to Sunday dinners with Mexican garment workers in Los Angeles and factory workers in El Paso. Since Teresa remains bilingual and bicultural throughout her life, her story reflects the constant struggle and resistance to maintain her Mexican identity, claiming a reality that is neither rewarded nor acknowledged as valid.

Teresa's account of her life as the maid's daughter is symbolic of the way that racial ethnics participate in the United States; sometimes we are included and other times excluded or ignored. Teresa's story captures the reality of social stratification in the United States, that is, a racist, sexist, and class-structured society upheld by an ideology of equality. I will analyze the experiences of the maid's daughter in an upper-middle-class neighborhood in Los Angeles to investigate the ways that boundaries of race, class, and gender are maintained or diffused in everyday life. I have selected various excerpts from the transcripts that illustrate how knowledge about a class-based and gendered, racist social order is learned, the type of information that is conveyed, and how the boundaries between systems of domination impact everyday life. I begin with a brief history of Teresa and her mother, Carmen.

Learning Social Boundaries: Background

Teresa's mother was born in Piedras Negras, a small town in Aguas Calientes in Mexico. After her father was seriously injured in a railroad accident, the family moved to a small town outside Ciudad Juarez . . . . By the time she was fifteen she moved to Juarez and took a job as a domestic, making about eight dollars a week. She soon crossed the border and began working for Anglo families in the country club area in El Paso. Like other domestics in El Paso, Teresa's mother returned to Mexico on weekends and helped support her mother and sisters. In her late twenties she joined several of her friends in their search for better-paying jobs in Los Angeles. The women immediately found jobs in the garment industry. Yet, after six months in the sweatshops, Teresa's mother went to an agency in search of domestic work. She was placed in a very exclusive Los Angeles

neighborhood. Several years later Teresa was born. Her friends took care of the baby while Carmen continued working; childcare became a burden, however, and she eventually returned to Mexico. At the age of thirty-six Teresa's mother returned to Mexico with her newborn baby. Leaving Teresa with her grandmother and aunts, her mother sought work in the country club area. Three years later Teresa and her mother returned to Los Angeles.

Over the next fifteen years Teresa lived with her mother in the employer's (Smith) home, usually the two sharing the maid's room located off the kitchen. From the age of three until Teresa started school, she accompanied her mother to work. She continued to live in the Smiths' home until she left for college. All of Teresa's live-in years were spent in one employer's household. The Smiths were unable to afford a full-time maid, however, so Teresa's mother began doing day work throughout the neighborhood. After school Teresa went to whatever house her mother was cleaning and waited until her mother finished working, around 4 or 6 P.M., and then returned to the Smiths' home with her mother. Many prominent families in the neighborhood knew Teresa as the maid's daughter and treated her accordingly. While Teresa wanted the relationship with the employers to cease when she went to college and left the neighborhood, her mother continued to work as a live-in maid with no residence other than the room in the employer's home; consequently, Teresa's social status as the maid's daughter continued . . . .

One of the Family

As Teresa got older, the boundaries between insider and outsider became more complicated, as employers referred to her and Carmen as "one of the family." Entering into an employer's world as the maid's daughter, Teresa was not only subjected to the rules of an outsider but also had to recognize when the rules changed, making her momentarily an insider. While the boundaries dictating Carmen's work became blurred between the obligations of an employee and that of a friend or family member, Teresa was forced into situations in which she was expected to be just like one of the employer's children, and yet she remained the maid's daughter . . . .

Living under conditions established by the employers made Teresa and her mother's efforts to maintain a distinction between their family life and an employer's family very difficult. Analyzing incidents in which the boundaries between the worker's family and employer's family were blurred highlights the issues that complicate the mother-daughter relationship. Teresa's account of her mother's hospitalization was the first of numerous conflicts between the two that stemmed from the live-in situation and their relationships with the employer's family. The following excerpt demonstrates the difficulty in interacting as a family unit and the degree of influence and power employers exerted over their daily lives:

When I was about ten my mother got real sick. That summer, instead of sleeping downstairs in my mother's room when my mother wasn't there, one of the kids was gone away to college, so it was just Rosalyn, David and myself that were home. The other two were gone, so I was gonna sleep upstairs in one of the rooms. I was around eight or nine, ten I guess. I lived in the back room. It was a really neat room because Rosalyn was allowed to paint it. She got her friend who was real good, painted a big tree and clouds and all this stuff on the walls. So I really loved it and I had my own room. I was with the Smiths all the time, as my parents, for about two months. My mother was in the hospital for about a month. Then when she came home, she really couldn't do anything. We would all have dinner, the Smiths were really, really supportive. I went to summer school and I took math and English and stuff like that. I was in this drama class and I did drama and I got to do the leading role. Everybody really liked me and Ms. Smith would come and see my play. So things started to change when I got a lot closer to them and I was with them alone. I would go see my mother everyday, and my cousin was there. I think that my cousin kind of resented all the time that the Smiths spent with me. I think my mother was really afraid that now that she wasn't there that they were going to steal me from her. I went to see her, but I could only stay a couple of hours and it was really weird. I didn't like seeing my mother in pain and she was in a lot of pain. I remember before she came home the Smiths said that they thought it would be a really good idea if I stayed upstairs and I had my own room now that my mother was going to be sick and I couldn't sleep in the same bed 'cause I might hurt her. It was important for my mother to be alone. And how did I feel about that? I was really excited about that [having her own room]—you know. They said, "Your mom she is probably not going to like it and she might get upset about it, but I think that we can convince her that it is ok." When my mom came home, she understood that she couldn't be touched and that she had to be really careful, but she wanted it [having her own room] to be temporary. Then my mother was really upset. She got into it with them and said, "No, I don't want it that way." She would tell me, "No, I want you to be down here. ¿Qué crees que eres hija de ellos? You're gonna be with me all the time, you can't do that." So I would tell Ms. Smith. She would ask me when we would go to the market together, "How does your mom seem, what does she feel, what does she say?" She would get me to relay that. I would say, "I think my mom is really upset about me moving upstairs. She doesn't like it and she just says no." I wouldn't tell her everything. They would talk to her and finally they convinced her, but my mom really, really resented it and was really angry about it. She was just generally afraid. All these times that my mother wasn't there, things happened and they would take me places with them, go out to dinner with them and their friends. So that was a real big change, in that I slept upstairs and had different rules. Everything changed. I was more independent. I did my own homework; they would open the back door and yell that dinner was ready—you know. Things were just real different.

The account illustrates how assuming the role of insider was an illusion because neither the worker's daughter nor the worker ever became a member of the white, middle-class family. Teresa was only allowed to move out of the maid's quarter, where she shared a bed with her mother, when two of the employer's children were leaving home, vacating two bedrooms . . . .

Teresa and Carmen did not experience the boundaries of insider and outsider in the same way. Teresa was in a position to assume a more active family role when employers made certain requests. Unlike her mother, she was not an employee and was not expected to clean and serve the employer. Carmen's responsibility for the housework never ceased, however, regardless of the emotional ties existing between employee and employers. She and her employers understood that, whatever family activity she might be participating in, if the situation called for someone to clean, pick up, or serve, that was Carmen's job. When the Smiths requested Teresa to sit at the dinner table with the family, they placed Teresa in a different class position than her mother, who was now expected to serve her daughter alongside her employer. Moving Teresa upstairs in a bedroom alongside the employer and their children was bound to drive a wedge between Teresa and Carmen. There is a long history of spatial deference in domestic service, including separate entrances, staircases, and eating and sleeping arrangements. Carmen's room reflected her position in the household. As the maid's quarter, the room was separated from the rest of the bedrooms and was located near the maid's central work area, the kitchen. The room was obviously not large enough for two beds because Carmen and Teresa shared a bed. Once Teresa was moved upstairs, she no longer shared the same social space in the employer's home as her mother. Weakening the bonds between the maid and her daughter permitted the employers to broaden their range of relationships and interaction with Teresa.

Carmen's feelings of betrayal and loss underline how threatening the employers' actions were. She understood that the employers were in a position to buy her child's love. They had already attempted to socialize Teresa into Euro-American ideals by planning Teresa's education and deciding what courses she would take. Guided by the importance they place on European culture, the employers defined the Mexican Spanish spoken by Teresa and her mother as inadequate and classified Castillan Spanish as "proper" Spanish. As a Mexican immigrant woman working as a live-in maid, Carmen was able to experience certain middle-class privileges, but her only access to these privileges was through her relationship with employers. Therefore, without the employers' assistance, she did not have the necessary connections to enroll Teresa in private schools or provide her with upper-middle-class experiences to help her develop the skills needed to survive in elite schools. Carmen only gained these privileges for her daughter at a price; she relinquished many of her parental rights to her employers. To a large degree the Smiths determined Carmen's role as a parent, and the other employers restricted the time she had to attend school functions and the amount of energy left at the end of the day to mother her own child.

Carmen pointed to the myth of "being like one of the family" in her comment, "¿Qué crees que eres hija de ellos? You're gonna be with me all the time, you can't do that." The statement underlines the fact that the bond between mother and daughter is for life, whereas the pseudofamily relationship with employers is temporary and conditional. Carmen wanted her daughter to understand that taking on the role of being one of the employer's family did not relinquish her from the responsibility of fulfilling her "real" family obligations. The resentment Teresa felt from her cousin who was keeping vigil at his aunt's hospital bed indicated that she had not been a dutiful daughter. The outside pressure from an employer did not remove her own family obligations and responsibilities. Teresa's relatives expected a daughter to be at her mother's side providing any assistance possible as a caretaker, even if it was limited to companionship. The employer determined Teresa's activity, however, and shaped her behavior into that of a middle-class child; consequently, she was kept away from the hospital and protected from the realities of her mother's illness. Furthermore, she was submerged into the employer's world, dining at the country club and interacting with their friends.

Her mother's accusation that Teresa wanted to be the Smiths' daughter signifies the feelings of betrayal or loss and the degree to which Carmen was threatened by the employer's power and authority. Yet Teresa also felt betrayal and loss and viewed herself in competition with the employers for her mother's time, attention, and love. In this excerpt Teresa accuses her mother of wanting to be part of employers' families and community:

> I couldn't understand it—you know—until I was about eighteen and then I said, "It is your fault. If I treat the Smiths differently, it is your fault. You chose to have me live in this situation. It was your decision to let me have two parents, and for me to balance things off, so you can't tell me that I said this. You are the one who wanted this." When I was about eighteen we got into a huge fight on Christmas. I hated the holidays because I hated spending them with the Smiths. My mother always worked. She worked on every holiday. She loved to work on the holidays! She would look forward to working. My mother just worked all the time! I think that part of it was that she wanted to have power and control over this community, and she wanted the network, and she wanted to go to different people's houses.

As employers, Mr. and Mrs. Smith were able to exert an enormous amount of power over the relationship between Teresa and her mother. Carmen was employed in an occupation in which the way to improve working conditions, pay, and benefits was through the manipulation of personal relationships with employers. Carmen obviously tried to take advantage of her relationship with the Smiths in order to provide the best for her daughter. The more intimate and interpersonal the relationship, the more likely employers were to give gifts, do favors, and provide financial assistance. Although speaking in anger and filled with hurt, Teresa accused her mother of choosing to be with employers and their families rather than with her own daughter.

Underneath Teresa's accusation was the understanding that the only influence and status her mother had as a domestic was gained through her personal relationships with employers. Although her mother had limited power in rejecting the Smiths' demands, Teresa held her responsible for giving them too much control. Teresa argued that the positive relationship with the Smiths was done out of obedience to her mother and denied any familial feelings toward the employers. The web between employee and employers' families affected both mother and daughter, who were unable to separate the boundaries of work and family.

Maintaining Cultural Identity

A major theme in Teresa's narrative was her struggle to retain her Mexican culture and her political commitment to social justice. Rather than internalizing meaning attached to Euro-American practices and redefining Mexican culture and bilingualism as negative social traits, Teresa learned to be a competent social actor in both white, upper-middle-class environments and in working- and middle-class Chicano and Mexicano environments. To survive as a stranger in so many social settings, Teresa developed an acute skill for assessing the rules governing a particular social setting and acting accordingly. Her ability to be competent in diverse social settings was only possible, however, because of her life with the employers' children. Teresa and her mother maintained another life—one that was guarded and protected against any employer intrusion. Their other life was Mexican, not white, was Spanish speaking, not English speaking, was female dominated rather than male dominated, and was poor and working-class, not upper-middle-class. During the week Teresa and her mother visited the other Mexican maids in the neighborhoods, on weekends they occasionally took a bus into the Mexican barrio in Los Angeles to have dinner with friends, and every summer they spent a month in Ciudad Juarez with their family . . . .

Teresa's description of evening activity with the Mexican maids in the neighborhood provides insight into her daily socialization and explains how she learned to live in the employer's home without internalizing all their negative attitudes toward Mexican and working-class culture. Within the white, upper-class neighborhood in which they worked, the Mexican maids got together on a regular basis and cooked Mexican food, listened to Mexican music, and gossiped in Spanish about their employers. Treated as invisible or as confidants, the maids were frequently exposed to the intimate details of their employers' marriages and family life. The Mexican maids voiced their disapproval of the lenient child-rearing practices and parental decisions, particularly surrounding drug usage and the importance of material possessions:

> Raquel was the only one [maid] in the neighborhood who had her own room and own TV set. So everybody would go over to Raquel's . . . . This was my mother's support system. After hours, they would go to different people's [maid's] rooms depending on what their rooms had. Some of them had kitchens and they would go and cook all together, or do things like play cards and talk all the time. I remember that in those situations they would sit, and my mother would talk about the Smiths, what they were like. When they were going to negotiate for raises, when they didn't like certain things, I would listen and hear all the different discussions about what was going on in different houses. And they would talk, also, about the family relationships. The way they interacted, the kids did this and that. At the time some of the kids were smoking pot and they would talk about who was smoking marijuana. How weird it was that the parents didn't care. They would talk about what they saw as being wrong. The marriage relationship, or how weird it was they would go off to the beauty shop and spend all this money, go shopping and do all these weird things and the effect that it had on the kids.

The interaction among the maids points to the existence of another culture operating invisibly within a Euro-American and male-dominated community. The workers' support system did not include employers and addressed their concerns as mothers, immigrants, workers, and women. They created a Mexican-dominated domain for themselves. Here they ate Mexican food, spoke Spanish, listened to the Spanish radio station, and watched novellas on TV. Here Teresa was not a cultural artifact but, instead, a member of the Mexican community.

In exchanging gossip and voicing their opinions about the employers' lifestyles, the maids rejected many of the employers' priorities in life. Sharing stories about the employers' families allowed the Mexican immigrant women to be critical of white, upper-middle-class families and to affirm and enhance their own cultural practices and beliefs. The regular evening sessions with other working-class Mexican immigrant women were essential in preserving Teresa and her mother's cultural values and were an important agency of socialization for Teresa. For instance, the maids had a much higher regard for their duties and responsibilities as mothers than as wives or lovers. In comparison to their mistresses, they were not financially dependent on men, nor did they engage in the expensive and time-consuming activity of being an ideal wife, such as dieting, exercising, and maintaining a certain standard of beauty in their dress, makeup, and hairdos. Unlike the employers' daughters, who attended cotillions and were socialized to acquire success through marriage, Teresa was constantly pushed to succeed academically in order to pursue a career. The gender identity cultivated among the maids did not include dependence on men or the learned helplessness that was enforced in the employers' homes but, rather, promoted self-sufficiency. However, both white women employers and Mexican women employees were expected to be nurturing and caring. These traits were further reinforced when employers asked Teresa to babysit for their children or to provide them with companionship during their husbands' absences.

So, while Teresa observed her mother adapting to the employers' standards in her interaction with their children, she learned that her mother did not approve of their lifestyle and understood that she had another set of expectations to adhere to. Teresa attended the same schools as employers' children, wore similar clothes, and conducted most of her social life within the same socioeconomic class, but she remained the maid's daughter—and learned the limitations of that position. Teresa watched her mother uphold higher standards for her and apply a different set of standards to the employers' children; most of the time, however, it appeared to Teresa as if they had no rules at all.

Sharing stories about the Smiths and other employers in a female, Mexican, and worker-dominated social setting provided Teresa with a clear image of the people she lived with as employers rather than as family members. Seeing the employers through the eyes of the employees forced Teresa to question their kindness and benevolence and to recognize their use of manipulation to obtain additional physical and emotional labor from the employees. She became aware of the workers' struggles and the long list of grievances, including no annual raises, no paid vacations, no social security or health benefits, little if any privacy, and sexual harassment. Teresa was also exposed to the price that working-class immigrant women employed as live-in maids paid in maintaining white, middle-class, patriarchal communities. Employers' careers and lifestyles, particularly the everyday rituals affirming male privilege, were made possible through the labor women provided for men's physical, social, and emotional needs. Female employers depended on the maid's labor to assist in the reproduction of their gendered class status. Household labor was expanded in order to accommodate the male members of the employers' families and to preserve their privilege. Additional work was created by rearranging meals around men's work and recreation schedules and by waiting on them and serving them. Teresa's mother was frequently called upon to provide emotional labor for the wife, husband, mother, and father within an employer's family, thus freeing members to work or increase their leisure time.

Discussion

Teresa's account offers insight into the ways racial ethnic women gain knowledge about the social order and use the knowledge to develop survival strategies. As the college-educated daughter of an immigrant Mexican woman employed as a live-in maid, Teresa's experiences in the employers' homes, neighborhood, and school and her experiences in the homes of working-class Mexicano families and barrios provided her with the skills to cross the class and cultural boundaries separating the two worlds. The process of negotiating social boundaries involved an evaluation of Euro-American culture and its belief system in light of an intimate knowledge of white, middle-class families. Being in the position to compare and contrast behavior within different communities, Teresa debunked notions of "American family values" and resisted efforts toward assimilation. Learning to function in the employers' world was accomplished without internalizing its belief system, which defined ethnic culture as inferior. Unlike the employers' families, Teresa's was not able to assume the taken-for-granted reality of her mother's employers because her experiences provided a different kind of knowledge about the social order.

While the employers' children were surrounded by positive images of their race and class status, Teresa faced negative sanctions against her culture and powerless images of her race. Among employers' families she quickly learned that her "mother tongue" was not valued and that her culture was denied. All the Mexican adults in the neighborhood were in subordinate positions to the white adults and were responsible for caring for and nurturing white children. Most of the female employers were full-time homemakers who enjoyed the financial security provided by their husbands, whereas the Mexican immigrant women in the neighborhood all worked as maids and were financially independent; in many cases they were supporting children, husbands, and other family members. By directly observing her mother serve, pick up after, and nurture employers and their families, Teresa learned about white, middle-class privileges. Her experiences with other working-class Mexicans were dominated by women's responsibility for their children and extended families. Here the major responsibility of mothering was financial; caring and nurturing were secondary and were provided by the extended family or children did without. Confronted with a working mother who was too tired to spend time with her, Teresa learned about the racial, class, and gender parameters of parenthood, including its privileges, rights, responsibilities, and obligations. She also learned that the role of a daughter included helping her mother with everyday household tasks and, eventually, with the financial needs of the extended family. Unlike her uncles and male cousins, Teresa was not exempt from cooking and housework, regardless of her financial contributions. Within the extended family Teresa was subjected to standards of beauty strongly weighted by male definitions of women as modest beings, many times restricted in her dress and physical movements. Her social worlds became clearly marked by race, ethnic, class, and gender differences.

Successfully negotiating movement from a white, male, and middle-class setting to one dominated by working-class, immigrant, Mexican women involved a socialization process that provided Teresa with the skills to be bicultural. Since neither setting was bicultural, Teresa had to become that in order to be a competent social actor in each. Being bicultural included having the ability to assess the rules governing each setting and to understand her ethnic, class, and gender position. Her early socialization in the employers' households was not guided by principles of creativity, independence, and leadership but, rather, was based on conformity and accommodation. Teresa's experiences in two different cultural groups allowed her to separate each and to fulfill the employers' expectations without necessarily internalizing the meaning

attached to the act. Therefore, she was able to learn English without internalizing the idea that English is superior to Spanish or that monolingualism is normal. The existence of a Mexican community within the employers' neighborhood provided Teresa with a collective experience of class-based racism, and the maids' support system affirmed and enhanced their own belief system and culture. As Philomena Essed (1991, 294) points out, "The problem is not only how knowledge of racism is acquired but also what kind of knowledge is being transmitted."

Teresa's life story lends itself to a complex set of analyses because the pressures to assimilate were challenged by the positive interactions she experienced within her ethnic community. Like other bilingual persons in the United States, Teresa's linguistic abilities were shaped by the linguistic practices of the social settings she had access to. Teresa learned the appropriate behavior for each social setting, each marked by different class and cultural dynamics and in which women's economic roles and relationships to men were distinct. An overview of Teresa's socialization illustrates the process of biculturalism—a process that included different sets of standards and rules governing her actions as a woman, as a Chicana, and as the maid's daughter . . . .

Notes

This essay was originally presented as a paper at the University of Michigan, "Feminist Scholarship: Thinking through the Disciplines," 30 January 1992. I want to thank Abigail J. Stewart and Donna Stanton for their insightful comments and suggestions.

1. The names are pseudonyms.

REFERENCE

Essed, Philomena. 1991. *Understanding Everyday Racism.* Newbury Park, Calif.: Sage Publications.

THINKING ABOUT THE READING

Teresa's childhood is unique in that she and her mother lived in the household of her mother's employer, requiring them to conform to the expectations of the employers even when her mother was "not at work." Her childhood was shaped by the need to read signals from others to determine her position in various social settings. What were some of the different influences in Teresa's early socialization? Did she accept people's attempts to mold her, or did she resist? How did she react to her mother's employers' referring to her as "one of the family"? Teresa came from a poor family, but she spent her childhood in affluent households. With respect to socialization, what advantages do you think these experiences provided her? What were the disadvantages? How do you think these experiences would have changed if she were a *son* of a live-in maid rather than a daughter? If she were a poor *white* girl rather than Latina?

Tiger Girls on the Soccer Field

Hilary Levey Friedman

(2013)

Charlotte, age 9, told me about her experiences playing competitive soccer: "At recess I'm like the only girl playing soccer. Everyone else is doing something else. So usually they call me a tomboy because I'm playing with the boys. But I'm NOT a tomboy. A tomboy is somebody who like wants to be a boy and is like always being with the boys and stuff. I have dolls and I like pink. I really like girl things, like I painted my nails."

To Charlotte, being a tomboy is a negative label. She is more eager to identify with her femininity, pointing out how she paints her nails and wears pink. She wants a strong femininity, the kind that lets her be an aggressive soccer player, too. "We play soccer against boys sometimes because it's better for the girls to learn to be more aggressive," she told me. While Charlotte thinks girls can be just as good as boys at soccer, she thinks they'll only improve if they become as tough as the boys.

Her mom Marie agrees. Looking ahead, she sees competitive sports as a way for her daughter to become aggressive—not just in the athletic arena, but also in life. Marie told me, "We have no illusions that our daughter is going to be a great athlete. But the team element [is important]. I worked for Morgan Stanley for 10 years, and I interviewed applicants, and that ability to work on a team was a crucial part of our hiring process. So it's a skill that comes into play much later. It's not just about ball skills or hand-eye coordination."

"When I was interviewing job candidates at Morgan Stanley," Marie, a white woman with two Ivy League degrees told me, "if I got a female candidate—because it's banking and you need to be aggressive, you need to be tough—if she played, like, ice hockey, *done*. My

daughter's playing, and I'm just a big believer in kids learning to be confidently aggressive, and I think that plays out in life assertiveness."

Many parents like Marie believe that being cutthroat and aggressive sets girls on a path to the corner office as a company executive. The higher up you go in the class hierarchy, the more likely you will encounter parents like Marie, who believe in teaching their daughters what I call "aggressive femininity." They are taught to be both physically and competitively forceful, actively subsuming aspects of their femininity; many of their parents define their daughters in opposition to "girly-girls."

As Sheryl Sandberg, CEO of Facebook and author of the bestseller, *Lean In,* declared, "Instead of calling our daughters bossy, let's say, 'My daughter has executive leadership skills!'" Girls today grow up in a world with an unprecedented set of educational and professional opportunities, and many look up to successful women like Sandberg. More girls will graduate from college and earn advanced degrees than ever before, and nearly all professions are open to them, even combat careers in the military.

Successful women want to raise daughters who share the qualities that have brought them success—qualities that some liken to bossiness.

Nice Girls Competing

When I studied 95 families with elementary school-age children who were involved in competitive afterschool activities—chess, dance, and soccer—I met parents like Marie who saw their kids' participation in competitive afterschool activities as a way to develop certain values and skills: the importance of winning; the ability to bounce back from a loss to win in the future; to perform within time limits; to succeed in stressful situations; and to perform under the gaze of others—what I call "Competitive Kid Capital."

One of the most striking findings was that upper-middle-class parents of girls often perceive a link between aggression and success in athletics, and are more likely to enroll their daughters in soccer or chess, rather than dance—activities that are deemed more cooperative and less competitive. Like Sheryl Sandberg, they believe that executive leadership skills can be effectively developed and honed on soccer fields and basketball courts, even when the competitors are wearing pink shoes and jerseys.

Malcolm, an African-American lawyer with three Ivy League degrees, believes that sports don't just steer his seven-year-old daughter toward assertiveness, they actively drive her away from more traditionally feminine pursuits. "She's a cute little girl, but I don't like her to be a girly-girl," he explained. "You know, I don't want her to be a cheerleader—nothing against that—but I want her to prepare to have the option, if she wants to be an executive in a company, that she can play on that turf. And if she's kind of a girly-girl, maybe she'll be a secretary. There's nothing wrong with that, but let her have the option of doing something else if she wants."

Malcolm thinks being a "girly-girl" means less desirable, more traditionally feminine occupations. The images he evokes related to being an executive, such as "play on that turf," suggests the importance he places on athletics to help his daughter follow a historically male career path. And he identifies cheerleading—which was once a male-dominated area and still has an athletic and competitive component, even as the athletes are now expected to wear make-up, curl their hair, and often bare their midriffs—as being too much of a girly-girl activity.

Sports Make the Girl

Today, sports are important element of American upper-middle-class culture and child-rearing practices. But as recently as a century ago, organized team sports were limited to males. Women and girls were generally seen as physically inferior and mentally unable to handle competition. Even when they were allowed to participate, competition was off-limits, and seen as damaging.

When New York City's Public Schools Athletic Girls League was founded in 1905, for example, the director was opposed to keeping records, arguing that girls could easily injure themselves if they got too aggressive or tried to break a record. All-girls' elite schools were among the first to break with this view of women and competition, though they called competitive organizations "associations" instead of "leagues," lest people complain a league was too masculine.

Much of this changed, along with social attitudes, after the passage of Title IX 40 years ago. With time, young women who had once been focused on the arts came, in the twenty-first century, to see athletics as especially important tools for development. Two recent studies, one by the Women's Sports Foundation and the other by the Oppenheimer Foundation, have found that 82 percent of executive businesswomen played organized sports in middle school and high school. Of female Fortune 500 executives, 80 percent said they were competitive tomboys during childhood. The Oppenheimer study also found that, while 16 percent of all American women describe themselves as athletic, among women who earn over $75,000 annually, the number rises to about 50 percent.

These conclusions are consistent with the studies like those of economist Betsy Stevenson, whose work on Title IX finds that participation in high school sports increases the likelihood that a girl will attend college, enter the labor market, and enter previously male-dominated occupations. She suggests that sports develops such skills as learning how to compete and how to become a team member, which are both key as women navigate the traditionally male-dominated labor market.

But competition, athletic or otherwise, is still seen as a masculine attribute. In 2010, the journal *Sex Roles* published a study on high school boys and girls that found that even today, "boys are 'trained' from an early age to be competitive . . . Research suggests that girls are less comfortable than boys in competitive circumstances and that girls are socialized to mask overt competitiveness and aggressiveness more generally." David Hibbard and Duane Buhrmester, both psychologists, argue that a mentality of "competing to win" is at odds with the "nice girl" ideal. Girls who engage in head-to-head competition may have more social difficulties, even as they become prepared for a fast-tracked, upper-middle-class life.

Pink Girls and Dancing Queens

Parents of chess-playing girls also encourage their daughters to be assertive and competitive. As one chess mom explained to me, "We're raising her . . . to be feminist. And so she says she wants to be a Grandmaster or the President [of the United States]. She doesn't have any ideas about gender limitations and I think that's a good thing."

Chess girls don't have to be as assertive as soccer girls like Charlotte. Partly because it is not a physical game, chess allows girls to be what one mother of two sons described to me as a "pink girl": "These girls have princess T-shirts on," she said. They have "rhinestones and bows in their hair—and they beat boys. And the boys come out completely deflated. That's the kind of thing I think is so funny. That girl Carolyn, I call her the killer chess player. She has bows in her hair, wears dresses, everything is pink, Barbie backpack, and she plays killer chess."

That a winning girl can look so feminine has an especially strong effect on boys, and sometimes their parents. Another chess mom told me how a father reacted negatively when his son lost to her daughter: "The father came out and was shocked. He said, 'You let a girl beat you!'"

In competitive dance, it's more common to see girls win, if only because the activity is dominated by girls. Dance is a physical activity that, like cheerleading, "no girly-girls" dad Malcolm would like his daughter to avoid. Competitive dancers are expected to wear make-up when they compete. While this has a practical purpose—to make sure the dancers' faces are not "washed out" by the stage lights—lipstick, blush, and mascara also accentuate feminine features—practices that are among those sociologist C. J. Pascoe would identify as part of "normative femininity."

As I sat in the audience at dance competitions, I often heard teachers and parents remark, "Wow, she looks beautiful up there," or, "They look very good." In addition to make-up, girl's dance costumes featured sequins, rhinestones, ribbons, and other decorative embellishments, and, at most competitions, costume and appearance are evaluated as part of the final score.

In contrast, in chess and soccer, appearance matters little to the outcome of the competition. Although soccer girls' appearances are regulated, it is done in a way that de-emphasizes femininity. Soccer girls must remove all jewelry (for safety reasons), and coaches direct girls to make sure all of their hair is out of their faces. To keep their view unimpeded, girls pull their hair back in ponytails, using headbands or elastic bands. This has become a fashion and identity statement itself—perhaps a way to assert femininity in a less-than-feminine environment, and to keep shorter hair and bangs off the face. And, of course, female soccer uniforms are not easily distinguishable from male uniforms. Many traditional markers of femininity are absent from the pitch.

It is not surprising, then, that although both soccer and dance parents mentioned lifelong fitness and health as a motivation for their young daughters' involvement with these activities, only dance moms linked their kids' participation to obesity and appearance. Dance mom Tiffany told me about her concerns about her daughter's future body: "My short-term goal for her is to keep, believe it or not, physically fit. Because, she's an eater, across the board . . . [Dance] keeps her at a nice weight.

You know what I mean? And she struggles with that [weight], that's going to be her struggle, I told her."

Gender Scripts and Classed Lessons

Another set of scripts—those about femininity—helps explain how parents (especially dance and soccer parents) choose among activities for their daughters. I call the dance script the "graceful girls," the soccer "aggressive girls," and the chess "pink warriors." When dance, soccer, and chess parents draw from different gender scripts, they are shaped by class, producing classed lessons in femininity for their girls.

Though nearly all of the families I met are part of the broadly defined middle class, parents higher up in the hierarchy of the middle class promote a more aggressive femininity, as seen in both soccer and chess families. Dance mothers, who generally have lower status than the chess and soccer parents, promote a femininity that is less competitively aggressive and prioritizes physical appearance. Lower-middle-class and working-class families place a greater emphasis on traditional femininity.

Among the 38 families I met who had competitive young girls, the vast majority of soccer families were upper-middle-class. None of the dance families were upper-middle-class, and over a third were lower-middle-class; dance was the only activity of the three that had any working-class participants. Chess families with daughters who compete tend to look the most like soccer families, as the majority of families are upper-middle-class.

These upper-middle-class families had at least one parent who has earned an advanced postgraduate degree and work in a professional or managerial occupation, and both parents had earned a four-year college degree. The lower-middle-class families have just one parent with a college degree; neither parent works in a professional or managerial occupation.

Recall Malcolm and Marie. The former is a lawyer, and the latter was an investment banker who recently stopped working to spend more time with her five children. Both attended elite universities, and were representative of the rest of the parents. Most of the soccer parents had similar occupations, or they were professors or doctors.

It is not surprising that these highly credentialed, competitive parents have similar occupational aspirations for their children, including their daughters. They are trying to impart particular skills and lessons to their daughters at a young age to help them succeed in the long term. As Malcolm made clear, upper-middle-class parents do not want their daughters to end up as secretaries, so participation in competitive activities, where aggression is inculcated, becomes a priority so the girls can maintain their family's status in the future.

Bossy Is Best?

Today, there are three times more female soccer players than Girl Scouts in the United States. This trend is due, in part, to the fact that upper-middle-class families are trying to strategically maintain their family's class position, preparing their daughters to enter what are traditionally male worlds. Parents are choosing afterschool activities that will give these girls an advantage in college admissions and beyond; they are more likely to have the resources to enable their daughters to travel and compete.

But aggressive femininity can come at a cost. A recent study of the long-term effects of sports participation on adolescent girls by psychologists Campbell Leaper and Elizabeth Daniels found that many girls "struggle to reconcile their athleticism with traditional standards of hegemonic femininity that emphasize maintaining a thin body ideal and adhering to a rigid definition of beauty." Aggressive and pink warrior girls, along with graceful girls, face what psychologist Stephen Hinshaw calls the "triple bind" of being supportive, competitive and successful—and effortlessly beautiful.

In her work on female litigators, sociologist Jennifer Pierce similarly found that successful women had to become either "very male" or "very caring." She describes this binary: "Whereas men are praised for using intimidation and strategic friendliness, women who are aggressive are censured for being too difficult to get along with, and women who are nice are considered 'not tough enough' to be good litigators." Women need to be aggressive to succeed, but not *so* aggressive that they get labeled bitchy. It's a delicate balancing act for women in the work force, and for parents who want to raise girls who can be the boss.

These classed gender ideals also have long-term implications for inequality. Girls from upper-middle-class families seem better equipped with the skills they need to succeed in more lucrative careers, and in leadership roles as adults. Better understanding socialization practices at the upper end of the class structure may open up real opportunities for others as well.

Sheryl Sandberg wasn't a soccer player. She wasn't even athletic, in an aggressive sense, at all. She was once an aerobics instructor who succeeded by leading others in a silver leotard. Her story suggests that soccer and contact sports aren't a direct path to the corner office, and that dance and cheerleading don't shut the door on success.

The future is not cast in stone: Tiffany's dancing daughter may yet become an executive, and Malcolm's daughter may become her assistant. That doesn't stop many affluent parents from being convinced that leaning in while wearing pink cleats produces girls with executive leadership skills.

THINKING ABOUT THE READING

The socialization process is one of the most important aspects of sociology because it allows us to understand how society reproduces itself and why it is constantly changing. How does Friedman's article on children's participation in afterschool activities contribute to the nature (genetic inheritance) versus nurture (environmental influence) debate? What does socialization in these various afterschool activities—chess, dance, soccer—teach children about their self and place in the social world? In your answer, consider terms from the article like *aggressive femininity, normative femininity,* and *competitive kid capital.* According to the author, how does time and place in history influence the content of these socialization messages? How might a person's place in her or his life cycle shape these messages and the tools available to achieve them? Do other factors besides social class and gender influence your socialization process? What about race and ethnicity? Sexuality? Religion? Physical and mental abilities?

Working 'the Code'

On Girls, Gender, and Inner-City Violence

Nikki Jones

(2008)

In mainstream American society, it is commonly assumed that women and girls shy away from conflict, are not physically aggressive, and do not fight like boys and men.

In this article, I draw on field research among African-American girls in the United States to argue that the circumstances of inner-city life have encouraged the development of uniquely situated femininities that simultaneously encourage and limit inner-city girls' use of physical aggression and violence. First, I begin by arguing that, in the urban environments that I studied, gender—being a girl—does not protect inner-city girls from much of the violence experienced by inner-city boys. In fact, teenaged boys and girls are both preoccupied with 'survival' as an ongoing project. I use my analysis of interviews with young people involved in violent incidents to demonstrate similarities in how young people work 'the code of the street' across perceived gender lines. This in-depth examination of young people's use of physical aggression and violence reveals that while young men and young women fight, survival is still a gendered project.

Race, Gender, and Inner-City Violence

Inner-city life has changed dramatically over the last century and especially over the last 30 years.

In his ethnographic account of life in inner-city Philadelphia, Elijah Anderson writes that the code of the street is 'a set of prescriptions and proscriptions, or informal rules, of behaviour organised around a desperate search for respect that governs public social relations, especially violence among so many residents, particularly young men and women' (Anderson, 1999, p. 10). Furthermore, the code is 'a system of accountability that promises "an eye for an eye," or a certain "pay back" for transgressions' (Anderson, 1999, p. 10). Fundamental elements of the code include respect and 'a credible reputation for vengeance that works to deter aggression' (Anderson, 1999, p. 10). According to Anderson, it is this complex relationship between masculinity, respect and violence that, at times, encourages poor, urban young men to risk their lives in order to be recognised and respected by others *as a man.*

Black feminist scholar Patricia Hill Collins considers Anderson's discussion of masculinity and the 'code of the street' in her recent analysis of the relationship between hegemonic (and racialised) masculinities and femininities, violence and dominance (Collins, 2004, pp. 188–212). Collins argues that the hyper-criminalisation of urban spaces is exacerbated by the culture of the code. As young men from distressed urban areas cycle in and out of correctional facilities at historically remarkable rates, she argues, urban public schools, street concerns and homes have become a '. . . nexus of street, prison and youth culture,' which exerts 'a tremendous amount of pressure on Black men, especially young, working class men, to avoid being classified as "weak"' (Collins, 2004, p. 211).

What About Girls?

Over the last few decades, feminist criminologists and gender and crime scholars have examined women's and girls' experiences with aggression and violence with increasing complexity. Emphasising how particular material circumstances influence women's and girls' relationship to violence shifts the focus from the consideration of dichotomous gender differences to the empirical examination of gender similarities and differences in experiences with violence among young women and men who live in poor, urban areas (Simpson, 1991). The analysis presented here follows in this tradition by recognising the influence of shared life circumstances on young people's use of violence.

The young people from Philadelphia's inner-city neighbourhoods that I encountered generally share similar life circumstances, yet how they respond to these structural and cultural circumstances—that is, how they work the code of the street—is also gendered in ways that reflect differences among inner-city girls' and boys' understanding of what you 'got to' do to 'survive.'

Methods

Each of the respondents featured in this study was enrolled in a city hospital-based violence intervention project that targeted youth aged 12 to 24 who presented in the emergency department as a result of an intentional violent incident and were considered to be at either moderate or high risk for involvement in future violent incidents. As a consequence of patterns of racial segregation within the city, almost the entire population of young women and men who voluntarily enrolled in the hospital's violence intervention project were African-American.

My fieldwork for this study took place in three phases over 3 years (2001–2003). During the first phase of the study, which lasted about a year and a half, I conducted 'ride alongs' with intervention counsellors who met with young people in their homes shortly after their initial visit to the emergency room. I also conducted a series of interviews with members of the intervention counselling staff. Most of the staff grew up in Philadelphia and were personally familiar with many of the neighbourhoods we visited. During this time and throughout the study, I also observed interactions in the spaces and places that were significant in the lives of the young people I met. These spaces included trolley cars and buses (transportation to and from school), a neighbourhood high school nicknamed 'the Prison on the Hill,' the city's family and criminal court, and various correctional facilities in the area. I also intentionally engaged in extended conversations with grandmothers and mothers, sisters, brothers, cousins and friends of the young people I visited and interviewed. I recorded this information in my fieldnotes and used it to complement, supplement, test and, at times, verify the information collected during interviews.

Shared Circumstances, Shared Code

While the problem of inner-city violence is believed to impact boys and men only, my interviews with teenaged inner-city girls revealed that young women are regularly exposed to many of the same forms of violence that men are exposed to in their everyday lives and are deeply influenced by its normative order. In the inner-city neighbourhoods I visited, which were often quite isolated from the rest of the city, I encountered young men and young women who could quickly recall a friend, relative or 'associate' who had been shot, robbed or stabbed. In the public high school I visited, I watched adolescent girls and boys begin their school day with the same ritual: they dropped their bags on security belts, stepped through a metal detector, and raised their arms and spread their legs for a police-style 'pat down' before entering the building. Repeatedly, I encountered teenaged girls who, like the young men they share space with in the inner city, had stories to tell about getting 'rolled on,' or getting 'jumped,' or about the 'fair one' gone bad. It is these shared circumstances of life that engender a shared understanding about how to survive in a setting where your safety is never guaranteed. In the following sections, I provide portraits of four young people involved in violent incidents in order to illustrate what was revealed to me during the course of field research and interviews: an appreciation of 'the code of the street' that cut across gender lines. The first two respondents, Billy and DeLisha, tell stories of recouping from a very public loss in a street fight. The second set of respondents, Danielle and Robert, highlight how even those who are averse to fighting must sometimes put forth a 'tough front' to deter potentially aggressive challenges in the future.

Billy and DeLisha: 'I'm Not Looking Over My Shoulder'

Billy was 'jumped' by a group of young men while in 'their' neighbourhood, which is within walking distance of his own. He tells me this story as we sit in the living room of his row home. Billy recently reached his 20s, although he looks older than his age. He is White but shares a class background that is similar to many of the young people I interviewed. His block, like most of the others I visited during this study, is a collection of row homes in various states of disrepair. Billy spends more time here than he would like. He is unemployed and when asked how best the intervention project he enrolled in could help him his request was simple: I need a job. As we talk, I think that Billy is polite—he offers me a drink (a beer, which I decline) before we begin our interview—and even quiet. He recalls two violent battles within the last year, both of which ended with him in the emergency room, without wavering too far from a measured, even tone. The first incident he recalls for me happened in South Philadelphia. He was walking down the block, when he came across a group of guys on the corner, guys who he had 'trouble' with in the past. As he stood talking to an acquaintance, Billy was approached from behind and punched in the back of the head. The force of the punch was multiplied exponentially by brass knuckles, 'splitting [his] head open.' Billy was knocked out instantly, fell face-first toward the ground and split his nose on a concrete step. The thin scar from this street-fight remains several months later.

In contrast to Billy's even tone, DeLisha is loud. She is thin with a medium-brown complexion. Her retelling of the story of her injury is more like a re-enactment as the adrenaline, anxiety and excitement of the day return. She comes across as fiercely independent, especially for a 17-year-old girl. DeLisha, a young mother with a 1-year-old daughter, has been unable to rely on her own drug-addicted mother for much of her life. After years of this independence, she is convinced that she does not need anyone's help to 'make it' in life. While she has been a 'fighter' for as long as she can remember, she was never hurt before. Not in school. Not in her neighbourhood, which is one of the most notorious in the city. And not like this. She had agreed to a fight with another neighbourhood girl. The younger girl, pressured by her family and peers to win the battle, shielded a box-cutter from DeLisha's sight until the very last minute. When it seemed that she would lose, the girl flashed the box-cutter and slashed DeLisha across the hand, tearing past skin and muscle into a tendon on her arm.

During my interviews with Billy and DeLisha, I asked each of them how these very public losses, which also resulted in serious physical injuries, would influence their mobility within the neighbourhood. Would they avoid certain people and places? Would or could they shrug their loss off or would they seek vengeance for their lost battle? Billy's and DeLisha's responses were strikingly similar in tone, nearly identical at some points, and equally revealing of two of the most basic elements of the code of the street: the commitment to maintaining a 'tough front' and 'payback.'

Billy: I mean, just like I say, I walk around this neighbourhood. I'm not looking over my shoulder . . . I'm not going to walk [and] look around my shoulder because I've got people looking for me. I mean you want me . . . you know where I live. They can call me at any time they want. That's how, that's how I think . . . . I'm not going to sit around my own neighbourhood and just say: 'Aww, I got to watch my back.' You want me? You got me.

DeLisha: I'm not a scared type . . . I walk on the streets anytime I want to. I do anything I want to, anytime I want to do it. It's never been a problem walking on the street 3.00 in the morning. If I want to go home 3.00 in the morning, I'm going to go home. I'm not looking over my shoulder. My grandma never raised me to look over my shoulder. I'm not going to stop because of some little incident [being cut in the hand with a box cutter].

Billy and DeLisha's strikingly similar responses reveal their commitment to a shared 'system of accountability,' the code of the street, which, as Anderson argues, governs much of social life, especially violence, in distressed urban areas (Anderson, 1999). Billy and DeLisha hold themselves accountable to this system ('I'm not going to . . . ') and are also aware that others will hold them accountable for their behaviours and actions. Billy and DeLisha are acutely aware that someone who 'looks over their shoulder' while walking down the street is perceived as weak, a moving target, and both are determined to reject such a fate. Instead, Billy and DeLisha remain committed to managing their 'presentation of self' (Goffman, 1959) in a way that masks any signs of vulnerability.

In addition to their commitment to 'not looking over their shoulder,' Billy and DeLisha are also sensitive to the fact that the fights they were in were not 'fair.' These street-level injustices inform Billy and DeLisha's expectations for retaliation. Consistent with the code, both Billy and DeLisha—equally armed with long fight histories—realise the importance of 'payback' and consider future battles with their challengers to be inevitable. When I asked DeLisha if she anticipated another fight with the young woman who cut her, she replied with a strong yes, 'because I'm taking it there with her.' Billy was also equally committed to retaliation, telling me: ' . . . one by one, I will get them.'

Danielle and Robert: 'Sometimes You Got to Fight'

In *Code of the Street* (1999), Anderson demonstrates how important it is for young people to prove publicly that they are not someone to be 'messed with.' One of the ways that young people prove this to others is by engaging in fights in public, when necessary. The following statements from Danielle and Robert, two young people who are adept at avoiding conflicts, illustrate teenaged girls' and boys' shared understanding of the importance of demonstrating that one is willing to fight as a way to deter ongoing challenges to one's well-being:

Danielle: 'cause sometimes you got to fight, not fight, but get into that type of battle to let them know that I'm not scared of you and you can't keep harassing me thinking that it's okay.

Robert: . . . you know, if someone keep picking on you like that, you gonna have to do something to prove a point to them: that you not going to be scared of them . . . So, sometimes you do got to, you do got to fight. Cause you just got to tell them that you not scared of them.

Like DeLisha and Billy, Danielle, a recent high-school graduate, and Robert, who is in the 11th grade, offer nearly identical explanations of the importance of physically protecting one's own boundaries by demonstrating to others that you will fight, if necessary. While neither Danielle nor Robert identify as 'fighters,' both are convinced that sometimes you 'got to fight.' Again, this shared language reveals an awareness and commitment to a shared system of accountability, 'the code of the street,' which encourages young people—teenaged girls and boys—to present a 'tough front' as a way to discourage on-going challenges to one's personal security. For the young people in this study, the value placed on maintaining a tough front or 'proving a point' cut across perceived gender lines.

In addition to possibly deterring future challenges, Anderson argues that presenting and ultimately proving oneself as someone who is not to be 'messed with' helps to build a young person's confidence and self-esteem: 'particularly for young men and perhaps increasingly among females . . . their identity, their self-respect, and their honor are often intricately tied up with the way they perform on the streets during and after such [violent] encounters' (Anderson, 1999, p. 76). Those young people who are able to perform well during these public encounters acquire a sense of confidence that will facilitate their movement throughout the neighbourhood. This boost to one's sense of self is not restricted to young men; young women who can fight and win may also demonstrate a strong sense of pride and confidence in their ability to 'handle' potentially aggressive or violent conflicts, as illustrated by the following interview with Nicole.

Nicole: 'I Feel Like I Can Defend Myself'

My conversation with Nicole typifies the confidence expressed by teenaged girls who can fight and win. Nicole is a smart, articulate young woman who attended some community college courses while still a senior in high school. She planned to attend a state university to study engineering after graduation. While in high school, she tells me, she felt confident in her ability to walk the hallways of her sometimes chaotic public school: 'I feel like I can defend myself.' Unlike some young women who walk the hallways constantly testing others, Nicole's was a quiet confidence: 'I don't, like, I mean, when I'm walking around school or something, I don't walk around talking about "yeah, I beat this girl up."' Nicole could, in fact, claim that she didn't beat up just one

girl but several, at the same time. Nicole explained to me how her most recent fight began:

> We [she and another young woman] had got into two arguments in the hallway and then her friends were holding her back. So I just said, 'Forget it. I'm just going to my class.' So I'm in class, I'm inside the classroom and I hear Nina say, 'Is this that bitch's class?' I came to the door and was like, 'Yes, this is my class.' And she puts her hands up [in fighting position] and she swings . . . And me and her was fighting, and then I got her on the wall, and then I felt somebody pulling my hair, and it turns out to be Jessica. Right? And then we fighting, and then I see Tasha, and it's me and all these three people and then they broke it all up.

Nicole's only injury in the fight came from the elbow of the school police officer who eventually ended the battle. As Nicole recalls this fight, and her performance in particular, I notice that she is smiling. This smile, together with the tone in which she tells the story of her earlier battle, makes it clear that she is proud of her ability to meet the challenge presented to her by these young women. Impressed at her ability to fight off three teenaged girls at the same time, I ask Nicole: 'How did you manage not to get jumped?' She quickly corrects my definition of the situation: 'No. I managed to beat them up.' After retelling her fight story, Nicole shakes her head from side to side and says: 'I had to end up beating them up. So sad.' I notice her sure smile return. 'You don't really look like you feel bad about that,' I say. 'I don't,' she replies.

The level of self-confidence that Nicole displays in this brief exchange contrasts with the passivity and submissiveness that is commonly expected of women and girls, especially white, middle-class women and girls (Collins, 2004). It is young men, not teenaged girls, who are expected to exude such confidence as they construct a 'tough front' to deter would-be challengers (Anderson, 1999). Nicole's confidence is also more than an expressive performance. Nicole knows that she is physically able to fight and win, when necessary, because she has done so in the past. For teenaged girls like Nicole and Sharmaine, whom I discuss below, this confidence is essential to their evaluation of how best to handle potential interpersonal conflicts in their everyday lives.

Sharmaine: '. . . I Have One Hand Left'

Sharmaine, an 8th grader, displayed a level of self-confidence similar to Nicole's after a fight with a boy in her classroom. Moments before the fight, the boy approached Sharmaine while she was looking out her classroom window, and 'whispered something' in her ear. Sharmaine knew that this boy liked her, but she thought she had made it quite clear that she did not like him. Sharmaine quickly told him to back off and then looked to her teacher for reinforcement. Her teacher, Sharmaine recalls, just laughed at the boy's advances. After he whispered in Sharmaine's ear a second time, she turned around and punched him in the face. Sharmaine later ended up in the emergency room with a jammed finger from the punch. I asked Sharmaine if she was concerned about him getting back at her when she returned to school. She tells me that someone in the emergency room asked her the same question. 'What did you say?' I ask. 'I told them no . . . because I have one hand left.'

For young women like Nicole and Sharmaine, the proven ability to defend themselves translates into a level of self-confidence that is not typically expected in girls and young women. Those girls who are confident in their ability to 'take care of themselves' become more mobile as they come to believe, as DeLisha says, that they can 'do anything [they] want to, anytime [they] want to do it.' Girls who are able to gain and maintain this level of self-confidence are able to challenge the real and imagined gendered boundaries on space and place in the inner city.

'Boys Got to Go Get Guns'

The need to be 'distinguished as a man'—a benchmark of hegemonic masculinity—often fosters adolescent boys' preoccupation with distinguishing themselves *from* women (Anderson, 1999; Collins, 2004, p. 210; Connell & Messerschmidt, 2005). This is a gendered preoccupation that was not revealed in urban adolescent girls' accounts of physical aggression and violence. The following statement from Craig, a young man who has deliberately checked his readiness to fight after being shot in the hip, illustrates how the need to 'be a man' influences young men's consideration of violence:

> Yeah, I don't fight no more. I can't fight [because of injury]. So, I really stop and think about stuff because it isn't even worth it . . . unless, I mean, you really want it [a fight] to happen . . . I'm going to turn the other cheek. But, I'm not going to be, like, wearing a skirt. That's the way you got to look at it.

While Craig is prepared to exit his life as a 'fighter,' he predicts that his newfound commitment to avoid fights will not stand up to the pressure of proving his manhood to a challenger. Craig is well aware of how another young man can communicate that he 'really want [a fight] to happen.' Once a challenger publicly escalates a battle in this way, young men like Craig have few choices. At this moment, a young man will have to demonstrate to his challenger, and his audience, that he isn't 'wearing a skirt.' Not only must he fight, he must also fight *like a man*.

Craig's admission is revealing of how a young man's concern with not being 'like' a woman influences his consideration of the appropriate use of physical aggression. While a similar type of preoccupation with intergender distinctions was not typically revealed in young women's accounts, I found that teenaged girls were generally aware of at least one significant difference in how young women and men were expected to work the code of the street.

As is revealed in my conversation with Shante, a teenaged girl who was hit in the head with a brick by a neighbourhood girl, young men are generally expected to use more serious or lethal forms of violence than girls or women. I asked Shante what people in her neighbourhood thought about girls fighting.

> 'Today,' she asked, 'you mean like people on the street?'
>
> 'Yeah.'
>
> 'If [a girl] get beat up, you just get beat up. That's on you.'
>
> 'Do you think it's different for boys?' I asked.
>
> 'Umm, boys got to go get guns. They got to blow somebody's head off. They got to shoot. They don't fight these days. They use guns.'

Shante's perception of what boys 'got to' do is informed by years of observation and experience. Shante has grown up in a neighbourhood marked by violence. Days before this interview, she saw a young man get shot in the head. She tells me he was dead by the time he hit the sidewalk. When I asked Shante whether or not girls used guns, she could recall just one young woman from the neighbourhood—the same young woman who hit Shante over the head with a brick—who had 'pistol whipped' another teenaged girl. While she certainly used the gun as a weapon, she didn't shoot her. These two incidents are actually quite typical of reported gender differences in the use of weapons in violent acts: boys and men are much more likely than girls and women to use guns to shoot and kill. Women and girls, like many of the young women I spoke with during this study, are far more likely to rely on knives and box-cutters, if they use a weapon at all (see also Miller, 1998 & 2001; Pastor, et al., 1996, p. 28). Those young women who did use a weapon, such as a knife or box-cutter, explained that they did so for protection. For example, Shante told me that she carried a razor blade, 'because she doesn't trust people.'

Takeya: 'A Good Girl'

In contrast to the commitment to protecting one's manhood, which Craig alludes to and Elijah Anderson describes in great detail (Anderson, 1999), the young women I spoke to did not suggest that they fought because that's what *women* do. Furthermore, while young women deeply appreciated the utility of a 'tough front,' they were unlikely to use phrases like 'I don't want to be wearing a skirt.' In fact, while young men like Craig work to prove their manhood by distinguishing themselves from women, many of the young women I spoke with—including the 'toughest' among them—embraced popular notions of femininity, 'skirts' and all. For many of the girls I interviewed, an appreciation of some aspects of hegemonic femininity modulated their involvement in violent interactions.

My conversation with Takeya sheds light on how inner-city girls attempt to reconcile the contradictory concerns that emerge from intersecting survival and gender projects. When I asked Takeya, a slim 13-year-old girl with a light-brown complexion, about her fighting history, she replied, 'I'm not in no fights. I'm a good girl.' 'You are a good girl?' I asked. 'Yeah, I'm a good girl and I'm-a be a pretty girl at 18.'

Takeya's concern with being a 'pretty girl' reflects an appreciation of aspects of hegemonic femininity that place great value on beauty. Her understanding of what it means to be beautiful is also influenced by the locally placed value on skin colour, hair texture and body figure. While brown skin and textured hair may not fit hegemonic (White, middle-class) conceptions of beauty, in this setting, a light-brown skinned complexion, 'straight' or 'good' hair, and a slim figure help to make one 'pretty' and 'good' (Banks, 2000). Yet, Takeya also knows that one's ability to stay pretty—to be a pretty girl at age 18—is directly influenced by one's involvement in interpersonal aggression or violence.

In order to be considered a 'pretty girl' by her peers, Takeya knows that she must avoid those types of interpersonal conflicts that tend to result in cuts and scratches to young women's faces, especially the ones that others consider beautiful (in *Code of the Street* [1999] Anderson writes that such visible scars often result in heightened status for the young women who leave their mark on pretty girls). Yet, Takeya is also aware that the culture of the code requires her to become an able fighter and to maintain a reputation as such. After expressing her commitment to being a 'good' girl, Takeya is sure to inform me that not only does she know how to fight, others also recognise her as an able fighter: 'I don't want you to think I don't know how to fight. I mean everybody always come get me [for fights]. [I'm] the number one [person they come to get].'

Takeya's simultaneous embrace of the culture of code and some aspects of normative femininity, Craig's concern with distinguishing himself from women, and Shante's convincing disclosure regarding what boys 'got to' do highlight how masculinity and femininity projects overlap and intersect with the project of survival for young people in distressed inner-city neighbourhoods. Both Craig and Takeya appreciate fundamental elements of 'the code,' especially the importance of being known as an able fighter. Yet, Craig's use of physical aggression is likely to be encouraged by his commitment to a distinctive aspect of hegemonic masculinity: being distinguished from a girl. Meanwhile, Takeya's use of physical aggression and violence is tempered—though not extinguished—by seemingly typical 'female' concerns: being a 'good' and 'pretty' girl. In contrast to the project of accomplishing masculinity, which overlaps and, at times, contradicts the project of survival for young men, the project of accomplishing femininity can, at times, facilitate young women's struggle to survive in this setting.

Gender, Survival, and 'the Code'

I have argued that gender does not protect young women from much of the violence young men experience in distressed inner-city neighbourhoods, and that given these shared circumstances, it becomes equally important for women and men to work 'the code of the street.' Like many adolescent boys, young women also recognise that reputation, respect and retaliation—the '3 Rs' of the code of the street—organise their social world (Anderson, 1999). Yet, as true as it is that, at times, young men and women work the code of the street in similar ways, it is also true that differences exist. These differences are rooted in the relationships between masculinity, femininity and the use of violence or aggression in distressed urban areas and emerge from overlapping and intersecting survival and gender projects.

In order to 'survive' in today's inner city, young women like DeLisha, Danielle, Shante and Takeya are encouraged to embrace some aspects of the 'code of the street' that organises much of inner-city life (Anderson, 1999). In doing so, these girls also embrace and accomplish some aspects of hegemonic masculinity that are embedded in the code. My analysis of interviews with teenaged girls and boys injured in intentional violent incidents reveals an appreciation of the importance of maintaining a tough front and demonstrating nerve across perceived gender lines. It is this appreciation of the cultural elements of the code that leads teenaged girls like Danielle to believe strongly that 'sometimes you got to fight.'

REFERENCES

Anderson, E. (1999). *Code of the street: Decency, violence and the moral life of the inner city.* New York: W. W. Norton.

Banks, I. (2000). *Hair matters: Beauty, power, and Black women's consciousness.* New York: New York University Press.

Collins, P. Hill. (2004). *Black sexual politics: African Americans, gender, and the new racism.* New York: Routledge.

Connell, R.W., & Messerschmidt, J.W. (2005). Hegemonic masculinity: Rethinking the concept. *Gender & Society,* 19(6), 829–859.

Goffman, E. (1959). *The presentation of self in everyday life.* New York: Anchor Books.

Miller, J. (1998). Up it up: Gender and the accomplishment of street robbery. *Criminology,* 36(1), 37–66.

Miller, J. (2001). *One of the guys: Girls, gangs, and gender.* Oxford: Oxford University Press.

Pastor, J., McCormick, J., & Fine, M. (1996). Makin' homes: An urban girl thing. In B. J. Ross Leadbeater & N. Way (Eds.), *Urban girls: Resisting stereotypes, creating identities.* New York: New York University Press.

Simpson, S. S. (1991). Caste, class, and violent crime: Explaining difference in female offending. *Criminology,* 29(1), 115–135.

THINKING ABOUT THE READING

This reading demonstrates that inner-city girls are also not as isolated from violence as is commonly thought. What are some of the reasons for their involvement with violence? What is the "code of the street"? How are violence and the "code" related to the ways in which these girls see themselves? How are they related to their survival? Does the way in which girls use and understand violence differ from the ways in which boys see it?

Supporting Identity

The Presentation of Self

6

Social behavior is highly influenced by the images we form of others. We typically form impressions of people based on an initial assessment of their social group membership (ethnicity, age, gender, etc.), their personal attributes (e.g., physical attractiveness), and the verbal and nonverbal messages they provide. These assessments are usually accompanied by a set of expectations we've learned to associate with members of certain social groups or people with certain attributes. Such judgments allow us to place people in broad categories and provide a degree of predictability in interactions.

While we are forming impressions of others, we are fully aware that they are doing the same thing with us. Early in life, most of us learn that it is to our advantage to have people think highly of us. In "The Presentation of Self in Everyday Life," Erving Goffman describes a process called *impression management* in which we attempt to control and manipulate information about ourselves to influence the impressions others form of us. Impression management provides the link between the way we perceive ourselves and the way we want others to perceive us. We've all been in situations— a first date, a job interview, meeting a girlfriend's or boyfriend's family for the first time—in which we've felt compelled to "make a good impression." What we often fail to realize, however, is that personal impression management may be influenced by larger organizational and institutional forces.

Impression management is used to control the assessment others make of us in relation to certain group memberships. For example, initial impressions are often formed around key facets of identity like race and social class. In "Blue Chip Blacks: Managing Race in Public Spaces," Karyn R. Lacy presents research based on interviews with middle-class blacks in Washington, D.C. Despite what the research literature on racial stigma theory has shown, these individuals use their agency and cultural capital to produce "public identities" and control interactions with whites that lead to positive outcomes in public arenas like shopping malls, real estate (house hunting), and the workplace. The use of public identities demonstrates how some middle-class blacks can define their situation and avoid racial discrimination through the manipulation of their public interactions with whites.

The third reading is likely to raise considerable discussion. Why do college-age men go on "girl hunts"? Sociologist David Grazian uses Goffman's framework to explain this behavior. He suggests that the urban nightlife girl-hunt scene is actually a ritual of male bonding and masculine identity building. Getting a girl is not really the goal. Hanging out and bonding with other men and reinforcing patterns of masculinity is the point of these ritual-like practices. If this is the case, then what are the implications for the perpetuation of cultural practices that build masculinity by objectifying women?

Something to Consider as You Read

As you read these selections on the presentation of self and identity, consider where people get their ideas about whom and what they can be in various settings. Consider a setting in which everyone present may be trying to create a certain impression because that's what they all think everyone else wants. What would have to happen for the "impression script" to change in this setting? In what ways do material resources and authority influence the impression we're able to make? Are there certain types of people who needn't be concerned about the impressions they give off? Compare and contrast the readings on public identities and the "girl hunt." Are there similar cultural scripts operating in both these scenarios?

The Presentation of Self in Everyday Life

Selections

Erving Goffman

(1959)

Introduction

When an individual enters the presence of others, they commonly seek to acquire information about him or to bring into play information about him already possessed. They will be interested in his general socio-economic status, his conception of self, his attitude toward them, his competence, his trustworthiness, etc. Although some of this information seems to be sought almost as an end in itself, there are usually quite practical reasons for acquiring it. Information about the individual helps to define the situation, enabling others to know in advance what he will expect of them and what they may expect of him. Informed in these ways, the others will know how best to act in order to call forth a desired response from him.

For those present, many sources of information become accessible and many carriers (or "sign-vehicles") become available for conveying this information. If unacquainted with the individual, observers can glean clues from his conduct and appearance which allow them to apply their previous experience with individuals roughly similar to the one before them or, more important, to apply untested stereotypes to him. They can also assume from past experience that only individuals of a particular kind are likely to be found in a given social setting. They can rely on what the individual says about himself or on documentary evidence he provides as to who and what he is. If they know, or know of, the individual by virtue of experience prior to the interaction, they can rely on assumptions as to the persistence and generality of psychological traits as a means of predicting his present and future behavior.

The expressiveness of the individual (and therefore his capacity to give impressions) appears to involve two radically different kinds of sign activity: the expression that he *gives,* and the expression that he *gives off.* The first involves verbal symbols or their substitutes which he uses admittedly and solely to convey the information that he and the others are known to attach to these symbols. This is communication in the traditional and narrow sense. The second involves a wide range of action that others can treat as symptomatic of the actor, the expectation being that the action was performed for reasons other than the information conveyed in this way. As we shall have to see, this distinction has an only initial validity. The individual does of course intentionally convey misinformation by means of both of these types of communication, the first involving deceit, the second feigning.

Taking communication in both its narrow and broad sense, one finds that when the individual is in the immediate presence of others, his activity will have a promissory character. The others are likely to find that they must accept the individual on faith, offering him a just return while he is present before them in exchange for something whose true value will not be established until after he has left their presence. (Of course, the others also live by inference in their dealings with the physical

119

world, but it is only in the world of social interaction that the objects about which they make inferences will purposely facilitate and hinder this inferential process.) The security that they justifiably feel in making inferences about the individual will vary, of course, depending on such factors as the amount of information they already possess about him, but no amount of such past evidence can entirely obviate the necessity of acting on the basis of inferences. As William I. Thomas suggested:

> It is also highly important for us to realize that we do not as a matter of fact lead our lives, make our decisions, and reach our goals in everyday life either statistically or scientifically. We live by inference. I am, let us say, your guest. You do not know, you cannot determine scientifically, that I will not steal your money or your spoons. But inferentially I will not and inferentially you have me as a guest.[1]

Let us now turn from the others to the point of view of the individual who presents himself before them. He may wish them to think highly of him, or to think that he thinks highly of them, or to perceive how in fact he feels toward them, or to obtain no clear-cut impression; he may wish to ensure sufficient harmony so that the interaction can be sustained, or to defraud, get rid of, confuse, mislead, antagonize, or insult them. Regardless of the particular objective which the individual has in mind and of his motive for having this objective, it will be in his interests to control the conduct of the others, especially their responsive treatment of him.[2] This control is achieved largely by influencing the definition of the situation which the others come to formulate, and he can influence this definition by expressing himself in such a way as to give them the kind of impression that will lead them to act voluntarily in accordance with his own plan. Thus, when an individual appears in the presence of others, there will usually be some reason for him to mobilize his activity so that it will convey an impression to others which it is in his interests to convey. . . .

I have said that when an individual appears before others his actions will influence the definition of the situation which they come to have. Sometimes the individual will act in a thoroughly calculating manner, expressing himself in a given way solely in order to give the kind of impression to others that is likely to evoke from them a specific response he is concerned to obtain. Sometimes the individual will be calculating in his activity but be relatively unaware that this is the case. Sometimes he will intentionally and consciously express himself in a particular way, but chiefly because the tradition of his group or social status require this kind of expression and not because of any particular response (other than vague acceptance or approval) that is likely to be evoked from those impressed by the expression. Sometimes the traditions of an individual's role will lead him to give a well-designed impression of a particular kind and yet he may be neither consciously nor unconsciously disposed to create such an impression. The others, in their turn, may be suitably impressed by the individual's efforts to convey something, or may misunderstand the situation and come to conclusions that are warranted neither by the individual's intent nor by the facts. In any case, in so far as the others act *as if* the individual had conveyed a particular impression, we may take a functional or pragmatic view and say that the individual has "effectively" projected a given definition of the situation and "effectively" fostered the understanding that a given state of affairs obtains. . . .

When we allow that the individual projects a definition of the situation when he appears before others, we must also see that the others, however passive their role may seem to be, will themselves effectively project a definition of the situation by virtue of their response to the individual and by virtue of any lines of action they initiate to him. Ordinarily the definitions of the situation projected by the several different participants are sufficiently attuned to one another so that open contradiction will not occur. I do not mean that there will be the kind of consensus that arises when each individual present candidly expresses what he really feels and honestly agrees with the expressed feelings of the others present. This kind of harmony is an optimistic ideal and in any case not necessary for the smooth working of society. Rather, each participant is expected to suppress his immediate heartfelt feelings, conveying a view of the situation which he feels the others will be able to find at least temporarily acceptable. The maintenance of this surface of agreement, this veneer of consensus, is facilitated by each participant concealing his own wants behind statements which assert values to which everyone present feels obliged to give lip service. Further, there is usually a kind of division of definitional labor. Each participant is allowed to establish the tentative official ruling regarding matters which are vital to him but not immediately important to others, e.g., the rationalizations and justifications by which he accounts for his past activity. In exchange for this courtesy he remains silent or noncommittal on matters important to others but not immediately important to him. We have then a kind of interactional *modus vivendi*. Together the participants contribute to a single overall definition of the situation which involves not so much a real agreement as to what exists but rather a real agreement as to whose claims concerning what issues will be temporarily honored. Real agreement will also exist concerning the desirability of avoiding an open conflict of definitions of the situation.[3] I will refer to this level of agreement as a "working consensus." It is to be understood that the working consensus established in one interaction setting will be quite different in content from the working consensus established in a different type of setting. Thus, between two friends at lunch, a reciprocal show of affection, respect, and concern for the other is maintained. In service occupations, on the other hand, the specialist often maintains an image of disinterested involvement in the problem of the client, while the client responds with a show of respect for the competence and integrity of the specialist. Regardless of such differences in content, however, the general form of these working arrangements is the same. . . .

. . . Given the fact that the individual effectively projects a definition of the situation when he enters the presence of others, we can assume that events may occur within the interaction which contradict, discredit, or otherwise throw doubt upon this projection. When these disruptive events occur, the interaction itself may come to a confused and embarrassed halt. Some of the assumptions upon which the responses of the participants had been predicated become untenable, and the participants find themselves lodged in an interaction for which the situation has been wrongly defined and is now no longer defined. At such moments the individual whose presentation has been discredited may feel ashamed while the others present may feel hostile, and all the participants may come to feel ill at ease, nonplussed, out of countenance, embarrassed, experiencing the kind of anomy that is generated when the minute social system of face-to-face interaction breaks down. . . .

We find that preventive practices are constantly employed to avoid these embarrassments and that corrective practices are constantly employed to compensate for discrediting occurrences that have not been successfully avoided. When the individual employs these strategies and tactics to protect his own projections, we may refer to them as "defensive practices"; when a participant employs them to save the definition of the situation projected by another, we speak of "protective practices" or "tact." Together, defensive and protective practices comprise the techniques employed to safe-guard the impression fostered by an individual during his presence before others. It should be added that while we may be ready to see that no fostered impression would survive if defensive practices were not employed, we are less ready perhaps to see that few impressions could survive if those who received the impression did not exert tact in their reception of it.

In addition to the fact that precautions are taken to prevent disruption of projected definitions, we may also note that an intense interest in these disruptions comes to play a significant role in the social life of the group. Practical jokes and social games are played in which embarrassments which are to be taken unseriously are purposely engineered.[4] Fantasies are created in which devastating exposures occur. Anecdotes from the past— real, embroidered, or fictitious—are told and retold, detailing disruptions which occurred, almost occurred, or occurred and were admirably resolved. There seems to be no grouping which does not have a ready supply of these games, reveries, and cautionary tales, to be used as a source of humor, a catharsis for anxieties, and a sanction for inducing individuals to be modest in their claims and reasonable in their projected expectations. The individual may tell himself through dreams of getting into impossible positions. Families tell of the time a guest got his dates mixed and arrived when neither the house nor anyone in it was ready for him. Journalists tell of times when an all-too-meaningful misprint occurred, and the paper's assumption of objectivity or decorum was humorously discredited. Public servants tell of times a client ridiculously misunderstood form instructions, giving answers which implied an unanticipated and bizarre definition of the situation.[5] Seamen, whose home away from home is rigorously he-man, tell stories of coming back home and inadvertently asking mother to "pass the fucking butter."[6] Diplomats tell of the time a near-sighted queen asked a republican ambassador about the health of his king.[7]

To summarize, then, I assume that when an individual appears before others he will have many motives for trying to control the impression they receive of the situation. This report is concerned with some of the common techniques that persons employ to sustain such impressions and with some of the common contingencies associated with the employment of these techniques. It will be convenient to end this introduction with some definitions. . . . For the purpose of this report, interaction (that is, face-to-face interaction) may be roughly defined as the reciprocal influence of individuals upon one another's actions when in one another's immediate physical presence. An interaction may be defined as all the interaction which occurs throughout any one occasion when a given set

of individuals are in one another's continuous presence; the term "an encounter" would do as well. A "performance" may be defined as all the activity of a given participant on a given occasion which serves to influence in any way any of the other participants. Taking a particular participant and his performance as a basic point of reference, we may refer to those who contribute the other performances as the audience, observers, or co-participants. The pre-established pattern of action which is unfolded during a performance and which may be presented or played through on other occasions may be called a "part" or "routine."[8] These situational terms can easily be related to conventional structural ones. When an individual or performer plays the same part to the same audience on different occasions, a social relationship is likely to arise. Defining social role as the enactment of rights and duties attached to a given status, we can say that a social role will involve one or more parts and that each of these different parts may be presented by the performer on a series of occasions to the same kinds of audience or to an audience of the same persons. . . .

Performances

Front

I [use] the term "performance" to refer to all the activity of an individual which occurs during a period marked by his continuous presence before a particular set of observers and which has some influence on the observers. It will be convenient to label as "front" that part of the individual's performance which regularly functions in a general and fixed fashion to define the situation for those who observe the performance. Front, then, is the expressive equipment of a standard kind intentionally or unwittingly employed by the individual during his performance. For preliminary purposes, it will be convenient to distinguish and label what seem to be the standard parts of front.

First, there is the "setting," involving furniture, décor, physical layout, and other background items which supply the scenery and stage props for the spate of human action played out before, within, or upon it. A setting tends to stay put, geographically speaking, so that those who would use a particular setting as part of their performance cannot begin their act until they have brought themselves to the appropriate place and must terminate their performance when they leave it. It is only in exceptional circumstances that the setting follows along with the performers; we see this in the funeral cortège, the civic parade, and the dreamlike processions that kings and queens are made of. In the main, these exceptions seem to offer some kind of extra protection for performers who are, or who have momentarily become, highly sacred. . . .

It is sometimes convenient to divide the stimuli which make up personal front into "appearance" and "manner," according to the function performed by the information that these stimuli convey. "Appearance" may be taken to refer to those stimuli which function at the time to tell us of the performer's social statuses. These stimuli also tell us of the individual's temporary ritual state, that is, whether he is engaging in formal social activity, work, or informal recreation, whether or not he is celebrating a new phase in the season cycle or in his life-cycle. "Manner" may be taken to refer to those stimuli which function at the time to warn us of the interaction role the performer will expect to play in the oncoming situation. Thus a haughty, aggressive manner may give the impression that the performer expects to be the one who will initiate the verbal interaction and direct its course. A meek, apologetic manner may give the impression that the performer expects to follow the lead of others, or at least that he can be led to do so. . . .

Dramatic Realization

While in the presence of others, the individual typically infuses his activity with signs which dramatically highlight and portray confirmatory facts that might otherwise remain unapparent or obscure. For if the individual's activity is to become significant to others, he must mobilize his activity so that it will express *during the interaction* what he wishes to convey. In fact, the performer may be required not only to express his claimed capacities during the interaction but also to do so during a split second in the interaction. Thus, if a baseball umpire is to give the impression that he is sure of his judgment, he must forgo the moment of thought which might make him sure of his judgment; he must give an instantaneous decision so that the audience will be sure that he is sure of his judgment.[9] . . .

Similarly, the proprietor of a service establishment may find it difficult to dramatize what is actually being done for clients because the clients cannot "see" the overhead costs of the service rendered them. Undertakers must therefore charge a great deal for their highly visible product—a coffin that has been transformed into a casket—because many of the other costs of conducting a funeral are ones that cannot be readily dramatized.[10] Merchants, too, find that they must charge high prices for things that look intrinsically inexpensive in order to compensate the establishment for expensive things like insurance, slack periods, etc., that never appear before the customers' eyes. . . .

Idealization

. . . I want to consider here another important aspect of this socialization process—the tendency for performers to offer their observers an impression that is idealized in several different ways.

The notion that a performance presents an idealized view of the situation is, of course, quite common. Cooley's view may be taken as an illustration:

> If we never tried to seem a little better than we are, how could we improve or "train ourselves from the outside inward"? And the

same impulse to show the world a better or idealized aspect of ourselves finds an organized expression in the various professions and classes, each of which has to some extent a cant or pose, which its members assume unconsciously, for the most part, but which has the effect of a conspiracy to work upon the credulity of the rest of the world. There is a cant not only of theology and of philanthropy, but also of law, medicine, teaching, even of science—perhaps especially of science, just now, since the more a particular kind of merit is recognized and admired, the more it is likely to be assumed by the unworthy.[11]

Thus, when the individual presents himself before others, his performance will tend to incorporate and exemplify the officially accredited values of the society, more so, in fact, than does his behavior as a whole.

To the degree that a performance highlights the common official values of the society in which it occurs, we may look upon it, in the manner of Durkheim and Radcliffe-Brown, as a ceremony—as an expressive rejuvenation and reaffirmation of the moral values of the community. Furthermore, insofar as the expressive bias of performances comes to be accepted as reality, then that which is accepted at the moment as reality will have some of the characteristics of a celebration. To stay in one's room away from the place where the party is given, or away from where the practitioner attends his client, is to stay away from where reality is being performed. The world, in truth, is a wedding.

One of the richest sources of data on the presentation of idealized performances is the literature on social mobility. In most societies there seems to be a major or general system of stratification, and in most stratified societies there is an idealization of the higher strata and some aspiration on the part of those in low places to move to higher ones. (One must be careful to appreciate that this involves not merely a desire for a prestigeful place but also a desire for a place close to the sacred center of the common values of the society.) Commonly we find that upward mobility involves the

presentation of proper performances and that efforts to move upward and efforts to keep from moving downward are expressed in terms of sacrifices made for the maintenance of front. Once the proper sign-equipment has been obtained and familiarity gained in the management of it, then this equipment can be used to embellish and illumine one's daily performances with a favorable social style.

Perhaps the most important piece of sign-equipment associated with social class consists of the status symbols through which material wealth is expressed. American society is similar to others in this regard but seems to have been singled out as an extreme example of wealth-oriented class structure—perhaps because in America the license to employ symbols of wealth and financial capacity to do so are so widely distributed. . . .

Reality and Contrivance

. . . Some performances are carried off successfully with complete dishonesty, others with complete honesty; but for performances in general neither of these extremes is essential and neither, perhaps, is dramaturgically advisable.

The implication here is that an honest, sincere, serious performance is less firmly connected with the solid world than one might first assume. And this implication will be strengthened if we look again at the distance usually placed between quite honest performances and quite contrived ones. In this connection take, for example, the remarkable phenomenon of stage acting. It does take deep skill, long training, and psychological capacity to become a good stage actor. But this fact should not blind us to another one: that almost anyone can quickly learn a script well enough to give a charitable audience some sense of realness in what is being contrived before them. And it seems this is so because ordinary social intercourse is itself put together as a scene is put together, by the exchange of dramatically inflated actions, counteractions, and terminating replies. Scripts even in the hands of unpracticed players can come to life because life itself is a dramatically enacted thing. All the world is not, of course, a stage, but the crucial ways in which it isn't are not easy to specify. . . .

When the individual does move into a new position in society and obtains a new part to perform, he is not likely to be told in full detail how to conduct himself, nor will the facts of his new situation press sufficiently on him from the start to determine his conduct without his further giving thought to it. Ordinarily he will be given only a few cues, hints, and stage directions, and it will be assumed that he already has in his repertoire a large number of bits and pieces of performances that will be required in the new setting. The individual will already have a fair idea of what modesty, deference, or righteous indignation looks like, and can make a pass at playing these bits when necessary. He may even be able to play out the part of a hypnotic subject[12] or commit a "compulsive" crime[13] on the basis of models for these activities that he is already familiar with.

A theatrical performance or a staged confidence game requires a thorough scripting of the spoken content of the routine; but the vast part involving "expression given off" is often determined by meager stage directions. It is expected that the performer of illusions will already know a good deal about how to manage his voice, his face, and his body, although he—as well as any person who directs him—may find it difficult indeed to provide a detailed verbal statement of this kind of knowledge. And in this, of course, we approach the situation of the straightforward man in the street. Socialization may not so much involve a learning of the many specific details of a single concrete part—often there could not be enough time or energy for this. What does seem to be required of the individual is that he learn enough pieces of expression to be able to "fill in" and manage, more or less, any part that he is likely to be given. The legitimate performances of everyday life are not "acted" or "put on" in the sense that the performer knows in advance just what he is going to do, and does this solely because of the effect it is likely to

have. The expressions it is felt he is giving off will be especially "inaccessible" to him.[14] But as in the case of less legitimate performers, the incapacity of the ordinary individual to formulate in advance the movements of his eyes and body does not mean that he will not express himself through these devices in a way that is dramatized and performed in his repertoire of actions. In short, we all act better than we know how.

When we watch a television wrestler gouge, foul, and snarl at his opponent we are quite ready to see that, in spite of the dust, he is, and knows he is, merely playing at being the "heavy," and that in another match he may be given the other role, that of clean-cut wrestler, and perform this with equal verve and proficiency. We seem less ready to see, however, that while such details as the number and character of the falls may be fixed beforehand, the details of the expressions and movements used do not come from a script but from command of an idiom, a command that is exercised from moment to moment with little calculation or forethought. . . .

Personality-Interaction-Society

In recent years there have been elaborate attempts to bring into one framework the concepts and findings derived from three different areas of inquiry: the individual personality, social interaction, and society. I would like to suggest here a simple addition to these inter-disciplinary attempts.

When an individual appears before others, he knowingly and unwittingly projects a definition of the situation, of which a conception of himself is an important part. When an event occurs which is expressively incompatible with this fostered impression, significant consequences are simultaneously felt in three levels of social reality, each of which involves a different point of reference and a different order of fact.

First, the social interaction, treated here as a dialogue between two teams, may come to an embarrassed and confused halt; the situation may cease to be defined. Previous positions may become no longer tenable, and participants may find themselves without a charted course of action. The participants typically sense a false note in the situation and come to feel awkward, flustered, and, literally, out of countenance. In other words, the minute social system created and sustained by orderly social interaction becomes disorganized. These are the consequences that the disruption has from the point of view of social interaction.

Secondly, in addition to these disorganizing consequences for action at the moment, performance disruptions may have consequences of a more far-reaching kind. Audiences tend to accept the self projected by the individual performer during any current performance as a responsible representative of his colleague-grouping, of his team, and of his social establishment. Audiences also accept the individual's particular performance as evidence of his capacity to perform the routine and even as evidence of his capacity to perform any routine. In a sense these larger social units—teams, establishments, etc.—become committed every time the individual performs his routine; with each performance the legitimacy of these units will tend to be tested anew and their permanent reputation put at stake. This kind of commitment is especially strong during some performances. Thus, when a surgeon and his nurse both turn from the operating table and the anesthetized patient accidentally rolls off the table to his death, not only is the operation disrupted in an embarrassing way, but the reputation of the doctor, as a doctor and as a man, and also the reputation of the hospital may be weakened. These are the consequences that disruptions may have from the point of view of social structure.

Finally, we often find that the individual may deeply involve his ego in his identification with a particular part, establishment, and group, and in his self-conception as someone who does not disrupt social interaction or let down the social units which depend upon that interaction. When a disruption occurs, then, we may find that the self-conceptions around which his personality has been built may become discredited. These are consequences that disruptions may have from the point of view of individual personality.

Performance disruptions, then, have consequences at three levels of abstraction: personality, interaction, and social structure. While the likelihood of disruption will vary widely from interaction to interaction, and while the social importance of likely disruptions will vary from interaction to interaction, still it seems that there is no interaction in which the participants do not take an appreciable chance of being slightly embarrassed or a slight chance of being deeply humiliated. Life may not be much of a gamble, but interaction is. Further, insofar as individuals make efforts to avoid disruptions or to correct for ones not avoided, these efforts, too, will have simultaneous consequences at the three levels. Here, then, we have one simple way of articulating three levels of abstraction and three perspectives from which social life has been studied.

Staging and the Self

The general notion that we make a presentation of ourselves to others is hardly novel; what ought to be stressed in conclusion is that the very structure of the self can be seen in terms of how we arrange for such performances in our Anglo-American society. . . .

The self, then, as a performed character, is not an organic thing that has a specific location, whose fundamental fate is to be born, to mature, and to die; it is a dramatic effect arising diffusely from a scene that is presented, and the characteristic issue, the crucial concern, is whether it will be credited or discredited.

In analyzing the self then we are drawn from its possessor, from the person who will profit or lose most by it, for he and his body merely provide the peg on which something of collaborative manufacture will be hung for a time. And the means for producing and maintaining selves do not reside inside the peg; in fact these means are often bolted down in social establishments. There will be a back region with its tools for shaping the body, and a front region with its fixed props. There will be a team of persons whose activity on stage in conjunction with available props will constitute the scene from which the performed character's self will emerge, and another team, the audience, whose interpretive activity will be necessary for this emergence. The self is a product of all of these arrangements, and in all of its parts bears the marks of this genesis.

The whole machinery of self-production is cumbersome, of course, and sometimes breaks down, exposing its separate components: back region control; team collusion; audience tact; and so forth. But, well oiled, impressions will flow from it fast enough to put us in the grips of one of our types of reality—the performance will come off and the firm self accorded each performed character will appear to emanate intrinsically from its performer.

Let us turn now from the individual as character performed to the individual as performer. He has a capacity to learn, this being exercised in the task of training for a part. He is given to having fantasies and dreams, some that pleasurably unfold a triumphant performance, others full of anxiety and dread that nervously deal with vital discreditings in a public front region. He often manifests a gregarious desire for teammates and audiences, a tactful considerateness for their concerns; and he has a capacity for deeply felt shame, leading him to minimize the chances he takes of exposure.

These attributes of the individual *qua* performer are not merely a depicted effect of particular performances; they are psychobiological in nature, and yet they seem to arise out of intimate interaction with the contingencies of staging performances.

And now a final comment. In developing the conceptual framework employed in this report, some language of the stage was used. I spoke of performers and audiences; of routines and parts; of performances coming off or falling flat; of cues, stage settings, and backstage;

of dramaturgical needs, dramaturgical skills, and dramaturgical strategies. Now it should be admitted that this attempt to press a mere analogy so far was in part a rhetoric and a maneuver. . . .

And so here the language and mask of the stage will be dropped. Scaffolds, after all, are to build other things with, and should be erected with an eye to taking them down.

This report is not concerned with aspects of theater that creep into everyday life. It is concerned with the structure of social encounters—the structure of those entities in social life that come into being whenever persons enter one another's immediate physical presence. The key factor in this structure is the maintenance of a single definition of the situation, this definition having to be expressed, and this expression sustained in the face of a multitude of potential disruptions.

A character staged in a theater is not in some ways real, nor does it have the same kind of real consequences as does the thoroughly contrived character performed by a confidence man; but the *successful* staging of either of these types of false figures involves use of *real* techniques—the same techniques by which everyday persons sustain their real social situations. Those who conduct face to face interaction on a theater's stage must meet the key requirement of real situations; they must expressively sustain a definition of the situation: but this they do in circumstances that have facilitated their developing an apt terminology for the interactional tasks that all of us share.

Notes

1. Quoted in E. H. Volkart, editor, *Social Behavior and Personality,* Contributions of W. I. Thomas to Theory and Social Research (New York: Social Science Research Council, 1951), p. 9.
2. Here I owe much to an unpublished paper by Tom Burns of the University of Edinburgh. He presents the argument that in all interaction a basic underlying theme is the desire of each participant to guide and control the responses made by the others present. A similar argument has been advanced

by Jay Haley in a recent unpublished paper, but in regard to a special kind of control, that having to do with defining the nature of the relationship of those involved in the interaction.

3. An interaction can be purposely set up as a time and place for voicing differences in opinion. But in such cases participants *must* be careful to agree not to disagree on the proper tone of voice, vocabulary, and degree of seriousness in which all arguments are to be phrased, and upon the mutual respect which disagreeing participants must carefully continue to express toward one another. This debaters' or academic definition of the situation may also be invoked suddenly and judiciously as a way of translating a serious conflict of views into one that can be handled within a framework acceptable to all present.

4. Goffman, *op. cit.*, pp. 319–27.

5. Peter Blau, "Dynamics of Bureaucracy" (Ph.D. dissertation, Department of Sociology, Columbia University, forthcoming, University of Chicago Press), pp. 127–29.

6. Walter M. Beattie, Jr., "The Merchant Seaman" (unpublished M.A. report, Department of Sociology, University of Chicago, 1950), p. 35.

7. Sir Frederick Ponsonby, *Recollections of Three Reigns* (New York: Dutton, 1952), p. 46.

8. For comments on the importance of distinguishing between a routine of interaction and any particular instance when this routine is played through, see John van Neumann and Oskar Morgenstern, *The Theory of Games and Economic Behaviour* (2nd ed.) (Princeton: Princeton University Press, 1947), p. 49.

9. See Babe Pinelli, as told to Joe King, *Mr. Ump* (Philadelphia: Westminster Press, 1953), p. *75*.

10. Material on the burial business used throughout this report is taken from Robert W. Habenstein, "The American Funeral Director" (unpublished Ph.D. dissertation, Department of Sociology, University of Chicago, 1954). I owe much to Mr. Habenstein's analysis of a funeral as a performance.

11. Charles H. Cooley, *Human Nature and the Social Order* (New York: Scribner's, 1922), pp. 352–53.

12. This view of hypnosis is neatly presented by T. R. Sarbin, "Contributions to Role-Taking Theory. I: Hypnotic Behavior," *Psychological Review,* 57, pp. 255–70.

13. See D. R. Cressey, "The Differential Association Theory and Compulsive Crimes," *Journal of Criminal Law, Criminology and Police Science,* 45, pp. 29–40.

14. This concept derives from T. R. Sarbin, "Role Theory," in Gardner Lindzey, *Handbook of Social Psychology* (Cambridge: Addison-Wesley, 1954), Vol. 1, pp. 235–36.

THINKING ABOUT THE READING

According to Goffman, why must everyone engage in impression management? What are some of the reasons we do this? What does he mean by the terms *definition of the situation, working consensus,* and *preventative strategies*? Consider a situation in which you were particularly aware of your own self-presentation. Do you think Goffman is interested primarily in the interactions between people or in their individual psychology? What is the source of the "scripts" that people use to determine what role they should play in a given situation or performance?

Blue Chip Blacks: Managing Race in Public Spaces

Karyn R. Lacy

(2007)

"They're trying to be like the whites instead of being who they are," Andrea Creighton, a forty-three-year-old information analyst with the federal government, told me when I asked whether she believed blacks had made it in the United States or still had a long way to go. Andrea is black, and she perceives irrepressible distinctions between middle-class blacks and whites, even though many aspects of her life appear to reflect membership in the suburban middle-class mainstream. She and her husband, Greg, have two teenage children: a girl, age seventeen, and a boy, age fifteen. They have lived on a quiet street in Sherwood Park, an upper-middle-class suburb of Washington, D.C., for seven years. Their four-bedroom home is an imposing red-brick-front colonial with shiny black shutters, nestled on an acre of neatly manicured lawn. The children are active members of the local soccer team, and Greg is one of the team's coaches. Andrea and her husband each drive midsize cars and have provided their daughter, who is old enough to drive unaccompanied by an adult, with her own car. At first blush, they seem nearly identical to their white middle-class counterparts. But unlike the nearly all-white neighborhood that the average middle-class white family calls home, the Creightons' upscale subdivision is predominantly black. Andrea and Greg are pleased that their children are growing up in a community filled with black professionals. The Creightons' residence in Sherwood Park is one indication of the kind of social differentiation Andrea employs to define her identity as a member of the black middle class. Though she shares many lifestyle characteristics with mainstream whites, she feels that middle-class blacks are not mirror images of middle-class whites, nor should they aspire to be.

In terms of occupational status, educational attainment, income, and housing, the top segment of the black middle class is equal to the white middle class. The key distinction between the white and black middle classes is thus a matter of degree. Middle-class whites fit the public image of the middle class and may therefore take their middle-class status for granted, but blacks who have "made it" must work harder, more deliberately, and more consistently to make their middle-class status known to others.

Instances of discrimination against blacks in stores, in the workplace, and in other public spaces occur every day, unobserved by potential sympathizers and unreported by black victims. As sociologist Joe Feagin's gripping study of the black middle-class experience shows, middle-class status does not automatically shield blacks from discrimination by whites in public spaces (Feagin 1991). His interviewees' reports of being denied seating in restaurants, accosted while shopping, and harassed by police officers lead Feagin to conclude that a middle-class status does not protect blacks from the threat of racial discrimination. Feagin's study documents the formal and informal mechanisms that contribute to persistent discrimination toward blacks in the public sphere. His perspective, which has been invaluable in shedding light on the dynamics of racial stratification in the United States, suggests that contemporary patterns of discrimination often prevent accomplished blacks from enjoying the taken-for-granted privileges associated with a middle-class status, such as a leisurely dinner out or a carefree shopping experience.

This study demonstrates that despite the ever-present possibility of stigmatization, not all middle-class blacks feel as overwhelmed by and as ill-equipped to grapple with perceived discrimination as racial stigma theory implies. Some perceive themselves as active agents capable of orchestrating public interactions with whites to their advantage in a variety of public settings. Study participants from Lakeview, Riverton, and Sherwood Park describe how the strategic deployment of cultural capital, including language, mannerisms, clothing, and credentials, allows them to create what I call *public identities* that effectively lessen or short-circuit potential discriminatory treatment.

White Americans typically equate race with class and then reflexively consign all blacks to the lowest class levels. The experiences of middle-class blacks in my study suggest that those who actively correct the misapprehensions of white strangers reduce the likelihood of discriminatory treatment. This invocation of a public identity is a deliberate, conscious act—one that entails psychological costs as well as rewards. As Charlotte, an elementary school teacher and Lakeview resident, explains, black people "have two faces," and learn to distinguish self-presentation strategies suitable in the white world from self-presentation strategies useful in the black world.

Most middle-class whites, on the other hand, pay little overt attention to their own race or class. For them, most activities such as shopping, working as a manager, or buying a house are routinized, psychologically neutral, and relatively conflict free. Public challenges to their class status are rare. Middle-class blacks face a different reality. When they leave the familiarity of their upscale suburban communities, many of the accoutrements associated with their middle-class lifestyle fade from view. Skin color persists. On occasions when race trumps class, blacks' everyday interactions with white store clerks, real estate agents, and office subordinates can become exercises in frustration or humiliation or both. Asserting public identities makes it possible for blacks to tip the balance of a public interaction so that class trumps race. Blacks who successfully bring their middle-class status firmly into focus pressure white strangers and workplace subordinates to adjust their own behaviors in light of this information. Public identities, then, are not so much prepared responses that permit individuals to skillfully avoid or ignore strangers or social deviants when in public as they are strategies for sustaining problem-free interactions involving strangers. The use of public identities allows some middle-class blacks to complete their shopping without being accosted by store clerks or security guards, to supervise workplace subordinates effectively, and to disarm hostile real estate agents.

Constructing Public Identities: Boundary-Work in the Public Sphere

A key component of the public identities asserted by middle-class blacks is based on class and involves differentiating themselves from lower-class blacks through what I call *exclusionary* boundary-work. Washington-area middle-class blacks are firm in their belief that it is possible to minimize the probability of encountering racial discrimination if they can successfully convey their middle-class status to white strangers. To accomplish this feat, interviewees attempt to erect exclusionary boundaries against a bundle of stereotypes commonly associated with lower-class blacks. Exclusionary boundary-work is most readily apparent when middle-class blacks are shopping or managing employees in the workplace. Middle-class blacks also engage in *inclusionary* boundary-work in order to blur distinctions between themselves and white members of the middle class by emphasizing areas of consensus and shared experience. Efforts to highlight overlaps with the white middle class are common when middle-class blacks engage in house-hunting activities.

The construction and assertion of public identities varies according to social context and the basis of perceived discrimination. In the context of shopping, the middle-class blacks in this study perceive that race bias is operational, that is, that there is a failure by others to distinguish· them from the black poor. Specifically, they know that whites wrongly assume that blacks are poor and that the poor are likely to be shoplifters. Consequently, when shopping, these middle-class blacks confront the stereotype of the street-savvy black shoplifter, which white store clerks often apply to blacks as a group. To disassociate themselves from this negative image and signal that they "belong" in the store (i.e., that they have money, can afford the merchandise, and have no need to steal), study participants report that they dress with care. "People make decisions about you based on how you're dressed and what you look like," Michelle says. "Because I know that," she elaborates, "I choose my dress depending on what the environment is." Interviewees contend that their decisions to eschew clothing associated with urban popular culture—for example, oversized gold earrings, baggy jeans, and designer tennis shoes—maximize their chances of enjoying a trouble-free shopping experience and signal their respectability to white strangers. This kind of exclusionary boundary-work helps middle-class blacks establish *social differentiation*—they make clear to store personnel that they are *not* like the poor.

Evidence of social differentiation emerges in the workplace as well. Just as the professions have used educational credentials to limit membership and to bring legitimacy to their discipline, professional blacks underscore their authority as managers by highlighting credentials such as job title and professional status. Holding positions of power, interviewees believe, makes them impervious to workplace discrimination.

In the context of house-hunting, middle-class blacks perceive that class, rather than race bias, operates. In order to maximize their range of residential options, public identities are constructed to be linked in an inclusionary

manner with their white counterparts. With the dominant cultural code in mind, middle-class blacks rely on mainstream language and mannerisms to carry out interactions with real estate agents. In cases in which these interactions break down, respondents use their own resources and social networks to find an acceptable home on their own. Put simply, middle-class blacks engage in inclusionary boundary-work to establish *social unity*—to show that middle-class blacks are much like the white middle-class. These identity construction processes are mutually reinforcing in that they each help to affirm respondents' position as legitimate members of the American middle class.

Cultural Capital and Cultural Literacy

Cultural capital, a key signifier of middle-class status, constitutes the means by which public identities are staked out. Cultural capital theorists argue that an important mechanism in the reproduction of inequality is a lack of exposure to dominant cultural codes, behaviors, and practices (Bourdieu and Passeron 1977). Middle-class blacks have obviously secured a privileged position in the occupational structure. But cultural capital differs from such economic capital in that cultural capital indicates a "proficiency in and familiarity with dominant cultural codes and practices—for example, linguistic styles, aesthetic preferences, styles of interaction" (Aschaffenburg and Maas 1997). These signifiers of middle-class status are institutionalized and taken for granted as normative, hence the underlying assumption that groups that cannot activate cultural capital fall victim to systematic inequality.

The majority of the blacks in this study are first-generation middle-class or grew up in working-class families; therefore, they could not acquire cultural capital through the process outlined by Bourdieu. They were not in a position to inherit from their parents the ability to signal their class position to whites via mainstream cultural resources because their parents either did not have access to middle-class cultural resources or they had views about black-white interaction that were informed by Jim Crow laws and other pillars of racial segregation. The few interviewees who did grow up in the middle class question how much their parents, who went about their everyday lives almost exclusively in black communities, could have effectively prepared them to negotiate routine interactions with whites as equals.

The blacks in my study were not endowed with the cultural capital useful in managing interactions with whites through their families of origin. As children, they were compelled to figure out these negotiations on their own through their immersion in white colleges, workplaces, and educational institutions, without involving their parents or other adults. They did so through two socialization processes that facilitate the construction of public identities: improvisation and script-switching.

Improvisations Socialization

During childhood, the blacks in this study were socialized into a set of informal strategies that allowed them to negotiate on their own the racial discrimination they faced at that time. In contrast to their parents' strategies of avoidance, deference, and unwillingness to confront authority, interviewees were more likely to fight back surreptitiously. For example, they often challenged indirectly the authority of white teachers and authority figures. When these middle-class blacks employed improvisational strategies, they left the impression that they were obeying the rules when they were, in fact, circumventing rules and established practices. This phenomenon is typified by Brad, who told me how a white guidance counselor had discouraged his applying to college: "My high school counselor told me that I should not go to Michigan because I probably wouldn't make it, and I should go to a trade school. [That way] I would have a job, [and] I could support my family." He pauses, visibly upset. Then, with sarcasm, he adds, "She was great."

I asked him, "This was a black woman telling you this?" He answered, "Uh-uh, she was a white woman. Miss Blupper. I remember her name." Miss Blupper's lack of confidence in Brad's intellectual ability made him even more determined to go to college. Brad acquired on his own a knowledge of college rankings and the admissions process that his guidance counselor was unwilling to provide. He ended up graduating from high school early to attend the University of Michigan and went on to become a judge.

In addition to being discouraged from pursuing a college track by high school teachers, middle-class blacks frequently faced white teachers who were heavily invested in symbolically maintaining the racial boundaries that had been dismantled by desegregation policy. Looking back on his tenure as class president during his junior year at the predominantly white high school, Greg remembers that the tradition dictating who should escort the homecoming queen was abandoned by his white teacher when she realized that he was slotted to escort a white girl:

> My junior year in high school there was always the tradition that the juniors put on the prom for the seniors. . . . I was the class president, and I was 'spose to escort the queen. . . . Well, they made an exception that year. [He laughs.] Basically they said, well, they'd let me and my date lead the parade, and the queen and everybody else [were to] follow behind. Well, you know how I am, I'm saying, "What's up with this?" I'm 'spose to walk the queen, but the queen's white. They didn't want me walking a white queen. I guess they didn't want this black guy walking in with this white queen. So it's really funny that the girl that I happened to be dating at that time, she had naturally red hair, and [she was] just as white as almost snow. But she was black! Yeah, she was a black girl! [He laughs.] . . . So, anyway, I said, "I'll take her to the prom. I'll fake 'em all out." So I'm leading the prom, me [and the girl], we're going to the prom together. So nobody knew anything; so me and [the girl] showed up, and my, my, my, you talking about fine [attractive]!

Greg decided to "pay back" the teacher not by using official channels and reporting her to higher authorities or by insisting that in fact he would escort the white queen as tradition dictated, but by devising a scheme on his own that would both expose the absurdity of the black-white boundary and preserve his dignity. Brad also circumvented official channels in his quest for a college education.

By the time he entered high school, Greg possessed an insider's knowledge of mainstream culture; he knew whites would be baffled by the apparent racial identity of his fair-skinned date. He acquired this familiarity with dominant codes and practices through exposure to white cultural norms in integrated settings, settings that required him to manage interactions with whites. Greg improvised strategies for managing these interactions as the specific conflict arose, yet these incidents prepared him, as I will demonstrate, for later experiences with racial discrimination.

Script-Switching

Script-switching processes refer to the strategies middle-class blacks employ to demonstrate that they are knowledgeable about middle-class lifestyles and to communicate their social position to others.

Scholars now recognize that blacks and whites tend to "behave" different kinds of scripts. For example, Thomas Kochman observed that blacks tend to communicate in an "emotionally intense, dynamic, and demonstrative" style, whereas whites tend to communicate in a "more modest and emotionally constrained" style (Kochman 1981:106). Of course, Kochman's schema is a generalization of these racial groups. There are whites and blacks who do not fit neatly into the categories he lays out. But these exceptions do not erase the powerful impact of these stereotypes on everyday interactions across the color line. Because public interactions are governed by mainstream scripts, middle-class blacks are compelled to switch from black scripts to white scripts in public spaces. Thus, public interactions require a different presentation of self than those asserted in majority-black spaces. In short, the middle-class blacks sometimes downplay their racial identities in public interactions with whites. Jasmine is short, with a bouncy haircut in the shape of a trendy bob. She seems taller than she actually is because she is extroverted and somewhat bossy, whereas her husband Richard is quiet and shy. Jasmine, now forty-five, describes how she felt compelled to script-switch as a teenager when her parents enrolled her in a predominantly white high school:

> I remember wanting to do "the white thing" when I was there. I had iodine and baby oil, trying to get a tan, and why wasn't [my] hair blowing in the wind? They [the white girls] would be shaving their legs and that type of thing, and most African American girls aren't that particular. I felt I needed to be a part of them, I needed to do their thing. . . . To this day, I think I made the blend [between two cultures] pretty decent because I have plenty of friends who just hate going back to our high school reunion. They just see no purpose [in going], but I enjoyed it because I participated in everything. . . . I was homecoming queen, I was in their beauty pageant when no other black person would dare to be in their pageant. I was like, "If you can do it, I can do it!"

Charlotte, speaking with admiration of a worker in a predominantly white school system with very few other black teachers, outlined how a black male art teacher who declined to script-switch was harassed by the white principal. "[The] white principal can't *stand* him, and I think it's because he's this big, black guy, and he's loud. You know, 'Hey, how ya doing!' Kind of like that. He's real down to earth, and I think they're kind of envious of him, because he's been in books, he's been in the [*Washington*] *Post*, he's been on TV, and they're trying to get their little doctorates. And they're always demeaning him. . . . They are just awful to him."

According to Charlotte, this teacher is subjected to a different set of evaluation criteria than the other teachers working at the school. But because Charlotte and the few other black teachers have not been mistreated in the ways that she observes the black male teacher has been, Charlotte feels that the white principal is reacting not so much to the art teacher's race as to his refusal to display the appropriate command of cultural capital—in short, to switch scripts. By Charlotte's account, the white principal interprets the art teacher's behavior as gauche, even though there may be no basis for this conclusion aside from the teacher's refusal to engage a white script. "He kinda doesn't make the—he's an artist, and he's eccentric, and he's just *him*, and he doesn't do the bullshit." Charlotte added parenthetically, "And see . . . they want that, they want him to do that."

As Charlotte's narrative makes clear, some middle-class blacks believe that social acceptance in the public sphere is contingent upon their ability to script-switch. They believe that they are less likely to be hassled in white settings if they are willing to script-switch. Blacks who refuse to do so or are uncomfortable doing so may be penalized, just as the teacher at Charlotte's school was targeted.

Asserting Public Identities

Undoubtedly, all persons attempting to cross class boundaries have to spend time thinking about clothing, language, tastes, and mannerisms; they risk being identified as a member of a lower class if they make a mistake. Concerns among the socially mobile about needing to properly appropriate the general skills and cultural styles of the middle class in a convincing way are well-documented in the sociological literature and in fictional accounts. However, middle-class blacks' ambiguous position in the racial hierarchy means that they have to spend more time thinking about what they will wear in public, work harder at pulling off a middle-class presentation of self, and be more demonstrative at it than white middle-class people who are also exhibiting their status and negotiating for deference. Moreover, while the

fault line for upwardly mobile whites today is strictly class, middle-class blacks must negotiate class boundaries as well as the stereotypes associated with their racial group. In this section, I demonstrate how public identities are put to work in three public spaces, each with its own distinct pattern of black-white interaction. While shopping and in the workplace, these middle-class blacks employ public identities to establish their distinctiveness from the black poor and from subordinate workers. In the context of house-hunting, middle-class blacks perceive that class bias operates; therefore, public identities are constructed to establish their overlap with the white middle class.

Exclusionary Boundary-Work

Shopping

An obvious way for middle-class blacks to signal their class position is through physical appearance.

In real terms, this would mean selecting clothing that contrasts sharply with the attire associated with black popular culture. Philip, who wears a suit to his job as a corporate executive, observed: "Being black is a negative, particularly if you're not lookin' a certain way. You . . . go in an elevator dressed in what I have on now [he is wearing a blue polo shirt and white shorts], white women start holding their pocketbooks. But if I'm dressed like I normally go to work, then it's fine."

Philip implies that he can control the extent to which he will be evaluated on the basis of whites' stereotypes about poor blacks by the type of clothing he decides to wear to the store. If Philip decides to assert his public identity, he will shop in his suit. Once he begins to make purchases, additional signifiers of his social status such as credit cards and zip code assure the store clerk that he is a legitimate member of the middle class. Through his performance, Philip believes that he annuls a stigmatized racial identity. He believes that when he is dressed as a professional, whites see his class status first and respond to him as a member of that social group.

The assurance of these additional middle-class signifiers allows middle-class blacks to occasionally engage in subversive expressions of their class identity, much to their delight. Terry complained that store clerks react negatively to blacks who are "dressed down" under the assumption that they cannot afford to buy anything. "Going into a store, somebody follows you around the store. But [store clerks] don't help you [at all] if you go into a specialty store. They just refuse to walk up to you. Then you see a white person walk in and they immediately run to help them." However, as a member of the middle class, Terry is pleased that she has the leisure time and the requisite skills to voice a complaint:

> Now lately I will write a complaint. I will find out who owns the store and write a complaint. Before I used to just tell the [salesperson, "I guess you didn't know who walked into your store. It's a shame that you treat people like this because you don't know how much money I have." I love going to expensive stores in jeans and a T-shirt. Because they don't know how much money you have. And, you know, I may have a thousand dollars to give away that day. [She laughs.] They just don't know. And the way people treat you, I think it's a shame, based on your appearance.

Convinced that a store clerk ignored her because her clothing belied her actual class status, Terry went on to test her suspicion by varying the style of clothing that she sports while shopping. Terry enjoys "dressing down," but this subversive presentation of self appears to be enjoyable precisely because she can shed this role at a moment's notice, reassuming her actual middle-class identity. She then drew on her resources as a member of the middle class to file a formal complaint.

Because their performance as members of the middle class is perceived as legitimate when they are clothed in a way that signifies their social status, these blacks believe that using this strategy helps them to avoid the discrimination that blacks of a lower-class status experience. This perception is illustrated by Michael, a stylish corporate manager who suggested that his appearance, coupled with his Sherwood Park zip code and his assets, lead others to draw the conclusion that he is middle-class. He boasted, "When I apply for anything [that requires using] credit, I just give my name, address. . . . You have to fill out the credit application . . . you put your address down there, then you put down your collateral, IRA, all that stuff. So I don't know if I've been discriminated against that way. I mean, I can go to the store and buy what I want to buy."

In cases of racial discrimination, blacks are typically precluded from achieving a desired goal, such as obtaining a desired product or entering a particular establishment. Since middle-class blacks in this study enter stores and "buy what they want to buy, (when they are dressed in a manner that reflects their social status), they conclude that they have not experienced racial discrimination.

This suggests that when interviewees "buy what they want to buy" without interference from whites, they have successfully conveyed their class position to store clerks.

Others also suggested that when middle-class blacks are dressed down, that is, not engaging public identities, their shopping experience is often extremely unpleasant. Michelle attempted to shop while dressed down, and was dismissed by the store clerk: "I went somewhere and they tried to tell me how I couldn't afford something . . . I was in the mood to buy. They were saying, "Well, it might cost this or that." I mean I went there seriously looking to shop. But I wasn't dressed that way." In response to my question, "Was it clothing or race?" Michelle looked slightly puzzled, as if she hadn't consider this possibility, then waffled as to the explanation for the store clerk's behavior.

> Probably a mixture of both, I don't know. See, I don't know what it's like to be white and dressed poorly and [to] try and buy something. I've always had in my mind where someone

told me that you could wear holey jeans as long as you have on two-hundred-dollar shoes. People know that you got money. That's when you're worried about what people think about you. But, you know, on a relaxed day, I don't care what they [white people] think. You either have the money or you don't.

Sorting out the store clerk's motivation is difficult for Michelle in part because whites' stereotypes of the face of poverty are conflated with race. When most whites think abstractly about the middle class, they see a white family, not a black one. This same image leads whites to associate poverty with blacks. In order for whites to believe that the blacks appearing before them are middle-class, they would have to erase the indelible image linking the concept "middle class" exclusively to whites. Middle-class blacks in the Washington, D.C., area convey this status by engaging their public identity, expressed through clothing that signals their middle-class status to others. In the workplace, middle-class blacks focus on a different form of cultural capital—professional title and credentials—to minimize racial tension in the workplace and to underscore their position as managers or supervisors.

The Workplace

Perhaps no public setting better reflects the cultural styles and preferences of the American mainstream than the corporate world. As Feagin and Sikes observe in *Living with Racism*, blacks "in corporate America are under constant pressure to adapt . . . to the values and ways of the white word" (Feagin and Sikes 1994: 135).

White colleagues and clients still register surprise when they encounter corporate blacks who speak intelligently about the topic at hand, black managers still confront "glass ceilings," and black managers still endure subjective critiques assessing their "fit" with the corporate culture. I focus here on two such problems faced by black managers today: managing white subordinates and negotiating racial disputes. Like shopping sites, workplace settings are characterized by a

low regard for black cultural styles. According to Mary Jackman, many whites perceive black cultural styles as "inappropriate for occupational tasks involving responsibility or authority" (Jackman 1994: 130). This means that black managers' credibility resides in their ability to switch to the script associated with white cultural styles. Therefore, in the workplace, black managers assert public identities by demonstrating their command of the cultural capital appropriate for their title or position. Indeed, they must, since the workplace experiences of middle-class blacks are characterized by frequent episodes of discriminatory treatment.

Michael, a corporate manager, has a dry sense of humor and enjoys putting people in their place. He established his role as an authority figure at the outset by highlighting impermeable boundaries between himself and his receptionist. One such boundary is the telephone. Clearly annoyed, Michael explained, "The receptionist, always bitches about answering telephones, but that's her job. She's the receptionist. I ain't never gonna answer the telephone." Michael does not answer his own telephone because his conception of a manager means that subordinates handle mundane details such as phone messages. Answering the phone would reduce his social status to that of a subordinate.

In his position as corporate manager, Michael says he has never experienced any racial discrimination. He attributes this feat to the weight of his title and his ability to utilize it. "On *this* job . . . I always came in with some authority. Hey, you know, like, 'I'm corporate manager. You all can do whatever you want to do, but remember, I'm the one that signs [off]. I'm the one that signs.' And, when you're the one that signs, you got the power. So even if they don't like you, they got to smile, which is okay by me." Greg used a similar strategy with white employees who resented having to work under him after his company was awarded a lucrative contract. He begins to smile as he remembers how he handled the conflict:

There are two folks that I know of that are stone redneck. I mean they're the biggest rednecks you ever did see. They now came over to work for me. They couldn't accept that. So we had several briefings and I said, "Okay, here's how we're gonna do this and here's how we're gonna work." Well, the people they work for . . . were also big rednecks, so they just sort of go along together. Well, they refused—not openly refused, but just subtly. They wouldn't come to meetings. . . . I ended up basically saying to them, "Look, y'all can do what you want to do. But when it comes time for bonuses, and it comes time for yearly wages and all that kind of stuff, now you can go to Jim [white supervisor who reports to Greg], and he can tell you what to do and y'all can go do it. But if he doesn't tell me that you did it, I won't know. So when it comes time for your annual evaluation, I'll just say, 'Didn't do nothing.' So, it's y'all's fault." Well, then they sort of opened up.

In contrast to previous studies of middle class blacks in the workplace, those surveyed here feel empowered to negotiate workplace discrimination. Situated in positions of power, middle-class blacks rely on public identities—for example, their role as supervisor or manager—to solidify their identities as persons of considerable social status. Once their status is established, these middle-class blacks are in a position to extinguish racial conflicts in the workplace. In other instances, middle-class blacks decide that such effort is "not worth it," and juxtapose the pleasant aspects of their high-status occupations against such racial incidents as they arise. Though racial discrimination in the workplace has hardly disappeared, black professionals have become more adept at using class-based resources to resolve these kinds of conflicts.

Inclusionary Boundary-Work

House-Hunting

In *American Apartheid*, Douglas Massey and Nancy Denton argue that middle-class blacks have not had the opportunity to live wherever they want, to live "where people of their means and resources usually locate" (Massey and Denton 1993:138). They conclude that a major factor in blacks' exclusion is racial discrimination by real estate agents, who serve as the "gatekeepers" of predominantly white neighborhoods to which blacks, even those with the requisite resources, seldom gain entry.

Yet middle-class blacks interviewed for this study insist that one of the benefits of being middle-class is the option of living in any neighborhood one desires. Their housing decisions are no longer restricted by the behavior of real estate agents. John, who chose the majority-black but upper-middle-class Sherwood Park community, explained, "We could have lived anywhere we wanted to. We could have afforded to live a lot of different places, but we chose here." He and most of the middle-class blacks in this study minimize the likelihood that they have experienced racial discrimination while house-hunting because, in so many other aspects of their lives, they use class-based resources to secure a desired good. How do blacks use their public identity while house-hunting? To manage their interactions with white real estate agents, these middle-class blacks place a good deal of emphasis on displays of cultural capital—particularly appropriate clothing, apt language, and knowledge of the housing market. Yet house-hunting is a more complicated site for the construction and use of public identity because in house-hunting, unlike shopping and the workplace, respondents are unsure as to whether real estate agents are responding to their race or their class.

The preoccupation with presenting a middle-class appearance is evident in Lydia's description of her experience while viewing a model home in a predominantly white suburban subdivision located in the same greater metropolitan area where she and her husband eventually bought a home.

In response to the question "Have you ever experienced racial discrimination while house-hunting?" Lydia replied:

I guess I never really thought about that in terms of racial, but economically, I think I have been. I tend not to be a person that dresses up. [She chuckles.] A couple times I've gone looking for houses and I'll just wear sweatpants. And you go out looking for a house that's in expensive neighborhoods, I don't know what they expect me to drive up in. That has nothing to do with how much money I have in the bank. And I've had that happen . . . a couple times. . . . I went to a house. . . . I don't know what we were driving, probably an old beat-up car. So I pull into the driveway, and I had on sweatpants, my [baseball] hat, I go in and see the house. I'd asked [the real estate agent] about the house, asked her for the information, and 1 said I wanted to take a tour. She immediately said to me, "Is this your price range?" [Dramatic pause.] I asked her how much was the house. She told me, and it was my price range, no big deal. I asked, "Was this a black real estate agent?" Lydia answered, "White. She wanted to discuss my income before she would show me the house. Basically, I told her I'll take a look at the house, and I'll let her know when I'm finished."

Lydia felt that the real estate agent was attempting to discourage her from viewing the house. However, she believed that her choice of clothing, her baseball hat, and her old car all signaled the wrong social class status to the agent—not that the agent objected to black home-seekers. I attempted to clarify the kind of discrimination Lydia felt she had experienced by posing a follow-up question: "Is that standard procedure? Do real estate agents normally ask you how much you make before they show you the house?" Lydia responded, shaking her head slightly from side to side, "No, no. I had been looking at lots and lots of houses. And I *knew* what she was doing. It was her way of saying, 'Oh, *God*, who is this person coming in here?' Because when I was there, a white couple came in, and I stopped to listen to what [the agent] would say to them. None of that, none of that."

I asked, "Did they have on sweatpants too?"

"No, they were dressed up," she laughed.

I persisted, "But you think it was because you had on sweatpants, not because you were a black person?"

"I think she probably, maybe looked at me and felt maybe I didn't make enough money to afford the house. That was part of it. I'm not sure, looking at houses, that we ever experienced any kind of *racial* discrimination. Because the real estate agents we had . . . they all took us to predominantly white neighborhoods. It wasn't that they were trying to steer us toward any type of neighborhood. They were willing to take our money anywhere." She burst into laughter.

I asked, "So do you think you could have actually bought one of those houses if you'd wanted to?"

"Oh yeah, oh yeah."

Lydia had an opportunity to test her suspicion that the real estate agent associated her with the poor when a white couple arrived to view the same home, even though the white couple had been well-dressed, not like her, and no comparison that controlled on clothing had been possible. Lydia concluded that the agent assessed the couple more favorably based on the quality of their clothing, and to support her position, Lydia identified occasions when white real estate agents had accepted her middle-class performance as a legitimate expression of who she is, showing her expensive homes in white neighborhoods.

Lydia's account illustrates the difficulty in pinpointing racial discrimination in the housing market. She did go on to view the model home. Though she was dressed in an overly casual way, Lydia used strong language to inform the real estate agent that she intended to tour the home. And the agent did not move to prevent her from walking through the model home. Consequently, in Lydia's view, the encounter did not qualify as a "racial" one. So long as they are permitted to view the homes of their choice, the middle-class blacks in this study do not perceive racial discrimination in the housing market as affecting their own housing choices.

For instance, Audrey, now sixty-four, remembers her disheartening experience with a real estate agent over twenty years ago, when she and her husband moved into the area from another city:

> The agent took us down south [of the city] mostly, to . . . where more of the blacks lived . . . where they seemed to be feeding the black people that came into the area. . . . And when she started out showing us property [south of the city] . . . we told her we wanted to be closer. The things she showed us [that were closer] . . . it was gettin' worse. The properties . . . weren't as nice. So when she showed us the properties [in a black and Hispanic low-income section], we kind of like almost accepted the fact that this was what you're going to be getting.

Audrey and her family moved into the undesirable housing, but "from that day on," she said, "we never stopped looking at houses. We took it upon ourselves to continue just to look, to explore different areas." A year later, they moved to a more attractive neighborhood. Now distrustful of real estate agents, Audrey drew on cultural knowledge she'd acquired on her own—about desirable neighborhoods, schools, and the housing market in general—to locate a home in a neighborhood more suited to her family's tastes. Acquiring this kind of detailed information takes leisure time and research skills.

Greg and his wife found that their real estate agent also directed them to undesirable housing when they returned to the United States from a work assignment in Taiwan. Greg remembers:

> The agent kept showing us older homes. . . . They were ten-year-old homes, twelve-year-old homes, and they just weren't our style. . . . Some of the homes, they had beautician shops in the basement, and she thought that was a great deal, you know, you could wash, you could style your hair. And I'm thinking, "I don't need that." So Andrea [his wife] just said, "I'm not interested in those." So we came here [to Sherwood Park] just on a whim, I guess. And they had a girl [real estate agent] named [Liz], she said, "Let me show you these," and we looked at 'em. We

went, "Oh," and, "Ah, yeah, okay." Then Andrea just said, "Hey, that's what I want."

In each of these examples, middle-class blacks confront discrimination from real estate agents. Audrey and her husband were steered to a section of the city where many blacks already lived. Greg and his wife were shown older, less attractive homes within their general area of choice. But the fact that these families were able to successfully find a home that did appeal to them leads them to the conclusion that widespread discrimination against blacks no longer effectively bars blacks of their social status from entering the neighborhood of their choice. Recall John's comment: "We could have lived anywhere we wanted to. . . . We chose here." When real estate agents fail them, middle-class blacks simply find an attractive home by driving around on their own. As Audrey made clear, they "never stop looking," or they happen to find a desirable home "on a whim," as Greg and his wife did.

In cases where respondents do recognize discriminatory practices, they rely on two strategies to secure desirable housing, both of which require middle-class blacks to assert public identities. Some blacks confront real estate agents directly, the option Lydia chose when she advised the agent that she would "take a look at the house, and . . . let her know when [she had] finished." Though she was "dressed down," Lydia used unmistakable language to articulate her middle-class identity to the agent. In short, Lydia attempted to show that she belonged there, viewing the model home, just as much as the well-dressed white couple. In doing so, she relied on the class conviction that her access to cultural capital effectively challenged the real estate agent's potential roadblock.

Other middle-class blacks forgo the agent-client relationship completely, locating homes on their own as they drive through potential neighborhoods. Many already have friends living in the neighborhoods where they find their homes. Through these social networks, they are made aware of homes coming up for sale. This strategy can be likened to the self-reliant script that middle-class blacks make use of in the workplace. In the workplace, these middle-class blacks place little faith in the EEOC to resolve racial conflicts; instead, they resolve them on their own. While house-hunting, they dispense with real estate agents who are unwilling to help them find adequate housing. To locate a home on one's own requires skill and resources: a car, a working knowledge of the area's neighborhoods, leisure time to search, and so on. Thus, the middle-class blacks in this study realize that racial discrimination persists in the housing market, but they do not feel that their housing options are severely limited by it. After all, in the end, Lakeview and Riverton residents do locate a home that pleases them, and because they have no way to systematically assess whether their housing search compares unfavorably to that of their white counterparts, they tend to wave off the practices of prejudicial real estate agents as inconsequential in their housing decisions. Relying on middle-class resources and networks to negotiate these public interactions and to secure their dream home is a reasonably satisfying solution.

Conclusion

Although what makes the evening news is corporate discrimination scandals—multimillion-dollar lawsuits filed against companies accused of engaging in various forms of modern racism—the everyday instances of racial discrimination experienced by middle-class blacks warrant additional attention from scholars and the public. Feagin's racial stigma theory suggests that a middle-class standing does not protect blacks from racial discrimination. However, I have shown that this conclusion may not be invariantly true. Middle-class blacks in the Washington, D.C., area use public identities to reduce the probability that racial discrimination will determine important outcomes in their lives. By examining how public identities are employed in various public settings, we gain insight into the informal strategies blacks develop as a result of their

experiences in a racialized society. These informal strategies are far more common than the occasional discrimination suits filed by blacks and profiled in the media.

Public identities constitute a form of cultural capital in which blacks with the knowledge and skills valorized by the American mainstream are in a position to manipulate public interactions to their advantage. Previous studies have not examined how high-status minority group members come to possess cultural capital. I introduced two conceptual devices to explain this process and to connect the acquisition of cultural capital to the construction and assertion of public identities in adulthood: improvisational processes and script-switching. To assert public identities, middle-class blacks first acquire cultural capital through their childhood introduction to integrated settings and through their ongoing interactions in the American mainstream, where white cultural styles rule the day. These improvisational and script-switching socialization processes allow middle-class blacks to demonstrate their familiarity with the cultural codes and practices associated with the white middle class. I also show that the cultural capital so critical to doing well in school is influential beyond the school setting as well: in shopping malls, the workplace, and to some extent, with real estate agents.

Among these middle-class blacks, projecting public identities is an opportunity to shore up their status as a group that is not merely black, but distinctly black and *middle-class*. Interviewees noted that "the world is not fair" and that "people will look at [them] in special ways because [they] are black." But these middle-class blacks also tend to associate persistent racial discrimination in public spaces with lower-class blacks, not their class grouping. As members of the middle class, they firmly believe in their ability to engage in strategies that minimize the amount and severity of discrimination directed toward their group. On the rare occasions when they believe that they do experience discrimination—from sales clerks, for example—middle-class blacks associate the incidents with an inability on their part to effectively signal their class position to store employees.

The findings presented in this chapter do not negate the racial stigma paradigm. Rather, these findings call attention to a neglected aspect of the model, namely, the mobilization of class-related strategies as a bulwark against racial discrimination. Indeed, the data suggest that social class may figure more centrally in middle-class blacks' subjective understanding of their public interactions than previous studies allow.

REFERENCES

Aschaffenburg, Karen, and Ineke Maas. 1997. "Cultural and Educational Careers: The Dynamics of Social Reproduction." *American Sociological Review* 62:573-87.

Bourdieu, Pierre, and Jean-Claude Passeron. 1977. *Reproduction in Education, Society, and Culture.* Beverly Hills, Calif.: Sage.

Feagin, Joe. 1991. "The Continuing Significance of Race: Antiblack Discrimination in Public Places." *American Sociological Review* 56: 101-16.

Feagin, Joe, and Melvin Sikes. 1994. *Living with Racism: The Black Middle-Class Experience.* Boston: Beacon Press.

Jackman, Mary. 1994. *The Velvet Glove.* Berkeley: University of California Press.

Kockman, Thomas. 1981. *Black and White Styles in Conflict.* Chicago: University of Chicago Press.

Massey, Douglas, and Nancy Denton. 1993. *American Apartheid.* Cambridge, Mass.: Harvard University Press.

THINKING ABOUT THE READING

According to Lacy, what was the key distinction between middle-class blacks and middle-class whites? What are public identities, and how did the study participants use these in their public interactions with whites? What is cultural capital, and how was it used in the creation of these public identities? What do the findings in the study mean for racial stigma theory? How might other minority groups use public identities in the architecture of their social environments?

The Girl Hunt

Urban Nightlife and the Performance of Masculinity as Collective Activity

David Grazian

(2007)

Young urbanites identify downtown clusters of nightclubs as direct sexual marketplaces, or markets for singles seeking casual encounters with potential sex partners (Laumann et al. 2004).

In this article I examine girl hunting—a practice whereby adolescent heterosexual men aggressively seek out female sexual partners in nightclubs, bars, and other public arenas of commercialized entertainment. In this article I wish to emphasize the performative nature of contemporary flirtation rituals by examining how male-initiated games of heterosexual pursuit function as strategies of impression management in which young men sexually objectify women to heighten their own performance of masculinity. While we typically see public sexual behavior as an interaction between *individuals,* I illustrate how these rituals operate as collective and homosocial group activities conducted in the company of men.

The Performance of Masculinity as Collective Activity

Girl hunting in nightclubs would not seem to serve as an especially efficacious strategy for locating sexual partners, particularly when compared with other methods (such as meeting through mutual friends, colleagues, classmates, or other trusted third parties; common participation in an educational or recreational activity; or shared membership in a civic or religious organization). In fact,

the statistical rareness of the one-night stand may help explain why successful lotharios are granted such glorified status and prestige among their peers in the first place (Connell and Messerschmidt 2005:851). But if this is the case, then why do adolescent men persist in hassling women in public through aggressive sexual advances and pickup attempts (Duneier and Molotch 1999; Snow et al. 1991; Whyte 1988), particularly when their chances of meeting sex partners in this manner are so slim?

I argue that framing the question in this manner misrepresents the actual sociological behavior represented by the girl hunt, particularly since adolescent males do not necessarily engage in girl hunting to generate sexual relationships, even on a drunken short-term basis. Instead, three counterintuitive attributes characterize the girl hunt. First, the girl hunt is as much *ritualistic* and *performative* as it is utilitarian—it is a social drama through which young men perform their interpretations of manhood. Second, as demonstrated by prior studies (Martin and Hummer 1989; Polk 1994; Sanday 1990; Thorne and Luria 1986), girl hunting is not always a purely heterosexual pursuit but can also take the form of an inherently *homosocial* activity. Here, one's male peers are the intended audience for competitive games of sexual reputation and peer status, public displays of situational dominance and rule transgression, and in-group rituals of solidarity and loyalty. Finally, the emotional effort and logistical deftness required by rituals of sexual pursuit (and by extension the public performance of masculinity itself) encourage some young men to seek out safety in numbers by participating in the girl hunt as a kind of *collective activity*, in which they enjoy the social and psychological resources generated by group cohesion and dramaturgical teamwork (Goffman 1959). Although tales of sexual adventure traditionally feature a single male hero, such as Casanova, the performance of heterosexual conquest more often resembles the exploits of the dashing Christian de Neuvillette and his better-spoken coconspirator Cyrano de Bergerac (Rostand 1897). By aligning themselves with similarly oriented accomplices, many young men convince themselves of the importance and efficacy of the girl hunt (despite its poor track record), summon the courage to pursue their female targets (however clumsily), and assist one another in "mobilizing masculinity" (Martin 2001) through a collective performance of gender and heterosexuality.

Methods and Data

I draw on firsthand narrative accounts provided by 243 heterosexual male college students attending the University of Pennsylvania, an Ivy League research university situated in Philadelphia. These data represent part of a larger study involving approximately 600 college students (both men and women).

Because young people are likely to self-consciously experiment with styles of public behavior (Arnett 1994, 2000), observing undergraduates can help researchers understand how young heterosexual men socially construct masculinity through gendered interaction rituals in the context of everyday life. But just as there is not one single mode of masculinity but many *masculinities* available to young men, respondents exhibited a variety of socially recognizable masculine roles in their accounts, including the doting boyfriend, dutiful son, responsible escort, and perfect gentleman. In the interests of exploring the girl hunt as *one among many types* of

social orientation toward the city at night, the findings discussed here represent only the accounts of those heterosexual young men whose accounts revealed commonalities relevant to the girl hunt, as outlined above.

The Girl Hunt and the Myth of the Pickup

It is statistically uncommon for men to successfully attract and "pick up" female sexual partners in bars and nightclubs. However, as suggested by a wide selection of mass media—from erotic films to hardcore pornography—heterosexual young men nevertheless sustain fantasies of successfully negotiating chance sexual encounters with anonymous strangers in urban public spaces (Bech 1998), especially dance clubs, music venues, singles bars, cocktail lounges, and other nightlife settings. According to Aaron, a twenty-one-year-old mixed-race junior:

> I am currently in a very awkward, sticky, complicated and bizarre relationship with a young lady here at Penn, where things are pretty open right now, hopefully to be sorted out during the summer when we both have more time. So my mentality right now is to go to the club with my best bud and seek out the ladies for a night of great music, adventure and female company off of the grounds of campus.

Young men reproduce these normative expectations of masculine sexual prowess—what I call *the myth of the pickup*—collectively through homosocial group interaction. According to Brian, a nineteen-year-old Cuban sophomore:

> Whether I would get any girl's phone number or not, the main purpose for going out was to try to get with hot girls. That was our goal every night we went out to frat parties on campus, and we all knew it, even though we seldom mention that aspect of going out. *It was implicitly known that tonight, and every night out, was a girl hunt.* Tonight, we were taking that goal to Philadelphia's nightlife. In the meanwhile, we would have fun drinking, dancing, and joking around. (emphasis added)

For Brian and his friends, the "girl hunt" articulates a shared orientation toward public interaction in which the group collectively negotiates the city at night. The heterosexual desire among men for a plurality of women (hot *girls,* as it were) operates at the individual and group level. As in game hunting, young men frequently evaluate their erotic prestige in terms of their raw number of sexual conquests, like so many notches on a belt. Whereas traditional norms of feminine desire privilege the search for a singular and specified romantic interest (Prince Charming, Mr. Right, or his less attractive cousin, Mr. Right Now), heterosexual male fantasies idealize the pleasures of an endless abundance and variety of anonymous yet willing female sex partners (Kimmel and Plante 2005).

Despite convincing evidence to the contrary (Laumann et al. 2004), these sexual fantasies seem deceptively realizable in the context of urban nightlife. To many urban denizens, the city and its never-ending flow of anonymous visitors suggests a sexualized marketplace governed by transactional relations and expectations of personal noncommitment (Bech 1998), particularly in downtown entertainment zones where nightclubs, bars, and cocktail lounges are concentrated. The density of urban nightlife districts and their tightly packed venues only intensifies the pervasive yet improbable male fantasy of successfully attracting an imaginary surplus of amorous single women.

Adolescent men strengthen their belief in this fantasy of the sexual availability of women in the city—the myth of the pickup—through collective reinforcement in their conversations in the hours leading up to the girl hunt. While hyping their sexual prowess to the group, male peers collectively legitimize the myth of the pickup and increase its power as a model for normative masculine behavior. According to Dipak, an eighteen-year-old Indian freshman:

> I finished up laboratory work at 5:00 pm and walked to my dormitory, eagerly waiting to "hit up a club" that night. . . . I went to eat with my

three closest friends at [a campus dining hall]. We acted like high school freshmen about to go to our first mixer. We kept hyping up the night and saying we were going to meet and dance with many girls. Two of my friends even bet with each other over who can procure the most phone numbers from girls that night. Essentially, the main topic of discussion during dinner was the night yet to come.

Competitive sex talk is common in male homosocial environments (Bird 1996) and often acts as a catalyst for sexual pursuit among groups of adolescent and young adult males. For example, in his ethnographic work on Philadelphia's black inner-city neighborhoods, Anderson (1999) documents how sex codes among youth evolve in a context of peer pressure in which young black males "run their game" by women as a means of pursuing in-group status. Moreover, this type of one-upmanship heightens existing heterosexual fantasies and the myth of the pickup while creating a largely unrealistic set of sexual and gender expectations for young men seeking in-group status among their peers. In doing so, competitive sexual boasting may have the effect of momentarily energizing group participants. However, in the long run it is eventually likely to deflate the confidence of those who inevitably continue to fall short of such exaggerated expectations and who consequently experience the shame of a spoiled masculine identity (Goffman 1963).

Preparing for the Girl Hunt Through Collective Ritual

Armed with their inflated expectations of the nightlife of the city and its opportunities for sexual conquest, young men at Penn prepare for the girl hunt by crafting a specifically gendered and class-conscious nocturnal self (Grazian 2003)—a presentation of masculinity that relies on prevailing fashion cues and upper-class taste emulation. According to Edward, a twenty-year-old white sophomore, these decisions are made strategically:

I hadn't hooked up with a girl in a couple weeks and I needed to break my slump (the next girl you hook up with is commonly referred to as a "slump-bust" in my social circle). So I was willing to dress in whatever manner would facilitate in hooking up.

Among young college men, especially those living in communal residential settings (i.e., campus dormitories and fraternities), these preparations for public interaction serve as *collective rituals of confidence building*—shared activities that generate group solidarity and cohesion while elevating the personal resolve and self-assuredness of individual participants mobilizing for the girl hunt. Frank, a nineteen-year-old white sophomore, describes the first of these rituals:

> As I began observing both myself and my friends tonight, I noticed that there is a distinct pre-going-out ritual that takes place. I began the night by blasting my collection of rap music as loud as possible, as I tried to overcome the similar sounds resonating from my roommate's room. Martin seemed to play his music in order to build his confidence. It appears that the entire ritual is simply there to build up one's confidence, to make one more adept at picking up the opposite sex.

Frank explains this preparatory ritual in terms of its collective nature, as friends recount tall tales that celebrate character traits commonly associated with traditional conceptions of masculinity, such as boldness and aggression. Against a soundtrack of rap music—a genre known for its misogynistic lyrics and male-specific themes, including heterosexual boasting, emotional detachment, and masculine superiority (McLeod 1999)—these shared ritual moments of homosociality are a means of generating group resolve and bolstering the self-confidence of each participant. Again, according to Frank:

> Everyone erupted into stories explaining their "high-roller status." Martin recounted how he spent nine hundred dollars in Miami one weekend, while Lance brought up his cousins

who spent twenty-five hundred dollars with ease one night at a Las Vegas bachelor party. Again, all of these stories acted as a confidence booster for the night ahead.

Perhaps unsurprisingly, this constant competitive jockeying and one-upmanship so common in male-dominated settings (Martin 2001) often extends to the sexual objectification of women. While getting dressed among friends in preparation for a trip to a local strip club, Gregory, a twenty-year-old white sophomore, reports on the banter: "We should all dress rich and stuff, so we can get us some hookers." Like aggressive locker-room boasting, young male peers bond over competitive sex talk by laughing about real and make-believe sexual exploits and misadventures (Bird 1996). This joking strengthens male group intimacy and collective heterosexual identity and normalizes gender differences by reinforcing dominant myths about the social roles of men and women (Lyman 1987).

After engaging in private talk among roommates and close friends, young men (as well as women) commonly participate in a more public collective ritual known among American college students as "pregaming." As Harry, an eighteen-year-old white freshman, explains,

> Pregaming consists of drinking with your "boys" so that you don't have to purchase as many drinks while you are out to feel the desired buzz. On top of being cost efficient, the actual event of pregaming can get any group ready and excited to go out.

The ritualistic use of alcohol is normative on college campuses, particularly for men (Martin and Hummer 1989), and students largely describe pregaming as an economical and efficient way to get drunk before going out into the city. This is especially the case for underage students who may be denied access to downtown nightspots. However, it also seems clear that pregaming is a bonding ritual that fosters social cohesion and builds confidence among young men in anticipation of the challenges that accompany the girl hunt. According to Joey, an eighteen-year-old white freshman:

> My thoughts turn to this girl, Jessica. . . . I was thinking about whether or not we might hook up tonight. . . . As I turn to face the door to 301, I feel the handle, and it is shaking from the music and dancing going on in the room. I open the door and see all my best friends just dancing together. . . . I quickly rush into the center of the circle and start doing my "J-walk," which I have perfected over the years. My friends love it and begin to chant, "Go Joey— it's your birthday." I'm feeling connected with my friends and just know that we're about to have a great night. . . . Girls keep coming in and out of the door, but no one really pays close attention to them. Just as the "pregame" was getting to its ultimate height, each boy had his arms around each other jumping in unison, to a great hip-hop song by Biggie Smalls. One of the girls went over to the stereo and turned the power off. We yelled at her to turn it back on, but the mood was already lost and we decided it was time to head out.

In this example, Joey's confidence is boosted by the camaraderie he experiences in a male-bonding ritual in which women— supposedly the agreed-upon raison d'être for the evening—are ignored or, when they make their presence known, scolded. As these young men dance arm-in-arm with one another, they generate the collective effervescence and sense of social connectedness necessary to plunge into the nightlife of the city. As such, pregaming fulfills the same function as the last-minute huddle (with all hands in the middle) does for an athletic team (Messner 2002). It is perhaps ironic that Joey's ritual of "having fun with my boys" prepares him for the girl hunt (or more specifically in his case, an opportunity to "hook up" with Jessica) even as it requires those boys to exclude their female classmates. At the same time, this men-only dance serves the same function as the girl hunt: it allows its participants to expressively perform hege-monic masculinity through an aggressive dis-play of collective identification.

During similar collective rituals leading up to the girl hunt, young men boost each other's confidence in their abilities of sexual persua-sion by watching films about male heterosex-ual exploits in urban nightlife, such as Doug Liman's *Swingers* (1996), which chronicles the storied escapades of two best friends, Mike and Trent. According to Kevin, an eighteen-year-old white freshman:

> I knew that [my friend] Darryl needed to calm down if he wanted any chance of a sec-ond date. At about 8:15 pm, I sat him down and showed him (in my opinion), the movie that every man should see at least once—I've seen it six times—*Swingers*. . . . Darryl imme-diately related to Mike's character, the self-conscious but funny gentleman who is still on the rebound from a long-term relationship. At the same time, he took Trent's words for scrip-ture (as I planned): "There's nothing wrong with showing the beautiful babies that you're money and that you want to party." His mind was clearly eased at the thought of his being considered "money." Instead of being too con-cerned with not screwing up and seeming "weird or desperate," Darryl now felt like he was in control. The three of us each went to our own rooms to get ready.

This collective attention to popular cul-tural texts helps peer groups generate common cultural references, private jokes, and speech norms as well as build in-group cohesion (Eliasoph and Lichterman 2003; Fine 1977; Swidler 2001).

Girl Hunting and the Collective Performance of Masculinity

Finally, once the locus of action moves to a more public venue such as a bar or nightclub, the much-anticipated "girl hunt" itself proceeds as a strategic display of masculinity best per-formed with a suitable game partner. According to Christopher, a twenty-two-year-old white senior, he and his cousin Darren "go out together a lot. We enjoy each other's company and we seem to work well together when trying to meet women." Reporting on his evening at a local dance club, Lawrence, a twenty-one-year-old white junior, illustrates how the girl hunt itself operates as collective activity:

> We walk around the bar area as we finish [our drinks]. After we are done, we walk down to the regular part of the club. We make the rounds around the dance floor checking out the girls. . . . We walk up to the glassed dance room and go in, but leave shortly because it is really hot and there weren't many prospects.

Lawrence and his friends display their elaborated performance of masculinity by making their rounds together as a pack in search of a suitable feminine target. Perhaps it is not surprising that the collective nature of their pursuit should also continue *after* such a prize has been located:

> This is where the night gets really interesting. We walk back down to the main dance floor and stand on the outside looking at what's going on and I see a really good-looking girl behind us standing on the other side of the wall with three friends. After pointing her out to my friends, I decide that I'm going to make the big move and talk to her. So I turn around and ask her to dance. She accepts and walks over. My friends are loving this, so they go off to the side and watch. . . .
>
> After dancing for a little while she brings me over to her friends and introduces me. They tell me that they are all freshman [*sic*] at [a local college], and we go through the whole small talk thing again. I bring her over to my two boys who are still getting a kick out of the whole situation. . . . My boys tell me about some of the girls they have seen and talked to, and they inform me that they recognized some girls from Penn walking around the club.

Why do Lawrence and his dance partner both introduce each other to their friends? Lawrence seems to gain almost as much plea- sure from his *friends'* excitement as from his own exploits, just as they are "loving" the vicar- ious thrill of watching their comrade succeed in commanding the young woman's attention,

as if their own masculinity is validated by his success.

In this instance, arousal is not merely individual but represents a collectively shared experience as well (Thorne and Luria 1986:181). For these young men the perfor- mance of masculinity does not necessarily require successfully meeting a potential sex partner as long as one enthusiastically par- ticipates in the ritual *motions* of the girl hunt in the company of men. When Lawrence brings over his new female friend, he does so to celebrate his victory with his buddies, and in return, they appear gratified by their *own* small victory by association. (And while Lawrence celebrates with them, perhaps he alleviates some of the pressure of actually con- versing with her.)

As Christopher remarked above on his relationship with his cousin, the collective aspects of the girl hunt also highlight the effi- cacy of conspiring with peers to meet women: "We go out together a lot. We enjoy each other's company and we seem to work well together when trying to meet women." In the language of the confidence game, men eagerly serve as each other's shills (Goffman 1959; Grazian 2004; Maurer 1940) and sometimes get roped into the role unwittingly with varying degrees of success.

Among young people, the role of the pas- sive accomplice is commonly referred to in contemporary parlance as a *wingman*. In pub- lic rituals of courtship, the wingman serves multiple purposes: he provides validation of a leading man's trustworthiness, eases the interaction between a single male friend and a larger group of women, serves as a source of distraction for the friend or friends of a more desirable target of affection, can be called on to confirm the wild (and frequently mislead- ing) claims of his partner, and, perhaps most important, helps motivate his friends by build- ing up their confidence. Indeed, men describe the role of the wingman in terms of loyalty, personal responsibility, and dependability, traits commonly associated with masculinity (Martin and Hummer 1989; Mishkind et al.

1986). According to Nicholas, an eighteen-year-old white freshman:

> As we were beginning to mobilize ourselves and move towards the dance floor, James noticed Rachel, a girl he knew from Penn who he often told me about as a potential girlfriend. Considering James was seemingly into this girl, Dan and I decided to be good wingmen and entertain Rachel's friend, Sarah.

Hegemonic masculinity is not only expressed by competitiveness but camaraderie as well, and many young men will take their role as a wingman quite seriously and at a personal cost to their relationships with female friends. According to Peter, a twenty-year-old white sophomore:

> "It sounds like a fun evening," I said to Kyle, "but I promised Elizabeth I would go to her date party." I don't like to break commitments. On the other hand, I didn't want to leave Kyle to fend for himself at this club. . . . Kyle is the type of person who likes to pick girls up at clubs. If I were to come see him, I would want to meet other people as well. Having Elizabeth around would not only prevent me from meeting (or even just talking to) other girls, but it would also force Kyle into a situation of having no "wing man."

In the end, Peter takes Elizabeth to a nightclub where, although he *himself* will not be able to meet available women, he will at least be able to assist Kyle in meeting them:

> Behind Kyle, a very attractive girl smiles at me. Yes Oh, wait. Damnit, Elizabeth's here. . . . "Hey, Kyle," I whisper to him. "That girl behind you just smiled at you. Go talk to her." Perhaps Kyle will have some luck with her. He turns around, takes her by the hand, and begins dancing with her. She looks over at me and smiles again, and I smile back. I don't think Elizabeth noticed. I would have rather been in Kyle's position, but I was happy for him, and I was dancing with Elizabeth, so I was satisfied for the moment.

By the end of the night, as he and Kyle chat in a taxi on the way back to campus, Peter learns that he was instrumental in securing his friend's success in an additional way:

> "So what ever happened with you and that girl?" I ask. "I hooked up with her. Apparently she's a senior." I ask if she knew he was a freshman. "Oh, yeah. She asked how old you were, though. I said you were a junior. I had to make one of us look older."

Peter's willingness to serve as a wingman demonstrates his complicity in sustaining the ideals of hegemonic masculinity, which therefore allows him to benefit from the resulting "patriarchal dividends"—acceptance as a member of his male homosocial friendship network and its attendant prestige—even when he himself does not personally seek out the sexual rewards of the girl hunt.

In addition, the peer group provides a readily available audience that can provide emotional comfort to all group members, as well as bear witness to any individual successes that might occur. As demonstrated by the preceding examples, young men deeply value the erotic prestige they receive from their conspiratorial peers upon succeeding in the girl hunt. According to Zach, a twenty-year-old white sophomore:

> About ten minutes later, probably around 2:15 am, we split up into cabs again, with the guys in one and the girls in another. . . . This time in the cab, all the guys want to talk about is me hooking up on the dance floor. It turns out that they saw the whole thing. I am not embarrassed; in fact I am proud of myself.

As an audience, the group can collectively validate the experience of any of its members and can also internalize an individual's success as a shared victory. Since, in a certain sense, a successful sexual interaction must be recognized by one's peers to gain status as an in-group "social fact," the group can transform a private moment into a celebrated public event—thereby making it "count" for the male participant and his cohorts.

A participant's botched attempt at an ill-conceived pickup can solidify the male group's bonds as much as a successful one. According to Brian, the aforementioned nineteen-year-old Cuban sophomore:

> We had been in the club for a little more than half an hour, when the four of us were standing at the perimeter of the main crowd in the dancing room. It was then when Marvin finished his second Corona and by his body gestures, he let it be known that he was drunk enough and was pumped up to start dancing. He started dancing behind a girl who was dancing in a circle with a few other girls. Then the girl turned around and said "Excuse me." Henry and I saw what happened. We laughed so hard and made so much fun of him for the rest of the night. I do not think any of us has ever been turned away so directly and harshly as that time.

In this instance, Marvin's abruptly concluded encounter with an unwilling female participant turns into a humorous episode for the rest of his peer group, leaving his performance of masculinity bruised yet intact. Indeed, in his gracelessness Marvin displays an enthusiastic male heterosexuality as emphasized by his drunken attempts to court an unsuspecting target before a complicit audience of his male peers. And as witnesses to his awkward sexual advance, Brian and Henry take pleasure in the incident, as it not only raises *their* relative standing within the group in comparison with Marvin but can also serve as a narrative focus for future "signifying" episodes (or ceremonial exchanges of insults) and other rituals of solidarity characteristic of joking relationships among male adolescents (Lyman 1987:155). Meanwhile, these young men can bask in their collective failure to attract a woman without ever actually challenging the basis of the girl hunt itself: the performance of adolescent masculinity.

In the end, young men may enjoy this performance of masculinity—the hunt itself—even more than the potential romantic or sexual rewards they hope to gain by its successful execution. In his reflections on a missed opportunity to procure the phone number of a law student, Christopher, the aforementioned twenty-two-year-old senior, admits as much:

"There's something about the chase that I really like. Maybe I subconsciously neglected to get her number. I am tempted to think that I like the idea of being on the look out for her better than the idea of calling her to go out for coffee." While Christopher's excuse may certainly function as a compensatory face-saving strategy employed in the aftermath of another lonely night (Berk 1977), it might also indicate a possible acceptance of the limits of the girl hunt despite its potential opportunities for male bonding and the public display of adolescent masculinity.

REFERENCES

Anderson, Elijah. 1999. *Code of the Street: Decency, Violence, and the Moral Life of the Inner City.* New York: Norton.

Arnett, Jeffrey Jensen. 1994. "Are College Students Adults? Their Conceptions of the Transition to Adulthood." *Journal of Adult Development* 1(4):213–24.

———. 2000. "Emerging Adulthood: A Theory of Development from the Late Teens through the Twenties." *American Psychologist* 55(5): 469–80.

Bech, Henning. 1998. "Citysex: Representing Lust in Public." *Theory, Culture & Society* 15(3–4): 215–41.

Berk, Bernard. 1977. "Face-Saving at the Singles Dance." *Social Problems* 24(5):530–44.

Bird, Sharon R. 1996. "Welcome to the Men's Club: Homosociality and the Maintenance of Hegemonic Masculinity." *Gender & Society* 10(2):120–32.

Connell, R. W. and James W. Messerschmidt. 2005. "Hegemonic Masculinity: Rethinking the Concept." *Gender & Society* 19(6):829–59.

Duneier, Mitchell and Harvey Molotch. 1999. "Talking City Trouble: Interactional Vandalism, Social Inequality, and the 'Urban Interaction Problem.'" *American Journal of Sociology* 104(5): 1263–95.

Eliasoph, Nina and Paul Lichterman. 2003. "Culture in Interaction." *American Journal of Sociology* 108(4):735–94.

Fine, Gary Alan. 1977. "Popular Culture and Social Interaction: Production, Consumption, and Usage." *Journal of Popular Culture* 11(2): 453–56.

Goffman, Erving. 1959. *The Presentation of Self in Everyday Life.* Garden City, NY: Anchor Books.

——. 1963. *Stigma: Notes on the Management of Spoiled Identity.* New York: Simon & Schuster.

Grazian, David. 2003. *Blue Chicago: The Search for Authenticity in Urban Blues Clubs.* Chicago: University of Chicago Press.

——. 2004. "The Production of Popular Music as a Confidence Game: The Case of the Chicago Blues." *Qualitative Sociology* 27(2):137–58.

Kimmel, Michael S. and Rebecca F. Plante. 2005. "The Gender of Desire: The Sexual Fantasies of Women and Men." In *The Gender of Desire: Essays on Male Sexuality,* edited by M. S. Kimmel. Albany: State University of New York Press.

Laumann, Edward O., Stephen Ellingson, Jenna Mahay, Anthony Paik, and Yoosik Youm, eds. 2004. *The Sexual Organization of the City.* Chicago: University of Chicago Press.

Lyman, Peter. 1987. "The Fraternal Bond as a Joking Relationship: A Case Study of the Role of Sexist Jokes in Male Group Bonding." In *Changing Men: New Directions in Research on Men and Masculinity,* edited by M. S. Kimmel. Newbury Park, CA: Sage.

Martin, Patricia Yancey. 2001. "'Mobilizing Masculinities': Women's Experiences of Men at Work." *Organization* 8(4):587–618.

Martin, Patricia Yancey and Robert A. Hummer. 1989. "Fraternities and Rape on Campus." *Gender & Society* 3(4):457–73.

Maurer, David W. 1940. *The Big Con: The Story of the Confidence Man.* New York: Bobbs-Merrill.

McLeod, Kembrew. 1999. "Authenticity within Hip-Hop and Other Cultures Threatened with Assimilation." *Journal of Communication* 49(4):134–50.

Messner, Michael A. 2002. *Taking the Field: Women, Men, and Sports.* Minneapolis: University of Minnesota Press.

Mishkind, Marc, Judith Rodin, Lisa R. Silberstein, and Ruth H. Striegel-Moore. 1986. "The Embodiment of Masculinity." *American Behavioral Scientist* 29(5):545–62.

Polk, Kenneth. 1994. "Masculinity, Honor, and Confrontational Homicide." In *Just Boys Doing Business? Men, Masculinities, and Crime,* edited by T. Newburn and E. A. Stanko. London: Routledge.

Rostand, Edmond. 1897. *Cyrano de Bergerac.*

Sanday, Peggy Reeves. 1990. *Fraternity Gang Rape: Sex, Brotherhood, and Privilege on Campus.* New York: New York University Press.

Snow, David A., Cherylon Robinson, and Patricia L. McCall. 1991. "'Cooling Out' Men in Singles Bars and Nightclubs: Observations on the Interpersonal Survival Strategies of Women in Public Places." *Journal of Contemporary Ethnography* 19(4):423–19.

Swidler, Ann. 2001. *Talk of Love: How Culture Matters.* Chicago: University of Chicago Press.

Thorne, Barrie and Zella Luria. 1986. "Sexuality and Gender in Children's Daily Worlds." *Social Problems* 33(3):176–90.

Whyte, William H. 1988. *City: Rediscovering the Center.* New York: Doubleday.

THINKING ABOUT THE READING

What is the "girl hunt"? According to the author, the purpose of the girl hunt is male social bonding. What does he mean by this? The author uses Goffman's framework as a way to understand why men engage in these activities. What are some of the interaction rituals and performances these young men engage in when they go out to clubs? What are the implications of this kind of research for understanding social issues such as gender, dating, and sexual violence?

Building Social Relationships

Intimacy and Family

7

In this culture, close, personal relationships are the standard by which we judge the quality and happiness of our everyday lives. Yet in a complex, individualistic society like ours, these relationships are becoming more difficult to establish and sustain. Although we like to think that the things we do in our relationships are completely private experiences, they are continually influenced by large-scale political interests and economic pressures. Like every other aspect of our lives, close relationships are best understood within the broader social context. Laws, customs, and social institutions often regulate the form relationships can take, our behavior in them, and even the ways in which we can exit them. At a more fundamental level, societies determine which relationships can be considered "legitimate" and therefore entitled to cultural and institutional recognition. Relationships that lack societal validation are often scorned and stigmatized.

If you were to ask couples applying for a marriage license why they were getting married, most, if not all, would no doubt mention the love they feel for one another. But, as Stephanie Coontz discusses in "The Radical Idea of Marrying for Love," love hasn't always been a prerequisite or even a justification for marriage. Until relatively recently, marriage was principally an economic arrangement, and love, if it existed at all, was a sometimes irrational emotion that was of secondary importance. In fact, in some past societies, falling in love before marriage was considered disruptive, even threatening, to the extended family. Today, however, it's hard to imagine a Western marriage that begins without love.

Speaking of love, gay fatherhood has presented a challenge to the socially constructed and legitimate images of paternity and masculinity in society. Even within the gay community, gay fatherhood has brought up questions around the sexual norms of gay culture. Stacey interviews gay fathers in Los Angeles to explore the growing social character of paternity and the deliberate as well as difficult terrain these men navigate as they become fathers. In the same way that Coontz shows how marriage has entered contested terrain, paths to "planned parenthood" for gay men are full of tensions as they negotiate both cultural and institutional recognition.

The covenant marriage movement developed as a response to what some U.S. religious leaders and organizations saw as the breakdown of the family, in large part attributed to the fracturing of heterosexual marriages. This cultural phenomenon became institutional as various states in the U.S. passed covenant marriage laws that were designed to make marriages stronger and deeper in their commitment. In "Covenant Marriage: Reflexivity and Retrenchment in the Politics of Intimacy," Dwight Fee uses the notion of reflexivity to understand the burgeoning covenant marriage movement. Although members of the movement steadfastly believe that they are revitalizing the belief in the sanctity of marriage, Fee points out that they might just be bucking tradition and custom, and opening up marriage to the possibility of transformation.

Something to Consider as You Read

Each of these selections emphasizes the significance of external or structural components in shaping family experiences. As you read, keep track of factors such as income level and job opportunities and consider how these factors affect the choices families make. Consider some of the ways in which household income might be related to family choices. For example, consider what choices a family with a high income might have regarding how best to assist an ailing grandparent or how to deal with an unexpected teen pregnancy or in providing children with extracurricular activities. Consider how these choices are related to the appearance of "traditional family values." How does legal marriage support families who have access to it? For instance, what kinds of benefits and social assistance do married couples receive that assists them in raising children? What kind of symbolic importance does legal marriage bestow? How might a redefinition of marriage impact different groups in society? How do different routes to parenthood affect the cultural and institutional recognition of families?

The Radical Idea of Marrying for Love

Stephanie Coontz

(2005)

The Real Traditional Marriage

To understand why the love-based marriage system was so unstable and how we ended up where we are today, we have to recognize that for most of history, marriage was not primarily about the individual needs and desires of a man and woman and the children they produced. Marriage had as much to do with getting good in-laws and increasing one's family labor force as it did with finding a lifetime companion and raising a beloved child.

Marriage, a History

Reviewing the role of marriage in different societies in the past and the theories of anthropologists and archaeologists about its origins, I came to reject two widespread, though diametrically opposed, theories about how marriage came into existence among our Stone Age ancestors: the idea that marriage was invented so men would protect women and the opposing idea that it was invented so men could exploit women. Instead, marriage spoke to the needs of the larger group. It converted strangers into relatives and extended cooperative relations beyond the immediate family or small band by creating far-flung networks of in-laws. . . .

Certainly, people fell in love during those thousands of years, sometimes even with their own spouses. But marriage was not fundamentally about love. It was too vital an economic and political institution to be entered into solely on the basis of something as irrational as love. For thousands of years the theme song for most weddings could have been "What's Love Got to Do with It?". . .

For centuries, marriage did much of the work that markets and governments do today. It organized the production and distribution of goods and people. It set up political, economic, and military alliances. It coordinated the division of labor by gender and age. It orchestrated people's personal rights and obligations in everything from sexual relations to the inheritance of property. Most societies had very specific rules about how people should arrange their marriages to accomplish these tasks.

Of course there was always more to marriage than its institutional functions. At the end of the day—or at least in the middle of the night—marriage is also a face-to-face relationship between individuals. The actual experience of marriage for individuals or for particular couples seldom conforms exactly to the model of marriage codified in law, custom, and philosophy in any given period. But institutions do structure people's expectations, hopes, and constraints. For thousands of years, husbands had the right to beat their wives. Few men probably meted out anything more severe than a slap. But the law upheld the authority of husbands to punish their wives physically and to exercise forcibly their "marital right" to sex, and that structured the relations between men and women in *all* marriages, even loving ones.

The Radical Idea of Marrying for Love

George Bernard Shaw described marriage as an institution that brings together two people "under the influence of the most violent, most insane, most delusive, and most transient of passions. They are required to swear that they will remain in that excited, abnormal, and exhausting condition continuously until death do them part."[1]

Shaw's comment was amusing when he wrote it at the beginning of the twentieth century, and it still makes us smile today, because it pokes fun at the unrealistic expectations that spring from a dearly held cultural ideal—that marriage should be based on intense, profound love and a couple should maintain their ardor until death do them part. But for thousands of years the joke would have fallen flat.

For most of history it was inconceivable that people would choose their mates on the basis of something as fragile and irrational as love and then focus all their sexual, intimate, and altruistic desires on the resulting marriage. In fact, many historians, sociologists, and anthropologists used to think romantic love was a recent Western invention. This is not true. People have always fallen in love, and throughout the ages many couples have loved each other deeply.[2]

But only rarely in history has love been seen as the main reason for getting married. When someone did advocate such a strange belief, it was no laughing matter. Instead, it was considered a serious threat to social order.

In some cultures and times, true love was actually thought to be incompatible with marriage. Plato believed love was a wonderful emotion that led men to behave honorably. But the Greek philosopher was referring not to the love of women, "such as the meaner men feel," but to the love of one man for another.[3]

Other societies considered it good if love developed after marriage or thought love should be factored in along with the more serious considerations involved in choosing a mate. But even when past societies did welcome or encourage married love, they kept it on a short leash. Couples were not to put their feelings for each other above more important commitments, such as their ties to parents, siblings, cousins, neighbors, or God.

In ancient India, falling in love before marriage was seen as a disruptive, almost antisocial act. The Greeks thought lovesickness was a type of insanity, a view that was adopted by medieval commentators in Europe. In the Middle Ages the French defined love as a "derangement of the mind" that could be cured by sexual intercourse, either with the loved one or with a different partner.[4] This cure assumed, as Oscar Wilde once put it, that the quickest way to conquer yearning and temptation was to yield immediately and move on to more important matters.

In China, excessive love between husband and wife was seen as a threat to the solidarity of the extended family. Parents could force a son to divorce his wife if her behavior or work habits didn't please them, whether or not he loved her. They could also require him take a concubine if his wife did not produce a son. If a son's romantic attachment to his wife rivaled his parents' claims on the couple's time and labor, the parents might even send her back to her parents. In the Chinese language the term *love* did not traditionally apply to feelings between husband and wife. It was used to describe an illicit, socially disapproved relationship. In the 1920s a group of intellectuals invented a new word for love between spouses because they thought such a radical new idea required its own special label.[5]

In Europe, during the twelfth and thirteenth centuries, adultery became idealized as the highest form of love among the aristocracy. According to the Countess of Champagne, it was impossible for true love to "exert its powers between two people who are married to each other."[6]

In twelfth-century France, Andreas Capellanus, chaplain to Countess Marie of Troyes, wrote a treatise on the principles of courtly love. The first rule was that "marriage is no real excuse for not loving." But he meant loving someone outside the marriage. As late as the eighteenth century the French essayist Montaigne wrote that any man who was in love with his wife was a man so dull that no one else could love him.[7]

Courtly love probably loomed larger in literature than in real life. But for centuries, noblemen and kings fell in love with courtesans rather than the wives they married for political reasons. Queens and noblewomen had to be more discreet than their husbands, but they too looked beyond marriage for love and intimacy.

This sharp distinction between love and marriage was common among the lower and middle classes as well. Many of the songs and stories popular among peasants in medieval Europe mocked married love.

The most famous love affair of the Middle Ages was that of Peter Abelard, a well-known theologian in France, and Héloïse, the brilliant niece of a fellow churchman at Notre Dame. The two eloped without marrying, and she bore him a child. In an attempt to save his career but still placate Héloïse's furious uncle, Abelard proposed they marry in secret. This would mean that Héloïse would not be living in sin, while Abelard could still pursue his church ambitions. But Héloïse resisted the idea, arguing that marriage would not only harm his career but also undermine their love.[8] . . .

"Happily Ever After"

Through most of the past, individuals hoped to find love, or at least "tranquil affection," in marriage.[9] But nowhere did they have the same recipe for marital happiness that prevails in most contemporary Western countries. Today there is general agreement on what it takes for a couple to live "happily ever after." First, they must love each other deeply and choose each other unswayed by outside pressure. From then on, each must make the partner the top priority in life, putting that relationship above any and all competing ties. A husband and wife, we believe, owe their highest obligations and deepest loyalties to each other and the children they raise. Parents and in-laws should not be allowed to interfere in the marriage. Married couples should be best friends, sharing their most intimate feelings and secrets. They should express affection openly but also talk candidly

about problems. And of course they should be sexually faithful to each other.

This package of expectations about love, marriage, and sex, however, is extremely rare. When we look at the historical record around the world, the customs of modern America and Western Europe appear exotic and exceptional. . . .

About two centuries ago Western Europe and North America developed a whole set of new values about the way to organize marriage and sexuality, and many of these values are now spreading across the globe. In this Western model, people expect marriage to satisfy more of their psychological and social needs than ever before. Marriage is supposed to be free of the coercion, violence, and gender inequalities that were tolerated in the past. Individuals want marriage to meet most of their needs for intimacy and affection and all their needs for sex.

Never before in history had societies thought that such a set of high expectations about marriage was either realistic or desirable. Although many Europeans and Americans found tremendous joy in building their relationships around these values, the adoption of these unprecedented goals for marriage had unanticipated and revolutionary consequences that have since come to threaten the stability of the entire institution.

The Era of Ozzie and Harriet: The Long Decade of "Traditional" Marriage

The long decade of the 1950s, stretching from 1947 to the early 1960s in the United States and from 1952 to the late 1960s in Western Europe, was a unique moment in the history of marriage. Never before had so many people shared the experience of courting their own mates, getting married at will, and setting up their own households. Never had married couples been so independent of extended family ties and community groups. And never before had so many people agreed that only one kind of family was "normal."

The cultural consensus that everyone should marry and form a male breadwinner family was like a steamroller that crushed every alternative view. By the end of the 1950s even people who had grown up in completely different family systems had come to believe that universal marriage at a young age into a male breadwinner family was the traditional and permanent form of marriage.

In Canada, says historian Doug Owram, "every magazine, every marriage manual, every advertisement . . . assumed the family was based on the . . . male wage-earner and the child-rearing, home-managing housewife." In the United States, marriage was seen as the only culturally acceptable route to adulthood and independence. Men who chose to remain bachelors were branded "narcissistic," "deviant," "infantile," or "pathological." Family advice expert Pat Landes argued that practically everyone, "except for the sick, the badly crippled, the deformed, the emotionally warped and the mentally defective," ought to marry. French anthropologist Martine Segalen writes that in Europe the postwar period was characterized by the overwhelming "weight of a single family model." Any departure from this model—whether it was late marriage, non-marriage, divorce, single motherhood, or even delayed childbearing—was considered deviant. Everywhere psychiatrists agreed and the mass media affirmed that if a woman did not find her ultimate fulfillment in home-making, it was a sign of serious psychological problems.[10]

A 1957 survey in the United States reported that four out of five people believed that anyone who preferred to remain single was "sick," "neurotic" or "immoral." Even larger majorities agreed that once married, the husband should be the breadwinner and the wife should stay home. As late as 1962 one survey of young women found that almost all expected to be married by age twenty-two, most hoped to have four children, and all expected to quit work permanently when the first child was born.[11]

During the 1950s even women who had once been political activists, labor radicals, or feminists—people like my own mother, still proud of her work to free the Scottsboro Boys from legal lynching in the 1930s and her job in the shipyards during the 1940s—threw themselves into homemaking. It's hard for anyone under the age of sixty to realize how profoundly people's hunger for marriage and domesticity during the 1950s was shaped by their huge relief that two decades of depression and war were finally over and by their amazed delight at the benefits of the first real mass consumer economy in history. "It was like a miracle," my mother once told me, to see so many improvements, so quickly, in the quality of everyday life. . . .

This was the first chance many people had to try to live out the romanticized dream of a private family, happily ensconced in its own nest. They studied how the cheery husbands and wives on their favorite television programs organized their families (and where the crabby ones went wrong). They devoured articles and books on how to get the most out of marriage and their sex lives. They were even interested in advertisements that showed them how to use home appliances to make their family lives better. . . .

Today strong materialist aspirations often corrode family bonds. But in the 1950s, consumer aspirations were an integral part of constructing the postwar family. In its April 1954 issue, *McCall's* magazine heralded the era of "togetherness," in which men and women were constructing a "new and warmer way of life. . . as a family sharing a common experience." In women's magazines that togetherness was always pictured in a setting filled with modern appliances and other new consumer products. The essence of modern life, their women readers learned, was "abundance, emancipation, social progress, airy house, healthy children, the refrigerator, pasteurised milk, the washing-machine, comfort, quality and accessibility."[12] And of course marriage.

Television also equated consumer goods with family happiness. Ozzie and Harriet hugged each other in front of their Hotpoint appliances. A man who had been a young father in the 1950s told a student of mine that he had no clue how to cultivate the family "togetherness" that his wife kept talking about until he saw an episode of the sitcom *Leave It to Beaver,* which gave him the idea of washing the car with his son to get in some "father son" time.

When people could not make their lives conform to those of the "normal" families they saw on TV, they blamed themselves—or their parents. . . . "Why didn't she clean the house in high heels and shirtwaist dresses like they did on television?"[13]

At this early stage of the consumer revolution, people saw marriage as the gateway to the good life. Americans married with the idea of quickly buying their first home, with the wife working for a few years to help accumulate the down payment or furnish it with the conveniences she would use once she became a full-time housewife. People's newfound spending money went to outfit their homes and families. In the five years after World War II, spending on food in the United States rose by a modest 33 percent and clothing expenditures by only 20 percent, but purchases of household furnishings and appliances jumped by 240 percent. In 1961, Phyllis Rosenteur, the author of an American advice book for single women, proclaimed: "Merchandise plus Marriage equals our economy."[14]

In retrospect, it's astonishing how confident most marriage and family experts of the 1950s were that they were witnessing a new stabilization of family life and marriage. The idea that marriage should provide both partners with sexual gratification, personal intimacy, and self-fulfillment was taken to new heights in that decade. Marriage was the place not only where people expected to find the deepest meaning in their lives but also where they would have the most fun. Sociologists noted that a new "fun morality," very different "from the older 'goodness morality,'" pervaded society. "Instead of feeling guilty for having too much fun, one is inclined to feel ashamed if one does not have enough." A leading motivational researcher of the day argued that the challenge for a consumer society was "to demonstrate that the hedonistic approach to life is a moral, not an immoral, one."[15]

But these trends did not cause social commentators the same worries about the neglect of societal duties that milder ideas about the pleasure principle had triggered in the 1920s. Most 1950s sociologists weren't even troubled by the fact that divorce rates were *higher* than they had been in the 1920s, when such rates had been said to threaten the very existence of marriage. The influential sociologists Ernest Burgess and Harvey Locke wrote matter-of-factly that "the companionship family relies upon divorce as a means of rectifying a mistake in mate selection." They expressed none of the panic that earlier social scientists had felt when they first realized divorce was a permanent feature of the love-based marital landscape. Burgess and Locke saw a small amount of divorce as a safety valve for the "companionate" marriage and expected divorce rates to stabilize or decrease in the coming decades as "the services of family-life education and marriage counseling" became more widely available.[16]

The marriage counseling industry was happy to step up to the plate. By the 1950s Paul Popenoe's American Institute of Family Relations employed thirty-seven counselors and claimed to have helped twenty thousand people become "happily adjusted" in their marriages. "It doesn't require supermen or superwomen to succeed in marriage," wrote Popenoe in a 1960 book on saving marriages. "Success can be attained by almost anyone."[17]

There were a few dissenting voices. American sociologist Robert Nisbet warned in 1953 that people were loading too many "psychological and symbolic functions" on the nuclear family, an institution too fragile to bear such weight. In the same year, Mirra Komarovsky decried the overspecialization of gender roles in American marriage and its corrosive effects on women's self confidence.[18]

But even when marriage and family experts acknowledged that the male breadwinner family created stresses for women, they seldom supported any change in its division of labor. The world-renowned American sociologist Talcott Parsons recognized that because most women were not able to forge careers, they might feel a need to attain status in other ways. He suggested that they had two alternatives. The first was to be a "glamour girl" and exert sexual sway over men. The second was to develop special expertise in "humanistic" fields, such as the arts or community volunteer work. The latter, Parsons thought, was socially preferable, posing less of a threat to society's moral standards and to a woman's own self-image as she aged. He never considered the third alternative: that women might actually win access to careers. Even Komarovsky advocated nothing more radical than expanding part-time occupations to give women work that didn't interfere with their primary role as wives and mothers.[19]

Marriage counselors took a different tack in dealing with housewives' unhappiness. Popenoe wrote dozens of marital advice books, pamphlets, and syndicated newspaper columns, and he pioneered the *Ladies' Home Journal* feature "Can This Marriage Be Saved?," which was based on case histories from his Institute of Family Relations. The answer was almost always yes, so long as the natural division of labor between husbands and wives was maintained or restored. . . .

In retrospect, the confidence these experts expressed in the stability of 1950s marriage and gender roles seems hopelessly myopic. Not only did divorce rates during the 1950s never drop below the highs reached in 1929, but as early as 1947 the number of women entering the labor force in the United States had begun to surpass the number of women leaving it.[20] Why were the experts so optimistic about the future of marriage and the demise of feminism?

Some were probably unconsciously soothed into complacency by the mass media, especially the new television shows that delivered nightly images of happy female homemakers in stable male breadwinner families. . . .

When divorce did occur, it was seen as a failure of individuals rather than of marriage. One reason people didn't find fault with the 1950s model of marriage and gender roles was that it was still so new that they weren't sure they were doing it right. Millions of people in Europe and America were looking for a crash course on how to attain the modern marriage. Confident that "science" could solve their problems, couples turned not just to popular culture and the mass media but also to marriage experts and advice columnists for help. If the advice didn't work, they blamed their own inadequacy.[21] . . .

At every turn, popular culture and intellectual elites alike discouraged women from seeing themselves as productive members of society. In 1956 a *Life* magazine article commented that women "have minds and should use them. . . so long as their primary interest is in the home.". . . Adlai Stevenson, the two-time Democratic Party candidate for president of the United States, told the all-female graduating class of Smith College that "most of you" are going to assume "the humble role of housewife," and "whether you like the idea or not just now," later on "you'll like it."[22]

Under these circumstances, women tried their best to "like it." By the mid-1950s American advertisers reported that wives were using housework as a way to express their individuality. It appeared that Talcott Parsons was right: Women were compensating for their lack of occupational status by expanding their role as consumer experts and arbiters of taste and style. First Lady Jackie Kennedy was the supreme exemplar of this role in the early 1960s.[23]

Youth in the 1950s saw nothing to rebel against in the dismissal of female aspirations for independence. The number of American high school students agreeing that it would be good "if girls could be as free as boys in asking for dates" fell from 37 percent in 1950 to 26 percent in 1961, while the percentage of those who thought it would be good for girls to share the expenses of dates declined from 25 percent to 18 percent. The popular image was that only hopeless losers would engage in such egalitarian behavior. A 1954 Philip Morris ad in the *Massachusetts Collegian* made fun of poor Finster, a boy who finally found a girl who shared his belief in "the equity of Dutch treat." As a result, the punch line ran, "today

Finster goes everywhere and shares expenses fifty-fifty with Mary Alice Hematoma, a lovely three-legged girl with side-burns."[24]

No wonder so many social scientists and marriage counselors in the 1950s thought that the instabilities associated with the love-based "near-equality" revolution in gender roles and marriage had been successfully contained. Married women were working outside the home more often than in the past, but they still identified themselves primarily as housewives. Men seemed willing to support women financially even in the absence of their older patriarchal rights, as long as their meals were on the table and their wives kept themselves attractive. Moreover, although men and women aspired to personal fulfillment in marriage, most were willing to stay together even if they did not get it. Sociologist Mirra Komarovsky interviewed working-class couples at the end of the 1950s and found that "slightly less than one-third [were] happily or very happily married." In 1957, a study of a cross section of all social classes found that only 47 percent of U.S. married couples described themselves as "very happy." Although the proportion of "very happy" marriages was lower in 1957 than it was to be in 1976, the divorce rate was also lower.[25]

What the experts failed to notice was that this stability was the result of a unique moment of equilibrium in the expansion of economic, political, and personal options. Ironically, this one twenty-year period in the history of the love-based "near-equality" marriage when people stopped predicting disaster turned out to be the final lull before the long-predicted storm.

The seeming stability of marriage in the 1950s was due in part to the thrill of exploring the new possibilities of married life and the size of the rewards that men and women received for playing by the rules of the postwar economic boom. But it was also due to the incomplete development of the "fun morality" and the consumer revolution. There were still many ways of penalizing nonconformity, tamping down aspirations, and containing discontent in the 1950s.

One source of containment was the economic and legal dependence of women. Postwar societies continued the century-long trend toward increasing women's legal and political rights outside the home and restraining husbands from exercising heavy-handed patriarchal power, but they stopped short of giving wives equal authority with their husbands. Legal scholar Mary Ann Glendon points out that right up until the 1960s, "nearly every legislative attempt to regulate the family decision-making process gave the husband and father the dominant role."[26]

Most American states retained their "head and master" laws, giving husbands the final say over questions like whether or not the family should move. Married women couldn't take out loans or credit cards in their own names. Everywhere in Europe and North America it was perfectly legal to pay women less than men for the same work. Nowhere was it illegal for a man to force his wife to have sex. One legal scholar argues that marriage law in the 1950s had more in common with the legal codes of the 1890s than the 1990s.[27]

Writers in the 1950s generally believed that the old-style husband and father was disappearing and that this was a good thing. The new-style husband, said one American commentator, was now "partner in the family firm, part-time man, part-time mother and part-time maid." Family experts and marital advice columnists advocated a "fifty-fifty design for living," emphasizing that a husband should "help out" with child rearing and make sure that sex with his wife was "mutually satisfying."[28]

But the 1950s definition of fifty-fifty would satisfy few modern couples. Dr. Benjamin Spock, the famous parenting advice expert, called for men to get more involved in parenting but added that he wasn't suggesting equal involvement. "Of course I don't mean that the father has to give just as many bottles, or change just as many diapers as the mother," he explained in a 1950s edition of his perennial bestseller *Baby and Child Care*. "But it's fine for him to do these things occasionally. He might make the formula on Sunday."[29]

The family therapist Paul Popenoe was equally cautious in his definition of what modern marriage required from the wife. A wife should be "sympathetic with her husband's work and a good listener," he wrote. But she must never consider herself "enough of an expert to criticize him."[30] . . .

Many 1950s men did not view male breadwinning as a source of power but as a burdensome responsibility made worthwhile by their love for their families. A man who worked three jobs to support his family told interviewers, "Although I am somewhat tired at the moment, I get pleasure out of thinking the family is dependent on me for their income." Another described how anxious he had been to finish college and "get to. . . acting as a husband and father should, namely, supporting my family." Men also remarked on how wonderful it felt to be able to give their children things their families had been unable to afford when they were young.[31]

A constant theme of men and women looking back on the 1950s was how much better their family lives were in that decade than during the Depression and World War II. But in assessing their situation against a backdrop of such turmoil and privation, they had modest expectations of comfort and happiness, so they were more inclined to count their blessings than to measure the distance between their dreams and their real lives.

Modest expectations are not necessarily a bad thing. Anyone who expects that marriage will always be joyous, that the division of labor will always be fair, and that the earth will move whenever you have sex is going to be often disappointed. Yet it is clear that in many 1950s marriages, low expectations could lead people to put up with truly terrible family lives.

Historian Elaine Tyler May comments that in the 1950s "the idea of 'working marriage' was one that often included constant day-to-day misery for one or both partners." Jessica Weiss recounts interviews conducted over many years in the Berkeley study with a woman whose husband beat her and their children. The wife often threw her body between her husband and the young ones, taking the brunt of the violence on herself because "I can take it much easier than the kids can." Her assessment of the marriage strikes the modern observer as a masterpiece of understatement: "We're really not as happy as we should be." She was not even indignant that her neighbors rebuffed her children when they fled the house to summon help. "I can't say I blame the neighbors," she commented. "They didn't want to get involved." Despite two decades of such violence, this woman did not divorce until the late 1960s.[32]

A 1950s family that looked well functioning to the outside world could hide terrible secrets. Both movie star Sandra Dee and Miss America of 1958, Marilyn Van Derbur, kept silent about their fathers' incestuous abuse until many years had passed. If they had gone public in the 1950s or early 1960s, they might not even have been believed. Family "experts" of the day described incest as a "one-in-a-million occurrence," and many psychiatrists claimed that women who reported incest were simply expressing their own oedipal fantasies.[33]

In many states and countries a nonvirgin could not bring a charge of rape, and everywhere the idea that a man could rape his own wife was still considered absurd. Wife beating was hardly ever treated seriously. The trivialization of family violence was epitomized in a 1954 report of a Scotland Yard commander that "there are only about twenty murders a year in London and not all are serious—some are just husbands killing their wives."[34] . . .

Still, these signs of unhappiness did not ripple the placid waters of 1950s complacency. The male breadwinner marriage seemed so pervasive and popular that social scientists decided it was a necessary and inevitable result of modernization. Industrial societies, they argued, needed the division of labor embodied in the male breadwinner nuclear family to compensate for their personal demands of the modern workplace. The ideal family—or what Talcott Parsons called "the normal" family—consisted of a man who specialized in the practical, individualistic activities needed for subsistence and a woman who took care of the emotional needs of her husband and children.[35]

The close fit that most social scientists saw between the love-based male breadwinner family and the needs of industrial society led them to anticipate that this form of marriage would accompany the spread of industrialization across the globe and replace the wide array of other marriage and family systems in traditional societies. This view was articulated in a vastly influential 1963 book titled *World Revolution and Family Patterns,* by American sociologist William F. Goode. Goode's work became the basis for almost all high school and college classes on family life in the 1960s, and his ideas were popularized by journalists throughout the industrial world.[36]

Goode surveyed the most up-to-date family data in Europe and the United States, the Middle East, sub-Saharan Africa, India, China, and Japan and concluded that countries everywhere were evolving toward a conjugal family system characterized by the "love pattern" in mate selection. The new international marriage system, he said, focused people's material and psychic investments on the nuclear family and increased the "emotional demands which each spouse can legitimately make upon each other," elevating loyalty to spouse above obligations to parents. Goode argued that such ideals would inevitably eclipse other forms of marriage, such as polygamy. Monogamous marriage would become the norm all around the world.

The ideology of the love-based marriage, according to Goode, "is a radical one, destructive of the older traditions in almost every society." It "proclaims the right of the individual to choose his or her own spouse. . . . It asserts the worth of the *individual* as against the inherited elements of wealth or ethnic group." As such, it especially appealed "to intellectuals, young people, women, and the disadvantaged.". . .

Despite women's legal gains and the "radical" appeal of the love ideology to women and youth, Goode concluded that a destabilizing "full equality" was not in the cards. Women had not become more "career-minded" between 1900 and the early 1960s, he said. In his 380-page survey of world trends, Goode did not record even one piece of evidence to suggest that women might become more career-minded in the future.

Most social scientists agreed with Goode that the 1950s family represented the wave of the future. They thought that the history of marriage had in effect reached its culmination in Europe and North America and that the rest of the world would soon catch up. As late as 1963 nothing seemed more obvious to most family experts and to the general public than the preeminence of marriage in people's lives and the permanence of the male breadwinner family.

But clouds were already gathering on the horizon.

When sustained prosperity turned people's attention from gratitude for survival to a desire for greater personal satisfaction. . .

When the expanding economy of the 1960s needed women enough to offer them a living wage. . .

When the prepared foods and drip-dry shirts that had eased the work of homemakers also made it possible for men to live comfortable, if sloppy bachelor lives. . .

When the invention of the birth control pill allowed the sexualization of love to spill over the walls of marriage. . .

When the inflation of the 1970s made it harder for a man to be the sole breadwinner for a family. . .

When all these currents converged, the love-based male-provider marriage would find itself buffeted from all sides.

Notes

1. Quoted in John Jacobs, *All You Need Is Love and Other Lies About Marriage* (New York: HarperCollins, 2004), p. 9.

2. William Jankowiak and Edward Fischer, "A Cross-Cultural Perspective on Romantic Love," *Ethnology* 31 (1992).

3. Ira Reiss and Gary Lee, *Family Systems in America* (New York: Holt, Rinehart and Winston, 1988), pp. 91–93.

4. Karen Dion and Kenneth Dion, "Cultural Perspectives on Romantic Love," *Personal Relationships* 3 (1996); Vern Bullough, "On Being a Male in the Middle Ages," in Clare Less, ed., *Medieval Masculinities* (Minneapolis: University of Minnesota Press, 1994); Hans-Werner Goetz, *Life in the Middle Ages, from the Seventh to the Thirteenth Century* (Notre Dame, Ind.: University of Notre Dame Press, 1993).

5. Francis Hsu, "Kinship and Ways of Life," in Hsu, ed., *Psychological Anthropology* (Cambridge, U.K.: Schenkman, 1972), and *Americans and Chinese: Passage to Differences* (Honolulu: University Press of Hawaii, 1981); G. Robina Quale, *A History of Marriage Systems* (Westport, Conn.: Greenwood Press, 1988); Marilyn Yalom, "Biblical Models," in Yalom and Laura Carstensen, eds., *Inside the American Couple* (Berkeley: University of California Press, 2002).

6. Andreas Capellanus, *The Art of Courtly Love* (New York: W. W. Norton, 1969), pp. 106–07.

7. Ibid., pp. 106–07, 184. On the social context of courtly love, see Theodore Evergates, ed., *Aristocratic Women in Medieval France* (Philadelphia: University of Pennsylvania Press, 1999); Montaigne, quoted in Olwen Hufton, *The Prospect Before Her: A History of Women in Western Europe, 1500–1800* (New York: Alfred A. Knopf, 1996), p. 148.

8. Betty Radice, trans., *Letters of Abelard and Heloise* (Harmondsworth, U.K.: Penguin, 1974).

9. The phrase is from Chiara Saraceno, who argues that until the end of the nineteenth century, Italian families defined love as the development of such feelings over the course of a marriage. Saraceno, "The Italian Family," in Antoine Prost and Gerard Vincent, eds., *A History of Private Life: Riddles of Identity in Modern Times* (Cambridge, Mass.: Belknap Press, 1991), p. 487.

10. Owram, *Born at the Right Time*, p. 22 (see chap. 13, n. 20); Elaine Tyler May, *Homeward Bound: American Families in the Cold War Era* (New York: Basic Books, 1988); Barbara Ehrenreich, *The Hearts of Men: American Dreams and the Flight from Commitment* (Garden City, N.Y.: Anchor Press, 1983), pp. 14–28; Douglas Miller and Marson Nowak, *The Fifties: The Way We Really Were* (Garden City, N.Y.: Doubleday, 1977), p. 154; Duchen, *Women's Rights* (see chap. 13, n. 28); Marjorie Ferguson, *Forever Feminine: Women's Magazines and the Cult of Femininity* (London: Heinemann, 1983); Moeller, *Protecting Motherhood* (see chap. 13, n. 22); Martine Segalen, "The Family in the Industrial Revolution," in Burguière et al., p. 401 (see chap. 8, n. 2).

11. Daniel Yankelovich, *New Rules: Searching for Self-Fulfillment in a World Turned Upside Down* (New York: Random House, 1981); Lois Gordon and Alan Gordon, *American Chronicle: Seven Decades in American Life, 1920–1989* (New York: Crown, 1990).

12. Alan Ehrenhalt, *The Lost City: Discovering the Forgotten Virtues of Community in the Chicago of the 1950s* (New York: Basic Books, 1995), p. 233; modernity quote from the French woman's magazine *Marie-Claire*, in Duchen, *Women's Rights and Women's Lives*, p. 73 (see chap. 13, n. 28).

13. Quoted in Ruth Rosen, *The World Split Open: How the Modern Women's Movement Changed America* (New York: Viking, 2000), p. 44.

14. Coontz, *The Way We Never Were*, p. 25; Rosenteur, quoted in Bailey, *From Front Porch to Back Seat*, p. 76 (see chap. 12, n. 11).

15. Martha Wolfenstein, "Fun Morality" [1955], in Warren Susman, ed., *Culture and Commitment, 1929–1945* (New York: George Braziller, 1973), pp. 84, 90; Coontz, *The Way We Never Were*, p. 171.

16. Ernest Burgess and Harvey Locke, *The Family: From Institution to Companionship* (New York: American Book Company, 1960), pp. 479, 985, 538.

17. Molly Ladd-Taylor, "Eugenics, Sterilisation and Modern Marriage in the USA," *Gender & History* 13 (2001), pp. 312, 318.

18. Nisbet, quoted in John Scanzoni, "From the Normal Family to Alternate Families to the Quest for Diversity with Interdependence," *Journal of Family Issues* 22 (2001); Mirra Komarovsky, *Women in the Modern World: Their Education and Their Dilemmas* (Boston: Little, Brown, 1953).

19. Talcott Parsons, "The Kinship System of the United States" in Parsons, *Essays in Sociological Theory* (Glencoe, Ill.: Free Press, 1954); Parsons and Robert Bales, *Family, Socialization, and Interaction Processes* (Glencoe, Ill.: Free Press, 1955).

20. *Historical Statistics of the United States: Colonial Times to the Present* (Washington, D.C.: U.S. Department of Commerce, Bureau of the Census, 1975); Sheila Tobias and Lisa Anderson, "What Really Happened to Rosie the Riveter," *Mss Modular Publications* 9 (1973).

21. Beth Bailey, "Scientific Truth. . . and Love: The Marriage Education Movement in the United States," *Journal of Social History* 20 (1987).

22. Miller and Nowak, *The Fifties*, pp. 164–65; Weiss, *To Have and to Hold*, p. 19 (see chap. 13, n. 29); Rosen, *World Split Open*, p. 41.

23. Glenna Mathews, *"Just a Housewife": The Rise and Fall of Domesticity in America* (New York: Oxford University Press, 1987); Betty Friedan, *The Feminine Mystique* (New York: Dell, 1963).

24. Bailey, *From Front Porch to Back Seat,* p. 111.

25. Mirra Komarovsky, *Blue-Collar Marriage* (New Haven: Vintage, 1962), p. 331. Mintz and Kellogg, *Domestic Revolutions,* p. 194; Norval Glenn, "Marital Quality," in David Levinson, ed., *Encyclopedia of Marriage and the Family* (New York: Macmillan, 1995), vol. 2, p. 449.

26. Mary Ann Glendon, *The Transformation of Family Law* (Chicago: University of Chicago Press, 1989), p. 88. On Europe, Gisela Bock, *Women in European History* (Oxford, U.K.: Blackwell Publishers, 2002), p. 248; Bonnie Smith, *Changing Lives: Women in European History Since 1700* (Lexington, Mass.: D. C. Heath, 1989), p. 492.

27. Sara Evans, *Tidal Wave: How Women Changed America at Century's End* (New York: Free Press, 2003), pp. 1–20; John Ekelaar, "The End of an Era?," *Journal of Family History* 28 (2003), p. 109. See also Lenore Weitzman, *The Marriage Contract* (New York: Free Press, 1981).

28. Ehrenhalt, *Lost City,* p. 233.

29. Quoted in Michael Kimmell, *Manhood in America: A Cultural History* (New York: Free Press, 1996), p. 246.

30. Ladd-Taylor, "Eugenics," p. 319.

31. Ibid., p. 32; Robert Rutherdale, "Fatherhood, Masculinity, and the Good Life During Canada's Baby Boom," *Journal of Family History* 24 (1999), p. 367.

32. May, *Homeward Bound,* p. 202; Weiss, *To Have and to Hold,* pp. 136–30.

33. Marilyn Van Derbur Atler, "The Darkest Secret," *People* (June 10, 1991); Dodd Darin, *The Magnificent Shattered Life of Bobby Darin and Sandra Dee* (New York: Warner Books, 1995); Elizabeth Pleck, *Domestic Tyranny* (New York: Oxford University Press, 1987); Linda Gordon, *Heroes of Their Own Lives: The Politics and History of Family Violence, 1880–1960* (New York: Viking, 1988).

34. Coontz, *The Way We Never Were,* p. 35; Leonore Davidoff et al., *The Family Story* (London: Longmans, 1999), p. 215.

35. Parsons, "The Kinship System of the United States"; Parsons, "The Normal American Family," in Seymour Farber, Piero Mustacchi, and Roger Wilson, eds., *Man and Civilization: The Family's Search for Survival* (New York: McGraw-Hill, 1965); Parsons and Bales, *Family, Socialization, and Interaction Processes.* For similar theories in British sociology, see Michael Young and Peter Willmott's *The Symmetrical Family* (London: Pelican, 1973), pp. 28–30; *Family and Kinship in East London* (Glencoe, Ill.: The Free Press, 1957); and *Family and Class in a London Suburb.*

36. The quotations and figures in this and the following paragraphs are from Goode, *World Revolution.*

THINKING ABOUT THE READING

According to Coontz, if not for romance, what are some of the common reasons throughout history that people marry? What are the characteristics of the "male bread-winner, love-based marriage"? What social conditions are necessary for this kind of family arrangement to prevail? Does Coontz think this family form is viable in the long-term future? Do you?

Gay Parenthood and the End of Paternity as We Knew It

Judith Stacey

(2011)

Because let's face it, if men weren't always hungry for it, nothing would ever happen. There would be no sex, and our species would perish.

—Sean Elder, "Why My Wife Won't Sleep With Me," 2004

Because homosexuals are rarely monogamous, often having as many as three hundred or more partners in a lifetime—some studies say it is typically more than one thousand—children in those polyamorous situations are caught in a perpetual coming and going. It is devastating to kids, who by their nature are enormously conservative creatures.

—James Dobson, "Same-Sex Marriage Talking Points"

Unlucky in love and ready for a family, [Christie] Malcomson tried for 4½ years to get pregnant, eventually giving birth to the twins when she was 38. Four years later, again without a mate, she had Sarah. "I've always known that I was meant to be a mother," Malcomson, 44, said. "I tell people, I didn't choose to be a single parent. I choose to be a parent."

—Lornet Turnbull, "Family Is. . . Being Redefined All the Time," 2004

Gay fathers were once as unthinkable as they were invisible. Now they are an undeniable part of the contemporary family landscape. During the same time that the marriage promotion campaign in the United States was busy convincing politicians and the public to regard rising rates of fatherlessness as a national emergency (Stacey 1998), growing numbers of gay men were embracing fatherhood. Over the past two decades, they have built a cornucopia of family forms and supportive communities where they are raising children outside of the conventional family. Examining the experiences of gay men who have openly pursued parenthood against the odds can help us to understand forces that underlie the decline of paternity as we knew it. Contrary to the fears of many in the marriage-promotion movement, however, gay parenting is not a new symptom of the demise of fatherhood, but of its creative, if controversial, reinvention. When I paid close attention to gay men's parenting desires, efforts, challenges, and achievements, I unearthed crucial features of contemporary paternity and parenthood more generally. I also came upon some inspirational models of family that challenge widely held beliefs about parenthood and child welfare.

The Uncertainty of Paternity

Access to effective contraception, safe abortions, and assisted reproductive technologies (ART) unhitches traditional links between heterosexual love, marriage, and baby carriages. Parenthood, like intimacy more generally, is now contingent. Paths to parenthood no longer appear so natural, obligatory, or uniform as they used to but have become voluntary, plural, and politically embattled. Now that children impose immense economic and social responsibilities on their parents, rather than promising to become a reliable source of family labor or social security, the pursuit of parenthood depends on an emotional rather than an economic calculus. "The men and women who decide to have children today," German sociologists Ulrich Beck and Elisabeth Beck-Gernsheim correctly point out, "certainly do not do so because they expect any material advantages. Other motives closely linked with the emotional needs of the parents play a significant role; our children mainly have 'a psychological utility.'" (Beck and Beck-Gernsheim 1995:105). Amid the threatening upheavals, insecurities, and dislocations of life under global market and military forces, children can rekindle opportunities for hope, meaning, and connection. Adults who wish to become parents today typically seek the intimate bonds that children seem to promise. More reliably than a lover or spouse, parenthood beckons to many (like Christie Malcomson in the third epigraph to this chapter) who hunger for lasting love, intimacy, and kinship—for that elusive "haven in a heartless world" (Lasch 1995).

Gay men confront these features of post-modern parenthood in a magnified mode. They operate from cultural premises antithetical to what U.S. historian Nicholas Townsend termed "the package deal" of (now eroding) modern masculinity—marriage, work, and fatherhood (Townsend 2002). Gay men who choose to become primary parents challenge conventional definitions of masculinity and paternity and even dominant sexual norms of gay culture itself.

Gay fatherhood represents "planned parenthood" in extremis. Always deliberate and often difficult, it offers fertile ground for understanding why and how people do and do not choose to become parents today. Unlike most heterosexuals or even lesbians, gay men have to struggle for access to "the means of reproduction" without benefit of default scripts

for achieving or practicing parenthood. They encounter a range of challenging, risky, uncertain options—foster care, public and private forms of domestic and 'international adoption, hired or volunteered forms of "traditional" or gestational surrogacy, contributing sperm to women friends, relatives, or strangers who agree to co-parent with them, or even resorting to an instrumental approach to old-fashioned heterosexual copulation.

Compared with maternity, the social character of paternity has always been more visible than its biological status. Indeed, that's why prior to DNA testing, most modern societies mandated a marital presumption of paternity. Whenever a married woman gave birth, her husband was the presumed and legal father. Gay male paternity intensifies this emphasis on social rather than biological definitions of parenthood. Because the available routes to genetic parenthood for gay men are formidably expensive, very difficult to negotiate, or both, most prospective gay male parents pursue the purely social paths of adoption or foster care (Brodzinsky, Patterson, and Vaziri 2002).

Stark racial, economic, and sexual asymmetries characterize the adoption marketplace. Prospective parents are primarily white, middle-class, and relatively affluent, but the available children are disproportionately from poorer and darker races and nations. Public and private adoption agencies, as well as birth mothers and fathers, generally consider married heterosexual couples to be the most desirable adoptive parents (Human Rights Campaign 2009). These favored straight married couples, for their part, typically seek healthy infants, preferably from their own race or ethnic background. Because there are not enough of these to meet the demand, most states and counties allow single adults, including gay men, to shop for parenthood in their overstocked warehouse of "hard to place" children. This is an index of expediency more than tolerance. The state's stockpiled children have been removed from parents who were judged to be negligent, abusive, or incompetent. Disproportionate numbers are children of color, and the very hardest of these to place are older boys with "special needs," such as physical, emotional, and cognitive disabilities.

The gross disjuncture between the market value of society's adoptable children and the supply of prospective adoptive parents allows gay men to parent a hefty share of them. Impressive numbers of gay men willingly rescue such children from failing or devastated families. Just as in their intimate adult relationships, gay men more readily accept children across boundaries of race, ethnicity, class, and even health.

The multi-racial membership of so many of gay men's families visually signals the social character of most gay fatherhood. In addition, as we will see, some gay men, like single-mother-by-choice Christie Malcomson, willingly unhitch their sexual and romantic desires from their domestic ones in order to become parents. For all of these reasons, gay men provide frontier terrain for exploring noteworthy changes in the meanings and motives for paternity and parenthood.

Finding Pop Luck in the City of Angels

Gay paternity is especially developed and prominent in L.A.—again, not the environment where most people would expect to find it, but which, for many reasons, became a multi-ethnic mecca for gay parenthood. According to data reported in Census 2000, both the greatest number of same-sex couple households in the United States and of such couples who were raising children were residing in Los Angeles County (Sears and Badgett 2004). It is likely, therefore, that the numbers there exceeded those of any metropolis in the world.

Local conditions in Los Angeles have been particularly favorable for gay and lesbian parenthood. L.A. County was among the first in the United States to openly allow gay men to foster or adopt children under its custody, and numerous local, private adoption agencies, lawyers, and services emerged that specialized in facilitating domestic and international

adoptions for a gay clientele. In 2001 California enacted a domestic-partnership law that authorized second-parent adoptions, and several family-court judges in California pioneered the still-rare practice of granting pre-birth custody rights to same-sex couples who planned to co-parent. The City of Angels became the surrogacy capital of the gay globe, thanks especially to Growing Generations, the world's first gay- and lesbian-owned professional surrogacy agency founded to serve an international clientele of prospective gay parents (Strah and Margolis 2003).

The gay men I studied were among the first cohort of gay men young enough to even imagine parenthood outside heterosexuality and mature enough to be in a position to choose or reject it. I intentionally over-sampled for gay fathers. Nationally 22 percent of male same-sex-couple households recorded in Census 2000 included children under the age of eighteen (Simmons and O'Connell 2003:10). However, fathers composed half of my sample overall and more than 60 percent of the men who were then in same-sex couples. Depending on which definition of fatherhood one uses, between twenty-four and twenty-nine of my fifty primary interviewees were fathers of thirty-five children, and four men who were not yet parents declared their firm intention to become so.[1] Only sixteen men, in contrast, depicted themselves as childless more or less by choice. Also by design, I sampled to include the full gamut of contemporary paths to gay paternity. Although most children with gay fathers in the United States were born within heterosexual marriages before their fathers came out, this was true for only six of the thirty-four children that the men in my study were raising. All of the others were among the pioneer generation of children with gay dads who chose to parent after they had come out of the closet. Fifteen of the children had been adopted (or were in the process of becoming so) through county and private agencies or via independent, open adoption agreements with birth mothers; four were foster-care children; five children had been conceived through surrogacy contracts, both gestational and "traditional"; and four children had been born to lesbians who conceived with sperm from gay men with whom they were co-parenting. In addition, five of the gay men in my study had served as foster parents to numerous teenagers, and several expected to continue to accept foster placements. Two men, however, were biological but not social parents, one by intention, the other unwittingly.[2]

The fathers and children in my study were racially and socially diverse, and their families, like gay-parent families generally, were much more likely to be multi-racial and multi-cultural than are other families in the United States, or perhaps anywhere in the world. Two-thirds of the gay-father families in my study were multi-racial. The majority (fifteen) of the twenty-four gay men who were parenting during the time of my study were white, but most (twenty-one) of their thirty-four children were not.[3] Even more striking, only two of the fifteen children they had adopted by 2003 were white, both of these through open adoption arrangements with birth mothers; seven adoptees were black or mixed race, and six were Latino. In contrast, nine of the twelve adoptive parents were white, and one each was black, Latino, and Asian American.

It is difficult to assess how racially representative this is of gay men, gay parents, and their families in the city, the state, or the nation. Although the dominant cultural stereotype of gay men and gay fathers is white and middle class, U.S. Census 2000 data surprisingly report that racial minorities represented a higher proportion of same-sex-couple-parent households in California than of heterosexual married couples (Sears and Badgett 2004). The vast majority of the children in these families, however, were born within their gay parents' former heterosexual relationship (Gates 2005). Contemporary gay paths to paternity are far more varied and complex.

Predestined Progenitors

Of the men I interviewed, eighteen who had become dads and four who planned to do so

portrayed their passion for parenthood in terms so ardent that I classify them as predestined parents. The following two stories illustrate typical challenges and triumphs of different paths to predestined parenthood. The first depicts another blessedly compatible and privileged couple, and the second is about a courageous, much less affluent gay man who was "single by chance, parent by choice."

Predestined Pairing

Eddie Leary and Charles Tillery, a well-heeled, white, Catholic couple, had three children born through gestational surrogacy. Their firstborn was a genetic half-sibling to a younger set of twins. The same egg donor and the same gestational surrogate conceived and bore the three children, but Charles is the genetic father of the first child, and Eddie's sperm conceived the twins. At the time I first interviewed them in 2002, their first child was three years old, the twins were infants, and the couple had been together for eighteen years. Eddie told me that they had discussed their shared desire to parent on their very first date, In fact, by then Eddie had already entered a heterosexual marriage primarily for that purpose, but he came out to his wife and left the marriage before achieving it. Directly echoing Christie Malcomson, Eddie claimed that he always knew that he "was meant to be a parent." He recalled that during his childhood whenever adults had posed the clichéd question to him, "What do you want to be when you grow up?" his ready answer was "a daddy."

Charles and Eddie met and spent their first ten years together on the East Coast, where they built successful careers in corporate law and were gliding through the glamorous DINC (double income, no children) fast lane of life. By their mid-thirties, however, they were bored and began to ask themselves the existential question, "Is this all there is?" They had already buried more friends than their parents had by their sixties, which, Eddie believed, "gives you a sense of gravitas." In addition, he reported, "My biological clock was definitely ticking." In the mid-1990s, the couple migrated to L.A., lured by the kind of gay family life style and the ample job opportunities it seemed to offer. They spent the next five years riding an emotional roller coaster attempting to become parents. At first Eddie and Charles considered adoption, but they became discouraged when they learned that then-governor Pete Wilson's administration was preventing joint adoptions by same-sex couples. Blessed with ample financial and social resources, they decided to shift their eggs, so to speak, into the surrogacy basket. One of Charles's many cousins put the couple in touch with her college roommate, Sally, a married mother of two in her mid-thirties who lived in Idaho. Sally was a woman who loved both bearing and rearing children, and Charles's cousin knew that she had been fantasizing about bestowing the gift of parenthood on a childless couple. Although Sally's imaginary couple had not been gay, she agreed to meet them. Eddie and Sally both reported that they bonded instantly, and she agreed to serve as the men's gestational surrogate.

To secure an egg donor and manage the complex medical and legal processes that surrogacy requires at a moment just before Growing Generations had opened shop, Eddie and Charles became among the first gay clients of a surrogate parenthood agency that mainly served infertile heterosexual couples. Shopping for DNA in the agency's catalog of egg donors, they had selected Marya, a Dutch graduate student who had twice before served as an anonymous donor for married couples in order to subsidize her education. Marya had begun to long for maternity herself, however, and she was loathe to subject her body and soul yet again to the grueling and hormonally disruptive process that donating ova entails. Yet when she learned that the new candidates for her genes were gay men, she found herself taken with the prospect of openly aiding such a quest. Like Sally, she felt an immediate affinity with Eddie and agreed to enter a collaborative egg-donor relationship with him and Charles. When she had served as egg donor for infertile married couples, Marya explained, "the mother there can get a little

jealous and a little threatened, because she's already feeling insecure about being infertile, and having another woman having that process and threatening the mother's role, I think is a big concern." With a gay couple, in contrast, "you get to be—there's no exclusion, and there's no threatened feelings."

Because Eddie is a few years older than Charles, he wanted to be the first to provide the sperm, and all four parties were thrilled when Sally became pregnant on the second in-vitro fertilization (IVF) attempt. Elation turned to despair, however, when the pregnancy miscarried in the thirteenth week. Eddie described himself as devastated, saying, "I grieved and mourned the loss of my child, just as if I'd been the one carrying it." In fact, Sally recovered from the trauma and was willing to try again before Eddie, who said, "I couldn't bear the risk of losing another of my children." Instead, Charles wound up supplying the sperm for what became the couple's firstborn child, Heather. Two years later, eager for a second child, the couple had persuaded both reluctant women to subject their bodies to one more IVF surrogacy, this time with Eddie's sperm. A pair of healthy twin boys arrived one year later, with all four procreative collaborators, as well as Sally's husband, present at the delivery to welcome the boys into what was to become a remarkable, surrogacy-extended family.

Occasionally Marya, the egg donor, continued to visit her genetic daughter, but Eddie and Sally quickly developed an extraordinary, deep, familial bond. They developed the habit of daily, long-distance phone calls that were often lengthy and intimate. "Mama Sally," as Heather started to call her, began to make regular use of the Leary-Tillery guest room, accompanied sometimes by her husband and their two children. Often she came to co-parent with Eddie as a substitute for Charles, who had to make frequent business trips. The two families began taking joint vacations skiing or camping together in the Rockies, and once Marya had come along. Sally's then ten-year-old daughter and eight-year-old son began to refer to Heather as their "surrogate sister."

Eddie and Charles jointly secured shared legal custody of all three children through some of the earliest pre-birth decrees granted in California. From the start, the couple had agreed that Eddie, a gourmet cook who had designed the family's state-of-the-culinary-art kitchen, would stay home as full-time parent, and Charles would be the family's sole breadwinner. After the twins arrived, they hired a daytime nanny to assist Eddie while Charles was out earning their sustenance, and she sometimes minded the twins when Eddie and Heather joined the weekly playgroup of the Pop Luck Club (PLC), composed of at-home dads and tots. Charles, for his part, blessed with Herculean energy and scant need for sleep, would plunge into his full-scale second shift of baby. Feedings, diapers, baths, and bedtime storytelling the moment he returned from the office. Although Eddie admitted to some nagging concerns that he "may have committed career suicide by joining the mom's club in the neighborhood," he also believed he'd met his calling: "I feel like this is who I was meant to be."

Parent Seeking Partner

Armando Hidalgo, a Mexican immigrant, was thirty-four years old when I interviewed him in 2001. At that point, he was in the final stages of adopting his four-year-old black foster son, Ramon. Armando had been a teenage sexual migrant to Los Angeles almost twenty years earlier. He had run away from home when he was only fifteen in order to conceal his unacceptable sexual desires from his large, commercially successful, urban Mexican family. The youthful Armando had paid a coyote to help him cross the border. He had survived a harrowing illegal immigration experience which culminated in a Hollywood-style footrace across the California desert to escape an INS patrol in hot pursuit. By working at a Taco Bell in a coastal town, Armando put himself through high school. Drawing upon keen intelligence, linguistic facility, and a prodigious work ethic and drive, he had built a stable career managing a designer

furniture showroom and he had managed to secure U.S. citizenship as well.

Four years after Armando's sudden disappearance from Mexico, he had returned there to come out to his family, cope with their painful reactions to his homosexuality and exile, and begin to restore his ruptured kinship bonds. He had made annual visits to his family ever since, and on one of these he fell in love with Juan, a Mexican language teacher. Armando said that he told Juan about his desire to parent right at the outset, and his new lover had seemed enthusiastic: "So, I thought we were the perfect match." Armando brought his boyfriend back to Los Angeles, and they lived together for five years.

However, when Armando began to pursue his lifelong goal of parenthood, things fell apart. To initiate the adoption process, Armando had enrolled the couple in the county's mandatory foster-care class. However, Juan kept skipping class and neglecting the homework, and so he failed to qualify for foster-parent status. This behavior jeopardized Armando's eligibility to adopt children as well as Juan's. The county then presented Armando with a "Sophie's choice." They would not place a child in his home unless Juan moved out. Despite Armando's primal passion for parenthood, "at the time," he self-critically explained to me, "I made the choice of staying with him, a choice that I regret. I chose him over continuing with my adoption." This decision ultimately exacted a fatal toll on the relationship. In Armando's eyes, Juan was preventing him from fulfilling his lifelong dream of having children. His resentment grew, but it took another couple of years before his passion for parenthood surpassed his diminishing passion for his partner. That is when Armando moved out and renewed the adoption application as a single parent.

Ramón was the first of three children that Armando told me he had "definitely decided" to adopt, whether or not he found another partner. His goal was to adopt two more children, preferably a daughter and another son, in that order. Removed at birth from crack-addicted parents, Ramón had lived in three foster homes in his first three years of life, before the county placed him with Armando through its fost-adopt program. Ramón had suffered from food allergies, anxiety, and hyperactivity when he arrived, and the social worker warned Armando to anticipate learning disabilities as well. Instead, after nine months under Armando's steady, patient, firm, and loving care, Ramón was learning rapidly and appeared to be thriving. And so was Armando. He felt so lucky to have Ramón, whom he no longer perceived as racially different from himself: "To me he's like my natural son. I love him a lot, and he loves me too much. Maybe I never felt so much unconditional love."

In fact, looking back, Armando attributed part of the pain of the years he spent struggling to accept his own homosexuality to his discomfort with gay male sexual culture and its emphasis on youth and beauty. "I think it made me fear that I was going to grow old alone," he reflected. "Now I don't have to worry that I'm gay and I'll be alone." For in addition to the intimacy that Armando savored with Ramón, his son proved to be a vehicle for building much closer bonds with most of his natal family. Several of Armando's eleven siblings had also migrated to Los Angeles. Among these were a married brother, his wife, and their children, who provided indispensable back-up support to the single working father. Ramón adored his cousins, and he and his father spent almost every weekend and holiday with them.

Ramón had acquired a devoted, long-distance *abuela* (grandmother) as well. Armando's mother had begun to travel regularly from Mexico to visit her dispersed brood, and, after years of disapproval and disappointment, she had grown to admire and appreciate her gay son above all her other children. Armando reported with sheepish pride that during a recent phone call his mother had stunned and thrilled him when she said, "You know what? I wish that all your brothers were like you. I mean that they liked guys." Astonished, Armando had asked her, "Why do you say that?" She replied, "I don't know. I just feel that

you're really good to me, you're really kind. And you're such a good father." Then she apologized for how badly she had reacted when Armando told the family that he was gay, and she told him that now she was really proud of him. "'Now I don't have to accept it,'" Armando quoted her, "'because there's nothing to accept. You're natural, you're normal. You're my son, I don't have to accept you.' And she went on and on. It was so nice, it just came out of her. And now she talks about gay things, and she takes a cooking class from a gay guy and tells me how badly her gay cooking teacher was treated by his family when they found out and how unfair it is and all."

Although Armando had begun to create the family he always wanted, he still dreamt of sharing parenthood with a mate who would be more compatible than Juan: "I would really love to meet someone, to fall in love." Of course, the man of his dreams was someone family-oriented: "Now that's really important, family-oriented, because I am very close to my family. I always do family things, like my nephews' birthday parties, going to the movies with them, family dinners, etcetera. But these are things that many gay men don't like to do. If they go to a straight family party, they get bored." Consequently, Armando was pessimistic about finding a love match. Being a parent, moreover, severely constrained his romantic pursuits. He didn't want to subject Ramón, who had suffered so much loss and instability in his life, to the risk of becoming attached to yet another new parental figure who might leave him. In addition, he didn't want Ramón "to think that gay men only have casual relationships, that there's no commitment." "But," he observed, with disappointment, "I haven't seen a lot of commitment among gay men." Armando took enormous comfort, however, in knowing that even if he never found another boyfriend, he will "never really be alone": "And I guess that's one of the joys that a family brings." Disappointingly, I may never learn whether Armando found a co-parent and adopted a sister and brother for Ramón, because I was unable to locate him again in 2008.

Adopting Diversity

While Eddie, Charles, and Armando all experienced irrepressible parental yearnings, they pursued very different routes to realizing this common "destiny." Gestational surrogacy, perhaps the newest, the most high-tech, and certainly the most expensive path to gay parenthood, is available primarily to affluent couples, the overwhelming majority of whom are white men who want to have genetic progeny. Adoption, on the other hand, is one of the oldest forms of "alternative" parenthood. It involves bureaucratic and social rather than medical technologies, and the county fost-adopt program which Armando and six other men in my study employed is generally the least expensive, most accessible route to gay paternity. Like Armando, most single, gay prospective parents pursue this avenue and adopt "hard-to-place" children who, like Ramón, are often boys of color with "special needs."

The demographics of contrasting routes to gay parenthood starkly expose the race and class disparities in the market value of children. Affluent, mainly white couples, like Charles and Eddie, can purchase the means to reproduce white infants in their own image, or even an enhanced, eugenic one, by selecting egg donors who have traits they desire with whom to mate their own DNA. In contrast, for gay men who are single, less privileged, or both, public agencies offer a grab bag of displaced children who are generally older, darker, and less healthy (U.S. Department of Health and Human Services 2003; Kapp, McDonald, and Diamond 2001). Somewhere in between these two routes to gay paternity are forms of "gray market," open domestic or international adoptions, or privately negotiated sperm-donor agreements with women, especially lesbians, who want to co-parent with men. Independent adoption agencies and the Internet enable middle-class gay men, again typically white couples, to adopt newborns in a variety of hues.

Price does not always determine the route to parenthood that gay men choose, or the race, age, health, or pedigree of the children

they agree to adopt. During the period of my initial research, only one white, middle-class couple in my study had chosen to adopt healthy white infants. Some affluent white men enthusiastically adopted children of color, even when they knew that the children had been exposed to drugs prenatally. Drew Greenwald, a very successful architect who could easily have afforded assisted reproductive technology (ART), was the most dramatic example of this. He claimed, "It never would have occurred to me to do surrogacy. I think it's outrageous because there are all these children who need good homes. And people have surrogacy, they say, in part it's because they want to avoid the complications of adoption, but in candor they are really in love with their own genes. . . . I just think there is a bit of narcissism about it."

Drew had opted for independent, open, transracial adoption instead. When I first interviewed him in 2002, he had just adopted his second of two multi-racial babies born to two different women who both had acknowledged using drugs during their pregnancies. Soon after adopting his first infant, Drew reunited with James, a former lover who had fallen "wildly in love" with Drew's new baby. James moved in while Drew was in the process of adopting a second child, and they have co-parented together ever since. Indeed, parenthood is the "glue" that cemented a relationship between the couple that Drew believed might otherwise have failed. Shared parenting provided them with a "joint project, a focus, and a source of commitment."

I was indulging in my guilty pleasure of reading the Style section of the Sunday *New York Times* one morning in the fall of 2008, when I stumbled across a wedding photo and announcement that Drew and James, "the parents of five adopted children," had just married. Several weeks later, on a conference trip to Los Angeles, I visited the bustling, expanded family household. I learned that the white birth mother of their second child had since had two more unwanted pregnancies, one with the same African American man as before and one with a black Latino. She had successfully appealed to Drew and James to add both of these mixed-race siblings to their family. After the first of these two new brothers had joined their brood, Drew and James began to worry that because only one of their children was a girl, she would find it difficult to grow up in a family with two dads and only brothers. And so they turned to the Internet, where they found a mixed-race sister for their first daughter. Three of the five children suffered from learning or attention-deficit difficulties, but Drew took this in stride. He was well aware, he said, that he and James had signed on "for all sorts of trauma, challenge, heartache" in the years ahead. He was both determined and financially able to secure the best help available for his children. Nonetheless, Drew acknowledged, "I fully expect that the kids will break my heart at some point in various ways, but it's so worth it." It was sufficiently worth it, apparently, that the year after my 2008 visit, I received an email from Drew announcing that their child head count had climbed to six, because their "jackpot birth mom" had given birth yet again. "We're up to four boys and two girls," Drew elaborated. "It's a lot, as you can imagine, but wonderful."

Situational Parents

Despite the fact that I over-sampled for gay parents, the majority of men in my study fell into the intermediate range on the passion-to-parent continuum. I would classify twenty-six of my fifty primary research subjects as having been situationally with or without children. Nine men whose personal desire to parent had ranged from reluctant, unenthusiastic, or indifferent to ambivalent, hesitant, or even mildly interested became situational parents after they succumbed to the persuasive entreaties of a fervently motivated mate, or if they fell in love with a man who was already a parent. Sixteen men who had remained childless expressed a similar range of sentiments, and in one case even a portion of regret. These men would have agreed to co-parent with a predestined partner or, in some cases, with

even just a willing one. They had remained childless, however, either because they were single or because their partners were refuseniks or other situationists." None of them had a passion for parenthood that was potent enough to overcome the resistance of a reluctant mate or to confront alone the formidable challenges that prospective parents, and especially gay men, must meet.

Persuasive Partner

Glenn Miya, a Japanese American who was thirty-six years old when we first met, liked children enough to spend his workday life as a pediatrician. Nonetheless, he had not felt an independent desire to fill his home life with them as well. His long-term partner, Steven Llanusa, a Cuban-Italian elementary school teacher, however, was a predestined parent who, eight years into their relationship, had given Glenn an ultimatum to co-parent with him or part. Glenn's initial misgivings had been serious enough to rupture the couple's relationship for several months. Looking backward on this period, Glenn thought that he had been "suffering a bit of pre-parental panic," while Steven felt that he "was being forced to make a choice between his partner or being a parent," just the way Armando had felt. Although Steve had not wanted to face this choice, he had been determined that he "was not going to renege" on his commitment to parenthood. Fortunately for both men and, as it turns out, for the three Latino brothers whom they later adopted, couples counseling helped Glenn to work through his reservations and to reunite the couple.

Their co-parenting career began, Glenn said, by "parenting backwards." First they had signed up with a foster-care-parent program and taken in several teenagers, including one who was gay. Both the positive and negative aspects of their experiences as foster parents convinced them that they were ready to make a more permanent commitment to children. The couple's combined income was clearly sufficient to cover the expense of independent adoption, and perhaps even surrogacy, had they wished to pursue these options. Instead, however, they had enrolled in the county's fost-adopt program, choosing "very consciously to adopt elementary-school-age kids," because they believed that they could not afford to stay home as full-time parents and did not want to hire a nanny to take care of infants or toddlers. They chose, in other words, to undertake what most authorities consider to be the most difficult form of adoptive parenthood. Nor had they chosen to start, or to stop, with one "difficult-to-place" child. Rather, they had accepted first a set of seven-year-old Mexican American twin boys and their five-year-old brother soon afterword. The county had removed the three boys from drug-addicted parents. Both twins had acquired learning disabilities from fetal alcohol syndrome, and one had a prosthetic leg. All three boys had suffered parental neglect and been physically abused by their father, who was serving a prison sentence for extensive and repeated domestic violence.

Despite the formidable challenges of transracially adopting three school-age abused and neglected children with cognitive, physical, and emotional disabilities, or perhaps partly because of these facts, the Miya-Llanusa family had become a literal California poster family for gay fatherhood. Both parents and their three sons played active leadership roles in the Pop Luck Club; they all participated in public education and outreach within the gay community and beyond; they spoke frequently to the popular media; they hosted massive community and holiday parties; and they served as general goodwill ambassadors for gay and multi-cultural family values in the boys' schools, sports teams, and dance classes and in their Catholic parish and their white, upper-middle-class suburban neighborhood.

Although Steve had been the predestined parent, and Glenn initially had been a reluctant, situational one, Glenn was the one who told me that he wouldn't mind emulating Eddie Leary's pattern of staying home to parent full-time, if his family had been able to afford

forgoing the ample income that his pediatric practice earned.

The Miya-Llanusa clan was still going strong and still going public with their enduring love and family story when I caught up with them again in October 2008. Love certainly had come first for this family, but it had taken twenty-two years before the state of California briefly allowed marriage to follow. In August 2008, Steve and Glenn had seized the moment and held a glorious, almost-traditional, religious and legal wedding ceremony, with all three, now teenage sons as ushers, and more than one hundred of their beaming family and friends in attendance. By then, Proposition 8 was on the California ballot, and Glenn and Steve had contributed their time, resources, and a photo-album slide show portraying the history of their love, marriage, and family to that unsuccessful political campaign to keep marriage legal for other California families like theirs.

Poly-Parent Families

Independent adoption often generates complex family ties. Many pregnant women choose this option so that they can select adoptive parents whom they like for their babies and who will maintain contact with them after the adoption has been finalized. That is one of the reasons for the steady growth in the number of children Drew and James were raising. Although there are no reliable data on this, gay men seem to have an advantage over lesbian or single straight women who seek gray-market babies, because some birth mothers find it easier to relinquish their babies to men than to women, just as Marya had felt about donating her eggs. A pregnant woman who chooses gay men to adopt her offspring can hold on to her maternal status and avoid competitive, jealous feelings with infertile, adopting mothers.

It is true that most of the men in my study who adopted children through the gray market wanted their children to stay in touch with their birth mothers, and sometimes with their birth fathers as well. Drew and James even chose to operate "on a first-name basis" with their six (so far!) adopted children in order to reserve the terms *Mommy and Daddy* for their children's various genetic parents. Poly-parenting families do not always spring from such contingencies, however. Pursuing parenthood outside the box inspires some people to create intentional multi-parent families.

Front House/Back House

After thirteen years of close friendship, Paul (a white gay man) and Nancy (a white lesbian) decided to try to start a family together through alternative insemination. The two self-employed professionals spent the next two years carefully discussing their familial visions, values, expectations, anxieties, and limits. In October 1999, when Nancy began attempting to conceive their first child, they composed and signed a co-parenting agreement. They understood that the document would lack legal force but believed that going through the process of devising it would lay a crucial foundation for co-parenting. This agreement could serve as a model of ethical, sensitive planning for egalitarian, responsible co-parenting. In fact, it has already done so for several lesbian and gay friends of Paul's and Nancy's, and for two of mine. I do not know of any heterosexual couples who have approached the decision to parent together so thoughtfully. Perhaps this agreement can inspire some of them to do so too. Nancy and Paul were delighted, devoted biological and legal co-parents of a preschool-age son and an infant daughter when I interviewed them in 2001. They were not, however, the children's only parents. Before Nancy became pregnant with their first child, Cupid tested Paul's ability to live up to the sixth of the pair's prenatal pledges. Nancy had met and entered a romantic relationship with Liza, a woman who long had wanted to have children. Paul had risen to the challenge of supporting and incorporating Liza into his parenting alliance with Nancy, and so their son

and daughter were born into a three-parent family. Nancy and Paul more than honored all of the pertinent terms in their shared parenting plan. Jointly they had purchased a duplex residential property. During the period of my study, Nancy and Liza lived together in the front house, Paul inhabited the back house, their toddler was sleeping alternate nights in each, and the breastfed infant still was sharing her two mothers' bedroom every night. Paul and Nancy, the two primary parents, were fully sharing the major responsibilities and expenses along with the joys of parenthood. Both had reduced their weekly work schedules to three days so that each could devote two days weekly to full-time parenting. A hired nanny cared for the children on the fifth day. Liza, who was employed full-time, did early evening child care on the days that Nancy and Paul worked late, and she fully co-parented with them on weekends and holidays.

This three-parent family enjoyed the support of a thick community of kith and kin. One of Paul's former lovers was godfather to the children, and he visited frequently. The three-parent family celebrated holidays with extended formal and chosen kin, including another gay-parent family.

The family was still intact when I contacted Paul and Nancy again 'in October 2008. Nancy and Liza had just celebrated their tenth anniversary as a couple, and Paul was still single.

Careful Fourplay

A second successfully planned poly-parent family included two moms, two dads, and two homes. Lisa and Kat, a monogamous, white lesbian couple, had initiated this family when after fifteen years together, they had asked their dear friend and former housemate, Michael Harwood, to serve as the sperm donor and an acknowledged father to the children they wished to rear. It had taken Michael, a white gay man who was single at that time, five years of serious reflection and discussions before he finally agreed to do so. "There is really no way to express the complexity of my journey," Michael related in an account he wrote for a gay magazine, "or to impart the richness of the experience. Given the rare opportunity to truly think about whether or not I wanted to be a parent (as opposed to having it sprung upon me), I left no rock unturned—no hiking trail was untread."[4]

Gradually Michael had realized that he did not wish to become a parent unless he too had a committed mate: "I told them that I could not do it alone (without a partner). I thought about what it would be like going through parenthood without a significant partner with whom to discuss and share things. It seemed too isolating."[5] Fortuitously, just when his lesbian friends were reaching the end of their patience, Michael met and fell in love with Joaquin, a Chicano, gay predestined parent who had always wanted children. The new lovers asked Lisa and Kat to give them a year to solidify their union before embarking on co-parenthood. Both couples reported that they spent that year in a four-way parental courtship:

> Joaquin and I had many talks and all four of us were, quite frankly, falling in love with each other in a way that can only be described as romantic love. There were flowers, there were candlelight dinners, and there were many beach walks and much laughter. There were many brave conversations about our needs and our fears and our excitement. There was nothing that could prepare us for the first night when Joaquin and I went to Lisa and Kat's home to make love and leave a specimen. . . . By the way, it is not a turkey baster but a syringe that is used. Love was the main ingredient, though, and Joaquin and I experienced a transcendent epiphany as we walked along the beach after the exchange. We knew that our lives and our relationship to Lisa and Kat would never be the same even if the conception did not happen. We shared, perhaps, the most intimate of experiences with Lisa and Kat.[6]

Since that magical night, the two couples also had shared many of the intimate joys and burdens of parenting two children. Unlike

Nancy and Paul, however, they did not try to equalize parental rights and responsibilities. Lisa and Michael are the children's biological and legal parents, with both of their names on both of the birth certificates. The children resided, however, with Lisa and Kat, who are their primary, daily caretakers and their chief providers. Lisa, who gave birth to and breast-fed both children, also spent the most time with them, primarily because Kat's employment demanded more time outside the home. Although Michael and Joaquin lived and worked more than seventy-five miles away, they had visited their children every single weekend of the children's lives as well as on occasional weeknights. They also conferred with the co-moms and spoke, sang, read, or sent emails to their preschooler almost daily. In addition, the adults consciously sustained, monitored, and nurtured their co-parenting alliance and friendship by scheduling periodic "parent time" for the four adults to spend together while the children slept.

This four-parent family, like the three-parent front-house/back-house family and like the surrogacy-extended family that Eddie and Mama Sally nurtured, regularly shared holidays and social occasions with a wide array of legal and chosen kin. They too were immersed in a large local community of lesbian- and gay-parent families, a community which Lisa had taken the initiative to organize. Three proud sets of doting grandparents were constantly vying for visits, photos, and contact with their grandchildren. In painful contrast, Kat's parents had rejected her when she came out, and they refused to incorporate, or even to recognize, their grandchildren or any of their lesbian daughter's family members within their more rigid, ideological understanding of family.

The Contingency of Contemporary Parenthood

This colorful quilt of lucky, and less lucky, gay pop stories from my research opens a window onto the vagaries of contemporary paths to parenthood generally and to paternity specifically. Because I intentionally over-sampled for fathers when I was recruiting participants for my study, I wound up including a disproportionate number of predestined parents. Their stories help us to understand some complex connections between romantic partnership and parenthood today. Most, if not all, of the fervently motivated dads strongly wished to combine the two forms of intimacy. Some even had made parenthood a pivotal courtship criterion, and the luckiest of these, like Eddie and Charles, found compatible predestined partners. However, if push comes to shove for a predestined parent, children will trump coupledom and can even thwart it, as we have seen. Although Armando deeply desired and attempted to combine partnership with parenthood, he was ultimately unwilling to sacrifice the latter on the pyre of adult intimacy. On the other hand, parenthood can prove a pathway to coupling for a fortunate few who, like Drew and Bernardo, find that their parental status enhances their appeal to other predestined parents.

There are numerous reasons to believe that fewer straight men than gay men feel a predestined urge to parent. For one thing, by definition, if not by disposition, gay men are already gender dissidents. Living without wives or girlfriends, they have to participate in caretaking and domestic chores more than straight men do and are less likely to find these activities threatening to their masculine identities. Second, gay men are more likely to be single than are straight men or than are women of whatever sexual orientation (Bell and Weinberg 1978). That translates into a higher percentage of men like Armando, who are apt to feel drawn to seek compensatory intimacy through parenthood. On the carrot side of the ledger, gay dads enjoy easier access than most straight dads do to primary parenting status and its rewards and to support networks for their families.

Gay men also face less pressure to conform to gender scripts for parenting or to defer to women's biological and cultural advantages for nurturing young children. Gay fatherhood, that is to say, occupies terrain more akin to conventional motherhood than to dominant forms of paternity.

The unmooring of masculinity from paternity exposes the situational character of contemporary fatherhood and fatherlessness. No longer a mandatory route to masculine adult social status, paternity today is increasingly contingent on the fate of men's romantic attachments. In fact, to attain any form of parenthood today requires either the unequivocal yearning of at least one adult or a more or less accidental pregnancy, like egg donor Marya's. In other words, contemporary maternity has also become increasingly situational, a fact that is reflected in declining fertility rates.

Nonetheless, the majority of women still skew toward the predestined pole of the desire-to-parent continuum. Men, in contrast, regardless of their sexual inclinations, generally cluster along the situational bandwidth. Heterosexual "situations" lead most straight men into paternity (and straight women to maternity). Homosexual situations, on the other hand, lead most gay men to forgo parenthood (Lesbian situations likely are somewhere in between) (Simmons and O'Connell 2003). If this contrast seems obvious, even tautological, it was not always the case. Instead, most contemporary gay fathers became parents while they were enmeshed in closeted homosexual "situations." The past few decades of hard-won gains in gay struggles for social acceptance have diminished the need for men with homo-erotic desires to resort to this ruse.

Paradoxically, the same shift from closeted to open homosexuality which has made gay fatherhood so visible might also reduce its incidence. Beyond the closet, far fewer gay men than before will become situational parents because they entered heterosexual marriages to pass as straight. Openly gay paternity, by definition, is never accidental. It requires the determined efforts of at least one gay man, like Armando, Eddie, whose passion for parenthood feels predestined—a man, that is, whose parental desires more conventionally might be labeled maternal rather than paternal.

The gay dads I studied did not feel that parenting made them less, or more, of a man. Instead, most felt free to express a full palette of gender options. As Drew put it, "I feel that I have a wider emotional range available to me than maybe most of the straight men I know. And I feel comfortable being mother, father, silly gay man, silly queen, tough negotiator in business. I feel like I'm not bound by rules." Rather than a bid for legitimate masculine status, or a rejection of it, intentional gay parenthood represents a search for enduring love and intimacy in a world of contingency and flux.

Of course, there is nothing distinctively gay or masculine about this quest. Heterosexual masculinity also no longer depends upon marriage or parenthood. Indirectly, therefore, gay male paths to planned parenthood highlight the waning of traditional incentives for pursuing the status of fatherhood as we knew it. Parenthood, like marriage and mating practices, has entered contingent terrain.

The fact that gay men now pursue parenthood outside social conventions of gender, marriage, and procreation catapults them into the vanguard of contemporary parenting. Just as gay men are at once freer and more obliged than most of the rest of us to craft the basic terms of their romantic and domestic unions, so too they have to make more self-conscious decisions about whether to parent, with whom, and how. I hope that the thoughtful, magnanimous, child-centered co-parenting agreement that Paul and Nancy devised will inspire throngs of prospective parents to undertake similar discussions before deciding whether baby should make three, or four or more, for that matter.

Notes

1. Twenty-four men were actively parenting children. In addition, two men were step-fathers to a partner's non-residential children; one man with his mother formerly co-foster-parented teenagers; four of the adoptive fathers had also formerly fostered teenagers, and two of these intended to resume this practice in the future; one man served as a known sperm donor for lesbian-couple friends; and one man was a genetic father who does not parent his offspring.

2. One man, a sperm dad who nicknamed himself a "spad," had facilitated a lesbian friend's desire to conceive a child with a donor willing to be an avuncular presence in her child's life. The other unwittingly impregnated a former girlfriend who chose to keep the child and agreed not to reveal its paternity.

3. Of the gay parents, five are Latino, three are black or Caribbean, and one is Asian American. Thirteen of the thirty-four children are white; nine are Latino; eight are black, Caribbean, or mixed race; and four are multi-racial Asian.

4. "Love Makes a Family," unpublished speech to a gay community group, on file with author. Additional information about this speech is withheld to protect the anonymity of my informant.

5. Ibid.

6. Ibid.

REFERENCES

Beck, Ulrich, and Elizabeth Beck-Gernsheim. 1995. *The Normal Chaos of Love.* Cambridge, UK: Polity.

Bell, Alan P., and Martin S. Weinberg. 1978. *Homosexualities: A Study of Diversity among Men and Women.* New York: Simon and Schuster.

Brodzinsky, David, Charlotte J. Patterson, and Mahnoush Vaziri. 2002. "Adoption Agency Perspectives on Lesbian and Gay Prospective Parents: A National Study." *Adoption Quarterly* 5(3): 5-23.

Gates, Gary. Distinguished Scholar at the Williams Institute, UCLA Law School, personal communication, May 17, 2005.

Human Rights Campaign. 2009. "Equality from State to State 2009." http://www.hrc.org/documents/HRC_States_Report_09.pdf.

Kapp, Stephen, Thomas P. McDonald, and Kandi L. Diamond. 2001. "The Path to Adoption for Children of Color." *Child Abuse and Neglect* 25(2): 215-229.

Lasch, Christopher. 1995. *Haven in a Heartless World: The Family Besieged.* New York: Norton.

Sears, R. Bradley, and M.V. Lee Badgett. 2004. "Same-Sex Couples and Same-Sex Couples

Raising Children in California: Data from Census 2000." Williams Project on Sexual Orientation and the Law, UCLA Law School.

Simmons, Tavia, and Martin O'Connell. 2003. "Married-Couple and Unmarried-Partner Households: 2000. U.S. Census Bureau, February.

Stacey, Judith. 1998. "Dada-ism in the Nineties: Getting Past Baby Talk about Fatherlessness." In *Lost Fathers: The Politics of Fatherlessness*, ed. Cynthia Daniels. New York: St. Matin's.

Strah, David, and Susanna Margolis. 2003. *Gay Dads*. New York: J.T. Tacher/Putnam.

Townsend, Nicholas. 2002. *The Package Deal: Marriage, Work, and Fatherhood in Men's Lives*. Philadelphia: Temple University Press.

U.S. Department of Health and Human Services, Administration for Children and Families, Administration on Children, Youth, and Families, Children's Bureau. 2003. *The AFCARS Report*. http://www.acf.hhs.gov/programs/cb/publications/afcars/report8.pdf.

THINKING ABOUT THE READING

According to Stacey, how do gay men who choose to parent challenge conventional definitions of masculinity and paternity? How have these men made the "social character of paternity" more visible? How do the stories of Stacey's interviewees compare with images of gay male families you have observed in the media? Stacey's interviewees all lived in Los Angeles, a city that she notes is one of the most favorable cities for the architectures of gay and lesbian parenthood. Due to different legal and social restrictions on gay parenthood and families in other areas of the United States, how might the experiences of gay men who wish to parent and form families be different in these places?

Covenant Marriage: Reflexivity and Retrenchment in the Politics of Intimacy

Dwight Fee

(2011)

In recent years, sociologists have pointed to many transformations in personal life. We have heard quite a bit about the "Questioning of tradition," the "redefinition of gender," the "reworking of relationships," or the "transformation of intimacy" and so on. Some sociologists have understood changes in private life in terms of an increase in "reflexivity" (see Giddens 1991, 1992; Beck and Beck-Gernsheim 1995; Swidler 2001; Weeks 1995; Weeks, Heaphy and Donovan 2001). Generally speaking, reflexivity means that, in a time of change and heightened social diversity, people no longer are able unconsciously to rely on traditions and customs to determine how they live. Applied to intimacy and sexuality, people are thrown back upon themselves to define their relationships and their identities within them. Crudely put, we must make decision for ourselves once ingrained institutions and traditions are questioned, or once it becomes harder to say, "That's just the way the world is."

Therefore, once traditions are questioned, conventional intimate arrangements assume the status of mere *choices* that exist among many other competing ones. Not everyone has the same choices or can act on them as easily as others, but nevertheless, most of the time choice rules. Of course, tradition "hangs around" among all the options—but that hardly sounds like a tradition.

The Travails of Reflexivity

Being thrown back upon oneself when figuring out relationships and sexuality is surely challenging. For example, it would stand to reason that "commitment" itself would have to be debated and defined within each relationship, rather than simply assumed across all of them. And because we can't assume much cultural uniformity about such things, how do we establish trust in our relationships? Perhaps more than anything else, *risk* comes to paint the entire landscape of intimate life.

Despite all of the problems and ambiguities, however, most of those researching the growing uncertainty surrounding intimacy are encouraged. After all, people have to talk more, figure things out together, "be open." Consider Beck and Beck Gernsheim's (1995: 5) view of the situation:

> [I]t is no longer possible to pronounce in some binding way what family, marriage, parenthood, sexuality, or love mean, or what they should or could be; rather, these vary in substance, exceptions, norms and morality from individual to individual and from relationship to relationship. The answers to the questions above must be worked out, negotiated, arranged and justified in all the details of how, what, why or why not, even if this might unleash the conflicts and devils that lie slumbering among the details and were assumed to be tamed. Increasingly, the individuals who want to live together are, or more precisely becoming, the legislators of their own way of life, the judges of their own transgressions, the priests who absolve their own sins, and the therapists who loosen the bonds of their own past . . . Love is becoming a blank that the lovers must fill in themselves, across the widening trenches of biography . . .

If these authors are right, even when we pick up the pieces of the old system we are patterning new relational forms, if only subtly. It may be that in many cases this reflexive work is opening up new avenues for autonomy in relationships, making our lives more "our own" and authentic, and, perhaps most crucially, making equality in relationships more possible.

Giddens (1992) calls this mode of relationality the "pure relationship." By calling it "pure" Giddens is suggesting that the viability of this type of relationship depends only on the people involved. The participants are the ones in charge; in this way it is "internally self-referential" through mutual disclosure. Reflexivity "disarms" those forming and moving through relationships. All that there is that other person and you—"free floating" as Giddens (1992) puts it. For some, it sounds a lot less romantic; for others, it is the beginning of possibility. For still others, as we will soon see, it reflects a moral decline, as relationships are seen as increasingly whimsical and self-serving.

Covenant Marriage: "Super-Sizing" Matrimony?

On Valentine's Day 2005, Governor Mike Huckabee (Republican-Arkansas) and his wife entered into a covenant marriage in front of about 6,400 onlookers. Already married for thirty years, the Huckabees took a new kind of plunge, one that was established to "inspire confidence" in marriage, and one usually discussed by proponents as important counter-strategies to the high divorce rate and to the "changing social values" that "threaten marriage." According to an Associated Press article in the *New York Times* (February 15 2005), the governor announced to the crowd: "There is a crisis in America. The crisis is divorce. It is easier to get out of a marriage than [to get out of a] contract to buy a used car." After the Huckabees renewed their vows, the governor instructed the couples in the audience to do the same - to face each other and to repeat the vows of the Governor and First Lady. Many

couples followed suit, crying, and then kissing after their spontaneous recitations.

Originally emerging from conservative Protestant churches in the late 1980s and early 1990s, the covenant marriage movement began as a response to a declared "divorce culture" and a "crisis of the family" in the U.S. Religious leaders and organizations quickly targeted legislative change so as to make the marriage bond a weightier, more durable (and, if only indirectly, religiously-based) commitment. The Covenant Marriage Law was first established in Louisiana in 1997, and similar laws were passed soon after in Arkansas and Arizona. While mainly in Southern states, there is now some kind of covenant marriage legislation afoot in some twenty states, including Minnesota, Iowa, Indiana, and Maryland, which is part of other widespread "divorce reform" legislative activity.

While there has been an increasing amount of public and media-based attention paid to covenant marriage since the Huckabee ceremony, it has so far fallen short of some proponents' early predictions that covenant marriage would "boom" and "could soon sweep the nation." Studies are scant, but the consensus seems to be that numbers are down, and were never really up. Of about 35,000 marriages in Arkansas in 2004, only 164 were of the covenant variety -mostly being conversions of existing marriages. According to Gilgoff (2005), rates are similar in Arizona and Louisiana—with no more than 2 percent of marriages being covenant. Still, it's worth considering what's going on here, now that covenant marriage has at least some salience within the broadening array of marriage debates. (Many proponents attribute the low numbers of covenant marriages to people simply not knowing about the option.)

Covenant marriage, of course, is more than a declaration of traditional marriage; it has very specific, legal dimensions. Advocates for covenant marriage want to offer an alternative to what they see as a blasé, or self-serving, or "test-drive" approach to marriage, since "no fault" divorce was ushered in during the 1970s. In the three states that have actually passed and instituted covenant marriage laws—Louisiana, Arkansas, and Arizona—couples are given a choice between standard marriage and the "CM" option. It's as easy as checking the appropriate box—for the court clerk - but, according to Nock, Wright, and Sanchez (1999), here are the differences for the CM couple:

- the couple will seek premarital counseling—which must include discussions of the seriousness of marriage—and have a signed affidavit (signed by the counselor and the couple) to prove their participation;
- likewise, divorce is only possible if the couple goes to counseling, and after a two year waiting or cooling-off period.
- dissolving a covenant marriage in less than two years requires that one person prove fault on the part of the other. Acceptable faults are felony convictions, abuse, abandonment or adultery. Irreconcilable differences ("we just don't get along") are not acceptable grounds for divorce before two years (2.5 years if you have kids);
- and, couples can "upgrade" to a CM, like Governor Huckabee and his wife.

At the root of CM is the hope of revitalizing a belief in marriage and its sanctity through critiquing the supposed "contract mentality" of recent years. As Gary Chapman argues in *Covenant Marriage: Building Communication and Intimacy* (2003), the legalistic side of marriage is surely important, but the contract mentality has replaced "as long as we both shall live" with "we are committed to each other so long as this relationship is mutually beneficial for us." By contrast, covenant marriage offers deep spirituality and (ideally) a life-long commitment to the other's well being that is "above one's self." As one Louisiana woman put it, "we know that if we have problems, we can't just say I'm leaving" (Loconte 1998).

Covenant Marriage: Political Statement or Personal Choice?

There are many debates around covenant marriage, and some center on the specific problems that exist, or potentially exist, inside of them. Obviously, the fact that it becomes harder to get out of this form of marriage is a major concern in cases of marital violence and abuse. The CM laws state that divorce can be granted in such situations, but many are skeptical that these instances will be "verified" by those charged with that responsibility, which we would presume are mostly pastors and other church-based counselors. (Remember that abuse must be "proved.") Whether women get trapped in CMs remains unclear. Given the recent instigation of covenant marriage, I have not seen any systematic research to argue the situation either way. Predictably, the little research that has been done on CM has unambiguously shown that the large majority of supporters hold highly traditional attitudes about gender and the roles of men and women within marriage (Nock, Wright, and Sanchez 1999), which could itself worry some critics when it comes to issues of abuse.

However, advocates are quick to argue that most marriages fall apart because of "low-level" conflict, where the couple drift apart, often without confronting their problems openly. In this sense, covenant marriage proponents say, "we're not erecting a barricade . . . we're just putting in some speed bumps" (Loconte 1998). They might also point out that the requirement to seek counseling before marriage—and subsequently, if problems arise—is not something men are often willing to do. As a progressive reform, CM could help men transcend "traditional" codes of masculinity by prompting them to develop effective communication and coping skills.

But then there is the larger issue of its cultural and political significance. On the one hand, proponents are right about the challenges of marriage; however, the supposed moral vacuum or "collapse" that they see behind it—as if statistics reflect ethical stances—has an obvious reactionary subtext. While covenant marriages are hardly widespread, it may not be going too far to say that we are witnessing the latest attempt to redefine marriage along religious and otherwise conservative lines.

According to the website ReligiousToler-ance.org, some states are considering abolishing conventional marriage and offering only the covenant version—and obviously this is just when debates about gay marriage are particularly salient. For many, it makes sense that covenant marriage would emerge in the wake of gay marriage initiatives and the passage of the Defense of Marriage Act. Even though we have to make a focused effort to find much in the rhetoric about gay marriage, it is easy to assume that the CM movement is only a knee-jerk political expression. Proponents, though, might say it is simply a way to exemplify God's vision of marriage: "one man, one woman, forever—above their own shifting desires." As far as I have been able to determine, the part about "one man, one woman" is written into the actual legislation that is on the books in Louisiana, Arkansas and Arizona. This wording, we must assume, reaches out beyond covenant marriage itself. From this perspective, then, it is no accident that the Huckabee ceremony and all of the subsequent journalistic coverage comes at a time when gay marriage has arguably become the most salient social issue thus far in twenty-first-century America. Gay groups, in fact, were in attendance at the Huckabee event, fundraising and raising awareness about how marriage—any kind of marriage—is not available to same-sex couples.

In this sense, covenant marriage is at least an *implicit* socio-political statement about a "return" to most traditional forms of heterosexual relations. Put another way, *personal understandings and choices about marriage are intersecting with (or becoming articulated within) discourses of social and political reform.* This is tricky because we are not always dealing with, on the one hand, people's solely "personal" concerns about their relationship choices, or on the other hand, an explicit and intentional political backlash. Covenant marriage, in the broadest sense, is a place where a multitude of personal and political strategies are at work—so much so that the two realms are often indistinguishable. Of course, this predicament is nothing new; it is what many theorists and researchers have discussed in terms of the displacement of the private onto the public

within the "politics of intimacy," or in debates about "sexual citizenship" and so on. Virtually all intimate choices now intertwine with various "culture wars" about sexuality, morality, and, if only indirectly, marriage itself. Even if covenant marriage only bears a kin-relationship to other more obvious political appropriations of marriage by conservatives, *covenant marriage is implicitly political, whether or not its supporters see themselves in such a light.*

Reflexivity and Retrenchment

Whatever the politics of CM supporters, there is something highly *performative* about covenant marriage from a sociological perspective: the willingness to step apart from the crowd, to make one's choice visible and different, to say (and to do so in an almost public way) "this particular alternative is the best way to go." In a strict sociological sense, this development is "anti-traditional," as it makes reflexivity and innovation central to decision-making about marriage. The centrality of therapy in covenant marriage makes it even more so—couples must deliberate, disclose their fears, and ostensibly work together. We might say it is "*doing* intimacy" in a world where virtually no one can simply blend into the background and not give voice to their choices (Seidman 2002). Covenant marriage is presumably about creating options, new possibilities, and, we would assume, the creation of more satisfying relationships. The equality piece is more ambiguous, but the innovation is there, whether or not one approves of the particular vision. As one advocate put it, "[covenant marriage] has everything to do with giving people more choices" (Nock, Wright, and Sanchez 1999). The difference here, however, is that reflexive processes are paradoxically moving, or hoping to move, in the direction of "tradition," or at least the way that tradition is being defined by the covenant marriage instigators.

This irony of providing more and more choices is not lost on some conservatives. We need only take note of the reactionary discourse about gay marriage to get the gist of the "slippery slope" argument: "so after gay marriage, what's next, marrying your cat?" If covenant marriage proponents take this view, we could easily grant covenant marriage the official status of *moral panic*. But it goes further: this slippery slope viewpoint is one reason why traditionalists themselves are part of the heretofore modest cultural impact of covenant marriage. When given the option of tinkering or not tinkering with marriage, many invested in orthodoxy and traditionalism will invariably side on the latter approach of sticking with the status quo. If something is so sacred and natural, there is something irreverent and contradictory about breaking it into differing levels and subcategories. It is here that the ironies of tradition/de-tradition come full circle: can reflexivity in intimate life be effectively used to reaffirm heteronormativity, which has historically thrived on the very *absence* of it? Can choice be used to fend off other choices seen as threatening or dangerous? In sum, how can the covenant marriage movement advocate a reflexive program when it comes very close to saying that reflexivity itself is the problem with marriage today?

REFERENCES

Associated Press (2005) "Thousands Renew Vows in Arkansas," New York Times, February 15.

Beck, U. and E. Beck-Gernsheim (1995) *The normal chaos of love*. Cambridge: Polity.

Chapman, G. (2003) *Covenant marriage: building communication and intimacy*. Nashville, TN: Broadman and Holman.

Giddens, A. (1991) *Modernity and self-identity: self and society in the late-modern world*. Stanford, CA: Stanford University Press.

———. (1992) *The transformation of intimacy: sexuality, love and eroticism in modern societies*. Stanford, CA: Stanford University Press.

Gilgoff, D. (2005) "Tying a right knot," *US News and World Report*, February 28.

Loconte, J. (1998) "I'll Stand Bayou: Louisiana couples choose a more muscular marriage contract," *Policy Review* 89 (5).

Nardi, P. (1999) *Gay men's friendships: invincible communities*. Chicago, IL and London: University of Chicago Press.

Nock, S., J. Wright, and L. Sanchez (1999) "America's Divorce Problem," *Society* (May-June) (36); 4.

Plummer, K. (2003) *Intimate citizenship: private decisions and public dialogues*. Seattle, WA and London: University of Washington Press.

Seidman, S. (2002) *Beyond the closet*. London and New York: Routledge.

Swidler, A. (2001) *Talk of love*. Chicago, IL: University of Chicago Press.

Weeks, J. (1995) *Invented moralities: sexual values in the age of uncertainty*. New York: Columbia University Press.

Weeks, J., B. Heaphy, and C. Donovan (2001) *Same-sex intimacies*. London and New York: Routledge.

THINKING ABOUT THE READING

Drawing on Fee's definition of reflexivity that refers to how we consciously think about something that we might otherwise take for granted, how, if at all, have you employed reflexivity in your relationships and identities within them (e.g. romantic relationships, friends, family members)? Do you rely on long-standing traditions and customs, or do you make other choices that challenge these traditions and customs? Fee suggests that it is important to note that not everyone has the opportunity to be as reflexive as the next person. In what situations might an individual feel restricted from making choices that challenge tradition and custom? Give some examples. Finally, taking the central example of covenant marriage, do you agree or disagree with Fee that the covenant marriage movement is advocating a reflexive program while simultaneously suggesting that reflexivity is the problem with marriage today? What if any concerns would you have with the equality issue in covenant marriages? Considering the steady and ongoing change in marriage and family forms in recent decades, is the covenant marriage movement a viable option for couples in contemporary society?

Constructing Difference

Social Deviance

8

According to most sociologists, deviance is not an inherent feature or personality trait. Instead, it is a consequence of a definitional process. Like beauty, it is in the eye of the beholder. Deviant labels can impede everyday social life by forming expectations in the minds of others. Some sociologists argue that the definition of *deviance* is a form of social control exerted by more powerful people and groups over less powerful ones.

At the structural level, the treatment of people defined as deviant is often more a function of *who* they are than of *what* they did. In particular, sex, age, class, ethnic, and racial stereotypes often combine to influence social reactions to individuals who have broken the law. In "Watching the Canary," Lani Guinier and Gerald Torres provide several explanations for the disproportionate number of black and brown young men in U.S. prisons. They examine the intersection of racial profiling tactics, the war on drugs, and our mass incarceration policies to illustrate why these men are at greater risk for arrest. On the basis of race, these men are already defined as deviant and often expected to be engaged in criminal activity.

The definitional process that results in the labeling of some people as deviant can occur at the institutional as well as the individual level. Powerful institutions are capable of creating a definition of deviance that the public comes to accept as truth. One such institution is the field of medicine. We usually think of medicine as a benevolent institution whose primary purpose is to help sick people get better. But in "Healing (Disorderly) Desire: Medical-Therapeutic Regulation of Sexuality," P. J. McGann shows how the medical institution shapes dominant images and expectations of gender and sexuality. She points to the way in which contemporary sexual difficulties have been defined as violations of culturally approved sexual rules. The medical-therapeutic profession made up of physicians, psychiatrists, psychologists, counselors, and other specialists serves as an agent of social control by enforcing these definitions at the cultural and individual levels.

Our perceptions of deviant social problems can also be influenced by the identities of people most closely associated with the behavior in question. The use of marijuana is frequently associated with the stereotype of the "pothead." Who uses marijuana for medical purposes, and how do these individuals negotiate the deviant identity and politics associated with its use? It may surprise readers to learn that this group consists of children and older people as well as individuals who might normally be seen as possible "pot" users. In "Patients, 'Potheads,' and Dying to Get High," Wendy Chapkis describes the various strategies that providers and users of medical marijuana engage in to offset the impression of the deviant "pothead."

Something to Consider as You Read

In reading and comparing these selections, consider who has the power to define others as deviant. Think about the role of social institutions in establishing definitions of deviance. For example, how does medicine or religion or law participate in describing certain behaviors as abnormal and/or immoral and/or illegal? Does it make a difference which social institution defines certain behaviors as deviant? Why do you think certain deviant behaviors fall under the domain of medicine and others fall under the domain of the law? And do these classifications change with time? For instance, during Prohibition, alcohol consumption was illegal; subsequent to its reinstatement as a legal substance, overconsumption among certain social classes symbolized depravity, and now alcohol abuse is often treated as a medical condition. Who makes the decisions to define certain behaviors not only as deviant, but as deviant within a particular social domain?

Watching the Canary

Lani Guinier and Gerald Torres

(2002)

"To my friends, I look like a black boy. To white people who don't know me I look like a wanna-be punk. To the cops I look like a criminal." Niko, now fourteen years old, is reflecting on the larger implications of his daily journey, trudging alone down Pearl Street, backpack heavy with books, on his way home from school. As his upper lip darkens with the first signs of a moustache, he is still a sweet, sometimes kind, unfailingly polite upper-middle-class black boy. To his mom and dad he looks innocent, even boyish. Yet his race, his gender, and his baggy pants shout out a different, more alarming message to those who do not know him. At thirteen, Niko was aware that many white people crossed the street as he approached. Now at fourteen, he is more worried about how he looks to the police. After all, he is walking while black.

One week after Niko made these comments to his mom, the subject of racial profiling was raised by a group of Cambridge eighth graders who were invited to speak in a seminar at Harvard Law School. Accompanied by their parents, teachers, and the school principal, the students read essays they had written in reaction to a statement of a black Harvard Law School student whose own arrest the year before in New York City had prompted him to write about racial profiling.[1] One student drew upon theories of John Locke to argue that "the same mindset as slavery provokes police officers to control black people today." Another explained a picture he had drawn showing a black police officer hassling a black woman because the officer assumed she was a prostitute. Black cops harass black people too, he said aloud. "It just seems like all the police are angry and have a

lot of aggression coming out." A third boy concluded that when the cops see a black person they see "the image of a thug." Proud that he knew the *American Heritage Dictionary*'s definition of a thug—a "cut-throat or ruffian"— he concluded that the cops are not the key to understanding racial profiling. Nor did he blame the white people who routinely crossed the street as he approached. If what these white people see is a thug, "they would normally want to pull their purse away." He blamed the media for this "psychological enslavement," as well as those blacks who allowed themselves to be used to "taint our image."

One boy spoke for fifteen minutes in a detached voice, showing little emotion; but he often strayed from his prepared text to describe in great detail the story of relatives who had been stopped by the police or to editorialize about what he had written. Only after all the students left did the professor discover why the boy had talked so long—and why so many adults had shown up for this impromptu class.

Several of the boys, including the one who had spoken at length, had already had personal encounters with the police. Just the week before, two of the boys had been arrested and had spent six hours locked in separate cells . . . .

Watching the Canary

Rashid and Jonathan (not their real names) are the sons of a lawyer and a transit employee, respectively. "Why don't you arrest *them*?" one of the boys asked the officer, referring to the white kids walking in the same area. "We only have two sets of cuffs," the officer replied.

These cops knew whom to take in: the white kids were innocent; the black boys were guilty.

In the words of one of their classmates, black boys like Rashid and Jonathan are viewed as thugs, despite their class status. Aided by the dictionary and the media, our eighth-grade informant says this is racial profiling. Racial profiling, he believes, is a form of "psychological enslavement." . . .

But these black boys are not merely victims of racial profiling. They are canaries. And our political-race project asks people to pay attention to the canary. The canary is a source of information for all who care about the atmosphere in the mines—and a source of motivation for changing the mines to make them safer. The canary serves both a diagnostic and an innovative function. It offers us more than a critique of the way social goods are distributed. What the canary lets us see are the hierarchical arrangements of power and privilege that have naturalized this unequal distribution.

. . . We have urged those committed to progressive social change to watch the canary—and to assure the most vulnerable among us a space to experiment with democratic practice and discover their own power. Even though the canary is in a cage, it continues to have agency and voice. If the miners were watching the canary, they would not wait for it to fall off its perch, legs up. They would notice that it is talking to them. "I can't breathe, but you know what? You are being poisoned too. If you save me, you will save yourself. Why is that mine owner sending all of us down here to be poisoned anyway?" The miners might then realize that they cannot escape this life-threatening social arrangement without a strategy that disrupts the way things are.

What would we learn if we watched these particular two black boys? First, we would discover that from the moment they were born, each had a 30 percent chance of spending some portion of his life in prison or jail or under the supervision of the criminal justice system . . . . Among black men between the ages of 18 and 30 who drop out of high school, more become incarcerated than either go on to attend college or hold a job[2] . . .

In the United States, if young men are not tracked to college and they are black or brown, we wait for their boredom, desperation, or sense of uselessness to catch up with them. We wait, in other words, for them to give us an excuse to send them to prison. The criminal justice system has thus become our major instrument of urban social policy.

David Garland explains that imprisonment has ceased to be the incarceration of individual offenders and has instead become "the systematic imprisonment of whole groups of the population"—in this case, young black and Latino males in large urban municipalities. Or as the political scientist Mary Katzenstein observes, "Policies of incarceration in this country are fundamentally about poverty, about race, about addiction, about mental illness, about norms of masculinity and female accommodation among men and women who have been economically, socially, and politically demeaned and denied."[3] . . .

But how does this "race to incarcerate" happen disproportionately to young black and Latino boys? Why is it that increasingly the nation's prisons and jails have become temporary or permanent cages for our canaries? One reason is that white working-class youth enjoy greater opportunities in the labor market than do black and Latino boys, owing in part to lingering prejudice . . . .

A second reason for the disproportionate impact of incarceration on the black and brown communities is the increased discretion given to prosecutors and police officers and the decreased discretion given to judges, whose decisions are exposed to public scrutiny in open court, unlike the deals made by prosecutors and police. Media sensationalism and political manipulation around several high profile cases (notably Willie Horton and Polly Klaas) led to mandatory minimum sentences in many states. Meanwhile, laws such as "three strikes and you're out" channeled unreviewable discretion to prosecutors, who decide which strikes to call and which to ignore . . . .

A third and, according to some commentators, the most important explanation for the disproportionate incarceration of black and Latino young men is the war on drugs. In this federal campaign—one of the most volatile issues in contemporary politics—drug users and dealers are routinely painted as black or Latino, deviant and criminal. This war metaphorically names drugs as the enemy, but it is carried out in practice as a massive incarceration policy focused on black, Latino, and poor white young men. It has also swept increasing numbers of black and Latina women into prison . . . .

Presidents Ronald Reagan and George Bush had a distinct agenda, according to Marc Mauer: to "reduce the powers of the federal government," to "scale back the rights of those accused of crime," and to "diminish privacy rights."[4] Their goal was to shrink one branch of government (support for education and job training), while enlarging another (administration of criminal justice). Mauer concludes that the political and fiscal agendas of both the Reagan and first Bush administrations were quite successful. They reduced the social safety net and government's role in helping the least well off. Their success stemmed, in part, from their willingness to "polarize the debate" on a variety of issues, including drugs and prison.

Racial targeting by police (racial profiling) works in conjunction with the drug war to criminalize black and Latino men. Looking for drug couriers, state highway patrols use a profile, developed ostensibly at the behest of federal drug officials, that suggests black and Latinos are more likely to be carrying drugs. The disproportionate stops of cars driven by blacks or Latinos as well as the street sweeps of pedestrians certainly helps account for some of the racial disparity in sentencing and conviction rates. And because much of the drug activity in the black and Latino communities takes place in public, it is easier to target . . . .

A fourth explanation for the high rates of incarceration of black and brown young men is the economic boon that prison-building has brought to depressed rural areas. Prison construction has become—next to the military— our society's major public works program. And as prison construction has increased, money

spent on higher education has declined, in direct proportion. Moreover, federal funds that used to go to economic or job training programs now go exclusively to building prisons . . . .

A fifth explanation is the need for a public enemy after the Cold War. Illegal drugs conveniently fit that role. President Nixon started this effort, calling drugs "public enemy number one." George Bush continued to escalate the rhetoric, declaring that drugs are "the greatest domestic threat facing our nation" and are turning our cities "into battlegrounds." By contrast, the use and abuse of alcohol and prescription drugs, which are legal, rarely result in incarceration . . . .

When drunk drivers do serve jail time, they are typically treated with a one- or two-day sentence for a first offense. For a second offense they may face a mandatory sentence of two to ten days. Compare that with a person arrested and convicted for *possession* of illegal drugs. Typical state penalties for a first-time offender are up to five years in prison and one to ten years for a second offense . . . .

We do not, by any means, claim to have exhaustively researched the criminal justice implications of racial profiling, the war on drugs, or our nation's mass incarceration policies. What we do claim is that canary watchers should pay attention to these issues if they want to understand what is happening in the United States. The cost of these policies is being subsidized by all taxpayers; one immediate result is that government support for other social programs has become an increasingly scarce resource.

Notes

1. Bryonn Bain, "Walking While Black," *The Village Voice*, April 26, 2000, at 1, 42. Bain and his brother and cousin were arrested, held overnight and then released, with all charges eventually dropped, after the police in New York City, looking for young men who were throwing bottles on the Upper West Side, happened upon Bain et al. as they exited a Bodega. Bain, at the time, had his laptop and law books in his backpack, because he was enroute to the bus station where he intended to

catch a bus back to Cambridge. Bain's essay in *The Voice* generated 90,000 responses.

2. Bruce Western and Becky Pettit, "Incarceration and Racial Inequality in Men's Employment," 54 *Industrial and Labor Relations Review* 3 (2000).

3. "Remarks on Women and Leadership: Innovations for Social Change," sponsored by Radcliffe Association, Cambridge, Massachusetts, June 8, 2001. In her talk, Katzenstein cites David Garland. "Introduction: The Meaning of Mass Imprisonment," 3(1) *Punishment and Society* 5–9 (2001).

4. Marc Mauer. (1999) *Race to Incarcerate*, New York: New Press.

THINKING ABOUT THE READING

Make a list of the social factors that Guinier and Torres link to the high incarceration rate of African American and Latino men. Discuss why these factors may affect these men more than white men. Do you think economic opportunity is related to these factors? In other words, are all African American and Latino men equally at risk for incarceration? What other factors do you think might be part of this equation? Groups who oppose the death penalty often argue that it is applied unevenly and discriminates among certain groups of people. Discuss this argument in light of what you have just read. As you think about this, consider each of the phases of the judicial process: processes of arrest, the decision to charge with a crime, availability of legal defense, jury selection, and sentencing guidelines. Who or what is making the decisions in each of these instances? Do you think the different people and agencies involved in each step of the process are all in agreement, or might there be disagreement between, say, the police, judges, and lawmakers? How might these relationships affect the likelihood of a defendant being treated "justly"?

Healing (Disorderly) Desire: Medical-Therapeutic Regulation of Sexuality[1]

P. J. McGann

(2011)

Sex matters—to individuals, to be sure, but also to social groups. Consequently all societies define and enforce norms of how to "do it," with whom, when, where, how often, and why. Yet how such sexual norms are enforced, indeed which acts are even considered to *be* sex ("it"), varies tremendously. In some cases sexual regulation is informal, as when girls or women admonish one another to control their sexual appetites lest one gain a "reputation." In others, regulation is more formal, as when a female prostitute is arrested and sentenced for her sexual misconduct. Of course, the legal system is not the only institution that formally regulates acceptable and unacceptable sexual practices. Religion also helps construct and enforce ideals of normal sex, defining some acts as sinful, others as righteous. In both cases, the moral language of sin and crime renders the social control aspects of legal and religious sexual regulation apparent.

But what of therapeutic approaches, as when a girl viewed as having "too much" sex is referred to juvenile court for "correction" of her incorrigibility? Is not intervention then for the girl's own good? Might it, for example, derail her developing delinquency, perhaps even prevent her subsequent involvement in prostitution? And what of the prostitute herself? What if rather than sending her to jail we instead direct her to therapy - based on the belief that a woman who sells her sexuality to others must, *obviously*, be sick? Do these therapeutic approaches also count as sexual regulation?

Here it is helpful to speak of social control, a broad concept that refers to any acts or practices that encourage conformity to and/ or discourage deviations from norms (Conrad and Schneider 1992). From this perspective a medical-therapeutic response to violations of sexual rules *is* a form of sexual social control. However, in contrast to the transparently moral language of law and religion—good/ bad, righteous/sinful, right/wrong—therapeutic regulation of sex relies on more opaque dichotomies of health and illness, normality and abnormality. Although such terms may camouflage the moral evaluation being made, the result is the same; whether the means are legal, religious, or therapeutic, a negative social judgment is made and a sexual hierarchy is produced (Rubin 1993). A dichotomy of good versus bad sexual practices, good versus bad "sexual citizens" (Seidman 2002), is thus created and enforced:

> Individuals whose behavior stands high in this hierarchy are rewarded with certified mental health, respectability, legality, social and physical mobility, institutional support, and material benefits. As sexual behaviors or occupations fall lower on the scale, the individuals who practice them are subjected to a presumption of mental illness, disreputability, criminality, restricted social and physical mobility, loss of institutional support, and economic sanctions.
>
> *(Rubin 1993: 12)*

Medical-therapeutic approaches—medicine, psychiatry, psychology, social work, and juvenile justice—are part of a web of practices that help define and enforce a society's sexual hierarchy and sexual norms. The "'helping" ethos of therapeutic approaches, however, disguises their regulatory dynamics and effects. An illness diagnosis provides a seemingly positive rationale for restricting or changing sexual behaviors found to be disturbing; intervention is, after all, *for our own good.* Even so, what is considered a sexual disorder may have disciplinary consequences. Whether or not a sexual activity is "really" a dysfunction or even causes distress for those diagnosed, individual sexual choices deemed non-typical are curtailed, and sexual culture is restricted in the name of health.

This chapter explores some of the politics of "healing" disorderly desire. Using three contemporary sexual difficulties—erectile dysfunction, gender identity disorder, and sexual addiction/compulsion—I show how medical-therapeutic approaches shape and direct sexual expression. Some forms of regulation are directly repressive; they limit or deny sexual options construed as unnatural, abnormal, or unhealthy. Other forms of medical-therapeutic regulation are more subtle; their "normalizing" dynamics work by producing cultural ideals of natural and healthy sexuality. The ostensibly objective medical model of sex is especially important in this regard. It provides both the taken-for-granted undemanding of what "sex" is (and is for) and the reference point from which sexual abnormality and sexual disorders are defined. As we shall see, this intertwining of the individual and cultural levels, and of repressive and normalizing forms of power, is a central dynamic in medical-therapeutic sexual regulation. Moreover, given that some individuals who "have" sexual disorders surfer neither distress nor impairment, it seems that diagnostic categories are not purely scientific entities, but social constructs that reflect social and political dynamics and concerns.

Medicalized Sex and Medical Social Control

When something is "medicalized" it is conceptually placed in a medical framework. The "problem" is then understood using medical language, typically as a disorder, dysfunction, disease, or syndrome, and is approached or solved via medical means (Conrad and Schneider 1992). A "sex offender," for example, might be sentenced to rehabilitative therapy rather than prison, or a man concerned about his homosexual desire might consult a psychiatrist rather than a priest. Although such medical-therapeutic regulation may be less punitive than criminal or religious sexual intervention, medicalizing sex produces positive and negative results.

On the plus side, defining sexual difficulties as medical problems may make it easier for people to talk more openly about sex and thus seek information and advice. Accordingly a medical approach to sex may enhance individual sexual pleasure. Yet medicalization also raises the possibility of "medical social control" (Conrad and Schneider 1992)—in this case, the use of medical means to increase conformity to sexual norms and/or to decrease sexual deviance. Prescription drugs, talk therapy, behavioral modification, negative or aversive conditioning, and/or confinement in a juvenile or mental health facility, can be enlisted to ensure adherence to sexual norms. Even without such direct medical intervention, viewing sex with a "medical gaze" often leads to a limited, biologically reductionist understanding. Stripped from its social context, sexual *difference* may become sexual *pathology*.

Medical social control sometimes has a slippery, elusive character. When individuals consult therapeutic professionals regarding sexual matters, they typically anticipate alleviation of sexual distress rather than restriction of sexual freedom. For their part psychiatrists, doctors, therapists, and social workers may neither intend nor understand their therapeutic practice as tools of sexual repression. Despite this mismatch of intent and effect, therapeutic intervention has regulatory consequences. The "promiscuous" girl can be held against her will in a mental or juvenile justice institution. The man who desires multiple sex partners might be forced to remain monogamous and to refrain from masturbation lest his sexual "addiction" overtake him.

Sexology and Its Legacies

Although some of our categories of sexual disease are new, medicine and sex have long been entangled in North America and Europe. Sexology, the science of sex, originated in mid-nineteenth-century Europe when physicians such as Magnus Hirschfeld, Richard von Krafft-Ebing, and Havelock Ellis turned their attention to sexual behavior. At the time Europe was caught up in a cultural mood of scientific rationality, evolutionism, and fantasies of white racial superiority. These currents inspired detailed scientific description of sexual diversity, and the delineation of sexual practices into normal and abnormal types. The latter were dubbed "perversions" and seen as sickness rather than sin. With the emergence of sexology, formal regulation of sexuality shifted from predominantly religious to secular modes of social control. Regulation of deviant sexuality thus became the province of medical authority (Foucault 1990).

Commonsense understandings of categories of disease view them as morally neutral descriptions of states of un-health. Yet even cursory consideration of the malleability of sexological categories shows that sexual disorders reflect more than just the accumulated sexual knowledge of the time. Forms of sexual behavior once considered abnormal and diseased are now "known" to be a normal part of sexual health. Some sexual illnesses reflect the normative standards of more powerful groups at the expense of those with differing sexual tastes and less power. And some sexual disorders seem more like reflections of prevailing cultural currents rather than actual sexual dysfunctions.

Masturbation, for example, was once the disease of "Onanism" (Conrad and Schneider 1992). A dangerous illness on its own, "self-abuse" was also a sort of gateway disease—a disorder that could so weaken the afflicted that he might fall prey to other perverse "infections" such as homosexuality or sadism. Now, though, masturbation is considered a "natural" (even if private) part of healthy sexuality; in fact, masturbation is prescribed as a therapeutic treatment for some sexual disorders, such as "premature ejaculation" (ejaculation that occurs before coitus) or "anorgasmia" (inability to orgasm). Healthy and normal sexual practices may also become disordered or unsavory over time. Visits to female prostitutes, for example, were once part of the prescribed treatment for male (but not female) "lovesickness." Massage of female external genitalia by a doctor or midwife was once the preferred treatment for "hysteria" (Maines 1999). However, in most locales today the former is illegal and the latter might be considered sexual misconduct or abuse. The female "psychopathic hypersexual" illustrates how disease categories reflect cultural concerns. Female sexual psychopaths "suffered" from an excessive amount of sexual desire at a time when it was "known" that girls and women were naturally modest and chaste, or at least sexually passive. Interestingly, the hypersexual female diagnosis emerged at the end of the Victorian era—a time of changing gender relations and rising anxiety over the increasing independence and agency of women. The psychopathic hypersexual diagnosis reflects these concerns and codifies the violation of normative gender standards as disease. Finally, the declassification of homosexuality as a mental disorder in response to social and political developments outside psychiatry is the example *par excellence* that disease categories rest on more than scientific facts (Conrad and Schneider 1992). One wonders: if historical categories of sexual disease are so obviously shaped by non-scientific factors, might the same be true of contemporary constructions of normal and abnormal, healthy and diseased sex?

The Medical Model of Sex

Although many concepts from classic sexology are no longer accepted, there are continuities between nineteenth- and twenty-first-century medical approaches to sex. The thrust to describe and delineate the diversity of sexual practices and types persists. So, too, does the "medical model" of sex. This view posits sex as an innate, natural essence or drive contained in and released from the body. Bodies, in turn, are understood as machine-like composites of parts. When the parts are in proper working order, bodies are able to achieve their functional purposes. Sexual organs become engorged as blood and other bodily fluids accumulate in anticipation of sexual activity. These changes, as well as sexual drives, patterns of sexual behavior, and even sexual types (bi, homo, hetero), are understood as universal properties of individuals independent of society. Cultural variation in sexual practice is seen as relatively superficial; changes in surface social details do not alter the deeper biological reality of sex (Tieffer 1995). Because reproduction is considered the natural function of sex, the medical model depicts heterosexuality as natural and neutral, not in need of explanation or scrutiny—unless, that is, something goes awry with the hydraulic sexual machine. Thus, nineteenth-century sexology and modern sexual science have mostly observed, described, and catalogued deviations from or problems with sex oriented toward reproduction.

The contemporary Human Sexual Response Cycle (HSRC) is the iconic embodiment of this approach. First conceived by Masters and Johnson in the 1960s, the HSRC describes a presumably universal pattern of physiological changes that occur during "sex": excitement, plateau, orgasm, and resolution. In the "excitement" stage, for example, penises become engorged with blood and vaginas lubricate in preparation for "sex." Most medical-therapeutic professionals concerned with sexual disorders now rely on a three-stage derivative model of desire, arousal, and orgasm. Despite its supposed scientific neutrality—the HSRC model was based on seemingly disinterested laboratory observation of heterosexual genital intercourse—the HSRC has been critiqued as heteronormative and androcentric, and for reifying a limited understanding of "sex" as the cultural sexual ideal (Tieffer 1995).

Although the array of potentially normal human sexual activity is vast, HSRC constructs only a narrow range of acts relating to coitus (penile-vaginal intercourse) as constituting "sex." Other forms of sexual activity are relegated to "foreplay"—preparatory, albeit pleasurable, preparations for the "real thing." Forms of sexual activity that do not culminate in coitus are viewed as perverse substitutions for, or distractions from, the real thing (Tieffer 1995). Oral sex followed by heterosexual coitus may be normal foreplay, for example, whereas oral sex in the absence of coitus is considered abnormal or dysfunctional. The HSRC thus constructs both what *should* and *should not* be done during normal sex. In so doing the HSRC helps constitute "sex" itself.

What, for example, comes to mind when one person says to another, "We had sex"? Despite the nearly endless possibilities (given the number of bodies and body parts that may or may not be involved, variations in sequence, pace, position, sexual aids or toys, and the like) the meaning of "We had sex" is typically unproblematic in everyday life. In fact, a common response might be a titillated "Really! How many times?" The answer to this question is also typically unproblematic, given that we know both what "sex" is and what "counts" as a time. Now, though, let's make it explicit that the two people who "had sex" are of the same sex. Did the meaning of "having sex" change in your mind? What counts as a "time" now? Will your answer change if our partners are male, female, or transgendered? What if we add a third or fourth participant? Is the sex that was had still the *normal* kind? Or does it now appear abnormal, maybe even *sick*, despite being consensual and mutually pleasurable?

The HSRC is also critiqued as androcentric (male-centered), given that the orgasm in question is the man's. Clinically, male ejaculation/orgasm marks the transition to the "resolution" stage. As such, male orgasm is the basis of counting how many "times" sex occurs, or even if sex is "had" at all. Moreover, although the HSRC codifies "foreplay" as an official part of sex, there is no category of "afterplay"—such as sexual activity focused on female orgasm after the man ejaculates. Even adding this concept, though, leaves coitus intact as the defining sexual moment. The (heterosexual) male's orgasmic experience thus defines "sex," whereas female orgasm is not considered. Indeed, female orgasmic pleasure is not a necessary part of real sex. Female orgasm does not count, at least not from the perspective of the supposedly universal and natural HSRC—unless, that is, the counting concerns "abnormal" female sex response. Since at least 70 percent of women do not achieve orgasm from penile-vaginal penetration alone, the HSRC focus on coitus and male ejaculation as the goal and purpose of "sex" renders most women sexually unhealthy, defective, disordered, or dysfunctional (Tieffer 1995). Despite these shortcomings, sexual activities that diverge from the HSRC are defined as abnormal, pathological, deviant, unnatural, dysfunctional, and disordered.

Sexual Disorder in DSM

"DSM" is short for *Diagnostic and Statistical Manual of Mental Disorder*. Published by the American Psychiatric Association, DSM is a professionally approved listing of diagnostic categories and criteria. It is the central text for those working in the mental and sexual health fields in the USA, and the key to second-party reimbursement for medical-therapeutic services. DSM has undergone four revisions since its initial publication in 1952. A roman numeral in the title denotes placement in the revision sequence: DSM-II in 1968, DSM-III in 1980, DSM-III-R in 1987, DSM-IV in 1994, and DSM-IV-TR in 2000. Categories of disease are refined and reconceptualized over the course of these editions. Sometimes this results in a disorder being relocated within DSM's typological system, as when homosexuality shifted from psychopathic personality disturbance (DSM-I) to type of sexual deviance (DSM-II); sometimes it leads to the complete removal of a disorder, as when homosexuality was left out of DSM-III.

The most recent DSM lists three major classifications of Sexual Disorder: Paraphilias, Sexual Dysfunctions, and Gender Identity Disorders. "Paraphilias" include exhibitionism, fetishism, frotteurism, pedophilia, sexual masochism, sexual sadism, transvestic fetishism, and voyeurism. (Many of these types were the original "perversions" described by nineteenth-century sexology.) "Sexual Dysfunctions" concern impairments or disturbances related to coitus. Three subtypes directly mirror the derivative HSRC model: disorders of desire, disorders of arousal, and disorders of orgasm. The fourth subtype, pain during coitus, also reflects the centrality of coitus in constructing the sexual dysfunctions. The last major classification of sexual disorder in DSM is "Gender Identity Disorders." With subtypes for adults and children, these disorders represent deviations from "normal" gender embodiment.

DSM facilitates communication among an array of sexual helping professionals with diverse training, specialization, and institutional placements and practices. Using DSM categories, individuals as varied as a social worker with one year of postgraduate academic training, a psychiatrist with over ten years of medical and clinical training, or a college intern working in a residential juvenile treatment program, can communicate with one another. This is helpful, to be sure. But the shared language of DSM may also make the sexual disorders seem less politically contested and more objectively real than they really are. This may, in turn, make it more difficult for practitioners to recognize the biases built into DSM diagnostic categories. Far from being neutral classifications, the major DSM categories of sexual disorder encode normative assumptions of sexuality. Paraphilias delineate that which we should do sexually; sexual dysfunctions reflect incapacities in what we *should* do; and gender identity disorders concern how we should appear and who we should be while doing it.

One way to avoid uncritically replicating these biases is to rename the major types of sexual disorder based on their ideological effects rather than naming the types based on their relationship to coitus. "Sexual dysfunctions," for example, seems a neutral and comprehensive term; in reality it is a specific reference to *hetero*sexual dysfunctions of penile-vaginal intercourse. Consider instead "disorders of prowess"—disorders based on one's compromised ability to engage in coitus. We could similarly disrupt the heteronormativity of HSRC and speak of "disorders of appetite"— disorders of too much or too little desire to engage in coitus, and/or having desires that do not include or that extend beyond coitus. Finally, "gender violations" seems an apt tag for forms of gender expression and embodiment that violate the traditional gender styles underpinning normative heterosexuality. Having linguistically interrupted diagnostic business as usual, I now turn to some specific disorders and consider how each reflects and reproduces dominant North American sexual norms and the sexual hierarchy built on them.

Sexual Disorders and the Maintenance of Ideal Sexuality

Some people do experience distress in relation to sexual matters. Treatment of sexual disorders may alleviate such distress and thereby enhance sexual pleasure. This does not mean, however, that medical-therapeutic intervention does not also produce negative consequences or operate in repressive fashion. Moreover, since some of the DSM's sexual disorders are not necessarily *dysfunctions* but violations of dominant sexual norms, therapeutic intervention may enforce conformity to the dominant sexual ideal. Sexual codes, though, are political, ethical, moral, and existential matters_not medical ones. While bringing one's sexual practices into line with prevailing sexual norms may alleviate individual distress, it also obscures the social, cultural, and ideological sources of sexual difficulties.

The Western sexual ideal has become less oriented to procreation and more pleasure-based over time. This new "relational" sexual code (Levine and Troiden 1988) understands sexual

activity as creating, expressing, and enhancing a couple's intimacy, and mutual sexual pleasure is accordingly thought of as a normal part of healthy sex. This does not mean, of course, that anything goes. Ideally sexual pleasure occurs within an on-going committed monogamous relationship between two conventionally gendered people of "opposite" sexes (Rubin 1993). In some locales homosexuality may be approaching this sexual ideal—provided, that is, the same-sex couple and their relationship is otherwise normal: the partners are committed to one another, their sex is an expression of love and caring, and they are, like heterosexuals, either masculine men or feminine women (Seidman 2002). Ideal sex occurs in private, is genitally centered (as per the HSRC construction of coitus as "sex"), and is caring rather than aggressive or violent (Rubin 1993). Individuals who engage in such normal sex are good sexual citizens, while those who engage in non-normative sex are thought of as bad. The latter are perceived as immoral, abnormal, unhealthy, diseased, perverted and socially dangerous (Seidman 2002).

Erectile Dysfunction: A Prowess Disorder

At first glance it may be hard to grasp how improving a man's erection may be a form of sexual regulation and repression. Certainly treatment of Erectile Dysfunction (ED) holds the promise of increased sexual pleasure! It also, however, channels pleasure toward particular sexual acts and body parts in a manner that reflects and reinforces the limited HSRC construction of coitus as the be-all and end-all of "sex." The focus on erections also helps reproduce traditional masculinity and associated stereotypes of "natural" male and female sexuality.

Previously known as the psychological and interpersonal disorder of "impotence," ED is now understood as a physiological impairment of arousal. ED has recently risen to prominence alongside the increased visibility of drug-based treatments; indeed, the discovery of a pharmacological treatment is intertwined with the discovery that impotence is "really" a hydraulic and mechanical disorder. In this, the "Viagra age" (Loe 2004) is emblematic of the biological reductionism that often results when sex is medicalized. The individualized focus removes sexual problems from their interpersonal, social, and cultural contexts. ED thus seems a purely medical rather than a political matter.

The proliferation of penile fixes—Viagra, Cialis, Levitra, and the like—has made it possible for many men to achieve the full, long-lasting erections they desire. The penile fix has also raised expectations and created new norms of male sexual performance. In the Viagra Age it is easy enough to rebuild him, make him bigger, harder, and get him that way faster regardless of his age, fatigue, or emotional state. With the little blue pill and some physical stimulation a real man can get the job done, whether or not his heart is in it. That the perfect penis is now but a swallow away reinforces the cultural understanding of male sexuality as machine-like, uncomplicated, straightforward, and readily available. This reinforces the commonsense view that men are "about" sex whereas women are "about" relationships, while constructing female sexuality as complicated and mysterious (Loe 2004). These contrasting images of male and female sexuality reflect the notion that men and women are "opposite" sexes. This gendered assumption in turn bolsters the seeming neutrality of heterosexuality as complementary opposites that "naturally" attract the other. In this way ED reflects and reinforces heteronormative cultural ideals of sexuality *and* gender.

The ED treatment focus on producing erections "sufficient" for penetration also disciplines the sexuality of individual men For starters, it directs attention to preparing the man for "sex"—understood, of course, as coitus. While this constructs sex in an image of male orgasm, it also constrains the realm of pleasurable and culturally valuable sexual activity. The phallic focus comes at the expense of the man's other body parts and their pleasures, and construes

other sexual activities, including other types of intercourse (anal or oral), as less than the real thing. The phallic focus even deflects attention from the wider possibilities of pleasure linked to other penile states (the soft penis, for example, or movements between soft and hard). Preoccupation with the size and "quality" of erections also reinforces a sexual "work ethic" that emphasizes active male performance rather than sexual enjoyment and/or receptivity. The man's sexuality is thus restricted and restrained, his potential pleasures lessened. Pharmaceutical ads disseminate these messages widely in their depictions of ED treatments as being for caring, committed heterosexual couples rather than, say, homosexual couples, single men, men who masturbate or use pornography, or men who engage in multiple-partner sex (Loe 2004).

Gender Identity Disorder: A Gender Violation

The gendered nature of ED and its treatment suggests the close coupling of traditional gender and normative sexuality. As Seidman (2002) points out, good sexual citizens are gender-normal citizens: their gender identities and expressions fit traditional gender images and understandings. Thus, normal sex occurs between individuals whose gender styles and gender identities are seen as appropriate for their sex category—men are masculine and see themselves as male; women are feminine and see themselves as female. The gender identity disorders reflect and reinforce these essentialist understandings of the "natural" relationship between sex category, gender identity, and gender embodiment, by pathologizing alternative configurations of sex and gender (McGann 1999). Non-normative ways of doing gender—a feminine man, for example—and atypical gender identities—such as a female-bodied person who identifies as male—are examples of clinical "gender dysphoria." Whether or not their ego functioning is impaired, they experience distress related to their condition, or other psychopathology exists, gender dysphoric individuals, including children, may be diagnosed with and treated for Gender Identity Disorder (GID). Although a GID diagnosis can have the positive result of facilitating access to medical technologies of bodily transformation, it does so by constructing gender difference as disease. GID thus also provides a rationale for medical social control of gender difference—an especially troubling possibility for gender-different children.

When GID first appeared in 1980, it included two types of diagnostic criteria. One concerned impairments in cognitive functioning centered on sexual anatomy, such as a boy thinking his penis ugly or wishing he did not have a penis, or a girl insisting that she could one day grow a penis. The other diagnostic criteria were thought to indicate the child's desire to "be" the other sex. In actuality, however, these criteria focused on cultural violations of gendered appearance or activity norms— boys who look and "act like" girls, for example. Although a child need not demonstrate distress regarding the condition—in fact, DSM notes that most children deny distress—a child had to demonstrate *both* the cognitive functioning and cultural criteria to be diagnosed. That is, a child could not be diagnosed with GID on the basis of cultural gender role violations alone. This two-tiered diagnostic requirement has weakened over subsequent DSM editions. Since 1994 (DSM-IV) it has been possible to diagnose a child as gender disordered based *only* on cultural criteria—that is, based only on the child's violations of social standards of traditional masculinity and femininity in the absence of demonstrated impairment of cognitive function. Thus, a girl with short hair, whose friends are boys, and who refuses to wear dresses, may now "have" GID. In effect, the diagnostic net has widened; a tomboy considered normal under DSM-III-R became abnormal in DSM-IV.

Interestingly, this expansion of GID has occurred alongside the removal of homosexuality from DSM-III and the increasing "normalization" of homosexuality in everyday life (Seidman

2002). None the less, organizations such as Focus on the Family publicize and support therapeutic treatment of gender-different children in order to stave off their future homosexuality. Because children can be and are diagnosed and treated solely for gendered appearance and role violations, GID enforces our cultural gender dichotomy and our understanding of hetero-sexuality as the natural attraction of gendered opposites (McGann 1999).

One need not be gender-dysphoric oneself to suffer GID's disciplinary effects. As noted earlier, medical judgments of health and illness influence everyday life understandings. In this case the construction of atypical gender as illness discourages gender openness and fluidity for all. GID also regulates sexual expression directly by limiting normal sex to that which occurs between traditionally gendered people; cross-dressing sex play by individuals who are otherwise gender-normal, for example, is "known" to be abnormal or perverse. The sexuality of gender-atypical but non-dysphoric people is also distorted by GID. The wholly normative heterosexual desire of a "tomboyish" woman may be invisible to her potential partner, for example. Alternatively, her erotic draw to males may be dismissed as unbelievable or insincere since she is, *obviously*, a lesbian, based on her appearance (McGann 1999).

Sexual Addiction/Compulsion: A Disorder of Appetite

At times the terms "sexual addiction" and "sexual compulsion" are used interchangeably; at times they refer to different disorders. Neither is currently listed as an official mental disorder in the DSM. None the less, patients are treated for sexual addiction/compulsion, books and articles are published on the disorder, practitioners are trained in its treatment modalities, therapeutic institutions specialize in it, and TV documentaries such as Discovery Health's *Sex Mania!* present it as a valid diagnostic category. Sexual addiction/compulsion is thought to be similar to other chemical or behavioral dependencies, such as those on alcohol or food. In practice, the diagnosis can refer to nearly any sexual behavior deemed "excessive" in the therapist's or clinician's professional judgment. In this, sexual addiction is a near-perfect obverse of the prevailing sexual ideal, the dark shadow of the good sexual citizen. As with GID, many individuals diagnosed with sex addiction deny that their disorder causes them distress or harm, and helping professionals often have to work long and hard to convince their "patients" that they are in fact "sick." For this reason sexual addiction aptly illustrates how disease categories crystallize political differences regarding sexual norms. It also shows how disease categories reflect the social currents and concerns of their origin.

Sexual addiction was "unthinkable" in the relatively sexually permissive, sex positive 1970s (Levine and Troiden 1988). At the time sex was seen in a more recreational, pleasure-based light and therapeutic concern consequently focused on "Inhibited Sexual Disorder" (Irvine 2005). But in the 1980s and the early days of the AIDS epidemic, fears of sexual chaos came to the fore and therapeutic attention turned instead to excessive thus dangerous sexual desire. As the dominant sexual ideal shifted from a recreational to a relational code, forms of sexual expression that had been normalized in the 1970s were pathologized as addictive and compulsive (Levine and Troiden 1988).

Gay men were at first thought to be especially prone to sex addiction. Indeed, the gay press worried that the diagnosis was a medical form of homophobia, a way to pathologize behavior construed as deviant by the hetero majority, but that was normative within some gay communities (Levine and Troiden 1988). While gay male acceptance of anonymous and/or public sex may have initially swelled the sex addict rank, heterosexuals also "suffer" from the disorder. Straight women who deviate from relationally-oriented monogamous sex may be considered addicts, for example. A broad range of sexual activity outside of coital monogamy is considered indicative of addiction/compulsion, including multiple partners (at the same time or as successive couplings),

"frequent" masturbation, the use of pornography, "recreational" sex (sex solely for pleasure), anonymous or public sex. Sex addiction also manifests within the otherwise sexually normal hetero couple, as when one partner desires coitus more frequently, and/or wants to engage in activities in addition to or instead of coitus. In these cases a therapist may rip the balance in favor of the more traditional partner by elevating one personal preference as "normal" while deeming the other compulsive or addictive. Here, use of the term "lust" rather than "desire" in the sex addiction literature reveals a moral evaluation masquerading as neutral medical description. Other morally charged "retro-purity" terms are also common in the sexual addiction literature, such as promiscuity, nymphomania, and womanizing (Irvine 2005).

Although the activities presumed indicative of sexual addiction or compulsion may be atypical, they are not inherently pathological. It seems, then, that medical ideology has retained the theme of morality but has done so in seemingly apolitical terms. The sex addict diagnosis codifies prevailing erotic values as health (Levine and Troiden 1988). This move privileges a certain style of sexual expression while marginalizing others. Indeed, the sex addict diagnostic guidelines read like a description of a dangerous sexual citizen. The construction of sexual activities not oriented toward coitus, polyamorous relationships, and non-relational, pleasure-based sex as illness ends political debate on these matters before it begins.

Sexual Disorders or Disorderly Sex?

Medicalized sex is not necessarily the enemy of pleasure. As Rachel Maines (1999: 3) documents regarding the preferred treatment of hysteria: "Massage to orgasm of female patients was a staple of medical practice among some (but certainly not all) Western physicians from the time of Hippocrates until the 1920s." This example is titillating, of course. It is also instructive: it points to the necessity of separating the therapeutic professional's *intent* from the potentially repressive *effects* of therapeutic intervention, and to the importance of viewing both in the context of cultural understandings of sex and eroticism. The clinical phenomenon of "hysterical paroxysm" certainly looks now to be orgasm. But in a cultural moment that understood vaginal penetration as necessary for "sex" to occur it was seen instead as the climax of illness. Just as the physician treating the hysterical patient did not necessarily intend to incite his patient's pleasure, contemporary helping professionals may not intend to restrict the sexual freedom of their patient-clients.

Medical-therapeutic sexual regulation works at the cultural level via a normalizing dynamic that constructs a limited range of sexual activity as healthy, natural, normal sex. Medical-therapeutic regulation also works repressively directly on individuals, limiting their sexual choices and/or serving as justification for coercive "therapeutic" responses to non-normative sexual variation. Both dynamics and more are apparent in the sexual disorders just discussed. Erectile dysfunction illustrates the strait-jacket that is the medical model of sex. It also shows the chameleon-like nature of medical social control; therapeutic response to a sexual problem can simultaneously enhance and reduce pleasure. GID demonstrates how medical constructions of "normality" at the cultural level intertwine with the individual level; the enforcement of normal gender on individuals reinforces the cultural concepts of gender that the naturalness of hetero-sexuality is built on. Together, ED and GID show that one need not be diagnosed to have one's sexuality regulated by medical-therapeutic approaches. Finally, much like the female hypersexual diagnosis, sexual addiction/compulsion demonstrates the political danger that arises when illness categories embody prevailing erotic ideals. At such times sexual disorder can be wielded as a "baton" to force erotically unconventional individuals to adhere to sexual norms (Levine and Troiden 1988). Perhaps then, rather than speaking of

sexual *disorders*—a term that suggests objective disease and dysfunction—we could more accurately speak of *disorderly* sex; sex that is socially disruptive, sex that disturbs the dominant cultural sexual ideal.

Culturally-defined sexual ideals regarding valid forms of sexual activity and relationship are institutionally supported (defining marriage as the union of two rather than three persons, for example); such institutionalization confers legitimacy, value, and power such that questioning or challenging the norm seems to threaten disorder.

Medical diagnoses may be preferable when other definitional options include depravity (you sinner! you freak!) or personal moral failing (how *could* you?). But medical neutrality is false neutrality given the negative social judgment that is illness (Irvine 2005; Conrad and Schneider 1992). The helping ethos and humanitarian ideal of medicine may obfuscate but does not negate the reality that therapeutic intervention in sexual matters has disciplinary effects. Disease categories are forms of power that enshrine and enforce prevailing sexual standards in the name of sexual health. Disorders of desire are thus as much about the *social* body as they are about the corporeal one. Medical-therapeutic discourse, though, disguises the ways in which the personal has always been political when it comes to sex.

Note

1. This work was supported in part by NIMH Grant T32MH19996. and benefited from many stimulating discussions with Kim Green as well.

REFERENCES

Conrad, Peter, and Joseph Schneider. 1992. *Deviance and Medicalization: From Badness to Sickness*. Philadelphia, PA: Temple University Press.

Foucault, Michel. 1990 (1978). *The History of Sexuality* New York: Vintage.

Irvine, Janice. 2005. *Disorders of Desire* (2nd ed). Philadelphia. PA; Temple University Press.

Levine, Martin P., and Richard R. Troiden. 1988 "The myth of sexual compulsivity." *Journal of Sex Research* 25, 3: 347—63.

Loe. Meika. 2004. *The Rise of Viagra: How the Little Blue Pill Changed Sex in America.* New York: NYU Press.

Maines, Rachel P. 1999. *The Technology of Orgasm "Hysteria," the Vibrator, and Women's Sexual Satisfaction.* Baltimore. MD: Johns Hopkins University Press

McGann. P. J. 1999. "Skirting the gender normal divide: a tomboy life story." In Mary Romero and Abigail J Stewart (eds), *Women's Untold Stories; Breaking Silence, Talking Back, Voicing Complexity.* New York. Routledge.

Rubin, Gayle S. 1993. "Thinking sex." In Henry Abelove. Michele Aina Barale, and David M. Halperin (eds), *The Lesbian and Gay Studies Reader.* New York: Routledge.

Seidman, Steven. 2002. *Beyond the Closet: The Transformation of Gay and Lesbian Life.* New York: Routledge.

Tieffer, Leonore. 1995. *Sex is Not a Natural Act and Other Essays.* Oxford: Westview Press.

THINKING ABOUT THE READING

According to McGann, how do the medical institution and other institutions (legal, religious, etc.) help create and enforce "normal" sexual activity and relationships? Taking one of the three examples McGann analyzes, explain how these definitions work at both cultural and individual levels. Taking McGann's definition of "disorderly sex," think of some examples of this concept beyond the ones she provides in this article.

Patients, "Potheads," and Dying to Get High

Wendy Chapkis

(2006)

The Wo/Men's Alliance for Medical Marijuana (WAMM) is an organization that is not easily classified. WAMM is not, as the federal Drug Enforcement Administration (DEA) might suggest, a cover for illicit drug dealing to recreational users, but neither is it properly characterized as a pharmacy dispensing physician-recommended medicine. In this article, I describe briefly the origins of WAMM and then discuss the problem of trying to divide medical marijuana users into "real patients" and "potheads." Such classification is complicated further by the relationship between medicinal cannabis use and the experience of getting "high."

What Is WAMM?

WAMM was founded in California in 1993 by medical marijuana patient Valerie Corral and her husband, Michael Corral, a master gardener. In April 2004, WAMM drew national and international attention when it successfully won a temporary injunction against the U.S. Justice Department; as a result, the alliance now operates the only nongovernmental legal medical marijuana garden in the country. The organization is unique in other respects as well. It is organized as a *cooperative*. Marijuana is grown and distributed collectively and *without charge* to the 250 patient participants. Instead of paying for their marijuana, members are expected, as their health permits, to contribute volunteer hours to the organization by working in the garden; assisting with fund-raising; making cannabis tinctures, milk, capsules, and muffins; or volunteering in the office.

Over a five-year period (from 1999 to 2004), I conducted more than three dozen interviews with WAMM members about their involvement with the organization and their therapeutic use of marijuana. The WAMM members interviewed for this article reported use of marijuana with a physician's recommendation for a range of conditions including nausea related to chemotherapy (for cancer and AIDS), spasticity (multiple sclerosis), seizures (epilepsy), and chronic and acute pain. In order to become members of WAMM, each of the patient participants had to discuss with his or her doctor the possible therapeutic value of marijuana and to have been told explicitly (and in writing) that cannabis might prove useful in managing the specific symptoms associated with his or her illness, disability, or course of treatment. The number of members the program can accommodate is limited by the amount of marijuana the organization is able to grow. There is an extensive waiting list to join the organization; with more than 80% of its members living with a life-threatening illness, the standing joke is that "people are literally dying to get into WAMM."

Financial support for the organization comes largely from external donations. In 1998, however, the federal government revoked WAMM's nonprofit status on the grounds that it was involved in supplying a federally prohibited substance. WAMM's struggle for survival further intensified in the fall of 2002 when the federal DEA raided the WAMM garden and arrested the two cofounders (to date, no charges have been filed against them). Despite these challenges, WAMM has continued to operate with the full support of California's elected officials and in close cooperation with local law enforcement. In April 2004, Judge Jeremy Fogel of the federal district court in San Jose (citing a recent Ninth Circuit Court of Appeals decision, *Raich v. Ashcroft,* soon to be reviewed by the U.S. Supreme Court) barred the Justice Department from interfering with the Corrals, WAMM patients, or the collective's garden. The federal injunction has provided at least temporary respite in the ongoing battle with the federal government.

Who Are the WAMM Members? "Worthy Patients" or "Unworthy Potheads"?

Dorothy Gibbs is the sort of patient voters are encouraged to imagine when the question of medical marijuana is before them. At ninety-four and confined to a bed in a Santa Cruz nursing home, this WAMM member is hardly the stereotypical "pothead" many critics believe to be hiding behind the medical marijuana movement. Cannabis, for Dorothy Gibbs, has never been anything but a medicine, a particularly effective analgesic that relieves severe pain associated with her post-polio syndrome:

> I never smoked marijuana before; I had no reason to. But the relief I got was wonderful and long lasting and pretty immediate, too. I didn't really have any misgivings about using marijuana; I figured it had to be better than what I'd got. They had me on lots of other medications, but I couldn't stand them; they made me so sick.

Most Americans (80% according to a recent CNN/Time poll; Stein, 2002) support the right of seriously ill patients like Dorothy Gibbs to access and use medical marijuana. This broad support is coupled, however, with lingering concerns that medical marijuana may be, as described in *Time* magazine, largely "a kind of ruse" (Stein). From this perspective, medical marijuana campaigns are seen as a cover for drug legalization and most, if not all, "medicinal use" as nothing more than

a recreational habit dressed up in a doctor's recommendation.

Tensions between medical and social uses of marijuana are unavoidable in a political context in which nonmedicinal use is at once widespread, formally prohibited, and often severely punished. Because of the social and legal penalties associated with recreational use, it is reasonable that some consumers would attempt to acquire a measure of legitimacy and protection by identifying a medical need for marijuana. Medical marijuana users, then, become divided in the public arena between patients, like Dorothy Gibbs, who have never used marijuana except as a medicine, and "pretenders" who have a social relationship to the drug. As with other discreditable identities (like the prostitute, the poor person, or the single mother), a line is then drawn between a small class of deserving "victims" and a much larger group of the willfully bad who are unworthy of protection or support.

Such divisions are both illusory and dangerous. In the case of marijuana use, the identities of medical and social users are not neatly dichotomous. Some medical users have had prior experience with marijuana as a means of enhancing pleasure before they had occasion to become familiar with its potential in relieving pain. Other patients discovered the reasons for the plant's popularity as a recreational drug only after being introduced to it for a more narrowly therapeutic purpose.

With the majority of WAMM members living with life-threatening conditions and many of the chronically ill confined to wheelchairs, this is an organization that presents the legitimate face of medical marijuana, the sick and dying who are widely seen as deserving of the drug. Yet even within this population, neat divisions between medical and social users are unworkable. "Di," for example, a WAMM member in her midforties living with AIDS, acknowledges,

> I'm just going to be totally honest—it wasn't AIDS that introduced me to pot. I had smoked marijuana as a kid and I liked it even then.

When I tested positive in 1991, I felt that it was kind of a benefit that I got to use the term "medical marijuana," but I didn't quite own it as medicine because it had just been my lifestyle. But then, a few years ago, I traveled out of state [without access to marijuana]. I spent a week traveling and then went to Florida with my mom. By the time we got there, I was in so much pain from the neuropathy, I couldn't get up. We went to Urgent Care and they gave me morphine. The pain just wouldn't go away. I took the morphine for a week until I got back to California. When I got home, I started smoking pot again as normal and it took about three or four days and I stopped taking the morphine. I realized I had probably kept myself from having this really severe nerve pain for a long time by smoking every day. It was like this big validation that I really was using good medicine.

"Maria," a fifty-two-year-old single mother living with metastatic ovarian cancer, had no current relationship to marijuana when she fell ill, but she did associate the drug with the recreational use of her youth. This past association made it difficult for her to accept that cannabis might have therapeutic value:

I don't even know if I would have believed [that marijuana was medicine] if I hadn't tried it for medical purposes myself. I hadn't smoked for many years since I had my daughter. But a good friend said that they had heard it was really good for the nausea [related to chemotherapy] and turned me on to WAMM .... What an incredible difference; the pharmaceuticals don't hold a candle [to marijuana] in terms of immediate relief . . . I don't think I would have believed it because it had always been recreational to me.

A Cover for Drug Dealing or an Alternative Pharmacy?

Because of confusions about the legitimacy of marijuana as medicine and of users as patients, provider organizations such as WAMM are often misunderstood as well. Even within communities largely tolerant of marijuana use, such as Santa Cruz, suspicions remain about the role of a provider organization. "Betty," now a WAMM volunteer, initially assumed WAMM was little more than a cover for recreational users to obtain their drug of choice:

A friend of the family developed stomach cancer, and when he got the prescription for marijuana he said to me, "I got into this organization; it's called WAMM." I had heard of WAMM but had never been involved with it or anything. Anyway, he says, "Everybody wants to be my caregiver but they all smoke and they're going to steal my pot. I know you don't do marijuana, so would you do this for me?" At first I said, "No, I don't think so." A couple of weeks later, he came back and asked again. So I said, "I'll tell you what—I'll go and check this out, but I'm not going to be sitting around with a bunch of potheads. I'm really not into that, I might as well be honest. But I'll go with you and check it out." So I went and I was really surprised at what I found. These people aren't potheads. These people aren't drug addicts. They're not derelicts. It's nothing like I had envisioned in my mind. I was very surprised . . . these people are really sick. And it's not like they all sit around and get stoned. I was amazed.

Similarly, "Hal," a seventy-year-old with severe neurological pain from failed back surgery, remembers that when a friend suggested he consider marijuana to manage the pain and WAMM as a way to access that marijuana, he was suspicious:

Right, "medical" marijuana, sure. But [after trying it] I couldn't deny I felt better. I didn't know anything about WAMM; I'd never even heard of a cannabis buying club. I just wasn't in that world. I immediately jumped to the wrong conclusion. I thought "you're a bunch of potheads who are scamming the system." Right? So I'll be a pothead and scam the system. I don't care because I need it. I need it.

Hal's suspicion that WAMM was largely a cover for drug dealing to recreational users was shattered only when he attended his first weekly membership meeting:

The first time I went to WAMM, with all these misconceptions in my mind, I looked around the room and thought, "My god, these people are really not well." I went home and said to my wife, "I'm going to have to rethink this whole thing. I'm going to have to stop jumping to conclusions here because this was an incredible experience."

Attending a WAMM meeting is indeed consciousness altering; new patients and guests enter expecting a room thick with marijuana smoke and instead find a room filled with human suffering and a collectively organized attempt to alleviate it. In fact, no marijuana is smoked at WAMM membership meetings. Rather, the hour-and-a-half gathering is spent building community: sharing news about the needs of the organization and the needs of the membership. Announcements are made not only about volunteer "opportunities" to work in the garden or the office, but also about members needing hospital visits, meals, or informal hospice support. Memorials are planned for those who have recently died, and holiday parties are organized for those with a desire to socialize and to celebrate. Information is exchanged about the practical dimensions of living with chronic or terminal illness and about coping with the often cascading challenges of pain, poverty, and social isolation. The meetings conclude with members picking up a week's supply of medical marijuana.

Neither Drug Dealing nor a Pharmacy: A New Model of Community Health Care

Although WAMM is not, then, a cover for recreational drug dealing, neither is it simply a pharmacy dispensing physician-recommended medicine. Indeed, by its very design, the organization does not "dispense" marijuana at all. Rather, members collectively grow, harvest, clean, and store the plants; transform them into tinctures, baked goods, and other products; and draw their share throughout the year

according to medical need. This is made all the more remarkable by the fact that WAMM never charges for that medicine. The paradigm-breaking phenomenon of patients collectively producing their own medicines not only challenges the "pharmaceuticalization" of healing, it also creates a therapeutic setting that effectively disrupts the atomized experience of illness and treatment characteristic of conventional medical practice. And, because WAMM members are on the front lines of legal and political battles around medical marijuana, the organization also necessarily facilitates civic engagement.

In short, WAMM approaches "health care" in the most expansive terms, addressing "afflictions" of the body, mind, and spirit, as well as those of the body politic. In this way, the organization more closely resembles women's health care cooperatives (originating in the feminist health care movement of the 1970s) and AIDS self-help and community support organizations (organized through the gay community in the 1980s and 1990s) than it does a pharmacy.

Like these earlier manifestations of community-based health initiatives, WAMM, too, deliberately challenges the monopoly of medical professionals, the pharmaceutical industry, and the state to determine the conditions of treatment, access to drugs, and even the terms of life and death. The objective of WAMM activists is not simply to add another drug to a patient's medicine cabinet but rather to create community. WAMM cofounder Valerie Corral observes:

> We came together around the marijuana, but it's not just the marijuana, it's the community. If the government has its way, and we have to go to a pharmacy to get our prescriptions filled, then we do it all alone. We would lack that coming together, and that is as important as anything else. Totally important. There is magic in joining together with other beings in suffering. That's the "joyful participation in the sorrows of the world" that the Buddhists talk about. It's how you recognize something is bigger than you and it's a paradigm breaker.

Patient participants initially may join WAMM for no other reason than to access doctor-recommended medication. But it is difficult for members to relate to the organization as nothing more than a dispensary. Weekly attendance at a ninety-minute participants' meeting is required for pickup of marijuana. At a minimum, this means that members must become familiar with each other's faces, witness each other's suffering, and confront repeated requests for assistance by both the organization and by individual participants. In other words, just because the marijuana in WAMM is free and organic doesn't make it without cost, at least in terms of emotional investment. For some, like thirty-seven-year-old "John," living with HIV, the price feels very high indeed.

> I've had a strange relationship to WAMM because a dispensary is really what I would have rather had it be. I'm a matter-of-fact kind of person, and if I have to have this condition, and I have to use a substance, I want to be able to get it and go and not be a part of anything. I don't want to know who my pharmacist is. That's exactly how I feel about WAMM. I go to the meetings because it is a requirement, but it's not necessarily what I would opt to do. I bet everybody who goes just wants to pick up their medicine and leave. Basically, what we want is our medicine and to get on with our lives.

Indeed, those "with a life" and, perhaps more important, an income may prefer a dispensary or buyers' club over a demandingly intimate self-help collective. But for many who remain members, marijuana becomes only one of a number of threads tying them to the organization. "Joe," a forty-year-old man with a severe seizure disorder, explains:

> The medicine is actually turning into a secondary or tertiary part of what WAMM is all about for me now. It's more about the group itself, the fellowship that goes on, the ways we help each other. Actually that's the biggest thing I want to rave about: that de-isolation that takes place. Isolation that accompanies illness gets to everybody eventually. Suddenly you are removed from any kind of social matrix, like

being in school or at work so you don't have the day-to-day contacts with people that make all the difference in your life. WAMM takes you out of that isolation by putting you in contact with other people, like it or not. That's what I really like about the requirement that you come every week to get what you need. You have to be there. That's the only rule actually, and that's what makes it work. People get there whether they'd rather stay at home and then they start finding things in themselves that relate to other people. It's a way for patients to get a hold of their own lives and feel whole, feel human.

One of the most distinctive features of belonging to the WAMM community is, in the words of one participant, the possibility of "dying in the embrace of friends." Because the majority of members are living with life-threatening illness, death is a close companion. For the most active members, this is both the source of great social cohesion and, simultaneously, an almost unbearably painful aspect of collective life. "Kurt," a forty-two-year-old living with AIDS, explains:

> At first I came because I heard that this Mother Teresa was giving out the best medicinal marijuana in the fucking world. And I wanted to know what this was about. What I found was a collective. WAMM has become the most unique group I've belonged to in my whole life. Sometimes it's hard for me, though, because it's a place for the sick and dying. And I'm sick but I'm not dying. I've pulled away from WAMM these past years because every time I become close to someone, they've died. And I was like "fuck this. I'm not going to go through this every time." But what WAMM has done for me—and for everybody they've supplied—is what nobody could do. Whether it's the marijuana or the tincture, or Valerie just coming and sitting by your side. So many people have died, but at least they had somebody sitting by their side.

Dying to Get High

Given decades of condemnation in this country of "reefer madness" and the supposedly dangerously intoxicating high produced by marijuana, it is not surprising that medical marijuana advocates have steered away from any discussion of the consciousness-altering properties of the substance. In an effort to distinguish medical from recreational use, the medical marijuana movement has focused almost entirely on the utility of medical marijuana in physical symptom management (that is, on its effects on nausea, pain, appetite, muscle spasms, ocular pressure, and seizure disorders). It is as if the "high" that inspires recreational use either disappears with medicinal use or, at best, is an unintended and unfortunate side effect. The medical marijuana movement, in other words, seems to have decided that talking about the psychoactive properties of cannabis will serve only to further discredit the drug, working against efforts to transform it into a "medicine."

WAMM cofounder Valerie Corral has resisted this impulse. In addition to gathering data on how marijuana affects members' physical symptom management, Valerie has been encouraging members to reflect on how marijuana might be affecting their psychospiritual well-being. Valerie observes:

> I've gotten criticism for even talking about "consciousness"—I think people are afraid it will be used against us. But I really think it's interesting that the government is so determined to take the "high" out of marijuana before they legalize it as a prescription medicine. You never hear them talking about taking the "low" out of opiates; we allow medicine that relieves pain and is addictive but puts a veil over consciousness. So why is it so important to remove access to a drug that relieves pain and allows for an opening of consciousness?

My interviews suggest that living with severe and chronic pain and with an enhanced awareness of death is, in itself, profoundly consciousness altering. Medical interventions that ignore this dimension are increasingly recognized as inadequate by those involved in palliative care. "Healing," in such situations, is necessarily distinct from "curing" and involves interventions in body,

mind, and spirit. Dr. Bal Mount, the founder and director of the Palliative Care Unit at the Royal Victorian Hospital in Montreal, argues, "Healing doesn't necessarily have to do with just the physical body. If one has a broader idea of what healing and wellness are, all kinds of people die as well people" (quoted in Webb, 1999, p. 317).

"Bill," a fifty-three-year-old gay man who has been a caregiver to several WAMM members living with and dying of AIDS, was a cofounder of the local AIDS project in the 1980s and has extensive experience with the medical use of marijuana. He reports:

> The gay community was well aware of marijuana, and early on in the AIDS epidemic we realized that it solved several major things: it solved problems of appetite when somebody wouldn't eat anymore; and it solved nausea, which I didn't think it would, but it did. And it seemed to really help somebody get past the stuck spot they were in of being sick and not being able to be helped, being in that all-alone space. Get them stoned and they got past that.

Deborah Silverknight, a fifty-one-year-old African American/Native American woman with chronic pain from a broken back, notes that this association between marijuana and a sense of enhanced well-being is an old one:

> My great-grandmother referred to marijuana as the "mother plant"—the one you smoke that helps you medicinally and spiritually. Marijuana is a meditative thing for me. It's not only about the physical pain, but relief of pain of the spirit. If I'm having a terrible back spasm, then it's mostly about the need for physical pain relief. But even then, it has that other dimension as well.

The psychospiritual effects of marijuana were frequently remarked upon by WAMM members who reported that the consciousness-altering properties of marijuana were a necessary component of its therapeutic value. Altered consciousness enhances physical symptom relief by helping them to deal with situational depression associated with chronic pain and illness.

"Barb," a forty-five-year-old white woman with post-polio syndrome, observes:

> When I get a pain flair, I smoke and it helps to relieve the pain and relieve the spasms but it also means I don't get as depressed. My attitude is more like, "oh, okay, I'm going to be in pain today, but I'm going to enjoy what I can enjoy and get through the day." Marijuana never fails to lift my mood. I smoke and think "okay, I'm just going to have to go with the pain today. It's beautiful outside and I'm going to go tool around the garden in my chair." It takes you to another level mentally of acceptance about being in this kind of pain. So when I'm in that "I can't handle this another minute stage," it produces a positive shift and I can go on to something else. The other drugs I'm prescribed have such major side effects, but if I smoke a joint, the biggest side effect is a mental lift. And that's a side effect I can live with.

"Hal," the seventy-year-old living with severe neuropathy, notes:

> When you are in constant pain, your focus is 100% on yourself: I can't move this way, I can't twist this way, I can't put my foot down that way. That kind of thing. It's terrible.
>
> I'd never been one who was self-absorbed to the extent that I would forget about other things. I became that way [because of the pain]. I don't know how my wife could stand it. But, I find at this point [with the marijuana], I am in a sense witnessing my pain; what's happened as a result is that I am no longer so absorbed in my pain. I can rise above it, and then I'm able to do whatever I have to do.

One common objection in antidrug literature to the "high" associated with psychoactive drug use is that it offers only a "distortion" or "escape" from reality. The implication is that escape is somehow unworthy or undesirable, and the "alternative reality" accessed through drugs is illegitimate. But, in the context of chronic pain or terminal illness, one might question whether, in the words of Lily Tomlin, reality isn't "greatly overrated."

Pamela Cutler, a thirty-eight-year-old white woman in the final stages of living with metastatic breast cancer, observes:

> Marijuana kind of helps dull the reality of this situation. And anyone who says it's not a tough reality . . . I mean your mind will barely even take it in. It does dull it, and I don't think there is anything wrong with that if I want to dull it. That's fine . . . was diagnosed with breast cancer and had a radical mastectomy . . . the whole thing was a big shock. I mean I was thirty-six. I was like, "What?" And ever since then it's been like a roller coaster: okay, it's spread to your bones, and then it's spread to my lungs, and then my liver . . . [Marijuana] makes it easier to take for me. It doesn't really take it away. It just dulls the sharpness of it— like "oh my god, I'm going to be dead." I just think that's just incredible.

Although most of the individuals I interviewed commented on the therapeutic value of the psychoactive properties of marijuana, a number were careful to make a distinction between the psychoactive effect of marijuana when used medicinally and the effects when used recreationally. For many of them, the contrast between "getting loaded for fun" and medicinal use was described as profound. In part, this difference may be a question of, as Norman Zinberg (1984) has phrased it, the effects of "set" (the user's mindset) and "setting" (the context in which the drug is taken). A substance taken in expectation of pleasurable intoxication by a healthy individual may produce a substantially different effect from that experienced by an individual living with a life-threatening illness or in chronic pain.

"Kurt," the forty-two-year-old white man living with AIDS, notes:

> I used to smoke recreationally, but it became a whole different thing when I became HIV positive and needed it as a medicinal thing. I had never had a life-threatening disease, and now I was watching everyone die in front of me. It wasn't just getting high anymore; it let me think about why I am still here after they are all gone.

Some individuals suggested that the different experience of marijuana when used medicinally was less about changed context and more about simple drug habituation. "Cheri," a fifty-two-year-old white woman with chronic pain and seizure disorder, reports:

I have to use marijuana every day to deal with pain. . . . I feel like I'm so habituated that it really doesn't do that much to my mood anymore or at least it's hard to tell. . . . It was more fun being a big pothead than it is being a medical user, for me. You get higher when you are a recreational user. Anytime you use something every day, your system almost naturalizes it. And frankly, I do not really feel stoned anymore unless I smoke because I am so habituated to eating it. And when I smoke, I remember how wonderful it was when marijuana actually got you high. It's like any drug; your body gets habituated.

Hal too reports a diminishing "high" as he became more accustomed to the drug:

After a couple of months, I found that I wasn't getting high as much as I was getting calm. It took a couple of months though. At first, I'd smoke and get really high and have a wonderful afternoon or evening or whatever. But then it started to change and I just got calm.

Hal's shift from "high" to "calm" may be the result not only of biochemical tolerance but also the effect of increased familiarity with the altered state so that it becomes the quotidian reality rather than the "alter."

Interview subjects who had a history of drug abuse and recovery were especially insistent on making a clear distinction between a recreational "high" and the effects of medicinal marijuana use. By drawing a clear line between "getting loaded" and "taking medicine," these individuals were able to maintain their sense of sobriety while using cannabis therapeutically. Inocencio Manjon-McFaline, a fifty-four-year-old African American/Latino man with cancer and a former cocaine addict who got sober in 1998, described the difference like this:

What's strange now is that I don't feel the effects [from marijuana] that I remember from when I would smoke it before, smoking to get loaded. It's a different time for me. I'm not smoking it looking for a high. Maybe it's just psychologically different knowing I'm smoking it for medicinal use. But I haven't felt loaded. I smoke only for the pain. It gets me out of there, out of that frame of mind. I'll smoke and I'll tend to focus on what I want to focus on. Generally, that's my breathing and my heartbeat. And I'll get really into plants. I just really get into that and forget about pain . . . . Every breath I take is a blessing. I don't fear death, but I don't look forward to it. I really treasure life.

Inocencio's comments raise an important question about what it means to get "high." Clearly he is no longer looking to "get loaded" and argues that he no longer gets "high." Yet, his description of his medicinal use suggests that the marijuana assists him not only in dealing with pain and nausea but also in "focusing" on his breath, on his heartbeat, on the blessings of being alive. This state may seem more "altered" when there are more conventional demands on one's time than when one is in a state of dying. The present-tense focus, which is an aspect of getting "high" that is often commented on, matches the needs of the end-of-life process and therefore may not feel "altering" but rather "confirming" or "enhancing."

Qualities associated with the psychoactive effects of cannabis—such as present-tense focus, mood elevation, and a deepened appreciation of the "minor miracles" of life—may be especially usefully enhanced in the face of anxiety over death or chronic pain. Given anti-drug rhetoric in our culture, it is not surprising that some medical marijuana patients may downplay the psychoactive effects of cannabis use. And certainly some medical marijuana users may become habituated to the effects of the THC and to the altered or enhanced state to which it provides access. But "habituation," "tolerance," or "familiarity" are not synonymous with "no effect." For those living with chronic pain, terminal illness, or both, the psychotherapeutic and metaphysical effects of marijuana may complement the mindset and setting in which the substance is used. As these accounts suggest, although medical marijuana use is most certainly not just about getting "loaded" in any conventional recreational sense, its therapeutic value may be strongly tied to the psychoactive properties of *the plant* (rather than "of canna- bis"). This suggestion has significant implica- tions for both the practice of medicine and the transformation of public policy.

REFERENCES

Stein, J. (2002, November 4). The new politics of pot. *Time*. Retrieved March 4, 2005, from http://www.time.com/time/archive/preview/ 0,10987,1101021104-384830,00.html
Webb, M. (1999). *The good death*. New York: Bantam.
Zinberg, N. (1984). *Drug, set, and setting*. New Haven, CT: Yale University Press.

THINKING ABOUT THE READING

People who routinely use marijuana are often considered socially deviant. How is this social conception of deviance applied to people who use marijuana for medical purposes? How do common conceptions of deviance affect the availability of medical marijuana? What are some of the strategies that health care providers and users of medical marijuana use to reduce the stigma? What are the factors that determine why some drugs are considered medicinal (and therefore legal) and others considered recreational (and therefore illegal)? Can you think of other types of activities that may be considered beneficial in one social situation and deviant in another?

PART III

Social Structure, Institutions, and Everyday Life

The Structure of Society

Organizations and Social Institutions

9

One of the great sociological paradoxes is that we live in a society that so fiercely extols the virtues of rugged individualism and personal accomplishment, yet we spend most of our lives responding to the influence of larger organizations and social institutions. These include both nurturing organizations, such as churches and schools, and larger, more impersonal bureaucratic institutions.

No matter how powerful and influential they are, organizations are more than structures, rules, policies, goals, job descriptions, and standard operating procedures. Each organization, and each division within an organization, develops its own norms, values, and language. This is usually referred to as organizational culture. Organizational cultures are pervasive and entrenched, yet, even so, individuals often find ways to exert some control over their lives within the confines of these organizations. Accordingly, organizations are dynamic entities in which individuals struggle for personal freedom and expression while also existing under the rules and procedures that make up the organization. Given this dynamic activity, an organization is rarely what it appears to be on the surface.

For example, many people are unaware of, and unconcerned with, the harsh conditions under which our most coveted products are made. William Greider, in "These Dark Satanic Mills," discusses the exploitative potential of relying on "third world" factories. He uses a particular tragedy, the 1993 industrial fire at the Kader Industrial Toy Company in Thailand, to illustrate how global economics create and sustain international inequality. Greider shows us the complex paradox of the global marketplace: Although foreign manufacturing facilities free factory workers from certain poverty, they also ensnare the workers in new and sometimes lethal forms of domination.

In "The Smile Factory," John Van Maanen examines the organizational culture of Disney theme parks. He finds that Disneyland and Disney World have a highly codified and strict set of conduct standards. Variations on tightly defined employee conduct is not tolerated. Van Maanen discovers that beneath the surface of the "happiest place on earth" lies a mosaic of distinct status groups with firm boundaries dividing them.

In her article "Cool Stores, Bad Jobs," Yasemin Besen-Cassino looks at the ways in which corporations like Starbucks and Banana Republic attract young people into low-wage, no-benefit jobs through the allure of working in trendy environments. These chains target affluent young people and market the jobs as fashionable and desirable.

Something to Consider as You Read

As you read these selections, think about a job you've had and the new procedures you had to learn when you started. Was the job just about the procedures, or did you also have to learn new (and perhaps informal) cultural norms? Think about some of the ways in which the organizational environment induces you to behave in ways that are very specific to that situation. As you read, compare some of these organizational environments to the ones discussed in this chapter. How might other social institutions such as sports and religion shape behavior and beliefs?

These Dark Satanic Mills

William Greider

(1997)

... If the question were put now to everyone, everywhere—do you wish to become a citizen of the world?—it is safe to assume that most people in most places would answer, no, they wish to remain who they are. With very few exceptions, people think of themselves as belonging to a place, a citizen of France or Malaysia, of Boston or Tokyo or Warsaw, loyally bound to native culture, sovereign nation. The Chinese who aspire to get gloriously rich, as Deng instructed, do not intend to become Japanese or Americans. Americans may like to think of themselves as the world's leader, but not as citizens of "one world."

The deepest social meaning of the global industrial revolution is that people no longer have free choice in this matter of identity. Ready or not, they are already of the world. As producers or consumers, as workers or merchants or investors, they are now bound to distant others through the complex strands of commerce and finance reorganizing the globe as a unified marketplace. The prosperity of South Carolina or Scotland is deeply linked to Stuttgart's or Kuala Lumpur's. The true social values of Californians or Swedes will be determined by what is tolerated in the factories of Thailand or Bangladesh. The energies and brutalities of China will influence community anxieties in Seattle or Toulouse or Nagoya.

... Unless one intends to withdraw from modern industrial life, there is no place to hide from the others. Major portions of the earth, to be sure, remain on the periphery of the system, impoverished bystanders still waiting to be included in the action. But the patterns of global interconnectedness are already the dominant reality. Commerce has leapt beyond social consciousness and, in doing so, opened up challenging new vistas for the human potential. Most people, it seems fair to say, are not yet prepared to face the implications ....

Two centuries ago, when the English industrial revolution dawned with its fantastic invention and productive energies, the prophetic poet William Blake drew back in moral revulsion. Amid the explosion of new wealth, human destruction was spread over England—peasant families displaced from their lands, paupers and poorhouses crowded into London slums, children sent to labor at the belching ironworks or textile looms. Blake delivered a thunderous rebuke to the pious Christians of the English aristocracy with these immortal lines:

> And was Jerusalem builded here
> Among these dark Satanic mills?

Blake's "dark Satanic mills" have returned now and are flourishing again, accompanied by the same question.[1]

On May 10, 1993, the worst industrial fire in the history of capitalism occurred at a toy factory on the outskirts of Bangkok and was reported on page 25 of the *Washington Post*. The *Financial Times* of London, which styles itself as the daily newspaper of the global economy, ran a brief item on page 6. The *Wall Street Journal* followed a day late with an account on page 11. The *New York Times* also put the story inside, but printed a dramatic photo on its front page: rows of small shrouded bodies on bamboo pallets—dozens of them—lined along the damp pavement, while dazed rescue workers stood awkwardly among the corpses. In the background, one could see the collapsed, smoldering structure of a mammoth factory where the Kader Industrial Toy Company of Thailand had employed three thousand workers manufacturing stuffed toys and plastic dolls, playthings destined for American children.[2]

The official count was 188 dead, 469 injured, but the actual toll was undoubtedly higher since the four-story buildings had collapsed swiftly in the intense heat and many bodies were incinerated. Some of the missing were never found; others fled home to their villages. All but fourteen of the dead were women, most of them young, some as young as thirteen years old. Hundreds of the workers had been trapped on upper floors of the burning building, forced to jump from third- or fourth-floor windows, since the main exit doors were kept locked by the managers, and the narrow stairways became clotted with trampled bodies or collapsed.

When I visited Bangkok about nine months later, physical evidence of the disaster was gone—the site scraped clean by bulldozers—and Kader was already resuming production at a new toy factory, built far from the city in a rural province of northeastern Thailand. When I talked with Thai labor leaders and civic activists, people who had rallied to the cause of the fire victims, some of them were under the impression that a worldwide boycott of Kader products was under way, organized by conscience-stricken Americans and Europeans. I had to inform them that the civilized world had barely noticed their tragedy.

As news accounts pointed out, the Kader fire surpassed what was previously the worst industrial fire in history—the Triangle Shirtwaist Company fire of 1911—when 146 young immigrant women died in similar circumstances at a garment factory on the Lower East Side of Manhattan. The Triangle Shirtwaist fire became a pivotal event in American politics, a public scandal that provoked citizen reform movements and energized the labor organizing that built the International Ladies Garment Workers Union and other unions. The fire in Thailand did not produce meaningful political responses or even shame among consumers.

The indifference of the leading newspapers merely reflected the tastes of their readers, who might be moved by human suffering in their own communities but were inured to news of recurring calamities in distant places. A fire in Bangkok was like a typhoon in Bangladesh, an earthquake in Turkey.

The Kader fire might have been more meaningful for Americans if they could have seen the thousands of soot-stained dolls that spilled from the wreckage, macabre litter scattered among the dead. Bugs Bunny, Bart Simpson and the Muppets. Big Bird and other *Sesame Street* dolls. Playskool "Water Pets." Santa Claus. What the initial news accounts did not mention was that Kader's Thai factory produced most of its toys for American companies—Toys "R" Us, Fisher-Price, Hasbro, Tyco, Arco, Kenner, Gund and J. C. Penney—as well as stuffed dolls, slippers and souvenirs for Europe.[3]

Globalized civilization has uncovered an odd parochialism in the American character: Americans worried obsessively over the everyday safety of their children, and the U.S. government's regulators diligently policed the design of toys to avoid injury to young innocents. Yet neither citizens nor government took any interest in the brutal and dangerous conditions imposed on the people who manufactured those same toys, many of whom were mere adolescent children themselves. Indeed, the government position, both in Washington and Bangkok, assumed that there was no social obligation connecting consumers with workers, at least none that governments could enforce without disrupting free trade or invading the sovereignty of other nations.

The toy industry, not surprisingly, felt the same. Hasbro Industries, maker of Playskool, subsequently told the *Boston Globe* that it would no longer do business with Kader, but, in general, the U.S. companies shrugged off responsibility. Kader, a major toy manufacturer based in Hong Kong, "is extremely reputable, not sleaze bags," David Miller, president of the Toy Manufacturers of America, assured *USA Today*. "The responsibility for those factories,"

Miller told ABC News, "is in the hands of those who are there and managing the factory."[4]

The grisly details of what occurred revealed the casual irresponsibility of both companies and governments. The Kader factory compound consisted of four interconnected, four-story industrial barns on a three-acre lot on Buddhamondhol VI Road in the Sampran district west of Bangkok. It was one among Thailand's thriving new industrial zones for garments, textiles, electronics and toys. More than 50,000 people, most of them migrants from the Thai countryside, worked in the district at 7,500 large and small firms. Thailand's economic boom was based on places such as this, and Bangkok was almost choking on its own fantastic growth, dizzily erecting luxury hotels and office towers.

The fire started late on a Monday afternoon on the ground floor in the first building and spread rapidly upward, jumping to two adjoining buildings, all three of which swiftly collapsed. Investigators noted afterwards that the structures had been cheaply built, without concrete reinforcement, so steel girders and stairways crumpled easily in the heat. Thai law required that in such a large factory, fire-escape stairways must be sixteen to thirty-three feet wide, but Kader's were a mere four and a half feet. Main doors were locked and many windows barred to prevent pilfering by the employees. Flammable raw materials—fabric, stuffing, animal fibers—were stacked everywhere, on walkways and next to electrical boxes. Neither safety drills nor fire alarms and sprinkler systems had been provided.

Let Some of the Survivors Describe What Happened

A young woman named Lampan Taptim: "There was the sound of yelling about a fire. I tried to leave the section but my supervisor told me to get back to work. My sister who worked on the fourth floor with me pulled me away and insisted we try to get out. We tried to go down the stairs and got to the second floor; we found

that the stairs had already caved in. There was a lot of yelling and confusion. . . . In desperation, I went back up to the windows and went back and forth, looking down below. The smoke was thick and I picked the best place to jump in a pile of boxes. My sister jumped, too. She died."

A young woman named Cheng: "There is no way out [people were shouting], the security guard has locked the main door out! It was horrifying. I thought I would die. I took off my gold ring and kept it in my pocket and put on my name tag so that my body could be identifiable. I had to decide to die in the fire or from jumping down from a three stories' height." As the walls collapsed around her, Cheng clung to a pipe and fell downward with it, landing on a pile of dead bodies, injured but alive.

An older woman named La-iad Nadsnguen: "Four or five pregnant women jumped before me. They died before my eyes." Her own daughter jumped from the top floor and broke both hips.

Chauweewan Mekpan, who was five months pregnant: "I thought that if I jumped, at least my parents would see my remains, but if I stayed, nothing would be left of me." Though her back was severely injured, she and her unborn child miraculously survived.

An older textile worker named Vilaiwa Satieti, who sewed shirts and pants at a neighboring factory, described to me the carnage she encountered: "I got off work about five and passed by Kader and saw many dead bodies lying around, uncovered. Some of them I knew. I tried to help the workers who had jumped from the factory. They had broken legs and broken arms and broken heads. We tried to keep them alive until they got to the hospital, that's all you could do. Oh, they were teenagers, fifteen to twenty years, no more than that, and so many of them, so many."

This was not the first serious fire at Kader's factory, but the third or fourth. "I heard somebody yelling 'fire, fire,'" Tumthong Podhirun testified, "... but I did not take it seriously because it has happened before. Soon I smelled smoke and very quickly it billowed inside the place. I headed for the back door but it was locked. . . . Finally, I had no choice but to join the others and jumped out of the window. I saw many of my friends lying dead on the ground beside me."[5]

In the aftermath of the tragedy, some Bangkok activists circulated an old snapshot of two smiling peasant girls standing arm in arm beside a thicket of palm trees. One of them, Praphai Prayonghorm, died in the 1993 fire at Kader. Her friend, Kammoin Konmanee, had died in the 1989 fire. Some of the Kader workers insisted afterwards that their factory had been haunted by ghosts, that it was built on the site of an old graveyard, disturbing the dead. The folklore expressed raw poetic truth: the fire in Bangkok eerily resembled the now-forgotten details of the Triangle Shirtwaist disaster eighty years before. Perhaps the "ghosts" that some workers felt present were young women from New York who had died in 1911.

Similar tragedies, large and small, were now commonplace across developing Asia and elsewhere. Two months after Kader, another fire at a Bangkok shirt factory killed ten women. Three months after Kader, a six-story hotel collapsed and killed 133 people, injuring 351. The embarrassed minister of industry ordered special inspections of 244 large factories in the Bangkok region and found that 60 percent of them had basic violations similar to Kader's. Thai industry was growing explosively—12 to 15 percent a year—but workplace injuries and illnesses were growing even faster, from 37,000 victims in 1987 to more than 150,000 by 1992 and an estimated 200,000 by 1994.

In China, six months after Kader, eighty-four women died and dozens of others were severely burned at another toy factory fire in the burgeoning industrial zone at Shenzhen. At Dongguan, a Hong Kong–owned raincoat factory burned in 1991, killing more than eighty people (Kader Industries also had a factory at Dongguan where two fires have been reported since 1990). In late 1993, some sixty women died at the Taiwanese-owned Gaofu textile plant in Fuzhou Province, many of them smothered in their dormitory beds by toxic fumes from burning textiles. In 1994, a shoe factory fire killed ten persons at Jiangmen; a textile factory fire killed thirty-eight and injured 160 at the Qianshan industrial zone.[6]

"Why must these tragedies repeat themselves again and again?" the *People's Daily* in Beijing asked. The official *Economic Daily* complained: "The way some of these foreign investors ignore international practice, ignore our own national rules, act completely lawlessly and immorally and lust after wealth is enough to make one's hair stand on end."[7]

America was itself no longer insulated from such brutalities. When a chicken-processing factory at Hamlet, North Carolina, caught fire in 1991, the exit doors there were also locked and twenty-five people died. A garment factory discovered by labor investigators in El Monte, California, held seventy-two Thai immigrants in virtual peonage, working eighteen hours a day in "sub-human conditions." One could not lament the deaths, harsh working conditions, child labor and subminimum wages in Thailand or across Asia and Central America without also recognizing that similar conditions have reappeared in the United States for roughly the same reasons.

Sweatshops, mainly in the garment industry, scandalized Los Angeles, New York and Dallas. The grim, foul assembly lines of the poultry-processing industry were spread across the rural South; the *Wall Street Journal's* Tony Horwitz won a Pulitzer Prize for his harrowing description of this low-wage work. "In general," the U.S. Government Accounting Office reported in 1994, "the description of today's sweatshops differs little from that at the turn of the century."[8]

That was the real mystery: Why did global commerce, with all of its supposed modernity and wondrous technologies, restore the old barbarisms that had long ago been forbidden by law? If the information age has enabled multinational corporations to manage production and marketing spread across continents, why were their managers unable—or unwilling—to organize such mundane matters as fire prevention?

The short answer, of course, was profits, but the deeper answer was about power: Firms behaved this way because they could, because nobody would stop them. When law and social values retreated before the power of markets, then capitalism's natural drive to maximize returns had no internal governor to check its social behavior. When one enterprise took the low road to gain advantage, others would follow.

The toy fire in Bangkok provided a dramatic illustration for the much broader, less visible forms of human exploitation that were flourishing in the global system, including the widespread use of children in manufacturing, even forced labor camps in China or Burma. These matters were not a buried secret. Indeed, American television has aggressively exposed the "dark Satanic mills" with dramatic reports. ABC's *20/20* broadcast correspondent Lynn Sherr's devastating account of the Kader fire; CNN ran disturbing footage. Mike Wallace of CBS's *60 Minutes* exposed the prison labor exploited in China. NBC's *Dateline* did a piece on Wal-Mart's grim production in Bangladesh. CBS's *Street Stories* toured the shoe factories of Indonesia.

The baffling quality about modern communications was that its images could take us to people in remote corners of the world vividly and instantly, but these images have not as yet created genuine community with them. In terms of human consciousness, the "global village" was still only a picture on the TV screen.

Public opinion, moreover, absorbed contradictory messages about the global reality that were difficult to sort out. The opening stages of industrialization presented, as always, a great paradox: the process was profoundly liberating for millions, freeing them from material scarcity and limited life choices, while it also ensnared other millions in brutal new forms of domination. Both aspects were true, but there was no scale on which these opposing consequences could be easily balanced, since the good and ill effects were not usually apportioned among the same people. Some human beings were set free, while other lives were turned into cheap and expendable commodities.

Workers at Kader, for instance, earned about 100 baht a day for sewing and assembling

dolls, the official minimum wage of $4, but the constant stream of new entrants meant that many at the factory actually worked for much less—only $2 or $3 a day—during a required "probationary" period of three to six months that was often extended much longer by the managers. Only one hundred of the three thousand workers at Kader were legally designated employees; the rest were "contract workers" without permanent rights and benefits, the same employment system now popularized in the United States.

"Lint, fabric, dust and animal hair filled the air on the production floor," the International Confederation of Free Trade Unions based in Brussels observed in its investigative report. "Noise, heat, congestion and fumes from various sources were reported by many. Dust control was nonexistent; protective equipment inadequate. Inhaling the dust created respiratory problems and contact with it caused skin diseases." A factory clinic dispensed antihistamines or other drugs and referred the more serious symptoms to outside hospitals. Workers paid for the medication themselves and were reimbursed, up to $6, only if they had contributed 10 baht a month to the company's health fund.

A common response to such facts, even from many sensitive people, was: yes, that was terrible, but wouldn't those workers be even worse off if civil standards were imposed on their employers since they might lose their jobs as a result? This was the same economic rationale offered by American manufacturers a century before to explain why American children must work in the coal mines and textile mills. U.S. industry had survived somehow (and, in fact, flourished) when child labor and the other malpractices were eventually prohibited by social reforms. Furthermore, it was not coincidence that industry always assigned the harshest conditions and lowest pay to the weakest members of a society—women, children, uprooted migrants. Whether the factory was in Thailand or the United States or Mexico's *maquiladora* zone, people who were already quite powerless were less likely to resist, less able to demand decency from their employers . . . .

After the fire Thai union members, intellectuals and middle-class activists from social rights organizations (the groups known in developing countries as nongovernmental organizations, or NGOs) formed the Committee to Support Kader Workers and began demanding justice from the employer. They sent a delegation to Hong Kong to confront Kader officials and investigate the complex corporate linkages of the enterprise. What they discovered was that Kader's partner in the Bangkok toy factory was actually a fabulously wealthy Thai family, the Chearavanonts, ethnic Chinese merchants who own the Charoen Pokphand Group, Thailand's own leading multinational corporation.

The CP Group owns farms, feed mills, real estate, air-conditioning and motorcycle factories, food-franchise chains—two hundred companies worldwide, several of them listed on the New York Stock Exchange. The patriarch and chairman, Dhanin Chearavanont, was said by *Fortune* magazine to be the seventy-fifth richest man in the world, with personal assets of $2.6 billion (or 65 billion baht, as the *Bangkok Post* put it). Like the other emerging "Chinese multinationals," the Pokphand Group operates through the informal networks of kinfolk and ethnic contacts spread around the world by the Chinese diaspora, while it also participates in the more rigorous accounting systems of Western economies . . . .

In the larger context, this tragedy was not explained by the arrogant power of one wealthy family or the elusive complexities of interlocking corporations. The Kader fire was ordained and organized by the free market itself. The toy industry—much like textiles and garments, shoes, electronics assembly and other low-wage sectors—existed (and thrived) by exploiting a crude ladder of desperate competition among the poorest nations. Its factories regularly hopped to new locations where wages were even lower, where the governments would be even more tolerant of abusive practices. The contract work assigned to foreign firms, including thousands of small sweatshops, fitted neatly into the systems of far-flung production of major brand names and distanced the capital owners from personal responsibility. The "virtual corporation" celebrated by some business futurists already existed in these sectors and, indeed, was now being emulated in some ways by advanced manufacturing—cars, aircraft, computers.

Over the last generation, toy manufacturers and others have moved around the Asian rim in search of the bottom-rung conditions: from Hong Kong, Korea and Taiwan to Thailand and Indonesia, from there to China, Vietnam and Bangladesh, perhaps on next to Burma, Nepal or Cambodia. Since the world had a nearly inexhaustible supply of poor people and supplicant governments, the market would keep driving in search of lower rungs; no one could say where the bottom was located. Industrial conditions were not getting better, as conventional theory assured the innocent consumers, but in many sectors were getting much worse. In America, the U.S. diplomatic opening to Vietnam was celebrated as progressive politics. In Southeast Asia, it merely opened another trapdoor beneath wages and working conditions.

A country like Thailand was caught in the middle: if it conscientiously tried to improve, it would pay a huge price. When Thai unions lobbied to win improvements in minimum-wage standards, textile plants began leaving for Vietnam and elsewhere or even importing cheaper "guest workers" from Burma. When China opened its fast-growing industrial zones in Shenzhen, Dongguan and other locations, the new competition had direct consequences on the factory floors of Bangkok.

Kader, according to the ICFTU, opened two new factories in Shekou and Dongguan where young people were working fourteen-hour days, seven days a week, to fill the U.S. Christmas orders for Mickey Mouse and other American dolls. Why should a company worry about sprinkler systems or fire escapes for a dusty factory in Bangkok when it could hire brand-new workers in China for only $20 a month, one fifth of the labor cost in Thailand?

The ICFTU report described the market forces: "The lower cost of production of toys in China changes the investment climate for countries like Thailand. Thailand competes with China to attract investment capital for local toy production. With this development, Thailand has become sadly lax in enforcing its own legislation. It turns a blind eye to health violations, thus allowing factory owners to ignore safety standards. Since China entered the picture, accidents in Thailand have nearly tripled."

The Thai minister of industry, Sanan Kachornprasart, described the market reality more succinctly: "If we punish them, who will want to invest here?" Thai authorities subsequently filed charges against three Kader factory managers, but none against the company itself nor, of course, the Chearavanont family.[9]

... The fire in Bangkok reflected the amorality of the marketplace when it has been freed of social obligations. But the tragedy also mocked the moral claims of three great religions, whose adherents were all implicated. Thais built splendid golden temples exalting Buddha, who taught them to put spiritual being before material wealth. Chinese claimed to have acquired superior social values, reverence for family and community, derived from the teachings of Confucius. Americans bought the toys from Asia to celebrate the birth of Jesus Christ. Their shared complicity was another of the strange convergences made possible by global commerce ....

In the modern industrial world, only the ignorant can pretend to self-righteousness since only the primitive are truly innocent. No advanced society has reached that lofty stage without enduring barbaric consequences and despoliation along the way; no one who enjoys the uses of electricity or the internal combustion engine may claim to oppose industrialization for others without indulging in imperious hypocrisy.

Americans, one may recall, built their early national infrastructure and organized large-scale agriculture with slave labor. The developing American nation swept native populations from their ancient lands and drained the swampy prairies to grow grain. It burned forests to make farmland, decimated wildlife, dammed the wild rivers and displaced people who were in the way. It assigned the dirtiest, most dangerous work to immigrants and children. It eventually granted political rights to all, but grudgingly and only after great conflicts, including a terrible civil war.

The actual history of nations is useful to remember when trying to form judgments about the new world. Asian leaders regularly remind Americans and Europeans of exactly how the richest nation-states became wealthy and observe further that, despite their great wealth, those countries have not perfected social relations among rich and poor, weak and powerful. The maldistribution of incomes is worsening in America, too, not yet as extreme as Thailand's, but worse than many less fortunate nations ....

Coming to terms with one's own history ought not only to induce a degree of humility toward others and their struggles, but also to clarify what one really believes about human society. No one can undo the past, but that does not relieve people of the burden of making judgments about the living present or facing up to its moral implications. If the global system has truly created a unified marketplace, then every worker, every consumer, every society is already connected to the other. The responsibility exists and invoking history is not an excuse to hide from the new social questions.

Just as Americans cannot claim a higher morality while benefiting from inhumane exploitation, neither can developing countries pretend to become modern "one world" producers and expect exemption from the world's social values. Neither can the global enterprises. The future asks: Can capitalism itself be altered and reformed? Or is the world doomed to keep renewing these inhumanities in the name of economic progress?

The proposition that human dignity is indivisible does not suppose that everyone will become equal or alike or perfectly content in his or her circumstances. It does insist that certain well-understood social principles exist internationally which are enforceable and ought to be the price of admission in the global system. The idea is very simple: every person—man, woman and child—regardless of where he or she exists in time and place or on the chain of economic development, is entitled to respect as an individual being.

For many in the world, life itself is all that they possess; an economic program that deprives them of life's precious possibilities is not only unjust, but also utterly unnecessary. Peasants may not become kings, but they are entitled to be treated with decent regard for their sentient and moral beings, not as cheap commodities. Newly industrialized nations cannot change social patterns overnight, any more than the advanced economies did before them, but they can demonstrate that they are changing.

This proposition is invasive, no question, and will disturb the economic and political arrangements within many societies. But every nation has a sovereign choice in this matter, the sort of choice made in the marketplace every day. If Thailand or China resents the intrusion of global social standards, it does not have to sell its toys to America. And Americans do not have to buy them. If Singapore rejects the idea of basic rights for women, then women in America or Europe may reject Singapore—and multinational firms that profit from the subordination of women. If people do not assert these values in global trade, then their own convictions will be steadily coarsened.

In Bangkok, when I asked Professor Voravidh to step back from Thailand's problems and suggest a broader remedy, he thought for a long time and then said: "We need cooperation among nations because the multinational corporations can shift from one country to another. If they don't like Thailand, they move to Vietnam or China. Right now, we are all competing and the world is getting worse. We need a GATT on labor conditions and on the minimum wage, we need a standard on the minimum conditions for work and a higher standard for children."

The most direct approach, as Voravidh suggested, is an international agreement to incorporate such standards in the terms of trade, with penalties and incentives, even temporary embargoes, that will impose social obligations on the global system, the firms and countries. Most of the leading governments, including the United States, have long claimed to support this idea—a so-called social clause for GATT—but the practical reality is that they do not. Aside from rhetoric, when their negotiators are at the table, they always yield readily to objections from the multinational corporations and developing nations. Both the firms and the governing elites of poor countries have a strong incentive to block the proposition since both profit from a free-running system that exploits the weak. A countering force has to come from concerned citizens. Governments refuse to act, but voters and consumers are not impotent, and, in the meantime, they can begin the political campaign by purposefully targeting the producers—boycotting especially the well-known brand names that depend upon lovable images for their sales. Americans will not stop buying toys at Christmas, but they might single out one or two American toy companies for Yuletide boycotts, based on their scandalous relations with Kader and other manufacturers. Boycotts are difficult to organize and sustain, but every one of the consumer-goods companies is exquisitely vulnerable.

In India, the South Asian Coalition on Child Servitude, led by Kailash Satyarthi, has created a promising model for how to connect the social obligations of consumers and workers. Indian carpet makers are notorious for using small children at their looms—bonded children like Thailand's bonded prostitutes—and have always claimed economic necessity. India is a poor nation and the work gives wage income to extremely poor families, they insist. But these children will never escape poverty if they are deprived of schooling, the compulsory education promised by law.

The reformers created a "no child labor" label that certifies the rugs were made under honorable conditions and they persuaded major importers in Germany to insist upon the label. The exporters in India, in turn, have to allow regular citizen inspections of their workplaces to win the label for their rugs. Since this consumer-led certification system began, the carpet industry's use of children has fallen dramatically. A Textile Ministry official in New Delhi said: "The government is now contemplating the total eradication of child labor in the next few years."[10]

Toys, shoes, electronics, garments—many consumer sectors are vulnerable to similar approaches, though obviously the scope of manufacturing is too diverse and complex for consumers to police it. Governments have to act collectively. If a worldwide agreement is impossible to achieve, then groups of governments can form their own preferential trading systems, introducing social standards that reverse the incentives for developing countries and for capital choosing new locations for production.

The crucial point illustrated by Thailand's predicament is that global social standards will help the poorer countries escape their economic trap. Until a floor is built beneath the market's social behavior, there is no way that a small developing country like Thailand can hope to overcome the downward pull of competition from other, poorer nations. It must debase its citizens to hold on to what it has achieved. The path to improvement is blocked by the economics of an irresponsible marketplace.

Setting standards will undoubtedly slow down the easy movement of capital—and close down the most scandalous operations—but that is not a harmful consequence for people in struggling nations that aspire to industrial prosperity or for a global economy burdened with surpluses and inadequate consumption. When global capital makes a commitment to a developing economy, it ought not to acquire the power to blackmail that nation in perpetuity. Supported by global rules, those nations can begin to improve conditions and stabilize their own social development. At least they would have a chance to avoid the great class conflicts that others have experienced.

In the meantime, the very least that citizens can demand of their own government is that it no longer use public money to finance the brutal upheavals or environmental despoliation that has flowed from large-scale projects of the World Bank and other lending agencies. The social distress in the cities begins in the countryside, and the wealthy nations have often financed it in the name of aiding development. The World Bank repeatedly proclaims its new commitment to strategies that address the development ideas of indigenous peoples and halt the destruction of natural systems. But social critics and the people I encountered in Thailand and elsewhere have not seen much evidence of real change.

The terms of trade are usually thought of as commercial agreements, but they are also an implicit statement of moral values. In its present terms, the global system values property over human life. When a nation like China steals the property of capital, pirating copyrights, films or technology, other governments will take action to stop it and be willing to impose sanctions and penalty tariffs on the offending nation's trade. When human lives are stolen in the "dark Satanic mills," nothing happens to the offenders since, according to the free market's sense of conscience, there is no crime.

Notes

1. William Blake's immortal lines are from "Milton," one of his "prophetic books" written between 1804 and 1808. *The Portable Blake,* Alfred Kazin, editor (New York: Penguin Books, 1976).

2. *Washington Post, Financial Times* and *New York Times,* May 12, 1993, and *Wall Street Journal,* May 13, 1993.

3. The U.S. contract clients for Kader's Bangkok factory were cited by the International Confederation of Free Trade Unions headquartered in Brussels in its investigatory report, "From the Ashes: A Toy Factory Fire in Thailand," December 1994. In the aftermath, the ICFTU and some nongovernmental organizations attempted to mount an "international toy campaign" and a few sporadic demonstrations occurred in Hong Kong and London, but there never was a general boycott of the industry or any of its individual companies. The labor federation met with associations of British and American toy manufacturers and urged them to adopt a "code of conduct" that might discourage

the abuses. The proposed codes were inadequate, the ICFTU acknowledged, but it was optimistic about their general adoption by the international industry.

4. Mitchell Zuckoff of the *Boston Globe* produced a powerful series of stories on labor conditions in developing Asia and reported Hasbro's reaction to the Kader fire, July 10, 1994. David Miller was quoted in *USA Today,* May 13, 1993, and on ABC News *20/20,* July 30, 1993.

5. The first-person descriptions of the Kader fire are but a small sampling from survivors' horrifying accounts, collected by investigators and reporters at the scene. My account of the disaster is especially indebted to the investigative report by the International Confederation of Free Trade Unions; Bangkok's English-language newspapers, the *Post* and *The Nation;* the Asia Monitor Resource Center of Hong Kong; and Lynn Sherr's devastating report on ABC's *20/20,* July 30, 1993. Lampan Taptim and Tumthong Podhirun, "From the Ashes," ICFTU, December 1994; Cheng: *Asian Labour Update,* Asia Monitor Resource Center, Hong Kong, July 1993; La-iad Nads-nguen: *The Nation,* Bangkok, May 12, 1993; and Chaweewan Mekpan: *20/20.*

6. Details on Thailand's worker injuries and the litany of fires in China are from the ICFTU report and other labor bulletins, as well as interviews in Bangkok.

7. The *People's Daily* and *Economic Daily* were quoted by Andrew Quinn of Reuters in *The Daily Citizen* of Washington, DC, January 18, 1994.

8. Tony Horwitz described chicken-processing employment as the second fastest growing manufacturing job in America: *Wall Street Journal,* December 1, 1994. U.S. sweatshops were reviewed in "Garment Industry: Efforts to Address the Prevalence and Conditions of Sweatshops," U.S. Government Accounting Office, November 1994.

9. Sanan was quoted in the *Bangkok Post,* May 29, 1993.

10. The New Delhi–based campaign against child labor in the carpet industry is admittedly limited to a narrow market and expensive product, but its essential value is demonstrating how retailers and their customers can be connected to a distant factory floor. See, for instance, Hugh Williamson, "Stamp of Approval," *Far Eastern Economic Review,* February 2, 1995, and N. Vasuk Rao in the *Journal of Commerce,* March 1, 1995.

THINKING ABOUT THE READING

Greider argues that the tragedy of the Kader industrial fire cannot be explained simply by focusing on greedy families and multinational corporations. Instead, he blames global economics and the organization of the international toy industry. He writes, "The Kader fire was ordained and organized by the free market itself." What do you suppose he means by this? Given the enormous economic pressures that this and other multinational industries operate under, are such tragedies inevitable? Why have attempts to improve the working conditions in "third world" factories been so ineffective?

The Smile Factory

Work at Disneyland

John Van Maanen

(1991)

Part of Walt Disney Enterprises includes the theme park Disneyland. In its pioneering form in Anaheim, California, this amusement center has been a consistent money maker since the gates were first opened in 1955. Apart from its sociological charm, it has, of late, become something of an exemplar for culture vultures and has been held up for public acclaim in several best-selling publications as one of America's top companies. . . . To outsiders, the cheerful demeanor of its employees, the seemingly inexhaustible repeat business it generates from its customers, the immaculate condition of park grounds, and, more generally, the intricate physical and social order of the business itself appear wondrous.

Disneyland as the self-proclaimed "Happiest Place on Earth" certainly occupies an enviable position in the amusement and entertainment worlds as well as the commercial world in general. Its product, it seems, is emotion—"laughter and well-being." Insiders are not bashful about promoting the product. Bill Ross, a Disneyland executive, summarizes the corporate position nicely by noting that "although we focus our attention on profit and loss, day-in and day-out we cannot lose sight of the fact that this is a feeling business and we make our profits from that."

The "feeling business" does not operate, however, by management decree alone. Whatever services Disneyland executives believe they are providing to the 60 to 70 thousand visitors per day that flow through the park during its peak summer season, employees at the bottom of the organization are the ones who

most provide them. The work-a-day practices that employees adopt to amplify or dampen customer spirits are therefore a core concern of this feeling business. The happiness trade is an interactional one. It rests partly on the symbolic resources put into place by history and park design but it also rests on an animated workforce that is more or less eager to greet the guests, pack the trams, push the buttons, deliver the food, dump the garbage, clean the streets, and, in general, marshal the will to meet and perhaps exceed customer expectations. False moves, rude words, careless disregard, detected insincerity, or a sleepy and bored presence can all undermine the enterprise and ruin a sale. The smile factory has its rules.

It's a Small World

. . . This rendition is of course abbreviated and selective. I focus primarily on such matters as the stock appearance (vanilla), status order (rigid), and social life (full), and swiftly learned codes of conduct (formal and informal) that are associated with Disneyland ride operators. These employees comprise the largest category of hourly workers on the payroll. During the summer months, they number close to four thousand and run the 60-odd rides and attractions in the park.

They are also a well-screened bunch. There is—among insiders and outsiders alike—a rather fixed view about the social attributes carried by the standard-make Disneyland ride operator. Single, white males and females in their early twenties, without facial blemish, of above average height and below average weight, with straight teeth, conservative grooming standards, and a chin-up, shoulder-back posture radiating the sort of good health suggestive of a recent history in sports are typical of these social identifiers. There are representative minorities on the payroll but because ethnic displays are sternly discouraged by management, minority employees are rather close copies of the standard model Disneylander, albeit in different colors.

This Disneyland look is often a source of some amusement to employees who delight in pointing out that even the patron saint, Walt himself, could not be hired today without shaving off his trademark pencil-thin mustache. But, to get a job in Disneyland and keep it means conforming to a rather exacting set of appearance rules. These rules are put forth in a handbook on the Disney image in which readers learn, for example, that facial hair or long hair is banned for men as are aviator glasses and earrings and that women must not tease their hair, wear fancy jewelry, or apply more than a modest dab of makeup. Both men and women are to look neat and prim, keep their uniforms fresh, polish their shoes, and maintain an upbeat countenance and light dignity to complement their appearance—no low spirits or cornball raffishness at Disneyland.

The legendary "people skills" of park employees, so often mentioned in Disneyland publicity and training materials, do not amount to very much according to ride operators. Most tasks require little interaction with customers and are physically designed to practically insure that is the case. The contact that does occur typically is fleeting and swift, a matter usually of only a few seconds. In the rare event sustained interaction with customers might be required, employees are taught to deflect potential exchanges to area supervisors or security. A Training Manual offers the proper procedure: "On misunderstandings, guests should be told to call City Hall.... In everything from damaged cameras to physical injuries, don't discuss anything with guests . . . there will always be one of us nearby." Employees learn quickly that security is hidden but everywhere. On Main Street security cops are Keystone Kops; in Frontierland, they are Town Marshalls; on Tom Sawyer's Island, they are Cavalry Officers, and so on.

Occasionally, what employees call "line talk" or "crowd control" is required of them to explain delays, answer direct questions, or provide directions that go beyond the endless stream of recorded messages coming from virtually every nook and cranny of the park. Because such tasks are so simple, consisting of little more than keeping the crowd informed and moving, it is perhaps obvious why management considers the sharp appearance and wide smile of employees so vital to park operations. There is little more they could ask of ride operators whose main interactive tasks with visitors consist of being, in their own terms, "information booths," "line signs," "pretty props," "shepherds," and "talking statues."

A few employees do go out of their way to initiate contact with Disneyland customers but, as a rule, most do not and consider those who do to be a bit odd. In general, one need do little more than exercise common courtesy while looking reasonably alert and pleasant. Interactive skills that are advanced by the job have less to do with making customers feel warm and welcome than they do with keeping each other amused and happy. This is, of course, a more complex matter.

Employees bring to the job personal badges of status that are of more than passing interest to peers. In rough order, these include: good looks, college affiliation, career aspirations, past achievements, age (directly related to status up to about age 23 or 24 and inversely related thereafter), and assorted other idiosyncratic matters. Nested closely alongside these imported status badges are organizational ones that are also of concern and value to employees.

Where one works in the park carries much social weight. Postings are consequential because the ride and area a person is assigned provide rewards and benefits beyond those of wages. In-the-park stature for ride operators turns partly on whether or not unique skills are required. Disneyland neatly complements labor market theorizing on this dimension because employees with the most differentiated skills find themselves at the top of the internal status ladder, thus making their loyalties to the organization more predictable.

Ride operators, as a large but distinctly middle-class group of hourly employees on the floor of the organization, compete for status not only with each other but also with other employee groupings whose members are hired for the season from the same applicant pool. A loose approximation of the rank ordering among these groups can be constructed as follows:

1. The upper-class prestigious Disneyland Ambassadors and Tour Guides (bilingual young women in charge of ushering—some say rushing—little bands of tourists through the park);

2. Ride operators performing coveted "skilled work" such as live narrations or tricky transportation tasks like those who symbolically control customer access to the park and drive the costly entry vehicles (such as the antique trains, horse-drawn carriages, and Monorail);

3. All other ride operators;

4. The proletarian Sweepers (keepers of the concrete grounds);

5. The sub-prole or peasant status Food and Concession workers (whose park sobriquets reflect their lowly social worth—"pancake ladies," "peanut pushers," "coke blokes," "suds divers," and the seemingly irreplaceable "soda jerks").

Pay differentials are slight among these employee groups. The collective status adheres, as it does internally for ride operators, to assignment or functional distinctions. As the rank order suggests, most employee status goes to those who work jobs that require higher degrees of special skill, [offer] relative freedom from constant and direct supervision, and provide the opportunity to organize and direct customer desires and behavior rather than

to merely respond to them as spontaneously expressed.

The basis for sorting individuals into these various broad bands of job categories is often unknown to employees—a sort of deep, dark secret of the casting directors in personnel. When prospective employees are interviewed, they interview for "a job at Disneyland," not a specific one. Personnel decides what particular job they will eventually occupy. Personal contacts are considered by employees as crucial in this job-assignment process as they are in the hiring decision. Some employees, especially those who wind up in the lower ranking jobs, are quite disappointed with their assignments as is the case when, for example, a would-be Adventureland guide is posted to a New Orleans Square restaurant as a pot scrubber. Although many of the outside acquaintances of our pot scrubber may know only that he works at Disneyland, rest assured, insiders will know immediately where he works and judge him accordingly.

Uniforms are crucial in this regard for they provide instant communication about the social merits or demerits of the wearer within the little world of Disneyland workers. Uniforms also correspond to a wider status ranking that casts a significant shadow on employees of all types. Male ride operators on the Autopia wear, for example, untailored jump-suits similar to pit mechanics and consequently generate about as much respect from peers as the grease-stained outfits worn by pump jockeys generate from real motorists in gas stations. The ill-fitting and homogeneous "whites" worn by Sweepers signify lowly institutional work tinged, perhaps, with a reminder of hospital orderlies rather than street cleanup crews. On the other hand, for males, the crisp, officer-like Monorail operator stands alongside the swashbuckling Pirate of the Caribbean, the casual cowpoke of Big Thunder Mountain, or the smartly vested Riverboat pilot as carriers of valued symbols in and outside the park. Employees lust for these higher status positions and the rights to small advantages such uniforms provide. A lively internal labor market exists wherein there is much scheming for the more prestigious assignments.

For women, a similar market exists although the perceived "sexiness" of uniforms, rather than social rank, seems to play a larger role. To wit, the rather heated antagonisms that developed years ago when the ride "It's a Small World" first opened and began outfitting the ride operators with what were felt to be the shortest skirts and most revealing blouses in the park. Tour Guides, who traditionally headed the fashion vanguard at Disneyland in their above-the-knee kilts, knee socks, tailored vests, black English hats, and smart riding crops were apparently appalled at being upstaged by their social inferiors and lobbied actively (and, judging by the results, successfully) to lower the skirts, raise the necklines, and generally remake their Small World rivals. . . .

Movement across jobs is not encouraged by park management, but some does occur (mostly within an area and job category). Employees claim that a sort of "once a sweeper, always a sweeper" rule obtains but all know of at least a few exceptions to prove the rule. The exceptions offer some (not much) hope for those working at the social margins of the park and perhaps keep them on the job longer than might otherwise be expected. Dishwashers can dream of becoming Pirates, and with persistence and a little help from their friends, such dreams just might come true next season (or the next).

These examples are precious, perhaps, but they are also important. There is an intricate pecking order among very similar categories of employees. Attributes of reward and status tend to cluster, and there is intense concern about the cluster to which one belongs (or would like to belong). To a degree, form follows function in Disneyland because the jobs requiring the most abilities and offering the most interest also offer the most status and social reward. Interaction patterns reflect and sustain this order. Few Ambassadors or Tour Guides, for instance, will stoop to speak at length with Sweepers who speak mostly among themselves or to Food workers. Ride operators, between the poles, line up in ways referred to above with only ride proximity (i.e., sharing a break area) representing a potentially significant intervening variable in the interaction calculation. . . .

Paid employment at Disneyland begins with the much renowned University of Disneyland whose faculty runs a day-long orientation program (Traditions I) as part of a 40-hour apprenticeship program, most of which takes place on the rides. In the classroom, however, newly hired ride operators are given a very thorough introduction to matters of managerial concern and are tested on their absorption of famous Disneyland fact, lore, and procedure. Employee demeanor is governed, for example, by three rules:

> First, we practice the friendly smile.
>
> Second, we use only friendly and courteous phrases.
>
> Third, we are not stuffy—the only Misters in Disneyland are Mr. Toad and Mr. Smee.

Employees learn too that the Disneyland culture is officially defined. The employee handbook put it in this format:

> Dis-ney Cor-po-rate Cul-ture (diz'ne kor'pr'it kul'cher) *n* 1. Of or pertaining to the Disney organization, as *a:* the philosophy underlying all business decisions; *b:* the commitment of top leadership and management to that philosophy; *c:* the actions taken by individual cast members that reinforce the image.

Language is also a central feature of university life, and new employees are schooled in its proper use. Customers at Disneyland are, for instance, never referred to as such, they are "guests." There are no rides at Disneyland, only "attractions." Disneyland itself is a "Park," not an amusement center, and it is divided into "back-stage," "on-stage," and "staging" regions. Law enforcement personnel hired by the park are not policemen, but "security hosts." Employees do not wear uniforms but check out fresh "costumes" each working day from "wardrobe." And, of course, there are no accidents at Disneyland, only "incidents." . . .

Classes are organized and designed by professional Disneyland trainers who also instruct a well-screened group of representative hourly employees straight from park operations on the approved newcomer training methods and materials. New-hires seldom see professional trainers in class but are brought on board by enthusiastic peers who concentrate on those aspects of park procedure thought highly general matters to be learned by all employees. Particular skill training (and "reality shock") is reserved for the second wave of socialization occurring on the rides themselves as operators are taught, for example, how and when to send a mock bobsled caroming down the track or, more delicately, the proper ways to stuff an obese adult customer into the midst of children riding the Monkey car on the Casey Jones Circus Train or, most problematically, what exactly to tell an irate customer standing in the rain who, in no uncertain terms, wants his or her money back and wants it back now.

During orientation, considerable concern is placed on particular values the Disney organization considers central to its operations. These values range from the "customer is king" verities to the more or less unique kind, of which "everyone is a child at heart when at Disneyland" is a decent example. This latter piety is one few employees fail to recognize as also attaching to everyone's mind as well after a few months of work experience. Elaborate checklists of appearance standards are learned and gone over in the classroom and great efforts are spent trying to bring employee emotional responses in line with such standards. Employees are told repeatedly that if they are happy and cheerful at work, so, too, will the guests be at play. Inspirational films, hearty pep talks, family imagery, and exemplars of corporate performance are all representative of the strong symbolic stuff of these training rites. . . .

Yet, like employees everywhere, there is a limit to which such overt company propaganda can be effective. Students and trainers both seem to agree on where the line is drawn, for there is much satirical banter, mischievous winking, and playful exaggeration in the classroom. As young seasonal employees note, it is difficult to take seriously an organization that provides its retirees "Golden Ears" instead of gold watches after 20 or more years of service. All newcomers are aware that the label "Disneyland" has both an unserious and artificial connotation and that a full embrace of the Disneyland role would be as deviant as its full rejection. It does seem, however, because of the corporate imagery, the recruiting and selection devices, the goodwill trainees hold toward the organization at entry, the peer-based employment context, and the smooth fit with real student calendars, the job is considered by most ride operators to be a good one. The University of Disneyland, it appears, graduates students with a modest amount of pride and a considerable amount of fact and faith firmly ingrained as important things to know (if not always accept). . . .

Employees learn quickly that supervisors and, to a lesser degree, foremen are not only on the premises to help them, but also to catch them when they slip over or brazenly violate set procedures or park policies. Because most rides are tightly designed to eliminate human judgment and minimize operational disasters, much of the supervisory monitoring is directed at activities ride operators consider trivial: taking too long a break; not wearing parts of one's official uniform such as a hat, standard-issue belt, or correct shoes; rushing the ride (although more frequent violations seem to be detected for the provision of longer-than-usual rides for lucky customers); fraternizing with guests beyond the call of duty; talking back to quarrelsome or sometimes merely querisome customers; and so forth. All are matters covered quite explicitly in the codebooks ride operators are to be familiar with, and violations of such codes are often subject to instant and harsh discipline. The firing of what to supervisors are "malcontents," "trouble-makers," "bumblers," "attitude problems," or simply "jerks" is a frequent occasion at Disneyland, and among part-timers, who are most subject to degradation and being fired, the threat is omnipresent. There are few workers who have not witnessed first-hand the rapid disappearance of a co-worker for offenses they would regard as "Mickey Mouse." Moreover, there are few employees who themselves have not violated a good number of operational and demeanor standards and anticipate, with just cause, the violation of more in the future. . . .

Employees are also subject to what might be regarded as remote controls. These stem not from supervisors or peers but from thousands of paying guests who parade daily through the park. The public, for the most part, wants Disneyland employees to play only the roles for which they are hired and costumed. If, for instance, Judy of the Jets is feeling tired, grouchy, or bored, few customers want to know about it. Disneyland employees are expected to be sunny and helpful; and the job, with its limited opportunities for sustained interaction, is designed to support such a stance. Thus, if a ride operator's behavior drifts noticeably away from the norm, customers are sure to point it out—"Why aren't you smiling?" "What's wrong with you?" "Having a bad day?" "Did Goofy step on your foot?" Ride operators learn swiftly from the constant hints, glances, glares, and tactful (and tactless) cues sent by their audience what their role in the park is to be, and as long as they keep to it, there will be no objections from those passing by.

> I can remember being out on the river looking at the people on the Mark Twain looking down on the people in the Keel Boats who are looking up at them. I'd come by on my raft and they'd all turn and stare at me. If I gave them a little wave and a grin, they'd all wave back and smile; all ten thousand of them. I always wondered what would happen if I gave them the finger? (Ex-ride operator, 1988)

Ride operators also learn how different categories of customers respond to them and the parts they are playing on-stage. For example, infants and small children are generally timid, if not frightened, in their presence. School-age children are somewhat curious, aware that the operator is at work playing a role but sometimes in awe of the role itself. Nonetheless, these children can be quite critical of any flaw in the operator's performance. Teenagers, especially males in groups, present problems because they sometimes go to great lengths to embarrass, challenge, ridicule, or outwit an operator. Adults are generally appreciative and approving of an operator's conduct provided it meets their rather minimal standards, but they sometimes overreact to the part an operator is playing (positively) if accompanied by small children. . . .

The point here is that ride operators learn what the public (or, at least, their idealized version of the public) expects of their role and find it easier to conform to such expectations than not. Moreover, they discover that when they are bright and lively others respond to them in like ways. This . . . balancing of the emotional exchange is such that ride operators come to expect good treatment. They assume, with good cause, that most people will react to their little waves and smiles with some affection and perhaps joy. When they do not, it can ruin a ride operator's day. . . .

By and large, however, the people-processing tasks of ride operators pass good naturedly and smoothly, with operators hardly noticing much more than the bodies passing in front of view (special bodies, however, merit special attention as when crew members on the subs gather to assist a young lady in a revealing outfit on board and then linger over the hatch to admire the view as she descends the steep steps to take her seat on the boat). Yet, sometimes, more than a body becomes visible, as happens when customers overstep their roles and challenge employee authority, insult an operator, or otherwise disrupt the routines of the job. In the process, guests become "dufusses," "ducks," and "assholes" (just three of many derisive terms used by ride operators to label those customers they believe to have gone beyond the pale). Normally, these characters are brought to the attention of park security officers, ride foremen, or area supervisors who, in turn, decide how they are to be disciplined (usually expulsion from the park).

Occasionally, however, the alleged slight is too personal or simply too extraordinary for a ride operator to let it pass unnoticed or merely inform others and allow them to decide what, if anything, is to be done. Restoration of one's respect is called for, and routine practices have been developed for these circumstances. For example, common remedies include: the "seatbelt squeeze," a small token of appreciation given to a deviant customer consisting of the rapid cinching-up of a required seatbelt such that the passenger is doubled-over at the point of departure and left gasping for the duration of the trip; the "break-toss," an acrobatic gesture of the Autopia trade whereby operators jump on the outside of a norm violator's car, stealthily unhitching the safety belt, then slamming on the brakes, bringing the car to an almost instant stop while the driver flies on the hood of the car (or beyond); the "seatbelt slap," an equally distinguished (if primitive) gesture by which an offending customer receives a sharp, quick snap of a hard plastic belt across the face (or other parts of the body) when entering or exiting a seat-belted ride; the "break-up-the-party" gambit, a queuing device put to use in officious fashion whereby bothersome pairs are separated at the last minute into different units, thus forcing on them the pain of strange companions for the duration of a ride through the Haunted Mansion or a ramble on Mr. Toad's Wild Ride; the "hatch-cover ploy," a much beloved practice of Submarine pilots who, in collusion with mates on the loading dock, are able to drench offensive guests with water as their units pass under a waterfall; and, lastly, the rather ignoble variants of the "Sorry-I-didn't-see-your-hand" tactic, a savage move designed to crunch a particularly irksome customer's hand (foot, finger, arm, leg, etc.) by bringing a piece of Disneyland property to bear on the appendage, such as the door of a Thunder Mountain railroad car or the starboard side of a Jungle Cruise boat. This latter remedy is, most often, a "near miss" designed to startle the little criminals of Disneyland.

All of these unofficial procedures (and many more) are learned on the job. Although they are used sparingly, they are used. Occasions of use

provide a continual stream of sweet revenge talk to enliven and enrich colleague conversation at break time or after work. Too much, of course, can be made of these subversive practices and the rhetoric that surrounds their use. Ride operators are quite aware that there are limits beyond which they dare not pass. If they are caught, they know that restoration of corporate pride will be swift and clean.

In general, Disneyland employees are remarkable for their forbearance and polite good manners even under trying conditions. They are taught, and some come to believe, for a while at least, that they are really "on-stage" at work. And, as noted, surveillance by supervisory personnel certainly fades in light of the unceasing glances an employee receives from the paying guests who tromp daily through the park in the summer. Disneyland employees know well that they are part of the product being sold and learn to check their more discriminating manners in favor of the generalized countenance of a cheerful lad or lassie whose enthusiasm and dedication is obvious to all.

At times, the emotional resources of employees appear awesome. When the going gets tough and the park is jammed, the nerves of all employees are frayed and sorely tested by the crowd, din, sweltering sun, and eyeburning smog. Customers wait in what employees call "bullpens" (and park officials call "reception areas") for up to several hours for a 3½ minute ride that operators are sometimes hell-bent on cutting to 2½ minutes. Surely a monument to the human ability to suppress feelings has been created when both users and providers alike can maintain their composure and seeming regard for one another when in such a fix.

It is in this domain where corporate culture and the order it helps to sustain must be given its due. Perhaps the depth of a culture is visible only when its members are under the gun. The orderliness—a good part of the Disney formula for financial success—is an accomplishment based not only on physical design and elaborate procedures, but also on the low-level, part-time employees who, in the final analysis, must be willing, even eager, to keep the show afloat. The ease with which employees glide into their kindly and smiling roles is, in large measure, a feat of social engineering. Disneyland does not pay well; its supervision is arbitrary and skin-close; its working conditions are chaotic; its jobs require minimal amounts of intelligence or judgment; and asks a kind of sacrifice and loyalty of its employees that is almost fanatical. Yet, it attracts a particularly able workforce whose personal backgrounds suggest abilities far exceeding those required of a Disneyland traffic cop, people stuffer, queue or line manager, and button pusher. As I have suggested, not all of Disneyland is covered by the culture put forth by management. There are numerous pockets of resistance and various degrees of autonomy maintained by employees. Nonetheless, adherence and support for the organization are remarkable. And, like swallows returning to Capistrano, many part-timers look forward to their migration back to the park for several seasons.

The Disney Way

Four features alluded to in this unofficial guide to Disneyland seem to account for a good deal of the social order that obtains within the park. First, socialization, although costly, is of a most selective, collective, intensive, serial, sequential, and closed sort. These tactics are notable for their penetration into the private spheres of individual thought and feeling. . . . Incoming identities are not so much dismantled as they are set aside as employees are schooled in the use of new identities of the situational sort. Many of these are symbolically powerful and, for some, laden with social approval. It is hardly surprising that some of the more problematic positions in terms of turnover during the summer occur in the food and concession domains where employees apparently find little to identify with on the job. Cowpokes on Big Thunder Mountain, Jet Pilots, Storybook Princesses, Tour Guides, Space Cadets, Jungle Boat Skippers, or Southern Belles of New Orleans Square have less difficulty on this score. Disneyland, by design, bestows identity through a process carefully set up to strip away the job relevance of other sources of identity and learned response and replace them with others of organizational relevance. It works.

Second, this is a work culture whose designers have left little room for individual experimentation. Supervisors, as apparent in their focused wandering and attentive looks, keep very close tabs on what is going on at any moment in all the lands. Every bush, rock, and tree in Disneyland is numbered and checked continually as to the part it is playing in the park. So too are employees. Discretion of a personal sort is quite limited while employees are "on-stage." Even "back-stage" and certain "off-stage" domains have their corporate monitors. Employees are indeed aware that their "off-stage" life beyond the picnics, parties, and softball games is subject to some scrutiny, for police checks are made on potential and current employees. Nor do all employees discount the rumors that park officials make periodic inquiries on their own as to a person's habits concerning sex and drugs. Moreover, the sheer number of rules and regulations is striking, thus making the grounds for dismissal a matter of multiple choice for supervisors who discover a target for the use of such grounds. The feeling of being watched is, unsurprisingly, a rather prevalent complaint among Disneyland people, and it is one that employees must live with if they are to remain at Disneyland.

Third, emotional management occurs in the park in a number of quite distinct ways. From the instructors at the university who beseech recruits to "wish every guest a pleasant good day," to the foremen who plead with their charges to, "say thank you when you herd them through the gate," to the impish customer who seductively licks her lips and asks, "what does Tom Sawyer want for Christmas?" appearance, demeanor, and etiquette have special meanings at Disneyland. Because these are prized personal attributes over which we normally feel in control, making them commodities can be unnerving. Much self-monitoring is involved, of course, but even here self-management has an organizational side. Consider ride operators who may complain of being "too tired to smile" but, at the same time, feel a little guilty for uttering such a confession. Ride operators who have worked an early morning shift on the Matterhorn (or other popular rides) tell of a queasy feeling they get when the park is opened for business and they suddenly feel the ground begin to shake under their feet and hear the low thunder of the hordes of customers coming at them, oblivious of civil restraint and the small children who might be among them. Consider, too, the discomforting pressures of being "on-stage" all day and the cumulative annoyance of having adults ask permission to leave a line to go to the bathroom, whether the water in the lagoon is real, where the well-marked entrances might be, where Walt Disney's cryogenic tomb is to be found, or—the real clincher—whether or not one is "really real."

The mere fact that so much operator discourse concerns the handling of bothersome guests suggests that these little emotional disturbances have costs. There are, for instance, times in all employee careers when they put themselves on "automatic pilot," "go robot," "can't feel a thing," "lapse into a dream," "go into a trance," or otherwise "check out" while still on duty. Despite a crafty supervisor's (or curious visitor's) attempt to measure the glimmer in an employee's eye, this sort of willed emotional numbness is common to many of the "on-stage" Disneyland personnel. Much of this numbness is, of course, beyond the knowledge of supervisors and guests because most employees have little trouble appearing as if they are present even when they are not. It is, in a sense, a passive form of resistance that suggests there still is a sacred preserve of individuality left among employees in the park.

Finally, taking these three points together, it seems that even when people are trained, paid, and told to be nice, it is hard for them to do so all of the time. But, when efforts to be nice have succeeded to the degree that is true of Disneyland, it appears as a rather towering (if not always admirable) achievement. It works at the collective level by virtue of elaborate direction. Employees—at all ranks—are stage-managed by higher ranking employees who, having come through themselves, hire, train, and closely supervise those who have replaced them below. Expression rules are laid out in corporate manuals. Employee time-outs intensify work experience. Social exchanges are forced into narrow bands of interacting groups. Training and retraining programs are continual. Hiding places are few. Although little sore spots and irritations remain for each individual, it is difficult to imagine work roles being more defined (and accepted) than those at Disneyland. Here, it seems, is a work culture worthy of the name.

THINKING ABOUT THE READING

What is the significance of the title "The Smile Factory"? What, exactly, is the factory-made product that Disney sells in its theme parks? How does the Disney organizational culture shape the lives of employees? Disney has been criticized for its strict—some would say oppressive—employee rules and regulations. Would it be possible to run a "smile factory" with a more relaxed code of conduct? Disney theme parks in countries such as France and Japan have not been nearly as successful as Disneyland and Disney World. What are some of the reasons why the "feeling business" doesn't export as well to other countries? Consider also the social rankings that employees create. Describe examples of social rankings in your own experience. What are the criteria for these rankings?

Cool Stores, Bad Jobs

Yasemin Besen-Cassino

(2013)

"I just came in to get coffee one day, but got a job with it." Josh, a 19-year-old college student, had settled into his dorm room and headed into town, figuring he might like to work where he usually hangs out. He wanted to make some money and hopefully some friends. After chatting with the shift manager about music and movies, he was offered a job—just like that.

Josh's new job at the Coffee Bean, a pseudonym for a national coffee chain, is typical of a part-time student job: it offers low pay, limited hours, no benefits, and non-standard shifts involving nights and weekends, but it's a job. You'd expect his coworkers would be other struggling students or "adults" who can't do any better. Instead, Josh is pretty much the norm. Affluent students like Josh, with his fashionable clothes, stylish haircut, and brand-new cell phone, are becoming typical workers in places like Coffee Bean.

According to the 2000 Department of Labor's Report on the Youth Labor Force, youth from higher socio-economic status backgrounds are *more* likely to work than their less affluent counterparts (40 percent of higher income 15-year-olds, compared to 32 percent from the lowest income quartile). According to the Current Population Survey, among older teenagers, those from the lowest income groups are the ones least likely to work. In fact, the lowest SES citizens are less likely to work at every age group.

We wouldn't be surprised to see that poor students must work to put themselves through school or to help with basic expenses. But why do affluent students like Josh choose to give up their free time to work in part-time jobs they don't really need?

To answer that question, I hung out at the Coffee Bean, interviewing current and former student workers—40 in all. I also interviewed dozens of college students about their work experiences, perception of brands and consumption habits, and experiences in the aftermath of the recent economic recession.

What I found is that young people see low-paid chain stores as places to socialize with friends away from watchful parental eyes. They can try on adult roles and be associated with their favorite brands. Corporations like Starbucks and Old Navy, in turn, target such kids, marketing their jobs as cool, fashionable, and desirable. Soon, their workers match their desired consumers.

"Every Shift Was Like a Party"

Jamie, a 19-year-old full-time student and the employee at the Coffee Bean, told me his work "is not something you do for money or experience, you know. It's where I hang out. And my parents are okay with it." Since he lives at home, work provides a central space to socialize and see friends without adult supervision, and his parents encourage his employment (though Jamie admits to using work as an excuse to get out of family obligations and house chores).

Not all parents are oblivious to such motives, however. Sarah started working at the Coffee Bean when she turned 18. Her mother knows she works at the coffee shop so that she can see her friends. Wiping dirty tables, washing dishes, carrying trash bags, and dealing with needy and annoying customers was not how she thought her daughter would develop her skills and utilize her knowledge. She characterized her daughter's time at the shop as a "waste of time," even as she admitted that the job kept Sarah "busy" and "out of trouble."

Suburbs are social wastelands for many young people, offering little public transportation and limited chances to hang out with friends or meet new people. Many young people turn to malls and shopping centers, socializing in front of stores and congregating in mall parking lots.

In response, many malls, shopping centers, and movie theaters recently began to ban unattended teenagers, implementing a "parental escort policy." While the owners seek out young customers, they see young people hanging out together as a "counter-productive activity" which can encourage illegal behavior, drug use, or alcohol consumption. It's closed off the few public spaces young people had for socializing outside of school.

Given limited public space for socializing in the suburbs, more and more young people are turning to work as a safe, central place to socialize, free of parental supervision and adult scrutiny.

Sarah loved the people she worked with and thought her job was fun. She scheduled her shifts so that she could work with her friends, and many acquaintances trickled in over the course of the day. She spent so much time at the coffee shop that she felt as though she lived there. Where else could she go that would both welcome her and her friends?

Jules, who is now in college, remembers that the high-end clothing store where she worked part-time during high school didn't even seem like a job. Instead, every shift was like a "party." She would schedule her shifts to see her friends, who were also employees. Her workplace was the place to be.

Representing the Brand That Represents You

Monica, the daughter of two doctors, grew up in an affluent suburb of a large city. When it

came to getting a job, she said she wouldn't work just anywhere. Individually owned, family businesses or "mom and pop" places were out of the question. They might offer more money and better working conditions, but in Monica's words: "[I]t's not the same." Her friends don't work at such places, and those shops don't have the right brand, the cool, desirable image she hoped she would gain by working at someplace hipper (like the one where she eventually did take a job).

Just as consuming certain brands distinguishes young people from others, so, too, does choosing a workplace. In addition to social benefits, well-known chains can offer social distinction and function as identity markers. When asked why she prefers one store's job over the other, Brianna, a 19-year-old college student, said, "[I] shop there." Like Josh, her motto is "[I]f I shop there, I'll work there." During the past few decades, as a result of unfettered markets, more and more aspects of life have become commodified, including social spaces in the suburbs. In late capitalism, young people search for identities through the brands of the products they buy—and sell. Many young affluent people also self-identify through the brands of the stores they work for: "I am a typical Coffee Bean guy." When working conditions are comparable, many young people gravitate toward those jobs they associate with better branding, or with their own "personal brand."

Employers use this hunt for social space and prestige to their advantage, advertising job openings so that they can target affluent young people. Companies can seek out workers to perform both basic tasks *and* aesthetic labor to represent their brand—workers who "look good and sound right," according to British scholars Dennis Nickson and Chris Warhurst. Many retail and service jobs now require their workers to embody the look of their brands.

For high-end clothing shops, sociologist Mary Gatta wrote in a 2011 article, the best workers are affluent, female workers who look and sound like potential consumers of the brand. Sociologist David Wright has described how bookstore employees are expected to seem like avid readers. The perfectly tailored workforce helps build authenticity and brand loyalty.

Making Bad Jobs Look Good

"What is it like to work at Starbucks?" asks a 2012 advertisement. "It is a lot like working with friends. For one thing, the people, who work here are not employees, we're partners . . . ." Instead of working conditions, pay, benefits, or advancement opportunities, the ad touts opportunity to work with friends. Spencer's, a store that specializes in retail and entertainment, ad emphasizes fun: "Join the Party!"

The thing is, it can be hard to recruit affluent, good looking, and social young people to work at relatively low-paying jobs that offer few advancement opportunities. So job ads must frequently emphasize the coolness and desirability of the brand. A 2011 Old Navy recruitment ad proclaims: "Cool Jobs are in our jeans." A job at Old Navy must be as cool as their denim. Another Old Navy ad reads: "If you love fashion and fun, you're in the right place." A 2012 H&M job ad tells prospective employees: "A great job is always in fashion." We're fashionable, the ad says, and if you work here, you can be, too.

Job advertisements market employment just as the stores market products. When Old Navy says "Try us on," they are suggesting young people can try on the job just as they try on the clothes in the store. Cotton On's 2012 ad compares the person and the product—"I am Cotton On, Are You? Be a Part of the Crew! Join us Today!"—explicitly reinforcing a link between the products and the workers: if you like to consume these goods, you'll like selling them.

By working there, young people are entitled to discounts, which further bolsters consumption of the brand. A 2012 employment ad for Express reads, "We're looking for people with style, people who love fashion and people who

want an Express discount. We're looking for people like you." By mentioning a store discount, stores show that they want to attract workers who already like and use their products. "Must Love Make-up," a 2012 Bare Escentuals ad reads, while H&M asks: "You Obviously like Shopping Here, Why not Work Here?"

Working for a retail shop often creates a high level of brand loyalty and insider status. If customers are trying to associate themselves with a desired brand (Ecko even offers additional discounts to customers if they can show off a tattoo—a real tattoo—of the company's logo), workers are associated with it even more strongly. As a 2012 Cache recruitment puts it: "Cache Careers: The only thing that is more amazing that shopping at Cache is working at Cache." By working at these stores, young people can become associated with a cool brand. Employee discounts create even greater brand loyalty.

Interviewing affluent young people, employers rarely ask about qualifications or talents, nor do they speak of the power or control these youth will enjoy on the job. Rather, they're asked about their favorite music and movies. It's all about the fun environment and the cool brand.

Branding the Self

Will, a 19-year-old white male, talks about Coffee Bean. "A typical employee," he says, "is usually a teenager or an adult in their early 20s, who feels they are more sophisticated for serving overpriced coffee." They did not see it as an opportunity to make money. They saw how popular Coffee Bean was and wanted to be a part of the popular chain of coffee shops.

A marker of identity, the job can help define the person—something many young people struggle to do. Ashley, a 19-year-old white female, notices that people working at the coffee shop have a certain look and personality. "They are artsy, somewhat nerdy. The guys that work there usually play the guitar.

Smart people usually work at Coffee Bean." For Ashley and other workers, this "vibe" is a social marker that says a lot about their own personalities as employees. Eric says the other Coffee Bean baristas "are classy hippies, who listen to the Grateful Dead and memorize the script to *Rent* and *Rocky Horror Picture Show*." And for Mike, Coffee Bean workers are, "liberal, artsy, upper-to middle class, earring, tattoos, drives a green car, hates the war and loves trees." Employees' interests, social and political preferences, and other consumption habits are all deduced from where they work.

"Fast Food Employees Are Dumb"

Of course not all working students are affluent. Mason is a 21-year-old social science major who resides in a predominantly African-American, low-income city. When he applied for jobs, he had difficulty finding a job in the stores affluent kids could work—he didn't have the "right" look. More economically disadvantaged youth like Mason often end up in fast food jobs. Keeping up with aesthetic demands alongside bills can require a hefty investment.

In fact, many students who work at the Coffee Bean and similar business do so to put themselves through school or help their families—they're not all like the young people I've described above, even though that is a growing segment of workers. But many employers prefer to hire the affluent students because they "look good and sound right."

Sociologists Christine Williams and Catherine Connell, in a 2010 article, reported that employers intentionally locate affluent workers by shutting less affluent workers out: they offer part-time jobs that pay too little to live on. They construct long interview processes (remember Josh's "interview-over-coffee," a wandering conversation that determined he would get a job at the Coffee Bean?) designed to weed out those who don't have time to wait.

So, even as more affluent young people use certain jobs to accumulate social prestige and see their friends, less affluent young people who really *need* these jobs are less likely to get them. More often, the lower-SES students will have to settle for the less desirable fast food jobs.

In the words of Sean, an affluent, white, 20-year-old male, "a typical [fast food] employee is a teenage student or an adult with problems and no education. Most [fast food] employees are dumb." When working at a particular store, however badly paid, is seen as a status marker, those who work in food service are believed to be inferior, lacking in requisite skills and intelligence. But even affluent workers report have trouble keeping up with the aesthetic requirements of their jobs, and sometimes chasing that cool factor plunges them into high levels of debt.

Jules, a white, 20-year-old female, remembers that the upscale clothing store where she worked during her high school years was *the* place to be seen. Working there meant that she was a part of an exclusive club. However, trying to keep up with the aesthetic requirements—she needed to look fashionable and put-together, and wearing the store's latest looks made them easier to sell (Oh, you like this shirt? We have it in green . . .) meant she would buy new clothes from the shop every week. Despite the employee discount, by the time she left the job, she had accumulated credit card debt that rivaled her student loans.

Affluent young workers, who think of their jobs as an extension of their social lives, are less likely to speak up when their jobs are problematic, when they experience sexual harassment, or when they see gender or racial discrimination. Viewing them as just "part-time jobs," as ways of associating themselves with a cool brand rather than support themselves or families, this growing group of affluent young workers is also less likely to complain about how little they're paid. These days, it's hip workers and their disdain for fast-food employees that are tilting the labor marker in unexpected ways.

THINKING ABOUT THE READING

Besen-Cassino focuses on contemporary corporations that target affluent youth as employees. What are some of the strategies these companies use to convince young people to work for low wages and few benefits, that is, what do these companies do to make bad jobs look cool? How does the company benefit from this arrangement? What about employees, do they benefit? How does a brand's popularity influence the choice to work for that company? When young people see their jobs as "cool" or as a party, how likely are they to speak up about poor working conditions? What might some of the social theorists say about these tactics and working conditions under capitalism?

The Architecture of Stratification

Social Class and Inequality

10

Inequality is woven into the fabric of all societies through a structured system of *social stratification.* Social stratification is a ranking of entire groups of people that perpetuates unequal rewards and life chances in society. The structural-functionalist explanation of stratification is that the stability of society depends on all social positions being filled—that is, there are people around to do all the jobs that need to be done. Higher rewards, such as prestige and large salaries, are afforded to the most important positions, thereby ensuring that the most qualified individuals will occupy the highest positions. In contrast, conflict theory argues that stratification reflects an unequal distribution of power in society and is a primary source of conflict and tension.

Social class is the primary means of stratification in American society. Contemporary sociologists are likely to define a person's class standing as a combination of income, wealth, occupational prestige, and educational attainment. It is tempting to see class differences as simply the result of an economic stratification system that exists at a level above the individual. Although inequality is created and maintained by larger social institutions, it is often felt most forcefully and is reinforced most effectively in the chain of interactions that take place in our day-to-day lives.

The media play a significant role in shaping people's perceptions of class. But instead of providing accurate descriptive information about different classes, the media—especially the news media—give the impression that the United States is largely a classless society. According to Gregory Mantsios in "Making Class Invisible," when different classes are depicted in the media, the images tend to hover around stereotypes that reinforce the cultural belief that people's position in society is largely a function of their own effort and achievement or, in the case of "the poor," lack of effort and achievement.

The face of American poverty has changed somewhat over the past several decades. The economic status of single mothers and their children has deteriorated while that of people older than age 65 has improved somewhat. What hasn't changed is the ever-widening gap between the rich and the poor. Poverty persists because in a free market and competitive society, it serves economic and social functions. In addition, poverty receives institutional "support" in the form of segmented labor markets and inadequate educational systems. The ideology of competitive individualism—that to succeed in life, all one has to do is work hard and win in competition with others—creates a belief that poor people are to blame for their own suffering. So, although the problem of poverty remains serious, public attitudes toward poverty and poor people are frequently indifferent or even hostile. Sociologists such as Fred Block and his colleagues call this attitude "the compassion gap." According to their research, this cultural attitude of indifference or disdain is rooted in individualism and a lack of understanding of economic conditions over time (e.g., the relative difficulty of owning a home today as compared with the period just after World War II when much government assistance was available). The authors see the "compassion gap" as an attitude that gets in the way of establishing more workable social policies for the poor.

This attitude extends to the ways in which we perceive people's status based on characteristics such as clothing, personal hygiene, and physical traits, such as scars or blemishes. In "Branded With Infamy" Vivyan Adair describes the various ways in which poor women's bodies are marked as "unclean" or "unacceptable." These markings are the result of a life of poverty: a lack of access to proper health care, nutrition, and shelter; and demanding physical and emotional labor. But instead of seeing the impact of economic circumstances on the lives of these women, more affluent people tend to view them (and their children) as members of an undesirable social class that should be disciplined, controlled, and punished.

In "The People of Wal-Mart," Nicholas Copeland and Christine Labuski take on the company's claim that it is lifting up its employees and providing access to the American Dream. The authors describe the ways in which the Wal-Mart proclaims a path to social mobility, only to thwart it continuously in its business practices and legal dealings with disgruntled employees. Rather than resolving poverty, as much of the company's advertising claims, the evidence indicates that Wal-Mart's practices actually deepen inequality.

Something to Consider as You Read

In reading these selections, pay careful attention to the small ways in which economic resources affect everyday choices and behavior. For instance, how might poverty, including the lack of access to nice clothing, affect one's ability to portray the best possible image at a job interview? Consider further the connection between media portrayals and self-image. Where do people get their ideas about their own self-worth, their sense of entitlement, and how they fit into society generally? How do these ideals differ across social class and how are they similar? Some observers have suggested that people in the United States don't know how to talk about class, except in stereotypical terms. How might this lack of "class discourse" perpetuate stereotypes and the myth that the poor deserve their fate? Consider examples of the "compassion gap" in your own life and as reflected in recent news and policy decisions. Does the compassion gap relate to the failure to fully understand social issues such as teenage pregnancy?

Making Class Invisible

Gregory Mantsios

(1998)

Of the various social and cultural forces in our society, the mass media is arguably the most influential in molding public consciousness. Americans spend an average twenty-eight hours per week watching television. They also spend an undetermined number of hours reading periodicals, listening to the radio, and going to the movies. Unlike other cultural and socializing institutions, ownership and control of the mass media is highly concentrated. Twenty-three corporations own more than one-half of all the daily newspapers, magazines, movie studios, and radio and television outlets in the United States. The number of media companies is shrinking and their control of the industry is expanding. And a relatively small number of media outlets is producing and packaging the majority of news and entertainment programs. For the most part, our media is national in nature and single-minded (profit-oriented) in purpose. This media plays a key role in defining our cultural tastes, helping us locate ourselves in history, establishing our national identity, and ascertaining the range of national and social possibilities. In this essay, we will examine the way the mass media shapes how people think about each other and about the nature of our society.

The United States is the most highly stratified society in the industrialized world. Class distinctions operate in virtually every aspect of our lives, determining the nature of our work, the quality of our schooling, and the health and safety of our loved ones. Yet remarkably, we, as a nation, retain illusions about living in an egalitarian society. We maintain these illusions, in large part, because the media hides gross inequities from public view. In those instances when inequities are revealed, we are provided with messages that obscure the nature of class realities and blame the victims of class-dominated society for their own plight. Let's briefly examine what the news media, in particular, tells us about class.

About the Poor

The news media provides meager coverage of poor people and poverty. The coverage it does provide is often distorted and misleading.

The Poor Do Not Exist

For the most part, the news media ignores the poor. Unnoticed are forty million poor people in the nation—a number that equals the entire population of Maine, Vermont, New Hampshire, Connecticut, Rhode Island, New Jersey, and New York combined. Perhaps even more alarming is that the rate of poverty is increasing twice as fast as the population growth in the United States. Ordinarily, even a calamity of much smaller proportion (e.g., flooding in the Midwest) would garner a great deal of coverage and hype from a media usually eager to declare a crisis, yet less than one in five hundred articles in the *New York Times* and one in one thousand articles listed in the *Readers Guide to Periodic Literature* are on poverty. With remarkably little attention to them, the poor and their problems are hidden from most Americans.

When the media does turn its attention to the poor, it offers a series of contradictory messages and portrayals.

The Poor Are Faceless

Each year the Census Bureau releases a new report on poverty in our society and its results are duly reported in the media. At best, however, this coverage emphasizes annual fluctuations (showing how the numbers differ from previous years) and ongoing debates over the validity of the numbers (some argue the number should be lower, most that the number should be higher). Coverage like this desensitizes us to the poor by reducing poverty to a number. It ignores the human tragedy of poverty—the suffering, indignities, and misery endured by millions of children and adults. Instead, the poor become statistics rather than people.

The Poor Are Undeserving

When the media does put a face on the poor, it is not likely to be a pretty one. The media will provide us with sensational stories about welfare cheats, drug addicts, and greedy panhandlers (almost always urban and Black). Compare these images and the emotions evoked by them with the media's treatment of middle-class (usually white) "tax evaders," celebrities who have a "chemical dependency," or wealthy businesspeople who use unscrupulous means to "make a profit." While the behavior of the more affluent offenders is considered an "impropriety" and a deviation from the norm, the behavior of the poor is considered repugnant, indicative of the poor in general, and worthy of our indignation and resentment.

The Poor Are an Eyesore

When the media does cover the poor, they are often presented through the eyes of the middle class. For example, sometimes the media includes a story with panhandlers. Rather than focusing on the plight of the poor, these stories are about middle-class opposition to the poor. Such stories tell us that the poor are an inconvenience and an irritation.

The Poor Have Only Themselves to Blame

In another example of media coverage, we are told that the poor live in a personal and cultural cycle of poverty that hopelessly imprisons them. They routinely center on the Black urban population and focus on perceived personality or cultural traits that doom the poor. While the women in these stories typically exhibit an "attitude" that leads to trouble or a promiscuity that leads to single motherhood, the men possess a need for immediate gratification that leads to drug abuse or an unquenchable greed that leads to the pursuit of fast money. The images that are seared into our mind are sexist, racist, and classist. Census figures reveal that most of the poor are white not Black or Hispanic, that they live in rural or suburban areas not urban centers, and hold jobs at least part of the year. Yet, in a fashion that is often framed in an understanding and sympathetic tone, we are told that the poor have inflicted poverty on themselves.

The Poor Are Down on Their Luck

During the Christmas season, the news media sometimes provides us with accounts of poor individuals or families (usually white) who are down on their luck. These stories are often linked to stories about soup kitchens or other charitable activities and sometimes call for charitable contributions. These "Yule time" stories are as much about the affluent as they are about the poor: they tell us that the affluent in our society are a kind, understanding, giving people—which we are not.[1] The series of unfortunate circumstances that have led to impoverishment are presumed to be a temporary condition that will improve with time and a change in luck.

Despite appearances, the messages provided by the media are not entirely disparate. With each variation, the media informs us what poverty is not (i.e., systemic and indicative of American society) by informing us what it is. The media tells us that poverty is either an aberration of the American way of life (it doesn't exist, it's just another number, it's unfortunate but temporary) or an end product of the poor themselves (they are a nuisance, do not deserve better, and have brought their predicament upon themselves).

By suggesting that the poor have brought poverty upon themselves, the media is engaging in what William Ryan has called "blaming the victim." The media identifies in what ways the poor are different as a consequence of deprivation, then defines those differences as the cause of poverty itself. Whether blatantly hostile or cloaked in sympathy, the message is that there is something fundamentally wrong with the victims—their hormones, psychological makeup, family environment, community, race, or some combination of these—that accounts for their plight and their failure to lift themselves out of poverty.

But poverty in the United States is systemic. It is a direct result of economic and political policies that deprive people of jobs, adequate wages, or legitimate support. It is neither natural nor inevitable: there is enough wealth in our nation to eliminate poverty if we chose to redistribute existing wealth or income. The plight of the poor is reason enough to make the elimination of poverty the nation's first priority. But poverty also impacts dramatically on the non-poor. It has a dampening effect on wages in general (by maintaining a reserve army of unemployed and underemployed anxious for any job at any wage) and breeds crime and violence (by maintaining conditions that invite private gain by illegal means and rebellion-like behavior, not entirely unlike the urban riots of the 1960s). Given the extent of poverty in the nation and the impact it has on us all, the media must spin considerable magic to keep the poor and the issue of poverty and its root causes out of the public consciousness.

About Everyone Else

Both the broadcast and the print news media strive to develop a strong sense of "we-ness" in their audience. They seek to speak to and for an audience that is both affluent and like-minded. The media's solidarity with affluence, that is, with the middle and upper class, varies little from one medium to another. Benjamin DeMott points out, for example, that the *New York Times* understands affluence to be intelligence, taste, public spirit, responsibility, and a readiness to rule and "conceives itself as spokesperson for a readership awash in these qualities." Of course, the flip side to creating a sense of "we," or "us," is establishing a perception of the "other." The other relates back to the faceless, amoral, undeserving, and inferior "underclass." Thus, the world according to the news media is divided between the "underclass" and everyone else. Again the messages are often contradictory.

The Wealthy Are Us

Much of the information provided to us by the news media focuses attention on the concerns of a very wealthy and privileged class of people. Although the concerns of a small fraction of the populace, they are presented as though they were the concerns of everyone. For example, while relatively few people actually own stock, the news media devotes an inordinate amount of broadcast time and print space to business news and stock market quotations. Not only do business reports cater to a particular narrow clientele, so do the fashion pages (with $2,000 dresses), wedding announcements, and the obituaries. Even weather and sports news often have a class bias. An all news radio station in New York City, for example, provides regular national ski reports. International news, trade agreements, and domestic policies issues are also reported in terms of their impact on business climate and the business community. Besides being of practical value to the wealthy, such coverage has considerable ideological value. Its message: the concerns of the wealthy are the concerns of us all.

The Wealthy (as a Class) Do Not Exist

While preoccupied with the concerns of the wealthy, the media fails to notice the way in which the rich as a class of people create and shape domestic and foreign policy. Presented as an aggregate of individuals, the wealthy appear without special interests, interconnections, or unity in purpose. Out of public view are the class interests of the wealthy, the interlocking business links, the concerted actions to preserve their class privileges and business interests (by running for public office, supporting political candidates, lobbying, etc.). Corporate lobbying is ignored, taken for granted, or assumed to be in the public interest. (Compare this with the media's portrayal of the "strong arm of labor" in attempting to defeat trade legislation that is harmful to the interests of working people.) It is estimated that two-thirds of the U.S. Senate is composed of millionaires. Having such a preponderance of millionaires in the Senate, however, is perceived to be neither unusual nor antidemocratic; these millionaire senators are assumed to be serving "our" collective interests in governing.

The Wealthy Are Fascinating and Benevolent

The broadcast and print media regularly provide hype for individuals who have achieved "super" success. These stories are usually about celebrities and superstars from the sports and entertainment world. Society pages and gossip columns serve to keep the social elite informed of each other's doings, allow the rest of us to gawk at their excesses, and help to keep the American dream alive. The print media is also fond of feature stories on corporate empire builders. These stories provide an occasional "insider's" view of the private and corporate life

of industrialists by suggesting a rags to riches account of corporate success. These stories tell us that corporate success is a series of smart moves, shrewd acquisitions, timely mergers, and well thought out executive suite shuffles. By painting the upper class in a positive light, innocent of any wrongdoing (labor leaders and union organizations usually get the opposite treatment), the media assures us that wealth and power are benevolent. One person's capital accumulation is presumed to be good for all. The elite, then, are portrayed as investment wizards, people of special talent and skill, who even their victims (workers and consumers) can admire.

The Wealthy Include a Few Bad Apples

On rare occasions, the media will mock selected individuals for their personality flaws. Real estate investor Donald Trump and New York Yankees owner George Steinbrenner, for example, are admonished by the media for deliberately seeking publicity (a very un-upper-class thing to do); hotel owner Leona Helmsley was caricatured for her personal cruelties; and junk bond broker Michael Milkin was condemned because he had the audacity to rob the rich. Michael Parenti points out that by treating business wrongdoing as isolated deviations from the socially beneficial system of "responsible capitalism," the media overlooks the features of the system that produce such abuses and the regularity with which they occur. Rather than portraying them as predictable and frequent outcomes of corporate power and the business system, the media treats abuses as if they were isolated and atypical. Presented as an occasional aberration, these incidents serve not to challenge, but to legitimate, the system.

The Middle Class Is Us

By ignoring the poor and blurring the lines between the working people and the upper class, the news media creates a universal middle class. From this perspective, the size of one's income becomes largely irrelevant: what matters is that most of "us" share an intellectual and moral superiority over the disadvantaged. As *Time* magazine once concluded, "Middle America is a state of mind." "We are all middle class," we are told, "and we all share the same concerns": job security, inflation, tax burdens, world peace, the cost of food and housing, health care, clean air and water, and the safety of our streets. While the concerns of the wealthy are quite distinct from those of the middle class (e.g., the wealthy worry about investments, not jobs), the media convinces us that "we [the affluent] are all in this together."

The Middle Class Is a Victim

For the media, "we" the affluent not only stand apart from the "other"—the poor, the working class, the minorities, and their problems—"we" are also victimized by the poor (who drive up the costs of maintaining the welfare roles), minorities (who commit crimes against us), and by workers (who are greedy and drive companies out and prices up). Ignored are the subsidies to the rich, the crimes of corporate America, and the policies that wreak havoc on the economic well-being of middle America. Media magic convinces us to fear, more than anything else, being victimized by those less affluent than ourselves.

The Middle Class Is Not a Working Class

The news media clearly distinguishes the middle class (employees) from the working class (i.e., blue collar workers) who are portrayed, at best, as irrelevant, outmoded, and a dying breed. Furthermore, the media will tell us that the hardships faced by blue collar workers are inevitable (due to progress), a result of bad luck (chance circumstances in a particular industry), or a product of their own doing

(they priced themselves out of a job). Given the media's presentation of reality, it is hard to believe that manual, supervised, unskilled, and semiskilled workers actually represent more than 50 percent of the adult working population. The working class, instead, is relegated by the media to "the other."

In short, the news media either lionizes the wealthy or treats their interests and those of the middle class as one and the same. But the upper class and the middle class do not share the same interests or worries. Members of the upper class worry about stock dividends (not employment), they profit from inflation and global militarism, their children attend exclusive private schools, they eat and live in a royal fashion, they call on (or are called upon by) personal physicians, they have few consumer problems, they can escape whenever they want from environmental pollution, and they live on streets and travel to other areas under the protection of private police forces.[2]

The wealthy are not only a class with distinct life-styles and interests, they are a ruling class. They receive a disproportionate share of the country's yearly income, own a disproportionate amount of the country's wealth, and contribute a disproportionate number of their members to governmental bodies and decision-making groups—all traits that William Domhoff, in his classic work *Who Rules America*, defined as characteristic of a governing class.

This governing class maintains and manages our political and economic structures in such a way that these structures continue to yield an amazing proportion of our wealth to a minuscule upper class. While the media is not above referring to ruling classes in other countries (we hear, for example, references to Japan's ruling elite), its treatment of the news proceeds as though there were no such ruling class in the United States.

Furthermore, the news media inverts reality so that those who are working class and middle class learn to fear, resent, and blame those below, rather than those above them in the class structure. We learn to resent welfare, which accounts for only two cents out of every dollar in the federal budget (approximately $10 billion) and provides financial relief for the needy,[3] but learn little about the $11 billion the federal government spends on individuals with incomes in excess of $100,000 (not needy), or the $17 billion in farm subsidies, or the $214 billion (twenty times the cost of welfare) in interest payments to financial institutions.

Middle-class whites learn to fear African Americans and Latinos, but most violent crime occurs within poor and minority communities and is neither interracial[4] nor interclass. As horrid as such crime is, it should not mask the destruction and violence perpetrated by corporate America. In spite of the fact that 14,000 innocent people are killed on the job each year, 100,000 die prematurely, 400,000 become seriously ill, and 6 million are injured from work-related accidents and diseases, most Americans fear government regulation more than they do unsafe working conditions.

Through the media, middle-class—and even working-class—Americans learn to blame blue collar workers and their unions for declining purchasing power and economic security. But while workers who managed to keep their jobs and their unions struggled to keep up with inflation, the top 1 percent of American families saw their average incomes soar 80 percent in the last decade. Much of the wealth at the top was accumulated as stockholders and corporate executives moved their companies abroad to employ cheaper labor (56 cents per hour in El Salvador) and avoid paying taxes in the United States. Corporate America is a world made up of ruthless bosses, massive layoffs, favoritism and nepotism, health and safety violations, pension plan losses, union busting, tax evasions, unfair competition, and price gouging, as well as fast buck deals, financial speculation, and corporate wheeling and dealing that serve the interests of the corporate elite, but are generally wasteful and destructive to workers and the economy in general.

It is no wonder Americans cannot think straight about class. The mass media is neither objective, balanced, independent, nor neutral. Those who own and direct the mass media are themselves part of the upper class, and neither they nor the ruling class in general have to conspire to manipulate public opinion. Their interest is in preserving the status quo, and their view of society as fair and equitable comes naturally to them. But their ideology dominates our society and justifies what is in reality a perverse social order—one that perpetuates unprecedented elite privilege and power on the one hand and widespread deprivation on the other. A mass media that did not have its own class interests in preserving the status quo would acknowledge that inordinate wealth and power undermines democracy and that a "free market" economy can ravage a people and their communities.

Notes

1. American households with incomes of less than $10,000 give an average of 5.5 percent of their earnings to charity or to a religious organization, while those making more than $100,000 a year give only 2.9 percent. After changes in the 1986 tax code reduced the benefits of charitable giving, taxpayers earning $500,000 or more slashed their average donation by nearly one-third. Furthermore, many of these acts of benevolence do not help the needy. Rather than provide funding to social service agencies that aid the poor, the voluntary contributions of the wealthy go to places and institutions that entertain, inspire, cure, or educate wealthy Americans—art museums, opera houses, theaters, orchestras, ballet companies, private hospitals, and elite universities.

2. The number of private security guards in the United States now exceeds the number of public police officers. (Robert Reich, "Secession of the Successful." *New York Times Magazine,* February 1991.)

3. A total of $20 billion is spent on welfare when you include all state funding. But the average state funding also comes to only two cents per state dollar.

4. In 92 percent of the murders nationwide the assailant and the victim are of the same race (46 percent are white/white, 46 percent are black/black), 5.6 percent are black on white, and 2.4 percent are white on black. (FBI and Bureau of Justice Statistics, 1985–1986, quoted in Raymond S. Franklin. *Shadows of Race and Class*, University of Minnesota Press, Minneapolis, 1991, p. 108.)

THINKING ABOUT THE READING

What kinds of messages do people get about wealth and social position from the media? What do these messages suggest about who is deserving and who is not? If these messages are based on inaccurate stereotypes, where can people get more accurate information? Do you think that people in different social classes view themselves and their lives differently based on how they are portrayed in the news and on television? If these portrayals are a significant source of information about one's place in society, do you think these media images affect a person's sense of self-worth and opportunity?

Branded With Infamy

Inscriptions of Poverty and Class in America

Vivyan Adair

(2002)

"My kids and I been chopped up and spit out just like when I was a kid. My rotten teeth, my kids' twisted feet. My son's dull skin and blank stare. My oldest girl's stooped posture and the way she can't look no one in the eye no more. This all says we got nothing and we deserve what we got. On the street good families look at us and see right away what they'd be if they don't follow the rules. They're scared too, real scared."

—Welfare recipient and activist, Olympia, Washington, 1998

I begin with the words of a poor, White, single mother of three. Although officially she has only a tenth-grade education, she expertly reads and articulates a complex theory of power, bodily inscription, and socialization that arose directly from material conditions of her own life. She sees what many far more "educated" scholars and citizens fail to recognize: that the bodies of poor women and children are produced and positioned as texts that facilitate the mandates of a . . . profoundly brutal and mean-spirited political regime. . . .

Over the past decade or so, a host of inspired feminist welfare scholars and activists have addressed and examined the relationship between state power and the lives of poor women and children. As important and insightful as these exposés are, with few exceptions, they do not get at the closed circuit that fuses together systems of power, the material conditions of poverty, and the bodily experiences that allow for the perpetuation—and indeed the justification—of these systems. They fail to consider what the speaker of my opening passage recognized so astutely: that systems of power produce and patrol poverty through the reproduction of both social and bodily markers. . . .

. . . [In this article I employ the theory of Michel Foucault to describe how the body is] the product of historically specific power relations. Feminists have used this notion of social inscription to explain a range of bodily operations from cosmetic surgery (Brush 1998, Morgan 1991), prostitution (Bell 1994), and Anorexia Nervosa (Hopwood 1995, Bordo 1993) to motherhood (Chandler 1999, Smart 1992), race (Stoler 1995, Ford-Smith 1995), and cultural imperialism (Desmond 1991). As these analyses illustrate, Foucault allows us to consider and critique the body as it is invested with meaning and inserted into regimes of truth via the operations of power and knowledge. . . .

Foucault clarifies and expands on this process of bodily/social inscription in his early work. In "Nietzsche, Genealogy, History," he positions the physical body as virtual text, accounting for the fact that "the body is the inscribed surface of events that are traced by language and dissolved by ideas" (1977, 83). . . . For Foucault, the body and [power] are inseparable. In his logic, power constructs and holds bodies. . . .

In *Discipline and Punish* Foucault sets out to depict the genealogy of torture and discipline as it reflects a public display of power on the body of subjects in the 17th and 18th centuries. In graphic detail Foucault begins his book with the description of a criminal being tortured and then drawn and quartered in a public square. The crowds of good parents and their growing children watch and learn. The public spectacle works as a patrolling image, socializing and controlling bodies within the body politic. Eighteenth century torture "must mark the victim: it is intended, either by the scar it leaves on the body or by the spectacle that accompanies it, to brand the victim with infamy . . . it traces around or rather on the very body of the condemned man signs that can not be effaced" (1984, 179). For Foucault, public exhibitions of punishment served as a socializing process, writing culture's codes and values on the minds and bodies of its subjects. In the process punishment . . . rearranged bodies.

. . . Foucault's point in *Discipline and Punish* is . . . that public exhibition and inscription have been replaced in contemporary society by a much more effective process of socialization and self-inscription. According to Foucault, today discipline has replaced torture as the privileged punishment, but the body continues to be written on. Discipline produces "subjected and practiced bodies, docile bodies" (1984, 182). We become subjects . . . of ideology, disciplining and inscribing our own bodies/minds in the process of becoming stable and singular subjects. . . . The body continues to be the site and operation of ideology. . . .

Indeed, while we are all marked discursively by ideology in Foucault's paradigm, in the United States today poor women and children of all races are multiply marked with signs of both discipline and punishment that cannot be erased or effaced. They are systematically produced through both 20th century forces of socialization and discipline and 18th century exhibitions of public mutilation. In addition to coming into being as disciplined and docile bodies, poor single welfare mothers and their children are physically inscribed, punished, and displayed as dangerous and pathological

"other." It is important to note when considering the contemporary inscription of poverty as moral pathology etched onto the bodies of profoundly poor women and children, that these are more than metaphoric and self-patrolling marks of discipline. Rather on myriad levels—sexual, social, material and physical—poor women and their children, like the "deviants" publicly punished in Foucault's scenes of torture, are marked, mutilated, and made to bear and transmit signs in a public spectacle that brands the victim with infamy. . . .

The (Not So) Hidden Injuries of Class

Recycled images of poor, welfare women permeate and shape our national consciousness.[1] Yet—as is so often the case—these images and narratives tell us more about the culture that spawned and embraced them than they do about the object of the culture's obsession . . . .

These productions orchestrate the story of poverty as one of moral and intellectual lack and of chaos, pathology, promiscuity, illogic, and sloth, juxtaposed always against the order, progress, and decency of "deserving" citizens. . . .

I am, and will probably always be, marked as a poor woman. I was raised by a poor, single, White mother who had to struggle to keep her four children fed, sheltered, and clothed by working at what seemed like an endless stream of minimum wage, exhausting, and demeaning jobs. As a child poverty was written onto and into my being at the level of private and public thought and body. At an early age my body bore witness to and emitted signs of the painful devaluation carved into my flesh; that same devaluation became integral to my being in the world. I came into being as disciplined body/mind while at the same time I was taught to read my abject body as the site of my own punishment and erasure. In this excess of meaning the space between private body and public sign was collapsed.

For many poor children this double exposure results in debilitating . . . shame and lack. As Carolyn Kay Steedman reminds us in

Landscape for a Good Woman, the mental life of poor children flows from material deprivation. Steedman speaks of the "relentless laying down of guilt" she experienced as a poor child living in a world where identity was shaped through envy and unfulfilled desire and where her own body "told me stories of the terrible unfairness of things, of the subterranean culture of longing for that which one can never have" (1987, 8). For Steedman, public devaluation and punishment "demonstrated to us all the hierarchies of our illegality, the impropriety of our existence, our marginality within the social system" (1987, 9). Even as an adult she recalls that:

> . . . the baggage will never lighten for me or my sister. We were born, and had no choice in the matter; but we were social burdens, expensive, unworthy, never grateful enough. There was nothing we could do to pay back the debt of our existence. (1987, 19)

Indeed, poor children are often marked with bodily signs that cannot be forgotten or erased. Their bodies are physically inscribed as "other" and then read as pathological, dangerous, and undeserving. What I recall most vividly about being a child in a profoundly poor family was that we were constantly hurt and ill, and because we could not afford medical care, small illnesses and accidents spiraled into more dangerous illnesses and complications that became both a part of who we were and written proof that we were of no value in the world.

In spite of my mother's heroic efforts, at an early age my brothers and sister and I were stooped, bore scars that never healed properly, and limped with feet mangled by ill-fitting, used Salvation Army shoes. When my sister's forehead was split open by a door slammed in frustration, my mother "pasted" the angry wound together on her own, leaving a mark of our inability to afford medical attention, of our lack, on her very forehead. When I suffered from a concussion, my mother simply put borrowed ice on my head and tried to keep me awake for a night. And when throughout elementary school we were sent to the office for mandatory and very public yearly checks, the school nurse sucked air through her teeth as she donned surgical gloves to check only the hair of poor children for lice.

We were read as unworthy, laughable, and often dangerous. Our school mates laughed at our "ugly shoes," our crooked and ill-serviced teeth, and the way we "stank," as teachers excoriated us for inability to concentrate in school, our "refusal" to come to class prepared with proper school supplies, and our unethical behavior when we tried to take more than our allocated share of "free lunch."[2] Whenever backpacks or library books came up missing, we were publicly interrogated and sent home to "think about" our offences, often accompanied by notes that reminded my mother that as a poor single parent she should be working twice as hard to make up for the discipline that allegedly walked out the door with my father. When we sat glued to our seats, afraid to stand in front of the class in ragged and ill-fitting hand-me-downs, we were held up as examples of unprepared and uncooperative children. And when our grades reflected our otherness, they were used to justify even more elaborate punishment. . . .

Friends who were poor as children, and respondents to a survey I conducted in 1998,[3] tell similar stories of the branding they received at the hands of teachers, administrators, and peers. An African-American woman raised in Yesler Terrace, a public housing complex in Seattle, Washington, writes:

> Poor was all over our faces. My glasses were taped and too weak. My big brother had missing teeth. My mom was dull and ashy. It was like a story of how poor we were that anyone could see. My sister Evie's lip was bit by a dog and we just had dime store stuff to put on it. Her lip was a big scar. Then she never smiled and no one smiled at her cause she never smiled. Kids called her "Scarface." Teachers never smiled at her. The princip[al] put her in detention all the time because she was mean and bad (they said).

And, a White woman in the Utica, New York, area remembers:

> We lived in dilapidated and unsafe housing that had fleas no matter how clean my mom tried to be. We had bites all over us. Living in our car between evictions was even worse—then we didn't have a bathroom so I got kidney problems that I never had doctor's help for. When my teachers wouldn't let me got to the bathroom every hour or so I would wet my pants in class. You can imagine what the kids did to me about that. And the teachers would refuse to let me go to the bathroom because they said I was willful.

Material deprivation is publicly written on the bodies of poor children in the world. In the United States poor families experience violent crime, hunger, lack of medical and dental care, utility shut-offs, the effects of living in unsafe housing and/or of being homeless, chronic illness, and insufficient winter clothing (Lein and Edin 1996, 224–231). According to Jody Raphael of the Taylor Institute, poor women and their children are also at five times the risk of experiencing domestic violence (Raphael, 2000).

As children, our disheveled and broken bodies were produced and read as signs of our inferiority and undeservedness. As adults our mutilated bodies are read as signs of inner chaos, immaturity, and indecency as we are punished and then read as proof of need for further discipline and punishment. When my already bad teeth started to rot and I was out of my head with pain, my choices as an adult welfare recipient were to either let my teeth fall out or have them pulled out. In either case the culture would then read me as a "toothless illiterate," as a fearful joke. In order to pay my rent and to put shoes on my daughter's feet I sold blood at two or three different clinics on a monthly basis until I became so anemic that they refused to buy it from me. A neighbor of mine went back to the man who continued to beat her and her children after being denied welfare benefits, when she realized that she could not adequately feed, clothe and house her family on her own minimum wage income.

My good friend sold her ovum to a fertility clinic in a painful and potentially damaging process. Other friends exposed themselves to all manner of danger and disease by selling their bodies for sex in order to feed and clothe their babies.

Exhaustion also marks the bodies of poor women in indelible script. Rest becomes a privilege we simply cannot afford. After working full shifts each day, poor mothers trying to support themselves at minimum wage jobs continue to work to a point of exhaustion that is inscribed on their faces, their bodies, their posture, and their diminishing sense of self and value in the world. My former neighbor recently recalled:

> I had to take connecting buses to bring and pick up my daughters at childcare after working on my feet all day. As soon as we arrived at home, we would head out again by bus to do laundry. Pick up groceries. Try to get to the food bank. Beg the electric company to not turn off our lights and heat again. Find free winter clothing. Sell my blood. I would be home at nine or ten o'clock at night. I was loaded down with one baby asleep and one crying. Carrying lots of heavy bags and ready to drop on my feet. I had bags under my eyes and no shampoo to wash my hair so I used soap. Anyway I had to stay up to wash diapers in the sink. Otherwise they wouldn't be dry when I left the house in the dark with my girls. In the morning I start all over again.

This bruised and lifeless body, hauling sniffling babies and bags of dirty laundry on the bus, was then read as a sign that she was a bad mother and a threat that needed to be disciplined and made to work even harder for her own good. Those who need the respite less go away for weekends, take drives in the woods, take their kids to the beach. Poor women without education are pushed into minimum wage jobs and have no money, no car, no time, no energy, and little support, as their bodies are made to display marks of their material deprivation as a socializing and patrolling force.

Ultimately, we come to recognize that our bodies are not our own; that they are rather public property. State mandated blood tests, interrogation of the most private aspects of our lives, the public humiliation of having to beg officials for food and medicine, and the loss of all right to privacy, teach us that our bodies are only useful as lessons, warnings, and signs of degradation that everyone loves to hate. In "From Welfare to Academe: Welfare Reform as College-Educated Welfare Mothers Know It," Sandy Smith-Madsen describes the erosion of her privacy as a poor welfare mother:

> I was investigated. I was spied upon. A welfare investigator came into my home and after thoughtful deliberation, granted me permission to keep my belongings. . . . Like the witch hunts of old, if a neighbor reports you as a welfare queen, the guardians of the state's compelling interest come into your home and interrogate you. While they do not have the right to set your body ablaze on the public square, they can forever devastate heart and soul by snatching away children. Just like a police officer, they may use whatever they happen to see against you, including sexual orientation. Full-fledged citizens have the right to deny an officer entry into their home unless they possess a search warrant; welfare mothers fork over citizenship rights for the price of a welfare check. In Tennessee, constitutional rights go for a cash value of $185 per month for a family of three. (2000, 185)

Welfare reform policy is designed to publicly expose, humiliate, punish and display "deviant" welfare mothers. "Workfare" and "Learnfare"—two alleged successes of welfare reform—require that landlords, teachers, and employers be made explicitly aware of the second class status of these very public bodies. In Ohio, the Department of Human Services uses tax dollars to pay for advertisements on the side of Cleveland's RTA busses that show a "Welfare Queen" behind bars with a logo that proclaims "Crime does not pay. Welfare fraud is a crime" (Robinson 1999). In Michigan a pilot program mandating drug tests for all welfare recipients began on October 1, 1999. Recipients who

refuse the test will lose their benefits immediately (Simon 1999). In Buffalo, New York, a County Executive proudly announced that his county will begin intensive investigation of all parents who refuse minimum wage jobs that are offered to them by the state. He warned: "We have many ways of investigating and exposing these errant parents who choose to exploit their children in this way" (Anderson 1999). And, welfare reform legislation enacted in 1996 as the Personal Responsibility and Work Opportunities Reconciliation Act (PRWORA), requires that poor mothers work full-time, earning minimum wage salaries with which they cannot support their children. Often denied medical, dental, and childcare benefits, and unable to provide their families with adequate food, heat, or clothing, through this legislation the state mandates child neglect and abuse. The crowds of good parents and their growing children watch and learn. . . .

Reading and Rewriting the Body . . .

The bodies of poor women and children, scarred and mutilated by state mandated material deprivation and public exhibition, work as spectacles, as patrolling images socializing and controlling bodies within the body politic. . . .

Spectacular cover stories of the "Welfare Queen" play and re-play in the national mind's eye, becoming a prescriptive lens through which the American public as a whole reads the individual dramas of the bodies of poor women and their place and value in the world. These dramas produce "normative" citizens as singular, stable, rational, ordered, and free. In this dichotomous, hierarchical frame the poor welfare mother is juxtaposed against a logic of "normative" subjectivity as the embodiment of disorder, disarray, and other-ness. Her broken and scarred body becomes proof of her inner pathology and chaos, suggesting the need for further punishment and discipline.

In contemporary narrative welfare women are imagined to be dangerous because they refuse to sacrifice their desires and fail to participate in legally sanctioned heterosexual relationships; theirs is read, as a result, as a selfish, "unnatural," and immature sexuality. In this script, the bodies of poor women are viewed as being dangerously beyond the control of men and are as a result construed as the bearers of perverse desire. In this androcentric equation fathers become the sole bearers of order and of law, defending poor women and children against their own unchecked sexuality and lawlessness.

For Republican Senator [now Attorney General] John Ashcroft writing in *The St. Louis Dispatch*, the inner city is the site of "rampant illegitimacy" and a "space devoid of discipline" where all values are askew. For Ashcroft, what is insidious is not material poverty, but an entitlement system that has allowed "out-of-control" poor women to rupture traditional patriarchal authority, valuation, and boundaries (1995, A:23). Impoverished communities then become a site of chaos because without fathers they allegedly lack any organizing or patrolling principle. George Gilder agrees with Ashcroft when he writes in the conservative *American Spectator* that:

> The key problem of the welfare culture is not unemployed women and poor children. It is the women's skewed and traumatic relationships with men. In a reversal of the pattern of civilized societies, the women have the income and the ties to government authority and support. . . . This balance of power virtually prohibits marriage, which is everywhere based on the provider role of men, counterbalancing the sexual and domestic superiority of women. (1995, B:6)

For Gilder, the imprimatur of welfare women's sordid bodies unacceptably shifts the focus of the narrative from a male presence to a feminized absence.

In positioning welfare mothers as sexually chaotic, irrational, and unstable, their figures are temporarily immobilized and made to yield meaning as a space that must be brought under control and transformed through public displays of punishment. Poor single mothers and children who have been abandoned, have fled physical, sexual, and/or psychological abuse, or have in general refused to capitulate to male control within the home are mythologized as dangerous, pathological, out of control, and selfishly unable—or unwilling—to sacrifice their "naturally" unnatural desires. They are understood and punished as a danger to a culture resting on a foundation of inviolate male authority and absolute privilege in both public and private spheres.

William Raspberry disposes of poor women as selfish and immature, when in "Ms. Smith Goes After Washington," he warrants that:

> . . . unfortunately AFDC is paid to an unaccountable, accidental and unprepared parent who has chosen her head of household status as a personal form of satisfaction, while lacking the simple life skills and maturity to achieve love and job fulfillment from any other source. I submit that all of our other social ills—crime, drugs, violence, failing schools . . . are a direct result of the degradation of parenthood by emotionally immature recipients. (1995, A:19)

Raspberry goes on to assert that like poor children, poor mothers must be made visible reminders to the rest of the culture of the "poor choices" they have made. He claims that rather than "coddling" her, we have a responsibility to "shame her" and to use her failure to teach other young women that it is "morally wrong for unmarried women to bear children," as we "cast single motherhood as a selfish and immature act" (1995, A:19).

Continuous, multiple, and often seamless public inscription, punishing policy, and lives of unbearable material lack leave poor women and their children scarred, exhausted, and confused. As a result their bodies are imagined as an embodiment of decay and cultural dis-ease that threatens the health and progress of our nation. . . . In a 1995 *USA Today* article entitled "America at Risk: Can We Survive Without Moral Values?" for example, the inner city is portrayed as a "*dark*" realm of "*decay* rooted in the *loss* of values, the *death* of work ethics, and the *deterioration* of families and communities."

Allegedly here, "all morality has *rotted* due to a *breakdown* in gender discipline." This space of disorder and disease is marked with tropes of race and gender. It is also associated with the imagery of "communities of women *without* male leadership, cultural values and initiative [emphasis added]" (1995, C:3). In George Will's *Newsweek* editorial he proclaims that "*illogical* feminist and racial *anger* coupled with *misplaced* American emotion may be part or a cause of the *irresponsible* behavior *rampant* in poor neighborhoods." Will continues, proclaiming that here "mothers *lack* control over their children and have *selfishly* taught them to embrace a *pathological* ethos that values *self-need* and *self-expression* over self-control [emphasis added]" (1995, 23).

Poor women and children's bodies, publicly scarred and mutilated by material deprivation, are read as expressions of an essential lack of discipline and order. In response to this perception, journalist Ronald Brownstein of the *L.A. Times* proposed that the *Republican Contract with America* will "*restore* America to its path, *enforcing* social *order* and common *standards* of behavior, and replacing *stagnation* and *decay* with *movement* and *forward* thinking *energy* [emphasis added]" (1994, A:20). In these rhetorical fields poverty is . . . linked to lack of progress that would allegedly otherwise order, stabilize, and restore the culture. What emerges from these diatribes is the positioning of patriarchal, racist, capitalist, hierarchical, and heterosexist "order" and movement against the alleged stagnation and decay of the body of the "Welfare Queen."

Race is clearly written on the body of the poor single mother. The welfare mother, imagined as young, never married, and Black (contrary to statistical evidence[4]), is framed as dangerous and in need of punishment because she "naturally" emasculates her own men, refuses to service White men, and passes on—rather than appropriate codes of subservience and submission—a disruptive culture of resistance, survival, and "misplaced" pride to her children (Collins 1991). In stark contrast, widowed women with social security and divorced women with child support and alimony are imaged as White, legal, and proper-tied mothers whose value rests on their abilities to stay in their homes, care for their own children, and impart traditional cultural morals to their offspring, all for the betterment of the culture. In this narrative welfare mothers have only an "outlaw" culture to impart. Here the welfare mother is read as both the product and the producer of a culture of disease and disorder. These narratives imagine poor women as powerful contagion capable of, perhaps even lying in wait to infect their own children as raced, gendered, and classed agents of their "diseased" nature. In contemporary discourses of poverty racial tropes position poor women's bodies as dangerous sites of "naturalized chaos" and as potentially valuable economic commodities who refuse their proper role.

Gary McDougal in "The Missing Half of the Welfare Debate" furthers this image by referring to the "crab effect of poverty" through which mothers and friends of individuals striving to break free of economic dependency allegedly "pull them back down." McDougal affirms—again despite statistical evidence to the contrary—that the mothers of welfare recipients are most often themselves "generational welfare freeloaders lacking traditional values and family ties who can not, and will not, teach their children right from wrong." "These women" he asserts "would be better off doing any kind of labor regardless of how little it pays, just to get them out of the house, to break their cycles of degeneracy" (1996, A:16).

In this plenitude of images of evil mothers, the poor welfare mother threatens not just her own children, but all children. The Welfare Queen is made to signify moral aberration and economic drain; her figure becomes even more impacted once responsibility for the destruction of the "American Way of Life" is attributed to her. Ronald Brownstein reads her "spider web of dependency" as a "crisis of character development that leads to a morally bankrupt American ideology" (1994, A:6).

These representations position welfare mothers' bodies as sites of destruction and as catalysts for a culture of depravity and disobedience; in the process they produce a reading of the writing on the body of the poor woman that calls for further punishment and discipline. In New York City, "Workfare" programs force *lazy* poor women to take a job—"any job"—including working for the city wearing orange surplus prison uniforms picking up garbage on the highway and in parks for about $1.10 per hour (Dreier 1999). "Bridefare" programs in Wisconsin give added benefits to *licentious* welfare women who marry a man—"any man"—and publish a celebration of their "reform" in local newspapers (Dresang 1996). "Tidyfare" programs across the nation allow state workers to enter and inspect the homes of poor *slovenly* women so that they can monetarily sanction families whose homes are deemed to be appropriately tidied.[5] "Learnfare" programs in many states publicly expose and fine *undisciplined* mothers who for any reason have children who don't (or can't) attend school on a regular basis (Muir 1993). All of these welfare reform programs are designed to expose and publicly punish the *misfits* whose bodies are read as proof of their refusal or inability to capitulate to androcentric, capitalist, racist, and heterosexism values and mores.

The Power of Poor Women's Communal Resistance

Despite the rhetoric and policy that mark and mutilate our bodies, poor women survive. Hundreds of thousands of us are somehow good parents despite the systems that are designed to prohibit us from being so. We live on the unlivable and teach our children love, strength, and grace. We network, solve irresolvable dilemmas, and support each other and our families. If we somehow manage to find a decent pair of shoes, or save our foodstamps to buy our children a birthday cake, we are accused of being cheats or living too high. If our children suffer, it is read as proof of our inferiority and bad mothering; if they succeed we are suspect for being too pushy, for taking

more than our share of free services, or for having too much free time to devote to them. Yet, as former welfare recipient Janet Diamond says in the introduction to *For Crying Out Loud*:

> In spite of public censure, welfare mothers graduate from school, get decent jobs, watch their children achieve, make good lives for themselves . . . welfare mothers continue to be my inspiration, not because they survive, but because they dare to dream. Because when you are a welfare recipient, laughter is an act of rebellion. (1986, 1)

. . . Because power is diffuse, heterogeneous, and contradictory, poor women struggle against the marks of their degradation. . . .

Poor women rebel by organizing for physical and emotional respite, and eventually for political power. My own resistance was born in the space between self-loathing and my love of and respect for poor women who were fighting together against oppression. In the throes of political activism (at first I was dragged blindly into such actions, ironically, in a protest that required, according to the organizer, just so many poor women's bodies) I became caught up in the contradiction between my body's meaning as despised public sign, and our shared sense of communal power, knowledge, authority, and beauty. Learning about labor movements, fighting for rent control, demanding fair treatment at the welfare office, sharing the costs, burdens, and joys of raising children, forming good cooperatives, working with other poor women to go to college, and organizing for political change, became addictive and life affirming acts of resistance.

Communal affiliation among poor women is discouraged, indeed in many cases prohibited, by those with power over our lives. Welfare offices, for example, are designed to prevent poor women from talking together; uncomfortable plastic chairs are secured to the ground in arrangements that make it difficult to communicate, silence is maintained in waiting rooms, case workers are rotated so that they do not become too "attached" to their clients, and, reinforced by "Welfare Fraud" signs covering industrially painted walls, we are daily reminded not to trust anyone with the details of our lives for fear of further exposure and punishment. And so, like most poor women, I had remained isolated, ashamed, and convinced that I was alone in, and responsible for, my suffering.

Through shared activism we became increasingly aware of our individual bodies as sites of contestation and of our collective body as a site of resistance and as a source power.

Noemy Vides in "Together We Are Getting Freedom," reminds us that "by talking and writing about learned shame together, [poor women] pursue their own liberation" (305). Vides adds that it is through this process that she learned to challenge the dominant explanations that decreed her value in the world,

> provoking an awareness that the labels— ignorant peasant, abandoned woman, broken-English speaker, welfare cheat—have nothing to do with who one really is, but serve to keep women subjugated and divided. [This communal process] gives women tools to understand the uses of power; it emboldens us to move beyond the imposed shame that silences, to speak out and join together in a common liberatory struggle. (305)

In struggling together we contest the marks of our bodily inscription, disrupt the use of our bodies as public sign, change the conditions of our lives, and survive. In the process we come to understand that the shaping of our bodies is not coterminous with our beings or abilities as a whole. Contestation and the deployment of new truths cannot erase the marks of our poverty, but the process does transform the ways in which we are able to interrogate and critique our bodies and the systems that have branded them with infamy. As a result these signs are rendered fragile, unstable, and ultimately malleable.

Notes

1. Throughout this paper I use the terms "welfare recipients," and "poor working women" interchangeably because as the recent *Urban Institute* study made

clear, today these populations are, in fact, one and the same. (Loprest 1999)

2. As recently as 1995, in my daughter's public elementary school cafeteria, "free lunchers" (poor children who could not otherwise afford to eat lunch, including my daughter) were reminded with a large and colorful sign to "line up last."

3. The goal of my survey was to measure the impact of the 1996 welfare reform legislation on the lives of profoundly poor women and children in the United States. Early in 1998 I sent fifty questionnaires and narrative surveys to four groups of poor women on the West and the East coasts; thirty-nine were returned to me. I followed these surveys with forty-five minute interviews with twenty of the surveyed women.

4. In the two years directly preceding the passage of the PRWORA, as a part of sweeping welfare reform, in the United States the largest percentage of people on welfare were white (39%) and fewer than 10% were teen mothers. (1994. U.S. Department of Health and Human Services, "An Overview of Entitlement Programs")

5. *Tidyfare* programs additionally required that caseworkers inventory the belongings of AFDC recipients so that they could require them to "sell-down" their assets. In my own case, in 1994 a HUD inspector came into my home, counted my daughter's books, checked them against his list to see that as a nine year old she was only entitled to have twelve books, calculated what he perceived to be the value of the excess books, and then had my AFDC check reduced by that amount in the following month.

REFERENCES

Abramovitz, Mimi. 1989. *Regulating the lives of women: Social welfare policy from colonial times to the present.* Boston: South End Press.
———. 2000. *Under attack, fighting back.* New York: Monthly Review Press.
Albelda, Randy. 1997. *Glass ceilings and bottomless pits: Women's work, women's poverty.* Boston: South End Press.
"America at risk: Can we survive without moral values?" 1995. *USA Today.* October, Sec. C: 3.
Amott, Teresa. 1993. *Caught in the crises: Women and the U.S. economy today.* New York: Monthly Review Press.

Anderson, Dale. 1999. "County to investigate some welfare recipients." *The Buffalo News.* August 18, Sec. B: 5.

Ashcroft, John. 1995. "Illegitimacy rampant." *The St. Louis Dispatch.* July 2, Sec. A: 23.

Bell, Shannon. 1994. *Reading, writing and rewriting the prostitute body.* Bloomington and Indianapolis: Indiana University Press.

Bordo, Susan, 1993. *Unbearable weight: Feminism, Western culture and the body.* Berkeley: University of California Press.

Brownstein, Ronald. 1994. "GOP welfare proposals more conservative." *Los Angeles Times,* May 20, Sec. A: 20.

———. 1994. "Latest welfare reform plan reflects liberals' priorities." *Los Angeles Times.* May 20, Sec. A: 6.

Chandler, Mielle. 1999. "Queering maternity." *Journal of the Association for Research on Mothering.* Vol. 1, no. 2, (21–32).

Collins, Patricia Hill. 2000. *Black feminist thought: Knowledge, consciousness, and the politics of empowerment.* New York: Routledge.

Crompton, Rosemary. 1986. *Gender and stratification.* New York: Polity Press.

Desmond, Jane. 1991. "Dancing out the difference; cultural imperialism and Ruth St. Denis's Radna of 1906." *Signs.* Vol. 17, no. 1, Autumn, (28–49).

Diamond, Janet. 1986. *For crying out loud: Women and poverty in the United States.* Boston: Pilgrim Press.

Dreier, Peter. 1999. "Treat welfare recipients like workers." *Los Angeles Times.* August 29, Sec. M: 6.

Dresang, Joel. 1996. "Bridefare designer, reform beneficiary have role in governor's address." *Milwaukee Journal Sentinel.* August 14, Sec. 9.

Dujon, Diane and Ann Withorn. 1996. *For crying out loud: Women's poverty in the Unites States.* South End Press.

Edin, Kathryn and Laura Lein. 1997. *Making ends meet: How single mothers survive welfare and low wage work.* Russell Sage Foundation.

Ford-Smith, Honor. 1995. "Making white ladies: Race, gender and the production of identity in late colonial Jamaica." *Resources for Feminist Research,* Vol. 23, no. 4, Winter, (55–67).

Foucault, Michel. 1984. Discipline and punish. In P. Rabinow (ed.) *The Foucault reader.* New York: Pantheon Books.

———. 1978. *The history of sexuality: An introduction.* Trans. R. Hurley. Harmondsworth: Penguin.

———. 1984. "Nietzsche, genealogy, history." In P. Rabinow (ed.) *The Foucault reader.* New York: Pantheon Books.

———. 1980. *Power/knowledge: Selected interviews and other writings 1972–1977.* C. Gordon (ed.). Brighton: Harvester.

Funiciello, Theresa. 1998. "The brutality of bureaucracy." *Race, class and gender: An anthology,* 3rd ed. Eds. Margaret L. Andersen and Patricia Hill Collins. Belmont: Wadsworth Publishing Company, (377–381).

Gilder, George. 1995. "Welfare fraud today." *American Spectator.* September 5, Sec. B: 6.

Gordon, Linda. 1995. *Pitied, but not entitled: Single mothers and the history of welfare.* New York: Belknap Press, 1995.

hooks, bell. "Thinking about race, class, gender and ethics" 1999. Presentation at Hamilton College, Clinton, New York.

Hopwood, Catherine. 1995. "My discourse/myself: Therapy as possibility (for women who eat compulsively)." *Feminist Review.* No. 49, Spring, (66–82).

Langston, Donna. 1998. "Tired of playing monopoly?" *In Race, class and gender: An anthology,* 3rd ed. Eds. Margaret L. Andersen and Patricia Hill Collins. Belmont: Wadsworth Publishing Company, (126–136).

Lerman, Robert. 1995. "And for fathers?" *The Washington Post.* August 7, Sec. A: 19.

Loprest, Pamela. 1999. "Families who left welfare: Who are they and how are they doing?" *The Urban Institute,* Washington, D.C. August, No. B-1.

McDougal, Gary. 1996. "The missing half of the welfare debate." *The Wall Street Journal.* September 6, Sec. A: 16 (W).

McNay, Lois. 1992. *Foucault and feminism: Power, gender and the self.* Boston: Northeastern University Press.

Mink, Gwendoly. 1998. *Welfare's end.* Cornell University Press.

———. 1996. *The wages of motherhood: Inequality in the welfare state 1917–1942.* Cornell University Press.

Morgan, Kathryn. 1991. "Women and the knife: Cosmetic surgery and the colonization of women's bodies." *Hepatia.* V6, no 3. Fall, (25–53).

Muir, Kate. 1993. "Runaway fathers at welfare's final frontier. *The Times.* Times Newspapers Limited. July 19, Sec. A: 2.

"An overview of entitlement programs." 1994. U.S. Department of Health and Human Services. Washington, DC: U.S. Government Printing Office.

Piven, Frances Fox and Richard Cloward. 1993. *Regulating the poor: The functions of public welfare.* New York: Vintage Books.

Raspberry, William. 1995. "Ms. Smith goes after Washington." *The Washington Post.* February 1, Sec. A: 19.

———. 1996. "Uplifting the human spirit." *The Washington Post.* August 8, Sec. A: 31.

Robinson, Valerie. 1999. "State's ad attacks the poor." *The Plain Dealer,* November 2, Sec. B: 8.

Sennett, Richard and Jonathan Cobb. 1972. *The hidden injuries of class.* New York: Vintage Books.

Sidel, Ruth. 1998. *Keeping women and children last: America's war on the poor.* New York: Penguin Books.

Simon, Stephanie. 1999. "Drug tests for welfare applicants." *The Los Angeles Times.* December 18, Sec. A: 1. National Desk.

Smart, Carol. 1997. *Regulating womanhood: Essays on marriage, motherhood and sexuality.* New York: Routledge.

———. *Disruptive bodies and unruly sex: the regulation of reproduction and sexuality in the nineteenth century.* New York: Routledge, (7–32).

Smith-Madsen, Sandy. 2000. "From welfare to academe: Welfare reform as college-educated welfare mothers know it." *And still we rise: Women, poverty and the promise of education in America.* Forthcoming. Vivyan Adair and Sandra Dahlber (eds.). Philadelphia: Temple University Press, (160–186).

Steedman, Carolyn Kay. 1987. *Landscape for a good woman.* New Brunswick, N.J., Rutgers University Press.

Stoler, Ann Laura. 1995. *Race and the education of desire: Foucault's history of sexuality and the colonial order of things.* Durham: Duke University Press.

Sylvester, Kathleen. 1995. "Welfare debate." *The Washington Post.* September 3, Sec. E: 15.

Tanner, Michael. 1995. "Why welfare pays." *The Wall Street Journal.* September 28, Sec. A: 18 (W).

Vides, Noemy and Victoria Steinitz. 1996. "Together we are getting freedom." *For crying out loud.* Diane Dujon and Ann Withorn (eds.). Boston: South End Press, (295–306).

Will, George. 1995. "Welfare gate." *Newsweek.* February 5, Sec. 23.

THINKING ABOUT THE READING

When we think of people's bodies being labeled as deviant, we usually assume the bodies in question either deviate from cultural standards of shape and size or are marked by some noticeable physical handicap. However, Adair shows us that poor women's and children's bodies are tagged as undesirable in ways that are just as profound and just as hard to erase. What does she mean when she says that the illnesses and accidents of youth became part of a visible reminder of who poor people are in the eyes of others? How do the public degradations suffered by poor people (for instance, having a school nurse wear surgical gloves to check only the hair of poor children for lice) reinforce their subordinate status in society? Why do you think Adair continually evokes the images of "danger," "discipline," and "punishment" in describing the ways non-poor people perceive and respond to the physical appearance of poor people? Explain how focusing on the "deviance" of poor people deflects public attention away from the harmful acts committed by more affluent citizens.

The People of Wal-Mart

Nicholas Copeland and Christine Labuski

(2013)

In March 2011, The Wal-Mart Foundation donated $2 million and six thousand items of business-wear to Dress for Success (DFS), a New York City-based organization whose mission is to assist low-income women prepare for the workplace. Wal-Mart's press release, which emphasized the "desperate" need of DFS's clients, as well as Wal-Mart's commitment to working women, was distributed widely; it was soon followed by a video, which was uploaded to the "Community Journal" page of Wal-Martnyc.com, the company website (now known as nyc.walmartcommunity.com) dedicated to "separating the facts from the fiction" about Wal-Mart's mostly unsuccessful attempts to establish stores in New York City. In addition to interviews with Joi Gordon, CEO of Dress for Success, and Mary Fox, Wal-Mart's Senior Vice President of Global Apparel Sourcing, the video prominently features one of the collaboration's greatest success stories—Lyneese Roldan. A stylish African-American woman in her early thirties who, according to Ms. Gordon, was "homeless" and "living couch-to-couch" prior to working with DFS, Lyneese is presented as living proof of the attainability of the American Dream for women of color willing to make the personal changes necessary for success. Through a DFS program called the *Going Places Network,* Ms. Roldan secured steady employment with cosmetics icon Bobbi Brown. For Lyneese, "[i]t was the greatest day of [her] life," and she tells the viewer, in no uncertain terms: "I am going places. And I know this. So I'm very grateful."

The *Going Places Network,* a 12-week skills enhancement course sponsored by Wal-Mart, is an extension of a pilot program that the company launched with DFS in 2009 "in response to [the country's] challenging economic climate." According to DFS's website, the Network is intended to "help unemployed and under-employed Dress for Success clients gain professional skills, accelerate their job search and build confidence through weekly training sessions, one-on-one career coaching and networking in a supportive environment." The pilot program was deemed successful enough for Wal-Mart to make their $2 million donation, enabling DFS to expand the program to 60 U.S. cities.

One of the earliest cities to receive a substantial sum of the money was Chicago. Though the city has very recently begun to open its borders to Wal-Mart, Chicago was slow to embrace the retail giant, due to the same kinds of concerns expressed by New Yorkers (Jones 2010). Wal-Mart used DFS to smooth their passage into both these cities through the bodies of these women, specifically their public displays of mobility and gratitude. By wearing suits manufactured for Wal-Mart, and by having their job training linked to the company's patronage, participants in the *Going Places Network* were repackaged as affective stakeholders in Wal-Mart's success. This philanthropy reinforced Wal-Mart's carefully cultivated self-image as a path to economic independence for impoverished, non-white women.

Less than two weeks after this media flurry, the United States Supreme Court heard opening arguments for a lawsuit known as *Wal-Mart v. Dukes.* Betty Dukes, the plaintiff, was then a 60-year-old African-American woman from California. Dukes has worked for Wal-Mart since 1994, and in 2001, along with four other former and current employees, she filed a sex discrimination suit that claimed she had been denied the training and opportunity she needed to advance within the company. The suit further alleged that "Wal-Mart discriminates against its female employees in making promotions, job assignments, pay decisions and training, and retaliates against women who complain against such practices." After Ms. Dukes' initial filing, 1.6 million additional women signed on, representing a substantial portion of the women who have worked for Wal-Mart since the cutoff date of December 26, 1998.

One key issue in the case was whether the women could sue the company as a "class"— that is, as a group of people who had been collectively injured by the same individual or organization. In order to be considered a class, the plaintiffs' attorneys had to demonstrate that Wal-Mart treated women *as a whole* differently than they did men—an allegation upheld by a previous court, which had found "significant proof of a corporate policy of discrimination," Not surprisingly, Wal-Mart vehemently disputed these allegations, and appealed the case all the way to the Supreme Court. Not only did Wal-Mart vigorously deny the charges of discrimination, they also insisted that their 4,000-plus stores are too different from one another—in size, location, workforce, and overall character—for the company to be guilty of the systematic behavior alleged by the plaintiffs.

In June 2011, The Supreme Court ruled against Betty Dukes and her peers, having decided that the plaintiffs had "little in common but their sex and their lawsuit." Though individual women are still free to sue the company of their own accord, the justices were unanimous that they could no longer proceed as a class. The Court was divided, however, about whether the company had engaged in widespread discrimination, and all three female justices (in addition to Justice Breyer) dissented from the majority opinion on that point. The decision was a clear financial and ideological victory for Wal-Mart. A successful class-action lawsuit could have not only cost the company billions of dollars, but might also have set a precedent affecting core elements of their business model, a model that relies heavily on the routine and systematic subordination of certain groups of people.

One of the most important sources of Wal-Mart's legitimacy is its democratic openness to poor shoppers from all social groups, an implicit promise to make the American Dream accessible to all. This openness has earned Wal-Mart criticism from those who believe themselves superior to the people at Wal-Mart, an elitism that strengthens the company's populist image. Furthermore, Wal-Mart presents itself as a ladder to success for its associates, many of whom come from disadvantaged backgrounds. Wal-Mart expresses eternal gratitude to their associates, and presents the opportunities they offer as a cancellation of their debt.

However, there is a wide gulf between Wal-Mart's self-image and the experience of many employees for whom Wal-Mart is a low paying and "dead end" job. These negative experiences reinforce a host of criticisms from progressive groups who allege that Wal-Mart intentionally discriminates against female and non-white employees, and others who contend that their business model relies on a low wage workforce that is disproportionately female and minority. This model, some contend, depresses wages throughout the economy, and cultivates a captive customer base who cannot afford to shop elsewhere. In response to these critiques, which complicate their efforts to expand into urban markets, Wal-Mart has engaged in a host of PR and philanthropic activities in order to more aggressively promote itself as a harmonious multicultural company interested in promoting the well-being of non-whites and women.

These representations obscure the company's chronic exploitation of structural inequalities; they also render the history and depth of these problems—along with more holistic, long term, and collective solutions to them—invisible. Wal-Mart's focus on individual market discipline as a solution for social inequality leaves these problems both unresolved and "normal." The question of whether or not Wal-Mart is "good for women" or other disadvantaged groups thus reveals tensions between group and individual identities. While Wal-Mart's solution might work for individual women, it comes at the expense of a collective that is left behind. Finally, the strategy of the Dukes case, while critical of Wal-Mart, reinforces the individual, market-based model of social advancement that acts as a horizon of possibility in the dominant political imaginary.

People of Wal-Mart

One truly democratic aspect of Wal-Mart is that virtually everyone is welcome as a customer. Wal-Mart's business model focused on poor, rural, white communities in its early years, and they continue to target poor, nonwhite, and urban customers. Wal-Mart also hires entry-level employees from all walks of life, many without college degrees. Approximately 57 percent of Wal-Mart's workforce is female, and the company is also one of America's largest private employers of racial minorities.

Some Americans think that the door at Wal-Mart is open too wide. Consider the popular website (and book) People of Wal-Mart, an expanding library of images, taken from Wal-Mart stores, of customers and employees who appear to be poor, rural, overweight, gay, lesbian, transgendered, unfashionable, costumed, or just plain bizarre. People of Wal-Mart encourages visitors to laugh at and judge a group of individuals depicted as ridiculous and pathetic. Although the individuals are of different ages and ethnicities, most "targets" share a low socioeconomic class.

Such criticisms only reinforce Wal-Mart's image as a champion for ordinary people. Wal-Mart's embrace of the poor and unsophisticated, however, while more inclusive than People of Wal-Mart, still reinforces a notion of social ranking. The company encourages "disadvantaged" people to engage in self-improvement and class mobility through aspirational consumption and savings. While some may see this as contrived, detractors often neglect the

concrete ways that Wal-Mart *is* improving the quality of many people's lives. "Save Money, Live Better" is not just a slogan, it is an experience shared by many shoppers. People *feel* things about Wal-Mart: loyal customers and employees repeatedly narrate not only a sense of belonging but also of accomplishment and efficiency in making financially-savvy enhancements to their daily routines. Through convenient locations, fully-stocked shelves, extended hours, lay-away plans, and reliable EDLP. Wal-Mart stores become places where shoppers of limited means can dream: of more Christmas presents under the tree, of a more elaborate welcome home party for a returning soldier, or of a meal with restaurant-quality ingredients for a family with limited disposable income. Indeed, many of the company's most vocal proponents are attentive consumers who understand themselves in the upwardly mobile terms of the American Dream.

Mom-Preneurs

Wal-Mart's practice of addressing their customers as individuals actively engaged in self-improvement through practical consumption is also evident with the "Wal-Mart Moms" featured on the company's website. This group was named by pollsters after they were identified in the 2004 presidential campaign as a key swing-voter group that leaned toward George W. Bush. Wal-Mart seized the opportunity to turn these women into a market demographic, conducting a great deal of research on their consumer preferences and habits, as well as their broader political and social outlook, and expressive repertoire. One way they have done this is by cultivating relationships with web-savvy moms who blog and tweet about the relationships between shopping and their everyday lives. This has included sponsored trips to Bentonville where moms sampled new products, met with the actor Harrison Ford, and networked with Wal-Mart-sponsored business connections.

The women claim authenticity: "We're real Moms. And we're bloggers. We've come together with Wal-Mart to celebrate Moms, share our experiences and create a community." According to their introductory group post, "We've been asked by Wal-Mart to simply represent the voice of all moms." The discussion topics are "lifestyle" focused, and include parenting, "green living," health, and politics. The "Moms on Politics" section reminds female consumers of their swing-voter significance and encourages their participation in upcoming elections. Wal-Mart is intensely interested in the unvarnished opinions of these women on a range of topics, as well as in convincing the public of their collective consumer wisdom.

For Wal-Mart, the blogs provide a wealth of information about women's shopping preferences, and enable Wal-Mart to further disseminate its brand of family-oriented, everyday, and practical provisioning. The site invites low- and middle-income women who surf it to see themselves as part of a broader community of "Wal-Mart moms" who face similar problems and concerns. The "mompreneurs," as they are cheerfully described on the company's website, epitomize the consumer-oriented version of the American Dream that Wal-Mart seeks to promote, and portray the company as a trusted partner in self-improvement. While the site appeals to "all moms," these blogs do *not* invite female readers to understand themselves in the terms of the 1.6 million women that sued Wal-Mart, i.e., as part of a collective subject seeking equality, though it is certain that a sizeable number of Wal-Mart's female consumers have experienced gender-based discrimination in their own lives.

Climbing the Wal-Mart Ladder

In the U.S., social hierarchy is typically understood through the metaphor of the ladder to success, and many of us view the climb as integral to achieving the Dream. Through faith in the existence of equal opportunity—often referred to as one's "shot" at the top—many Americans believe that effort determines rank, and that individuals choose their social position, regardless of background. In this imaginary, disciplinary self-fashioning becomes the ideal site and measure of citizenship. One downside in keeping with this narrative is that it leads many of us to turn to beliefs about the qualities and capabilities of "women and minorities" in order to explain their so-called failure to climb the ladder.

The most explicit way that Wal-Mart markets its vision of social mobility is by promoting the legend of Sam Walton, whose life the company narrates as one of hard work, tenacity, and the ultimate attainment of the American Dream. This carefully constructed biography studiously avoids the elements of his success that were not the result of individual effort. By relegating these factors to the background, Wal-Mart's official "story" of social mobility is substantiated—even glorified—while the more complex one of pervasive social inequality remains untold. Indeed, Sam Walton is presented as a role model for everyone, especially Wal-Mart associates, regardless of his or her race, class, or gender.

Wal-Mart's commercial advertising aggressively promotes this vision, using members of minority groups to foreground the opportunities for social mobility offered by the company. In television, internet, and print promotions, Wal-Mart celebrates its ability and willingness to create good, meaningful jobs, particularly those that advance the careers of women and minority groups. A typical television spot features Tejas, a recent Indian immigrant who works as a customer service manager in Idaho. As we watch the smiling Tejas interact with various customers, the shift manager's voice tells us that Tejas has been named "associate of the month" more than once, due to the ways that he "exemplifies respect for the individual." The manager tells us that Tejas was promoted into management after only six months, while yet another voice adds: "He looks at his job as if it is a privilege to be here, which makes it a privilege for us to work with him." For his part, Tejas only reinforces this message of mobility: "There is definitely 100 percent opportunity [here]. If you work, you will get rewarded. As everybody knows, America is the land of opportunity."

Another commercial features an associate named Noemi, a middle-aged Latina from Texas who tells the viewer that she raised her sons on welfare during the 1980s. However, Noemi says that "After [she] got the job at Wal-Mart, things started changing." She explains: "I wrote a letter to the food stamp office, [saying] 'Thank you very much, I don't need you anymore.'" In this ad, receiving resources through governmental redistribution is presented as a reason for shame, a sign of personal failure and dependency. Visibly choking up, Noemi continues: "You know, now I can actually say I bought my home. I know that the more I dedicated, the harder I worked, this is going to benefit my family." As Noemi speaks, we see a picture of her alongside Sam Walton. The commercial posts a statistic claiming that "73 percent of Wal-Mart's store management team started as hourly associates," but does not reveal the percentage of hourly associates that "make it" into management (the substance of *Wal-Mart v. Dukes* and a figure that the company does not make available). At the end of the commercial, Noemi introduces her son, Mario, who also works at Wal-Mart; she beams: "I believe Mario is following in my footsteps."

Though we are meant to feel as if we "know" something about Noemi through this intimate portrait, we are not privy to the details of Noemi's life that allowed her to say "No thank you" to the government assistance that helped her raise her children. As with the edited version of Sam's biography, the elements of Noemi's "success story" that are not derived from her relationship with capitalist free enterprise are downplayed, if not erased entirely. This narrative is misleading and very important to disrupt. Though Wal-Mart claims to have freed Noemi from her dependence on food stamps, there is ample evidence that many of the company's employees require government assistance—specifically food stamps—in order to make ends meet. Furthermore, by taking sole credit for assisting Noemi, Wal-Mart

trivializes the fact that this woman successfully raised a family with help from a meager federal assistance wage. Wal-Mart's representation also presents Noemi's capacity to "work hard" solely in terms of her labor for the company, and omits what she *has already accomplished* on behalf of her two sons, one of whom now "follow[s] in [her] footsteps." Though government assistance had long helped to stabilize Noemi's life, Wal-Mart's re-packaging of her story treats such assistance as an impediment—rather than a facilitator—of social mobility and financial independence.

These commercials encourage us to celebrate the small number of Wal-Mart employees who "make it," and to ignore the great majority who are routinely passed over. Wal-Mart's success stories are carefully selected to emphasize the company's "truth": that individual hard work is the only path to upward mobility and full (consumer) citizenship. Furthermore, in a powerful sense, this opportunity at social mobility is presented as canceling the debt that Wal-Mart owes to their associates.

Complicating Wal-Mart's Mobility Narrative

Missing from Wal-Mart's inclusion narrative are the structural realities and historical processes through which certain groups became disadvantaged. For African-Americans, for example, this includes the slave trade, lynching, segregation, restrictive zoning, gentrification, predatory lending, the war on drugs, and negative media representations; for women the list might include a gendered division of labor, sexual assault and rape, objectification, and their systematic exclusion from positions of authority. Furthermore, both women and racial minorities have been, in the aggregate and individually, uniquely disadvantaged by neoliberal economic policies that have decreased public spending and social protections. In addition, Wal-Mart's definition of social exclusion, and the individualized, market based solutions they recommend, ignore the forms of collective social and political agency, such as labor unions and the progressive movements of the 1960s and 70s, that sought to address the structural roots of inequality. These groups and their many contemporary manifestations, like Occupy Wall Street and Rebuild the Dream, focus on leveling the playing field and promoting more access to material resources for marginalized populations. In this way, Wal-Mart's representational strategy reproduces a central tenet of neoliberal thought, that of rendering progressive movements irrelevant, and proposing market mechanisms as the sole means to resolving social inequality.

Also absent in this characterization is the role that Wal-Mart's business model plays in constructing and maintaining these inequalities. Numerous critics highlight the disparity between Wal-Mart's promise of social mobility and the reality of its "dead end" jobs. Wal-Mart, for its part, takes no responsibility for low wages, insisting that: "retail and service wages *are what they are.*" This narrative normalizes Wal-Mart's pay structure and treats wages as a free-floating fact, unaffected by the company's business model and the neoliberal regulatory framework as a whole. It also ignores numerous lawsuits that implicate Wal-Mart in wage violations and outright wage theft, and the fact that Wal-Mart's associates are some of the lowest paid employees in the United States. Sales associates currently average $8.81 per hour (Moberg 2011), and a recent study concludes that Wal-Mart pays average wages significantly lower than any other retail or big box. These rates are compounded by the company's history of pushing experienced (and better paid) employees out in order to reduce labor costs.

Nelson Lichtenstein likens Wal-Mart's pay and promotion structure to "a short stack of pancakes with a long thin strawberry perched in the middle." And while corporate attention is focused on the strawberries—individuals like Tejas and Noemi—stories of "the rest," i.e., the millions of disaffected, betrayed, injured, exhausted, and still-struggling employees for whom Wal-Mart's promise remains unrealized, crowd the internet on sites like Working at

WAL-MART and Wal-MartSucks.org. For the majority, advancement is arduous and elusive.

As with other putatively meritocratic organizations, promotions at Wal-Mart are based on allegedly neutral standards related to experience, training, and personal characteristics, such as leadership skills and decision-making ability. Normalizing these standards, however, distracts our attention away from other dynamics. First, although only a very limited number of salaried positions exist, employees who are not promoted are framed as having not performed adequately. Second, certain factors, such as a college education, that are more likely to correlate with one's ability to meet such standards are more consistent with particular demographic categories, i.e., white and middle-class, which already enjoy greater amounts of social privilege. Through these "objective" criteria, Wal-Mart reproduces, rather than resolves, larger patterns of social exclusion.

Moreover, numerous lawsuits strongly indicate that promotion standards are not always applied evenly, due to either overt discrimination or, more commonly, to the ways that many of us reflexively associate qualities such as "leadership potential" with certain *types* of people, particularly men. Indeed, Betty Dukes' initial complaint stemmed from a comment made by her then-manager: "People like you don't get promoted." Though her manager did not clarify his remark, we, like Dukes, can easily imagine that her race and gender were possible "character defects" that interfered with her promotion. Though rarely cited as the formal reason for non-promotion, there is ample evidence of discrimination at Wal-Mart, and that sexist and racist thinking often explains structural inequality in terms of personal failure.

Wal-Mart's mobility narrative also does not address the fact that their business model depresses wages throughout the economy: most competitors have lowered wages in order to stay alive in Wal-Mart's shadow. The company's model also affects the supply chain. A new report by the National Employment Law Project argues that Wal-Mart's squeeze has lowered wages and motivated a shift to temporary and immigrant labor throughout the "multilayered and hydra headed" supply chain.

Wal-Mart is notable for their role in generating an economic underclass, and for their simultaneous—and almost unprecedented—insistence that they are a path to social mobility for their cherished associates. Most Wal-Mart associates are, by necessity, Wal-Mart customers; Wal-Mart's low wage model creates a captive audience of consumers who cannot afford to shop anywhere else. Betty Dukes remarked on Wal-Mart's practice of "setting up right in Poorville," even placing ads in the local paper when welfare checks were issued. Whether intentional or incidental, Wal-Mart's sales increase under grim economic circumstances, including the U.S.'s recent recession. Some have even argued that, in effect, Wal-Mart depends on poverty to grow.

Wal-Mart's critics invite us to reflect upon the neoliberal perversion of the American Dream, in which the concentration of wealth at the top of our society corresponds with ever larger groups of ordinary citizens fighting for basic living standards at the bottom. Despite the fact that each of us knows scores of "deserving" people who remain in this ever-widening bottom, in spite of their hard work, we maintain a tenacious faith in upward mobility. In neoliberal times marked by downward mobility and growing economic disparities, most of us still believe in the possibility of the *climb* rather than the brokenness of the ladder. Wal-Mart's hopeful self-presentation fortifies the "cruel optimism" that leaves many of us attached to dreams of mobility, even as they become more impossible to realize.

For or Against Collective Empowerment?

Circulating reports about Wal-Mart's low wages fuel the ambivalence we feel toward Wal-Mart. While consumers appreciate EDLP, they are often simultaneously aware that the prices are virtually incompatible with the promise of liberal inclusion. These reports foster the nagging concern that Wal-Mart preys on a permanent low wage workforce, that they are an agent in the disempowerment of groups of people, e.g., racial minorities, women, and the less educated. These perceptions and doubts create problems as Wal-Mart seeks inroads with non-white communities and women in the U.S. and abroad. As an attempt to manage and contain this ambivalence, Wal-Mart projects an image of interracial and multicultural harmony, and has aggressively promoted itself as actively engaged in uplifting disadvantaged populations. Toward this end, in 2003, Wal-Mart created an Office of Diversity aimed at streamlining the transition of minority employees into management, and mounted a more robust affirmative action program in 2005. Indeed, part of why Wal-Mart gained permission to expand into Chicago was because they agreed to hire women and people of color to build their stores.

And the company is not shy about showcasing their successes: in addition to the "leaked" video of their Hurricane Katrina relief efforts, when the contract for the construction of Chicago's first Wal-Mart store was awarded to a company owned by a local African-American woman, Wal-Mart took out a full-page ad in *Ebony* magazine. Moreover, recent ASMs prominently featured entertainers of color, including Will Smith, the Black-Eyed Peas, Alicia Keys, Juanes, and Lionel Richie. A lengthy segment by Rosalind Brewer, the African-American female President and CEO of Sam's Club, at the 2012 ASM was followed by a video describing three African-American women—a grandmother, mother, and daughter—who were all Wal-Mart associates. These women described how the company had helped them to get ahead, one of them remarking: "It's a great company! What more could we ask for?" as if women of color had never asked for more from the company, and perhaps had no right to.

Just as Wal-Mart's victory in the Dukes case resurrected their image as a redneck—and legally untouchable—boys club, new corporate initiatives strike a decidedly feminist chord. The Global Women's Economic Empowerment Initiative highlights the company's efforts to promote women's employment on farms and factories, gender diversity in Wal-Mart accounts, job training and education for women, as well as sourcing from women owned businesses. This initiative was launched in 2011 and counts Secretary of State Hillary Clinton (the first female member of Wal-Mart's board) as a partner, signifying the potential to win over some of the store's more established feminist critics.

These philanthropic efforts and programs often depart from the neoliberal narrative of individual mobility in the sense that they single out women and minority groups for a helping hand. As was the case with Katrina, Wal-Mart frequently appears as a benevolent governmental agency tasked with helping disadvantaged groups *en masse*. But Wal-Mart's efforts are very selective. For example, if Wal-Mart is interested in "empowering" their global and primarily female supply chain workers, as well as the "disadvantaged" clients of Dress for Success, why does the company object to making life easier for their own associates? We believe Wal-Mart's resistance to unions or class actions constitutes a refusal to recognize their employees as a group whose self-defined interests diverge from their own and threaten their bottom line. This aversion toward contentious groups ultimately succeeded in the Betty Dukes case: while female associates remain free to sue Wal-Mart as individuals, their affiliation with a self-defined group, i.e., women who claim systematic discrimination, remains unrecognized.

Discrimination: Dukes and Beyond

In essence, *Wal-Mart v. Dukes* hinged on one very important disparity in the professional aspirations of Betty Dukes and her peers: between how high they *imagined* they could climb, and how high they (now) believe they were *allowed* to climb. The plaintiffs in the Dukes case alleged that female employees were systematically denied equal pay, promotions, and training. Many also claimed that they were subjected to workplace retaliation because of their gender. They argued that Wal-Mart's strong, centralized structure fosters or facilitates gender stereotyping and discrimination, that the policies and practices underlying this discriminatory treatment are consistent throughout Wal-Mart stores, and that this discrimination is common to all women who work or have worked at Wal-Mart. They argued that these acts of discrimination were a large part of why, although over 70 percent of Wal-Mart's employees are female, nearly two-thirds of its managers are male.

Lawyers representing these women argued that, in addition to the fact that their clients were singled out for different and inferior treatment because of their gender, they were also disadvantaged by a corporate culture that systematically holds women back. They claimed that Wal-Mart's family model of management relegated women to a complementary yet subordinate role; by deploying a family metaphor within the company, Wal-Mart's corporate culture naturalized the hierarchy between their (mostly) male managers and a (mostly) female workforce. The attorneys' argument was shaped by the case's expert witness: a sociologist named William Bielby who specializes in gender and workplace discrimination. Guided by a theory of "cognitive bias," Bielby determined that "subjective and discretionary features of the Wal-Mart personnel system created systematic barriers to the career advancement of women".

Wal-Mart's legal strategy was two pronged. First, they argued that the 1.6 million litigants were too diverse to constitute a "class"; second, they purported that the company was too de-centralized and the stores too diverse for that many women to have been so uniformly affected. In short, Wal-Mart argued that they were too big to be sued in a class-action lawsuit, one of the only legal strategies available to "ordinary" people who cannot afford to hire their own attorney.

Although Wal-Mart ultimately prevailed, the door to collective action against the company is not completely closed. The company recently settled with a group of African American truck drivers with similar claims of discrimination.

The outcome of the Dukes case was predictably hailed and decried by various Wal-Mart proponents and detractors, but we are more interested in Dukes' strategy than in her defeat. By claiming that Wal-Mart imposed limits on their professional opportunities, Betty Dukes and her fellow litigants defined their ability to be "successful" in terms that were quintessentially American. By arguing that their presence near the bottom of a hierarchy was due to unfair treatment at the hands of sexist managers—and not to structural obstacles—the lawsuit affirmed the existence of a fair and functioning ladder to social mobility, a supposedly neutral standard by which many Americans gauge their individual success and self-worth.

Wal-Mart v. Dukes reminds us that discrimination remains an impediment to social mobility; the Supreme Court did not unanimously reject the plaintiffs' evidence, but rather could not agree on whether 1.6 million women suffered the same experience. But even if it had succeeded, the suit would have reinforced the dominant narrative of social mobility by positing the act of discrimination as the only barrier to getting ahead in the U.S.—an exception to the rule of equal opportunity. But structural impediments to social mobility do exist, even without discrimination. Even were Dukes victorious, it would not change the situation of a textile worker in Bangladesh, for example, who has been sewing garments for Wal-Mart's suppliers since the age of thirteen, and who might question Wal-Mart's "commitment to working women." What do we imagine about these "supply chain workers" and how might they interpret the phrase "*Yes you can!*"—the phrase that Wal-Mart has asked them to sew into the lining of each and every suit jacket fashioned for Dress for Success, a jacket they cannot even afford? The idea of a ladder normalizes the belief that full citizenship can and must be earned, and that those on the bottom need only wait their turn. In this vision, someone is always, *necessarily,* on the bottom, working their way up. The detail that this vision obscures, however, is that some never even get a turn at all.

Conclusion

Wal-Mart spends millions in advertising telling the stories of Lyneese, Tejas, and Noemi in order to distract us from a low-wage, pyramid shaped, and patriarchal business model that preys on poverty and constrains real social mobility. But this ladder metaphor conveniently ignores the simple reality that "[s]omeone still ha[s] to stock the shelves", and that someone is far more likely to be non-white, female and less educated. Stories about disadvantaged individuals successfully "climbing the ladder" limit our frame of reference to market based, individual models of advancement and relegate direct, collective, political efforts to resolve social hierarchies outside the realm of the thinkable.

Wal-Mart presents their path to social mobility as a cancelation of the debt they owe their employees for their hard work, as well as for a social debt created by historical injustice and present day discrimination. However, their repayment does not resolve inequality or poverty and tends to make these problems worse. Wal-Mart ignores how the question of debt is framed by their critics, including many of their own associates. Lawsuits like the Dukes case blame discriminatory treatment at Wal-Mart for preventing the ladder from functioning properly. Other critics emphasize how inequality is built into our society and how it has been exacerbated by free market policies. Many accuse Wal-Mart of spearheading these trends: fighting against living wages, benefits, and unionization, and sending a powerful ripple throughout the market. Many critics also emphasize the need for a significant redistribution of material resources in order to overcome social exclusion. Such demands and the groups that make them are rendered incoherent, invisible, or harmful in Wal-Mart's representational strategy, yet persist as a consistent reminder of the contradiction between the company's self-image as a social leveler, and the concrete effects of its business practices.

THINKING ABOUT THE READING

Copeland and Labuski write that Wal-Mart works hard to foster an image as a ladder to success for employees. What are some of the strategies the company uses to give the impression that it is a path to the American Dream? Are these images accurate reflections of real employee experiences? What are some of the differences between the Wal-Mart public image and actual work conditions? How is it possible for a company to sustain an image that is so distinct from reality? Why do so many of us buy into it?

The Architecture of Inequality

Race and Ethnicity

The history of race in the United States is an ambivalent one. Cultural beliefs about equality conflict with the experiences of most racial and ethnic minorities: oppression, violence, and exploitation. Opportunities for life, liberty, and the pursuit of happiness have always been distributed along racial and ethnic lines. U.S. society is built on the assumption that different immigrant groups will ultimately assimilate, changing their way of life to conform to that of the dominant culture. But the increasing diversity of the population has shaped people's ideas about what it means to be an American and has influenced our relationships with one another and with our social institutions.

Sociologists tell us that race is not a biological characteristic but rather a social construction that can change across time and from culture to culture. The socially constructed nature of race is illustrated in "Racial and Ethnic Formation" by Michael Omi and Howard Winant. However, the authors are quick to point out that just because race is socially created doesn't mean it is insignificant. Indeed, our definitions of race are related to inequality, discrimination, and cultural dominance and resistance. Race may not be a purely biological trait, but it is an important part of every social institution.

It has been said that white people in the United States have the luxury of "having no color." When someone is described with no mention of race, the default assumption is that he or she is white. In other words, *white* is used far less often as a modifying adjective than *black, Asian,* or *Latino.* As a result, "whiteness" is rarely questioned or examined as a racial or ethnic category. In her article "Optional Ethnicities," Mary C. Waters argues that unlike members of other groups, U.S. whites can choose whether or not to include their specific ancestry in descriptions of their own identities. For whites of European descent, claiming an ethnic identity is a voluntary "leisure-time activity" with few social implications. Indeed, the option of being able *not* to claim any ethnicity is available only to the majority group in a society.

In the final reading for this chapter, Sociologist Maxwell Leung focuses on the hype surrounding basketball player Jeremy Lin. Stereotypes of the Asian "model minority" factor significantly into the media coverage of Lin's success.

Something to Consider as You Read

As you read these selections, consider the differences between individual prejudice and institutional racism. Is it possible for someone not to be racist and still participate in practices that perpetuate racism? Compare these readings with those in other chapters. Consider the connections between access to economic resources, social class, and race. How might socioeconomic status influence attitudes and behaviors toward others who may share your ethnicity but not your class position? Think also about how you identify your own race or ethnicity. When you fill out a questionnaire that asks you to select a racial/ethnic category, do you think the category adequately reflects you? When you go somewhere, do you assume you will easily find others of your own race or ethnicity? When you watch television or a movie, how likely is it that the central characters will be people who share your racial background? Practice asking yourself similar questions as a way of enhancing your racial awareness.

Racial and Ethnic Formation

Michael Omi and Howard Winant

(1994)

In 1982–83, Susie Guillory Phipps unsuccessfully sued the Louisiana Bureau of Vital Records to change her racial classification from black to white. The descendant of an 18th-century white planter and a black slave, Phipps was designated "black" in her birth certificate in accordance with a 1970 state law which declared anyone with at least 1/32nd "Negro blood" to be black.

The Phipps case raised intriguing questions about the concept of race, its meaning in contemporary society, and its use (and abuse) in public policy. Assistant Attorney General Ron Davis defended the law by pointing out that some type of racial classification was necessary to comply with federal record-keeping requirements and to facilitate programs for the prevention of genetic diseases. Phipps's attorney, Brian Begue, argued that the assignment of racial categories on birth certificates was unconstitutional and that the 1/32nd designation was inaccurate. He called on a retired Tulane University professor who cited research indicating that most Louisiana whites have at least 1/20th "Negro" ancestry.

In the end, Phipps lost. The court upheld the state's right to classify and quantify racial identity.[1]

Phipps's problematic racial identity, and her effort to resolve it through state action, is in many ways a parable of America's unsolved racial dilemma. It illustrates the difficulties of defining race and assigning individuals or groups to racial categories. It shows how the racial legacies of the past—slavery and bigotry—continue to shape the present. It reveals both the deep involvement of the state in the organization and interpretation of race, and the inadequacy of state institutions to carry out these functions.

It demonstrates how deeply Americans both as individuals and as a civilization are shaped, and indeed haunted, by race.

Having lived her whole life thinking that she was white, Phipps suddenly discovers that by legal definition she is not. In U.S. society, such an event is indeed catastrophic.[2] But if she is not white, of what race is she? The *state* claims that she is black, based on its rules of classification,[3] and another state agency, the court, upholds this judgment. But despite these classificatory standards which have imposed an either-or logic on racial identity, Phipps will not in fact "change color." Unlike what would have happened during slavery times if one's claim to whiteness was successfully challenged, we can assume that despite the outcome of her legal challenge, Phipps will remain in most of the social relationships she had occupied before the trial. Her socialization, her familial and friendship networks, her cultural orientation, will not change. She will simply have to wrestle with her newly acquired "hybridized" condition. She will have to confront the "Other" within.

The designation of racial categories and the determination of racial identity is no simple task. For centuries, this question has precipitated intense debates and conflicts, particularly in the U.S.—disputes over natural and legal rights, over the distribution of resources, and indeed, over who shall live and who shall die.

A crucial dimension of the Phipps case is that it illustrates the inadequacy of claims that race is a mere matter of variations in human physiognomy, that it is simply a matter of skin color. But if race cannot be understood in this manner, how *can* it be understood? We cannot

271

fully hope to address this topic—no less than the meaning of race, its role in society, and the forces which shape it—in one chapter, nor indeed in one book. Our goal in this chapter, however, is far from modest: we wish to offer at least the outlines of a theory of race and racism.

What Is Race?

There is a continuous temptation to think of race as an *essence,* as something fixed, concrete, and objective. And there is also an opposite temptation: to imagine race as a mere *illusion,* a purely ideological construct which some ideal non-racist social order would eliminate. It is necessary to challenge both these positions, to disrupt and reframe the rigid and bipolar manner in which they are posed and debated, and to transcend the presumably irreconcilable relationship between them.

The effort must be made to understand race as an unstable and "decentered" complex of social meanings constantly being transformed by political struggle. With this in mind, let us propose a definition: *race is a concept which signifies and symbolizes social conflicts and interests by referring to different types of human bodies.* Although the concept of race invokes biologically based human characteristics (so-called "phenotypes"), selection of these particular human features for purposes of racial signification is always and necessarily a social and historical process. In contrast to the other major distinction of this type, that of gender, there is no biological basis for distinguishing among human groups along the lines of race.[4] Indeed, the categories employed to differentiate among human groups along racial lines reveal themselves, upon serious examination, to be at best imprecise, and at worst completely arbitrary.

If the concept of race is so nebulous, can we not dispense with it? Can we not "do without" race, at least in the "enlightened" present? This question has been posed often, and with greater frequency in recent years.[5] An affirmative answer would of course present obvious practical difficulties: it is rather difficult to jettison widely held beliefs, beliefs which moreover are central to everyone's identity and understanding of the social world. So the attempt to banish the concept as an archaism is at best counterintuitive. But a deeper difficulty, we believe, is inherent in the very formulation of this schema, in its way of posing race as a *problem,* a misconception left over from the past, and suitable now only for the dustbin of history.

A more effective starting point is the recognition that despite its uncertainties and contradictions, the concept of race continues to play a fundamental role in structuring and representing the social world. The task for theory is to explain this situation. It is to avoid both the utopian framework which sees race as an illusion we can somehow "get beyond," and also the essentialist formulation which sees race as something objective and fixed, a biological datum.[6] Thus we should think of race as an element of social structure rather than as an irregularity within it; we should see race as a dimension of human representation rather than as an illusion. These perspectives inform the theoretical approach we call racial formation.

Racial Formation

We define *racial formation* as the sociohistorical process by which racial categories are created, inhabited, transformed, and destroyed. Our attempt to elaborate a theory of racial formation will proceed in two steps. First, we argue that racial formation is a process of historically situated *projects* in which human bodies and social structures are represented and organized. Next we link racial formation to the evolution of hegemony, the way in which society is organized and ruled. Such an approach, we believe, can facilitate understanding of a whole range of contemporary controversies and dilemmas involving race, including the nature of racism, the relationship of race to other forms of differences, inequalities, and oppression such as sexism and nationalism, and the dilemmas of racial identity today.

From a racial formation perspective, race is a matter of both social structure and cultural representation. Too often, the attempt is made to understand race simply or primarily in terms of only one of these two analytical dimensions.[7] For example, efforts to explain racial inequality as a purely social structural phenomenon are unable to account for the origins, patterning, and transformation of racial difference.

Conversely, many examinations of racial difference—understood as a matter of cultural attributes á la ethnicity theory, or as a society-wide signification system, á la some poststructuralist accounts—cannot comprehend such structural phenomena as racial stratification in the labor market or patterns of residential segregation.

An alternative approach is to think of racial formation processes as occurring through a linkage between structure and representation. Racial *projects* do the ideological "work" of making these links. A *racial project is simultaneously an interpretation, representation, or explanation of racial dynamics, and an effort to reorganize and redistribute resources along particular racial lines.* Racial projects connect what race *means* in a particular discursive practice and the ways in which both social structures and everyday experiences are racially *organized*, based upon that meaning. Let us consider this proposition, first in terms of large-scale or macro-level social processes, and then in terms of other dimensions of the racial formation process.

Racial Formation as a Macro-Level Social Process

To interpret the meaning of race is to frame it social structurally. Consider for example, this statement by Charles Murray on welfare reform:

> My proposal for dealing with the racial issue in social welfare is to repeal every bit of legislation and reverse every court decision that in any way requires, recommends, or awards differential treatment according to race, and thereby put us back onto the track that we left in 1965. We may argue about the appropriate limits of government intervention in trying to enforce the ideal, but at least it should be possible to identify the ideal: Race is not a morally admissible reason for treating one person differently from another. Period.[8]

Here there is a partial but significant analysis of the meaning of race: it is not a morally valid basis upon which to treat people "differently from one another." We may notice someone's race, but we cannot act upon that awareness. We must act in a "color-blind" fashion. This analysis of the meaning of race is immediately linked to a specific conception of the role of race in the social structure: it can play no part in government action, save in "the enforcement of the ideal." No state policy can legitimately require, recommend, or award different status according to race. This example can be classified as a particular type of racial project in the present-day U.S.—a "neoconservative" one.

Conversely, *to recognize the racial dimension in social structure is to interpret the meaning of race.* Consider the following statement by the late Supreme Court Justice Thurgood Marshall on minority "set-aside" programs:

> A profound difference separates governmental actions that themselves are racist, and governmental actions that seek to remedy the effects of prior racism or to prevent neutral government activity from perpetuating the effects of such racism.[9]

Here the focus is on the racial dimensions of *social structure*—in this case of state activity and policy. The argument is that state actions in the past and present have treated people in very different ways according to their race, and thus the government cannot retreat from its policy responsibilities in this area. It cannot suddenly declare itself "color-blind" without in fact perpetuating the same type of differential, racist treatment.[10] Thus, race continues to signify difference and structure inequality. Here, racialized social structure is immediately linked to an interpretation of the meaning of race. This example too can be classified as a particular type of racial project in the present-day U.S.—a "liberal" one.

To be sure, such political labels as "neoconservative" or "liberal" cannot fully capture the complexity of racial projects, for these are always multiply determined, politically contested, and deeply shaped by their historical context. Thus, encapsulated within the neoconservative example cited here are certain egalitarian commitments which derive from a previous historical context in which they played a very different role, and which are rearticulated in neoconservative racial discourse precisely to oppose a more open-ended, more capacious conception of the meaning of equality. Similarly, in the liberal example, Justice Marshall recognizes that the contemporary state, which was formerly the architect of segregation and the chief enforcer of racial difference, has a tendency to reproduce those patterns of inequality in a new guise. Thus he admonishes it (in dissent, significantly) to fulfill its responsibilities to uphold a robust conception of equality. These particular instances, then, demonstrate how racial projects are always concretely framed, and thus are always contested and unstable. The social structures they uphold or attack, and the representations of race they articulate, are never invented out of the air, but exist in a definite historical context, having descended from previous conflicts. This contestation appears to be permanent in respect to race.

These two examples of contemporary racial projects are drawn from mainstream political debate; they may be characterized as center-right and center-left expressions of contemporary racial politics.[11] We can, however, expand the discussion of racial formation processes far beyond these familiar examples. In fact, we can identify racial projects in at least three other analytical dimensions: first, the political spectrum can be broadened to include radical projects, on both the left and right, as well as along other political axes.

Second, analysis of racial projects can take place not only at the macro-level of racial policy-making, state activity, and collective action, but also at the micro-level of everyday experience. Third, the concept of racial projects can be applied across historical time, to identify racial formation dynamics in the past. We shall now offer examples of each of these types of racial projects.

The Political Spectrum of Racial Formation

We have encountered examples of a neoconservative racial project, in which the significance of race is denied, leading to a "color-blind" racial politics and "hands off" policy orientation; and of a "liberal" racial project, in which the significance of race is affirmed, leading to an egalitarian and "activist" state policy. But these by no means exhaust the political possibilities. Other racial projects can be readily identified on the contemporary U.S. scene. For example, "far right" projects, which uphold biologistic and racist views of difference, explicitly argue for white supremacist policies. "New right" projects overtly claim to hold "color-blind" views, but covertly manipulate racial fears in order to achieve political gains.[12] On the left, "radical democratic" projects invoke notions of racial "difference" in combination with egalitarian politics and policy.

Further variations can also be noted. For example, "nationalist" projects, both conservative and radical, stress the incompatibility of racially defined group identity with the legacy of white supremacy, and therefore advocate a social structural solution of separation, either complete or partial.[13] . . . Nationalist currents represent a profound legacy of the centuries of racial absolutism that initially defined the meaning of race in the U.S. Nationalist concerns continue to influence racial debate in the form of Afrocentrism and other expressions of identity politics.

Taking the range of politically organized racial projects as a whole, we can "map" the current pattern of racial formation at the level of the public sphere, the "macro-level" in which public debate and mobilization takes place.[11] But important as this is, the terrain on which racial formation occurs is broader yet.

Racial Formation as Everyday Experience

At the micro-social level, racial projects also link signification and structure, not so much as efforts to shape policy or define large-scale meaning, but as the applications of "common sense." To see racial projects operating at the level of everyday life, we have only to examine the many ways in which, often unconsciously, we "notice" race.

One of the first things we notice about people when we meet them (along with their sex) is their race. We utilize race to provide clues about *who* a person is. This fact is made painfully obvious when we encounter someone whom we cannot conveniently racially categorize—someone who is, for example, racially "mixed" or of an ethnic/racial group we are not familiar with. Such an encounter becomes a source of discomfort and momentarily a crisis of racial meaning.

Our ability to interpret racial meanings depends on preconceived notions of a racialized social structure. Comments such as, "Funny, you don't look black," betray an underlying image of what black should be. We expect people to act out their apparent racial identities; indeed we become disoriented when they do not. The black banker harassed by police while walking in casual clothes through his own well-off neighborhood, the Latino or white kid rapping in perfect Afro patois, the unending *faux pas* committed by whites who assume that the non-whites they encounter are servants or tradespeople, the belief that non-white colleagues are less qualified persons hired to fulfill affirmative action guidelines, indeed the whole gamut of racial stereotypes—that "white men can't jump," that Asians can't dance, etc., etc.— all testify to the way a racialized social structure shapes racial experience and conditions meaning. Analysis of such stereotypes reveals the always present, already active link between our view of the social structure—its demography, its laws, its customs, its threats—and our conception of what race means.

Conversely, our ongoing interpretation of our experience in racial terms shapes our relations to the institutions and organizations through which we are imbedded in social structure. Thus we expect differences in skin color, or other racially coded characteristics, to explain social differences. Temperament, sexuality, intelligence, athletic ability, aesthetic preferences, and so on are presumed to be fixed and discernible from the palpable mark of race. Such diverse questions as our confidence and trust in others (for example, clerks or salespeople, media figures, neighbors), our sexual preferences and romantic images, our tastes in music, films, dance, or sports, and our very ways of talking, walking, eating, and dreaming become racially coded simply because we live in a society where racial awareness is so pervasive. Thus in ways too comprehensive even to monitor consciously, and despite periodic calls—neoconservative and otherwise—for us to ignore race and adopt "color-blind" racial attitudes, skin color "differences" continue to rationalize distinct treatment of racially identified individuals and groups.

To summarize the argument so far: the theory of racial formation suggests that society is suffused with racial projects, large and small, to which all are subjected. This racial "subjection" is quintessentially ideological. Everybody learns some combination, some version, of the rules of racial classification, and of her own racial identity, often without obvious teaching or conscious inculcation. Thus are we inserted in a comprehensively racialized social structure. Race becomes "common sense"—a way of comprehending, explaining, and acting in the world. A vast web of racial projects mediates between the discursive or representational means in which race is identified and signified on the one hand, and the institutional and organizational forms in which it is routinized and standardized on the other. These projects are the heart of the racial formation process.

Under such circumstances, it is not possible to represent race discursively without simultaneously locating it, explicitly or implicitly, in a social structural (and historical) context. Nor is it possible to organize, maintain, or transform social structures without simultaneously engaging, once more either explicitly or implicitly, in racial signification. Racial formation, therefore, is a kind of synthesis, an outcome, of the interaction of racial projects on a society-wide level. These projects are, of course, vastly different in scope and effect. They include large-scale public action, state activities, and interpretations of racial conditions in artistic, journalistic, or academic fora,[15] as well as the seemingly infinite number of racial judgments and practices we carry out at the level of individual experience.

Since racial formation is always historically situated, our understanding of the significance of race, and of the way race structures society, has changed enormously over time. The processes of racial formation we encounter today, the racial projects large and small which structure U.S. society in so many ways, are merely the present-day outcomes of a complex historical evolution. The contemporary racial order remains transient. By knowing something of how it evolved, we can perhaps better discern where it is heading . . . .

Notes

1. *San Francisco Chronicle,* 14 September 1982, 19 May 1983. Ironically, the 1970 Louisiana law was enacted to supersede an old Jim Crow statute which relied on the idea of "common report" in determining an infant's race. Following Phipps's unsuccessful attempt to change her classification and have the law declared unconstitutional, a legislative effort arose which culminated in the repeal of the law. See *San Francisco Chronicle,* 23 June 1983.

2. Compare the Phipps case to Andrew Hacker's well-known "parable" in which a white person is informed by a mysterious official that "the organization he represents has made a mistake" and that " . . . [a]ccording to their records . . . , you were to have been born black: to another set of parents, far from where you were raised." How much compensation, Hacker's official asks, would "you" require to undo the damage of this unfortunate error? See Hacker, *Two Nations: Black and White, Separate, Hostile, Unequal* (New York: Charles Scribner's Sons, 1992) pp. 31–32.

3. On the evolution of Louisiana's racial classification system, see Virginia Dominguez, *White By Definition: Social Classification in Creole Louisiana* (New Brunswick: Rutgers University Press, 1986).

4. This is not to suggest that gender is a biological category while race is not. Gender, like race, is a social construct. However, the biological division of humans into sexes—two at least, and possibly intermediate ones as well—is not in dispute. This provides a basis for argument over gender divisions—how "natural," etc.—which does not exist with regard to race. To ground an argument for the "natural" existence of race, one must resort to philosophical anthropology.

5. "The truth is that there are no races, there is nothing in the world that can do all we ask race to do for us . . . . The evil that is done is done by the concept, and by easy—yet impossible—assumptions as to its application." (Kwame Anthony Appiah, *In My Father's House: Africa in the Philosophy of Culture* [New York: Oxford University Press, 1992].) Appiah's eloquent and learned book fails, in our view, to dispense with the race concept, despite its anguished attempt to do so; this indeed is the source of its author's anguish. We agree with him as to the non-objective character of race, but fail to see how this recognition justifies its abandonment. This argument is developed below.

6. We understand essentialism as *belief in real, true human, essences, existing outside or impervious to social and historical context.* We draw this definition, with some small modifications, from Diana Fuss, *Essentially Speaking: Feminism, Nature, & Difference* (New York: Routledge, 1989) p. xi.

7. Michael Omi and Howard Winant, "On the Theoretical Status of the Concept of Race," in Warren Crichlow and Cameron McCarthy, eds., *Race, Identity, and Representation in Education* (New York: Routledge, 1993).

8. Charles Murray, *Losing Ground: American Social Policy, 1950–1980* (New York: Basic Books, 1984) p. 223.

9. Justice Thurgood Marshall, dissenting in *City of Richmond v. J. A. Croson Co.*, 488 U.S. 469 (1989).

10. See, for example, Derrick Bell, "Remembrances of Racism Past: Getting Past the Civil Rights Decline," in Herbert Hill and James E. Jones, Jr., eds., *Race in America: The Struggle for Equality* (Madison: The University of Wisconsin Press, 1993) pp. 75–76; Gertrude Ezorsky, *Racism and Justice: The Case for Affirmative Action* (Ithaca: Cornell University Press, 1991) pp. 109–111; David Kairys, *With Liberty and Justice for Some: A Critique of the Conservative Supreme Court* (New York: The New Press, 1993) pp. 138–41.

11. Howard Winant has developed a tentative "map" of the system of racial hegemony in the U.S. circa 1990, which focuses on the spectrum of racial projects running from the political right to the political left. See Winant, "Where Culture Meets Structure: Race in the 1990s," in idem, *Racial Conditions: Politics, Theory, Comparisons* (Minneapolis: University of Minnesota Press, 1994).

12. A familiar example is use of racial "code words," recall George Bush's manipulations of racial fear in the 1988 "Willie Horton" ads, or Jesse Helms's use of the coded term "quota" in his 1990 campaign against Harvey Gantt.

13. From this perspective, far right racial projects can also be interpreted as "nationalist." See Ronald Walters, "White Racial Nationalism in the United States," *Without Prejudice* Vol.1, no. 1 (Fall 1987).

14. To be sure, any effort to divide racial formation patterns according to social structural location—"macro" vs. "micro," for example—is necessarily an analytic device. In the concrete, there is no such dividing line. See Winant, "Where Culture Meets Structure."

15. We are not unaware, for example, that publishing this work is in itself a racial project.

THINKING ABOUT THE READING

What do Omi and Winant mean when they say that "race is always historically situated"? What do they mean when they say that everyone learns a system of rules and routines about race that become common sense? Consider some examples of these commonsense rules in contemporary society. How do people learn these rules? How do they unlearn them? Is the idea that race is "natural" one of the rules of the current "race project" in this society? If so, how does this particular rule contribute to social inequality?

Optional Ethnicities

For Whites Only?

Mary C. Waters

(1996)

What does it mean to talk about ethnicity as an option for an individual? To argue that an individual has some degree of choice in their ethnic identity flies in the face of the common-sense notion of ethnicity many of us believe in—that one's ethnic identity is a fixed characteristic, reflective of blood ties and given at birth. However, social scientists who study ethnicity have long concluded that while ethnicity is based on a *belief* in a common ancestry, ethnicity is primarily a *social* phenomenon, not a biological one (Alba 1985, 1990; Barth 1969; Weber [1921] 1968, p. 389). The belief that members of an ethnic group have that they share a common ancestry may not be a fact. There is a great deal of change in ethnic identities across generations through inter-marriage, changing allegiances, and changing social categories. There is also a much larger amount of change in the identities of individuals over their lives than is commonly believed. While most people are aware of the phenomenon known as "passing"—people raised as one race who change at some point and claim a different race as their identity—there are similar life course changes in ethnicity that happen all the time and are not given the same degree of attention as "racial passing."

White Americans of European ancestry can be described as having a great deal of choice in terms of their ethnic identities. The two major types of options White Americans can exercise are (1) the option of whether to claim any specific ancestry, or to just be "White" or American, (Lieberson [1985] called these people "unhyphenated Whites") and (2) the choice of which of their European ancestries to choose to include in their description of their own identities. In both cases, the option of choosing how to present yourself on surveys and in everyday social interactions exists for Whites because of social changes and societal conditions that have created a great deal of social mobility, immigrant assimilation, and political and economic power for Whites in the United States. Specifically, the option of being able to not claim any ethnic identity exists for Whites of European background in the United States because they are the majority group—in terms of holding political and social power, as well as being a numerical majority. The option of choosing among different ethnicities in their family backgrounds exists because the degree of discrimination and social distance attached to specific European backgrounds has diminished over time . . . .

Symbolic Ethnicities for White Americans

What do these ethnic identities mean to people and why do they cling to them rather than just abandoning the tie and calling themselves American? My own field research with suburban Whites in California and Pennsylvania found that later-generation descendants of European origin maintain what are called "symbolic ethnicities." Symbolic ethnicity is a term coined by Herbert Gans (1979) to refer to ethnicity that is individualistic in nature and without real social cost for the individual. These symbolic identifications are essentially leisure-time activities, rooted in nuclear family traditions and reinforced by the voluntary enjoyable aspects of being ethnic (Waters 1990). Richard Alba (1990) also found later-generation Whites in Albany, New York, who chose to keep a tie with an ethnic identity because of the enjoyable and voluntary aspects to those identities, along with the feelings of specialness they entailed. An example of symbolic ethnicity is individuals who identify as Irish, for example, on occasions such as Saint Patrick's Day, on family holidays, or for vacations. They do not usually belong to Irish American organizations, live in Irish neighborhoods, work in Irish jobs, or marry other Irish people. The symbolic meaning of being Irish American can be constructed by individuals from mass media images, family traditions, or other intermittent social activities. In other words, for later-generation White ethnics, ethnicity is not something that influences their lives unless they want it to. In the world of work and school and neighborhood, individuals do not have to admit to being ethnic unless they choose to. And for an increasing number of European-origin individuals whose parents and grandparents have intermarried, the ethnicity they claim is largely a matter of personal choice as they sort through all of the possible combinations of groups in their genealogies . . . .

Race Relations and Symbolic Ethnicity

However much symbolic ethnicity is without cost for the individual, there is a cost associated with symbolic ethnicity for the society. That is because symbolic ethnicities of the type described here are confined to White Americans of European origin. Black Americans, Hispanic Americans, Asian Americans, and American Indians do not have the option of a symbolic

ethnicity at present in the United States. For all of the ways in which ethnicity does not matter for White Americans, it does matter for non-Whites. Who your ancestors are does affect your choice of spouse, where you live, what job you have, who your friends are, and what your chances are for success in American society, if those ancestors happen not to be from Europe. The reality is that White ethnics have a lot more choice and room to maneuver than they themselves think they do. The situation is very different for members of racial minorities, whose lives are strongly influenced by their race or national origin regardless of how much they may choose not to identify themselves in terms of their ancestries.

When White Americans learn the stories of how their grandparents and great-grandparents triumphed in the United States over adversity, they are usually told in terms of their individual efforts and triumphs. The important role of labor unions and other organized political and economic actors in their social and economic successes are left out of the story in favor of a generational story of individual Americans rising up against communitarian, Old World intolerance, and New World resistance. As a result, the "individualized" voluntary, cultural view of ethnicity for Whites is what is remembered.

One important implication of these identities is that they tend to be very individualistic. There is a tendency to view valuing diversity in a pluralist environment as equating all groups. The symbolic ethnic tends to think that all groups are equal; everyone has a background that is their right to celebrate and pass on to their children. This leads to the conclusion that all identities are equal and all identities in some sense are interchangeable—"I'm Italian American, you're Polish American. I'm Irish American, you're African American." The important thing is to treat people as individuals and all equally. However, this assumption ignores the very big difference between an individualistic symbolic ethnic identity and a socially enforced and imposed racial identity.

My favorite example of how this type of thinking can lead to some severe misunderstandings between people of different backgrounds is from the *Dear Abby* advice column. A few years back a person wrote in who had asked an acquaintance of Asian background where his family was from. His acquaintance answered that this was a rude question and he would not reply. The bewildered White asked Abby why it was rude, since he thought it was a sign of respect to wonder where people were from, and he certainly would not mind anyone asking HIM about where his family was from. Abby asked her readers to write in to say whether it was rude to ask about a person's ethnic background. She reported that she got a large response, that most non-Whites thought it was a sign of disrespect, and Whites thought it was flattering:

> Dear Abby,
> I am 100 percent American and because I am of Asian ancestry I am often asked "What are you?" It's not the personal nature of this question that bothers me, it's the question itself. This query seems to question my very humanity. "What am I? Why I am a person like everyone else!"
> Signed, A REAL AMERICAN

> Dear Abby,
> Why do people resent being asked what they are? The Irish are so proud of being Irish, they tell you before you even ask. Tip O'Neill has never tried to hide his Irish ancestry.
> Signed, JIMMY.
> (Reprinted by permission of Universal Press Syndicate)

In this exchange Jimmy cannot understand why Asians are not as happy to be asked about their ethnicity as he is, because he understands his ethnicity and theirs to be separate but equal. Everyone has to come from somewhere—his family from Ireland, another's family from Asia—each has a history and each should be proud of it. But the reason he cannot understand the perspective of the Asian American is that all ethnicities are not equal; all are not

symbolic, costless, and voluntary. When White Americans equate their own symbolic ethnicities with the socially enforced identities of non-White Americans, they obscure the fact that the experiences of Whites and non-Whites have been qualitatively different in the United States and that the current identities of individuals partly reflect that unequal history.

In the next section I describe how relations between Black and White students on college campuses reflect some of these asymmetries in the understanding of what a racial or ethnic identity means. While I focus on Black and White students in the following discussion, you should be aware that the myriad other groups in the United States—Mexican Americans, American Indians, Japanese Americans—all have some degree of social and individual influences on their identities, which reflect the group's social and economic history and present circumstance.

Relations on College Campuses

Both Black and White students face the task of developing their race and ethnic identities. Sociologists and psychologists note that at the time people leave home and begin to live independently from their parents, often ages eighteen to twenty-two, they report a heightened sense of racial and ethnic identity as they sort through how much of their beliefs and behaviors are idiosyncratic to their families and how much are shared with other people. It is not until one comes in close contact with many people who are different from oneself that individuals realize the ways in which their backgrounds may influence their individual personality. This involves coming into contact with people who are different in terms of their ethnicity, class, religion, region, and race. For White students, the ethnicity they claim is more often than not a symbolic one—with all of the voluntary, enjoyable, and intermittent characteristics I have described above.

Black students at the university are also developing identities through interactions with others who are different from them. Their identity development is more complicated than that of Whites because of the added element of racial discrimination and racism, along with the "ethnic" developments of finding others who share their background. Thus Black students have the positive attraction of being around other Black students who share some cultural elements, as well as the need to band together with other students in a reactive and oppositional way in the face of racist incidents on campus.

Colleges and universities across the country have been increasing diversity among their student bodies in the last few decades. This has led in many cases to strained relations among students from different racial and ethnic backgrounds. The 1980s and 1990s produced a great number of racial incidents and high racial tensions on campuses. While there were a number of racial incidents that were due to bigotry, unlawful behavior, and violent or vicious attacks, much of what happens among students on campuses involves a low level of tension and awkwardness in social interaction.

Many Black students experience racism personally for the first time on campus. The upper-middle-class students from White suburbs were often isolated enough that their presence was not threatening to racists in their high schools. Also, their class background was known by their residence and this may have prevented attacks being directed at them. Often Black students at the university who begin talking with other students and recognizing racial slights will remember incidents that happened to them earlier that they might not have thought were related to race.

Black college students across the country experience a sizeable number of incidents that are clearly the result of racism. Many of the most blatant ones that occur between students are the result of drinking. Sometimes late at night, drunken groups of White students coming home from parties will yell slurs at single Black students on the street. The other types of incidents that happen include being singled out for special treatment by employees, such as

being followed when shopping at the campus bookstore, or going to the art museum with your class and the guard stops you and asks for your I.D. Others involve impersonal encounters on the street—being called a nigger by a truck driver while crossing the street, or seeing old ladies clutch their pocketbooks and shake in terror as you pass them on the street. For the most part these incidents are not specific to the university environment, they are the types of incidents middle-class Blacks face every day throughout American society, and they have been documented by sociologists (Feagin 1991).

In such a climate, however, with students experiencing these types of incidents and talking with each other about them, Black students do experience a tension and a feeling of being singled out. It is unfair that this is part of their college experience and not that of White students. Dealing with incidents like this, or the ever-present threat of such incidents, is an ongoing developmental task for Black students that takes energy, attention, and strength of character. It should be clearly understood that this is an asymmetry in the "college experience" for Black and White students. It is one of the unfair aspects of life that results from living in a society with ongoing racial prejudice and discrimination. It is also very understandable that it makes some students angry at the unfairness of it all, even if there is no one to blame specifically. It is also very troubling because, while most Whites do not create these incidents, some do, and it is never clear until you know someone well whether they are the type of person who could do something like this. So one of the reactions of Black students to these incidents is to band together.

In some sense then, as Blauner (1992) has argued, you can see Black students coming together on campus as both an "ethnic" pull of wanting to be together to share common experiences and community, and a "racial" push of banding together defensively because of perceived rejection and tension from Whites. In this way the ethnic identities of Black students are in some sense similar to, say, Korean students wanting to be together to share experiences. And it is an ethnicity that is generally much stronger than, say, Italian Americans. But for Koreans who come together there is generally a definition of themselves as "different from" Whites. For Blacks reacting to exclusion there is a tendency for the coming together to involve both being "different from" but also "opposed to" Whites.

The anthropologist John Ogbu (1990) has documented the tendency of minorities in a variety of societies around the world, who have experienced severe blocked mobility for long periods of time, to develop such oppositional identities. An important component of having such an identity is to describe others of your group who do not join in the group solidarity as devaluing and denying their very core identity. This is why it is not common for successful Asians to be accused by others of "acting White" in the United States, but it is quite common for such a term to be used by Blacks and Latinos. The oppositional component of a Black identity also explains how Black people can question whether others are acting "Black enough." On campus, it explains some of the intense pressures felt by Black students who do not make their racial identity central and who choose to hang out primarily with non-Blacks. This pressure from the group, which is partly defining itself by not being White, is exacerbated by the fact that race is a physical marker in American society. No one immediately notices the Jewish students sitting together in the dining hall, or the one Jewish student sitting surrounded by non-Jews, or the Texan sitting with the Californians, but everyone notices the Black student who is or is not at the "Black table" in the cafeteria.

An example of the kinds of misunderstandings that can arise because of different understandings of the meanings and implications of symbolic versus oppositional identities concerns questions students ask one another in the dorms about personal appearances and customs. A very common type of interaction in the dorm concerns questions Whites ask Blacks about their hair. Because Whites tend to know little about Blacks, and Blacks know a lot about Whites, there is a general asymmetry in the level of curiosity people have about one another. Whites, as the numerical majority, have had little contact with Black culture; Blacks, especially those who are in college, have had to develop bicultural skills—knowledge about the social worlds of both Whites and Blacks. Miscommunication and hurt feelings about White students' questions about Black students' hair illustrate this point. One of the things that happens freshman year is that White students are around Black students as they fix their hair. White students are generally quite curious about Black students' hair—they have basic questions such as how often Blacks wash their hair, how they get it straightened or curled, what products they use on their hair, how they comb it, etc. Whites often wonder to themselves whether they should ask these questions. One thought experiment Whites perform is to ask themselves whether a particular question would upset them. Adopting the "do unto others" rule, they ask themselves, "If a Black person was curious about my hair would I get upset?" The answer usually is "No, I would be happy to tell them." Another example is an Italian American student wondering to herself, "Would I be upset if someone asked me about calamari?" The answer is no, so she asks her Black roommate about collard greens, and the roommate explodes with an angry response such as, "Do you think all Black people eat watermelon too?" Note that if this Italian American knew her friend was Trinidadian American and asked about peas and rice the situation would be more similar and would not necessarily ignite underlying tensions.

Like the debate in *Dear Abby*, these innocent questions are likely to lead to resentment. The issue of stereotypes about Black Americans and the assumption that all Blacks are alike and have the same stereotypical cultural traits has more power to hurt or offend a Black person than vice versa. The innocent questions about Black hair also bring up a number of asymmetries between the Black and White experience. Because Blacks tend to have more knowledge about Whites than vice versa, there is not an even exchange going on; the Black freshman is likely to have fewer basic questions about his White roommate than his White roommate has about him. Because of the differences historically in the group experiences of Blacks and Whites there are some connotations to Black hair that don't exist about White hair. (For instance, is straightening your hair a form of assimilation, do some people distinguish between women having "good hair" and "bad hair" in terms of beauty and how is that related to looking "White"?) Finally, even a Black freshman who cheerfully disregards or is unaware that there are these asymmetries will soon slam into another asymmetry if she willingly answers every innocent question asked of her. In a situation where Blacks make up only 10 percent of the student body, if every non-Black needs to be educated about hair, she will have to explain it to nine other students. As one Black student explained to me, after you've been asked a couple of times about something so personal you begin to feel like you are an attraction in a zoo, that you are at the university for the education of the White students.

Institutional Responses

Our society asks a lot of young people. We ask young people to do something that no one else does as successfully on such a wide scale—that is to live together with people from very different backgrounds, to respect one another, to appreciate one another, and to enjoy and learn from one another. The successes that occur every day in this endeavor are many, and they are too often overlooked. However, the problems and tensions are also real, and they will not vanish on their own. We tend to see pluralism working in the United States in much the same way some people expect capitalism to work. If you put together people with various interests and abilities and resources, the "invisible hand" of capitalism is supposed to make all the parts work together in an economy for the common good.

There is much to be said for such a model—the invisible hand of the market can solve complicated problems of production and distribution better than any "visible hand" of a state plan. However, we have learned that unequal power relations among the actors in the capitalist marketplace, as well as "externalities" that the market cannot account for, such as long-term pollution, or collusion between corporations, or the exploitation of child labor, means that state regulation is often needed. Pluralism and the relations between groups are very similar. There is a lot to be said for the idea that bringing people who belong to different ethnic or racial groups together in institutions with no interference will have good consequences. Students from different backgrounds will make friends if they share a dorm room or corridor, and there is no need for the institution to do any more than provide the locale. But like capitalism, the invisible hand of pluralism does not do well when power relations and externalities are ignored. When you bring together individuals from groups that are differentially valued in the wider society and provide no guidance, there will be problems. In these cases the "invisible hand" of pluralist relations does not work, and tensions and disagreements can arise without any particular individual or group of individuals being "to blame." On college campuses in the 1990s some of the tensions between students are of this sort. They arise from honest misunderstandings, lack of a common background, and very different experiences of what race and ethnicity mean to the individual.

The implications of symbolic ethnicities for thinking about race relations are subtle but consequential. If your understanding of your own ethnicity and its relationship to society and politics is one of individual choice, it becomes harder to understand the need for programs like affirmative action, which recognize the ongoing need for group struggle and group recognition, in order to bring about social change. It also is hard for a White college student to understand the need that minority students feel to band together against discrimination. It also is easy, on the individual level, to expect everyone else to be able to turn their ethnicity on and off at will, the way you are able to, without understanding that ongoing discrimination and societal attention to minority status makes that impossible for individuals from minority groups to do. The paradox of symbolic ethnicity is that it depends upon the ultimate goal of a pluralist society, and at the same time makes it more difficult to achieve that ultimate goal. It is dependent upon the concept that all ethnicities mean the same thing, that enjoying the traditions of one's heritage is an option available to a group or an individual, but that such a heritage should not have any social costs associated with it.

As the Asian Americans who wrote to *Dear Abby* make clear, there are many societal issues and involuntary ascriptions associated with non-White identities. The developments necessary for this to change are not individual but societal in nature. Social mobility and declining racial and ethnic sensitivity are closely associated. The legacy and the present reality of discrimination on the basis of race or ethnicity must be overcome before the ideal of a pluralist society, where all heritages are treated equally and are equally available for individuals to choose or discard at will, is realized.

REFERENCES

Alba, Richard D. 1985. *Italian Americans: Into the Twilight of Ethnicity.* Englewood Cliffs, NJ: Prentice Hall.

———. 1990. *Ethnic Identity: The Transformation of White America.* New Haven: Yale University Press.

Barth, Frederick. 1969. *Ethnic Groups and Boundaries.* Boston: Little, Brown.

Blauner, Robert. 1992. "Talking Past Each Other: Black and White Languages of Race." *American Prospect* (Summer): 55–64.

Feagin, Joe R. 1991. "The Continuing Significance of Race: Anti-Black Discrimination in Public Places." *American Sociological Review* 56: 101–17.

Gans, Herbert. 1979. "Symbolic Ethnicity: The Future of Ethnic Groups and Cultures in America." *Ethnic and Racial Studies* 2: 1–20.

Lieberson, Stanley. 1985. *Making It Count: The Improvement of Social Research and Theory.* Berkeley: University of California Press.

Ogbu, John. 1990. "Minority Status and Literacy in Comparative Perspective." *Daedalus* 119: 141–69.

Waters, Mary C. 1990. *Ethnic Options: Choosing Identities in America.* Berkeley: University of California Press.

Weber, Max. [1921]/1968. *Economy and Society: An Outline of Interpretive Sociology.* Eds. Guenther Roth and Claus Wittich, trans. Ephraim Fischoff. New York: Bedminister Press.

THINKING ABOUT THE READING

What is "symbolic ethnicity" according to Waters? Why is this form of ethnic expression optional for some and not others? Based on Waters's thesis, would a campus club for Norwegian Americans be the same as one for African Americans? Consider the slogan "different but equal." Do you think this idea can be applied to racial and ethnic relations in contemporary society? Why are some ethnic and racial groups the subject of discrimination and oppression while others are a source of group membership and belonging? When might an ethnic identity be both? How would you describe the ethnic and racial climate of your college campus?

Jeremy Lin's Model Minority Problem

Maxwell Leung

(2013)

By the time the New York Knicks and Los Angeles Lakers faced off in New York last February, breakout star Jeremy Lin had led the Knicks to a phenomenal three-game winning streak. Less than four minutes into the first quarter, the Knicks were leading 7-4, and Lin threw a perfect half-court pass to Tyson Chandler for an easy two-point slam. As fans in Madison Square Garden cheered the offensive attack, Lin mouthed the words "Come on!" The Knicks pressed their defensive attack, and a player from the Lakers dropped the ball.

The crowd sensed another quick score. Lin scooped up the ball and drove in for an easy lay-up. The Lakers called a time out and the fans erupted. Less than five minutes in, the Knicks had an uncontested 10-point run. Lin already had 9 points and 2 assists.

That night, a thousand miles away at Grinnell College in Iowa, I joined students from the Asian and Asian American Alliance to cheer on Jeremy Lin. Although we were unaware of it at the time, the game against the Lakers was one of the high points of what came to be known as "Linsanity"—the global cultural phenomenon that accompanied Lin's meteoric rise from an unknown player to an international star.

The excitement began with Lin's first game as a Knick in February 2012 and ended with the announcement of a season-ending knee injury only a month later. Since, Lin has left the Knicks to join the Houston Rockets and has struggled as a player. The national adulation that surrounded his breakout performance has largely faded.

The story of how Jeremy Lin became an NBA star is one of denied opportunities, enduring racism, and barrier-breaking in professional sports. Although his star has dimmed, Lin's story is worth our attention.

The Model Minority—Again

Jeremy Lin's success in the face of daunting obstacles both challenges the prevailing racial narrative of basketball and reinforces it, offering Asian Americans the chance to see themselves as something other than doctors, engineers, or accountants, while also affirming the belief that they are high achievers. In effect, Linsanity affirmed the myth of Asian Americans as the "model minority." Through hard work and perseverance, Asian Americans supposedly show how any minority can overcome institutionalized inequality. At the same time, Lin's achievements alone could do little to undo understandings of Asian men, exemplified by the docile honor student, that are at odds with male achievement in sports.

The model minority trope is taken for granted in U.S. media. In June 2012 the Pew Research Center released a report titled "The Rise of Asian Americans," and it was big news. The report *should* have given Asian Americans—who comprise nearly six percent of the national population—a reason to celebrate. Sampling more than 3,500 people from six of the largest Asian ethnic groups (Chinese-, Filipino-, Indian-, Vietnamese-, Korean-, and Japanese-Americans), Pew's report portrayed Asian Americans as an immigrant group that has successfully broken many social, political, and economic barriers. On the whole, Pew found, Asian Americans are highly educated, possess an admirable work ethic, and earn higher-than-average incomes.

The report goes on to describe Asian Americans' strong family ties and high levels of happiness: "Most Asian Americans feel good about their lives in the U.S. They see themselves as having achieved economic prosperity on the strength of hard work, a character trait they say is much more prevalent among Asian Americans than among the rest of the U.S. population. Most say they are better off than their parents were at a comparable age. And among the foreign born, very few say that if they had to do it all over again, they would stay in their home country rather than emigrate to the U.S."

Scholars, Asian American organizations, and advocacy groups—from the Japanese American Citizens League to the National Council of Asian Pacific Americans—criticized the report as "one-dimensional," "exclusionary," and full of "over-generalizations" that portrayed Asian Americans as the torchbearers of American exceptionalism. California Congresswoman Judy Chu, who chairs the Congressional Asian Pacific American Caucus stated, "I would strongly caution against using the data [in the report] to validate the 'model minority' myth." As she pointed out, "Our community is one of stark contrasts, with significant disparities within and between various subgroups."

For example, another recent report, this time from the Asian American Center for Advancing Justice, showed that while Asian Americans are successful in terms of educational achievement compared to whites, specific ethnic groups (such as Hmong, Cambodian, Laotian, and Vietnamese Americans) have high school graduation rates as low as 61 percent and even lower rates of college graduation—numbers comparable to Latinos and African Americans. The Pew Report had lumped all these groups together as "Asian American," ignoring some of the most distressed communities and the economic, health, and other challenges they face.

When research and portraits of Asian Americans are consistently framed this way, Asian Americans are almost always seen as superior to other minority groups in terms of educational achievement, economic stability, and social acceptance. Supposed exemplary Asian cultural values—hard work, perseverance, strong family traditions, a reverence for education, self-reliance, even self-sacrifice—are portrayed as unique among ethnic groups. As this story goes, even when Asian Americans face cultural and linguistic barriers, institutional racism, and other dramatically unequal treatment, they will not only overcome the obstacles, but do so without protest or complaint.

Popular culture has long portrayed Asian American men as geniuses, overachievers, computer geeks, or nerds. They're shy and docile, humble and passive. If Asian American women are presented as exotic and hypersexualized, men are rendered effete, weak, and physically and sexually inferior. Examples range from the insufferable Long Duk Dong in the 1984 film *Sixteen Candles* to William Hung, famous for his cringeworthy rendition of "She Bangs" on *American Idol* in 2008. The character Raj on the hugely popular sitcom *The Big Bang Theory* is the most recent example of an image of a socially dysfunctional Asian American man. Such representations leave Asian Americans to struggle against broad stereotypes that are as inaccurate as they are negative—especially in a culture that prizes traditional masculinity.

Jeremy Lin's breakout success gave Asian American men a striking respite from these oppressive images. Lin is tall, strong, aggressive, and physically gifted. Far from shy or quiet, he's a powerful player in a physically demanding sport, displaying style and swagger on a huge media stage. The Linsanity phenomenon marked more than just the international embrace of a spectacular new Asian American sports star—it posed a challenge to emasculating stereotypes.

At the same time, Lin could be the poster child for the Pew Report. He was smart and driven, but overlooked by college recruiters and the NBA draft, and he bounced from team to team. His hard work and focus—model behavior—paid off in the form of a phenomenal ascent to the upper echelons of a multi-billion dollar sport.

Invisible Man?

The myth of the model minority is central to understanding the story of Jeremy Lin's encounter with discrimination and his subsequent success as a professional basketball player. Likely because he did not fit expectations about what an elite basketball player looks like, Lin was a talented player but flew under the radar. The fact that many college coaches and recruiters later admitted that they'd failed to recognize Lin's talents suggests they couldn't see "past" his Asian features.

As Lin himself said in an interview with EPSN in 2012, "I was very disappointed, discouraged. I'm undrafted, I'm out of Harvard. 'Asian American.' That was kind of the perception everyone had of me and that was kind of the perception I had of myself. And when everyone thinks that, then it's hard to break that."

Yet Asians and Asian Americans who play basketball are not a wholly new phenomenon. There have been Asian players in the NBA—most notably Yao Ming of the Houston Rockets and Wataru Misaka, the first Japanese American to play professional basketball with the New York Knicks in 1947. There have also been standout Asian American college players such as Raymond Townsend, part-Filipino, who played for UCLA in the 1970s; Corey Gaines, part-Japanese, who played for Loyola Marymount University in the '80s and Rex Walters, part-Japanese, who played for Kansas in the early '90s.

As Lin's remarks on ESPN and in a more recent television interview suggest, he *is* the first professional basketball player to deliberately and comfortably claim his Asian American heritage and be acknowledged as such by his fans. He has directly confronted the experience of social invisibility he experienced on his way up. And yet Lin's success as a Knick is still couched in the default language of the model minority: he worked very hard to get to the top. He's got intelligence—not just talent. If African American point guards are the norm in basketball, then Jeremy Lin is an anomaly whose existence almost demands explanation.

In his second career appearance against the Houston Rockets, Lin had an impressive showing, even though his Knicks trailed throughout the game and eventually lost. Late in the third quarter, one of the television sports show hosts commented about Lin's overall performance: "He's a hustler; he runs the show. Very intelligent player. Does the fact that he went to Harvard help that? Absolutely!"

But what *does* Lin's intelligence or Harvard degree have to do with his basketball skills? One could say that all professional athletes need intelligence to perform exceptionally. One might also observe that playing point guard requires especially intelligent play—a successful player in this role must read defenses, make plays, and provide assists. But in relation to race, "intelligence" is a loaded word.

According to sociologist Douglas Hartmann, "because of sport's *de facto* association with bodies and the mind/body dualisms . . . African American athletic excellence serves to reinforce racial stereotypes by grounding them in essentialized, biological terms." He continues: "Athletic prowess is believed to be inversely associated with intellectual and/or moral excellence." Reporting and commentary about black basketball players, for example, often refers not to their formal education, but to an "urban experience" of playing basketball in the streets.

In contrast, Lin's "intelligence" on the court was tied explicitly to his Ivy League education, even though Lin began playing the game at his local YMCA and on neighborhood playgrounds in Palo Alto, California. It's the model minority discourse at work: educational achievements are primary, and the physical experience of playing ball is less central.

In the Lin narrative, basketball is a meritocracy based on skill, and those who rise to the top earn their rewards. This reaffirms the classic American story that those "who work hard and possess the right stuff will always prevail"—and *deserve* to, according to sociologist of sport Susan Birrell. Conversely, those who try and fail? They didn't work hard enough.

Trying to Flip the Script

Despite the Asian American basketball players who came before Jeremy Lin, his stunning performance on the national stage confirmed something Asian Americans know, but had rarely witnessed: We can jump, drive, and shoot the ball. According to sociologist Oliver Wang, Linsanity made Asian Americans playing professional basketball "a national concept." Lin's triumph resonated with Asian Americans and many others, and it led some to believe Lin could present a real challenge to longstanding stereotypes.

Not only do Asian Americans hope that Lin is the real deal, a truly talented basketball player of NBA caliber, we also want to see the devotion he has generated translate into real changes in perceptions of Asian Americans. For us, it is hard to overestimate the pure euphoria of seeing this man lead on the court, outmaneuver defenders, and make clutch plays—all with confidence, bravado, and off-court dignity.

This year, the documentary *Linsanity*, directed by Evan Jackson Leong, premiered at the Sundance Film Festival and opened San Francisco's Center for Asian American Media's annual film festival. Audiences cheered, giving it a standing ovation. An inspirational basketball story told through Jeremy Lin's eyes, the film documents his rise to stardom.

Although Linsanity lasted just three glorious weeks, Jeremy Lin still offers a powerful new image of Asian American male sport prowess that both challenges and reaffirms the model minority myth. His success offers a critical commentary on how we understand the contradictory and often frustrating place of Asian Americans in American culture.

In March 2013, *Wall Street Journal* columnist Jeff Yang, discussing the Leong documentary, told eager readers: "Keep your eyes peeled, sports fans. Linsanity may well end up having a sequel." Although Jeremy Lin has faded from basketball stardom, his story, by reaffirming some stereotypes while calling others into question, gives us a way to understand Asian Americans' complicated relationship to American cultural values.

THINKING ABOUT THE READING

Although Linsanity lasted just three glorious weeks, Jeremy Lin offered a powerful new image of Asian American male sport prowess that both challenged and reaffirmed the model minority myth. What is the model minority myth, and how did Lin's performance challenge it? The author writes that Lin's success both challenges the prevailing racial narrative of basketball and reinforces it. What is the racial narrative in basketball (and other sports)? According to the author, Lin offers Asian Americans the chance to see themselves as something other than doctors, engineers, or accountants, while also affirming the belief that they are high achievers. In addition to high-profile sports, what are some of the other sources of the stereotypes we have about race and performance?

The Architecture of Inequality

Sex and Gender

12

In addition to racial and class inequality, gender inequality—and the struggle against it—has been a fundamental part of the historical development of our national identity. Gender ideology has influenced the lives and dreams of individual people, shaped popular culture, and created or maintained social institutions. Gender is a major criterion for the distribution of important economic, political, and educational resources in most societies. Gender inequality is perpetuated by a dominant cultural ideology that devalues women on the basis of presumed biological differences between men and women. This ideology overlooks the equally important role of social forces in determining male and female behavior.

Gender inequality exists at the institutional level as well, in the law, in the family (in terms of such things as the domestic division of labor), and in economics. Not only are social institutions sexist, in that women are systematically segregated, exploited, and excluded, but they are also gendered. Institutions themselves are structured along gender lines so that traits associated with success are usually stereotypically male characteristics: tough-mindedness, rationality, assertiveness, competitiveness, and so forth.

Women have made significant advances politically, economically, educationally, and socially over the past decades. The traditional obstacles to advancement continue to fall. Women have entered the labor force in unprecedented numbers. Yet despite their growing presence in the labor force and their entry into historically male occupations, rarely do women work alongside men or perform the same tasks and functions.

Bart Landry explores the intersections of race and gender in "Black Women and a New Definition of Womanhood." Landry examines the difficulties black women have faced throughout history in being seen by others as virtuous and moral. This article provides a fascinating picture of women's struggle for equality from the perspective of black women, a group that is often ignored and marginalized in discussions of the women's movement. Although much of the article focuses on black women's activism in the 19th century, it provides important insight into the intersection of race and gender today. Landry raises an important contrast between the way in which 19th-century middle-class white women and middle-class black women framed the relationship between family and public life.

Jobs within an occupation still tend to be divided into "men's work" and "women's work." Such gender segregation has serious consequences for women in the form of blocked advancement and lower salaries. But looking at gender segregation on the job as something that happens only to women gives us an incomplete picture of the situation. It is just as important to examine what keeps men out of "female" jobs as it is to examine what keeps women out of "male" jobs. The proportion of women in male jobs has increased over the past several decades, but the proportion of men in female jobs has remained virtually unchanged. In "Still a Man's World," Christine L. Williams looks at the experiences of male nurses, social workers, elementary school teachers, and librarians. She finds that although these men do feel somewhat stigmatized by their nontraditional career choices, they still enjoy significant gender advantages.

Bodily transformation practices like plastic surgery, tattooing, and weight lifting have become widespread practices across society, but new technologies are taking this transformation process to another level. In "New Biomedical Technologies, New Scripts, New Genders," Eve Shapiro uses case studies to explore the connection between new biomedical technologies and gendered bodies and identities. She illustrates how the somatechnic frontier is giving individuals the opportunity to construct new bodies to fit *and* contest existing social scripts for women and men.

Something to Consider as You Read

While reading these selections, think about the significance of gender as a social category. A child's gender is the single most important thing people want to know when it is born. "What is it?" is a commonly understood shorthand for "Is it a boy or a girl?" From the time children are born, they learn that certain behaviors, feelings, and expectations are associated with the gender category to which they have been assigned. Think about some of the behaviors associated with specific gender categories. Make a list of stereotypical gender expectations. Upon reflection, do these seem reasonable to you? What are some recollections you have about doing something that was considered inappropriate for your gender? Think about ways in which these stereotypical expectations affect people's perceptions, especially in settings such as school or jobs.

Black Women and a New Definition of Womanhood

Bart Landry

(2000)

A popular novel of 1852 chirped that the white heroine, Eoline, "with her fair hair, and celestial blue eyes bending over the harp. . . really seemed 'little lower than the angels,' and an aureola of purity and piety appeared to beam around her brow."[1] By contrast, in another popular antebellum novel, *Maum Guinea and Her Plantation Children* (1861), black women are excluded from the category of true womanhood without debate: "The idea of modesty and virtue in a Louisiana colored-girl might well be ridiculed; as a general thing, she has neither."[2] Decades later, in 1902, a commentator for the popular magazine *The Independent* noted, "I sometimes hear of a virtuous Negro woman, but the idea is absolutely inconceivable to me. . . .I cannot imagine such a creature as a virtuous Negro woman."[3] Another writer, reflecting early-twentieth-century white male stereotypes of black and white women, remarked that, like white women, "Black women had the brains of a child, [and] the passions of a woman" but, unlike white women, were "steeped in centuries of ignorance and savagery, and wrapped about with immoral vices."[4]

Faced with the prevailing views of white society that placed them outside the boundaries of true womanhood, black women had no choice but to defend their virtue. Middle-class black women led this defense, communicating their response in words and in the actions of their daily lives. In doing so they went well beyond defending their own virtue to espouse a broader conception of womanhood that anticipated modern views by more than half a century. Their vision of womanhood combined the public and the private spheres and

eventually took for granted a role for women as paid workers outside the home. More than merely an abstract vision, it was a philosophy of womanhood embodied in the lives of countless middle-class black women in both the late nineteenth and the early twentieth centuries.

Virtue Defended

Although black women were seen as devoid of all four of the cardinal virtues of true womanhood—piety, purity, submissiveness, and domesticity—white attention centered on purity. As Hazel Carby suggests, this stemmed in part from the role assigned to black women in the plantation economy. She argues that "two very different but interdependent codes of sexuality operated in the antebellum South, producing opposite definitions of motherhood and womanhood for white and black women which coalesce in the figures of the slave and the mistress."[5] In this scheme, white mistresses gave birth to heirs, slave women to property. A slave woman who attempted to preserve her virtue or sexual autonomy was a threat to the plantation economy. In the words of Harriet Jacobs's slave narrative, *Incidents in the Life of a Slave Girl* (1861), it was "deemed a crime in her [the slave woman] to wish to be virtuous."[6]

Linda Brent, the pseudonym Jacobs used to portray her own life, was an ex-slave struggling to survive economically and protect herself and her daughter from sexual exploitation. In telling her story, she recounts the difficulty all black women faced in practicing the virtues of true womanhood. The contrasting contexts of black and white women's lives called for different, even opposite, responses. While submissiveness and passivity brought protection to the white mistress, these characteristics merely exposed black women to sexual and economic exploitation. Black women, therefore, had to develop strength rather than glory in fragility, and had to be active and assertive rather than passive and submissive. . . .

Three decades later, in the 1890s, black women found reasons to defend their moral integrity with new urgency against attacks from all sides. Views such as those in *The Independent* noted earlier were given respectability by a report of the Slater Fund, a foundation that supported welfare projects for blacks in this period. The foundation asserted without argument, "The negro women of the South are subject to temptations. . . which come to them from the days of their race enslavement. . . .To meet such temptations the negro woman can only offer the resistance of a low moral standard, an inheritance from the system of slavery, made still lower from a lifelong residence in a one-room cabin."[7]

At the 1893 World Columbian Exposition in Chicago, where black women were effectively barred from the exhibits on the achievements of American women, the few black women allowed to address a women's convention there felt compelled to publicly challenge these views. One speaker, Fannie Barrier Williams, shocked her audience by her forthrightness. "I regret the necessity of speaking of the moral question of our women," but "the morality of our home life has been commented on so disparagingly and meanly that we are placed in the unfortunate position of being defenders of our name."[8] She went on to emphasize that black women continued to be the victims of sexual harassment by white men and chided her white female audience for failing to protect their black sisters. In the same vein, black activist and educator Anna Julia Cooper told the audience that it was not a question of "temptations" as much as it was "the painful, patient, and silent toil of mothers to gain title to the bodies of their daughters."[9] Williams was later to write on the same theme.

"It is a significant and shameful fact that I am constantly in receipt of letters from the still unprotected women in the South, begging me to find employment for their daughters. . . to save them from going into the homes of the South as servants as there is nothing to save them from dishonor and degradation."[10] Another black male writer was moved to reveal in *The Independent:* "I know of more than one colored woman who was openly importuned by White women to become the mistress of their husbands, on the ground that they, the white wives, were afraid that, if their husbands did not associate with colored women they would certainly do so with outside white women. . . .And the white wives, for reasons which ought to be perfectly obvious, preferred to have all their husbands do wrong with colored women in order to keep their husbands *straight!*"[11] The attacks on black women's virtue came to a head with a letter written by James Jacks, president of the Missouri Press Association, in which he alleged, "The Negroes in this country were wholly devoid of morality, the women were prostitutes and all were natural thieves and liars."[12] These remarks, coming from such a prominent individual, drew an immediate reaction from black women throughout the country. The most visible was Josephine St. Pierre Ruffin's invitation to black club women to a national convention in Boston in 1895; one hundred women from ten states came to Boston in response. In a memorable address to representatives of some twenty clubs, Ruffin directly attacked the scurrilous accusations:

> Now for the sake of the thousands of self-sacrificing young women teaching and preaching in lonely southern backwoods, for the noble army of mothers who gave birth to these girls, mothers whose intelligence is only limited by their opportunity to get at books, for the cultured women who have carried off the honors at school here and often abroad, for the sake of our own dignity, the dignity of our race and the future good name of our children, it is "meet, right and our bounden duty" to stand forth and declare ourselves and our principles, to teach an ignorant and

suspicious world that our aims and interests are identical with those of all good, aspiring women. Too long have we been silent under unjust and unholy charges. . . .It is to break this silence, not by noisy protestations of what we are not, but by a dignified showing of what we are and hope to become, that we are impelled to take this step, to make of this gathering an object lesson to the world.[13]

At the end of three days of meetings, the National Federation of Afro-American Women was founded, uniting thirty-six black women's clubs in twelve states.[14] The following year, the National Federation merged with the National League of Colored Women to form the National Association of Colored Women (NACW).

Racial Uplift: In Defense of the Black Community

While the catalyst for these national organizations was in part the felt need of black women to defend themselves against moral attacks by whites, they soon went beyond this narrow goal. Twenty years after its founding, the NACW had grown to fifty thousand members in twenty-eight federations and more than one thousand clubs.[15] The founding of these organizations represented a steady movement by middle-class black women to assume more active roles in the community. Historian Deborah Gray White argues that black club women "insisted that only black women could save the black race," a position that inspired them to pursue an almost feverish pace of activities.[16]

These clubs, however, were not the first attempts by black women to participate actively in their communities. Since the late 1700s black women had been active in mutual-aid societies in the North, and in the 1830s northern black women organized anti-slavery societies. In 1880 Mary Ann Shadd Cary and six other women founded the Colored Women's Progressive Franchise Association in Washington, D.C. Among its stated goals were equal rights for women, including the vote, and

the even broader feminist objective of taking "an aggressive stand against the assumption that men only begin and conduct industrial and other things."[17] Giving expression to this goal were a growing number of black women professionals, including the first female physicians to practice in the South.[18] By the turn of the twentieth century, the National Business League, founded by Booker T. Washington, could report that there were "160 Black female physicians, seven dentists, ten lawyers, 164 ministers, assorted journalists, writers, artists, 1,185 musicians and teachers of music, and 13,525 school instructors."[19]

Black women's activism was spurred by the urgency of the struggle for equality, which had led to a greater acceptance of black female involvement in the abolitionist movement. At a time when patriarchal notions of women's domestic role dominated, historian Paula Giddings asserts, "There is no question that there was greater acceptance among Black men of women in activist roles than there was in the broader society."[20] This is not to say that all black men accepted women as equals or the activist roles that many were taking. But when faced with resistance, black women often *demanded* acceptance of their involvement. In 1849, for example, at a black convention in Ohio, "Black women, led by Jane P. Merritt, threatened to boycott the meetings if they were not given a more substantial voice in the proceedings."[21]

In the postbellum period black women continued their struggle for an equal voice in activities for racial uplift in both secular and religious organizations. . . .These women's organizations then played a significant role not only in missionary activities, but also in general racial uplift activities in both rural and urban areas.[22]. . .

Black Women and the Suffrage Movement

In their struggle for their own rights, black women moved into the political fray and eagerly joined the movement for passage of a constitutional amendment giving women the right to vote. Unlike white women suffragists, who focused exclusively on the benefits of the vote for their sex, black women saw the franchise as a means of improving the condition of the black community generally. For them, race and gender issues were inseparable. As historian Rosalyn Terborg-Penn emphasizes, black feminists believed that by "increasing the black electorate" they "would not only uplift the women of the race, but help the children and the men as well."[23]

Prominent black women leaders as well as national and regional organizations threw their support behind the suffrage movement. At least twenty black suffrage organizations were founded, and black women participated in rallies and demonstrations and gave public speeches.[24] Ironically, they often found themselves battling white women suffragists as well as men. Southern white women opposed including black women under a federal suffrage as a matter of principle. Northern white women suffragists, eager to retain the support of southern white women, leaned toward accepting a wording of the amendment that would have allowed the southern states to determine their own position on giving black women the vote, a move that would have certainly led to their exclusion.[25]

After the Nineteenth Amendment was ratified in 1920 in its original form, black women braved formidable obstacles in registering to vote. All across the South white registrars used "subterfuge and trickery" to hinder them from registering, including a "grandmother clause" in North Carolina, literacy tests in Virginia, and a $300 poll tax in Columbia, South Carolina. In Columbia, black women "waited up to twelve hours to register" while white women were registered first.[26] In their struggle to register, black women appealed to the NAACP, signed affidavits against registrars who disqualified them, and finally asked for assistance from national white women suffrage leaders. They were especially disappointed in this last attempt. After fighting side by side with white women suffragists for passage of the Nineteenth Amendment, they were rebuffed by the National Woman's Party leadership with the argument that theirs was a race rather than a women's rights issue.[27] Thus, white women continued to separate issues of race and sex that black women saw as inseparable.

Challenging the Primacy of Domesticity

A conflicting conception of the relationship between gender and race issues was not the only major difference in the approaches of black and white women to their roles in the family and society. For most white women, their domestic roles as wives and mothers remained primary. In the late nineteenth century, as they began increasingly to argue for acceptance of their involvement on behalf of child-labor reform and growing urban problems, white women often defended these activities as extensions of their housekeeping role. Historian Barbara Harris comments, "The [white women] pioneers in women's education, who probably did more than anyone else in this period to effect change in the female sphere, advocated education for women and their entrance into the teaching profession on the basis of the values proclaimed by the cult of true womanhood. In a similar way, females defended their careers as authors and their involvement in charitable, religious, temperance, and moral reform societies."[28] Paula Giddings notes that in this way white women were able "to become more active outside the home while still preserving the probity of 'true womanhood.'"[29] From the birth of white feminism at the Seneca Falls Convention in 1848, white feminists had a difficult time advancing their goals. Their numbers were few and their members often divided over the propriety of challenging the cult of domesticity. . . .

In the late nineteenth century the cult of domesticity remained primary even for white women graduates of progressive women's colleges such as Vassar, Smith, and Wellesley. For them, no less than for those with only a high-school education, "A Woman's Kingdom" was "a well-ordered home."[30] In a student essay, one Vassar student answered her rhetorical question, "Has the educated woman a duty towards the kitchen?" by emphasizing that the kitchen was "exactly where the college woman belonged" for "the orderly, disciplined, independent graduate is the woman best prepared to manage the home, in which lies the salvation of the world."[31] This essay reflects the dilemma faced by these young white women graduates. They found little support in white society to combine marriage and career. . . . Society sanctioned only three courses for the middle-class white woman in the Progressive period: "marriage, charity work or teaching."[32] Marriage and motherhood stood as the highest calling. If there were no economic need for them to work, single women were encouraged to do volunteer charity work. For those who needed an independent income, teaching was the only acceptable occupation.

Historian John Rousmaniere suggests that the white college-educated women involved in the early settlement house movement saw themselves as fulfilling the "service norm" so prominent among middle-class women of the day. At the same time, he argues, it was their sense of uniqueness as college-educated women and their felt isolation upon returning home that led them to this form of service. The settlement houses, located as they were in white immigrant, working-class slums, catered to these women's sense of noblesse oblige; they derived a sense of accomplishment from providing an example of genteel middle-class virtues to the poor. Yet the settlement houses also played into a sense of adventure, leading one resident to write, "We feel that we know life for the first time."[33] For all their felt uniqueness, however, with some notable exceptions these women's lives usually offered no fundamental challenge to the basic assumptions of true womanhood. Residency in settlement houses was for the most part of short duration, and most volunteers eventually embraced their true roles of wife and mother without significant outside involvement. The exceptions were

women like Jane Addams, Florence Kelley, Julia Lathrop, and Grace Abbott, who became major figures in the public sphere. Although their lives disputed the doctrine of white women's confinement to the private sphere, the challenge was limited in that most of them did not themselves combine the two spheres of marriage and a public life. Although Florence Kelley was a divorced mother, she nevertheless upheld "the American tradition that men support their families, their wives throughout life," and bemoaned the "retrograde movement" against man as the breadwinner.[34]

Most college-educated black middle-class women also felt a unique sense of mission. They accepted Lucy Laney's 1899 challenge to lift up their race and saw themselves walking in the footsteps of black women activists and feminists of previous generations. But their efforts were not simply "charity work"; their focus was on "racial uplift" on behalf of themselves as well as of the economically less fortunate members of their race.[35] The black women's club movement, in contrast to the white women's, tended to concern themselves from the beginning with the "social and legal problems that confronted both black women and men."[36] While there was certainly some elitism in the NACW's motto, "Lifting as We Climb," these activists were always conscious that they shared a common experience of exploitation and discrimination with the masses and could not completely retreat to the safe haven of their middle-class homes.[37] On the way to meetings they shared the black experience of riding in segregated cars or of being ejected if they tried to do otherwise, as Ida B. Wells did in 1884.[38] Unlike white women for whom, as black feminist Frances Ellen Watkins Harper had emphasized in 1869, "the priorities in the struggle for human rights were sex, not race,"[39] black women could not separate these twin sources of their oppression. They understood that, together with their working-class sisters, they were assumed by whites to have "low animalistic urges." Their exclusion from the category of true womanhood was no less complete than for their less educated black sisters.

It is not surprising, therefore, that the most independent and radical of black female activists led the way in challenging the icons of true womanhood, including on occasion motherhood and marriage. Not only did they chafe under their exclusion from true womanhood, they viewed its tenets as strictures to their efforts on behalf of racial uplift and their own freedom and integrity as women. In 1894 *The Woman's Era* (a black women's magazine) set forth the heretical opinion that "not all women are intended for mothers. Some of us have not the temperament for family life. . . . Clubs will make women think seriously of their future lives, and not make girls think their only alternative is to marry."[40] Anna Julia Cooper, one of the most dynamic women of the period, who had been married and widowed, added that a woman was not "compelled to look to sexual love as the one sensation capable of giving tone and relish, movement and vim to the life she leads. Her horizon is extended."[41] Elsewhere Cooper advised black women that if they married they should seek egalitarian relationships. "The question is not now with the woman 'How shall I so cramp, stunt, and simplify and nullify myself as to make me eligible to the honor of being swallowed up into some little man?' but the problem. . . rests with the man as to how he can so develop. . . to reach the ideal of a generation of women who demand the noblest, grandest and best achievements of which he is capable."[42]

. . . Black activists were far more likely to combine marriage and activism than white activists. . . .Historian Linda Gordon found this to be the case in her study of sixty-nine black and seventy-six white activists in national welfare reform between 1890 and 1945. Only 34 percent of the white activists had ever been married, compared to 85 percent of the black activists. Most of these women (83 percent of blacks and 86 percent of whites) were college educated.[43] She also found that "The white women [reformers], with few exceptions, tended to view married women's economic dependence on men as desirable, and their employment as a misfortune. . . ."[44] On the other hand, although there were exceptions, Gordon writes, ". . . most black women activists projected a favorable view of working women and women's professional aspirations."[45] Nor could it be claimed that these black activists worked out of necessity, since the majority were married to prominent men "who could support them."[46]

Witness Ida B. Wells-Barnett (married to the publisher of Chicago's leading black newspaper) in 1896, her six-month-old son in tow, stumping from city to city making political speeches on behalf of the Illinois Women's State Central Committee. And Mary Church Terrell dismissing the opinion of those who suggested that studying higher mathematics would make her unappealing as a marriage partner with a curt, "I'd take a chance and run the risk."[47] She did eventually marry and raised a daughter and an adopted child. Her husband, Robert Terrell, a Harvard graduate, was a school principal, a lawyer, and eventually a municipal court judge in Washington, D.C. A biographer later wrote of Mary Terrell's life, "But absorbing as motherhood was, it never became a full-time occupation."[48] While this could also be said of Stanton, perhaps what most distinguished black from white feminists and activists was the larger number of the former who unequivocally challenged domesticity and the greater receptivity they found for their views in the black community. As a result, while the cult of domesticity remained dominant in the white community at the turn of the twentieth century, it did not hold sway within the black community.

Rejection of the Public/Private Dichotomy

Black women of the nineteenth and early twentieth centuries saw their efforts on behalf of the black community as necessary for their own survival, rather than as noblesse oblige. "Self preservation," wrote Mary Church Terrell in 1902, "demands that [black women] go among the lowly, illiterate and even the vicious, to whom they are bound by ties of race and sex. . . to reclaim them."[49] These women rejected the confinement to the private sphere mandated by the cult of domesticity. They felt women could enter the public sphere without detriment to the home. As historian Elsa Barkley Brown has emphasized, black women believed that "Only a strong and unified community made up of both women and men could wield the power necessary to allow black people to shape their own lives. Therefore, only when women were able to exercise their full strength would the community be at its full strength. . . ."[50]

In her study of black communities in Illinois during the late Victorian era (1880–1910), historian Shirley Carlson contrasts the black and white communities' expectations of the "ideal woman" at that time:

The black community's appreciation for and development of the feminine intellect con trasted sharply with the views of the larger society. In the latter, intelligence was regarded as a masculine quality that would "defeminize" women. The ideal white woman, being married, confined herself almost exclusively to the private domain of the household. She was demure, perhaps even self-effacing. She often deferred to her husband's presumably superior judgment, rather than formulating her own views and vocally expressing them, as black women often did. A woman in the larger society might skillfully manipulate her husband for her own purposes, but she was not supposed to confront or challenge him directly. Black women were often direct, and frequently won community approval for this quality, especially when such a characteristic was directed toward achieving racial uplift. Further, even after her marriage, a black woman might remain in the public domain, possibly in paid employment. The ideal black woman's domain, then, was both the private and public spheres. She was wife and mother, but she could also assume other roles such as schoolteacher, social activist, or businesswoman, among others. And she was intelligent.[51]

. . . Although many black males, like most white males, opposed the expansion of black women's roles, many other black males supported women's activism and even criticized their brethren for their opposition. Echoing Maggie Walker's sentiments, T. Thomas Fortune wrote, "The race could not succeed nor build strong citizens, until we have a race of women competent to do more than hear a brood of negative men."[52] Support for women's suffrage was especially strong among black males. . . .Black men saw women's suffrage as advancing the political empowerment of the race. For black women, suffrage promised to be a potent weapon in their fight for their rights, for education and jobs.[53]

A Threefold Commitment

An expanded role for black women did not end at the ballot box or in activities promoting racial uplift. Black middle class women demanded a place for themselves in the paid labor force. Theirs was a threefold commitment to family, career, and social movements. According to historian Rosalyn Terborg-Penn, "most black feminists and leaders had been wives and mothers who worked yet found time not only to struggle for the good of their sex, but for their race." Such a threefold commitment "was not common among white women."[54]

In her study of eighty African American women throughout the country who worked in "the feminized professions" (such as teaching) between the 1880s and the 1950s, historian Stephanie Shaw comments on the way they were socialized to lives dedicated to home, work, and community. When these women were children, she indicates, "the model of womanhood held before [them] was one of achievement in *both* public and private spheres. Parents cast domesticity as a complement rather than a contradiction to success in public arenas."[55]. . .

An analysis of the lives of 108 of the first generation of black clubwomen bears this out. "The career-oriented clubwomen," comments Paula Giddings, "seemed to have no ambivalence concerning their right to work, whether necessity dictated it or not."[56] According to Giddings, three-quarters of these 108 early clubwomen were married, and almost three-quarters worked outside the home, while one-quarter had children.

A number of these clubwomen and other black women activists not only had careers but also spoke forcefully about the importance of work, demonstrating surprisingly progressive attitudes with a very modern ring. "The old doctrine that a man marries a woman to support her," quipped Walker, "is pretty nearly thread-bare to-day."[57] "Every dollar a woman makes," she declared in a 1912 speech to the Federation of Colored Women's Clubs, "some man gets the direct benefit of same. Every woman was by Divine Providence created for some man; not for some man to marry, take home and support, but for the purpose of using her powers, ability, health and strength, to forward the financial. . . success of the partnership into which she may go, if she will. . . ."[58] Being married with three sons and an adopted daughter did not in any way dampen her commitment to gender equality and an expanded role for wives.

Such views were not new. In a pamphlet entitled *The Awakening of the Afro-American Woman,* written in 1897 to celebrate the earlier founding of the National Association of Colored Women, Victoria Earle Matthews referred to black women as "co-breadwinners in their families."[59] Almost twenty years earlier, in 1878, feminist writer and activist Frances Ellen Harper sounded a similar theme of equality when she insisted, "The women as a class are quite equal to the men in energy and executive ability." She went on to recount instances of black women managing small and large farms in the postbellum period.[60]

It is clear that in the process of racial uplift work, black middle-class women also included membership in the labor force as part of their identity. They were well ahead of their time in realizing that their membership in the paid labor force was critical to achieving true equality with men. For this reason, the National Association of Wage Earners insisted that all black women should be able to support themselves.[61]. . .

As W. E. B. DuBois commented as early as 1924, "Negro women more than the women of any other group in America are the protagonists in the fight for an economically independent womanhood in modern countries. . . .The matter of economic independence is, of course, the central fact in the struggle of women for equality."[62]

Defining Black Womanhood

In the late 1930s when Mary McLeod Bethune, the acknowledged leader of black women at the time and an adviser to President Franklin Roosevelt on matters affecting the black community, referred to herself as the representative of "Negro womanhood" and asserted that black women had "room in their lives to be wives and mothers as well as to have careers," she was not announcing a new idea.[63] As Terborg-Penn emphasizes:

> . . . most black feminists and leaders had been wives and mothers who worked yet found time not only to struggle for the good of their sex, but for their race. Until the 1970s, however, this threefold commitment—to family and to career and to one or more social movements—was not common among white women. The key to the uniqueness among black feminists of this period appears to be their link with the past. The generation of the woman suffrage era had learned from their late nineteenth-century foremothers in the black women's club movement, just as the generation of the post World War I era had learned and accepted the experiences of the preceding generation. Theirs was a sense of continuity, a sense of group consciousness that transcended class.[64]

This "sense of continuity" with past generations of black women was clearly articulated in 1917 by Mary Talbert, president of the NACW. Launching an NACW campaign to save the home of the late Frederick Douglass, she said, "We realize today is the psychological moment for us women to show our true worth and prove the Negro women of today measure up to those sainted women of our race, who passed through the fire of slavery and its galling remembrances."[65] Talbert certainly lived up to her words, going on to direct the NAACP's antilynching campaign and becoming the first woman to receive the NAACP's Spingarn Medal for her achievements.

What then is the expanded definition of true womanhood found in these black middle-class women's words and embodied in their lives? First, they tended to define womanhood in an inclusive rather than exclusive sense. Within white society, true womanhood was defined so narrowly that it excluded all but a small minority of white upper- and upper-middle-class women with husbands who were able to support them economically. Immigrant women and poor women—of any color—did not fit this definition. Nor did black women as a whole, regardless of class, because they were all seen as lacking an essential characteristic of true womanhood—virtue. For black women, however, true womanhood transcended class and race boundaries. Anna Julia Cooper called for "reverence for woman as woman regardless of rank, wealth, or culture."[66] Unlike white women, black women refused to isolate gender issues from other forms of oppression such as race and nationality, including the struggles of colonized nations of Africa and other parts of the world. Women's issues, they suggested, were tied to issues of oppression, whatever form that oppression might assume. . . .

The traditional white ideology of true womanhood separated the active world of men from the passive world of women. As we have seen, women's activities were confined to the home, where their greatest achievement was maintaining their own virtue and decorum and rearing future generations of male leaders. Although elite black women did not reject their domestic roles as such, many expanded permissible public activities beyond charity work to encompass employment and participation in social progress. They founded such organizations as the Atlanta Congress of Colored Women, which historian Erlene Stetson claims

was the first grassroots women's movement organized "for social and political good."[67]

The tendency of black women to define womanhood inclusively and to see their roles extending beyond the boundaries of the home led them naturally to include other characteristics in their vision. One of these was intellectual equality. While the "true" woman was portrayed as submissive ("conscious of inferiority, and therefore grateful for support"),[68] according to literary scholar Hazel Carby, black women such as Anna Julia Cooper argued for a "partnership with husbands on a plane of intellectual equality."[69] Such equality could not exist without the pursuit of education, particularly higher education, and participation in the labor force. Cooper, like many other black women, saw men's opposition to higher education for women as an attempt to make them conform to a narrow view of women as "sexual objects for exchange in the marriage market."[70] Education for women at all levels became a preoccupation for many black feminists and activists. Not a few—like Anna Cooper, Mary L. Europe, and Estelle Pinckney Webster—devoted their entire lives to promoting it, especially among young girls. Womanhood, as conceived by black women, was compatible with—indeed, required—intellectual equality. In this they were supported by the black community. While expansion of educational opportunities for women was a preoccupation of white feminists in the nineteenth century, as I noted above, a college education tended to create a dilemma in the lives of white women who found little community support for combining marriage and career. In contrast, as Shirley Carlson emphasizes, "The black community did not regard intelligence and femininity as conflicting values, as the larger society did. That society often expressed the fear that intelligent women would develop masculine characteristics—a thickening waist, a diminution of breasts and hips, and finally, even the growth of facial hair. Blacks seemed to have had no such trepidations, or at least they were willing to have their women take these risks."[71]

In addition to women's rights to an education, Cooper, Walker, Alexander, Terrell, the leaders of the National Association of Wage Earners, and countless other black feminists and activists insisted on their right to work outside the home. They dared to continue very active lives after marriage. Middle-class black women's insistence on the right to pursue careers paralleled their view that a true woman could move in both the private and the public spheres and that marriage did not require submissiveness or subordination. In fact, as Shirley Carlson has observed in her study of black women in Illinois in the late Victorian period, many activist black women "continued to be identified by their maiden names—usually as their middle names or as part of their hyphenated surnames—indicating that their own identities were not subsumed in their husbands."[72]

While the views of black women on womanhood were all unusual for their time, their insistence on the right of all women—including wives and mothers—to work outside the home was the most revolutionary. In their view the need for paid work was not merely a response to economic circumstances, but the fulfillment of women's right to self-actualization. Middle-class black women like Ida B. Wells-Barnett, Margaret Washington, and Mary Church Terrell, married to men who were well able to support them, continued to pursue careers throughout their lives, and some did so even as they reared children. These women were far ahead of their time, foreshadowing societal changes that would not occur within the white community for several generations. . . .

Rather than accepting white society's views of paid work outside the home as deviant, therefore, black women fashioned a competing ideology of womanhood—one that supported the needs of an oppressed black community and their own desire for gender equality. Middle-class black women, especially, often supported by the black community, developed a consciousness of themselves as persons who were competent and capable of being influential. They believed in higher education as a means of sharpening their talents, and

in a sexist world that looked on men as superior, they dared to see themselves as equals both in and out of marriage.

This new ideology of womanhood came to have a profound impact on the conception of black families and gender roles. Black women's insistence on their role as co-breadwinners clearly foreshadows today's dual-career and dual-worker families. Since our conception of the family is inseparably tied to our views of women's and men's roles, the broader definition of womanhood advocated by black women was also an argument against the traditional family. The cult of domesticity was anchored in a patriarchal notion of women as subordinate to men in both the family and the larger society. The broader definition of womanhood championed by black middle-class women struck a blow for an expansion of women's rights in society and a more egalitarian position in the home, making for a far more progressive system among blacks at this time than among whites.

Notes

1. Quoted in Hazel V. Carby, *Reconstructing Womanhood: The Emergence of the Afro-American Woman Novelist* (New York: Oxford University Press, 1987), p. 26.
2. Ibid.
3. Quoted in Paula Giddings, *When and Where I Enter: The Impact of Black Women and Race and Sex in America* (New York: Bantam Books, 1985), p. 82.
4. Ibid., p. 82.
5. Carby, *Reconstructing Womanhood,* p. 20.
6. Harriet Jacobs, *Incidents in the Life of a Slave Girl,* L. Baria Child, ed. (1861; paperback reprint, New York: Harcourt Brace Jovanovich, 1973), p. 29.
7. Quoted in Giddings, *When and Where I Enter,* p. 82.
8. Ibid., p. 86.
9. Ibid., p. 87.
10. Ibid., pp. 86–87.
11. Ibid., p. 87.
12. Quoted in Sharon Harley, "Black Women in a Southern City: Washington, D.C., 1890–1920," pp. 59–78 in Joanne V. Hawks and Sheila L. Skemp,

eds., *Sex, Race, and the Role of Women in the South* (Jackson, Miss.: University Press of Mississippi, 1983), p. 72.

13. Eleanor Flexner, *Century of Struggle: The Woman's Rights Movement in the United States* (Cambridge: Harvard University Press, 1959), p. 194.

14. Giddings, *When and Where I Enter*, p. 93.

15. Ibid., p. 95. For a discussion of elitism in the "uplift" movement and organizations, see Kevin K. Gains, *Uplifting the Race: Black Leadership, Politics, and Culture in the Twentieth Century* (Chapel Hill, N.C.: University of North Carolina Press, 1996). Black reformers, enlightened as they were, could not entirely escape being influenced by Social Darwinist currents of the times.

16. Deborah Gray White, *Too Heavy a Load: Black Women in Defense of Themselves, 1894–1994* (New York: W. W. Norton & Company, 1999), p. 36.

17. Quoted in Giddings, *When and Where I Enter*, p. 75.

18. Ibid.

19. Ibid.

20. Ibid., p. 59.

21. Ibid.

22. Evelyn Brooks Higginbotham, *Righteous Discontent: The Women's Movement in the Black Baptist Church, 1880-1920* (Cambridge: Harvard University Press, 1993).

23. Rosalyn Terborg-Penn, "Discontented Black Feminists: Prelude and Postscript to the Passage of the Nineteenth Amendment," pp. 261–278 in Lois Scharf and Joan M. Jensen, eds., *Decades of Discontent: The Woman's Movement, 1920–1940* (Westport, Conn.: Greenwood Press, 1983), p. 264.

24. Ibid., p. 261.

25. Ibid., p. 264.

26. Ibid., p. 266.

27. Ibid., pp. 266–267.

28. Barbara J. Harris, *Beyond Her Sphere: Women and the Professions in American History* (Westport, Conn.: Greenwood Press, 1978), pp. 85–86.

29. Giddings, *When and Where I Enter*, p. 81.

30. John P. Rousmaniere, "Cultural Hybrid in the Slums: The College Woman and the Settlement House, 1889–1984," *American Quarterly* 22 (Spring 1970): p. 56.

31. Ibid., p. 55.

32. Rousmaniere, "Cultural Hybrid in the Slums," p. 56.

33. Ibid., p. 61.

34. Quoted in Linda Gordon, "Black and White Visions of Welfare: Women's Welfare Activism, 1890–1945," *Journal of American History* 78 (September 1991): 583.

35. Giddings, *When and Where I Enter*, p. 97.

36. Estelle Freedman, "Separatism as Strategy: Female Institution Building and American Feminism, 1870–1930," pp. 445–462 in Nancy F. Cott, ed., *Women Together: Organizational Life* (New Providence, RI: K. G. Saur, 1994), p. 450; Nancy Forderhase, "'Limited Only by Earth and Sky': The Louisville Woman's Club and Progressive Reform, 1900–1910," pp. 365–381 in Cott, ed. *Women Together: Organizational Life* (New Providence, RI: K. G. Saur, 1994); . . . Mary Dell Brady, "Kansas Federation of Colored Women's Clubs, 1900–1930," pp. 382–408 in Nancy F. Cott, *Women Together.*

37. Higginbotham, *Righteous Discontent*, pp. 206–207.

38. Giddings, *When and Where I Enter*, p. 22.

39. Terborg-Penn, "Discontented Black Feminists," p. 267.

40. Giddings, *When and Where I Enter*, p. 108.

41. Ibid., pp. 108–109.

42. Ibid., p. 113.

43. Linda Gordon, "Black and Whites Visions of Welfare," p. 583.

44. Ibid., p. 582.

45. Ibid., p. 585.

46. Ibid., pp. 568–69.

47. Ibid., p. 109.

48. Quoted in Giddings, ibid., p. 110.

49. Ibid., p. 97.

50. Elsa Barkley Brown, "Womanist Consciousness: Maggie Lena Walker and the Independent Order of Saint Luke," *Signs: Journal of Women in Culture and Society* 14, no. 3 (1989): 188.

51. Shirley J. Carlson, "Black Ideals of Womanhood in the Late Victorian Era," *Journal of Negro History* 77, no. 2 (Spring 1992): 62. Carlson notes that these black women of the late Victorian era also observed the proprieties of Victorian womanhood in their deportment and appearance but combined them with the expectations of the black community for intelligence, education, and active involvement in racial uplift.

52. Quoted in Giddings, *When and Where I Enter*, p. 117.

53. See Rosalyn Terborg-Penn, *African American Women in the Struggle for the Vote, 1850–1920* (Bloomington, Ind.: Indiana University Press, 1998).

54. Rosalyn Terborg-Penn, "Discontented Black Feminists," p. 274.

55. Stephanie J. Shaw, *What a Woman Ought to Be and to Do: Black Professional Women Workers During the Jim Crow Era* (Chicago: University of Chicago Press, 1996), p. 29. Shaw details the efforts of family and community to socialize these women for both personal achievement and community service. The sacrifices some families made included sending them to private schools and sometimes relocating the entire family near a desired school.

56. Giddings, *When and Where I Enter,* p. 108.

57. Brown, "Womanist Consciousness," p. 622.

58. Ibid., p. 623.

59. Carby, *Reconstructing Womanhood,* p. 117.

60. Quoted in Giddings, *When and Where I Enter,* p. 72.

61. Brown, "Womanist Consciousness," p. 182.

62. Quoted in Giddings, *Where and When I Enter,* p. 197.

63. Quoted in Terborg-Penn, "Discontented Black Feminists," p. 274.

64. Ibid., p. 274.

65. Quoted in Giddings, *Where and When I Enter,* p. 138.

66. Quoted in Carby, *Reconstructing Womanhood,* p. 98.

67. Erlene Stetson, "Black Feminism in Indiana, 1893–1933," *Phylon* 44 (December 1983): 294.

68. Quoted in Barbara Welter, "The Cult of True Womanhood: 1820–1860," p. 318.

69. Carby, *Reconstructing Womanhood,* p. 100.

70. Ibid., p. 99.

71. Carlson, "Black Ideals of Womanhood in the Late Victorian Era," p. 69. This view is supported by historian Evelyn Brooks Higginbotham's analysis of schools for blacks established by northern Baptists in the postbellum period, schools that encouraged the attendance of both girls and boys. Although, as Higginbotham observes, northern Baptists founded these schools in part to spread white middle-class values among blacks, blacks nevertheless came to see higher education as an instrument of their own liberation (*Righteous Discontent,* p. 20).

72. Ibid., p. 67.

THINKING ABOUT THE READING

How were the needs and goals of black women during the 19th-century movement for gender equality different from those of white women? How did their lives differ with regard to the importance of marriage, motherhood, and employment? What does Landry mean when he says that for these women, "race and gender are inseparable"? What was the significance of the "clubs" for these black women? How does this article change what you previously thought about the contemporary women's movement?

Still a Man's World

Men Who Do "Women's Work"

Christine L. Williams

(1995)

Gendered Jobs and Gendered Workers

A 1959 article in *Library Journal* entitled "The Male Librarian—An Anomaly?" begins this way:

> My friends keep trying to get me out of the library....Library work is fine, they agree, but they smile and shake their heads benevolently and charitably, as if it were unnecessary to add that it is one of the dullest, most poorly paid, unrewarding, off-beat activities any man could be consigned to. If you have a heart condition, if you're physically handicapped in other ways, well, such a job is a blessing. And for women there's no question library work is fine; there are some wonderful women in libraries and we all ought to be thankful to them. But let's face it, no healthy man of normal intelligence should go into it.[1]

Male librarians still face this treatment today, as do other men who work in predominantly female occupations. In 1990, my local newspaper featured a story entitled "Men Still Avoiding Women's Work" that described my research on men in nursing, librarianship, teaching, and social work. Soon afterwards, a humor columnist for the same paper wrote a spoof on the story that he titled, "Most Men Avoid Women's Work Because It Is Usually So Boring."[2] The columnist poked fun at hairdressing, librarianship, nursing, and babysitting—in his view, all "lousy" jobs requiring low intelligence and a high tolerance for boredom. Evidently people still wonder why any "healthy man of normal intelligence" would willingly work in a "woman's occupation."

In fact, not very many men do work in these fields, although their numbers are growing. In 1990, over 500,000 men were employed in these four occupations, constituting approximately 6 percent of all registered nurses, 15 percent of all elementary school teachers, 17 percent of all librarians, and 32 percent of all social workers. These percentages have fluctuated in recent years: As Table 1 indicates, librarianship and social work have undergone slight declines in the proportions of men since 1975; teaching has remained somewhat stable; while nursing has experienced noticeable gains. The number of men in nursing actually doubled between 1980 and 1990; however, their overall proportional representation remains very low.

Very little is known about these men who "cross over" into these nontraditional occupations. While numerous books have been written about women entering male-dominated occupations, few have asked why men are underrepresented in traditionally female jobs.[3] The underlying assumption in most research on gender and work is that, given a free choice, both men and women would work in predominantly male occupations, as they are generally better paying and more prestigious than predominantly female occupations. The few men who willingly "cross over" must be, as the 1959 article suggests, "anomalies."

Popular culture reinforces the belief that these men are "anomalies." Men are rarely portrayed working in these occupations, and when they are, they are represented in extremely stereotypical ways. For example, in the 1990 movie *Kindergarten Cop*, muscle-man Arnold

Table 1 Men in the "Women's Professions": Number (in thousands) and Distribution of Men Employed in the Occupations, Selected Years

Profession	1975	1980	1990
Registered Nurses			
Number of men	28	46	92
% men	3.0	3.5	5.5
Elementary Teachers[a]			
Number of men	194	225	223
% men	14.6	16.3	14.8
Librarians			
Number of men	34	27	32
% men	18.9	14.8	16.7
Social Workers			
Number of men	116	134	179
% men	39.2	35.0	21.8

Sources: U.S. Department of Labor, Bureau of Labor Statistics, Employment and Earnings 38, no. 1 (January 1991), table 22 (employed civilians by detailed occupation), p. 185; vol. 28, no. 1 (January 1981), table 23 (employed persons by detailed occupation), p. 180; vol. 22, no. 7 (January 1976), table 2 (employed persons by detailed occupation), p. 11.

[a]Excludes kindergarten teachers.

Schwarzenegger played a detective forced to work undercover as a kindergarten teacher; the otherwise competent Schwarzenegger was completely overwhelmed by the five-year-old children in his class. . . .

[I] challenge these stereotypes about men who do "women's work" through case studies of men in four predominantly female occupations: nursing, elementary school teaching, librarianship, and social work. I show that men maintain their masculinity in these occupations, despite the popular stereotypes.

Moreover, male power and privilege is preserved and reproduced in these occupations through a complex interplay between gendered expectations embedded in organizations, and the gendered interests workers bring with them to their jobs. Each of these occupations is "still a man's world" even though mostly women work in them.

I selected these four professions as case studies of men who do "women's work" for a variety of reasons. First, because they are so strongly associated with women and femininity in our popular culture, these professions highlight and perhaps even exaggerate the barriers and advantages men face when entering predominantly female environments. Second, they each require extended periods of educational training and apprenticeship, requiring individuals in these occupations to be at least somewhat committed to their work (unlike those employed in, say, clerical or domestic work). Therefore I thought they would be reflective about their decisions to join these "nontraditional" occupations, making them "acute observers" and, hence, ideal informants about the sort of social and psychological processes I am interested in describing.[4] Third, these occupations vary a great deal in the proportion of men working in them. Although my aim was not to engage in between-group comparisons, I believed that the proportions of men in a work setting would strongly influence the degree to which they felt accepted and satisfied with their jobs.[5]

I traveled across the United States conducting in-depth interviews with seventy-six men and twenty-three women who work in nursing, teaching, librarianship, and social work. Like the people employed in these professions generally, those in my sample were predominantly white (90 percent). Their ages ranged from twenty to sixty-six, and the average age was thirty-eight. I interviewed women as well as men to gauge their feelings and reactions to men's entry into "their" professions. Respondents were intentionally selected to represent a wide range of specialties and levels of education and experience. I interviewed students in professional schools, "front line" practitioners, administrators, and retirees, asking them about their motivations to enter these professions, their on-the-job experiences, and their opinions about men's status and prospects in these fields. . . .

Riding the Glass Escalator

Men earn more money than women in every occupation—even in predominantly female jobs (with the possible exceptions of fashion modeling and prostitution).[6] Table 2 shows that men outearn women in teaching, librarianship, and social work; their salaries in nursing are virtually identical. The ratios between women's and men's earnings in these occupations are higher than those found in the "male" professions, where women earn 74 to 90 percent of men's salaries. That there is a wage gap at all in predominantly female

professions, however, attests to asymmetries in the workplace experiences of male and female tokens. These salary figures indicate that the men who do "women's work" fare as well as, and often better than, the women who work in these fields. . . .

Hiring Decisions

Contrary to the experience of many women in the male-dominated professions, many of the men and women I spoke to indicated that there is a *preference* for hiring men in these four occupations. A Texas librarian at a junior high school said that his school district "would hire a male over a female":

[CW: Why do you think that is?]

Because there are so few, and the. . . ones that they do have, the library directors seem to really. . . think they're doing great jobs. I don't know, maybe they just feel they're being

Table 2 Median Weekly Earnings of Full-Time Professional Workers, by Sex, and Ratio of Female: Male Earnings, 1990

Occupation	Both	Men	Women	Ratio
Registered Nurses	608	616	608	.99
Elementary Teachers	519	575	513	.89
Librarians	489	—*	479	—
Social Workers	445	483	427	.88
Engineers	814	822	736	.90
Physicians	892	978	802	.82
College Teachers	747	808	620	.77
Lawyers	1,045	1,178	875	.74

Source: U.S. Department of Labor, Bureau of Labor Statistics, Employment and Earnings 38, no. 1 (January 1991), table 56, p. 223.

*The Labor Department does not report income averages for base sample sizes consisting of fewer than 50,000 individuals.

progressive or something, [but] I have had a real sense that they really appreciate having a male, particularly at the junior high. . . .As I said, when seven of us lost our jobs from the high schools and were redistributed, there were only four positions at junior high, and I got one of them. Three of the librarians, some who had been here longer than I had with the school district, were put down in elementary school as librarians. And I definitely think that being male made a difference in my being moved to the junior high rather than an elementary school.

Many of the men perceived their token status as males in predominantly female occupations as an *advantage* in hiring and promotions. When I asked an Arizona teacher whether his specialty (elementary special education) was an unusual area for men compared to other areas within education, he said,

Much more so. I am extremely marketable in special education. That's not why I got into the field. But I am extremely marketable because I am a man.

. . . Sometimes the preference for men in these occupations is institutionalized. One man landed his first job in teaching before he earned the appropriate credential "because I was a wrestler and they wanted a wrestling coach." A female math teacher similarly told of her inability to find a full-time teaching position because the schools she applied to reserved the math jobs for people (presumably men) who could double as coaches. . . .

. . . Some men described being "tracked" into practice areas within their professions which were considered more legitimate for men. For example, one Texas man described how he was pushed into administration and planning in social work, even though "I'm not interested in writing policy; I'm much more interested in research and clinical stuff." A nurse who is interested in pursuing graduate study in family and child health in Boston said he was dissuaded from entering the program specialty in favor of a concentration in "adult nursing." And a kindergarten teacher described his difficulty finding a job in his specialty after graduation: "I was recruited immediately to start getting into a track to become an administrator. And it was men who recruited me. It was men that ran the system at that time, especially in Los Angeles."

This tracking may bar men from the most female-identified specialties within these professions. But men are effectively being "kicked upstairs" in the process. Those specialties considered more legitimate practice areas for men also tend to be the most prestigious, and better-paying specialties as well. For example, men in nursing are overrepresented in critical care and psychiatric specialties, which tend to be higher paying than the others.[7] The highest paying and most prestigious library types are the academic libraries (where men are 35 percent of librarians) and the special libraries which are typically associated with businesses or other private organizations (where men constitute 20 percent of librarians).[8]

A distinguished kindergarten teacher, who had been voted citywide "Teacher of the Year," described the informal pressures he faced to advance in his field. He told me that even though people were pleased to see him in the classroom, "there's been some encouragement to think about administration, and there's been some encouragement to think about teaching at the university level or something like that, or supervisory-type position."

The effect of this "tracking" is the opposite of that experienced by women in male-dominated occupations. Researchers have reported that many women encounter "glass ceilings" in their efforts to scale organizational and professional hierarchies. That is, they reach invisible barriers to promotion in their careers, caused mainly by the sexist attitudes of men in the highest positions.[9] In contrast to this "glass ceiling," many of the men I interviewed seem to encounter a "glass escalator." Often, despite their intentions, they face invisible pressures to move up in their professions. Like being on a moving escalator, they have to work to stay in place. . . .

Supervisors and Colleagues: The Working Environment

. . . Respondents in this study were asked about their relationships with supervisors and female colleagues to ascertain whether men also experienced "poisoned" work environments when entering nontraditional occupations.

A major difference in the experience of men and women in nontraditional occupations is that men are far more likely to be supervised by a member of their own sex. In each of the four professions I studied, men are overrepresented in administrative and managerial capacities, or, as in the case of nursing, the organizational hierarchy is governed by men. For example, 15 percent of all elementary school teachers are men, but men make up over 80 percent of all elementary school principals and 96 percent of all public school superintendents and assistant superintendents.[10] Likewise, over 40 percent of all male social workers hold administrative or managerial positions, compared to 30 percent of all female social workers.[11] And 50 percent of male librarians hold administrative positions, compared to 30 percent of female librarians, and the majority of deans and directors of major university and public libraries are men.[12] Thus, unlike women who enter "male fields," the men in these professions often work under the direct supervision of other men.

Many of the men interviewed reported that they had good rapport with their male supervisors. It was not uncommon in education, for example, for the male principal to informally socialize with the male staff, as a Texas special education teacher describes:

> Occasionally I've had a principal who would regard me as "the other man on the campus" and "it's us against them," you know? I mean, nothing really that extreme, except that some male principals feel like there's nobody there to talk to except the other man. So I've been in that position.

These personal ties can have important consequences for men's careers. For example, one California nurse, whose performance was judged marginal by his nursing superiors, was transferred to the emergency room staff (a prestigious promotion) due to his personal friendship with the physician in charge. And a Massachusetts teacher acknowledged that his principal's personal interest in him landed him his current job:

> [CW: You had mentioned that your principal had sort of spotted you at your previous job and had wanted to bring you here [to this school]. Do you think that has anything to do with the fact that you're a man, aside from your skills as a teacher?]
>
> Yes, I would say in that particular case, that was part of it. . . . We have certain things in common, certain interests that really lined up.
>
> [CW: Vis-à-vis teaching?]
>
> Well, more extraneous things—running specifically, and music. And we just seemed to get along real well right off the bat. It is just kind of a guy thing; we just liked each other. . . .

Interviewees did not report many instances of male supervisors discriminating against them, or refusing to accept them because they were male. Indeed, these men were much more likely to report that their male bosses discriminated against the *females* in their professions. . . .

Of course, not all the men who work in these occupations are supervised by men. Many of the men interviewed who had female bosses also reported high levels of acceptance—although the level of intimacy they achieved with women did not seem as great as with other men. But in some cases, men reported feeling shut-out from decision making when the higher administration was constituted entirely by women. I asked this Arizona librarian whether men in the library profession were discriminated against in hiring because of their sex:

> Professionally speaking, people go to considerable lengths to keep that kind of thing out of their [hiring] deliberations. Personally, is

another matter. It's pretty common around here to talk about the "old girl network." This is one of the few libraries that I've had any intimate knowledge of which is actually controlled by women. . . . Most of the department heads and upper level administrators are women. And there's an "old girl network" that works just like the "old boy network," except that the important conferences take place in the women's room rather than on the golf course. But the political mechanism is the same, the exclusion of the other sex from decision making is the same. The reasons are the same. It's somewhat discouraging. . . .

Although I did not interview many supervisors, I did include twenty-three women in my sample to ascertain their perspectives about the presence of men in their professions. All of the women I interviewed claimed to be supportive of their male colleagues, but some conveyed ambivalence. For example, a social work professor said she would like to see more men enter the social work profession, particularly in the clinical specialty (where they are underrepresented). She said she would favor affirmative action hiring guidelines for men in the profession, and yet, she resented the fact that her department hired "another white male" during a recent search. I confronted her about this apparent ambivalence:

> [CW: I find it very interesting that, on the one hand, you sort of perceive this preference and perhaps even sexism with regard to how men are evaluated and how they achieve higher positions within the profession, yet, on the other hand, you would be encouraging of more men to enter the field. Is that contradictory to you, or. . . ?]
> Yeah, it's contradictory. . . .

Men's reception by their female colleagues is thus somewhat mixed. It appears that women are generally eager to see men enter "their" occupations, and the women I interviewed claimed they were supportive of their male peers. Indeed, several men agreed with this social worker that their female colleagues had facilitated their careers in various ways

(including college mentorship). At the same time, however, women often resent the apparent ease with which men seem to advance within these professions, sensing that men at the higher levels receive preferential treatment, and thus close off advancement opportunities for women.

But this ambivalence does not seem to translate into the "poisoned" work environment described by many women who work in male-dominated occupations. Among the male interviewees, there were no accounts of sexual harassment (indeed, one man claimed this was a disappointment to him!). However, women do treat their male colleagues differently on occasion. It is not uncommon in nursing, for example, for men to be called upon to help catheterize male patients, or to lift especially heavy patients. Some librarians also said that women asked them to lift and move heavy boxes of books because they were men. . . .

Another stereotype confronting men, in nursing and social work in particular, is the expectation that they are better able than women to handle aggressive individuals and diffuse violent situations. An Arizona social worker who was the first male caseworker in a rural district, described this preference for men:

> They welcomed a man, particularly in child welfare. Sometimes you have to go into some tough parts of towns and cities, and they felt it was nice to have a man around to accompany them or be present when they were dealing with a difficult client. Or just doing things that males can do. I always felt very welcomed.

But this special treatment bothered some respondents: Getting assigned all the violent patients or discipline problems can make for difficult and unpleasant working conditions. Nurses, for example, described how they were called upon to subdue violent patients. A traveling psychiatric nurse I interviewed in Texas told how his female colleagues gave him "plenty of opportunities" to use his wrestling skills. . . .

But many men claimed that this differential treatment did not distress them. In fact, several said they liked being appreciated for the special traits and abilities (such as strength) they could contribute to their professions.

Furthermore, women's special treatment of men sometimes enhanced—rather than detracted from—the men's work environments. One Texas librarian said he felt "more comfortable working with women than men" because "I think it has something to do with control. Maybe it's that women will let me take control more than men will." Several men reported that their female colleagues often cast them into leadership roles. . . .

The interviews suggest that the working environment encountered by "nontraditional" male workers is quite unlike that faced by women who work in traditionally male fields. Because it is not uncommon for men in predominantly female professions to be supervised by other men, they tend to have closer rapport and more intimate social relationships with people in management. These ties can facilitate men's careers by smoothing the way for future promotions. Relationships with female supervisors were also described for the most part in positive terms, although in some cases, men perceived an "old girls'" network in place that excluded them from decision making. But in sharp contrast to the reports of women in nontraditional occupations, men in these fields did not complain of feeling discriminated against because they were men. If anything, they felt that being male was an asset that enhanced their career prospects.

Those men interviewed for this study also described congenial workplaces, and a very high level of acceptance from their female colleagues. The sentiment was echoed by women I spoke to who said that they were pleased to see more men enter "their" professions. Some women, however, did express resentment over the "fast-tracking" that their male colleagues seem to experience. But this ambivalence did not translate into a hostile work environment for men: Women generally included men in their informal social events and, in some ways, even facilitated men's careers. By casting men into leadership roles, presuming they were more knowledgeable and qualified,

or relying on them to perform certain critical tasks, women unwittingly contributed to the "glass escalator effect" facing men who do "women's work."

Relationships With Clients

Workers in these service-oriented occupations come into frequent contact with the public during the course of their work day. Nurses treat patients; social workers usually have client case loads; librarians serve patrons; and teachers are in constant contact with children, and often with parents as well. Many of those interviewed claimed that the clients they served had different expectations of men and women in these occupations, and often treated them differently.

People react with surprise and often disbelief when they encounter a man in nursing, elementary school teaching, and, to a lesser extent, librarianship. (Usually people have no clear expectations about the sex of social workers.) The stereotypes men face are often negative. For example, according to this Massachusetts nurse, it is frequently assumed that male nurses are gay:

> Fortunately, I carry one thing with me that protects me from [the stereotype that male nurses are gay], and the one thing I carry with me is a wedding ring, and it makes a big difference. The perfect example was conversations before I was married. . . .[People would ask], "Oh, do you have a girlfriend?" Or you'd hear patients asking questions along that idea, and they were simply implying, "Why is this guy in nursing? Is it because he's gay and he's a pervert?" And I'm not associating the two by any means, but this is the thought process.

. . . It is not uncommon for both gay and straight men in these occupations to encounter people who believe that they are "gay 'til proven otherwise," as one nurse put it. In fact, there are many gay men employed in these occupations. But gender stereotypes are at least as responsible for this general belief as any "empirical" assessment of men's sexual lifestyles. To the degree that men in these professions are perceived as not "measuring up" to the supposedly more challenging occupational roles and standards demanded of "real" men, they are immediately suspected of being effeminate—"like women"—and thus, homosexual.

An equally prevalent sexual stereotype about men in these occupations is that they are potentially dangerous and abusive. Several men described special rules they followed to guard against the widespread presumption of sexual abuse. For example, nurses were sometimes required to have a female "chaperone" present when performing certain procedures or working with specific populations. This psychiatric nurse described a former workplace:

> I worked on a floor for the criminally insane. Pretty threatening work. So you have to have a certain number of females on the floor just to balance out. Because there were female patients on the floor too. And you didn't want to be accused of rape or any sex crimes.

Teachers and librarians described the steps they took to protect themselves from suspicions of sexual impropriety. A kindergarten teacher said:

> I know that I'm careful about how I respond to students. I'm careful in a number of ways—in my physical interaction with students. It's mainly to reassure parents. . . .For example, a little girl was very affectionate, very anxious to give me a hug. She'll just throw herself at me. I need to tell her very carefully: "Sonia, you need to tell me when you want to hug me." That way I can come down, crouch down. Because you don't want a child giving you a hug on your hip. You just don't want to do that. So I'm very careful about body position.

. . . Although negative stereotypes about men who do "women's work" can push men out of specific jobs, their effects can actually benefit men. Instead of being a source of negative discrimination, these prejudices can add to the "glass escalator effect" by pressuring men to move *out* of the most feminine-identified areas and *up* to those regarded as more legitimate for men.

The public's reactions to men working in these occupations, however, are by no means always negative. Several men and women reported that people often assume that men in these occupations are more competent than women, or that they bring special skills and expertise to their professional practice. For example, a female academic librarian told me that patrons usually address their questions to the male reference librarian when there is a choice between asking a male or a female. A male clinical social worker in private practice claimed that both men and women generally preferred male psychotherapists. And several male nurses told me that people often assume that they are physicians and direct their medical inquiries to them instead of to the female nurses.[13]

The presumption that men are more competent than women is another difference in the experience of token men and women. Women who work in nontraditional occupations are often suspected of being incompetent, unable to survive the pressures of "men's work." As a consequence, these women often report feeling compelled to prove themselves and, as the saying goes, "work twice as hard as men to be considered half as good." To the degree that men are assumed to be competent and in control, they may have to be twice as incompetent to be considered half as bad. One man claimed that "if you're a mediocre male teacher, you're considered a better teacher than if you're a female and a mediocre teacher. I think there's that prejudice there.". . .

There are different standards and assumptions about men's competence that follow them into nontraditional occupations. In contrast, women in both traditional and nontraditional occupations must contend with the presumption that they are neither competent nor qualified. . . .

The reasons that clients give for preferring or rejecting men reflect the complexity of our society's stereotypes about masculinity and femininity. Masculinity is often associated with competence and mastery, in contrast to femininity, which is often associated with instrumental incompetence. Because of these stereotypes, men are perceived as being stricter disciplinarians and stronger than women, and thus better able to handle violent or potentially violent situations. . . .

Conclusion

Both men and women who work in nontraditional occupations encounter discrimination, but the forms and the consequences of this discrimination are very different for the two groups. Unlike "nontraditional" women workers, most of the discrimination and prejudice facing men in the "female" professions comes from clients. For the most part, the men and women I interviewed believed that men are given fair—if not preferential—treatment in hiring and promotion decisions, are accepted by their supervisors and colleagues, and are well-integrated into the workplace subculture. Indeed, there seem to be subtle mechanisms in place that enhance men's positions in these professions—a phenomenon I refer to as a "glass escalator effect."

Men encounter their most "mixed" reception in their dealings with clients, who often react negatively to male nurses, teachers, and to a lesser extent, librarians. Many people assume that the men are sexually suspect if they are employed in these "feminine" occupations either because they do or they do not conform to stereotypical masculine characteristics.

Dealing with the stress of these negative stereotypes can be overwhelming, and it probably pushes some men out of these occupations.[14] The challenge facing the men who stay in these fields is to accentuate their positive contribution to what our society defines as essentially "women's work." . . .

Notes

1. Allan Angoff, "The Male Librarian—An Anomaly?" *Library Journal*, February 15, 1959, p. 553.
2. *Austin-American Statesman*, January 16, 1990; response by John Kelso, January 18, 1990.
3. Some of the most important studies of women in male-dominated occupations are:

Rosabeth Moss Kanter, *Men and Women of the Corporation* (New York: Basic Books, 1977); Susan Martin, *Breaking and Entering: Policewomen on Patrol* (Berkeley: University of California Press, 1980); Cynthia Fuchs Epstein, *Women in Law* (New York: Basic Books, 1981); Kay Deaux and Joseph Ullman, *Women of Steel* (New York: Praeger, 1983); Judith Hicks Stiehm, *Arms and the Enlisted Woman* (Philadelphia: Temple University Press, 1989); Jerry Jacobs, *Revolving Doors: Sex Segregation and Women's Careers* (Stanford: Stanford University Press, 1989); Barbara Reskin and Patricia Roos, *Job Queues, Gender Queues: Explaining Women's Inroads into Male Occupations* (Philadelphia: Temple University Press, 1990).

Among the few books that do examine men's status in predominantly female occupations are Carol Tropp Schreiber, *Changing Places: Men and Women in Transitional Occupations* (Cambridge: MIT Press, 1979); Christine L. Williams, *Gender Differences at Work: Women and Men in Nontraditional Occupations* (Berkeley: University of California Press, 1989); and Christine L. Williams, ed., *Doing "Women's Work": Men in Nontraditional Occupations* (Newbury Park, CA: Sage Publications, 1993).

4. In an influential essay on methodological principles, Herbert Blumer counseled sociologists to "sedulously seek participants in the sphere of life who are acute observers and who are well informed. One such person is worth a hundred others who are merely unobservant participants." See "The Methodological Position of Symbolic Interactionism," in *Symbolic Interactionism: Perspective and Method* (Berkeley: University of California Press, 1969), p. 41.

5. The overall proportions in the population do not necessarily represent the experiences of individuals in my sample. Some nurses, for example, worked in groups that were composed almost entirely of men, while some social workers had the experience of being the only man in their group. The overall statistics provide a general guide, but relying on them exclusively can distort the actual experiences of individuals in the workplace. The statistics available for research on occupational sex segregation are not specific enough to measure internal divisions among workers. Research that uses firm-level data finds a far greater degree of segregation than research that uses national data. See William T. Bielby and James N. Baron, "A Woman's Place Is with Other Women: Sex Segregation within Organizations," in *Sex*

Segregation in the Workplace: Trends, Explanations, Remedies, ed. Barbara Reskin (Washington, D.C.: National Academy Press, 1984), pp. 27–55.

6. Catharine MacKinnon, *Feminism Unmodified* (Cambridge: Harvard University Press, 1987), pp. 24–25.

7. Howard S. Rowland, *The Nurse's Almanac,* 2d ed. (Rockville, MD: Aspen Systems Corp., 1984), p. 153; John W. Wright, *The American Almanac of Jobs and Salaries,* 2d ed. (New York: Avon, 1984), p. 639.

8. King Research, Inc., *Library Human Resources: A Study of Supply and Demand* (Chicago: American Library Association, 1983), p. 41.

9. See, for example, Sue J. M. Freeman, *Managing Lives: Corporate Women and Social Change* (Amherst: University of Massachusetts Press, 1990).

10. Patricia A. Schmuck, "Women School Employees in the United States," in *Women Educators: Employees of Schools in Western Countries* (Albany: State University of New York Press, 1987), p. 85; James W. Grimm and Robert N. Stern, "Sex Roles and Internal Labor Market Structures: The Female Semi-Professions," *Social Problems* 21(1974): 690–705.

11. David A. Hardcastle and Arthur J. Katz, *Employment and Unemployment in Social Work: A Study of NASW Members* (Washington, D.C.: NASW, 1979), p. 41; Reginald O. York, H. Carl Henley and Dorothy N. Gamble, "Sexual Discrimination in Social Work: Is It Salary or Advancement?" *Social Work* 32 (1987): 336–340; Grimm and Stern, "Sex Roles and Internal Labor Market Structures."

12. Leigh Estabrook, "Women's Work in the Library/Information Sector," in *My Troubles Are Going to Have Trouble with Me,* ed. Karen Brodkin Sacks and Dorothy Remy (New Brunswick, NJ: Rutgers University Press, 1984), p. 165.

13. Liliane Floge and D. M. Merrill found a similar phenomenon in their study of male nurses. See "Tokenism Reconsidered: Male Nurses and Female Physicians in a Hospital Setting," *Social Forces 64* (1986): 931–932.

14. Jim Allan makes this argument in "Male Elementary Teachers: Experiences and Perspectives," in *Doing "Women's Work": Men in Nontraditional Occupations,* ed. Christine L. Williams (Newbury Park, CA: Sage Publications, 1993), pp. 113–127.

THINKING ABOUT THE READING

Compare the discrimination men experience in traditionally female occupations to that experienced by women in traditionally male occupations. What is the "glass escalator effect"? In what ways can the glass escalator actually be harmful to men? What do you suppose might happen to the structure of the American labor force if men did in fact begin to enter predominantly female occupations in the same proportion as women entering predominantly male occupations?

New Biomedical Technologies, New Scripts, New Genders

Eve Shapiro

(2010)

In 1939, soon after graduating from St Anne's College of the University of Oxford, England, Lawrence Michael Dillon became the first transsexual man to undergo physical transition from female to male. Dillon had lived as a masculine woman during college and experienced discrimination for years because of his gender presentation. While Dillon came to a masculine identity during his college years, he had long looked and acted masculine and expressed desires to be a man. Even though Dillon knew himself to be a man, albeit one hidden within a female body, he had no social support and no social scripts with which he could make sense of his situation. He was without any language to talk about gender non-conformity or transgenderism; indeed the word 'transsexual' had yet to be coined, and there was certainly no discussion of any difference between sex and gender. Dillon was unable to find anyone who would either support his gender identity or enable the physical changes he required to live as a man, and he struggled to make sense of these desires.

Michael Dillon's life story stands in stark contrast to the contemporary experiences of many young female-to-male transgender people. A feature article in the *New York Times Magazine* on March 16, 2008, for example, included a profile of Rey, an 18-year-old White female-to-male transgender college student (Quart 2008). In this *New York Times Magazine* article Rey reflects on growing up a masculine child, being mistaken for a boy, and coming out as transgender to himself at 14 and to his family at the age of 17.

Rey's story is similar in part to Michael Dillon's; both grew up masculine and developed a gender identity as a boy/man, at a young age. But while Michael Dillon negotiated an identity without a language for gender non-conformity, Rey not only gained language and learned social scripts to describe who he was from other transgender people, he was able to do so at a relatively young age. Specifically, he heard a transgender man speak at a Gay Straight Alliance meeting at his high school and immediately went home and ran a Google Internet search for the word 'transgender.' In another illustration of the online identity work that was discussed in the last chapter, Rey elaborated that, "The Internet is the best thing for trans people . . . Living in the suburbs, online groups were an access point [for me]" (Quart 2008:34). Unlike Michael Dillon, who had no access to information about transgenderism, Rey was able to find and use a wide array of information and support resources to validate, define, and negotiate his own masculine identity and female body.

The ability to communicate with other transgender individuals, learn about treatments for transsexualism, and engage with others as a boy online, all helped Rey redefine his identity. Advances in communication helped Rey understand and define his gender identity, while developments in medical technology, allowed Rey to reshape his body to reflect his gendered identity. Whether and how new social scripts emerge in response to technological innovations in fields dealing with human anatomy can be illuminated by examining how individuals use biomedical means to know and construct their bodies.

New Body Technologies

Notwithstanding issues of transgenderism, the ability for and acceptability of body modification has also changed, as demonstrated by the rise and social acceptance of bodily transformation practices such as plastic surgery, use of pharmaceuticals, weightlifting, tattooing, shaving, and hair dyeing. More so now than ever before, it is common practice for individuals to produce and refine their gendered bodies in ways that both reinforce and contest normative social scripts for women's and men's bodies.

While body work is transformative and often purposeful on the part of individuals, these changes, whether by chance, social structure, or agency of the individual, are always already shaped by social norms and historical context. When an individual chooses to get a tattoo, for example, they may do so for any of a variety of reasons including an effort to adorn their body, mark a significant event, or signal participation in a community or identity category. But this agentic choice is informed by and given meaning through gendered societal beliefs about tattoos and their significance, body and beauty scripts, and the dominant societal paradigms. Approaching the body from the perspective of being something both shaped by and actively shaping identity as well as society allows a better understanding of how new technologies are dynamically engaged with gendered bodies.

In this chapter I examine a number of case studies to make sense of how gendered bodies and identities both inform and respond to these new biomedical technologies. Using a sociological approach to map the intricate, multiple connections between embodied identities, technologies, and social gender paradigms, I examine how the ability to construct new bodies is changing who people think they are and can be.

Somatechnics: Technologies and the Body

Biomedical technology has become the medium through which we know and intervene into our bodies, and genetic testing, body scans, surgery, and medication are just a few examples. A term that emerged in the 1970s to reflect the increasingly technological approaches to biology and medicine, 'biotechnology' brings engineering and technological theories in disciplines including agriculture, medicine, genetics, and physiology to bear on natural systems. In other words, biotechnology refers to any intentional manipulation of organic processes/ organisms.

Of particular relevance to this discussion is biomedical technology, or technologies that are directed at maintaining and/or transforming the human body. This includes genetic testing and manipulation, pharmacology, surgery including microsurgery, imaging, cloning, synthetic drugs, hormones and vaccines, prosthetics, and implants, to name a few. Moving beyond discovery for its own sake as a motivation for scientific research, the profitability of biotechnology has led to the development of numerous attendant industries centered on body work. Rates of plastic surgery, 'lifestyle drug' use, genetic engineering, and 'medi-spa' treatments have increased dramatically over the last 20 years. The hugely profitable biotechnological industry in the United States generated 58.8 billion U.S. dollars in health care revenue in 2006 alone. In Canada biotechnology firms generated 4.2 billion Canadian dollars of revenue in 2005. This exponential growth in the techniques of biomedical intervention and their acceptance also signals a source of social change for institutions and individuals.

Recently, some scholars have used the term *somatechnics* to describe human-body focused technologies and to distinguish them from agricultural and/or animal-focused biotechnologies.

Somatechnics

Technologies of the body. More specifically, an understanding that the body and technology are always and already interrelated and mutually constitutive. Technologies shape how we know, understand, and shape the body, and the body is always a product of historically and culturally specific transformative practices.

Nikki Sullivan, one of the pioneers of this concept, has focused on body modification like tattooing to make sense of how body technologies are both shaped by and an intentional engagement with social scripts for gendered bodies. Others have done work in a similar vein, including Susan Stryker, who has explored the social and technological history of transsexualism, and Samantha Murray, whose work focuses on fatness and the emergence of bariatric surgery. Research by each of these scholars demonstrates that modern embodied identities are always already in dynamic relationship to technologies, and more specifically that technologies are used to construct, maintain, and transform gendered bodies and identities.

Somatechnics and Social Norms

One very timely example of the dynamic relationship between somatechnics and social norms is bariatric (i.e. weight loss) surgery. With weight loss surgery, individuals—mostly women—are using biomedical technologies to reshape their bodies in dramatically increasing numbers. Many individuals benefit from this surgery, which can reduce health problems, raise self-esteem, and facilitate alignment between body and identity.

Even though versions of the surgery have been used for more than 50 years, widespread access to this biomedical technology was limited. During the 11-year period from 1995-2006 bariatric surgery rates skyrocketed by 800 percent; estimates suggest that in 2008 more than 200,000 surgeries were performed in the United States alone. What makes bariatric surgery such an interesting case study is that the highly contentious debates about the surgery engage directly with contemporary body and gender paradigms and social scripts. These debates take place within both medical circles and larger

society as they manifest in and through the bodies and identities of individuals. Dominant body paradigms posit the idea that fat bodies are inherently unhealthy, undesirable, and a sign of internal character failings, which legitimates biomedical intervention.

Societal body norms have a direct effect on what individuals do to reshape their bodies. Both men and women are pressured to change their bodies, and are stigmatized if they do not conform to these demands. Although the scientific research and development of weight loss technologies may be seen as unbiased, the emphasis on that objective revolves around contemporary body and gender paradigms. These societal forces are joined with contemporary advances in medical technology to form the foundation of a phenomenally profitable weight-loss industry—just think of how many diet and body shaping products you can name—and that industry puts even more pressure on individuals to conform to physical ideals.

The debate playing out around bariatric surgery is over the nature of the body. Dominant paradigms view thinness as natural and achievable through discipline and in turn discount the need for surgery. Slowly challenging this (aided by bariatric surgery, weight loss drugs like Alii, and the hunt for a 'fat gene') is a paradigm that views fatness as disease and therefore a malady worthy of medical intervention and treatment. Finally, the recent emergence of fat-positive activism has challenged social paradigms regarding body size. Groups like the National Association to Advance Fat Acceptance (NAAFA) take issue with dominant medical and social paradigms that link health to thinness and fat to disease. These organizations point toward historical and cultural variation in body size scripts, and stress that research reveals a wide range of differences in health and body size; not all large bodies are unhealthy and not all thin bodies are healthy. For many individuals whose bodies do not conform to normative body scripts, the presence of a counter-hegemonic paradigm reinforces their own positive social body and identity scripts. In other words, the debate about 'normal' bodies is in fact a debate over the dominant body paradigm, and it is taking place in part through debates about biomedical 'treatments' for obesity. This new technology of bariatric surgery is reshaping individual bodies and identities while the application of the technology is simultaneously responding to and reshaping societal body paradigms (paradigms such as what constitutes a healthy body) and social scripts for 'normal' embodied identities.

A number of social scientists have studied this emerging soma-technical phenomenon and found that weight loss surgery is altering individual gendered identities and bodies. For example, as Patricia Drew documents in her research, part of how bariatric advocates have tried to legitimize this new biomedical intervention has been to first create scripts for the ideal patient that draw on and reinforce hegemonic body paradigms and then require the adoption of these scripts in order to access bariatric surgery. This gate-keeping requires that individuals adopt (or, at the very least, pretend to adopt) particular physiological, behavioral, and attitude scripts (much like transsexual scripts to access 'sex-reassignment surgery'). This ideal patient script is shaped by the controversial history of the technology, a history in which early versions led to high rates of complication and death. It is, in turn, reshaping dominant body paradigms and scripts, offering a fine example of how technological development can interact with social scripts and bodies. Paradigm shifts in the perception of fatness as a disease can both be shaped by the increase in bariatric surgery, and, simultaneously, further legitimize the biomedical intervention. Similarly, the dominant belief that the internal self is reflected in the body compels individuals to change their body to match their internal identity, and simultaneously reinforces body scripts that devalue fat bodies (often decreasing people's estimation of the worth of their own inner selves). These dynamics are also gendered; fat male bodies are viewed as feminized while fat female bodies are de-feminized, particularly in terms of sexuality. Body scripts

shape the identities and bodies of individuals by demanding particular gendered scripts and body practices from individuals, as in turn the bodies and identities present in a context reinforce or challenge existing social scripts.

In her study, Patricia Drew found that the very public medical debates about weight loss surgery shaped the ways one could be an acceptable patient by constructing ideal patient scripts, while these same scripts shaped individuals in significant ways. Drew's interviews with patients revealed that most individuals incorporated into their own story the key narrative elements of the dominant script, elements such as viewing themselves as empowered through the use of weight loss surgery, and as responsible for their body. At the same time, those whose narrative did not contain the key elements of the acceptable script still used it strategically to access surgery. What Drew concludes is that these ideal patient scripts, or discourses-in-practice, learned in part through mandatory support group meetings, which afforded discursive practice, helped individuals negotiate between larger social body paradigms and individual identity. Most patients adopted the ideal patient scripts in part or full, and in the process, hegemonic body paradigms. Concomitantly, the social scripts rooted in those ideologies shaped the bodies and identities of participants.

In addition to this clear example of how technologies are in dynamic relationship to social scripts, ideologies, bodies and identities, bariatric surgery is a compelling case study for another reason: it is deeply gendered. According to the U.S. Centers for Disease Control, while women make up 59 percent of the obese population they account for 85 percent of weight loss surgery patients. If surgery was simply the product of obesity, then men and women would be accessing surgery at rates equal to the ratio of obesity in the general population, that is, statistically only 59 percent of patients should be women. These numbers suggest that people use this new technology of weight loss surgery based on gendered ideologies and gendered social scripts for ideal patients. Thus the technology is gendered and it produces gendered outcomes and societal changes.

Patricia Drew concludes that weight loss surgery is deeply gendered because of four intersecting gendered paradigms and scripts. First, as many scholars have documented, North American societies' gendered body and beauty paradigms place higher demands on women, and place more stringent sanctions on them for deviating from normative beauty standards. Women are expected to go to greater lengths and exercise more discipline upon themselves and their bodies than men are (McKinley 1999). Second, as Nelly Oudshoorn argued with regard to birth control, part of why women are held more accountable is that when the male body is held as a normal baseline, the female body is resultantly seen as more in need of intercession, and as a more legitimate target for biomedical intervention. Women are more likely to seek any medical care, which is, in itself, a product of gendered body and health paradigms, and this holds true for weight loss surgery. Third, weight loss surgery requires participation in support groups, groups that our society views as largely the domain of women. Finally, these gendered dynamics shape the social scripts disseminated by medical and media sources about weight loss surgery. In her analysis of hundreds of brochures, advertisements, and websites about weight loss surgery, Drew found that publicity materials pictured women much more often than men. For example, in 21 issues of *Obesity Help*, with a total of 80 advertisements, only nine of the ads featured men as patients. Drew concludes that not only do dominant ideologies shape the ideal patient scripts, but they also shape whether and how individuals use the new technologies. This, in turn, inspires change in both men's and women's bodies and identities, and reinforces the ideologies and scripts that produced these bodies and identities in the first place. These dynamically intertwined relationships are just one example of how individuals both reinforce and contest paradigms and scripts for femininity and masculinity as they use somatic technologies.

Technology and Body Work

It is now possible to alter the look of one's body through myriad technologies, just a few of which are plastic surgery, steroids, growth hormones, hair dye, permanent makeup, hair transplants, sub-cultural body modification practices like tattoos and scarification, laser hair removal, machine-enhanced exercise regimens, and spa treatments.

For individuals who want and have the means to engage in this transformative work, the ability to embody new identities, in order to either manifest what was previously consigned to one's existing inner selfhood or produce a body that matches a sought after inner identity, is increasingly possible. This holds true for both normative and non-normative bodily changes; individuals can become more masculine men (for example through steroid use or testosterone shots), more feminine women (through breast augmentation and laser hair removal, as examples), as well as transverse gender norms to become more feminine men, masculine women, or more androgynous male, female, or transgender individuals. All of this work is *body work*. 'Body work' refers to both the intentional nature of interventions into the body and to the technological and personal labor involved in those transformations.

Gendered Selves, Gendered Bodies

Anne Balsamo published a groundbreaking book in 1996, *Technologies of the Gendered Body*, which explored how body technologies in the late twentieth century were shaped by, and in turn reproduced, dominant gender paradigms and inequalities. Examining primarily media and cultural products, she analyzed technological interventions into the body, and concluded that these technologies are "ideologically shaped by the operation of gender interests, and consequently . . . serve to reinforce traditional gendered patterns of power and authority" (Balsamo 1996:10).

In other words, what Balsamo is saying is that body technologies are developed and used in tandem with hegemonic gender paradigms to reproduce gender inequality and maintain the status quo. Later work has taken both a more empirical approach to studying gendered technologies by relying more on examination of individuals' lived experiences rather than on textual analysis, and a more liberatory view of technological intervention. However, Balsamo's scholarship captures the central connection between gender ideologies and scripts and somatechnics that I have been examining. In her analysis of body technologies and gender, she asserts that technologies shape and are shaped by dominant gender paradigms and that these together reshape gendered bodies and identities.

How Are Biomedical Technologies Shaping Gendered and Raced Bodies?

When scholars speak about biomedical technologies and gender, they are referring to a wide range of bodily interventions that are a subset of the range of biomedical technologies we discussed earlier. Gendered technologies include hormone manipulation (estrogen and testosterone for both men and women, birth control pills, hormone blockers, synthetic thyroid medications, steroids, etc.), non-surgical body modification (tattoos, hair dye, weight lifting, dieting, piercing, dress, etc.), and surgical body modification (plastic surgery, weight-loss surgery, sex-reassignment surgery, breast augmentation, etc.). These technologies can be used, as I explore below, in both liberating and regressive ways. In all of the cases that follow, many individuals benefit from biomedical technologies like plastic and bariatric surgery. My intent here is not to argue these technologies are good or bad, but to bring complexity to their analysis.

While both men and women are using gendered technologies to shape their bodies in a variety of ways, these changes are neither evenly distributed among men and women, nor gender neutral in their consequences. By way of illustrating this uneven distribution, consider the example of gender distribution among plastic surgery recipients. According to 2008 data from the American Society of Plastic Surgeons, almost 11 million cosmetic procedures in the United States were performed on women, compared to 1.1 million procedures on men. This amounts to women comprising a staggering 91 percent of all plastic surgery cases. While the rates of invasive cosmetic procedures like liposuction have held relatively stable over the last few years, the rise in minimally invasive procedures such as Botox injection has been astronomical. This increase marks not only a remarkable increase in the overall number of cosmetic procedures, but also a significant statistical increase of women as recipients in proportion to men. In 2000, women comprised 86 percent of all procedures, but between 2000 and 2008 there was a 72 percent increase in procedures for women whereas there was only a 9 percent increase in rates for men.

Examining this demographic data alongside ethnographic accounts of plastic surgery use, it is evident that plastic surgery is being used to construct explicitly gendered bodies and identities. These are products of social scripts, gender paradigms, and available technologies, and are often hyper-normative. For example, the most common surgical cosmetic procedures for women are breast augmentation and liposuction, both of which are invasive methods to produce hyper-normative femininity: thinness, and large breasted-ness. This gendered aspect is not lost on patients; in her interviews with women patients, Debra Gimlin found that plastic surgery was a deeply gendered endeavor deployed by women to "make do" within a sexist and beauty-obsessed culture. In the personal narratives Gimlin collected, she found that the body work women engaged in was a conscious part of negotiating a gendered identity within the constraints of gender, class, and race norms.

The ability to produce socially valued bodies, bodies that possess the ideal skin color, facial features, and so forth, rests not only in the production of normative gender, but also requires race- and class-based privileges. Indeed, women of color in North America face unattainable expectations because social scripts include very racialized ideal beauty norms. As societies, North America prizes White features, and this list of prized features is limited to characteristics natural only in some White phenotypes. Similarly, body size is intertwined with social class; a well toned body is often a mark of wealth since cheap food is more fattening and promotes poor health, and the time and means to exercise is often a class-based privilege. When women use plastic surgery they are constructing a racialized, gendered, and classed body and they often do so in line with a narrow ideal characterized by features such as blond flowing hair, a thin nose, almond-shaped eyes, large breasts, a small waist, and broad hips. And as Balsamo pointed out, just as gender inequality affects somatechnics, racism affects the technologies that are developed and used.

Women of color are increasingly turning to cosmetic surgery; in 2008 White men and women made up 73 percent of patients, which was a significant decrease from 2000 when 86 percent of patients were White. In fact, while cosmetic procedures decreased 2 percent for White people in 2008, they increased 11 percent for men and women of color. Looking at trends over the last eight years, in the United States between 2000 and 2008 there was a 161 percent increase in cosmetic procedures among African-Americans, 227 percent among Hispanics, and 281 percent for Asian Americans compared to an increase of 63 percent among White individuals. Moreover, the most common cosmetic surgery procedures for people of color are nose reshaping, eyelid surgery, and breast augmentation, which are all procedures that alter racialized facial and body features to better match White norms (American Society of Plastic Surgeons 2009b).

The racial disparities in the statistics among cosmetic procedures suggest a trend by women of color toward using these technologies to mediate radicalized gender beauty norms. In this process, these women reaffirm the hegemony of White body and beauty paradigms. Eugenia Kaw's 1991 study of plastic surgery and race in San Francisco is a strong example of these processes. Kaw interviewed Asian American women, asking questions about why they used plastic surgery and what it meant to them. In these interviews women described plastic surgery as a way to better meet societal beauty scripts. In her interviews it was also clear that, like Gimlin found in her study of mostly White women, these Asian American women were conscious about what they were doing and how it mattered. For example, 'Jane' commented,

> Especially if you go into business, whatever, you kind of have to have a Western facial type and you have to have like their features and stature—you know, be tall and stuff. In a way you can see it is an investment in your future. (Kaw 1993: 78)

While the women Kaw spoke with were all vocal about their pride at being Asian, they also understood, as 'Jane' summarized, that White features were viewed more positively in society. The plastic surgeons that Kaw interviewed expressed very similar views, while also revealing how racialized gender scripts not only shape individuals, but whether and how technologies may be used. For instance, Kaw notes that doctors couched their racialized cosmetic procedures as efforts to help women achieve a look that is 'naturally' more beautiful, implying that White features are objectively more attractive. For example, one doctor stated that, "90 percent of people look better with double eyelids. It makes the eye look more spiritually alive." (Kaw 1993:81). Through these and other compelling examples Kaw builds a substantial analysis of how plastic surgery is being used to produce particular raced and gendered bodies concurrently.

Based on these interviews, Kaw suggests that social and ideological changes have coincided with the increased acceptance of plastic surgery in recent years to encourage surgical body work among Asian women and that this body work, in turn, constrains available scripts for femininity by erasing racialized differences among women's bodies. What Kaw concluded was that plastic surgery is, "a means by which the women can attempt to permanently acquire not only a feminine look considered more attractive by society, but also a certain set of racial features considered more prestigious." In other words, experiences of body work were gendered and racialized in such a way that while plastic surgery was simultaneously liberating on the individual level, it was detrimental on the societal level as social scripts for normatively gendered bodies became even more ethnocentric.

Hegemonic Race and Gender Norms Are Reproduced Through Body Work

Across the board women's bodies are more subject to body work than men's are. Many cultural critics have argued that new media technologies are creating unrealistic ideals for bodies and that these unattainable body scripts affect women disproportionately.

Although photographic images are still commonly viewed as factual evidence, recent technological advancements in print and film now allow imperceptible alterations to these images. Because of the ability to alter media images to create features like smaller pores, bigger eyes, thinner legs, larger breasts, and more defined muscles, published and broadcast representations of idealized beauty are themselves fictions. Recent resistance to this manipulation on the part of some actresses has made public how even thin and normatively beautiful actresses are subject to body-editing. For example, Keira Knightley, whose breasts were digitally enhanced in publicity for the 2004 movie *King Arthur*, refused similar manipulation for the 2008 movie *The Duchess*, and the ensuing tension between the actress and the movie studio was played out in the media. Kate Winslet publicly critiqued the manipulated images of her legs in *GQ* magazine in 2003, an edit she was not consulted about." These and similar examples point to how no bodies—not even famous ones prized for their sex-appeal—meet the ideal without somatechnic manipulation.

Although beauty scripts place a greater burden on women to meet bodily expectations, men are also subject to gendered scripts that suggest the need to technologically enhance their masculinity. Recent revelations about the seemingly omnipresent use of steroids by male athletes are signs of scripts that declare that men's bodies are inadequate in their unenhanced state. The use of steroids in U.S. Major League Baseball has become so expected that revelations of use do little to damage the careers of players like Alex "A-Rod" Rodriguez and Barry Bonds. The investigatory "Mitchell Report," submitted to the Commissioner of Major League Baseball, quotes National League Most Valuable Player Ken Caminiti as stating in 1992 that in his estimate, "at least half" of Major League players were using anabolic steroids (Mitchell 2007:60-61). This widespread use of steroids and the subsequent bodily changes in baseball players have shifted body scripts for athletes so much that unenhanced bodies stand little chance of competing.

Similarly, the increasing attention paid to men's bodies and the rising rates of eating disorders among boys suggest that boys and men are increasingly subject to gendered body pressures. Television shows like "Queer Eye for the Straight Guy" and men's magazines such as *GQ* all capitalize on the rise of the 'metrosexual,' a masculinity rooted in high levels of body work. This body work encompasses not only pursuits of traditional male attributes by means such as working out and sculpting efforts, but also includes practices formerly confined to the pursuit of feminine ideals, such as shaving, waxing, dyeing, plucking, and renewed attention to clothing.

Recent scholarship by Jennifer Wesely offers a rich example of how individuals are intentionally using biomedical technologies to construct hegemonically gendered and raced bodies. Wesely interviewed 20 women in the southwest of the United States to examine how women working in a strip club used body technologies to construct profitable bodies, and to negotiate multiple identities: for example to demarcate their true self as separate from their stripper self. What she found was that the women engaged in a wide variety of often dangerous and painful technologies like drug use, plastic surgery, waxing, and diuretics in order to produce the idealized femininity they felt was expected of them. Moreover, this gendered body work became a central focus of their lives. Wesely found that, "As dancers, these women relied on their bodies in ways that necessitated their constant critique, attention, and maintenance, leading to more body technologies." The pervasive use of these body technologies erased differences in bodies through implants, hair dye, tanning, and dieting, and reinforced hegemonic beauty scripts such that the ideal to which the women held themselves accountable was one which is now biomedically constructed. Samantha Kwan and Mary Nell Trautner summarize this process as it functions in society at large and conclude that, "Women's effortless authentic beauty is thus far from it. Beauty work is in large part this process of transforming the natural body to fit the cultural ideal, altogether while concealing the process and making it seem natural." In the case of Wesely's study, the intentionally constructed nature of gendered bodies was rendered invisible and assumed to be natural because body work was ubiquitous at the strip club, and produced bodies that aligned with idealized femininities.

One particularly insightful part of Wesely's research is her investigation of how these bodily changes function in conversation with the multiple layers of identity that the dancers (and everyone else) construct and employ through body technologies. Wesely found that the dancers' bodies and identities were in dynamic relationship to one another. What is key here is the complexity by which this happens. First of all, these women are not dupes; they are intentionally crafting their bodies because it makes dancing more profitable. By the same token, however, these choices, which make sense within the world of strip clubs, set these women apart from mainstream society. The choices the strippers make about body work are shaped and constrained by their context. Further, their choices have meaning and import beyond the personal level; the more the women shape their bodies to match an unrealistic feminine ideal, the more masked the constructed nature of femininity becomes, and the more normative, or, rather, hyper-normative the feminine body and identity scripts supported at the clubs become. The technologically enhanced bodies that the women who work at the strip club construct, shaped in line with the particular norms within that narrow context, are more feminine, more sexual, and more gendered than our broader society's normative scripts demand.

Through her ethnographic research, Wesely is able to document how the women experienced identity changes as the product of these technological interventions. The more technologies the women used to produce ideal bodies, the more wedded they became to their 'stripper' identities. Even though the women often wanted to separate their 'true identity' from their 'dancer identity,' body technologies such as breast enhancement, genital piercing, and hair dyeing would not allow them to leave the dancer-life behind. As one dancer commented, "In real life, when we're dressing in clothes . . . if you've got huge tits you look awful during the day. They look good only in a G-string in a strip club." In other words, some body technologies used by the women met beauty scripts only in the strip club, but the women had to 'wear' them all the time, which limited their ability to cast off a 'stripper identity' at the end of the day. Simultaneously, Wesely found that the women engaged in other technological interventions in an effort to cordon off their 'true' identities from their 'stripper' identities (for example through different clothing, by shaving, and through drug use).

Along with altering their bodies, then, the women tried to walk the line between producing a marketable body and maintaining a body that was a meaningful reflection of their internal sense of self. The women made choices about their bodies, but did so within a context that limited their options and as a result often were unable to embody their 'inner selves.' As Wesely concludes:

> Although body technologies have the potential to destabilize or challenge constructions of gendered bodies and related identity, this is even more difficult in a context that capitalizes on very limited constructions of the fantasy feminine body. Indeed, the women in the study felt tremendous pressure to conform to body constructions that revolve around extreme thinness, large breasts, and other features that conform to a "Barbie doll" image. (Wesely 2003: 655)

The consequences of these choices, as Wesely suggests, are significant. A number of scholars have documented how women who embody hegemonic femininity earn more money for stripping, and the women Wesely talked with acknowledged that normative gender scripts alongside financial, peer, and managerial pressure, directly informed the changes they made in their bodies.

On the personal level, this body work affects the identities of the women. They engage in body work that is encouraged within the context of their occupation, and which is aimed at producing femininities in line with the dominant gender paradigms of the strip club. In due course, this body work, in tandem with each individual's personal biography, shapes their identity. On an institutional level, the outcome of the biomedical construction of hyper-normative femininities by the women was an erasure of difference. By producing a very narrow set of femininities in line with hegemonic paradigms and gendered body scripts, the women naturalized a feminine body that was virtually unattainable without the use

of body technologies, and in this process they erased the very real differences that had existed between each of their bodies. Predictably, the somatechnical changes the women manifested were not only gendered, but also raced; the women of color at the clubs Wesely studied spoke about how they had to look *more* sexy, and produce a *more* ideal femininity than White women to be seen as acceptable by both management and customers. These findings are in line with what Eugenia Kaw found in her study of Asian American women. A consequence of this body work, then, was the reproduction of racist beauty norms, and the re-entrenchment of phenotypically White bodies as the only ideal body type.

The Complexities of Body Work

It is important to remember, however, that while each technology may have the possibility of reifying gender scripts, it can also open up potential for new gendered bodies. Females can lift weights, play sports, and cut their hair; males can don makeup, wear high heels, and dance ballet. Multiple mundane technologies can be, and are, deployed to create new masculinities and femininities. Technologies can and do have multiple, contradictory personal and social implications. For instance, hair removal and surgical technologies are used by members of the transgender community in order to manipulate public perception of their bodies so that this perception matches their gender identities. Plastic surgery is neither good nor bad; it is a technology engaged by individuals in complex ways within particular social contexts.

Alongside these circumstantial changes, new technologies are allowing people to intervene into the shape, function, and appearance of their bodies in transformative ways. The ability to manifest, in an embodied fashion, chosen identities and/or appearance norms is significant, and these technologies are working hand-in-hand with existing body and gender paradigms and scripts to refashion people's lives. Returning to the stories of Michael Dillon and Rey demonstrates how these dynamics bear on the lives of individuals; these two men came of age in two very different historical moments, and the gender paradigms, scripts, and technologies of their day and the social contexts within which they were situated crafted radically different paths for each of them.

Michael Dillon came of age in the early 1930s, in England. At the same moment that Michael Dillon was struggling to make sense of his own gender non-conformity Radcliffe Hall was embroiled in an obscenity trial that catapulted language and knowledge of lesbianism and gender non-conformity into the public sphere. In Radcliffe Hall's *Well of Loneliness*, the gender and sexuality of the main character, Steven, are conflated such that Steven was understood as lesbian because of his gender non-conformity. This became one of the only places Dillon saw himself reflected and it was through this public debate that he learned about gender non-conformity. But, just as Radcliffe Hall's *Well of Loneliness* was about gender non-conformity that was culturally understood as homosexuality, Michael Dillon was told to make sense of his own gender non-conformity as homosexuality by the few people in whom he confided.

Michael Dillon spent years trying to situate himself within society and ultimately sought medical intervention so he could manifest socially his internal gender identity. His quest for help, however, was thwarted, in part because there was no gender paradigm within which transgenderism could fit. When Dillon's search for medical help failed, he became a doctor in his own right in order to support his own and others' bodily changes. He began taking testosterone in 1939 and by 1944 had legally changed his gender after both hormonal and surgical 'sex-reassignment' efforts. Just eight years after Lib Elbe's publicized sex-reassignment surgery (she is credited with being the first male-to-female person to medically change her sex) and 11 years before Christine Jorgensen's public coming out after her surgery, Dillon became the first female-to-male (FTM) person on record to change

his sex. He was finally able to bring his gender identity as a man into more alignment with his public role and body. Over the next 20 years, Dillon wrote about what would eventually be termed transsexuality (see, for example, his book *Self: A Study in Endocrinology and Ethics*), and struggled to make a life for himself. Dillon intentionally cultivated a hetero-normative life, and in fact took on a misogynist persona as part of constructing his masculinity. After being publicly outed as transsexual in 1958, Dillon retreated to a life of monasticism in Tibet, and died in 1962 aged 47.

Rey's story is not yet fully written—he is, after all, only 18—but already there is much more to tell about his path toward social masculinity than there was for Dillon. At age 18, after coming out to his family and starting college, Rey pursued hormone therapy and began to live his life in his chosen gender. Within a few months he began taking testosterone to produce masculine secondary sex characteristics like facial and body hair and a deeper voice. He also had 'top surgery' which included a double mastectomy alongside the construction of a male-appearing chest. Compared to Michael Dillon's long wait and multiple surgeries (surgeries which were often failures—Dillon endured more than 13), Rey was able to engage in body-altering procedures with relative ease. Rey is part of a growing population of young transgender and transsexual individuals who have both the ability and social support to reshape their bodies and identities.

A number of things are significant about Rey's experience and the magazine article that profiled it. First, Rey's ability to manifest his chosen gender, in a bodily fashion, is remarkable. Compared to Michael Dillon's multi-year struggle to physically change his sex, Rey's ability to do so as soon as he turned 18 (the point at which he no longer needed parental consent) marks a significant shift in accessibility, education, and legitimacy. Second, the respect and acumen with which Alissa Quart constructed her story on Rey and other young transgender individuals is heartening. In the span of 50 years, social scripts have expanded significantly such that they reflect a familiarity with the language and complexity of gender non-conformity; for example the *New York Times Magazine* used terms like transgender, transmale, and genderqueer that were unfamiliar or non-existent during Dillon's lifetime.

These changes suggest that the possible ways of being sexed and gendered in the world have expanded. While I am not claiming that transgenderism has been incorporated as normative into North American cultures, I am suggesting that progress has been made. New technologies have been developed that range from the simple expansion of language to cutting edge surgeries that allow and facilitate precise bodily changes. Dominant gender paradigms have shifted to include transgenderism as a possibility hand-in-hand with these technologies. Alternative gender scripts have proliferated making it possible for individuals—including young people like Rey—to access information about transgenderism more readily and to construct more diverse gender identities and sexed bodies than ever before. Indeed, the life-stories of Michael Dillon and Rey reveal significant change in gender scripts over the past 50 years. And, Dillon's and Rey's experiences reveal how these changes in gender paradigms, scripts, technologies, and embodied selves matter in the everyday lives of individuals.

Like the stories of Dillon and Rey, all of the case studies I have discussed in this chapter have demonstrated significant relationships between social scripts, individual bodies and identities, and social paradigms. As embodied gender continues to change, I suspect that it will fuel ongoing transformation of social scripts and paradigms. I would expect, for example, a shift in gender norms alongside more diversity of bodies. But, as established in Chapter 1, technology is neither Utopian nor regressive. Technologies are being used to transform bodies in both non-normative ways and in ways that reinforce expectations about gendered bodies. Further, new bodies and identities can

both support and inhibit social change, provoke normative identity re-entrenchment and spark an expansion in social scripts, regardless of the desire or intention of individuals. Personal meaning making around one's body or identity does not exist in a vacuum.

We are clearly living in a moment where gender paradigms, scripts, bodies, and identities are all being simultaneously refined and renegotiated. New technologies are being deployed to re-entrench hegemonic masculinities and femininities and erase race and gender differences in bodies. Hormonal birth control places the burdens of sexual decisions on women and genital surgeries such as 'hymenorrhaphy' (hymen reconstruction) reinforce the importance of virginity in women. Conversely, these same biomedical technologies such as testosterone and estrogen regimens and genital construction methods are allowing individuals to shape their bodies in new ways that create more diverse pairings of sex and gender, and these new embodied genders are significant.

We must recognize the social gender paradigms and scripts tied up with biomedical innovation and attune ourselves to whether, and how, these new technologies are disciplining, regulating, and transforming the gendered body in new ways. Are we on the brink of a new gender order? Somatechnic frontiers are certainly reshaping the body in previously unknown ways, and this process challenges gender norms and scripts to make space accordingly. The documented expansion of gender possibilities—for both transgender and cisgender individuals—certainly suggests that gender ideologies and scripts are being reworked. But just as information technologies are not moving North American societies unidirectionally toward expanded identity possibilities, biomedical technologies are used in some ways that encourage expansion of gender possibilities while in others they help to resist this process. If, however, we take as true the dynamic and reciprocal relationships between technology, ideology, scripts, bodies and identities, then gender is now and will continue to transform itself alongside technological innovation.

REFERENCES

American Society of Plastic Surgeons. 2009b. "Cosmetic Procedures Up in All Ethnic Groups Except Caucasians in 2008." Arlington Heights, IL: Society of Plastic Surgeons. Retrieved May 26, 2009 (http://www.plasticsurgury.org/Media/Press_Realease/Cosmetic_Procedures_Up_in_All_Ethnic_Groups_Excpet_Caucasians_in_2008.html).

Balsamo, Anne. 1996. *Technologies of the Gendered Body: Reading Cyborg Women.* Durham, NC: Duke University Press.

Kaw, Eugenia. 1993. "Medicalization of Racial Features: Asian American Women and Cosmetic Surgery." *Medical Anthropology Quarterly* 7(1):74–89.

McKinley, Nita Mary. 1999. "Women and Objectified Body Consciousness: Mothers' and Daughters' Body Experience in Culture, Developmental, and Familial Context." *Developmental Psychology* 35:760–769.

Mitchell, George J. 2007. "Report to the Commissioner of Baseball of an Independent Investigation into the Illegal Use of Steroids and Other Performance Enhancing Substances by Players in Major League Baseball." New York, NY: Office of the Commissioner of Baseball. Retrieved March 8, 2009 (http://files.mlb.com/mitchrpt.pdf).

Quart, Alissa. 2008. "When Girls Will Be Boys." *New York Times Magazine*, March 16, pp. 32–37.

Wesely, Jennifer. 2003. "Exotic Dancing and the Negotiation of Identity: The Multiple Use of Body Technologies." *Journal of Contemporary Ethnography* 32(6):643–669.

THINKING ABOUT THE READING

According to Shapiro, how have biomedical technologies affected gender paradigms, scripts, bodies, and identities? How has Shapiro's discussion of her case studies and other research impacted your understanding of gender? Shapiro notes that forms of body transformation have become very socially acceptable in society. Besides reinforcing and contesting gendered bodies, how have race and class privileges operated in body transformation procedures to produce "natural beauty"? What roles have the media and business played in the production of socially valued bodies and scripts?

Global Dynamics and Population Demographic Trends

13

In the past several chapters, we have examined the various interrelated sources of social stratification. Race, class, and gender continue to determine access to cultural, economic, and political opportunities. Another source of inequality that we don't think much about, but one that has enormous local, national, and global significance, is the changing size and shape of the human population and how people are distributed around the planet. Globally, population imbalances between richer and poorer societies underlie most if not all of the other important forces for change that are taking place today. Poor, developing countries are expanding rapidly, while the populations in wealthy, developed countries have either stabilized or, in some cases, declined. When the population of a country grows rapidly, the age structure is increasingly dominated by young people. In slow-growth countries with low birthrates and high life expectancy, the population is much older. Countries with different age structures face different challenges regarding the allocation of important resources.

Globalization also contributes to significant shifts in local economies and shifts employment opportunities, sometimes in surprising ways. Surrogate motherhood is increasingly popular among many Indian women who find this form of employment less strenuous and more satisfying than work in sweatshops. Sharmila Rudrappa chronicles the stories of some of these women in "India's Reproductive Assembly Line."

Some other large-scale demographic phenomena affect people regardless of their age. Take, for instance, immigration. As social and demographic conditions in poor, developing countries grow worse, pressures to migrate increase. Countries on the receiving end of this migration often experience high levels of cultural, political, and economic fear. Immigration—both legal and illegal—has become one of the most contentious political issues in the United States today. While politicians debate proposed immigration restrictions, people from all corners of the globe continue to come to this country looking for a better life. An informed understanding of this phenomenon requires an awareness of the reasons for migration and the connection between the choices individuals make to immigrate and larger economic conditions that reflect global markets.

As Arlie Russell Hochschild points out in "Love and Gold," immigration can create serious problems in the families people leave behind. Many destitute mothers in places such as the Philippines, Mexico, and Sri Lanka leave their children for long periods of time to work abroad because they cannot make ends meet at home. Ironically, the jobs these women typically take when they leave their families—nannies, maids, service workers—involve caring for and nurturing other people's families. So while migrant women provide much-needed income for their own families and valuable "care work" for their employers, they leave an emotional vacuum in their home countries. Hochschild asks us to consider the toll this phenomenon is taking on the children of these absent mothers. Not surprisingly, most of the women feel a profound sense of guilt and remorse that is largely invisible to the families they work for.

Another form of demographic segregation that people may be less aware of is age segregation—the culture and institutional separation of people of different ages. Social demographers point out that cultural survival is dependent not only on older people sharing traditions and knowledge with younger people, but also on reverse knowledge sharing whereby young people help older people keep up with cultural changes. Current social processes of work/education separation, high rates of mobility, etc., have resulted in a pattern of extreme age segregation in developed countries. Young people rarely interact in a sustained way with older people unless they are related through family ties. Uhlenberg and Jong Gierveld ask how integrated we are across age differences. Using a study based on a Dutch survey, they explore this question by examining personal networks. How many people of varying ages are in your personal network? Although this study is based in the Netherlands, it has strong relevance to most Western nations.

Something to Consider as You Read

Global or demographic perspectives are big-picture perspectives. As you read these selections, practice thinking about the ways that demographic and global processes may shape individual experiences and choices. For example, consider your personal networks. Do they show signs of age segregation? How has immigration affected your everyday life? Do you know the story of how your family arrived in this country? How many generations have they been here? Is there a substantial immigrant population in your hometown? How has their presence been received by others? How do your personal experiences with immigrants compare to the largely negative images that are often presented in the media? Beyond immigration, think about the ways in which big economic and political changes affect the choices individuals make. Now, add wealth and technology to the equation and consider which countries are going to be in the best position to adjust to these global changes. Who is going to be most affected, possibly even exploited, in this global adjustment?

India's Reproductive Assembly Line

Sharmila Rudrappa

(2012)

"If you asked me two years ago whether I'd have a baby and give it away for money, I wouldn't just laugh at you, I would be so insulted I might hit you in the face," said Indirani, a thirty-year old garment worker and gestational surrogate mother. "Yet, here I am today. I carried those twin babies for nine months and gave them up." Living in the southern Indian city of Bangalore, married at 18, and with two young children of her own, she had delivered twins a month earlier for a Tamil couple in the United States.

I met Indirani when she was still pregnant and living in a dormitory run by Creative Options Trust for Women, Bangalore's only surrogacy agency at the time. COTW works with infertility specialists who rely on the Trust to recruit, house, care for, and monitor surrogate mothers for their clients. Straight and gay couples arrive from all over India and throughout the world to avail themselves of Bangalore's expertise in building biological families. Indirani and other mothers introduced me to 70 other surrogates whom they had gotten to know through their line of work. Some of them, including Indirani herself, double as recruiting agents, bringing new laborers into Bangalore's reproductive assembly line.

India is emerging as a key site for transnational surrogacy, with industry profits projected to reach $6 billion in the next few years, according to the Indian Council for Medical Research. In 2007, the *Oprah* show featured Dr. Nayna Patel in the central Indian town of Anand, Gujarat, who was harnessing the bodies of rural Gujarati women to produce babies for American couples. Subsequent newspaper articles and TV shows, as well as blogs by users of surrogacy, popularized the nation as a surrogacy destination for couples from the United States, England, Israel, Australia and to a lesser extent Italy, Germany, and Japan.

The cities of Anand, Mumbai, Delhi, Hyderabad and Bangalore have become central hubs for surrogacy due to the availability of good medical services, inexpensive pharmaceuticals, and, most importantly, cheap and compliant labor. The cost of surrogacy in India is about $35,000-40,000 per baby, compared to the United States, where it can run as high as $80,000, which it makes it particularly appealing to prospective parents. It is working class women that make India's reproductive industry viable. In Bangalore, the garment production assembly line is the main conduit to the reproduction assembly line, as women move from garment factories to selling their eggs, to surrogacy.

Indirani's life typifies that of other women in Bangalore's garment factories. Paid low wages, she works intermittently, in one of the city's many garment factories. She quit when she became pregnant, and joined the line again when her two children attended school, taking time away when she was sick, or to care for sick family members. Bangalore's reproduction industry affords women like her the possibility of extracting greater value from their bodies once they have been deemed unproductive workers in garment factories. Because of its life affirming character, Indiriani and others see surrogacy, however exploitative, as a more meaningful and creative option than factory work.

Disposable Workers

The popular understanding is that women who have large debt burdens and are destitute opt to become surrogate mothers. But while they are in debt, the seventy mothers I met were not among the poorest in Bangalore. Many were part of dual, or multiple income households, and tended to be garment workers who earn more than the average working woman in the city.

Former surrogate mothers, who also work as recruiting agents, have extensive networks among women in prime reproductive age in their own extended families, and among neighbors and friends who work as maids, cooks, street sweepers, or construction workers. Because cuts in food, education, and medical subsidies due to state divestment, along with volatile markets and global financial crises lead to unsteady factory work and low wages, their greatest recruiting success is among garment workers.

Like garment workers in sweatshops across the world, women in Bangalore are underpaid and overworked. In order to meet short production cycles set by global market demands, they work at an inhumanely fast pace, with few or no breaks. They frequently suffer from headaches, chest pain, ear and eye pain, urinary tract infections, and other health problems. Sexual harassment and abuse are rampant on the production line. The supervisors, almost all men, castigate women in sexually derogatory terms when they do not meet production quotas and often grope the women as they instruct them how to work better. "Sometimes," says Indirani, "I wouldn't take a lunch break when pieces piled up. I didn't want to be shamed in front of everyone. I would go to any length to avoid calling the supervisor's attention to me."

Indirani earned $100 to $110 monthly, depending upon her attendance, punctuality, and overtime hours. Frequently, she and her co-workers were unable to meet the inordinately high production targets and were required by supervisors to stay past regular working hours to meet their quota. "Playing" catch-up, however, did not necessarily result in overtime pay. Indirani's husband became suspicious if her paycheck did not reflect her overtime hours. He wondered whether she was really at the factory, or whether she was cavorting with another man. Indirani, like many of the women I interviewed, reported that she felt debased at work and at home.

Prior research on Bangalore's female garment workers suggests that they work an average of sixteen hours a day in the factory and at home doing laundry, cooking, taking care of children, and commuting to work. Working in the factory all day, and then returning home to complete household tasks was absolutely exhausting. Indirani's friend Suhasini, who was also a surrogate mother, avoided garment work altogether. Her mother, sister, and other women family members had worked the line, and she knew it was not what she wanted for her life. "But I need money," she told me. "For us," she says, "surrogacy is a boon." She describes Mr. Shetty who started COTW, as "a god to us." When I met her again in December 2011, Suhasini was receiving hormonal injections so that she could be a surrogate mother the second time around.

For much of her working life Indirani has been intermittently employed in one of Bangalore's many garment factories. She quit when pregnant, and joined the line again when her two children attended school. She also stopped factory work when she was sick, or had to care for sick family members. From the perspective of the garment factories, when Indirani is healthy she is a valuable worker for the firm. But during her pregnancies and illnesses, or has to attend to her family's needs, she loses her value as a worker, and the company replaces her. She is, as anthropologist Melissa Wright calls it, a "disposable worker." Upon recovering her health, or managing family chores efficiently, Indirani cycles back into the garment factory again, this time miraculously having regained her value for the production process. Over her working life Indirani has shifted from being valuable, to becoming an undesirable worker who must seek other forms of employment to help support her family.

Making Babies

Indirani and her auto-rickshaw worker husband have struggled for much of their married life to make ends meet, and to support their small children. Indirani's husband did not earn much money as an auto-driver. He rented his vehicle from an acquaintance, and the daily rental and gasoline costs cut significantly into the household income. So Indirani and he decided to borrow money from her cousin to purchase an auto-rickshaw of their own. Their troubles worsened when they were unable to pay back the loan, and the cousin would often arrive at their door, demanding his money and screaming expletives at them. He would come to the factory on payday and take Indirani's entire paycheck. She said, "I'd work hard, facing all sorts of abuse. And at the end of it I wouldn't even see any money. I felt so bad I contemplated suicide." When a friend at work suggested that she sell her eggs to an agency called COTW for approximately $500, Indirani jumped at what she perceived as a wonderful opportunity. After "donating" her eggs, Indirani decided to try surrogacy; she became pregnant with twins on her first attempt.

When I asked Indirani whether the hormonal injections to prepare her for ova extraction, and subsequently for embryo implantation were painful or scary, she avoided answering directly. "*Aiyo akka*," she said. "When you're poor you can't afford the luxury of thinking about discomfort." When I told her about the potential long-term effects of hyper-ovulation she shrugged. Her first priority was getting out of poverty; any negative health threats posed by ova extraction or surrogacy were secondary.

Indirani did not find surrogacy to be debasing work. She earned more money as a reproduction worker than she did as a garment worker, and found the process much more enjoyable. She was exhausted physically and emotionally working as a tailor in the factory and then cleaning, cooking, and taking care of her family. Upon getting pregnant, however, Indirani lived in the COTW dormitory. At first she missed her family, often wondering what her children were doing. Was her mother-in-law taking care of them? "I was in a different place surrounded by strangers," she recalled. But soon she began to like the dormitory. She didn't have to wake up by 5 am to prepare meals for the family, pack lunches for everyone, drop the children off at the bus stop so they could get to school, and then hop onto the bus herself to get to the garment factory. Instead, she slept in, and was served breakfast when she wanted. She had no household obligations, and no one made demands on her time and emotions. Surrogacy afforded her the luxury of being served by others. She did not remember a time in her life when she felt so liberated from all responsibilities.

Surveillance and Sisterhood

As she got to know the other women in the COTW dormitory, Indirani began to feel as though she was on vacation. For Indirani and many of the surrogate mothers I interviewed, it was easier to talk with the friends they made in COTW than with childhood friends and relatives; they felt they had more common with one another. Through the surrogacy process, many women told me, they lost a baby but gained sisters for life.

Indirani's husband brought the children over to visit on some weekday evenings, and her daughter stayed overnight with her on weekends. Her older sister Prabha, also a garment worker who was similarly strapped for cash, joined her at COTW two months after Indirani arrived, becoming a gestational surrogate for a straight, white couple. Like most surrogates, she had no idea where they were from, or where her contract baby would live.

Noting the closed circuit cameras that monitored the mothers' every move in the dormitory, I asked how they felt about them. Indirani said they didn't bother her; in fact, most of the mothers did not register the cameras' presence. While this initially surprised me, I soon realized that they were accustomed to surveillance in their everyday lives. Living under the gaze of relatives and inquisitive neighbors, and housed in one-two room homes where it was common for six to eight households to share a bathroom, notions of privacy were quite foreign. Surveillance at the dormitory was benign in comparison to the surveillance and punishment meted out for supposed infractions on the garment shop floor, where long conversations with teammates, taking a few minutes of rest, or going on breaks were all curtailed. In comparison, surveillance at COTW, designed to check on whether the women were having sex with their men folk who visited the facilities, seemed relatively banal.

The surrogate mothers delivered their babies through caesarian surgeries between the 36th and 37th week of gestation in order to conform to the scheduling needs of potential parents. Indirani was initially fearful of going under the knife, but she saw many mothers survive caesarians and she was no longer anxious. In the end, she found the caesarian method of delivering the twins she had carried easier than the vaginal births of her own two children.

The $4000 Indirani earned was far less than the $7000 the surrogacy agency charged for the children. While she was legally entitled to a larger amount because she carried twins, Indirani made no more money than those mothers pregnant with singletons. Her take-home pay actually ended up being less than $4000 after she paid the recruiting agent $200 and bought small, obligatory gifts for the COTW staff for having taken care of her during her pregnancy. Indirani had the option of staying on in the dormitory for up to two months after delivering her twins, but like all the mothers I interviewed, she chose not to do so because COTW charged for post-natal care, and for food and board. She could not afford to lose her hard-earned money on what she perceived as a luxury, so she returned home within days of delivery to all the household work that waited. Within a week of returning home, her remaining earnings went directly to her cousin, the moneylender. Still, knowing her debts were paid off gave her peace of mind.

Indirani claimed she does not feel any attachment to the twins she had carried. "They were under contract. I couldn't bring myself to feel anything for them," she told me. "They were never mine to begin with, and I entered into this knowing they were someone else's babies." It is hard enough for her to take care of her own two children, she said. "Why do you think I'm going through all this now? What would I do with two more? They are burdens I cannot afford." On the other hand, some mothers professed deep attachments to the babies they had given up. Roopa, a divorced mother who gave birth to a baby girl three years ago, always celebrated her contract baby's birthday. "June 21st *akka*," she said, "I cook a special meal. My daughter doesn't know why we have a feast, but it's my way of remembering my second child. I still cry for that little girl I gave away. I think about her often. I could never do this again."

Life out of Waste

Regardless of how they felt about the babies they had given up, the women almost all said they derived far more meaning from surrogacy than they did working under the stern labor regimes of the garment factory. In our conversations, time and again, women described the many ways they are deemed worthless in the garment factory. Their labor powers exhausted, their sexual discipline suspect, their personal character under question, they are converted to waste on the shop floor, until they are eventually discarded. On the other hand, Bangalore's reproduction industry, they said, gave them the opportunity to be highly productive and creative workers once more.

Indirani contrasted the labor processes in producing garments and producing a baby: the latter was a better option, she said. "Garments? You wear your shirt a few months and you throw it away. But I make you a baby? You keep that for life. I have made something so much bigger than anything I could ever make in the factory." Indirani observed that while the people who wore the garments she'd worked on would probably never think about her, she was etched forever in the minds of the intended parents who took the twins she bore.

Indirani and the other mothers I met did not necessarily see selling eggs or surrogacy as benign processes. Nor did they misread their exploitation. However, given their employment options and their relative dispossession, they believed that Bangalore's reproduction industry afforded them greater control over their emotional, financial, and sexual lives. In comparison to garment work, surrogacy was easy.

Surrogacy was also more meaningful for the women than other forms of paid employment. Because babies are life affirming in ways garments are obviously not, surrogacy allowed women to assert their moral worth. In garment work their sexual morality was constantly in question at the factory and at home. At the dormitory, in contrast, they were in a women-only space, abstaining from sex, and leading pure, virtuous lives.

Through surrogacy, Indirani said, she had built a nuclear family unit and fulfilled one infertile woman's desire to be a mother. In the process, she had attempted to secure the future of her own family and her own happiness. As a garment worker Indirani felt she was being slowly destroyed, but as a surrogate mother she said she was creating a new world. She was ready to go through surrogacy once again to earn money for her children's private schooling. The last time we met in December 2011, Indirani asked me, "If anyone you know wants a surrogate mother, will you think of me? I want to do this again."

THINKING ABOUT THE READING

Sharmila Rudrappa studies surrogacy from a sociological perspective. According to her research, why do so many women in India become surrogate mothers? What are the social and economic reasons that lead them to this path? Why does she refer to it as "India's reproductive assembly line"? How does it reinforce these ideals? When sociologists study the choices of people in other cultures, they must be careful not to impose their own cultural-ethnic biases. In thinking about the experiences of these women and their families, how might someone from another (more affluent) culture judge them? How does this form of surrogacy challenge traditional ideas about family? Consider other choices people are making across the world as a result of shifting economic conditions in their local environment—for example, women who leave their children at home in poorer countries to seek employment in wealthy locations.

Love and Gold

Arlie Russell Hochschild

(2002)

Whether they know it or not, Clinton and Princela Bautista, two children growing up in a small town in the Philippines apart from their two migrant parents, are the recipients of an international pledge. It says that a child "should grow up in a family environment, in an atmosphere of happiness, love, and understanding," and "not be separated from his or her parents against their will ..." Part of Article 9 of the United Nations Declaration on the Rights of the Child (1959), these words stand now as a fairy-tale ideal, the promise of a shield between children and the costs of globalization.

At the moment this shield is not protecting the Bautista family from those human costs. In the basement bedroom of her employer's home in Washington, D.C., Rowena Bautista keeps four pictures on her dresser: two of her own children, back in Camiling, a Philippine farming village, and two of her children she has cared for as a nanny in the United States. The pictures of her own children, Clinton and Princela, are from five years ago. As she recently told *Wall Street Journal* reporter Robert Frank, the recent photos "remind me how much I've missed." She has missed the last two Christmases, and on her last visit home, her son Clinton, now eight, refused to touch his mother. "Why," he asked, "did you come back?"

The daughter of a teacher and an engineer, Rowena Bautista worked three years toward an engineering degree before she quit and went abroad for work and adventure. A few years later, during her travels, she fell in love with a Ghanaian construction worker, had two children with him, and returned to the Philippines with them. Unable to find a job in the Philippines, the father of her children went to Korea in search of work and, over time, he faded from his children's lives.

Rowena again traveled north, joining the growing ranks of Third World mothers who work abroad for long periods of time because they cannot make ends meet at home. She left her children with her mother, hired a nanny to help out at home, and flew to Washington, D.C., where she took a job as a nanny for the same pay that a small-town doctor would make in the Philippines. Of the 792,000 legal household workers in the United States, 40 percent were born abroad, like Rowena. Of Filipino migrants, 70 percent, like Rowena, are women.

Rowena calls Noa, the American child she tends, "my baby." One of Noa's first words was "Ena," short for Rowena. And Noa has started babbling in Tagalog, the language Rowena spoke in the Philippines. Rowena lifts Noa from her crib mornings at 7:00 A.M., takes her to the library, pushes her on the swing at the playground, and curls up with her for naps. As Rowena explained to Frank, "I give Noa what I can't give to my children." In turn, the American child gives Rowena what she doesn't get at home. As Rowena puts it, "She makes me feel like a mother."

Rowena's own children live in a four-bedroom house with her parents and twelve other family members—eight of them children, some of whom also have mothers who work abroad. The central figure in the children's lives—the person they call "Mama"—is Grandma, Rowena's mother. But Grandma works surprisingly long hours as a teacher—from 7:00 A.M. to 9:00 P.M. As Rowena tells her story to Frank, she says little about her father, the children's grandfather (men are discouraged from participating actively in child rearing in the Philippines). And Rowena's father is not much involved with his grandchildren. So, she has hired Anna de la Cruz, who arrives daily at 8:00 A.M. to cook, clean, and care for the children. Meanwhile, Anna de la Cruz leaves her teenage son in the care of her eighty-year-old mother-in-law.

Rowena's life reflects an important and growing global trend: the importation of care and love from poor countries to rich ones. For some time now, promising and highly trained professionals have been moving from ill-equipped hospitals, impoverished schools, antiquated banks, and other beleaguered workplaces of the Third World to better opportunities and higher pay in the First World. As rich nations become richer and poor nations become poorer, this one-way flow of talent and training continuously widens the gap between the two. But in addition to this brain drain, there is now a parallel but more hidden and wrenching trend, as women who normally care for the young, the old, and the sick in their own poor countries move to care for the young, the old, and the sick in rich countries, whether as maids and nannies or as day-care and nursing-home aides. It's a care drain.

The movement of care workers from south to north is not altogether new. What is unprecedented, however, is the scope and speed of women's migration to these jobs. Many factors contribute to the growing feminization of migration. One is the growing split between the global rich and poor . . . .

[For example] domestic workers [who] migrated from the Philippines to the United States and Italy [in the 1990s] had averaged $176 a month, often as teachers, nurses, and administrative and clerical workers. But by doing less skilled—though no less difficult—work as nannies, maids, and care-service workers, they can earn $200 a month in Singapore, $410 a month in Hong Kong, $700 a month in Italy, or $1,400 a month in Los Angeles. To take one example, as a fifth-grade dropout in Colombo, Sri Lanka, a woman could earn $30 a month plus room and board as a housemaid,

or she could earn $30 a month as a salesgirl in a shop, without food or lodging. But as a nanny in Athens she could earn $500 a month, plus room and board.

The remittances these women send home provide food and shelter for their families and often a nest egg with which to start a small business. Of the $750 Rowena Bautista earns each month in the United States, she mails $400 home for her children's food, clothes, and schooling, and $50 to Anna de la Cruz, who shares some of that with her mother-in-law and her children. As Rowena's story demonstrates, one way to respond to the gap between rich and poor countries is to close it privately—by moving to a better paying job. . . .

The International Organization for Migration estimates that 120 million people moved from one country to another, legally or illegally, in 1994. Of this group, about 2 percent of the world's population, 15 to 23 million are refugees and asylum seekers. Of the rest, some move to join family members who have previously migrated. But most move to find work.

As a number of studies show, most migration takes place through personal contact with networks of migrants composed of relatives and friends and relatives and friends of relatives and friends. One migrant inducts another. Whole networks and neighborhoods leave to work abroad, bringing back stories, money, know-how, and contacts. Just as men form networks along which information about jobs are passed, so one domestic worker in New York, Dubai, or Paris passes on information to female relatives or friends about how to arrange papers, travel, find a job, and settle. Today, half of all the world's migrants are women. . . .

The trends outlined above—global polarization, increasing contact, and the establishment of transcontinental female networks—have caused more women to migrate. They have also changed women's motives for migrating. Fewer women move for "family reunification" and more move in search of work. And when they find work, it is often within the growing "care sector," which, according to the economist

Nancy Folbre, currently encompasses 20 percent of all American jobs.

A good number of the women who migrate to fill these positions seem to be single mothers. After all, about a fifth of the world's households are headed by women: 24 percent in the industrial world, 19 percent in Africa, 18 percent in Latin America and the Caribbean, and 13 percent in Asia and the Pacific. . . .

Many if not most women migrants have children. The average age of women migrants into the United States is twenty-nine, and most come from countries, such as the Philippines and Sri Lanka, where female identity centers on motherhood, and where the birth rate is high. Often migrants, especially the undocumented ones, cannot bring their children with them. Most mothers try to leave their children in the care of grandmothers, aunts, and fathers, in roughly that order. An orphanage is a last resort. A number of nannies working in rich countries hire nannies to care for their own children back home either as solo caretakers or as aides to the female relatives left in charge back home. Carmen Ronquillo, for example, migrated from the Philippines to Rome to work as a maid for an architect and single mother of two. She left behind her husband, two teenagers—and a maid.

Whatever arrangements these mothers make for their children, however, most feel the separation acutely, expressing guilt and remorse to the researchers who interview them. Says one migrant mother who left her two-month-old baby in the care of a relative. "The first two years I felt like I was going crazy. You have to believe me when I say that it was like I was having intense psychological problems. I would catch myself gazing at nothing, thinking about my child." Recounted another migrant nanny through tears, "When I saw my children again, I thought, 'Oh children do grow up even without their mother.' I left my youngest when she was only five years old. She was already nine when I saw her again, but she still wanted me to carry her."

Many more migrant female workers than migrant male workers stay in their adopted countries—in fact, most do. In staying, these mothers remain separated from their children, a choice freighted, for many, with a terrible sadness. Some migrant nannies, isolated in their employers' homes and faced with what is often depressing work, find solace in lavishing their affluent charges with the love and care they wish they could provide their own children. In an interview with Rhacel Parreñas, Vicky Diaz, a college-educated school teacher who left behind five children in the Philippines, said, "the only thing you can do is to give all your love to the child [in your care]. In my absence from my children, the most I could do with my situation was to give all my love to that child." Without intending it, she has taken part in a global heart transplant.

As much as these mothers suffer, their children suffer more. And there are a lot of them. An estimated 30 percent of Filipino children—some eight million—live in households where at least one parent has gone overseas. These children have counterparts in Africa, India, Sri Lanka, Latin America, and the former Soviet Union. How are these children doing? Not very well, according to a survey Manila's Scalabrini Migration Center conducted with more than seven hundred children in 1996. Compared to their classmates, the children of migrant workers more frequently fell ill; they were more likely to express anger, confusion, and apathy; and they performed particularly poorly in school. Other studies of this population show a rise in delinquency and child suicide. When such children were asked whether they would also migrate when they grew up, leaving their own children in the care of others, they all said no.

Faced with these facts, one senses some sort of injustice at work, linking the emotional deprivation of these children with the surfeit of affection their First World counterparts enjoy. In her study of native-born women of color who do domestic work, Sau-Ling Wong argues that the time and energy these workers devote to the children of their employers is diverted from their own children. But time and energy are not all that's involved; so, too, is love. In this sense, we can speak about love as an unfairly distributed resource—extracted from one place and enjoyed somewhere else.

Is love really a "resource" to which a child has a right? Certainly the United Nations Declaration on the Rights of the Child asserts all children's right to an "atmosphere of happiness, love, and understanding." Yet in some ways, this claim is hard to make. The more we love and are loved, the more deeply we can love. Love is not fixed in the same way that most material resources are fixed. Put another way, if love is a resource, it's a *renewable* resource; it creates more of itself. And yet Rowena Bautista can't be in two places at once. Her day has only so many hours. It may also be true that the more love she gives to Noa, the less she gives to her own three children back in the Philippines. Noa in the First World gets more love, and Clinton and Princela in the Third World get less. In this sense, love does appear scarce and limited, like a mineral extracted from the earth.

Perhaps, then, feelings *are* distributable resources, but they behave somewhat differently from either scarce or renewable material resources. According to Freud, we don't "withdraw" and "invest" feeling but rather *displace* or redirect it. The process is an unconscious one, whereby we don't actually give up a feeling of, say, love or hate, so much as we find a new object for it—in the case of sexual feeling, a more appropriate object than the original one, whom Freud presumed to be our opposite-sex parent. While Freud applied the idea of displacement mainly to relationships within the nuclear family, it seems only a small stretch to apply it to relationships like Rowena's to Noa. As Rowena told Frank, the *Wall Street Journal* reporter, "I give Noa what I can't give my children."

Understandably, First World parents welcome and even invite nannies to redirect their love in this manner. The way some employers describe it, a nanny's love of her employer's child is a natural product of her more loving Third World culture, with its warm family ties, strong community life, and long tradition of patient maternal love of children. In hiring a nanny, many such employers implicitly hope

to import a poor country's "native culture," thereby replenishing their own rich country's depleted culture of care. They import the benefits of Third World "family values." Says the director of a coop nursery in the San Francisco Bay Area, "This may be odd to say, but the teacher's aides we hire from Mexico and Guatemala know how to love a child better than the middle-class white parents. They are more relaxed, patient, and joyful. They enjoy the kids more. These professional parents are pressured for time and anxious to develop their kids' talents. I tell the parents that they can really learn how to love from the Latinas and the Filipinas."

When asked why Anglo mothers should relate to children so differently than do Filipina teacher's aides, the nursery director speculated, "The Filipinas are brought up in a more relaxed, loving environment. They aren't as rich as we are, but they aren't so pressured for time, so materialistic, so anxious. They have a more loving, family-oriented culture." One mother, an American lawyer, expressed a similar view:

> Carmen just enjoys my son. She doesn't worry whether... he's learning his letters, or whether he'll get into a good preschool. She just enjoys him. And actually, with anxious busy parents like us, that's really what Thomas needs. I love my son more than anyone in this world. But at this stage Carmen is better for him.

Filipina nannies I have interviewed in California paint a very different picture of the love they share with their First World charges. Theirs is not an import of happy peasant mothering but a love that partly develops on American shores, informed by an American ideology of mother-child bonding and fostered by intense loneliness and longing for their own children. If love is a precious resource, it is not one simply extracted from the Third World and implanted in the First; rather, it owes its very existence to a peculiar cultural alchemy that occurs in the land to which it is imported.

For María Gutierrez, who cares for the eight-month-old baby of two hardworking professionals (a lawyer and a doctor, born in the Philippines but now living in San Jose, California), loneliness and long work hours feed a love for her employers' child. "I love Ana more than my own two children. Yes, more! It's strange, I know. But I have time to be with her. I'm paid. I am lonely here. I work ten hours a day, with one day off. I don't know any neighbors on the block. And so this child gives me what I need."

Not only that, but she is able to provide her employer's child with a different sort of attention and nurturance than she could deliver to her own children. "I'm more patient," she explains, "more relaxed. I put the child first. My kids, I treated them the way my mother treated me."

I asked her how her mother had treated her and she replied:

> My mother grew up in a farming family. It was a hard life. My mother wasn't warm to me. She didn't touch me or say "I love you." She didn't think she should do that. Before I was born she had lost four babies—two in miscarriage and two died as babies. I think she was afraid to love me as a baby because she thought I might die too. Then she put me to work as a "little mother" caring for my four younger brothers and sisters. I didn't have time to play.

Fortunately, an older woman who lived next door took an affectionate interest in María, often feeding her and even taking her in overnight when she was sick. María felt closer to this woman's relatives than she did to her biological aunts and cousins. She had been, in some measure, informally adopted—a practice she describes as common in the Philippine countryside and even in some towns during the 1960s and 1970s.

In a sense, María experienced a premodern childhood, marked by high infant mortality, child labor, and an absence of sentimentality, set within a culture of strong family commitment and community support. Reminiscent of fifteenth-century France, as Philippe Ariès describes it in *Centuries of Childhood*, this was a childhood before the romanticization of the child and before the modern middle-class ideology of intensive mothering. Sentiment wasn't the point; commitment was.

María's commitment to her own children, aged twelve and thirteen when she left to work abroad, bears the mark of that upbringing. Through all of their anger and tears, María sends remittances and calls, come hell or high water. The commitment is there. The sentiment, she has to work at. When she calls home now, María says, "I tell my daughter 'I love you.' At first it sounded fake. But after a while it became natural. And now she says it back. It's strange, but I think I learned that it was okay to say that from being in the United States."

María's story points to a paradox. On the one hand, the First World extracts love from the Third World. But what is being extracted is partly produced or "assembled" here: the leisure, the money, the ideology of the child, the intense loneliness and yearning for one's own children. In María's case, a premodern childhood in the Philippines, a postmodern ideology of mothering and childhood in the United States, and the loneliness of migration blend to produce the love she gives to her employers' child. That love is also a product of the nanny's freedom from the time pressure and school anxiety parents feel in a culture that lacks a social safety net—one where both parent and child have to "make it" at work because no state policy, community, or marital tie is reliable enough to sustain them. In that sense, the love María gives as a nanny does not suffer from the disabling effects of the American version of late capitalism.

If all this is true—if, in fact, the nanny's love is something at least partially produced by the conditions under which it is given—is María's love of a First World child really being extracted from her own Third World children? Yes, because her daily presence has been removed, and with it the daily expression of her love. It is, of course, the nanny herself who is doing the extracting. Still, if her children suffer the loss of her affection, she suffers with them. This, indeed, is globalization's pound of flesh.

Curiously, the suffering of migrant women and their children is rarely visible to the First

World beneficiaries of nanny love. Noa's mother focuses on her daughter's relationship with Rowena. Ana's mother focuses on her daughter's relationship with María. Rowena loves Noa, María loves Ana. That's all there is to it. The nanny's love is a thing in itself. It is unique, private—fetishized. Marx talked about the fetishization of things, not feelings. When we make a fetish of an object—an SUV, for example—we see that object as independent of its context. We disregard, he would argue, the men who harvested the rubber latex, the assembly-line workers who bolted on the tires, and so on. Just as we mentally isolate our idea of an object from the human scene within which it was made, so, too, we unwittingly separate the love between nanny and child from the global capitalist order of love to which it very much belongs.

The notion of extracting resources from the Third World in order to enrich the First World is hardly new. It harks back to imperialism in its most literal form: the nineteenth-century extraction of gold, ivory, and rubber from the Third World. . . . Today, as love and care become the "new gold," the female part of the story has grown in prominence. In both cases, through the death or displacement of their parents, Third World children pay the price.

Imperialism in its classic form involved the north's plunder of physical resources from the south. Its main protagonists were virtually all men: explorers, kings, missionaries, soldiers, and the local men who were forced at gunpoint to harvest wild rubber latex and the like. . . .

Today's north does not extract love from the south by force: there are no colonial officers in tan helmets, no invading armies, no ships bearing arms sailing off to the colonies. Instead, we see a benign scene of Third World women pushing baby carriages, elder care workers patiently walking, arms linked, with elderly clients on streets or sitting beside them in First World parks.

Today, coercion operates differently. While the sex trade and some domestic service is brutally enforced, in the main the new emotional imperialism does not issue from the barrel of a gun. Women choose to migrate for domestic work. But they choose it because economic pressures all but coerce them to. That yawning gap between rich and poor countries is itself a form of coercion, pushing Third World mothers to seek work in the First for lack of options closer to home. But given the prevailing free market ideology, migration is viewed as a "personal choice." Its consequences are seen as "personal problems.". . .

Some children of migrant mothers in the Philippines, Sri Lanka, Mexico, and elsewhere may be well cared for by loving kin in their communities. We need more data if we are to find out how such children are really doing. But if we discover that they aren't doing very well, how are we to respond? I can think of three possible approaches. First, we might say that all women everywhere should stay home and take care of their own families. The problem with Rowena is not migration but neglect of her traditional role. A second approach might be to deny that a problem exists: the care drain is an inevitable outcome of globalization, which is itself good for the world. A supply of labor has met a demand—what's the problem? If the first approach condemns global migration, the second celebrates it. Neither acknowledges its human costs.

According to a third approach—the one I take—loving, paid child care with reasonable hours is a very good thing. And globalization brings with it new opportunities, such as a nanny's access to good pay. But it also introduces painful new emotional realities for Third World children. We need to embrace the needs of Third World societies, including their children. We need to develop a global sense of ethics to match emerging global economic realities. If we go out to buy a pair of Nike shoes, we want to know how low the wage and how long the hours were for the Third World worker who made them. Likewise, if Rowena is taking care of a two-year-old six thousand miles from her home, we should want to know what is happening to her own children.

If we take this third approach, what should we or others in the Third World do?

One obvious course would be to develop the Philippine and other Third World economies to such a degree that their citizens can earn as much money inside their countries as outside them. Then the Rowenas of the world could support their children in jobs they'd find at home. While such an obvious solution would seem ideal—if not easily achieved—Douglas Massey, a specialist in migration, points to some unexpected problems, at least in the short run. In Massey's view, it is not underdevelopment that sends migrants like Rowena off to the First World but development itself. The higher the percentage of women working in local manufacturing, he finds, the greater the chance that any one woman will leave on a first, undocumented trip abroad. Perhaps these women's horizons broaden. Perhaps they meet others who have gone abroad. Perhaps they come to want better jobs and more goods. Whatever the original motive, the more people in one's community migrate, the more likely one is to migrate too.

If development creates migration, and if we favor some form of development, we need to find more humane responses to the migration such development is likely to cause. For those women who migrate in order to flee abusive husbands, one part of the answer would be to create solutions to that problem closer to home—domestic-violence shelters in these women's home countries, for instance. Another might be to find ways to make it easier for migrating nannies to bring their children with them. Or as a last resort, employers could be required to finance a nanny's regular visits home.

A more basic solution, of course, is to raise the value of caring work itself, so that whoever does it gets more rewards for it. Care, in this case, would no longer be such a "pass-on" job. And now here's the rub: the value of the labor of raising a child—always low relative to the value of other kinds of labor—has, under the impact of globalization, sunk lower still. Children matter to their parents immeasurably, of course, but the labor of raising them does not earn much credit in the eyes of the world. When middle-class housewives raised children as an unpaid, full-time role, the work was dignified by its aura of middle-classness. That was the one upside to the otherwise confining cult of middle-class, nineteenth- and early-twentieth-century American womanhood. But when the unpaid work of raising a child became the paid work of child-care workers, its low market value revealed the abidingly low value of caring work generally—and further lowered it.

The low value placed on caring work results neither from an absence of a need for it nor from the simplicity or ease of doing it. Rather, the declining value of child care results from a cultural politics of inequality. It can be compared with the declining value of basic food crops relative to manufactured goods on the international market. Though clearly more necessary to life, crops such as wheat and rice fetch low and declining prices, while manufactured goods are more highly valued. Just as the market price of primary produce keeps the Third World low in the community of nations, so the low market value of care keeps the status of the women who do it—and, ultimately, all women—low.

One excellent way to raise the value of care is to involve fathers in it. If men shared the care of family members worldwide, care would spread laterally instead of being passed down a social class ladder. In Norway, for example, all employed men are eligible for a year's paternity leave at 90 percent pay. Some 80 percent of Norwegian men now take over a month of parental leave. In this way, Norway is a model to the world. For indeed it is men who have for the most part stepped aside from caring work, and it is with them that the "care drain" truly begins.

In all developed societies, women work at paid jobs. According to the International Labor Organization, half of the world's women between ages fifteen and sixty-four do paid work. Between 1960 and 1980, sixty-nine out of eighty-eight countries surveyed showed a growing proportion of women in paid work. Since 1950, the rate of increase has skyrocketed in the United States, while remaining high in Scandinavia and the United Kingdom and moderate in France and Germany. If we want developed societies with women doctors, political leaders, teachers, bus drivers, and computer programmers we will need opportunal people to give loving care to their children. And there is no reason why every society should not enjoy such loving paid child care. It may even be true that Rowena Bautista or María Guttierez are the people to provide it, so long as their own children either come with them or otherwise receive all the care they need. In the end, Article 9 of the United Nations Declaration on the Rights of the Child—which the United States has not yet signed—states an important goal. . . .It says we need to value care as our most precious resource, and to notice where it comes from and ends up. For, these days, the personal is global.

THINKING ABOUT THE READING

Why do women leave their own families to work in other countries? Why is there such great demand for nannies and other care workers in some countries? Discuss the concept of carework as a commodity available for sale on a global market. What other services are available on a global market that used to be considered something one got "for free" from family members? Before such services were hired out, who, traditionally, was expected to provide them? What has changed? Discuss some reasons why women make up so much of the global labor force today. If these trends in global labor continue, what do you think families will look like in the near future?

Age-Segregation in Later Life

An Examination of Personal Networks

Peter Uhlenberg and Jenny de Jong Gierveld

(2004)

Introduction

Margaret Mead (1970) argued that in societies where change is slow and imperceptible, knowledge and culture are passed on from older generations to younger ones. In these traditional settings, she suggested, it is essential for older people to teach newcomers how to function in the society. In contrast, in modern societies where social and technological change is pervasive, it also is necessary for younger people to teach the old. If older people do not interact with and learn from younger people, they risk becoming increasingly excluded from contemporary social developments as they age through later life. Older people may not need or want to know everything that younger ones know, but acquiring some new knowledge is essential to avoid becoming marginalised in later life. The most common example of what the young can currently teach the old is how to use email and the Internet, but many other areas of new knowledge created by cultural change could be described. In either traditional or modern societies, therefore, age-integration is needed if all generations are to be productive participants in the society. Of course there are additional reasons why it would be mutually beneficial for older and younger people to interact with each other. Older people may have resources that could promote the well-being of younger people (and *vice versa*). The absence of interaction, or age-segregation, promotes ageism and insensitivity to the challenges faced by others who differ in age. In general, it seems likely that age-integration promotes a more civil society. In this paper we take the perspective of older people and explore the level of their integration with, or segregation from, younger adults.

One way to examine the level of age-segregation of older people from younger ones in contemporary society is to examine the age-composition of personal social networks. How diverse are the ages of those with whom individuals interact most frequently and most significantly? Age-integration at the level of personal networks is relevant because network members play an important role in integrating individuals (of any age) into the larger society. Through network members, information and ideas are shared, new ways of thinking and living are discussed, and advice is exchanged. Network members exchange social, emotional, material and informational support that promotes well-being. Through networks individuals are recruited into social movements and organisations, which provide further opportunities for developing personal bonds (Marsden 1988; McPherson, Smith-Lovin and Cook 2001). Thus it is likely that older people whose personal networks lack younger members may be excluded from full participation in the society in which they live.

Forces Promoting Age Homophily in Networks

The social forces that have produced the institutionalisation and age-related stages of the life course over the past two centuries are also likely to have led to widespread age-segregation in social networks (Kohli 1988). Consider, for example, the structured social contexts from which network members might be drawn. A structured pattern of age-segregation begins early in life, for educational institutions use single years of age to group most children throughout childhood, while nurseries and day-care anticipate the age-homogeneity of the school environment from soon after birth. Sports and music for children are often tied to school, and result in age-segregated activities after school and on weekends. Churches imitate schools by establishing Sunday schools, where children are taught in age-homogeneous groups. Laws forbid children to participate in work settings. Specialised doctors see children; specialised therapists counsel and work with children; and special courts deal with children. The separation into homogeneous age groupings is further promoted by television, movies and other forms of entertainment that target children of particular ages. Quite similar institutional forces now largely segregate adolescents and young adults to age-homogeneous networks and activities (Lofland 1968). In these ways a culture that emphasises age-homogeneous groups is established early in life, so that one expects to find a deficit of older people in the personal networks of children and young adults, and *vice versa*. In somewhat similar ways, the age-segregated social institutions encountered by older people encourage age-homogeneity in personal networks through later life.

Work organisations tend to exclude people past age 60 or 65 years from a significant life activity, excluding them from one mechanism that promotes integration and some cross-age interactions with younger adults. Old people continue to be excluded from mainline educational settings (Hamil-Luker and Uhlenberg 2002). When efforts are made to involve older people in educational activities, they often operate from an age-segregationist principle, with separate programmes for old people. Many older people report that participating in

church or other religious activity is their most significant social activity outside the family. But in church people often are grouped on the basis of age for activities, so older churchgoers interact with other old people, and their social networks remain age-homogeneous. Participating in a senior centre or other age-restricted organisation may increase social activity and help expand social networks, but also reinforce age-segregated interactions. Similarly, nursing homes, retirement homes and retirement communities promote extreme age-segregation towards the end of life. In many ways, therefore, older people encounter a society that restricts opportunities for developing age-integrated personal social networks.

Although age-composition has seldom been the focus of studies of personal social networks, several report interesting findings on age homophily (and homogeneity) in networks. A recent review of the literature on homophily in social networks concludes that age consistently creates strong divisions in personal networks (McPherson et al. 2001). In his studies of Detroit men and Northern California residents, Fischer (1977, 1982) reported striking age-homogeneity in non-kin friendship networks. Indeed, 72 per cent of the close friends of the Detroit men were within eight years of their own ages. Similarly, Feld (1984), analysing the Northern California data, found that approximately half of all non-family associates with whom respondents were sociable or discussed problems were within five years of their age. In her analysis of friendship structure, Verbrugge (1977) reported that half of the friends identified by Detroit men occupied the same 10-year age category as the respondent, as did over 40 per cent of the friends of respondents in a German survey. And, as noted above, the GSS study of discussion-partner networks found most non-kin partners to be similar in age (Burt 1991; Marsden 1988). In general, studies have found age-homogeneity in non-kin networks across respondents of all ages, although it is stronger among younger than older people.

As already suggested, however, much less age-homogeneity is observed in kin networks (Burt 1991). This is not surprising, because older people often identify the relationships with their adult children, who tend to be 20 to 40 years younger than themselves, as very important. The 1988 *National Survey of Families and Households* showed that two-thirds of older women in the United States who had children visited a child at least once a week, and over 80 per cent had weekly contact with a child (Uhlenberg and Cooney 1990). Not only do inter-generational ties involve a high level of communication, but also these relationships are generally reported to be emotionally close and significant for instrumental support (for a review see Lye 1996). Furthermore, other kin (parents, aunts and uncles, siblings, cousins, grandchildren, and nieces and nephews) of diverse ages are frequently cited as significant network members. Thus one would expect the age-heterogeneity of personal networks to vary by the number of kin who are included in the network. The primary factor affecting the number of kin in a network is kinship composition. Other family-related events may affect how often older people include kin in their personal networks. In particular, partner status and partner history are relevant, e.g., adult children tend to intensify social interactions with a recently widowed parent who had been in a first marriage (Lopata 1996; Wolf, Freedman and Soldo 1997), and an earlier parental divorce reduces the likelihood that adult children interact frequently with their fathers in later life (Doherty, Kouneski and Erickson 1998; Dykstra 1998; Furstenberg, Hoffman and Shrestha 1995; Jong Gierveld and Dykstra 2002; Lye et al. 1995).

One would expect, of course, that the probability of a network including younger non-kin would increase with the total number of non-kin in the network. More interesting, it is likely that older people have more opportunities to recruit network members of diverse ages when they are active in social contexts that include younger adults. Therefore we anticipate that employed people are more likely than the retired to identify younger non-kin as network members. Similarly, attending church regularly or engaging in volunteer activities might promote greater age- integration, if these occur in age-heterogeneous contexts. The age-composition of the neighbourhood could also be a factor influencing the likelihood of interacting with younger adults. In addition to these structured settings for recruiting non-kin network members, current and past family context may also be relevant. Marital and partner status might be related to the size and intensity of non-kin network relationships. Older adults who are embedded in a large kinship circle, including a partner, children, children-in-law, grandchildren and siblings, need to invest a lot of time in maintaining these social and supportive relationships. In general, therefore, they have less time and energy than others to invest in a varied set of non-kin contacts (Dykstra 1995). Some widowed older adults who live without a partner may intensify contacts with their children, but others may revive latent bonds with others. The latter are to an extent building a new social network of people outside their own household that includes non-kin relationships. Indeed, success has been reported for a special training programme to support widowed older adults to begin new relationships (Stevens 2001). It is not yet known how age-heterogeneous the new relationships formed by widowed persons are.

Adults who divorce and remain without a partner may also compensate for the reduction in the size of the social networks. Personal contacts with new friends, with people 'in the same boat,' may be established in order to rebuild a social network. Those who never formed a partner union and the childless are however in a different position and do not experience the same transition. They often rely on siblings, friends, neighbours and other kin and acquaintances (such as colleagues and co-members of sport and hobby clubs) to maintain social participation and integration (Dykstra 1995). The never-married especially have been found to have a varied network of long-standing non-kin relationships (Wagner, Schütze and Lang 1999).

This interpretation of the literature on networks, kinship and ageing leads to several hypotheses. First, we expect that young adults are under-represented in the personal networks of older people. Second, that the presence of young adults in the personal networks of older people becomes increasingly rare at the more advanced ages. Third, it is expected that a disproportionate number of the younger network members of older people will be kin rather than non-kin. Fourth, the number of living children should be positively associated with having younger kin network members, but not with having younger non-kin network members. Fifth, the likelihood of having younger non-kin network members is higher for those who are employed, attend church, do volunteer work or live in age-integrated neighbourhoods. Sixth, the likelihood of having younger non-kin network members is higher for currently widowed and divorced older adults, who may have renewed and broadened their personal networks, than for those who are currently married, who tend to maintain their past couple-oriented social contacts. Seventh, the larger the number of friends, neighbours and other non-kin in an older person's network, the more likely that there will be young non-kin in the network.

As this study is exploratory, we also include in the analysis two variables of interest but without hypotheses of their effect, namely sex and the educational level of the respondent. One might expect older women from these Dutch cohorts to have less non-family social interaction than men, and hence to have less age diversity in their non-kin networks, but it is also possible that women possess superior social skills that allow them to bridge age barriers more easily than men. Higher levels of educational attainment are associated with higher levels of geographical mobility, so may reduce the breadth of network members that develop over time in a small community. But more education could also be associated with less ageism and greater acceptance of cross-age relationships.

Discussion

Despite the potentially significant implications, previous research has not examined the extent to which people in later life regularly interact with young adults. Using data from The Netherlands, this study has provided evidence on the extent to which older people have age-integrated or age-segregated personal social networks. Further, it has explored the factors associated with diversity in the age-composition of the networks of older people. Several interesting and provocative findings have emerged, and it is hoped that they will stimulate further research.

First, there clearly is a deficit of young adults in the networks of older people. People aged 55–64 years have significantly fewer young adult network members than would be expected if age were not a factor in selection, and the deficit grows even larger for people over the age of 65 years. For example, those aged 75–89 years had only about one-fifth of the number of network members aged less than 35 years that would be expected with complete age-integration. In fact, 68 per cent of the population older than 75 years did not identify any network member younger than 35 years of age.

Second, an overwhelming proportion of the younger network members identified by older people were kin. About 90 per cent of the network members aged less than 45 years old who were reported by people past age 65 years were kin, and a large majority of older people reported no non-kin less than 45 years of age in their networks. Most neighbours, friends and other non-kin associates of older people were old themselves. Thus the most crucial determinant of having younger network members is the size of the kin group, and especially the number of living children. Family building in the young adult phase of the life course turns out to be the major determinant of age-integrated or age-segregated personal networks in late life.

Third, although no segment of the older population appeared to be well integrated with younger adults outside of family relationships, several factors did increase the likelihood that an older person had some significant cross-age interactions. These included participation in organisations that had members of different ages (e.g., work and volunteer settings), and living in a neighbourhood with a high proportion of non-old adults. A plausible explanation for the significance of these factors is that a necessary condition for forming cross-age associations is the opportunity for meeting people of different ages. The failure of church activity to foster more age-heterogeneous relationships may be because church attendance in The Netherlands is much higher among older than younger age groups. In other words, churches may not be strongly age-integrated settings. It also may be that simply occupying common space is insufficient to promote the development of cross-age relationships. Relationships develop when structures promote mutual interaction around a meaningful activity, so while sitting side-by-side in a church service may have no effect, working together on a common project may be highly effective. Further, cultural norms are almost certainly important. When age differences are emphasised and age-stereotypes are prevalent, a significant barrier exists for forming friendships and close associations between young and old people.

Fourth, specific life course events, in particular divorce followed by living alone, increased the likelihood that an older person had some significant cross-age interactions with non-kin. Several studies have shown that shortly after divorce there tends to be a reduction in the number of personal relationships (DeGarmo and Kitson 1996). As time passes after a divorce, however, new relationships are formed. In this process of forming replacement relationships, there is an opportunity for younger non-kin to join the network.

Looking ahead, we anticipate two changes that could significantly increase the age-segregation of the personal networks of older people in The Netherlands. First is the ageing of the population, which will decrease the relative supply of younger adults as potential network members and increase the relative supply of older ones. Around the time of the NESTOR survey, about 34 per cent of the population aged over 20 years was in the age group 20–35 years, while 17 per cent was aged 65 or more years. By 2050, these two percentages will be reversed—21 per cent of the adult population will be aged 20–35 years, and 33 per cent will be 65 or more years. The second and related change in future cohorts will be a significant decline in the average number of adult children. Because children are the major source of young adult network members, a decline in the number of children could have a large effect. Those aged 65 or more years in 1992 lived out their reproductive years when the Total Fertility Rate exceeded 3.0, but the cohorts entering old age in the near future will have completed family sizes of only about half that level. Further, the increasing prevalence of divorce in future cohorts entering old age may lead to a weakening of the tie between parent and adult child for an increasing proportion of older people (Cooney and Uhlenberg 1990; Dykstra 1998; Jong Gierveld and Peeters 2003). The increase in the number of younger non-kin that is associated with divorce is far smaller than the loss of children from the network. Thus, unless other changes occur, older people in the future are likely to have even less interaction with young adults than they currently do—and as shown above, current levels of interaction are extremely low.

This prospect provokes the question of what changes might divert a trend towards even greater age-segregation of older people. If, as argued in this paper, non-kin network members tend to be recruited from structured social contexts such as workplaces, volunteer settings, educational organisations and neighbourhoods, more attention might be given to increasing the involvement of older people in social structures that include people of various ages. This line of thinking leads directly to the issue of institutional age-segregation, as occurs when chronological age is used as a criterion for participation. Matilda Riley called attention to the structural lags in major social institutions which denied opportunities to healthy and skilled people reaching old age to engage productively in society (Riley, Kahn and Foner 1994). The institutions which are most clearly structured by age are schools and places of work, but the rules and practices of many others create age-group separation. Age is embedded in the formulation and implementation of many social welfare policies and programmes, e.g., nutrition, housing, protective services and recreation. Concerns related to the old often fall under different government programmes and offices than do matters related to children and youth (Hagestad 2002). Even academic disciplines (such as gerontology) tend to sustain separation by age. There is, however, some evidence that the use of chronological age to structure the life course may have peaked.

A recent tendency to break down structural age barriers has been noted in both work and education (Riley and Riley 2000). Retirement in the United States has recently become more flexible, allowing an increasing number of older people to participate in the labour force. The long trend towards earlier age at retirement stopped in the mid 1980s in the United States, and since then labour force participation rates among those aged 55 or more years have been gradually increasing (Clark and Quinn 2002). The long-discussed idea of lifelong learning may now be happening, as an increasing number of people in mid and later life learn alongside younger people (Davey 2002). There are interesting examples in the United States of breaking down the age barriers around schools and creating community learning-centres open to all ages (US Department of Education 2000). In academic programmes, traditional gerontological approaches are being challenged by a life course perspective that views ageing as a lifelong process. If, as suggested by these examples, institutional age-segregation is declining, opportunities for cross-age interaction should increase.

Related to institutional age-segregation is cultural age-segregation, as reflected in age stereotypes and ageist language. In addition to removing the barriers to cross-age interaction, a reduction in ageism and cultural age-stereotyping could facilitate age-integration. The prevalence of age-stereotypes in society hinders the formation of close non-kin relationships between older and younger people (Bytheway 1995; Hummert et al. 1994; Nelson 2002). There is of course some circularity in this association, because age-segregation is a root cause of age-stereotypes. Nevertheless, educational programmes and media efforts to combat ageist stereotypes and language might play a role in increasing understanding and empathy between disparate age groups. Similar efforts to reduce racism and sexism are generally considered to have produced positive results.

Attention is being given not only to ways of reducing structural and cultural barriers between older and younger people, but also to inter-generational programmes that purposely bring diverse ages together. In The Netherlands, a co-ordinated effort to bring older people into age-integrated settings is occurring through an inter-generational neighbourhood development programme at *The Netherlands Institute for Care and Welfare* (Penninx 1999). A notable initiative from this inter-generational programme has involved the Dutch Guilds that exist in about 90 municipalities. People who are aged 50 or more years and who are willing to share their knowledge and skills can form a guild that anyone can contact for assistance free of charge. A request for help, e.g., with car repair, tutoring in school, business advice or care for a disabled child, is referred to an appropriate guild member who then responds directly to the individual needing assistance. Through this matching process, older volunteers and younger people are brought together in a context that is likely to promote positive inter-generational interaction. Other inter-generational programmes described by Penninx include: children visiting older people living in age-segregated institutional settings, older people helping children in local schools, adolescent choreteams helping older neighbourhood residents with various household chores, and older people meeting with immigrant youth to promote their successful integration into Dutch society. Similar inter-generational programmes are developing in other countries. Careful evaluations of the various types of deliberate efforts to bridge age gaps would provide useful information on what structures actually facilitate age-integration.

REFERENCES

Burt, R. S. 1991. Measuring age as a structural concept. *Social Networks, 13*, 1–34.

Bytheway, B. 1995. *Ageism.* Open University Press, Buckingham.

Clark, R. L. and Quinn, J. F. 2002. Patterns of work and retirement for a new century. *Generations, 22*, 17–24.

Cooney, T. M. and Uhlenberg, P. 1990. The role of divorce in men's relations with their adult children after mid-life. *Journal of Marriage and the Family, 52*, 677–88.

Davey, J. A. 2002. Active aging and education in mid and later life. *Ageing & Society, 22*, 95–113.

DeGarmo, D. S. and Kitson, G. C. 1996. Identity relevance and disruption as predictors of psychological distress for widowed and divorced women. *Journal of Marriage and the Family, 58*, 983–97.

Doherty, W. J., Kouneski, E. F. and Erickson, M. F. 1998. Responsible fathering: an overview and conceptual framework. *Journal of Marriage and the Family, 60*, 277–92.

Dykstra, P. A. 1995. Network composition. In C. P. M. Knipscheer, J. de Jong Gierveld, T. G. van Tilburg and P. A. Dykstra (eds), *Living Arrangements and Social Networks of Older Adults.* VU University Press, Amsterdam, 97–114.

Dykstra, P. A. 1998. The effects of divorce on intergenerational exchanges in families. *The Netherlands Journal of Social Sciences, 33*, 77–93.

Feld, S. L. 1984. The structured use of personal associates. *Social Forces, 62*, 640–52.

Fischer, C. S. 1977. *Networks and Places: Social Relations in the Urban Setting.* Free Press, New York.

Fischer, C. S. 1982. *To Dwell Among Friends: Personal Networks in Town and City.* University of Chicago Press, Chicago.

Furstenberg, F. F. Jr., Hoffman, S. D. and Shrestha, L. 1995. The effect of divorce on intergenerational transfers: new evidence. *Demography, 32*, 319–33.

Hagestad, G. O. 2002. Personal communication.

Hamil-Luker, J. and Uhlenberg, P. 2002. Later life education in the 1990s: increasing involvement and continuing disparity. *Journal of Gerontology: Social Sciences, 57B*, S324–31.

Hummert, M. L., Garsta, T. A., Shaner, J. L. and Strahm, S. 1994. Stereotypes of the elderly held by young, middle-aged, and elderly adults. *Journal of Gerontology: Psychological Sciences, 49*, P240–9.

Jong Gierveld, J. de and Dykstra, P. A. 2002. The long-term rewards of parenting: older adults' marital history and the likelihood of receiving support from adult children. *Ageing International, 27*, 49–69.

Jong Gierveld, J. de and Peeters, A. 2003. The interweaving of repartnered older adults' lives with their children and siblings. *Ageing & Society, 22*, 1–19.

Kohli, M. L. 1988. Social organization and subjective construction of the life course. In A. B. Sorensen, F. E. Weiner and L. R. Sherrod (eds), *Human Development and the Life Cycle.* Erlbaum, Hillsdale, New Jersey, 271–92.

Lofland, J. 1968. The youth ghetto. *Journal of Higher Education, 39*, 121–43.

Lopata, H. Z. 1996. *Current Widowhood: Myths and Realities.* Sage, Thousand Oaks, California.

Lye, D. N. 1996. Adult child-parent relationships. *Annual Review of Sociology, 22*, 79–102.

Lye, D. N., Klepinger, D. H., Hyle, P. D. and Nelson, A. 1995. Childhood living arrangements and adult children's relations with their parents. *Demography, 32*, 261–80.

Marsden, P. V. 1988. Homogeneity in confiding relationships. *Social Networks, 10*, 57–76.

McPherson, M., Smith-Lovin, L. and Cook, J. M. 2001. Birds of a feather: homophily in social networks. *Annual Review of Sociology, 27*, 415–44.

Mead, M. 1970. *Culture and Commitment: A Study of the Generation Gap.* Natural History Press, Garden City, New York.

Nelson, T. D. (cd) 2002. *Ageism, Stereotyping and Prejudice against Older Persons.* MIT Press, Cambridge, Massachusetts.

Penninx, K. 1999. *DeBuurt voor Alle Leeftijden [The Neighbourhood of All Ages].* NIZW Uitgeverij, Utrecht, The Netherlands.

Riley, M. W. and Riley, J. W. Jr. 2000. Age-integration: conceptual and historical background. *The Gerontologist, 40,* 266–70.

Riley, M. W., Kahn, R. L. and Foner, A. 1994. *Age and Structural Lag: Society's Failure to Provide Meaningful Opportunities in Work, Family, and Leisure.* Wiley, New York.

Stevens, N. 2001. Combating loneliness: a friendship enrichment programmc for older women. *Ageing & Society, 21,* 183–202.

Uhlenberg, P. and Cooney, T. M. 1990. Family size and mother-child relations in later life. *The Gerontologist, 30,* 618–25.

US Department of Education 2000. *Schools as Centers of Community: A Citizen's Guide for Planning and Design.* US Department of Education, Washington, DC.

Verbrugge, L. M. 1977. The structure of adult friendship choices. *Social Forces, 56,* 576–97.

Wagner, M., Schütze, Y. and Lang, F. R. 1999. Social relationships in old age. In P. B. Baltes and K. U. Mayer (eds), *The Berlin Aging Study: Aging from 70 to 100.* Cambridge University Press, Cambridge, 282–301.

Wolf, D. A., Freedman, V. and Soldo, B. J. 1997. The division of family labor: care for elderly parents. *The Journals of Gerontology, 52B,* special issue, 102–9.

THINKING ABOUT THE READING

What is age segregation? According to the authors, what are some of the reasons for age segregation? What are some of the everyday consequences of age segregation? Draw a diagram of your personal networks (e.g., the people you see daily, people you spend holidays with, people you work with). What is the age range of the people in your networks? How many older people do you know who are not your relatives? This reading uses information from a study of Dutch people. How would the findings compare to other cultures? In which social settings would you expect to find the *least* age segregation?

The Architects of Change

Reconstructing Society

14

Throughout this book, you've seen examples of how society is socially constructed and how these social constructions, in turn, affect the lives of individuals. It's hard not to feel a little helpless when discussing the control that culture, massive bureaucratic organizations, social institutions, systems of social stratification, and population trends have over our individual lives. However, social change is as much a part of society as social stability. Whether at the personal, cultural, or institutional level, change is the preeminent feature of modern societies. Social change occurs in many ways and on many levels (e.g., through population shifts and immigration, as illustrated in the previous chapter). Sociologists are also interested in specific, goal-based social movements. Who participates in social movements? What motivates this participation? How successful are they? Social movements range from neighborhood organizers seeking better funding for schools to large-scale religious groups seeking to influence law and politics regarding issues such as abortion, same-sex marriage, and immigration. Social movements come in all shapes and sizes. The readings in this final chapter provide three examples of different forms of social movements.

Sociologist William I. Robinson suggests that the current immigrant labor protests reflect more than temporary opposition to immigration policies. According to Robinson, these protests are indicative of a growing awareness regarding global capitalism and the exploitation of immigrant labor. Robinson traces the necessity of immigrant labor in the new global markets and asks us to consider the possibility that a global social movement is forming based on the issue of immigrant labor rights.

A small community working-class group sheds new light on the usefulness of a direct action model in comparison to the modes of resistance utilized by large, established worker unions. In "The Seattle Solidarity Network: A New Approach to Working Class Social Movements," Walter Winslow shows how SeaSol has taken a very specific philosophy and applied it toward the plight of workers and tenants who have experienced discrimination in their workplace and homes.

In the final reading, "Challenging Power: Toxic Waste Protests and the Politicization of White, Working-Class Women," Celene Krauss examines the process by which women with very traditional ideas about government and family became the leading activists in the toxic waste movement. She shows that these women were not motivated by the ideology of environmental movements, but rather by direct health threats to their children.

Something to Consider as You Read

As you read these selections, consider the connection between people's ideas, beliefs, and goals and the motivation to become involved in social change. Participation in a social movement takes time and resources. What do you care enough about to contribute your time and money? In thinking about the near future, which groups do you think are "worked up" enough about something to give a lot of time and energy in trying to create social change? If these groups prevail, what do you think the future will look like?

"Aquí Estamos y No Nos Vamos!"

Global Capital and Immigrant Rights

William I. Robinson

(2006)

A spectre is haunting global capitalism—the spectre of a transnational immigrant workers' uprising. An immigrant rights movement is spreading around the world, spearheaded by Latino immigrants in the US, who have launched an all-out fight-back against the repression, exploitation and racism they routinely face with a series of unparalleled strikes and demonstrations. The immediate message of immigrants and their allies in the United States is clear, with marchers shouting: "*aquí estamos y no nos vamos!*" (we're here and we're not leaving!). However, beyond immediate demands, the emerging movement challenges the very structural changes bound up with capitalist globalisation that have generated an upsurge in global labour migration, thrown up a new global working class, and placed that working class in increasingly direct confrontation with transnational capital.

The US mobilisations began when over half a million immigrants and their supporters took to the streets in Chicago on 10 March 2006. It was the largest single protest in that city's history. Following the Chicago action, rolling strikes and protests spread to other cities, large and small, organised through expanding networks of churches, immigrant clubs and rights groups, community associations, Spanish-language and progressive media, trade unions and social justice organisations. Millions came out on 25 March for a "national day of action." Between one and two million people demonstrated in Los Angeles—the single biggest public protest in the city's history—and millions more followed suit in Chicago, New York, Atlanta, Washington DC, Phoenix, Dallas, Houston, Tucson, Denver and dozens of other cities. Again, on 10 April, millions heeded the call for another day of protest. In addition, hundreds of thousands of high school students in Los Angeles and around the country staged walk-outs in support of their families and communities, braving police repression and legal sanctions.

Then on the first of May, International Workers' Day, trade unionists and social justice activists joined immigrants in "The Great American Boycott 2006/A Day Without an Immigrant." Millions—perhaps tens of millions—in over 200 cities from across the country skipped work and school, commercial activity and daily routines in order to participate in a national boycott, general strike, rallies and symbolic actions. The May 1 action was a resounding success. Hundreds of local communities in the south, midwest, north-west and elsewhere, far away from the "gateway cities" where Latino populations are concentrated, experienced mass public mobilisations that placed them on the political map. Agribusiness in the California and Florida heartlands—nearly 100 per cent dependent on immigrant labour—came to a standstill, leaving supermarket produce shelves empty for the next several days. In the landscaping industry, nine out of ten workers boycotted work, according to the American Nursery and Landscape Association. The construction industry suffered major disruptions. Latino truckers who move 70 per cent of the goods in Los Angeles ports did not work. Care-giver referral agencies in major cities saw a sharp increase in calls from parents who needed last-minute nannies or baby-sitters. In order to avoid a total shutdown of the casino mecca in Las Vegas—highly dependent on immigrant labour—casino owners were forced to set up tables in employee lunch-rooms and hold meetings to allow their workers to circulate petitions in favour of immigrant demands. International commerce between Mexico and the United States ground to a temporary halt as protesters closed Tijuana, Juarez-El Paso and several other crossings along the 2,000-mile border.

These protests have no precedent in the history of the US. The immediate trigger was the passage in mid-March by the House of Representatives of HR4437, a bill introduced by Republican representative James Sensenbrenner with broad support from the anti-immigrant lobby. This draconian bill would criminalise undocumented immigrants by making it a felony to be in the US without documentation. It also stipulated the construction of the first 700 miles of a militarised wall between Mexico and the US and would double the size of the US border patrol. And it would apply criminal sanctions against anyone who provided assistance to undocumented immigrants, including churches, humanitarian groups and social service agencies.

Following its passage by the House, bill HR4437 became stalled in the Senate. Democrat Ted Kennedy and Republican John McCain co-sponsored a "compromise" bill that would have removed the criminalisation clause in HR4437 and provided a limited plan for amnesty for some of the undocumented. It would have allowed those who could prove they have resided in the US for at least five years to apply for residency and later citizenship. Those residing in the US for two to five years would have been required to return home and then apply through US embassies for temporary "guest worker" permits. Those who could not demonstrate that they had been in the US for two years would be deported. Even this "compromise" bill would have resulted in massive deportations and heightened control over all immigrants.

Yet it was eventually jettisoned because of Republican opposition, so that by late April the whole legislative process had become stalled. In May, the Senate renewed debate on the matter and seemed to be moving towards consensus based on tougher enforcement and limited legalisation, although at the time of writing (late May 2006) it appeared the legislative process could drag on until after the November 2006 congressional elections.

However, the wave of protest goes well beyond HR4437. It represents the unleashing of pent-up anger and repudiation of what has been deepening exploitation and an escalation of anti-immigrant repression and racism. Immigrants have been subject to every imaginable abuse in recent years. Twice in the state of California they have been denied the right to acquire drivers' licences. This means that they must rely on inadequate or non-existent public transportation or risk driving illegally; more significantly, the drivers' licence is often the only form of legal documentation for such essential transactions as cashing cheques or renting an apartment. The US-Mexico border has been increasingly militarised and thousands of immigrants have died crossing the frontier. Anti-immigrant hate groups are on the rise. The FBI has reported more than 2,500 hate crimes against Latinos in the US since 2000. Blatantly racist public discourse that, only a few years ago, would have been considered extreme has become increasingly mainstreamed and aired in the mass media.

More ominously, the paramilitary organisation Minutemen, a modern day Latino-hating version of the Ku Klux Klan, has spread from its place of origin along the US-Mexican border in Arizona and California to other parts of the country. Minutemen claim they must "secure the border" in the face of inadequate state-sponsored control. Their discourse, beyond racist, is neo-fascist. Some have even been filmed sporting T-shirts with the emblem "Kill a Mexican Today?" and others have organised for-profit "human safaris" in the desert. One video game discovered recently circulating on the internet, "Border

Patrol," lets players shoot at Mexican immigrants as they try to cross the border into the US. Players are told to target one of three immigrant groups, all portrayed in a negative, stereotypical way, as the figures rush past a sign that reads "Welcome to the United States." The immigrants are caricatured as bandolier-wearing "Mexican nationalists," tattooed "drug smugglers" and pregnant "breeders" who spring across with their children in tow.

Minutemen clubs have been sponsored by right-wing organisers, wealthy ranchers, businessmen and politicians. But their social base is drawn from those formerly privileged sectors of the white working class that have been "flexibilised" and displaced by economic restructuring, the deregulation of labour and global capital flight. These sectors now scapegoat immigrants—with official encouragement—as the source of their insecurity and downward mobility.

The immigrant mobilisations have seriously threatened ruling groups. In the wake of the recent mobilisations, the Bush administration stepped up raids, deportations and other enforcement measures in a series of highly publicised mass arrests of undocumented immigrants and their employers, intended to intimidate the movement. In April 2006 it was revealed that KBR, a subsidiary of Halliburton—Vice-President Dick Cheney's former company, which has close ties to the Pentagon and is a major contractor in the Iraq war—won a $385 million contract to build large-scale immigrant detention centres in case of an "emergency influx" of immigrants.

Latino immigration to the US is part of a worldwide upsurge in transnational migration generated by the forces of capitalist globalisation. Immigrant labour worldwide is conservatively estimated at over 200 million, according to UN data.[1] Some 30 million are in the US, with at least 20 million of them from Latin America. Of these 20 million, some 11–12 million are undocumented (south and east Asia are also significant contributors to the undocumented population), although it must be stressed that these figures are low-end

estimates. The US is by far the largest immigrant-importing country, but the phenomenon is global. Racist attacks, scapegoating and state-sponsored repressive controls over immigrants are rising in many countries around the world, as is the fightback among immigrant workers wherever they are found. Parallel to the US events, for instance, the French government introduced a bill that would apply tough new controls over immigrants and roll back their rights. In response, some 30,000 immigrants and their supporters took to the streets in Paris on 13 May 2006 to demand the bill's repeal.

The Global Circulation of Immigrant Labour

The age of globalisation is also an age of unprecedented transnational migration. The corollary to an integrated global economy is the rise of a truly global—although highly segmented—labour market. It is a global labour market because, despite formal nation state restrictions on the free worldwide movement of labour, surplus labour in any part of the world is now recruited and redeployed through numerous mechanisms to where capital is in need of it and because workers themselves undertake worldwide migration, even in the face of the adverse migratory conditions.

Central to capitalism is securing a politically and economically suitable labour supply, and at the core of all class societies is the control over labour and disposal of the products of labour. But the linkage between the securing of labour and territoriality is changing under globalisation. As labour becomes "free" in every corner of the globe, capital has vast new opportunities for mobilising labour power where and when required. National labour pools are merging into a single global labour pool that services global capitalism. The transnational circulation of capital induces the transnational circulation of labour. This circulation of labour becomes incorporated into the process of restructuring the world economy. It is a mechanism for the provision of labour to transnationalised circuits of accumulation and constitutes a structural feature of the global system.

While the need to mix labour with capital at diverse points along global production chains induces population movements, there are sub-processes that shape the character and direction of such migration. At the structural level, the uprooting of communities by the capitalist break-up of local economies creates surplus populations and is a powerful push factor in outmigration, while labour shortages in more economically advanced areas is a pull factor that attracts displaced peoples. At a behavioural level, migration and wage remittances become a family survival strategy (see below), made *possible* by the demand for labour abroad and made increasingly *viable* by the fluid conditions and integrated infrastructures of globalisation.

In one sense, the South penetrates the North with the dramatic expansion of immigrant labour. But transnational migratory flows are not unidirectional from South to North and the phenomenon is best seen in global capitalist rather than North-South terms. Migrant workers are becoming a general category of super-exploitable labour drawn from globally dispersed labour reserves into similarly globally dispersed nodes of accumulation. To the extent that these nodes experience labour shortages—skilled or unskilled—they become magnets for transnational labour flows, often encouraged or even organised by both sending and receiving countries and regions.

Labour-short Middle Eastern countries, for instance, have programmes for the importation (and careful control) of labour from throughout south and east Asia and north Africa. The Philippine state has become a veritable labour recruitment agency for the global economy, organising the export of its citizens to over a hundred countries in Asia, the Middle East, Europe, North America and elsewhere. Greeks migrate to Germany and the US, while Albanians migrate to Greece. South Africans move to Australia and England, while Malawians, Mozambicans and Zimbabweans

work in South African mines and the service industry. Malaysia imports Indonesian labour, while Thailand imports workers from Laos and Myanmar and, in turn, sends labour to Malaysia, Singapore, Japan and elsewhere. In Latin America, Costa Rica is a major importer of Nicaraguan labour, Venezuela has historically imported large amounts of Colombian labour, the Southern Cone draws on several million emigrant Andean workers and an estimated 500,000 to 800,000 Haitians live in the Dominican Republic, where they cut sugar cane, harvest crops and work in the *maquiladoras* under the same labour market segmentation, political disenfranchisement and repression that immigrant workers face in the United States and in most labour-importing countries.

The division of the global working class into "citizen" and "non-citizen" labour is a major new axis of inequality worldwide, further complicating the well-known gendered and racialised hierarchies among labour, and facilitating new forms of repressive and authoritarian social control over working classes. In an *apparent* contradiction, capital and goods move freely across national borders in the new global economy but labour cannot and its movement is subject to heightened state controls. The global labour supply is, in the main, no longer coerced (subject to extra-economic compulsion) due to the ability of the universalised market to exercise strictly economic discipline, but its movement is juridically controlled. This control is a central determinant in the worldwide correlation of forces between global capital and global labour.

The immigrant is a juridical creation inserted into real social relations. States create "immigrant labour" as distinct categories of labour in relation to capital. While the generalisation of the labour market emerging from the consolidation of the global capitalist economy creates the conditions for global migrations as a world-level labour supply system, the maintenance and strengthening of state controls over transnational labour create the conditions for immigrant labour as a distinct category of labour. The creation of these distinct categories ("immigrant labour") becomes central to the global capitalist economy, replacing earlier direct colonial and racial caste controls over labour worldwide.

But why is this juridical category of "immigrant labour" reproduced under globalisation? Labour migration and geographic shifts in production are alternative forms for capitalists to achieve an optimal mix of their capital with labour. State controls are often intended *not to prevent* but to *control* the transnational movement of labour. A *free* flow of labour would exert an equalising influence on wages across borders whereas state controls help reproduce such differentials. Eliminating the wage differential between regions would cancel the advantages that capital accrues from disposing of labour pools worldwide subject to different wage levels and would strengthen labour worldwide in relation to capital. In addition, the use of immigrant labour allows receiving countries to separate reproduction and maintenance of labour, and therefore to "externalise" the costs of social reproduction. In other words, the new transnational migration helps capital to dispose of the need to pay for the reproduction of labour power. The inter-state system thus acts as a condition for the structural power of globally mobile transnational capital over labour that is transnational in actual content and character but subjected to different institutional arrangements under the direct control of national states.

The migrant labour phenomenon will continue to expand along with global capitalism. Just as capitalism has no control over its implacable expansion as a system, it cannot do away in its new globalist stage with transnational labour. But if global capital needs the labour power of transnational migrants, this labour power belongs to human beings who must be tightly controlled, given the special oppression and dehumanization involved in extracting their labour power as non-citizen immigrant labour. To return to the situation in the US, the immigrant issue presents a contradiction for political and economic elites: from the vantage points of dominant group interests, the dilemma is how to deal with the new "barbarians" at Rome's door.

Latino immigrants haw massively swelled the lower rungs of the US workforce. They provide almost all farm labour and much of the labour for hotels, restaurants, construction, janitorial and house cleaning, child care, gardening and landscaping, delivery, meat and poultry packing, retail, and so on. Yet dominant groups fear a rising tide of Latino immigrants will lead to a loss of cultural and political control, becoming a source of counter-hegemony and instability, as immigrant labour in Paris showed itself to be in the late 2005 uprising there against racism and marginality.

Employers do not want to do away with Latino immigration. To the contrary, they want to sustain a vast exploitable labour pool that exists under precarious conditions, that does not enjoy the civil, political and labour rights of citizens and that is disposable through deportation. It is the *condition of deportability* that they wish to create, or preserve, since that condition assures the ability to super-exploit with impunity and to dispose of this labour without consequences should it become unruly or unnecessary. The Bush administration opposed HR4437 not because it was in favour of immigrant rights but because it had to play a balancing act by finding a formula for a stable supply of cheap labour to employers with, at the same time, greater state control over immigrants.

The Bush White House proposed a "guest worker" programme that would rule out legalisation for undocumented immigrants, force them to return to their home countries and apply for temporary work visas, and implement tough new border security measures. There is a long history of such "guest worker" schemes going back to the *bracero* programme, which brought millions of Mexican workers to the US during the labour shortages of the Second World War, only to deport them once native workers had become available again. Similar "guest worker" programmes are in effect in several European countries and other labour-importing states around the world.

The contradictions of "immigrant policy reform" became apparent in the days leading up to the May 1 action, when major capitalist groups dependent on immigrant labour—especially in the agricultural, food processing, landscaping, construction, and other service sectors—came out in support of legalisation for the undocumented. Such transnational agro-industrial giants as Cargill, Swift and Co, Perdue Farms, Tyson Foods and Goya Foods, for instance, closed down many of their meat-packing and food processing plants and gave workers the day off.

Neoliberalism in Latin America

If capital's need for cheap, malleable and deportable labour in the centres of the global economy is the main "pull factor" inducing Latino immigration to the US, the "push factor" is the devastation left by two decades of neoliberalism in Latin America. Capitalist globalisation—structural adjustment, free trade agreements, privatisations, the contraction of public employment and credits, the break-up of communal lands and so forth, along with the political crises these measures have generated—has imploded thousands of communities in Latin America and unleashed a wave of migration, from rural to urban areas and to other countries, that can only be analogous to the mass uprooting and migration that generally take place in the wake of war.

Just as capital does not stay put in the place it accumulates, neither do wages stay put. The flip side of the intense upsurge in transnational migration is the reverse flow of remittances by migrant workers in the global economy to their country and region of origin. Officially recorded international remittances increased astonishingly, from a mere $57 million in 1970 to $216 billion in 2005, according to World Bank data. This amount was higher than capital market flows and official development assistance combined, and nearly equalled the total amount of world FDI (foreign direct investment) in 2004. Close to one billion people, or one in every six on the planet, may receive some support from the global flow of remittances, according to senior World Bank economist Dilip Ratha.[2] Remittances have become an economic mainstay for an increasing number of countries. Most of the world's regions, including Africa, Asia, Latin America and southern and eastern Europe, report major remittance inflows.

Remittances redistribute income worldwide in a literal or geographic sense but not in the actual sense of *redistribution*, meaning a transfer of some added portion of the surplus from capital to labour, since they constitute not additional earnings but the separation of the site where wages are earned from the site of wage-generated consumption. What is taking place is a historically unprecedented separation of the point of production from the point of social reproduction. The former can take place in one part of the world and generate the value—then remitted—for social reproduction of labour in another part of the world. This is an emergent structural feature of the global system, in which the site of labour power and of its reproduction have been transnationally dispersed.

Transnational Latino migration has led to an enormous increase in remittances from Latino ethnic labour abroad to extended kinship networks in Latin America. Latin American workers abroad sent home some $57 billion in 2005, according to the Inter-American Development Bank.[3] These remittances were the number one source of foreign exchange for the Dominican Republic, El Salvador, Guatemala, Guyana, Haiti, Honduras, Jamaica and Nicaragua, and the second most important source for Belize, Bolivia, Colombia, Ecuador, Paraguay and Surinam, according to the Bank. The $20 billion sent back in 2005 by an estimated 10 million Mexicans in the US was more than the country's tourism receipts and was surpassed only by oil and *maquiladora* exports.

These remittances allow millions of Latin American families to survive by purchasing goods either imported from the world market or produced locally or by transnational capital. They allow for family survival at a time of crisis and adjustment, especially for the poorest sectors—safety nets that replace governments and fixed employment in the provision of economic security. Emigration and remittances also serve the political objective of pacification. The dramatic expansion of Latin American emigration to the US from the 1980s onwards helped to dissipate social tensions and undermine labour and political opposition to prevailing regimes and institutions. Remittances help to offset macroeconomic imbalances, in some cases averting economic collapse, thereby shoring up the political conditions for an environment congenial to transnational capital.

Therefore, bound up with the immigrant debate in the US is the entire political economy of global capitalism in the western hemisphere—the same political economy that is now being sharply contested throughout Latin America with the surge in mass popular struggles and the turn to the Left. The struggle for immigrant rights in the US is thus part and parcel of this resistance to neoliberalism, intimately connected to the larger Latin American—and worldwide—struggle for social justice.

No wonder protests and boycotts took place throughout Latin America on May 1 in solidarity with Latino immigrants in the US. But these actions were linked to local labour rights struggles and social movement demands. In Tijuana, Mexico, for example, *maquiladora* workers in that border city's in-bond industry marched on May 1 to demand higher wages, eight-hour shifts, an end to "abuses and despotism" in the *maquila* plants and an end to sexual harassment, the use of poison chemicals and company unions. The workers also called for solidarity with the "Great American Boycott of 2006 on the other side of the border" and participated in a protest at the US consulate in the city and at the main crossing, which shut down cross- border traffic for most of the day.

The Nature of Immigrant Struggles

Labour market transformations driven by capitalist globalisation unleash what McMichael calls "the politics of global labor circulation"[4] and fuel, in labour-importing countries, new nativisms, waves of xenophobia and racism against immigrants. Shifting political coalitions scapegoat immigrants by promoting ethnic-based solidarities among middle classes, representatives of distinct fractions of capital and formerly privileged sectors among working classes (such as white ethnic workers in the US and Europe) threatened by job loss, declining income and the other insecurities of economic restructuring. The long-term tendency seems to be towards a generalisation of labour market conditions across borders, characterised by segmented structures under a regime of labour deregulation and racial, ethnic and gender hierarchies.

In this regard, a major challenge confronting the movement in the US is relations between the Latino and the Black communities. Historically, African Americans have swelled the lower rungs in the US caste system. But, as African Americans fought for their civil and human rights in the 1960s and 1970s, they became organised, politicised and radicalised. Black workers led trade union militancy. All this made them undesirable labour for capital—"undisciplined" and "noncompliant."

Starting in the 1980s, employers began to push out Black workers and massively recruit Latino immigrants, a move that coincided with deindustrialisation and restructuring. Blacks moved from super-exploited to marginalized—subject to unemployment, cuts in social services, mass incarceration and heightened state repression—while Latino immigrant labour has become the new super-exploited sector. Employers and political elites in New Orleans, for instance, have apparently decided in the wake of Hurricane Katrina to replace that city's historically black working class with Latino immigrant labour. Whereas fifteen years ago no one saw a single Latino face in places such as Iowa or Tennessee, now Mexican, Central American and other Latino workers are visible everywhere. If some African Americans have misdirected their anger over marginality at Latino immigrants, the Black community has a legitimate grievance over the anti-Black racism of many Latinos themselves, who often lack sensitivity to the historic plight and contemporary experience of Blacks with racism, and are reticent to see them as natural allies. (Latinos often bring with them particular sets of racialised relations from their home countries.)[5]

White labour that historically enjoyed caste privileges within racially segmented labour markets has experienced downward mobility and heightened insecurity. These sectors of the working class feel the pinch of capitalist globalisation and the transnationalisation of formerly insulated local labour markets. Studies in the early 1990s, for example, found that, in addition to concentrations in "traditional" areas such as Los Angeles, Miami, Washington DC, Virginia and Houston, Central American immigrants had formed clusters in the formal and informal service sectors in areas where, in the process of downward mobility, they had replaced "white ethnics," such as in suburban Long Island, the small towns of Iowa and North Carolina, in Silicon Valley and in the northern and eastern suburbs of the San Francisco Bay Area.[6]

The loss of caste privileges for white sectors of the working class is problematic for political elites and state managers in the US, since legitimation and domination have historically been constructed through a white racial hegemonic bloc. Can such a bloc be sustained or renewed through a scapegoating of immigrant communities? In attempting to shape public discourse, the anti-immigrant lobby argues that immigrants "are a drain on the US economy." Yet, as the National Immigrant Solidarity Network points out, immigrants contribute $7 billion in Social Security a year. They earn $240 billion, report $90 billion, and are only reimbursed $5 billion in tax returns. They also contribute $25 billion more to the US economy than they receive in health-care and social services.

But this is a limited line of argument, since the larger issue is the incalculable trillions of dollars that immigrant labour generates in profits and revenue for capital, only a tiny proportion of which goes back to them in the form of wages.

Moreover, it has been demonstrated that there is no correlation between the unemployment rate among US citizens and the rate of immigration. In fact, the unemployment rate has moved in cycles over the past twenty-five years and exhibits a comparatively lower rate during the most recent (2000–2005) influx of undocumented workers. Similarly, wage stagnation in the United States appeared, starting with the economic crisis of 1973, and has continued its steady march ever since, with no correlation to increases or decreases in the inflow of undocumented workers. Instead, downward mobility for most US workers is positively correlated with the decline in union participation, the decline in labour conditions and the polarisation of income and wealth that began with the restructuring crisis of the 1970s and accelerated the following decade as Reaganomics launched the neo-liberal counterrevolution.

The larger backdrop here is transnational capital's attempt to forge post-Fordist, post-Keynesian capital-labour relations worldwide, based on flexibilisation, deregulation and deunionisation. From the 1970s onwards, capital began to abandon earlier reciprocities with labour, forged in the epoch of national corporate capitalism, precisely because the process of globalisation allowed to it break free of nation state constraints. There has been a vast acceleration of the primitive accumulation of capital worldwide through globalisation, a process in which millions have been wrenched from the means of production, proletarianised and thrown into a global labour market that transnational capital has been able to shape. As capital assumed new power relative to labour with the onset of globalisation, states shifted from reproducing Keynesian social structures of accumulation to servicing the general needs of the new patterns of global accumulation.

At the core of the emerging global social structure of accumulation is a new capital-labour relation based on alternative systems of labour control and diverse contingent categories of devalued labour—sub-contracted, outsourced, casualised, informal, part-time, temp work, home-work, and so on—the essence of which is cheapening and disciplining labour, making it "flexible" and readily available for transnational capital in worldwide labour reserves. Workers in the global economy are themselves, under these flexible arrangements, increasingly treated as a sub-contracted component rather than a fixture internal to employer organisations. These new class relations of global capitalism dissolve the notion of responsibility, however minimal, that governments have for their citizens or that employers have towards their employees.

Immigrant workers become the archetype of these new global class relations. They are a naked commodity, no longer embedded in relations of reciprocity rooted in social and political communities that have, historically, been institutionalised in nation states. Immigrant labour pools that can be super-exploited economically, marginalised and disenfranchised politically, driven into the shadows and deported when necessary are the very epitome of capital's naked domination in the age of global capitalism.

The immigrant rights movement in the US is demanding full rights for all immigrants, including amnesty, worker protections, family reunification measures, a path to citizenship or permanent residency rather than a temporary "guest worker" programme, an end to all attacks against immigrants and to the criminalisation of immigrant communities. While some observers have billed the recent events as the birth of a new civil rights movement, clearly much more is at stake. In the larger picture, this goes beyond immediate demands; it challenges the class relations that are at the very core of global capitalism. The significance of the May 1 immigrant rights mobilisation taking place on international workers'

day—which has not been celebrated in the US for nearly a century—was lost on no one.

In the age of globalisation, the only hope of accumulating the social and political forces necessary to confront the global capitalist system is by transnationalising popular, labour and democratic struggles. The immigrant rights movement is all of these—popular, pro-worker and democratic—and it is by definition transnational. In sum, the struggle for immigrant rights is at the cutting edge of the global working-class fight-back against capitalist globalisation.

Notes

1. Manuel Oruzco, "Worker remittances in an international scope," *Working Paper* (Washington, DC, Inter-American Dialogue and Multilateral Investment Fund of the Inter-American Development Bank, March 2003), p. 1.

2. For these details, see Richard Boudreaux, "The new foreign aid; the seeds of promise," *Los Angeles Times* (14 April 2006), p. 1A.

3. Inter-American Development Bank, *Remittances 2005: promoting financial democracy* (Washington, DC, IDB, 2006).

4. Philip McMichael, *Development and Social Change: A Global Perspective* (Thousand Oaks, CA, Pine Forge Press, 1986), p. 189.

5. In a commentary observing that mainstream Black political leaders have been notably lukewarm to the immigrant rights movement, Keeanga-Yamahtta Taylor writes: "The displacement of Black workers is a real problem—but not a problem caused by displaced Mexican workers . . . if the state is allowed to criminalize the existence [of] immigrant workers this will only fan the flames of racism eventually consuming Blacks in a back draft of discrimination. How exactly does one tell the difference between a citizen and a non-citizen? Through a massive campaign of racial profiling, that's how . . . In fact, the entire working class has a stake in the success of the movement." She goes on to recall how California building owners and labour contractors replaced Black janitors with largely undocumented Latino immigrants in the 1980s. But after a successful Service Employees International

Union drive in the "Justice for janitors" campaign of the late 1980s and 1990s, wages and benefits went up and the union's largely Latino members sought contractual language guaranteeing African Americans a percentage of work slots. See Taylor, "Life ain't been no crystal stair: Blacks, Latinos and the new civil rights movement," *Counterpunch* (9 May 2006), downloaded 18 May 2006 <http://www.counterpunch.org/taylor0508 2006.html>.

6. See the special issue of NACLA *Report on the Americas,* "On the line: Latinos on labor's cutting edge" (Vol. 30, no. 3, November/December 1996).

THINKING ABOUT THE READING

What is the "global circulation of immigrant labor"? What are some of the issues and concerns that face immigrant workers? According to Robinson, recent immigrant labor demonstrations reflect the growing consciousness of a "global working class." Who or what are the "global working class" described in this reading? What are some of the ways they resist global capitalism? What will be some of the implications of these strategies if they are successful?

The Seattle Solidarity Network: A New Approach to Working Class Social Movements

*Walter Winslow**

(2011)

The Future of Working Class Social Movements

The winter of 2011 proved timely for examining social movements in the United States. As an active member of The Seattle Solidarity Network (SeaSol), a small Seattle based network of working class individuals that fight for tenant and worker rights in their community, I saw first hand the two very different approaches that large seasoned unions and small community working class support groups utilized to collectively fight for rights in the workforce. In Renton, Washington, SeaSol was in the midst a bitter campaign against a small Italian restaurant in an effort to recover a waitress' unpaid wages. At the same time, in Madison, Wisconsin, a Republican governor was trying to push through legislation intended to quash public sector unions in the State while tens of thousands of people protested at the Capitol building. The stark contrast between the all but unknown conflict SeaSol was battling in Renton and the much-publicized protests in Wisconsin at the same time can be seen as parallel harbingers of two very different futures for working-class social movements in the United States: extinction or rejuvenation. The juxtaposition of these two specific events provides a useful starting point for understanding how SeaSol's approach differs from that of the mainstream political Left in the United States.

The Future From Madison, Wisconsin

On February 11th, 2011, Governor Scott Walker of Wisconsin introduced a new "budget repair bill" designed to strip Wisconsin's 283,351 public employees (WTA 2011) of their collective bargaining rights and greatly weaken public sector unions in the state. The proposed bill was designed to eliminate the automatic deduction of union dues from union employees' pay and mandatory union membership, limit labor contracts to one year, remove the right to collective bargaining entirely in some industries while strictly limiting it in others, and require public unions to run a campaign to be successfully re-certified in a National Labor Relations Board election every year (State Legislature of Wisconsin 2011).

The proposed bill was a litmus test for the strength of public sector unions across the nation as much of the country watched and waited to see what would happen. Despite their strength is numbers, Wisconsin's public sector unions and their supporters struggled to prevent the bill from becoming law. Thousands of protesters occupied the Capitol Rotunda in Madison, demanding that the bill be scrapped. Wisconsin's Democratic state lawmakers physically fled to Illinois in order to prevent the state senate from having the necessary quorum to vote on the bill, and a variety of private

---

*Editors' note: This article is based on original research conducted by the author for his honors thesis in sociology. This version is extracted from the original thesis and has been edited by Jennifer Hamann for this reader.

and public unions organized solidarity rallies at every state capital in the country. The cross-country reactions to the bill captured major media attention that pushed unions into the spotlight, questioning their effectiveness not only in Wisconsin, but across the United States. Though the demonstrations and media frenzy made for good television, it gave the protestors no real leverage. On March 11, 2011, Governor Walker signed the bill into law (Bauer 2011, Davey 2011, Haas 2011, Ramirez 2011).

As a result of the new law, public sector unions across the country may soon be faced with similar measures—possibly marking another step towards the complete extinction of unions as a serious social force in the United States. In the wake of this disaster for organized labor, Wisconsin's protesters and their sympathizers across the nation have been left wondering: is there anything else they could have done?

There is at least one compelling answer to this question: the unions and their supporters could have used sustained direct action tactics to put pressure on Governor Walker. In the ensuing protests, teachers from across the State called in "sick" to attend demonstrations at the Capitol building in a brash wildcat strike. In Madison alone, forty percent of the districts' teachers phoned in sick, causing the entire school district to cancel classes (DeFour 2011). However, the unions' own leaders moved quickly to stop the strikes. The Madison Teacher's union, Madison Teacher's Inc (MTI), The Milwaukee Teacher's Association, and the State's largest teacher's union, the Wisconsin Education Council Association (WEAC) consistently issued statements urging union workers to continue to report for work and reassuring them that they had the situation well in hand (Bell 2011, WISC-TV 2011). Union leaders made it clear that determining appropriate strategies for resisting the bill was their purview.

Instead of direct action, union leaders funneled popular anger into more passive modes of resistance; they urged supporters to sign petitions outside the capitol and brought in speakers from across the country to condemn Republicans and extol the Democrats. The Reverend Jesse Jackson led one group of protestors in a chant: "When we vote, we win! When we vote, we win!" (Wisconsin Reporter 2011). Jackson's message was simple: Governor Walker's bill should be dealt with using only the proper channels of legal and electoral processes.

Public sector unions utilized the same tired strategies the Left has been relying on for decades: public demonstrations, legal battles, and continued support of the Democratic Party. Any divergent strategies that were utilized were proactively suppressed and union members were urged to remain at work. These traditional approaches failed to stop the budget repair bill in Wisconsin and they have failed to slow the general decline of unions at large across the country. As unions have become less participatory and increasingly executive, they have not been able to mobilize the popular support necessary to stop corporate offensives at the bargaining table or in Congress. A union's greatest strength is the ability to unite workers to take action on the job that directly disrupts business. Today however, unions fail to utilize this power. In its place, America's unions continue to languish in a willful state of institutional bondage. As the most historically significant form of working-class social movement, the obvious impotency of unions as demonstrated in Wisconsin has grim implications for the future.

The Seattle Solidarity Network: An Alternative Approach

The Seattle Solidarity Network (SeaSol) is a small but growing grassroots mutual support organization for workers and tenants. The five young men who founded SeaSol in December of 2007, all members of the Industrial Workers of the World (IWW), wanted to find a way to contribute to rebuilding a revolutionary working-class social movement by winning tangible victories with a small number of supporters. Ultimately, they were interested in the potential of unions to serve as a mechanism to eventually overturn capitalist social relations entirely. As their idea of forming some sort of mutual support network began to take shape in late 2007, they decided to include tenants' issues in their project, an issue that is often left out of a union's scope of support. Their class politics prompted them to view tenants' and workers' issues as inextricably linked and they hoped that by engaging with both, they would be able to ensure a higher and broader level of activity for their new organization.

Despite the revolutionary ambitions of many of its members, SeaSol does not base its day-to-day activities on any grandiose vision of the future and does not have any official political agenda or affiliation. Instead, SeaSol exists to achieve immediate material gains for low-wage workers and tenants in the here and now. Since its formation three and a half years ago, SeaSol has successfully resolved approximately twenty-five specific housing and job-related issues while growing to nearly one hundred members. In the absence of effective legal remedies and strong workers' or tenants' unions, SeaSol members work to protect one another from employer or landlord abuses by carrying out escalating campaigns of public protest.

This research examines both why this unique organization is experiencing growing success and how its members are politicized as a direct result of their participation. SeaSol's approach is especially notable because it defies prevailing ideologies surrounding social change by operating outside the paradigm of contemporary progressive organizations. SeaSol is unique in that it:

- Is entirely support by volunteers
- Adheres to no explicit political ideology
- Does not rely on lawyers or other professionals
- Does not involve itself in electoral politics
- Is not a legally recognized non-profit organization
- Is funded exclusively by small individual donations

This article reveals how working-class people do not necessarily need to depend on politicians or non-profit organizations to improve their lives. In Seattle, they are coming together as equals to directly improve their lives using only their own collective power and imagination. SeaSol's present activities are limited, but the wider implications of the organization's strategy for social change are boundless.

The Future From Renton, Washington

The winter of 2011 also tested worker's rights in the suburb of Renton, Washington just outside of Seattle. SeaSol was leading their last picket outside of a Bella Napoli Italian restaurant because its owner, Ciro Donofrio, had fired a waitress named Ramona and was refusing to pay her for her last month of work. Ramona describes what happened to her in an article on SeaSol's website:

> For the entire month of September I worked for Ciro Donofrio at his Italian Restaurant in Renton, Bella Napoli. During this time, Ciro was verbally abusive towards his employees and even customers. He would throw temper tantrums in front of tables and claim we were out of things on the menu simply because he did not feel like making them . . . I still had to pay rent so I continued to work for Ciro. Things got hairy when I had $110 of my bank "disappeared" one night when only he and I were working. Also, I needed my check and Ciro claimed that he only paid his employees at the end of every month. I thought this was strange, especially after I had seen him give a check to the cook, but I dismissed it. What was he going to do, not pay me? (The Seattle Solidarity Network, 2011)

Refusing to pay her was exactly what Donofrio ended up doing after firing Ramona. Ramona decided to file a claim against Donofrio with the Department of Labor and Industries (L&I), but quickly became frustrated with the slow and impersonal nature of the process. As a result, when Ramona's friend told her about a poster she had seen promoting SeaSol, Ramona decided to contact the organization.

Ramona brought her case to the next weekly SeaSol meeting where members voted to initiate a direct action campaign against Donofrio. Shortly after, forty SeaSol supporters marched into Bella Napoli restaurant with Ramona and delivered a letter to Donofrio telling him that he had 14 days to pay her the wages he owed before they would take further action. When he failed to pay Ramona's wages after two weeks, SeaSol began an escalating campaign that involved flyer distribution, posters and two and half months of picketing Donofrio and his restaurant. Despite the rainy cold winter weather, roughly thirty individuals consistently showed up for the evening pickets at Bella Napoli, a location that was also a good twenty minute drive from Seattle. We paraded up and down the sidewalk in front of the restaurant carrying signs and chanting, "Work for Ciro, get paid zero!" while he eyed us angrily from inside his empty restaurant. After about half an hour, as it became obvious that no one was going to cross the picket line that night, Donofrio decided to close his restaurant for the night. A week later, Donofrio was forced to close the doors to his business.

The fight was a milestone for SeaSol in many ways. For the first time, the network had the strength and numbers to force an employer to choose between paying what he owed or closing the doors of his business permanently. The amount of money at stake was small and the number of people involved was nothing compared to the tens of thousands who were protesting in Wisconsin at about the same time. However, despite the insignificance of the campaign on a grand scale, SeaSol's victory in Renton clearly demonstrated the organization's growing power.

Ramona did eventually receive a check through the Department of Labor and Industries for approximately half of the amount she was actually owed, but when she attempted to cash it the check bounced. Ramona remained unclear as to exactly why this was, but she said that after speaking with L&I it seemed to have something to do with the fact that L&I had not actually secured payment from Donofrio before issuing the check. SeaSol was also unable to secure payment from Donofrio, but when asked if she would remain involved in SeaSol anyway Ramona said:

> Definitely it's just the justice, it's just seeing a group of people stand beside you and support you and tell you it's ok, I've been through this, it'll get better and we'll stand up to them and they won't win.

The sort of success SeaSol experienced in Ramona's campaign, small though it may be, provides on example of the possibility that powerful working class social movements can still be rebuilt in the United States. Moreover, the campaign proved that organized members of the working-class are capable of identifying and defeating their own enemies without legal or professional assistance.

An Egalitarian Organization

SeaSol is comprised of three groups of volunteers denoting three different levels of activity and commitment to the organization: organizers, members, and supporters. Anyone may become an organizer if they are willing, at a minimum, to commit to attend SeaSol's weekly planning meetings and to call ten to twenty SeaSol members every time the organization utilizes its phone-tree. People who volunteer at this level are more likely to be ideologically motivated. SeaSol's membership is defined as everyone who has agreed to receive notification about every SeaSol action. Individuals who may want to work with SeaSol in order to get help dealing with a specific job or housing issue are required to become involved at this level. Supporters are those who are interested in the organization but want to be notified less frequently, typically only about SeaSol's largest or most important actions. The organization is presently comprised of approximately sixteen organizers, ninety members, has over two hundred people on its phone-tree, and over five hundred supporters on its largest email list.

SeaSol has no formalized leadership structure and the organization's weekly meetings are open to the public. Typically twenty to thirty people attend these weekly meetings. Many members who are not organizers regularly attend, but it is less common for supporters to attend. The group makes all of its decisions during these weekly meetings by taking a simple majority vote after a period of discussion; anyone present at a meeting is permitted to vote. The primary purpose of these meetings is to plan SeaSol's activities for the coming week and to delegate logistical responsibilities.

The organization has successfully taken on a variety of workers' and tenants' issues including wage theft, landlord neglect, deposit theft, unfair fees, and predatory lawsuits. SeaSol carries out public campaigns designed to force the employer or landlord to meet a specific demand using escalating amounts of social and economic pressure. In the past three and a half years SeaSol has undertaken a wide array of tactics as part of these campaigns. A far from comprehensive list of direct action tactics. Includes storming into offices en masse to deliver written demands, putting up posters telling would-be renters or customers not to do business with a given company, picketing storefronts and other businesses, picketing public events connected with the employer or landlord, and putting up posters around the employer's or landlord's neighborhood or workplace.

SeaSol's tactics are intended not just to achieve the desired results, but also to do so in a way that empowers those who participate in SeaSol campaigns. This is one reason the organization does not seek legal help with its campaigns. The most active participants in SeaSol believe that legal processes are slow, biased, ineffectual, costly, and passive for the participant. SeaSol has only sought legal representation one time in order to defend itself in court against a lawsuit brought against them by a major Seattle real estate developer that they were pressuring. Additionally, as a rule of thumb, the organization only takes on cases that they feel are going to be empowering for the participants. For the same reason, SeaSol only takes on fights with people who are willing and able to take a leading role in their own campaign and seem genuinely interested in joining and helping others.

Their overall success rate is notably high, winning twenty-one of twenty-five fights in the past three years. It is no accident that SeaSol finds success in such a high percentage of their campaigns, rather, it is the direct result of one of the organizations most basic principles: "winnability."

Winnability

When asked why SeaSol had decided to take on Ramona's wage-theft, one organizer noted the following:

> The fact that it was very winnable, we had a lot of leverage on the business, we had the power to put this company out of business—so we ought to be able to win this fight!

Another SeaSol organizer expanded on the same idea in greater detail:

> Winnability is one of our basic principles. It is this concept that is really important and kind of straight forward and seems kind of silly to talk so explicitly about, but really I think it is kind of ignored by other activist groups generally and that is: can you win what you are trying to get? Can you get your demand? Could you do it? Is it possible? And while you can never know that concretely, you never know for sure, but you can use rational thinking about what that person [the employer or landlord] values and how they've been acting in the past.

This is probably the single most important principle SeaSol emphasizes in its internal trainings and public presentations. Every SeaSol fight is based around a specific concrete demand. If the organization does not feel like this concrete demand can be met, it will not take on the case. As simple and "silly to talk so explicitly about" as this idea may seem, the truth is that winnability is something many activists rarely consider. Many activist organizations rally around a specific issue, such as globalization, but never take the time to honestly ask themselves, for example: what would it really take to transform or dismantle the IMF and World Bank? What sort of popular movement would be needed to force the U.S. to restructure how it conducts world trade? Does the Left in this country really have the power to achieve this outcome?

SeaSol organizers seriously consider relevant power dynamics before they decide to begin a new campaign. The organization is open about its unwillingness to take on fights they do not believe they can win, regularly voting not to take on certain campaigns because they do not feel that they are winnable. One organizer explained how just recently the group had voted to take on a small time landlord who had stolen several tenants' deposits but then changed their mind when further research indicated that it was probably unwinnable:

> [S]he had stolen their deposit and we really wanted to take on the fight and we thought she had this moving company we might be able to target, but even when we took it on we weren't sure. Then after doing more research and finding out she actually isn't even in the State three weeks out of the month and she has no other economic targets and no vacancies and has no reputation in the neighborhood—it made it seem like a very unwinnable campaign so we decided not to take it on after all.

These kind of pragmatic ideas about what SeaSol can and cannot accomplish form a major part of the organization's culture. Multiple informants reported that this simple pragmatism was part of what made SeaSol so distinct when compared to other activist groups. One organizer who also works as a paid union organizer said that compared to her paid work:

> Working with SeaSol has just kind of kept me sane . . . I don't really think that a lot of activism is really leading to anything whereas with SeaSol I feel it can be very empowering for people.

Several other informants reported that SeaSol's pragmatic approach was actually part of a conscious strategy to build a larger and more powerful movement to accomplish greater goals. Many informants reported that they had become demoralized by the repeated failures they had experienced working with other organizations in the past that had tried to implement sweeping social changes that they did not have the power to make—like ending the US wars in the Middle East or stopping governmental budget cuts to health and human services.

While SeaSol organizers believe that it is useful to understand social problems on a systemic level, they also understand that it is foolhardy at this point in time to think the Left can attack those systems directly with any success. To be able to do that successfully SeaSol organizers reason that they need to work on dramatically increasing their numbers through practical activity rather than through propaganda. All four SeaSol organizers interviewed said that this was why they thought winning campaigns was so crucial, every victory proves that SeaSol's approach really works. All six SeaSol contacts, including two members who did not initially get involved with SeaSol for any sort of ideological reasons, reported that they wanted SeaSol to continue to grow in order to successfully take on larger and more significant social problems such as "Chase" bank, "capitalism," "the State," and even "industrial aqua-culture." In one SeaSol organizer's words, "the basic motif of SeaSol that I know is we do what we can today so we can do what we want to tomorrow."

To quote another SeaSol organizer:

> The question, the difficult part, is how do you get from nobody to hundreds of thousands of people? How do you get that force so that it can operate well? So that it can operate sustainably and in a progressively better way? The answer to that for me, is what we're doing."

There is no doubt that SeaSol is effectively winning the small fights. However, the more important question is whether these victories will actually spawn the larger movement everyone involved in SeaSol hopes for?

Strength in Numbers

Between the spring of 2010 and the spring of 2011, SeaSol's organizing committee grew from eight members to sixteen. Attendance at weekly meetings also increased from the low teens to the mid twenties during the same period. One of the most interesting ways SeaSol continues to grow is based around the organization's concept of mutual aid. A strong willingness to join SeaSol and a verbal agreement to continue to support the organization in the future is required before SeaSol will agree to take on a campaign for an outsider. One organizer's description of her first impression of a woman dealing with a landlord issue after their first meeting illustrates this point:

> She said, "I don't want them [the property management company] to do this to someone else," which is something that is really important for me to hear from someone. There is some enlightened self-interest involved, or a lot actually, but the fact that she's thinking about other people and recognizes that she is connected to other people, that others are like me, is a really good sign. She just really wanted to fight back, so it wasn't just, oh, I feel sorry for this woman, it was like, oh, I really feel for her but I also have a lot of respect for her. She's ready to fight back against this huge company. She doesn't have any experience that I ever got out of her doing this, so I had a lot of admiration for that.

SeaSol is making a conscious effort to distinguish itself from social service agencies. They don't want to provide direct action casework for someone who is not interested in passing on the support to the next worker or tenant in need. SeaSol wants to retain their permanent involvement. The woman made it clear that she did not want to have a passive role in her campaign. The organizer did not only feel sorry for the woman—she respected her—and left the meeting feeling excited to work with her side by side. In this case, SeaSol ended up launching a successful six-week campaign with the woman in the spring of 2011 to force her landlord to drop several hundred dollars in unjust fees and return her stolen security deposit. The woman has remained a SeaSol member and continues to attend actions when she can.

SeaSol is successfully retaining the participation of people who initially become involved in order to resolve their own problems. However, it is self-evident that a mass movement will never be built one person at a time and this is not the primary way SeaSol has grown in the past few years. SeaSol's success or failure at building a larger working-class social movement depends on its ability to get more than one person involved at a time. One organizer described his thoughts about SeaSol's growth this way:

> When I say "gathering people" there are sort of two things that go on with that in any given fight. There are the people that come into it because they are at the center of a fight and then there are the people that come into it because there is a fight going on and they want to help out. For that latter group, I have seen more people come on from that group in labor fights—because labor fights involve big actions that you want to have as many people as possible at and really landlord fights don't.

Another organizer echoed the idea that labor fights are ideal for strengthening SeaSol. When I asked him if he thought Ramona's campaign helped the organization grow, he commented:

> It brought in Ramona and some of Ramona's friends, but mainly it was a great fight because it gave us a lot of picketing opportunities. It gave us opportunities for fun and exciting actions that lots of people can participate in and that had an immediate and powerful impact—and people could see the power in that it actually destroyed the business. It gave people an opportunity to come out and picket that was real, not just symbolic.

Getting the maximum number of people involved is something SeaSol considers when deciding what campaigns to take on and what tactics to use. The more SeaSol has taken on compelling campaigns that have required multiple mass actions, the more the organization has grown. One organizer described how while in one campaign against a landlord SeaSol had largely relied on smaller groups informally heading out to put up "Do Not Rent Here" posters around properties owned by the landlord, the organization adapted its strategy in a later fight to involve more people:

> Everything in Nelson [the later campaign] was just a better job of what we did in George's fight [the previous campaign]. By having different groups go poster around different neighborhoods as one big action instead of just informally mobilizing for it . . .

In this case SeaSol intentionally adapted its strategy to involve more people not because it was necessarily more effective at getting the posters put up, but rather because it was a way of allowing more people to help take action against the landlord. SeaSol's continued growth is very much dependent on the amount the organization can find ways to effectively mobilize larger groups of people in a meaningful way.

One of the most important elements of recruitment involves basic training. SeaSol provides first hand training on how to effectively fight back against employers and landlords. One organizer described the importance of this kind of growth like this:

> Well in the short term obviously, we have these very small issue based economic fights, and you know it's helping people tackle, engaging people in struggle in their own life and then helping them actually win. In the long term I see it as helping people develop themselves as organizers, develop organizing skills, both for themselves and then just for everybody that is involved because it is such a collaborative and cooperative effort.

Every organizer hopes that SeaSol can provide practical training for people that will stay with them for the rest of their lives. This means training not only the individuals at the center of a specific campaign in how they can successfully face down their employer or landlord, but also providing useful experience for everyone involved in the campaign. A different

organizer described what this might look like in more specific terms:

> My hope is that we can build it [SeaSol] into a stronger and stronger force and it can lead to having a large number of people who are competent and confident at organizing and doing direct action, we can hopefully branch out from the types of fights we are doing and organize groups of workers in workplaces and tenants in apartment buildings.

This sort of transition is vital to SeaSol's future growth. Everyone who is heavily involved in SeaSol recognizes that the organization's present model is not going to be able to build a truly mass movement. Instead, they want to use SeaSol's current activities as a springboard to expose people to direct action and inspire people to want to organize on their job at work or as tenants in their buildings. The organization hopes to continue evolving not only so that it can become more effective at what it is already doing, but more importantly so it can increasingly transition to taking actions that involve larger and larger numbers of people—perhaps into new kinds of workers' and tenants' unions. As one of SeaSol's founders put it, he hoped SeaSol could, "serve as the foundation for a broader working class movement."

The Process of Politicization

Nearly all of the most active participants in SeaSol identify as revolutionaries. In its only written statement regarding its long-term political ambitions SeaSol states in a pamphlet describing the organization that it hopes to someday create "a world without bosses or landlords." As one SeaSol organizer described it, she believed that SeaSol is ultimately trying to:

> . . . build up enough people who are serious about taking control of their lives and who don't think bosses and landlords are necessary. To build up a militant, conscious, organized Left to take over, immediately, the sources of capitalism and that State that interfere the most

directly in our own lives and to take control of our own lives . . .

SeaSol is not only concerned with delivering immediate material victories to people. The organization is also passionately concerned with achieving these goals in a way that transforms people's opinions about society and empowers them to feel that the working-class could one day actually overturn the power relations that so utterly define their lives. First and foremost, SeaSol attempts to prefigure how such a society might work by focusing on how the organization is internally structured. This is why SeaSol is all volunteer and directly democratic. There is little difference between the ideological and practical reasoning for this. One of SeaSol's founding organizers explained the importance of SeaSol's decision-making process this way:

> To avoid authoritarianism is practical. It's sort of an ideological way of putting it, but it is a shorthand way of saying something that's practical that's much harder to describe in words. If we got in a situation where some individual or clique who isn't accountable to anyone else was able to force their will on the majority, force other people to do things that they didn't want to do rather than being free and democratic, then I don't think it would be possible to pursue the type of organizing we are trying to do. I think it would change the organizing model because our whole model is based on encouraging people to take action on their own because they want to.

SeaSol's organizers want to build a cooperative and egalitarian working-class movement to do away with those who they believe exercise illegitimate authority over other people's lives—namely bosses and landlords. Not only SeaSol's decision-making process, but also its entire strategic approach is intended to empower and politicize the people who become involved in the organization. This is one reason why SeaSol relies on direct action instead of legal or political action. They want to prove that when people are well organized, they can solve their own problems directly

and effectively. The overwhelming majority of SeaSol's organizers have backgrounds in various types of activism and became involved in SeaSol for precisely these reasons. But to what extent does SeaSol actually transform how those people who become involved for entirely practical reasons feel about contemporary society? Ramona from Renton said:

> I felt like to L&I I am just like another case number and it's very impersonal and with SeaSol I just met a lot of people that I just really related to, that made me feel welcome, that made me feel like my voice was important, and really supported me.

Another informant named George joined SeaSol to fight unjust charges brought against him by his former landlord regarding a bedbug infestation. He had similar reasons for deciding to join SeaSol:

> I know a little bit about the legal system and I know that attorneys are expensive and the legal process is—unfortunately—the landlord has a lot of money and a mansion you know and I can't afford to put myself in court against this man. It ain't gonna happen, I'm not gonna win. I had no resources to fight someone like that.

Both Ramona and George felt that their legal options were entirely inadequate. This frustration with their "official" options is undoubtedly what initially made SeaSol's approach so attractive to them, but their subsequent participation in a SeaSol campaign had a major impact on their personal beliefs about their own position in society. This does not mean that George or Ramona would now describe themselves as anarchists, as many SeaSol organizers and members do, and this is certainly not what SeaSol is trying to accomplish. Instead, SeaSol believes that taking action is a much more radicalizing experience than talking about politics in the abstract. This shared willingness to take direct action does not require everyone to share all of the same political beliefs. SeaSol's priority at this time is simply to build a shared culture of resistance for working-class power. One SeaSol organizer and anarchist who had confronted her own boss in the past as part of a union drive described the power of that kind of confrontational experience this way:

> I mean once you've marched on your own boss for instance, and I imagine it is the same for anybody who goes and confronts their landlord, it doesn't sound like a big deal handing this letter and saying, look, I demand what's right and I'm going to claim my right as another individual who should have equal power to you. It's definitely transformative. It is scary as hell and it's a huge moment of growth for people and it stays with you. It really does stay with you forever.

It was clear that Ramona and George were first brought into the organization by desperate circumstances and a willingness to try a different approach, but both of them said that they plan to remain permanently involved. Ramona described her opinion of SeaSol in these words:

> It's a really amazing organization that's really changed my whole perspective on things . . . it is like a family, I love it and I will always remain involved in SeaSol. I feel like I belong and I feel like it helps everyone feel like they belong, it's like a home.

It is significant that even though SeaSol was unable to recover her stolen wages, this did not taint her opinion of the organization. What was important to her was how her participation in the group made her feel. It made her feel that she belonged and that she does not have to face the injustices in her life alone. Ramona did not join SeaSol because she had read the theories of Bakunin or Marx and was inspired by their ideas, Ramona joined SeaSol because Ciro Donofrio stole her wages and she thought SeaSol could help. She remains involved with SeaSol not because she has adopted an anarchist or a Marxist position, but because she wants to be part of SeaSol where she feels a sense of empowerment and belonging. George

recalled similar sentiments in his experience with SeaSol:

> It really saved my ass because the landlord would have sent it to collections- and it made me believe in other human beings in the world . . . I was very happy to get help from SeaSol and you know I feel like I can help and that's the nice thing about Seattle Solidarity. They helped me and I'm trying to help, what I can, back, because I like what they're doing number one and plus I feel like I owe Seattle Solidarity for the help.

One organizer noted:

> It [SeaSol] gives me a sense of something I've always been wanting . . . it's like we are making better lives for ourselves as immediately as possible and for people after us. To me that is meaning in itself and it's also a group of people who is also ready to be solid for you . . . to me building that up and making it more powerful is the most important thing I can think of to do to change what I think is wrong with the world.

SeaSol gives people at all levels of participation hope and a sense that they just might be able to change working-class issues that are close to home. Whether SeaSol's long-term strategy will work or not, there is little doubt that SeaSol has greatly influenced how its participants view the world. SeaSol is not a mass revolutionary working-class social movement at the moment, but it is undoubtedly reaching new people and exposing them to experiences that makes them believe in the power of their own united effort.

Conclusion

SeaSol is an extraordinary example of radical political praxis. The success of SeaSol's practical approach should give pause to those who believe revolutionary ideologies are irrelevant in the contemporary United States. SeaSol's revolutionary members are not only finding common ground with typical members of the working-class, they are taking common action, action that is delivering real material gains to SeaSol's members while forging new social relationships based on shared struggles. SeaSol has had enough success in the past three years to begin attracting the attention of other activists both nationally and internationally. Solidarity networks have begun to emerge across the country as a direct result of people learning about SeaSol's activities. Presently, solidarity networks have been formed in the cities of Atlanta, Boston, Iowa City, New York, Oakland, San Diego, San Francisco, and Santa Cruz. Internationally, people have been inspired by SeaSol's work to start their own solidarity networks in Canada, England, Scotland, Australia, and New Zealand. It is much too soon to say whether this model will grow into an actual popular movement in the United States or remain simply the obscure activity of a few scattered groups of like-minded individuals. Nevertheless, the continuing development of this new kind of working-class social movement demands further research and deserves to be followed closely in the coming years.

REFERENCES

Bauer, Scott, Todd Richmond. 2011. "Thousands protest Wisconsin's anti-union bill." MSNBC Online, February 17. Retrieved April 9, 2011 (http://www.msnbc.msn.com/id/41624142/ns/politics-more_politics/)

Bauer, Scott. 2011. "Scott Walker Signs Wisconsin Union Bill Into Law." The Huffington Post, March 11. Retrieved June 29, 2011 (http://www.huffingtonpost.com/2011/03/11/scott-walker-signs-wiscon_n_834508.html)

Bell, Mary. 2011. "Statement from WEAC President Mary Bell." Washington Education Association Council, March 9, 2011. Retrieved June 29, 2011 (http://www.weac.Org/news_and_publications/11-03-09/Statement_from_WEAC_President_Mary_Bell_on_Senate_vote.aspx)

Davey, Monica. 2011. "Republican Tactics End Wisconsin Stalemate." The New York Times, March 9. Retrieved June 30, 2011 (http://www.nytimes.com/2011/03/10/us/10wisconsin.html?_r=1)

DeFour, Matthew. 2011. "Madison schools closed Wednesday due to district wide teacher sickout." Wisconsin State Journal, February 16. Retrieved June 29, 2011 (http://host.madison.com/wsj/news/local/education/local_schools/article e3cfe584-3953-11eO-9284-001cc4c03286.html)

Haas, Kevin, Greg Stanely. 2011. "Wisconsin Democrats Flee to Clock Tower." Rockford Register Star, February 17. Retrieved April 9, 2011 (http.7/www.rrstar.com/carousel/x43522562/Wisconsin-Democrats-flee-to-Rockford-to-block-anti-union-bill)

Mayers, Jeff. 2011. "Divided Supreme Court Upholds Wisconsin Law." Reuters, June 14. Retrieved June 29, 2011 (http://www.reuters.com/article/2011/06/15/us-wisconsin-unions-idUSTRE75D6O520110615)

MSNBC. 2011. "Wisconsin Protesters Vacate Capitol After Judge Orders Them Out." MSNBC.com. Retrieved June 29, 2011 (http://www.msnbc.msn.com/id/41884135/)

Ramirez, Antonio. 2011. "Wisconsin Solidarity Rallies Today in all 50 States." Change.org. Retrieved April 9, 2011 (http://news.change.org/stories/wisconsin-solidarity-rallies-today-in-all-50-states).

Seattle Solidarity Network. 2010. "Problems with your Boss or Landlord?" Outreach poster.

Seattle Solidarity Network. 2011. "Three month fight puts thieving restaurant out of business." Retrieved May 30, 2011 (www.seasol.net).

State of Wisconsin. 2011-2012 State Legislature. 2011. "Bill." Madison, Wisconsin: January 2011 Special Session. Retrieved April 9, 2011 (http://bloximages.chicago2.vip.townnews.com/host.madison.com/content/tncms/assets/editorial/f/8c/e99/f8ce991a-3612-11e0-97f9-001cc4c03286 revisions/4d558a5d60362.pdf.pdf)

WISC-TV. 2011. "Senate Votes to Strip Collective Bargaining Rights." Channel300.com (http://www.channel3000.com/politics/27138601/detail.html)

Wisconsin Reporter. 2011. "Jesse Jackson Outside Capitol Part One." Retrieved June 29, 2011 (http://www.wisconsinreporter.com/jesse-jackson-outside-capitol-pt-2)

Wisconsin Taxpayers Alliance. 2011. "The Wisconsin Taxpayer." The Wisconsin Taxpayer's Alliance. Retrieved April 9, 2011 (http://www.wistax.org/taxpayer/10Wiwo283.pdf)

THINKING ABOUT THE READING

Describe the principles and strategy of the working-class social movement known as the Seattle Solidarity Network (SeaSol). How does Winslow contrast SeaSol with larger working-class social movements like unions? What are their similarities? What are their differences? According to Winslow, why is SeaSol experiencing success and how are its members politicized from their participation? What was the motivation for the founding of SeaSol? How has SeaSol influenced its participants in the architecture of their own lives?

Challenging Power

Toxic Waste Protests and the Politicization of White, Working-Class Women

Celene Krauss

(1998)

Over the past two decades, toxic waste disposal has been a central focus of women's grassroots environmental activism. Women of diverse racial, ethnic, and class backgrounds have assumed the leadership of community environmental struggles around toxic waste issues (Krauss 1993). Out of their experience of protest, these women have constructed ideologies of environmental justice that reveal broader issues of inequality underlying environmental hazards (Bullard 1990, 1994). Environmental justice does not exist as an abstract concept prior to these women's activism. It grows out of the concrete, immediate, everyday experience of struggles around issues of survival. As women become involved in toxic waste issues, they go through a politicizing process that is mediated by their experiences of class, race, and ethnicity (Krauss 1993).

Among the earliest community activists in toxic waste protests were white, working-class women. This [article] examines the processby which these women became politicized through grassroots protest activities in the 1980s, which led to their analyses of environmental justice, and in many instances to their leadership in regional and national toxic waste coalitions. These women would seem unlikely candidates for becoming involved in political protest. They came out of a culture that shares a strong belief in the existing political system, and in which traditional women's roles center around the private arena of family. Although financial necessity may have led them into the workplace, the primary roles from which they derived meaning, identity, and satisfaction are those of mothering and taking care of family. Yet, as we shall see, the threat that toxic wastes posed to family health and community survival disrupted the taken-for-granted fabric of their lives, politicizing women who had never viewed themselves as activists. . . .

This [article] shows how white, working-class women's involvement in toxic waste issues has wider implications for social change. . . . These women . . . fought to close down toxic waste dump sites, to prevent the siting of hazardous waste incinerators, to oppose companies' waste-disposal policies, to push for recycling projects, and so on. Their voices show us . . . that their single-issue community protests led them through a process of politicization and their broader analysis of inequities of class and gender in the public arena and in the family. Propelled into the public arena in defense of their children, they ultimately challenged government, corporations, experts, husbands, and their own insecurities as working-class women. Their analysis of environmental justice and inequality led them to form coalitions with labor and people of color around environmental issues. These women's traditional beliefs about motherhood, family, and democracy served a crucial function in this politicizing process. While they framed their analyses in terms of traditional constructions of gender and the state, they actively reinterpreted these constructions into an oppsitional ideology, which became a resource of resistance and a source of power in the public arena.

Subjective Dimensions of Grassroots Activism

In most sociological analysis of social movements, the subjective dimension of protest has often been ignored or viewed as private and individualistic. . . . [Contemporary theories] show us how experience is not merely a personal, individualistic concept: it is social. People's experiences reflect where they fit into the social hierarchy. . . . Thus, white, working-class women interpret their experience of toxic waste problems within the context of their particular cultural history, arriving at a critique that reflects broader issues of class and gender. . . .

. . . This article focuses on the subjective process by which white, working-class women involved in toxic waste protests construct an oppositional consciousness out of their everyday lives, experiences, and identities. As these women became involved in the public arena, they confronted a world of power normally hidden from them. This forced them to re-examine their assumptions about private and public power and to develop a broad reconceptualization of gender, family, and government.

The experience of protest is central to this process and can reshape traditional beliefs and values (see Thompson 1963). My analysis reveals the contradictory ways in which traditional culture mediates white, working-class women's subjective experience and interpretation of structural inequality. Their protests are framed in terms of dominant ideologies of motherhood, family, and a deep faith in the democratic system. Their experience also reveals how dominant ideologies are appropriated and reconstructed as an instrument of their politicization and a legitimating ideology used to justify resistance. For example, as the political economy of growth displaces environmental problems into their communities, threatening the survival of children and family and creating everyday crises, government toxic waste policies are seen to violate their traditional belief that a democratic government will protect their families. Ideologies of motherhood and democracy

become political resources which these women use to initiate and justify their resistance, their increasing politicization, and their fight for a genuine democracy.

Methodological Considerations

My analysis is based on the oral and written voices of white, working-class women involved in toxic waste protests. Sources include individual interviews, as well as conference presentations, pamphlets, books, and other written materials that have emerged from this movement. Interviews were conducted with a snowball sample of twenty white, working-class women who were leaders in grassroots protest activities against toxic waste landfills and incinerators during the 1980s. These women ranged in age from twenty-five to forty; all but one had young children at the time of their protest. They were drawn from a cross section of the country, representing urban, suburban, and rural areas. None of them had been politically active before the protest; many of them, however, have continued to be active in subsequent community movements, often becoming leaders in state-wide and national coalitions around environmental and social justice issues. I established contact with these women through networking at activist conferences. Open-ended interviews were conducted between May 1989, and December 1991, and lasted from two to four hours. The interview was designed to generate a history of these women's activist experiences, information about changes in political beliefs, and insights into their perceptions of their roles as women, mothers, and wives.

Interviews were also conducted with Lois Gibbs and four other organizers for the Citizens Clearinghouse for Hazardous Wastes (CCHW). CCHW is a nation-wide organization created by Gibbs, who is best known for her successful campaign to relocate families in Love Canal, New York. Over the past two decades, this organization has functioned as a key resource for community groups fighting around toxic waste issues in the United States. Its leadership and staff are composed primarily of women, and the organization played a key role in shaping the ideology of working-class women's environmental activism in the 1980s. . . .

The Process of Politicization

Women identify the toxic waste movement as a women's movement, composed primarily of mothers. As one woman who fought against an incinerator in Arizona and subsequently worked on other anti-incinerator campaigns throughout the state stressed: "Women are the backbone of the grassroots groups, they are the ones who stick with it, the ones who won't back off." Because mothers are traditionally responsible for the health of their children, they are more likely than others within their communities to begin to make the link between toxic waste and their children's ill health. And in communities around the United States, it was women who began to uncover numerous toxin-related health problems: multiple miscarriages, birth defects, cancer, neurological symptoms, and so on. Given the placement of toxic waste facilities in working-class and low-income communities and communities of color, it is not surprising that women from these groups have played a particularly important role in fighting against environmental hazards.

White, working-class women's involvement in toxic waste issues is complicated by the political reality that they, like most people, are excluded from the policy-making process. For the most part, corporate and governmental disposal policies with far-reaching social and political consequences are made without the knowledge of community residents. People may unknowingly live near (or even on top of) a toxic waste dump, or they may assume that the facility is well regulated by the government. Consequently, residents are often faced with a number of problems of seemingly indeterminate origin, and the information withheld from them may make them unwitting contributors to the ill health of their children.

The discovery of a toxic waste problem and the threat it poses to family sets in motion a process of critical questioning about the relationship between women's private work as mothers and the public arena of politics. The narratives of the women involved in toxic waste protests focus on political transformation, on the process of "becoming" an activist. Prior to their discovery of the link between their family's health and toxic waste, few of these women had been politically active. They saw their primary work in terms of the "private" sphere of motherhood and family. But the realization that toxic waste issues threatened their families thrust them into the public arena in defense of this private sphere. According to Penny Newman:

> We woke up one day to discover that our families were being damaged by toxic contamination, a situation in which we had little, if any, input. It wasn't a situation in which we chose to become involved, rather we did it because we had to . . . it was a matter of our survival. (Newman 1991, 8)

Lois Gibbs offered a similar account of her involvement in Love Canal:

> When my mother asked me what I wanted to do when I grew up, I said I wanted to have six children and be a homemaker. . . . I moved into Love Canal and I bought the American Dream: a house, two children, a husband, and HBO. And then something happened to me and that was Love Canal. I got involved because my son Michael had epilepsy . . . and my daughter Melissa developed a rare blood disease and almost died because of something someone else did. . . . I never thought of myself as an activist or an organizer. I was a housewife, a mother, but all of a sudden it was my family, my children, and my neighbors. . . .

It was through their role as mothers that many of these women began to suspect a connection between the invisible hazard posed by toxic wastes and their children's ill health, and this was their first step toward political activism. At Love Canal, for example, Lois Gibbs's fight to expose toxic waste hazards was triggered by the link she made between her son's seizures and the toxic waste dump site. After reading about toxic hazards in a local newspaper, she thought about her son and then surveyed her neighbors to find that they had similar health problems. In Woburn, Massachusetts, Ann Anderson found that other neighborhood children were, like her son, being treated for leukemia, and she began to wonder if this was an unusually high incidence of the disease. In Denver, mothers comparing stories at Tupperware parties were led to question the unusually large number of sick and dying children in their community. These women's practical activity as mothers and their extended networks of family and community led them to make the connection between toxic waste and sick children—a discovery process rooted in what Sara Ruddick (1989) has called the everyday practice of mothering, in which, through their informal networks, mothers compare notes and experiences, developing a shared body of personal, empirical knowledge.

Upon making the link between their family's ill health and toxic wastes, the women's first response was to go to the government, a response that reflects a deeply held faith in democracy embedded in their working-class culture. They assumed that the government would protect the health and welfare of their children. Gibbs (1982, 12) reports:

> I grew up in a blue-collar community, I was very patriotic, into democracy . . . I believed in government. . . . I believed that if you had a complaint, you went to the right person in government. If there was a way to solve the problem, they would be glad to do it.

An Alabama activist who fought to prevent the siting of an incinerator describes a similar response:

> We just started educating ourselves and gathering information about the problems of incineration. We didn't think our elected officials knew. Surely, if they knew that there was already a toxic waste dump in our county, they would stop it.

In case after case, however, these women described facing a government that was indifferent, if not antagonistic, to their concerns. At Love Canal, local officials claimed that the toxic waste pollution was insignificant, the equivalent of smoking just three cigarettes a day. In South Brunswick, New Jersey, governmental officials argued that living with pollution was the price of a better way of life. In Jacksonville, Arkansas, women were told that the dangers associated with dioxin emitted from a hazardous waste incinerator were exaggerated, no worse than "eating two or three tablespoons of peanut butter over a thirty-year period." Also in Arkansas, a woman who linked her ill health to a fire at a military site that produced Agent Orange was told by doctors that she was going through a "change of life." In Stringfellow, California, eight hundred thousand gallons of toxic chemical waste pumped into the community [water supply] flowed directly behind the elementary school and into the playground. Children played in contaminated puddles yet officials withheld information from their parents because "they didn't want to panic the public."

Government's dismissal of their concerns about the health of their families and communities challenged these white, working-class women's democratic assumptions and opened a window on a world of power whose working they had not before questioned. Government explanations starkly contradicted the personal, empirical evidence which the women discovered as mothers, the everyday knowledge that their children and their neighbors' children were ill. Indeed, a recurring theme in the narratives of these women is the transformation of their beliefs about government. Their politicization is rooted in a deep sense of violation, hurt, and betrayal from finding out their government will not protect their families. Echoes of this disillusionment are heard from women throughout the country. In the CCHW publication *Empowering Women* (1989, 31) one activist noted:

> All our lives we are taught to believe certain things about ourselves as women, about democracy and justice, and about people

in positions of authority. Once we become involved with toxic waste problems, we need to confront some [of] our old beliefs and change the way we view things.

Lois Gibbs summed up this feeling when she stated:

There is something about discovering that democracy isn't democracy as we know it. When you lose faith in your government, it's like finding out your mother was fooling around on your father. I was very upset. It almost broke my heart because I really believed in the system. I still believe in the system, only now I believe that democracy is of the people and by the people, that people have to move it, it ain't gonna move by itself.

These women's loss of faith in "democracy" as they had understood it led them to develop a more autonomous and critical stance. Their investigation shifted to a political critique of the undemocratic nature of government itself, making the link between government inaction and corporate power, and discovering that government places corporate interests and profit ahead of the health needs of families and communities. At Love Canal, residents found that local government's refusal to acknowledge the scope of the toxic waste danger was related to plans of Hooker Chemical, the polluting industry, for a multi-million dollar downtown development project. In Woburn, Massachusetts, government officials feared that awareness of the health hazard posed by a dump would limit their plans for real-estate development. In communities throughout the United States, women came to see that government policies supported waste companies' preference of incineration over recycling because incineration was more profitable.

Ultimately, their involvement in toxic waste protests led these women to develop a perspective on environmental justice rooted in issues of class and a critique of the corporate state. They argued that government's claims—to be democratic, to act on behalf of the public interest, to hold the family sacrosanct—are false. One woman who fought an incinerator in Arizona recalled:

I believed in government. When I heard EPA, I thought, "Ooh, that was so big." Now I wouldn't believe them if they said it was sunny outside. I have a list of the revolving door of the EPA. Most of them come from Browning Ferris or Waste Management, the companies that plan landfills and incinerators.

As one activist in Alabama related:

I was politically naive. I was real surprised because I live in an area that's like the Bible belt of the South. Now I think the God of the United States is really economic development, and that has got to change.

Another activist emphasized:

We take on government and polluters.... We are up against the largest corporations in the United States. They have lots of money to lobby, pay off, bribe, cajole, and influence. They threaten us. Yet we challenge them with the only things we have—people and the truth. We learn that our government is not out to protect our rights. To protect our families we are now forced to picket, protest and shout. (Zeff, 1989, 31)

In the process of protest, these women were also forced to examine their assumptions about the family as a private haven, separate from the public arena, which would however be protected by the policies and actions of government should the need arise. The issue of toxic waste shows the many ways in which government allows this haven to be invaded by polluted water, hazardous chemicals, and other conditions that threaten the everyday life of the family. Ultimately, these women arrived at a concept of environmental injustice rooted in the inequities of power that displace the costs of toxic waste unequally onto their communities. The result was a critical political stance that contributed to the militancy of their activism. Highly traditional values of democracy and motherhood remained central to their lives: they justified their resistance as mothers protecting their children and working to make the promise of democracy real. Women's politicization around toxic waste protests led them to transform their traditional beliefs into resources of opposition which enabled them to enter the public arena and challenge its legitimacy, breaking down the public/private distinction.

Appropriating Power in the Public Arena

Toxic waste issues and their threat to family and community prompted white, working-class women to redefine their roles as mothers. Their work of mothering came to extend beyond taking care of the children, husband, and housework; they saw the necessity of preserving the family by entering the public arena. In so doing, they discovered and overcame a more subtle process of intimidation, which limited their participation in the public sphere.

As these women became involved in toxic waste issues, they came into conflict with a public world where policy makers are traditionally white, male, and middle class. The Citizen's Clearinghouse for Hazardous Waste, in the summary of its 1989 conference on women and organizing, noted:

> Seventy to eighty percent of local leaders are women. They are women leaders in acommunity run by men. Because of this, many of the obstacles that these women face as leaders stem from the conflicts between their traditional female role in the community and their new role as leader: conflicts with male officials and authorities who have not yet adjusted to these persistent, vocal, head-strong women challenging the system. . . . Women are frequently ignored by male politicians, male government officials and male corporate spokesmen.

Entering the public arena meant overcoming internal and external barriers to participation, shaped by gender and class. White, working-class women's reconstructed definition of

motherhood became a resource for this process, and their narratives reveal several aspects of this transformation.

For these women, entering the public arena around toxic waste issues was often extremely stressful. Many of them were initially shy and intimidated, as simple actions such as speaking at a meeting opened up wider issues about authority, and experiences of gender and class combined to heighten their sense of inadequacy. Many of these women describe, for example, that their high-school education left them feeling ill-equipped to challenge "experts," whose legitimacy, in which they had traditionally believed, was based on advanced degrees and specialized knowledge.

One woman who fought to stop the siting of an incinerator in her community in Arizona recalled: "I used to cry if I had to speak at a PTA meeting. I was so frightened." An activist in Alabama described her experience in fighting the siting of an incinerator in her community:

> I was a woman . . . an assistant Sunday School teacher. . . . In the South, women are taught not to be aggressive, we're supposed to be hospitable and charitable and friendly. We don't protest, we don't challenge authority. So it was kind of difficult for me to get involved. I was afraid to speak. And all of a sudden everything became controversial. . . . I think a lot of it had to do with not knowing what I was. . . . The more I began to know, the better I was . . . the more empowered.

Male officials further exacerbated this intimidation by ignoring the women, by criticizing them for being overemotional, and by delegitimizing their authority by labeling them "hysterical housewives"—a label used widely, regardless of the professional status of the woman. In so doing, they revealed an antipathy to emotionality, a quality valued in the private sphere of family and motherhood but scorned in the public arena as irrational and inappropriate to "objective" discourse.

On several levels, the debate around toxic waste issues was framed by policy makers in such a way as to exclude women's participation, values, and expression. Women's concerns about their children were trivialized by being placed against a claim that the wider community benefits from growth and progress. Information was withheld from them. Discourse was framed as rational, technical, and scientific, using the testimony of "experts" to discredit the everyday empirical knowledge of the women. Even such details as seating arrangements reflected traditional power relations and reinforced the women's internalization of those relations.

These objective and subjective barriers to participation derived from a traditional definition of women's roles based on the separation of the public and private arenas. Yet it is out of these women's political redefinition of the traditional role of mother that they found the resources to overcome these constraints, ultimately becoming self-confident and assertive. They used the resources of their own experience to alter the power relations they had discovered in the public arena.

The traditional role of mother, of protector of the family and community, served to empower these activists on a number of levels. From the beginning, their view of this role provided the motivation for women to take risks in defense of their families and overcome their fears of participating in the public sphere. A woman who fought the siting of an incinerator in Arkansas described this power:

> I was afraid to hurt anyone's feelings or step on anyone's toes. But I'm protective and aggressive, especially where my children are concerned. That's what brought it out of me. A mother protecting my kids. It appalled me that money could be more important than the health of my children.

A mother in New Jersey described overcoming her fear in dealing with male governmental officials at public hearings, "When I look at a male government official, I remember that he was once a little boy, born of a woman like me, and then I feel more powerful." In talking about Love Canal, Lois Gibbs showed the power of motherhood to carry women into activities alien to their experience:

> When it came to Love Canal, we never thought about ourselves as protestors. We carried signs, we barricaded, we blocked the gates, we were arrested. We thought of it as parents protecting our children. In retrospect, of course, we were protesting. I think if it had occurred to us we wouldn't have done it.

In these ways, they appropriated the power they felt in the private arena as a source of empowerment in the public sphere. "We're insecure challenging the authority of trained experts," notes Gibbs, "but we also have a title of authority, 'mother.'"

Working-class women's experiences as organizers of family life served as a further source of empowerment. Lois Gibbs noted that women organized at Love Canal by constantly analyzing how they would handle a situation in the family, and then translating that analysis into political action. For example, Gibbs explained:

> If our child wanted a pair of jeans, who would they go to? Well they would go to their father since their father had the money—that meant we should go to Governor Carey.

Gibbs drew on her own experience to develop organizing conferences that helped working-class women learn to translate their skills as family organizers into the political arena.

> I decided as a housewife and mother much of what I learned to keep the household running smoothly were skills that translated very well into this new thing called organizing. I also decided that this training in running a home was one of the key reasons why so many of the best leaders in the toxic movement—in fact, the overwhelming majority—are women, and specifically women who are housewives and mothers. (Zeff 1989, 177)

Of her work with the CCHW, Gibbs stated:

> In our own organization we're drawing out these experiences for women. So we say, what do you mean you're not an organizer? Are you a homemaker—then God damn it you can organize and you don't know it. So, for example,

when we say you need to plan long-term and short-term goals, women may say, I don't know how to do that. . . . We say, what do you mean you don't know how to do that? Let's talk about something in the household—you plan meals for five, seven, fourteen days—you think about what you want for today and what you're going to eat on Sunday—that is short-term and long-term goals.

Movement language like "plug up the toilet," the expression for waste reduction, helped women to reinterpret toxic waste issues in the framework of their everyday experience. "If one does not produce the mess in the first place, one will not have to clean it up later," may sound like a maternal warning, but the expression's use in the toxic waste context implies a radical economic critique, calling for a change in the production processes of industry itself.

As women came to understand that government is not an objective, neutral mediator for the public good, they discovered that "logic" and "objectivity" are tools used by the government to obscure its bias in favor of industry, and motherhood became a strategy to counter public power by framing the terms of the debate. The labels of "hysterical housewives" or "emotional women," used by policy makers to delegitimize the women's authority, became a language of critique and empowerment, one which exposed the limits of the public arena's ability to address the importance of family, health, and community. These labels were appropriated as the women saw that their emotionalism, a valued trait in the private sphere, could be transformed into a powerful weapon in the public arena.

> What's really so bad about showing your feelings? Emotions and intellect are not conflicting traits. In fact, emotions may well be the quality that makes women so effective in the movement. . . . They help us speak the truth.

Finally, through toxic waste protests, women discovered the power they wield as mothers to bring moral issues to the public, exposing the contradictions of a society that purports to value motherhood and family, yet creates social policies that undermine these values:

> We bring the authority of mother—who can condemn mothers? . . . It is a tool we have. Our crying brings the moral issues to the table. And when the public sees our children it brings a concrete, moral dimension to our experience. . . . They are not an abstract statistic.

White, working-class women's stories of their involvement in grassroots toxic waste protests reveal their transformations of initial shyness and intimidation into the self-confidence to challenge the existing system. In reconceptualizing their traditional roles as mothers, these women discovered a new strength. As one activist from Arizona says of herself, "Now I like myself better. I am more assertive and aggressive." These women's role in the private world of family ultimately became a source of personal strength, empirical knowledge, and political strategy in the public sphere. It was a resource of political critique and empowerment which the women appropriated and used as they struggled to protect their families.

Overcoming Obstacles to Participation: Gender Conflicts in the Family

In order to succeed in their fights against toxic wastes in their homes and communities, these women confronted and overcame obstacles not only in the public sphere, but also within the family itself, as their entry into the public arena disrupted both the power relationships and the highly traditional gender roles within the family. Divorce and separation were the manifestations of the crises these disruptions induced. All of the women I interviewed had been married when they first became active in the toxic waste movement. By the time of my interviews with them, more than half were divorced.

A central theme of these women's narratives is the tension created in their marriages by participation in toxic waste protests. This aspect of struggle, so particular to women's lives, is an especially hidden dimension of white, working-class women's activism. Noted one activist from New York:

> People are always talking to us about forming coalitions, but look at all we must deal with beyond the specific issue, the flack that comes with it, the insecurity of your husband that you have outgrown him. Or how do you deal with your children's anger, when they say you love the fight more than me. In a blue-collar community that is very important.

For the most part, white, working-class women's acceptance of a traditional gendered division of labor has also led them to take for granted the power relations within the family. Penny Newman, who was the West Coast Director of CCHW, reflected on the beginnings of her community involvement:

> I had been married just a couple of years. My husband is a fireman. They have very strict ideas of what family life is in which the woman does not work, you stay at home. . . . I was so insecure, so shy, that when I finally got to join an organization, a woman's club, . . . it would take me two weeks to build up the courage to ask my husband to watch the kids that night. I would really plan out my life a month ahead of time just to build in these little hints that there is a meeting coming up in two weeks, will you be available. Now, if he didn't want to do it, or had other plans, I didn't go to the meeting. (Zeff 1989, 183)

Involvement in toxic waste issues created a conflict between these traditional assumptions and women's concerns about protecting their children, and this conflict made visible the power relations within the family. The CCHW publication *Empowering Women* (1989, 33) noted that:

> Women's involvement in grassroots activism may change their views about the world and their relations with their husbands. Some husbands are actively supportive. Some take no stand: "Go ahead and do what you want. Just

make sure you have dinner on the table and my shirts washed." Others forbid time away from the family.

Many of these women struggled to develop coping strategies to defuse conflict and accommodate traditional gender-based power relations in the family. The strategies included involving husbands in protest activities and minimizing their own leadership roles. As Lois Gibbs commented: "If you bring a spouse in, if you can make them part of your growth, then the marriage is more likely to survive, but that is real hard to do sometimes." Will Collette, a former director at CCHW, relates the ways in which he has observed women avoiding acknowledged leadership roles. He described this encounter with women involved in a toxic waste protest in New York:

> I was sitting around a kitchen table with several women who were leading a protest. And they were complaining about how Lou and Joe did not do their homework and weren't able to handle reports and so on. I asked them why they were officers and the women were doing all the work. They said, "That's what the guys like, it keeps them in and gives us a little peace at home."

In a similar vein, Collette recalled working with an activist from Texas to plan a large public hearing. Upon arriving at the meeting, he discovered that she was sitting in the back, while he was placed on the dais along with the male leadership, which had had no part in the planning process.

As the women became more active in the public arena, traditional assumptions about gender roles created further conflict in their marriages. Women who became visible community leaders experienced the greatest tension. In some cases, the husbands were held responsible for their wives' activities, since they were supposed to be able to "control" their wives. For example, a woman who fought against an incinerator in Arkansas related:

> When the mayor saw my husband, he wanted to know why he couldn't keep his pretty little

wife's mouth shut. As I became more active and more outspoken, our marriage became rockier. My husband asked me to tone it down, which I didn't do.

In other cases, women's morals were often called into question by husbands or other community members. Collette relates the experience of an activist in North Dakota who was rumored to be having an affair. The basis for the rumor, as Collette describes, was that "an uppity woman has got to be promiscuous if she dares to organize. In this case, she was at a late-night meeting in another town, and she slept over, so of course she had to have had sex."

Toxic waste issues thus set the stage for tremendous conflict between these women and their husbands. Men saw their roles as providers threatened: the homes they had bought may have become valueless; their jobs may have been at risk; they were asked by their wives to take on housework and child care. Meanwhile, their wives' public activities increasingly challenged traditional views of gender roles. For the women, their husbands' negative response to their entry into the public sphere contradicted an assumption in the family that both husband and wife were equally concerned with the well-being of the children. In talking about Love Canal, Gibbs explained:

> The husband in a blue-collar community is saying, get your ass home and cook me dinner, it's either me or the issue, make your choice. The woman says: How can I make a choice, you're telling me choose between the health of my children and your fucking dinner, how do I deal with that?

When women were asked to choose between their children and their husbands' needs, they began to see the ways in which the children had to be their primary concern.

At times this conflict resulted in more equal power relations within the marriages, a direction that CCHW tried to encourage by organizing family stress workshops. By and large, however, the families of activist women did not tolerate this stress well. Furthermore,

as the women began openly to contest traditional power relations in the family, many found that their marriages could not withstand the challenges. As one activist from Arkansas described:

> I thought [my husband] didn't care enough about our children to continue to expose them to this danger. I begged him to move. He wouldn't. So I moved my kids out of town to live with my mom.

All twenty women interviewed for this article were active leaders around toxic waste issues in their communities, but only two described the importance of their husband's continuing support. One white woman who formed an interracial coalition in Alabama credited her husband's support in sustaining her resolve:

> I've had death threats. I was scared my husband would lose his job, afraid that somebody's going to kill me. If it weren't for my husband's support, I don't think I could get through all this.

In contrast, most of these activists described the ongoing conflict within their marriages, which often resulted in their abandoning their traditional role in the family, a process filled with inner turmoil. One woman described that turmoil as follows:

> I had doubts about what I was doing, especially when my marriage was getting real rocky. I thought of getting out of [the protest]. I sat down and talked to God many, many times. I asked him to lead me in the right direction because I knew my marriage was failing and I found it hard leaving my kids when I had to go to meetings. I had to struggle to feel that I was doing the right thing. I said a prayer and went on.

Reflecting on the strength she felt as a mother, which empowered her to challenge her government and leave her marriage, she continued:

> It's an amazing ordeal. You always know you would protect your children. But it's amazing to find out how far you will go to protect your own kids.

The disruption of the traditional family often reflected positive changes in women's empowerment. Women grew through the protest; they became stronger and more self-confident. In some cases they found new marriages with men who respected them as strong individuals. Children also came to see their mothers as outspoken and confident.

Thus, for these women, the particularistic issue of toxic waste made visible oppression not only in the public sphere, but also in the family itself. As the traditional organization of family life was disrupted, inequities in underlying power relations were revealed. In order to succeed in fighting a toxic waste issue, these women had also to engage in another level of struggle as they reconceptualized their traditional role in family life in order to carry out their responsibilities as mothers.

Conclusion

The narratives of white, working-class women involved in toxic waste protests in the 1980s reveal the ways in which their subjective, particular experiences led them to analyses that extended beyond the particularistic issue to wider questions of power. Their broader environmental critique grew out of the concrete, immediate, everyday experience of struggling around survival issues. In the process of environmental protest, these women became engaged with specific governmental and corporate institutions and they were forced to reflect on the contradictions of their family life. To win a policy issue, they had to go through a process of developing an oppositional or critical consciousness which informed the direction of their actions and challenged the power of traditional policy makers. The contradiction between a government that claimed to act on behalf of the family and the actual environmental policies and actions of that government were unmasked. The inequities of power between white, working-class women and middle-class, male public officials were made visible. The reproduction within the

family of traditional power relationships was also revealed. In the process of protest these women uncovered and confronted a world of political power shaped by gender and class. This enabled them to act politically around environmental issues, and in some measure to challenge the social relationships of power, inside and outside the home.

Ideologies of motherhood played a central role in the politicizing of white, working-class women around toxic waste issues. Their resistance grew out of an acceptance of a sexual division of labor that assigns to women responsibility for "sustaining the lives of their children and, in a broader sense, their families, including husband, relatives, elders and community." . . .

The analysis of white, working-class women's politicization through toxic waste protests reveals the contradictory role played by dominant ideologies about mothering and democracy in the shaping of these women's oppositional consciousness. The analysis these women developed was not a rejection of these ideologies. Rather, it was a reinterpretation, which became a source of power in the public arena. Their beliefs provided the initial impetus for involvement in toxic waste protests, and became a rich source of empowerment as they appropriated and reshaped traditional ideologies and meanings into an ideology of resistance. . . .

REFERENCES

Bullard, Robert D. 1990. *Dumping in Dixie: Race, Class and Environmental Quality.* Boulder, CO: Westview Press.

Bullard, Robert D. 1994. *Communities of Color and Environmental Justice.* San Francisco: Sierra Club Books.

Citizen's Clearing House for Hazardous Wastes. 1989. *Empowering Women.* Washington, DC: Citizen's Clearinghouse for Hazardous Wastes.

Krauss, Celene. 1993. "Women and Toxic Waste Protests: Race, Class and Gender as Resources of Resistance." *Qualitative Sociology* 16(3): 247–262.

Newman, Penny. 1991. "Women and the Environment in the United States of America." Paper presented at the Conference of Women and the Environment, Bangladore, India.

Ruddick, Sara. 1989. *Maternal Thinking: Towards a Politics of Peace*. New York: Ballantine Books.

Thompson, E. P. 1963. *The Making of the English Working Class*. New York: Pantheon Books.

Zeff, Robin Lee. 1989. "Not in My Backyard/Not in Anyone's Backyard: A Folklorist Examination of the American Grassroots Movement for Environmental Justice." Ph.D. dissertation, Indiana University.

THINKING ABOUT THE READING

Krauss describes how ordinary women became mobilized to construct a movement for social change when they felt their children's health was being threatened. Did their traditional beliefs about motherhood and family help or hinder their involvement in this protest movement? What effect did their participation have on their own families? Why do the women Krauss interviewed identify the toxic waste movement as a women's movement? Why don't men seem to be equally concerned about these health issues? How did the relative powerlessness of their working-class status shape the women's perspective on environmental justice?

Credits

Chapter 1

Chapter 2

Chapter 3

Chapter 4

Chapter 5

Chapter 6

Chapter 7

Chapter 8

Chapter 9

Chapter 10

Chapter 11

From "Racial and Ethnic Formation" from *Racial Formation in the United States: From the 1960's to the 1990's,* 2nd edition, by Michael Omi and Howard Winant. Copyright © 1994 by Michael Omi and Howard Winant. Reprinted with permission from Routledge.

From "Optional Ethnicities" by Mary Waters from *Origins and Destinies: Immigration, Race, and Ethnicity in America,* 1st edition. Edited by Pedraza and Rumbaut. Copyright © 1996 South-Western, a part of Cengage Learning, Inc. Reproduced by permission, www.cengage.com/permissions.

From "Jeremy Lin's Model Minority Problem" by Maxwell Leung. *Contexts,* Summer 2013, Vol. 12, No. 3, pp. 52–56.

Chapter 12

From "Black Women and a New Definition of Womanhood" by Bart Landry from *Black Working Wives: Pioneers of the American Family Revolution* by Bart Landry. Copyright © 2000 by the Regents of the University California. Reprinted by permission of the University of California Press.

Excerpts from "*Still a Man's World: Men Who Do 'Women's Work'*" by Christine L. Williams. Copyright © 1995 by the Regents of the University California. Reprinted by permission of the University of California Press.

From "New Biomedical Technologies, New Scripts, New Genders" by Eve Shapiro in *Gender Circuits: Bodies and Identities in a Technological Age.* Copyright © 2010 Taylor & Francis. Reprinted with permission.

Chapter 13

From "India's Reproductive Assembly Line" by Sharmila Rudrappa. *Contexts.* Spring 2012, Vol. 11, No. 2, pp.22-27.

From "Love and Gold" by Arlie Russell Hochschild from *Global Woman: Nannies, Maids, and Sex Workers in the New Economy* by Barbara Erhrenreich and Arlie Russell Hochschild. Copyright © 2002 by Barbara Ehrenreich and Arlie Russell Hochschild. Reprinted by permission of Henry Holt and Company, LLC.

From "Age-Segregation in Later Life: An Examination of Personal Networks" by Peter Uhlenberg and Jenny DeJong Gierveld from *Ageing and Society,* Vol. 24, No: 1. pp. 5–28.

Chapter 14

From "'Aquí Estamos y No Nos Vamos!' Global Capital and Immigrant Rights" by William Robinson from *Race & Class* Vol. 48, No. 2, 2006.

From "The Seattle Solidarity Network: A New Approach to Working Class Social Movements" by Walter Winslow.

From *Community Activism and Feminist Politics: Organizing Across Race, Class, and Gender* by Nancy A. Naples. Copyright © 1998 by Routledge. Reproduced by permission of Routledge/Taylor & Francis Books, Inc

$SAGE research**methods**

The essential online tool for researchers from the world's leading methods publisher

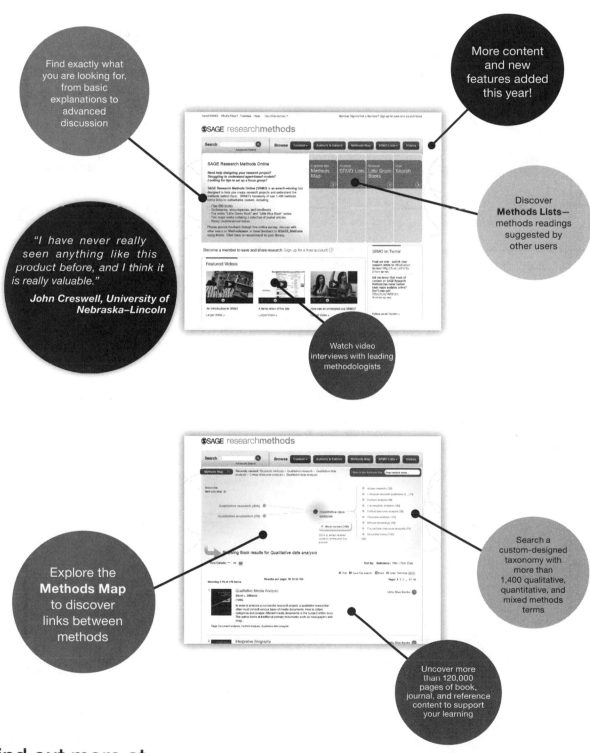

Find exactly what you are looking for, from basic explanations to advanced discussion

More content and new features added this year!

"I have never really seen anything like this product before, and I think it is really valuable."

John Creswell, University of Nebraska–Lincoln

Discover **Methods Lists**— methods readings suggested by other users

Watch video interviews with leading methodologists

Explore the **Methods Map** to discover links between methods

Search a custom-designed taxonomy with more than 1,400 qualitative, quantitative, and mixed methods terms

Uncover more than 120,000 pages of book, journal, and reference content to support your learning

Find out more at
www.sageresearchmethods.com

STUDIES IN BAPTIST HISTORY AND THOUGHT
VOLUME 33

A Dictionary of European Baptist Life and Thought

STUDIES IN BAPTIST HISTORY AND THOUGHT
VOLUME 33

A full listing of titles in this series
appears at the end of this book

This volume is published in co-operation with the
International Baptist Theological Seminary, Prague,
Czech Republic

STUDIES IN BAPTIST HISTORY AND THOUGHT
VOLUME 33

A Dictionary of European Baptist Life and Thought

General Editor John H.Y. Briggs

Foreword by David Coffey

Paternoster:
thinking faith

MILTON KEYNES · COLORADO SPRINGS · HYDERABAD

British Library Cataloguing in Publication Data
A catalogue record for this book is available from the British Library

ISBN 978-1-84227-535-1

Typeset by Philip Alexander
Printed and bound in Great Britain
by AlphaGraphics Nottingham

Series Preface

Baptists form one of the largest Christian communities in the world, and while they hold the historic faith in common with other mainstream Christian traditions, they nevertheless have important insights which they can offer to the worldwide church. Studies in Baptist History and Thought will be one means towards this end. It is an international series of academic studies which includes original monographs, revised dissertations, collections of essays and conference papers, and aims to cover any aspect of Baptist history and thought. While not all the authors are themselves Baptists, they nevertheless share an interest in relating Baptist history and thought to the other branches of the Christian church and to the wider life of the world.

The series includes studies in various aspects of Baptist history from the seventeenth century down to the present day, including biographical works, and Baptist thought is understood as covering the subject-matter of theology (including interdisciplinary studies embracing biblical studies, philosophy, sociology, practical theology, liturgy and women's studies). The diverse streams of Baptist life throughout the world are all within the scope of these volumes.

The series editors and consultants believe that the academic disciplines of history and theology are of vital importance to the spiritual vitality of the churches of the Baptist faith and order. The series sets out to discuss, examine and explore the many dimensions of their tradition and so to contribute to their on-going intellectual vigour.

A brief word of explanation is due for the series identifier on the front cover. The fountains, taken from heraldry, represent the Baptist distinctive of believer's baptism and, at the same time, the source of the water of life. There are three of them because they symbolize the Trinitarian basis of Baptist life and faith. Those who are redeemed by the Lamb, the book of Revelation reminds us, will be led to 'fountains of living waters' (Rev. 7.17).

Series Editors

Anthony R. Cross, Fellow of the Centre for Baptist History and Heritage, Regent's Park College, Oxford, UK

Curtis W. Freeman, Research Professor of Theology and Director of the Baptist House of Studies, Duke University, North Carolina, USA

Stephen R. Holmes, Lecturer in Theology, University of St Andrews, Scotland, UK

Elizabeth Newman, Professor of Theology and Ethics, Baptist Theological Seminary at Richmond, Virginia, USA

Philip E. Thompson, Assistant Professor of Systematic Theology and Christian Heritage, North American Baptist Seminary, Sioux Falls, South Dakota, USA

Series Consultants

David Bebbington, Professor of History, University of Stirling, Scotland, UK

Paul S. Fiddes, Professor of Systematic Theology, University of Oxford, and Principal of Regent's Park College, Oxford, UK

Ken R. Manley, Distinguished Professor of Church History, Whitley College, The University of Melbourne, Australia

Stanley E. Porter, President and Professor of New Testament, McMaster Divinity College, Hamilton, Ontario, Canada

To the memory of Wiard Popkes, a great European Baptist New Testament scholar, who was part of the original editorial team for this volume but who was tragically taken from us before it was completed

and

To the students and faculty of IBTS 1949-2009

Foreword

I am delighted to commend this Baptist initiative in 'compact' theology - some 700 articles from Advent to Zwingli, embracing both theological and pastoral topics as well as informative articles on Baptist life in every part of the EBF.

This is a book written by Baptists for Baptists. The Editors' aims have been to provide from European resources, and from a European perspective, an account of both contemporary Baptist life and thought, and of the heritage that stands behind it. This should both provide European Baptists, especially in Eastern Europe where bibliographic resources are limited, with an authoritative reference work to assist them to nourish their own constituencies in Baptist identity, as well as making available a useful reference work for non-Baptists, or Baptists in other parts of the world, anxious to ascertain Baptist attitudes – varied though they may be – on particular issues.

The volume aims to embrace a wide variety of viewpoints amongst the European Baptist family, as it also tackles a wide and diverse range of topics in an attempt to help its readers at least start on the task of learning more. Themes engaged include aspects of ecclesiology, liturgy and worship, community service, and mission. Theological subjects are not neglected and neither are issues in ethics and the history and heritage of our churches. Ecclesiastical organisations receive due attention as does Baptist witness in the various countries within the EBF.

I am sure that the wide distribution of this book amongst our constituency and beyond will be of great advantage to our nurture and our witness.

David Coffey
President, Baptist World Alliance
May 2009

inclined to suggest questions than to lay down rules, or offer final answers.

[2] THE AIM OF THE PROJECT was therefore the preparation of a one-volume scholarly book in the English language, with entries arranged in alphabetical order, giving an account of both contemporary Baptist life and thought and of the heritage that stands behind this. In its turn the hope is that this work will promote scientific research into different aspects of the European Baptist tradition, strengthen the identity of its members and reveal both the strengths and weaknesses of its present witness potentials, thereby encouraging future development of this part of Christ's church in the territories covered by Baptist unions belonging to the EBF. It is hoped that it will become a principal standard reference source for Baptists and non-Baptists interested in the history, theology and practice of European Baptists and their service in the world.

[3] SCOPE OF THE WORK: The adjective European plays a key part in describing this book's contents. Other geographical areas have different histories and may indeed have different emphases in thought and practice. This dictionary is about European Baptists working in their own area of witness. Their influence has been felt all round the world and they too have received help from other regions, but the detail of such matters is not the subject of attention here. However, we do have to admit that the EBF's activities are not limited by continental boundaries but extend to those Asiatic territories which were parts of the former Soviet Union and to the countries of the Near East. The territorial borders of the work are, therefore, identical with those of the EBF. Subject-wise the dictionary does not confine itself to any one particular discipline of analysis – biblical, theological, historical and practical – or any one aspect of Baptist witness. Rather we have sought to make it as comprehensive as possible; having in mind that perhaps it might be the only theological dictionary on the bookshelf of a Baptist pastor, for example, somewhere in Siberia. Since Baptists would not want to claim special theological emphases in all areas of Christian belief and practice, a number of entries connected with the major emphases of the Christian faith are not covered as extensively here as in some other dictionaries because Baptists do not differ from the classical teaching of the Christian Church on these basic doctrines.

[4] METHOD OF WORKING: The direction of the work has been undertaken by a small editorial committee. The original plan was to have a general editor who would be assisted by a number of section editors, but for a number of practical reasons that did not prove possible. For example, part way through the process the project was deprived of the weight of Professor Wiard Popkes' scholarship by his premature death but not happily before he had completed most of the articles that had been assigned to him. We would want to take this opportunity to pay tribute to his contribution and his encouragement of the project at the editorial meetings he was able to attend. We deeply regret that he has not been able to complete the journey with us to see the volume published. Because so many of the original sectional editors were unable to

serve, the direction of the project has become more centred on the general editor and the staff of IBTS than they would have wished. The selection of articles was determined by identifying nine general areas of interest within which to seek and secure entries:

Ecclesiology
Worship and Liturgy
Theology
Diakonia
Mission
Ethics
History and Heritage
Organisations
Biography

Some thought that we had some topics under the wrong headings, but that did not matter, for the only purpose of the sectional lists was to secure as comprehensive a coverage of topics as possible. The only difficulty is that for some topics we have received more than one entry and when this has happened we have either edited them into one entry or have decided to publish both.

In addition to topics identified within the nine chosen themes there are national entries for all countries represented in the membership of the Federation, together with entries for all their theological institutions.

In editing the entries the editors have been mindful of the book's intended readership. Accordingly some articles which were more concerned with technical issues of biblical interpretation, issues in themselves very important and undergirding the interpretation here offered, have had to be edited in favour of exposition and analysis of more general significance. Others which may have over represented a particular national viewpoint/situation have had to be 'Europeanised', indeed a number of authors themselves requested that this be done. In other cases there was a need to harmonise entries. Further since many readers would read the articles as representative of Baptist views in Europe in general, which of course are far from being uniform, some further central editing has had to take place so that the volume may be owned by the whole family. Regrettably, since the project had no dedicated secretariat, only that tasked with caring for all IBTS activities, it has not been possible to refer back to authors to discuss these changes.

[5] BIOGRAPHIES: It became apparent to the editorial committee that the nominations for biographical entries from the different countries were far too uneven to proceed with this part of the enterprise, whilst it was too late to return to the constituency to secure a more even spread of entries. It was therefore decided with some regret that all but a minimum of biographical entries should not be published in the main dictionary but would be published later in a *Biographical Dictionary of European Baptists*. Those retained are

those from outside the Baptist tradition who have made a significant impact on Baptist history, some of the founders of the movement and those who had a Europe-wide significance.

[6] SPONSORING INSTITUTION: The initiative for producing this dictionary has been closely connected with the International Baptist Theological Seminary in Prague, as the main educational institution serving the whole of the EBF family. It is fitting that it should appear both in the year in which Baptists are celebrating the 400th anniversary of their separate existence and the 60th anniversary of IBTS which was founded in Rüschlikon, Switzerland in 1949 and relocated to Prague, Czech Republic in 1996-97.

[7] ACKNOWLEDGMENTS: A volume of this kind obviously depends on the work of the many scholars that our authors and editors have consulted and to which they are deeply indebted. They apologise for any unintended use of other people's writings not properly acknowledged. The whole enterprise has benefited enormously from the energies of the staff of the IBTS, and in particular to successive personal assistants to the rector, the late Maureen White, Lina Andronovienė, and Vanessa Lake, who have all cheerfully and professionally handled a mass of amorphous writings in several languages, and have helped by their tact and discretion to keep the project moving forward. For the last stage of the project, profound thanks needs to be expressed to Phil Alexander for preparing the text for the publishers. Additionally we would want to express our thanks to Dr. Anthony R. Cross for shepherding us in this exciting venture, innovatory both for those who have attempted to translate a vision into a volume, and for Paternoster as publishers.

John H.Y. Briggs
For the Editorial Team

List of Contributors

EDITORIAL GROUP

(JHYB) Briggs, John H.Y. (United Kingdom) General editor.
Director of the Centre for Baptist History and Heritage, Regent's Park College, University of Oxford. Research Professor in Baptist history, International Baptist Theological Seminary, Prague, Czech Republic.

(KGJ) Jones, Keith G. (United Kingdom)
Rector, International Baptist Theological Seminary, Prague, Czech Republic.

(IMR) Randall, Ian M. (United Kingdom)
Senior Research Fellow in Baptist and Anabaptist Studies, International Baptist Theological Seminary, Prague, Czech Republic. Director of Research, Spurgeon's College, London.

(PAE) Eidberg, Peder A. (Norway)
Retired lecturer in Baptist History, Stabbek Seminary, Oslo.

(SVS) Sannikov, Sergei V. (Ukraine)
Director of Theological Education for the Ukrainian Evangelical Christian-Baptists. Executive director, the Euro Asiatic Accrediting Association.

(TP) Pilli, Toivo (Estonia)
Rector, the Baptist Theological Seminary, Tartu, Estonia.

(WP) Popkes, Wiard (who died during the work of compilation)
Research Professor in Biblical Studies, International Baptist Theological Seminary, Prague, Czech Republic. Professor of Biblical Studies, University of Hamburg.

CONTRIBUTORS

(AA) Ajaj, Azar (Israel) Lecturer of Nazareth Evangelical Theological School.

(AAD) Antonio Albert Dominguez (Spain) Pastor of Pueblo Nuevo Baptist Church in Madrid. Librarian for the Spanish Religious Evangelical Entities Federation (FEREDE). Alumnus, IBTS, Prague, Czech Republic.

(AAP) Peck, Anthony A. (United Kingdom) General Secretary, EBF.

(AB) Bârzu, Adrian (Romania) Alumnus, IBTS, Prague, Czech Republic. Pastor Baptist Union of Romania.

(AD) Dügeroglu, Ayhan (Turkey) Pastor, Izmir Independent Protestant Church.

(AG) Gilmore, Alec (United Kingdom) Lecturer in Theology, IBTS, Prague, Czech Republic. Former Director, Eurolit.

(AK) Kravtsev, Andrei (Russia) Alumnus, IBTS, Prague Czech Republic. Principal of the North Caucasus Bible Institute, Prohladny.

(AlG) Golloshi, Alfred (Albania) Alumnus, IBTS, Prague, Czech Republic. Pastor, Freedom Baptist Church, Tirana.

(ALa) Latuzis, Albertas (Lithuania) Director Baptist and Anabaptist Research Centre, Klaipeda. Former President of Lithuanian Baptists.

(AL) Lohikko, Anneli (Finland) Alumna of IBTS, Prague, Czech Republic. Finnish Baptist Union (Finnish-Speaking)

(AN) Nahapetyan, Asatur (Armenia) General Secretary, Union of Evangelical Christian Baptist Churches of Armenia. Alumnus, IBTS, Prague, Czech Republic.

(AP) Popov, Alexander (Russia) Moscow Baptist Seminary. Research Student, IBTS, Prague, Czech Republic

(ARC) Cross, Anthony R. (United Kingdom) Director Elect of the Centre for Baptist History and Heritage, Regent's Park College, University of Oxford.

(AS) Szirtes, András (Hungary) (deceased) Former Lecturer at the Hungarian Baptist Theological Seminary.

(BB) Bjelajac, Branko (Serbia) Serbian Historian from the Church of the Nazarene, lecturing in Novi Sad Seminary.

(BBow) Bowers, Brian (United Kingdom) Retired Curator, The Science Museum, London. Life Deacon and former Treasurer, Bloomsbury Central Baptist Church, London.

(BH) Hylleberg, Bent (Denmark) Danish Baptist Historian. Principal of the Danish Baptist Seminary.

(BJS) Stanley, Brian J. (United Kingdom) Professor of World Christianity, New College, Edinburgh. Director of the Centre for the Study of Christianity in the Non-Western World, Edinburgh.

(BT) Talbot, Brian (Scotland) Minister, Broughty Ferry Baptist Church, Dundee, Scotland.

(BTar) Tarranger, Billy (Norway) Former General Secretary and Former Rector of the Baptist Theological Seminary, Stabekk, Norway.

(CJMG) Gorton, Catriona J.M. (United Kingdom) Minister at Hugglescote Baptist Church, East Midlands, UK. Alumna of Northern Baptist College, Manchester.

(CP) Prokhorov, Constantine (Russia) Lecturer in Church History, Omsk Theological Baptist Seminary. Research Student, IBTS, Prague, Czech Republic.

(DA) Adam, Dejan (Serbia) Research Student, IBTS, Prague, Czech Republic.

(DBM) Murray, Derek B. (Scotland) Retired Baptist Minister. Former College Tutor, Scottish Baptist College. Now resident in Aberdeenshire, Scotland.

(DDC) Chetti, Daniel D. (Lebanon) Arab Baptist Theological Seminary.

(DDM) Morgan, D. Densil (Wales) Professor of Theology, University of Bangor. Warden, Y Coleg Gwyn, the North Wales Baptist College, Bangor.

(DH) Howell, David (United Kingdom) Centre for Youth Ministries.

(DJ) Jackson, Darrell (United Kingdom) Baptist Minister. Director of Nova Research Centre. Tutor in European Studies, Redcliffe College, Gloucestershire, UK.

(DJT) Tidball, Derek J. (United Kingdom) Former Principal of the London School of Theology. Former Head of the Department of Mission, BUGBI.

(DaL) Lagergren, David (Sweden) Former Missionary to the Congo. Former Rector of Bethel Theological Seminary, Stockholm. Former General Secretary of the Baptist Union of Sweden. President of EBF, 1983-85.

(DL) Lütz, Dietmar (Germany) Pastor of Johann-Gerhard-Oncken-Congregation, Hamburg.

(DP) Peterlin, Davorin (Croatia) New Testament Scholar. Former Director of the Keston Institute, Oxford, UK.

(DT) Tomasetto, Domenico (Italy)

(DW) Weiand, Dietrich
EBM Latin America
Mission Secretary.

(EL) Lucas, Ernest
(United Kingdom)
Vice Principal, Bristol
Baptist College, UK.

(EM) Mazis, Edgars
(Latvia)
Baptist Pastor, Riga.
Alumnus, IBTS, Prague,
Czech Republic.

(EP) Pilli, Einike
(Estonia)
Development Officer,
Open University Centre,
University of Tartu.
Member Tartu Salem
Baptist Church, Estonia.

(EV) Várady, Endre
(Hungary)
Lecturer in New
Testament, Baptist
Theological Seminary,
Budapest.

(FE) Emeish, Fawaz
(Jordan)
President of the Board,
The Baptist School of
Amman, Jordan.

**(FGS) Graf-Stuhlhofer,
Franz** (Austria)
Austrian Baptist
Historian and
Theologian. Lecturer at
University of Vienna.

(FH) Haddad, Fuad
(Israel)
Chairman of the
Association of Baptist
Churches in Israel.

**(FMM) Méndez-
Moratalla, Fernando**
(Spain)
Seminario Teológico,
UEBE, Madrid.

**(FS) Scaramuccia,
Franco** (Italy)

**(FWB) Bowers, Faith
W.** (United Kingdom)
Member of Bloomsbury
Central Baptist Church,
London. A director of
the London Baptist
Association. Former
member of BUGBI
Council. Sub-editor,
Baptist Quarterly.

**(GA) Ashworth,
Graham** (United
Kingdom)
Former Pro Vice-
Chancellor, the
University of Salford.
President of BUGB,
2000-01. Research
Professor IBTS, Prague,
Czech Republic –
President, Federation of
Environmental
Education. Trustee, the
John Rae Initiative.

**(GAW) Abraham-
Williams, Gethin**
(Wales)
Baptist Minister. Former
General Secretary,
CYTUN, Church
Together in Wales.

(GB) Balders, Günter
Former Lecturer in
Church History, German
Baptist Seminary, Elstal,
Berlin.

(GJ) Göran Janzon
(Sweden)
Lecturer in Mission
Studies and former
Principal, Örebro
Theological Seminary
(1978-81, 1985-98)

(GL) Lie, Geir
(Norway)
Historical Theology
scholar and lecturer.

(GLN) Nichols, Gregory L. (USA)
Research Student, IBTS, Prague, Czech Republic.

(HG) Guderian, Hans (Germany)
Baptist Pastor, Berlin. Former General Secretary of EBM.

(IB) Benedetti, Italo (Italy)
Pastor, via del Teatro Valle Baptist Church, Rome.

(IH) Hoskins, Iain (United Kingdom)
Tutor, Bristol Baptist College.

(IN) Noble, Ivana (Czech Republic)
Senior Research Fellow, IBTS, Prague, Czech Republic. Docent, Evangelical Faculty of Theology, Charles University, Prague, Czech Republic.

(IS) Shehadeh, Imad (Jordan)
President, Jordan Evangelical Seminary.

(JAK) Kirk, J. Andrew
Former Dean and Head of the School of Mission and World Christianity, Selly Oak Colleges. Senior Research Fellow, IBTS, Prague, Czech Republic.

(JB) Biggs, John (United Kingdom)
Former Lecturer in Chemistry, the University of Hull, UK. President of BUGB (1989-90). Moderator of the Free Church Council in the UK.

(JD) Dyck, Johannes (Germany)
Computer consultant. Alumnus, IBTS, Prague, Czech Republic.

(JDW) Weaver, John D.
Principal of South Wales Baptist College.

(JE) Edström, Jan (Finland)
Baptist Pastor. Former General Secretary, Finnish Ecumenical Council.

(JFVN) Nicholson, John F.V. (United Kingdom)
Former North Eastern Area Superintendent, BUGB.

(JGMP) Purves, James G.M. (Scotland)
Pastor, Bristo Baptist Church, Edinburgh, Scotland. Lecturer in Theology, IBTS, Prague, Czech Republic.

(JJS) Skarre, Jan Jørgen (Norway)
Organist of Eben Ezer, Drammen Baptist Church, Drammen, Norway.

(JS) Sæthre, Jan (Norway)
President of the Baptist Union of Norway. Chair of Finance Committee, EBF.

(KES) Smith, Karen E.
Tutor in Church History and Spirituality, South Wales Baptist College. Pastor, Orchard Place Baptist Church, Neath, Wales.

(KJ) Jarosz, Katarzyna (Poland)
Alumna, IBTS, Prague, Czech Republic. Research Student, Queen's University, Belfast, UK.

(KTB) Bakke, Kai Torre (Norway)
Assistant Professor, Baptist Theological Seminary of Norway, Stabbekk

(LA) Andronovienė, Lina (Lithuania)
Director, the Non-Residential Bible School of the Baptist Union of Lithuania. Course Leader, Applied Theology, IBTS, Prague, Czech Republic.

(LB) Bethell, Lauran (USA)
Global Mission Coordinator on Trafficking and Prostitution, American Baptist Churches – International Ministries.

(LEH) Holmqvist, Leif-Erik (Finland)
Finnish Baptist Union (Finnish-Speaking).

(LK) Kucová, Lydie
Registrar and Lecturer in Old Testament, IBTS, Prague, Czech Republic.

(LM) Mikhovich, Leonid (Belarussia)
Rector, Baptist Theological Seminary, Minsk. Research Student, IBTS, Prague, Czech Republic.

(LN) Nittnaus, Lothar (Switzerland)
Retired minister.

(MB) Banfield, Michael (United Kingdom)
Baptist Minister. Senior Chaplain, London Luton Airport.

(MD) Dowling, Maurice (United Kingdom)
Lecturer, Irish Baptist College, Belfast, UK.

(MEW) Whalley, Mary E. (United Kingdom)
Deacon, Blenheim Baptist Church, Leeds, UK. Lecturer in Early Learning, Leeds Metropolitan University.

(MHT) Taylor, Michael H. (United Kingdom)
Retired Professor of Social Theology, University of Birmingham, UK. Former Director of Christian Aid, UK.

(MI) Ivanov, Mikahil (Russia)
Lecturer at Moscow Baptist Theological Seminary.

(MIB) Bochenski, Michael I. (United Kingdom)
Former Rector, Warsaw Baptist Seminary, Warsaw. Pastor, Rugby Baptist Church, UK.

(MKi) Michael Kisskalt (Germany)
Professor of Missiology, Elstal Baptist Theological Seminary, Berlin.

(MK) Karetnikova, Marina (Russia)
Baptist Historian.

(MN) Nersisyan, Mihran (Armenia)

(MR) Remmel, Meego (Estonia)
President of the Union of Free Evangelical and Baptist Churches of Estonia.

(MS) Songulashvili, Malkhaz (Georgia)
Baptist (Arch)bishop, the Evangelical Baptist Church of Georgia.

(NC) Csényi, Norbert (Hungary)
Research Student, IBTS, Prague, Czech Republic.

(NFS) Skarre, Niels F. (Norway)
Lecturer in Sociology, Oslo, Norway.

(NGW) Wright, Nigel G. (United Kingdom)
Principal, Spurgeon's College, London.

(NJW) Wood, Nick J.
(United Kingdom)
Lecturer, Regent's Park
College, Oxford.
Director of MTh Studies
and the Oxford Centre
for Christianity and
Culture.

(NK) Kember, Norman
(United Kingdom)
Retired Professor of
Biophysics. Member,
Harrow Baptist Church,
London. Committee
Member and former
President, Baptist Peace
Fellowship.

(OAJ) Joø, Odd A.
(Norway)
Senior Pastor of Baerum
Baptist Church, Stabekk,
Norway. Lecturer in
Historic and Systematic
Theology, Baptist
Theological Seminary,
Stabekk, Norway

(OB) Bunaciu, Otniel
(Romania)
President of the Baptist
Union of Romania.
Professor, Baptist
Theological Faculty,
University of Bucharest.

**(OES) Szebeni, Oliver
E.** (Hungary)
Baptist Theological
Seminary, Budapest.

(OJ) Olegs Jermolajevs
(Latvia)
Principal, Latvian
Baptist Seminary, Riga.
Alumnus, IBTS, Prague,
Czech Republic.

**(OL) Lundergaard,
Ole** (Denmark)
Baptist Pastor and
scholar.

**(OR) Raychynets,
Oksana** (Ukraine)
Lecturer, Ukraininan
Evangelical Theological
Seminary, Kiev.
Alumna, IBTS, Prague,
Czech Republic.

(PaS) Sanders, Paul
(Lebanon)
Chancellor, Arab Baptist
Theological Seminary,
Lebanon.

(PeM) Petr Macek
(Czech Republic)
Docent, Protestant
Theological Faculty,
Charles University,
Prague, Czech Republic.

**(PBM) Beasley-Murray,
Paul** (United Kingdom)
Senior Minister, Central
Baptist Church,
Chelmsford, UK.
Former Principal,
Spurgeon's College.

(PC) Clarke, Peter
(United Kingdom)
Retired Baptist Minister.
Former Chaplain,
Mildmay Mission
Hospital, London.

(PF) Fiddes, Paul
(United Kingdom)
Professorial Research
Fellow, Regent's Park
College, University of
Oxford.

(PFP) Penner, Peter F.
(Germany)
Course Leader in
Biblical Studies, IBTS,
Prague, Czech Republic.

(PFW) Walker, Paul F.
(United Kingdom)
Minister, Highgate
Baptist Church,
Birmingham, UK.
Lecturer, the Urban
Theology Unit,
University of
Birmingham, UK.

(PG) Goodliff, Paul
(United Kingdom)
Head of the Department
of Ministry, BUGB.
Former Senior Regional
Minister, Central Baptist
Association, UK.

(PH) Halliday, Philip
(United Kingdom)
Regional Secretary for
Europe, BMS World
Mission.

(PJM) Morden, Peter J. (United Kingdom) Tutor at Spurgeon's College, London.

(PM) Montacute, Paul (United Kingdom) Director, Baptist World Aid, BWA, Falls Church, Virginia, USA.

(PMi) Midteide, Per (Norway) Pastor, Skien Baptist Church, Norway.

(PMIL) Liland, Peder M.I. (Norway) Pastor/lecturer Lillesand.

(PO) Osenenko, Pavel (Belarus) Lecturer in Baptist History, Minsk Theological Seminary, Belarus.

(PRP) Parushev, Parush R. (Bulgaria) Pro-Rector, IBTS, Prague, Czech Republic.

(PS) Shepherd, Peter (United Kingdom) Minister, Broadway Baptist Church, Derby, UK. President, Baptist Historical Society, UK.

(PV) Veselá, Petra (Czech Republic) Kvestorká, IBTS, Prague, Czech Republic.

(PZ) Zvagulis, Peter (Latvia) Research Student, IBTS, Prague, Czech Republic.

(RH) Hayden, Roger (United Kingdom) Archivist, Bristol Baptist College, UK. Former President, Baptist Historical Society, UK. Former Area Superintendent, BUGB.

(RK) Knežević, Ruben Author in Biblical Studies and Baptist History scholar.

(RNS) Shuff, Roger N. (United Kingdom) Retired Baptist Minister.

(SCJ) Jewery, Sue-Clements (United Kingdom) Marriage Guidance Counsellor. Member, New North Road Baptist Church, Huddersfield, UK.

(SH) Holmes, Stephen (United Kingdom) Baptist Minister. Lecturer in Systematic Theology, St Mary's College, the School of Divinity, University of St Andrews.

(SS) Stiegler, Stefan (Germany) Chaplain, Albertinien Hospital, Hamburg. Former rector, Elstal Baptist Theological Seminary, Berlin.

(SV) Verhaeghe, Samuel (Belgium) President of the Union of Baptists in Belgium.

(TaP) Petrova, Tanya (Bulgaria) Lecturer and Former Rector, Bulgarian Evangelical Theological Institute, Sofia.

(TvdL) Tuen Van der Leer (Netherlands) Rector, Dutch Baptist Seminary, Barnveldt, Netherlands.

(TB) Bergsten, Torsten (Sweden) Member, Valsätra United Congregation Uppsala, Sweden.

(TBO) Oprenov, Teodor B. (Bulgaria) General Secretary of the Baptist Union of Bulgaria.

(TFTN) Noble, Timothy F.T. (United Kingdom) Course Leader for Magister of Theology and Contextual Missiology (MTh) degree programmes, IBTS, Prague, Czech Republic.

(TG) Grass, Tim (United Kingdom) Associate Lecturer, Spurgeon's College, London.

(TKJ) Jones, Timothy K. (United Kingdom) Deacon, Bloomsbury Central Baptist Church, London. Climate Change Policy Officer, the World Development Movement.

(TVC) Cheprasov, Timofey V (Russia) Research Student, IBTS, Prague, Czech Republic.

(VS) Spangenberg, Volker (Germany) Rector, Elstal Baptist Theological Seminary, Berlin.

(WJA) Allen, W. (Bill) J. (United Kingdom) Former Regional Minister, Yorkshire Baptist Association and Tutor at Spurgeon's College, London.

(WH) Huizing, Wout (Netherlands) Lecturer, Dutch Baptist Seminary, Netherlands.

(YP) Pusey, Yona (Wales) Former Chairperson, European Baptist Women's Union

(ZW) Wierzchowski, Zbigniew (Poland) Pastor, Glogow Baptist Church, Poland. Research Student, IBTS, Prague, Czech Republic.

A

ABC-USA
See *American Baptist Churches, USA*.

Abortion
[See also *Birth Control*]
Arising from the conviction that life begins at the moment of conception, and is given by God, voluntary abortion would be seen as morally wrong fairly universally among European Baptists, with possible exceptions, in some communities, in the case of rape or a woman's life being in danger, or indeed as a result of discovering the unborn child is extremely likely to have a severe genetic disability which would lead to a very poor quality of life for both the child and the wider family.

An additional set of questions has been added with the development of genetic research and technological progress such as in the selective reduction of multiple embryos in the treatment of infertility, stem cell research, and so on. However, public debate on these issues has to date not been prominent among Baptists in Europe.

LA

Absolution
Absolution follows *confession* of *sin*, and if appropriate, restitution. It is when Zacchaeus (Lk 19:1-10) prepares to return stolen *property* and give half of his goods to the *poor* that *Jesus* declares that *salvation* has come to his house. In Baptist *tradition* absolution may be described as the assurance of the *forgiveness* of sins after confession, and 1Jn 1:9 'if we confess our sins, he is faithful and just to forgive us our sins' has often been quoted as a reassurance of such pardon, always recognising that forgiveness belongs to God alone.

In *Catholic* practice absolution is given by the priest who has heard such individual confession along with the demand for the performance of stated penances. In Baptist and *Protestant* practice it is usually seen as a personal transaction between the believer and the Saviour. In more recent worship books, the leader may pronounce absolution after the *Prayers* of Confession, as in the 1994 *Book of Common Order of the Church of Scotland*, or offer forgiveness in more general terms. The 2005 British Baptist book of *Worship*, *Gathering for Worship*, p.44, has prayers after confession in which the leader offers absolution but this is not done on the basis of *apostolic ordination* to priestly office.

Discipline has played an important part in the life of Baptist churches, and exclusion from the *Lord's Table* because of flagrant sin and disobedience and lack of subsequent *repentance* has been a powerful agent in preserving purity in the Church. There are however instances in Church Books of sinners repenting and being received back into full *fellowship*, and this represents a process of absolution, although that may not be the word used. As with confession so with absolution we may need to re-interpret unfamiliar concepts to deepen our individual spiritual lives and strengthen the fellowship of our churches by losing our fear of sharing intimate details of our lives with a trusted other person.

DBM

FURTHER READING: John Colwell, *Promise and Presence* (esp. ch. 8 'The Sacrament of Cleansing'), Paternoster, Carlisle, 2005. Christopher Ellis and Myra Blyth (eds) for the Baptist Union of Great Britain, *Gathering for Worship*, Canterbury, Norwich, 2005. P. Sheppy, 'Penance' in A.R. Cross and Philip Thompson, *Baptist Sacramentalism, II*, Paternoster, Carlisle, 2006

ACT International
[See also *Emergency/Disaster Relief*]
ACT (Action by Churches Together) International, formed in 1995 and based in the *WCC* complex in Geneva brings together Christian humanitarian and development agencies and partner churches throughout the world. It enables a common ground for cooperation and coordination amongst such organisations and with related Christian denominations.

The organisation involves an Emergency Committee (or *General Assembly*) which comprises 30 elected members from around the world who meet annually to shape ACT policies. An Executive Committee comprising six of the elected members, and one person each representing the *WCC* and the *Lutheran* World Federation (Lutherans have been responsible for funding of the work) meets several times a year to oversee the implementation of policies and mandates of the ACT CO.

Amongst ACT International *membership* are European churches, national aid and development agencies such as *Christian Aid* (*United Kingdom*), *Danchurch Aid* (*Denmark*), Finnchurch Aid (*Finland*), Brot für die Welt [*Bread for the World*] (*Germany*) and also more denominational agencies such as *Hungarian Baptist Aid. Ecumenical* in formation, Baptists often participate in the work of ACT International through their *national council of churches.*

ET

Administrators, European Baptists in the 20th and 21st centuries

The gift of administration is one of the *gifts* of the *Holy Spirit* to which the *Apostle* Paul specifically refers in 1Co 12. However, amongst many Christians the *work* of administration in regional, national or continental spheres is seen much more as a 'necessary evil' compared to *preaching*, engaging in *mission*, teaching *theology*, leading *choirs* and so on, which are seen by many as higher gifts. Nevertheless, European Baptists have been blessed in the past century by gifted individuals who have placed gifts of administration in finance, building projects, organisational structures and the like at the disposal of Baptist communities, often with great effect.

In the realm of finance David E. Nixon and later Jan Sæthre have developed the work of the *EBF* Finance Committee and offered advice and skills to those responsible for finance in member bodies. Lawyers who have contributed to wider European Baptist life have been John V. Beaumont, Peter D. Deutsch and Petra Veselá, developing legal frameworks for the development of European Baptist institutions as legal entities.

Administrators of note who have served the wider community have included Barbara Askew, Maureen White, Karin Schaffrik, Helle

Liht and Gergana Atanassova.

Undoubtedly the succession of EBF General Secretaries have had this gift and placed it at the disposal of the whole European Baptist family – W.O. Lewis, Henry Cook, Erik Rudén, C. Ronald Goulding, Gerhard Claas, Knud Wümpelmann, Karl Heinz Walter, Theodor Angelov and Anthony A. Peck.

KGJ

Advent

This is a four week period of the year set aside as a preparation for the celebration of the incarnation, or the nativity. In the West Advent begins on the fourth Sunday before *Christmas* (late Nov or very early Dec). The name is derived from the Latin root meaning 'coming' or 'arrival'.

The early western church from the 6th century onwards had a period of six weeks of *fasting* and penitence before Christmas. The reduction to four weeks was a gradual development, but is now almost universally accepted. Today, the accent of the Advent season is on 'getting ready' for the coming of *Christ* – at Bethlehem, into our prepared lives and the final coming of Christ in glory. There are a variety of interpretations about the themes to emphasise for each Advent Sunday and these are reflected throughout Europe. One Baptist *worship* resource has Advent 1 as the Advent hope itself. Advent 2 refers to the *Bible* and in some parts of Europe is recognised as Bible Sunday. Advent 3 focuses on the heralds of the Messiah, such as John the Baptist and Advent 4 on our own calling to reflect the light of Jesus in a dark world.

Others arrange the order as:

Advent 1	God's people waiting expectantly
	The Eschatological Hope, the Hope of Christ's return in glory [see *Eschatology*]
	The God who comes
Advent 2	The prophets
	The Announcement of the coming of the Messiah
	The God who speaks
Advent 3	John the Baptist
	The call to *repentance*
	The Forerunner (John the Baptist)
Advent 4	*Mary, the Mother of Jesus*

The Annunciation to Mary
Mary's *Faith*

Each option has a logic and there is certainly no uniformity of application and in some communities no such clear four week theme is used.

Typically Baptist order or liturgy includes for the Sundays of Advent a wreath of live seasonal greenery with four strongly coloured candles, often in an appropriate seasonal colour of maroon or royal purple and with a larger central white candle representing the birth of Christ which is lit at the Christmas Eve *Eucharist*, or on Christmas morning. There is often a local custom of the appropriate number of candles being lit each Sunday by a different group or family within the church community and with the pastor lighting the central candle at the Christmas worship. Some people will not sing traditional Christmas songs or decorate the worship room beyond the Advent ring until the fourth Sunday of Advent, linking back to the past tradition of reflective preparation, whilst others have decorated and illuminated Christmas trees, stable scenes, Christingle stars and a display of poinsettia plants from the first Advent Sunday.

KGJ

Advent Testimony
See *Dispensationalism*.

Afterlife
See *Heaven, Hell and the Future Life*.

Agapê
See *Love*.

Agape Meal
The *agapê* (Agape Meal/Love Feast) is rooted in the *ministry* of *Jesus*. According to Ac 2:42-47; 4: 32-35, the first Christians continued the practice of eating together and sharing their goods. In its fullest sense the agape meal is part of the economic solidarity that characterised at least part of the earliest church. The *Didache* and the writings of the early Church Fathers like Tertullian and Ignatius testify to its importance among Christians in the early centuries AD. It was celebrated in conjunction with the sharing of the cup and the bread [see *Communion and Intercommunion*; *Eucharistic Liturgy*; *Sacrament, Sign and Symbol*]. From the 4th century onwards the practice was largely given up, apparently because of disorder at the celebration. It survived, however, in some places within the Eastern Church. During the 16th century various *Anabaptist* groups to whom it became a most important token of communal *love* and caring revived the practice. Wesley and *Methodism* adopted it from the *Moravians*, and today it is practiced among many Church groups, including Baptists, though in most places without an emphasis on economic sharing. It has sometimes been used in *ecumenical* situations to provide an occasion for sharing in love without involving the difficult issues of intercommunion. Some Baptists would argue that there has been a false separation of the Holy Communion from the Agape sharing, and have accordingly devised new ways of reuniting these practices of the Ancient Church.

OL

Agricultural mission
From the development of Baptist *mission* and the pioneer work of *William Carey* in Serampore, there has been a concern that the gospel should be imparted to people in a *holistic* way, thus alongside those engaged in pastoral and *evangelistic* mission, there have been from the earliest years *educational* and medical missionaries. From the beginning Carey observed the farming patterns of those amongst whom he lived and sought to experiment with introducing new crops, or developing more sophisticated farming techniques to improve the harvest potential and thus feed more adequately those amongst whom he was living and seeking to share the gospel.

This approach to mission is replicated in the Baptist mission agencies emerging out of European Baptist life and working cross-culturally, especially in Asia, Africa and Latin America. Those called to serve as agricultural missionaries have been fully committed to giving testimony to their *faith* in classic verbal ways, but have also sought to express the *love* and compassion of *Christ* through this desire to assist in the development of farming techniques, use and care of the land, seeking to identify ways of producing additional protein for those without adequate food.

This mission work has often had a special attraction to those from farming communities and been supported in specific ways. For instance, special activities in support of agricultural mission at harvest time, or the collecting of used farm and agricultural implements of a basic kind to ship to those struggling to have the appropriate farming tools. Occasionally these initiatives had specific names, such as 'Operation Agri' amongst British Baptists, but generally such mission work has been seen as part of the overall approach of a cross-cultural mission agency, as has medical and educational work.

KGJ

AIDS
See *HIV-AIDS*.

Albania, Baptist history in
Evangelical missionaries, practicing believers' *baptism*, have worked in Albania from 1936 with the first known baptismal service taking place in 1937. The Conservative Baptist Foreign Missionary Society inherited the *property* of the former Albanian Evangelical Mission after the conclusion of WWII, and the *Southern Baptist Convention* Foreign Mission Board engaged in daily Albanian radio broadcast during the latter years of oppression.

Mainstream Baptist work in Albania started in the autumn of 1992 by Chris and Mairi Burnett, a Scottish couple sent to the country by the *Baptist Missionary Society*. In 1993, in the capital city, Tirana, the *European Baptist Federation* established the Baptist Centre that was planned to become the hub for Baptist witness. The first *worship* service took place 11 Sep 1993, and the Way of Hope Baptist church was established 5 Jun 1994. The EBF took a co-ordinating role, and its mission efforts were assisted by other organisations like the Foreign Mission Board (later International Mission Board) of the SBC, the Italian Baptist Union, the *Co-*

operative Baptist Fellowship and the Baptist Missionary Society. Slightly later, Brazilian and Canadian Baptist missionaries became involved.

Since the mid-1990s the Baptist work has continued to grow fast, with a focus on church planting. Baptist churches have been planted in Lezhe and Burrell, as well as at Bergu i Lumit in the outskirts of the capital. In Tirana, Freedom Baptist Church emerged in 1996, and Light of the World Baptist church in 2000. The Baptist Union of Albania was founded in 1999. In 2003 there were six churches in the *union*. Besides this, there are several independent Baptist churches, mostly planted by missionaries from the USA. Albanian Baptists co-operate with the wider evangelical movement in the country in the field of evangelism. There is a continuous challenge to find creative ways of reaching out to society, fostering spiritual growth, and training young church leaders.

AlG

Albertinen-Diakoniewerk Hamburg
[See also *Deaconesses*]
On 1 May 1907 Albertine Assor (1863-1953) together with eight other deaconesses founded the *Diakonissenverein Siloah* in Hamburg-Eimsbüttel and began welfare and social work for the *sick* and disadvantaged in private homes in Hamburg. In 1912 Albertine Assor, a very modern leader, rented a house in Malente (Holstein) for retreats and use as a vacation home for her deaconesses and in 1914 all the deaconesses of Siloah were enrolled in a private pension scheme. The work was growing fast and the deaconesses worked more and more in *hospitals* in and around Hamburg. In 1927 they rented a building and established their first hospital *Am Weiher* under their own management with 73 beds and opened their own School of Nursing.

In 1930 *Pastor* Hans Fehr became 'Inspektor', later Director, and the name of the organisation was changed to *Diakonissenhaus Siloah e.V.* In 1938 they bought the *Klinik Johnsallee* (45 beds) from the *Jewish* physician Dr. Calmann – the *Israelitische Krankenhaus* in Hamburg. In 1940 the name of the organisation was changed again into

Albertinen-Haus, Mutterhaus für Evangelische Diakonie und Krankenanstalten e.V. In 1941 'Oberin' Albertine Assor retired and Martha Kropat became Mother Superior.

In 1962 the Albertinen-Haus moved to Hamburg-Schnelsen (Süntelstraße 11A) and the deaconesses began a *youth work* programme, which later became the foundation of the Baptist Church Hamburg-Schnelsen. 1 Oct 1964 the new building of the *Albertinen-Krankenhaus* (first stage: 210 beds) was opened and Pastor Walter Füllbrandt became Director. In 1970 the second stage, again with 210 beds was added and the structure of the organisation changed, so that *men* and married persons [see *Marriage*] could now also become members of the Albertinen-Haus. In 1973 the Baptist Church Hamburg-Schnelsen became an independent member of the German Baptist *Union* (now more than 300 baptised *members* [see *Baptism*]).

In 1980 the Centre of Geriatrics and Gerontology (Sellhopsweg 18-22) including 150 apartments for *elderly* residents was opened, sponsored by the government of *Germany*, and five years later the Bobath Training Centre opened. In 1986 the name changed to *Albertinen-Diakoniewerk e.V.*; the Centre for Geriatrics and Gerontology is now called Albertinen-Haus. In 1996 Prof. Dr. Fokko ter Haseborg became Director of the Albertinen-Diakoniewerk e.V. Today, Albertinen includes two hospitals: the Albertinen-Krankenhaus in Hamburg-Schnelsen and the *Evangelische Amalie Sieveking-Krankenhaus* in Hamburg Volksdorf; the *Albertinen-Haus – Zentrum für Geriatrie and Gerontologie* in Hamburg-Schnelsen including the *Max Herz-Haus* (a centre for Alzheimer's care), the *Residenz am Wiesenkamp* – a home for the elderly in Hamburg-Volksdorf, two Kindergarten operations, the Albertinen Nursing School offering a Bachelor's Degrees in Nursing in cooperation with the Hamburg University of Applied Sciences, the *Abertinen-Akademie* and the *Diakonie-Hospiz Volksdorf* opened in Apr 2008.

The various departments of the Albertinen Group include more than 1,000 hospital-beds, about 2,800 employees and care for 70,000 patients annually in accordance with its *mission*: 'We help each other act as *Jesus* said: "In everything, do to others what you would have them do to you!" (Mt 7:12)'. Through the Albertinen-Foundation various national and international projects are supported, e.g. the *Herzbrücke*, which enables *children* from Afghanistan to come to Germany for life-saving heart surgery.

SS

FURTHER READING: www.albertinen.de.

Alcohol
[See also *Alcoholism*]
Alcohol has been associated with the Christian *Church* from the very beginning, especially in the fermented fruit of the vine. Christians recall that *Jesus* turned water into *wine* at Cana in Galilee and that the *Eucharist* was instituted around the second wine cup of blessing from *Jewish* celebratory events, possibly the *Passover* meal. One of the staple activities in medieval monastic communities has been the production of wine, mead and beer. Alcohol content in fermentation, brewing and distillation has for centuries been a way of ensuring the ability to drink fluids when supplies of clean drinking water or other palatable drinks were not available. In the *sacrament*, to accompany eating and as part of social life, alcohol has been a part of the European Christian story from the very beginning. The key accent has been on liturgical [see *Liturgy*], refectory and relaxed social settings for the consumption of alcoholic beverages in moderation.

However, the misuse and over use of alcohol has certainly always been frowned upon by the Christian Church and because of misuse some Baptist communities have advocated total abstinence, others have reserved use to wine in the liturgy and others have advocated *temperance*. In some north European countries the abuse of alcohol and the growth of the incidence of alcoholism in deprived industrial urban societies, has been a cause of alarm and of action by Baptists and others. In some countries Baptist churches in particular, have campaigned for teetotalism. By contrast in southern Europe churches were more at home with the fruit of the vine and were less negative in their approach to alcohol. In general, Baptists are more tolerant of wine and beer than so-called 'hard' spirits.

The use of wine at the Eucharist is common throughout Baptist communities in Europe, though some in parts of Scandinavia and the isles substitute unfermented grape juice or even blackcurrant juice, which is viewed with astonishment by most Baptists in Eastern Europe who see that as a serious departure from scriptural [see *Bible*] norms.

ET

Alcoholism

[See also *Alcohol*]

In some north European countries the abuse of alcohol in deprived industrial urban societies, especially before the coming of the *welfare state* when the principle victims were the drunkard's family, led to Christian communities, and Baptist churches in particular, widely adopting and campaigning for teetotalism. By contrast in southern Europe churches were more at home with the fruit of the vine and were less negative in their approach to alcohol.

The misuse of alcohol causes great concern to many Baptists and others concerned for community and social life. But such binge drinkers, and the small sad 'street' alcoholic group, mask the number of persons who secretly abuse alcoholic drinks. Alcoholics not only seriously endanger their own *health* and careers but also affect their families and friends. Alcohol is a depressant *drug* that disturbs coordination, speech, vision and mental competence. Over indulgence can lead to unconsciousness and complications that could lead to *death*. Over indulgence is associated with crime, *violence* and promiscuity. What begins as recreational can lead to a dependency. Alcoholism is a serious problem in many parts of northern Europe, soaking up resources to control drunken behaviour and robbing society of valuable human resources.

Observers have noticed that individuals indulge in alcoholic drinks in the first place to socialise. Singles culture rates clubs and bars as places of enjoyment and excitement where youngsters and the not-so young may meet and connect meaningfully with a partner. However, peer pressure can influence people with poor decision-making skills to over-indulge, especially those who have a

low self-image. Others turn to drink to ease the pains of life. Anger, fear and rejection can drive some to deaden the pain by over indulgence. There are a few who through ignorance of the dangers of alcohol begin to drink heavily. The drinks business is a powerful and *wealthy* industry expertly advertising its wares and claiming that drinking will guarantee excitement, confirm manhood (and womanhood) and open up lasting and happy relationships. Over indulgence is recognised as a problem by society which seeks to regulate the sale and consumption of alcoholic drinks. Some European countries have strong laws to attempt to protect the young and road users. Both OT and NT passages indicate the problem of over-indulgence and insist that the 'moderate' person is wise. The example of *Jesus* emphasises the principle that no one lives to themselves but all have responsibilities to their neighbours and especially to children. The new birth/*conversion* opens up the possibility to the 'repentant sinner' (including alcoholics) of a radical transformation through the power of God's *love*. *Discipleship* is to be clearheaded, compassionate, and committed to honour God, and not to abuse either mind or body. Christians have an obligation to obey the law of the land concerning drink, i.e. no drinking and driving. Christians are taught that to witness effectively their lifestyle should involve moderation in all areas, a conscientious *work* ethic [see *Protestant Work Ethic*] and being an example to children and neighbours.

Practically, some Baptist churches run programmes which encourage and support individuals who have a calling and the necessary skills to rehabilitate alcoholics. Such initiatives exist in *Slovakia* and the *United Kingdom*.

PC & ET

Alienation

In Ge 3 alienation, estrangement, broken relationships are depicted as the consequences of human *sin* and rebellion against God. Originally, humanity was created to live in *fellowship* with its Creator, but since the *Fall humankind* has been alienated from God. Not only so but as the subsequent narrative makes clear, alienation from God necessarily leads on to an estrangement from his *creation*, so that *work* now easily becomes toil in a land 'east of Eden', and it is not long before envy between brothers leads to the breaking of fraternal relationships, as jealousy leads on to murder. In due course the breaking of the *covenant* will lead to exile in Egypt and later in Babylon, for Israel as a *nation* in experiences of servitude to a foreign monarchy, which spell out the depth of alienation possible within human history, with which all who experience it may rightly identify. When – through the means of Divine *grace* – this alienation is overcome, the sinner is said to be reconciled to God (Col 1:21-22). Eph 2 offers three phrases to express the condition of those needing *salvation*: 'separation from *Christ*'; 'alienation form the commonwealth of Israel'; 'strangers to the covenants of promise', all of which are contrasted with being 'brought near to Christ' there to be made part of a new creation, 'no longer strangers and sojourners' but 'fellow citizens with the *saints* and members of the household of God' (v12-19). In a parallel passage in Col 1, Paul indicates that there is a moral dimension to *reconciliation*, for the aim of the exercise is to present the once-estranged as 'holy [see *Holiness*], blameless and irreproachable [see *Forgiveness*]', before Christ, which makes it necessary for them to 'continue in the faith, stable and steadfast not moving from the hope of the gospel' (v21-23). In recent years, *Marxists* have had much to say about a worker's alienation from his *work* in the modern *capitalist* system of production. Such an understanding may be agreed by Christians but with *justification* coming not from a particular reading of history and economics but from a *theological* understanding of the Creation story. Thus in scripture will be found both explanation for this aspect of human malaise and its remedy.

EV & ET

All-Union Council of Evangelical Christians-Baptists (AUCECB)

[See also *Reform Baptists*]

The All-Union Congress (Conference) of Evangelical Christians and Baptists in the *Soviet Union* was held in Oct 1944. The All-Union Council of Evangelical Christians-

Baptists dates from that point. The Baptists and the *Evangelical* Christians, although holding similar beliefs, had somewhat separate stories in *Russia*. They had been united for a short time in the early 20th century but in 1944 they merged – or rather, they were forcibly merged by the *state*. However, there were steps which led to this from within the two groups.

In 1942 a letter – 'A Proclamation to all Baptists and Evangelical Christians in the *USSR*' – was circulating in local evangelical communities. This letter, calling believers to fight *fascism*, was probably initially written by four people: two Baptists and two Evangelical Christians. A Temporary Council of Evangelical Christians and Baptists was formed and this became the AUCECB. At the 1944 Congress the participants approved a resolution which asserted: 'Having forgotten all differences in opinions in the past we decide to create from two *Unions* one Union: the Union of Evangelical Christians and Baptists with the All-Union Council as its *authority* which will reside in Moscow city.'

During the Congress the members of the AUCECB were elected. The key positions were held by Y. Zhidkov (president), A. Karev (secretary), M. Goltayev and M. Orlov (vice-presidents), P. Malin (treasurer), and A. Andreyev, F. Patkovsky and N. Lavinadto (members). Although the members of the executive board were drawn in equal proportions from the Baptists and the Evangelical Christians the most important positions were granted to those from an Evangelical Christian background. A few weeks after the Congress the AUCECB received permission to issue a *magazine*, *Bratsky Vestnik* (*BV*). The first editorial announced that articles would include religious and patriotic articles; *sermons* and devotional articles; material on the history of the Evangelical Baptist movement in the USSR and on the history of Christianity; biographies of Evangelical Christians and Baptists; reports on the life and activity of the AUCECB and of local communities; and correspondence.

The activity of the AUCECB in its early years consisted mainly in bringing together and seeking to unify various evangelical churches. The Union was expanding both in its territory and its denominational variety. Supervisors were appointed. By the beginning of 1947 these numbered more than 50 people. They were appointed by the Council and carried out its wishes. There was much disquiet at local level about joining the apparently pro-government Union [see *Separation of Church and State*], but most churches accepted the realities of the situation. Many 100s of the churches were registered under the umbrella of the AUCECB.

The AUCECB expanded into the *Baltic* countries that were occupied by the Soviet troops. While the churches of Central Russia, *Belarus*, *Ukraine*, the Caucasus, and Siberia were culturally and linguistically homogeneous and shared the same history, there were significant differences between Russian speakers and Baltic peoples. Maybe an even more difficult task consisted in attaching *Pentecostals* to the Union of the ECB. However, the only way by which Pentecostals could gain state registration was to become a part of the AUCECB. At a later stage the *Mennonites* joined the Union.

In 1948 an extended session of the Council of the AUCECB took place. The Council summed up the results of the first four years and the process of legalisation of local communities of the ECB. However, following this, the authorities clamped down. After 1948 any developments for Evangelicals in the Soviet Union became impossible for a relatively long period. The second issue of *BV* in 1949 became its last issue until the *death* of Stalin in 1953.

After Stalin's death came the so-called Khrushchev Thaw. For the AUCECB this meant gaining permission to publish Bibles (1957) and *Hymnals* (1956). But by the end of the 1950s the USSR was experiencing a new anti-religious programme. There were mass closures of churches, the expulsion of believers from educational institutes, and the creation of a network of spies. By the end of this period the AUCECB was about to cease its activities because of the impossibility of continuing under the immense pressure of state interference.

The dissent in the Union at the beginning of the 1960s attracted the attention of many in the West. Its importance was seen as consisting of a clear demonstration of the discontent of the Soviet believers with the religious policy of the USSR. The AUCECB split into the official Union and a 'reform'

Union which considered that too many compromises with the state had taken place. Dissent became a real problem for the AUCECB after the 'underground' Council began to play a role on the international scene and the problems in the Union could not be kept hidden any longer.

In 1964 Khrushchev was dismissed as General Secretary of the *Communist* Party and was followed by Brezhnev. This period gained the name 'stagnation' and this stagnation lasted practically until the days of perestroika. This societal stagnation also affected the life of the AUCECB. The beginning of the Brezhnev period coincided with the leaders of the Union entering old age. In the second half of the 1960s, however, a new generation of Baptist leaders took over. The period from 1965-70 was a period of stabilisation of relations between the Communists and the AUCECB. The Union was given certain freedoms (e.g. in 1968 it received permission to start training *ministers* in the Correspondence Bible Institute).

1971 was a turning point in the history of the AUCECB, with the death of the General Secretary, Alexander Karev. The new board of the AUCECB consisted of leaders for whom the Union of Evangelical Christians-Baptists was the only form of Evangelical movement they knew. The foreign affairs of the AUCECB in the 1970s and 80s were very important parts of its activities. The AUCECB became an active participant in the life of the *Baptist World Alliance* and the *European Baptist Federation*. When the major shift in Soviet policy toward religion occurred in 1988 most of the believers were not prepared for such changes. In 1990, however, the AUCECB organised the 44th All-Union Congress and the AUCECB opened the way for the gradual deconstruction of the previous system of organisation of the Union. With the demise of the USSR the Union, although it existed until the end of 1993, was a nominal organisation. The next Congress, in 1993, was a Congress of the ECB in Russia only.

AP

Alpha and related evangelistic strategies

Alpha leads a family of evangelistic products

informed by *UK* research conducted in 1990 (later published in *Finding Faith Today*, 1992). It confirmed initial suspicions that for the majority, Christian **conversion** was a process rather than a crisis. Longer established products, including *MasterLife*, assumed that *discipleship* was the process, finding *faith* a crisis. Indeed *Alpha*, in 1977, was an introductory discipleship course for the **Anglican** church of Holy Trinity, Brompton, in west London. With Nicky Gumbel's arrival at the church in 1986 *Alpha* became a 15-session introduction to the Christian faith for non-Christians, featuring weekly small group meals and a residential weekend.

Alternatives began to emerge in the mild 1990s as a response to perceived inadequacies of *Alpha*. *Emmaus* (1996) reflected a broader Anglican approach, mainstream **evangelicals** published the 10-session *Christianity Explored* (2001), and the 8-session *Y-course* (1998), whilst the 6-session *Start!* (2003) was written for those less literate.

Alpha courses are widespread in churches, prisons, the armed forces, universities, and the workplace, supported by promotional videos, DVDs, books, and posters. By 2005, 6,336 courses had been run in 41 continental European countries with 7,234 in the UK. A third of UK Baptist churches have run *Alpha* courses, though other European Baptists remain wary of charismatic elements, may incorrectly perceive it as **Roman Catholic**, or criticise its lack of attention to **baptism**, **church membership** and **holistic** community discipleship. The 2003 **EBF Home Mission** Secretaries' Conference addressed these concerns although data from the Baptist Union of Great Britain in 2002 suggested that churches running *Alpha* (or *Emmaus*) courses were more likely to experience increasing numbers of baptisms and church members.

The success of Alpha and related approaches probably lies in the centrality of small groups, journeying in faith, eating together, open discussion and exploration, and the importance of a transformational encounter with God through the living *Christ*.
DJ

FURTHER READING: John Finney, *Finding Faith Today*, British and Foreign Bible Society, Swindon, 1992. Stephen Hunt, *The Alpha Enterprise*, Ashgate, Aldershot, 2004. Darrell Jackson, *The Impact of Alpha on Baptist Churches*, Baptist Union of Great Britain, Didcot, 2002. www.missiologist.net.

American Baptist Churches, USA (ABC-USA)

This is a *fellowship* of approximately 5,800 Baptist churches with a **membership** in excess of 1,484,000 people drawn from throughout the United States of America, though principally the States north of the Mason-Dixon line. ABC-USA is the oldest continuing body of Baptist Christians in North America and one of the oldest Baptist bodies in the world and was a founding member of the **Baptist World Alliance** in 1905. The first church of ABC-USA was formed in Providence, Rhode Island in 1638.

The critical point in the creation of what we now know as ABC-USA, was the **mission** imperative focused in the support of Adoniram and Ann Judson and Luther Rice who went from the USA and began north American international Baptist mission work in Asia. Rice helped establish in 1814 the General Missionary Convention of the Baptist Denomination in the United States for Foreign Missions (also known as the Triennial Convention).

In 1907 this body, by now renamed the American Baptist Foreign Mission Society, became a constituent part of the Northern Baptist **Convention**. A **Southern Baptist Convention** had previously been formed in 1845. The division into two conventions from the original Triennial Convention for mission derives from differing attitudes to slavery and the African-American population. American Baptists developed a wide range of mission boards and agencies in **theological education**, **home mission**, publications (the Judson Press), social and welfare ministries, chaplaincies and all the usual instruments of denominational support. Their attitude from the beginning was to cooperate with others in mission and witness and so they have been members of the **National Council of Churches** in the USA and of the **World Council of Churches**, whilst also maintaining, active involvement with the National Association of **Evangelicals** in the USA.

ABC-USA, through its earlier mission boards, has always taken a constructive attitude to partnership with European Baptist *unions* and maintains a Regional Mission Office at the *European Baptist Centre* in Prague. ABC-USA has a national resource building at Valley Forge in Pennsylvania and counts ten seminaries as partners or member bodies including Eastern, Northern, Colgate Rochester, Andover-Newton, Central and American Baptist Seminary of the West.

KGJ

FURTHER READING: William H. Brackney *The Baptists,* Greenwood, Connecticut, 1988. William H. Brackney, *Baptist Life and Thought: A Source Book,* Judson, Valley Forge, 1998. www.abc-usa.org.

Amnesty International

[See also *Human Rights Advocacy*; *Religious Liberty*]

Amnesty International was founded in 1961 by a British lawyer and won the Nobel *Peace* Prize in 1977. By the 1990s it had over a million members and subscribers scattered all over the world, working with around 6,000 volunteers in 162 countries investigating some 4,000 cases a year. Non-aligned and independent of all governments, and *political* parties, it plays a major part in campaigning for human rights as spelt out in the1948 *United Nations* Universal Declaration of Human Rights, and undertakes education to secure a right appreciation of such issues. In particular it works for the release of prisoners of *conscience* whether imprisoned for their political convictions, religious beliefs or because of their colour or race. It undertakes advocacy for those held without charge, seeks fair and speedy trials of all political prisoners, opposing torture, degrading treatment and the use of the death penalty. It also investigates 'disappearances', political killings and the treatment of refugees Whilst its London office evaluates reports received from all round the world, the credibility of its work depends on thorough, impartial and objective research, which is never published anonymously but always in its own name. More recently it has turned its attention to human rights abuses by armed opposition groups, and since 1989 has established groups in Central and Eastern Europe as well

as in Africa and Asia. It has formal representation at the UN, UNESCO and the *Council of Europe*.

JHYB

Anabaptism

The widely agreed historical starting point for Anabaptism (sometimes generically also referred to as belonging to the 'radical' or the 'left wing' of the *Reformation*) is Jan 1525 when the first believers' *baptism* of modern times took place in Zürich. However, the way for this was paved by certain events in the early Reformation, especially Zwinglian reforms [see *Zwingli*], interest in the Biblical texts, increasing criticism of medieval ecclesial patterns of church life and the spread of humanist views across Europe. This led to an increasing conviction that the mainstream or magisterial reformers – that is reformers acting at the wills of local rulers rather than representing popular sentiment – stopped part-way and did not take ecclesiastical changes as far as they should have done to return to NT norms. In spite of persecution, and in some cases because of this, Anabaptists spread comparatively quickly. In the 16th century Anabaptist work clustered in *Switzerland* and Southern *Germany*, Moravia, Northern Germany and *Holland*. Early Anabaptist leaders, such as *Balthasar Hubmaier* and Pilgram Marpeck, helped to shape early Anabaptist *theology* whilst Michael Sattler helped to formulate the Schleitheim Articles (1527), a confession of agreed faith [see *Creeds, Covenants and Confessions of Faith*] and practice which helped to unite Early Anabaptism. It emphasised believers' baptism, committed *discipleship, church discipline*, the *ethics* of *love* and separation from earthly government structures. Perhaps the most important Anabaptist distinctive was their ecclesiology – the church (brotherhood) consisted only of spiritually renewed persons who voluntarily join the *fellowship*.

However, all the Anabaptist groups had also their own characteristics. The majority of Anabaptists were peaceful and refused to take oaths and bear arms, but there were also revolutionary groups. Some Anabaptist groups, especially the Hutterites, inspired by Jacob Hutter, made serious efforts to live a communitarian life. Hutterite communities continue to exist today in some parts of the world, mainly in North America. Some extreme apocalyptic expectations, partly influenced by Melchior Hofmann, led to an attempt to establish by force an Anabaptist Jerusalem on earth, which ended in the Münster fiasco of 1534, in which extreme and violent Anabaptist rule in the city led to government authorities throughout Europe identifying Anabaptism with *political* sedition, and instituting persecution accordingly. As a consequence, Menno Simons, a second generation Anabaptist leader, devoted his life to re-building and encouraging Anabaptist communities in North Germany/Holland after the Münster events, and to make it quite clear that they stood for *non-violence*. In the later history, especially because of persecution and restrictions on the practice of their *faith*, many Anabaptist communities spread further and further east in Europe and beyond: 'Eternal Abrahams' they settled in Transylvania, *Poland*, *Ukraine*, and later the Americas, wherever they found a ruler who would tolerate them and allow their communities to develop unmolested. The largest 'brotherhood' of Anabaptist descent today is the *Mennonites*, who are actively involved in peacemaking and conflict resolution as well as disaster relief projects.

The second half of the 20th century saw a considerable resurgence of Anabaptist ideas and values on the wider theological and church scene. A number of Anabaptist *scholars* (e.g. John Howard Yoder, Alan Kreider and Ron Sider) have made serious efforts to interpret the Anabaptist heritage in light of the new challenges for the Christian church in a world (at least the European and American world) which was moving from modernism to post-modernism. The legacy of Anabaptism has also inspired Baptists who are seeking to implement the values of Christian community, committed discipleship and the ethics of *Jesus* in the life of a believer. In addition there are other elements in the 'Anabaptist vision', to use the term associated with Harold Bender which they also wanted to honour: witness to *peace* as an inseparable part of the gospel, commitment to religious liberty, and seeking for alternative patterns of being a church, especially when compared to *Christendom* mod-

els. There has also been questioning about the extent to which Anabaptism has influenced the Baptist story. In *Britain*, *E.A. Payne* stood for a theory of spiritual 'soul-friendship' between Anabaptists and Baptists, believing that 'ideas have wings'. Later, B.R. White argued that there is little evidence of direct encounter of the Anabaptist and Baptist traditions in the 17th century, and, of course, because of Münster, the early English Baptists, in their writings, were anxious to distance themselves as far as possible from those continental Anabaptists who had provoked such universal ire. However, there were financial links continuing in the 17th century between English Baptists and Dutch Mennonites, and when the *Baptist Missionary Society* was founded in 1792, Mennonite congregations in Europe were duly canvassed for support, which perhaps explains why John Rippon in the *Baptist Annual Register* at the end of the 18th century lists the Mennonite Congregations in Europe as Baptist congregations. It is not surprising therefore that on the mainland of Europe, in the 19th and 20th century, particularly in *Russia* and Ukraine, there was much mutual influence between Mennonites and Baptists.

TP

FURTHER READING: Keith G. Jones, *A Believing Church: Learning from Some Contemporary Anabaptist and Baptist Perspectives*, Baptist Union of Great Britain, Didcot, 1998. C. Arnold Snyder, *Anabaptist History and Theology: An Introduction*, Pandora and Herald, Kitchener, Ontario and Scottdale, Pennsylvania, 1995. C. Arnold Snyder, *Following in the Footsteps of Christ: The Anabaptist Tradition*, Darton, Longman and Todd, London, 2004. George H. Williams, *The Radical Reformation* (3rd ed.), Sixteenth Century Journal Publishers, Kirksville, Mo., 1992.

Anglicanism, Baptists and

[See also *Bilateral Conversations*]
The language of the 'Anglican Communion' came into use in the second half of the 19th century when it was realised that those 'duly constituted dioceses, provinces or regional churches in *communion* with the see of Canterbury' had no means of discussing matters of mutual concern, and this was urgent because of disputed jurisdictions in South Africa. It was then that the Canadian

Church proposed a common conference 'of the members of our Anglican Communion' which led to the convoking of the first Lambeth Conference in 1867. At the time of the **Reformation** there was one Church in **England** and **Wales** (without national distinction) and from 1612, following the amalgamation of the English and the Scottish crowns in **Scotland** also. However, after the so-called 'Glorious Revolution' the established Church in Scotland reverted to being **Presbyterian** and a non-established Episcopal Church of Scotland was founded in **communion** with Canterbury. By legislation in 1867 the Church in **Ireland**, no longer representing the population which was predominantly **Catholic** in the south, became disestablished in 1871, as did the Welsh Church in 1920 following legislation in 1914/19.

After the American War of Independence, when the now independent colonists [see **Colonialism**] wanted to have **bishops** in good order it was hardly possible for the Archbishop of Canterbury to consecrate Samuel Seabury, the first bishop consecrated for service outside the British Isles, without securing his oath of allegiance to George III. This made necessary; a journey to Aberdeen where he was consecrated by three Scottish Bishops.

As British people became dispersed around the world as plantation owners, bankers, railway builders, traders, etc., or for less honourable reasons, such as accounted for the convict communities in Australia, so there was need for **overseas chaplains**, a need largely met through the agencies of the Society for the Promotion of Christian Knowledge (1699) and the Society for the Propagation of the Gospel (1701), or indeed by secular companies like the East India Company. Later more deliberate endeavours were directed towards the non-Christian populations of Asia and Africa in the great Protestant **missionary** advance of the 19th century through societies such as the Church Missionary Society (1799), operating throughout many parts of the British Empire. Everywhere churches were being established and bishops consecrated. Gradually this family of churches became known as the Anglican Communion, the presiding bishops in other countries relating to the Archbishop of Canterbury now recognised as the head of the Anglican Communion.

Throughout the mainland of Europe Anglican churches are not common. There is a Diocese in Europe, with a Cathedral in Gibraltar (and Pro-Cathedrals in **Malta** and Brussels), within the Church of England, but in most countries (44) on the European mainland parishes are limited to major cities and are generally formed of expatriate communities of both the Church of England and the American Episcopal Church. There are indigenous episcopal churches in **Spain** along with the Lusitanian Church in **Portugal** which are members of the Anglican Communion.

Even though from the 17th to the early 20th century Baptists suffered disadvantages in **education** and other areas as over against the privileges of the **State Church**, Baptists have secured increasing respect from their Anglican colleagues. The **ecumenical** outreach of the Anglican Communion was clearly laid out in the so-called **Lambeth Quadrilateral** of 1888, which in 1920 was incorporated in the Lambeth Conference's Appeal to All Christian People' to both of which the Baptist Union made firm but courteous replies, as later they did when Archbishop Fisher in his 1946 Cambridge University **sermon** invited the **Free Churches** in England 'to take episcopacy into their own systems', drawing attention to the fact that such matters could not be considered in isolation from the **fellowship** they enjoyed with other Baptists in Europe and other parts of the world. More recently Baptists in the UK have engaged in a useful consistent **dialogue** with the Church of England for over a decade. Baptists in England and Wales work with Anglicans in the national ecumenical councils, whilst there are also local congregations in England and Wales involving Anglicans and Baptists in what are called **Local Ecumenical Partnerships**. Certain cathedrals (e.g. Worcester, Norwich) have benefited from the advice and fellowship of Baptist **ministers** by appointing them Honorary Canons.

Internationally, the **Baptist World Alliance** conducted conversations with the Anglican Communion between 2000 and 05. Differences between the traditions focus on **ecclesiology**, the practice of **baptism** and liturgical forms of *worship*.

KGJ

FURTHER READING: *Conversations Around the World 2000-2005: The Report of the International Conversations between the Anglican Communion and the Baptist World Alliance*, The Anglican Communion Office, London, 2005. *Pushing at the Boundaries of Unity: Anglicans and Baptists in Conversation*, Church House, London, 2005.

Annihilation and Universalism

As Christian thinkers in the 19th century contemplated the nature of judgment in the after-life, a variety of revisions were canvassed. Most radically, some called Universalists, were convinced that eventually all would be saved. Samuel Cox, Baptist minister in Nottingham, England, in his two books *Salvator Mundi, or is Christ the Saviour of All Men?* (1877) and *The Larger Hope* (1883) argued that in his judgment this did not diminish the doctrine of the *Atonement* but rather made *the cross* the source of even more *grace*, taking 1Ti 4:10 as his text. Although Cox sought scriptural warrant for his ideas which were reverentially presented, his works were strongly criticised by other Baptists. Cox writes, 'We still believe in the Atonement, that the forgiving and redeeming *love* of God is revealed in the life, death and passion of Our Lord *Jesus Christ*, but we also believe in an Atonement of wider scope that Christ will see of the travail of his soul and be satisfied in a larger and diviner way than some of our *theologians* have supposed.' *Spurgeon* was not impressed and referred to such ideas as a species of 'post mortem *salvation*.' Some argued that after *death* there would be a further opportunity for *repentance* and *conversion*.

Even such a figure as the *Anglican Evangelical*, T.R. Birks, Professor of Moral Philosophy at Cambridge, and sometime Secretary of the *Evangelical Alliance*, championed the notion of eventual universal restitution after a period of punishment, views which forced his resignation from the Secretaryship but not from the Alliance itself. Defining *Hell* as separation from God, there has been an increasing emphasis on self-judgement and a person placing himself apart from God rather than God exercising judgment upon the individual.

Others simply argued that *eternal life* was for believers only and others would simply be extinguished at the grave. This is the position described as annihilation, or sometimes referred to as 'conditional immortality' which had been advanced by John Foster, a Baptist minister who spent most of his career as a Christian journalist, who queried the justice of applying eternal torment for temporal *sin*, and whether this really reflected the Divine Goodness. Those who hold to the traditional view of judgement argue that these revisionist views do not take sin seriously enough nor do they respect human freedom to reject God.

The entry in the *New Bible Dictionary of Theology* on *Eschatology* interestingly notes that the notion of Hell involves separation from God, and comments 'Whether this involves eternal conscious torment (the traditional Christian view) or the cessation of existence (as taught by advocates of 'conditional immortality') is a matter of ongoing debate.

ET

FURTHER READING: Samuel Cox, *Salvator Mundi, or is Christ the Saviour of All Men?*, C. Keegan Paul, London, 1880. Samuel Cox, *The Larger Hope*, Keegan Paul, Trench and Co., London, 1883. G. Rowell, *Hell and the Victorians: a study of nineteenth-century controversies covering eternal punishment and the future life*, Clarendon, Oxford, 1974. M.J. Harris, *Raised Immortal*, Marshall Morgan and Scott, London, 1983. S.H. Travis, *Christian Hope and the Future of Man*, Inter-Varsity, Leicester, 1980.

Anniversaries

Anniversaries are generally perceived within baptistic communities in Europe as being liturgical events associated with the recalling of important dates within the stories of specific Baptist communities – Churches, *Associations* and *Unions*.

As in the secular world, so in the Christian world, there is generally a desire to more specifically celebrate anniversaries occurring after a decade or multiple decades. So, for instance, European Baptists in 2009 celebrate the 400th anniversary of the founding of the first 'English' Baptist church in Amsterdam in 1609.

In some countries special services to celebrate the anniversary of the **Sunday School** were also high points in the Baptist church year. Often there can be invitations to former **scholars** to return to their school, special choirs and **preachers** and festal meals. This was perhaps experienced at its most intense in the midlands and north of England in the 20th century when Sunday School Anniversaries were almost *the* most important point in the church year. Church Anniversaries have never been so significant, but it is common enough for a specific Sunday in the year to be classified as the Church Anniversary Sunday and **members** encouraged to be sure to attend **worship** on that day. In some churches it is an occasion for a community meal and the renewal of any **covenant** for participation in membership that the church might have.

The celebration of the anniversary of the **pastor** can also be an event celebrated with real enthusiasm in certain parts of Europe. Again, this is often done by inviting a guest preacher, having a celebratory meal and making some gift to the pastor especially in significant milestone years of the pastorate – five, ten or fifteen years.

KGJ

Anointing of the Sick

The practice of anointing the sick with oil and praying for **healing** is based primarily upon the words of Jas 5:14-16, and alluded to in Mk 6:13. Throughout Church history there are scattered references to the practice in the Eastern as well as the Western Church. In the Catholic Church of the Middle Ages it was administered as the sacrament of Extreme Unction to the sick and the dying. Since the Second **Vatican** Council it has again been practised in the **Roman Catholic** Church as an anointing of the sick. During the 16th century it was used by some **Anabaptist** groups as an instrument of care and prayer for the sick but the mainstream reformers tended to see it as a **ministry** confined to the **apostolic** era. Among the **Mennonites** it has continued to be practised. During the 20th century it became a prominent feature in **Pentecostal** and **Charismatic** communities, and more widely amongst those churches that see a ministry of **healing** as part of their Christian witness, e.g. several

modern Prayer Books within the **Anglican** Communion provide liturgies for this purpose. Likewise some **Lutheran** and **Presbyterian** Churches make provision for this.

The extent to which Baptist Churches exercise this ministry is more difficult to discern especially amongst those churches which do not use worship manuals. However, as examples the Estonians have a service entitled 'prayer with anointing', for those who are sick, dated 1998, mainly used by pastors in prayers in the home, and the British Baptists' *Gathering for Worship*, 2005, has such a form which makes provision for both the laying on of hands and the anointing with oil. More generally Baptists would wish to affirm the need for a **holistic** approach to healing embracing both the ministry of those in the medical profession and the prayers of the Church, including appropriate symbolic actions.

OL

Anthropology, Theological

Denominated the 'doctrine of man' by earlier writers, Christian anthropology is rooted in the stories of **creation** in the OT. Man was created by God – **humankind** is his creature, created in the image of God (Ge 1:26, *Imago Dei*). There is disagreement over what the Imago Dei actually constitutes. Some have thought it to be something unique to humanity such as human consciousness of its self identity, **free will**, the ability to communicate with God or the ability to show **love**. To confine its meaning too narrowly is not consistent with the holistic Hebrew view of the person as a unified self, embracing both soul and body. The Hebrew understanding of a unified self of soul and body has been contested primarily because of the use of terms like *pneuma* [spirit], *psyche* [soul] and *sarx/soma* [body] in the NT. Apollinaris of Laodocea introduced the trichotomic view, with a three-part division consisting of body, mind (or spirit), and soul, but this view was later condemned at the 4th Council of Constantinople (869-79 AD).

The context of Ge 1:26 suggests that Imago Dei is to be understood as a question of the exercising of similar roles: just as God is presented as the one arranging the creation in a divine order, man is given the high responsibility to ruling over the created order on God's behalf. This stresses the co-operative understanding of humankind as part of the created world, further developed in the creation of man 'out of earth', brought into being by 'the breath of life', in Ge 2:7. It suggests both a fundamental dependence on God and a responsibility for the created world. Humankind has no life independent of the will and spirit of God and the authority exercised within the created order is the delegated *authority* of a steward [see *Stewardship*] – Adam's *fall* can be seen not only as an act of disobedience but as a grasping after a supposed moral autonomy apart from the purposes of the Creator.

Humankind is also created as both man and woman. The representation of the Imago Dei is not confined to the individual human, but is manifest in a completeness of human experience embracing different sexes, races and ages. Indeed some *scholars* think therefore that the Imago Dei relates to the relational ability of human beings.

Christian anthropology needs to be set in the context not only of Creation but of *Incarnation*: the *Word* made flesh, the God who takes the initiative in the re-creation of fallen humanity, that is to say the incarnate Christ not only exemplifies true humanity but through his sacrificial *death* provides the means to renew what has been corrupted, the drawing anew of the divine image in human life [see *Atonement*; *Salvation and Soteriology*]. Thus Paul's ambition for the Ephesian church when he prays 'for the equipment of the *saints*,...for the building up the *body of Christ* until we all attain to the *unity* of the *faith*, and of the knowledge of the Son of God, to mature manhood, to the measure of the stature of the fullness of Christ' (Eph 4:12-13). Here is the promise of Adam's fall reversed.

KTB & ET

Antinomianism

Antinomianism (derived from Greek words meaning 'beyond the law') represents the view that Christians are released by *grace* form the obligation to observe the moral law. Historically, some *Anabaptists*, who were worried by legalism in the church, were accused of this, as was *Luther* for his emphasis on *justification* by *faith* alone. To this he replied that he had not forbidden good works but saw them not as a cause of *salvation*, but consequential of it. Antinomianism came to be used as a term of abuse to decry the high-*Calvinist* who places all his confidence in his being numbered amongst the elect [see *Election*], without any attention to behaviour befitting a member of *Christ*'s *church*, or differently put, places his trust in *membership* of the invisible church whilst not bothering to live a life appropriate to a member of the visible church. Antinomianism emphasises the Christian's freedom from the condemnation of the law, at the expense of commitment to living a disciplined Christian life in this world. In other words, justification was stressed at the expense of the need for *sanctification*. Tobias Crisp, a 17th-century Church of England clergyman, who taught a form of hyper-Calvinism, had a considerable influence amongst English Baptists such as John Skepp, though *scholars* have successfully defended John Gill and John Brine against this charge. Andrew Fuller [see *Fullerism*] wrote a tract against Antinomianism, which he introduces with the notion that 'Irreligion is not so dangerous as false religion' which attacked the *evangelical* faith whilst its preachers were doing battle with Arianism and Socinianism, 'under the names and forms of *orthodoxy*.' Fuller sees the root of the problem in a false experience of *conversion*; true conversion consists of '*repentance* toward God, and faith toward our Lord Jesus Christ.' Not being under the law does not absolve Christians from the obligation to love God with all their heart and mind and soul and their neighbour as themselves. Contrary to antinomian assertions true faith always entails a strong moral dimension.

JHYB

Anti-Semitism and the Holocaust
[See also *Judaism, Baptists and*]
Anti-Jewish sentiment, partly ethnic and partly confessional, has existed from ancient times, becoming visible in physical action at a number of junctures in history. In the early Christian period this antagonism found *theological* focus as the Jews were labelled

'*Christ*-killers' provoking the ironic distinction of a requirement to love Jesus but to hate Jews, now often seen to be under the curse of God. After Christianity became the established imperial religion in the time of Constantine, church councils began repeatedly to issue Anti-Semitic statements, so that Anti-Semitism became part of medieval ecclesiastical reality. Later came forced *conversions*, the Inquisition, and the Anti-Semitic writings of *Martin Luther*.

Towards the end of the 19th century this antagonism accelerated and in 1879 the term Anti-Semitism was coined just at the time when agitation and pogroms in Eastern Europe led to the westward *migration* of 1,000s of Yiddish people to the western democracies and the USA, which eventually found their evil fulfilment in the Holocaust and the Final Solution. The word Holocaust derives from the LXX version of the OT where it means a wholly consumed burned offering. In the 1950s it began to be applied to the extermination of some six million Jews (or one third of Europe's Jewish population) in death camps for which the name Auschwitz has become symbolic, for which there was little precedent save the genocide of over a million Armenians living in the Turkish Empire during WWI. The Holocaust has prompted writers to ask, 'Where was God in Auschwitz?' whilst for some this has been a cause of loss of belief others such as Jürgen Moltmann suggest that he was in the camp participating in the *suffering* of the victims because he is the crucified God, not the impassable God of traditional *theology*.

Since the war, Western Christianity, including Baptist churches, have experienced *guilt* for their inactivity on behalf of the suffering Jews. Undoubtedly there are heroic stories of Baptists putting their lives at risk to help and aid Jews, but there was a more general silence which may not be sufficiently excused by claims to ignorance. Later interchurch bodies saw the need to condemn Anti-Semitism as a 'sin against God and man'.

ET

Apartheid

The word 'apartheid', which literally means 'separateness', refers to the racial policies implemented by a variety of Acts such as the Population Registration Act and the Pass Laws by the Afrikaner National Party after it came to power in South Africa in 1948. Not only did this enforce segregation, culminating in the establishment of separate Bantustans or 'independent homelands', but it ensured that the black population remained economically deprived. The Dutch *Reformed Church* which from the 19th century onwards had established congregations of specific ethnic identity underwrote the apartheid policies with a neo-*Calvinist theology* of a divinely determined separation of the races. Whilst resistance to Apartheid, spearheaded by the African National Congress was initially peaceful, after the Sharpville massacre of 1960 *state* repression provoked violent resistance leading up to the Soweto uprising of 1976 which, in turn, provoked the *United Nations* to designate Apartheid as a 'crime against humanity'. In 1990 the banning of the liberation movements marked a change in government policy paving the way for non-racial elections in 1994 won by the ANC under the leadership of Nelson Mandela. Churches in membership with the South African Council of Churches, supported by the wider church, played a major part in resisting racial injustice. Baptists however were suspicious of *ecumenical* activity especially of a *political* kind and were slow to engage with the issue.

ET

Apathy

The word is derived from the Greek *apathes* meaning 'without feeling'. The reverse of enthusiasm or partisanship or commitment, it describes a situation in which people lack the passion to take up a position. It came into the English language in the 17th century after Europe had become exhausted from the religious wars of the previous century. More recently it has come to describe the European *mission* field where people are not so much opposed to religion but so imbedded in a material culture that they choose not to engage with the purposes of life or to ask ultimate questions. It is the attitude of 'don't care' which politely ignores the mission of the church in all its forms.

JHYB

Apologetics

Christian witness involves the rebuttal of falseness and the clarification of misunderstandings. This arises from the fact that we proclaim *Jesus* as 'the light of the world' and that 'the light shines in the darkness' (Jn 8:12, 1:5), and not only from a logical or pragmatic point of view. The contradictions between the Gospel and other truth claims, and between the Christian way of living and other ways of living are inevitable (cf. Mt 10:24f; Jn 15:18ff; 1Pe 4:4). Paul's testimonies were often defences (Greek *apologia*) against different charges (e.g. Ac 22:1ff, 26:1ff; 2Ti 4:16). Peter looks on authentic Christian life as a good apologia (1Pe 2:11-12).

Historically, apologetics has focused on various issues: the relationship with philosophy and other religions, evidences for the existence of God, miracles, God and *suffering* (theodicy), etc. These days the main issues are post-modern claims on the nature of truth and knowledge, religious pluralism (e.g. *Islam* in Europe), encountering the scientific world-view [see *Science; Science and Faith*], and new religiosity (e.g New Age). Some apologists presuppose that there are common starting-points (a belief, an experience, existential questions, the created order, etc.) with other world-views as witnesses ('an unknown god', Ac 17:23), while others reject this.

Polemics as related to apologetics deal with denominational controversies. Baptist polemics usually centre on the nature of the church and *baptism*.

Apologetics is unthinkable without a proper knowledge of rivalling truths and generous behaviour towards others (2Ti 2:24-25). Nevertheless one should remember that it is pointless without the awakening and persuading work of the *Holy Spirit*: no apologia can create a living *faith*.

AS

Apostles

Jesus appointed a group of twelve apostles to be his closest companions and to carry on his work after he returned to the Father. The apostles are identified by name and were given by Jesus authority to *preach*, to *heal* and to cast out demons (Mk 3:13-19; Mt 10:1-4). The essential task of the apostles is implied in the meaning of the word: to be sent, specifically to be sent as messengers with a purpose. The original twelve apostles, reconstituted after the defection of Judas by the addition of Matthias (Ac 1:26), were also qualified by virtue of having accompanied Jesus in his *ministry* and pre-eminently by being witnesses to the *Resurrection* (Ac 1:21-22). As an exceptional case, Paul was also reckoned among the apostles (1Co 15:7-9). Whereas these stipulations clearly set an historic limit to who may be regarded as apostles, the NT also applies the word to a wider band of early Christian leaders engaged in *mission* work and *church planting*, including Barnabas (Ac 14:4, 14), Andronicus and Junia (Ro 16:7) and, possibly, Silvanus and Timothy (1Th 2:7). Subsequent generations of ministries may be considered apostolic in so far as they continue the mission of the first apostles. The word might also appropriately, if reservedly, be applied in its broader meaning to significant pioneers who engage in mission and church planting, particularly when this involves breaking new ground. *Charles Haddon Spurgeon* in London and *Johann Gerhard Oncken* in Hamburg would be significant 19th-century European Baptist examples of this.

In some *restorationist* church structures, apostles are to be found who exercise spiritual *authority* over other *ministers*. Such practices are at odds with classical Baptist *ecclesiology* where ministers under God are responsible to *church meeting* and to church meeting alone, unimpeded by any other authority.

NGW & ET

Apostolicity

Alongside *unity, holiness* and *catholicity*, Apostolicity is one of the four marks of the church listed in the Nicene Creed. Tertullian in the second century described the church as being built upon the foundation of the Apostles (Eph 2:19f) and maintaining the doctrines and practices of the early or primitive church. Apostolicity, then, is a way of referring to those churches who have the marks of the primitive churches who were in *communion* with one another.

The idea of apostolicity became a topic for *theological* debate at the time of the *Reformation* when there was an attempt to determine which churches might rightly claim to be 'true churches'.

For the *Roman Catholic* Church apostolicity is built upon the succession of *Bishops* of Rome from Peter until today. For Baptists and other churches in the *reformed* tradition apostolicity depends much more on the particular congregations of believers taking proper regard to the *faith* once delivered to the primitive churches and seeking to live out the life of faith now by reference back to the faith of the church as recounted in *scripture* and without falling into the problem of giving a high regard to subsequent traditions of the churches, but trying in all ways to remodel the church in the form of the primitive church under the guidance of the *Holy Spirit*.

KGJ

Applied Theology

See *Practical Theology*.

Arab Baptist Theological Seminary, Beirut

Soon after WWII when *Southern Baptist missionaries* began their pioneering work in the Middle East, the need for trained national • church leaders became apparent. Temporary training programs were carried out for a number of years in various places. In 1953, Finlay Graham began *theological* training classes in his home in north Beirut with three *students*, and the next year three more were added. In 1956, William Hem began similar classes in Ajloun, Jordan.

In the late 1950s, a theological committee of the Arab Baptist General Mission recommended that a seminary be established for the training of Christian workers throughout the Arab world. Beirut was chosen as the location and Dr. Graham was elected to be the first president. Classes met in rented apartments during the first school year, 1960-1961, moving in Oct 1961 to the newly-constructed campus located in Mansourieh-Maten overlooking the city and the Mediterranean.

Lebanon, the historic gateway between the Arab World and the West, embracing as it does a cosmopolitan intersection of languages, cultures and peoples, was a strategic place for the Arab Baptist Theological Seminary (ABTS) to be located.

Dr. Graham served as ABTS President until 1977 and was succeeded by Dr. Emmett Barnes until 1993. In 1993, the ABTS management was completely transferred to a regional board of Trustees and Revd Dr. Ghassan Khalaf was elected as the President. In 1998 ABTS came under the legal ownership of the Lebanese Society for Educational and Social Development (LSESD). The Seminary celebrated its 40th anniversary in 2000 and inaugurated its new Learning Resource Centre and renovated campus in 2004, in the presence of the *European Baptist Federation* Council.

At the time of writing, ABTS has graduated over 230 students who are serving in ministries throughout the Middle East and North Africa as well as in the Arabic-speaking communities of the Western world. In addition, over 250 other students have studied at the Seminary for periods from one semester or more. Students are serving in a wide-variety of ministries, as pastors, church planters, evangelists, leaders of Christian organisations and 'lay' pastors. ABTS considers its graduates and alumni as its most precious treasure and clearest manifestation of the impact of the Seminary in the worldwide *ministry* of the Gospel of *Jesus Christ*.

PaS

Architecture

[See also *Chapels*; *Church Building (Sanctuary)*]

At the beginning of Baptist history, believers gathered in private homes for *Bible studies*, prayers and *fellowship*. Most importantly these were gatherings of 'true believers' in contrast to, and opposition to the general congregations of the established churches which made few demands upon those assembled. Lack of economic means with little thought for the need for specially dedicated assembly houses made these private assemblies sufficient for a long time.

As development continued and congregations increased, the place where *worship* took place became more important, though there was to be no simple copying of parish churches whether in style or in worship Baptists wanted worship places which reflected their *ecclesiology*, so simple chapels or buildings of some religious character were raised. Such buildings were intended to present Baptist beliefs and practice as offering an alternative Christian denomination, equal to other churches. Chapels were often designated with biblical names with some Christian symbols appearing on them to identify their function.

Whereas in the **United Kingdom** a distinct style of dissenting architecture had emerged in the 18th century, in other parts of Europe, e.g. in *Scandinavia* it was not until the first half of the 19th century that this happened and then mainly in towns where more deliberately planned Baptist places of worship began to emerge.

Churches were growing and **members** became more concerned about their meeting places as places of worship. Their lay-out was, therefore, to display the distinctive elements of Baptist worship. Accordingly there developed a focus on the *pulpit*, the baptising pool, and the **communion** table. These were religious buildings different from those built for secular purposes. Since the worship of God was the most important event in the lives of the believers the place of worship had to reflect that importance and suggest something of the majesty of God. In spite of lack of bells and spires, churches became often an important part of town scenery. Many good examples are to be seen even today. When in the 19th century other denominations were turning to the Gothic as the ideal style for places of worship, many Baptists rejected this, initially, as too closely associated with **Roman Catholicism** and the unreformed worship of the middle ages. By contrast the neo-classical style was much used by Baptists, not least because it seemed to have the blessing of *C.H. Spurgeon*, because it was in this style that he built the Metropolitan Tabernacle. Resistance to the Gothic did not last long, because in the public mind it represented the style in which a church ought to be built, that is to say it was thought of as 'Christian' architecture, and more prosperous Baptists wanted to worship in 'a proper church'. More modern churches

have been built in a style which is hardly distinguishable from that of other denominations, at least as far as external appearance is concerned.

Consequently, we cannot talk about typical Baptist architecture. There were no manuals of Baptist architecture prescribing what the style ought to be though individual architects did develop what they thought to be an appropriate style for Baptist churches As ministers and church members have become accustomed to more travel in Europe and beyond so ideas on how to design a church have been influenced by these experiences. Sometimes, however, municipal authorities, concerned with the townscape of strategic central sites have insisted that Baptists build in what they perceive to be an appropriate ecclesiastical style which means that a new church has to conform to the norms of the established church or even Catholic norms. Modern congregations need church buildings not only for their Sunday morning worship, but also rooms for several group activities throughout the week. Another possible reason for the need of such buildings is to achieve a higher status 'building-wise', to give the impression of a serious church organisation and life compared to other churches.

Economical development made it possible to erect church buildings which even today give the impression that Baptists are an important group of free churches with their own status, their own practice separated from others, but united in international **unity** of churches through the **European Baptist Federation** and/or the **Baptist World Alliance**.

Today certain churches of high aesthetic quality are preserved as national monuments. In the Baptist family one can find a variety of both older churches in the Gothic Revival, late Romanesque and Art Nouveaux styles as well as examples of new churches of good architectural quality with detailed, professional plans for the church building, equipment and decorations.

JJS & ET

Armenia, Baptist history in

Armenia, a country squeezed between *Georgia*, *Azerbaijan*, Iran and *Turkey*, has a venerable Christian history. The Armenian Apostolic (Gregorian) Church traces its tradition back to the early centuries after *Christ*; Christianity became the official religion in the Armenian areas in the 4th century. In the 1820s, *evangelical* ideas reached the country due to the *preaching* and *educational* work of *Protestant missionaries* Felician Zaremba and August Dietrich from the Basel Mission in *Switzerland*. Zaremba and Dietrich preached in Shushi (Karabakh region), Alexandrapol (Gyumri or Kumayri) and Yerevan. Though their work was stopped in 1835 by the opposition from the Armenian Apostolic Church, the evangelical vision continued to live among small groups of people of Protestant leanings who emphasised the *authority* of the *Bible* for *faith* and life, though they practised *infant baptism*. Parts of the New Testament, distributed by the Russian Bible Society, increased interest in the Bible amongst the population. Besides this, some preachers, such as Abraham Amirkhanyan, who viewed the Early Church as his model, spread Protestant views. Evangelical tradition in Armenian territory was expanded in the 1880s when Baptist preachers came to Armenia from Tiflis (Tbilisi), which then had a considerable Armenian community both in the city and in the local Baptist church. In 1890, in the town of Shushi, a small Baptist congregation of approximately 50 *members* was established. Andrei Mazaev, a deacon from the Tiflis church, blessed the Shushi church leaders, A. Davydov and A. Agarunov, for *ministry*. In 1917 there were Baptist groups in Stepanavan, Gyumri, Yerevan and the village of Urut. In the 1920s, during a brief period of relative freedom for Soviet evangelicals, Russian Evangelical Christian evangelists were active in the Trans-Caucasus region. However, the Baptist work in Armenia remained comparatively spontaneous and weakly organised. This was probably one reason why in the 1930s, in the purges of Stalin's repressions, Baptist work was practically wiped out. In 1944, the Soviet religious policy again allowed Baptist work, though merged with other evangelical churches, which together belonged to the *All-Union Council of Evangelical Christians-Baptists*. Some Protestant groups, such as the Ararat Brotherhood which was a fruit of the 19th century Basel Mission work, also merged

with the Baptists. In Soviet Armenia, Baptist activities remained modest, with the Yerevan church being the central venue for Baptist life. The Yerevan church, which included a number of Protestant believers who had repatriated to Armenia after WWII, joined the Union of Evangelical Christian-Baptists in 1947, after long conversations about the issue of *baptism*. The Protestant group gradually accepted the principle of believers' baptism by immersion. Since the collapse of the Soviet Union in the early 1990s, Armenian Baptists, with a young and energetic leadership, have seen phenomenal revitalisation and *growth* spreading all over the country. Charity work and literature distribution have been re-established and a theological seminary has been founded [see *Armenian Baptist Theological Seminary*]. Missionary ministries have been started in Edjmiadzin, Sisian, Artashat, Hrazdan, Ijevan, Armavir, Ashtarak, Kyavar, Goris, Metsamor, Urut, Talin, etc. The Baptist movement, which in 1991 had only six congregations, established new churches in Ararat, Arevshat, Stepanavan, Vanadzor, Gyumri, Yerevan and Abovyan. Today, The Union of Evangelical Christian Baptist Churches of Armenia, which was established in 1998, incorporates about 120 churches and *mission stations* with a total membership of approximately 3,400, and there are plans for further growth. The Union is a member of both *EBF* and *BWA*.

AN & MN

Armenian Baptist Theological Seminary

In 1992, a Nazarene *theological* school, 'Emmanuel' Bible College, with a four-year Bachelor's degree programme, was established in *Armenia*. Baptists co-operated in this project. In 1996 the first 12 *students* graduated from the school. Several Baptists who studied at this college now serve in Baptist churches as pastors. In 1997 the work further developed out of this beginning with the founding of the *Evangelical* Theological Seminary, and this institution, offering *education* from a wider *Protestant* basis, continues to operate. However, the developing Baptist movement in Armenia saw a need for its own school and in 1998 the Armenian Baptist Theological Seminary was founded. At the meeting of the Baptist Union in the same year, Asatur Nahapetyan was entrusted with the leadership of the seminary. In 1999 the first enrolment took place and in Oct 2001 the first group of students graduated from the seminary, which offers a three-year Bachelor's level theological education. By 2005, 95 students had graduated from the seminary. Today there are approximately 50 students who study in the departments of Pastoral Training and Christian Education.

AN

Arminianism

[See also *Calvinism*; *Election*; *Predestination*]

Arminianism is the word normally used to describe those who reject the confining of *salvation* to a predetermined number of the elect predestined before the foundation of the world. Rather Arminians focus on the exercise of human *free will*, promoted by the *Spirit*, in responding to the call of *Christ*. This way of systematising *theology* [see *Systematic Theology*] has played a large part in Baptist thought, especially in English-speaking countries. The General Baptists of *England* and the Free-Will Baptists of North America are both distinguished by their Arminian theology from those much more numerous Baptists who hold to an *orthodox* Calvinism.

Jacobus Arminius (or Jacob Harmenz, 1559-1609) was a Dutch *Reformed pastor* who had studied at Leiden, Marburg and in Geneva under Beza, who commended him back to the Dutch Church. He served as a pastor in Amsterdam from 1588 before becoming a professor at Leiden in 1603. Older historians were of the view that Arminius was initially an orthodox Calvinist and only later developed his revisionist views, but Bangs, his foremost biographer, argues, with the support of modern scholarship, that reformed theology was only slowly developing an orthodoxy and that in the second half of the 16th century there was a considerable amount of permitted theological flexibility. Indeed Arminius's conflict with the authorities was one of the causes célèbre which served to reduce this, for reformed theology

as defined by the Synod of Dort (1618-9) clearly excluded his views of free will as heterodox. Arminius's orthodoxy had been under question from the time of a sermon he preached in Amsterdam in 1591. Because he wrote little, it was difficult to focus the issue until he set out his views for his *students* in 1604, after his appointment to the theology chair at Leiden. Here, he came out against both supra and infralapsarian versions of the doctrine. By now however other issues were involved: the mandatory status of *confessions* and *catechisms* as rules of *faith*, and the legitimacy of the intervention of the civil magistracy in religious affairs, the former of which Arminius questioned and the latter of which he championed.

His concern was essentially *Christological*, his problem being that if people's destiny was already determined before the foundation of the world, the work of Christ was confined to effecting a salvation already determined, that is to say his work was confined to a subordinate aspect of human redemption. Accordingly Arminius places emphasis on God's foreknowledge rather than his prior determination of the fate of individuals. His part here was to determine the categories of persons to be saved or damned, that is to receive into favour those who believed and to exclude those who did not. Another way of expressing this is to say that Arminius reversed the orders of election and *grace*; for reformed orthodoxy the operation of grace was dependent on election, but for Arminius election was subsequent to grace seen in God's determination to save all who repent and believe. Salvation then becomes dependent on *humankind*'s response to the gospel which was an act of free choice though prompted by the Spirit not something coerced by irresistible grace. This response, God in his wisdom wholly foresaw, and thus his ability to count all such amongst the names of the elect. At the same time there is clear rejection here of any idea of a limited *atonement*.

After his death his sympathisers drew up the Remonstrance to the States General asking for a revision of the Belgic Confession. The five points of Arminianism were:

(1) Predestination is conditional on a person's response, being grounded in God's foreknowledge.

(2) Christ died for all humanity, but nobody enjoys the *forgiveness* of *sins* except the believer.

(3) *Humankind* has not saving grace of himself, for in a state of sin he cannot do anything good, so he must be born again of the Spirit.

(4) The grace of God is the beginning, continuing and the accomplishing of all good, so all that a regenerate person succeeds in doing must be ascribed to the grace of God in Christ. However, this grace is not irresistible because *scripture* speaks of those who resisted the Holy Ghost.

(5) In Christ and through his life-giving Spirit, the believer is equipped with all things necessary to resist temptation if only he/she will seek his assistance.

These propositions were condemned at the Synod of Dort in 1618-19, where a Calvinist orthodoxy was established.

The English General Baptists are often said to be Arminian in theology, though there are other sources for their free will beliefs, such as the teaching associated with the name of Peter Baro in Cambridge, and more generally an *Anabaptist* rejection of predestinarian formulae. The term is also unhelpful in that in England it becomes associated with Archbishop Laud's attempts to restore catholic *worship*, something sternly resisted by all Baptists. In the earliest years it is also argued that the issue existed as a divisive issue within congregations, such as that of Thomas Lambe in London, as much as between them, though after the civil war the division of Baptists into two doctrinal families had become fairly clear. The Orthodox Creed published in London by the General Baptists in 1679, states in article 18: 'And Christ died for all humanity, and there is a sufficiency in his death and merits for the sins of the whole world, and hath appointed the gospel to be preached unto all, and hath sent forth his spirit to accompany the word in order to beget repentance and faith: so that if any do perish, it's not for the want of the means of grace manifested by Christ to them, but for the non-improvement of the grace of God, offered freely to them through Christ in the gospel.'

Scholars have distinguished between a 17th-century Arminianism 'of the head' and an 18th-century Arminianism 'of the heart' as incarnated in the Wesleyan *revival*, which served to revive so-called Arminian emphases among *Evangelical* Baptists not only with the founding of the New Connexion of General Baptists in 1770 but with a moderating of a received Calvinism amongst many Particular Baptists. In the 19th century the fact of revivalism seemed to challenge all restricted views of the exercise of God's grace. In the writings of Jonathan Edwards it led to widespread amendment of Bezan Calvinism and in the thinking of Charles Finney it found ample justification in an updated version of Evangelical Arminianism. Many Baptists, especially in large parts of Eastern Europe, however, believe such classifications of theological opinion create artificial systems which are unhelpful amongst those searching for a lively Biblical way of understanding the mind of God for humankind and its salvation.

DBM & JHYB

FURTHER READING: Carl Bangs, *Arminius: A Study in the Dutch Reformation*, Abingdon, Nashville, Tn., 1971. James R. Coggins, *John Smyth and his Congregation*, Herald, Waterloo, Ontario, 1991. Stephen Wright, *The Early English Baptists, 1603-1649*, Boydell, Woodbridge, UK, 2006.

Ascensiontide

This day celebrates the Ascension of *Jesus Christ*, or his return to his Father, which, according to Ac 1:3, took place on the 40th day after the *Resurrection*. Accounts of worship in the early church during the 4th century in the *Apostolic Constitutions* recall the development of special commemorative liturgies to celebrate this day, at least in the Antioch – Constantinople region. Initially in some places the Ascension and *Pentecost* were closely related together. *Theologically* the Ascension marks the end of Jesus' earthly appearances to the disciples: the beatitude given to Thomas is relevant here: 'Thomas, because you have seen me you have found *faith*: blessed are they who never saw me and yet come to faith'. This is the birth of spiritual religion.

Amongst Baptists special services for Ascensiontide are quite rare, though within the context of the main Sunday *liturgy* attention may be drawn to the season with most Baptist hymn-books [see *Hymnals*] providing hymns for use at this season. *Easter* and Pentecost are more widely recognised and celebrated within baptistic communities. However, in some countries of central and Eastern Europe, e.g. in Transylvania, special Ascension Day services will be held with appropriate *preaching* relating to the theme of the day. The proper emphasis of such services will be the entry of Christ into His kingly office at the right hand of the Father.

KGJ

Ash Wednesday

This day marks the beginning of *Lent*. This first day of *fasting* makes it possible to maintain the Quadragesima, or forty days before the events of *Easter*. In certain Christian traditions in the special worship of this day associated with the beginning of Lent it is traditional to have the imposition of ashes on the foreheads of believers recalling how in the *Bible* they are used as a sign of purification (Nu 19:9, 17f; Heb 9:13) and of penitence (Jnh 3:6; Lk 10:13). In some traditions those ashes are formed by burning the Palm crosses distributed to the congregation on *Palm Sunday* the previous year. This practice no doubt developed in about the 10th century.

Whilst some Baptist congregations undoubtedly mark the formal beginning of Lent with special services, there are few, if any instances, where the imposition of ashes would take place.

KGJ

Assembly, General – as governing body of Union

[See also *Ecclesiology (Church Polity)*; *Unions/Conventions*]
Baptists are *congregationalists* at every level of their life together. A synodical [see *Synod*] form of government is foreign to the Baptist understanding of the church. Just as the *church meeting* is the final *authority* under God in the life of a local Baptist church, so the general assembly of churches should be the final authority under God in the life of a Baptist *union* or convention. The chief purpose of a Baptist assembly is not to provide inspiration, but to seek direction for the life and *mission* of the union or convention. By definition, therefore, a Baptist assembly is a deliberative assembly. So the distinguished British Baptist, George Gould, declared at the 1879 Norwich Assembly of the Baptist Union of *Great Britain and Ireland*: 'We meet as a deliberative body of Christians, who, agreeing in the belief of *evangelical* truth, and desiring to maintain the ordinances of the Gospel as our Lord hath delivered them to us, take counsel together that we may act, as far as possible, in concert for the furtherance of the Gospel of *Christ*, and in promotion of the efficiency of our body through its various organisations'.

Inevitably much of the day-to-day business of the union or convention will be delegated, either to its staff or to appropriate committees and councils – just as much of the day-to-day business of a *local church* will be delegated to *ministers*, *elders*, *deacons*, and other groups. However, delegation always implies accountability. Final authority lies with the Assembly.

The principle underlying such congregationalism may be found in the Council of Jerusalem where the issue of circumcision was decided not by the *apostles* and elders alone, but together with the church (Ac 15:22).

PBM

Associations and Associating

The first *Anabaptist* communities in central Europe were noted for their conviction that local gathering communities of believers had within their ecclesial realities the full possibility of understanding and determining the mind of *Christ* and could, therefore, be described as being autonomous [see *Autonomy*] in their community life and decision-making. However, at the same time, as John Howard Yoder and others have shown, these gathering communities wanted to relate to other like-minded communities for mutual support, to share concerns and to discuss together matters of mutual import. This associating was thus a deep conviction and was based in part on their understanding of how the NT churches were interrelated.

Associating in this way was carried forward and was a feature of the first Baptist communities. The General Baptists associated together and the first Particular Baptists did likewise [see *England*]. Moreover some of the earliest churches had congregations in several neighbouring locations so that they themselves were like a mini-association. Even if there was at first no formal association amongst some of the early congregations, there was correspondence and the intention of associating together with other like-minded groups. Early *confessions of faith*, such as the London Confession of 1644, in Article XLVII, follows the 1596 confession and bears testimony to the duty of associating with other like-minded congregations as a tool for building up the *Body of Christ* in diverse places. So, Baptist and baptistic *ecclesiology* from the beginning was against absolute independency or isolationism and for interdependency under the associating principle.

Associating, as developed by both General and Particular Baptists, was to be of like-minded congregations who could send messengers to meetings in an Association. These gatherings of messengers in assembly were for mutual help, edification, counsel, *unity* in action and the furtherance of *mission*. An economic element came forward with the development of joint missionary activity within the association and, later, in the English Northamptonshire Association, *William Carey* advanced his convictions about world mission.

It is thus an impossibility and a denial of Baptist ecclesiology to attach the two words 'Baptist' and 'Independent' in the same sentence. Our ecclesiology understands the mission of the NT church as embodying the associating principle and from the first Baptist churches until today this *theological* disposition has been a bedrock of Baptist ecclesiology, although there have always been Baptist churches which have impoverished their witness by their isolationist stance. These have often been churches of an extreme theological orientation who have been worried by 'the *guilt* by association' argument of relating to any body that did not think exactly as they did. Often quite large they have not been persuaded of the need for *fellowship* with and support from the larger body. Associating begins in a local

confined geographical area, has a national expression in a *union* or a *convention*, a continental expression as in the *European Baptist Federation* and a global dimension in the *Baptist World Alliance*.

It would be wrong to think that the principle of associating should stop at Baptist boundaries. For the sake of mission and as a demonstration that Baptists are not *sectarian* but recognise other denominations as true parts of Christ's world-wide church (sometimes called 'catholic' in the best sense of this word), they have engaged in wider inter-church relationships.

KGJ

FURTHER READING: E.A. Payne, *The Fellowship of Believers: Baptist Thought and Practice, Yesterday and Today* (Enlarged Ed.), Kingsgate, London, 1952. A. Gilmore (ed), *The Pattern of the Church: a Baptist view*, Lutterworth, London, 1963. B.R. White, 'The Practice of Association', in D. Slater, (ed) *A Perspective on Baptist Identity*, Mainstream, 1987. www.ebf.org.

Assurance of Forgiveness
See *Absolution*.

Atonement

What *Christ* achieved through his death on the cross, lies at the centre of Christian *faith*, for the universal sinfulness of *humankind* presents a basic dilemma, which humanity does not have the capacity to resolve, thus requiring God's gracious initiative. Although fundamental to the nature of Christian belief, the atonement has also been the focus of considerable debate over Christian history. This goes back to the perceived meaning of the Hebrew word, *kaphar* [atone], in the OT. The debate has turned around whether the word primarily signifies an atoning action directed towards God, that is an act which re-secures his favour, for which the English word is 'propitiation', or whether it is something done with regard to offences committed, covering them or blotting them out ('expiation'). This distinction should not, however, be pressed too hard, for different translations of *scripture* use both words almost indiscriminately to translate the Hebrew or the Greek, thus 1Jn 4:10; Ro 3:25; 1Jn 2:2 have 'propitiation' in the

the suffering of God the Father in the cross of Jesus in sympathy with the Son

AV but 'expiation' in the RSV. This suggests a danger in over-pressing different, apparently contradictory, explanations of what is involved in the atonement. It is better to try and hold differing models together, so that the death of Christ is seen as substitution, ransom, sacrifice, victory and example, all at the same time. All of this must be interpreted within a framework of Trinitarian *theology* [see *Trinity*], and must be free of interpretations based on how particular systems of law operated. Thus it is better not to ask 'to whom the ransom is paid?' for some forensic and transactional notions of the atonement seem to make the Son the one who appeases the Father, when it is God who is in Christ reconciling the world to himself (2Co 5:19); the Father who so loved the world that he gave his only begotten Son (Jn 3:16); whilst the Father sends his own Son in the likeness of sinful flesh to deal with *sin*, passing *judgement* against sin within that very nature, in order that the just requirements of the law might be fulfilled in us, whose conduct is no longer controlled by the old nature but by the *Spirit*.

Many Baptists have clearly followed *Calvin* in their understanding of the atonement in believing that in the atonement Christ takes upon himself the penalty of human sin, Christ bearing in his own body on the Cross the wrath of God, in our place standing condemned, and bearing our punishment [see *Calvinism*]. In this *tradition* there has been division amongst Baptists from the very earliest years between those who believe that Christ's death was for all who will turn to Christ in saving faith, and those who limit God's purposes only to the elect [see *Election*] (since a *Sovereign* God cannot be gainsaid and must be able to do all that he wishes to do). The first position clearly endorses the *missionary* task whilst the second stresses the divine initiative, which the first group would see as being in balance with the need for identified human response. Over time both positions have been modified. Under the influence of the *Methodist* Revival, Daniel Taylor restated the case for general *redemption* echoing the warm-hearted *evangelical preaching* of John Wesley, whilst Andrew Fuller [see *Fullerism*] restated the Calvinist faith that he had inherited in a way which underlined the obligation to engage energetically in missionary endeavour both in this country and in pagan lands abroad.

At the very beginning of the 20th century the British Baptist, T. Vincent Tymms, Principal of Rawdon College, wrote *The Christian Idea of the Atonement* in which he warned against 'all attempts to frame an intellectual theory of Atonement. It is enough to believe that Christ suffered on our behalf, and that in his name repentance is granted and remission of sins to every creature.' But he then proceeded to argue, 'Should a fresh review of Scripture bring to light a doctrine of Atonement which preserves all that is precious in the Gospel, that "God loved us and sent his Son...to be the propitiation of our sins", whilst excluding from its interpretation every element which is incongruous with the Fatherhood of God and the spontaneity and freeness of His mercy, it will do more than anything else to add boldness and fervour to many preachers.' That said he opposed all theories which focussed on an angry deity to be appeased by the imposition of punishment, which he believed to be incompatible with the life and teaching of Jesus. The essence of his thinking is expressed in the sentence: 'It was emphatically our sin not our punishment that bowed his soul in Gethsemane and ruptures his surcharged heart at Calvary. The *sufferings* of Christ are thus traced to man's iniquity, not to Divine anger: to man's injustice, not God's justice.' Tymms thus shares with the medieval *theologian*, Peter Abelard, in pointing to the moral influence of the atonement: 'the disclosure of God's *love* in the cross has the power to create love within our loveless hearts' But he goes beyond Abelard in affirming 'the need for Christ to endure the suffering and death which is the consequence of sin, in order to make clear the grief of God over human sin and the costliness to God in offering *forgiveness*.'

H. Wheeler Robinson, who joined the staff of Rawdon two years after Tymms retired, towards the end of his life developed these ideas further. Both men, according to Paul Fiddes, 'affirm the suffering of God the Father in the cross of Jesus in sympathy with the Son, both emphasise that Christ endured in himself the terrible consequences of human sin, and both find atonement to lie in the power of the cross to transform human lives in the present.' Robinson argues that at the cross the suffering caused by sin is changed into the power of forgiveness. Thus he writes, 'By the actuality of a divine transformation of the consequences of sin upon the cross of Christ there are liberated the spiritual energies and influences which eventually transform *men* from being enemies into being friends and servants of God.'

Fiddes himself argues that Baptists' special contribution to the theology of the Atonement is to bring Calvinist and *Arminian* traditions together in affirming 'the enduring of sin and divine wrath by Christ (Calvinist tradition), while also affirming the central place of human response and human transformation (Arminian tradition)' bringing together both 'the objective initiative of God's *grace* together with the 'existential' stress on personal response' which he sees as 'an understanding of atonement that does justice to the New Testament witness', linking together 'human response in the present with the act of God in the past.'

Some become so attached to a particular view of the Atonement that they believe that their understanding of it is the only form sanctioned by scripture, that indeed that the words in the theory are themselves part of scripture rather than a suggested interpretation of it. Thus, when in recent years, the Baptist Evangelical, Steve Chalke, suggested that extreme theories of penal substitution could logically bring an accusation of child-abuse against God., controversy filled the air, though the outcome of the debate was to show that there was room for differences of opinion amongst Evangelicals on the theory, but not on the central affirmation of the importance of the atonement.

ET

FURTHER READING: T. Vincent Tymms, *The Christian Idea of the Atonement*, MacMillan, London and New York, 1904. Paul Fiddes, *Past Event and Present Salvation: The Christian Idea of Atonement*, John Knox, Westminster, 1989. Paul Fiddes, *Tracks and Traces: Baptist Identity in Church and Theology*, Paternoster, Carlisle, 2003. Stephen R. Holmes, *The Wondrous Cross: Atonement and Penal Substitution in the Bible and History*, Paternoster, Milton Keynes, 2007

AUCECB
See *All-Union Council of Evangelical Christians-Baptists*.

Auricular Confession
Confession of *sin* secretly before God, without an intermediary, has been one of the popular tenets of *Protestant* devotional practice. In reaction to the elaborate and sometimes corrupt penitential system of the medieval church a more immediate access to God was emphasised at the *Reformation*. The practice of auricular confession, that is confession to an authorised person in a one-to-one setting continued in the *Roman Catholic* tradition and was revived in the Anglo-Catholic movement in the Church of England. The ultra-Protestant polemic directed at the priest in Confession gave rise to suspicion and indeed fear of such intimate revelation of sins and weaknesses. The rugged individualism of Protestant spirituality certainly did not provide a fertile soil for any sort of auricular confession. The exhortation of Jas 5:16, 'therefore confess your sins to one another', although it is in the context of *healing*, has been used to confine the use of confession, if it is used at all, to small meetings of Christians.

General Confession has been permitted in the Roman Catholic Church in recent years, under strict conditions, and there has been a decline in auricular confession. At the same time other Christians, Baptists among them have rediscovered the need for individual counselling. Many have discovered the value of a 'soul-friend' or a spiritual director, bound by the rules of confidentiality, with whom sins and sorrows may be discussed, and by whom words of *absolution* may be spoken. The various schools of Psychoanalysis provide a secular equivalent seen by some to be more appropriate to present-day life and problems.

In the *liturgy* of the *Church* there must be room for *prayers* of general confession of sins both of commission and of omission, for confession is an activity of the *fellowship* as well as an individual matter. This is closely allied to *Church discipline*, for it is on confession of wrongdoing in the presence of the church that the sinner can be offered a restoration of fellowship.

DBM

FURTHER READING: John Colwell, *Promise and Presence* (esp. Ch. 8, 'The Sacrament of Cleansing'), Paternoster, Carlisle, 2005.

Austria, Baptist history in

During the *Reformation* era, there were many *Anabaptists* in Austria, but the Habsburgs exterminated or expelled them. It is estimated that about 600 Anabaptists were burnt or drowned there, including two famous leaders: *Balthasar Hubmaier* (burnt in Vienna, 1528) and Jakob Huter (burnt in Innsbruck, 1536).

After the great fire in Hamburg in 1842, many workmen came from the heartlands of the Habsburg Empire as part of the rebuilding programme and some of them were converted in the congregation of *Johann Gerhad Oncken*. In 1846 they went back home, taking with them their new-found *faith*. This spreading of the Baptist movement within the Habsburg Empire was supported by some Baptist co-workers of the British and Foreign Bible Society, such as Edward Millard. The first Austrian congregation was founded in 1869 in Vienna; it was also the first free church in Austria (later came the *Methodists* and the Adventists, after WWI, came the *Pentecostals*, and after WWII, came the *Mennonites*). This first congregation was the starting point for congregations around the Habsburg Empire, continuing in Bratislava, Prague, Zagreb, Budapest, etc. At first the Baptists in these cities were *members* of the Viennese congregation, which had more than 200 members by 1900. The possibility of having public assemblies was restricted for all non-acknowledged churches such as the Baptists. Accordingly, they had a lot of problems with the police and some Baptists were even imprisoned. After WWI and the *peace* treaty of Saint Germain (in 1919) there was *religious freedom* in Austria. At the same time Austria became a small independent country with its capital, Vienna, now at its eastern border. Baptists, however, were not acknowledged as a church, so their rights were more restricted than the larger churches. In 1998 a lesser status of recognition, 'Bekenntnisgemein-

schaft', was created and the Baptists were given this status.

The new freedom after WWI allowed a church house to be built at Mollardgasse 35, Vienna in 1924 at which the oldest Austrian congregation still meets. In the years 1929-60 the German Baptist preacher, Arnold Köster, served there. The 1930s saw the beginning of new home *Bible study* groups in the east and centre of Austria, especially in Vienna-Hütteldorf and in Salzburg. During WWII, Köster criticised aspects of National Socialism in his sermons. In 1953 the 'Bund der Baptistengemeinden in Österreich' (Union of the Baptist Congregations in Austria) was founded. At the present time there are about 1300 Baptists in Austria.

FGS

FURTHER READING: Franz Graf-Stuhlhofer et al (eds), 'Frisches Wasser auf dürres Land. Festschrift zum 50-jährigen Bestehen des Bundes der Baptistengemeinden in Österreich', *Baptismus-Studien* 4, Oncken-Verlag, Kassel, 2004.

Authority in the Church

For Baptist communities authority in the church is firmly focused in the *Lord of the Church, Jesus Christ* himself. Baptists are not convinced there are other major significant authorities – *Scripture, Tradition*, hierarchy. As Christocentric communities it is to Christ we look. As the British Baptist Declaration of Principle pronounces 'Jesus Christ himself is the Head of the *Church*.' Of course, this fine declaration has practical implications for baptistic ecclesia in the discernment of the mind of Christ for the authentic life of the church.

So, the principal authority in Baptist churches lies with the community of baptised believers [see *Baptism*] gathering together in the presence of the *Holy Spirit* to study the scriptures, pray and seek together to discern the will of Christ for the community. Such a gathering is the formative place for authority in the life of the Church. It has, since the mid 1800s, been adapted almost universally throughout Europe, from the original vision to a more formal '*Church meeting*' with minutes being taken and votes cast, but in more authentic and historic form the discerning of the mind of Christ and identifying Authority in the Church took place in the context of a service of *worship* during which the community sought to discern in *prayer* and study what the life and witness of the church should be like.

The Church meeting may, and generally does, assign some responsibilities to *Deacons* and/or *Elders* and/or a *Pastor*, but it is always clear this is a derived authority from the *gathering community* of believers gathered by the Holy Spirit.

The Church rarely, if ever, gives any significant and regular authority to wider ecclesial bodies such as associations, *unions* and federations; however *local churches* will expect such wider representative assemblies to act on their behalf in promoting *mission*, representing the churches to wider society and government and in the promotion and protection of *human rights* and *religious freedom*.

In some countries, because of the legal status of churches, there is another form of authority- the foundation document, charter, trust deed or statutes of the church. These documents with a legal status might be required for the foundation and registration of the church and their articles will have an on-going authority in determining the general life of the church (or the use of the building in which the church gathers) from generation to generation.

The historic *creeds* of the church and, in some countries, the general statement of belief of Baptist churches associating together will be taken as significant documents having an important role in setting out the general parameters of the belief, practice and authority within Baptist churches, but only rarely will they be taken as having so much authority as to override the living authority of Christ seen and recognised through the Holy Spirit as a local church meeting seeks to meet in prayer and study to discern the mind of Christ.

KGJ

FURTHER READING: Brian Haymes, Ruth Gouldbourne, and Anthony R. Cross, *On Being the Church: Revisioning Baptist Identity*, Paternoster, Carlisle, 2008.

Autonomy of the local church
[See also *Local Church*]
Baptist understanding of *ecclesiology* places the key emphasis on the *theology* of the church in the local *gathering community* of believers. It is a universal Baptist conviction that God is gathering *women* and *men* into communities of *faith* around a *covenant*. Such bodies are answerable only to the *Lord of the Church* [see *Authority*] and not to the demands of the *state* or ruler or to the dictates of some higher ecclesial authority. Theologically the Triune God [see *Trinity*] draws people in *repentance* and by faith through the waters of *baptism* and into a community ecclesial experience. Theologically, it follows that such communities covenanted together and sharing their convictions have a freedom and a responsibility in the setting of their *worship* and *prayer* to determine the mind of *Christ* for their life together, and to support, encourage and admonish one another in each individual journey of *discipleship* as it seems good to the *Holy Spirit* and to the whole community.

This theological understanding means that each gathering church is 'autonomous'; it has all the gifts that God so richly gives to be the *Body of Christ* in that place. Those covenanted together have a responsibility to participate in meetings to discern the mind of Christ. It is not an optional extra. This responsibility laid upon a local church is not because it has within its own rights the power and authority to ignore everyone else, but because the community understands the Triune God has drawn them into a body together and they are placed in God's *sovereign* will. However, such churches understand that though they have the responsibility to determine the mind of Christ as it applies to them, generally it is right and proper, in following the pattern of the NT churches, to associate with other like-minded congregations on matters of mutual concern and interest, to take counsel and to engage together in *mission* [see *Associations and associating*].

The concept of the autonomy of the local church has been expounded strongly by Baptists ever since *Thomas Helwys*'s Confession of 1611 where he commented in Article 10 'the *Church* of Christ is a company of faithful people, separated from the world by the word and Spirit of God, being knit together unto the Lord and unto one another, by baptism, upon their own confession of faith and (*confession* of) sins.' It is not to be confused with independency, which is not a Baptist belief.

KGJ

Awakening
See *Great Awakening*; *Renewal*.

Azerbaijan, Baptist history in
While the other two Trans-Caucasian countries, *Georgia* and *Armenia*, are historically Christian, Azerbaijan differs by having a predominantly *Muslim* population. *Protestant missionaries* from the Basel *Mission* worked in the Caucasus in the 1820s and 1830s, thus preparing the soil for later *evangelical* seeds. As a result of their work, the Shemakha brotherhood, a group with Protestant *theological* leanings, emerged. However, the Baptist mission which started in the 1870s, advanced slowly. Baptist work centered mostly in Baku, where Vassilii Ivanov, later known as an editor of the publication *Baptist* (in Russian), initiated a Baptist church around 1880. In 1884, at a Russian Baptist conference, Ivanov was elected as an evangelist for the Caucasus region. After his exile to Slutsk in 1895, for his missionary activities, Ivanov returned to Baku, and served the Baku church as minister from 1900-17. Another outstanding figure in the Azerbaijan Baptist story was Vasilii Pavlov, who learned the local Azeri language and worked in the Caucasus in the 1870s and 1880s, as well as later, around 1923. Pavlov's mission to preach the Gospel to the Caucasian Muslims was not fully carried out, as he died in Baku in 1924. Nevertheless, smaller Baptist groups, predominantly Russian-speaking, emerged in the course of time in Hatshmass, Lenkoran, Kedabaks and other locations. During the Soviet years, another Baptist church was founded in Sumgait. In 1989 there were six Baptist churches in the country, with a total *membership* of more than 600 believers. The rise of religious activity at the beginning of the 1990s, and the coming of *political* independence for Azerbaijan, had a double effect. On the one hand Baptist work intensified and new churches were planted. On the other hand, many church members belonging to ethnic *.ies* emigrated from the country because of the increasingly difficult political and economic situation. In 2006, the Union of Evangelical Christians-Baptists of Azerbaijan, a member of *EBF*, consisted of 22 churches with the total number of church members reaching 3,000. There have been attempts to expand the predominantly Russian-speaking Baptist work to reach local Azeris. Part of the worship in the Baku Church now embraces the Azeri language and there are Azeri-speaking congregations in other city centres.

TP

B

Balkan States, Baptist history in the

See *Albania*; *Bosnia and Herzegovina*; *Bulgaria*; *Croatia*; *Macedonia*; *Serbia, Baptist history in*.

Baltic States, Baptist history in the

See *Estonia*; *Latvia*; *Lithuania, Baptist history in*.

Bangor Baptist College

The first college established in north *Wales* for the training of Baptist *ministers* was at Llangollen, Denbighshire, in 1862. Its principal was John Pritchard, minister of the town's Baptist church, who was succeeded in the principalship by Hugh Jones, his co-pastor, in 1866. Under the leadership of Gethin Davies, appointed principal in 1883, the college moved in 1892 to the city of Bangor, Caernarfonshire, where the second constituent college of the new University of Wales had been founded eight years earlier.

The leading personality in the Bangor college was Silas Morris, professor of the NT and principal between 1886 and 1923. The OT professor was Thomas Witton Davies, a *student* of Georg Heinrich Ewald at Göttingen, who transferred from the Baptist College to the chair in Semitics at Bangor University. Both men were keen to fuse critical scholarship with the *evangelicalism* in which they had been raised.

For the rest of the 20th century the college was served by a secession of able teachers including John Gwili Jenkins, J. Williams Hughes and D. Eirwyn Morgan, with some 500 students having trained there between 1892 and the present. The college still serves its primary constituency, namely the Welsh-speaking churches of the Baptist Union of Wales.

DDM

Baptism

[See also *Sacrament, Sign and Symbol*; *Baptism and Christian initiation liturgy*]

In NT times there were *no* unbaptised believers (1Co 12:13, note 'all'): the Christian *church* was the baptised community. The predecessor of Christian baptism was John's baptism of *repentance* and *confession* (Mt 3:1-2, 6, 11) which anticipated *Pentecost* when the *Spirit* would come upon the disciples (Mt 3:11; Mk 1, 4-5, 7-8; Lk 3:16). *Jesus'* baptism at John's hands was one of identification with humanity and a *revelation* to John and others that the Son of God had come (Mk 1:9-11).

Christian baptism originates in the post-*resurrection* command of the exalted Christ (hence '*ordinance*', i.e., that which is ordained by Christ) to 'Go and make disciples of all nations, baptising...and teaching them...' (Mt 28:19-20) and in the *apostolic* church it was an integral and essential part of the *preaching* of the gospel/the *kerygma* (cf. below on 1Co 1:17). All those who repented and accepted Christ were baptised immediately (see Ac 8:12; 36-38; 10:44-48; 16:14-15, 31-33; 18:8) and were assured that in this expression of their *faith* they would receive the *forgiveness* of their *sins* and the gift of the life-giving Spirit (Ac 2:38, 41). NT baptism was *conversion*-baptism/conversion-initiation into the triune God [see *Trinity*]. New converts were then discipled [see *Discipleship*] in their faith both in what they should believe (doctrine) and how they should live as followers of Christ (*ethics*, cf. Ro 6:3-4, 'live a new life'). Baptism is, therefore, inseparably linked with discipleship, and disciplined Christian living. Because baptism is an ordinance of Christ and the God-ordained response to the preaching of the gospel it is not an optional extra. Often people say 'I'm not ready to be baptised' or 'I am waiting for Jesus to tell me to be baptised' or 'It's not my kind of thing'. This is largely due to Baptists having a low view of baptism and not including it in preaching. Spiritualising the process of becoming a Christian, Baptists have separated Spirit- and water-baptism in a way that is untrue to the NT (see Ac 2:38; 1Co 12:13; Jn 3:5). This separation did not begin to happen until the 4th century, when the spirit-matter dualism characteristic of the Hellenistic world in general and Gnosticism in particular invaded *theology*. By contrast a healthy view of God as creator [see *Creation*], and matter as the means in and through which he works for the *salvation* of his bodily creation, humanity, must be emphasised. With this understanding of the goodness of God's creation and the way he uses ordinary, material means as vehicles of his gracious working, baptism becomes the meeting place of the initiating divine-human encounter (the *grace* of God meeting the faith of the repentant believer).

The word that gives us 'baptism'/'baptise' comes from the Greek word meaning 'to dip, to plunge' and this is why baptism is by total immersion, expressing the dying and rising of the Lord Jesus. This is in full accord not just with the meaning of the Greek but also with the practice of the NT: both Philip and the Ethiopian eunuch 'went *down* into the water' (Ac 8:38), while Jesus 'went *up* out of the water' (Mt 3:16). The physical going down into the water, being immersed into it and the being raised up from it provides baptism with its powerful *symbolism*. Paul uses the symbolism of a watery grave to show us that 'all of us who were baptised into Christ Jesus were baptised into his death' and were 'buried with him through baptism into death in order that, just as Christ was raised from the dead...we too may live a new life' (Ro 6:3-4). It also ties in with baptism in the NT being the occasion where the forgiveness of sins is first experienced (Ac 2:38) and the believer is washed clean by the working of the Spirit (Tit 3:5).

But baptism is more than a symbol, it is an *effective* symbol (the understanding of baptism as an ordinance does not exclude it being also a sacrament) because it is a divinely appointed *means of grace*. NT baptism is faith-baptism and this is clearly shown in the fact that the full range of the gifts of salvation that are attributed to faith in the NT are also attributed to baptism (see: forgiveness, cf. Ro 4:5-7 with Ac 2:38; justification, cf. Ro 3:28 with 1Co 6:11; sonship, cf. Jn 1:12 with Gal 3:26-27; being filled with the *Holy Spirit*, cf. Gal 3:2-5, 14 with Ac 2:38 and 1Co 12:13; entry into the church, cf. Gal 3:6-7 with Gal 3:27). However, this is *not* to succumb to the idea that baptism acts automatically for faith is always essential, otherwise the actions are meaningless. Any suggestion of mechanical operation of baptism is excluded in key NT passages. E.g. in 1Pe 3:21 we read that 'baptism now saves you' but it is 'not the removal of dirt' as happens in an ordinary bath, but it is 'the pledge/prayer of a good *conscience* towards God'. In fact, 'It saves...by the *resurrection* of Jesus Christ'. Elsewhere, Paul tells us that we are 'saved...through the washing of rebirth and *renewal/regeneration* by the Holy Spirit' who is poured out through Jesus Christ so that 'having been justified by his grace, we might become heirs having the hope of *eternal life*' (Tit 3:5-7; regeneration is Paul's expression for what John records as rebirth/birth from above, cf. Jn 3:3, 5).

Baptism normally takes place in the *baptistry* in a *church building*, but it can also take place in a river, lake or the sea, wherever there is running water. The place is not as important as the fact that baptism takes place amidst the *gathered* people of God for baptism is not a private ceremony but something which belongs to the whole church. Sometimes, however, immersion is not possible. In areas where there is drought, e.g., valid baptisms have been performed where there is no water at all, or, if only a little water is available, baptism can be performed by affusion/pouring (this was, in fact, the mode the first Baptists used 400 years ago before a deeper understanding of the NT led them to the practice of full immersion). Further, baptism is into the name of the triune God (Mt 28:19) and Baptists often use this as a baptismal formula spoken at the moment of immersion; in baptism a person is brought into an existence that is fundamentally determined and ruled by God—Father, Son and Spirit. There are some who baptise 'into the name of (the Lord) Jesus Christ' and this is quite legitimate. The norm for Baptists appears to be a single act of immersion using the trinitarian formula of Mt 28:19, but it can equally be a threefold immersion with each person of the Trinity named at the corresponding immersion, a practice which has ancient precedent.

Baptism is an occasion where the baptised believer professes/confesses faith in Christ (e.g., Ro 10:9-10; 1Ti 6:12), and this is why the baptised believer either responds to questions and/or gives their testimony of how they came to faith in Christ, so providing an evangelistic opportunity for the preaching of the gospel [see *Evangelism*].

This raises the question of the age for baptism. In the NT's faith-baptism it is not age which is critical, but whether those seeking baptism have come to faith in Christ. Many Baptists insist that baptism should not be administered until teenage years, sometimes early (13 or 14), sometimes later (17 or 18). But this upper age range changes baptism altogether from believers' baptism to adult baptism. Many people become Christians before their teenage years – sometimes much earlier. If this is the case then, as far as the NT is concerned, they are eligible for baptism. To separate baptism from conversion is to depart from NT baptism. However, the younger the child the more complicated matters become pastorally, requiring knowledge of the young person, discernment as to whether their request comes from a true commitment to Christ or from peer pressure, the desire for attention or some other reason. If the young person comes from a Christian family then the pastoral decision can be more straight forward than if the young person comes from a family where either one or neither of the parents are believers. In all such cases, the *pastor* and the church need to consult both with the parents and the candidate before the decision to baptise is taken. There might also be legal reasons why care needs to be taken. There are other reasons often given as to why baptism should be postponed. If it is because 'They are too young to be baptised', then the answer is 'If they are old enough to believe in Christ they are old enough to be baptised'. If it is 'because it will mean more to them when they are older', this is to divorce baptism from conversion and it thereby becomes something other than NT baptism. Sometimes young people are deferred from baptism on the grounds that they might backslide, but this is true of anyone at any age in life.

Baptism normally takes place within the church's *worship* thereby underlining its corporate dimension—it is not just an individual's act. According to Paul, 'we [are] all baptised by one Spirit into one body' (1Co 12:13) and enter God's family ('children of God through faith in Christ Jesus', Gal 3:26;

cf. Eph 2:19, 'members of God's household'). Baptism is the initiating rite, through which believers enter the church. Here Baptists have frequently understood baptism in *covenantal* terms. Believers are in covenantal relationship with the triune God and in and through this relationship they are in covenantal relationship with all other members of the Body of Christ. This is a great privilege, but with it comes responsibility to be fully committed to the work of Christ in the *local church*. This is why Baptists have frequently practised closed *membership* – though there have always been Baptists who have not excluded others who understand baptism differently. John Bunyan is perhaps the best known example of somebody who pastored a 'mixed congregation'. In NT times, however, when all believers were conversion-baptised, it was true that baptism was initiatory into the Body of Christ, the Church, but as soon as baptism is separated from conversion (by paedobaptists [see *Infant Baptism*] who put it before conversion, and by most Baptists who put it after conversion and baptism) then it becomes less easy to claim the fullness of the NT theology of baptism.

ARC

FURTHER READING: G.R. Beasley-Murray, *Baptism in the New Testament*, Macmillan, London, 1962. G.R. Beasley-Murray, *Baptism Today and Tomorrow*, Macmillan, London, 1966. O.S. Brooks, *The Drama of Decision: Baptism in the New Testament*, Hendrickson, Peabody, Ma., 1987. J.E. Colwell, *Promise and Presence: An Exploration of Sacramental Theology*, Paternoster, Milton Keynes, 2005. A.R. Cross, *Baptism and the Baptists: Theology and Practice in Twentieth-Century Britain*, Paternoster, Carlisle, 2002. Paul S. Fiddes (ed.), *Reflections on the Water: Understanding God and the World through the Baptism of Believers*, Regent's Park College and Smyth and Helwys, Oxford and Macon, Ga., 1996. S.K. Fowler, *More Than a Symbol: The British Baptist Recovery of Baptismal Sacramentalism*, Paternoster, Carlisle, 2002. S.E. Porter and A.R. Cross (eds), *Baptism, the New Testament and the Church: Historical and Contemporary Studies in Honour of R.E.O. White*, Sheffield Academic Press, Sheffield, 1999. S.E. Porter and A.R. Cross (eds), *Dimensions of Baptism: Biblical and Theological Studies*, Sheffield Academic Press, Sheffield, 2002. T.R. Schreiner and S.D. Wright (eds), *Believers' baptism: Sign of the New Covenant in Christ*, Broadman and Holman, Nashville, Tn., 2006. R.E.O. White, *The Biblical*

Doctrine of Initiation, Hodder and Stoughton, London, 1960. R.E.O. White, *Believing and Being Baptized: Baptism, So-called Re-baptism and Children in the Church*, Baptist Union of Great Britain, Didcot, 1996. *Conversations Around the World, 2000–2005: The Report of the International Conversations between The Anglican Communion and The Baptist World Alliance*, The Anglican Communion Office, London, 2005. *Pushing at the Boundaries of Unity: Anglicans and Baptists in Conversation*, Church House, London, 2005.

Baptism and Christian initiation liturgy

[See also *Baptism*; *Christian Initiation*; *Sacrament, Sign and Symbol*]

In Baptist churches believers' baptism generally takes place within the main service on Sunday. This service often includes the *eucharist* and reception into *membership* of those baptised, though in some circumstances, for want of time, the eucharist and reception into membership takes place on a later occasion. Baptism without incorporation into a local *gathering church* is not an authentic *ecclesiological* or *theological* position as far as Baptists are concerned.

Most Baptist churches are equipped with a *baptistry* in the church *worship* room, either at the entrance to the worship room, reminding us that baptism is entry into the *Church* of Christ, or at the centre, or front of the worship room in front or behind the *communion* table [see *Architecture*; *Church building (Sanctuary)*]. It is not common in Europe to follow the practice of many North American churches in having the baptistry on the wall behind the communion table at some height so that the immersion, or submersion, can be more effectively observed. Europeans tend to want to keep some spatial relationship between the believing community, the baptistry, the table and the *pulpit*. Some communities baptise in the open air when this is practicable, in the sea, a river or swimming pool. It is hoped thereby to provide an *evangelistic* opportunity.

Baptism is generally by immersion, or submersion, rather than by affusion, or sprinkling, or the imposition of water with the sign of the cross. It is normally at the climax of a service in which there has been *prayer*, the reading of *scripture* and *preaching* and normally the candidate(s) for baptism will give their testimony or respond to a series of questions about their *faith*.

The baptistry or baptismal pool, is prepared before worship. In some instances there is a continuing flow of running water to signify the onward journey of *discipleship*. After the *confession of faith* by the candidate(s), and often a prayer over the baptistry praying for the renunciation of evil, the *pastor* and those baptising the candidate(s) enter the water. Baptism is then conducted with a Trinitarian formula [see *Trinity*]. Baptism takes place generally by taking people back into the water, symbolically [see *Sign and Symbol*] taking up the imagery of Ro 6 of dying and rising to *Christ*, but some baptise by asking people to kneel and then pushing their heads under water in a forward motion.

Whilst in the baptistry there is normally a prayer for the infilling of the *Holy Spirit* on the one baptised, often with the *laying on of hands,* which has been a practice in many Baptist churches since the early 1600s.

The decision to baptise is invariably made by the meeting of members after hearing a report of the faith of those seeking baptism, given by visitors who have been appointed by the church meeting to meet with the candidate to explore such issues. The appointment of those who will baptise again, is normally by the *church meeting*, though usually the pastor and/or one or more *elders* or *deacons* participate.

A typical contemporary liturgy for baptism might be:

Call to worship
Praise and Thanksgiving
Reading of the Word
Proclamation of the Word
Testimony of the Candidate(s)
Renunciation of evil
Blessing of the baptistry
Baptism
Laying on of hands
Prayers of intercession
Reception into membership
The Peace
The Eucharist
Dismissal.

KGJ

FURTHER READING: A.R. Cross, *Baptism and the*

Baptists, Paternoster, Carlisle, 2002. Stanley K. Fowler, *More than a Symbol*, Paternoster, Carlisle, 2002.

Baptism, Eucharist and Ministry (BEM)

[See also *Baptism*; *Communion and Inter-communion*; *Eucharistic Liturgy*; *Ministry*; *Sacrament, Sign and Symbol*]
This was one of several documents produced by the Faith and Order Commission of the *World Council of Churches* to see how far there could be agreement between the churches on major matters of Christian *faith* and practice. The final text, after more than 20 years of study and conversation with the churches, was agreed in Lima, Peru, in Jan 1982, and so also the accompanying script for an agreed form of Eucharistic celebration which is often known as the Lima Liturgy. Those participating in the process embraced *Protestants*, including a number of Baptists (e.g. Morris West of *Bristol* and Günter Wagner of *Rüschlikon*), *Orthodox* and *Roman Catholics*. The BEM document communicates, confusingly, at two levels, first the approved text but alongside this an accompanying commentary where some of the difficulties of the document are to be found. BEM does not represent a complete statement of Christian truth in the designated areas; 'the churches remain entirely free to accept, correct or reject the text'. But the document is conceived of as a tool to be used in Christian *education*, in articulating a large measure of *unity* within the *Church*, helping different traditions both locally and globally to understand what they believe and practice in common, and perhaps to provoke liturgical reform [see *Liturgy*].

The actual text makes many robust affirmations that Baptists are able to agree with, e.g. the paragraphs on the institution and meaning of baptism with their recognition of the vital link between baptism and faith, that baptism is symbolic [see *Sign and Symbol*] of new life in union with *Christ*, the need for *conversion* prior to baptism, the anticipation in baptism of the coming of the *Spirit*, and the ethical demands properly made of the newly baptised [see *Ethics*]. Indeed so strong is the language here deployed that Baptists are agnostic as to how it can in

any way be applied to *infant baptism*. The statement that 'Any practice which might be interpreted as "rebaptism" must be avoided' has been almost universally rejected by Baptists.

The response to the document, now published in six volumes edited by Max Thurian was overwhelming. European Baptists (BUGB, the Scottish and Covenanted Welsh Baptists, Baptists in East *Germany*, *Denmark*, *Sweden* and *Russia*) showed themselves more ready to respond than the rest of the Baptist Community for only the responses from Burma and the *American Baptist Churches* have to be added for the rest of the family, though Günter Wagner also cites a response from the *Baptist World Alliance*, as also responses from *Italy* and West Germany that do not appear in the published volumes. Of the responding *unions* those from *Scotland*, Sweden and the two Germanies were not members of the World Council of Churches

In general Baptists welcomed the appearance of the document and the processes of deepening mutual understanding that this represented, and commended some of its central statements which seemed to affirm the historical Baptist position. There were worries about the ambiguity of language deployed, e.g., did a phrase like the *apostolic* faith mean the faith statements contained in the NT, the faith embodied in the historic *creeds*, or both these as continued in the *traditions* of the *church*? Indeed there was general concern to protect the sufficiency of *scripture* as alone the *authority* for all matters of faith and practice. British Baptists expressed some general disquiet in attributing to the sign what they believed to be the benefits of that which was being signified. Thus of baptism it is said, it 'gives', 'initiates', 'unites', 'effects', but if this relates merely to the performance of the rite, they term it 'at best hyperbole and at worst objectionable'; but if the reference is to the total work of Christ, here symbolised, then these words possess true meaning. But if that is so then it could be that those central affirmations would make a better starting point for *ecumenical* explorations than the *ecclesiological* concerns of BEM. If the church is defined as the community of the baptised, what is this saying about children in the church, and those who do not come to live out their baptism on the one hand, and faithful members of the *Salvation Army* and the *Society of Friends* on the other?

Whilst the paragraphs on the Eucharist contained many emphases that Baptists were ready to underwrite, acknowledging that they express them in a way helpful to confessional convergence, the overall emphasis of these paragraphs disturbed them, because once more meaning was being attributed to the sign rather than to the reality being symbolised. There was also a tendency to see every aspect of Christian *worship* as Eucharistic, creating what one respondent called 'an intolerable theological overload' with Eucharistic celebration eclipsing all other aspects of Christian worship. Otherwise the fear was of a dominating sacramentalism, and a sacramentarian *theology* of *grace*, with an unhelpful emphasis on a theology of the elements rather than a theology of action, and on the failure of the document clearly to allow for duly authorised lay *presidency*.

The setting of the ordained ministry [see *Ordination*] in the context of the total ministry and *mission* of the whole people of God, itself founded in the total ministry, mission and work of Jesus Christ, was widely welcomed, though the subsequent focus on a hierarchically ordained ministry was greatly regretted. Similarly the emphasis on *apostolic* succession being found in the faithful life of the whole church seems subsequently to be overtaken by a concern for clerical functions.

Baptists were happy to see the document to be a challenge to more effective ecumenical working and indeed to examine their own practice in these areas, though, as the East Germans pointed out, their hope of improved relationships came from sharing in the unity of the Spirit. There was widespread concern that the documents were overly concerned with, and gave priority to, the church and ecclesiology rather than issues of *salvation* and relationship to Christ. The Russian response boldly suggested that the order in the document – 'first comes the church and then Christ' – was back to front.

JHYB

FURTHER READING: *Baptism, Eucharist and Ministry*, Faith and Order Paper, no 111, 1982. Tho-

mas F. Best and Tamara Grdzelidze (eds), *BEM at 25: Critical insights into a continuing legacy*, WCC Publications, Geneva, 2007. William R. Estep, 'A Baptist World Alliance Response to Baptism, Eucharist and Ministry and Order Paper No 111', Jul 1986 in W.H. Brackney and R.J. Burke (eds), *Faith, Life and Witness*, Samford University, 1990. M. Thurian (ed), *Churches respond to BEM*, volume I, 1986 [BUGBI]. M. Thurian (ed), *Churches respond to BEM*, volume III, 1987, [AUCECB in the USSR, Scotland, Denmark, Covenanting Churches in Wales]. M. Thurian (ed), *Churches respond to BEM*, volume IV, 1987, [Union of Evangelical Free Churches (Baptist) in the GDR, Sweden]. Günter Wagner: *A survey of Baptist Responses to BEM*, Sep 1986, [Typescript deposited in the IBTS Library, Prague].

Baptist Missionary Society (BMS)

The Baptist Missionary Society was founded in Kettering, Northamptonshire, *England*, on 2 Oct 1792, and was the first of the *missionary* societies founded as a result of the *Evangelical Revival*. Formed by a group of Particular Baptists including Andrew Fuller (1754-1815) [see *Fullerism*], who was appointed secretary, and *William Carey (1761-1834)*, its original name was 'The Particular-Baptist Society for Propagating the Gospel among the Heathen'. The original base of the society was in the Baptist churches of the East Midlands, and a London office was not opened until 1819. BMS sent its first missionaries, John Thomas and William Carey, to Bengal in 1793. With William Ward (1769-1823) and Joshua Marshman (1768-1837), Carey developed church, *educational*, and *translation* work based at Serampore, north of Calcutta, and expanded the *mission* eastwards into what is now Bangladesh and up the Ganges valley to the north-west. After the *death* of Andrew Fuller, relationships between the Serampore missionaries and the society at home deteriorated, so that from 1827-37 the Serampore mission operated independently from BMS.

BMS also began work in Sri Lanka (1812) and the Caribbean, beginning with Jamaica in 1814, where its missionaries, notably William Knibb (1803-45), were instrumental in securing the abolition of slavery in 1834. The Baptist cause among the former slaves flourished as a result, and black Jamaican Baptists played a key role in initiating BMS mission in Cameroon in 1841. Following the German annexation of Cameroon, this mission was handed over to the Basel Mission in 1886. The Congo mission (1879) was maintained with lavish financial support from the Leeds philanthropist, Robert Arthington (1823-1900), for whom the rapid Baptist advance up the Congo River was part of a wider vision for the *evangelisation* of central Africa. BMS began work in China in 1859, where Timothy Richard (1845-1919) developed broadly conceived mission strategies which challenged many of the evangelical *orthodoxies* of the day. In 1891 the smaller General Baptist Missionary Society (formed in 1816), which worked mainly in Orissa, merged with BMS as part of the coming together of the previously separate General (*Arminian*) and Particular (*Calvinistic*) strands of Baptist life in England.

BMS missionary numbers reached their peak in 1921-22. As a result of the society's work, Baptist Christians are now particularly numerous in North-East India (Orissa and Mizoram), Jamaica, the Democratic Republic of Congo, and Angola. BMS also assists Baptist communities planted by other missions, as in Brazil, which it entered in 1953. Since the late 1980s, the society has been increasingly active in a number of European countries, and also in South-East Asia and Central America.

BMS in the 20th century has combined participation in *ecumenical* mission bodies with a firmer commitment to evangelistic priorities than has been true of some of the historic *Protestant* mission agencies. This commitment has strengthened in recent years in response to the *conservative evangelical* resurgence among British Baptists. BMS remains active as a voluntary society supported by Baptists in England, *Wales* and *Scotland*.

BJS

FURTHER READING: Catherine Hall, *Civilising subjects: metropole and colony in the English imagination, 1830-1867*, Polity, Cambridge, 2002. E. Daniel Potts, *British Baptist Missionaries in India 1793-1837: The History of Serampore and its Missions*, Cambridge University Press, London, 1967. Brian Stanley, *The History of the Baptist Missionary Society 1792-1992*, T&T Clark, Edinburgh, 1992.

Baptist Response – Europe (BR-E)

Baptist Response- Europe was an initiative of the *European Baptist Federation* following the collapse of the Berlin Wall (1989) and the implosion of the *communist political* regimes in Eastern and Central Europe. In the aftermath of these events and for much of the 1990s the political and social repercussions were immense and Baptist communities throughout Central and Eastern Europe were faced with stark new realities, both in the opportunities for *mission, church planting* and church development open to them, and to the changes in civic and social life around them.

In Western Europe and the developed 1st world, there was a strong desire to assist sisters and brothers in Central and Eastern Europe in taking full advantage of the possibilities opening up to them. This led to an outpouring of money and materials. At the same time the North Atlantic Treaty Organisation (NATO) powers and the Warsaw Pact (former communist) powers were reconfiguring to an anticipated more peaceful era. This meant reducing military resources in the Central Corridor, especially in *Germany* (former East and former West).

In these circumstances vehicles, *hospital* supplies and many other items related to the former military infrastructure were released, or indeed, abandoned and were obtained by church organisations at modest prices or in some cases without cost.

Baptist Response – Europe, created out of a consultation at Dorfweil, Germany, in 1990, was formally constituted by the EBF Council in Sep 1990. It soon became a Committee of the EBF drawing together interested *unions* and mission agencies to collect requests for assistance, to seek resources to meet those requests, and in some instances to acquire vehicles and other means of transporting the supplies and equipment to Baptist groups in Central and Eastern Europe. Early work of BR-E was meeting immediate humanitarian needs in *Bulgaria* and *Romania*. At its height the budget of Baptist Response – Europe exceeded the budgets of most western unions and mission agencies. The EBF General Secretary of the time, Dr. Karl Heinz Walter, assisted by his office staff in Hamburg, undertook an amazing task in responding to requests and identifying resources.

However, by the late 1990s the situation had changed dramatically. Countries in Central Europe joined NATO and later the *European Union*, whilst individual Baptist unions and mission agencies created more direct partnerships, without the same desire to have recourse to the EBF and resources began to dry up as the focus of attention in the developed world shifted to the Middle East and Africa.

Baptist Response – Europe was a vehicle which achieved much in a decade of hyperactivity. By the early part of the 21st century it had achieved its aim and was ultimately replaced by a different form of organisation, *European Baptist Aid*.

KGJ

Baptist Scholars, European, in the 20th and 21st centuries

See *Biblical Scholars*; *Historians*; *Liturgists*; *Missiologists*; *Theologians, European Baptists in the 20th and 21st centuries*; *Ecumenical Movement, European Baptist contributors in the 20th and 21st centuries*.

Baptist Women's Day of Prayer

[See also *Women in Baptist life*]
During the founding meeting of the European Baptist Women's Union in 1948 it was realised that communication and *fellowship* through opportunities for *prayer* were the best means of maintaining contact in a Europe fragmented by WWII. As well as the encouragement it gave to women who were physically separated from other Christians, prayer provided an opportunity for a collective seeking of God's presence, power and glory in local and international issues and situations.

The original plan was for a prayer week in Nov each year, but within two years this had become focussed in a single day – the first Monday in Nov. During those two years organised work among *women* also spread from Europe across the Atlantic, and an office set up within the *BWA* took on the responsibility of producing an annual theme and outlining suggestions for prayer services. An offering became part of the celebration,

and until very recently that offering has provided the entire budget for the Women's department of the BWA. In Europe e.g., the offering is divided – half going to the Women's Department, the remaining half to the European Baptist Women's Union (EBWU) committee expenses and officers' travel, as well as conferences and various projects within the member *unions*. The committee have never ceased to be thankfully amazed at how much the offering accomplishes!

The practice of holding the prayer day spread throughout the world, and the work of production and despatch has become a huge task. Added to this is the time and effort of translators worldwide, and also of local groups who adapt the programme to local needs. During the last decade the continental union women's committees have shared in the production of *Bible* passages, creative *worship* and distinctive inclusions.

The day is marked in many different ways – from small home groups to large regional gatherings – but everywhere women are encouraged in their local situations and inspired by the sense of the international family to which they belong.

YP

Baptist World Aid (BWAid)

[See also *Emergency and Disaster Relief*]
This is the relief and development arm of the *Baptist World Alliance*. For almost 85 years, Baptists have been caring for those in need through Baptist World Aid, irrespective of their race, creed or colour. Funds have been used to provide food, medicines and medical equipment, to support agricultural and *educational* projects, to build churches and seminaries have been built and to distributed Bibles.

BWAid was formed in 1920 to assist in the rebuilding of Europe in general, and Baptist facilities in particular. During WWII, a further impetus led to new work, particularly among *refugees*. In recent years, BWAid has helped those affected by war and genocide as well as numerous natural disasters.

Today, BWAid seeks to entrust, empower and enable over 200 BWA member bodies in their relief and development programs. Many have their own BWAid type organisation through which they work in their own countries, while others also work abroad. Work has also begun in many closed countries (e.g. North Korea) as the Baptist understanding of an *holistic* gospel has led to new challenges in living out the call of *Christ*.

PM

FURTHER READING: www.bwanet.org/bwaid.

Baptist World Alliance (BWA)

The BWA was founded at an inaugural Congress convened in London, England in 1905. Other denominations had begun to form world alliances; e.g. *Anglican bishops* met together in the first Lambeth conference in 1867, world *Presbyterians* had their first world gathering in 1875, the *Methodists* in 1881, and the *Congregationalists* in 1891. *John Clifford* attended as a visitor and the hope was expressed (but not fulfilled) that the other half of the Congregational family (the Baptists) would soon join with them. British Baptists at the beginning of the 20th century were also increasingly aware of a threefold bond of *fellowship*: to Baptist churches in the British Empire and other English-speaking *conventions*, to churches associated with the work of the *Baptist Missionary Society*, and Baptist churches in Europe. In 1900, e.g., the British Baptist *Union* was in conversation with the *Evangelical Alliance* as to how best to assist the *Stundists* in *Russia*, and in the following year representatives of five European countries came as fraternal delegates to the BU Council Meetings in Edinburgh. But some more broadly-based and continuing organisation was needed and this the more than 3,000 delegates who came to London in 1905 set up, an organisation all too soon to be challenged by war in Europe, though it was to more than prove its value in channelling aid to a continent torn apart by conflict in the immediate post-war years, a process to be repeated in the aftermath of WWII.

The Preamble to the Constitution, as currently amended (2005) states, 'The Baptist World Alliance, extending over every part of the world, exists as an expression of the essential oneness of Baptist people in the Lord *Jesus Christ*, to impart inspiration to the fellowship, and to provide channels for sharing concerns and skills in witness and *ministry*. This Alliance recognises the traditional autonomy and interdependence of Baptist churches and member bodies.' Eight objectives are then listed:

1. To promote Christian fellowship and cooperation among Baptists throughout the world.
2. To bear witness to the Gospel of Jesus Christ and assist member bodies in their divine task of bringing all people to God through Jesus Christ as Saviour and Lord.
3. To promote understanding and cooperation among Baptist bodies and with other Christian groups, in keeping with our *unity* in Christ.
4. To act as an agency for the expression of Biblical *faith* and historically distinctive Baptist principles and practices.
5. To act as an agency of reconciliation seeking *peace* for all persons, and uphold the claims of fundamental *human rights*, including full *religious liberty*.
6. To serve as a channel for expressing Christian social concern and alleviating human need.
7. To serve in cooperation with member bodies as a resource for the development of plans for *evangelism*, *education*, *church growth*, and other forms of *mission*.
8. To provide channels of communication dealing with work related to these objectives through all possible media.

The Alliance works through four divisions – Evangelism and Education, Study and Research, Promotions and Development, and *Baptist World Aid*, and three auxiliaries, *Women*'s, *Men*'s and *Youth*. It also embraces five regional organisations, some of which have an autonomous existence: the *European Baptist Federation*, the All-Africa Baptist Fellowship, the Asia Pacific Baptist federation, the Caribbean Baptist Fellowship, the Union of Baptists in Latin America and the North American Baptist Fellowship.

Under its terms of reference the BWA has conducted conversations with *Roman Catholics*, *Lutherans*, Reformed Churches, the *Mennonites* and Anglicans towards better mutual understanding. Preliminary conversations have also been held with the *Ecumenical* Patriarchate of the *Orthodox*

Church. By its terms of reference the Alliance cannot be a member of the *World Council of Churches* but it takes a full part in the meetings of *Christian World Communities*.

Even following the withdrawal of the *Southern Baptist Convention* with its *membership* of some 16 million in 2004, churches in membership with the BWA number around 35 million members and a community strength of more than a 100 million as of 2005.

ET

FURTHER READING: R.V. Pierard (Gen ed) *Baptists Together in Christ 1905-2005*, BWA, Falls Church, VA., 2005.

Baptistry

[See also *Baptism*; *Baptism and Christian initiation liturgy*; *Church Building (Sanctuary)*]
In the early church baptism was performed outdoors. As church buildings became common, we find baptistries included for the immersion of adults. When *infant baptism* became the dominant practice, the mode became affusion (sprinkling/pouring) instead of immersion and the baptistry was replaced by the baptismal font designed for affusion.

When baptism by immersion of adult believers became the required practice in some churches after the *Reformation*, there was a demand for a deep baptismal pool or grave as the whole body needed to be immersed in water. This mode of baptism has both *theological* and practical implications. Churches had to be supplied with a baptismal grave (baptistry) for baptism to be properly performed. Baptism should be organised as a presentation towards the congregation in a public Sunday service.

In many Baptist churches the baptistry is located at the front of the church under the floor. Part of the floor then has to be removed and arranged especially for the occasion of baptism. But more recently open baptistries have become more common making them one of the obvious features of a Baptist church's interior which marks it as different to church buildings of other denominations [see *Architecture*]. This also helps to make baptism a constant focus of

Baptist *worship*. There are even baptistries in existence with running water, signifying the church's constant readiness to baptise new believers.

JJS

Belarus, Baptist history in

The Baptist movement in Belarus arose out of the *evangelical* awakening that spread across the Russian Empire in the second half of the 19th century, reaching Belarus a little later than other parts, in the 1880s. Different social groups played their part: German settlers, mostly *Mennonites*, introduced some Belarusian peasants, who had migrated to other areas looking for employment, to evangelical ideas. After returning to Belarus, they shared their new religious insights in their villages. This is how Baptist beliefs spread in the southeast of Belarus, especially in the Gomel region.

Some returning home from *work* in Western Europe and America, as Baptists, became enthusiastically involved in *mission* work in their homeland. At the turn of the 20th century in Belarus, Bible *colporteurs*, such as Gerasim Andruhov from Minsk, played an important role in distributing Bibles and evangelical literature, and giving evangelical witness. In spite of obstacles from *Orthodox* clergy and believers, as well as from the imperial government, evangelical ideas spread to the Vitebsk, Mogilyov and Minsk provinces in the 1880s. In Polotsk Baptist worship services started in 1883. Baptist *preachers* from the *Baltic* countries brought their message to the city of Grodno. In the Brest area the evangelical church appeared in 1905.

After the revolution of 1905, Baptist believers appeared in Gomel, Bobruisk, Cherikov, Mogilev and other towns and villages. Later some war refugees during WWI met Baptist communities near Omsk and Tomsk, whilst some prisoners of war had come into contact with Baptists in *Germany* and *Austria*; on returning home they began sharing 'the new *faith*' with others. However, before 1917 only a few Baptist churches were officially registered; the Baptist churches in Ut village in the Gomel region and in Vitebsk were the exceptions. Preachers gathered around two *unions* formed in

Russia: the Baptist Union and the Union of Evangelical Christians, with central headquarters in Moscow and in St. Petersburg respectively. The *socialist* revolution of 1917 brought some *religious freedom* for evangelicals for a short time, when in many areas new Baptist churches emerged. In these years, Anton Kirtsun and Peter Krashenin worked in Grodno, Daniel Jasko in Slonim and Luka Dzekuts-Malej in Brest. Minsk Baptist church was led by a talented leader, Boris Cheberuk. In 1923, the Minsk Evangelical Christian church, led by Victor Chechnev, was formed, only to be closed by the Soviet authorities 10 years later. In the second half of the 1920s, numerous *baptisms* took place in Vitebsk, and also in Slutsk, where the largest Baptist church in Belarus emerged. However, from a greater perspective, *political* developments affected Baptist work. The Polish-Soviet war (1919-20) and the treaty of Riga (1921) partitioned the country. In general, the western Belarusian sector had more freedom for religious activities, while the eastern sector, under Soviet rule, was, from 1929, subject to severe religious persecution. Churches were closed, *church buildings* confiscated, and believers arrested. The German occupation (1941-44) brought some relief. Notwithstanding the war, Baptist churches made attempts to continue *worship* services and give *pastoral care* to their *members*. During the German occupation, the pastor of the Minsk Baptist church, A. Ketsko, and some other believers, risking their lives, rescued *Jewish* children from a number of *orphanages* [see *Anti-Semitism*]. Surprisingly, in Jun 1944, the German authorities gave permission to Belarusian Baptists to hold a conference in Minsk.

In 1944, the Evangelical Christians and the Baptists were united by requirement of the *state* into the *All-Union Council of Evangelical Christians-Baptists*. Viktor Chechnev became the senior presbyter in Belarus, serving from 1944-57, assisted by regional senior presbyters. Konstantin Veliseichik became senior presbyter in 1957, on the eve of Khrushchev's intensified atheistic pressure, and was followed by Ivan Bukaty in 1977.

The first change for the better came in 1988, when the Millennium of Christianity was celebrated in Russia. New opportunities for *preaching* the gospel were gradually opened up: *Sunday Schoolss* for children were organised, *evangelism* was intensified, new Baptist groups and churches were planted, and *theological* training was developed in different forms. In 1989, the first Bible Courses in Minsk were opened, and in 1990, the Union of Evangelical Christians-Baptists in Belarus was registered as an independent union. In 1994, Alexander Firisiuk became the leader of the Belarusian Union, serving in this capacity until 2002. In 1994, the publication *Krinitsa Zhitsia* [Source of Life] began to appear, and in 1997, the Minsk Theological Seminary was opened. Over the period 1990-2002, 177 new churches were opened in different towns and villages. At present, the Union of Evangelical Christians-Baptists in Belarus consists of more than 290 churches and *mission stations*, with approximately 14,000 members.

PO

Belgium, Baptist history in

The Baptist movement in Belgium owes its existence to the efforts of the French Baptist Federation [see *France*] in the 19th century. From its early days, the French Baptist Federation had a concern to carry the Gospel to its northern neighbours. The first conversions on Belgian soil took place among miners from Liege. After these new converts visited the Baptist church in Denain, France, the first Baptist church was established, probably in 1892, also in the Liege province, in Ougrée. Through the witness and the *evangelism* of the French Baptists, soon the second Baptist church in Belgium was established in Péruwelz, in the province of Henegouwen. This church undertook a building project and their building was finished in 1903. The embryonic state of the Belgian churches led the French Baptist Federation to extend their support by helping them with evangelism. For many years they sent their pastors to Belgium, though their work was limited to the French-speaking South. Baptist work in Flanders only began in the 1980s.

Baptist work developed sufficiently for the Belgian Baptist churches to form their own *union* in 1922. They encountered considerable difficulties and misunderstandings as in the wider society they were considered to be a *sect*. Until 1987, the Union of Baptists in Belgium was comprised of approximately nine churches that operated within the framework of the *European Baptist Federation*. In 1986, the first Flemish-speaking Baptist church, established in 1983 and situated in Middelkerke in the province of West Flanders was accepted into the *union*. From 1987, the Union of Baptists made great efforts to become officially recognised as a church. The recognition finally came in 1998. A partnership document was signed with the United *Protestant* Church in Belgium, with whom there is a very good working relationship.

The Belgian Baptist churches emphasise freedom of *conscience*, *mission*, believers' *baptism*, scriptural *authority* [see *Bible*], the *separation of church and state*, the *autonomy of the local church* and the mutual and reciprocal dependence of all the churches within the union. The Belgian Baptists belong to and co-operate with the European Baptist Federation and the *Baptist World Alliance*. The Union of Baptists in Belgium has grown from nine churches in 1987 to 30 churches in 2004, with a total *membership* of more than 1,000.

SV

Believers' Baptism

See *Baptism; Baptism and Christian initiation liturgy; Baptism, Eucharist and Ministry; Christian Initiation; Sacrament, Sign and Symbol*.

Believers' Church and *Volkskirche*

Unlike the great *state churches* of Europe, Baptist churches stand in the *Anabaptist* tradition of being believers' churches. In Baptist *ecclesiology* a church is made up of believers, who have committed themselves to *Christ* and to one another. The world may contain both 'wheat' and 'weeds', but the church is a foretaste of the *kingdom of God* and is therefore made up of 'children of the kingdom' (see Mt 13:38).

A believers' church normally practices believers' *baptism*. Generally speaking, for Baptists entry into a believers' church is through believers' baptism. Although some

Baptists have over-individualised the rite of baptism and reduced it to just a personal *confession of faith* (1Ti 6:12), rightly understood baptism is also a rite of incorporation into the Body of Christ, the *Church* (see 1Co 12:13; Gal 3:26-28). Baptism is a sign of commitment to Christ and to one another. For this reason, baptism and *church membership* belong together. And since for Baptists baptism is by definition the baptism of believers only (Ac 2:37, 38; 8:37; 18:8; etc.), the church is inevitably made up of believers alone.

A believers' church is a *fellowship* of believers. In entering into church membership, Baptists enter into a '*covenant*' with one another, which involves a mutual sharing of life with one another. Church membership for Baptists has a dynamic quality, in which members commit themselves to love one another, care for one another, encourage one another, pray for one another, and stand by one another, whatever the cost (e.g., Jn 13:34; 1Co 12:25; 1Th 5:11; Jas 5:16). Not surprisingly one of the most popular hymns [see *Hymnody*] at Baptist meetings is 'Blest be the tie that binds our hearts in Christian love'.

A believers' church is a *priesthood of all believers*. In a Baptist church there is no 'hierarchy': all are equal before the Lord and before one another (1Pe 2:4-5). So in the *church meeting*, the members (and not just the leaders) come together to discern the mind of Christ for their life together (Ac 13:1-2; 15:22, etc.). Similarly at the *Lord's Supper*, there is no dependence upon a 'priest' [see *Priesthood (hierarchical)*] (1Ti 2:5): members serve one another bread and *wine*. Although an *elder* or *minister* may preside, there is no 'priestly' *prayer* of consecration – instead a simple prayer of thanksgiving.

A believers' church entails the *ministry* of all believers. The membership roll is a ministry roll! Every member is called to serve God, both within the church (1Co 12:12-26) and in the wider world. Inevitably the ministry of all believers entails the *mission* of all believers. Every Baptist has good news to share (Mt 28:19). In the words of *J.G. Oncken*, 'Every Baptist is a missionary'.

A believers' church entails the 'sainthood' of all believers (Ro 1:7; Eph 4:1) [see

Saints]. In this regard the exercise of *church discipline* is a means of maintaining the 'purity' or '*holiness*' of a believers' church (Mt 18:15-20; 1Co 5:1-5). In many Baptist churches *discipline* relates not just to matters of gross immorality, but also to other life-style issues such as drink [see *Alcohol; Alcoholism*] and debt.

A believers' church is a *covenant* community gathered out of the world by *grace* and *faith*. It is the fruit of the work of the *Spirit* and thus cannot be under the control of a monarch or parliament. For them the intervention of the *state* is a fundamental offence against 'The *Crown Rights of the Redeemer*', Christ's Lordship in his church [see *Separation of Church and State*]. It is the fruit of each individual making a confession of faith and is far removed from the 'volkskirchen' or 'landeskirchen' born out of the Augsburg formula of 'cuius regio, eius religio'. In its spiritual, voluntary, faith nature it finds its home within the traditions of the Radical *Reformation*.

PBM

FURTHER READING: Donald F. Durnbaugh, *The Believers' Church*, Herald, Scottdale, Pa.,1985.

BEM

See *Baptism, Eucharist and Ministry*.

Bible, Baptist Understanding of the

General attitude towards the Bible. The understanding of the Bible among Baptists becomes manifest, first of all, in their practice. Throughout Baptist history, it has been their reading of scripture (though in fact the NT has usually played the more important part) that has been the mandate for founding congregations, for adopting the practice of believers' *baptism*, for their insistence on the need for personal belief, for establishing *missions* and championing of high ethical standards. A theory about the Bible is a secondary step. It is not even formulated in all of the *Confessions of Faith*; sometimes they simply presuppose its *authority* (e.g. London 1644; London 1660; Short Confession 1691). In all statements the supreme authority of the Bible becomes evident (cf. Cook, pp.13-

24). This unites Baptists of all times and places, however different they may otherwise appear. *Theological* debates inside and with other denominations or civil authorities are carried out on the basis of scriptural evidence.

Baptists have been a community of the book, upholding the authority of 'sola Scriptura'. At the same time, they have considered personal *faith* in *Jesus Christ* 'solus Christus' as decisive. Holy Scripture, in particular the NT, essentially testifies to Christ and his work of *salvation*, after all. The Bible thus is God's means of *revelation*, not revelation itself. But there is no revelation without the Bible, nor is their revelation outside it. This has made Baptists reluctant to accept any form of spiritualism or the adoption of inferences from a theory of sacred history which would come up with insights beyond the scriptural testimony. *Tradition*, important as it is, is not regarded as a source of revelation. In this sense, Baptists are a part of *Protestantism*. Confessions of Faith are considered as explanations of the Biblical teaching, not as revelatory statements in their own right.

The place of the Bible in Baptist life is reflected in its study by all people, organised in a regular form, within congregations, both for adults and for children. Equally, *preaching* is seen as essentially the exposition of scripture. A profound knowledge of the Bible forms the basis of Baptist life and practice.

Doctrinal formulations; controversial issues. In many ways the early confessions express what, by and large, became the standard Baptist position. The Second London Confession (SLC) of 1677 (Particular Baptists [see *England*]), largely based on the Westminster Confession, begins with an extensive chapter (I) 'Of the Holy Scriptures', stating (art. 1) that 'the Holy Scripture is the only sufficient, certain, and infallible rule of all saving knowledge, faith, and obedience'; God chose this way 'for the better preserving, and propagating of the Truth, and for the more sure establishment and comfort of the *Church* against the corruption of the flesh and the malice of *Satan*, and of the world'. The SLC then (2) lists the books of the OT and NT, (3) excludes the Apocrypha, proclaiming it to be of 'no authority to the

Church of God'. The Bible's authority (4) depends on God 'the author thereof; therefore it is to be received' as the Word of God. Art. 5 states that 'our full persuasion, and assurance of the infallible truth [see *Infallibility and Inerrancy*], and divine authority thereof, is from the inward work of the *Holy Spirit*, bearing witness by and with the Word in our hearts'. The Bible contains (6) 'all things necessary for [God's] glory, man's salvation, faith and life'. Although (7) 'all things in Scripture are not alike plain in themselves, or alike clear unto all; yet those things which are necessary to be known, believed, and observed for salvation, are so clearly opened...that not only the learned, but the unlearned, in a due use of ordinary means, may attain to a sufficient understanding of them'. The (8) OT in Hebrew and the NT in Greek, having been by God's 'singular care and *providence* kept pure in all ages, are therefore authentic'. For the benefit of all people 'they are to be translated into the vulgar language of every nation' [see *Bible Translation*]. The SLC concludes by saying that (9) 'the infallible rule of interpretation of Scripture is the Scripture itself'; and (10) it is 'the supreme judge by which all controversies of religion are to be determined'.

The 'Orthodox Creed' of 1679 (General Baptists) places the article 'Of the sacred Scripture' near its end (XXXVI). It is less detailed than the SLC, though following the same direction, emphasising the 'authority of God...therein'. The Bible contains 'all things necessary for salvation'; it has to be distinguished from 'pretended immediate inspiration' and 'natural religion'. It is 'sufficient to inform man of Christ the mediator, or of the way to salvation, and *eternal life*'. It is to be used by people 'in their mother tongue' for 'edification, and comfort...to frame their lives...both in faith and practice'. It 'ought to be interpreted according to the analogy of faith, and is the best interpreter of itself'. The holy scriptures are understood as 'the canonical books of the old and new testament', listing them, with the remark 'all which are given by the inspiration of God, to be the rule of faith and life'.

The New Hampshire Confession of 1833 is rather concise in stating: 'We believe, that the Holy Bible was written by *men* divinely inspired, and is a perfect treasure of *heavenly* instruction; that it has God for its author, salvation for its end, and truth, without any mixture of error, for its matter; that it reveals the principles by which God will judge us; and therefore is, and shall remain to the end of the world, the true centre of Christian union, and the supreme standard by which all human conduct, creeds, and opinions should be tried.'

The salient points thus are (cf. Hays and Steely pp.43-47): (1) *authority*, as God reveals himself in the Bible, it gives testimony to Christ; (2) *sufficiency*, functionally understood, for all matters of faith especially salvation; (3) *clarity*, scripture contains all that is necessary for faith and life; it interprets itself; no expert knowledge is required for its understanding; (4) *practicability*, scripture leads to a life according to God's will; (5) *canonical*, it comprises the OT and NT books, not the Apocrypha; (6) *exclusivity*, over against the claims of natural religion, the tradition of the church, and other forms of extra Biblical inspiration.

Critical issues: (1) Baptists cannot be said to have developed any considerable theory of inspiration. It seems enough to express the belief that the 'holy books...are truly inspired by the Holy Spirit' (*Poland* 1930, similar *Romania* 1974), or that 'this work, written by divinely inspired men, was put together...under the impulse and guidance of the Holy Spirit' (*Hungary* 1967). The Basis of Doctrine of the Baptist Union of *Ireland* speaks of 'verbal inspiration'. In general, Baptists have 'declined to commit themselves to any specific theory of Inspiration. They unite in accepting the fact, but they differ as to the method' (Cook pp.27f). (2) Terms like 'infallible' or 'without error' occur occasionally only (cf. the careful wording adopted in Hungary in 1967: 'The providence of God has saved the holy scripture – both in its origin and in its transmission – from all essential errors'). The SLC speaks of the pure transmission of the texts in their original languages, but does not extend this aspect to inerrancy, as was done in the USA in the late 20th century (cf. Ammerman pp.80-87). Scripture is 'certain' (SLC); it reveals God's truth. There is no doubt about this, hence it needs not be counter-argued or delineated.

After some debates, Norwegian Baptists in 1966 accepted a Statement Concerning the Bible which in five points sums up what is beyond controversy, viz. that (1) scripture 'is the final content of God's revelation'; (2) it has Jesus Christ 'as its highest authority'; (3) it leads to 'a true understanding of the great truth of salvation'; (4) 'the Holy Spirit is the Word's life principle'; (5) 'the gospel is God's offer of salvation'.

Biblical Interpretation. Interpretation is rather easy if an idea or institution, 'so far from finding any warrant for its existence in Scripture, seems in fact to contradict its plain and simple sense' (Cook, p.15). The 'plain and simple sense' is not always immediately obvious, however. Problems arise (1) in the assessment of the historical and cultural settings in which the books and their language/terminology originated; (2) by apparent differences, if not contradictions, between its various parts; (3) in relating the divine message to the human context, in particular in areas not covered directly by the Bible. Certain guidelines of interpretation have proved helpful among Baptists. Scripture is primarily interpreted by scripture itself; it is clear in its basic and essential message ('claritas Scripturae'). Under the guidance of the Holy Spirit every congregation (and individual: *Great Britain* 1888) has the liberty and duty to interpret the Bible. This can be done even by 'the unlearned, in a due use of ·ordinary means' (SLC). Baptists are 'not afraid that modern methods of critical study will in any way damage their fundamental convictions' (Cook, p.22). 'Biblical research and interpretation are...helpful in discovering the depth and riches of the biblical message' (*BWA*/Lutheran World Federation [LWF] 1990). The understanding of the Bible is a growing process, 'because God by His Spirit has taught us to see in Him [Christ] treasures of wisdom and power that our fathers did not discover' (Cook, p.22; cf. *BF&W* p.58). The Bible witnesses to historical events; Jesus Christ became a human person in history. Therefore, we 'must read and interpret the biblical writings not only in light of their historical context, but also in light of our own experience and historical circumstances, in order to allow the divine message to become a living reality ever again (BWA/LWF 1990, no. 13). 'The historical interpretation of Scripture takes into account the working of the Holy Spirit, both in originating and expounding the Holy Scriptures' (*Austria/Germany/Switzerland* 1977, I/vi). With the message of the Bible standing 'over against us in *grace* and in judgment, we seek to protect the divine message from human distortions' (BWA/LWF 1990, no. 14).

WP

FURTHER READING: Nancy Tatom Ammerman, *Baptist Battles: Social Change and Religious Conflict in the Southern Baptist Convention*, Rutgers University, New Brunswick, 1995. William H. Brackney and L.A. Cupit (eds), *Baptist Faith and Witness*, The Papers of the Study and Research Division of the BWA 1990-1995, McLean (BWA) 1995. Henry Cook, *What Baptists Stand for*, Kingsgate, London, 1947. Brooks Hays and John E. Steely, *The Baptist Way of Life: What it means to live and worship as a Baptist*, Mercer, Mason, 1974. William L. Lumpkin, *Baptist Confessions of Faith*, Judson, Valley Forge, 1980. G. Keith Parker, *Baptists in Europe: History and Confessions of Faith*, Broadman, Nashville, 1982.

Bible, Infallibility and Inerrancy of the
See *Infallibility and Inerrancy of the Bible*.

Bible, Inspiration of the
See *Inspiration of the Bible*.

Bible Readers
[See also *Bible, Baptist understanding of the*]
Baptists have always encouraged people to learn to read so that they could study the Bible for themselves. In their *evangelical* outreach in the 19th century, they supplied Bibles, tracts and 'good books' to the *poor*. In this they were aided by various societies set up to provide Bibles and other Christian literature. Bible readers went to the illiterate: the artist, Gustave Doré, depicted a scripture reader at work in the dormitory of a London refuge for the *homeless. Colporteurs* (suppliers of Christian literature) were widely used by Baptists; *C.H. Spurgeon* made considerable use of colportage.

Mrs Ellen Ranyard, a Bible Society agent in London, realised that only 'native agents' could hope to penetrate the worst slums The distinction between the voluntary labours of the middle-class lady superintendents and the working-class *women* they employed reflected the social divisions of the age. The Baptist ministers of Bloomsbury Chapel provided Mrs Ranyard with her first Bible Woman in 1857: Marian Bowers, a poor Christian woman living in the slum district who could read and was willing to sell Christian literature. She found that practical help with housekeeping and nutrition helped win women's confidence. Before working for Mrs Ranyard she had done similar work for the *Domestic Mission* of Bloomsbury Baptist Church. By 1860 Mrs Ranyard's Bible and Domestic Female Mission had 134 Bible Women in London and was spreading elsewhere. Some trained as Bible Women-nurses, one of the precursors to District Nursing. Their work must have influenced the formation of the Baptist Order of *Deaconesses* which originated in the same part of London later in the century. Some historians credit Mrs Ranyard with employing the first paid social workers.

FWB

Bible Societies

[See also *Bible, Baptist understanding of the*; *Bible Translation*]

The oldest Bible Society was the 'Cansteinsche Bibelanstalt' founded in Berlin in 1710. C.H. von Canstein began by distributing Bibles among the *children* in the classrooms of A.H. Francke's school in Berlin, itself one of the fruits of the *Pietist Revival*. By the end of the 18th century the society had distributed some three million low-cost Bibles and NTs amongst *Germany*'s poor.

The British Foreign Bible Society was founded in London in 1804, with the intention of not only making Bibles available 'without note or comment' but also to secure the widest possible support, both in *Britain*, and throughout Europe and the British Empire. But maintaining *Evangelical unity* was not easy: in India the *BMS missionaries* insisted on translating the Greek *baptizo* using the language of immersion to which the *paedobaptist* denominations, especially the *Church of England*, objected indicating that the word should not so much be translated

as transcribed. This led to the Baptists founding their own Bible Translation Society, even though the secretary of the BFBS, Joseph Hughes, was himself a Baptist *minister*. In *Scotland* in the 1820s, Robert Haldane objected to the BFBS circulating versions of the scriptures which contained the Apocrypha and in the next decade there was concern about Unitarian support for the BFBS, leading to the founding of the Trinitarian Bible Society, which was more discriminating both in the support it cultivated and the texts that it circulated.

Across Europe the Bible Society became not only an agency for spreading the scriptures, but as *women* and *men* read what was made available to them, so under the nurture of Bible Society *colporteurs* came into being. Thus agents of the different Bible societies played an important part in the story of the spread of Baptist beliefs. Very early on in 1808 the BFBS opened a Bible-depot in Paris to promote a difficult mission in *France*. Again, *Johann Oncken* was an agent of the Edinburgh Bible Society before becoming a Baptist pastor.

Edward Millard, who began to exercise a strategic *ministry* in Vienna from 1851 with the British and Foreign Bible Society and August Meereis, who began to work as a colporteur from 1872 and who later moved to Vienna, were both Baptist figures who played a significant role in helping to encourage Baptist mission and the development of Baptist churches across Central Europe. Millard was born in Bath, *England*, and was a teacher in the *Netherlands* from 1839-45. During this period he had an *evangelical conversion*, in the German city of Elberfield, and he later became an employee of the Bible Society in Cologne. In 1851 he was transferred to Vienna. Under his enthusiastic direction the Austro-Hungarian Division of the BFBS issued over three million copies of the Bible. As well as working for the Bible Society locally and then more broadly, Millard was able to encourage Baptist advance. Over the course of a few months he drew a number of Baptists together, holding meetings in his home. In the summer of 1852, however, he was forced to leave Vienna when the police closed the Bible depot. But concern for Vienna did not fade and he returned a decade later. Once again he started home meetings for *worship* and *Bible study*, until eventually, in Dec 1869, the first Baptist church was formed. This was also the first *free church* established in *Austria*.

In the early 1870s Baptist *witness* in the northern part of Transylvania (in present-day *Romania*), was also dependent on the initiative of Bible Society workers. Anton Novák, who came from Stajerország had already met Johann Rottmayer (who had been converted in the Baptist church in Hamburg) through working in Budapest. They were both carpenters and, as well as working together, they developed a friendship which led to the conversion of Novák and his wife to the evangelical *faith*. The Nováks then left Budapest and Anton became a colporteur in Transylvania with the British and Foreign Bible Society, starting work in 1865. In Nagyszalonta the Nováks met members of a Bible study group composed of people who were dissatisfied with the *preaching* in the local *Reformed Church*. At the same time as Novák started work with the BFBS, Johann Rottmayer found himself looking for work, as his carpenter's workshop suffered decline. Novák brought Rottmayer and the BFBS into contact with each other and this resulted, in 1866, in Rottmayer being offered a post as a colporteur, based in Kolozsvár (today's Cluj), in Transylvania. Rottmayer was to exercise a remarkable ministry. In a single year in Kolozsvár he had been able to sell more than 10,000 Bibles. The region he covered was extensive, and although he travelled long distances – walking or travelling by horse and cart – he realised that he needed help. Among those who were recruited by the BFBS, at Rottmayer's suggestion, several became involved in the emerging Baptist mission. Anton Novák's ministry resulted in a number of people in Nagyszalonta asking to be baptised as believers [see *Baptism*]. Novák met Heinrich Meyer from Budapest in 1875 at a BFBS conference and Meyer responded to Novák's request to come to Nagyszalonta and baptise eight people who were, as Novák put it, willing to receive baptism according to the teaching of the NT which marked an important step forward for Baptist mission among Hungarian-speaking people, since the Baptist witness up to that point had largely been among the German-speaking popula-

tion.

Millard, Novák and Rottmayer illustrate how closely related were the origins of so many Baptist churches in Eastern Europe with the work of Bible Society colporteurs and agents. Many others such as Jabob Klundt of Catalui in Romania, already a refugee from the Kherson province of *Ukraine* could be cited. Ordained by Augustus Liebig as a Baptist pastor, he was appointed a colporteur by Alexander Thomason who from 1860 was head of the British and Foreign Bible Society in the Ottoman Empire. Klundt, working first in Thessaloniki, Greece, and then in Skopje, *Macedonia*, was imprisoned several times and on three occasions was almost killed by Albanian robbers. Later he had periods of service in *Montenegro* – in Podgoritza and Cettinje – and in Scutari (now Üsküdar), a district of Istanbul. Others associated with the Catalui church from which Baptist work in Bulgaria sprang also became colporteurs. The BFBS also employed two Polish Baptists from Prussian *Poland* as colporteurs in north-eastern *Bulgaria*, one of whom, Kristian Krzossa, was head of the BFBS depot in Russe from 1872 to the early 20th century.

A region of significant Baptist growth in Ukraine was the Zaporozhye area, in the south-eastern part (east of Kherson). Again a factor in Baptist emergence here was the activity of the Bible Society. Tsar Alexander II gave freedom for the BFBS to spread the Bible in *Russia* and gave permission for the Russian Bible Society to take up its work again. One of the greatest pioneers was John Melville (known as Vasiliy Ivanovitch), a Scottish missionary with the BFBS. By 1870, as a result of the work of P. Kulish, the Pentateuch and the four gospels had been translated into Ukrainian. Yakov Deliakov, the colporteur who had introduced Voronin to Kalweit in Tiflis (Tbilisi), was by now active in Ukraine. Although Deliakov was then a Presbyterian by conviction, he contributed significantly to Baptist life. Through his ministry in Novo-Vasilievka and Astrahanka, a *Molokan* leader, Zinoviy Zaharov came to evangelical beliefs. Many of Zacharov's followers later became Baptists. The modern Russian Bible, the so-called synod-edition, was published in 1876 and was very important in the life of Evangelical Christians in

Russia.

The growing need for popular Bibles all round the world argued for the union of the separate publishing offices, such as the American Bible Society, BFBS, National Bible Societies of Scotland, the Netherlands Bible Society and the German Württemberg Bible Society. for collaboration in the spreading of the holy scriptures The United Bible Societies, established in 1946, when approximately 1,000 translations were in circulation, linked together some 137 societies in over 200 countries by 2000. Today the written word is supplemented by audiocassettes and videos and other electronic forms. One small example of the fruits of this collaboration is the sum of 2 million Chinese Bibles produced annually in cooperation with the Amity Foundation in China. Today, Bible Societies undertake the printing and circulating of the Bible in as many languages as possible in locally acceptable versions at favourable prices. At the moment there are 42 states in Europe and within those at least as many as 50 ethnic languages, some of them not wholly identified (e.g. there are three different *Roma* languages). To find a technical solution is not enough, there needs to be local involvement in production.

Recent years have seen greater participation by *Roman Catholics* and *Orthodox* in Bible production and circulation. Other Bible-related organisations include the International Bible Society that produced the NIV, Living Bible International, with similar purposes, the Gideons, concerned to make available Bibles in public places, the Scripture Gift Mission, the Scripture Union and the International Bible Reading Association concerned with helping people to read the Bible systematically, and the Wycliffe Bible Translators with their special techniques for making translations into languages which often do not as yet have a systematic grammar.

OES & ET

Bible study meetings
[See also *Bible, Baptist understanding of the*]
Baptist *spirituality* and understanding of *discipleship* has highlighted two aspects: *fellowship* and focus on the Bible. Baptist *ecclesiology* stresses the importance of the visible church, a fellowship, that gathers in the name of the Lord and meets around the Word. Bible study groups, often meeting on a weekly basis, are one manifestation of this focus. Sometimes these meetings take the form of congregational Bible study with a *preacher* or a lay leader leading the expository Bible study. Sometimes smaller groups for Bible study meet in homes. In many Baptist churches, especially since the 1970s, this form of mid-week meeting has replaced a central meeting for *Prayer*/Bible study, sometimes called the mid-week service. Mutual encouragement, communal interpretation of *scripture* and supporting group members is carried out through the practices of Bible study and fellowship in Baptist life. This basic focus on the Bible and fellowship is a good foundation for other forms of group meetings. E.g., a kind of Christian ABC course, *Alpha*, though originating from *Evangelical Anglicanism*, has been well received in many European Baptist churches, as an effective form of contact *evangelism*.

ET

Bible Translation
[See also *Bible, Baptist understanding of the*]
Bibles have always been important to Baptists in Europe and though for obvious reasons their involvement in translation has been limited, their commitment to the Bible's availability and distribution has always been a matter of high priority, many of the churches owing their origins to the work of Bible *colporteurs*.

Bibles first came to Europe with early *missionaries* or with business travellers and consequently few reached private hands. Change came with the invention of printing, with increasing literacy and (most of all) with the increased appetite for the scriptures born of the *Reformation*.

Early translations included *Bishop* Wulfila's 4th-century translation into Gothic, a 9th-century translation by Cyril and Methodius from Rome who introduced Christianity to *Czechoslovakia* and paved the way for a number of other translations, both partial and complete: a 14th-century translation from the Vulgate by unknown *scholars* into

Middle High German and Wycliffe's translation into English, also from the Vulgate around the same time.

By the 14th-century Czechoslovakia had a complete Bible, thanks to the influence of Jan Hus, and *Poland* had a slavish imitation of it known as the Sáruspatak Bible (1455). The first printed Bible in *Holland* was an incomplete version (1477) based on 14th and 15th-century manuscripts.

Of the post-Reformation translations the two most outstanding were *Luther*'s German translation, from the Hebrew and Greek, completed in 1534, which stimulated and provided a base for versions in other languages, both *Catholic* and *Protestant*, and the Authorised Version (sometimes known as the King James Version) in *Britain*, 1611, which had similar results. *France*, which never produced a comparable standard version, had a multiplicity of translations none of which achieved dominant status, the two which came nearest being the *Lovain Bible* (1578) for Catholics and the *Geneva Bible* (1588) for Protestants. Most recently came *La Bible de Jérusalem* (1946), which subsequently provided the basis for the Jerusalem Bible, an English translation from the original languages (1966). Antonio Brucioli, a layman, was responsible for the first complete Bible from the original languages in *Italy* and in *Spain,* where the Inquisition held the line against all Bible translation until the middle of the 16th century, the first complete translation (which included the Apocrypha) in Spanish appeared in Basle (1569). *Sweden* was the first country in Scandinavia to get a complete Bible with Gustav Vasa's translation (1541), the 'authorised version' and the main church Bible for centuries, followed by the Christian Bible III (1550) in *Denmark*.

From the Reformation until the end of the 18th century most people in Eastern Europe, from the Baltic to the Adriatic, spoke one of a variety of Slavonic languages and the Reformation provided a spur to translate the Bible into the vernacular.

Until the end of the 19th century in the *Soviet Union* the Bible was only available in a Slavonic version, first published in 1581. In the early 19th century a Russian Bible Society was set up with the protection of the Czar, to distribute portions of scripture and to translate the Bible into modern Russian, a programme subsequently taken over by the Russian *Orthodox Church* which insisted that many archaisms found in the Old Church Slavonic liturgical language be retained. The first Russian translation, which may be regarded as an 'authorised version' and still in use today, dates from 1876 and in 1988, to celebrate the millennium of the Christianisation of Russia, permission was given to print 100,000 Bibles with plans for a co-operative venture between the Russian Orthodox Church and the United Bible Society to produce a modern translation. In 1956 the *All-Union Council of Evangelical Christians-Baptists* secured permission for a printing of 10,000 copies of the NT. Other officially published translations of the Bible in the Soviet Union since 1956 include Georgian (1963, 1982), Armenian (1970, 1974-75, 1981), Latvian (1960, 1970), and Lithuanian (1973), with permission given to *Estonia* in 1971.

In Czechoslovakia the two principle translations were the Kralice Bible (six volumes), the work of the *Moravian* Brethren (1579-93 with revised editions in 1596 and 1613), universally acknowledged as the finest example of the old Czech language, and the St Wenceslas Bible (three volumes), the work of Jesuits (1715), based on the Vulgate but taking account of earlier translations including even the 'heretical' Kralice Bible, which by then had established itself as the 'authorised version' for a minority of Czechs who used it regularly in church and home in the 17th century and also for the Slovaks in the 18th century. The first major Protestant translation was an *ecumenical* translation in 1979.

Inspired by the Luther Bible the first complete Bible in *Hungary* was a translation by Károlyi (1590), a Reformed clergyman, widely distributed and soon established as the 'authorised version' of Hungarian Protestantism. A *Roman Catholic* translation by Káldi came in 1626. Both were extensively revised in the 20th century with a completely new Roman Catholic translation in 1973 and a new Protestant translation published by the Hungarian Bible Council (an affiliate of UBS) in 1975.

The first complete Bible in Poland was a Roman Catholic translation from the Vulgate (1561), soon overshadowed by the more scholarly Protestant translation from the original languages by **Calvinists** and Socinians (1563) and printed in Lithuania, but the two most commonly used Bibles over 300 years were the Catholic Wujek Bible (1599) and the more scholarly Protestant Gdansk Bible (1632). More recently a modern Polish NT appeared in 1966 followed by the complete Bible in 1975 to be followed by a further translation after the style of the Good News Bible.

In **Romania,** where Christianity arrived with the Roman armies in the 2nd century, the Romanian Orthodox Church claims 75% of the population. Baptists, who arrived in the 19th century, established a Baptist **union** (1919) and are now reckoned to be the fastest growing church in the country, are regarded as 'neo-Protestants', as opposed to the Protestant Churches (**Lutheran** and **Reformed**) and the Roman Catholic Church. The Orthodox Church has a substantial publishing house and a Bible publishing programme in collaboration with the UBS, the most recent complete Bible translation being in 1944, with revised editions in 1968, 1975 and 1982. Romanians have never been accustomed to a variety of translations and Baptists, who question its language and some of the language translations of this version (e.g. **'priest'** rather than **'elder'** or 'presbyter'), have adopted a more recent Protestant version which the Orthodox regard as inauthentic, hence, some of the Bible controversies of the **Cold War** years.

In the latter half of the 20th century the Bible was printed in **Yugoslavia**, in both Roman and Cyrillic script, with all the major languages in Yugoslavia freely available and translation carried out on an international basis. The first edition of the *Living New Testament* (called *The Book About Christ*) and intended for the secular market appeared in Croatian in 1982. A translation of the OT into Macedonian together with the Macedonian NT (1967) formed the first complete Bible in Macedonian in the late 1980s and the Protestants produced a 20-volume NT commentary by William Barclay, the result of a £4,000 grant from EUROLIT.

No production of Bibles was possible in **Bulgaria** from 1945-83 when a slightly revised edition of the Bulgarian Bible appeared, printed by the Orthodox Church on paper supplied by the UBS.

The first complete Bible in Lithuanian (1735) was actually printed in London.

With their strong commitment to the Bible and biblical scholarship [see **Biblical Scholars**] Baptists have not been slow to engage in Bible translation, particularly in Britain where they produced a long line of distinguished OT scholars in the late 19th and 20th centuries several of whom made a contribution in this field.

Benjamin Davies of **Regent's Park College**, and F.W. Gotch of **Bristol College** were involved in the revision of the OT and Joseph Angus of Regent's Park the NT in the Revised Version (1870) and Angus and Gotch also served at the same time as revisers and translators of the English Bible in America. L.H. Brockington and T.H. Robinson (Regent's park), A.R. Johnston (Cardiff University) and H.H. Rowley (Manchester University) worked on the translation of the OT for the New English Bible (1970), R.A. Mason (Regent's park) served similarly on the panel for the Revised English Bible (1989) and one or two others (including the present writer) served on the Anglicisation of the Good News Bible when it came from America.

One of the more popular translations at the beginning of the 20th century was *Weymouth's New Testament* (1903), reprinted several times as *The New Testament in Modern Speech* and published by James Clarke and Co. R.F. Weymouth (1822-1902) was a Baptist and distinguished NT scholar whose *Resultant Greek Testament*, on which his translation was based, reflected the greatest measure of agreement on the Greek text among 19th-century scholars. Complete with a critical apparatus and several distinguishing features, he also served as a consultant on *The Twentieth Century New Testament* (1902).

AG

FURTHER READING: S.L. Greenslade (ed), *Cambridge History of the Bible: The West from the Reformation to the Present Day*, Cambridge University, Cambridge, 1963. Philip Walters (ed), *World Christianity: Eastern Europe*, MARC, Eastbourne, 1988. Sabrina, Petra Ramet (ed), *Protestantism and Politics in Eastern Europe and Russia, The Communist and Post-Communist Eras: Chris-*

tianity Under Stress, Vol III, Duke University, Durham and London, 1992.

Bible Women
See *Bible Readers*.

Biblical Scholars, European Baptists in the 20th and 21st centuries

Baptist and baptistic communities in Europe have produced a significant number of Biblical Scholars in the last 100 years. This might be thought natural given the importance Baptists have placed on using the **Bible** at the core of the life of our churches.

Amongst those from European Baptist communities who have attained international recognition and have had influence beyond their own immediate sphere of work were Günter Wagner and George Beasley-Murray (1916-2000) both of whom, one-time members of the staff of **Rüshlikon**, as NT **scholars**, engaged with other Christian **traditions** around the NT understanding of **baptism**. Wagner also served for many years on the **World Council of Churches Faith and Order Commission**, along with British Baptist scholar, W. Morris S. West.

In the field of OT, or First Testament studies outstanding scholars from Europe have included Aubrey Johnson and his work on sacral kingship in ancient **Israel**, and T.H. Robinson, distinguished for his work on **prophecy**, both Professors at Cardiff, **Wales**. H.H. Rowley (1890-1969), one time editor of Peake's one volume commentary, H. Wheeler Robinson (1872-1945), G. Henton Davies (1906-98) whose commentary on Genesis fell victim to the **fundamentalist** resurgence in the **Southern Baptist Convention** and was withdrawn by the publishers, Broadman. Hans Harald Mallau (d.2006), from **Germany**, served in Argentina, then at **IBTS** as OT Professor. Stefan Stiegler was OT Professor and later Rector at **Elstal**. J.N. Schofield, in the University of Cambridge, was a prolific writer and was followed by R.E. Clements, who later held a chair in OT at King's College, London, writing commentaries on Deuteronomy, Ezekiel and Isaiah. Rex Mason, successively tutor at **Spurgeon's** and

Regent's Park College, was a pillar of OT studies at Oxford, where he successfully related OT research to **preaching**.

In the field of apocalyptic David S. Russell made a major contribution and in more recent times Stephen Finamore, Principal of **Bristol Baptist College**, has continued in this tradition.

In the NT, or Second Testament arena, without doubt Wiard Popkes (1937-2007), connected with both Elstal and IBTS, made a major contribution to research, especially on a NT understanding of the **church**. Marie Isaacs has done significant work on Hebrews and Davorlin Peterlin from **Croatia**, on Philippians. Johnny Jonsson of Stockholm has a reputation in the field of NT **ethics**, especially in relationship to **peace** studies. Biblical scholarship from a **conservative evangelical** perspective was consistently provided by the pen of Prof. Ralph Martin (of the London Bible College, Manchester and Fuller Seminary) and the widely read Donald Guthrie also of the London Bible College who also served as visiting lecturer at the *Freie Theologische Akademie*, Seeheim, in Germany. More recently Max Turner has achieved academic distinction at the London School of Theology.

KGJ

Bilateral Conversations
[See also *Ecumenical Movement; Leuenberg Confession Conversations on Baptism*]

Bilateral conversations, sometimes also-called bilateral **dialogue**, are so-called in contrast to multi-lateral conversations where more than two partners are involved. Bilateral conversations can be either on a world confessional level, or can be more regionally based. Such discussions can simply embrace a process of mutual education to overcome estrangement and ignorance, and negate old anathemas. Or they can lead to the affirmation of certain common concerns or core doctrines. Or most significantly of all they can lead to full **intercommunion**, or indeed the establishment of a united or uniting **church**.

Baptists have on the whole not been engaged in the last category of conversation. The only united church which has a Baptist presence is the Church of North India. Conversations which have more limited goals, however, still have their value. E.g. the Baptist-*Lutheran* conversations (1986-89) did lead to each side recognising each others' churches as true churches. The Baptist-*Reformed* Dialogue (1973-77) was seen as significant as spanning churches of the classic and the radical *reformations*. It has, therefore, been deemed momentous in stressing the importance of the radical tradition within the ecumenical encounter, and, for reformed Christians, the need not only to dialogue with more hierarchical and clerically-focused bodies, but with those who more radically amended the inherited concepts of *Christendom*. Following on the conversations some Reformed Churches have adopted the so-called dual practice which leaves the parents to choose either *infant baptism* or a service of thanksgiving/*dedication* leaving to the children themselves to ask for *baptism* when they have consciously made a decision to follow *Christ*. Baptist – *Roman Catholic* conversations [see *Roman Catholics, Baptist relations with*] took place between 1984 and 88 under the overall theme of 'Christian Witness in Today's World'. Two meetings were held in Europe, one in Berlin and one in Rome, with topics ranging from respect for *religious freedom* and the distinction between *evangelism* and *proselytism*. Baptists have also dialogued with the Disciples and the *Mennonites* with whom they have more common ground. Conversations with the *Anglicans*, focussing on different patterns of Christian initiation, have just been completed but attempts at conversations with the *Orthodox* were suspended very early in the process.

Such conversations and relationships are hardly new. Within the history of the Reformation itself Marburg and Ratisbon have an important place even though in the event neither was successful. Marburg, 1529, secured agreement by the churches of the Reformation on 14 out of 15 articles of *faith*, but failed to obtain consent on the nature of the *Eucharist*. Hopes of overcoming the breach in Christendom at Ratisbon were exaggerated even if Cardinal Contarini and *Luther*'s representative, Philip Melanchthon, did come near to one another on *Justification* by Faith, but the *papacy* and transub-

stantiation were obstacles which could not be overcome.

Bilateral and multilateral processes cannot be absolutely isolated, because all bilateral conversations have implications for other partners. E.g. the Leuenberg Agreement of 1973 provided for *pulpit* and table *fellowship* between Lutherans and Reformed in Europe, leading to the setting up of a Leuenberg Fellowship of *protestant* churches in Europe to which *EBF* was, for a time, an observer.

JHYB

Bioethics

Bioethics (derived from Greek words *bios*, 'life' and *ethos*, 'habit') is a relatively new field in contemporary applied *ethics*. Emerging from the late 1960s bioethics is addressing many questions as old as medicine, at the same time facing brand new moral problems of biotechnology, genomics, *environment* as well as issues of life and death in the context of *science*, *politics*, law, philosophy, and *theology*. Out of the Nuremberg War Crime Trials between 1946 and 49 the Nuremberg Code was drafted as a set of standards for judging physicians and scientists who had conducted biomedical experiments on concentration camp prisoners. In harmony with the Universal Declaration of *Human Rights*, adopted by *UN* in 1948, and the Convention on Human Rights and Biomedicine, adopted by the Council of Europe in 1997, modern European bioethical thinking and decision-making is guided by a common interpretation of a number of universal principles: e.g. the need to respect the voluntary consent of human subjects, thereby ruling out older paternalistic approaches in the treatment of human beings. In 2005 UNESCO adopted the Universal Declaration on Bioethics and Human Rights 'to provide a universal framework of principles and procedures to guide States in the formulation of their legislation, policies or other instruments in the field of bioethics.' The document states that 'independent, multidisciplinary and pluralist ethics committees should be established, promoted and supported at the appropriate level.' Christian bioethicists are to be involved in those 'pluralist ethics committees' while pointing out that 'a universal framework of principles and procedures' may not be enough. Different convictional communities of *faith* may reason differently. Ethics committees are established on the expectation that committee members, whether experts or laymen, should be able to make responsible decisions in borderline bioethical cases as well as to create certain precedents and practices according to the moral perspective about the kind of human beings to which civilised societies aspire. Thus an ideal type of the virtuous character as the object for the good life has become equally important as the globally acceptable standards of excellence aiming to solve the most complicated cases of bioethical challenges. Baptist vision, as the American *theologian*, James William McClendon, has argued, is about envisioning and embodying communal practices today as we discern them in our reading of scripture. Baptistic churches as convictional communities of faith look at the realities of bioethics always in connection with the Creator of human beings and the living world of creatures. *Christ*-like stewardship of life and life sciences cannot separate what the Creator has put together. Thus it is equally important to develop a virtuous approach to bioethics with personal integrity, communal responsibility, professional competency and unconditional faithfulness to the dignity of human life according to the image of God.

MR

FURTHER READING: Stephen E. Lammers and Allen Verhey (eds), *On Moral Medicine: Theological Perspectives in Medical Ethics*, Wm. B. Eerdmans, Grand Rapids, Mi. and Cambridge, 1998. Tom Beauchamp and James Childress, *Principles of Biomedical Ethics*, Oxford University, Oxford and New York, 2001. www.cec-kek.org/content/bioethicsconf.shtml – Human life in our hands? Churches and Bioethics (Reports from the consultation organised by the CEC Church and Society Commission in Strasbourg, 27-29 Nov 2003).

Birth Control

Birth control, or contraception, refers to various means used to prevent pregnancy and, in the case of Baptists, is usually discussed in the framework of the *ethics* of family life. European Baptist views on the topic have to be assessed keeping in mind the long shadow of the teachings held up until the 20th century by virtually all Christian denominations as they saw procreation to be the primary, if not the only, function of sexual intercourse, and indeed of *marriage* itself. With the development of chemical and biological research, the *Protestant* view began to diverge from the *Catholic* (and, in many instances, though less explicitly and consistently, *Orthodox*) insistence of the immorality of any contraceptive means, except natural forms of family planning by fertility awareness, etc. Baptist views have been affected by their dominating ecclesial [see *Ecclesiology*] contexts, though in practice it has been rarely discussed publicly, leading to many young people being ill-educated in this area. The teaching available has been dependent on the (often discreet) advice of the leaders of a particular community or the counsel of their peers and older relatives.

The spectrum of views on contraception can be seen in the variations of the average number of children in Baptist families across Europe, which is a helpful tool in the light of the scarcity of explicit discussions on the topic, of discerning what the local teaching is. Some very *conservative* pockets of eastern Baptists would hold that families should have as many children as possible in fulfilment of God's command to 'be fruitful and multiply' (Ge 1:28) and therefore would not approve of any family- planning methods. The reduction in the size of families within these communities would seem to indicate, however, that some methods of birth control are being increasingly practiced.

Other Eastern Baptist communities and most western Baptists stress human responsibility in family planning. Accepted methods would include all forms of natural family planning, but due to their low reliability, barrier and hormonal contraception would be more common, with the exclusion of post-intercourse contraception. Sterilisation has also been generally accepted, although its largely permanent effect makes it less popular than other pre-fertilisation methods. Coitus interruptus, or withdrawal, has been a common practice in both Eastern and Southern Europe, though increasingly less prevalent due to the availability of more reliable means.

The whole issue turns on what is deemed 'natural' and therefore 'God-given', and what is perceived to be humanly contrived, or trespassing on the divine determination of the patterns of human life. However, many would see the discoveries of medical science also as God's gift to his people. Perceptions of what is legitimate or illegitimate have also been influenced by the problem caused by unlimited population growth in the developing world and whether this challenges Christians to use medical science to discipline this situation.

LA

Bishop

The word Bishop derives from the Latin *biscopus* and is a translation from the Greek *episkopos,* an overseer, which appears in various NT documents. The development of the specialist role of the bishop from the local congregation, to the responsibility for congregations in a geographical area and the development of the work of the Bishop connected to a Cathedral, or mother church of a group, or diocese of churches and the place of a bishop within the Empire after the adoption of Christianity as the official religion of the Roman Empire is a major topic of reflection by Christian *historians* and *scholars*. Amongst the majority of Baptists the word has not been used because of the style of bishop which developed in medieval times involving the exercise of civil and ecclesial power and authority. Some early *Anabaptist* communities did use the word. However, a small number of Baptist communities in Eastern Europe have continued to use the word. Perhaps the earliest usage of the title of bishop was with the first Latvian Baptist leader, Revd Adams Gertners (1829-75), by Memel Baptist church in 1866. However while *Latvia* was an independent country (1918-40), the Head of the Baptist Union was instead called 'President'. The title 'Bishop' was again used during and after WWII. And later during the Soviet occupation of Latvia this title was used in opposition to the Soviet government and *AUCECB* of the USSR. Since Baptists generally refused to use hierarchical titles, the Latvian situation is almost unique. For many years Latvia

was the only country in the world where Baptists called their leaders 'Bishop'. However, Baptists in **Moldova** and **Georgia**, as well as the United Church of North India and a number of African countries, have also used this title. In both Moldova and Georgia it has referred to the presiding presbyter. More recently in Georgia several bishops have been ordained, including a woman and the presiding bishop has been re-titled archbishop, for which there is no Scriptural equivalent. The current *ecumenical* situation in Latvia and Georgia favours using this title since Baptists are one of the *state*-recognised traditional denominations. At the same time the title does not bestow hierarchical authority within the Latvian or Moldovan Baptist Unions as it does in many Episcopal churches. In Latvia the Bishop is elected for one or two 4-year periods by the Baptist Congress. In Georgia no time limit is set. In Moldova there is re-election. The function of a Baptist Bishop includes the representation of the Baptist Union before the state and society, helping congregations in solving doctrinal and spiritual questions, giving advice when congregations are seeking new *ministers* and acting as coordinator of the different activities of the Baptist Union. The bishop is not seen as benefiting from *apostolic* succession and there is nothing that he or she does which could not be done by any other pastor within the relevant *union*. In Latvia and Moldova exercising *ministry* in a local congregation continues to be an important task. In Georgia, with several bishops, the Archbishop does not exercise such weekly ministry, though he is attached to the Cathedral Baptist Church in Tbilisi. It must not be thought that those *unions/conventions* that do not use the title 'Bishop' have abandoned the Biblical concept of *episcope* or oversight; to see how they work this out see the separate article on *Episcope*.

EM & ET

Bivocational Ministries

This is a new title for something which has a long history as indicated by the title 'tent-maker ministries' formerly used of this work. Until the last century the number of *ministers* who could be wholly supported by their congregations was relatively few: the image of **William Carey**, the cobbler-pastor, is pertinent here. The most common way of funding the needs of the ministerial family was often the running of a school which a number of notable pastors did (James Hinton, John Ryland). Such functions as funded itinerancy work, or college, or denominational duties also helped to produce an adequate income.

In the second half of the 20th century, some of those graduating from college felt a call to work with smaller churches and, to lighten the burden upon them, agreed to continue in secular **work** as Ac 18 suggests Paul may have done at some stage in his **ministry**. But the concern is not only financial; from a **mission** point-of-view there is a good argument for a minister sharing with his/her people in being engaged in the workaday world of employment, and viewing ministry from that perspective. Increasingly in the mission field, the missionary combines gospel advocacy with such tasks as medical, **educational** or agricultural work, and is to that extent bivocational. Alongside career missionaries there are an increasing number of committed believers who deliberately take secular employment in the mission field in order to help the development of younger churches, sometimes operating in countries where full-time missionaries would not be allowed visas. All this helps to break down a false distinction between people and clergy, emphasising that all believers belong to the people of God without distinction.

JHYB

Black Theology
[See also *Theology*]
This is a form of **contextual theology** which first emerged amongst oppressed African-Americans, took root in Africa, in African **Diaspora** communities, and has now spread to other contexts and social groups across the world. Its development is thus inseparable from Black History. Its modern origins lie in the Civil Rights movement in the USA, led by the Baptist preacher, Martin Luther King Jr, during the 1950s and 1960s, supported by fellow Baptists such as Howard Thurman (1900-81). During slavery Black people's oppression was justified using the

Bible and Christian theology – Christianity was seen as having exclusive association with white culture and white people, failing even to recognise black people as fellow human beings. Black pastors began to ask how the Gospel of **Jesus Christ** speaks to black **men** and **women** struggling for freedom in such a racist society and so developed this alternative Christian response to the experience of being black in a post-slave society. The publication of Joseph Washington's *Black Religion* in 1964 was important, but the works of James Cone, especially *Black Theology and Black Power* (1969), *A Black Theology of Liberation* (1970) and *God of the Oppressed* (1975) were the most influential. Cone, initially rather belligerent, in his later work tempered his earlier militancy. In the 1970s, with the rise of the Black Power Movement, strongly influenced by Malcolm X, Black Theology began to drift away from its origins in Luther King's non-violent and integrationist approach towards a more aggressive and black **nationalistic** view. Black Theology is influenced by and closely connected with **Liberation Theology**, both of which make extensive use of motifs from the Exodus, whilst Black Theology also has deep roots in 19th-century slave narratives, slave resistance and the words of negro spirituals. By 1970 Black Theology had begun to influence **theologians** in an **Apartheid**-dominated South Africa, In South Africa, Black Theology and African Theology fused, with the one emphasis criticising the other. Here, Luther King's non-violent model as described by the Baptist, Louise Kretschmar, persisted. Not all Black Christians espouse Black theology; for the great majority the forces shaping their lives and thinking are **evangelical** and **Pentecostal**, but even here black identity and a consciousness of marginalisation have become increasingly significant.

PFW

Blessing of Children
See *Children, Blessing of.*

BMS
See *Baptist Missionary Society.*

Body of Christ
See *Church, The*.

Bosch, David J. (1929-92)
The South African *missiologist* David Jacob Bosch is well known for his compendium, *Transforming Mission: Paradigm Shifts in Theology of Mission* (1991) that has been translated into a number of languages. He has written six other books and edited many more, authored more than 150 articles, initiated many movements, was editor of *Theologia Evangelica* and *Missionalia*, the journal of the Southern African Missiological Society (SAMS) whose foundation he initiated. In South Africa he was both an eminent *scholar* in the university and an activist in the anti-*apartheid* movement. It was this latter work which led him to decline prestigious invitations to continue his work in the USA, where he was offered every opportunity to advance his research and writing. He is known and respected as a missiologist by both *conservative evangelicals* and those deeply involved in the *ecumenical movement*.

Having grown up in a pro-apartheid environment, he soon realised its sinfulness and, following his European and especially his *missionary* experience in the Transkei, Bosch become a spokesperson against apartheid. Later he was involved in the *reconciliation dialogue*, that Annemie, his wife, continued after his *death* in 1992. His connections with *anabaptistic* communities, resulting in a call for reshaping *ecclesiology* toward a radical alternative community modelled by these groups, became obvious not only in his book *The Church as the Alternative Community* (1982) but also in *Transforming Mission*.

PFP

Bosnia and Herzegovina, Baptist Bible Institute of
[See also *Bosnia and Herzegovina, Baptist history in*]
The Baptist Bible Institute, located in Sarajevo, established by the Baptist Church of Bosnia and Herzegovina in Sep 2001, is the only Baptist *educational* institution in the country. Its purpose is to train and equip the current and next generation of Bosnian indigenous leaders, *pastors*, and *missionaries*, in order to support the mission of the Baptist Church in Bosnia and Herzegovina. The Bible Institute offers theological *education* at diploma level, with an ambition to add degree level courses as soon as is practical. Courses in *theology* as well as practical *ministry* assignments are designed to provide *students* with knowledge and skills to minister in the multi-*faith* context of Bosnia and Herzegovina. The curriculum has been designed to meet the requirements of the *Euro-Asian Accrediting Association* for Theological Education. At present, the Institute relies heavily on visiting lecturers from Europe and the USA, and on missionary workers within the country.

OR

Bosnia and Herzegovina, Baptist history in
Probably the first Baptists in Bosnia and Herzegovina were Franc and Maria Tabory, a Hungarian couple from Novi Sad. Baptised in 1862 in the German Baptist Church in Bucharest, they moved to Sarajevo as *missionaries*. Franc Tabory was employed as a Bible *colporteur* by British and Foreign Bible Society. In 1863, he formed a small group of believers, mainly of German-speaking foreigners. During his missionary trip in 1868, August Liebig, a German Baptist missionary in Southeast Europe, baptised several converts in Lukavac, who soon moved to Sarajevo and there joined the existing Baptist congregation, the first Baptist church in Bosnia and Herzegovina. Later, Adolf Hempt, a Baptist Bible colporteur, and Edward Millard, who is known for his work as a missionary and the British and Foreign Bible Society agent in Vienna, became involved in its activities. August Liebig (in Bucharest) and Heinrich Meyer (in Budapest) continued to help in establishing the organisational patterns for the church. Baptist mission progressed mostly among the German-speaking population. By the beginning of the 20th century, there were five German-speaking Baptist congregations in Bosnia and Herzegovina, including those in Brezovo Polje, Franz Josefsfeld (later Kraljevičevo) and Bjelina.

Between the two world wars, the Baptist mission on the Balkans was revitalised and various language groups of Baptists emerged. However, the German mission, now supported also by German Baptist Conference in North America, was continuously influential in Bosnia and Herzegovina. Carl and Johan Sepper, Phillip Scherer, Károly Tary and Adolf Lehotsky all worked with good results. In 1924, the German Baptist church leaders established an umbrella-organisation, the German Baptist Conference, in Novi Sad. *Der Evangeliumsbote* (The Gospel Messenger) began to be published at this time. From 1924-44, the German churches maintained steady *growth*.

In 1919, in response to the *Baptist World Alliance*'s suggestion, the Foreign Mission Board of the *Southern Baptist Convention*, USA, started to work in parallel with the German Baptists. Their first missionary, Jovo Jekič, a Yugoslav immigrant to the USA, was soon accompanied by Vinko Vacek. Their goal was to solidify Baptist fellowships in Yugoslavia. In Mar 1922, the Baptist Union of Yugoslavia was founded. It included representatives from all Slavic Baptist ethnic associations: *Croatia*, *Serbia*, *Slovakia*, *Czech Republic*, and *Slovenia*'s language groups. Union leaders, such as Jovo Jekič, Vinko Vacek, Vaclav Horak and Josip Černy maintained close contacts with congregations in Bosnia and Herzegovina. Since 1923, the *union* has published a *magazine Glas Evanđelja* (Voice of the Gospel) in Serbo-Croatian. In 1925, all Baptist churches were recognised by the *state* law. However, discriminatory policies against Baptists were still pursued both by *political* and religious authorities. In this period, the two Baptists organisations, German and Slavic, existed in Bosnia and Herzegovina side by side in a spirit of cooperation.

During WWII the Baptist Union of Yugoslavia practically stopped all of its work. In 1944, the entire German population was forced to leave so the German Baptist Conference lost almost all its *members*. In autumn 1945, the Baptist Union of Yugoslavia was re-established. The Baptist churches of Bosnia and Herzegovina were part of it. During *Communism*, the number of Baptists in Bosnia and Herzegovina declined. Several dynamic *mission stations* from the pre-war

years were turned into small groups, while others disappeared. Urbanisation, started in the 1950s, weakened churches in rural areas, and Baptist work continued mainly in cities. Baptist mission work was revitalised during and after the Sarajevo Winter Olympics in1984. Thus, the work in Sarajevo was continued by a missionary Boris Kočarevic, and in Banja Luka by Milan Tovarloza. The outbreak of civil war in Bosnia in 1992 stopped any kind of Christian work once more.

After the Civil War the country suffered political and economic collapse and people felt hopeless. The same situation existed in Baptist churches. Although the Baptists in Bosnia had existed for almost 150 years, by the time the war ended, there were less than a dozen believers in the country. In 1997, the Croatian Baptist Union sent a missionary couple, Tomislav and Lidia Dobutovic to work in Sarajevo. In Mar 1998, Tomislav was ordained as *pastor* of Sarajevo Baptist Church, and by his efforts in 2000, the Baptist Church in Bosnia and Herzegovina was founded. In 2001 the union was accepted into the *European Baptist Federation*. The same year, the newly established Bible Institute of the Baptist Church in Bosnia and Herzegovina, invited Fedir Raychynets, a Ukrainian missionary, to help in organising the institute's *educational ministry*. Today, The Baptist Church of Bosnia and Herzegovina brings together 12 congregations (Sarajevo, Novi Travnik, Tuzla, Zenica, Gorazda, Banja Luka, Foca, and others) with approximately 250 church members in total.

OR

FURTHER READING: Oksana Raychynets, 'Baptist Mission Efforts in Bosnia-Herzegovina: 150 Years of Discontinuity and Struggle', Keith G. Jones and Ian M. Randall (eds), *Counter-Cultural Communities*, Paternoster, Carlisle, 2008.

Boy's Brigades and Girl's Life Brigades

William Smith (1854-1914), a Glasgow *Sunday School* teacher, was worried that all too many boys left the Sunday School at an early age. To retain their interest and to create an *esprit de corps* among them, in 1883 he created a uniformed organisation which focussed on weekly drill, gymnastics, working for awards and promotion to senior ranks, summer camps and Sunday *Bible* Class. There were regular Church Parades when the company, led by its drum and bugle band, would march around the neighbourhood and then into church where its flags would be received by the pastor. Its object was 'the advancement of *Christ*'s kingdom [see *Kingdom of God*] among boys and the promotion of habits of obedience, reverence, discipline, self-respect and all that tends towards a true Christian manliness'. The word 'manliness' provides the context of a period in history when manliness was closely related to godliness. The movement was distinctly military, seeking cultural relevance by attempting to sanctify something of the jingoism or chauvinism of late Victorian *Britain*. The uniform was a simplified version of one of the current military uniforms and the boys originally carried rifles. Not all were happy about this, though impressed by the usefulness of Smith's movement, for work with which he was knighted in 1909. Accordingly, a parallel organisation, the Boy's Life Brigade, imitated the Boy's Brigade but did not carry arms. Both soon developed organisations for girls whilst younger boys were invited to join the Life Boys. Brigades and Life Brigades were amalgamated in 1926 with the female organisation retaining the title of being a Life Brigade. The important feature about the BB/BLB was that, unlike the Boy Scouts, who originated in a manual written by Baden Powell, originally all companies had to be church-related. In *England* this meant mainly to one of the *Free Churches*. Brigades were very popular amongst Baptist Churches in the earlier years of the 20th century but found it difficult to adapt to the greater informality of life as the century came to an end. The movement did become worldwide though its quasi-military form meant it could not be easily transposed into some societies and so its principal strength remained in the United Kingdom.

JHYB

FURTHER READING: B. Fraser and M. Hoare, *Sure and Stedfast: a history of the Boys' Brigade, 1883–1983* (ed J. Springhall), Collins, London, 1983. D.M. Macfarlan, *First for Boys: the story of the Boys' Brigade, 1883-1983*, Collins, Glasgow 1982.

BR-E

See *Baptist Response – Europe*.

Bread for the World [Brot für die Welt]

Founded in 1959 as a response to the help that *Germany* had received in the immediate post-war period, Bread for the World is the relief agency of all *protestant* churches in Germany. Part of its income comes from an annual collection for its work and enables it literally to offer food aid, but also medical services, agricultural assistance and other help with vocational training as well as emergency relief. In fulfilling its mandate it works in cooperation with the *World Council of Churches* and the *Lutheran* World Federation. It does not fund *evangelism* but does support *mission* agencies in their social outreach. It has been a leading European Christian development agency, not least in the drawing together of other such agencies from Western Europe in APRODEV (Association of Protestant Relief and Development Agencies), together with the British *Christian Aid*.

ET

Brethren

This branch of *Protestant* Christianity, which earlier works refer to as 'Plymouth Brethren' or 'Open' and 'Exclusive' Brethren, that has become universally known as 'Brethren' and sometimes 'Christian Brethren' (despite a consistent reluctance until recent years to accept any appellation) shares with Baptists the conviction that the *local church* is a gathered *communion* of the redeemed [see *Redemption*], and the principle of the *priesthood of all believers*. Brethren, however, reject the concept of an ordained *ministry* [see *Ordination*], and collective *worship* in both the independent (or 'open') and connexional (or 'exclusive'/'Darbyite') streams of the movement has been characterised traditionally by the relative informality that marks their weekly celebration of the *Lord's Supper*.

Brethren origins lie in the discontent with established denominations that manifested itself particularly in *Britain*, Ireland and French-speaking *Switzerland* in the first third of the 19th century. The energy and determined expansion of the movement across most of Europe during the remainder of that century and beyond necessarily had an impact upon Baptist life. J.N. Darby (1800-82), perhaps Brethren's most prominent pioneer, was an early influence in the spiritual life of J.C. Philpot who later became an influential leader among Strict Baptists in *England*.

Prominent British Baptists such as *C.H. Spurgeon* were known to deprecate Brethrenism's strident critique of all other patterns of church life. Spurgeon also condemned Darby's *'dispensational'* scheme of biblical interpretation, insisting: 'Difference of dispensation does not involve a difference of *covenant*; and it is according to the covenant of *grace* that all spiritual blessings are bestowed.' Similarly those arguing for an *Evangelical Alliance* initially coupled Plymouth Brethrenism with Popery [see *Papacy*] and Puseyism as things to be opposed, though it was not long before Brethren were seen as valuable allies in the promotion of *evangelical* values. Many Baptists, like other evangelicals, were inspired by the Open Brethren leader, George Müller, and his huge *orphanage* ministry in Bristol; the concept of 'faith missions' owes much to Müller. By the early decades of the 20th century Brethren were to be found from the Low Countries to *Russia* and from *Germany* to the Balkans, *Italy* and the Iberian peninsula.

Although many connexional Brethren maintained a distinctively separatist position, the 20th century saw a notable degree of blurring of identity between Brethren and Baptists across Europe. In continental Europe this occurred to a significant extent under the external pressure of persecution from communist authorities in the East, as well as in Nazi Germany, where the Union of Evangelical Free Church Congregations still embraces both Baptist and Brethren congregations. In Russia, the late 19th century saw rapid *growth* among the aristocracy downwards of Brethren-type congregations known as 'Pashkovites', as a result of the work of Lord Radstock, an English aristocrat loosely associated with independent Brethren, and under Tsarist persecution these congregations (later known as 'Evangelical Christians') were accepted into the *union* of Russian Baptists from 1903, with full integration

occurring under Stalin in 1944.

In England in the post WWII period the resurgence of British evangelicalism, often in a guise ironically that betrayed the impact of Brethren ideals, has led to an ongoing drift from Brethren towards other evangelical groups. Significant numbers of former members of Brethren assemblies in Britain joined Baptist churches and a number of these became Baptist *pastors* and leaders in the denomination. Some thriving congregations once identified as independent Brethren are barely distinguishable from Baptist churches. Across mainland Europe (including parts of *Scandinavia*) Brethren groups continue in greater strength alongside Baptists. In the broadest terms the evangelical heritage that Brethren and Baptists share has with time become more significant than the *ecclesiological* distinctions between them.

For a quite different group sometimes referred to as Brethren see the entry on the *Church of the Brethren*.

RNS

FURTHER READING: D.W. Bebbington (ed), *The Gospel in the World: International Baptist Studies*, Paternoster, Carlisle, 2002. F.R. Coad, *A History of the Brethren Movement*, Regent College, Vancouver, 2001. D.G. Fountain, *Lord Radstock of Mayfield*, Mayflower Christian Books, Southampton, 1984. T. Grass, *Gathering to his Name*, Paternoster, Carlisle, 2006. R. Shuff, *Searching for the True Church: Brethren and Evangelicals in Mid- Twentieth-Century England*, Paternoster, Carlisle, 2005.

Bristol Baptist College

Towards the end of the 17th century there was a sense among some Baptists that, with the increasing age and death of *pastors* who had been university trained and the closure of the universities to *nonconformists*, it would be appropriate for those recognised as ministers among them to have some training particularly in the biblical languages, but in other aspects of thought and practice as well. In 1679, in an attempt to meet this need, Edward Terrill, a member of Broadmead Church in Bristol, made a deed, donating money to the church to be used to support a minister who was skilled in the biblical languages and would help to prepare *men* for the *ministry*.

The money did not become available until 1720, at which point Bernard Foskett was appointed as one of the ministers at Broadmead, with this responsibility. Gradually, drawing from *Wales*, and the south west of *England*, a steady stream of young *men* came for training. In 1770, the financial base of the institution was broadened with the founding of 'The Bristol Education Society', looking to the other churches for support as well. The Bristol connection was important since unlike the London leadership of the denomination it never became captive to high-*Calvinism* but instead consistently nurtured an *evangelical* Calvinism, well exhibited in the life of John Sutcliffe who with the non-college trained *Carey* and Fuller [see *Fullerism*] founded the *Baptist Missionary Society*.

In 1811, the College moved into purpose-built accommodation, and developed an existence separate from that of the Broadmead Church. Connections with Bristol University, a much younger body which became an independent institution in 1909, developed, so that early in the 20th century, *students* shared in classes at the University *theology* faculty.

In 1902 a site was purchased near the university, and in 1919 a new building was opened. Patterns changed towards the end of the 20th century. The teaching in the university faculty moved in different directions, so that by the 1990s, the College was once more trying to teach a degree in Christian doctrine independent of, but validated by Bristol University. In order to do this, a partnership with Trinity College, an evangelical *Anglican* college, was formed.

In 1996, the building was moved again, to near Bristol Downs, this time a non-residential building, reflecting the different patterns of training that had begun to emerge. At the same time, the College began a fruitful partnership with a course in *youth work* and theology.

As the oldest continuing *Free-Church* college in the world, Bristol Baptist College maintains its aim to produce 'able, evangelical, lively and zealous ministers of the gospel' – statement originating with the Education Society in 1770.

RH

Britain, Baptist history in
See *England*; *Ireland*; *Scotland*; *Wales, Baptist history in*.

Brot für die Welt
See *Bread for the World*.

Bucharest Baptist Theological Institute
During the first Congress of the Baptist Union of *Romania* in 1920, one of the leaders of the *union* proposed the establishment of a *mission* school that would be 'a good tool...and a workshop for training and testing the *ministers* of the Gospel'. The Baptist witness in Romania was almost 50 years old at that time and there was a lack of adequate leadership. The participants accepted the idea and decided that the school should operate out of the Baptist church in Buteni, Transylvania. On 1 Sep 1921 six-month-long Bible courses were begun with nine *students* and three teachers. The school was called the Baptist Seminary. Its first president was I.R. Socaciu who had been trained at Southern Baptist Seminary in Louisville, Kentucky. Because of persecution from the local police, the seminary had to move to a church in the city of Arad after six weeks. However, after only another two weeks, local police closed the seminary in Arad and it moved to Bucharest in Nov 1921 where it was housed by the German Baptist Church. In 1922 the duration of the courses was extended to four years while in 1924 the seminary's own building was erected on land that had been purchased for them by the Foreign Mission Board of the *Southern Baptist Convention*. In the following two years a second building, the 'Women's School', was constructed thanks to the generosity of Mrs C. James. Prior to 1928 the seminary had accepted *women* for training but, after it opened in 1930, women were able to attend a 2-year training programme in the James Memorial Training School.

The dictatorial regime under which Romania existed during WWII caused the closing of the seminary in Mar 1942 and on 28 Aug 1943 the buildings were confiscated though they were returned after the end of the war. In Nov 1946 the Baptist Seminary began its work again in Buteni and, the following year, moved back to Bucharest. When the *communist* regime passed a new law for religions in 1948, the Baptist Seminary was included in this law giving it a legal basis to exist. During the communist years the seminary was allowed to function but with a number of restrictions. The number of students admitted had to be approved by the Department of Religious Affairs and on one occasion only four students were permitted on the entire 4-year programme. The printing of textbooks was also almost impossible. In spite of these difficulties, the seminary continued with its mission to provide trained Christian leaders for the Romanian Baptist churches. With the single exception of 1969 when permission to accept students was not granted, the seminary always had a number of students in training. The seminary buildings were severely damaged by the 1977 earthquake, requiring general repairs. Planning permission for these repairs was hard to obtain but eventually it was granted and the buildings were consolidated with the help of funds from *BWA* and *EBF*.

Following the fall of communism in 1989 the seminary was granted provisional accreditation under the name of the 'Baptist Theological Institute of Bucharest' and it received full accreditation in 2005. In the same year it started a distance-learning degree programme to complement its existing ministerial training degree. The Baptist Theological Institute was instrumental in the founding of the *Baptist Theological Faculty of the University of Bucharest*. The two schools use the same facilities and work together sharing staff and offering complementary programmes. The Baptist Theological Institute has developed relations with *Regent's Park College, Oxford* which offers training and research resources for the development of teaching staff. It is also a member of the *Consortium of European Baptist Theological Schools* of EBF.

OB

Bucharest University, Baptist Theological Faculty

The Baptist Theological Faculty of the University of Bucharest was founded in 1991 as a result of the joint efforts of the *Bucharest Baptist Theological Institute*, the University of Bucharest and the Baptist Union of *Romania*. Following the anti-*communist* revolution of 1989, the opportunity was created for theological schools to join the existing *state* universities. The Baptists were the only *evangelicals* who were able to meet the requirements and start such a college.

The Faculty began by offering three joint honours programmes: *Theology* and Social work, Theology and Romanian language and literature as well as Theology and Foreign languages and literature (English, German, French and Russian). Male and female *students* from all evangelical denominations (as well as a few *Orthodox* and *Catholics*) attended the college which was fully accredited in 1995. The graduates often go on to serve in secular jobs such as teaching, social work, and translation but also in *mission* and *bivocational ministry*.

The Faculty operates in accommodation provided by the Bucharest Baptist Theological Institute and the Baptist Union of Romania. Most of its teachers are *pastors* and also teach for the Baptist Theological Institute. Since it was the first accredited evangelical college in Romania, the Faculty helped to organise final exams for the other Baptist and Evangelical colleges seeking accreditation. Without such assistance and validation the degrees offered by these colleges would not have been recognised by the state.

As a consequence of the Bologna Agreement, the Faculty is no longer able to offer joint honours degrees and it therefore now offers a theology degree with three certified areas of study: Mission, Counselling and Communication, and Management of *Non-Governmental Organisations*. The college was able to start a Master of Theology programme in 2005 and also has had a doctoral programme since 2000.

Since the founding of the Baptist Theological Faculty in Bucharest, *Regent's Park College* of Oxford University and TCM International Institute *Austria* have been instrumental in providing training and research resources for the development of teaching staff and for research projects of doctoral students. The Faculty is an associate member of the *Consortium of European*

Baptist Theological Schools of the *European Baptist Federation*.

OB

Budapest, Baptist Theological Seminary

Following the organisation of some shorter courses in 1896-1901, Hungarian Baptists, under the leadership of the Hamburg-graduated *pastor* András Udvarnoki, founded their own seminary – often called 'the heart of *mission*' – in 1906. Subsequent to Hamburg and Stockholm, it was the third Baptist Seminary in Europe. During its history the Seminary faced great problems – lack of proper buildings, financial pressures and *political* restrictions (e.g. the number of students was limited by the government in the *socialist* era) – yet it has been working continuously for 100 years.

The 1990s saw great developments in the Seminary's life with the renovation of its former buildings. With some 200 full-time and part-time students from different denominations, it offers a Bachelor of Divinity programme (training pastors), two Bachelor of *Theology* programmes (training church and social workers) and a Bachelor in *Church Music* programme. Degrees are officially accredited by the Hungarian *state*.

AS

BUild (Baptist Union Initiative with people with Learning Disabilities)

[See also *Disabilities, Work with those with severe*]

On 22 Nov 1983 a group of English Baptists concerned for people with developmental and learning disabilities met together and decided to form a network which would gather information and encourage churches to engage in active *ministry* with such people. This network became 'BUild' – the Baptist Union Initiative with people with Learning Disabilities. The closure of big *hospitals* for the 'subnormal' and moves to 'community care' gave a sense of urgency to this. Meanwhile developments in secular *education* for those with special needs raised questions for Christians: a few churches were

already pioneering special teaching and *worship* ministries.

BUild has encouraged churches to be aware of local possibilities, to form special groups and also to include those with learning disabilities in many church activities, both devotional and social. BUild has addressed *pastoral* needs, protection of vulnerable adults and advocacy, has explored *theological* issues, and has shared ideas for teaching and other activities. It has worked mainly through publications, sending speakers to churches and colleges, and arranging day conferences. An increasing number of those with considerable learning disabilities have come to *faith* and have found their own ways to *witness* to *Christ*. They have presented *music* and drama at BUGB assemblies. BUild members have also worked with Baptists in *Poland* to help initiate special ministries there.

FWB

Building (Sanctuary)

See *Church Building (Sanctuary)*.

Bulgaria, Baptist history in

The first *Protestants* to work systematically in the Bulgarian lands were the *Methodists* and the *Congregationalists* in the 1850s. Their work preceded the appearance of the first Baptist communities in Bulgaria by a quarter of a century. There were other factors that influenced the beginning of Baptist work in Bulgaria. Firstly, in the second half of the 19th century, British and Foreign Bible Society's *colporteurs*, such as Kristian Krzossa, Martin Heringer, M. Herboldt and Jacob Klundt, distributed *scripture* in territories then under Ottoman control. In 1868, the Society established a depot in Ruschuk (today's Russe) on the river of Danube. The colporteurs' work increased the interest of the population in the reading and study of the *Bible*. Secondly, a settlement of 37 Baptist families, German-Russians from Neu Danzig and Rorbach in Southern *Russia*, who were fleeing religious persecution, was established in 1866 in the village of Katalui, 14 km from Tulcha in the northeast corner of Bulgaria. *Johann Gerhard Oncken* visited

Katalui and Tulcha in 1869, and probably the first Baptist church in the Ottoman Empire was founded in Katalui, though some sources speak of Tulcha. From this region, the Baptist message spread in the surrounding areas. Thirdly, there were a number of Bulgarians who had come into contact with Baptists outside Bulgaria. Four of them, Vasil K. Marchev, Vasil Kiyosev, Peter Doychev and Georgi Chomonev, upon their return home, played a significant role in the growth of Baptist work in Ruschuk, Lompalanka (today Lom), Chirpan and Berkovitsa.

The first Bulgarian-speaking Baptist church on the territory of today's Bulgaria was established in Kazanluk, a town in central Bulgaria, after Ivan Kargel baptised five people there, on 7 Sep 1880. This *baptism* was an answer to an appeal by a small group who were convinced of believers' baptism already in 1876 Soon other congregations were formed: in Ruschuk (1882), Lompalanka (1884) and Sofia (1888). By the turn of the century there were more than 100 Baptists in Bulgaria, *worshipping* in four churches and a number of branches attached to each one of them. Though these Baptist groups were comparatively small, they continued to grow and in 1918, despite the negative effect of WWI, there were 261 Baptists. By that time four new churches had been founded: in Chirpan (1903), Guliantsi (1915), Aski-Zagre (today Stara Zagora) and in the village of Golintsi, near Lompalanka. The latter was the first *Roma* Baptist Church in the world. The Bulgarian Baptist Union was established on 15 May 1905 in Ruschuk.

Between 1918 and 44 Bulgarian Baptists grew to almost 1,000 in 23 congregations. Of crucial assistance in the development of the Baptist work was the assignment of the Bulgarian *mission* (in 1920) to the Baptist Union of *Germany* and the General Missionary Society of the German Baptist General Conference of the USA (later North American Baptist Conference). With their assistance, vital support was secured for native *pastors*, and a number of *church buildings* (Baptist chapels) were erected, e.g., in Kostenets (1920), Berkovitsa (1921), Sofia (1923), Golintsi (1930), and Lom (1930). A key role in this development was played by missionaries Jacob Klundt as well as by Karl Grabain, a German-Russian, who came to Bulgaria in

1911 and had an influential *ministry* in Lompalanka. Evgeniy Herrasimenko, a missionary of the Romanian Bulgarian Association and pastor of Ruschuk Baptist Church, and Carl E. Petrick, a missionary of the American Baptist Foreign Mission Society who moved to work in Bulgaria in 1914 and who had a great influence in the church in Sofia, must be mentioned. During the period between the wars, the Baptist Union published its own periodical *Evangelist*, organised *women*'s ministry and societies for social work, established *children's work* and *Sunday School* programmes in most of the churches. Well-known leaders of these days were Spass Raichev, Sava Lechov, Zaprian Vidolov, Dimitur Hristov, Georgi Vassov, Nikola Mihailov and Trifon Dimitrov.

Baptists in Bulgaria faced vicious persecution under *communist* rule from 1945-1989. Activities were severely restricted, children's and youth work was forbidden, Bible training and conferences were outlawed. Many church buildings were confiscated or demolished. The communist regime sentenced 12 Baptist pastors each for 8-12 years imprisonment as a result of two instigated false trials in 1949. The heavy persecution of *church members* and the devastating loss of leadership resulted in a decrease in membership, especially in the first 15-20 years of communism. At least two of the pastors, Ivan Angelov and Ivan Igoff, went back into ministry after their release from prison. The commitment of pastors such as Georgi Todorov, Yordan Gospodinov, Dimitur Nikov, Dimitur Apostolov and Ivan Odjakov as well as the ministry of lay leaders, such as Vasil Vangelov, helped the church to overcome the darkest period of its history and to meet the democratic changes of 1989 with 600 members, 10 churches and four pastors.

The 1990s brought *religious freedom* which made possible open-air meetings; women's, children's and youth ministries, and the training of church leaders. Confiscated church buildings were returned to the Baptists and new church buildings could once more be built. The Baptist Union had its first congress in 45 years in May 1991. This congress reported 26 Baptist congregations with 1,350 members. The same year, the Baptist Union was again officially recognised by the *state*. Some of the most influential leaders of the new time were Dr. Theodor Angelov, who served as president of the Bulgarian Baptist Union (1990-98) and General Secretary of the **European Baptist Federation** (1999-2004), Bojidar Igoff, General Secretary of the **union** (1990-97), the Baptist Union's first full time **evangelist**, Vasil Vangelov, who is the current union president, and Dimitur Podgorski, a leader in South West Bulgaria. Through the work of missionaries from the Foreign Mission Board (International Mission Board) of **SBC** the Baptist Theological Institute was established in 1992. Later, with help from the **European Baptist Convention**, and most recently the **Baptist Missionary Society** and the **American Baptist Churches**, Baptist work grew rapidly both among Bulgarians and among the **Roma minority**, expanding also to Bulgarian **Muslims**. A vast humanitarian and social work was developed and many new church buildings were erected, e.g., in Varna (1991), Sandanski (1991), Montana (1996), Dupnitsa (1995), Sliven (1998), Guliantsi (2004) and Berkovitsa (2003). At present, the union has 75 congregations, 31 pastors and 11 lay preachers with about 5,000 members.

TBO

FURTHER READING: T. Angelov, 'The Baptist Movement in Bulgaria', *Journal of European Baptist Studies*, Vol. I, No 3, May, 2001, pp.8-18. Teodor Oprenov, 'The Theology of Baptist Believers in Bulgaria as Reflected in the Publication *Evangelist* (1920-1939)', Keith G. Jones and Ian M. Randall (eds), *Counter-Cultural Communities*, Paternoster, Carlisle, 2008. A.W. Wardin, 'The Baptists in Bulgaria', *The Baptist Quarterly*, Vol. 34 (1991-4), pp.145-158.

Bulgarian Evangelical Theological Institute

Prior to WWII the so-called American College in Sofia-Simeonovo offered **education** to the entire family of **Evangelical** churches in **Bulgaria**. In Dec 1941 the Bulgarian government declared war on the United States and although the desire of the government was for the American teachers to stay, in the autumn of 1942 the demand of the Nazi Commander in Sofia was for them to leave within 48 hours. After the war the school's operation was not re-instated. During the **Communist** era in Bulgaria no formal train-

ing in connection with any of the Evangelical churches was permitted.

With the changes sweeping Eastern Europe in 1989 the Baptist believers within the family of Evangelical churches looked forward to a new stage of their work in Bulgaria. In 1992 the Bulgarian Baptist Union began the Bulgarian Baptist Theological Institute (BBTI). More than 20 **pastors**, along with 20 other **students**, enrolled in the programme. The basic curriculum consisted of 16 courses, which could be completed in four years, if one enrolled in and satisfied the requirements of every course. The courses were usually taught by lecturers/professors from **Germany**, **Britain**, or America. Courses taught by non-Bulgarian speakers were translated, and material was provided. For each course students earned a minimum of one-hour academic credit for each course, or a maximum of two hours. Courses were taught on a one-week intensive basis four times a year, and consisted of a minimum of 32 lecture hours over five days.

The school operated in Sofia on various rented facilities. Directors of BBTI were Doc. Dr. Parush Parushev then Revd Stoicho Apostolov, followed by Revd Theodor Oprenov and Doc. Dr. Milcho Angelov. The last course in the curriculum was offered in Dec 1995. 25 of the students completed enough of the courses to receive a 'Certificate' at a ceremony during the Mar 1996 meeting of the Bulgarian Baptist Conference. By then five extension centres were also added to the programme (Montana, Sandanski, Sofia, Varna and Sliven) with an enrolment of more than 100 participants who continued with their studies under the supervision of the Bulgarian Baptist Union.

Laws passed in 1949 which could have provided for an Evangelical Academy proved ineffective and it was not until the new constitution of 1990 was passed that **denominational leaders** could begin to negotiate for such provision which still took seven years to achieve but finally in 1998 a govenment-recognised school for Evangelicals was finally secured. The founders chose to name the school Bulgarian Evangelical Theological Institute (BETI). The Bulgarian Baptist Union was one of the founding members of BETI (est. 1999) and with the beginning of operation of the new institute the BBTI merged along with Logos Bible Academy to establish the United Theological Faculty of BETI as one of four Evangelical *theological* faculties. BETI is one of the unique theological training institutes around the globe with its currently four theological faculties serving Baptist, *Congregationalist*, and *Pentecostal* churches.

Distinguished leaders and faculty members among the Bulgarian Baptists who aided in the establishment of BETI are Theodor Angelov, Nikolay Nedelchev, Theodor Oprenov, Milcho Angelov and Parush Parushev. Prof. Dr. Roger Capps, a Baptist *missionary* to Bulgaria in 1999 was the vice-president for academic affairs of BETI, *doctor honoris causa* (2008) of BETI for his academic and leadership contribution to the educational work in Bulgaria. BETI has an established partnership relationship for exchange of faculty with the *International Baptist Theological Seminary* in Prague, *Czech Republic*.

TaP & PRP

Bunyan, John (1628-88)

John Bunyan has three claims on Baptist attention. First there is his work as an author. Amidst his vast output, *Grace Abounding to the Chief of Sinners* (1666) is deservedly famed as an outstanding spiritual autobiography, *The Holy City* (1665), represents his interpretation of church history from the *apostolic* period through his own life-time to the end of the ages, whilst *The Holy War* (1682) moved with ease from historical conflict and threat (largely seen in a potential papal [see *Papacy*] takeover of *Protestant England*) to spiritual warfare. The *violence* depicted in the book was a damning indictment of the Tory regime in England. The Baptist historian, Richard Greaves, argues that 'Bunyan's message was a call to resistance, but not insurrection, a summons to the faithful to stand resolutely for their *faith* in the face of a *state* determined to crush *nonconformity* and impose a *Catholic* sovereign on the country.'

Bunyan's most famous work, however, was *The Pilgrim's Progress* (1678.) which is probably the most distinguished religious allegory ever written, tracing as it does the journey of 'Christian' from the City of De-

struction to the Celestial City, a journey in which he encounters such expertly depicted figures as 'Mr. Talkative the son of Mr. Saywell', 'Mr. Worldly-Wiseman', and 'Mr. Facing-both-ways' but is supported by 'Greatheart', as on his pilgrimage he travels through such testing locations as 'Vanity Fair', the 'Slough of Despond' and the 'Hill Difficulty'. Pilgrim's Progress was followed two years later by its sequel *The Life and Death of Mr Badman*, 'a series of snapshots depicting the commonplace attitudes and practices against which Bunyan regularly *preached*.' In all his writings Bunyan lastingly communicates the reformed faith, and its practical demands rather more forcefully than any learned treatise or so many quickly forgotten sermons. *The Pilgrim's Progress* has been translated into well over 100 languages, and next to the *Bible* it became the most commonly possessed book in English homes, where its artless forms, its concrete images, and its sympathetic understanding of the strengths and weaknesses of ordinary people helped to shape the religious outlook of Britain's Protestant population for more than two centuries. It was also widely received throughout Europe.

The debate on whether Bunyan was a Baptist has attracted various antagonists. Certainly he was baptised as an adult believer [see *Baptism*] some time between 1651 and 53 by John Gifford, *minister* of the meeting house in Bedford, the congregation which set Bunyan apart to the task of *ministry* in 1656, first to labour in the surrounding villages then in Bedford itself form Jan 1672. That church had only slowly moved to *separatism* – Gifford combined his ministry there with a parish incumbency – but by the time of Bunyan's baptism was thus described: '*Calvinist* in *theology*, *Congregational* (or Independent) in *government*, this church generally followed the principle of believers' baptism following *conversion* to newness of life.' It was thus an independent church which practiced Believers' Baptism but not exclusively so. *A Confession of my Faith* (1672), in Greaves' judgment, 'established Bunyan as an *open-membership*, *open-communion* Baptist with *Reformed predestinarian* views.' In Bunyan's own words, the baptismal candidate 'must be a visible *Saint* before, else he ought not to be baptised'. Such views he made abundantly clear in his *Differences in Judgment about Water-Baptism, No Bar to Communion* (1673), in which he defends mixed congregations where both forms of baptism were practiced. Bunyan's legacy was to leave a **tradition** in Bedfordshire and neighbouring counties of a common Congregationalism, in which paedo-Baptists [see **Infant Baptism**] communed and held **membership** alongside those who confined baptism to believers only.

Bunyan's third significance for Baptists is a life of faithfulness notwithstanding persecution for his forthright advocacy of **puritan** doctrine and separatist practice and inner attacks from forces of mental and spiritual depression. He was long imprisoned for his faith, for most of the years between 1660 and 72 with only temporary release in 1668. So is formed the picture of the Bedfordshire tinker, who 'strives to mend souls as well as kettles and pans' in his prison cell. There he cultivated a profound **spirituality**, developed his gifts of creative writing, which also found fruit in his passionate defence of the **poor** and the oppressed, and his unqualified commitment to the belief that truth must be free.

JHYB

FURTHER READING: J.D. Ban, 'Was John Bunyan a Baptist?', *The Baptist Quarterly*, Oct 1984. R.L. Greaves, 'A Tinker's Dissent: a Pilgrim's Conscience' in *Church History*, vol 5, 1987. R.L. Greaves, *John Bunyan and English Nonconformity*, Humbledon, London, 1992. R.L. Greaves, *Glimpses of glory: John Bunyan and English Dissent*, Stanford University Press, Stanford, Ca., 2002. Michael Mullett, 'John Bunyan in Context' in *Church History*, vol 66, no. 3, 1997. R. Sharrock, *John Bunyan*, Hutchinson's University Library, London and New York, 1954.

Burials
See **Funerals**.

BWA
See **Baptist World Alliance**.

BWAid
See **Baptist World Aid**.

Byelorussia, Baptist history in
See **Belarus, Baptist history in**.

C

Call/Calling

[See also *Pastoral Call; Vocation*]

The call of God is a familiar theme in *scripture* whether to individuals or groups – e.g. the nation of *Israel* in the OT, or to the disciples to become 'fishers of men', or as expressed by the *apostle* the need for constant rejoicing by the believer that God has called them 'out of darkness into his wonderful light,' (1Pe 2:9). It is the verb which demonstrates how the concept of *election* comes to fruition in the life of individual Christians, for the elect are those whom God has called into his service. The stress is always on the divine initiative – that God has chosen us not, we who have chosen him. However, with that choice comes obligation, hence, Paul's instruction to Christian leaders 'to walk worthy of their calling (Eph 4:1).

As Baptists understand it, believers' baptism represents the essential response to that calling in the *Church* today, representing the believer identifying with the dying and rising of their *Saviour* and taking for themselves all that Christ has done for them, the objective aspects of the *sacrament*, as well as signifying their desire to serve him, which is the subjective aspect. In the sense that Baptism signifies an acceptance of that calling, it represents the *ordination* of every believer to Christian service (thus echoing *Oncken*'s commissioning of all *church members* to the *missionary* task, as many years earlier *Luther* spoke of *The Vocation of the Christian Man,* making it quite clear that a Christian could live out his/her vocation as a parent, a workman, a market trader, etc. in the secular world, for all these are tasks to be undertaken for the glory of God.

More precisely reference is made to the call to *ministry* which needs to be tested before a candidate is accepted for ministerial training. This is a process which starts in the *local church*, is confirmed by regional and national groupings of Baptist churches, by the institute involved in training, and finally once more by the local church, for in normative practice ordination is only offered once the individual's sense of call, tested in community, is ratified as a local church invites the trained individual to undertake the pastoral office among them, exercising a ministry of word and sacrament. All this is important for only a sense of this call of God can sustain a life-long ministry, that is to say that ministers in their daily activities are not merely exercising a career choice, or a task of compassionate service but they are where they are because they are so constrained by the compulsion of God's calling.

In the modern church the model has become more complicated as diversity of ministry has emerged, e.g. youth ministry, a ministry of *music*, a ministry of *education*, whilst some ministers are called to exercise their ministry through denominational administration, college functions, chaplaincy work and a variety of supra-congregational tasks, all now seen as legitimate aspects of Christian ministry for which ordination is appropriate, different ways in which to be obedient to the ministerial call.

ET

Calvin, Jean (1509-64)

[See also *Calvinism*]

Jean Calvin, French *Protestant* reformer [see *Reformation*] whose theology greatly influenced many Baptist groups, was born in Noyon, France in Jul 1509. Prepared for an ecclesiastical career from a very early age, he received a humanist education at the University of Paris securing BA and MA degrees. After this he undertook legal studies at Orleans and Bourges where he first came into contact with reformed thinking. He revealed his humanist interests by publishing a Latin commentary on Seneca's *De Clementia*. His *conversion* experience which was followed by his public declaration of his Protestant persuasion has been dated between 1530 and 34. He was very conscious of the way God had intervened in his life in this experience, as indeed he was to do subsequently in the way Calvin became committed to the Genevan reformation: he used the Latin tag, *Deus subiegit* [God subdued me]. Because of severe persecutions against French Protestants he was forced into exile. He spent a short time in Basel, where he published the first Latin edition of his *Institutes of the*

Christian Religion (1536), his major work, which he would considerably expand over the following decades. In the same year, he was persuaded by Guillaume Farel to assist with the reformation in Geneva which, despite periods of exile, was to become his life work. In 1538 he published his *Ordonnances Ecclésiastique* in which he set out the way in which a reformed church should be ordered and governed. Returning from three year's exile in Strasbourg in 1541, for the rest of his life he exercised wide powers in the city, shaping through the city council, the religious and moral life of the citizens, **preaching** and teaching regularly, making Geneva the centre of the new reform movement. Calvin, an outstanding and systematic **theologian** [see **Systematic theology**] as well as a great **Biblical scholar**, became a spiritual father of Reformed theology, and his ideas reached far beyond Geneva. His theological thinking followed Augustine and was greatly indebted to **Luther**, Melanchthon and Bucer, and to a lesser degree to **Zwingli**. His theology has the **Sovereign** God and His glory at the centre, and all the other doctrines evolve around this majestic theme. In 1553 he became embroiled in the Servetus affair. Michael Servetus was already known as an anti-trintarian [see **Trinity**] on which he had written a youthful treatise in 1531 after which he took up medicine. He was in correspondence with Calvin and could not therefore have been in any doubt that Calvin totally repudiated his views which he amplified in a major work published anonymously in 1553. Imprisoned by the Inquisition he escaped to Geneva where Calvin realised he had to act firmly lest the Inquisition identify the whole reformation movement with clear **heresy**. Servetus was burnt as a heretic in Geneva in Oct 1553. On **communion** Calvin took a median position between Luther and Zwingli rejecting both **Lutheran** consubstantiation and the idea that the bread and **wine** in the communion were mere **symbols**, regarding a **sacrament** as a visible **sign** of an invisible grace. He often stated that the body of **Christ** on which the believer feeds remains in **heaven** and that, therefore, in the sacrament the believer is raised to heaven to feed on Christ.

The influence of Calvin's theology (often through later developments of Calvinism) on European Baptist life and thought has been significant.

AB

Calvinism
[See also *Calvin, Jean (1509-64)*]

Calvinism, sometimes too simply identified as '*Reformed* Theology', is a robustly debated theological system amongst Baptists. The terms derives from the work of **scholars** who followed and developed the work of Jean Calvin (1509-64) in the 50 years after his death, especially enumerating the five points (or tulip) of Calvinism at the Synod of Dort, convened by the States General of the **Netherlands** and held from 13 Nov 1618 to 9 May 1619 to try to resolve controversy within the reformed churches regarding the teaching of the **Arminians**. The 'tulip' arising from this meeting, defining 'five-point Calvinism', focused on:

Total **Depravity**
Unmerited Favour
Limited **Atonement**
Irresistible **Grace**
Perseverance of the Saints

This systematisation of Calvin's thought was worked out by Calvin's disciples who may have gone further than him in applying strict logic to defining some of these emphases. Calvinism is frequently identified with the idea of the **predestination** of the elect [see **Election**] only to benefit from the **salvation** secured by **Christ**'s **death**, with the implication that all others are predestined to damnation. Many, however, would argue that ideas of predestination are secondary to Calvin's insistence on the **Sovereignty** of God, from which all his theology derives. Calvin's thinking found support early in French-speaking **Switzerland**, **France**, parts of **Germany**, **England**, Holland, **Hungary** and **Scotland**.

17th-century British Particular Baptists were Calvinists in their basic beliefs as revealed by their early **confessions of faith**. The first London Baptist Confession (1644) and the Second London Confession (1677), demonstrated their fundamental solidarity with the wider Calvinist community. In the Second Confession the articles are substantially and deliberately similar to the statements in the Presbyterian Westminster Confession (1646) and *Congregationalist* Savoy Declaration (1658).The form of Calvinism embodied in these confessions was not extreme but late in the century some London *pastors* developed from this Calvinist inheritance a form of high Calvinism that thought it trespassing on the role of the *Holy Spirit* in *preaching* to offer Christ's *salvation* to sinners [see *Sin*], who, of their own capacities, had no ability to respond. Reacting against the stultifying impact of high Calvinism by the late 1700s a modified form of *evangelical* Calvinism, most conspicuously seen in the writings of Andrew Fuller [see *Fullerism*], predominated amongst English Baptists and from within that tradition emerged the *missionary* impetus associated with *William Carey. C.H. Spurgeon*, though a Calvinist, was of this modified tendency being remembered (at least in legend) as declaring 'Lord bring in your elect, and then elect some more' and testifying to this evangelical Calvinism by his approach to *evangelism* and social *ministries*. In the 19th century Calvinists and Evangelical Arminians united around this evangelical missionary imperative to such an extent that differences between the two traditions became less and less important as both sides became ever more committed to evangelism at home and abroad.

Similarly *Johann G. Oncken*, who fathered so much Baptist witness across Europe was basically Calvinist in his theology though always prioritising mission and evangelism. Whilst many countries contained Baptists of both a Calvinist and an Arminian persuasion, some countries such as *Ukraine*, have always been firmly Arminian in their basic doctrine of the *grace* of God

There are those from North America who believe five-point Calvinism in its pure form is the only authentic Baptist theology, but generally European Baptists do not take such a view by virtue of history and by the continuing desire to engage in evangelical mission within this broader spectrum of evangelical Calvinism and Trinitarian Arminianism.

KGJ

Capital Punishment

Whilst now abolished in most countries,

Christian bodies were slow to question the legitimacy of capital punishment, considering it simply a matter of *state* security. Nevertheless, many Christians came to see it as a contradiction to the 6th commandment and joined forces with others, like *Amnesty International*, who saw it as a cruel and inhuman punishment that in its finality made no allowance for either wrongful conviction or *repentance*. The movement to abolish the death penalty has especially attacked its arbitrary use, raising serious questions about the legal systems of those countries that retain it. Supporters of the death penalty, whilst reducing the number of crimes punishable by *death*, still believe, that murderers that are proven guilty, do not deserve to live.

Portugal was the first country in Europe to abolish the death sentence in 1867, substituting life imprisonment for it. Shortly after WWII most European countries abolished the death penalty. Britain abolished it for murder in 1965, but kept it till 1998 for the rare occurrences of treason, piracy and military crimes, though the last execution in the UK took place in 1964, 13 years prior to the last execution in the European Comunity which took place in *France* in 1977. The *European Union* has since 1995 required the abolition of or a moratorium on the death sentence as a condition for membership. Only *Belarus* in Europe still retains capital punishment; *Russia* currently has a moratorium on its use. By 2000, 90% of all judicial executions took place in four countries: the USA, China, Iran and Indonesia. The UN Commission on *Human Rights* has since 1997 adopted annual resolutions calling for a moratorium of all judicial executions, pending their eventual abolition in all countries.

PMIL

Capitalism

Subsistence economies produce little if anything that is surplus to immediate requirements, whilst capitalist economies accumulate *wealth* and re-invest it for profit in manufacturing, trading and other enterprises. Modern capitalism emerged with industrialisation in the 18th century (see Smith), though Weber speculates that *Calvin's Protestantism*, if not its cause, provided fertile territory on which capitalism could flourish where hard work and modest, not to say ascetic, life-styles were virtues, money-making was a vocation, and *prosperity* a sign of one's *election*.

With the demise of the alternative, *socialist*, *state*-centred economies in the late 20th century and the spread of Western capitalism (a major feature of *'globalisation'*) until its influence, for good or ill, was felt almost everywhere, capitalism came to be regarded as the only viable, if not the ultimate, economic system. Its triumph has been described as 'the end of history' (Francis Fukuyama).

Capitalism, especially in Europe, dramatically improved the standard of living for vast numbers of people, so much so that many countries in the East and the South readily embraced it as their own model of economic development and their most hopeful route out of poverty.

Capitalism is closely associated with the 'free market' and free trade and a form of liberalism which insists that business should be free (`laissez-faire`) from government interference and control. This was in part a moral argument upholding the freedom of the individual but one which also reflected the belief that the laws of supply and demand, if left to themselves, would ensure efficient and profitable production on the one hand, and low prices benefiting the consumer on the other.

Nowadays it is generally agreed that the market cannot simply be left alone to be governed by some `hidden hand`. The interaction of various self-interests does not necessarily produce the best possible outcomes. Rising individualism undermines the mutual trust and regard which early capitalism assumed. No market is `free` in the sense that it offers a level playing field and an equal opportunity for everyone to succeed. Some enter it with advantages (inherited wealth e.g., or social influence, or appropriate knowledge and skills) over others. The market is competitive by definition. It readily creates winners and losers, gaps between rich and poor, imbalances and monopolies of economic power. Free-market capitalism promotes individualism rather than community, competition rather than cooperation, greed rather than sharing. It is far bet-

ter at creating wealth than distributing it fairly. Above all perhaps, the market is reluctant to provide essential goods and services which are not obviously profitable, such as universal education and *health* care, social services and support for the weaker and more vulnerable members of society.

These and other concerns have given rise to recurring debates about how markets should be regulated and the appropriate role of the state. Pure laissez-faire policies on the one hand and thoroughgoing socialist economies on the other may be seen as the two theoretical extremes: one controlling nothing and the other controlling everything. In practice they have rarely been adopted. Instead the state has acted as a referee in the market place to a greater or lesser extent. It has promoted the welfare of all its citizens by taxation e.g.. It has stimulated or slowed down economic activity. It has explored ways in which private enterprise can contribute to public services. Such endeavours have created the more nuanced versions of capitalism with which we are familiar, including the Social Market, the *Welfare State* and Public-Private Partnerships where the skills and resources of private enterprise contribute directly to social projects.

The debate about capitalism has often been polarised. Christian writers and institutions have adopted a whole range of views. Western *Protestant* Christianity has generally been sympathetic towards it (*Roman Catholicism* less so), adjusting traditional teaching (e.g. on *usury*) to its realities. Its *missionary* movements were often inseparably bound up with colonialism and capitalism as they spread across the globe.

The Liberation *Theologians* [see *Liberation Theology*] of the Global South, often drawing on the prophetic insights of Karl Marx (see Marx's *Capital*), have been harshly critical of what they judged to be an oppressive economic order from which the *poor* needed to be set free. Even in the West, Christians have been critical of its individualism, its competitive rather than communal spirit, and its tendency to promote greed and materialism. Most seriously, they have spoken out against the injustice (whether to industrial workers in English cotton towns or to 'poor' countries and people exploited for their cheap labour and raw materials) which has so often followed in its wake. At their most extreme, Christians have denounced capitalism as a *'heresy'* because it inevitably oppresses the poor and is therefore contrary to the gospel.

A good deal of contemporary Christian opinion lies between uncritical acceptance of capitalism and its outright rejection. It recognises what capitalism has achieved and that ideas, such as individual freedom and social solidarity, enterprise and cooperation, efficiency and compassion, profitability and justice are not necessarily mutually exclusive. It looks for better ways of combining the strengths of good government and private enterprise and is aware that other issues, such as sustainability, the care of the earth, and *spirituality*, which have not featured historically in debates about capitalism, are now very much on the agenda.

MHT

FURTHER READING: Ulrich Duchrow, *Global Economy: A Confessional Issue for the Churches?*, WCC Publications, Geneva, 1987. Francis Fukuyama, *The End of History and the Last Man*, Maxwell Macmillan International, New York, 1992. Ronald H. Preston, *Religion and the Persistence of Capitalism*, SCM, London, 1979. Adam Smith, *The Wealth of Nations*, London, 1776. Max Weber, *The Protestant Ethic and the Spirit of Capitalism* (ed and with foreword by R.H. Tawney), G. Allen and Unwin, London, 1930.

Care for the Elderly
See *Elderly, Care for the*.

Carey, William (1761-1834)
As the principal founder of the *Baptist Missionary Society*, Carey helped to initiate a movement which gave rise to similar societies in *Britain*, Europe, and America. Carey was a shoe-maker and largely self-educated. His interest in *missions* owed much to the accounts of the South Sea voyages of Captain James Cook, and also to the pioneering work of the *Moravians*. He wrote a pamphlet urging the obligation of Christians to spread the gospel *overseas*, *An Enquiry into the Obligations of Christians to Use Means for the Conversion of the Heathens* (1792), which led to the formation of the (Particular) Baptist Missionary Society. Carey offered

to go as one of the society's first two missionaries to Bengal, where he and his family arrived in Nov 1793. His wife, Dorothy, had been unwilling to go to India, and soon developed acute mental illness. She died in 1807. Carey later married twice more. In 1800 he moved to the Danish settlement of Serampore, north of Calcutta. The work of the 'Serampore Trio' of Carey, Joshua Marshman, and William Ward attracted widespread admiration. The first Hindu convert was baptised in 1800, but the rate of *conversion* was slow. Carey's later years were marred by poor relationships with the Baptist Missionary Society. His lasting achievement was as a *Bible translator* and linguist. He and his Indian pandits were responsible for the translation of the entire *Bible* into six Indian languages – and of parts of it into a further 29 languages. His encouragement of the Bengali language contributed to a Bengali cultural renaissance.

BJS

FURTHER READING: S.P. Carey, *William Carey, DD*, Hodder and Stoughton, London, 1923. E.D. Potts, *British Baptist Missionaries in India, 1793-1837*, Cambridge University Press, London, 1967.

Catechisms
See *Catechumenate; Ecclesiology*.

Catechumenate
This word derives from the Greek word *katecheo* which literally means 'to teach by word of mouth'. In the early church it was used to describe the state of new converts [see *Conversion*] who were being prepared for *baptism* by instruction in the Christian *faith*. Not yet full *members* of the *church*, as members of the catechumenate they had status within its family. To begin with such converts were often taught by laymen, but by the 4th century, the clergy had taken over the task with the *bishop* personally responsible for the concentrated teaching immediately before baptism. After the bishop had explained the fundamental teaching of the church, often focussing on the *creed*, the Lord's Prayer and the Ten Commandments, and the catechumens had memorised it, they were required to 'give it back' in a later

ceremony by replying to set questions. Thus some have suggested that *catechesis* might be translated as 'echo', for candidates sometimes sang out the answers to these questions. Oral teaching was the most common method for this instruction in the post-*apostolic* church, because few Christians could read and written texts were beyond the reach of even most literate Christians.

Later, catechetical schools were formed for those who tried to reconcile Christianity with the philosophies of their culture, and became the places where church leaders were trained. The first catechetical school was opened in the year 179 by Pantaenus in the large Christian community in Alexandria, Egypt, where Clement and Origen were later to become leaders. Other schools in Caesarea, Antioch, Edessa, Nisibis, Jerusalem, and Carthage, followed.

This reflects the radical change which came over the church with the increasing practice of *infant baptism*. The catechumenate were now those who had been baptised as children but who were now being prepared for confirmation of the promises made on their behalf. At the time of the *reformation* the reformers laid stress on the process of catechesis as necessary to the nurture of an intelligent church membership. The Czech *theologian*, J.A. Comenius, in particular sought more meaningful methods of communication, including the use of pictorial material, to ensure that the process was something more than rote learning and that real understanding was secured.

In the 18th century older catechical schools, which confined their work to members of church families, gave way to the *Sunday School* movement, which combined the process of educating the church's own young with a more out-going evangelistic [see *Evangelism*] purpose. By the early 19th century it had spread from the *UK* to *Germany*, *Holland* and *Switzerland* and thence to the rest of Europe.

The language of catechist and catechumenate has been revived in the modern church especially in the two-thirds world where new converts are instructed in the faith as they are prepared for baptism, with an increasing emphasis on contextualising the teaching in the local situation. Though the language is strange and not often used

by Baptists the idea of the catechumenate has poignant significance for Baptists because of their insistence on delaying baptism until faith has been personally confessed. The catechumenate expresses the way in which children belong within the church family even though not church members.

G.W. Rusling of *Spurgeon's College* argued the usefulness of the concept in the *Baptist Quarterly* (Vol XVIII, p246-8) as long ago as 1960, when he argued that a worshipping child of a Christian family, who was learning the faith in Sunday School, was, in fact, participating in a 'prolonged catechumenate', prolonged in that it extended from infancy to adolescence, as compared with the brief period of instruction undergone by a new convert in the early church. In both cases the instruction took place in the context of the hope that the person concerned would in due course experience *repentance*, faith and baptism. Rusling argued that Baptists were very familiar with the pastoral experience of the catchumenate but confessed, 'what we have not done is to make allowance for the idea of it in our *theology* of the Church'. But to do so would be to indicate to others that there was a way for a child to relate to the church before confessing the faith in believers' baptism. Here was a way of affirming that persons in this category were 'in a creative relationship with the Body of Christ.' Just because Baptists both believe in a regenerate church membership with the restriction of baptism to those who believe, and maintain that the church has an evangelistic vocation, 'the church must always have a catechumenate in its midst'. Such a catechumenate is constantly changing as members move on to baptism and full church membership, but the need for such a category remains constant. Indeed, a church without a catechumenate is in a perilous position.

George Beasley-Murray in 1966 affirmed that position, arguing that the catechumenate needed to be 'treated with utmost seriousness'. 'Its abolition after the Constantinian settlement when the masses swept into the church, and infant baptism became the accepted practice, was of untold loss to the church.' In caring for the young the catechumenate, 'or in modern terms, in an adequate system of Christian *education*', was the secret that explained both the way in which children and those coming to faith related to the church as well as providing the context within which the faith of an applicant for baptism could be discerned. Morris West was to affirm the same concern: 'The word "catechumenate" may not be widely accepted by Baptists for reasons which are not always clear. But the concept of it must be. *Church growth* comes about as much by the gradual incorporation of families into its life as by sudden conversions.'

Both were agreed that baptism should not be seen as the end of the catechetical process because the very concept of *discipleship* suggested a commitment to what educationists call life-long learning. Learning about *Jesus* can never come to an end. Examining people's theological knowledge and life-style before entering into membership may also carry an idea that baptism is like a final exam and after that you have your 'final degree' in Christian belief and experience. The emphasis should instead be upon the newly baptised entering into a community of learners.

In the case of children there needs to be the fullest possible cooperation between the church and the Christian home. Today, a purely didactic methodology is not considered appropriate and teachers are called to concentrate more upon what children actually experience and the questions they ask.

The need for the proper preparation of those wishing to join the church has never been more important. The secularisation of the life-style of even professing Christians is endangering distinctive patterns of Christian living, while the agnostic influences of *New Age* thinking confuse people's understanding of Christian teaching. Becoming a full member of the Christian community is also threatened by the phenomena called 'believing without belonging', where people, disappointed in their experiences of the institutional church in its several manifestations, form alternative communities, or more commonly distance themselves from all Christian institutions without renouncing the faith. Designing a more appropriate catechumenate could be crucial in holding such people in a meaningful relationship with God and his Church.

Baptists have used catechisms both for evangelism and educational activities. Of the several catechisms they have written that by the late 17th-century English pastor, Benjamin Keach (1640-1704), was very influential especially in North America Different catechisms have been written by Baptists to suit different contexts and people. Whatever the target groups, these catechisms carry the strong indication, that while explaining the Christian message, it should always be done by taking into consideration the learners and their context.

EP

Catholic/Catholicism
See *Roman Catholic*; *Roman Catholicism, Baptist relations with*; *Roman Catholicism, Baptists and*.

Catholicity
Catholicity is the notion that the *church* has a universality and comprehensiveness which includes all true believers in the Triune God [see *Trinity*] who are *orthodox* in their belief and faithful in their *discipleship*. The ancient *creeds* of the church express as key concepts for true communities of Christians both orthodoxy in belief and catholicity in community. If catholicity ever existed in both a spiritual [see *Spirituality*] and bodily way then this was in the early centuries of the church. Beyond that time and the time of the great *ecumenical* councils such as Nicea and Chalcedon, catholicity as originally intended no longer existed. Division within the Eastern church, the division of the Western church from the Eastern, the *reformation* and the radical reformation are all important moments marking the disintegration of catholicity as originally envisaged.

Some parts of the divided church, for instance the *Roman Catholic* Church, have sought to lay claim to universal catholicity, but this claim is spurious by their own standards in a true understanding, given the divisions of the church and the lack of *intercommunion* between the Roman Catholic Churches, the churches of the *Protestant* and Radical Reformations and the *Orthodox Churches*. Indeed, it can only be maintained by denying the validity of the churches in all other *Christian World Communions*, arguing that they only possess partial aspects of being church. This is the position adopted by the Roman Catholic Church.

Baptists, who have a less rigid view of catholicity, affirm they belong to the one true catholic, *apostolic* and universal church of *Jesus Christ*. They do so on the basis that Baptists are orthodox in belief, catholic and universal in presence throughout the world, and generally have an open *eucharistic* table for all those who love the Lord Jesus Christ and desire to be His true disciples [see *Open Communion*]. This more generous catholicity would be the mark of the majority of Baptist communities in Europe, though some would say their own way of being church was the only true way and that catholicity must be more narrowly defined. By refusing *fellowship* to others they *de facto* deny their own Christian status, and thus are in danger of losing their own churchly status and becoming a mere *sect*.

KGJ

CBF

See *Cooperative Baptist Fellowship*.

CEBTS

See *Consortium of European Baptist Theological Schools*.

CEC

See *Conference of European Churches*.

Celtic Spirituality

[See also *Intentional Communities; Spirituality*]

In many parts of Europe today there is today an increasing interest in Celtic spirituality. As well as the famous Iona community off the west coast of *Scotland* there are now others such as the Northumbrian Community, of which Roy Searle, a Baptist *minister* is one of the leaders. The Christian *faith* developed in a number of Celtic regions. In Gaul, Martin of Tours, with his monastic *mission* in the 4th century, was probably an influence on the whole of Celtic Christian-

ity. Followers of Martin came to *Wales*. The monastic style began and this influenced mission. There were also missions to Scotland. *Tradition* says that Patrick (c 390 461) came to *Ireland* and spread the Christian message through the whole country. A leading missionary to the Scottish Picts was Ninian (c.360-432) who was deeply influenced by Martin. He founded his 'Candida Casa' [White House] at Whithorn, dedicating it to Martin. Columba (521-597) carried on this work. Aidan (d651), who was at Iona, went to Northumbria in 633. He established a monastery at Lindisfarne. Cuthbert (c.634-687) was also an important influence.

The interest today in Celtic spirituality has involved a desire to see faith as having a relationship with the whole of *creation*: For the Celts, all of life had the presence of God in it. There is a deep love of the natural world in Celtic spirituality. *Worship* often took place in the open air. Central to that worship was *prayer*, which among the Celtic Christians was connected with daily life. Work was surrounded by prayer. The place of miracles was also significant: There are many accounts of miracles in the records of the Celtic *saints*. Finally, the way in which Celtic Christians such as Patrick undertook mission seems to have been sensitive to culture and community-based.

A number of the books on Celtic Christianity are rather simplistic. There is a tendency to idealise this period in the history of the church or to create the Celtic Christians in an image that is desired in the contemporary world. But there is also a serious concern – to learn from those Christians who lived in such a way as to make an impact on North-West Europe, and beyond, over the course of at least two centuries.

IMR

Central Asia, Baptist history in

[See also *Kazakhstan; Kyrgyzstan; Tajikistan; Turkmenistan; Uzbekistan, Baptist history in*]

Baptist origins and development in Central Asia (during the period of the Russian Empire the whole region was called Turkistan), had a dramatic context – the downfall of the Russian Empire, Civil War and the establishment of Soviet power. However, the first evangelical churches had already been established in the territory of contemporary Kyrgyzstan by the end of the 19th century. In 1882, German settlers from Southern **Ukraine** founded a **Mennonite** church in the Talas Valley. Other Mennonite churches soon also emerged in the region. In 1892, the first **evangelical** church with Baptist leanings, including both Russian and Armenian **members**, was founded near Ashkhabad (in present day Turkmenistan). In 1897, a Russian Baptist evangelist, Mihail Chechetkin, came from the Far East to the area of Central Asia. He planted Baptist churches in a number of Molokan villages in the Syr-Darya region. Chechetkin's work was continued in that region by S. Skorodumov.

During the first decades of the 20th century Baptist **revival** and *'church planting'* occurred in many towns and villages in Central Asia: Baptist churches were established in Tashkent (1902), Aktyubinsk (1906), Bishkek (1907), Ashkhabad (1908), Almaty (1917), Fergana (1922), Dushanbe (1929) and Karaganda (1931). Two evangelists of the All-Russian Baptist Missionary Society (founded in 1907), M. Shiruev and P. Demakin, undertook a **missionary** journey to Central Asia in 1908. They preached in Tashkent, Samarkand, Andizhan, and in many smaller towns and villages. They conducted **baptisms** and helped the first Central Asian Baptists to organise churches. In 1917, the Baptists in Central Asia working together with **Mennonite Brethren** established the Central Asian division of the All-Russian Baptist Union. A serious drawback in the **evangelism** of the early Baptist movement in Central Asia was the tendency to reach only two groups – Russians and Germans – while neglecting the majority of the population, the indigenous peoples.

As a result of Stalin's repressions in the 1930s, many convicted prisoners and exiled Christians, among them a number of ethnic Germans, were sent to Central Asia as in the tsarist times. They, illegally, started new churches: **Lutheran**, Mennonite and Baptist. The latter soon began to include Russians amongst those they attracted. Today, the time of exile is seen by many Central Asian Baptists as an act of divine **providence**. The Baptist work in Central Asia developed in the context of a culture characterised by strong patriarchal family traditions and local religious rituals, often mixed with **Muslim** beliefs. Today, Baptist missionaries **preach** in rural areas in 'missionary yurtas', which are more attractive constructions to the indigenous people than traditional **church buildings**. As an **apologetic** argument, they also refer to the Christian (Nestorian) presence in the region before the Muslim invasion of the 9th-12th centuries. In recent years, many books of **scripture** have been translated into Central Asian languages.

Because of the strengthening of Islamic influence, often supported by **political** preferences, Baptist work has become difficult in several regions in Central Asia. In Turkmenistan, all **Protestant** churches have been closed. A small number of Baptists in Turkmenistan meet persecution that is at times more severe than in the **Communist** era. In Uzbekistan, the Baptists, with approximately 3,000 members in 59 churches and groups, do not have any freedom for missionary activity. Kazakhstan, Tajikistan and Kyrgyzstan, have relative religious freedom, which gives certain stability to Baptist work. The number of Baptists in these three countries is comparable with the period before the fall of the **USSR**: approximately 15,000 in Kazakhstan, 3,000 in Kyrgyzstan and 500 in Tajikistan. However, during the 15 years prior to the publication of this volume, the number of Baptist emigrants from the five former Soviet republics of Central Asia has been greater than 50,000, a considerable number of which have been **ministers**. Only the significant influx of new **members** during the years of *perestroika* has prevented Baptist work from disappearing in the region. Baptist churches or groups are usually small in these countries with many Russian-speaking members. However, serious attempts are being made to reach local people. E.g., in Kyrgyzstan 14% of Baptist church members are Kyrgyz, while 20 years ago it was exceptional to have Kyrgyz members in the Baptist churches. Besides Russian, the Central Asian Baptists use local languages in their **worship**. The Central Asian Baptists have undertaken a number of educational and publishing projects. There are some Baptist schools using distance learning to train pastors and other Christian workers in the region; two such schools exist in Kazakhstan, one in Uzbekistan and one in Kyrgyzstan.

CP

Chapels

[See also *Architecture*; *Church Building (Sanctuary)*]

It is not hair-splitting to object to the use of the big word '*church*' for the place where Baptists meet, for 'church' belongs essentially to people, not bricks and mortar. Thus the usage seen in x: 'The Meeting Place of 'y' Baptist Church', clarifies the differential deployment of language. In fact a variety of words, including 'church', have been used for Baptist buildings. The oldest is probably 'Meeting House'. In the 18th and 19th centuries, 'Tabernacle' was sanctified by both Whitefield and *Spurgeon*. 'Chapel' has commonly been used and there have been 'Prayer Houses', 'Temples', a title favoured by some (e.g. William Fetler) and most recently the unecclesiastical 'Church Centres'. Popularly churches have also been known by their dedications especially the OT, 'Zions', 'Salems' and 'Ebenezers', and the NT 'Christchurches' and 'Emmanuels'. Some dedications reflect historical consciousness with 'Tyndale' and 'Wycliffe' common and *Carey* the most popular of Baptist designations.

The earliest Meeting Houses were domestic in scale, indeed many were converted houses and others have reverted to that function. The *pulpit* – the place from which the *sermon* would be delivered – was set in the middle of the longest wall, normally immediately opposite the entrance. In front of it was set the *communion* table, around which was the big pew, beyond which were the congregational pews all set around the Open Word of *scripture* and the *Lord's Table*. No organ pipes intruded at this date as organs smacked of *Catholic* ceremony, nor were there facilities for *baptisms* for these would take place outdoors, either in the neighbouring river, or occasionally in a specially constructed *baptistry*. These were essentially buildings for the theologically literate who met in covenant *fellowship* to wait on that 'more of truth and light' which the Lord would 'break forth from his Word.' The great *preaching* houses of the late 18th and 19th centuries were quite different for they were built to enable the untutored masses of the new industrial cities to congregate under the sound of the gospel. The *preacher* is now 'six foot above contradiction', lifted high above the congregation on the ground floor, for to exploit the space available great galleries have been added and the preacher needs to be visible to all. Increasingly, the organ pipes which are of no liturgical significance have been added and alongside the organist, the front part of the gallery may be set aside for the use of a *choir*. The communion table is still there. Indeed in front of it was located what was called the penitent's bench when appeals for gospel responses became a regular part of Baptist *liturgy*. Baptisms were now possible inside the *sanctuary* in a subterranean tank built beneath the place where the table stands. Later the desire for the baptistry to be always visible as a witness to Baptist beliefs will raise questions as to how to handle the threefold focus of Baptist *worship*: pulpit, table and pool. Sometimes as is common in the USA, the baptistry is set high up on the far wall so that the congregation can clearly see all that takes place both above and in the water. The shape of the sanctuary was initially an oblong, and the style first domestic and then classical (sanctified by Spurgeon) and only slowly Gothic, which had earlier been thought too catholic. With the Gothic style came transepts and chancels and vast lofty roof spaces none of which reflected *Puritan* worship needs, only a burden of upkeep on subsequent congregations, raising the issue of the life span of church buildings as they relate to mobile populations with changing liturgical needs.

The interior of the building, apart from those organ pipes, will have little by way of *decoration*, though some of the earliest chapels had superbly crafted hanging chandeliers, with the woodwork and glazing of the best quality as befitted the House of God. The Puritan *faith* of the worshippers was reflected in a constrained, even severe, interior. During the 19th century, the appetite for decoration grew, and stained glass offered a ready medium for this. Stencilled texts were also added, indicating either a call to worship or some central affirmations of the faith. Sometimes the design was abstract, fearing any bodily representations, but bolder spirits did use their windows to illustrate scripture, both OT narrative and NT miracle and parable. Some churches even used the visual images of *The Pilgrim's Progress* whilst others have tried to depict representative *saints* of every age to extend the narrower definition of sainthood within the catholic tradition. A fall on the pulpit has provided an opportunity to display other symbols, with the α and ω of scripture sometimes used, or the χρ (*Jesus Christ*) or a *cross* and IHS (In this sign)] of the early church, embroidered on it. Elsewhere the decoration is the cup and plate used in the communion service: the original of these could also be examples of the finest craftsmanship. Pictures have not commonly been seen in church but of recent years, whilst pulpits and pews have been increasingly banished to provide more flexible space, banners hung from the ceiling have become very common. The organ pipes are disappearing fast and in their place has come the screen on which to project the words and images that now accompany worship, produced by a variety of musicians, no longer the solitary organist. At the same time older *consciences* about candles have become less compelling and never did have the force in *Scandinavia* or Eastern Europe they had in *Great Britain*. The *Advent* wreath/candles and the Moravian Christingle Service, together with the appeal of candle-lit carol services, are all now very common. Crosses in churches, rarely seen in earlier years have become more common, but they would take the form of the empty cross of the Risen Lord not a crucifix. Two other features may be encountered – the first are memorials to those who contributed to the past heritage of the church, especially much-beloved pastors, and the second would be the war memorials which commemorate the tallies in young lives wreaked by major conflicts [see *Remembrance Day*].

In the 19th century the church often acquired separate buildings in which to conduct *Sunday Schools*. These were sometimes built on a separate site, but were often built adjacent to the sanctuary, spelling out the church's commitment to serve the community with a variety of services from coffee shops to counselling facilities. Also adjacent to a number of older chapels would be the Baptist burial ground, most of which have long since ceased to be used as they have been filled up, but sometimes exhibiting

interesting iconography and poetic celebration of a **theology** of **death**.

JHYB

Chaplaincy

Chaplaincy, also called Sector Ministry, is a lay [see *Laity*] or ordained [see *Ordination*], full or part time *ministry* to sectors of the community beyond the normal range of local church *mission* initiatives. Chaplains may work out their ministry in *hospitals*, universities and colleges, prisons, the armed forces, the emergency services, *sport*, shopping centres, railways, airports, ports, town centres, civic offices, industry and many other places of work. They engage with both the people and the issues found there, linking *faith* and work – *church* and world.

Chaplaincy is a way of living the Gospel in the contemporary world, without expecting people to leave their own familiar territory in order to encounter it. It is both mission and *pastoral* ministry, representing *Christ* in the places where life is lived out - and challenges, hurts, problems, questions, beliefs, and aspirations are worked through.

Chaplains are in some countries usually appointed ecumenically [see *Ecumenical Movement*], in other countries with an established church, this type of ministry is reserved for the established church. Chaplains find themselves at the edges of both the church which appoints them and the institution to which they minister – and the effect is of becoming a '*participant observer*' or '*resident alien*' in both. They are neither the creatures of management nor the representatives of trade unions. Yet this '*in between*' existence creates great *freedom* of opportunity for the Chaplain to build relationships, establish trust, and offer varied pastoral care. Some Chaplains also lead *worship* - in *Chapels* or *Prayer* Rooms at airports, hospitals, prisons, universities, or shopping centres.

Sector ministry recognises '*the sacrament of the present moment*' in every encounter with people. Through presence, support and involvement, the Chaplain is a constant reminder of the *love* of Christ and His Church for people in the midst of daily life and work - and therefore a sign of the *Kingdom*.

MB

FURTHER READING: Giles Legood (ed), *Chaplaincy, the Church's Sector Ministries*, Cassell, London, 1999. Michael Banfield, *Introducing the Airport Chaplaincy*, www.workplaceministry.org.uk/herts&beds/newsletter/25024%20Chaplaincy%20l onfl'ttp df, 2003.

Charisma
See *Glossolalia*.

Charismatic Movement
[See also *Charismatics*; *Pentecostalism*]
The charismatic movement, perhaps better called the neo-Pentecostal movement, originated in the USA in 1959-60 as a grassroots *renewal* movement within the historical non-Pentecostal denominations. The movement was and is characterised by its emphasis on and practice of what its adherents believe to be supernatural abilities bestowed upon them by the *Holy Spirit*, notably *speaking in tongues*, interpretation, *prophecy* and the exercise of gifts of *healing*.

The charismatic movement has its predecessor in the Pentecostal movement, founded by Charles Fox Parham (1873-1921) in 1901. While the original Pentecostal movement to a large extent appealed to the disinherited, the charismatic renewal attracted middle-class support. During the late 1950s the *Catholic* researcher Peter D. Hocken identified 'a considerable Pentecostal stirring reaching beyond the Pentecostal churches'. (*NIDPCM*, 2002 p.479) Both the Post-WWII Healing Revival (1946-59) and the two organisations, Camps Farthest Out (CFO) and Full Gospel Business Men Fellowship International (FGBMFI), were pre-charismatic initiatives outside of a strictly Pentecostal setting which introduced many believers to healing *prayer* and glossolalia.

However, it was through Episcopalian *minister*, Dennis Bennett (1917-91) that the emerging charismatic renewal attracted the media's attention. After notifying his parish *members* at St. Mark's Episcopal Church in Van Nuys, California on 3 Apr 1960 of his recent '*baptism* with the Holy Spirit', he was asked to resign as vicar of the church. Inducted to the benefice of St. Luke's Episcopal Church in Seattle, he became instrumental in igniting a charismatic renewal among non-Pentecostal ministers and laymen alike. 'Speaking in tongues is no longer a phenomenon of some odd *sect* across the street', a *Time* journalist announced: 'Now glossolalia seems to be back in US churches..., not only in the uninhibited Pentecostal sects but even among *Episcopalians*, who have been called God's frozen people.' (*Time* 15 Aug 1960, p.55)

Through parish member, Jean Stone, at St. Mark's Church and her *Trinity* journal subscribers were informed about the most recent occurrences within charismatic renewal in the historical churches. Significant non-Episcopalian leaders within the movement included Larry Christenson and Herbert Mjorud (American *Lutheran* Church), Donald Photenhauer and Rodney Lensch (the Lutheran Church – Missouri Synod), Robert Whitaker and J. Rodman Williams (United *Presbyterian* Church) and Howard Ervin (American Baptist Church). In 1967, Catholic *scholars* William Storey and Ralph Keifer became catalysts for a charismatic renewal within the Catholic Church. Spreading from Duquesne University to Notre Dame University and Michigan State University, the Catholic charismatic renewal distinguished itself from its *Protestant* counterpart in its initiating phase appealing exclusively to an academic audience.

A new phase within the history of the charismatic renewal was initiated when *Orthodox* minister Athanasius Emmert in 1972 prayed for *theologian* Eusebius A. Stephanou with the laying on of hands that the latter might receive his personal '*Pentecost*'. One year later the first Orthodox-charismatic conference was arranged in Ann Arbor, Michigan with some 100 participants. Stephanou has continued to proliferate his charismatic message through his monthly *magazine Logos* and via his Orthodox Renewal Center of St. Symeon the New Theologian in Florida. Orthodox-charismatic renewal is also proliferated through the *Theosis* journal, which, in turn, is connected with the Service Committee for Orthodox Charismatic Renewal.

Simultaneously with the numerical increase of charismatic believers within the non-Pentecostal denominations a new tendency developed during the 1970s as both independent churches and networks of churches which phenomenologically were charismatic chose not to affiliate with either the Pentecostal movement or with any non-Pentecostal denomination. Previously it had been customary to distinguish between 'Pentecostals' and 'charismatics' the term used to describe 'Pentecostal renewal' within the non-Pentecostal denominations and churches. During the 1970s and 80s 'Pentecostal' and 'charismatic' became synonymous terms. Both Pentecostalism and the charismatic renewal originated in the US Both movements, nonetheless, are global in nature and are among the fastest growing religious movements in Asia, Africa and Latin America, a process documented in the *New International Dictionary of the Pentecostal and Charismatic Movements* though its statistics are unreliable.

From the 1960s a number of Baptists in Europe became involved in charismatic renewal. One of the first was Douglas McBain, then minister in **Scotland**. In 1963 McBain began to speak in tongues and he became central to charismatic renewal in Baptist circles. Another was David Pawson, minister of Gold Hill Baptist Church, Buckinghamshire, and later of the Millmead Centre, a large Baptist church in Guildford. The Fountain Trust was formed in 1964 as an agency for pan-denominational charismatic renewal and attracted to its conferences Anglicans, Baptists, **Brethren**, Presbyterians, Pentecostals and Roman Catholics. Jim Graham, who succeeded Pawson as minister of Gold Hill, was among a number of Baptist ministers who saw considerable **growth** as a result of charismatic renewal. Other churches, however, split over the issues of speaking in tongues, prophecy and healing. Some new charismatic fellowships emphasised very strong leadership, and this attracted some Baptists.

For a number of Baptists in Europe, what John Wimber from California brought was an intensified form of charismatic renewal in the 1980s. This was true of Ansdell Baptist Church in the north-west of **England**. Nigel Wright, the minister, was deeply influenced. By this time charismatic renewal was having a significant impact on a number of Baptist communities in Europe – notably in **Germany** and **France**. Among some Baptists, however, the charismatic emphases were seen as incompatible with Baptist life. Tensions were exacerbated in the mid-1990s by 'the **Toronto Blessing**', which originated at a Vineyard Christian Fellowship in Toronto, Canada, and crossed to Europe. People began to 'laugh in the Spirit', exhibit physical contortions, and even make animal noises. David Coffey, the General Secretary of the Baptist Union of **Great Britain**, urged deeper biblical, historical and **theological** reflection among Baptists, and above all called for spiritual renewal that led to full-orbed **mission**: 'We know from the past', he wrote, 'that Renewal which goes deep into the life of the church possesses a reforming zeal which is personal, ecclesiastical and social in its dimension.' It was this kind of renewal that many Baptists welcomed.

GL & ET

FURTHER READING: Stanley M. Burgess and Eduard M. van der Maas (eds), *New International Dictionary of the Pentecostal and Charismatic Movements*, Zondervan, Grand Rapids, Mi., 2002.

Charismatics

[See also **Charismatic Movement**]

The usage derives from the NT Greek term *charismata* which describes the gifts of the **Holy Spirit**. It gained currency from the 1950s in order to describe recipients of Pentecostal experiences [see **Pentecost**] within the mainline denominations where for the most part it has been successfully harnessed within their structures. The charismatic movement exercised considerable influence throughout the second half of the 20th century to the point that there are now estimated to be between 500 and 600 million charismatics with continuing **growth** forecasted. Although more recent than the growth of **Pentecostalism** itself, charismatics, sometimes called 'neo-Pentecostals', look back to the recovery of charismatic experiences in the first decade of the 20th century through the **Welsh Revival** in 1904 and the Los Angeles Asuza Street revival in 1906. From these have stemmed the denominations of 'classic Pentecostalism' with their emphasis on **baptism** of the Spirit as a post-**conversion** experience evidenced by **speaking in tongues**. Subsequent movements such as the '**Signs and Wonders**' emphasis and the 'Toronto Blessing', have followed in the wake of this. Baptist responses to the charismatic movement have varied from whole-hearted embrace to outright rejection. This has to some extent been along geographical lines, with Westerners being more open to accept, and those in Eastern Europe more likely to reject charismatic experiences. Often, such responses have reflected previously held positions towards Pentecostalism as well as *theological* concerns, e.g., about the cessation of the charismata after the *apostolic* age.

NGW

Charter Oecumenica

[See also *Ecumenical Movement*]

Charter Oecumenica is an ecumenical agreement between the *Conference of European Churches* and the Council of European Bishops' Conferences of the *Roman Catholic* Church (CCEE) to maintain *koinonia* (fellowship) and to seeks all possible ways of working co-operatively as Christians in Europe in *mission* and in common life. The movement towards such an agreement arose out of the first two European Ecumenical Assemblies (EEA) held in Basel (1989) and Graz (1998). The Charter was signed in Strasbourg in 2001 on behalf of CEC-KEK by Metropolitan Jeremie (Romanian *Orthodox*) President of CEC and by Cardinal Vlk, Archbishop of Prague, then Chair of CCEE. The Charter, which grounds the common *faith* of European Christians in the Nicene-Constantinopolitan *Creed* of 381, declares the urgent need for common witness in Europe, asks for sharing information about plans for *evangelisation* and avoiding any form of pressure to make people convert [see *Conversion*] from one form of Christianity to another. It calls for a humble move from confrontation to cooperation and to ecumenical reflection and *education* to remove prejudices and misunderstandings. It calls for a continuing pattern of European Ecumenical Assemblies (a third such Assembly was held in Sibiu, *Romania* in 1998) and for churches to *pray* for one another. Other sections of the Charter refer to the relationship of the churches to *political* Europe, the respecting of diversity in culture, care for *creation*, opposing *anti-semitism* and intensify-

ing *dialogue* in Europe with *Judaism*. Whilst the Charter has not featured much within Baptist communities, several **unions** in **membership** with CEC-KEK did engage in the process of the creation of the Charter (*Great Britain* and *Sweden* offering significant comments) and Baptists on the whole have found the Charter more acceptable than some other ecumenical agreements because it puts the emphasis on **unity** in our declaration of a common faith (the 381 Creed) and not on 'our common **baptism**', which Baptists interpret as excluding them from ecumenical encounter.

KGJ

Child protection

[See also *Children's Work*]

Baptist *gathering churches* have, from *Spurgeon* onwards, had a concern for the protection of vulnerable children in society. In so doing he was entering an older tradition associated with the *Pietist* movement for the Francke Orphanage in Halle dates back to 1696 whilst the Foundling Hospital in London was founded in 1739 They have understood the words of *Jesus* in the gospels to indicate children being a proper concern of the *church* and their protection from harm and abuse a duty of the disciples of Jesus.

For Spurgeon and many others the first priority was to provide homes – *orphanages* – for children who either lost their parents through *death* or were abandoned by their parents, three years after the Scottish Baptist businessman, William Quarrier, had pioneered similar work in *Scotland*. This approach continues to this day and Baptists in more recent times have established important work amongst orphans and those without adequate home backgrounds in *Bulgaria*, *Romania*, *Ukraine* and many other European countries, adding to the earlier growth of such work in Western Europe.

More recently, it has been recognised that even the church community is not always a safe place for children. Christians have on occasions naively allowed people to work with and abuse children sexually in what should be the safe environs of the Christian community. So, today, many Baptist *unions* and churches have established guidelines to assist *local churches* develop safe environments for children. This has included requiring those who work with children to be vetted as to their suitability and trained in ways to protect children and in not countenancing only one adult to work with a group of children, as was often permitted in the old *Sunday School* movement.

Sometimes these developments have been reinforced by government regulation, even in some cases in response to the media's reporting of the abuse of children which has occurred in some Christian churches and this has prompted a proper desire to make sure child safety is not only believed in, but firmly acted out in European baptistic communities.

ET

Childlessness and Fertility Treatment

Scripture itself bears testimony to the disappointment and frustration that comes to childless couples, and nobody who has not had that experience should seek in any way to downplay such emotions. In times past, the answer would have been that such withholding of children was God's will and should be accepted as such. The question that arises in the 21ˢᵗ century is the extent to which medical science can be invoked to remedy this situation. Is there something irreverent about seeking the help of the medical scientist in aiding birth, when few would question the use of the very best surgical skills or *drug* therapy to eliminate or control a vicious cancer? Different people would draw the line of acceptability at different points. E.g. whilst the *Roman Catholic* Church pronounced against artificially assisted reproduction in 1987 some *Protestants* and *Evangelicals* would accept artificial insemination with the husband's sperm fertilised *in vitro,* but would be unhappy with the use of a donor sperm which has its origin outside the marital union, and would certainly oppose all use of artificial means to create a pregnancy outside of a properly ordered *marriage*. The use of the adverb 'artificially' is of interest, suggesting that all other births are natural, when we know in fact that there is very little that is natural about

the way we live our lives in the modern world which is so very much the construct of a diversity of scientific breakthroughs. A child brought to birth with the aid of the very latest medical techniques is as much a child of God as one which enters the world in a more traditional fashion. It is that new life, however brought to birth, and its nurture that is central to the process. Christian doctrine gives no support to the notion that to have children is a normative human right. Whilst sophisticated societies in the north rightly afford every encouragement to medical scientists to reduce childlessness to the minimum, in the south the problem is of a wholly different order, namely how to sustain those that have been born, often beyond the capacity of the immediate family to render support, so the ethical question [see *Ethics*] becomes one of limiting rather than assisting births.

JHYB

Children, Blessing of

Baptist *gathering* churches offer *baptism* to believers only with such baptisms normally taking place from puberty, onwards, though in the United States there are instances of much younger children being baptised (see the survey done by the Doctrine and Inter-Church Cooperation Commission of the *BWA* in 1998). However, parents and churches often want to mark the birth of a child within the believing community. It is unclear when such practices began; though the theory that its origination belongs to British Baptist, *John Clifford*, is now generally discounted, with evidence of such services being traced back to the 18ᵗʰ century. Certainly, from the mid-1800s onwards a variety of practices have developed whereby a church community and a family give thanks to God for the gift of a child and offer corporate *prayers* that the child might grow up in a setting where, in due time, the child might come to a personal profession of *faith* in *Jesus Christ* and be baptised as a believer.

The title for this short act of *worship*, which generally takes place within the main Sunday *liturgy* of the church, varies from place to place and from generation to generation; thus some speak of a service of

Thanksgiving for the birth of a child whilst commonly such services have been called Dedication services though some prefer to reserve the word dedication for those bringing the child to church and thereby dedicating themselves to the sacred task of parenthood. Like *weddings* and *funerals*, there are no strict Biblical grounds for holding such a service within the context of public worship. What Biblical *authority* has been sought has generally been found in the account of Jesus blessing children (Mt 19:13-15; Mk 10:13-16; Lk 18:15-17). Traditionally there have been three aspects – thanksgiving, dedication of the parents and the church and the blessing of the child. The accent of the liturgy also varies from simple thanksgiving, to dedication of the parents and, now rarely, to the dedication of the child. The church community often makes promises to assist the family, especially in the Christian upbringing of the child and in some cases the name of the child is entered on a special Cradle Roll as a focus of prayer and concern. The ceremony normally involves the child being presented to the church by the parents, brief promises about the upbringing of the child by the parents and congregation and then the pastor, or an appointed church official, blessing the child, normally with the Aaronic blessing.

In some instances *members* of the congregation offer prayers of thanksgiving [see *Prayers in Worship*] and these prayers can be accompanied by the giving of small gifts to the child as symbols of the prayers that have been offered, sometimes a Bible or Testament, or a candle.

Many argue that the practice is in search of a *theology*. For behind this event there are important questions about the status and place of children, both of believers and those who are not regular worshippers but seek such a service for their children from a gathering Baptist community which practises the baptism of believers only. Many congregations, as part of their *missionary* task to the community in which they are set, have had to adapt their liturgy to a form that is both honest and meaningful to those who are not fully committed. In 1966 British Baptists produced a report, *The Child and the Church*, which sought to address these concerns and advocated the re-introduction of

the early church concept of the *catechumenate*, with, possibly, this ceremony marking entry to that. However, the report was not taken up. In the mid-1990s the Theology and Education Division of the EBF did some provisional work on this topic and a draft report was presented to the EBF Council in Hamburg in 1999, but no further work was done. More recently the 1999 Whitley Lecture argued that children suffer marginalisation in Baptist communities and once again, the idea of a catechumenate was promoted.

KGJ

Children's Work

European Baptists have traditionally developed specialised church *ministries*, such as *music* ministries, youth and children's work. Jesus' words 'Let the little children come to me, and do not hinder them, for the *kingdom of God* belongs to such as these' (Mk 10:14) and, to a lesser extent, Moses instruction to Israelites to teach their children about God (Dt 6:6-7) have highlighted a Biblical [see *Bible*] motivation and justification for Baptist work with children. Even if children, who have not yet been baptised by immersion upon the confession of their faith [see *Baptism*], are not full *members* of the *local church*, they are seen as integral part of the church family. The Dedication or *Blessing of children*, in which both parents and church offer *prayers* of thanksgiving for the gift of children, pray for the appropriate gifts to nurture the young child in the *faith* until such time as he/she will seek baptism as a believer, usually in the context of congregational *worship*, is one sign of this conviction. Different activities in Baptist churches involve children: excursions and camps, children's worship services (children's church), *educational* and *sports* activities, and other special programmes for and with children. The goal of Christian children's work is to see and serve a child in a *holistic* way, taking into account emotional, physical, religious, social and intellectual aspects.

The main venue for Baptist children's work in Europe has been the *Sunday School*, a gathering for Bible stories, prayer, and play. Sunday School, usually organised by the local church, is arranged in a way that enables age-appropriate methods and materials to be used. More recently, Baptists have developed children's work activities which reach beyond the local congregational setting, and are addressed towards the wider community: some churches organise children's day care, (especially important for those families where mothers need to work) with mother and toddler clubs, after-school homework clubs, run or support orphanages, or offer help in other areas of work with children. Sometimes Baptists co-operate in areas where the main responsibility lies with the local city government who sometimes provide the funds for local churches to engage in this ministry.

Baptist children's work has made efforts to develop an awareness of the age-related specifics of a child's faith development and of children's *theology*. This has influenced educational and pedagogical methods used in Baptist Sunday Schools. On the other hand, some Baptist *theologians*, such as Haddon Willmer, have made efforts to find fresh ways of theological thinking by 'placing the child in the midst', even if such a movement as Child Theology is not exclusively Baptist.

TP

FURTHER READING: Scottie May, Beth Posterski et al, *Children Matter: Celebrating Their Place in the Church, Family, and Community*, Eerdmans Grand Rapids, Mi. and Cambridge, U.K., 2005. Robert J. Choun and Michael S. Lawson, *The Christian Educator's Handbook on Children's Ministry: Reaching and Teaching the Next Generation*, Baker, Grand Rapids, Mi., 2002. Michael J. Anthony (ed), *Evangelical Dictionary of Christian Education*, Baker Academic, Grand Rapids, Mi., 2001. John H.Y. Briggs, 'The Baptist Contribution to the Sunday School Movement in the Nineteenth Century' in Stephen Orchard and John H.Y. Briggs (ed), *The Sunday School Movement – Studies in the Growth and Decline of Sunday Schools*, Paternoster, Milton Keynes, 2007.

Choirs
See *Church Music*.

Christ Jesus
See *Incarnation*; *Jesus Christ*; *Logos*; *Lord of the Church and the Crown Rights of the Redeemer*.

Christendom
The definition of Christendom is part geographical, designating that part of the world inhabited by Christian peoples, as over against the pagan world beyond, part cultural signifying a prevailing Christian civilisation in which *faith* and culture interacted to such an extent that the distinction between church and civil society [see *Separation of Church and State*] became very indistinct, and part *political* indicating measures of social or legal compulsion to secure this unitary society. By contrast, the witness of the *apostolic* church was not set in such a society but in a pluralistic world of competing confessions and jurisdictions. The great change came with the Emperor Constantine, when *Catholic* Christianity moved from being a persecuted *sect* to being a tolerated religious option to becoming a dominating Church operating as the exclusive moral arm of the Empire, with *membership* of church and *state* coterminous so that it has been argued that *infant baptism* was a *baptism* into citizenship as well as admission to the *church*.

With the rise of *Islam* and the curtailment of Christendom's boundaries in North Africa, there was ever increasing emphasis on the idea of Christendom. Notwithstanding some challenges, both from outside and from within, such a society prevailed until the time of the *Reformation* and the rise of the *nation* state when the universal catholic faith of Europe gave way to national churches, each espousing its own confessional identity [see *Creeds, Covenants and Confessions of Faith*].

In the 1920s and 30s, confronted with the rise of both national socialism and *Marxism*, certain *Anglican* thinkers in *England* campaigned for a restoration of Christendom which found its most notable expression in the poet, T.S. Eliot's *The Idea of a Christian Society* (1939).Baptists in the tradition of the Radical Reformation and the *Free Churches* had little sympathy with such a compact with civic authority.

Since then, changing demographics and a rising secularism [see *Secularisation*] have arguably seen Europe move into a post-Christendom phase. But it is argued that the whole Christendom model must bear some responsibility for this change; for 'the coercion, control and domination that were part of the Christendom model of church and *mission* carried within themselves the seeds of the modern repudiation of Christianity in Europe'

JHYB

Christian Aid

The aid and development arm of over 40 Christian denominations in the British Isles (Great Britain and the Republic of *Ireland*). Founded after WWII as an *ecumenical* agency working with others to assist in the refugee crisis in Europe, the work soon expanded to take on aid and development concerns throughout the two-thirds world, working in about 50 countries. Christian Aid has always had warm support from British Baptists working with the Baptist *unions* in *England*, *Scotland* and *Wales*, who are normally represented on its governing board by a senior staff member of one of the unions. It works co-operatively with the other *Protestant* Relief and Development agencies (APRODEV) in northern Europe and more recently with the British *Catholic* aid agencies. British Baptist minister, Michael H. Taylor, served as Director from 1985-97 and other Baptists have served in senior positions with the agency. It has championed the move from the provision of aid to more long-term investment in development work, enabling two-thirds world communities to help to solve their own problems. It has also challenged the traditional views of a charity by campaigning for *political* change in economic relationships most notably in the debt redemption and fair trade campaigns of recent years.

KGJ

FURTHER READING: www.christianaid.org.uk.

Christian Brethren
See *Brethren*.

Christian Calendar
See *Christian Year*.

Christian Church, The
See *Churches of Christ*.

Christian Communal Living

Christian Communal Living can be defined as an outward and visible manifestation of the transforming initiative of the good news of *Jesus*, as like-minded sisters and brothers, who are walking in the footsteps of Christ on the same journey with their companions, join together to promote and live out the values of the *kingdom* of *Heaven* here in this world. In the word 'companion', 'pan' derives from the Latin word for 'bread', which gives a very particular connotation to the idea of Christian communal living, that is to say it revolves around believers joining together to break bread regularly, in both meals and *sacrament*, gathered around a common table [see *Baptism, Eucharist and Ministry; Communion and Intercommunion; Sacrament, Sign and Symbol.*]. Being a part of such an intentional community also implies working now for God's embassy, while believing and hoping that one day, on Earth, the kingdom will come to all *women* and *men* working for God's justice and galvanised by His *love* for all *creation*. However, living in a Christian community is not an easy task due to the fact that such a lifestyle calls for openness on the part of each and every individual, challenging, examining and changing personal convictions, even though this is often difficult. A person interested in Christian communal living must be led from imperfect human justice to the perfect justice of Christ. Such a person should, no doubt, be ready to face a permanent battle between the head and philosophical logic on one hand, and heart and *faith* on the other, by believing that in the end faith and love will win, regardless of periods when the head and logic control actions. Thus, communal living, centred on Christ, points to connecting Christian convictions with Christian living through fulfilling God's objective in this activity – to be affiliated with a group of reconciled disciples who enjoy *fellowship* with the Holy *Trinity*, with one another, and eventually with all creation. Just how difficult this is to achieve in practice can be traced in Peter Mommsen's moving description of the tensions in the Bruderhof movement in his biography of his grandfather, J. Heinrich Arnold, which in passing refers to *koinonia*, a faith-based co-operative defying the segregation of black and white workers on a peanut farm – 'a seminary in a cotton patch' in Georgia (USA) founded by radical **Southern Baptist**, Clarence Jordan, which soon suffered bombings and boycotts from outraged white segregationists. Another example of Baptist experimentation in this area is provided by Paul Dekar, this time from Australia.

DA

FURTHER READING: Paul R. Dekar, *Community of the Transfiguration: the Journey of a New Monastic Community*, Cascade Books, Eugene, Or., 2008. Peter Mommsen, *Homage to a Broken Man*, Plough Publishing House, Rifton, NY, 2004.

Christian Endeavour

Christian Endeavour, often referred to as 'CE', was founded by Francis E. Clark, a **Congregational Minister**, in the state of Maine in 1881 'to promote earnest Christian life' and to promote training for Christian service. Prioritising '**Christ** and his **Church**', it was a membership-based organisation constituted upon the signing of a pledge (cf Total Abstinence Movements): 'Trusting in the Lord Jesus Christ for strength I promise him that I will strive to do whatsoever he would have me do'. Such a pledge, renewed at the monthly 'Consecration' Meeting, led to very deliberate training programmes. This was achieved by allocating every member to a committee with specific tasks – from supporting **missionary** activity, seeking new members, care of the aged, concern for seamen, to training in the delivery of short addresses to the recording of decisions through minute taking. With many individuals called upon to convene, to record and to report, all were made to develop a sense of self-esteem. Active membership, or animated **laity**, was the movement's key concern. In some senses it may be seen to have consecrated bureaucracy to this end, and thus struggled to maintain its influence in the more informal society of the second half of the 20th century. The movement became international in 1885 and by 1910 had 3.5 million members world-wide with perhaps two-thirds of its membership in North America, but it was widely spread in Baptist Churches in **Britain**, **Germany** and **Scandinavia**, and Baptists afforded the movement many of its most dynamic leaders. Christian Endeavour also played its part in bringing Christian young people across the **protestant** denominations together and was one of the collaborating bodies that supported the Amsterdam Conference of Christian Youth in 1939. It is also credited as one on those **evangelical** bodies which played a significant part in the 'Epiphany of **Women**'. Those assisted in their Christian **discipleship** by CE often developed a very deep attachment to the movement and thus although essentially a youth movement it had to develop a branch for those beyond the age range of junior and senior branches who called themselves 'Comrades of Christian Endeavour'.

JHYB

Christian Initiation

[See also **Baptism and Christian initiation liturgy**; **Sacrament, Sign and Symbol**]

For many years Christians have understood **conversion** to happen at a specific, datable moment in time. But for such a view the records of the conversions in the book of Acts have always been problematic. Which is the normative order of conversion: **repentance**, water-**baptism**, **forgiveness** and reception of the **Spirit** (Ac 2:28, 41); or believing, water-baptism, the **laying on of hands** and reception of the Spirit (Ac 8:12-17); or reception of the Spirit, speaking in tongues and water-baptism (Ac 10:44-48); or believing and water-baptism (Ac 16:31-33); or believing, water-baptism, laying on of hands, reception of the Spirit and **speaking in tongues** (Ac 19:1-6; see also 9:17-18; 22:16)? But when it is recognised that becoming a Christian is a process, a journey, that is conversion-initiation, then such questions lose their relevance, as the **sovereign** activity of the Spirit of God is recognised in the various ways he works in bringing people to new life in **Christ**.

For an increasing number of Baptists, Christian initiation is expressed in the **liturgy** of baptism, acceptance into **membership** of the **local church** and Eucharistic sharing. This pattern can take place in a single **worship** service, or in a morning then evening service on the same Sunday, or over two weeks. However, expressing a pattern of initiation is not possible when baptism has been separated from conversion by a period that can extend from several months to decades, or when believers participate in the **Lord's Supper** before they have been baptised. This is most clearly seen in open membership churches, but is not uncommon in closed membership churches, not least because the majority of Baptists have separated baptism from conversion both in time and liturgy. Whilst Christian initiation in **paedobaptist** churches begins with infant baptism, Baptists have a service for the dedication/presentation/**blessing of children** in which thanks is given to God for the life of the child, prayers are offered for the child, their growth into Christian **faith** and for their parents, and promises are made by parents and the local church to continue to pray for and nurture the child in the Christian faith.

Christian initiation has also contributed towards Baptists' relationship with those from paedobaptist traditions. Various proposals have been offered over the years. There is the position that infant baptism is no baptism at all and that all paedobaptists are unbaptised. There are those who reject infant baptism and believe that membership of a Baptist church should be closed, that is, only those baptised as believers are accepted into membership. Others practice open membership where the question of baptism, as a believer or infant, is not essential for membership and people are sometimes accepted who have never been baptised by any means. Other open membership Baptist churches accept those from non-Baptist churches into membership on profession of faith, but those from within the Baptist tradition are not accepted into membership until they have been baptised. The **World Council of Churches' Baptism, Eucharist and Ministry** sought the recognition of 'common baptism'/equivalent alternatives whereby infant baptism completed in confirmation is seen as equivalent to believers' baptism. However, in recent years Baptist-**Anglican** conversations [see **Bilateral conversations**] have proposed 'common initiation' in which baptism (of believers or infants) is seen as one moment in a larger process of initiation. In all this, whatever position is adopted, respect for the convictions of others is necessary, even, and perhaps especially, when there is disagreement

on baptism.

ARC

Christian Socialism

Christian Socialism was essentially a response to the emergence of working-class and **socialist** movements in the mid 19th century which seemed to indicate the failure of the **church** to penetrate both this newly emerging social grouping seen in such events as the emergence of the Chartist movement, and later the spread of a wholly new ideology in the **political** world. The Chartists were not without their Christian champions, the most famous of whom was Thomas Cooper, one-time atheist who became a New Connexion General Baptist Evangelist [see **England**] in later life. There were also such phenomenon as Chartist Churches but these were few in number: that in Birmingham, with its **minister**, Arthur O'Neill, converted entirely to becoming a Particular Baptist congregation. Both Cooper and O'Neill were imprisoned for their Chartism and that is where their life-long friendship began. The Christian socialists, so-called, were led by F.D. Maurice, whose incarnational **theology** [see **Incarnation**], with its emphasis on the **kingdom** of **Christ**, was their inspiration. Charles Kingsley, the novelist, promoted the movement through fiery tracts, whilst Thomas Hughes, novelist and lawyer, was a powerful advocate and the movement's educationalist. J.M.F. Ludlow, who was responsible for the organisational ideas of the movement, had been in Paris at the time of the 1848 Revolution and was keen both to 'christianise the un-Christian socialists and to socialise the unsocialist Christians' in **England**, no easy task when the established church seemed to be allied to landed **wealth** and other conservative forces [see **Church and State**]. Experiments were made in co-operative production, which largely failed because of over-much idealism. More successful endeavours were made in working-class adult **education** for both **women** and **men**, and the securing of a proper legal framework for working-class organisations through the reform of friendly society legislation. The movement re-emerged in the 1870s and 1880s with the founding of the Anglo-Catholic Guild of St Matthew (1877) and the Christian Social Union (1889). These were essentially *Anglican* movements, though *John Clifford* sought to establish a similar organisation amongst *Free Church* ministers with the founding of 'The Ministers' Union' in 1893 for 'ministers who feel that the Gospel has a Social message today' which the following year became the Christian Socialist League (Brotherhood after 1900) with Clifford serving as Chairman/President. In 1894 he declared 'The country cannot accurately be called Christian so long as the people in their collective arrangements practically deny the fatherhood of God and the brotherhood of men. The members of the Christian Socialist League believe that the principles of Jesus Christ are directly applicable to all social and economic questions, and that such application to the conditions of the times demand the reconstruction of society upon a basis of association and fraternity.' Clifford's own writings were very influential amongst Baptists because he enjoyed a large influence both at home and abroad through his presidency of the *BWA*. He also wrote several tracts for the (socialist) Fabian Society, for membership of which he was proposed by the acerbic playwright, George Bernard Shaw. There were similar Christian socialist movements among *Lutherans* in *Germany* and *Denmark* and *Roman Catholics* in *Hungary* but of a fairly conservative order. The first Swedish Baptists were noted as supporting a universal franchise but their successors were more conservative. Another forceful voice in this area was the German American Baptist, Walter Rauschenbusch who published his *Christianity and the Social Crisis* in 1907 and *Christianizing the Social Order* in 1912. Like Clifford he shared an interest in social affairs with a concern for personal *evangelism*.

JHYB

Christian World Communions

Originally simply designated world confessional groups or bodies, in 1967 the language for international confessional organisations became World Confessional Families, which in 1979 was changed again to Christian World Communions. The *Orthodox* and *Catholic* Families would not immediately see their international compass or *catholicity* as of the same order as other church groups, still arguing some degree of exclusive claims for their own churchmanship. The first pan-*orthodox* conference was held in 1961 in Rhodes to discuss the relationship between the two great orthodox families, the Eastern and the Oriental Orthodox (Armenian, Syrian – both in the Middle East and in India, Coptic, and Ethiopian Orthodox). Otherwise the movement dates back to the late 19th and early 20th century.

The first Lambeth Conference, bringing *bishops* from every province in the world together, occurred in 1867. However, it was not until 1908 that the first of the less frequent *Anglican* Congresses, in which there was lay representation, was held. In 1875 the Alliance of the *Reformed Churches* was established for Presbyterians to which was added in 1949 the International Congregational Council. These two bodies joined together in 1970 to form the World Alliance of Reformed Churches (WARC). The Evangelical Church of the *Czech Brethren*, The Mission Covenant Church in *Sweden* and the *Waldensians* all have *membership* of WARC. The World *Methodist* Conference dates to 1881 but with a more formal structure from 1951. Our own *Baptist World Alliance* was formed in 1905. The *Lutheran* World Federation (Convention, 1923) which was formed in 1947, the best endowed of all the world families, has a large and well-funded organisation with headquarters at the Ecumenical Centre in Geneva. Its definition of 'Lutheran' – as spelt out in the Augsburg Confession and *Luther*'s Small Catechism – is tight, and, therefore, generally excludes those churches which include elements of the United and the Reformed traditions. None of these bodies is all embracing; there are significant numbers of congregations/*unions*, normally of a *conservative* persuasion, that do not belong to the world body. Of the world bodies LWF and WARC have the closest relationship with the *WCC*.

The Society of Friends (*Quakers*) (1920), *Mennonites* (1925), Disciples (1930), *Pentecostals* (1947) have all developed international organisations. Some churches in the two-thirds world have not always been happy with the existence of CWCs and regard them as unnecessarily perpetuating confessionalism. Others, by contrast would argue that through especially the promotion of *bilateral conversations* between confessions they serve the interests of the *ecumenical movement*. Moreover since 1957 the secretaries of the Christian World Communions have met annually together with representatives of the *Salvation Army*, the Seventh Day Adventists, and the Reformed Ecumenical Council (Synod). Since 1968 the *Vatican* Secretariat for Promoting Christian *Unity* has been represented at their meetings.

JHYB

Christian Year, The

The extent to which Baptist Christians follow the so-called Christian Year varies from country to country in Europe. At an extreme, there are those who mirror the attitude prevalent during the time of the English Commonwealth in the 1600s that every day is lived as a day of the Lord and no special note should be taken of any one day as having a significance for the Christian (Oliver Cromwell and the Parliament banned even the celebration of the *Incarnation*). Others objected to the celebration of the Christian Year as something developed by the Roman Church and expanded with its observation of specifically *Catholic* festivals and *saints* days. However, this is generally a minority view and most Baptist communities follow the main pattern of the Christian year as it has developed over the centuries. This varies depending on whether they are situated in an *Orthodox* setting in the East, in which case the Orthodox calendar is used, or in central and western areas where the Latin calendar is used.

This restricted entry does not permit a rehearsal of Christian understanding of time, but most Baptist communities in Europe would operate with an annual cycle of the year as a way of recalling God's *creation*, the anticipation of the coming of a Messiah, the incarnation, the life, death and *Resurrection* of *Jesus*, his *ascension* and the giving of the *Holy Spirit* to his followers. Such a year might be deemed to start at the end of the recreation or vacation season with the first Sunday in Sep. This is the point when we note the recommencement of many Church-centred activities with a focus on the created order, perhaps the celebration of the gift of creation itself. In some communities there is now at this time an emphasis on our responsibility as stewards to safeguard the creation and in certain countries the notion of *Eco-congregations* has begun to develop. In Eastern Europe, to a greater extent than in urbanised Western Europe especially the autumn months will see churches celebrating *Harvest* Thanksgiving with great enthusiasm and most congregations also prepare for the *Christmas* season with a special focus on the four Sundays before Christmas and the anticipation of the incarnation in the development of *Advent* services. The eastern churches celebrate the incarnation at *Epiphany* or the Festival of the Kings. Again, the marking of the change of the calendar, though not strictly part of an annual Christian cycle, is an occasion for late night, historically called 'watch-night', services in many churches. In some communities this is an occasion for the renewal of *church membership* and reciting of a Church *Covenant,* though there is no special covenant *liturgy* as in *Methodism*. Around this time of year a number of churches celebrate the Moravian Christingle service.

An increasing number of churches mark the beginning of *Lent* with events around 'Fat Tuesday' (*Poland*) or 'Pancake Tuesday' and *Ash Wednesday* (*UK*). In Latin countries Baptists have reacted strongly against the excesses of Mardi Gras and everywhere the general Lenten theme has increased spiritual discipline, participating in extra study groups [see *Bible study meetings*] or taking on some additional devotional reading.

Palm Sunday, Holy Week, Institution of the *Eucharist* or *Maundy Thursday*, (sometimes with *Passover* liturgies and *foot washing*), and *Good Friday* are all widely observed and some Baptists have special periods of preparation for Easter services.

Easter Day is widely marked, often with services of Believers' *Baptism* and a minority of churches also practice holding a service of *prayers* and readings around the *baptistry* and the renewal of baptismal vows on Holy Saturday or *Easter Eve*.

In certain communities Ascension Day is marked often with special preaching services and most congregations observe *Pentecost* as a special season.

It is not common for Baptists to mark days of commemoration for noted Christians of the past, though some churches do observe *Reformation* Sunday, Martin Luther King day and, of course *Baptist World Alliance* day.

Many find the celebration of the Christian Year a useful way of ensuring that there is annual reflection on some of the most important aspects of the *faith*. This is done in the reading of *scripture*, in *hymnody* and within a disciplined teaching *ministry*.

KGJ

Christmas

This period of two days – Christmas Eve and Christmas Day, is now almost universally observed by Baptists, with those in Western Europe doing so on the 24 and 25 Dec and most of those in Eastern Europe following the *Orthodox* liturgical calendar and doing so on 6 and 7 Jan. The adoption of the pagan winter festivals as the time to commemorate the birth of *Christ* no doubt had occurred amongst Christians in Rome by 354AD. In recent centuries the accent on celebration within the secular world has led to a complex interaction of myth and fable alongside the desire by Christians to recall the birth narratives of Jesus, though few Baptists today would resist the celebration of Christmas as something too 'Catholic', though this was known in earlier centuries.

On Christmas Eve many churches will hold special celebrations, including the *Eucharist*, often at midnight. This will be the main celebration of Christmas in Central Europe and the *Baltic* nations, whilst in some other parts of Europe the principal celebration will be on Christmas Day. Christmas Day services frequently have an accent on the *children*, who often come with gifts they have received to show to the congregation.

Christmas cribs will be found in the entrance to many *chapels* and worship rooms and *worship* can often include a nativity play or other seasonal drama. Most countries have special Christmas songs, or carols, which are sung in worship during this season and on Christmas Eve the great white candle in the *Advent* ring is lit. This represents the *incarnation*.

Congregation *choirs* or special groups of young people will often visit *elderly* or housebound *members* of the congregation to sing Christmas carols in their homes and a significant minority of churches will organise special Christmas meals open to the *homeless* or those with no family to celebrate the Christmas season with. Sometimes carols are sung in the streets either as an act of *witness* or to raise funds for a good cause.

The Germanic practice, dating from perhaps 1605, of having a decorated evergreen tree in the worship room is found in many places and elaborate stories are recounted to justify something which may actually have its roots in pagan yule celebrations. A common past practice of having the tree decorated with apples and confectionery relating to Adam and Eve has given way to coloured decorations, angels and lights supposedly signifying the *Christbaum* – the Christ Child's tree of life.

Baptists would tend to follow national practice with regard to special foods eaten on this celebration – e.g. Carp in the *Czech Republic*, Goose or Turkey, together with Christmas Pudding, Mince Pies and special Christmas cake, in the *UK*, pork and sausages in *Germany* and the Baltic countries.

In Western Europe in countries influenced by the Unitas Fraterum (*Moravians*) the practice of having a Christmas star or lighting special candles during Advent and the Christmas season is also common. A growing practice, which seems to have its roots in the USA, is for decorations in worship rooms to include bright red poinsettia plants.

In celebration of God's gift of his Son to sinful *men* and *women*, and also recognising the fact that the Magi brought gifts to Jesus, Christian people often give gifts to one another at Christmas; more recently from this has developed the habit of making gifts (e.g. goat, cattle, a water supply money for a clinic or towards the salary of a teacher) for the *poor* of the world either instead of, or in addition to, gifts to one another. Christmas is generally also the time for sending cards and exchanging family news with those one has not seen for a long time.

KGJ

Christology

[See also *Incarnation*; *Jesus Christ*; *Logos*; *Lord of the Church and the Crown Rights of the Redeemer*]

Issues of Christology are central to a Trinitarian [see *Trinity*] *faith*. It is just as important to be clear about whom Jesus is, as it is warmly to affirm the work of the *Holy Spirit*. These are, however, doctrines to be experienced in relationship and in the living out of the faith not merely to be assigned to some credal statement [see *Credalism*; *Creeds, Covenants and Confessions of Faith*]. Questions over the relationship of divinity to humanity within the person of Jesus Christ proved a focal issue of debate from the 3rd-5th centuries AD, when a dominant philosophy of Platonic *dualism* forced a focus on either the divinity of Jesus or his humanity, but found these hard to hold together. An attempt to resolve this led to the Christological formations of the Council of Chalcedon in 451AD. This provided the basis for *Christendom*'s understanding of Christology, the doctrine of the person of Christ, affirming both his full divinity and his full humanity in the classic language of 'One person in Two Natures'.

John Smyth puts it like this in his Short Confession of Faith of 1610: 'That Jesus Christ is true God and true man; viz., the Son of God, taking to himself, in addition the true and pure nature of a man, out of a true rational soul, and existing in a true human body.' Subsequent statements of Baptist belief have also adopted a high Christology, thus the Confession of Faith of the Swedish Baptists of 1861, affirms 'that our Lord Jesus Christ in his one person united true Godhead and true manhood' BUGBI's Declaratory Statement of 1888 combines the person and work of Christ in declaring belief in 'the Deity, the Incarnation, the *Resurrection* of the Lord Jesus Christ, and His Sacrificial and Mediatorial Work.' In the 20th century the *Evangelical* Association of French Baptists in 1924 adopted a rather older statement of faith which again is quite unambiguous in what it believes about Jesus, thus it avows: 'We believe that Jesus, the Word made flesh, the only mediator between God and men, is from all eternity the unique Son of God. We believe that Jesus, conceived by the power of the Holy Spirit and born of a virgin, was just

as truly man as he was truly God...'

Among *Anabaptists*, Chalcedonian Christology was less important than the *call* to imitation of, and conformity to, Christ. The call to conformity to Christ is known as Christomorphism. Here, the focus of interest lies in what the incarnate Christ was able to achieve whilst here on earth, rather than in static, descriptive categories. In recent years, resurgent interest in radical *discipleship* has led to increased dissatisfaction with the static categories of Chalcedonian Christology and has brought fresh concern as to how God's intention and Jesus' fulfilment of this in his *ministry* can be replicated in our humanity, that is how the sacrificial love of Jesus can be reformed in the lives of those who follow him.

In certain parts of the Baptist/Anabaptist constituency Christology has from time to time presented problems. E.g. early Polish (and some other Eastern European) Anabaptists adopted Socinian views of the Godhead, whilst Melchior Hoffman persuaded the Dutch Mennonites that Jesus' body only passed through the body of the virgin Mary as 'water passes through a pipe'. This view, which discounted Jesus' true humanity, was a view subsequently adopted by some (but not all) General Baptists in the south east of *England*. However, within a few years they had gone to the opposite extreme of denying his true divinity. Nor were Particular Baptists altogether immune to these tendencies, though Andrew Fuller [see *Fullerism*], in presenting a renewed Evangelical *Calvinism*, wrote strenuously against them. And even hyper-Calvinist Strict Baptists could dispute the details of the eternal generation of the Son, robustly upheld by the *Gospel Standard* but called both a 'figment' and 'a piece of twaddle' by the other Strict Baptist periodical, the *Earthen Vessel*.

The basic difficulty arose from attempting to read *scripture* without the benefit of the doctrinal defences hammered out by the Patristic Church in its battle with early *heresy*. Sometimes the line between *orthodoxy* and heterodoxy was very finely drawn. This history may well explain why Alexander McLaren asked the inaugural *BWA* Congress in 1905 to repeat the *Apostles'* Creed, as he said to ensure that there was no doubt as to the denomination's orthodoxy.

Recent *ecumenical dialogue* has added interest with its concern to understand both the nature of Christ's humanity, and the whole area of theological *anthropology*. Where Augustine of Hippo's understanding of Original *Sin* permeated Western *Catholic* thought, limiting expectation as to our potential similitude to Christ, Orthodoxy's ownership of Irenaeus of Lyon's more optimistic anthropology has led to a reappraisal of how humanity is recapitulated and reconciled to God through the eternal Word's assumption of human flesh, and His bodily resurrection.

JGMP & ET

Church, The

In *scripture* the Church is variously described as the Body of Christ, the New Israel, Christ's little flock, the People of God, and the Bride of Christ, all of which images shed light on its purpose and function. In *ecumenical* doctrine the Church is defined by its 'notes' from the Niceano-constantinopolitan creed, and by its 'marks' from *Reformation* discussions. The Church is 'one, holy, *catholic* and *apostolic*', and known by the pure *preaching* of the Word and the right administration of the *sacraments*. Baptists would not want to deny either of these claims (although their definition of the *notae ecclesiae* might be unusual), and would want to recover the third Reformation mark, the faithful application of *church discipline*. However, Baptist thinking about the Church has tended to start from the existence and faithfulness of the local congregation rather than any account of the universal church. *John Smyth* asked 'Is not the visible church of the NT with all the ordinances thereof the chief and principal part of the Gospel?' and defined that 'visible church' as 'two, three, or more *Saints* joined together by *covenant* with God and themselves, freely to use all the holy things of God, according to the word, for their mutual edification, and God's glory...'

The Reformation heritage, of a focus on preached scripture and sacrament is clear enough in this, as is the *holiness* of the church, maintained by church discipline (which is a more serious Baptist distinctive

in some parts of Europe, particularly the former Soviet states, than others). It may be more difficult to see how such local congregations can be regarded as 'one, catholic and apostolic'. *Unity* for Baptists is understood as a *theological* reality (we are all one in *Christ*) with structural implications. These include the formation of *associations*, *unions*, *Bunden*, and other translocal Baptist bodies, but also include less formal fraternal arrangements between churches, and an impetus to cross-denominational relationships where another church body can be recognised (so Baptists have often been at the forefront of founding alliances of *Evangelical* churches in parts of Europe). *Catholicity* would be understood similarly, although it is perhaps the attribute of the church taken least seriously by Baptists.

The church is 'apostolic', for Baptists, in part because it maintains and teaches the apostolic doctrine. Our distinctive contribution to doctrines of apostolicity, however, has been the recognition and stress that continuing the apostolic *mission*, of preaching the gospel in all nations, is a part of what it means for the church to be properly apostolic. *J.G. Oncken*'s great rallying cry, 'Every Baptist a missionary!' is echoed in different ways throughout Baptist life.

A final feature of Baptist *ecclesiology*, increasingly important in Europe, is a commitment to *religious liberty* for all. The *state* has no power under God to command, compel or forbid religious practice, and states which seek to claim such power must be opposed as transgressing beyond their realm of competence.

SH

Church: Universal, Triumphant, Invisible

Manifest in diverse local congregations which themselves display all the characteristics of God's new Israel, and therefore themselves called 'church', this same church has a larger reality as *universal* in time and space. Both these usages are employed by Baptists who do *not*, unlike other denominations, use the language of church to describe national *unions*. The *Church* as the Body of Christ must be one, confessing one *faith*, practicing one *baptism*, obedient to one Lord : divided it is unable to witness to God's reconciling *love*, divided it fails to be itself. To call the church *universal* is to underline that it cannot exclude from its *membership* anybody who genuinely confesses *Christ* as Lord. From the earliest years of the denomination's existence, its leaders were profoundly aware of the need to defend its distinctives, but at the same time of the dangers of separating from other Christians to such an extent that they could be correctly called *sectarian*, or even more disturbingly discovering themselves unchurching the rest of *Christendom*. 'Catholicity' in space is related to a catholicity across time, the church of today existing in vital *fellowship* with the church of the *apostles* and the church fathers as well as the church yet-to-be. There is also the distinction often made between the church *militant* that is the church at work in the world today, and the church *triumphant*, literally the church victorious, that is to say the *heavenly* church that has come through all the trials and tribulations of life in this world. The other distinction often made is that between the 'visible' and 'invisible' church. The 'visible' church is the church as seen by human beings, with all its ambiguity of faith and failure, service and *sin*, commitment and corruption, wheat and tares growing together. The 'invisible' church is the church as God sees it, still made up of fallible sinners, but those who have been redeemed by Christ [see *Redemption*], those whose names appear in the Lamb's book of life (Rev 21:27), those whom God has chosen. On the one hand, this means that membership of a *local church* does not of itself guarantee *salvation*, but on the other it is hard to see how a claim to be a member of the invisible church can be maintained which totally ignores the life of the visible church locally gathered.

JHYB

Church and State

See *National Church*; *Separation of Church and State*; *State, Baptist approaches to the*.

Church Building (Sanctuary)

[See also *Architecture*; *Chapels*; *Church Decoration*]

The interiors of the meeting houses of the emerging Baptists were very simple in the beginning, with their emphasis on a central *pulpit* surrounded by the big pew in front of the congregation, normally in the middle of the longest wall. The location was determined by the importance attributed to the *Bible* and the *sermon*. Accompanied by *hymns*, scripture readings and *prayers* the sermon was the most important part in the morning *worship*. For acoustic reasons the pulpit dominated the church's interior – placed on a higher level than the congregation. Respect for the *preacher* enhanced his elevated state. In front of the pulpit surrounded by the big pew was the *communion* table often set with a copy of the open scriptures, and it was around this open word that the *theologically* literate congregation met to seek the mind of *Christ* both in worship and in *church meeting*.

Under the influence of the *evangelical* revival the shape of the sanctuary altered with the pulpit moving to the middle of the shortest wall and now elevated 'six foot above contradiction'. The new imperative was on giving opportunity to as many as possible to hear the preached word and so the seating at ground level was supplemented by the building of galleries. Since the preaching now would be looking for conviction and a *faith* response there would also be a focus in front of the communion table for penitent sinner [see *Sin*] to make response to the preached word

Early Baptists were not happy about using the word 'church' for a place of worship. For the bricks and mortar the correct language was 'meeting house' or later 'chapel' or later still 'church centre'. Thus there were notice boards which proudly indicated 'The Meeting House of x Baptist Church'. Church language was descriptive of *people* not *plant*. Later generations have been less scrupulous and for more than 100 years the word church has been used for buildings without any great difficulty.

Baptist Churches today have at least three main objects in the sanctuary: the Big pew and/or pulpit, the Lord's Table and the *Baptistry*. These three religious objects remind the worshipper of belief, baptism and church. The baptistry would originally have been outside the church, perhaps in a local river. Later it was under the floor in the sanctuary and more recently 'an open baptistry' presented a symbol of the church's specific Baptist faith. The Lord's Table is normally freestanding with the vessels used for the Lord's Supper placed on it. In different countries there are different practices. Sometimes flowers may be placed on the table, as well as the Bible, the offering plate (after the financial gifts have been received) and sometimes candles but without any suggestion of special sanctity as signified in more *Catholic* styles of worship.

Decorations are often modest or minimal partly for economic reasons, partly from a suspicion of lavish external decorations which in the *puritan* worship tradition are replaced by the morally well furnished lives of the believers. Nevertheless some churches are decorated with rich stained glass and other paintings depicting Biblical scenes. More recently, churches have decorated their interiors with banners depicting scriptural themes. Organs have been placed in a variety of places – behind the pulpit, or to one side of pulpit and table or sometimes in a rear gallery. With *music* groups increasingly popular, a number of churches have removed their organs. In like fashion high pulpits are sometimes thought too remote and are accordingly abandoned and sometimes removed. The third item of historic furnishing under contemporary threat is the pews. Arguably uncomfortable they do not allow for experimentation in worship or the use of the sanctuary for other purposes in service of the community during the week

Older churches often had biblical verses or specially constructed words expressing the *mission* of the *local church* on the wall(s).

The most used symbol is the Christian *Cross* in Latin form, though an older generation thought even an empty cross too Catholic. We may also find symbols of God (e.g. depictions of the *Holy Spirit* or the *Trinity* in various parts of the sanctuary.

JJS & ET

Church Centres
See *Chapels*.

Church Council
See *Synod/Church Council*.

Church Decoration
[See also *Church Building (Sanctuary)*]
Baptist church interiors are generally not highly decorated though some have impressive facades, and interiors enhanced by well designed stained glass windows depicting Biblical images and stories. The chief decorative features are the focal points of Baptist *worship*: the *pulpit*, the *communion* table with chairs for the presiding *minister/pastor* and *deacons*, (for this is a table set for a meal not an altar on which to sacrifice), and the *baptistry*, though this is often concealed below the floor. Historically very often the organ has been visually dominant. Floral displays are common, with more elaborate displays on occasions such as *Christmas*, *Easter* and *Harvest*. At Harvest there will be major displays of fruit and vegetable produce in most parts of Europe, though this custom has all but died out in the isles. Older decorative features were confined to the inscribing of biblical texts, relevant to worship and the church's basic affirmations, on the church's walls. An open *Bible* and the vessels used for communion are often a focus of attention on the communion table. Certain *faith* symbols such as a descending dove, a *cross* accompanied by the letters IHS [standing for the Latin for 'In this sign'], PX [Greek letters standing for 'Christ the King'] A and Ω, [The Beginning and the End], communion cups (in the Czech lands) appear on pulpit falls and other similar places. More recently a variety of banners have been deployed in church, sometimes changing with the different seasons of the *Christian Year*. Sometimes displays of work done by *Sunday School* members are exhibited. Newer Churches often display some form of cross both internally and externally but not a crucifix since belief in a risen *Christ* would seem to indicate that the cross is now empty. Baptists differ as to the appropriateness of burning candles in church. In *Scandinavia* this may be taken to signify the presence of the *Holy Spirit* but in countries where the dominant culture is *Roman Catholic* they are often looked upon with suspicion. How-

ever, during Advent candles may be lit throughout European Baptist churches as they prepare to celebrate the coming of Christ. What is never present, unlike Baptist churches in the USA, is the national flag as there is a very strong refutation of *nationalism* in most European Baptist communities.

JHYB

Church Discipline

In Baptist traditional thought, church discipline has been seen as necessary to keep the church pure or to make the visible church as much like the invisible church as possible in any given locality, for only a church which is serious about *holiness* can represent *Christ* in the world. It is part of the nurture which encourages all believers to grow in the Christian life. Thus its ultimate goal is the development of a Christ-like community.

The concept of church discipline has been drawn from several Biblical texts (e.g. Mt 18:15-18; Lk 17:3; Jn 20:22-23; Ro 16:17; 1Co 5; 2Co 2:5-9; Gal 6:1; 2Th 3:6, 14; 2Ti 3:2-5; Tit 3:10; etc.). The text from Mt is often viewed as the key text that informs and shapes the practice of 'conflict resolution' or 'caring confrontation'. It suggests the following pattern of action:

- Every *member* of the community has the right and responsibility to confront the offender, thus church discipline is not a prerogative confined to church leaders.
- The practice of church discipline is not limited to personal offences – any *sin* should not be overlooked. Thereby Christians should not grade sins into more or less serious, since there are no 'trivial' offences, but at the same time there is nothing unforgivable [see *Forgiveness*].
- The process should begin at a very personal level, as when two church members meet to seek to iron out a difference that has arisen between them. If the issue is not resolved it may become necessary to appoint mediators who must have the confidence of both sides. In the unlikely event of this not resolving the issue resort could be made by laying the matter before the whole community of believers; certainly a

gathering of all the members would be the highest *authority* in determining the issue.

- Finally, if the offender does not listen to the community, according to the text he or she should be treated as 'a pagan or a tax collector'. Yet the question of how 'pagans and tax collectors' should be treated can yield two possible answers: follow the Pharisaic pattern of not associating with them, or Jesus' way – showering those concerned with *love* and care.

Although discipline should have a positive focus, the term 'church discipline' often evokes negative reactions, suggesting oppression, punishment and exclusion, and thus perceived as unloving.

The afore mentioned biblical texts suggest different ways of dealing with conflict, failure and offence within the community, making clear a preference for the way to *reconciliation* and *restoration* of the erring member, although the exclusion or separation of the sinner from the community must remain as a final sanction lest one individual spoil the *witness* of the whole church. Because such action always takes place in a particular cultural or historical context, the appearance of rather different ways of proceeding has been and is present in Baptist communities: ranging from almost total absence of any church discipline when *pastors* and lay-members [see *Laity*] of congregations find it difficult or almost inappropriate to interfere with the lives of their fellow Christians, to churches which seem over-involved in every area of the life of an individual Christian, directing or controlling their every activity in what is sometimes called 'heavy shepherding', the *pastoral* team deploying the very real threat of banning those who do not co-operate from participation in the *Eucharist*, or even excommunication from the community.

Very often the practice of 'discipling' (the word differs so little from 'disciplining' – both derive from the Latin root, *discere* –to learn), that is helping people to be disciples [see *Discipleship*], is turned into a practice of 'keeping the church pure from sin' by expelling sinners from the midst of the 'holy ones'. Since the 19th century such an attitude has been more evident among the Baptist churches of Eastern Europe, where church discipline is more often exercised and is mainly concerned with judging, condemning and penalising sin, expecting that the punishment would lead the sinner to repentance. Excommunication from the community is the most severe form of punishment. Based on Mathew's words (18:18) 'whatever you bind on earth will be bound in *heaven*', it is sometimes expected that excommunication from the church ultimately means expulsion of the believer from God's 'book of life', unless the sinner repents and is forgiven by the community. Ironically the most common cause of discipline is repeated absence from *worship* and communion, which is a form of self-excommunication prior to any intervention by the church. Often most attention is given to sexual trespasses including premarital sex, adultery and *divorce* as well as certain 'cultural sins' (e.g. the consumption of *alcohol*, the use of *tobacco*, cosmetics or wearing certain types of clothes). Churches in Western Europe in exercising discipline would omit some of the cultural sins just enumerated but would add business irregularities such as bankruptcy. When church discipline requires punishment or the purification of the church, it can open the door to abuse, church leaders becoming authoritarian tyrants and churches turning into narrow-minded and closed communities where any actions/thinking that does not correspond with the position of those in leadership positions is prohibited. This explains how initially positively-focused practices can gain negative connotations: in some periods of the history of the Church in various areas of European church discipline has been associated with repression, punishment and witch-hunting.

Yet church discipline is not essentially about the punishment of sins, large or small, however defined by the *local church*. It is about the whole community practicing brotherly and sisterly love, engaging in a *ministry* of mutual encouragement so that all may experience spiritual growth in Christ. This highlights the importance of the existence of an intentional community of believers bound by *covenantal* relationships as a necessary condition for the ability of both the church and individual Christians to

practice church discipline. This community has to have relationships that are deep enough to allow its members to be seriously involved in the lives of one another, without such action being considered intrusive. At the same time there has to be space for individual *freedom*. People need to be able to choose whether they want to belong to the community or not – participation has to be their choice, which is the best defence against the community becoming an oppressive and controlling agent.

TVC

FURTHER READING: John Howard Yoder, *Body Politics*, Discipleship Resources, Nashville, Tn., 1992.

Church Government
See *Assembly, General – as governing body of Union*; *Church Meeting*; *Consensus*; *Ecclesiology (Church Polity)*; *Unions/Conventions*.

Church Growth – theory and practice
Church Growth is sometimes labelled either 'autogenous' or 'allogenous', that is to say it either occurs within the families of existing *church members* by a process sometimes called biological church growth, or, by contrast through allogenous growth outside church families through *conversion* growth. Biological growth then concerns the ability of the church to win and retain all those born into Christian families, conversion growth its ability to attract those with no church connexions to *faith* in *Christ*. Another distinction sometimes made is between endogenous factors, basically attempts by Christian people by their own policy decisions, programmes and commitment to extend the work of the church, and those forces deemed exogenous, that is contextual forces, like war and *peace*, economic prosperity or depression, un/sympathetic cultures, etc., which either aid or impede church growth. Sometimes it has been argued that exogenous factors have made recruitment to faith all but impossible, though contrary to this it has also been argued that persecution purifies the church and over the

long term prepares for growth. Others have argued that the church needs to be constantly seeking to create a wide periphery of those with indirect church connexions as it is this pool which contains those most likely to respond to **mission** activity, whilst its absence is perceived to lead relentlessly to decline.

Donald McGavran (1897-1990) established Church Growth as a **missiological** discipline, developed its foundational principles, and instituted it as a movement. After 30 years' mission experience in India (1923-53), plus research in seven countries, he concluded that the essential task of mission was the, 'discipling [see **Discipleship**] of the peoples of the earth' and wrote *Bridges of God* (1955), the Movement's foundational text. In 1961 he founded the Institute of Church Growth, then became founding Dean of the Fuller School of World Mission in 1965.

McGavran identified three core principles for Church Growth theory and practice. First, effective **evangelism** meant proclaiming the Gospel with the goal of reconciling **women** and **men** to God and initiating them into the disciple-making **Church** of Jesus Christ. Secondly, existing churches and societal networks both hinder and assist effective mission. Empirical research, adopting analytical tools from social and behavioural science, was used to identify factors promoting Gospel receptivity and the rapid growth of the church. Thirdly, strategies and targets were needed to initiate a mass movement of conversions and the multiplication of churches [see **Church Planting**]. This was most likely to occur within a people group sharing common cultural, linguistic, religious, and other characteristics.

Understanding Church Growth (1970) is McGavran's *magnum opus* and provided the research methodology for over 1,000 doctoral students, including Rick Warren, Baptist pastor and author of *The Purpose-driven Church*. Whilst McGavran prioritised the needs of **overseas mission**, the task of applying Church Growth theory to North America was taken up by his colleague, Peter Wagner.

Within Europe, William Wagner applied church growth theory to church decline and Gospel receptivity. As the former FMB Consultant for Evangelism and Church Growth, he wrote two books of importance for Euro-

pean Baptists; *New Move Forward in Europe: German-speaking Baptists in Europe* (1978), and *Eight Growing Baptist Churches in Western Europe* (1989). In the latter he outlined 10 principles characteristic of growing Baptist Churches.

Paul Beasley-Murray, in *Turning the Tide* (1981), concluded that Peter Wagner's 'Seven Vital Signs' had applicability for British Baptist Churches, yet rejected the suggestion that church growth principles implied a mechanistic paradigm. In practice it has proven difficult for church growth exponents to dispel this suspicion and Church Development models popular in Europe now tend to emphasise church health rather than church growth.

DJ

FURTHER READING: Paul Beasley-Murray, *Turning the Tide*, Bible Society, London, 1981. Donald McGavran, *Bridges of God*, Friendship, New York, 1955. Donald McGavran, *Understanding Church Growth*, Eerdmans, Grand Rapids, Mi., 1970. C. Peter Wagner, *Your Church can grow*, Regal Books, Ventura, Ca., 1976. William Wagner, *New Move Forward in Europe: German-speaking Baptists in Europe*, William Carey Library, South Pasadena, Ca., 1978. William Wagner, *Eight Growing Baptist Churches in Western Europe*, Brentwood, Columbus, Ga., 1989. Rick Warren, *The Purpose-driven Church*, Zondervan, Grand Rapids, Mi., 1995.

Church Historians, European Baptists in the 20th and 21st centuries

Baptist and baptistic communities in Europe have produced a significant number of historians in the last 100 years. The British Baptist Historical Society was founded in 1908 and marked a moment when, serious **scholars** engaged in historical reflection, began to cooperate together.

The founding of the Institute of Baptist and **Anabaptist** Studies at **IBTS** in **Rüschlikon** in 1984 by Dr. H.W.W. Pipkin marked another seminal moment in the development of the pursuit of Baptist and baptistic historical studies across Europe. His own work on **Hubmaier** and on the Anabaptist movement more generally are worthy of note. A steady flow of Baptist historians now come from the specialist programmes of IBTS ensuring that there will be a continuing stream of recording and analysis of Baptist life in Europe and the Middle East.

Amongst those from European Baptist communities who have attained international recognition we might count the following key people as having made important contributions to the exploration of baptistic history in Europe.

The founding father of European Baptist historians was W.T. Whitley (1861-1947), whose *History of British Baptists* (1923/32), regional history of Baptists in the North West of *England*, and role in founding the Baptist Historical Society and editing its journal for more than 20 years is unsurpassed. Not only was he energetic in research but he provided a series of tools to enable others to undertake research, notably his edition of *The Minutes of the General Baptists, 1654-1811* (1909-10), his edition of *The Works of John Smyth* (2 vols., 1915) and his two volumes of *Baptist Bibliography* (1916/22). His ministries in England, then in Australia (where a Baptist College is named after him) and the lectures named after him to promote scholarship in succeeding generations have created an atmosphere conducive to the promotion of historical study amongst European Baptists. Almost as significant is Ernest A. Payne (1902-80), who engaged in promoting interest in the connection of ideas between the Anabaptists and the Baptists, making significant links with *Mennonite* historians and, by his writing, laying foundations for later exploration of the notion of baptistic roots amongst European Baptist scholars. Payne's biographer, W.M.S. West was also no mean historian. B.R. White produced a seminal, if not now wholly accepted, work on early English Baptist beginnings, challenging the connection of ideas made by Payne on the influence of the Anabaptists on English Baptist origins. Raymond Brown, D.B. Murray, A.R. Cross and Brian Talbot have all written on aspects of British Baptist history.

Günter Balders, historian at the *Elstal* Seminary in *Germany*, is noted for his masterly life of *Oncken* and his work in collecting hymnody used by Baptists across Europe. From *Scandinavia*, the Danes, Johanees Norgaard and Bent Hylleborg may be mentioned, as also the Swedes, Prof. Gunnar

Westin and David Lagergren, who also served as General Secretary of the Swedish *Union*, whose *Mission and State in the Congo* (1970) makes a critical contribution to *mission* history. Peder Edberg, for many years on the staff of the Norwegian seminary, has written more generally on Baptists in Scandinavia and for the countries of the former *USSR* Sergei V. Sannikov, responsible for *theological education* in the *Ukraine*, has engaged in a monumental recording of church history for the Slavic peoples. In the *Netherlands*, Olof de Vries holds a Professorship in History at the University of Utrecht.

J.H.Y. Briggs and Ian M. Randall have also been conspicuous producers of books and articles about different groups of Baptists and *evangelicals* across Europe. The place of the *missionary* enterprise, especially of the British *BMS* has been analysed in a masterly way by Brian Stanley. Sebastian Fath has reflected on the development of Baptist life in *France* and Toivo Pilli and Meego Remmel have been doing similar work in the *Baltic* lands, especially *Estonia*. David W. Bebbington, Professor of History at the University of Stirling, has led the Scottish Baptist history project, as well as contributing to a wider understanding of the history of evangelicalism across Europe. In *Wales*, Prof. Sir Glanmor Williams achieved major recognition as a social and religious historian, Densil D. Morgan , Professor at Bangor, has ranged widely over Baptist and Evangelical history. Karen Smith has done work on *covenant* and Baptist *spirituality* among 18th-century Particular Baptists, and Ruth M.B. Gouldbourne and Martin Rothkegel, who has take over responsibility for historical lecturing at Elstal, are younger scholars working in important areas of Anabaptist studies. Magnus Lindvall from *Sweden* has done work on both the Anabaptists and the history of Baptist life in Sweden, whilst Bernard Green and Keith G. Jones have recorded the story of the *EBF,* the latter providing an examination of *ecclesiology* of *association* among European Baptists. Raymond Brown, formerly principal of *Spurgeon's College*, amongst his other writings, has written sensitively on the 18th century whilst Anthony Cross has married theological to historical insights with great success in his various studies of Baptist *Sacra-*

mentalism, and of Baptist attitudes to *Baptism*, in particular. He is also the inspirer and administrative *tour de force* behind Paternoster's *Studies in Baptist History and Thought* which has done so much to disseminate Baptist scholarship in recent years.

ET

Church Meeting

[See also *Ecclesiology (Church Polity)*]
The Church Meeting is both an occasion and an event. As an occasion it is the time when church business is transacted, though this should not be too narrowly interpreted in terms of agendas and minutes, but should certainly include *worship* and *prayer*, whilst the agenda should not be narrowly confined to legal, budget and fabric issues, but should involve the reviewing of all the church's *mission* and *ministry* and the setting, under God, of strategic goals in every vital area. As an event the church meeting represents an opportunity to meet – to meet with one another and to meet with God – that is the church meeting, and it is out of this encounter that the life of the church springs. All too easily made mundane by insensitive planning, the church meeting is in fact the highest *authority* in the life of the church and that is why it should take place around the open book, itself a witness to the authority of the Incarnate Word [see *Christology*], and in an atmosphere of prayerful waiting for the understanding of *scripture* and the inspiration of the *Spirit*. There is no higher authority, neither that of monarch or other magistrate or *bishop* or *church council* or '*apostle*' set within the restorationist tradition. Under the Lordship of Christ, the church meeting is *sovereign*. That does not mean it should covet isolation or fail to seek the advice of the wider church. But that is the point: it may be advised, not instructed, though it may enter into *covenant* relationship with regional *associations*, national *unions*, continental fellowships and worldwide alliances the better to fulfil its missionary function. To associate is fundamental to Baptist churchmanship. Certain matters may be delegated to the *deacons* or to other committees, but these should always report back to the church meeting for final decision making. Its business should be conducted in

an orderly fashion and proper records kept. The taking of frequent votes is not helpful but a wise chairman/moderator will seek to discern the mind of the meeting and thereby secure its consent to such actions as need to be taken, on which hopefully a consensus will arise. The church meeting must take all necessary actions for the vigorous prosecution of the church's mission and it is the church meeting that votes to appoint a *pastor*, to elect deacons/elders and to receive into *membership* those whose profession of *faith* has been duly investigated in an orderly fashion, and who thereby enter into covenant relationship with both the *Lord of the Church* and its several members.

ET

Church Membership

Sociologists place Baptists in the family of *sect*-type churches over against those in the parish-type category. The latter type of church emphasises the inclusiveness of the *church* with all in a given area included in its orbit, thus *Anabaptists* in Zürich referred to the *state church* as 'everybody's church'. Churches of such traditions do not normally have a finite membership with the church very often defined by the *ministry* rather than by the membership. By contrast Baptists are exclusive in so far as they uphold the ideals of the *'Believers' Church'*, that is, they are exclusive, in that church membership is only for those who have made a commitment to *Christ*. Indeed in order for the church to be church it must have a regenerate membership. Baptist churches have a finite membership with precise methods for entry, the maintenance of high standards of *holiness* as becomes the body of Christ here on earth so there need to be mechanisms for disciplining the membership [see *Church Discipline*]. With a precise membership Baptists in church *covenants* spell out what the privileges and responsibilities of membership are. It has however to be confessed that a high standard of membership has sometimes had the effect of churches having a large number of adherents who may be regular in *worship*, generous in their giving, but who are wary of taking on the responsibilities of membership. In modern language they are happy to be in the church but wary of belonging to it.

ET

Church Music

[See also *Hymnody*; *Musical instruments in worship*]

Music is so deeply woven into Baptist life that without it, **worship** is hardly imaginable, though the earliest congregations did not use it. Music, often used to prepare the congregation for worship, is interspersed with the spoken word throughout worship, and usually continues after the 'amen'; it accompanies less formal gatherings for midweek **prayers** or **Bible study**, birthday celebrations, etc. The significance of music for Baptist church life is reflected in the histories of local communities which next to **ministers** would characteristically list their musicians and choir directors.

There is some use of non-vocal music in Baptist churches, such as in the use of organ voluntaries, or music played by a quartet or larger musical ensemble. Even then there is often some verbal association linked to the melody in the minds of the hearers. Most of the music used by Baptists, however, takes the form of songs, sung either congregationally, as a solo/group or by a choir. Some churches only sing or listen to one piece at a given time while others have a longer section devoted to worship through a series of songs. The interplay between lyrics and melody is a subject in its own right. As many testimonies would recount, metaphors, symbols, melody and harmony have a power of affecting the dispositions more profoundly than propositions alone. However, as far as reflecting on it **theologically**, music might be one of the most neglected aspects of Baptist worship, often approached in pragmatic terms (even seen as preliminary to 'more important' parts of the service such as the **sermon**). Yet not only does music shape the believers' religious understanding, but it also reflects and articulates their beliefs, embodying the spectrum of believers' experience of life with God often more clearly and accurately than many sermons or pamphlets.

As with the communicating of other forms of art, music is intrinsically connected with yearning for beauty, which does not so much have to do with the quality of the creating and performing as with the participants' awareness of being made in the image of God, the Creator, and the duty therein contained to use this gift of God. As music is the main form of art employed in Baptist churches, it may also help to account for its centrality in the church life. It points to an embedded notion that as an expression of God-ingrained creativity, music *does* something: i.e., it does not merely adorn worship, but is a part of the believers' participating in life with Christ. The participatory aspect of music traditionally is a strong one, with concern often expressed lest 'worship turns into a concert' (whether or not this is always avoided is a different matter). It is also here that the instances of the dissonances between the life proclaimed in worship and life actually lived by the community are most painfully felt.

Besides congregational singing, choirs have played a key role in virtually all European Baptist contexts. Bigger churches would often have more than one choir (e.g. **men**'s, mixed, **children** or **youth** choirs and smaller ensembles). By contrast with the United States, most European Baptist choirs would not be robed, though some colour coordination would be expected, especially for more festive occasions. Their placement in the worship room would vary, also depending on the **architecture** of the meeting place, thus in some cases it would be at the very front behind, or next to the **pulpit** or **communion** table, in some others at the back in a balcony; or on one of the sides.

Choirs played an especially important part in the life of churches in Eastern Europe during **communist** rule, when choir rehearsals and performances often served as a way of legitimising worship gatherings beyond the Sunday service. Various additional activities would take place besides singing, and as many **members** as possible were frequently recruited, at times resulting in the congregation consisting *mostly* of the choir. Though this could have affected the quality of the music performed, Eastern European Baptists have many excellent choirs, especially in larger congregations or in joint choirs drawn from several congregations. As the religious instruction of youth and children was prohibited by the authorities, youth choirs also served a function similar to **Sunday School**.

Since the *ministry* of the choir director embraced explicit spiritual responsibilities, candidates were carefully scrutinised. With *political* change and the arrival of new styles of music, choirs have begun to lose their significance, presenting a particular struggle to those who have witnessed their earlier, indeed, vital role.

In other parts of Europe the role of choirs had diminished even earlier, especially around the 1970s. In many parts of Europe instead of the choir leading congregational singing, this is done by smaller worship groups and individual singers/musicians. The changes taking place are also linked to the significant shifts in the sung repertoire which have been a cause for a number of debates and clashes, typically but not exclusively between older and younger generations. In a number of situations currently there is an apparent over-reliance on contributions from the United States and *Great Britain*; nevertheless, some *unions* (perhaps most notably in the Middle East and among Eastern Slavs) have a strong heritage of characteristically indigenous music.

LA

FURTHER READING: Keith G. Jones and Parush R. Parushev (eds), *Currents in Baptistic Theology of Worship Today*, International Baptist Theological Seminary, Prague, 2007.

Church of England
See *Anglicanism, Baptists and*.

Church of the Brethren, Baptists and the
The Church of the Brethren can be considered the *Anabaptists* of the *Pietist* movement of the early 18th century, that is they were essentially pietists who developed baptistic views and practised believers' *baptism* by immersion, though some claim for them continuity with the Zwickau prophets of the 16th century.

In the context of the crisis situation existing in both *church and state* in the Palatinate at the beginning of the 18th century, eight people in Schwarzenau in central *Germany*, to the north west of Frankfurt, in 1708 entered into a church state through

establishing a *covenant*, before making confession of their *faith* in believers' baptism. Led by Alexander Mack (1679-1735), a miller whose family came from the Heidelberg area, they soon encountered bitter persecution from their opponents who labelled them Dunkers or 'New Baptists' (Neutäufer). The community early developed a *missionary* spirit and set about spreading their ideas to surrounding territories and countries. By contrast with the *Mennonites* who kept within their distinct family groupings, the brethren sought to evangelise in territories of nominal *state church* confessions, whether *Lutheran* or *Reformed*. Christian Liebe took the faith to Berne in *Switzerland* where he was captured and sold by the city fathers as a galley slave to the King of Sicily. Others migrated to the textile manufacturing town of Krefeld on the lower Rhine when toleration in Marienborn was withdrawn, but persecution soon followed them there.

Thus in 1719 a first group of the brethren migrated to Pennsylvania, others followed ten years later and by 1735 most of them had left Europe for America. Their first *minister* in America was Peter Becker (1687-1758) who undertook baptisms and presided at love feasts, their language for *communion*, which also embraced *foot washing*, the kiss of *peace*, an *agape meal* and the taking of the eucharistic elements.

One of their leading *members* in America was Conrad Beissel (1690-1768) who, after a period as a hermit, split off from the main group and established the Ephrata Community, which developed thriving mills, printing presses, handicrafts, schools and choral *music*. Sabbatarians there developed both male and female celibate orders living a community life in separate monastic halls: their *chapel* was the largest in Pennsylvania in the early 18th century. After Beissel's death there was less *growth*. Their care of soldiers in the Revolutionary wars brought typhoid into the community which did much to destroy it physically because buildings had to be burnt to limit the contagion. A rump of married members continued their *worship* and witness throughout the 19th century.

In the 1880s the movement suffered further splits: a *conservative* group of c.5,000 (the Old Order, or Old German Baptist Brethren) resisted all change and a liberal group, also c.5,000, (The Progressives or the Brethren Church) were expelled. The moderate group, some 60,000 strong and initially known as the German Baptist Brethren, but since 1908 as the Church of the Brethren, now number over 215,000. The focus of membership is principally in North America but with sizeable followings in India, now part of the United Church of North India, Nigeria, where they are around 50,000 strong, and Ecuador, where their members now form part of the United Evangelical Church of Ecuador, the fruit of mission labours.

The Church of the Brethren is both an historic *Peace Church* and committed to *Believers' Church* principles. It enjoys fraternal relations with the *American Baptist Churches*.

JHYB

FURTHER READING: Donald Durnbaugh, *The Believers' Church*, Herald, Scottdale, Pa., 1985. Donald Durnbaugh (ed), *European Origins of the Brethren*, Brethren, Elgin, 1958. Donald Durnbaugh (ed), *The Church of the Brethren: Past and Present*, Brethren, Elgin, 1971. Ans J. van der Bent (ed), *Handbook Member Churches*, World Council of Churches, Geneva, 1982.

Church Planting

The planting of new churches has characterised the Baptist movement since its beginnings. This has been a vital ingredient in Baptist growth over the course of four centuries. Historically, *church growth* and church planting have gone hand in hand. Often those involved in starting new churches have been pioneers who have been highly motivated. Often the new churches planted have seen significant growth, although this is not always the case. An outstanding example of church planting in Europe was the German Baptist movement of the 19th century, led by *Johann Gerhard Oncken*. In this case – as in others – Baptist expansion to new geographical areas was intimately related to planting new churches. This can operate as churches are planted across national boundaries but can also happen more locally. At least in the past, people have not wanted or have not been able to travel long distances to get to church. Therefore there have been programmes of church planting to ensure that all communities have a local congregation. However, this has been subject to change, with people willing to travel longer distances by car to reach the 'church of their choice'.

Those who have invested energy in church planting have argued that in many cases it is easier to plant a new church and see it grow, than to change an old church into a growing community. New churches can also inspire the old ones, and can give hope for the future and provide inspiration for new forms and methods in *evangelism*. In addition, church planting can help to keep the church contextualised. A new church is likely to feel the challenge of speaking the language of the people, as they seek to attract the unchurched. The fresh *theological* insights of the new churches can help to keep the whole Christian body – Baptists and other denominations - vibrant.

There has also been significant interest among European Baptists in recent years in the planting of churches among different ethnic groups. Church planting can be cross-cultural or can take place entirely within the same ethnic group through the leadership of those who may have come from other parts of the world to Europe. In a number of Western, Southern and Northern European countries, the planting of churches among immigrant groups has produced rapidly growing Baptist communities.

In Eastern Europe, in the years following the end of *Communist* rule, many new Baptist churches have been planted. Significant Baptist growth has taken place in countries like *Ukraine*, *Armenia*, *Georgia*, *Moldova* and elsewhere. The *European Baptist Federation* has, as a body, been sponsoring church planters in many different countries since 2002. This programme is called The Indigenous *Missionaries* Program. EBF sponsors the church planters for five years, and expects the churches to be self-sustaining thereafter. The program has been successful thus far, with many new churches planted.

BTar & ET

Church Polity

See *Assembly, General – as governing body of Union; Ecclesiology (Church Polity); Unions/Conventions.*

Churches of Christ

This denomination which shares many common concerns with Baptists has its origins in America, first in the work of Barton Stone, a *Presbyterian minister* who was convinced that Christian *mission* was being impeded by the divisions in the church. He wanted to see all church structures abolished and all become simply 'Christians'. A parallel movement was led by Thomas Campbell and his son, Alexander, recent immigrants from *Ireland* who also came to baptistic beliefs from a Presbyterian background. From 1813 the Campbells were associated with the Pennsylvania Baptists, but in 1827 they formed their own separate movement which joined with Stones' followers in 1832 to become the Christian Church (Disciples of Christ), believing that separated churches could be reunited by an earnest search for the nature of the primitive church, which meant that the only *authority* for the new denomination was to be the NT. Thus their two special concerns were a search for the primitive church and for Christian *unity*.

The Campbellites, as they were sometimes known, shared with the *Scotch Baptists* an appreciation of the Glassites who had also earlier withdrawn from the Presbyterians. For about four years William Jones, leader of the Scotch Baptists in *Britain*, co-operated with Campbell until Jones had doubts about Campbell's unwillingness to underwrite doctrine which did not have specific and explicit scriptural authority [see *Bible*]. Whilst Jones withdrew from Campbell, not all Scotch Baptists did the same. Thus James Wallis and Jonathan Hine came to establish what was, in effect, the first Church of Christ in Great Britain in Nottingham at the end of 1836 which soon attracted the support of others seeking a restoration of the primitive church. Their historian points out that, sharing with the *Plymouth Brethren* an emphasis on weekly *communion* and believers' *baptism*, in the tracing of the development of particular congregations, it is difficult to see why one group found their future with the Brethren and another with the Churches of Christ. However, by 1842 a connexion of some 50 churches had developed.

In Great Britain they never secured the strength they obtained in the USA though they did spread to the white dominions, with missionary activity in Africa, Asia and the Pacific. At the founding congress of the *Baptist World Alliance* in 1905, J.H. Shakespeare, in computing the world-wide numbers of Baptists, added to Baptist numbers some 1.25 million Disciples of Christ whom, he argued, 'correspond with us in *faith* and practice'. In 1930 they established their own world body though the shape of its constitution shows some derivation from that of the BWA. Their peak of *membership* in the 1930s was some 16,600 members in the UK.

Conversations on closer relationships with the Baptists in the UK, started during WWII, foundered on the Baptists having many churches which practised open membership. However, some individuals and individual churches did transfer across. After WWII they were attracted by the United Reformed Church's commitment to the search for unity but negotiations were not easy and in the end the Association of Churches of Christ had to be dissolved in 1980 in order to allow those churches that wished, to join the URC, taking with them into that church their commitment to believers' baptism. Those who declined to take that action became the Fellowship of Churches of Christ which rather later formed an alliance with the Mission Department of BUGB.

JHYB

Churches of the Leuenberg Confession

See *Community of Protestant Churches in Europe*.

City Missions, Baptists and

This movement was founded by Scottish *Congregationalist*, David Nasmith (1799-1839). The first city mission was established in Glasgow in 1826, followed by Dublin 1828, New York, in 1830, then by a further 16 North American cities that year. 1832 saw the formation of a city mission in Edinburgh and Paris. It is probable, though, that the most influential one ever established opened in London ·in 1835. The majority of the directors and workers in the *United Kingdom* missions belonged to the Established

Church, *Anglican* in *England* and *Presbyterian* in Scotland. There were, though, a number of Baptists committed to this *evangelistic* work. In Glasgow Robert Kettle, a cotton yarn merchant, was a Vice-President of the Mission in the late 1840s and into the 1850s and was an active supporter throughout his life. His *pastor* James Paterson, minister of Hope Street Baptist Church, was a former mission agent (1828-29), and in subsequent years a regular subscriber. In Edinburgh William Innes, minister of Dublin Street Baptist Church, was an examiner of the city mission in the 1850s and lawyer Charles Spence, a *member* of James Haldane's Tabernacle Church, was the *mission* secretary.

One of the most prominent early supporters of the London City Mission (LCM) was Anglican clergyman Baptist Noel. His 1835 pamphlet, The *Unity of the Church*, commended full cooperation between the Dissenters and the Established Church, a policy carried out by the LCM. Noel became a Baptist in 1848. Baptist examiners of the LCM missionaries included William Murch, President of Stepney Baptist College, and Edward Steane, founder-pastor of Denmark Place Baptist Church, Camberwell. Other Baptists that were notable supporters of this agency were *Charles Spurgeon*, and F.B. Meyer. Spurgeon was the minister of New Park Street Baptist Church. A LCM missionary was attached to his church during his early ministry in London and he was a regular speaker at mission events. Meyer was also a prominent speaker at LCM meetings and had a close involvement with several of the missionaries during his pastorates in London at Regent's Park Chapel and Christ Church, Lambeth, between 1888 and 1920.

Baptists were involved in the work of the Birmingham Town Mission, but were accused by Anglican supporters of using the agency for 'sectarian' purposes. It appears that John Ham, minister of New Hall Street Baptist Church, was the main target of their criticism in 1838. There was, at least from the 1850s, a determined attempt to balance the number of Anglican and Dissenting ministers on the Management Committee of the Town Mission. The Manchester City Mission (Manchester and Salford Town Mission until 1850) first annual report of 1838 noted that its *missionaries* belonged to 'the Established Church, the *Methodists*, the *Moravians* and the Baptists.'

City Missions have also existed in a similar way, principally in Western European capital cities such as Stockholm and Berlin. The City Mission has not been a common feature of Southern Europe and naturally is unknown in the former *communist* countries where such forms of *missionary* work were prohibited.

These examples illustrate that Baptists, though less prominent than some other *Protestant* denominations, were committed to the work of the Town and City Missions from their establishment in the 19th century. Most city missions engaged in holistic mission amongst the neediest as well as *evangelistic* endeavours to particular trades and localities, often focussing on a mission hall where non-denominational worship became the norm.

BT

Civil Religion

Although the concept was mainly developed in the USA in the second half of the 20th century, its origins go back to the writings of Rousseau, who believed that belief in God, the life to come, the reward of virtue and the punishment of vice together with the rejection of religious intolerance – all these rather than the role of the institutional church – were necessary for the smooth running of the *state*. In 1967 Richard Bellah, a *sociologist* of religion, in an article on 'Civil Religion in America' noted that there existed a well-established religious dimension independent of the life of the churches which served to legitimate the authority of civil institutions, and to provide the *nation* with a common set of moral values which bind its peoples together in one common outlook. Developed to serve the purposes of governments or states, it may derive elements of its beliefs and practices from Christianity (or indeed any other *faith* system) but it cultivates generalised attitudes as over against the particularity of Christian doctrine, and judges things in terms of social utility rather than *theological* truth. Civil religion can be seen to be operating in various US presidential speeches which affirm the purposes and (manifest) destiny of the nation, calling for a commitment to patriotic values often presented in terms employing Biblical imagery. Such ideas are seductive, confusing as they do the Biblical *revelation* with inferior deductions which derive from other non-Biblical sources. Prime examples of where a species of civil religion has had a disastrous impact on human society can be seen in the religious myth-making that was made to surround both Hitler's National Socialism and the Afrikaner defense of *Apartheid* in South Africa. Such patterns of thinking are more civil *heresies* than civil religion, glorifying as they do the idol of the *state*.

JHYB

Clerical Dress

On first comment, most Baptist communities in Europe would claim to have not given much attention to formal patterns of dress expected or required of those called to the *ministry* of *Word* and *Sacrament*. The argument would have been stated that there is no special dress for those called to *preach* and preside at the table. However, this is a facile judgement, which a more careful examination of the actual reality across Europe and the Middle East would soon dispose of.

Historically, many Baptist *pastors* took great care in their apparel for Sunday *worship*, especially. There were norms and standards promoted by senior pastors and church leaders. Formal dark suits, or a morning coat with striped trousers, white shirts with cravat and appropriate formal hat for walking to the *chapel* building would have been the norm for male pastors during the 1800s and early 1900s. *C.H. Spurgeon*, Alexander McLaren and *J.G. Oncken* all prepared very formally for their Sunday responsibilities in choice of dress. In some parts of Europe the even more formal attire of the *Reformed* tradition was adopted and certainly in north and west Europe, in the middle of the last century, black academic or preaching robes, white bands, clerical collar and, where possessed, academic hood, would have been acceptable, if not required, especially in chapels in city centres and large towns. In some congregations *pulpit* attire was more a kind of academic dress rather than anything specifically clerical.

Today, though these approaches continue in many parts of north America, they are not so common in Western Europe. Certainly, the clerical collar is not uncommon in North West Europe and *Scandinavia*, especially for *ecumenical* occasions, for work in *hospitals* and other forms of *chaplaincy*. Amongst female pastors tailored suits or sober dresses, perhaps with a white blouse, were considered appropriate. Female *Deacons* also had distinctive dress in former years: e.g. a blue velvet band gathering up a silver silk veil flowing from the head to the neck, corresponding to more formal dress deployed by nursing sisters at that time. .In Slavic countries generally the pastor (always male, until recently) would be expected to be attired in a dark (black or dark blue, not brown) lounge suit, with a white shirt and sober coloured tie.

One previously common tradition was the wearing of black waders and a black gown for the celebration of *baptism*, but this approach has been challenged in many parts of Europe and more commonly now either informal white trousers and a shirt or the white cassock alb is to be seen as appropriate pastoral wear for the baptism of believers, the latter reflecting the liturgical dress emanating from the ecumenical community at Taize in *France*. In *Georgia*, for reasons of *contextual missiology*, a more general tradition of clerical dress exists with the use of coloured cassocks by pastors and more ornate liturgical vestments by the *bishops* and archbishop of the Georgian Evangelical Baptist Church. In the *United Kingdom* within the last decade of the 20th century and the first decade of the 21st century, many younger ministers, both female and male, have dispensed with more sober wear and an increased casualness is to be seen in the attire of both ministers and congregation.

KGJ

Clifford, John (1836-1923)

'For 60 years' it is claimed, 'he held high place in the *Evangelical* movement'. Happy to be associated with the *Evangelical Alliance*, he also believed that there was a social dimension to Christian commitment and that integrity of mind involved new accommodations of both scientific understanding and critical method. Whist in many respects the antithesis of **Spurgeon**, there was no personal antipathy between them. The most articulate of the New Connexion General Baptists [see **England**], (**Arminian** in **theology**, born out of the experience of the **Methodist Revival**), Clifford who was born at Sawley, Derbyshire, on 16 Oct 1836, had little formal **education** before aged 11 going to work 16 hours a day in a lace mill. Converted in Nov 1850 he was baptised [see **Baptism**] seven months later as a mark of his personal commitment to the service of **Christ**. His subsequent **call** to the **ministry** was followed by study at the Midland Baptist College.

During the early years of his only pastorate at Praed Street, Paddington, (subsequently Westbourne Park), London, the largely self-educated Clifford successfully completed his studies in arts, **science** and law through London University. Westbourne Park became the archetypal 'Institutional Church' sponsoring a diversity of programmes – philanthropic, educational, recreational, cultural and spiritual –all of which attracted a large, intelligent and influential **membership**. So extensive was its educational work that it was known as a 'people's university'. Clifford was instrumental in securing the full integration the New Connexion and the Particular Baptists within the life of the Baptist Union of **Great Britain and Ireland** which he twice served as President.

Clifford's *The Inspiration and Authority of the Bible*, first published in 1892, guardedly sought to show an evangelical openness to reverent criticism. He first used the language of '*social gospel*' as a campaigning slogan in addressing the Baptist Union in 1888: sacred was not to be separated from secular, rather God's **sovereignty** extended over the whole realm of human activity, for every social problem had a spiritual dimension. But the **church** was not to be taken over by mere **socialist** utopian talk: **political** change could do so much for **humankind** but could never do all it needed.

Politically, Clifford worked through the Liberal Party which he saw as best instrument for implementing the **Nonconformist Conscience**, whether in terms of a moral foreign policy abroad, or issues of social purity or confessional education at home.

Critical of **theologians** who thought they could exhaust the meaning of the **atonement** in wordy definitions, worked out in their 'verbal controversies and **creed**-fights', he nevertheless rejoiced in 'the free and full pardon it offers and the **hope** it creates'.

As the first President of the **Baptist World Alliance** (1905-11) he was a familiar figure in Europe. E.g. in 1907 he led a delegation to **Hungary** in an attempt to reconcile the two Baptist groups then in conflict there. Active at the European Congresses in Berlin in 1908 and Stockholm in 1913, he also travelled in the cause of European **Peace**. In 1920, he chaired the important London Conference on Baptist reconstruction and **mission** in Europe. Committed throughout his life to the **evangelistic** imperative – 'Our first business is to make men see Christ' – it was in fact during a debate on this in which he intended to speak, that he died at Baptist Church House on 20 Nov 1923.

JHYB

FURTHER READING: D.N.B., *Baptist Handbook*, 1925. J.H.Y. Briggs 'John Clifford' in T. Larsen (ed) *Biographical Dictionary of Evangelicals*, Inter-Varsity, Leicester and Downers Grove, Il., 2003. Sir James Marchant, *Dr. John Clifford, C.H., Life, Letters and Reminiscences*, (contains bibliography of Clifford's writings), Cassell, London and New York, 1924.

Climate change .

Climate change in the present context is the process by which the average temperature of the Earth is rising due to the increase of greenhouse gases which warm the Earth by absorbing radiation from the sun which bounces off the Earth's surface before returning to space. Whilst, greenhouse gases occur naturally, through the burning of fossil fuels (coal, oil and gas) and deforestation, humans are increasing the concentration of greenhouse gases in the atmosphere. The largest increase is in the levels of carbon dioxide, a significant greenhouse gas.

In the 20th century average global temperatures increased by 0.7°C. Even if drastic action is taken to reduce human-caused greenhouse gas emissions, scientists predict that temperatures are almost certain to increase by at least a further 1.3°C before the end of the 21st century. Depending on the extent to which humans seek to limit greenhouse gas emissions, temperatures could rise by between 2°C and 6°C.

The impacts of climate change will be felt across the Earth, but will impact the *poorest* people and countries the most. Depending on the extent of temperature increases, it is possible that glaciers on which over 1 billion people depend for dry-season water supplies could disappear. Drought and famine in regions such as southern Africa are predicted to increase in frequency and intensity, whilst flooding in countries like Bangladesh and many island states will also increase in frequency and intensity.

Historically, rich countries are responsible for 80% of carbon dioxide emissions. Currently, rich countries in which 15% of the world's population live are responsible for 50% of carbon dioxide emissions. The highest emitters of carbon dioxide are the United States, China, the *European Union*, India, *Russia* and Japan. However, this masks the fact that on a per person basis, rich countries are by far the highest emitters. The United States emits 20.2 tonnes of carbon dioxide per person and the EU 8.8 tonnes. This compares with 3.6 tonnes per person in China and 1 tonne in India.

Whilst the governments of all major emitters of greenhouse gas emitters now accept the reality of climate change, international agreement to reduce greenhouse gas emissions has so far been limited. The Kyoto Protocol was agreed in 1997 to set obligations on rich countries to reduce emissions by the small amount of 5 per cent by 2012. However, the US and Australia refused to sign the protocol as it excludes developing countries. Developing counties such as China and India say they will not accept any obligation to reduce emissions whilst their per-person emissions are still far lower than rich countries; and until they see rich countries taking action to significantly reduce emissions first.

From a *theological* point of view, it is argued that climate change is occurring because of the failure on the part of *humankind* to take seriously their *stewardship* of *creation*, and instead exploiting it to the jeopardy of future generations.

TKJ

Cloning

Cloning (derived from Greek *klon* – 'twig' or 'branch') describes the process in which an identical copy of something is made. In biology the term may describe processes used to create copies of DNA fragments (molecular cloning), cells (cell cloning), or organisms. It is also used to indicate asexual reproduction of organisms. The possibility of human cloning was raised in 1997 when the Scottish scientists at the Roslin Institute propagated the sheep, Dolly, the first mammal to be cloned from adult DNA. Quickly, in 1998, the Council of Europe agreed on the Additional Protocol to the Convention for the Protection of *Human Rights* and Dignity of the Human Being with regard to the Application of Biology and Medicine, which aimed at securing protection for the dignity and identity of all human beings; it states that 'any intervention seeking to create a human being genetically identical to another human being, whether living or dead, is prohibited.' In 2000 the European Parliament banned also so-called 'therapeutic cloning', which involves the creation of human embryos solely for research purposes since it 'poses a profound ethical dilemma [see *Ethics*], irreversibly crosses a boundary in research norms, and is contrary to public policy as adopted by the *European Union*.' The *UK* was called to review its position on human embryo cloning, and rejected a proposal to permit research using embryos created by cell nuclear transfer when it was laid before them. The voices of the churches were in tune with the European Parliament. In the science of cloning more pessimistic overtones have been heard since 2003 when Dolly's life had to be terminated by lethal injection because she was suffering from lung cancer and crippling arthritis.

While cloning is still a debatable issue today both in science and *bioethics*, the very latest adult skin stem cell research results show alternative possibilities for creating and developing much more personally fitting human organ transplants from a patient's own skin cells. If this proved successful many medical problems of transplantation, like need for immunosuppressive *drugs*, and bioethical questions concerning human cloning would be removed. Such potential alternative ways of developing new organs without the need for classical cloning methods could help to justify the traditional Christian critique of human cloning. Baptists, while open to new developments in biosciences, have always stressed that human beings, created by God according to his own image, should never be depersonalised, since every person embodies a unique dignity before the Lord. Nobody can play the role of God in his *creation*, but every person should be a good *steward* for the Lord of all creation.

MR

FURTHER READING: 'Cloning Animals and Humans' (online doc from 'Human life in our hands? Churches and Bioethics. Reports from the consultation organised by the CEC Church and Society Commission in Strasbourg, 27-29 Nov 2003'), www.cec-kek.org/content/bioethicsconf.shtml.

Closed Communion
See *Strict Communion*.

Cold War
This is the term that has been applied to the protracted state of tension between the international superpowers of USA and the former *Soviet Union* and their allies, after WWII. The term in this sense was first used in the US Congress in 1947 when Baptist Harry S. Truman was president. The superpowers engaged in intense military, *political*, economic and ideological competition spreading their geopolitical influence around the world.

The US reacted to the Soviet military expansion after 1945 with the Truman doctrine of containment. The Soviets signalled their hostility by creating the Iron Curtain, a political, military and ideological barrier to isolate itself and its Eastern-European allies from the West. The foreign policies of the USSR were oriented towards spreading the ideology of global class struggle, supporting *communist* revolution around the world, controlling trade in the Soviet dominated areas. Soviet leadership applied a doctrine of the right to military intervention if communism was threatened in its satellite countries (*Hungary* 1956; *Czechoslovakia* 1968; Afghanistan 1978). The early communist ideology insisted on the incompatibility of two systems: liberal democracy and totalitarian communism. In the late stages of the Cold War, East-West *dialogue* provided a new vision of peaceful coexistence.

The Cold War antagonism between the two systems was formalised by creating two opposing military alliances, NATO (1949-50) and the Warsaw Pact (1955). The world was divided into three parts consisting of the two blocks and so-called unaligned two-thirds world countries. The Cold War was characterised by mutual fear of nuclear annihilation. The arms race stimulated technological advances, including exploration of space. The superpowers mostly avoided direct military confrontation, fighting so-called proxy wars by supporting their allies in conflicts in other countries. The US was directly involved in the Korean War (1950-53), the Vietnam War (1959-75). During the Cold War there were periods of improved relations (as Détente after the 1969 SALT talks) and crises: the Greek Civil War (1946-49), the Berlin Blockade (1948-49), and the Cuban missile crisis (1962).

Given the official atheism of the Soviet Union, religion played an important role in the Cold War as a means of defining Western identity: The US and its allies saw themselves as representing the values of Judeo-Christian *freedom* over against atheist totalitarian slavery. The communists severely limited *religious freedom* and persecuted many Christians. A Polish Catholic priest named Popeliuszko was murdered by the communist security services. The stories of many imprisoned believers remain untold. Soviet ideological warfare also included atheist propaganda and monitoring of western 'clerical propaganda' broadcasts by Radio *Vatican*, Radio Free Europe, VOA, – as a part of the KGB's larger effort to 'combat bourgeois ideological diversions'(1967-1989).

Jimmy Carter, a devout Baptist layman [see *Laity*], as president of the USA successfully capitalised on the Helsinki Final Act (1975) negotiated by his predecessor Gerald Ford and signed by the USSR. Carter's foreign policy emphasis on individual *human rights* and rights for self-determination by all peoples strengthened the internal opposition in the USSR from both dissidents and the pro-independence movements in the republics. A number of underground Baptists in

Russia, *Ukraine*, *Belarus* and the *Baltic states* engaged in non-violent resistance. In 1975 major western TV networks aired a documentary on the conditions in the Soviet GULAG camps produced and smuggled to the West by a group of Latvian Baptists. The support provided by a Polish-born *Pope*, John Paul II, to the Solidarity movement in *Poland* in the 1980s, added to the international pressure on the Soviet regime. The Cold War gradually came to an end when the last Soviet leader, Mikhail Gorbachev, introduced his reforms (1987-88), Perestroika (reconstruction) and Glasnost (transparency).

The active phase of the Cold War ended in 1989 with the fall of the Berlin Wall and the end of communist regimes in Eastern Europe; the formal end of hostilities was signed in 1990 at the CSCE in Helsinki; the final 'point of no return' was reached in 1991 with the collapse of the USSR.

PZ

Collection

See *Offerings/Collection*; *Tithing*.

Colonialism

Colonialism describes those spheres of influence in the wider world created by the empire-building powers of the developed *nations* of the northern hemisphere. Those empires could be either formal, when *political* control was secured by governmental devices, or informal, when similar influence was secured through politico-economic influence, as exercised, e.g. by the superpowers of the last century. This became the context in which *overseas missions* took place, with missionaries sometimes called the agents of empire. In some cases this was undoubtedly true as some saw the establishment of secure government and the development of viable economies as necessary preconditions to effective mission, so David Livingstone's deliberate advocacy of a programme in Central Africa that linked together Christianity and Commerce, believing that only good trade could drive out bad trade, that is the slave trade. But in other situations missionaries were in constant conflict with Euro-

pean settlers and seen as the defenders of native rights, e.g. in the activities of *men* like Knibb and Phillippo and other *BMS* missionaries in Jamaica in their fight against slavery there. In India, *Carey* was so opposed by the governing East India Company that he had to settle in Danish territory at Serampore, and his campaigning against infanticide and suti (the burning of Indian widows on their husband's funeral pyres) was denounced in the British parliament as an unwarranted intrusion into local cultural practices. Ironically when Carey later raised funds for *Bible translation* by teaching at the Company College in Calcutta he was criticised by the society's home committee. Elsewhere it was missionaries, including the Swedish Baptist, E.V. Sjöblom, who were in the vanguard of campaigns against unjust colonial rule, as e.g. in the Leopold II's personal kingdom in the Congo where rubber workers suffered great abuses. In the two World Wars, Asian and African forces gained respect as they fought alongside their European counterparts. In Asia, where strong *nationalist* movements date back at least to the beginning of the 20th century, the encouragement of resistance forces against Japanese occupation in WWII, cultivated a leadership which, once anti-Japanese, could easily become anti-colonial. Accordingly, after WWII, colonial powers began to extract themselves from their imperial commitments as nation after nation secured their independence. The challenge for the missionary societies was to move from a mentality which split the world into sending and receiving nations into a world of partnership between older churches and their newer, often more robust, offspring in the developing world, as the centre of gravity of *Christendom* moved to the south. The dismantling of formal empires has been more easily achieved than the changing of the terms of trade in a globalised world [see *Globalisation*], still marked by great inequities between rich and poor nations.

JHYB

FURTHER READING: Brain Stanley, *The Bible and the Flag: Protestant Imperialism and British Imperialism in the 19th and 20th Centuries*, Apollos, Leicester, 1990.

Colportage/Colporteurs

From the beginning of the 19th century colporteurs were employed to sell the *scriptures* or gospel tracts in the manner of an itinerant peddler. The word, of French origin, means 'to carry from a pack slung around the neck'. Colporteurs, mainly males, were committed members of that great *missionary* endeavour which campaigned to see the scriptures broadcast across the face of Europe. In this process colporteurs travelled endless miles to ensure the *Bible* reached Europe's unchurched millions, often facing persecution in the process. The British Foreign Bible Society (BFBS) which prohibited its agents from selling any other books besides the Holy Scriptures, employed hundreds of people to distribute the Bible, or portions of the Bible, at affordable prices both in towns and in the countryside. The salary of the colporteurs was a small percentage of what they obtained from the copies they sold. Priest and clergymen did not accept them always cordially. Therefore they suffered abuse and sometimes had to appear at police stations for tribunal interrogations.

The colporteurs were not always Baptist missionaries, the Bible Societies employing *men* with different religious backgrounds, but the Baptists were the most diligent in the task of distributing the scriptures. One of them, Mihály Kornya (1844-1917) as colporteur and senior *pastor* of a Baptist congregation in *Hungary* baptised more than 11,000 believers in 44 years. Very often the reading of scripture distributed by a colporteur proved to be the vital to the starting of a new Baptist work.

OES

Comity

Comity has been defined as 'the mutual division of the world into spheres of work by *mission* societies, and non-interference in one another's affairs', more briefly designated 'denominationalism by geography'. The term was essentially North American and worked between denominations and within denominations. Thus it appears on the Agenda for the first *BWA* Congress in 1905 and for a while determined which areas were to be missioned by the *Southern Bap-*tist Convention* and which by the predecessors of *American Baptist Churches*, on the basis of comity agreements entered into by the two parts of the Baptist family from the late 19th century onwards. Such principles were reaffirmed in 1925 but by 1951 Southern Baptists were unwilling to accept any limitations to their missionary labours within the USA. For Baptists then comity started as a way of the Northern and Southern Conventions dealing with an expanding USA.

Deployed by all *Protestant* denominations, it was used to determine missionary policy in Central America and the Caribbean. Haphazard missionary expansion had led to chaotic and competing strategies which could only confuse those being *evangelised*. In the mission field the advocacy of comity dated back to the late 19th-century missionary conferences that led up to *Edinburgh 1910* which gave an added push to the co-operative principles that lay behind comity. The *World Evangelical Alliance*, the predecessor of the relatively recent organised World Evangelical Fellowship (1951), 'encouraged co-operative missionary work and facilitated "comity".' Comity thinking also lay behind *BMS* withdrawal from certain fields e.g. the Cameroon in 1886 with the unsuccessful attempt to transfer the work to the Basle Mission, and *Italy* in 1921. Comity broke down not so much because missionary societies did not hold to historical agreements but because of developing patterns of *migration* amongst those evangelised. It was a strategy of the era of missionary societies but, with the emergence of national churches, different strategies of cooperation were required.

JHYB

Commissioning of Missionaries
[See also *Mission*]

The commissioning or setting apart of missionaries is the corresponding act to ordination of a person entering the home ministry. The difference arises because in the case of missionaries there is not normally a call from a *local church* to *ministry* which is the normal prerequisite to *ordination*. This distinction, however, should not be pushed too far. Andrew Fuller [see *Fullerism*] in an interesting passage compared the *apostolic* origins of both *pastors* or *elders elected by* local churches and missionaries commissioned *to establish* churches. Fuller argues that, in the labours of missionaries seeking to plant new churches [see *Church Planting*] and encourage their *growth*, were to be seen 'all the leading characteristics of apostolic practice'. Later it would be the task of the churches to identify those who had appropriate gifts to be missionaries, to prepare them for service through appropriate instruction and then to send them out to *preach* the gospel in much the same way as *Jesus* himself commissioned the *apostles* with prayers that they might be filled with the *Holy Spirit* for the task they were about to undertake [see *Great Commission*]. 'The first missionaries to a heathen country could not be chosen by those to whom they were sent, but by him or them who sent them; nor could their influence be confined to a single congregation, but, by a kind of parental *authority*, would be extended to all the societies that might be raised by means of their labours' Succeeding pastors would be expected to be appointed by local churches on the normal principle. Apostolic practice according to Fuller justified both a church planting ministry with appointment from external agencies, and a ministry in already planted churches in which case it was appropriate for that company of God's people to choose and ordain its own pastors.

Another perceived difficulty was that not all missionaries were called to fulfil pastoral duties, and since teachers, *health* workers, agricultural developers and administrators were not ordained at home, why should they be ordained for work *overseas*? A service of commissioning for service in which the responsibilities of the sending church, as well as those of the individuals being commissioned, were spelt out, seemed more appropriate.

Today, we no longer live in a situation of foreign missions which determine the pattern of Christian witness in overseas countries; or, indeed, of *sending* churches in the north and *receiving* churches in the south. Instead there is a greater sense of mutuality and partnership with missionaries travelling from the south to the north as well as vice versa. Fully independent churches also

rightly wish to have a say in approving incoming missionaries, objecting to any notions of overseas personnel being forced upon them. Moreover there would seem to be an element of *theological* tension in an external church ordaining a minister for service in a different church. Rather the true nature of mission partnership needs to be recognised in services which recognise the setting aside of individuals to serve overseas.

HG

Common Market
See *European Union/Common Market*.

Communal Living
See *Christian Communal Living*.

Communion, Holy
See *Baptism, Eucharist and Ministry*; *Communion and Intercommunion*; *Eucharistic Liturgy*; *Sacrament, Sign and Symbol*.

Communion and Intercommunion
[See also *Eucharistic Liturgy*; *Koinonia*; *Open Communion*; *Strict Communion*]
This theological concept is an important one *ecclesiologically*. From the early days of the *church* it has been important for local communities of believers to identify those with whom they shared a common *faith* in *Jesus* the crucified messiah and now the risen and exalted Lord. This essential attribute of the *unity of the church* local with other churches in diverse places has focused for many around a sense of shared *koinonia* in the one faith so that believers in one congregation might participate in the *sacramental* services, especially the *Eucharist*, of another congregation, without any bar or hindrance. The original understanding of communion relates to the reception of the bread and *wine* by participants in the Eucharistic services, thereby entering into communion with each other and with Christ. In Baptist communities communion is always in both kinds – bread and *wine* separately, but in some Christian traditions only one

kind, bread, is normally received by the congregation whilst in others, including some Baptist churches, the bread is dipped in the wine (intinction). In other churches the bread is placed on a spoon so that the faithful may commune.

With the division of the one church and the loss of full unity between the *bishops* of the eastern *orthodox* churches and the western *catholic* churches and with the development of the denominations of the *reformation* and radical reformation, the issue of identifying which believers might commune has become an important point of *ecclesiology* and *church discipline*. Historically, the Eucharist was a closed service for believers only, but with the development of public *worship* after the Edict of Milan, the concern to guard the Eucharist against those who might receive inappropriately or in breach of the discipline of the church has become an important issue.

In Baptist churches the invitation to commune is generally given to all *members* in good standing. There is a difference of practice between those who have a closed membership of baptised believers [see *Baptism*] only and those who have *open membership*. Closed communion or *Strict communion* was commonly practised by Baptists in the 17th century, but a more open attitude exists today in many parts of the European Baptist family and in many churches the challenge is put upon the communicant as to whether they believe they are in a good relationship with Christ and fit to receive. Thus what used to be known as 'fencing the table', i.e. indicating who may participate, is done by the invitation which may be issued in terms such as 'The Lord Jesus invites all those who love him and desire to be his true disciples to meet him around his table.'

Intercommunion is the attempt to establish relationships between different denominational churches (generally specific *unions*, conventions or confessional families within a *nation*) to create conditions whereby members of one church can be regarded as having sufficient unity with members of another church to receive the Eucharistic elements in the worship of the second church. There are some general and easy arrangements in this way. For instance Baptists and *Mennonites,* as believer baptisers,

generally permit intercommunion between their members. In certain European countries the *evangelical* churches or *free churches*, *Methodists, Congregational* and Baptists would enjoy a measure of informal intercommunion. This has also been true in certain countries between Baptists and the national or *state church* where good *ecumenical* relations exist and has been achieved without the existence of formal and comprehensive agreements on doctrine.

A wider scheme of intercommunion in Europe has been based around the *Leuenberg* agreement creating the *Community of Protestant Churches in Europe* which provides intercommunion for a wide range of *Lutheran, Reformed,* Methodist and minority evangelical churches of the reformation and post reformation era. Another common arrangement is known as 'eucharistic hospitality' whereby one denomination invites communicant members of another denomination to participate fully in its communion without necessarily accepting the validity of the religious orders of other denominations – that is to say they would not welcome clergy of another denomination to share in presiding at the table.

An attempt was made by the *World Council of Churches* Faith and Order Commission to create a process which might lead to greater intercommunion in the Lima Document on *Baptism, Eucharist and Ministry*. The *Anglican* Churches have attempted to create sufficient common unity with the Lutheran, Reformed and *Moravian* churches in Europe to permit intercommunion in the *Meissen, Porvoo and Fetter Lane agreements* respectively. Baptists have generally stood apart from such dialogues because of the prior issue of *infant baptism*. However, more recently the *European Baptist Federation* and CPCE did have a helpful series of meetings to see whether church fellowship and intercommunion were possible. The conclusion was that there was not, as yet, sufficient 'church fellowship' (the CPCE *theological* term) to permit this.

It should be noted that some contemporary *scholars* have attempted to enlarge the definition of communion to include all elements of *liturgy, theology,* doctrine and *koinonia* and the attempt to obtain sufficient unity about them for deep conciliar fellowship between the *Christian World Communions,* but this seems to stretch the original understanding of the word too far.

KGJ

Communism/Socialism/Marxism

The classic definition of socialism argues that the means of production, distribution and exchange should be owned or regulated by the community as a whole, not by *wealthy* individuals or corporations beholden to their shareholders, representing the forces of private wealth and *capitalism*. Some would argue that such a concern for a society upholding common ownership, campaigning for justice for the oppressed and working for universal human brotherhood has its inspiration in *scripture*, and on this basis it has been developed in *Christian Socialist* programmes. In the Labour movement in many countries a form of socialism emerged which was not Marxist, but still looking to develop the collectivist *state* in which laissez faire was curbed and the market made to serve social interests, especially in the development of the *welfare state*, concerned with the development of *educational*, employment and recreational opportunities for all its citizens.

Marx's critique of capitalism, especially in the modern world, so largely shaped by the free-market forces of industrialisation and urbanisation, now aided by the processes of *globalisation*, is based on the notion that 'exploitation is built into the capitalist system of production, because labour is bound to sell its power to the market but after that has no say over what is produced, how it is produced or where the profit goes. The class associated with the ownership or control of profit makes capital at the expense of the class which has nothing to lose but its chains', often referred to as the proletariat.

The Marxist analysis of history attributes great power to the role of class, and the forces of economic determinism, minimising the role of the individual, with ultimately a waiting upon the *violence* of class warfare to bring in through revolution the promised millennium of a classless society. However since Marx's day other forces have to be put alongside class as obstructing human aspirations, such as race, colour and gender. For many, Marxism came to have a quasi-religious power, operating amongst its followers very much as a belief system, but with humanity rather than God at the centre of the system.

Whereas Marx dismissed Christianity philosophically with some passion, many of his followers, having secured *political* power, have extended his hostility to religion to active persecution of those involved in church life, Christian *faith* being identified with an unsocial otherworldliness, the so-called 'opium of the people.' Accordingly the Marxist *creed* has been used to underwrite the story of the oppression of the church in countries of Eastern Europe, in China, in North Korea, and other such countries, where a controlled collective economy has been married to militant atheism. In the former *Soviet Union* the building of socialism necessitated the centralisation of economic activity over a vast area by the establishment of state monopolies with the nationalisation of industry, the collectivisation of agriculture with the Party controlling all aspects of life, cultural, educational and social as well as political. The dictatorship of the proletariat became the dictatorship of the Communist Party, but all too soon this became the dominance of the Central Committee, then of the Kremlin, then of the party leader himself, making government wholly totalitarian. Whilst rule was exercised in the name of the working class, a new ruling bureaucracy emerged which sought to dominate communism internationally This history makes it difficult to disassociate Marxism as a system of thought from Communism as a coercive form of government, set on anti-Christian goals, as manifestly illustrated in the histories of *Russia* and China where those who wished to maintain Christian witness had to choose between courageous dissent and an easily misunderstood measure of collaboration.

However in the 1950s and 1960s dialogue did take place between a select number of Christian and Marxist thinkers both in Europe and North America, though a thorough-going Christian critique of capitalism, as much as of Marxism, remained undeveloped. After Warsaw Pact forces marched into *Czechoslovakia* in 1968 such conversations rapidly came to a halt, as also did related conversations in the Christian *Peace* Movement. Some have claimed that the conversations were in fact relocated to Latin America, re-emerging in *Liberation Theology*, with its use of Marxist tools of analysis to illuminate the nature of the human condition within poor societies whose economies are dominated by *trans-national companies*. Once again certain 'Marxist' themes such as *alienation*, exploitation and *praxis* were seen to have Christian significance, with the debate now as to how far Christians and Marxists could co-operate to secure a voice for the marginalised in societies governed by irresponsible and oppressive plutocracies. The misuse of power is a theme running through much modern history with large parts of the population having no access to how such power is used, no voice where issues are debated and decisions made. Just as the Christian *Church* suffers from its divisions, so modern socialism is divided by factions of both analysis and action, which can easily evacuate the term of all meaning. For all its faults the continued attractiveness of the Marxist creed in many places exists as a challenge to Christian societies to 'do' peace, justice and *creation* care with greater determination and intelligence, indeed, as the jargon has it, to exercise 'a *preferential option for the poor*'.

JHYB

Community of Protestant Churches in Europe (CPCE)

[See also *Leuenberg Confession Conversations on Baptism*]

CPCE is a family of *Protestant Reformation* churches in Europe signatories to the Leuenberg Concordat of 1973 and seeking to be a 'Protestant Reformation voice' in Europe.

At the conclusion of WWII doctrinal conversations began in Europe between the *Lutheran* and *Reformed Churches*, stimulated by the then new *World Council of Churches* and its *Faith and Order* Commission. These early conversations entered a new phase in 1960 in what became known as the Schauenberg Conversations between the Lutheran World Federation and the World Alliance of Reformed Churches. The outcome of these conversations was the pos-

sibility that an agreement might be reached about a common understanding of the gospel and the development of church fellowship, that is to say, *koinonia* in *word* and *eucharist* including mutual recognition of *ordination*.

In 1973 upon the Leuenberg near Basle in *Switzerland* an agreement was entered into between a wide group of magisterial reformation Lutheran and Reformed churches in Europe and the proto-reformation *Waldensian* Church, together with the Church of the *Czech Brethren* and certain Union churches in Germany. By 1993 there were 85 member churches from throughout Europe, but including, perversely the *Evangelical* Church of the River Plate (Argentina), the Evangelical Waldensian Church of Uruguay and Argentina and the Reformed Church of Argentina (these churches all having historic links to mother churches in Europe). In Europe, Protestant churches in the isles, *Scandinavia*, the *Baltic States*, Western and Southern Europe, Central Europe and *Romania* were all in membership. The name was changed from Leuenberg Church Fellowship to CPCE in 2003. There are currently 105 member Churches.

In 1994 agreement was reached with *Methodists* in Europe to be admitted to the Leuenberg Concordat on special terms and this was implemented in 1999. In 2000 informal *dialogue* began between representatives of CPCE and European Baptists, resulting in more formal dialogue between 2002 and 04 between the *EBF* and CPCE with an official report being issued in 2005. It did not prove possible for CPCE to see in European Baptists all those marks of the church which would permit them to enter church fellowship.

KGJ

FURTHER READING: *Agreement between Reformation Churches in Europe (Leuenberg Agreement)* (trilingual ed.), Verlag Otto Lembeck, Frankfurt, 1993. *Leuenberg, Meissen, Porvoo: Consultation between the Churches of the Leuenberg Church Fellowship and the Churches involved in the Meissen Agreement and the Porvoo Agreement)*, Verlag Otto Lembeck, Frankfurt, 1995. *Dialogue Between the community of Protestant Churches in Europe (CPCE) and the European Baptist Federation (EBF) on the Doctrine and Practice of Baptism.*

Community of Women and Men in the Church

Concern about this issue dates from the beginning of the 20th century and in part from even earlier – e.g. In the acceptability of *women* to serve as *missionaries* and if to serve, then on an equal basis with their brothers? The issue was already on the agenda of the *Faith and Order* movement from 1927 where questions were raised about barriers raised against women's service in the life of the *church*. In part, this was a question of justice, in part, it was a question of whether the churches could afford not to release such enormous reserves of personnel for more effective *witness* and service. Women were already in pain from what they saw as the *sufferings* of exclusion, being silenced, underestimated or just unheard. Technically the language of the Community of Women and *Men* in the Church is the title of a programme of the *World Council of Churches* which convoked an important international consultation on the subject in Sheffield, *England* in 1981. The letter to the churches from that Sheffield meeting spoke of 'how deep are the emotions involved in any reflection on our being as women and men', 'how hard it is to address and envision God in ways that respect the Christian understanding of personhood rather than suggesting male superiority', 'how great is the need for education' in this area, and 'how radical may be the changes needed'. The same concerns exist within our European Baptist family but clearly this is potentially a contentious and divisive issue, which requires careful discussion giving full respect to different *theological* convictions and cultural contexts.

Today, in most parts of the *EBF* family it is clear that women form a majority of committed members of *local churches*. It is also clear that they spearhead the mission advance of the churches through their involvement in various forms of outreach and service. It is less clear that all Baptist communities properly value the missional and diaconal *ministries* of women and the majority of Baptist *unions* will not permit women to be ordained [see *Ordination*] to the ministry of *Word* and *Sacrament*. Many communities in which language is gender exclusive have a preference for 'brothers' over 'sisters'; even in the title of some unions and gender-inclusive or gender-affirmative language belongs almost exclusively to Baptist unions in *Scandinavia* and Western Europe.

ET

Comparative Religion

This has more recently been redesignated as Religious Studies or the Study of Religion/s. This discipline emerged as part of the development of the social sciences during the late 19th and early 20th centuries, often using material garnered by European colonists [see *Colonialism*], explorers and *missionaries*. Therefore the discipline has been subject to the criticism of Orientalist bias, in that the comparison in question was usually unfavourable in relation to European (Christian) Culture. The subject gradually developed more rigorous and objective approaches and in *Germany* for a period was known as the 'science of religion' (*Religionswissenschaft*). Various disciplinary forms emerged: linguistic, as in the work of the German-born Oxford *scholar* F. Max Mueller (1823-1900) who edited the influential series *Sacred Texts of the East*; anthropological, such as the work of Oxford's Edward Burnett Tylor (1832-1917), who in 1884 became the first British university appointment in *Anthropology*, and Cambridge's James G. Frazer (1854-1941), whose multi-volume *The Golden Bough* ran into numerous printings. *Sociological* approaches were pioneered through the work of the French secular *Jewish* scholar, Emile Durkheim (1858-1917), who in 1913 became the first holder of a Chair in Sociology in *France* (at the Sorbonne) and German protestant Max Weber (1864-1920), professor at Vienna and Munich. Psychological approaches were developed by, and in reaction to, the work of the pioneering Viennese psychotherapist, Sigmund Freud (1856-1939), and his Swiss protégé, Carl Gustav Jung (1875-1961).

Baptists often encountered other religions through the work of their *missions* and the early work of the Serampore Trio (*W. Carey*, J. Marshman and W. Ward) included some of the first translations into English of Hindu texts such as the *Ramayana* and the

Mahabharata, which incorporates the influential *Bhagavad-Gita*. Born in India, **BMS** missionary, Lewis Bevan-Jones (1880-1960), was instrumental in interpreting **Islam** for a Christian audience through works such as *The People of the Mosque* (1932).

Other Baptists came to Comparative Religion through their study of Christian **theology**. Henry Wheeler Robinson (1872-1945), the British OT **scholar** and **theologian**, was influenced by psychological approaches, especially in developing the notion of corporate personality in relation to the OT, and like a number of Baptist scholars made significant contributions to the understanding of Hebrew religion (e.g. H.H. Rowley, T.H. Robinson, A.R Johnson). Robinson's protégé, Ernest A. Payne (1902-80), although best known as a church historian and **ecumenical** statesman, also held the post of University Lecturer in Comparative Religion while senior tutor at **Regent's Park College**, Oxford, and in 1933 published a commentary on the *Shaktas*, a Hindu sacred text, as well as supervising research for emerging scholars such as the **Anglican** Islamicist, Kenneth Cragg (b1913). Another Regent's graduate, originally a Baptist but later an Anglican priest, was T.O. (Trevor) Ling (1920-95) who, after Baptist pastorates in London, became Professor of Comparative Religion in Leeds and Manchester during the 1960s and 1970s and in Singapore during the 1980s; he wrote widely on **Marxism**, Buddhism and Indian traditions and produced an influential text book *A History of Religion East and West* (1968).

During the 1970s phenomenological approaches were pioneered from the centre at Lancaster University under the leadership of Ninian Smart (1927-2004), whilst the American anthropologist, Clifford Geertz (b1926), developed cultural analysis. Current trends have seen issues of gender and questions of 'insider/outsider' perspective come to the fore.

In more recent years a small group of British Baptist scholars have been researching and teaching in this area including Clinton Bennett (b1955) who spent some time teaching at Baylor in the USA, Paul Weller (b1956) Derby University, and Nicholas Wood (b1954) Oxford University.

NJW

FURTHER READING: F. Max Mueller, *Introduction to the Science of Religion*, [s.n.], London, 1873. E. Sharpe, *Comparative Religion: A History*, Scribner's, New York, 1975. E. Said, *Orientalism*, Pantheon Books, New York, 1978. C. Bennett, *In Search of the Sacred: Anthropology and the Study of Religions*, Cassell, New York, 1996. N. Smart, *Dimensions of the Sacred*, HarperCollins, London, 1996; D. Pals, *Seven Theories of Religion*, Oxford University Press, New York, 1996. J. Hinnells (ed), *The Routledge Companion to the Study of Religion*, Routledge, London and New York, 2005.

Conference of European Churches (CEC/KEK)

The Conference of European Churches, which had its roots in **ecumenical** developments following the end of the WWII, was founded in 1959 arising out of an earlier ecumenical event held in 1957 at Liselund, **Denmark**. The word 'Conference' rather than '**Council**' in the title reflects something of the nervousness of relationships in the **Cold War** years. The 1959 'Nyborg 1' meeting attracted 40 denominations from 20 countries. Some groupings, such as the **EBF**, appointed observers and some countries, such as **Great Britain**, were represented through their Council of Churches, rather than directly by individual denominations. Initially, amongst Baptists, there was a certain suspicion of this organisation seeking to bring together **Protestants** and **Orthodox**. Initially, the members were drawn from what we now think of as the **Leuenberg** church **fellowship**, together with some Orthodox churches. During the Cold War it was difficult for Protestant churches in Eastern Europe to play a full part in the development of CEC. CEC has had increasingly close contacts with the **Roman Catholic** Council of European Bishop's Conferences (CCEE) and this contact has led to the joint acceptance of the **Charta Oecumenica** (2001). It is a regional organisation relating to the **World Council of Churches**. Two joint assemblies between CEC and CCEE have been held, the so –called European assemblies at Basel in 1989 and Graz in 1997.

The principal work of the CEC has involved fostering ecumenical **dialogue**, engaging with the European institutions such as the Council of Europe and the **European Union**, reflecting on issues of **church** and society and participating in reflection on the Helsinki final acts, not least in the areas of **human rights** and **religious liberty**.

Individual Baptists have always played a prominent part in the life of CEC, though only a few member bodies of the EBF have been full members. Two General Secretaries of the CEC have been Baptists. Revd Dr. Glen Garfield Williams from Wales (1961-86) and Revd Dr. Keith H. Clements from England (1997-2005).

More recently, the EBF has become an associate member of the CEC and several more **unions** have joined the CEC, so that of the 41 Baptist unions within the boundaries of CEC, about 30% are members.

KGJ

FURTHER READING: www.cec-kek.org.

Conference on Christian Politics, Economics and Citizenship (COPEC)

[See also **Politics, Baptists and**]
There was debate in the 1920s among Baptists in some parts Europe about the extent to which politics had any place in Baptist churches. This represented a striking contrast to earlier **Free Church** confidence and involvement. Some **ministers** were saying that political statements belonged outside the **pulpit**, since ministers lacked the knowledge to make pronouncements and often their hearers had more expertise. Others, especially those who were sympathetic to the growing socialist mood of the times, argued that **faith** must be lived out in the political area. Some politically active Baptists shared in 1924 in COPEC (the Conference on Politics, Economics and Citizenship), which drew together 1,400 people from a wide range of denominations.

COPEC was held in Birmingham, **England** under the overall chairmanship of William Temple, then Bishop of Manchester and later Archbishop of Canterbury. Indeed Temple was the inspiration for the conference. There was great opposition among those present to laissez faire economics and there was general affirmation of the British Labour Government under Ramsay MacDonald. For Temple there was no tension between **evangelism** and social action. One

important network for Temple and others at COPEC, which expressed this **holistic** understanding of Christian faith, was the **Student Christian Movement** (SCM).

Among Baptists involved at COPEC was Hugh Martin, a British Baptist minister who was active in SCM, who chaired the COPEC executive. J. Ivory Cripps, minister of the Church of the Redeemer (Baptist), Birmingham, and then West Midland Baptist Superintendent (who had been Emmeline Pankhurst's **chaplain** during her hunger strike in prison on behalf of suffragettes), also played a full part in COPEC. But not everyone was convinced. Despite the many papers at COPEC, some of which would contribute to the thinking that produced the **Welfare State** in Britain, the social tradition was beginning to fade in many Baptist churches.

IMR

Confession
See **Auricular Confession**.

Confessions of Faith
See **Creeds, Covenants and Confessions of Faith**; **New Covenant, The**.

Congregational Polity
See **Church Meeting**; **Ecclesiology (Church Polity)**.

Congregationalism
Congregationalism has its origins amongst those **puritan** groups in **England**, then known as Independents, who separated from the established church in the early 17th century. It is a system of **church government** which locates decision making in the local gathered congregation, duly assembled in **church meeting** under the guidance of the **Holy Spirit** and gathered under the **authority** of the open **Bible**. The church meeting has the power to appoint the church's own **ministers** and make decisions about its **ministry** and **mission**. Such a congregation is composed of believers only, who join one another in **covenant** relationship, both with one another and with and before Almighty

God. Not simply a form of ecclesiastical democracy, in church meeting, whilst all may
contribute, the focus of attention is on
prayerfully [see *Prayer*] seeking to discern
the mind and will of *Christ* who is *sovereign*
in his church.

Congregationalism is thus to be distinguished from such other systems as *Episcopacy* (where *bishops* represent ecclesiastical
authority), *Presbyterianism* or Connexionalism (where that same authority is located in
centralised *church councils*). It also represents a coming together of the people of God
in a free but committed *association*, which
is of a different quality from churches
formed on the parish system in *state* or folk
or established churches which operate under
a measure of state control and intervention.

Congregationalism is not, however, isolationist but embraces the principle of associating with other congregations locally, regionally and nationally for the purposes of
fellowship and the prosecution of mission
both at home and abroad. The *local church*
may seek advice and guidance from the
wider fellowship which may also serve as an
instrument for stronger churches to make
ministry possible in less well resourced sectors of the community. In some countries
such councils may share authority with the
local church, even as there are Baptist bishops though these do not stand in an *apostolic* succession, exercising a function akin
to that of a superintending minister having
been elected by representatives of the
churches. Baptists as a congregational denomination are close relations of other Congregationalist denominations in the reformed tradition.

JHYB

Conscience

The English (as also French) term 'conscience' is a direct derivation from the Latin
conscientia which is equivalent to the Greek
syneidesis/syneidos. The basic meaning is
'co-knowledge' (cf. Italian *coszienza*, Dutch
geweten, German *Gewissen*), usually understood as 'an inner knowledge about oneself'.
The concept has its place in *anthropology*:
the individual has the capacity to know and
to reflect about what he/she does; hence it is
an important element in making ethical de-

cisions [see *Ethics*]. Conscience has been
defined as an inner court where accusing
and defending arguments are voiced (cf. Ro
2:15; 1Co 4:1-5). Although other cultures
and languages than the Graeco-Roman one
have their own ways of expressing such a
human (apparently universal) capacity, the
traditional Western concept is rooted in a
particular culture. There is no Hebrew
equivalent; the word 'heart' is most often
the location of such decisions (cf. 1Jo 3:19f).
This is reflected also by the fact that the 30
occurrences in the NT are found in the more
Hellenistic writings (Jn, Ac, Ro, 1-2Co, 1-2Ti,
Tit, Heb, 1Pe). Conscience indicates an ethical problem for the individual; there is a
conflict between the norms of the individual
and those of the society in which they live
(usually representing tradition and culture).
Theologically, conscience brings conviction
of *sin* (Jn 8:9; Heb 10:2). Conscience is not
identical to God's voice, as it cannot make
final judgment (1Co 4:4; even pagans have
one, viz. a consciousness of right and wrong:
Ro 2:14f.). A conscience can be 'weak' (1Co
8:7-13), i.e. not yet in accord with the norms
of *Christ*'s *kingdom*. The aim is to have a
'good' or 'pure'/'clean' conscience (e.g. Ac
23:1; 1Pe 3:16-21; 1Ti 1:19, 3:9; Tit 1:15,
parallel to 'mind') indicating that the individual norms are in accord with those of
Christ's kingdom (cf. Heb 13:18; parallel
'good conduct') which accord is a sign of
wholeness. Truthfulness is attested by a 'conscience in the *Holy Spirit*' (Ro 9:1; cf. 2Co
1:12, 4:12 'in truth recommend to every
conscience'). In practice, conflicts of conscience are usually caused by different demands from different 'social contexts' which
is the classic background of problems between *church and state*/society. Insofar as
religious convictions are involved, the Christian stance follows Ac 5:29, 'We must obey
God more than the humans'. Baptists have
always been aware of this conflict, claiming
the prevalence of conscientious decisions;
God's word and will must have preference.
The London Confession of 1644 conceived
of Christians as '...bound to defend...all civil
Laws, although...not actively submitting to
some Ecclesiastical Laws, which...our consciences could not submit to...' (article 49).
To take a more recent example, the *Confession of Faith* of the Baptist Churches in *Po-*

land, 1930 affirmed: 'We feel obliged to be absolutely obedient to all their [civil authority's] rules, providing they do not limit us in our endeavours to fulfil all our Christian duties...We do not see any hindrance – so far as our conscience is concerned – to hold any office with the civil authorities' (article 13).

WP

Conscientious Objectors
[See also *Pacifism and Peace Churches*; *Passive Resistance*]
Conscientious Objectors are persons with a pacifistic conviction, who refuse to enter military training or service, when subjected to compulsory conscription. The term refers positively to the matter of *conscience*, which is central to the universal declaration of *human rights*. Pacifist views may be derived from the ancient texts of Buddhism, Greek Stoicism or Christianity, and since the *Reformation* pacifism has had a number of spokesmen in Europe, not just within the historic peace churches.

Conscious opposition to participating in military service has gradually led to a legal recognition of the right to uphold a pacifist position in most European countries, whether it is for religious, philosophical or political reasons, allowing such persons to serve society in alternative ways, even during war time, when countries often practice general conscription. *Sweden*, a *nation* that since 1814 has followed the doctrine of 'nonalignment in *peace*, aiming at neutrality in war', recognises all types of conscientious objection but a non-combatant civil defence service is compulsory for everyone except for Jehovah's Witnesses.

PMIL

Consecration
See *Dedication*.

Consensus
Consensus can refer to both a concept and a process. In the first it refers to such a basic sharing in doctrine and experience as is necessary to enable joint Christian endeavour to take place. It is a sharing in *Christ* which

recognises each partner as, in some way, part of his great *church*, which both enables and requires witness together.

It also indicates a way of determining policy. Much Christian decision-making, whilst purporting to reflect a process of seeking the mind of Christ, works to parliamentary procedures of proposing and amending motions, adversarial speech-making, and the taking of votes. In recent years such procedures have been queried and it has been suggested that policy making should arrive out of a process of trying to secure consensus, rather than by voting. Voting necessarily sets up antipathy between those in the majority and those in the minority especially when this latter group seems to be in a permanent minority. To secure consensus it may be necessary to repeat a process of debate, having worked on identifying where areas of difficulty lie. Equally it may be agreed by all that the matter can be put to one side rather than dividing the body. Clearly the process needs perceptive moderating gifts so that the person moderating the process is sensitive to different interest groups. Deciding by consensus does not necessarily require unanimity because a group, clearly in the minority, may wish to respond to the interest of the majority by not pressing its point to a division. Agreement to adopt decision-making by consensus has been one way used by the *World Council of Churches* to retain the support of some *Orthodox Churches*.

JHYB

Conservative Evangelicalism
[See also *Evangelical/Evangelicalism – the use of the word in Europe*; *Evangelicalism, Baptists and*]
Although evangelicalism as a movement was shaped in the 18th century, it has always been a coalition of different groups rather than a movement in which participants have been agreed on all issues. In the 19th century evangelicals were often deeply divided over issues of *church and state*. The early 20th century saw an increasing fear among many evangelicals in the USA and *Britain* of the rise of a *social gospel* which, it was suggested by some, might take the place of the evangelical gospel of the *grace* of God. Another

contentious issue was the degree to which Biblical criticism helped in revealing the true meaning of **scripture**, or the extent to which, especially when allied to extreme **liberal theology**, it was used to corrode Biblical **authority**, now seen as offering only human insight. Evangelicals in England were also put on the defensive by the growth of Anglo-Catholic influence.

However, some evangelicals welcomed the possibility of a broader evangelicalism, one which was open to insights from other Christian traditions. These evangelicals became known as 'liberal', by contrast with 'conservative' evangelicals. The more conservative evangelicals looked to the Inter-Varsity Fellowship (IVF – later UCCF), formed in 1928, as a grouping that offered them hope. However, more liberal and more conservative evangelicals continued to work together in the **Evangelical Alliance**. On the whole Baptists have sought to avoid the labels 'liberal' or 'conservative'.

In the period immediately after WWII, there was considerable American interest in the creation of a pan-evangelical body to represent conservative evangelicals. At a conference at Gordon Divinity School in Boston, USA, in 1950, it was recommended to set up an International Association of Evangelicals. The agreed purpose of this body was:

(1) to witness to evangelical and historic Christianity,

(2) to encourage and promote **fellowship** among Evangelicals, and,

(3) to stimulate evangelism and promote united evangelical action in all spheres. A statement of **faith** was produced.

A year later, at a conference at Woudschoten in the Netherlands, the **World Evangelical Fellowship** (WEF) was set up. One of the speakers at Woudschoten was John Stott, who had become Rector of All Souls Church, Langham Place, London, in 1950. John Stott was to become the best-known leader of the world evangelical movement. By this time the labels 'liberal' and 'conservative' were commonly being used to define approaches to scripture rather than to denote differences over other issues. John Stott represented an evangelicalism which was to be conservative in its view of biblical authority, but also open in **ecumenical dialogue** and to social action.

But some conservatives believed that any cooperation with non-evangelicals was to be avoided. Martyn Lloyd-Jones, minister of Westminister Chapel, London, championed, from the 1960s, a **separatist** agenda. The Evangelical Alliances in Europe have sought, by contrast, to foster an inclusive vision among evangelicals. The 21st century saw conservatives insisting on the penal substitutionary theory of the **atonement** as essential to authentic evangelical belief, with more 'open' (now the preferred term – rather than 'liberal') evangelicals, such as a British Baptist, Steve Chalke, arguing for a more flexible theological approach. The differing strands in evangelicalism have continued to be in tension.

Another important line of distinction, especially in North America, is that which distinguishes evangelical from **fundamentalist**, a distinction which because of **mission** activity has also been brought to European shores. The most obvious distinction here is between the **sectarianism** of the fundamentalists who deny the validity of the faith of those who differ from them and the conservative evangelicals who may agonise over the perceived infidelity of those with different emphases, but can still see them as part of the world-wide family of **Jesus Christ**.

IMR

FURTHER READING: D.W. Bebbington, *Evangelicalism in Modern Britain: A History from the 1730s to the 1980s*, Routledge, London, 1995. D.W. Bebbington and Mark A. Noll (eds), *Biographical Dictionary of Evangelicals*, InterVarsity, Leicester and Downers Grove, Il., 2003. J.M. Gordon, *Evangelical Spirituality*, SPCK, London, 1991. C. Price and I.M. Randall, *Transforming Keswick*, OM, Carlisle, 2000. I.M. Randall, *Evangelical Experiences: A Study in the Spirituality of English Evangelicalism, 1918-1939*, Paternoster, Carlisle, 1999. I.M. Randall, *What a Friend we have in Jesus*, DLT, London, 2005.

Consortium of European Baptist Theological Schools (CEBTS)

CEBTS was established at **IBTS**, Prague in 2001. This development marked a significant moment of growth from dependency to interdependency for Baptist **theological education** in Europe. With the collapse of **communism** in 1989 both the **Baptist World**

Alliance and *European Baptist Federation* put in place Theological Assistance Groups to seek to provide help and support to emerging seminaries and theological institutions in Eastern Europe. This help was both financial and professional as lecturers were recruited from western institutions to teach at emerging schools in the East. The move to establish CEBTS in 2001 signified a coming of age of many institutions and a shift from a dependency culture to one of mutual support and encouragement. Today over 28 institutions in Europe and the Middle East are members and engaged in active mutual co-operation, making it a unique *covenanted* organisation concerned with theological education in the Baptist world family.

A general Forum of all the members is held at least once every two years and in between time the work of the organisation is carried forward by an action group. CEBTS promotes exchanges of lecturers, curricula development, transfer of students, organises specialist subject seminars, training of seminary officers – Rectors, Kvestors, Deans and Librarians. CEBTS promotes conferences on theological education and has developed a series of guidelines documents on sabbaticals, terms of employment, e-learning and the *EU* Bologna process.

Particularly successful has been the development within CEBTS of close partnerships between two or more member institution in different parts of Europe and the Middle East.

KGJ

FURTHER READING: Peter F. Penner, *Theological Education as Mission,* IBTS, Prague and Neufeld Verlag, Schwarzenfeld, Germany, 2005. www.cebts.eu. www.ebf.org/about-ebf/divisions/theology-education.php. www.ibts .cz/academics.

Contextual Missiology

[See also *Contextual Theologies; Contextualisation; Missiology; Mission*]

Contextual missiology has the mandate to contextualise the missionary endeavours of the *church*. As the church is taken into the mission of God, it needs to cross various boundaries: geographical, *political*, *sociological*, economic, confessional and many others. The so-called *Great Commission* sends the church out to make *disciples* among all ethnic groups. *Christ*'s disciples model for the missionary church this mission to the different ethnic groups in different contexts. The *incarnation* of Christ demonstrates how the Gospel is embedded in culture, showing Christ as being born into a specific culture, ethnic group, social setting and geo-political situation. Contextual missiology teaches that mission does not consist of taking the gospel, as received in one's own context, and simply imposing it on another context. Being sent with a mission into a specific context, the sent individual/community needs to develop a certain dynamic between the biblical text [see *Bible*], specific context and the faith community in order to be relevant. Contextual missiology is not a colonising concept, bringing all under a uniform model of *faith* in the triune God [see *Trinity*] and his *salvation*. It respects and cares for the God-given multi-contextual world, witnessing to it in a way that is authentic, as a gospel that can be understood and experienced in any context in any situation by any and every person. Such mission leads to an understanding and experience of salvation in any specific context. It forms disciples of the triune God, capable both of ongoing indigenous mission as well as having the capacity to cross borders to continue the mission of God in new situations, a task in which all – every individual believer and every *local church* – are included.

PFP

Contextual Theologies

[See also *Contextual Missiology; Contextualisation; Theology*]

Contextualisation, which began to be applied to theological reflection and the *mission* of the *Church* in the 1970s, represents a significant shift of emphasis in the methods used to think theologically and discern *missiologically* the life and work of the Christian community. From the early 1960s a new way of doing theology was emerging among non-Western churches. Rather than starting with the *dogmatic* tradition elaborated over many centuries in classical theologies, *theologians* from Africa, Asia and Latin America began to experiment with a method that responded to current social, political and cultural concerns as its first priority. Not only were there new regional perspectives but also theologies embracing specific ethnic and gender perspectives (e.g. **Black Theology** and **Feminist Theology**)

Theology, although rooted in and inspired by the **Word of God**, because it is a human endeavour, has always been contextual. It is the attempt to understand and articulate the purposes of God, as these flow from God's nature and activity in the natural world and human history. Although sometimes this elaboration has over-emphasised abstract and theoretical concepts, it has usually reflected particular situations, which have influenced (sometimes unconsciously) the theologies in question. It is often possible to detect, by careful historical analysis, the contemporary considerations which provoked specific theological treatises.

Western theology from the **Reformation** has had to respond to changing intellectual cultures from the scientific revolution of the 17th century through the challenge of the **Enlightenment** to the expansion of knowledge in the 19th century and more particularly the atheistic philosophies of Marx, Nietzsche and Freud. More recently the challenge has come from existential thinkers such as Heidegger, Sartre, Camus, and Jaspers. The cultural shift from confidence in the universal project of modernity to the relativist and **pluralist** musings of the postmodern condition has similarly stimulated a flurry of theological writings. A notable example of theological interest in secular philosophical trends has been the appropriation of ideas in the philosophy of language associated with names like Lévi-Strauss, Wittgenstein and Austin.

Whilst such considerations illustrate the way in which external intellectual developments have provided the context in which the Christian message has to be communicated and understood, the challenge has also come from social and political developments. The most notorious, perhaps, was the Barmen Declaration of 1934, a notable rejoinder to the threat posed by the Nazi regime to the Christian confession of the one Lord, **Jesus Christ**. Earlier the movement known as **Christian socialism** had advocated a political programme, based on socialist principles, to eradicate the degradation of

poverty. Between the wars, culminating in the Oxford Conference of 1938, the **ecumenical** project known as **Life and Work** was engaged in serious theological consideration of issues in **social ethics**.

So, in spite of the impression that is sometimes given, theology in the West was not all centred on internal debates within the Christian community. It reached beyond to address questions of relevance to the whole of society. More recently, Western theologians have turned their attention to issues of the **environment**, conflict and **peace**, multiculturalism, **politics** and the **state**, crime and punishment, *inter alia.* Nevertheless, the irruption of the Church of the non-Western world has significantly altered the whole conceptualisation of theology. In the late 1960s, theologians in direct contact with the living conditions of the **poorest** sectors of society in Latin America began to articulate a theology of liberation [see **Liberation Theology**]. Thinking about the implications for the gospel and the Church of human communities divided by extremes of affluence and misery, led them to conclude that the existence of the poor was a scandal that demanded a strategy of justice rather than a misfortune that called forth charity. Through fresh readings of the Bible and a socio-political analysis based on a neo-**Marxist** critique of economic structures, they argued that God took a **preferential option for the poor** which could be best realised through a socialist-inspired programme of reform. Whilst many of the writers were **Roman Catholic** the Latin American Theological Fraternity addressed the same issues from an **Evangelical** perspective.

Thus was born the famous **hermeneutical** circle, characterised by one theologian as 'the liberation of theology.' According to this approach, there are four principal elements in any authentic process of doing theology. There is the specific context in which the Church finds itself. There is the text of scripture which is the authoritative witness [see **Authority**] to God's acts in **creation**, **redemption** and transformation. Then, between the context and the text, there are crucial tools of interpretation: on one side, the social sciences; on the other, the theological disciplines. Added to these elements is, of course, the interpreter or interpreting community. Genuine theological reflection arises from Christians who are actively engaged with situations that need changing.

Now, this new contextual theology differed from the Western theological tradition in its assessment of the purpose of theology. Whereas the latter was concerned about right theoretical procedures and correct theological foundations (*orthodoxy*), when engaging with the context, the former insisted that discerning right action (*orthopraxis*) was the overriding consideration. Thus theology does not exist to provide just a correct theory or analysis of reality, but as a means of orienting and supporting the Christian community in its walk of obedience in the ways of the Lord. Liberation theology saw itself as a means of reading the signs of the times, i.e. of understanding, in the light of concrete realities, the *calling* of God to context-specific discipleship.

Soon, other theologies employing similar methods arose in other parts of the world. During the *apartheid* regime in South Africa, a liberation theology was developed, which saw institutional racism as the overriding focus for authentic theological work. As one writer put the matter, the challenge of enforced separate development of different races marked 'the end of innocence' for theology. In other parts of Africa, issues of culture became central to the theological agenda. Questions were raised about *healing*, the ancestors, family life, nation-building, and the nature of Christ in Africa. In Asia, Minjung Theology in Korea, the Theology of Struggle in the Philippines, Dalit Theology in India all addressed the issue of the poor and the oppressed. Hugely significant has been the debate about how the Christian community should relate to other *faith* communities. Fundamental questions about mission, *evangelism*, *dialogue* and collaboration have become a major preoccupation of theological thought.

Contextual theologies relate to at least two aspects of Christian life and thought held dear in the *Anabaptist* tradition: theology is the task of the whole community and theology has to be reflection on the meaning of radical *discipleship*. Theology should not be confined to an exercise that is located primarily in academic institutions. In so far as Christians are relating their fundamental

convictions to their experience of life, they are engaging in a theological task. As they reflect on the Christian basis for their practice, their theology is by nature contextual. Discipleship is an exploration of what is involved in following in the way of Jesus Christ. Intrinsically it is committed to action as the way of obedience to Jesus' call to 'come', 'see', 'follow' and 'go'. Thus, theology is authentic, only in so far as it is rooted in and accountable to a community committed to serving the nations through evangelism, prophetic witness [see *Prophecy*] and a *ministry* to the poor, the outcast and the victimised.

JAK

Contextualisation

[See also *Contextual Missiology*; *Contextual Theologies*]

Contextualisation derives from the conciliar debates within the **World Council of Churches** in the 1970s; the Theological **Education** Fund published a document entitled *s* in 1972 following on a consultation at the **Ecumenical** Institute at Bossey in 1971 on '*Dogmatic* or Contextual *Theology*?' In the context of the postcolonial era [see *Colonialism*] ways were sought as to how to do and to live theology in any context, an appropriate search given Christianity's *incarnational* origins. Hand in hand with this evaluation of context, there emerged local theologies, starting in the former colonies with different varieties of *liberation theology* at the forefront. In spite of the critical response that most *conservative evangelicals* gave it at first, the concept found its way also into the groups that belong to the **Lausanne movement**. They speak about it in terms of culture and context. Indeed, the goal of contextualisation has an *evangelical* tone, for its aim is that 'in so far as is humanly possible, an understanding of what it means that *Jesus Christ*, the Word is authentically experienced in each and every human situation'.

Contextualisation questions any monopolar reading of the biblical text [see *Bible*] from which an *orthodox* theology is developed that is to be once and for ever fixed and universally valid that, at most, may need to be adapted to a specific culture and context. Contextual epistemology goes beyond adaptation to the culture; it calls for a multi-linear reading of the text and a contextual, local theology. Contextualisation of theology is, then, not static but dynamic, being embedded in a concrete local situation and specific time. Local contextualised interpretations of the gospel should then lead, as Paul Hiebert and other *missiologists* suggest, to a global interpretation in a *dialogue* between the local and the global.

Other concepts, related to contextualisation, are referred to as incarnational theology or missiology. The term incarnational refers to the prologue of John's gospel where the Logos becomes flesh and lives in a concrete culture, time, context and geography. In this concept, it is expected that there is a core of belief/theology that needs to be retained and that needs to find its way into any culture. Another term, coming originally from the *Catholic* context, is the term inculturalisation. Here the Gospel is presented in a specific culture and goes beyond accommodation of the Gospel. The translational model attempts to communicate the message of the Gospel as close as possible to the original while translating it into contextually understandable ways. This and other terms are present buzz words, and with their attempts to contextualise the gospel and, at the same time, not to lose track, becoming dominated by theology or by context and slipping into *syncretism* or dogmatism.

PFP

Contraception
See *Birth Control*.

Conventions
See *Assembly, General – as governing body of Union*; *Ecclesiology (Church Polity)*; *Unions/Conventions*.

Conversion
[See also *New Birth*; *Regeneration*]
David Bebbington makes Conversionism, alongside Biblicism [see *Bible*], Crucicentrism [see *Atonement*] and Activism, a vital aspect of his *Evangelical* quadrilateral. That means that at the heart of the Evangelical experience there is need for a well-defined

change of life – a *repentance* of *sin* and a commitment to *Christ* as personal Saviour – which, whilst it may be the culmination of a longer process, marks the beginning of an individual's Christian biography. Such an emphasis came out of the *revivalist* movements of the 18th century: whereas in the earlier period, the *Puritan* home nurtured growth into Christian maturity. The emphasis was now on the possibility of somebody entering church as a most profane sinner and leaving it saved from sin, and thereafter for ever one of God's *saints* [see *Salvation and Soteriology*]. This was to be an experience endlessly repeated at home in the fruits of revival and *mission*, as it was also at the centre of the modern missionary movement: *Carey*'s heart was set on the 'conversion of the heathens'.

In the NT, the keynote to all Jesus' teaching was the double command 'Repent and Believe', that is, the *call* is to turn *from* sin and to turn *to* God. Thus *metanoia* ['repentance' or 'turning round'] means much more than just a change of mind; rather it indicates a fundamental re-orientation of the whole personality. Response to this summons is itself the gift of God rather than any human achievement (Ac 5:31). Thus it can also be regarded as the human experience that corresponds to the divine process of *regeneration*; as we turn to God, so he in his *grace* takes that turning and creates out of it a new life in Christ. In the NT these two processes come together in the *baptism* of the new believer, a *sacrament* which symbolises [see *Sign and Symbol*] both the turning to Christ, and the new birth/new life which God in his grace gives to the one who in a watery grave testifies to the *death* of a sinful and selfish past, from which, forgiven, they rise to incorporation into Christ, and the gift of the *Spirit* for the new life ahead. Thus it is claimed that conversion is completed in regeneration, which itself is revealed in the living of a holy life [see *Holiness*], which has constantly to be renewed.

Whether conversion is experienced suddenly, or whether it is the fruit of some longer process of seeking or maturation, it is 'an indispensable foundation to Christian believing'. Contrary to the hyper-*Calvinism* of a by-gone age, which taught that *preaching* for conversions was to steal the prerogative of the Holy Spirit, the NT witness is that the demand for personal conversion was at the heart of *apostolic* preaching, and that it is therefore a crucial task for today's *church*.

Conversion has also its community and moral dimensions. Whilst a personal experience is intrinsic to the understanding of conversion, and conversion has to do with the individual receiving the gift of eternal salvation, the converted sinner is immediately made a *member* of the community of the church, and there becomes part of a corporate identity which is set on *kingdom* work – to work for the establishment of the rule of Christ in the life of this world. Even as the converted sinner must always be different from what he or she was prior to conversion, so the new saint is also called to change the world, for it too needs conversion, to reflect more completely the will of God here on earth as it is manifested in *heaven*.

JHYB

FURTHER READING: W. Barclay, *Turning to God*, Westminster, Philadelphia, 1964. D.W. Bebbington, *Evangelicalism in Modern Britain*, Unwin Hyman, London and Boston, 1992.

Cooperative Baptist Fellowship (CBF)

This is a fellowship of approximately 1,800 Baptist churches with a *membership* in excess of 250,000 people drawn from throughout the United States of America. The CBF Mission statement is 'serving Christians and Churches as they discover and fulfil their God-given *mission*'. It came into being in 1990 out of the *Southern Baptist Convention* and originally consisted of churches and individuals who had become concerned at the direction, leadership style and mission policies developed following on from what is often described as the '*fundamentalist* resurgence' within the SBC. One of the original and deciding factors in the establishment of the CBF was the decision of some Southern Baptist Missionaries to resign from the Foreign Mission Board in the light of the defunding of the Seminary at *Rüschlikon, Switzerland*, breaking an earlier agreement with the *European Baptist Federation*. The CBF was formed to raise money to employ them as missionaries in Europe and to create

a support structure for them.

From the beginning the CBF was a mission agency supporting workers in the USA and *overseas* and serving as a place for encouragement and renewal of those hurt or disenfranchised by the new SBC leadership. It soon developed beyond that initial activity into a *fellowship* enabling mission in a wide variety of ways. Through a Coordinating Council elected by an annual Assembly the CBF encouraged the formation of, and has provided support for, new centres of *theological* formation in the USA as well as the *IBTS* seminary of the EBF. Within a few years CBF gained recognition by the US Government for the accreditation of *chaplains* to the Armed Forces, and they also began accrediting chaplains in medical work and other significant areas. Through mission work in the USA, new churches were established relating only to the CBF.

The organisation developed a resource centre in Atlanta and continued supporting mission work in Europe and has been a prime partner in the EBF Indigenous Missionary Project. In 2003 the CBF became a member body of the *Baptist World Alliance*. It holds an annual Assembly and publishes a *magazine* bi-monthly called *Fellowship!*

KGJ

FURTHER READING: www.thefellowship.info.

COPEC

See *Conference on Christian Politics, Economics and Citizenship*.

CPCE

See *Community of Protestant Churches in Europe*.

Council of Europe

The Council of Europe was an idea promoted by the late Sir Winston Churchill in a famous speech in Zürich in 1946. Drawing together 49 member states in 'geographic' Europe, it is much larger than the *European Union*. Founded in 1949 in the aftermath of WWII, its mission is to seek to develop throughout Europe common and democratic principles based on the European Convention on *Human Rights* and other reference texts on the protection of individuals. It draws together Parliamentarians and government ministers firstly in an assembly, and then in ministerial meetings. It aims to protect human rights, promote *pluralist democracies* and the rule of just laws. It seeks to promote awareness and encouragement of the development of Europe's cultural identity and diversity whilst seeking to find commonly acceptable solutions to the challenges facing European society, such as discrimination against *minorities*, xenophobia, intolerance, terrorism, trafficking in human beings, organised crime and corruption, cybercrime, and *violence* against *children*. It is trying to lay down ground rules whereby issues in *bioethics*, such as *cloning*, may be handled. It is concerned to consolidate democratic stability in Europe by backing *political*, legislative and constitutional reform. The current Council of Europe's political mandate was defined by the third Summit of Heads of State and Government, held in Warsaw in May 2005. Most countries in geographic Europe are members, except *Belarus*, which has applicant status. Baptists have valued the council as being a wider forum especially concerned with human rights and *religious freedom*, bringing together former soviet bloc countries and Western liberal democracies. The *EBF* in more recent years, using its status as a Swiss-registered Verein, has sought to engage with the Council of Europe as a recognised *non-governmental organisation*.

KGJ

FURTHER READING: www.coe.int.

Councils
See *Synods and Church Councils*.

Councils of Churches
See *National Councils of Churches*.

Covenants, Theology of
[See also *Creeds, Covenants and Confessions of Faith*; *New Covenant, The*; *Theology*]
The idea of 'covenant' [*berit*] took various forms in the *faith* of Ancient *Israel*, as found in the OT. A basic conviction was that God had initiated an agreement with persons for their benefit, and so covenant is an expression of God's loving mercy [*hesed*]. While covenant was thought to apply normatively to the nation of *Israel* or its representatives, some Israelite *traditions* apply it to all created beings (Ge 8:16). Some covenants were portrayed as unconditional from God's side, such as those with Abraham and the Davidic kings (Ge 12:1-4; 2Sa 7) while others were presented as conditional on human response, such as the tradition of the covenant made at Sinai through Moses. However, differences about covenant tended to merge, since God is portrayed by the Israelite prophets [see *Prophecy*] as willing to re-make a conditional covenant broken from the human side, and unconditional covenants still require human obedience. The growing conviction, especially within the 'Deuteronomic' movement, that human beings were unable to keep the covenant requirements, led to the *eschatological hope* of a 'new covenant' in which God would enable human hearts to respond to God's offer of life (Jer 31:31-4; Dt 30:5-6). NT writers see this promise fulfilled through the *death* and *resurrection* of *Christ* (2Co 3:6). At the centre of the *Lord's Supper*, in particular, is the announcement of a new covenant between God and all humanity sealed through the blood of Christ (Mk 14:24; 1Co 11:25).

At the time of the *Reformation*, the concept of covenant was widely used to express the relation of God with individual believers, local congregations and *national churches*. Reflecting the biblical [see *Bible*] diversity over covenant, *Calvinists* tended to stress the unconditional nature of God's covenant with the elect [see *Election*], while *Arminians* stressed that the covenant was conditional on human response, but these approaches also overlapped (Brachlow, 1988: pp.31-55). During the period of the English Reformation, supporters of the established church tended to appeal to the unconditional nature of covenant to affirm that God was sustaining a relation with the *national church*, while *Separatists* and Dissenters – Baptists among them – judged that the covenant with the existing church was conditional, broken and void, so that new congregations needed to be founded which were living in obedience to God's will

Four basic strands of the covenant idea can be discerned in the rich tapestry of thought among **Puritans** and Dissenters at that time, and they are still valuable for covenant theology today. First, 'covenant' referred to an eternal covenant of *grace* which God has made with human beings for their *salvation* in Jesus Christ. *Calvin* was influential in developing this idea, which for him included the restriction of the covenant to the elect. Second, the divine covenant referred to a kind of 'transaction' between the Persons of the triune God [see *Trinity*], in which the Son was envisaged as consenting to the will of the Father to undertake the work of salvation. Third, the term could refer to an agreement which God makes corporately with the **Church**, or with particular churches. Here writers often appealed to the covenant formula of God with Israel – 'I will be their God and they shall be my people'.

These three aspects of covenant all have a 'vertical' direction, between God and *humankind*, but a fourth introduced a 'horizontal' aspect between believers themselves. Separatists and Dissenters introduced the idea of a covenant as an agreement entered upon by **church members** when a particular *local church* was founded, and subsequently by new members on joining it. A local church covenant thus typically combined the third and fourth dimensions of covenant, with members promising to 'give themselves up to God' and to 'give themselves to each other', to 'walk in the ways of the Lord' and to 'walk together'. *John Smyth* (c.1570-1612) defines a church by this way of gathering it: 'A visible **communion** of Saincts [see *Saints*] is of two, three or more Saincts joyned together by covenant with God and themselves' (Smyth, 1915 [1607]: p.252). Already before Smyth, in the thought of the Separatist Robert Browne (1550-1633), God's making of a covenant with God's church is simultaneous with the making of covenant *by* the church, so that the act of local covenant-making is not simply a human promise, but is the gracious act of God to take the church 'to be his people' and God's 'promise to be our God and Saviour' (Browne, 1953 [1582]: pp.422-3).

This integration between divine and human making of covenant is the basis for the Baptist conviction that through covenant a local community is under the direct rule of Christ, and so has been given the 'seals of the covenant' – that is, the power to elect its own **ministry** to celebrate the **sacraments** of **baptism** and the Lord's Supper, and to administer spiritual **discipline**. These privileges are also a sharing in the threefold ministry of Christ as prophet, priest and king. They do not derive from any human view of the '**autonomy**' of a local church (which is not a traditional Baptist concept) but from being under the rule of Christ as covenant-maker.

John Smyth, and later Baptists, took a creative step beyond the fusing of the third and fourth aspects of covenant by integrating these with the first sense as well, God's eternal covenant of grace. As B.R. White maintains, 'it seems that for [Smyth], in the covenant promise of the local congregation the eternal covenant of grace became contemporary, and [human] acceptance of it was actualised in history' (White, 1971: p.128). Benjamin Keach in the later 17th century commends the idea that the church covenant is an occasion for the believer to 'enter personally' into the eternal covenant, while on God's part the church covenant is a 're-newing of the same [eternal] covenant'. (Keach, 1698: pp.211, 296). The two sides of this mystery of divine grace and human free response [see *Free Will*; *Freedom of Conscience*] were also, of course, kept in balance by the act of believers' baptism. On the one hand this was a 'seal' of the covenant given graciously to the church by God; on the other hand there was need to 'seal back the covenant unto the Lord' by personal faith and consent (Smyth, 1915 [1609]: p.645). This led Baptists such as Smyth to rule out **infant baptism**, whereas paedobaptists appealed to a different theology of a covenant, in which infant baptism was a sign of a covenant promised by God to the **children** of faithful parents.

The integration of the 'eternal' covenant with the local should also lead us to reconsider the second aspect of covenant, an eternal covenant within God's own triune life. As developed in the later Calvinist tradition, we may agree with Karl Barth that it gives an undesirable picture of two divine subjects having legal dealings with each other over a 'transaction' of **atonement**, which undermines the nature of atonement as a dynamic act of forgiving *love* [see *Forgiveness*]. But we might also think, with Barth, that God's making of covenant with created sons and daughters eternally shapes the relations between Father and Son in the love of the *Spirit*, so that the covenant of grace with human beings is inseparable from the communion between the Persons (Barth, 1974[1953]: pp.22-44, 54-66). Unlike Barth, we might call this a 'covenant in God' (Fiddes, 2003: pp.33-7). Such a vision deepens the first and third aspects of covenant, and when they are integrated with the fourth (the church covenant) it should be clear that the Baptist idea of the church as a covenant community is not that of a merely 'voluntary society'. It is a *'gathered* community' because God has gathered it, in accord with the scriptural witness to a God who has taken the initiative in making covenant.

Early Baptists used the 'covenant' idea to support their claim for continuity with the people of God in Israel and the early church. But, while the concept is rooted in scripture, we can see that they were using it in new and creative ways. Indeed, the very diversity of biblical ideas about covenant underlines that covenant is not a legal contract, but a relationship of trust in which there must be an openness to the future. In modern times Baptists have continued to develop the concept of covenant, and in particular to use the concept for the *associating* of churches together. Churches are increasingly conceived as covenanting together at a regional and national level, just as members covenant in a local community (BUGB Faith and Unity Executive, 1994: pp.4-14). While this extension of covenant is not found directly among early Baptists, they did think of churches as living under the 'one rule' of Christ as covenant-maker.

PF

FURTHER READING: Karl Barth, *The Doctrine of Reconciliation. Church Dogmatics*, IV, 1, T&T Clark, Edinburgh, 1974. Stephen Brachlow, *The Communion of Saints. Radical Puritan and Separatist Ecclesiology 1570-1625*, Oxford University Press, Oxford, 1988. Faith and Unity Executive Committee, *The Nature of the Assembly and the Council of the Baptist Union of Great Britain*, BUGB, Didcot, 1994. Paul S. Fiddes, *Tracks and Traces. Baptist Identity in Church and Theology*, Paternoster, Milton Keynes, 2003. Benjamin Keach, 'The Display of Glorious Grace, Or, the Covenant of Peace Opened', London, 1698. A. Peel and L. Carson (eds), *The Writings of Robert Harrison and Robert Browne*, Allen and Unwin, London, 1953. B.R. White, *The English Separatist Tradition. From the Marian Martyrs to the Pilgrim Fathers*, Oxford University Press, Oxford, 1971. W.T. Whitley (ed), *The Works of John Smyth*, 2 Volumes, Cambridge University Press, Cambridge, 1917.

Creation

[See also *Creation and Science*]

In the OT the word *bara* is used meaning 'to create'. The word is exclusively used for a divine creation. The equivalent word in the NT is *ktizein*, which is used both for the creation of the world, and the new creation in *Christ*.

Both the OT and NT offer many stories of how the world was created, providing at least four different aspects of creation. Central to all of them is that the creative initiative is a wholly divine initiative:

(1) God is presented as the almighty creator in Ge 1:1-2, 3 creating the world systematically by uttering his word. **Humankind** is portrayed as the climax of creation. The story is told through a week, legitimating the celebration of the **Sabbath** as part of the created order.

(2) In Ge 2:4-25 the creation is presented in the shape of a garden metaphor, stressing the earthliness of humankind and the cooperation of God and man in the creation and naming of the animals.

(3) In addition the creation can also be related to the conflict between God and evil [see **Devil**]. Ps 74:12-17 typically associates creation with the killing of Leviathan.

(4) Finally, the NT stresses Jesus' part as sharing in the processes of creation (Jn 1:1-3). This is probably derived from the portrayal of wisdom in Pr 8:22-31 and the Logos in Greek thought.

Discussion has often centred on whether creation was *ex nihilo* ['out of nothing'] or not. Both alternatives may be adduced from the **Bible**. The Logos rhetoric of Jn 1:1-3 implies that creation ultimately was *ex nihilo* since the Logos, along with God, is discerned from creation as a creative power, and not being created material. But especially the above mentioned 'fight metaphor', and (if Ge 1:1 is read as a headline for the whole text) the first creation story, opens with a creation on the basis of matter already existing.

The creation can also be seen as God rearranging chaos into cosmos. This is clearly the case in Ge 1:1-2, 3 where creation is neatly presented as a one week tidying up project, creating a sustainable *environment*, a cosmos. This is also the case with the story of Leviathan. Significantly the use of this motif in scripture presents the ordering of the cosmos as an ongoing endeavour by the Creator; he is still dividing the seasons (Ps 74:17) and controlling the ocean (Pr 8: 29).

This leads on to a picture of a present, personal Creator taking responsibility for his creation. The *universalism* of this message is apparent. The exilic community embraced this as an important message confronting the massive cultural and religious powers of their time. DeuteroIsaiah especially stresses the presence of the Creator, who supports the exilic community against their oppressors (Isa 43:1). Our existence as created beings can also be seen as an ethical imperative [see *Ethics*] demanding our acknowledgment of God as creator [see *Natural Law*].

The created order is, according to the NT, genuinely good (1Ti 4:4), but it is *suffering* under the paradigm of evil, groaning for the *eschatological* liberation to come Ro 8:19-23. This liberation, also part of the OT message (Isa 65:17), is portrayed as a new creation in Christ (Rev 21:1). In this way the message of the OT and NT starts and ends with creation.

KTB

FURTHER READING: Bernhard W. Anderson, *Creation versus chaos: the reinterpretation of mythical symbolism in the Bible*, Fortress, Philadelphia, 1987. Richard J. Clifford and John J. Collins (eds), 'Creation in the Biblical Traditions' in *The Catholic Biblical Quarterly: Monograph series; 24*, Catholic Biblical Association of America, Washington, DC, 1992.

Creation and Science

[See also *Creation*; *Science and Faith*]
The biblical account [see *Bible*] presents us with a universe that is ordered; good; the creation of a faithful God whose character and *grace* are revealed in all that he has made. The first account culminates in *worship* and the second in relationship. After the *Fall* and the Noah flood God made a *covenant* with Noah and all of creation, which is celebrated in worship.

The climax of God's initial acts of creation are human beings [see *Humankind*]. They are created male and female; in the image of God, *imago Dei*; from the material of creation; they are In-breathed by God; and are commissioned as stewards [see *Stewardship*] and co-creators.

From a theological standpoint we assert: creation is *ex nihilo*; God is revealed as omnipotent and omniscient; God is transcendent and immanent. He is Alpha and Omega, before the beginning and after the end of the universe as we know it.

We recognise a sacramental universe, that is to say, the universe is a visible expression of God's power, faithfulness, grace and *love*. Such a view supports a natural *theology* that maintains that we can learn about God from our observations of the universe (see Ro 1:20).

Our scientific understanding of creation is complementary, often supporting our theological affirmations, but also challenging us to discover more about the God whom we worship.

The scientific theory of a Big Bang beginning to the universe, confirms that time and space come into being with creation, which accords with the views of Augustine, and does not therefore intrinsically conflict with the biblical record, operating as it does at a different level of cause and effect. Science also recognises that the universe will come to an end as an environment in which carbon-based life may survive. The end of the universe will either be collapse as gravity overcomes expansion or a continued expansion through which all energy is used up.

Science has recognised that the universe has clear evidence of design and a fine tuning of the conditions that led to its origin. Cosmologists speak of an Anthropic Principle, which suggests that the universe had to be as old as it is, as big as it is, and with the evolving history that is observed, for human beings to have developed on planet Earth.

Creationism is an aspect of Christian belief that considers the Genesis account of creation to be an accurate history of the first six days of the universe's story. Considering the chronology of events in the OT, the universe is considered to have been brought into being some 6,000-8,000 years ago. Apart from the discrepancies with scientific research, there are a number of important biblical and theological questions raised by the claims of Creationism. Some of the most important are:

- The interpretation of Ge 1-11, which is taken to be literally true. Biblical interpretation of these chapters would suggest that they are poetic or hymnic, making polemical and theological statements in opposition to the contemporary Babylonian, Canaanite, Ugaritic and Egyptian myths.

- The suggestion of a universe and Earth that are merely 8,000 years old contradicts all the evidence that comes from scientific research. If we accept the creationist argument that God created a universe which appeared to be old, we are in danger of finding God to be deceitful. If on the other hand we accept the argument that before the Noah flood the creative processes were very fast, but that since the flood they have operated at the speeds we now observe, we are in danger of positing a God who is unfaithful.

- If we take the view that the variety of animals and plants did not evolve but were the special creations of God, we are in danger of suggesting an interventionist model of God. The problem raised by a God who intervenes, is the question of why he does not intervene to prevent an Auschwitz or an Asian Tsunami.

There is no conflict between science and *faith*, their observations of the universe in which we live are complementary. To use Albert Einstein's words: 'Religion without science is blind, and science without religion limps.'

JDW

FURTHER READING: John Weaver, *In the Begin-*

ning God, Smith and Helwys, Macon, Ga. and Regent's Park College, Oxford, 1994. John Weaver, *Earthshaping, Earthkeeping: A Doctrine of Creation*, SPCK/Lynx, London,1999.

Credalism

For Baptists the negative form of this term – non-credalism – has been of great importance. Reflecting on the fact that *creeds* had been used to expel them from *state churches* and then to persecute their tender *consciences*, Baptists became suspicious of the role played by creeds in the life of the church – as a criterion for disciplining those who did not conform. To make matters worse they observed that some of those who subscribed formally to the articles of the church did not in practice adhere to these positions and were left alone by the *bishops* so whilst *state churches* were patronised by latitudinarians, that is those with minimum belief commitments, *nonconformists* suffered from their conscientious upholding of what they saw as gospel truth. The great Salters Hall Debate of 1719 added another note: some of those present, including nearly all the Particular Baptists were prepared to subscribe trinitarian [see *Trinity*] articles, but there were those including nearly all the General Baptists [see *England*] who said that the *scriptures* themselves were their only standard of belief: a creed said, with the *authority* of the *church*, either less than or more than scripture; in both of which cases they preferred to take their stand with scripture rather than with the decrees of human *synods* or councils. Later as *theologians* began to explore the nature of religious language even devout believers began to be worried about the ability of language to convey the experience of God's *grace* and encounter with his *Spirit*: spiritual reality went beyond the capacities of human language to explain or convey it.

On the other hand Baptists have developed their own confessions of faith and covenants stating both the beliefs and practices of the church. One of these, the so-called Orthodox Creed of the General Baptists of 1678, stated in Article XXXVIII that the three creeds of the church – the *Apostles*, Nicene and Athanasian –'ought thoroughly to be received and believed.', as consonant with scripture and for the edification of the Christian family. In the same vein Alexander McLaren called on the delegated to the first Congress of the *Baptist World Alliance* in 1905 to join with him in reciting the Apostle's Creed 'to rid the world of considerable misunderstanding about the Baptists and stop a good deal of slander'. Dissenters they might be but they wanted to make public their claim to be part of the worldwide Church of *Jesus Christ* through the ages.

JHYB

Creeds, Covenants and Confessions of Faith

[See also *New Covenant, The*]

Whilst Baptists have produced many covenants and confessions of faith, they have been suspicious of creeds per se [see *Credalism*]. The early confessions of faith composed by Baptists in the 17th century were as much concerned to show how much they shared with the mainstream churches as to spell out the areas in which they differed. Thus the 1644 Confession is titled 'the confession of Faith of those churches which are commonly (though falsely) called *Anabaptists*.' It was republished in 1646, 1651, 1652, and 1653, and revised in 1677, taking advantage of the Westminster Confession as the best statement of the *reformed faith* in *England*, becoming known as the Second London Confession, which secured approval by the Particular Baptist Assembly in 1689. General Baptist Confessions appeared in 1651, 1654 and 1660 and in 1678 they produced The Orthodox Creed, so-called, which is clearly concerned to spell out their *Christological* and Trinitarian [see *Trinity*] commitment.

The concept of Covenant is an important Biblical concept [see *Bible*]. Unlike a human contract this cannot be negotiated but represents God's gracious initiative moving towards his people in promise at successive junctures in *Jewish* history, though successively Israel proves unfaithful and breaks the terms of the covenant. These failing covenants of the OT are replaced in the NT by the everlasting covenant sealed in *Christ*'s blood. All this is background to what happens when believers covenant together to form a *local church*, or a group of local churches seek *fellowship* with one another in forming an *association*. There is considerable overlap between covenants and confessions, with many covenants embracing a confession of faith before moving into laying down the ground rules as to how a covenant community is to govern its corporate life. The American Charles Deweese defines a church covenant as 'a series of written pledges based on the Bible which *church members* voluntarily make to God and to one another regarding their basic moral and spiritual commitments and the practice of their *faith*.' New members were often required to recite this on being admitted into membership and very often the whole church would recite the covenant on say the first *communion* of a new year and re-pledge their commitment to it. Matters dealt with on the *discipleship* side of a covenant would be to obey the commandments, maintain the faith, to do everything possible to uphold the *ministry* and *mission* of the church, to be regular in *worship* especially the celebration of the Lord's Supper, to respect the *Sabbath* day, to make appropriate financial commitment to the church including the maintenance of the ministry [see *Tithing*], at the same time pledging *prayer* support and loyalty to the *pastor*. Church members were to undertake mutual *pastoral* concern for fellow believers in the local church, making practical provision for the *poor* and bearing one another's burdens, to give a good example of godliness within the family, to engage in hospitality, always 'to walk in a way and manner becoming to the gospel', maintaining the strictest honesty in business, to eschew 'vain amusements and diversions', and finally 'to receive such, and only such, into communion with us as in a judgment of charity we think are born again.'

Many *unions*/conventions in the *EBF* have their own confessions and covenants – in addition to the early British confessions Lumpkin reproduces confessions from *Germany* (1944), *Sweden* (1861), *France* (1879/1924), the *Netherlands* and *Russia* (1884), and Deweese cites covenants from France (1879) and Sweden (1974) together with a statement on the obligations of church members from Russia (1985).

JHYB

FURTHER READING: Charles W. Deweese, *Baptist Church Covenants*, Broadman, Nashville, Tn., 1990. W.L. Lumpkin, *Baptist Confessions of Faith*, Judson, Valley Forge, Pa., 1969.

Cremation
See *Funerals*.

Croatia, Baptist history in

The roots of Croatian Baptists are to be found in the work of Bible *colporteurs*, some of whom were part of *J.G. Oncken*'s *missionary* outreach. The first gatherings in homes in Zagreb, led by Heinrich Meyer, were documented in 1872-73. In 1883, a group met in Daruvar under the leadership of Johann (not Filip as some authors suggest) Lotz. The first Baptist church, though not officially recognised, was founded in 1891 in Zagreb by Ivan Zrinšćak, Stjepan Bedeković and others. Paradoxically, WWI helped to spread Baptist convictions, for some soldiers (Aleksa Novak, Đuro Vezmar, Josip Baluban) who had served in *Hungary* and *Russia*, returned home as Baptists and shared their new-found *faith*. Some former American immigrants, Jovo Jekić and Milan Brkić, also returned as Baptists. The first Serbo-Croatian conference, charged with developing a structure for future work, was held in Daruvar in 1921. Better organisation in the years 1922-39 led to an expansion of the work under the leadership of Vinko Vacek, sponsored by the *SBC* Foreign Mission Board, after Vacek returned from the USA in 1922, when the number of Croatian Baptists grew from 70 to 600. Croatian Baptists participated in the Yugoslavian Baptist Union from its foundation in1922 with Vacek becoming its leader, travelling extensively throughout the country to found churches and *mission stations* with the first Baptist *chapels* built in Mošćenica (1924) and Mačkovec (1926).

During WWII, when Baptists were outlawed, some buildings were closed and destroyed. Whilst, the majority of Croatian Baptists continued to meet secretly, the forced expulsion of all ethnic German Baptists in 1944 greatly weakened them. After the war, Baptist work within the Serbo-Croatian Conference of the Yugoslavian Baptist Union resumed under the leadership of Josip Horak and Franjo Klem, but the *Communist* government determinedly attempted to limit the influence of religion, imprisoning some Baptists as spies. In 1953, however, the government abandoned its rigid religious policy.

During the rapid process of post-war urbanisation, Baptists were able to establish new churches and missions in growing industrial centres such as Sisak, Rijeka, Karlovac, and Osijek. The Baptist Seminary opened in Zagreb in 1954, moved to Daruvar in 1955, and finally moved to Novi Sad (Serbia) in 1957. Since 1955, youth congresses have been held regularly. Croatian Baptists have been involved in publication work and participated in indigenous mission projects within the Yugoslavian Baptist Union. In the 1970s and 80s Croatian Baptists became increasingly recognised by both *Catholic* and secular institutions, partly due to *Billy Graham*'s visit to Zagreb in 1967 and the *evangelistic* project, EURO 70. Cooperation with other *Protestant* churches developed and in 1976 Baptists and *Lutherans* founded the Protestant *Theological* Faculty in Zagreb. Several new churches both in the countryside and on the Adriatic Coast were opened in these years. Theological differences (concerning Biblical interpretation [see *Bible*], *ecumenical* cooperation and the *charismatic movement*) and tensions relating to the vision of future mission work persisted among various ethnic groups within the Yugoslavian Baptist Union until the end of the Yugoslavian Federation.

When, in 1991 the Yugoslavian Baptist Union ceased, by common consent of all its members, to exist, an independent Croatian Baptist Union was formed. In the new *political* context Croatian Baptists made efforts to both establish new churches and support existing ones, as well as being involved in relief work among war refugees. Welcome assistance came from the wider Baptist family, including the Canadian Baptists, the Southern Baptists (USA), the *European Baptist Federation* and the *Baptist World Alliance*. Today, the *union* has approximately 2,100 members in 60 churches and mission stations. The priorities of the union are theological *education* and *women's* and *youth work*, but several churches are also active in publishing, humanitarian and other social projects.

RK

Cross, The
See *Atonement*.

Crown Rights of the Redeemer
See *Lord of the Church and the Crown Rights of the Redeemer*.

Crucifixion, The
See *Atonement*.

Crusade Evangelism
[See also *Evangelism and Baptist Churches; Evangelism, Theology of; Evangelist*]
Crusade evangelism has its roots in the evangelical *revival* of the 18th century. Renewal movements, whether *Methodist, Pietist* or Baptist, used this approach to evangelise nominal Christians to lead them back to a personal relationship with God. The term 'crusade evangelism' has nothing to do with the crusades organised by the *Roman Catholic* Church in the Middle Ages. European languages, other than English, do not at all use the term crusade for such events, but translate it as mass evangelism, tent evangelism, etc. The language of evangelistic campaigns has similar military overtones and is equally unhelpful.

These evangelistic campaigns have played a key role in the development of the *conservative evangelical* movement in Europe and throughout the whole world. Travelling evangelists often preached outside of traditional *church buildings*, in the city, on a field, in a city hall, in theatres, and later in tents and on *sports* fields among other places where very large audiences could be gathered to listen to evangelistic *preaching* which looked for a visible response from those convicted of *sin* and seeking *salvation*. Such an approach was very different from the reticence of the high-*Calvinists* of an earlier period who were very reluctant to

invite individuals to respond to the gospel message lest not all present could be numbered amongst the elect [see *Election*], whilst they also believed that the task of alerting the human soul to its need essentially belonged to the *Holy Spirit* not any human preacher.

The concept of mass evangelisation was very powerful in the 19th and the first part of the 20th centuries with its methodology developed and given focus by North American evangelists who developed it to perfection as a key evangelistic strategy. Charles Finney, one of its great preachers, provided the movement with an essentially *Arminian theology*. *Missionaries* and famous international evangelists, sometimes taking the name of revivalists, and increasingly coming from the USA, travelled through different countries and continents 'conducting revivals' and proclaiming the Gospel, inviting and leading hundreds and thousands and even millions to *faith* in *Christ*. Amongst the most famous were D.L. Moody and R.A. Torrey, who with their accompanying musicians, Sankey and Alexander also developed a new *hymnody* for evangelism.

The most famous evangelist of the second half of the 20th century was the Baptist, *Billy Graham*. He visited many countries of the world, including various parts of Europe. Graham was involved in Western Europe soon after WWII and received permission to hold evangelistic mass meetings in Central and Eastern Europe even before the *Communist* regimes had collapsed. He always worked with *local church* leaders and secured remarkably wide support from the leaders of all denominations. His preaching and the ordering of his meetings always avoided the excesses associated with some evangelists who have been accused of sensationalism and the attempted psychological manipulation of those present. Throughout the centuries Europeans have also had their own national evangelists, usually working on a smaller scale. Technology has helped to moderate increasingly larger meetings. Such crusades could be organised by a single denomination but since most evangelists operated through para-church organisations they most often have had interdenominational support. Local churches have played their part by engaging in advance preparation for the event and in follow-up work with the new converts [see *Conversion*] after the evangelist has moved on. Such events helped to cross denominational boundaries and were a mark of the *unity of the church*, fulfilling Jesus' prayer for the unity of his disciples [see *Discipleship*] 'so that the world might believe.' As crusades became less and less effective, more and more emphasis was placed on thorough preparation for an evangelistic crusade and especially on the follow-up.

When Central and Eastern European countries relaxed their regulations and permitted various evangelistic activities, many Western European and especially US parachurch groups began to conduct crusades in these countries' large sport stadia and city halls. Some organised series of evangelistic crusades for an entire geographic region, such as the Volga Mission or Siberian Mission. The outcomes of these efforts remained quite modest as so often western organisers did not consider contextual spirituality [see *Contextualisation*] and failed to include or train local church leaders in the disciplines of proper follow-up. Because the initiative came from outside, vital contact with local churches, who did not fully own this activity was weak. Nevertheless, evangelistic mass meetings are still considered part of parachurch and church activities in evangelism. In some European contexts the method still produces good results. But for most places in Europe, it has lost its attractiveness and effectiveness and much effort and creativity is needed to make such events worthwhile.

The recent decades have seen TV evangelists appear on our screens and take a similar approach to crusade evangelism. Often there is an overlap between the traditional mass evangelism meeting and evangelistic preaching into the private living room in order to reach the laid back generation. A well designed programme, an appealing stage and an evangelistic sermon at the heart of a TV show extend the evangelistic crusade concept and utilise it with modern tools. Internet may be another evangelistic medium and where, at a time convenient for the recipient, such event can be viewed. In Europe, such evangelistic programmes are usually operated with USA TV evangelists; sometimes national evangelists are involved.

A mixture of local evangelistic events and an interactive *dialogue* is another attempt to further develop the classical evangelism crusade. In some Western and Central European countries ProChrist represents such an approach, where mass meetings are organised in selected cities and then transmitted to local churches via satellite technology in their national languages together with interviews with and testimonies from celebrities from *sport*, *politics*, religious life, etc. All this can be screened in local churches where local singing, praying and conversation take place and those who decide to accept Christ as their saviour are able to receive personal counselling. Such technological setups create both a local-communal and a global experience and offer a network that connects centres and places throughout different countries in Europe. Taking into account all creative attempts to find new ways of using the classical evangelistic crusade method, the last decades increasingly demonstrate that such events have success only if local Christians take courage to be witnesses outside such events and communicate their faith to relatives, neighbours and colleagues in both word and deed.

PFP

Czech Brethren and the Czech Reformation

[See also *Czech Republic, Baptist history in*; *Reformation*]

The Czech Reformation has its origins in the movement led by Jan Hus (c.1369-1415), a contemporary of John Wycliffe, some of whose writings were already known in Prague and were translated by Hus into Czech. Hus graduated with a Master's degree from Prague University in 1396, was ordained a *priest* [see *Ordination*] in 1400 and became Rector of the University in 1402. His reformist teachings, influenced by Wycliffe's writings, were swiftly condemned in Rome in 1407 and three years later the *Vatican* forbade his *preaching* at the Bethlehem Chapel in Prague before excommunicating him in 1411. Safe conduct for him to appeal to the Council of Constance was not honoured and he was burnt at the stake on 6 Jul 1415.

The church in the Czech lands was now

deeply divided, and the reformers, fortified by several **martyrs**, won the support of a substantial part of the Czech **nation**. They were known by different names – the Utraquists, because they insisted that in **communion** both bread and **wine** should be received by the **laity**, the Unitas Fratrum, and the Bohemian Brethren. Amongst them there developed more conservative and more radical **traditions**, the latter following the teaching of Peter Chelcicky (c.1380 - c.1460), perhaps the most original and challenging thinker of the Hussite era. Personal study of the **Bible**, combined with study of **Waldensian** thought and of the writings of John Wycliffe and of some Czech forerunners of the reformation (including Hus himself) led Chelcicky to champion a gospel of **peace**, an exclusively 'spiritual warfare', and a church entirely free of **state** control [see **Separation of Church and State**]. Other radical proposals included the rejection of the feudal division of society into three classes (nobility, clergy, and the common people) as incompatible with the **love** of God, an egalitarian social vision, which he combined with an uncompromising refusal to recognise theological defences of the state and its power structures, an emphasis which finds expression in his best-known theological work, *The Net of Faith* (c.1440). Thus Chelcicky became the recognised spiritual 'father' of those radical groups among the Czech Brethren, especially the Unity of the Brethren, who implemented his legacy.

By the beginning of the 17th century the reformers, notably the Czech Brethren or Unity of the Brethren, had the support of 90% of the population but after 1620 they became outlawed even in their homeland – the choices before them were **conversion** to **Catholicism** or banishment. The most famous person to go into exile was J.A. Comenius, the last of the church's **bishops**. Almost 100 years later in 1721 remnants of the **refugee** community were invited by Count von Zinzendorf, who had been brought up in the German **pietist** tradition, to settle on his estates at Herrnhut where they were reorganised as the **Moravian** Brethren, the origins of the worldwide family of Moravian churches.

When in 1781 the Emperor of **Austria** allowed a measure of toleration to **Protestants** within the Empire, this was only to those who belonged to the **Lutheran** or **Reformed Churches**, and so other Czech Protestants secured toleration under these labels. In 1918, however, these came together to form the **Evangelical** Church of the Czech Brethren. The church today has a presbyterian **ecclesiology**, and exercises a lively diaconal **ministry** and since 1989 has been enabled to exercise a public ministry through **chaplaincy** work in institutions such as the army and **prisons**. Training takes place in the Evangelical Theological Faculty at the Charles University. The church today numbers more than 100,000 **members** in more than 250 congregations served by some 230 clergy just over a quarter of whom are **women**.

Of a quite different origin and different outlook is the Czechoslovak Hussite Church which was founded in 1920 with its roots going back to those Roman Catholic priests of a **modernist** theological persuasion, who were campaigning in the late 19th century for a **liturgy** in the Czech language, the abolition of clerical celibacy and a place for the laity in the governance of the church, all of which reforms were rejected by the Vatican in 1919. It is suggested that the Hussite Church never commanded the support of more than 5% of the population and today has little more than 100,000 members (down from 500,000 in 1982) with 241 **pastors** of whom 107 are women. Its taking of the Hussite name is indicative of its **nationalist** outlook; in **theology** and ecclesiology it seeks to occupy a middle ground between Catholic and Protestant.

ET

Czech Republic, Baptist history in
[See also **Slovakia, Baptist history in.**]
Baptist work appeared on the territory of the former Czechoslovakia (the unified **state** of the Czech and Slovak Republics from 1918-92) in the late 1850s. Magnus Knappe, a Baptist **missionary** from **Germany**, and August Meereis, a missionary and **colporteur** of Czech descent from Volhynia (then Tsarist **Russia**), became the pioneers of the Baptist work in this country. Knappe, who worked among German inhabitants, performed the first **baptism** in 1867, while the first Czechs

were baptised by Meereis in 1877. Revd Henry Novotny (1846-1912), a former *preacher* of the Free *Reformed Church* in Prague, became the pastor of the first Baptist congregation in Bohemia, established in 1885 in Hledsebe, a small village north of Prague. The congregation then moved to the capital where it called itself the Prague Congregation of Christians Baptised in Faith. In the Austro-Hungarian Empire, Baptists were the target of public insult and slander, and the state authorities themselves severely hampered all local mission activities. In fact, their very *worship* services were considered illegal and had to be held under the protective name of another organisation. After the formation of independent Czechoslovakia in 1918 the situation changed. In 1919 in the Slovakian village of Vavrisovo, Baptists formed the Chelcicky Unity of Brethren, an association of Baptist congregations named after an influential Hussite radical of the 15th century, who is usually identified with the precursors of the Radical *Reformation*. The *union* included 15 Bohemian, Moravian, Slovak, German, and Hungarian congregations. American and British Baptists provided most of the initial support. In 1921 a seminary was established in Prague and two periodicals, *Chelcicky* and *Rozsievac* [*The Sower*], began their circulation. WWII brought some stagnation, but after the war a new upsurge of Baptist activity occurred from 1945-47, thanks largely to returning emigrants, primarily from Russia and *Poland*. However, the *Communist* regime, which took power in 1948, limited all activities and contacts of the churches and Baptist leaders were, together with *Roman Catholics*, among the most heavily persecuted. The seminary was closed in 1951 (future pastors received their *education* mostly in *Protestant* theological institutions in Czechoslovakia), and some Baptist *property* in *Slovakia* confiscated. Publication was practically reduced to an annual collection of devotionals and even that was censored by the state authorities. In the 1960s the Baptists, who by now had dropped 'Chelcicky' in favour of simply 'Baptist' in their name, divided their union into two regional sections – Bohemian-Moravian and Slovak. Though the situation began to improve – first during the short-lived 'Prague Spring' of 1968 and then

toward the end of the 1980s – new and exciting possibilities appeared only after the 'Velvet Revolution' in 1989. Although relations with the larger Baptist family in the world were never totally interrupted (and the work and representation of both Dr. Jindrich Prochazka and Stanislav Svec in the international bodies was indeed very valuable) only then could there be real and full partnership and participation extended at all levels. In 1992 a *Bible* school specialising in diaconal *ministries* was founded in the old Moravian capital of Olomouc, and Prague became the home of the respected *International Baptist Theological Seminary*. With the division of Czechoslovakia into two independent states, the Czech Republic and the Slovak Republic, in 1993, a corresponding division also occurred in the Baptist Union, although the two 'daughter' associations remain in close contact.

PeM

Czechoslovakia, Baptist history in
See *Czech Republic*; *Slovakia, Baptist history in*.

D

DanChurchAid, Denmark

[See also *Human Rights Advocacy*]

DanChurchAid is one of the major Danish humanitarian *non-governmental organisations*, working with churches and non-religious civil organisations to assist the poorest of the *poor*. DanChurchAid carries out its work with the objective: 'To help and be advocates of oppressed, neglected and marginalised groups in poor countries and to strengthen their possibilities of a life in dignity'. The organisation is one of a series of *national church* aid and development agencies in Europe such as *Christian Aid* (*United Kingdom*) and *Bread for the World* (*Germany*). *Ecumenical* in formation, Baptists generally participate as one of the supporting *Christian world communions* where such organisations exist.

It works co-operatively with the other Protestant Relief and Development agencies (APRODEV) in northern Europe and also with *ACT International* .These organisations often have the common strap line, 'we believe in life before death', and affirm that all human beings are created in the image of God and are therefore equal; that even the poorest of the poor have capacities to build on, and that assistance should be given regardless of race, religion and *political* affiliation.

ET

Danish Baptist Theological Seminary

Danish Baptists placed their theological Seminary in Tølløse, west of Copenhagen in 1928, when they built a *Folk High School* in the same location. On the campus they also placed a graduation school in order to gather together all forms of educational training on the same site. The buildings were renewed and enlarged in Tølløse in 1969 with support from both the *American Baptist Churches* and the *Southern Baptist Convention*. By 2000, more than 100 *pastors* had been trained for *ministry* at the Seminary. Until 1986 the Seminary and the Folk High School worked closely together in an additional training programme for lay people [see *Laity*]. In the 1990s it became evident that the small Union could not afford to maintain its own Seminary without cooperation with other partners. The Baptist Boarding School bought the property and the Seminary became the most prominent partner of the new Scandinavian Academy of Leadership and *Theology* (*SALT*), which was formed with Danish and Swedish partners in 2000 in Copenhagen and Malmø, *Sweden*.

BH

Deaconesses

The work of deaconesses in Baptist life owes something to examples that were offered in *Lutheranism* and *Anglicanism*. In the 19th century German Baptist leaders wished to encourage *ministries* carried out by *women*. German Baptists were led into the area of diaconal ministry carried out by women through the influence of Eduard Scheve and they established *Haus Bethel* in 1887 as a focus for the ministry of deaconesses. Their work developed in such areas as nursing, social work, care for *orphans* – often in the homes of Baptists – and larger homes for the aged [see *Elderly*].

In *England*, F.B. Meyer, who combined a strong emphasis on spiritual life with a commitment to socio-*political* involvement, secured a house for the use of Baptist deaconesses in 1890 and in announcing this he invited women who were willing to contribute towards their own maintenance as deaconesses to write to him. A number of Baptist women responded. Initially the 'Sisters' (as they were called), since they had to support themselves financially, were drawn from *wealthy* families. Later, churches employing deaconesses were asked to pay for their upkeep. Four sisters and a lady superintendent began their work, concentrating on the needs of the *poor* in London, especially in Leather Lane, Holborn and Gray's Inn. In 1894 the Baptist Deaconesses' Home and Mission was launched. Baptists beyond the English and German-speaking communities did not adopt the idea of a separated order of Deaconesses, though many women in *local churches* did take on specific ministries of social concern and action.

In the early 20th century period in England a close association with Bloomsbury Central Baptist Church was formed. Deaconesses formed an integral part of the Bloomsbury team. It seems that by 1907 there were about 20 deaconesses working with Baptist churches. In this period Sister Lizzie Hodgson, a deaconess at West End Baptist Chapel, Hammersmith, London, was attracting 500 each week to her women's meeting. More remarkably, she was also *preaching* on Sunday nights in the Lyric Theatre, Hammersmith, which seated 1,400 people, and was filling it, with two-thirds of the audience present being *men*. Another example of dynamic female leadership in Baptist life was Hettie Rowntree Clifford, who in 1914 was often preaching to 900 people at the West Ham Central Mission in London.

Meanwhile, in *Germany* there were further developments when in 1907 Albertine Assor founded *Diakonissenverein Siloah*, now known as the *Albertinen* order of Deaconesses in Hamburg, Germany. They engaged in a wide variety of social work, moving into major *hospital* work in 1964 under the leadership of Prof. Walter Füllbrandt.

In both *Britain* and Germany the Deaconess movement continued to grow in the 1920s. In England, Havelock Hall was opened as a Women's Training College for deaconesses in 1920. At the 1925 Baptist *Assembly*, Hettie Rowntree Clifford spoke about the role of deaconesses: there were over 40, and a few were taking charge of churches. The Lancashire and Cheshire *Association* appointed an itinerant Sister to help smaller churches. Birmingham's *Daily Mail* reported in 1924 on Sister Ida Evans, in Birmingham, who was making 3,000 visits each year in the slums. At Bloomsbury Baptist Church, London the deaconesses took on much of the daily work of the church.

There was a trend in the 1930s for deaconesses in England to take on church leadership. Fred Cawley, Principal of *Spurgeon's College, London*, argued in 1951 that the status of deaconesses should be equal to that of *ministers*. Two decades later, a Baptist *Union* of Great Britain report proposed that all deaconesses became ministers. There was no parallel movement in Germany, where the separate order continues. In 1974 the

British deaconesses voted on whether they supported this move and they accepted that their function had become ministerial. In Jun 1975 all serving deaconesses in the Baptist Union of Great Britain were transferred to the accredited list of ministers. Addressing an audience before the Baptist Assembly in 1977, as he was about to become Union President, Ernest Payne saw it as significant that 'at last the Christian *church* is ready to give a much more adequate recognition to women'.

IMR

FURTHER READING: Ruth M.B. Gouldbourne, *Reinventing the Wheel: Women and Ministry in English Baptist Life*, Whitley, Oxford, 1997. Nicola Morris, *Sisters of the People: The Order of Baptist Deaconesses 1890-1975*, CCSRG Research Paper 2, Bristol, 2002.

Deacons and Elders

Baptists have usually adopted a two-fold order of *ministry*, the oversight (*episkope*) exercised by ministers or pastors, or sometimes by a group of elders, and the service (*diakonia*) of deacons. At *baptism* we are all commissioned to Christian service, but then some are called [see *Call/Calling*] by their churches to special responsibilities as deacons, sharing in leadership of the *local church*. Deacons are chosen and commissioned by the local church for service in that church, whereas the pastor, while called to a particular ministry, is usually recognised as a leader by other churches too.

Churches do not all adopt identical leadership patterns. Many Baptist churches have one or more pastors supported by a team of deacons. Some churches are led by a group of elders. Others have one pastor and a team of elders and deacons. Where there are both elders and deacons, deacons usually look after practical administration, including the care of money and buildings, while elders major on spiritual and pastoral [see *Pastoral Care*] matters, but all church business requires a measure of spirituality so there is always some overlap. Usually pastors are paid a stipend by the church, elders and deacons are not.

The deacons' ministry has usually included care of the fellowship, especially the *poor*, but as churches grew and acquired *property*, administrative matters occupied them increasingly. Their responsibilities also include care of the minister, and sharing in *worship*, especially in *prayer* and serving at the *Lord's Table*. If they have suitable gifts, they share in *preaching* and teaching. They are expected to participate in deacons' meetings and in *church members'* meetings [see *Church Meeting*].

Among early English Baptists, some churches appointed *men* and also some *women* as deacons, finding women good at caring for the poor and sick. Later practice normally restricted the role to men until the 20ᵗʰ century. Many English and Welsh churches now have men and women on the diaconate, although a few churches resist this.

The number of deacons varies. Some churches have chosen seven, as in Ac 6:3; others have had 12, the number of *apostles*. The size of church, availability of suitable members, and amount of work to be covered are often determining factors.

Deacons in Western Europe are usually now elected for a given period, but may then be re-elected. In many parts of Eastern Europe Deacons are ordained and generally serve without re-election as long as they are physically able. Some countries have both women and men Deacons, though certain Slavic countries in particular would only call brothers to the office of Deacon. Some Western European churches require a break between periods of service. Many deacons, especially those who take particular responsibilities as church secretaries and treasurers or for the care of *buildings*, give many hours of largely unseen service to their churches.

BBow

Death

Death (Heb: *maweth*) may initially be described as the opposite of life. In the OT *humankind* is created by God blowing life into Adam. Death may also be described in similar terms: when God takes away human breath, people die, and return to dust (Ps 104:29). In this way both life and death is in the hands of God.

In the OT only Enoch and Elijah are described as not dying. But these are clear exceptions. Death is seen as a normal way to end life. There is no attempt to hide away the death of important persons like Abraham, Moses and David. Death is in this way a natural prerequisite of living. However, there are both good and bad ways to die. To die a good death is to die at an old age with sufficient offspring (Ge 15:15). A bad death on the other hand is a sudden and unnatural death (Isa 38:10). In the NT only God is said to be immortal (1Ti 6:16). Humans are on the other hand mortals (1Co 15:22), but shall be made immortal through the gift of *Christ* at the Parousia.

Interestingly to die is sometimes described in the OT as 'going to your fathers', but also as being 'cut off from the land of the living', (Isa 53:8) a kind of being after death which is only a shadow life, lived in a shadow land (Job 10:21-22), sometimes called the underworld (Pr 5:5 – *She'ol*). This She'ol is for every one (Job 30:23), both the righteous and the unrighteous. Death is a place where the relationship with God through his *revelation* and our praise, cannot be continued (Ps 88:9-12) and hence is anticipation with fear (Ecc 12:1-8) and groaning (Ps 6).

The OT does not sentimentalise death as a necessary part of the natural order. On the contrary, death is unnatural and arises out of a disordered society, spoilt by human *sin* and rebellion as described in Ge 3. This is further developed in the NT where death, and associated with it *alienation* from God, is clearly the result of sin (Ro 6:23). Here the deeds of Adam and Christ are contrasted: Death came into the world through the sin of Adam (Ro 5:12), but the second Adam (Christ) will be a life-giver (1Co 15:45). The abolition of death is the main purpose of Christ's *incarnation*, for in Christ the immortal God has tasted death and in so doing has destroyed it. Death is not any longer able to separate us from Christ (Ro 8:38-39). The sting of death is gone (1Co 15:55). In this way death becomes something positive, and can be paralleled as being 'at home with the Lord' (2Co 5:8). Beyond the *Good Friday* of Death lies an *Easter Day* of *Resurrection*, not only for the Christ but for those who put their trust in him. All this is symbolised in Believers' *Baptism*: descent into a watery grave followed by rising to new life in Christ (Ro 6 and Col 2).

Finally a second death is mentioned a few times in Rev (2:11). This second death is reserved for the *Devil* and his associates, and must be seen as the final destruction of all that belongs to evil.

KTB

FURTHER READING: Lloyd R. Bailey Sr., *Biblical perspectives on death*, Fortress, Philadelphia, 1979. J.M. Bremer, Th.P.J. van den Hout and R. Peters (eds). *Hidden futures : death and immortality in Ancient Egypt, Anatolia, the classical, biblical and Arabic-Islamic world*, Amsterdam University Press. Amsterdam, 1994.

Death Penalty
See *Capital Punishment*.

Debt, Two-Thirds World
See *Jubilee and Two-Thirds World Debt*.

Decorations
See *Church Decorations*.

Dedication

Baptist gathering churches have no universal practice or *theology* of Dedication as applied to buildings or furnishings of buildings. The general theological construct of dedication amongst Christians is that something or somebody is formally made over to God. Some Baptist communities have services of dedication when a new *building* for *worship* is completed. Still others will have liturgical acts [see *Liturgy*] of dedication for particular items within a worship space such as a musical instrument, *communion* table or some other item of furnishing which has been given by a specific donor. Some communities also dedicate church officers to their task, but for most the more appropriate theological and liturgical construct is a service of *commissioning* or *ordination* of a person to a particular *vocation* or *ministry* within or beyond the community of the church.

Many Baptists have held liturgical services for the *dedication of children*, but this is less common in Europe today and has generally been superseded by services of Thanksgiving for or Blessing of Children, which may involve the dedication of the parents to do all in their power to bring the child up in a *Christ*-like way and to understand the Gospel. In not dedicating the child this avoids important theological issues about *free will* and the rights of children.

Baptists generally do not then treat such dedicated buildings and artefacts as being especially holy [see *Holiness*], nor in any mystical way set aside. Consequently generally there are no theological problems at a later point if a building or an artefact is no longer used for the purpose to which it was dedicated.

KGJ

Dedication of Children
See *Children, Blessing of*.

Deism
See *Theism and Deism*.

Democracy

The word has two Greek components *dēmos* [the people] and *kratia* [power or rule] and therefore has come to mean 'rule by the people', but the people properly ordered, following a process of thoughtful engagement, as over against the demagogic rantings which arise from mob rule, which has little, if anything, in common with true democracy. It has wisely been observed that whilst the tyranny of a *minority* is bad, the tyranny of a majority is worse; for a majority is so much more secure than a minority, hence the need for education in democracy that the process may be wisely handled.

Whilst some city states in the ancient world practiced a measure of male democracy, it has only slowly become the preferred mode of government in larger *states* over the last 250 years. Accordingly the NT does not say very much about democracy. Rather Paul teaches his readers how to live responsibly within the existing *political* regime, whilst John in Revelation warns of the possibilities of the rise of regimes with intrinsically evil intent (cf. Ro 13 and Rev 13).

One of the first modern advocates of democracy was Rousseau, famous for the dictum, 'Man is born free but everywhere he is in chains'. Christian thinkers of the same period also affirmed that *humankind*, born in the image of God, was born free. Thus the Baptist *preacher*, Robert Hall, believed that man was born with 'natural liberty'. This, he believed, was an important aspect of the Christian doctrine of *creation*, arguing against all forms of tyranny that held *men* and *women* in subjection. It was, therefore, increasingly seen as a matter of justice, that what concerned all should be considered and approved by all. This means that justice demands of a *nation*'s politics that it be participatory, all citizens sharing in decision-making, and, therefore, owning for themselves the decisions taken, and consequently willingly taking part in their implementation.

Beyond politics, and perhaps more profoundly, the principle of participation needs to be extended to economic activity where ordinary people should, as of right, play their part in the setting of targets, and choosing the strategy by which these should be achieved. The search for democracy has necessarily involved other subsidiary goals, such as working for decolonisation [see *Colonialism*], the defence of *human rights*, the establishment of racial equality, the rights of women, and the agreement to discipline a nation's common life in such a way as to sustain ongoing life upon the planet. In the end all such questions have to do with the exercise of power – who has access to its levers and who are permanently excluding from access to the same, and how can they be empowered? A democratic society will therefore seek to pass laws which secure the welfare of all members of society, with a bias towards policies which place a priority on advancing the standard of living of the *poor* and marginalised.

Part of the problem with democracy is that there seems to be an ever-widening gap between the ideal, and the stale reality of the way democracy is realised in most modern states, where the politicians are less than ideal representatives of the people, and their policies seem mainly designed to keep themselves in power. Accordingly people are looking for new ways in which to make their politicians properly accountable.

JHYB

Denmark, Baptist history in

Danish Baptists, who date their origins to the 1830s, arose out of a religious awakening within the *Lutheran state church*. Such a group of awakened Christians came together under the leadership of P.C. Mønster and were brought into the Baptist family when Julius Købner visited Copenhagen in the summer of 1839. Købner was a converted Danish *Jew* who had become *Oncken*'s co-worker in Hamburg. When Oncken baptised [see *Baptism*] a dozen believers in Copenhagen on 27 Oct 1839, the first Danish Baptist Church was founded. Immediately Mønster wrote the very first application for *religious freedom* for all Danes, but the authorities paid no attention to his petition. As a free church they played their part in securing a paragraph on religious liberty in the new Danish Constitution of 1849 which brought to an end penal action against the Baptists.

From 1849, when Baptists numbered about 1,000, to 1888 Danish Baptists belonged to the German Baptist Union. This was unfortunate for the *mission* of the churches since in this period there were two Danish-German Wars which led to a loss of some 25% of the *membership* through *emigration* to the USA. From 1888 Danish Baptists looked to the Northern Baptists in the USA for inspiration and assistance for it was there that the emigrating Danish Baptists had found *fellowship*. Thus e.g. in 1888 the New Hampshire Confession was substituted for the German Baptist Confession as expressing the theological outlook of the *union*. *Pastors* began to be trained in Chicago, and when they returned to Europe the Danish Union began to grow once more.

In the 1920s Danish Baptists built a *Folk High School* and the *Danish Baptist Theological Seminary* outside Copenhagen. Foreign mission work was focused in Burundi and Rwanda, where they have been working in cooperation with independent churches since 1960. Because they have always been a small minority in a dominantly Lutheran folk-church society – about one Baptist for every 1,000 Danes – Danish Baptists have been anxious to exploit international relations. They have been part of the *Evangelical Alliance*, participants in the *BWA* from its beginning in 1905, and also of the *EBF* from 1948. Founder members of The *World*

Council of Churches since 1948, they have also been active in the *Lausanne Movement* for World *Evangelization*. Quite remarkably they have played a part in the various agencies of co-operative Christianity within Denmark (e.g. Bible Society, Dan Church Aid, Danish Mission Council) well beyond their numerical strength. Although originally practicing *Strict Communion* and *Calvinist* views of Particular *redemption* they have more recently developed a more open attitude to fellow Christians, practicing *open communion* since the 1930s and transferred membership from infant-baptising traditions [see *Infant Baptism*] since the 1980s. Today they number about 5,000 members in 50 congregations, with a *ministry* in a post-Christian multi-religious setting where Baptists from all round the world, seeking *sanctuary* as refugees, are enriching the life of the churches.

BH

Denominational Leaders, European Baptists in the 20th and 21st centuries

Baptist *unions* and conventions in Europe are normally led by a President and General Secretary. Presidents (or *Bishops*, National Leaders, Superintendents) are generally elected for a fixed term varying between one and five years, General Secretaries normally serve longer periods of time. In the last century some national leaders (a term with which many Baptists have difficulty, implying some form of *hierarchy*) have occupied important roles on the wider stage, either *ecumenically* or internationally.

The *International Baptist Theological Seminary* has furnished a succession of people who have served with prominence in the *Baptist World Alliance* including two General Secretaries, Josef Nordenhaug and Denton Lotz. German Baptist and EBF Secretary Gerhard Claas also served as BWA General Secretary in the 1980s and earlier in the 20th century *John Clifford*, J.H. Rushbrooke and Arnold T. Ohrn all served. BWA Presidents have included from Europe John Clifford, J.H. Rushbrooke, F. Townley Lord, Knud Wümplemann and David R. Coffey. Treasurers of the BWA have included the

following Europeans – Herbert Marnham, C.T. LeQuesne, Donald Finnemore and George Polson.

In the *World Council of Churches* Ernest A. Payne, David S. Russell, J.H.Y. Briggs, W.M.S. West and Ruth A. Bottoms have held important positions within the Executive Committee and in the Commissions of the WCC. Simon J. Oxley held a senior staff post from the 1990s through until 2008.

The *Conference of European Churches* has had two European Baptists as General Secretary, Glen Garfield Williams and Keith W. Clements.

Within the *European Evangelical Alliance* Nikolai Nedelchev, Theo Angelov and Hans Henrik Lund, have played prominent roles, whilst in the *World Evangelical Fellowship* Henri Blocher from *France* has served and in the European Evangelical Accrediting Association Paul Sanders has been a key member.

KGJ

Depravity, Human
See *Fall, The*.

Devil, The
The concept of 'The Devil' or 'Satan' is not fully developed in the OT. The Hebrew word *satan* refers to an 'accuser'/'adversary', or even 'enemy' (Ps 109:6). The NT uses the transliteration *satanos*, but the main word is *diabolos*.

Satan acts as a supernatural accuser three times in the OT, confronting Job (Job 1-2), David (1Ch 21:1) and Joshua, the high priest (Zec 3:1-10). But, Satan is in these instances still in the court of *heaven* acting as one of the sons of God. In early *Jewish* thought there is no room for an independent or autonomous adversary to God. God is the source of all action, both good and bad (Isa 45:7). But in the confrontation with David there is an interesting development. In the earlier version of the story in 2Sa 24:1 God is tempting David. But in the Chronicler's account Satan has become the tempter. This might be the first step towards an individual evil power.

Satan has also been identified with creatures like Leviathan (Ps 104:26), and the snake in the garden of Eden. As a matter of fact Wis 2:23-24 identifies the snake in the garden as the Devil. This is also the case in the NT (2Co 11:3).

The picture of an independent evil power with his own court and his own kingdom developed between the two testaments. In the NT Satan has become the main opponent of *Jesus* – it is he who tests Jesus in the wilderness (Mt 4), he who presides over the kingdom of evil (Mt 12:26), who causes disease (Lk 13:16) and who is the source of *sin* in the lives of people as varied as Peter, Judas and Ananias. Depicted as the force behind cosmic evil, the world of 'principalities and powers' (Eph 6:11-12), Christ has to destroy him (Heb 2:14). Whilst the Devil has been defeated by Christ's death on the *Cross*, he continues to act as if, falsely, he still possessed controlling power, but at the end of time his defeat will be made clear (Col 2:15). This is seen in Revelation as the writer depicts a crescendo of cosmic warfare ending in the final destruction of Satan in the second death, and the victory of Christ (Rev 20:14).

Whilst all talk of the satanic and demonic has been attacked by *liberal* theologians, thinkers of the order of E.L. Mascall argue that only some form of evil agency properly designated by the classic terms of *scripture* can account for our experience of the dimensions of sickness, disaster and evil.

KTB

Devotional Life

See *Spirituality/Devotional Life*.

Diakonia

The Greek word means service – 'the responsible service of the Gospel by deeds and by words performed by Christians in response to the needs of the people'. The practice of such diakonia is modelled on the *ministry* of *Jesus* and his care of both soul and body. In the early church, collections were taken for the relief of those in need and an order of '*deacons*' ordained [see *Ordination*] to this ministry of care, which became a major function of the medieval monastery. With the dissolution of the monasteries this offering of service fell into some disarray, though the reformers [see *Reformation*] were quick to stress its importance, whilst radical groups like the *Mennonites* established impressive care programmes, as did some of the new *Roman Catholic* orders.

In the 19th century, *pietist* groups, like the deaconesses of Kaiserwerth in *Germany*, became more systematically involved in the training of *women* for the diaconal ministry, whilst stressing that *evangelisation* and diakonia were part of a single unity of Christian ministry and *mission*. In this context, German Baptists developed their own deaconess movement supporting a considerable number of *hospitals* and other institutions. In the 20th century diakonia was manifestly an activity that churches could undertake together and so the rise of the different *ecumenical* aid societies such as *Bread for the World*, Danchurch Aid, *Christian Aid* and the *evangelical Tearfund*, reclaiming that tradition's social ministry in the previous ministry associated with names like Lord Shaftesbury, Dr. Barnado, and George Müller. Baptists have made major contributions to both ecumenical and evangelical aid organisations, as well as working through their own agencies such as *Baptist World Aid*. In nearly every country in Europe Baptists run *orphanages*, old people's homes [see *Elderly, Care for the*] and sometimes specialised facilities for those with particular problems: *drugs*, drink [see *Alcoholism*], *violence* in the home, etc.

WWII challenged the Christian Churches to new endeavours in diakonia with the demands for relief, reconstruction and the handling of millions of people who found themselves refugees because of invading armies and changed *political* boundaries. Following such endeavours relief agencies have been constantly active in dealing with successive world disasters leading to there being more refugees in the world today than there were in 1945-46. Whilst in emergencies immediate relief is the only proper response, Christians have become increasingly aware that aid can enpauperise and that there is a need to move clients from aid programmes to development programmes so that they can begin to participate in their own stabilisation. At the same time aid agencies have campaigned for fairer terms of world trade that do not unfairly work against third-world producer nations. In the past there was very much a division between givers and receivers, but now the emphasis on partnership arrangements with all partners having equal access to the table. The total contribution of the churches to diakonia is difficult to measure for whilst national and international work is easy to record, the myriad acts of compassion springing out of the witness of the local church defy measurement.

JHYB

Dialogue

The Dialogue approach to those of other *faiths*, coined at the World Parliament of Religions (Chicago, 1893), became popular during the 1960s, being used primarily of *Inter-Faith Dialogue* since the New Delhi Assembly of the *WCC* (1961). The WCC desk or unit for dialogue set up 10 years later held a consultation on 'Dialogue in Community' in Chiang Mai, Thailand in 1977, leading on to the publication of *Guidelines on Dialogue* (1979), which affirmed that: 'dialogue is neither a betrayal of *mission* or a "secret weapon" of *proselytism*, but a way "in which *Jesus Christ* can be confessed in the world today"'. Although initially the subject of controversy because of potential *syncretism*, dialogue has come to be recognised as an essential component of the life and *witness* of the *church* in the 21st century in engaging with cultural diversity and religious *pluralism*. The 13 recommendations of the original WCC Guidelines have been adapted to various contexts. The British Churches summarised them into Four Principles of Dialogue:

(1) Dialogue begins when people meet each other;
(2) Dialogue depends upon mutual understanding and mutual trust;
(3) Dialogue makes it possible to share in service to the community;
(4) Dialogue becomes the medium of authentic witness.

(*In Good Faith*, 1992, CTBI)

The British Baptist 'Joppa Group', formed in 1985 in order to address questions of *religious liberty* and Christian witness in an increasingly plural society, responded to this, positively but not uncritically, with the booklet *A Baptist Perspective on Interfaith Dialogue* (1992). This tried to engage with these principles from the point of view of five Baptist distinctives summarised as:

(i)   the primacy of *scripture*;
(ii) *liberty of conscience* and religious practice;
(iii) the Church as a fellowship of believers;
(iv) centrality of witness to Jesus as Lord;
(v)   a life of baptised *discipleship* [see *Baptism*];

which Paul Weller has developed at greater length.

Developments critical for the recognition of the importance of dialogue include: increasing contact between the 'Christian' West and the rest of the world during the rise and fall of the colonial era [see *Colonialism*]; the 'Renaissance' of Eastern traditions and the resurgence of *Islam* together with the recognition of the limitations of the Western intellectual tradition; the presence of Asian religions in western countries as a result of patterns of *migration*: all this coincided with the rejection of authoritarian approaches and more recently the development of post-modernity, and the adoption of more open-ended attitudes.

Nevertheless there has been considerable discussion as to the nature of dialogue and especially its relationship to confessional approaches and for Baptists the centrality of Christian witness to people of all faiths and none. Some have argued, with *scholars* like John Hick (b1922), that dialogue must always be towards truth, whereas others have sided with people like Lesslie Newbigin (1909-98), that dialogue is always confessional in nature. Others have recognised that dialogue is complex and multi-faceted, with differing emphases in different contexts.

There have been various attempts to delineate the scope of dialogue, many of them variations on the influential typology of Eric Sharpe (b1933). A scholar of *Comparative Religion,* he identifies four distinct types of dialogue:

1. Discursive dialogue – deliberate meeting for intellectual enquiry. This recognises that faith traditions have a distinctive worldview, which is frequently underpinned by sophisticated philosophical systems. This requires a certain

technical expertise in at least one's own tradition and is likely to be mainly the sphere of the expert or the religious professional. It will also mean deliberate or set-piece meetings, which are likely to have agreed 'agendas' and procedures. Through such a process a clearer picture can emerge both of a religion's own distinctive features, and of those things which might be held in common between traditions.

2. Human dialogue – which arises from encounter in ordinary relationships. This recognises that religion is frequently not so much about belief as practice, which is as much the concern of the ordinary believer as it is of the expert. Such dialogue is about the ordinary and everyday and occurs not in deliberate meetings of experts but in the accidental encounters of people in the meetings of everyday life. It may be that 'encounter' is really a better word than 'dialogue' here yet out of such encounter there should be no doubt that genuine relationships can be formed and searching dialogue can take place.

3. Secular dialogue – in which people of different traditions co-operate in matters of common concern. Because of the territorial problems that the meeting of faiths can produce, the neutral realm of the secular world can often provide the forum for constructive meeting of different faith communities. There are often matters of concern within a community, which may involve people of all faiths and none. Such things might be cooperation over events or facilities, sharing in the life of a school or community association, local *politics* and so forth. Sharing a common purpose is a strong base for building good relationships and offers the possibility of developing trust in addressing faith questions.

4. Interior dialogue – which focuses on the spiritual elements within various traditions. This recognises the centrality of the spiritual quest in religious traditions, and offers the possibility of a depth of encounter to the devout practitioner of faith, whether expert or simply a devout believer.

(*Truth and Dialogue*, pp.77-95)

This might suggest that dialogue is fundamentally about *agreement*, whereas in the experience of some it is equally as significant for its recognition of *difference*. John V. Taylor (1914-2001), 'The Theological Basis of Inter-Faith Dialogue' suggests that: 'Dialogue is a sustained conversation between parties who are not saying the same thing and who recognise and respect the differences, the contradictions and the mutual exclusions between their various ways of thinking. The object of this dialogue is understanding and appreciation, leading to further reflection about the implications for one's own position on the convictions and sensitivities of other faith traditions' (*Christianity and Other Religions*, p.212).

NJW

FURTHER READING: M. Braybrooke, *A Pilgrimage of Hope: 100 Years of Interfaith Dialogue*, SCM, London, 1992. CCBI, *In Good Faith: The Fours Principles of Interfaith Dialogue*, CCBI, London, 1992. K. Cracknell, *Towards a New Relationship*, Epworth, Westminster, London, 1986. M. Forward, *Inter-Religious Dialogue: A Short Introduction*, Oneworld, Oxford, 2001. J. Hick (ed), *Truth and Dialogue*, Westminster, Philadelphia, 1974. J. Hick and B. Hebblethwaite (eds), *Christianity and Other Religions*, Fortress, Philadelphia, 1980. Joppa Group, N. Wood (ed), *A Baptist Perspective on Interfaith Dialogue*, Joppa Publications, Alcester, 1992. WCC, *Guidelines on Dialogue with People of Living Faiths and Ideologies*, WCC, Geneva, 1979. P. Weller, 'Freedom and Witness in a Multi-Religious Society: A Baptist Perspective' in *Baptist Quarterly* Vol. XXXIII Nos.6 and 7, Apr and Jul 1990. P. Weller 'Baptist Principles as they relate to 'The Four Principles of Dialogue' in *Discernment* Vol. 5 no. 3, 1992.

Diaspora churches in Europe
[See also *Migration*]

Baptist life in Europe has been influenced by social and *political* movements which have resulted in significant numbers of one cultural, ethnic, or national group finding themselves a *minority* in another country or culture. An early 20th-century example occurred in 1920 when as a consequence of WWI by the Treaty of Trianon the Hungarian *Nation* shrank to a third of its size. This resulted in significant numbers of Hungarian Baptist 'diaspora' Churches in *Romania*,

Serbia, *Slovakia* and *Ukraine* which retain the Hungarian language and culture until the present time.

In the period after WWII American Servicemen who were Baptists found themselves stationed in Europe. With the help of the **Southern Baptist Convention** of the USA the European Baptist Convention was established to begin English-language churches near American Military bases. Renamed the **International Baptist Convention** in 2003 it has concentrated since the 1990s in planting English-speaking international multi-cultural churches in the capital cities of Europe [see *Church Planting*].

Since the ending of **Communism** in Eastern Europe in 1989-90 there has been freedom for new movements of people, especially economic migrants from East to West Europe. This has resulted in significant numbers of Romanian, Ukrainian and Moldovan Baptists churches in countries such as **Spain**, **Portugal** and **Italy**.

From the 1960s, increasing numbers of people from the Caribbean began to come to Europe to fill vacant places in **hospitals**, industries etc. Many came from Baptist churches but found that they were not always made to feel fully welcome in Baptist churches in the towns and cities where they had made their new homes. They for their part often found the services too formal and lacking in the vibrancy to which they were accustomed. Some did become valuable members of Baptist churches, some of which because of the changing ethnicity of their catchment areas became mainly black churches. Others founded black-led **pentecostal**-type churches such as the New Testament Church of God, or the Church of God of Prophecy, most often practicing believers' **baptism**.

Another movement which has intensified since the 1990s has been the flow of *refugees* into Europe; the Baptist **Union** of **Norway** (Refugees), e.g., has Burmese and Vietnamese churches in its membership. Former colonial links [see *Colonialism*] have led to significant numbers of Africans setting up 'baptistic' churches in London, Paris, Brussels, Rome, and other European cities, often subsequently applying for membership to the national Baptist union as a 'family' of churches. In 2007 the largest **membership** church in the Baptist Union of **Great Britain** was a church started in the 1980s by a Ghanian **pastor** mainly consisting of West Africans.

The most recent factor since 2004 has been the opening up of national borders with the enlargement of the **European Union**, giving all citizens the right to work anywhere within the EU. So e.g. by 2007 there were 600,000 Polish migrant workers in the UK, and discussions were taking place between the British and Polish Baptist Unions about the possibility of a Polish pastor to minister to these workers.

All these movements of people have presented new opportunities and challenges in the **mission** work of the Baptist unions of Europe. Positively it has encouraged cooperation between 'sending' and 'receiving' unions in ministering to diaspora groups. Some Baptist unions have faced the challenge of integrating diaspora churches into their union by forming a special department for this within their union structure. Often differences of **theology** and church culture have to be overcome e.g. on the question of the **ordination** of **women** to the **ministry**.

These developments also raise important questions about the nature of local Baptist churches [see *Local Church*], notably as to whether the ultimate goal should be mono-ethnic churches or multi-ethnic churches or whether the former is an important stage on the way to the latter. The presence of refugees, within Baptist congregations has sometimes involved Baptist churches and unions becoming involved in questions of justice for immigrants and asylum-seekers [see *Sanctuary*].

AAP

Disabilities, Work with those who have severe

[See also *BUild*]

Churches usually want to make appropriate **pastoral** response to people who have severe disabilities, but their attempts may be clumsy. Practical provision, like ramps, good lighting and hearing loops can make **church buildings** and **worship** more accessible to those with mobility and sensory disabilities. As such provision can be expensive; sadly it is sometimes done only when enforced by government requirements on all public buildings. Beyond such adaptations, sensitive inclusion involves attitudes even more than the provision of mechanical aids. The will to include everyone and sympathetic help can do much to overcome poor physical provision. Many churches depend on the gifts and faithful service of people whose physical disabilities could have been a reasonable excuse for a more passive *discipleship*.

With intellectual impairment (severe learning disability) there is a particular challenge in making the gospel known where words communicate poorly. Many can be brought to life-changing *faith*, partly by special teaching but mainly by experiencing the *love* and *grace* of God as it is reflected in the lives of *Christ*'s people. In *Britain* the work of BUild (the *B*aptist *U*nion *i*nitiative with people with *l*earning *d*isabilities) has helped churches develop effective *ministry* in this area. Baptists in *Poland* are doing similar work. It is rather easy for Baptists, with their stress on believers' baptism, to seek intellectual understanding which some can never achieve; but belief is about spiritual understanding which does not require an intelligence test.

Even the barrier of autism, a condition which involves social disability, puts up barriers to making human relationships and appears to counter everything the church offers, can be penetrated by the grace of God.

Where prenatal screening and the offer of *abortion* is available for some disabling conditions, like Down's Syndrome and spina bifida, the church should be sensitive to the need to support both the person with the disability and the parents, siblings and other carers. It is easy to urge pro-life policies, but the church should recognise what disability entails and expect to provide considerable on-going support for the families concerned.

FWB

Disarmament

[See also *Peace, Baptists and*]

Whilst efforts to secure disarmament between the two World Wars failed in their general aims because of the response of the emerging fascist powers to the Versailles settlement, and the reaction of the democracies to their strategies, the Geneva protocols of 1925 did ban the use of chemical and biological weapons as well as gas warfare. The statistics for post-1945 loss of life are horrendous; UNICEF puts the figure in excess of 23 million for the period 1945-92, the majority of whom were *women* and *children* civilians. Since 1959 the *UN* has been working for total disarmament, though its member governments are only prepared to think in terms of 'arms control'.

Meanwhile unimaginable sums are spent on weapon production, though happily that budget fell significantly in the last two decades of the 20th century. Notwithstanding the Non-Proliferation Treaty of 1968 the accord has hardly been successful in its desire 'to achieve at the earliest possible date the cessation of the nuclear arms race, and to undertake effective measures in the direction of nuclear disarmament.' In the context of increased hostility between *Islamic* and Christian *nations*, not to mention *Israel*'s perceptions of her need to defend her international position, uncertainty in the nuclear arms race remains and continues to menace world peace.

The Canberra Assembly of the *WCC* in 1991 called for the phased elimination of nuclear weapons, but the churches have yet to put their muscle behind that ambition. Indeed as the ending of the *cold war* reduced the perceived threat of nuclear war, the churches have moved their attention to restricting the conventional arms trade, opposition to land mines, with their long post-conflict after life, and restriction of trade in small arms. Nevertheless because of the relative cheapness of many weapons, – assault rifles can be bought for 'the price of a chicken or a bag of maize' – and their ready availability – more than half the trade in these weapons is legal – the world remains an exceedingly dangerous place, especially as the churches remain divided between *pacifist* and *just war* approaches to issues of war and peace.

Baptists have been divided in their opinions about the right, indeed some would say duty, of the *state* to be armed and to protect citizens. Some Baptists would be against nations having nuclear arms and arguing strongly for this type of disarmament and others for more general disarmament. Unions such as *Sweden* and *Great Britain* have passed resolutions against the arms trade. The *EBF* itself has passed no less that six resolutions supporting Nuclear Disarmament in the period 1977-87.

JHYB & KGJ

Disaster Relief
See *Emergency/Disaster Relief.*

Discipleship
Discipleship lies at the heart of the *church* in *mission*. It is a NT word used primarily in the Gospels and in the Acts of the Apostles. Disciples in the NT are followers of *Christ*, learners of his ways. The Latin noun *discere* means 'to learn'. The disciples are those who learn while Christ leads them through a journey. The *Great Commission* in Mt 28 sees discipleship as the main task of the church – 'therefore, disciple all nations' – while indicating by way of three Greek participles what the task may include:

(1) going forth
(2) baptising them [see *Baptism*] (in the name of the Father, and of the Son and of the *Holy Spirit)*
(3) teaching them (to keep all (things) that I commanded you).

Evangelicals have often separated the task into at least two parts. They speak of *evangelism* followed by *conversion* as one task, conducted by a specific evangelistic group or an individual, the evangelist, and then of discipleship, following on conversion and hopefully leading into *church membership*. In baptistic churches this will find focus in baptism after pre-baptismal teaching. However, the commission as given by Jesus does not break up the task into parts but sees it as one whole which is to be the task of the whole church.

Usually the task is seen chronologically with evangelism preceding discipleship. This chronological approach is also used by those who misinterpret the text by seeing each task in v.19 as separate tasks. But the text gives no evidence for this. Rather it sees the call to discipleship as a lifelong *vocation*.

Whilst in the process there is a specific moment of turning to Christ, manifested in baptism, this is only one early stage of the process of discipleship which has to be a life-long commitment. The going, or crossing of borders and boundaries in order to disciple others, the teaching and the learning must continue throughout a disciple's life.

Discipleship, as Mathew formulates it, has two additional ingredients of central value, which are often missed when vv.19-20 are read without the context of vv.16-20. The context points to Christ being at the centre of discipleship. The church is called to make disciples of the triune God [see *Trinity*] and not of any human leader. These disciples and the process of discipleship remain under the transforming power of Christ (v.16) and are informed by his presence among the disciples, by the presence of the promised Immanuel – God being in the midst of his disciples for all time.

PFP

Disciples of Christ
See *Churches of Christ.*

Discipline
See *Church Discipline.*

Discretion and Valour
Discretion and Valour: Religious Conditions in Russia and Eastern Europe was the fruit of a working group set up by the British Council of Churches which met intensively from 1971-73. Those involved included Sir John Lawrence, Revd Michael Bourdeaux, Revd Paul Oestreicher, Dr. Ernest Payne together with Revd Trevor Beeson, who wrote up their findings in the published volume in 1974. Dr. Ronald Goulding of the *EBF* was a consultant to the project which was concerned to discover just what the situation in Eastern Europe was some 30 years after the end of WWII. They were reassured that the situation was not as dire as it had been in the '50s even though full freedom was denied in many places. There was a perceived need for an authoritative account, free of the rancour often fostered by churches in exile,

which would bring out the differences in different countries, and between different churches. That the volume was so well received showed a deep concern in the West for the welfare of Christians in Eastern Europe. The title was well chosen: it was important to suggest that 'discretion' as much as 'valour' could be part of gospel obedience. Thus Sir John Lawrence wrote in the Foreword to the first edition, 'We do not accept that the only authentic Christianity is underground' (p.10). After warning about people in free states too readily passing judgment, Beeson boldly affirms, 'The Moscow Patriarchate, the All Union Council of Baptists, and the *Jewish* Rabbinate, e.g., have probably been no less heroic in shouldering the agony and the burden of accommodation than *Orthodox* resisters, Baptist reformers and spokesman of the new voice of *Soviet* Jewry have been in their refusal to yield any ground to the totalitarian claims of the *state*' (p.25).

The book was quickly translated into French, German and Finnish and chapters circulated in *Russia* in *samizdat* form – that is distributed in typescript or as material produced on illegal presses. The present writer has been at international conferences where copies of the book were eagerly passed from Western to Eastern delegates. The second revised edition, published in 1982, is perhaps a little milder than the original volume. E.g. after a discussion of how the *Lutheran* and *Reformed Churches* in *Hungary* took up a stance near to that of government, the first edition concludes with this comment, 'churches can become so deeply compromised that they cease to be signs and servants of the Gospel, and the benefits of freedom to *preach* and *worship* are in such circumstances published at too high a price' (p.247). That judgment is gone in the 1982 edition: instead there is an account of *Billy Graham*'s 1977 visit to Hungary.

One thing is abundantly clear in Beeson's account: as far as Baptists are concerned persecution existed long before a number of these Eastern European countries came under *communist* control. The account of relationships between the All Union Council and the *initsiativniki* found in the volume is eminently fair.

JHYB

Dispensationalism

Dispensationalism, a variant of the premillennial view of the Second Advent, was largely shaped by the early *Brethren* leader John Nelson Darby. It argued that God dealt with people in different ways in different eras ('dispensations') of history. Darby's *shema* was to be popularised by C.I. Scofield (*Congregational Minister* associate of D.W. Moody) in his Reference Bible of 1909. Crucially, Darby suggested that there would be a 'secret rapture' of the *church* at the return of *Christ*, which could take place 'at any moment', and that Christ would subsequently come back *with* his *saints* in a public appearance to reign for 1,000 years, in accordance with Rev 20. Much attention was given to issues connected with the interpretation and fulfilment of *prophecy* by a number of *evangelicals* in the 19th century. One view, the 'futurist' view, was that Revelation referred to events that were still in the future. Futurist premillennial interpreters were themselves divided, with some following Darby's ideas about a 'secret rapture'. Others, including a number of Baptists who embraced premillennialism, rejected Darby's scheme and expected a period of severe *suffering* for believers, 'the great tribulation', before Christ's visible return. The hope of the secret rapture was one that promised that true believers would be exempt from the sufferings of the great tribulation. Prophecies about the *kingdom of God* were, according to the logic of Dispensationalism, to be fulfilled, largely through the *Jews*, in the millennial age that would follow the advent. Dispensationalism has been more prevalent among American Baptists than in Europe, but it is to be found among European Baptists, in part because of American influence, and in those Baptist circles in *Britain* which have welcomed ex-Brethren into *membership*.

IMR

FURTHER READING: R.G. Clouse (ed), *The Meaning of the Millenium: Four Views*, Inter-Varsity, Downers Grove, Il., 1977. M. Williams, *This World is not my Home: The Origins and Development of Dispensationalism*, Christian Focus Publications, Fearn, Scotland, 2003.

Distance Learning, Theological

See *Theological Education by Extension*.

Diversity of Ministries

See *Ministries, Diversity of*.

Divorce and Remarriage

[See also *Marriage/Matrimony*]

Most Baptists would support the statement in the Latvian Baptist Union's 1998 Confession when it states, 'We **preach** the purity of family life based on the faithful marriage of one man and one woman, understanding the family as established by God with its norms clearly outlined in the NT which are binding on all people in all ages. The strength of the family is rooted in the godly behaviour and mutual *love* exhibited by its members.' That is the ideal; the difficult pastoral issue turns around what are the possibilities when, in a far from perfect world, that ideal relationship, solemnised with vows and promises as well as the invocation of God's blessing, breaks down, especially since the marriage relationship as spelt out in the NT is portrayed as mirroring the love of *Christ* for the *Church*. Many would therefore take the 'indissolubilist' position, namely that there are no circumstances in which such a marriage can be dissolved, with a consequent ruling out of any possibility of remarriage.

The teaching in the synoptic gospels on this is disputed: whilst some argue that Jesus, contrary to contemporary *Jewish* practice, totally forbade divorce, others argue that he conceded it as a permissible evil in a sinful world [see *Fall*; *Sin*]. Whilst arguing that the marriage bond *should* not be broken, they allow that, because of the persistent power of sin in a fallen world, it *can* be embraced as the lesser evil than that involved in perpetuating a harming and even demeaning relationship. That is to say they recognise that it is possible for a marriage to die and that because the gospel is about compassion, *forgiveness* and new beginnings, it is possible for Christian people to make, and the Church to recognise, a new start in a second marriage. This must not be lightly undertaken and only when all other possibilities

have been finally exhausted. This is one area of church life where a higher standard may be required of *pastors*/ministers than that required on lay members, for many Baptist Unions would at least require some disciplining of a pastor whose own failure has contributed to a marriage break-down, before continuing in *ministry*, even if that were ever to be allowed.

The problem may need to be taken further back, for one of the causes of divorce, even amongst *Evangelical* Christians, may be imperfect instruction about the nature of Christian marriage and the responsible handling of human sexuality in the first place, with the advice that most marriages will face difficult periods, or areas of tension, which need to be dealt with sensitively and compassionately by both partners, and indeed other members of the family, as well as by the *local church*, which needs to develop skills in caring for people living in or suffering from bruised relationships, as well as *children* growing up in such circumstances.

When prayerfully [see *Prayer*] a pastor, with the support of his or her *deacons*, has decided that a second marriage, following divorce, is the right way to proceed, there remains the problem of not allowing the exception to move or change the norm, that is to say the ministry of compassion has always to be exercised alongside a concern to maintain the institution of marriage and nurturing the highest standards within it. Few pastors in our age will enjoy the luxury of ministering to a congregation that does not contain or does not attract some divorced persons. Unlike the *Catholic Church*, Baptists would not engage in the need to show in a quasi-legal manner that the first marriage had somehow been inadequate, and therefore could be 'annulled', nor, as until recently in many *Anglican* churches, require the couple starting on a second marriage to secure this in a civil ceremony before receiving a blessing in church. Rather Baptists, when they judge it right to do so, would offer a second marriage in church.

JHYB

Dogmatics

Dogmatics is that branch of *Systematic Theology* wherein the central, core convictions of Christian *faith* are set out and related to one another. Christian dogmatics seeks to identify and set out the major areas of theological understanding, the foundation for constructing all other theological statements.

European Baptistic understandings of Christian Dogmatics have been affected by the varied contexts and cultures in which Baptists have formed their roots. For some, this lies in the *theology* of *Jean Calvin*. Thus a major Particular Baptist Confession in *England* in the 17th century drew, to a significant extent, from the *Presbyterian* (*Calvinistic*) Westminster Confession. Others have been more affected by the traditions of the Radical *Reformation* and the General Baptists, who also produced important *Confessions* in the 17th century such as the Orthodox Creed On the whole, the early Baptists tended to emphasise and combine central *scriptural* tenets, linking these with core convictions and their implications for the life of the *local church*.

In the 20th century many *Protestants* (and some *Catholics*) in Europe were profoundly affected by the theology of the Swiss theologian, Karl Barth. His thinking was expressed most fully in his 13-volume work, significantly entitled the *Church Dogmatics* [Ger. *Kirchliche Dogmatik*]. Barth published the *Dogmatics* over a period of nearly 40 years, until his death in 1968. Barth provides one outstanding example of how robust Christian doctrine could be set out in a relevant way, and it is significant for Baptists that the centre of Barth's theology was *Jesus Christ*.

For Baptists, the dogmatic core of Christian faith lies in the reality that the 'Word became flesh' (Jn 1:14), that is the Living Word in Christ, in his life, *death* and *resurrection*, is the final *authority* for the Christian community. Baptists believe that the appearance of God in human flesh, revealing the true character of God through a human being, is of fundamental importance. It is this commitment of God towards our humanity, foundationally expressed not only in the *Incarnation* but carried on throughout the life, teachings and *ministry* of Jesus Christ into His atoning death [see *Atonement*], resurrection, ascension and glorification, that allows valid explanation and application of Christian truths into different contexts and cultures.

This prioritisation of Jesus Christ carries implications for any schematisation of Baptist dogmatics, and this is being more fully explored today. The *church* is the visible, *gathered* community of believers. As God has expressed His full *revelation* to and through the humanity of Christ, so it is in and among the community of those who seek to follow Christ in their humanity that the presence and person of Jesus Christ is made known. It follows that the church is a voluntaristic community, constituted by those who intentionally profess Jesus Christ as Lord. The volitional and intentional nature of this profession is acknowledged through the practice of believers' *baptism*. Likewise, in that Jesus Christ is now glorified in the presence of God our Father, so the church receives and experiences the presence and empowering of the *Holy Spirit*, enabling her to live in the faith of Jesus Christ, to the glory of God our Father.

This is not to play down Trinitarian theology [see *Trinity*]. Baptists affirm in their dogmatics *reconciliation* to God our Father through Jesus Christ, enablement and empowerment by the Holy Spirit, and the expression of ministry through the local church. At the same time this leaves freedom for the development of theology in a way true to the context and culture in which the local church lives and seeks to act as a *missional* community. Baptistic churches seek to relate their present *witness* to that of the believing community that is witnessed to in the NT. In this regard, a dogmatic schema developed out of a convictional core is well suited to the post-modern era, where the focus of theology has moved from mapping out generalised, foundational meta-narratives to seeking to work out the implications of the Christian gospel within the local contexts where Christians find themselves. The development of a dogmatic model serves in developing theological suppositions that can be tested and reappraised in the light of scriptural witness and relevance to the church's life, witness and mission.

JGMP & ET

Domestic Missions

Christians, including Baptists, in 19th-century cities realised that the dense slums close to their churches presented a *mission* challenge comparable to the foreign missions they supported so enthusiastically. Domestic Missions addressed pressing social and spiritual needs close to home. The pioneering Bloomsbury Chapel Domestic Mission in central London left records that show the range of work undertaken. Even before a church was formed, William Brock came in 1848 to *preach* in the new *chapel*, bringing with him a young *temperance* missionary, George Wilson M'Cree, to lead the Domestic Mission. A man of great energy and 'consecrated commonsense', M'Cree was a homely preacher, an effective lecturer, a compassionate *pastor*, and persuasive *evangelist* and fund-raiser. He was helped by teams of district visitors, lay preachers [see *Laity*], teachers, doctors, and others from the Chapel, volunteering their time as well as money to improve the lives of the very poor. Ancillary societies encouraged self-help by making available subsidised food, clothing, blankets, coal, books, medicine, basic *education*, etc. at affordable prices. In this they co-operated with other churches and Christian bodies, including the London *City Mission*, the Ragged Schools, and Parish Dispensary. Although such a Mission only covered a small area, it transformed many lives, physically and spiritually. Articulate volunteers, often employers who now saw for themselves what poverty was like, helped to improve conditions, demanding clean water supplies, better housing and better working hours and conditions for employees.

FWB

Drugs

The general public are usually confronted with the drug culture either when a young person tragically dies due to an overdose or some large haul of drugs has been seized by Customs and Excise. There is a large population involved in illegal drug use. *Health* care professions are highly regulated by various Medicines Acts although abuse still occurs. The illegal use of drugs is big business and the Misuse of Drugs Act 1971 in the *UK*, gives law enforcement agencies powers to investigate and prosecute those who possess, deal or manufacture drugs illegally. The power and penalties vary dependent on the class of drug concerned. Drugs may be misused by smoking or snorting, by oral digestion or by injecting the drug into a vein. Crime is involved in smuggling drugs into Europe for illegal use and those addicted, are drawn into an underworld of *violence*, sickness and theft. Illegal drug trafficking is an international trade and consumes large resources to intercept dealers as they seek to outwit the law enforcement agencies to sell their cargos of misery mainly to young people in society and indeed to those associated with our churches.

The reasons why individuals are drawn into experimenting with illegal drugs use are complex. Many claim they started indulging for recreational reasons. They may be looking for relaxation or for excitement. Others are drawn in by the influence of friends or out of a sense of curiosity or adventure. Some are simply bored with their lives. However, it has been observed that there is a significant group that turn to drug use because they feel like failures; socially and/or *educationally*. A proportion whose lives are damaged by abuse and/or *poverty* also find solace in illegal drug use. Drugs can slow down, speed up or distort perceptions and fall into one of four groups:

- The *depressants* depress physical and brain function making the user feel relaxed and uninhibited, e.g. cannabis and *alcohol*.
- The *stimulants* excite the bodily systems making the user feel more energetic, e.g. cocaine and *tobacco*.
- The *hallucinogens* alter perception distorting the senses, e.g. ecstasy and cannabis.
- The *painkillers* numb pain, e.g. heroin.

Clearly, these drugs produce unwanted and adverse effects. Illegal drugs are known on the streets by a variety of names such as speed, coke, weed, smack and acid. One group that has particular fascination for young people is solvents that can be inhaled, but recent legislation in the UK prohibits their sale to customers under 18 years of age.

Although there are believed to be over 600 references to alcohol in the *Bible*, there are no clear references to drugs as we know them. However, Christians who base their lives on the Bible are committed to the principle of care – for self and for others. For the Christian the human body (as well as the Christian community) are vessels for God's ***Holy Spirit*** (Ac 2) while Paul describes the members of the Corinthian congregation as temples were God's Spirit lives (1Co 3:16-17) and Peter counsels Christians to be clear minded and self controlled (1Pe 4:7). All this implies a policy of no physical abuse so that nothing mars believers' ***witness*** and ***worship***. Pro 31:1-9 is advice given to a good King who uses alcohol (a depressant drug) wisely to ease the pains of terminal illness and grief and not to abuse it and so forget the law, and thereby failing the oppressed and denying justice to the needy.

George Ruston (a Baptist) of HOPE UK and Ken Walker of the Kaleidoscope Baptist Mission in London, are examples of good practice and a compassionate Christian response. Both offer resources for training in awareness and care. The rehabilitation of those addicted to the use of illegal drugs is a long-term commitment and needs to be given by skilled, caring and professionally-trained people. Such work, as a Christian ***calling***, should be supported by the churches. Prevention through the provision of clear information deserves church support. They should also consider ways to influence legislation so that better laws are drafted to frustrate the drug traffickers and to help rehabilitate addicts. The example of the Christian community, as members work out fulfilled and purposeful lives, can be a good advert to attract potential drug users to consider the Christian path as opposed to the destructive way of illegal drugs.

PC

Dual Alignments

See ***Ecumenical covenants and partnerships***.

Dualism

Dualism may seem a remote philosophical concept but wrongly understood it can have a profound impact on Christian ***discipleship***. Part of the difficulty is that it is sometimes used as an argument for a proper differentiation of concepts, sometimes for a false attribution of wholly independent forces. E.g. in the doctrine of ***Creation*** it is crucial to distinguish creator from that which is created. Nevertheless, just because the created order is God's creation it has profound moral worth, and thus material things are certainly not intrinsically evil. The material world exists to be enjoyed and to sustain life, but not to be selfishly exploited to the detriment of the whole human community and the created order itself. Any attempts at an otherworldly asceticism or ultra-***puritanism***, as practiced by some ***sects*** and orders, are therefore based on profound theological error. Another manifestation of dualism has been the heretical [see ***Heresy***] proposal that there exist in the world autonomous principles of good and evil, a teaching which is more Zoroastrian than Christian. In the Biblical record [see ***Bible***] ***sin*** enters the human condition as a consequence of a God-given ***freedom*** attributed to Adam to choose and make moral choices. As a consequence of the choice he makes original righteousness gives way through the ***Fall*** to the vitiating principle of 'original' sin. However, the emphasis of scripture is that Evil and ***Satan***, whilst tremendously powerful, are always subordinate to the one creator God and that the consequences of sin have been overcome through the work of ***Christ***. Other dualisms that need to be preserved are that between soul/mind and body – it is the whole person that is redeemed [see ***Redemption***] by Christ's ***death*** on the ***cross*** not some disembodied spirit – and that between reason and ***revelation***, which have their own separate functions.

KTB & ET

E

EAAA
See *Euro-Asian Accrediting Association*.

Easter Day
[See also *Easter liturgies*]
The climax of *Holy Week* celebrations comes with services in recognition of *Christ*'s *Resurrection* on Easter Day. Many Baptist churches have early morning sunrise services on local high points where the first 'Hallelujahs' of Easter are sung. Other congregations have early morning *Eucharist* celebrations followed by breakfast.

Normally, the main service of the day is one of the best attended of the year and if there has not been a baptismal service [see *Baptism*] as a conclusion to the *Easter Eve* service then it would be common for such a service to form part of the main celebratory *worship* service.

Baptists drawn from the wide musical resources [see *Church Music*] of the whole Christian family to celebrate on Easter Day and the worship might often include special contributions from choirs or music groups, drama and special presentations by the *children*.

Many Baptist churches in Eastern Europe *traditionally* commemorate the fact that the first witnesses to the empty tomb of the Resurrected Jesus were the *women* by having the *Word* broken open [see *Sermon*] by a female *church member*.

It is not unknown for the morning worship to conclude with a community lunch [see *Agape meal*].

KGJ

Easter Eve
[See also *Easter liturgies*]
This is the day in the Easter season, historically associated with vigil for those preparing to be baptised [see *Baptism*], with the renewal of baptismal vows, and with waiting for news of the resurrected *Christ*. The development of the vigil through the centuries of Christian Europe is a complicated story for the historical liturgist. Today, the accent is on waiting, *renewal* and preparation for those to be baptised on *Easter Day*, when many Baptist churches hold baptismal services.

Some Baptists, as in *Georgia*, have an overnight vigil on Easter Eve, through until Easter Day. Whilst others, in *England* for instance, will hold a midnight vigil with the renewal of baptismal vows and *prayers* around the *baptistry*, then go home, returning for an Easter Day sunrise service – often outdoors on an area of high ground – before the main service of Easter Day Liturgy with Baptisms.

The Easter vigil generally includes the reading of *scripture* expounding the narrative of God's saving acts with his people from *creation*, through the exodus, to a recounting of the life, *death* and *resurrection* of Jesus. The *worship* follows a pattern of the reading of selected scriptures followed by silent meditation. Elements in the service often reflect wider *ecumenical* tradition including the renewal of baptismal vows, lighting the Easter candle, preparing the baptistry for a baptismal service and sharing in the first *Eucharist* of Easter after midnight.

It is not common for Baptists to have other symbolic features in the service such as the lighting of the new fire, which is practiced by *Catholics* and others, though it is not totally unknown in some more liturgical [see *Liturgy*] Baptist congregations.

KGJ

Easter liturgies
[See also *Liturgy*]
The Easter liturgies generally refer to those special acts of *worship* occurring between *Palm Sunday* and the evening of *Easter Day*. This period of seven days has always been an important period within the cycle of worship in the *Christian Year*.

Significant liturgies during this period will include commemoration of the triumphal entry into Jerusalem by *Jesus* on Palm Sunday. Monday, Tuesday and Wednesday often have special services of reflection in what is called *Holy Week*, focusing on penitence, obedience and renewal.

On the Thursday of Holy Week [see *Great Thursday*] many churches remember the institution of the *Eucharist* with a special service including a celebration of the *Lord's Supper*. On the Friday [see *Great Friday*] most churches will hold a service of *prayer* and reflection recalling the events on the *cross*. Some churches hold a three hour vigil in the afternoon. Others will take part in open air services of *witness* where these are permitted. A smaller number of churches will hold an Easter Vigil on Saturday evening [see *Easter Eve*], but many more churches will hold a Sunrise service early in the morning of the Sunday, possibly on a local area of high ground, or in the centre of a city at some place of importance, e.g. in Prague, where the service is normally at the foot of the famous statue of Wenceslas. Such services are often followed by a breakfast in church premises. At the climax of Holy Week a wide range of services are held on the day of *resurrection*, Easter Day. These often include services of believers' *baptism*.

KGJ

Easter Saturday

See *Easter Eve*.

EBC

See *International Baptist Convention*.

EBF

See *European Baptist Federation*.

EBM

See *European Baptist Mission (EBM) – history and work*.

EBWU

See *Women in Baptist life; Women's work*.

Ecclesiology (Church Polity)

[See also *Assembly, General – as governing body of Union; Church, The; Unions/Conventions; Worship (Ecclesiology)*]

Ecclesia, from the Greek εκκλησια, the congregation of those called together, is in the NT a designation of the Christian Church, local as well as universal. Ecclesiology is the doctrine of the *church*. Different Christian traditions have developed this doctrine in various directions. Ecclesiology concerns both the nature of the church and church polity, or the way in which any group organises itself.

For Baptists the doctrine of the church is the foundation on which the understanding of *mission*, the *ordinances/sacraments* and *ecumenical* relations are all based. Historically it was the understanding of the church as the community of confessing and baptised believers [see *Baptism*] which led to the organisation of the first Baptist church, in Amsterdam 1609. The reading of the NT led the early Baptists to focus on the local congregation, but also to recognise the universal church as the communion of all of God's people. This understanding is already reflected in Baptist *confessions of faith* from the earliest in the 17th century.

According to normative Baptist ecclesiology, then, the local church is not a geographically defined entity, a parish. But neither is it a society of likeminded individuals banding together to promote common interests. As The Council of the Baptist Union of *Great Britain and Ireland* said in 1948: 'It is in *membership* of a local church in one place that the *fellowship* of the one holy catholic Church becomes significant. Indeed, such gathered companies of believers are the local manifestation of the one Church of God on earth and in *heaven*...Such churches are gathered by the will of *Christ* and live by the indwelling of His *Spirit*. They do not have their origin, primarily, in human resolution.' None the less, membership in the local church is on the basis of a conscious and deliberate acceptance of Jesus Christ as Saviour and Lord by each person. Entirely separate from the life of the *state* [see *Separation of Church and State*], the local church consists of people who through *faith* and *baptism*, upon a personal confession of this faith, have become members of the body of Christ, his Church.

Baptists hold that the NT is normative in matters of church polity. The centre of church polity is the local congregation. The church members, not a superior external *authority*, make the decisions regarding doctrinal matters, leadership, cooperation with other bodies and the range of *ministries* to be exercised by the church. It is they who, in *church meeting*, appoint the officers of the church including the *pastor*. This *autonomy* is expressed, e.g. in the adoption of a confession of faith indicating the church's theology, a *covenant* determining the responsibilities and rights of the members, and a constitution which regulates the administration of the church.

However, in the Baptist tradition these autonomous churches are not independent but interdependent. By the middle of the 17th century, permanent *associations* of churches were formed among English Baptists, both General and Particular. These early Baptist, in the words of W.T. Whitley, 'deliberately linked their churches, both to steady one another in doctrine and explain themselves unitedly to the world, to aid one another in time of need, and especially to propagate their views.' This development was not purely pragmatic and therefore accidental to the understanding of the church; rather it was based on the reading of the NT.

The associational principle has followed mainstream Baptists everywhere, and has developed into *unions* or conventions, which on a national level have been invested with much of the same authority and functions as the regional associations.

In summary the Baptist ecclesiology is: a regenerate church membership, baptism on personal confession of faith, the autonomy of the local church but churches combining in associations expressed through district associations and state and national conventions and unions, separation of church and state, with its corollary: *freedom of conscience* and *religious liberty* for all.

PAE

FURTHER READING: Paul S. Fiddes, *Tracks and Traces*, Paternoster, Carlisle and Waynesboro, Ga., 2003. Ernest A. Payne, *The Fellowship of Believers*, Kingsgate, London, 1952. Nigel G. Wright, *Free Church, Free State*, Paternoster, Milton Keynes and Waynesboro, Ga., 2005.

Eco-seminaries and Eco-congregations

[See also *Ecology and the Environment*]
Christians have always properly understood themselves to be stewards [see *Stewardship*] of God's magnificent *creation*. In traditional

theology, especially within **Orthodox** communities, a strong doctrine of the created order and the responsibility of **humankind** to take good care of creation in all its variety and magnificence has been properly emphasised within the totality of the life and work of the churches. However, such doctrinal affirmations have not always resulted in clear approaches and strategies within the life of believing communities. The **Anabaptist** communities of Moravia in the 1500s took a great concern in restoring the vineyards of the Lords of Lichtenstein, their landlords and in a proper concern for the care of the land and in husbandry of animals. However, the general attitude in later **Protestantism** nuanced stewardship towards exploitation of the abundance of the created order for the advancement of civilisation, the development of manufacturing activity and the pursuit of economic advance without much regard to the extensive use of non-renewable features of the creation such as oil, coal and valuable minerals and precious metals.

In recent years there has been increasing recognition within the Christian churches that such wanton exploitation of the created order has costs in terms of despoliation of the environment, the loss of animal and plant species because of lack of protection, the creating of unsustainable amounts of waste, leading to further pressure on the fragile balanced structure of the created order. In such circumstances the response has been a re-focusing on the earlier doctrines of creation, on the need for the use of the resources of the earth in a sustainable way, even if this involves limits to economic growth. If the major ways to achieve this demand action by governments, industry and international regulators, Christians are committed to action in local communities of believers. So, in Baptist communities and seminaries across Europe a movement has developed since the mid 1990s of Eco-seminaries and Eco-congregations where positive and consistent reflection and action is taken on a more adequate understanding of Christian stewardship for sustainability involving deliberate programmes of Biblical reflection [see *Bible*], emphasis in *worship* and practical action. Amongst principal areas of affirmative action to be noted are – insulation of buildings, reduction of use of energy, turning to sustainable and renewable forms of energy, programmes of planting and enhancing the environment, recycling schemes, waste reduction programmes, cleaning up and improving the built environment, reducing travel by car in favour of energy-efficient public transport. In several European countries schemes to develop Eco-congregations exist with Baptist churches taking part enthusiastically.

In 2006 *IBTS* hosted a major conference on the place of Environmental Theology in the seminary and a report has been issued and distributed to all seminaries in Europe. This explored how the theme of environmental theology could be introduced into every aspect of the life of the seminary – in worship, lectures and lifestyle. Prominent European Baptists are at the forefront in the drive towards development of environmentally-friendly initiatives including Sir John Houghton (*climate change*), Professor Graham W. Ashworth (environmental education), Dr. John Biggs (Eco-congregations), JUDr. Petra Veselá (European Environmental law), Revd Dr. John Weaver (environmental theology).

PV & KGJ

FURTHER READING: *Eco-congregation: The Churches' Environmental Programme*, Churches Together in Britain and Ireland, London, 2000. John Weaver and Margot R. Hodson (eds), *The Place of Environmental Theology: A guide for seminaries, colleges and universities*, IBTS, Prague, 2007.

École Pastorale, Massy, France

The Pastoral School at Massy, near Paris, *France* is a permanent institution for practical *theology*. Set up by Baptists and other *Free Churches*, it welcomes those coming from other churches as well. The aim of the school is to contribute to the practical theological formation and development of *pastors*. It is open to all who already exercise *ministry* to help them to reflect theologically on their practice and equip them to enhance this ministry. Sessions are always participatory. The intention is to discover the diversity of current trends and sensitivities and try to develop some cohesion. This brings pastors to a deeper understanding of the context and communities in which they work. The school offers a variety of special courses and theological days, and help in developing responsible *church members*. Papers from these courses appear as the *Cahiers de l'École Pastorale*, and these can be found on the internet.

FWB

FURTHER READING: www2.ecolepastorale.com/cahiers.

Ecology and the Environment

[See also *Climate Change; Justice, Peace and the Integrity of Creation*]
Baptist Christians, along with all other mainstream believers, have always asserted the theological conviction that God created the whole cosmos and set human beings to be stewards [see *Stewardship*] of the created order [see *Creation*]. However, whilst the *Anabaptist* communities in Moravia, *Slovakia* and elsewhere were noted for their concern for, and careful restoration of creation, for most Baptists beyond the theological assertions of the importance of God's world and the *call* to stewardship, little, if anything emerged from this until the end of the last century.

Individual Baptists with a background in biology, environmental studies and related disciplines began to speak out on the topic of the abuse of creation and the need for a commitment to sustainable development and not wanton destruction of the good earth in the wake of a more general concern for the degradation of the ecology in many parts of Europe and beyond. Particular concern was expressed about the pollution of rivers and land, the ill effects of acid rain on countries innocent of its production, the rise in so-called 'greenhouse gases' and the mountains of waste produced by a throw-away society which were being poured into land-fill sites.

In more recent years Baptist *politicians* and academics have given distinguished leadership to the Europe-wide campaign which seeks to address this issue. Baptist communities in Western Europe have joined with others in campaigns and direct action to lay these issues before politicians and to join in the demand for development of renewable energy, the abandonment of the reliance of fossil fuels, the importance of recycling and desire to live more simply so that those in the developing world may simply live.

Beyond the general, there is continuing debate about particular actions Baptist communities might take. So, there has been in some places action by local congregations and theological seminaries to work towards becoming *eco-communities*. Some Baptist Unions such as *Sweden* and *Great Britain* have developed whole programmes of practical and theological *education* in this area. Some individual congregations have engaged in programmes to reduce energy consumption, use 'greener' forms of energy, develop recycling programmes and work at a reduction of pollution in their locality.

More controversial have been attempts at direct action campaigns by some Baptists in protesting against airport expansion, programmes to build new coal-fired or nuclear power stations or to participate in direct action campaigns for the increased use of bicycles over against cars. Here, Baptist communities have found it more difficult to be of a common mind.

Meanwhile, in Central and Eastern Europe it would be fair to say that for most Baptists the topic is not yet on the agenda and it is at best a novelty and at worst an attack on individual freedom to suggest taking action to reduce reliance on fossil fuel, to engage in campaigns to clean up the environment or to abandon consumer goods and excessive packaging only recently available after the collapse of totalitarian regimes.

KGJ

Ecstatic speech
See *Glossolalia*.

Ecumenical/Ecumenical (Oecumenical) Movement
[See also *Ecumenical covenants and partnerships/Union Churches/Dual Alignments*; *Ecumenical Movement, European Baptist contributors in the 20ᵗʰ and 21ˢᵗ centuries*; *Oikoumene*; *Unity of the Church*; *World Council of Churches*]
The adjective 'ecumenical' derives from the

Greek *oikoumene*, which means the whole inhabited world. Its older usage was to describe the universal in the early church thus it is used of those councils which have been accepted as authoritative for all the ancient strands of Christianity. However the number of councils so accepted varies from church family to church family. Thus the Oriental *Orthodox Churches* (Armenians, Copts and Syrian Orthodox) only accept the first three, disagreeing with the way the Council of Chalcedon (451) spoke of the person of *Christ*, whilst the *Roman Catholic* and Eastern Orthodox Churches accept the *authority* of the first seven councils. The adjective is also used to describe the Patriarch of Constantinople amongst Eastern Orthodox Christians recognising his pre-eminence among, but not his jurisdiction over, other Orthodox churches.

More recently the Ecumenical Movement is that movement concerned to give new expression to the unity of the church. Part of the inspiration for this goes back to the experience of *Evangelical* Christians working across denominational boundaries in such activities as the work of the *Bible Society*, the *Sunday School* movement, the *YMCA/YWCA* , work with *students,* etc. as well as, on a pan-*protestant* basis, in the *Evangelical Alliance* and the emergence of the modern *missionary* movement. Given these roots it is perhaps a little surprising that some later evangelicals, including what Bebbington calls the 'Baptist fringe', were so hostile to giving organisational focus to the movement with the founding of the World Council of Churches in 1948. By then there had been other streams flowing in, e.g. the Malines Conversations between groups of *Anglican* and Roman Catholic theologians in the 1920s. There was also the quite remarkable Encyclical issue by the Ecumenical Patriarchate in 1920 'to all the *Churches* of Christ, wheresover they be', significant because notwithstanding Orthodoxy's exclusive claims to churchly status, it addressed other Christian bodies frankly and courteously as churches.

Thus a number of forces were at work within what was coming to be known as the ecumenical movement – such as the interdenominational concern for *Life and Work* (1925), and *Faith and Order* (1927), the *In-*

ternational Missionary Council (1921) and the World Council of Christian Education. Within *nations*, the *Free Churches* were increasingly collaborative both for defence, and for strength of *witness*. Dating back to the 1860s there was also the birth of organisations representing the various World Christian families, now known as *Christian World Communions*, the *Baptist World Alliance* being founded in 1905. At another level, *national councils*, and regional councils of churches have also become the norm. All are part of the ecumenical movement of which the WCC is but one expression. Indeed more recently this body has become content to sit alongside a more broadly-based Global Christian Forum which has strong evangelical, independent and *Pentecostal*, as well as Roman Catholic participation.

JHYB

Ecumenical communities
See *Intentional Communities*; *Oikoumene*.

Ecumenical covenants and partnerships
[See also *Ecumenical/Ecumenical (Oecumenical) Movement*; *Ecumenical Movement, European Baptist contributors in the 20th and 21st centuries*; *Oikoumene*; *Unity of the Church*; *World Council of Churches*]
All these words relate to churches which seek to relate to more than one denomination. In *Britain* the *tradition* goes right back to Baptist origins when some independent (congregational) churches only slowly moved to a Baptist position and therefore contained both those baptised as infants and those baptised as believers [see *Baptism*; *Infant Baptism*]. *John Bunyan* addressed this issue in his 1673 tract, *Differences in Judgment about Water-Baptism No Bar to Communion*. This both argued for *open communion* and formed the basis of cooperation in Bedfordshire and the surrounding counties of Baptists and *Congregationalists*.

This found institutional form, in the new context of the *Evangelical Revival*'s itinerant outreach to the rural world, with the establishment of the Bedfordshire Union of Christians in 1797. Churches relating to both Baptist and Congregational *unions* came to be known as 'Union Churches' and their number was increased with the planting of united *free-church* congregations in some of the 'garden cities' and new suburbs of the late 19th and early 20th centuries. Amalgamation of congregations because of war damage or changing population movements added to their number in the second half of the 20th century. This is not uniquely a British phenomenon for in *Sweden*, e.g., there are congregations that are dually aligned to the Baptist Union and to the Mission Covenant Church.

More recently the *ecumenical movement* has challenged the different denominations to provide local symbols of the *church*'s *unity*. From 1973 such ecumenical experiments were called Local Ecumenical Projects, but by the 1990s they were called Local Ecumenical Partnerships (LEPs). Some exist at the level of a general *covenant* committing the member churches in a given area to co-operative action, but others involve the sharing of *buildings*, *ministry*, *worship*, and *witness*, and the development of joint *membership* rolls. In 2001 some 750 such partnerships existed with Baptist participation in just under a third of these, that is, about 12% of churches in the Baptist Union of Great Britain were in ecumenical partnerships. One of the areas where these developments have progressed most comprehensively is the new town of Milton Keynes where there is an 'ecumenical moderator' for the whole area. Currently, and for the second time, this post is occupied by a Baptist *minister*. The existence of such united churches has challenged the Baptist Union to negotiate with other denominations methods whereby a member of an LEP, persuaded by their own conscience to seek believers' baptism, may do so. It has also challenged Baptists to consider how other patterns of initiation into church membership may be regarded, even as other churches have taken into their systems aspects of congregational church government which were previously under-developed.

JHYB

Ecumenical Movement, European Baptist contributors in the 20th and 21st centuries

[See also *Ecumenical/Ecumenical (Oecumenical) Movement; Oikoumene; Unity of the Church; World Council of Churches*]

European Baptist communities have provided a number of individuals who have made outstanding contributions to the effectiveness of the ecumenical movement. Wherever there is an effective *Free-church* movement Baptists will have been to the fore both in founding and sustaining it, and the experience gained there in cooperative church work has often been subsequently invested in wider ecumenical relations. As an example the Free Church Council in *England* was led by three successive Baptist ministers from 1970-99 whilst the British Council of Churches had a Baptist chairman of its executive from 1956-71.

The work of *Faith and Order* received sustained support from W.T. Whitley, C.T. Le Quesne, M.E Aubrey, W.M.S. West (who played a notable part in the production of the *Baptism Eucharist and Ministry* report), K.W. Clements, and Paul S. Fiddes as well as Gunther Wagner from *Rüschlikon*.

M.E. Aubrey played a significant part in drafting the constitution of the *World Council of Churches* which has had in its employ Revd Victor Hayward, Revd Gwynneth Hubble, Revd Myra Blyth and Revd Simon Oxley whilst E.A. Payne served both as Vice Moderator of the Central Committee and a president of the Council. Also serving on the Central Committee of the Council have been Alexei Bischkov from *Russia*, Janos Viczian from *Hungary*, Rasmus Hylleberg from *Denmark* and David S. Russell, David R. Goodbourn and John H.Y. Briggs from *Britain*, who also served on the Executive, chaired several committees, and acted as Rapporteur to the Council's Special Commission on relations with the *Orthodox* as well as being an editor of volume III of *A History of the Ecumenical Movement*. His successor on the Central Committee, Revd Ruth A. Bottoms provided outstanding service as Moderator of the unit responsible for the work of the Conference of World Mission and Evangelism (CWME), leading the team that organised the World Conference of CWME in Athens, the first to be held in an Orthodox country.

Others have made their contribution through national and international *evangelical* organisations: Robert Amess and Derek J. Tidball, as leaders within the British *Evangelical Alliance* exercised considerable influence, the latter also as Principal of the London School of *Theology*. Nikolai Nedelchev in *Bulgaria* was President of the *European Evangelical Alliance* for some years whilst Henri Blocher from *France* was much involved in the World Evangelical Federation's Theological Commission.

In the aid world Per Midtiede served as Secretary of *Norwegian Church Aid* and Michael H. Taylor as Director of *Christian Aid*. The Ecumenical Councils in *Finland* and Denmark both had Baptist Secretaries in Jan Edstrom and Holger Lam. Quite remarkably two of the four General Secretaries of the *Conference of European Churches* have been Baptists: Drs Glen Garfield Williams and Keith Clements. In *Wales* Revd Gethin Abraham-Williams served as secretary of Churches Together in Wales [*Cytun*], whilst David Goodbourn, a Baptist layman [see *Laity*], has served as General Secretary of Churches Together in Britain and *Ireland*.

In broadcasting and publishing distinguished service was provided by Hugh Martin, one of the founders of the Religious Book Club and for many years Editor/Managing Director of the *SCM* Press, which published a number of Faith and Order documents as also the preparatory material for the WCC Assembly in Amsterdam in 1948, and Edwin Robertson, who whilst on the staff of the BBC helped to found the World Association of Christian Communication. Both men were vitally connected with reconstruction work in Europe after 1945. Martin was one of the architects of the *Conference on Politics, Economics and Citizenship*, which was chaired by William Temple, served on a number of Baptist *Union* and Missionary Society Committees, and like his friend, E.A. Payne, received the rare honour of being made a Companion of Honour, for his work for the Free Churches and the infant British Council of Churches, whilst Robertson was one of the few Free Churchmen to receive a *Lambeth* doctorate from the Archbishop of Canterbury. His service to the denomination was to *Regent's Park College, Oxford* and as a *local church pastor* over almost 70 years, from 1938 until his *death* in harness as pastor at Hampstead, London, in 2007.

A number of Europeans also gave conspicuous service to the *Baptist World Alliance*. Serving as President have been *John Clifford*, J.H. Rushbrooke, F. Townley Lord, Knud Wümpelmann, and David Coffey and as secretaries, J.H. Shakespeare, J.H. Rushbrooke, Arnold Ohrn, Josef Nordenhaug, and Gerhard Class. Henry Cook, Eric Ruden, Ronald Goulding, Reinhold Kerstan, Archie Goldie, (both originally from Europe), Paul Montacute, Douglas Inglis, Joel Sorenson, Adolf Klaupiks, Regina Class have also served on the BWA staff. Serving as Vice Presidents have been K.O. Broady, *Sweden*; Marius Larsen, Denmark; J.G. Lehmann, Germany; H. Novotny, *Austria*-Hungary; J.A. Ohrn, *Norway*; E. Paschetto, *Italy*; B. Rocles, *Netherlands*; Reuben Saillens, France; Baron Uixhiull, *Estonia*; George White, MP, UK; I.S. Prokhanoff, Russia; B. Werts, *Germany*; C.E. Benander, Sweden; F.W. Simoleit, Germany, N.J. Nordstrom, Sweden; Hans Luckey, Germany, Johannes Norgaard, Denmark; H. Prochazka, *Czechoslovakia*; M. Ronchi, Italy; Per Gunnar Westin, Sweden; Jakob Meister, West Germany; Yakov Zhidkov, Russia; Henri Vincent, France; Aleksander Kircun, *Poland*, E.A. Payne, UK; Janos Laczkovski, Hungary; Rudolf Thaut, West Germany; David Largergren, Sweden; Michael Zhidkov, *Soviet Union*; A.S. Clement, UK; Rolf Dahmmann, East Germany; Josip Horak, *Yugoslavia*; Birgit Karlsson, Sweden; Irmgaard Class, Germany; Janos Viczian, Hungary; Mona Khauli, *Lebanon*; Gregory Komendant, *Ukraine*; Branko Lovrec, *Croatia*; Theo Angelov, Bulgaria; Jorge Pastor, *Spain*; Billy Taranger, Norway.

JHYB

Edinburgh 1910 – World Missionary Conference

The World Missionary Conference held at Edinburgh in Jun 1910 was not the first international *Protestant missionary* conference, but it remains the most important. It expressed the confidence of the Protestant churches at the time that the world could be converted to *Christ* through western missionary agency. The conference is also generally recognised as the source of the modern *ecumenical movement*. The 1,216 official delegates represented missionary societies rather than churches. Baptist participants included C.E. Wilson and W.Y. Fullerton of the *Baptist Missionary Society*, T.S. Barbour, foreign secretary of the American Baptist Foreign Mission Society, and the leading British Baptist layman [see *Laity*], Sir George W. Macalpine, who was vice-chairman of the Commission on 'The Home Base of Missions'. There were two representatives of the *Mission der deutschen Baptisten* (Hoefs and Mascher). The 17 Asian delegates (no Africans attended) included five Baptists, all delegates of the American Baptist Foreign Mission Society.

Modern historiography has, however, rightly become suspicious of the significance attributed to the Edinburgh Conference of 1910, so often perceived as the catalyst for the modern ecumenical movement. Two aspects of Edinburgh narrow its embrace. First, of the 1,216 delegates exactly 1,000 came from the *UK* and North America, some 171 from continental Europe but only 17 from the non-western world, of whom 5 – almost a third – were Baptists. Secondly, whilst the gathering was primarily of western Protestants, to retain *Anglican* involvement, the subject of discussion was restricted to missionary endeavour among 'non-Christian peoples' thereby excluding all activity in '*Catholic*' and '*Orthodox*' Europe, as well as Latin America and the Caribbean. The real division was between those who defined Christian identity primarily in terms of an act of personal commitment to Christ and those who thought in terms of belonging by territorial and baptismal [see *Baptism*] affiliation to the church catholic. The Edinburgh Conference was, therefore, set within the old context of *Christendom* and the dangerous world of 'canonical territories.' Protestant leaders accepted such a compromise in order to secure Anglican support, for without it the Anglo-Catholics would have withdrawn.

In a context no less complex, a follow up conference for 2010 is to consider the many missiological challenges of the 21st century.

BJS

Education – kindergarten, primary, secondary

'Education' is the means by which a society hands down from one generation to the next its knowledge, culture, and values. The individual being educated develops physically, mentally, emotionally, morally, socially and spiritually. Teachers or pedagogues who are specially trained for the task are usually responsible for formal education within schools.

The educational systems in Europe have been influenced by two main sources. Firstly, the *Jewish* tradition of education, both in its original form from the OT, the Torah and the Talmud and in the version modified by Christianity. Indeed, many monasteries or monastic schools as well as municipal and cathedral schools were founded during the centuries of early Christian influence across Europe. The second influence is that of education in ancient Greece, where Aristotle, Plato and other thinkers viewed education as producing intellectually well-rounded young people to take leading roles in the activities of the *state* and of society. The thinking of Jean Jacques Rousseau (1712-78), a French philosopher and social and *political* theorist, although strongly atheistic, has also been highly influential in the development of early educational theory.

All European countries now offer pre-school (kindergarten), primary (or elementary) and secondary school state provision or the equivalent in a grade system. This tripartite division is based largely on the work of the Swiss psychologist, Jean Piaget (1896-1980). His theory outlining the stages of intellectual development in *children* has had a major impact on the fields of both psychology and education. Across Europe, many church groups are involved in providing both premises and developmentally appropriate pre-school programmes for young children.

Within the *United Kingdom*, the *tradition* of the *free churches*, including Baptist, involvement in public education is rooted in the 18th century provision of charity schools and *Sunday Schools* which offered to teach reading, writing and basic mathematics alongside simple *Bible* instruction to all children free of charge. State-funded elementary education for all children from the ages of 5-14 was established by the Foster Act of 1870, with schools provided by both public boards and churches. However, by the beginning of the 20th century, there was concern and fierce opposition from many Baptists and other *Nonconformist* Christians that the introduction of free, compulsory Christian education for all school children (Balfour Act, 1902) was unduly influenced by providers of *Anglican* and *Roman Catholic* schools and posed a threat to basic *religious freedom*. Few Nonconformists would consider sending their children to church schools, though towards the end of the 20th century, this trend changed significantly.

By the time of the 1944 Education Act, in fact, there were fewer church schools and more state schools and, whilst both the compulsory provision of religious education and the provision of a daily act of collective *worship* remained in place, these were to be non-denominational. Subsequent acts have done little to change this legislation, other than to add that both religious education and collective worship are to be predominately Christian. The content of religious education is determined in state schools by a local authority Standing Advisory Council on Religious Education (SACRE). Many Baptist Christians serve on their local SACRE.

The wider debate concerning the influence of the church on education has echoes in other parts of Europe. During *Communist* times, in Eastern Europe, the curricula did not include any religious education, and public education was a strong tool of atheistic brainwashing. This transmissional model of education can still be seen in the schools of post-Communist countries, even if the method is not used for the goals of atheism or political indoctrination. Baptists and other *evangelicals* have joined their efforts (e.g. in *Lithuania*) to offer alternative forms of education where the activity of children and interactive teaching is more valued and Christian teaching is provided. At present, teaching Religious or Christian Education in secular state-funded schools varies enormously across Europe and often the choice is between denominational 'catecheses' or phenomenological 'religious studies' where Christianity is exposed among other religions as one possible option. Accordingly the post-Christian setting of many European countries leaves the main responsibility of Christian teaching to the *local church*. In adult education there remains scope for Christian initiatives both in face to face encounter and distance-learning packages.

MEW & ET

Education by Extension, Theological

See *Theological Education by Extension*.

Egypt, Baptist history in

Egypt is a predominantly *Islamic* country. However, the Christian tradition dating back to the Early Church, is represented in Egypt by the Coptic Church (c.17% of the population), while other Christian denominations have considerably shorter histories. Baptists reached Egypt in 1931 when Seddik Girgis, who had converted to Baptist beliefs [see *Conversion*] while abroad, returned to Egypt and began to share his views with others. American *Southern Baptists* played an important role in the early stages of Baptist witness in Egypt. Girgis studied at Southwestern Baptist Theological Seminary (Fort Worth, Texas) and at Texas Christian University. Ordained in Texas, he became a key figure for Baptist development in Egypt. His method of spiritual work was personal *evangelism*, and as a result of this, and his organisational skills, in the 1960s there were six Baptist churches in Egypt with a total *membership* of approximately 250. Girgis founded a Baptist *magazine*, and was president of the General Baptist Evangelical Convention, which was organised in the late 1960s. From the 1960s-80s, the Foreign Mission Board (International Mission Board) of the Southern Baptist Convention, USA, supported Baptist work in Egypt with financial resources, advisers and *missionaries*. Also other mission organisations, such as Baptist International Missions and Baptist Bible Fellowship International, have for certain periods of time been present in Egypt. Today, Egyptian Baptists more consciously seek for their own identity, while, in a dozen churches with a total membership of 1300, they face various challenges. Possibilities of

reaching out to Muslims are restricted for *proselytism* is prohibited. New church members usually come from a Christian background. Attempts have been made to organise *Bible study* in small house groups, to develop *Sunday School* work and to expand Biblical knowledge with the help of *Theological Education by Extension* materials.

TP

Elderly, Care for the

The care for the vulnerable within Christian communities has always been of paramount importance ever since the first church in Jerusalem set aside *deacons* (*diakonie* – servants) to take care of the widows and see they were not neglected within the gathering community of believers. In early *Anabaptist* communities in Moravia, the *Netherlands* and elsewhere, this concern for the vulnerable and often with a focus on widows and the elderly, has been a feature of baptistic communities. In modern European societies the *state* or local government or private companies make such provision with supportive care, warden-controlled housing schemes and care in nursing homes. All form part of the provision available within modern states and communities. Nevertheless, in many countries, Baptist churches, or *associations* of churches, continue to make provision for care of the elderly who might not have family near at hand or who prefer to live residentially or in housing schemes with a deliberate and sustained Christian ethos.

In general, such provision by Baptist churches has sought to comply with the best standards of professional supportive care for the elderly and the frail, but with the add-on of a clear Christian ethos, *prayers* and *worship* being held on regular patterns in community meeting rooms, visitation of residents by local *church members* and the like. Some *unions*, or special associations within Baptist unions, have made significant contributions to the provision of responsible, competent and *Christ*-like care of the elderly. Examples would be in *Germany*, *Great Britain* and *Scandinavia*. With an ever-increasing proportion of the population living beyond the age of 70, it becomes a critical task for the *local church* to reassess how it can best carry out its **mission** and **ministry** to the elderly, and how the resources represented by such people can best be used in the life of the local church.

KGJ

Elders

See **Deacons and Elders**.

Election

[See also **Arminianism**; **Calvinism**]
This doctrine relates to whether people are to be considered as beneficiaries or recipients of the **salvation** that comes in and through **Jesus Christ**. The doctrine is often juxtaposed with the concept of free choice [see **Freedom of Conscience**]. Whether or not people are elect might best be understood as a question of soteriological focus affected by two issues.

(1) whether knowledge of salvation should be properly theocentric or homocentric
(2) the scope of the saving work of Jesus Christ

Theocentric or Homocentric. Where Baptist soteriology has identified with soteriological roots in either **Puritan** Reformed or Wesleyan thinking, it has adopted a homocentric epistemology. That is, the emphasis is on our human appropriation: '(Jesus came) *to save me*'. Consequently, the approach to determining election has been to look for a sense of assurance of salvation in the believer.

Puritan Reformed thought approached this in a rational way, through use of the logical syllogism: if you saw the evidence of salvation in the fruit of your life, you could take it that you were saved and one of the elect. Wesleyan thought approached the question experientially: if you feel an inner testimony that Christ is your Saviour, you are saved and one of the elect. The emphasis is that salvation is rooted in the human beneficiary of God's electing *grace*.

Orthodox and **Roman Catholic** theologies, rooted in an earlier age, prioritise a theocentric epistemology. The focus is more '*Jesus came to save* (me)'. The emphasis is upon divine beneficence. Salvation flows to all who come to receive **ministry** in the name of Jesus Christ, through the agency of the **church**. This approach is theocentric, in that it perceives the issue of election from the perspective of God the Giver.

The scope of the saving work of Jesus Christ. Western **theology** followed Augustine's emphasis on the universal sinfulness and depravity of **humankind** [see **Fall**; **Sin**], stressing Christ's sinless humanity separated from the sinfulness of humankind. This has reinforced a homocentric perspective to the saving work of Christ, taking focus away from a common humanity shared with our Saviour. This reinforced a western tendency to determine salvation not by what is manifest in Christ, but by either a hidden decree or human choice.

Baptists throughout Europe reflect, in their theology of election, this confusion of theological thought. It remains to be seen whether new dialogues with the Orthodox tradition will lead to new perspectives on how election is to be understood.

JGMP

Elstal Baptist Theological Seminary

See **German Baptist Theological Seminary Elstal**.

Emanuel University, Oradea, Romania

Emanuel had its origins in the pressing need for pastoral training during the late **Communist** era. In 1985, Josif Tson, then **minister** of Emanuel Baptist Church, Oradea, oversaw the commencement of a covert programme. With the end of the Ceauçescu régime, this emerged into the open and developed as an independent institution. Emanuel Bible Institute was thus founded in 1990.

In 1998, the name was changed to Emanuel University, reflecting the development of other departments within the Faculty of **Theology** in such fields as **Music**, Management and Social Work; these later became separate faculties, and have been joined by a Graduate School in Theology. The University received government accreditation in 2002, and **students** come from throughout Eastern Europe and beyond.

Like many such institutions, Emanuel

has relied heavily on intensive short courses taught by visiting teachers from the West, but now has an increasing number of Romanian staff. Its ethos is fairly traditional Baptist, and it has received academic and financial support from the **Southern Baptist** constituency and from **Conservative Evangelicals** in Western Europe and Canada (it receives no government funding or subsidies). In a fast-changing society and theologically-maturing church, it faces the challenge of developing indigenous responses to local issues as it seeks to equip Christians to play their part in the development of post-Communist society.

TG

Emergency/Disaster Relief

Whilst there has been a general movement from aid programmes to those which nurture development and self-sustaining economic enterprise, the world still needs the means to respond to sudden emergencies such as war, earthquakes, hurricanes, floods, etc. Other problems such as that associated with caring for *refugees*, which it was once thought could be eliminated, have in fact been perpetuated by new crises which continue to demand an immediate response from the churches as also other relief agencies. In fact the response to international emergencies is now on a scale which could not even have been conceived of in former years with **ACT International** (1995) providing the consolidated instrument for applying such human and financial resources, where speed of action is of the essence of effectiveness. Within the Baptist family the global spread of Baptist communities enables **Baptist World Aid** to apply such resources as it can command swiftly and immediately to crisis situations.

ET

Emigration Societies

[See also *Migration*]

Emigration Societies were born out of the *Temperance* Movement. Those working in this area, which included members of downtown Baptist churches, following pioneering work by the **Salvation Army**, became conscious that some *children* had little hope of normal healthy growth because of their

home environment where the domestic budget was overwhelmingly corrupted by parental addiction to *alcohol* [see *Alcoholism*]. Accordingly, they took the hard decision that it was in the best interests of such children to be separated from their parents and they made arrangements for children from these homes to have a new start in North America or one of the white dominions in an alcohol-free environment.

JHYB

England, Baptist history in

Of all members of the Baptist family, English Baptists have the longest history and are thus to some degree the parents of the whole movement. Beyond that there is much debate as to whether the movement is directly born out of continental **Anabaptism** or more precisely is an offshoot of 17th-century **Separatism**, in which case Baptists can be regarded as **Puritans** in one of their most radical forms. The issue is complicated by the fact that after what happened in Münster in 1534-35 there was a vigorous attempt by all English Baptists to disavow any links with the dangers seen to be inherent in continental Anabaptism. Two distinct streams in English Baptist life emerged, one of which came to be seen as **Arminian** in **theology** whilst the other remained strictly **Calvinist**. The General Baptists, who were seen to espouse a general **atonement**, were initially led by **John Smyth**, formerly a Cambridge academic, and **Thomas Helwys**, a lawyer. Smyth was known as the Se-baptist because, persuaded that all branches of the Christian **church** were corrupt, he first baptised himself and then baptised Helwys [see **Baptism**]. Smyth came to think his judgement in this matter mistaken and so, much to Helwys' annoyance, sought, with those who agreed with him, to join the **Mennonite** Waterlander Church in Amsterdam. Helwys, convinced of the need for a radical new beginning in the life of the church, returned to England, and formed the first Baptist Church on British soil in 1612, but Helwys was soon imprisoned for his advocacy of religious toleration where he died shortly afterwards.

By 1638, at the latest, some London separatist churches had come to adopt believers' baptism and herein are to be found the origins of the Particular Baptists – churches which believed in particular redemption as described within a moderate Calvinist theological scheme. These emerging Baptist groups, with a further group of Seventh Day Baptists, soon had to deal with all the problems thrown up by the English Civil War – the respective realms of **church and state**, the theological bases for opposition to the ruling monarch, how God's purposes could be seen to be working out in the pages of human history. In the process a king was executed and various attempts of less than general acceptability made to find an alternative form of government within the Commonwealth and Protectorate periods. These impinged on the emerging Baptist denomination both positively and negatively. Positively the movement of the army around the **nation** helped to propagate the new ideas, though few Baptists were prepared to accept state financed clergy posts. Negatively, the disruptions in society gave rise to a movement known as Fifth Monarchism, which persuaded its devotees, who included a number of Baptists, that by determined action they could hasten the second coming [see **Christology**] by rash **political** action. At the same time Quaker discontent with all forms of institutional religion attracted a number of General Baptist congregations to join the Society of Friends

These movements put a break on Baptist **growth** so that by 1660 Baptists numbered only about 300 churches, which after the restoration of the Stuart monarchy faced a generation of intermittent persecution. The 'Glorious Revolution' of 1688 which saw the accession of the **protestant** monarchs, William and Mary, brought only partial toleration. But more than that they also suffered from internal problems as on the one hand many General Baptists developed aberrant views of **Christ**'s divinity, and on the other amongst the Particular Baptists a hyper-Calvinism, that so stressed the **sovereignty** of God that it jeopardised both ideas of moral responsibility and effective **evangelism**, became increasingly prevalent. Churches within the orbit of the **Bristol** Academy, however, consistently maintained an **evangelical** Calvinism.

By 1750 English Baptists had experienced little growth with only modest prospects for the future. All that changed as the liveliness of the Evangelical **Revival** began to make its mark on the denomination. In 1770 some from a **Methodist** and Countess of Huntingdon background formed the New Connexion of General Baptists espousing an **orthodox** and evangelical Arminianism which soon attracted most of those churches in the old connexion which has remained orthodox. At the same time a number of those influenced by George Whitefield entered the Baptist **ministry** and a reading of Jonathan Edwards led men of the calibre of Andrew Fuller [see **Fullerism**] to articulate a new Evangelical Calvinism which developed a new vision of world **mission**. Out of this emerged the founding of the **Baptist Missionary Society** in 1792 with **William Carey** and his colleagues setting up the first overseas **mission station** in Danish territory at Serampore, India. In the event **overseas mission** revolutionised the church at home with the founding of the Itinerant Society ushering in a remarkable period of church growth: Particular Baptist churches grew from around 400 in 1789 to more than 1,000 by 1835. At the same time the life of **local churches** became much more varied. **Worship** services now pretty universally embraced **hymn** singing though still climaxed in the **preaching** of the sermon. Most churches now operated **Sunday Schools** which sometimes had almost an autonomous existence sometimes with separate **buildings**. At the end of the century specialised youth organisations were developed with the founding of mutual improvement societies, **Boys Brigades and Girls Life Brigades**, **Christian Endeavour**, and more locally organised societies which were all part of what came to be known as the 'institutional church' providing for **church members** a complete slate of social, recreational and cultural organisations that were **chapel**-based. Baptists were also responsible for a formidable array of philanthropic endeavours on behalf of the disadvantaged (e.g. **orphans**, slum dwellers, and the **elderly**).

Such growth was in part the fruit of united evangelical endeavour, which led Robert Hall to ponder how it could be right for Christians to be united in mission but to separate at the **Lord's Table**, and hence his advocacy of **open communion**. In this period of growth Baptists developed new *educational* institutions; alongside a rejuvenated Bristol Academy, newly focused on ministerial formation, new colleges emerged at Rawdon (Leeds); Stepney (London) [see *Regent's Park College*], Bury/Manchester in Lancashire [see *Northern Baptist College*], together with Pastors', later *Spurgeon's*, College, in South London. A better educated society argued the need for a better-trained ministry.

In 1813 a first Baptist *union* serving the whole nation was founded but within 20 years it was remodelled to allow evangelical General Baptists Churches to become members a process which came to full fruition in 1891when the two streams of Baptist life fully united. From 1809, *The Baptist Magazine* provided Baptists with a monthly journal, and from 1855 *The Freeman* provided them with a weekly newspaper.

Notwithstanding increased numbers and *wealth*, Baptists were second-class citizens suffering penal legislation until 1828 when the Test and Corporation Acts limiting their ability to take civil offices were repealed. Until 1868 there remained a liability to pay church rate for the upkeep of the parish church, and until 1871 religious tests remained in force in the ancient universities of Oxford and Cambridge. As Baptists, alongside other nonconformists eliminated a number of disabilities so they were very conscious of the need to exploit their new opportunities, and thus to press for the exercise of conscience – the *nonconformist conscience* – in both local and national government. Out of this arose campaigns for Sunday observance and against sexual alliance, for *temperance* and against *gambling*, and to secure the elimination of their remaining disabilities. They soon came up against other issues – slavery in the colonies [see *Colonialism*], poverty, the exploitation of labour, the provision of decent housing and educational opportunities for all – which required major changes in the exercise of power.

At the time of the launching of the 1833 Union, there were at most 70,000 Baptists in England. This had risen to just short of 411,000 with some 570,000 Sunday School *scholars* enrolled, by the high point of 1906, but by 1991 this had fallen back to c160,000 members (or rather less than a quarter of a million if strict, and independent Baptists and those in *Wales, Scotland* and *Ireland* are added in) with some 136,000 associated young people.

Superficially the two most significant figures in Baptist life in the 19th century, *Charles Haddon Spurgeon* and *John Clifford*, might be seen to represent the old Particular and General Baptist traditions; both of them in their differing ways helped the denomination to engage with the emerging urban industrial culture. Spurgeon, ever anxious to defend the faith of the Puritans, did so with homely interpretation of scripture, bringing the great doctrines of the faith within the reach of the large congregations that filled his Metropolitan Tabernacle Sunday by Sunday. Beyond that this great church supported a battery of agencies and organisations which sought to meet the social and spiritual needs of the people of South London. Whilst John Clifford was deemed to hold advanced views in many areas of theology, wrote *socialist* tracts for the Fabian Society and led the 'Passive Resistance Movement' against the British government's determination to give rate aid to denominational schools, both were passionately committed to the promotion of personal evangelism.

In more recent years Baptists have emerged as a bridge denomination between the mainstream denominations with their *ecumenical* concerns and the world of Evangelical religion. Ecumenically they have taken a leading role in the several councils of the *Free Churches* in England, and were founding members of both the British Council of Churches (as later of Churches Together in England, and in Britain and Ireland) and the *World Council of Churches*. At the same time many Baptists have given service to the *Evangelical Alliance* of which body many Baptist churches are members.

Denominational agencies/departments are now more developed than in 1900, offering resources to the local church in various areas of ministry and mission. A system of regional ministry seeks to interpret the principles of *episcope* within a free-church context with particular emphases on the *pastoral care* of ministers and equipping the churches for mission each in its own locality. Worship patterns have changed with the denomination open to *charismatic* influences and enriched by them. A further change is the way in which the so-called 'mission fields' of Asia, Africa and Latin America have come to Britain with the largest congregations in the nation representing their *diaspora* communities.

JHYB

FURTHER READING: J.H.Y. Briggs, *The English Baptists of the Nineteenth Century*, Baptist Historical Society, Didcot, 1994. Raymond Brown, *English Baptists of the Eighteenth Century*, Baptist Historical Society, Didcot, 1986. Roger Hayden, *English Baptist history and heritage*, Baptist Union of Great Britain, Didcot, 1990. Ian M. Randall, *English Baptists of the Twentieth Century*, Baptist Historical Society, Didcot, 2005. B.R. White, *English Baptists of the Seventeenth Century* (2nd Ed.), Baptist Historical Society, London, 1985.

Enlightenment

The Enlightenment [German: *Aufklärung*] or 'Age of Reason' – a period that extends from the Glorious Revolution in England (1688) to the conclusion of the Napoleonic Wars in Europe – represents a significant development in the intellectual history of the West. Whilst the period did witness *science* emerging as a force that authenticated ideas in the way that once only religion had done, not all the changes in the ferment of the mind in the period were hostile to religious belief. The movement had Christian roots, encapsulated in the Cambridge Platonist affirmation, 'The mind of man is the candle of the Lord', an affirmation of the importance of the rationalism that underlay the Enlightenment.

A number of key traits can be identified within the movement:

(1) reason as the final arbiter of truth and falsehood;

(2) a stress on nature and an appeal to what is natural – thus Pope's couplet:
  Nature and Nature's Laws lay hid in Night:
  God said, 'Let Newton be' and all was light.
  Nature was not capricious but worked to regular rhythms which it was open to the human mind to detect and analyze. Newton, for instance, was not hostile to Christianity and wrote books of speculative *theology* alongside his scientific studies.

(3) Belief in Progress – the development of history from the primitive to the more sophisticated and more particularly the growth of freedom as a developing theme in history;

(4) Tradition's loss of *authority* – the justification of institutions by their utility not their antiquity. Enlightenment man believed himself to be growing up into new freedom, confident of new resources within the self. The new critical temper looked at the *scriptures* with judgmental eyes, miracles were made subject to rational investigations, whilst the **Roman Catholic** Church and its supporting sacerdotalism received hostile comment. The culture of suspicion born of the Enlightenment required religion to justify itself in a radically new way.

In two respects the impact of the Enlightenment on Christian *witness* was negative. First, it is associated with the names of a number of critics of Christian *revelation*, such as Kant and Lessing, Gibbon and Hume, Voltaire and Rousseau, whilst other writers such as Leibnitz and Locke sought to base Christian belief on new rational grounds, which changed the nature of the *faith* thus affirmed. At a more practical level, it was from the Enlightenment that the ethic of exploitation of natural resources to the maximum advantage of present users was derived now leading to global *ecological* crisis. On the other hand, the Enlightenment encouraged such changes as the end of witch-hunting and the upholding of *religious liberty* rather than the enforcing of a privileged *orthodoxy*.

Whilst some religious thinkers essentially reacted against the Enlightenment, elsewhere there was continuity between the Enlightenment and the work of *Evangelical* apologists [see *Apologetics*]. This, e.g., has been argued for much Evangelical writing, and at its best the late 18th-century *nonconformist pulpit* was both rational and evangelical, able to relate to the changing cultural context, whilst demonstrating that the exploration of revelation required hard intellectual analysis.

JHYB

Environment

See *Ecology and Environment*.

Epiphany

The 12th day after *Christmas* is celebrated as the feast of Epiphany in the West. Of course, it coincides with the celebration of Christmas in *Orthodox* Eastern Europe. The word itself means 'Manifestation' and might historically be interpreted as the manifestation of the *revelation* of God to the world in *Jesus Christ*, though some people see it more narrowly as the manifestation of Christ to the Gentiles. Since about the 5th century it has also been linked to the visit of the Magi, hence some countries refer to Epiphany as the celebration of the 'Three Kings'.

There is a complicated relationship between the celebration of the *incarnation* by the West on 25 Dec and Epiphany on 6 Jan, which is beyond the scope of this Dictionary and has not been an issue for Baptists.

Contemporary celebration of the event in the West links it to the visit of the Magi and at this point special Christmas *decorations* are taken out of *worship* rooms and homes. In some traditions the six Sundays of Epiphany are used to further develop the theme of 'Manifestation' as witnessed by the *baptism* of Jesus by John, in calling the first disciples, in the performing of miracles, especially that at Cana of Galilee, the cleansing of the temple, the exposition of the wisdom of God and the Parables as representative of how Jesus manifest his purposes to the people. In the Orthodox East the celebration is subsumed within the celebration of the incarnation.

KGJ

Episcopalianism, Baptists and

See *Anglicanism, Baptists and*.

Episcope

The Greek word means literally 'watching over'. It only occurs twice in the NT (Ac 1:20 and 1Ti 3:1) and the proper noun derived from it only five times (Ac 20:28, Php 1:1, 1Ti 3:2, Tit 1:7 and 1Pe 2:25). In two places it is linked with shepherding, and thus suggests primarily *pastoral care* and leadership. The most accurate English translation is '*bishop*', and the bishop traditionally has a crook.

Baptists however have generally avoided that translation, because of its hierarchical and sacerdotal connections. Because of their doctrine of the *church*, they have applied it primarily to the *pastor* of the *local church*. The C17 English Particular Baptist Confessions do not use the term, but the 1678 Orthodox Creed of General Baptists writes of three orders of *ministry*: bishops or messengers; elders or pastors; *deacons* or overseers of the *poor* [see *England*]. Thomas Grantham however, one of their leaders, uses bishop of the second order, equivalent to elder, and describes the first order as *apostles* or messengers.

Baptists have always acknowledged a wider dimension beyond the local church, but not until the C20 have they wrestled with episcope in that wider body. *Associations* had officers, but they were not given *theological* significance. In 1916 J.H. Shakespeare, General Secretary of the Baptist Union of *Great Britain and Ireland*, an *ecumenical* pioneer, proposed dividing the *union* into 10 Areas, each to have a General Superintendent. These originally had an administrative role, regarding ministerial settlement and financial grants, but fairly quickly came to be seen by both ministers and churches as filling a need for episcope. Rather strangely they were always agents of the union rather than of regional Associations. As the ecumenical movement developed they were recognised by church leaders in other denominations as their equivalent.

In 2000 two important changes were made in this episcope beyond the local church by BUGB. The title 'superintendent' was dropped and replaced by 'regional minister', responsible not to the union, but to the local Association. The number of these was drastically reduced to correspond roughly with the former Areas. At the same time episcope in each became collegial, rather than personal. Each Association has at least two, but the number and role varies within each Association. This change corresponds with a similar development in leadership in many local churches where elders have been introduced to complement deacons, and the pastor shares his episcopal role with them, and, in larger churches, with a ministry team. The corporate nature of episcope as residing in the *church meeting* has always been predominant in the local church, but Associations and Unions have not found it easy to exercise this at their levels.

Elsewhere in Europe the term 'superintendent' has been adopted in some Unions. In *Estonia* the title used was 'Senior Presbyter'. In others, especially in Eastern Europe countries such as *Latvia*, *Moldova* and *Georgia* have preferred the Biblical [see *Bible*] title 'bishop'. In Latvia the bishop is elected every three years, is recognised by the Government alongside the other church leaders, and is seeking to give a lead in *church planting*.

JFVN

Eschatology

Eschatology [*eschatos* – 'last (things)'] is for many Baptists, especially those in *conservative* churches, an important and sensitive issue for irreconcilable views here have sometimes resulted in church splits. There is significant diversity not only between the OT and NT, but also between different authors in the same testament. Such interesting peculiarities derived from a variety of texts cannot be captured in an overview entry such as this. An emphasis on the last things, the end to which all time is moving, together with an understanding of *creation* as the starting point of the whole cosmic process, spell out a unified view of history and time. While some religious traditions offer a cyclical explanation of creation and life on earth, all Abrahamic traditions (*Judaism*, Christianity and *Islam*) follow a linear model, pointing to a finite beginning and a definite conclusion in both human and cosmic history, with Christianity leading on to the final establishment of the new order of the everlasting *kingdom of God*, the *hope* that awaits fulfilment in the end times, for which all Abrahamic traditions long.

The Hebrew Bible/OT provides the oldest texts offering through prophetic [see *Prophecy*] and apocalyptic materials a colourful picture of hope set in the end times when the day of the Lord will dawn. After Israel has failed to follow God's commands to promote *peace* and justice, their misbehaviour led to their being taken into captivity. Canonical and extra-canonical prophetic and apocalyptic literature look to the day of Yahweh, when a Davidic, but at the same time a Messianic kingdom will be established, where all will live in safety and enjoy justice. Beside the Davidic ruler, who represents the rule of God over Israel and all humanity, there are other figures who feature in the end times, such as the Son of man, the end-time prophet, a priestly figure, and even a *suffering* servant. The eschatological sequence of events will start with the final *judgment* which will lead on to the new age of God's *salvation*. This end time hope found in the OT gave birth to the hope of *resurrection* after *death*. But this hope of restoration seems to envisage a new life not only for *Israel* but for all the nations of the earth. Inter-testamental literature picks up and creatively develops this hope, adding Hellenistic ideas, as well as expanding this eschatological perspective through *Jewish* rabbinic, apocalyptic and prophetic materials.

The NT develops the theme of eschatology using OT texts primarily as its starting point. *Jesus* is at the centre of the fulfilment of the eschatological hope in the NT, thereby confronting 1st-century Jewish messianic expectations. Instead of a mighty and powerful Messiah who would free the Jews from Roman occupancy, Jesus challenges the corrupt Jewish elite and acts on behalf of the *poor* and the marginalised, in much the same way as OT prophets spoke in favour of living according to God's justice, establishing a new order ruled by messianic values. Such an eschatology focuses on the crucified Messiah, who died and rose again as the first fruit of the promised eschatological kingdom of God. With these events in Jerusalem fulfilling OT expectations, the disciples of Christ were empowered to proclaim the good news first to the Jews and then to all the nations. Such proclamation is itself another part of the fulfilment of ancient prophecy. Until these final eschatological events happen, Jesus' followers live in an only partially-fulfilled end time, living with the mystery of 'already' and 'not yet', that is to say the *incarnate* Christ has already instituted God's coming kingdom, but its full implementation has still to be awaited, for *sin* and evil, death and disease, remain part of human experience. The *Spirit* of God as the sign of the beginning of the end times came at *Pentecost* to prepare all humanity for the coming Day of God, building and adding to the *church* which itself is another eschatological reality. The Day of God is at once a day of judgment and salvation, when those who have chosen it, separate themselves from God in the experience called Hell, whilst the faithful enter into their heavenly reward, that is to be with God for ever for that is the essence of *Heaven*. In it God's intentions are made clear in the *forgiveness* of sins, the conquest of evil, the establishment of a new order, discontinuous with the course of present history, which turns the old order of selfish power structures on its head. The Baptist NT *scholar*, George Beasley-Murray, who was at one time a member of the *Rüschlikon* faculty, made eschatology the subject of his first and his last major publications: *Jesus and the Future* (1954) and *Jesus and the Last Days* (1993).

The Christian church lives in the eschatology of the 'already' and 'not yet'; the new age has already started while the old has not yet passed away. As the church anticipates the return of the Christ who ascended to heaven, the followers of Jesus gather in eschatological communities of hope both witnessing to the Christ events of the past and anticipating the consummation of God's purposes in the end time. Thus whenever Christians meet at the table they break bread and pour out *wine* [see *Communion and Intercommunion; Eucharistic liturgy; Sign, Sacrament and Symbol*] in celebration of the death and resurrection of Jesus but they do this 'until he comes', spelling out their future hope. Issues which often cause discussions and disagreements in the church, due to differing views on the details of such final events as the parousia (the second coming of Christ), rapture, tribulation, millennium, Israel and the church, etc. are important issues that require a continuing dialogue but cannot become reasons for parting ways, for different groups of Baptists, *theologians* and lay people [see *Laity*], share a variety of often contradicting positions on those issues.

It seems that, as the Jewish community was surprised by the first coming of Jesus as the Messiah, so will the church be at his second coming. The eschatological hope has always encouraged the church to be involved in God's *mission*, to emphasise the need to always be ready for his coming with patterns of holy living [see *Holiness*]. Such hope has, throughout history been responsible for the vital and pulsating life of the church as the church has tried to 'seek first the kingdom of God and its righteousness'. As it approaches the eschaton, the church needs also to be involved in caring for and reconciling the whole creation to God, by responsible Christian living, caring for God's creation, and continuing God's mission in striving for peace and justice as visible signs of the kingdom that is already there, and yet is still to come in all its fullness. At the end of time the Christian hope is that God's purposes for his creation will be wholly vindicated, in his people, in the world, and in the whole created order.

PFP

FURTHER READING: G. Beasley-Murray, *Jesus and the Future*, MacMillan, London, 1954. G. Beasley-Murray, *Jesus and the Last Days*, Hendrickson, Peabody, Ma., 1993. E. Brunner, *Eternal Hope* [E.T.], Lutterworth, London, 1954. D.Gowan, *Eschatology of the Old Testament*, Philadelphia, 1986. C. Holman, *Till Jesus Comes*, Hendrickson, Peabody, Ma., 1996. E.P. Sanders, *Jesus and Judaism*, Fortress, Philadelphia, 1985. H. Travis, *The Pauline Eschatology*, Zondervan, Grand Rapids, Mi., 1987. B. Witherington, *Jesus, Paul and the End of the World*, InterVarsity, Downers Grove, Il., 1992.

Estonia, Baptist history in

The first Baptist church in Estonia was established in Haapsalu on the west coast in 1884. Adam Reinhold Schiewe, a German Baptist *pastor* from St. Petersburg, conducted the baptismal service [see *Baptism*] for candidates who had become awakened in a wave of a *pietistic revival*, initiated by Swedish *Lutheran missionaries*, which emphasised *repentance* from *sin*, *conversion* and a changed lifestyle. Gradually separating from the Lutheran church, and being under pressure both from the *state* and the majority churches (Lutheran and *Orthodox*), some of these revivalist groups, in their search for new ecclesiastical structures, had made contacts with Baptists. In the same year, other Baptist churches were founded in Tallinn, the capital city, as well as in Kärdla on the island of Hiiumaa (Dagö). Julius Herrmann, a German Baptist from Riga, *Latvia* was instrumental in founding a Baptist congregation in Pärnu in the south-west. These early churches in Estonia, where often the German pastors had to be translated into Estonian, all built upon the *spirituality* of the *Moravians* (Herrnhuters) and revivalist trends. Though this early Baptist movement attracted mostly farmers and workers, some individuals from *Baltic* German nobility, such as Manfred von Glehn and Woldemar von Üksküll, also converted to Baptist *faith*. The latter, being well known beyond Estonia, then still a part of Tsarist *Russia*, represented Baptists of Russia at the First Baptist World Congress in 1905.

As a result of spontaneous *evangelistic* efforts, the Estonian Baptist movement grew significantly at the end of the 19th and the beginning of the 20th century. By 1900 there were nine Baptist churches and seven *mission stations* with a total *membership* of 1,434; by 1920 there were 25 churches and 2,657 members. From the beginning, Estonian Baptists had their own indigenous leaders, though Schiewe functioned as a superintendent for Estonian churches until 1895. Founded in 1904, the publication *Teekäija* [The Pilgrim], whilst nurturing church members spiritually, also created *theological* unity and gave church members a sense of belonging together. *Sunday Schools* for *children*, a *music* ministry and work with choirs, as well as first attempts to organise short-term training for preachers and pastors, became characteristic of Baptist life. After 1908, when two Baptists, Andres Tetermann and Johannes Felsberg, established a printing press in Tallinn, publishing was intensified. Publications included translations of some of *Spurgeon*'s volumes, music with notes, a survey of the first 25 years of Estonian Baptist history, and other literature. When compared to other *free churches* that emerged in Estonia before WWI, Baptists, even in these early years, had strong *local church* structures and a variety of *ministries*.

In 1920, the Estonian Baptist Union was registered according to the laws of the young republic, and two years later, a Preachers' Seminary, later renamed the *Estonian Baptist Theological Seminary*, was established. In the 1920s and 1930s, the Estonian Baptists, focusing on ministerial training, publishing activities as well as evangelism, were less active in social work, though a small *orphanage* existed in Haapsalu and Adam Podin's personal ministry in caring for those suffering from leprosy, which still existed in Estonia in the 1930s, was remarkable. Theologically, Estonian Baptists increasingly emphasised personal *sanctification*, witnessing lifestyle and were challenged by *holiness* and *pentecostal* ideas about the *Holy Spirit*. In missionary work, with *Egypt* as its main focus, Estonian Baptists co-operated with the Evangelical Christian Free Church, from whom they differed mainly in *ecclesiology*. In the 1930s, Estonian Baptists achieved wider recognition in society: the president of the *union* from 1933-44, Karl Kaups, was elected a member of the Estonian Parliament (1938-40). Membership had grown to 7,549 by the year 1939 and when children and youth are included then the community strength was well over 10,000. Baptists hoped to step out of the shadow of being thought of as a *sect*, an accusation which was frequently heard in the predominantly Lutheran society.

Following the Soviet occupation in 1940, all churches, including Baptists, suffered from atheistic restrictions: publications were not allowed and the seminary was closed, pastors were threatened, some leaders arrested, and *property* seized. WWII brought a great deal of material and human loss for Estonian Baptists. In 1944, Karl Kaups, Evald Mänd and some other key Baptist figures emigrated to *Sweden*, along with a number of general church members. In 1945, under pressure from the Soviet state authorities, four free churches in Estonia (Baptists, *Pentecostals*, the Evangelical Christian Free Church and the Revivalist Free Church) were merged into one union, which now was supervised by the *All-Union Council of Evangelical Christians-Baptists* in Moscow. Theologically this union maintained a Baptist profile. Johannes Lipstok, who had been in the Baptist Union leadership before WWII, was nominated the Senior Presbyter of the Estonian Evangelical Christian-Baptist churches, with a recorded membership of 9,751 in 1946.

In the atheistic context, Baptists focused on maintaining *fellowship* between local churches, offering semi-legal opportunities for pastoral training in the form of supervised self-study or short-term courses, and encouraged personal evangelism. Robert Võsu, in the position of Senior Presbyter from 1970-85, travelled extensively to local churches and made every effort to encourage a new generation of presbyters. Osvald Tärk, presbyter of Oleviste Church (formed in 1950 of eight free churches and using the impressive cathedral-like church in Tallinn), was known throughout the whole *Soviet Union* for his theological contribution to Soviet Baptists. In 1975 a Baptist *hymnal*, *Evangeelsed Laulud* [*Evangelical Hymns*], was published, after almost 30 years of waiting for permission from the state. In the 1980s, a typewritten publication, *Logos*, in spite of its limited circulation, helped to unite Estonian Baptists.

At the end of the 1980s, in an atmosphere of growing *religious freedom*, the Union of Evangelical Christians-Baptists of Estonia re-opened the Theological Seminary, which soon moved from Tallinn to Tartu. Children's and youth work began to flourish, becoming one of the strongest ministries in the union. The union was challenged to find its place within wider Estonian culture, to define or re-define its relationships with traditional churches as well as new movements, including *charismatic* forms of Christianity, and to become involved in social and mission work. Membership, which had declined through the Soviet period, stabilised. Today, the Union of Evangelical Christian and Baptist Churches of Estonia, has a membership of 6,000 in 84 churches. The union is a member of the Estonian Council of Churches, as well as the *EBF* and *BWA*. Particularly close relations have developed with Baptist and Evangelical Free Churches in Nordic countries.

TP

FURTHER READING: Toivo Pilli, 'Baptists in Estonia 1884-1940', *The Baptist Quarterly* Vol.XXXIX, No.1, January 2001, pp.27-34. Toivo Pilli, 'Union of Evangelical Christians-Baptists of Estonia, 1945-1989: Survival Techniques, Outreach Efforts, Search for Identity', *Baptist History and Heritage* Vol. XXXVI, Nos. 1 and 2, (Winter/Spring 2001), pp.113-135. T. Pilli, *Dance or Die: The Shaping of Estonian Baptist Identity under Communism*, Paternoster, Milton Keynes, 2008.

Estonian Baptist Theological Seminary

[See also *Estonia, Baptist history in*]
The Seminary was established in 1922 in Keila (Kegel), not far from Tallinn. This arose out of the decisions made at the London Conference of 1920, which brought together Baptist leaders both from Europe and North America to facilitate Baptist work and *mission* in post-war Europe. The Estonian seminary, supported by British and American Baptists and working under the leadership of Adam Podin, moved to Tallinn in 1931. In the 1930s, the weight of theological as over against general subjects increased. In 1938, Osvald Tärk, after his theological studies at Andover Newton Theological Institute and Union Seminary, USA, became director of the seminary, which, unfortunately, was closed in 1940 by the *communist* authorities. Some of the seminary graduates were to make major contributions to Baptist life in Estonia during the atheistic pressure of the Soviet years. Estonian Baptists, in spite of atheistic restrictions, tried to keep alive the tradition of theological *education* and ministerial training, offering short-term courses and encouraging self-study. In 1956-60, a semi-legal distance training course for younger generations of Baptist presbyters (*pastors*) was organised in Tallinn. However, it was not until 1989 that the Theological Seminary was re-established. The first post-Soviet seminary rector was Dr. Peeter Roosimaa, who, together with two other Estonians, had studied *theology* at Buckow Theological Seminary in the German Democratic Republic in 1979-82. Today, the Seminary operates from the university city of Tartu, offering a 3-year course in accordance with the European requirements for basic theological education. In addition, working closely with the *local churches* and Baptist Union leadership, the seminary regularly organises training courses and continuing education opportunities, and is involved in theological reflection related to issues par-

ticularly relevant to Estonian Baptists.

TP

Eternal Life
[See also *Annihilation and Universalism; Heaven, Hell and the Future Life*]
The Hebrew word *'olam* was originally a secular word meaning time without limit, but under prophetic usage it come to mean that which belongs to God alone and thus the nature of his care for Israel, though it never quite breaks from its time significance. The Greek word in the NT is *aiōn,* which again, in secular literature, does not have any special **theological** meaning. But in the gospels the word is given a special meaning through the life, **death** and **resurrection** of **Jesus**. Thus 'eternal' becomes a quality, not merely, a time word, and is not simply a synonym for 'everlasting', though clearly the connection between the two terms is close. So when in Jn 6:47 Jesus says that the believer will have eternal life, John Marsh makes it clear 'This does not mean that such persons will continue in this mortal, temporal existence for ever; it means that by a new relationship to God set up through Jesus Christ, a new dimension of life is opened to man, eternal life. This is not life without temporal limits, but life-in-Christ and Christ-in-life. The transition to this eternal life can be made in time; but the temporal boundaries of human life do not affect it.' The fourth gospel is teaching very clearly the possibility of the Christian believer having eternal life as a present possession, but when this present world, corrupted by evil [see **Fall**], comes to an end, then the eternal will endure free of **sin** and death. The relationship between the eternal and present experience is important, because whilst death marks a major discontinuity, teaching on eternal life guarantees a continuity of relationship with Christ beyond the grave. But the eternal not only projects forward into God's future but is beyond time in terms of an existence before the foundations of the world, thus in his high priestly **prayer** Jesus prays for those 'given him by the Father before the world began' (Jn 17:24), Paul speaks of God's wisdom 'framed from the very beginning to bring us to our full glory' (1Co 2:7); John of 'a lamb slain from the foundation of the world' (Rev 13:8).

ET

Ethical Investments
[See also *Ethics*]
Ethical Investments identify the precepts which enable us to match our ideals and principles with our investments. Companies and governments are evaluated not only for their investment potential, but also in accordance with specific ethical criteria.

Ethical Investments can be divided into three categories. The first category is based on international norms as reflected in key **UN** conventions and declarations. Included are *Human Rights principles*. Business should support and respect the protection of internationally proclaimed **human rights** within their sphere of influence; and make sure that they are not complicit in human rights abuses. In the realms of *Labour standards*, businesses should uphold the freedom of association and the effective recognition of the right to collective bargaining, work for the elimination of all forms of forced and compulsory **labour**, and the effective abolition of child labour. They should seek to eliminate all discrimination in respect of employment and occupation. Out of respect for the *Environment* businesses should support a precautionary approach to **environmental** challenges, undertake initiatives to promotes greater environmental responsibility, and encourage the development and diffusion of environmentally friendly technologies.

The second category concerns business involvement. This includes companies that are principally engaged in the sale or production of **tobacco** or **alcohol**, **gambling** services, military industries, pornography and pornographic publishing, or that are publicly recognised as having a clear presence in these activities. There are differing views based on culture as to whether alcohol production should be included or not in this list. Excluded are also companies connected to corruption.

The third category concerns refraining from investing in the bonds of governments and *states* that retain the **death penalty**.

In practice there are three different methods, separately or jointly, by which to manage ethical investments:

- Set and enforce a minimum ethical standard based on the investment criteria.
- Carefully research and select a list of positive companies and markets in which to invest.
- Focus on **dialogue** with the aim of improving the ethical standard of the business in general.

JS

Ethics

Ethics [Greek *cthos*] is a philosophical activity that studies, systematises and attempts to justify moral reasoning. If constrained exclusively by rational premises it is the domain of moral philosophy. Morality [Latin: *mos, moris* – 'custom or usage for actual human conduct'] is a central concern of organised social and religious life. Part of Christian theological undertaking is to study the morality of Christian communities. In the modern disciplinary divide of the complex theological task, it is called theological ethics or moral **theology**.

The principle categories of ethical discourse were developed by the thinkers of the Classical Hellenistic period, particularly in the search for purpose or true ends of things [*telos*] and the virtues of human life. Aristotle is credited as developing the teleological approach to moral discourse. Things have purpose and this can be determined by rational reflections on their nature and place in the order of things. Order brings harmony and is inherently good. To be good or virtuous is to acquire a quality of character that enables the person to attain that person's ultimate end which is *eudemonia* [roughly meaning 'living a good life with integrity or in happiness']. Much philosophical and theological moral thought squared on **natural law**/natural order discourse builds on this assumption. Thomas Aquinas' synthesis of natural and revealed 'cardinal virtues' aimed at securing the ultimate happiness of Christians' everlasting life [see **Eternal Life**] with God and still provides grounds for much **Roman Catholic** moral teaching. Re-

cently, teleological ethics is in resurgence contributing to some of the chief advances in contemporary ethics. When centred on ends which are worth striving for, teleological ethics justifies moral actions as right or wrong depending on their contribution to the progression towards desirable consequences (thus consequential ethics). The ends alone (not the means) justify the course of moral actions.

It is widely agreed that the early Christian moral discourse drew from two intellectual sources: Hebrew thought and the Hellenistic philosophical tradition. Already in the **apologetic** writings of Paul there are traces of the philosophical conventions of his time. By the time of the Post-Nicaean fathers, philosophical conceptualisation was making a strong imprint on Christian moral thought. By the time of the Middle Ages the divide between philosophical and theological ethics had become practically non-existent: the two traditions of intellectual reflections were so comprehensively intertwined.

The **Enlightenment** brought a sharp separation of intellectual thought from religious activities and established the dominance of philosophical ethics in the moral thinking of the western world. Philosophical ethics had to distinguish itself from traditional Judaeo-Christian moral thinking. The upheaval in Europe caused by protracted religious wars in the wake of the **Reformation** brought about the belief that turning to reason as the sole common foundation for personal and social life would secure **peace** and universal consensus on moral, socio-**political** and economic matters. The search for moral foundations went in several different directions. Two schools of modern philosophical thought gained prominence and exercised considerable influence on the development of Christian ethics: the ethics of obligation (deontological or Kantian) and the ethics of the greatest happiness (utilitarianism).

Deontological ethics [Greek stem: *deont-*, meaning 'binding') emphasises binding moral precepts or imperatives. It originates with Immanuel Kant and reflects a Platonic understanding of the existence of some transcendental ideal state of affairs – categorical imperatives (therefore universal and assessable by reason) above and beyond particular life situations. From this moral perspective there is no real distinction between being rational and being moral. The intuition behind it centres on the fact that a person often knows what the person's moral duty is quite apart from calculating the consequences of moral actions, and even in the face of unfavourable consequences. The purpose of moral reasoning is to distinguish the one truly good thing (e.g. moral rules or principles, **human rights**, divine commands, etc.) and to direct human will to act so that one person's action could be willed to become the universal rule for all persons to be followed in like circumstances. Much of **Protestant** and **Evangelical** moral theology is strongly influenced by deontological moral reasoning.

Utilitarianism is an ethical position that assumes that one ought to direct one's will to act in a particular way (act utilitarianism) or to follow the rule of conduct (rule utilitarianism) that brings about the greatest good (pleasure, happiness, welfare) for the greatest number of people. By its nature utilitarian morality is insensitive or hostile to minority concerns. This moral perspective originates with Jeremy Bentham and John Stuart Mill and in spite of difficulties in formulating what constitutes the greatest good, it appeals to the 'natural' reasoning in moral matters of secular and **Marxist** ideologies. When the greatest good is defined with the emphasis on the outcomes of a particular situation it leads to situationist ethics. Utilitarianism may be looked at as a form of a pragmatic teleological ethics (Stassen and Gushee, p.119).

Modern ethical reasoning has made a significant shift away from the classical Hellenic and Judaeo-Christian moral thinking by stressing the role of human will and by changing the focus of ethical discourse from what constitutes a good (moral) person or community to how an autonomous person makes rational decisions when faced with moral dilemmas. Morality consists in directing human will in decision-making. Some French existentialists (Jean-Paul Sartre) pressed the modern preoccupation with moral decision-making to its ultimate logical extent by locating morality not in what is decided but purely and simply in the very process of deciding.

Christian ethicists in most cases have appropriated dominant patterns of ethical reasoning instigated by modern moral philosophers and put them to use theologically. Until recently, two types of reasoning strategies have notably been employed in Christian moral discourse. One is to base ethics upon principles with universal validity supposedly derived from biblical texts [see **Bible**] and usually articulated in propositional form following a deontological line of reasoning. The other one is closely related to the notion of values either individual or shared. Christian value theorists differ in the way they bring values under moral considerations. Value ethic theories can either centre on one particular value (e.g. hedonism, eudamonia, power, etc.) or hold to plurality of values (e.g. knowledge, truth, pleasure, beauty, friendship, harmony, virtue, self-expression, etc.). Commonly value theorists employ teleological, particularly utilitarian, lines of reasoning.

The confidence in the universal validity of philosophical methodologies was severely undermined by the post-modern cultural and intellectual shift. Philosophers like Ludwig Wittgenstein, J.L. Austin, W.V.O. Quine, Alasdair MacIntyre, Michael Walzer, Bernard Williams, Charles Taylor, Paul Ricoeur, Hans-Georg Gadamer challenged the framework of modern philosophical thought by providing alternative ways of conceptualising the use of language, the coherence of knowledge and the formation of human morality. Furthermore, they stress the essential role of intellectual and moral traditions in ethical discourse: Autonomous 'pure reason' is unable to generate a uniquely rational moral system. Rational acceptability of a moral precept can be determined only in relation to a context of the inherited assumptions of a given moral tradition. Even the old dividing line between philosophy as dependant on purely unaided human reason, and theology accepting as a given the **revelation** of the scripture, is now blurred. This opens up a possibility for developing holistically a system of moral thought and belief. Following the trend, some recent **theologians** (e.g. George Lindback, John Howard Yoder, James Wm. McClendon, Jr., Stanley Hauerwas, Nancey Murphy, Glen Stassen, Brad Kallenberg) seek to return to the emphases on the moral community, character formation and virtue, as emphasised in the biblical narrative, to secure adequate tools for Christian moral reflections. Baptist ethicists McClendon and Stassen undertook a thoroughgoing revision of the source and the structure of Christian moral theology. They locate the source of Christian ethics in the moral discourse of the Bible and its structure as integrated enquiry into the existential, corporate and inspirational force of scripture's moral (*Kingdom*) vision. McClendon locates the thrust of ethical discourse in the biblical story as 'realistic' or 'history-like' narrative shared in a certain ongoing real life-story. The task of Christian ethics is 'the discovery, understanding, and creative transformation of a shared and lived story (of a Christian individual or community), one whose focus is Jesus of Nazareth and the kingdom he claims – a story that on its moral side requires such...[ethics] to be true to itself' (McClendon, p.330). Stassen emphasises the ethics of *incarnational discipleship* as the basis for the formation of holistic Christian character by participation in transforming initiatives (conviction-forming practices) of communal living outlined by Jesus in the Sermon on the Mount and elsewhere in scripture (Stassen and Gushee, p.58).

PRP

FURTHER READING: Stanley Hauerwas, *Vision and Virtue: Essays in Christian Ethical Reflection*, Fides, Notre Dame, 1974. Alasdair MacIntyre, *After Virtue: A Study in Moral Theory* (2nd ed.), University of Notre Dame Press, Notre Dame, 1984. Alasdair MacIntyre, *Three Rival Versions of Moral Enquiry: Encyclopaedia, Geneology, and Tradition*, University of Notre Dame Press, Notre Dame, 1990. James Wm. McClendon, Jr., *Ethics: Systematic Theology, Volume one* (2nd rev. ed.), Abingdon, Nashville, Tn., 2002. Nancey Murphy, *Anglo-American Postmodernity: Philosophical Perspectives on Science, Religion, and Ethics*, Westview, Boulder, 1997. Glen Stassen and David Gushee, *Kingdom Ethics: Following Jesus in Contemporary Context*, InterVarsity, Downers Grove, Il., 2003.

Eucharist

See *Baptism Eucharist and Ministry*; *Communion and Intercommunion*; *Eucharistic liturgy*; *Open Communion*; *Ordinance and Sacrament*; *Sacrament, Sign and Symbol*; *Strict Communion*.

Eucharistic liturgy

[See also *Baptism Eucharist and Ministry*; *Church architecture*; *Communion and Intercommunion*; *Liturgy*; *Open Communion*; *Ordinance and Sacrament*; *Sacrament, Sign and Symbol*; *Strict Communion*]

In Baptist churches the Eucharist/Lord's Supper/Communion generally takes place within the main *worship* service on Sunday. The frequency of the service varies from church to church. There are those who believe the *scriptural* pattern set out in the Acts of the Apostles (Ac 2:47) means that the principal service each Lord's Day should be eucharistic. Others take their concerns from *Calvin* who argued that infrequent communion was the invention of the *devil*. Still others have inherited a pattern of infrequent communion based on later *Calvinistic* developments in *Switzerland* and *Scotland*. If there are two services on a Sunday, then some celebrate twice in a month, once in a morning and once in an evening. Others have a monthly celebration. The pattern of the old *Reformed* approach of quarterly communion with a special season of preparation is not as common as it was in the 18th and 19th centuries.

Most Baptists refer to the meal as the Lord's Supper, but there is an increased use of the word Eucharist, given its place in the NT and the accent on thanksgiving, or *eucharista*, for the redeeming work of *Christ*. The practice of some Baptists in former times of making the Communion a separate short act of worship following on after the dismissal of the congregation at the end of the main Sunday service is now largely discredited and a comprehensive liturgy of the Word and Eucharist is the norm in Europe. In the Eucharist, or Communion three tenses are to be observed – the past tense celebrating the finished work of Christ, the present tense as the people of God make rendezvous with the Risen Christ, and the future tense as we anticipate the completion of the *kingdom* when Christ returns in majesty.

A typical outline of a Eucharistic celebration would be:
Call to Worship
Praise and General Thanksgiving
Confession
Reading of the Word

Sermon
Response in *prayer* and intercession
The Peace
The Offering
Invitation to the table
Great Prayer of Thanksgiving
Breaking and Sharing
Dismissal.

Some traditions retain the pattern of separate prayers for the bread and the *wine*, led by a *Deacon* or Elder, but many others have adopted one thanksgiving prayer, often led by the *pastor*, as a result of the liturgical movement and reception of the BEM process and reflection on the Lima Liturgy.

Normally the pastor of a *local church* presides at the table, but many congregations, especially in Western Europe, hold to the tradition that the *church meeting* can appoint whoever it wills to preside and there are those who are anxious to maintain the witness to lay presidency [see *Laity*] at the table. In Eastern Europe generally a Eucharistic service can only take place when there is an ordained pastor [see *Ordination*] to preside.

In most churches the single cup and a single leavened loaf are used. In Eastern and Southern Europe wine is normally used, whereas in parts of Western and Northern Europe unfermented grape juice or cordial is substituted and distribution takes place using small individual communion glasses, which unfortunately breaks down the symbolism. This development arose out of the *Temperance* movement in the 19th century.

It is typical for communicants to remain seated for the distribution which is done either by deacons or elders passing the plate and cup, or by communicants serving each other.

In most Baptist churches the 'table is fenced'. That is to say, there is an injunction against improper reception of the bread and wine. This can either be a relatively open invitation to 'all those who love or Lord Jesus Christ and desire to be His true disciples', through all those who have been baptised [see *Baptism*], to the narrower all those who have been baptised as believers and are in *membership* with the local *covenanted* community.

Generally, the *children* of believers would not receive communion until they have been baptised but in a few instances a blessing is offered to children present. There are also rare examples of bread being dipped in milk and honey then offered to children. This mirrors the idea of the promise to the Hebrew people that they would cross the Jordan and enter a land flowing with milk and honey. So for the children there is an anticipation of the eucharistic meal after they have passed through the waters of baptism.

KGJ

FURTHER READING: Stanley K. Fowler, *More than a Symbol*, Paternoster, Carlisle, 2002. Michael H. Taylor, *Variations on a Theme*, Galliard, London, 1973.

Euro-Asia Accrediting Association (EAAA)

The EAAA is the youngest accreditation association in the family of *evangelical* agencies which are involved in the accreditation of Christian *educational* institutions.

Beginning in 1989 when perestroika began to have a serious impact on the church life of the *Soviet Union*, *theological* colleges, schools and seminaries of a new type arose in numerous locations. The first of such seminaries arose in Odessa in August 1989, known today as the *Odessa Theological Seminary*. In 1990 in Belorechisk (Kransodar krai) an institute began which would later become the St. Petersburg Christian University. In 1991 a Bible School was organized in Donetsk, known today as the Donetsk Christian University. Near Kiev the work of the Irpen Biblical Seminary began, along with many other schools. All of them worked independently of one another. However, their understanding of Christian *unity* compelled them to seek a way of working together.

The first serious attempt to organise a meeting of representatives of the theological and biblical schools was undertaken by the 'Association for Spiritual Renewal' which was working in Moscow under the leadership of the late Peter Petrovich Deyenka. From 10-12 Feb 1993, around 40 representatives of *Bible* courses, colleges, institutes and seminaries from various *Protestant* confessions (Baptists, *Pentecostals*, Adventists among others) gathered in Moscow. In Feb 1994, seven schools with formal programmes of *educa-*

tion which had been in existence for no less than one year took an important step: they decided to found their own Accrediting As-sociation. In order to create the Association, both legally and practically, a new committee was formed consisting of leaders of the above mentioned schools. Sergei V. Sannikov was chosen as the chairman of the Preparatory Committee.

On 13 Oct 1997, in Moscow, the final session of the EAAA Preparatory Committee was held and on 14 Oct in Mitishchi (near Moscow) the EAAA was constituted. There were 37 organisations which were the founding members of the EAAA, of which 31 were theological schools including 15 from *Russia*, 13 from *Ukraine*, and one each from *Moldova*, *Kazakhstan* and *Uzbekistan*. Six organisations became Associate members of the Association. The EAAA Board was chosen consisting of 12 members. A.I. Melnichuk was chosen the Chairman of the Board, his assistant P.F. Penner, and the Executive Director, S.V. Sannikov. One of the main achievements of this conference was the approval of accreditation Standards for schools having a formal mode of education.

Today the EAAA unites 50 educational institutions and two other organisations which have an interest in Christian education in the area of the former Soviet Union, or programmes related to it.

SVS

EUROLIT

History. The origins of EUROLIT lie back in 1977 after David Russell (General Secretary of the Baptist Union of *Great Britain*) returned from visiting *Bulgaria* with a concern for *theological education* and the need for mini libraries with standard works and accompanying study courses and Gerhard Claas (General Secretary of the *European Baptist Federation*) invited Alec Gilmore, then editor of Lutterworth Press, to the EBF Council in *Italy*, with theological education high on the agenda.

At the same time Denton Lotz (an American Baptist *missionary* in Europe) was in correspondence with David Russell, John David Hopper (a *Southern Baptist* American missionary) and Stanislav Vec (General Secretary of the Baptist Union of *Czechoslova-*

kia) on similar lines which led to a proposal at the EBF Council in Paris, 1980, for the formation of a Books and Translations Committee with David Russell as Chairman (1979-87).

David Russell wanted to raise funds in the *UK* but was prevented from creating a special fund by his official position but by this time Alec Gilmore who shared all their concerns had become Director of *Feed the Minds*, a UK *ecumenical* charity specialising in Christian education, literature, publishing and distribution working mainly in the two-thirds world. He wanted to develop FTM projects in Eastern Europe but lacked the contacts. The two collaborated. Feed the Minds opened a special fund, EUROLIT, to raise contributions, David Russell arranged contacts and introductions, gave advice and promoted the fund in Baptist circles, and Barbara Askew, secretary to Ronald Goulding, received the funds in the UK and channelled these through EUROLIT. Feeds the Minds in turn promoted the fund among other churches and handled administration. Alec Gilmore made extensive visits to Eastern Europe, assessing needs, offering information and arranging grants, becoming a member of the Books and Translations Committee and subsequently Chairman (1987-92) until the Committee came to an end in 1992 as a result of restructuring.

Objectives. The principle objectives were:
(1) to help churches in Eastern Europe to develop Christian literature.
(2) to stimulate Christians in the West to learn more about Eastern Europe, to *pray* more intelligently and to give more generously.
(3) to work openly, respecting the laws of other countries and to seek to work with them.

In common with the *BWA* and the EBF, EUROLIT visits were always arranged at the invitation of the churches and with the approval of the secular authorities, and projects were often discussed with other church leaders and government officials.

Programme. Throughout the 80s the programme developed in three stages:
- Stage One provided theological textbooks for seminaries, mainly (as far as Baptists were concerned) through the Books and Translations Committee.

Grants for seminaries enabled librarians and faculty to choose the books they needed, students were given the benefit of the FTM/EUROLIT Student Book awards at the beginning of their *ministry* and seminaries had full and free access to the FTM Book Service to fill gaps in their shelves with used but still much needed titles, and received free distribution of the *Theological Book Review* to keep abreast of what was being published in the west.

Along with the Books and Translation Committee Denton Lotz had also initiated the Summer Institute of Theological Education (SITE) which brought a selection of pastors from Eastern Europe to *Rüschlikon* for a month every summer for intensive theological education at the end of which EUROLIT ensured that they had a collection of titles, chosen by their teachers and relating to their studies, which they could take home for their personal use.

- Stage Two (which complemented Stage One without destroying it) took the form of cash for paper, small machinery, printing and publishing costs. This included funding paper for the Baptists of *Hungary* to produce a hymnbook [see *Hymnody*], including tunes by Hungarian musicians based on themes of Hungarian composers such as Bartok and Kodally, and paper and publishing rights to the *Reformed Church* of Hungary and the *Lutheran* Church of *Poland* to produce their own translation of a Bible Encyclopaedia for children with colour illustrations.

Small printing machinery was made available to Baptists in Moscow and financial support was given for the translation and publication of a series of the Layman's Bible Commentary in *Yugoslavia* and Barclay Daily Bible Studies in Warsaw and Budapest. Other grants provided resources for a variety of hymnbooks, lexicons, concordances, religious education books, visual aids for children's *magazines* and mini libraries for young people.

- Stage Three focused on training programmes initially for writers and translators with more long-term plans for a greater professionalism in publishing and distribution with a view to more rewarding cooperation with the western publishing world when the opportunity came. Four major Workshops were held, two in Oxford for Baptist *scholars*, academics and publishers, one for translators on the occasion of the EBF Council in Glasgow, 1987, and a larger ecumenical one for translators and publishers in Rüschlikon, 1988.

In the days immediately after the end of the *Cold War* Alec Gilmore led a weekend training course for Russian Baptists in Moscow and a week's training session for the Latvian Baptists and their publisher, Bishop Janos Eisans, who then spent a week at the SCM Press in London getting acquainted with western publishing.

With the end of the Cold War, however, when the doors were opening for easier relationships and the opportunities greater than ever structural changes within the EBF led to closing down the Books and Translation Committee, transferring literature and publishing matters to the new Theology and Education Division.

Though in many respects it was a Baptist operation with most of the money coming from Baptist sources there was always an ecumenical slant. Knud Wumpelman, General Secretary of the EBF, warmly welcomed this emphasis and British Baptists found no difficulty with the fact that their contributions though mainly going to Baptist work could be used wherever EUROLIT felt the need was greatest.

This led EUROLIT into a fruitful development with the Reformed Church in Hungary, which worked closely with the United Bible Societies and had very professional publishing department, when towards the end of the Cold War permission was given for religious education in schools and the Reformed Church was made responsible for providing the text books. The opportunity was great and had to be seized but the Church had no expertise or resources and at that point EUROLIT was able to help in both areas. Similarly, in Romania, thanks to the good offices of Ioan Bunaciu, then Principal of the Baptist College in Bucharest, a good relationship also developed with the *Ortho-*

dox Publishing House, also responsible for all religious publishing including Bibles. No grants were made but the contact proved beneficial in other ways and Father Verzahn, their publisher, attended the Translators' Workshop in Rüschlikon (1988) and made himself at home in what was predominantly a Baptist event.

In the early 90s due to the restructuring within the EBF, the changing demands from Eastern Europe and changes of personnel EUROLIT went into remission.

AG

FURTHER READING: Stanley Crabb, *Our Favourite Memories, 1949-1999*, European Baptist Federation, Hamburg, 1999. Bernard Green, *Crossing the Boundaries: a History of the European Baptist Federation,* Baptist Historical Society, Didcot, 1997.

European Baptist Centre, Prague

[See also *European Baptist Federation; International Baptist Theological Seminary*]
The European Baptist Centre is a campus site located in the Jenerálka, Praha 6 suburb of the capital city of the *Czech Republic*. It is the campus base of several European Baptist Federation institutions and is wholly owned by the Swiss-based Verein of the EBF. The Centre houses the offices of the EBF, the International Baptist Theological Seminary, the Hotel Jenerálka, Šárka Valley Community Church (a member church of the Czech Baptist Union, BJB) and the European regional offices of *American Baptist Churches-USA* International Ministries and Canadian Baptist ministries.

The campus was purchased from the Czech Government in 1994, initially with the purpose of housing IBTS and, ultimately, the offices of the EBF. The site was designated the European Baptist Centre in 2004 when the EBF offices moved to the campus as a permanent location after a period in Sofia, and prior to that, Hamburg, Copenhagen and London.

The campus has a very long and interesting history, the main building dating from 1828. It witnessed infamous events during the time of the Nazi occupation of the Czech lands and the post WWII *communist* regime, when it served both as an interrogation centre and as a secret research centre.

KGJ

FURTHER READING: Petra Veselá, *Fit for a King,* IBTS, Prague, 2004. www.ibts.eu. www.ebf.org. www.hotel-jeneralka.cz. www.svcc.cz

European Baptist congregations/associations in North America
See *European Churches in America*.

European Baptist Convention (EBC)
See *International Baptist Convention*.

European Baptist Federation (EBF)
The EBF exists to bring together Baptists in Europe and the Middle East for *fellowship*, cooperation in *mission*, concern for *human rights* and *religious freedom*, *theological education*, and humanitarian aid. In 2008 the EBF consisted of 52 member Baptist *unions* and three Affiliated Churches. The EBF is affiliated to the *Baptist World Alliance* as a Regional Fellowship. It is an Associate member of the *Conference of European Churches*.

The EBF was formed in Paris (1950), though there had long been the vision for such an organisation within in the BWA (founded 1905) especially in the mind of British Baptist, J.H. Rushbrooke, who was Baptist Commissioner to Europe from 1920 and later General Secretary of the BWA.

The devastation of WWII in Europe brought a new impetus to the desire for a body which would bring together Baptists to work together for the relief and reconstruction of Baptist life in Europe as well as cooperation for effective mission. Mission agencies based in the USA, especially the Foreign Mission Board (FMB) of the *Southern Baptist Convention* and *American Baptist Churches*, played a significant role. Two related developments in 1948 were the creation of a *European Baptist Women's Union* and the establishment by the SBC of the USA of the *International Baptist Theological Seminary* in *Rüschlikon, Switzerland*.

The original Constitution (1950) states the purpose of the EBF as fourfold: 'to promote fellowship among Baptists in Europe; to stimulate and coordinate *evangelism* in

Europe; to provide a board of consultation and planning for Baptist mission in Europe; to stimulate and coordinate where desirable the *missionary* work of the European Baptists outside Europe.' The last named objective found its expression in the establishment of the European Baptist Missionary Society, later the *European Baptist Mission* in 1954.

The Paris Council of 1950 planned the first of the EBF Conferences (later known as Congresses) for 1952, and these were held at regular intervals until the Congress in Lillehammer, *Norway* in 1994. These have proved important and memorable occasions to gather European Baptists together. After a gap of some years a significant event is being planned for 2009 in Amsterdam, *Netherlands*, to celebrate the 400th Anniversary of the beginning of Baptist life.

At the time of the EBF's formation the 'Iron Curtain' had descended on Eastern Europe making life very difficult for Baptist Churches in Warsaw Pact countries. Much of the EBF's energies in the first 30 years were spent supporting Baptist believers facing persecution under *Communism*. An important initiative was the work of the Books and Translations committee under the able leadership of Alec Gilmore and David S. Russell, which provided much needed *Bible* commentaries and theological books for Russian-speaking pastors in Eastern Europe. EBF leaders were also active in defending the human rights and religious freedom of Baptists subject to pressure and persecution by Communist governments.

The full-time leadership of the Federation was provided for the first five years by the BWA Associate Secretary for Europe, W.O. Lewis but from 1959 onwards the EBF appointed its own General Secretary, beginning with Erik Ruden from *Sweden*. The working office of the General Secretary was in London for the first 25 years of the EBF's existence, thereafter being situated in the country of the current General Secretary before being, permanently located in 2004 in the newly-established *European Baptist Centre* in Prague, *Czech Republic*. For a full list of EBF General Secretaries see below.

From the establishment of the EBF a President has been elected from among the leaders of the member unions to serve for two years. In the early years, with the difficulties of communication with unions in Warsaw Pact countries, it was inevitable that Presidents would mainly be from Western Europe but in recent years EBF Presidents have been drawn from all regions of Europe. In 1994 the EBF elected its first woman President, Birgit Karlsson of Sweden.

The Council of the EBF, consisting of representatives of member unions, meets annually and is the main expression of its corporate life and an important forum for fellowship, discussion and planning for the future. An Executive meets twice a year.

The EBF was the first of the Regional Fellowships affiliated to the BWA to become self-supporting, and according to its current Statutes it is a legally independent body registered as a *verein* [charitable trust] in Switzerland. It has been customary for the EBF General Secretary also to be appointed as a Regional Secretary by the BWA and successive General Secretaries have been fully involved in the life of the Alliance.

After the collapse of communism in Central and Eastern Europe (1989-90) the EBF was active in providing much-needed Humanitarian Aid to the countries emerging from 50 years of oppression. A new organisation, *Baptist Response-Europe* was formed by the EBF, *Baptist World Aid* and the British *Baptist Missionary Society* to coordinate the work of providing practical relief from hunger and *poverty*. This evolved in 2007 to become European Baptist Aid, (EBAid) a consortium of Baptist Aid organisations engaged in longer-term development projects as well as emergency relief.

From the outset the EBF has been very concerned to support its member unions in mission and evangelism. In 2003 the EBF initiated the Indigenous Mission Project whereby gifted *men* and *women* are financially supported to plant new churches in their own countries and cultures [see *Church Planting*]. Significant Financial support has come from EBF partner mission agencies and in 2008 there were 60 indigenous missionaries in 25 countries, with much success being seen in terms of new believers and churches.

In human rights and religious freedom the EBF has, post-communism, concentrated on evaluating new laws on Religious Freedom, some of which have proved disadvantageous to Baptist and other minority churches. The question of the official registration of Baptist churches has often proved to be difficult. Relationships with *state churches*, especially *Orthodox Churches*, have sometimes become strained and in 1992 the EBF produced a Statement, *What are Baptists?*, to explain the identity of European Baptists to government authorities and state churches.

In 2005 the EBF took a significant step in its concern for the Human Trafficking of young women and girls across Europe who are then forced into *prostitution*. An Anti-Trafficking network was formed, giving help and resources to the member unions to engage in both 'prevention' projects and care for the victims of what is considered a modern form of slavery.

In theological education an important moment came in 1989 when IBTS in Switzerland was formally handed over by the FMB of the SBC to the ownership of the EBF. Since moving to Prague in 1996 it has become the centre of a *Consortium of European Baptist Theological Schools* seeking to help, resource and encourage the many Baptist Seminaries and Bible Schools in the EBF region, especially those established from the 1990s onwards

The EBF has been very well served by many people not all of whom can be listed but it is appropriate to list here the succession of Presidents and General Secretaries.
Presidents: Bredahl Petersen, *Denmark*, 1950-52; Henry Cook, *UK*, 1952-54; Manfredi Ronchi, *Italy*, 1954-56; Hans Luckey, *Germany*, 1956-58; Eric Rudén, Sweden, 1958-59; F. Ernst Huizinga, Netherlands, 1959-60; Ronald Goulding, UK, 1960-62; Baungaard Thomsen, Denmark, 1962-64; Jacob Broertjes, Netherlands, 1964-66; Michael Zhidkov, *Russia*, 1966-68; Rudolf Thaut, Germany, 1968-70; Andrew McRae, *Scotland*, 1970-72; Claus Meister, Switzerland, 1972-74; José Goncalves, *Portugal*, 1974-76; Alexej Bichkov, Russia, 1976-78; Knud Wümpelmann, Denmark, 1978-80; David Russell, UK, 1980-81; Stanislaw Sveč, Czech Republic, 1981-83; David Lagergren, Sweden, 1983-85; Pierro Bensi, Italy, 1985-87;Vasile Talpos, *Romania*, 1987- 89; Peter Barber, Scotland, 1989-91; John W. Merritt, *EBC*, 1991-93; Birgit Karlsson, Sweden, 1993-

95; Theodor Angelov, *Bulgaria*, 1995-97;David Coffey, UK, 1997-99; Ole Jørgensen, Denmark, 1999-01; Gregory Komendant, *Ukraine*, 2001-03; Billy Taranger, Norway, 2003-05; Helari Puu, *Estonia*, 2005-07; Toma Magda, *Croatia*, 2007-09.
General Secretaries: W.O. Lewis, USA, 1950-55; Henry Cook (acting), UK, 1955-59; Erik Ruden (the first secretary to be appointed by the EBF), Sweden, 1959-68; Ronald Goulding, UK, 1968-76; Gerhard Claas, Germany, 1976-80; Knud Wumpelmann, Denmark, 1980-89; Karl-Heinz Walter, Germany, 1989-99; Theo Angelov, Bulgaria, 1999-2004; Anthony Peck, UK, 2004-present.

AAP

FURTHER READING: European Baptist Federation, *What are Baptists?*, EBF, 1992. Keith G. Jones, *The European Baptist Federation 1950-2006: a case study in interdependency*, Paternoster, Milton Keynes, 2009.

European Baptist Mission (EBM) – history and work

The history of the EBM officially begins with its foundation in Sep 1954, with an inaugural meeting in Zürich when representatives from the *EBF* as well as church *unions* from *Germany*, *France* and *Switzerland* were present. EBM has been a registered society under Swiss law since then with its legal seat in Zürich. But there is an important pre-history to EBM which is to be found in correspondence in Dec 1951 between Jacob Meister, the chairman of the board of the German Union and Henri Vincent, the President of the French Baptist Union in which the German Baptists asked the French Baptists to support them in starting German *mission* work in Cameroon. In his response Henri Vincent doubted whether the French colonial [see *Colonialism*] authorities would approve of a German mission. Then in a letter of 28 Dec 1951 he made this revolutionary, pioneering proposal:

> If the idea of a unified Europe is to grow and become a reality, it is very likely that all barriers will fall between our nations, and we may then be able to think on [in] all matters, including missions, in terms, not of Germany or France, but of Europe.

I do pray for it. In that case, would it not be possible to organise a European Baptist Missionary Society, including French and German, and sending missionaries wherever it wants?

Here were the beginnings of a great vision – only a short period after the end of WWII. In its meetings in Rome in Sep 1953 and in München in Sep 1954, the EBF began to put this vision into action, thereby passing on the challenge to successive generations, with the first Council in Jan 1955 sending French missionaries into Northern Cameroon, where two years later the Union of Evangelical Baptist Churches in the Cameroon was brought into being after more than a century of Baptist missionary activity in the Cameroon. In 1965 the mission took over historic work formerly undertaken by the *BMS* in Sierra Leone which in 1974 was organised into the Baptist Union in Sierra Leone.

Originally, South America was never in EBM's line of sight. Africa was thought to be enough of a challenge! When German pastor, Horst Borkowski, received an invitation to South America in 1969 to *evangelise* German-speaking peoples in Argentina and Southern Brazil during the 'Campaña de las Americas', nobody would have guessed that an EBM branch would develop. This *crusade* first led to an independent movement named MASA (Missionary Activities in South America) in 1972, which in 1979 became a branch of EBM, with new work in Peru added the following year together with work in Bolivia from 1992. Six years later missionary help was sent to Cuba with work established in both the west and east of the island. Thus in Latin America MASA supports *children*'s homes, a Day-Care-Centre in Sao Paulo/Brazil, *theological education* and evangelistic work amongst native Indians.

In Africa, the Baptist Union of Central Africa (1984), and the Baptist Union of Mozambique (1992), became partner unions as did the well-established Baptist Convention of South Africa (1994) whilst new work was pioneered in Equatorial Guinea from 1993, and in Malawi from 1997. The work in Africa is focussed on *church growth* and evangelism, theological education, support for schools and Vocational Training Centres (with more than 9,000 *students*), medical work and hunger relief work.

EBM supported church growth projects by local missionaries in *Ukraine* and in *Georgia* for a short period of time in the 1990s. EBM is also partnered with another organisation to support work in Gotlam, India.

Currently some 17 European Baptist Unions are members of EBM: *Austria*, *Belgium*, *Czech Republic*, *Finland* (Finnish-speaking), France, Germany, *Hungary*, Hungarian Baptists in *Romania*, *International Baptist Convention*, *Italy*, *Netherlands*, *Norway*, *Poland*, *Portugal*, Romania, *Spain* and Switzerland. EBM co-operates with seven partner unions in Africa: Sierra Leone, Cameroon, Central African Republic, Equatorial Guinea, Mozambique, South Africa and Malawi. Through MASA, it is involved in five Latin-American countries: Argentina, Brazil, Peru, Bolivia and Cuba; as well as offering support to a children's Home in Porto, Portugal, until 2010. Worldwide the Mission deploys some 50-60 missionaries (long-term and short-term co-workers) working alongside c.300 national (indigenous) mission co-workers. Although registered in Switzerland its offices are located in at the Baptist Centre in Elstal near Berlin.

Today, European Baptists are challenged to participate in an even wider worldwide partnership in world missions, embracing more Baptist unions from Europe and co-operating with unions and conventions in Africa, Latin America and Asia on the basis of sending and receiving missionaries, sharing resources in an equal way, seeking to develop a truly worldwide European Baptist Mission.

HG & DW

European Baptist Women's Union
See *Women in Baptist life*; *Women's work*.

European Churches in North America
The earliest Baptists in North America had fled there under the pressure of *political* persecution in the 17th century but they were mainly English-speaking though there were also some early Welsh-speaking congrega-

tions. From the late 18th century economic pressures as well as continued persecution drove large numbers of people from the continent to seek a new start in America but these groups were not English-speaking and so they did not immediately integrate into existing church groups but instead founded new churches of their own which both preserved their language heritage and their different national cultures. Thus Norwegian, Swedish Danish and especially German churches were founded. Moreover since successive waves of migrants arrived over a long period of history the language and culture was refreshed notwithstanding the problems of the acculturation of earlier waves of migrants reflected, e.g., in such things as a younger generation marrying outside the community. Though individual churches are older the following is a list of the dates when these churches began to form national *unions*, some existing in both the USA and Canada:

1891   The English and French-Speaking Baptist Conference of New England (some authorities give 1895)
1891   The Italian Baptist Association
1891   The Finnish Baptist Union of America
1891   The American Magyar (Hungarian) Baptist Union
1891   The Danish Baptist General Conference of America. Dissolved in the 1950s and absorbed into the Northern Convention.
        The Norwegian Baptist Conference of America [some authorities give 1864] Dissolved in the 1950s and absorbed into the Northern Convention.
1891   The Czecho-Slovak Conference
        The Polish Baptist Conference (some authorities give 1909)
1913   The Rumanian Baptist Association of America
1914   The Swedish Baptist General Conference of America (originated 1869, but certain churches date back to 1852)
1919   The German Baptist Churches of North America (also 1865, but origins date back to 1850)
        The Russian Baptist Conference (The Russian and Ukrainian Evangelical Baptist Union)
        The Portuguese Baptist Conference
1919   The Ukrainian Evangelical Baptist Convention
1930   The Latvian Baptists

It is interesting that the German churches are shown as associating at a relatively late date. In fact the years of WWI were particularly difficult for Germans in the USA. Accordingly in that context many German congregations abandoned their native language in *worship* lest they be thought to be un-American. On the other hand during and after the war they played a crucial part in sustaining *mission* work in *Germany*'s former African colonies. During WWII, again for obvious reasons they dropped the adjective German from their title and became The North American Baptist Conference (1944). It does not take much imagination to understand the problems associated with such a haemorrhaging of *membership* from young churches in Europe, the importance of lively networking for the *pastoral care* of new arrivals and the importance of these *diaspora churches* in supporting parent churches facing difficulties in Europe.

                                            JHYB

European Evangelical Alliance

[See also *Evangelical Alliance*; *World Evangelical Alliance/Fellowship*]

When the Evangelical Alliance was formed in London in 1846 representatives came from across mainland Europe. Of the 922 people who signed as attendees 84% were from Britain and over 7% were from other European countries. National Evangelical Alliances were formed in a number of European countries and major conferences were held over succeeding decades in Western European cities. After WWII steps were taken to set up an international *evangelical* body, with much of the initiative for this coming from the USA. In 1950 a conference was held in *England* which drew together representatives from 12 Evangelical Alliances in Europe and delegates from the National Association of Evangelicals in America. Further steps were taken at a conference at Gordon Divinity School in Boston, USA, later in the same year. It was recommended that there should be an International Association of Evangelicals. The agreed purpose of this body was:

(1) to witness to evangelical and historic Christianity;
(2) to encourage and promote *fellowship* among Evangelicals, and;
(3) to stimulate *evangelism* and promote united evangelical action in all spheres.

At a meeting held in the *Netherlands* in 1951 a World Evangelical Fellowship was formed. Although most delegates at that conference affirmed the need for a worldwide fellowship of evangelicals, there was not unanimity. When the vote was taken, representatives from *Germany* abstained, and *France*, *Denmark*, *Norway* and *Sweden* opposed the proposal. One of the main concerns among the European Alliances was that the word 'infallible' in the Basis of Faith implied too mechanical an understanding of biblical inspiration [see *Infallibility and Inerrancy of the Bible*; *Inspiration of the Bible*]. There were also concerns that cooperation with those who might not hold to the Basis of Faith in its entirety was being prohibited. The background was that the *World Council of Churches* had been formed in 1948 and there was a fear among some Europeans that American evangelicals wanted to form a rival, anti-*ecumenical* body. There was some hesitation among representatives of the British Evangelical Alliance, but they decided to join nonetheless, as did the Spanish Evangelical Alliance.

In 1952 representatives from several European countries met in Germany and established their own separate European Evangelical Alliance (EEA). The breach with WEF was not healed until 1968, up to which point WEF was able to make little headway in Europe. However, gradually the EEA gained momentum. A new evangelical impetus took place across Europe in the late 1980s and early 90s. In the East, national Evangelical Alliances that had been outlawed were formed once more. In *Albania*, e.g., an Alliance which had first been formed in 1892 was re-established in 1992 and played a part in the formation of a new constitution for the country. Other developments in former *communist* countries have been similar. A Bulgarian Alliance was formed and became a member of the EEA in 1993, and a Bulgarian Baptist *pastor*, Nik Nedelchev, became

EEA President. In 2006, of the 37 national Alliances that were EEA members, 14 were from former communist countries. The growing number of evangelicals from Central and Eastern Europe have played a crucial role in the new Europe, with the EEA operating as an important channel for evangelical cooperation.

The EEA office has been in London, at the British Evangelical Alliance office, but the EEA also set up an office in Brussels in 1994, and has sought to influence *European Union* policy in areas such as religious freedom and treatment of refugees. E.g. in 1996 the European Parliament determined to pass a resolution which had negative implications for *religious freedom*. However, by working with Christian parliamentarians, the EEA succeeded in changing the text. The final resolution was amended to make specific reference to the importance of religious freedom and the European Convention of *Human Rights*. The EEA has sought to work with others over a number of EU issues to co-ordinate Christians responses and has encouraged Christians in each European country to continue talking to their governments to persuade them to be aware of the situations of the faith communities.

IMR

FURTHER READING: I.M. Randall and D. Hilborn, *One Body in Christ: The History and Significance of the Evangelical Alliance*, Paternoster, Carlisle, 2001. I.M. Randall, 'Evangelical and European Integration' in *European Journal of Theology*, Vol. 14, No. 1 (2005), pp.17-26.

European Union (EU)/Common Market

Two world wars left statesmen in Europe intent on engineering structures which would make further conflict impossible. Accordingly a number of institutions – *political*, economic, juridical, military – were brought into being, most of which, whilst they reduced the significance of boundaries within Western Europe, tended to exaggerate the divisions between West and East. Another question raised was the extent to which this was a rich man's club consolidating and strengthening its position against poorer producer *nations*. In the event it has established good formal relations with the

ACP (African, Caribbean and Pacific nations) working through a body called the Parity Assembly.

The oldest of the many European institutions is the *Council of Europe*, formed in London in 1949, and with its headquarters in Strasbourg, with the requirement that all member *states* recognise the rule of law and guarantee their citizens the enjoyment of *human rights* and fundamental freedoms. It works through a committee of ministers advised by a parliamentary assembly. It seeks to foster cooperation in *education*, justice, *sport*, and *environment*. It has also developed policies on *migration* and local and regional development.

Earlier defence groupings such as the Western Europe Union have been absorbed into NATO (North Atlantic Treaty Organisation), founded in 1949. In the legal field the European Convention on Human Rights came into being in 1953 and the European Court of Justice in 1959 to which appeal from national jurisdictions can be made.

The European Economic Community has its roots in reconstruction in Europe after WWII aided as it was by the USA's Marshall Plan funding of European recovery. The initial concerns were to work together on coal, iron and steel supplies to protect and coordinate heavy engineering in Europe (1951). From this emerged the Organisation for European Economic Cooperation (OEEC: 1948) which in 1961 became the Organisation for Economic Cooperation and Development (OECD). By then the Treaty of Rome (1957) had established the European Economic Community (EEC), initially comprising *France*, *Germany*, *Italy* and the BENELUX countries (*Belgium*, *Luxembourg*, the *Netherlands*), a central concern being the establishment of a 'Common Market', with most of the remaining countries in Western Europe forming EFTA (European Free Trade Association, 1959).

The EU has complex mechanisms of government – it has a Council of Ministers, a high-powered Commission combining Commissioners responsible for different functional areas of operation but acting together under the Presidency of the Commission, all located in Brussels so hence the name 'Brussels' in common speech often stands for the power/bureaucracy of the EU.

In 1959 a European Parliament, which meets in Strasbourg, was added with the first direct elections taking place in 1979.

In 1972, after French opposition had been countered, the *UK*, *Ireland* and *Denmark* entered the Union, the first extension of the community's membership. Greece joined in 1981. *Portugal* and *Spain* joined in 1986. *Austria*, *Finland*, *Sweden* were admitted in 1995. A further major admission was made of several nations in 2004 of two Mediterranean islands and several post-communist states of Central Europe – Cyprus, *Czech Republic*, *Estonia*, *Hungary*, *Latvia*, *Lithuania*, *Malta*, *Poland*, *Slovakia* and *Slovenia*. In 2007 *Bulgaria* and *Romania* also joined.

Other nations applying include *Croatia* and the former-Yugoslav Republic of *Macedonia*. *Norway*, *Switzerland* and *Iceland* participate in many areas of EU life, but not as members, rather as client states. *Russia* has expressed concern about the enlargement of the European Union into Central and South Eastern Europe. Other issues raised have been the extent to which a Christian heritage is essential to the nature of European institutions and therefore whether it would be appropriate to offer membership to *Turkey*, a secular *Islamic* state; whilst some are hesitant others sees this as an exercise in bridge-building between the West and the Islamic world. The Maastricht Treaty (1992) was a pivotal moment binding the existing members together in important areas of monetary policy and bringing about the single European currency, the Euro. Nations who were members prior to that point claimed opt-out arrangements from certain parts of the Maastricht Treaty including the Euro. Nations joining since that time have only been able to build in delays to adopting all the previsions of Maastricht. More recently further development and refinement of the operations of the EU have been agreed in the Lisbon Treaty (2007) awaiting full ratification by the Czech Republic and Republic of Ireland.

The pace at which nations sought further integration and the extent to which they wished to reserve powers to national parliaments caused considerable tensions within the Union, which to a degree were about how far economic cooperation could be married to continued political autonomy. E.g. when the European Monetary System came into being in 1977 (with the common currency established as the Euro), some nations in membership postponed joining. Similarly Britain and Ireland have not joined the Schengen agreement of open borders within the European Union, though countries outside full membership of the EU such as Switzerland have joined the border-free Europe created by the Schengen Treaty (1995).

Because all of these institutions have a major impact on the lives of people across Europe the churches have been concerned to establish a Christian presence in Brussels and Strasbourg, the locations of most of the decision-making. Baptists tend to have two attitudes to the EU. Those who see great value in continental cooperation, not least in creating a peaceful, border-free place where citizens and subjects of individual nations can benefit from employment, health care and security without an individual nation imposing restrictions or treating individuals as of lesser value than others, in some ways mirroring the ideals of the first *Anabaptists* who were not bound by 'territory' in the way of most other Christians. Others oppose the whole EU enterprise, seeing it as linked to an agenda designed to ensure secular domination of Europe.

ET

Euthanasia

Euthanasia (derived from Greek words *eu* [good] and *thanatos* [death]) is a controversial technical term in contemporary *bioethics* both in terms of concept and in possible practice. In the Parliamentary Assembly of the Council of Europe it has been defined as 'any medical act intended to end a patient's life at his or her persistent, carefully considered and voluntary request in order to relieve unbearable *suffering*', and/or 'in his/her obvious interest'. This formulation suggests that euthanasia may be conducted with consent as voluntary euthanasia or without consent as involuntary euthanasia. Also, ethicists [see *Ethics*] have argued that there are different forms of euthanasia: it could be conducted passively, non-aggressively or aggressively. Passive euthanasia would entail the withholding of common

treatments (such as antibiotics, or surgery) or the distribution of a medication (such as morphine) to relieve pain, knowing that it may also result in *death* as a double effect. Non-aggressive euthanasia would entail the withdrawing of life support. Aggressive euthanasia would entail the use of lethal substances or forces in order to kill. Aggressive euthanasia is illegal in most countries, but not in all (e.g. *Belgium* and the *Netherlands*). The Church and Society Commission of the *Conference of European Churches* (CSC of CEC) has stated: 'All churches agree that the deliberate killing of suffering and dying human beings is a grave *sin*. All churches underline the need for the maintenance of good terminal care, including the offer of *pastoral care*. The problem of euthanasia normally comes up in a situation where, at least, two important principles of medical ethics collide or at least are at odds: protection of human life and the alleviation of pain and distress'. A grey area would be in case of refusing or resigning from further medical treatment and restricting oneself to the alleviation of pain and distress which may result in a shortening of life or, rather, accelerating of the process of dying. CSC of CEC recognises 'a broad agreement in the churches that there is no virtue in the prolongation of dying by means of medical "high technology" and that there is no *theological* difficulty in allowing a terminal patient to die naturally' since 'Christian *faith* implies that we trust in God who is with us in life and death', and 'belief in *resurrection* means that the "sting" of death is removed (1Co 15:54ff).' A more general issue would be defining the concept of 'natural' in bioethics since medical care is often 'unnatural' in a sense. CSC of CEC emphasises: 'Medical technology itself may entail difficult end of life decisions, for instance in the case of tube-feeding treatment to stroke patients with dysphagia (swallowing disorder). If no tube treatment is given, the patient may die a natural death, but without having a chance of the improvement of his/her situation. However, if the tube is removed after it has become clear that it has had no therapeutical value at all, the patient will die. The question remains if we can call it a natural death.' Baptists stress the dignity of human life. Based on this conviction, one may consider a death to be 'unnatural' if it is caused by withdrawing what is biologically necessary to sustain human life (e.g. air, water, nutrients, warmth). Even a healthy human or animal would die if deprived of biologically essential substances. Baptist bioethical convictions could not countenance the unnatural death of a person. At the same time, no treatment should add suffering. Appropriate to the human beings as the good stewards [see *Stewardship*] of God's *creation* would be to accept and execute the euthanasia of animals, but in a way that is not 'unnatural' or causing suffering. Behind all such questions in medical ethics lies a fear that scientific innovations may be trespassing on areas which are rightly within the divine prerogative. On the other hand it is a God-given intelligence which the devout scientist would argue should be exploited to the extent of the gifting that God has given. More crudely some would try and make distinctions between what is natural and what is unnatural, but there is very little in 21st-century urban industrial culture which is not the fruit of 100s of human interventions to make life as humanity most wants it to be. Complicated ethical decisions in this area need to be made with as clear and calm and reverent a mind as is possible.

MR

FURTHER READING: Stephen E. Lammers and Allen Verhey (eds), *On Moral Medicine. Theological Prespectives in Medical Ethics* (2nd ed.), Eerdmans, Grand Rapids, Mi., and Cambridge, 1988. www.cec-kek.org/content/bioethicsconf.shtml.

Evangelical/Evangelicalism – the use of the word in Europe

[See also *Evangelicalism, Baptist approach to*]

The word 'evangelical', which might be understood simply enough in many parts of the world when applied to Christians, is much more complicated to understand and nuance in the European scene, especially in certain of the significant European languages such as German and Russian. It is also problematic in Czech, Lithuanian and other less dominant languages within the continent.

No doubt the oldest use, generally, belongs within the context of describing *Lu-*

theranism as the 'Evangelical Church'. By this is meant that it is not *Catholic* and belongs to the understanding of Christianity arising out of the Magisterial *Reformation*. So, there are in many European countries 'Evangelical Churches' which are, in some form, churches of the Magisterial Reformation, but might, for instance, have within them a variety of *theological* positions, some of which might be classified as '*liberal*'. Thus its use is as part of a formal title of a significant church rooted in the Reformation and not as denoting churches, or individuals, holding a certain prescribed set of theological tenets.

In Tsarist *Russia*, *France* and *Spain*, the word 'Evangelical' was and is used by Baptists as part of their official title and in some instances this may be more to do with the desire of baptistic groups not to be seen as narrow *sects*, but belonging, in some way, to the larger *Protestant* Reformation world.

The other use of the word is that associated in the Anglo-Saxon world with a form of Christianity which, renewed by experience of the *Great Awakening* and Evangelical *Revival* of the 18th century, emphasises conversionism [see *Conversion*], activism, biblicism [see *Bible*] and crucicentrism [see *Atonement*].

Such evangelicalism exists within and outside the churches of the magisterial reformation and can be further subdivided into a range of groupings including *conservative evangelicalism*, radical evangelicalism and liberal evangelicalism. In most European countries many churches and organisations within these groupings belong to a national *Evangelical Alliance*, which, in turn, is normally part of the *European Evangelical Alliance* and the *World Evangelical Fellowship*.

The attempt to clarify definitions has proved difficult with linguists in some countries not agreeing to two words to differentiate the two notions and Christians in other countries declining to use the word 'Protestant' in place of 'Evangelical', especially where the dominant non-Catholic or *Orthodox* community is the 'Evangelical Church'.

KGJ & LA

FURTHER READING: D.W. Bebbington, *Evangelicalism in Modern Britain: A History from the*

1730's to the 1980's, Unwin Hyman, London, 1989.

Evangelical Alliance

[See also *European Evangelical Alliance*; *World Evangelical Alliance/Fellowship*]

John Angell James, a *Congregational* minister in Birmingham, *England*, proposed in 1842 an alliance of *Free Church* and *Anglican evangelicals*. In the same period Free Church leaders, including leading English Baptists such as J.H. Hinton, then the Secretary of the Baptist Union, J.P. Mursell of Leicester, and Charles Stovel of East London, were campaigning for members of Free Churches to work together for religious equality. In Aug 1846 the conference that brought the Evangelical Alliance into being met in London. Of the 922 attendees at the founding conference, 84% came from Britain, over 8% from the USA and 7% from European continental countries – including European Baptist figures such as *Johann Oncken*. The Alliance affirmed the divine *inspiration*, *authority* and sufficiency of *scripture*; the *unity* of the Godhead, and the *Trinity* of Persons; the depravity of human nature in consequence of the *Fall*; the *incarnation* of the Son of God and his work of atonement for sinners [see *Sin*]; *justification* by *faith* alone; the work of the *Holy Spirit* in *regeneration* and *sanctification*; the right and duty of private judgement in the interpretation of scripture; and the divine institution of the Christian *ministry* and the *ordinances* of *baptism* and the *Lord's Supper*. There had been a hope that a worldwide Alliance could be formed, but British evangelicals in particular, including notable Baptists, insisted that they could not be in *fellowship* with evangelicals in America who were slave-owners. Thus national Evangelical Alliances were formed. They became active in pursuing issues such as *religious freedom*, e.g. freedom for evangelicals in predominantly *Roman Catholic* and *Orthodox* countries. In the 1950s a *World Evangelical Fellowship* and a European Evangelical Alliance were formed. Baptists have actively participated in national Alliances since their foundation, and there is strong Baptist involvement in the European Evangelical Alliance.

IMR

FURTHER READING: J.B.A. Kessler, *A Study of the Evangelical Alliance in Great Britain*, Oosterbaan and Le Cointre, Goes, Netherlands, 1968. I.M. Randall, 'American influence on Evangelicals in Europe: A comparison of the founding of the Evangelical Alliance and the World Evangelical Fellowship', in H. Krabbendam and D. Rubin, (eds), *Religion in America: European and American Perspectives*, VU University Press, Amsterdam, 2004, pp.263-74. I.M. Randall and D. Hilborn, *One Body in Christ: The History and Significance of the Evangelical Alliance*, Paternoster, Carlisle, 2001.

Evangelical Christian Union, Russia

The Evangelical Christian Union was founded in St. Petersburg in 1909 by Ivan Stepanovich Prokhanov and merged in 1944 with the Russian Baptist Union to form the *All-Union Council of Evangelical Christians-Baptists*, which was an umbrella organisation for practically all *Soviet evangelicals*.

The roots of the Evangelical Christian Union are in the Victorian Evangelical *preaching* of Lord Radstock beginning in 1874 in St. Petersburg which emphasised *revival*, *sanctification*, and Christian *unity*. In 1878, under the leadership of V.A. Pashkov, the movement became known as 'Pashkovism' and developed ties with the *Evangelical Alliance*. The *political* pressure of Pobedonostsev, the Ober-Prokuror of the Holy *Synod*, forced Pashkov into exile in 1884, causing *Ivan Kargel* to take on the leadership of the group. During the Pobedonostsev period, the movement was limited to *evangelistic* house groups scattered throughout the Russian Empire and an informal *Bible* school lead by Kargel in St. Petersburg. Pashkovism spread both in the 'lower' and 'higher' ranks of Tsarist Russian society. The 'Pashkovites' were *orthodox* in their Christian belief, emphasising the Bible, conversionism [see *Conversion*], and Christian unity. They did not ordain leaders [see *Ordination*], practice *baptism*, nor maintain *membership* rolls.

Ivan Prokhanov, of Russian Molokani extract, had been baptised in 1887 by the fledging Baptist Church of Tiflis (now Tblisi). Prokhanov was a man of immense drive who had been influenced by his studies at *Bristol College* and his exposure to the Evangelical Alliance. In 1898, he moved to St. Petersburg to assist Kargel with the leadership of the loosely connected group of Pashkovites. Prokhanov laboured to organise and unite the Pashkovites and draw them into a *fellowship* with all evangelical believers throughout the Russian Empire. In his work for Christian unity, he did not regard Christian practices such as baptism, *communion* or styles of church leadership to be issues which should divide the organisation.

In 1909, Prokhanov united the former Pashkovites as well as some other evangelical believers into the 'Union of Evangelical Christians'. This group soon connected with the *Baptist World Alliance* of which Prokhanov became a vice-president in 1911. The Evangelical Christian Union remained distinct from the Russian Baptist Union (formed in 1884) over issues of the need for ordination, *closed communion*, and the *laying on of hands*, all of which the Russian Baptist Union insisted upon as well as a certain doctrinal clarity which Prokhanov was not willing to force upon the Evangelical Christian Union. There were multiple attempts at a merger but ultimately it was the pressure of the Soviet *state* which forced the two groups to unite.

GLN

Evangelicalism, Baptists and

[See also *Evangelical/Evangelicalism – the use of the word in Europe*]
Evangelicalism is a pan-denominational movement within *Protestantism* which took shape in the 18th century and was particularly associated with *revival* in *Britain*, led by John Wesley and George Whitefield, with awakening in North America, where Jonathan Edwards was the leading thinker, and with the *Moravian movement* in Central Europe. David Bebbington, in *Evangelicalism in Modern Britain*, has spoken of conversionism [see *Conversion*], Biblicism [see *Bible*], crucicentrism [see *Atonement*] and activism as the four distinctives of evangelicalism. He argues that the decade beginning in 1734 'witnessed in the English-speaking world a more important development than any other, before or after, in the history of Protestant Christianity: the emergence of the movement that became Evangelicalism'. Mark Noll, in *The Rise of Evangelicalism*, notes that Baptists were the 'great benefici ary' of the *Great Awakening* in New England. This movement has had a profound effect on Baptist life.

English Baptists were to be affected in the area of conversionist thinking and practice through energetic younger 18th-century leaders such as the *Calvinistic* Baptist *minister*, Andrew Fuller [see *Fullerism*], who became the Secretary of the *Baptist Missionary Society*, and the General Baptist leader [see *England*], Dan Taylor. In 1785 Fuller published (the argument is that he had completed the writing rather earlier) his ground-breaking theological work, *The Gospel Worthy of all Acceptation*, which argued for 'the free offer of the gospel' to all sinners [see *Sin*], and rejected the non-evangelistic 'high Calvinism' which had been prevalent in Particular Baptist spirituality in the earlier 18th century, especially in London. By contrast churches in the orbit of the *Bristol College* were less influenced by such high Calvinism. English Baptists took up the evangelical conversionist message and found in it a source of spiritual renewal and growth. The influence continued. *Charles Haddon Spurgeon*, who became known as the Prince of Preachers of the Victorian era, described his own conversion in classic evangelical terms as an encounter with *Jesus*.

In evangelicalism there is a strong focus on individual Bible reading and serious attention to biblical *preaching* as means of spiritual growth. Preaching has always been central to Baptist life and this has resonated with evangelical priorities. In the 19th century, as Baptist congregations in Britain and America grew, great pulpiteers became prominent. Spurgeon attracted so many people to his preaching in London that the Metropolitan Tabernacle, accommodating 5,000 people, was built to house his congregation. Other famous British pulpiteers were Alexander McLaren and *John Clifford*. Reading of scripture and hearing preaching is to deepen a relationship with Christ. Spurgeon rejected any sermon 'which does not lead to Christ, or of which Jesus Christ is not the top and the bottom'. As John Stott, an international evangelical leader of the 20th century, put it, 'to be a Christian is to live...through, on, in, under, with, for and like Jesus Christ'. Evangelicalism has also linked spiritual vibrancy with the proper handling of the Bible. Another British evangelical leader, Martyn Lloyd-Jones, minister of Westminster Chapel, London, spoke of preaching as '*theology* on fire'. One of the most famous phrases about the Bible came from the American evangelist, *Billy Graham*, a Baptist. For him what was important was what 'the Bible says'.

Seeing the *cross* of Christ as at the heart of the experience of personal *salvation*, evangelicals went on to view the Christian life as one in which disciples of Christ were called to give up their own way and follow the crucified Saviour. This is the life of *holiness*. There have been different views about how such holiness is to be achieved. Andrew Fuller typically held that holiness was fostered by the Bible. He wrote: 'The more we read the holy Scriptures, the more we shall imbibe their spirit and be formed by them as a model.' The Keswick Convention's approach to *spirituality* [see *Keswick Spirituality*], expressed at the annual Convention held in the English Lake District from 1875, helped to shape the prevailing pattern of *piety* within English-speaking evangelicalism for a good part of the 20th century. The emphasis was on the 'deeper Christian life'. *Anglicans* predominated at Keswick, but Baptist ministers such as F.B. Meyer and Graham Scroggie were sigificant. Meyer also spoke at many holiness meetings across continental Europe. The best known *hymn*-writer of the Keswick movement was Frances Ridley Havergal, one of the greatest evangelical hymn-writers of the 19th century.

A final feature of evangelicalism has been active engagement in *evangelism*, aimed at bringing people to an experience of conversion. The 18th-century evangelical awakenings also led directly to evangelistic and missionary endeavours by Protestants. In 1732 the Moravians, at Herrnhut, Germany, committed themselves to what proved to be a remarkable Protestant missionary work, reaching places such as Greenland and Lapland. Jonathan Edwards' book *An Humble Attempt*, with its vision of 'the Advancement of Christ's Kingdom on Earth', was crucial in

the story of evangelical – not least Baptist - developments. A 'Prayer Call' in 1784 by the Northamptonshire Association of Baptist Churches was part of the missionary thrust and a further consequence was the formation in October 1792 of the Baptist Missionary Society. It is not possible to understand Baptist world missionary endeavour without taking account of the impact of evangelicalism.

A prime mover behind the formation of the BMS was William Carey, a young Baptist minister. His spiritual vision was set out in a book and a sermon. The book, published in 1792, was *An Enquiry into the Obligation of Christians, to Use Means for the Conversion of the Heathen*. Carey argued that Roman Catholic missionaries had surmounted great obstacles in their missionary endeavours, and he then talked about the example of the Moravians. He concluded: 'But none of the moderns have equalled the Moravian Brethren in this good work.' The sermon ('Expect great things...') was delivered on 30 May 1792 to the Northamptonshire Baptist Association. On the following day the business of the *Association* continued, but *Carey* was insistent, asking: 'Is nothing to be done?' It was decided, despite reluctance on the part of some, to act. In the 19th century European Baptists became, in a more intentional way, a missionary body, and this was summed up best by Johann Oncken, the father of European Baptists, who spoke of 'every (Baptist) member a missionary'.

Evangelical mission has also involved social action. F.B. Meyer became well known for his contribution to social improvement in the 1880s and in the decades that followed, for instance the rehabilitation of offenders. During his *ministry* in Leicester (in the English Midlands) in the 1880s, in a Baptist church which he began, he discovered that *men* coming out of prison were quickly drawn back into crime. With the cooperation of the governor, he visited the prison daily, taking discharged prisoners to a coffee house for a plate of ham. Meyer also found ex-prisoners employment. He claimed that many were converted and the prison population was reduced. Meyer, who spoke of how the gospel could be 'incarnated' in the community, involved his congregations in ministry – to the city of Leicester and then later to South London when he moved there. Baptists took up and re-moulded typical evangelical emphases. This has continued as Baptists such as Steve Chalke in the later 20th century became known for their entrepreneurial social initiatives. Baptists have been and are conversionist, biblicist, cross-centred and activist.

IMR

FURTHER READING: D.W. Bebbington, *Evangelicalism in Modern Britain: A History from the 1730s to the 1980s*, Routledge, London, 1995. D.W. Bebbington and Mark A. Noll (eds), Biographical dictionary of Evangelicals, InterVarsity, Leicester and Downers Grove, Il., 2003. J.M. Gordon, *Evangelical Spirituality*, SPCK, London, 1991. C. Price and I.M. Randall, *Transforming Keswick*, OM, Carlisle, 2000. I.M. Randall, *Evangelical Experiences: A Study in the Spirituality of English Evangelicalism, 1918-1939*, Paternoster, Carlisle, 1999. I.M. Randall, *What a Friend we have in Jesus*, DLT, London, 2005.

Evangeliska Frikyrkan
See *InterAct*.

Evangelism, The theology of
[See also *Evangelism and Baptist churches*; *Evangelism and the media*; *Evangelist*; *Theology*]
The Greek NT has provided the current terms for evangelism. The *euangelion* is the good news that leads to human happiness. To spread or proclaim the good news means to evangelise (*euangelizo*), and the one who does it is called an *evangelist* (*euangelistes*). It is a term that goes back to *Jesus* and his usage, as his reading of the Isaiah text demonstrates (Lk 4:16-21). Through frequent use in the Synoptics, in Acts and in the Epistles the concept of spreading the good news is dominant in the whole NT. The *euangelion* is the news about the fulfilment of predictions made by OT prophets [see *Prophecy*] and of humanity's deepest longings. John, who does not use this word in his writings, mentions instead the term 'to witness' (*martyreo*). The one who witnesses to Christ and to the life Christ offers gives witness (*martyria*) to it. The content of the good news is the message of the coming *kingdom* and God's reign, what leads to *salvation*, justice

and righteousness.

The present day use of the term is probably influenced primarily by Paul who employs it as a key term in his theology. At the heart of the good news is the *revelation* that God became human, lived, suffered, died and rose from the dead and that through this salvation has been made available to all humanity. The Reformers [see *Reformation*], noting Paul's frequent reference to the gospel followed him in placing it over against the law, with a corresponding new stress on *grace* and *faith* rather than deeds.

Present day *evangelicals* have often reduced the term evangelism to proclaiming a spiritual salvation from personal *sin*, calling those outside Christian communities to *conversion*. In this way, the *ethics* of the kingdom, that both Jesus and Paul proclaimed, have become separated from the good news of *forgiveness* and the *love* of God. But the good news is not only grace by faith, it is a call to live according to God's righteousness in spreading the good news as the Radical Reformers pointed out, the emphasis not only on '*justification* by faith' but also on 'faith that obeys'.

In the 20th century there has been debate between evangelicals and those engaged in the *ecumenical movement* as to the use of the terms *mission* and evangelism. *David J. Bosch* in his compendium defines them as many would do today: 'I perceive mission to be wider than evangelism...Mission denotes the total task God has set the church for the salvation of the world, but always related to a specific context of evil, despair, and lostness (as Jesus defined his "mission" according to Lk 4:18f)...Mission is the *church* sent into the world, to love, to serve, to *preach*, to teach, to *heal*, to liberate...Evangelism should therefore not be equated with mission...[but] viewed as an essential "dimension of the total activity of the Church"...evangelism involves witnessing to what God has done, is doing and will do...Evangelism does aim at a response...is always invitation...[and] remains an indispensable ministry...' George W. Peters defines evangelism for the *conservative evangelicals*: 'It is the authoritative [see *Authority*] proclamation of the gospel of Jesus Christ as revealed in the *Bible* in relevant and intelligible terms, in a persuasive manner with the definite purpose of making Christian converts. It is a presentation-penetration-permission-confrontation that not only elicits but demands a decision.' Together with Bosch and others he perceives mission much wider than evangelism.

A third term of the mission debate of the 20th century needs to be introduced as connected to mission and evangelism: namely, the social responsibility of the church. It seems that social responsibility is part of both, of evangelism and of the mission of the church, according to NT writings; it reflects kingdom ethics as a result of conversion and becoming a disciple of Christ to follow his way. The *apostle* John's focus on witness underlines the way in which right proclamation and right living belong together as part of the good news. As demonstrated and proclaimed by Christ, individual Christians and the whole church are called to evangelism that points to the good news in Christ. Through his life Christ offered an example and through his *death* and *resurrection* he made possible forgiveness, a changed life through the *Holy Spirit*, reconciliation both with God and other people, healing wounds, and bringing together *peace*, justice and righteousness. This leads to holy living [see *Holiness*] in a community of the followers of the new way that continues to be a witness as salt and light to the world that suffers from sin, injustice, war, poverty, and many more signs of life without God. Evangelism is the good news that God can change a hopeless situation as he invites everyone into his kingdom.

PFP

Evangelism and Baptist churches
[See also *Evangelism, The theology of*; *Evangelism and the media*; *Evangelism, The theology of*; *Evangelist*]
For Baptists a commitment to the *missionary* task is definitive of the nature of the church; without this commitment the *church* is not fulfilling its proper *calling*. How this is worked out in practice takes many different forms. The strategy has often been to surround the church with an attached group of persons (*Sunday School* parents, persons using the church's premises,

extended families, etc.) who form its natural mission field. If such a group falls to too small a number then the *evangelistic* task is imperilled, since people in this group can be shown to have been the best respondents to the church's missionary endeavours, such as their participation in campaign evangelism, seeker-friendly, and other special services, etc. Sunday School activities, especially activity with its older members, have provided opportunities for direct evangelism, as have the various youth groups, formal and informal, sponsored by the church. In some parts of Europe, especially in the north and east, *choirs* of different kinds have provided similar opportunities even in the days of *communist* oppression. Special evangelistic activities have been undertaken for different gender and even class groups. Sometimes churches have organised open-air witness, proclaiming the gospel in both song and personal testimony, often using the occasion to invite people to discover more through coming to church services. In many churches, baptismal services [see *Baptism*; *Baptism and Christian initiation liturgy*], in which appeals for personal commitment to *Christ* are made, have also served to focus the church's outreach into the local community. More recently the promotion of such things as *Alpha*, Emmaus and similar courses have been used to bring people to a point of commitment, whilst many churches would stress the importance of the church's regular pattern of *preaching* and *communion* as vital evangelistic witness. By contrast others judge the cultural gap between the church and secular society too great and so have turned to the exploitation of café and pub churches and even the development of cyber-churches, but some question the latter can truly be called church.

ET

Evangelism and the media
[See also *Evangelism, The theology of*; *Evangelism and Baptist churches*; *Evangelist*]
Evangelism through the media is the propagation of good news by means of modern mass media: print, TV, radio, direct distribution of audio/video material, and internet. The use of written texts, even though cum-

bersomely written, in spreading the Christian teachings dates back to the 1st century AD; the invention of the printing press by Johannes Gutenberg in 1450 made the *Bible* available to a wider society and constituted the first use of mass media in a modern sense of the term. Radio evangelism first spread in the US in the late 1920s and into the 30s. TV evangelism first appeared in 1950s and drew large audiences. Due to the more complex nature of the medium and higher cost of broadcasting, only few of the radio *evangelists*, such as *Billy Graham*, were able to successfully switch to TV evangelism. While Christian media experts like Malcolm Boyd believe that Christians have to communicate their *faith* by all means available, including electronic media, TV evangelism has drawn some criticism from Christians who believe that spreading the good news electronically alienates [see *Alienation*] people from their real church communities and sacramental practices, and lacks the personal encounter essential to true evangelism. Also scandals in the 1980s involving some of the TV-evangelists have cast some doubt among the general public about the motivations of TV evangelism. Today the televised evangelical message has diversified, using formats from conversational talk-show-like format to fictionalised entertainment series. Use of the telephone, distribution of audio and video recordings with Christian *music* and Gospel readings are other forms of electronic evangelism. The internet is a new multi-medium that combines elements of all of the electronic media with the print medium. It has become the most egalitarian of all media and besides its global reach brings a new capability of interactivity. E-preaching and e-congregations have become familiar terms. Similarly as with the earlier debate about TV, e-preaching has its supporters and opponents. Opponents believe that the virtual nature of the World Wide Web prevents people from developing real communal relationships at their local congregations and may keep them away from participating in the *communion*. The supporters of on-line evangelism maintain that the Internet gives a unique chance to reach people who would otherwise be left in the dark. There is also plenty of testimony to those who find spiritual nourishment and the development of deep friendship through belonging to an e-congregation. While the development of electronic media brings new possibilities in disseminating the Christian message, the traditional print format remains a very important part of the evangelisation effort.

PZ

Evangelist

[See also *Evangelism, The theology of; Evangelism and Baptist churches; Evangelism and the media*]

In Eph 4:11 Paul refers to the *ministry* of an evangelist [*euangelistes*] and places this activity as part of the core *ministries* of the *church*. This underlines the key importance of an evangelist in and for the church. Biblically [see *Bible*] speaking, this ministry is mainly a ministry of the proclamation of the good news (1Co 9:16). But in Eph 4:12-13 it seems that the evangelist has also training and up-building responsibilities. This means that besides reaching out and sharing the good news, an evangelist needs to build up others, explain to those within the church what the good news [*euangelion*] is all about, and train members for this ministry in the church and in the world. In the different uses of the NT it seems that the role of an evangelist includes the role of a defender or *apologist* of the good news (Php 1) as well as someone pointing to the origins of the good news as coming from God (Gal 1).

The early church knew this ministry and we can see many evangelists in *praxis* (Ac 21:8 and 2Ti 4:5) which may explain why so very few definitions of what an evangelist is are given and what this ministry includes. Because the ministry of an evangelist was so familiar to early churches, it is not even listed as a spiritual gift in the NT. Even though it is a distinct core ministry, as Eph 4:11 clearly points out, it seems that the sharing of the good news is a responsibility of everyone who is part of the body of Christ, and the praxis of the early church demonstrates this. It is not just a ministry of Christ's *apostles*, but it is the key task of every believer. The fact that Paul lists the evangelist among other key leaders of the church demonstrates its importance for the church and not only for the world. Throughout history evangelists have spread the good news, developed training institutions for evangelists, brought about revival and **renewal** inside the church and contextualised the good news for different situations and cultures [see **Contextualisation**]. In different **unions** within Europe the relationship between the ministry of a separate order of evangelists as over against the settled ministry of a local congregation has been frequently debated. Itinerant societies at the end of the 18th century tried to appoint village evangelists but were more successful in persuading settled **ministers** to give some of their time to this work. The Baptist Union of **Great Britain** at the beginning of the 20th century once more maintained a separate list of evangelists, and more recently one of its colleges has mounted a special stream in ministerial training for evangelists and church planters.

As we analyse this ministry today, we observe it exercised not only in and by the church but mainly by para-church structures, such as monasteries in the past or, as in the **free church** tradition, by para-church organisations. This sometimes causes separation between the church and evangelistic ministries. Instead of integrating evangelists into the church and this way engaging the whole church in a ministry that brings vitality to the church, evangelists are often not an integral part of the church. As in the past, churches need evangelists with special giftedness and calling, and the 20th century can point to a number of such evangelists who contributed to the life of the church. But as in the early days of the church everyone in the church was involved in witnessing to the good news, it is important today that, according to Eph 4:11-13, the whole church is directly involved in the sharing of the good news, reaching out and fulfilling that which is the main reason of the church's existence. With this **Oncken**'s famous slogan 'every Baptist a missionary' may be readily associated.

PFP

Evangelistic Campaigns
See *Crusade Evangelism*.

Evolution
[See also *Creation*; *Creation and Science*; *Science*; *Science and Faith*]

Darwin's theory of evolution (*The Origin of the Species*, 1859) was a direct challenge to the dominant scientific theory of the early 19th century. Most scientists maintained that species were individual creations of God, although Lamarck (1809) had suggested the transmutation of species, based on a model of increasing complexity and a capacity to inherit acquired characteristics that were useful to the particular environment.

The writings of Charles Lyell (*Principles of Geology*, 1830-33) advocating the principle of uniformitarianism, that is, that past processes operated in the same way as those observed in the world today, and Malthus' essay on population growth (published 1838) led Darwin to recognise that 'only organisms well adapted to their environments and to reproduction would survive the struggle for existence'. This was in contrast to William Paley's view that the complexities of fossil and living species were explained as individual works of the divine creator. Although Darwin's theory does not strictly contradict the existence of God, it did undermine what was then the prevailing argument for God's existence based on the adaptation of organisms to their environment.

Neither Lamarck nor Darwin was able to show how characteristics of the favoured species were passed on from one generation to another. It was the Abbot of Brunn, Gregor Johann Mendel (1822-84) in Moravia, breeding garden peas in a monastery garden, who arrived at the concept of dominant and recessive genes, and formulated the laws of heredity. Mendelian genetics combined with Darwinian natural selection provided the means by which evolution might be understood to progress.

The modern revolution of molecular biology began in 1953 with the elucidation of the structure of DNA by James Watson and Francis Crick. At this level, inherited characteristics can be said to be determined by the genes carried by an individual.

The fossil record presents a picture of evolving life forms, from simple algal life in the oceans about 3,200 million years ago to the variety of simple and complex life forms we see in our world today. These include *Homo sapiens*, who is the only life form, as far as is known, with a consciousness that is able to perceive the story of the universe. Consciousness is associated with seeing necessary truths; it appears to be the element in the brain which allows us to see and appreciate what mathematical truth is, and this in itself demonstrates that the brain is not a computer. Our perception of aesthetic beauty in art, music, and nature, and our emotions of hope, fear, anxiety or despair, support this view. The presence in the universe of a conscious mind requires explanation. Today, cosmologists speak of an apparent design within the universe that is suggestive of purpose, and some scientists suggest that biological evolution requires a guiding mechanism, beyond the process of natural selection through non-random survival, to enable it to reach its goal in human beings.

Nancey Murphy states that much of the resistance to evolutionary biology can be traced to the limited views of divine action. The natural laws recognised by science were seen as a denial of divine action, and so evolution was seen as natural rather than God working out his creative purpose through the evolutionary process. It is the level of explanation that is important, and Murphy claims that biological evolution requires the higher level of explanation which only *theology* can give.

The *Bible* may not be a scientific textbook, but it does provide the answers to the questions that science poses concerning the origin, meaning and purpose of the world in which we live, and of the place of human life within that universe. We do not have a ready-made world, but the Bible presents a picture of an emerging creation. We can see evolution as a God-given capacity, the same as fruitfulness, fertility and development. The danger arises when evolution leads us into a reductionism of nothing but physics and chemistry.

The animal relationship of *humankind* is inescapable. We share all but 0.7% of the DNA of the two extant chimpanzee species. We are closer in relation to the chimps than the two species of Gibbon are to each other (they differ by 2.2% of their DNA). But there is a clear distinction between the most intelligent primates and human beings, as we are

able to shape our own evolution by shaping our own environment.

We are linked to natural creation: created on the same day (Gen 1); and of the same substance (Gen 2). But we are also distinct: *imago Dei* (Gen 1); and with God's spirit/breath (Gen 2).

Intelligent design is presented as an alternative view by William Dembski. He is concerned that modern theology, 'mistakenly', has a theology of nature that rules out intervention. Intelligent design is defined as design, which is due to an actual intelligence, but the attributes of that intelligence are open.

Dembski sets chance, necessity and contingency in nature in opposition to God's activity, and consistently places intelligent design in opposition to Darwinism. He fears that if we do not exclude evolution from the debate the result will be that 'the unchanging God of traditional theology gives way to the evolving God of process theologies. Thus traditional *theism* with its strong transcendence gives way to panentheism, with its modified transcendence wherein God is inseparable from and dependent on the world.' However, we should note that this emphasis on transcendence runs the danger of being contrary to the *revelation* of God in scripture, who is both transcendent and immanent.

Dembski presents the classic Enlightenment argument that we must choose either nature (naturalism, Darwinism) or God (intelligent design). I consider that this is a false dichotomy, as it is possible that God works through the natural laws that are his own creation. The biblical picture is of human beings being intimately involved in God's creation, and being given freedom by God to respond to his *love* displayed through his self revelation in creation, in his dealings with his people, and in the *Incarnation of Christ*.

JDW

FURTHER READING: Denis Alexander and Robert S. White, *Beyond Belief. Science, faith and ethical challenges*, Lion, Oxford, 2004. R.J. Berry, *God and the Biologist*, Apollos, Leicester, 1996. William A. Dembski, *The Design Revolution. Answering the toughest questions about intelligent design*, IVP, Downers Grove, Il., 2004. Malcolm Jeeves and R.J. Berry, *Science, Life and Christian*

Belief, Apollos, Leicester, 1998. Nancey Murphy, *Reconciling Theology and Science*, Pandora, Kitchener, On., 1997.

Exegesis
See *Hermeneutics*.

Exorcism
This topic at once raises a number of important questions – the relationship between illness and **sin** (the fact that **Jesus** denied a direct connection in a particular case – Jn 9:1-3 – does not necessarily mean that there is no connection at all in other cases) the interaction between divine power and that of evil spirits, especially in the light of Jesus' conquest of **Satan** (Mk 3:22ff; Eph 1:20-22 and Col 2:15) and the distinction between a proper recognition of God's power in his world, and practices which amount to little more than acts of petty superstition.

The **Jews**, like their pagan neighbours, developed various ways for expelling or overcoming the activities of evil spirits especially as represented in the language of 'demon possession'. The gospels contain a number of examples of Jesus engaging in exorcism, calling demons out of individuals (e.g. Mt 10; 17:14ff, Mk 5, Lk 11:14ff) and in Acts, the **apostles** continued this **ministry** (16:18 and 19:13ff). The dimensions of wickedness seen in some people's lives provide convincing evidence that, even though ultimately defeated, the Devil still exercises considerable power even in our modern sophisticated technological world. Moreover, since he exercises a spiritual tyranny, only spiritual forces can liberate those held in his thraldom. It is, therefore, appropriate that a prayerful [see **Prayer**] unsensational service, ordered in the name of Jesus, be deployed as part of the **church**'s **pastoral care** in dealing with individuals burdened with serious crippling forces apparently beyond their control or medical cure occasioning deep spiritual distress.

The presence of African **diaspora churches in Europe** has led to some unwelcome publicity given to fierce and unloving attempts to exorcise young children which have given rise to cases of punitive child abuse of the most serious order, which are not only religiously perverse, but represent clear criminal acts which the secular authority rightly pursues with vigour. Exorcism in the name of Jesus must be conducted with great care and restraint and in a way and manner which is harmonious with his mission and person, and respectful of the vulnerability of a person clearly suffering deep emotional trauma.

ET

F

Faculta Valdesa di Teologia, Rome

See *Waldensian Faculty of Theology, Rome*.

Faith

Faith is a critical word in Christian understanding. E.g. 'believers', those exercising faith, is one of the earliest titles given to Christians. In the synoptic gospels faith is portrayed as a vital factor in some of the miracles, whereas by contrast the scepticism of the people amongst whom *Jesus* grew up in Nazareth meant that he was unable to do any mighty acts among them, a vivid underlining of the power of unbelief. Already it can be seen that the word 'faith' operates through a number of different meanings, e.g. extending to faith as commitment, the faith as a synonym for *apostolic* doctrine, and faith as a way of life and *hope* as in the phrases 'communities of faith' and 'other living faiths'.

In the great chapter on faith, Heb 11, the writer writes of a panoply of faith heroes who turned belief into action. In the midst of this, in summary fashion, he asserts: 'without faith it is impossible to please God, for whoever would approach him must believe that he exists and rewards those that approach him.' The chapter certainly concerns those who shared a belief system, but it is essentially about having sufficient confidence in those beliefs to act upon them. This was the faith that was at the heart of the *Reformation* which forms part of that misleading tag, '*justification* by faith', which fatally leaves out the *grace* that gives validity to that faith (Eph 2:8). *Luther* himself distinguishes two kinds of faith by using two Latin words; *assensus* meaning mental assent, and *fiducia* meaning trusting action, and it is clearly the second that is at the heart of his classic restating of *evangelical* truth. This distinction is not dissimilar from that which distinguishes 'belief in' from 'belief that', with the suggestion that the former, with its emphasis upon subscribing to a

number of propositional truths, was favoured by the *Catholic* Church, whereas the latter, stressing that faith is essentially willingly responding to what God has done in Christ in his personal self-giving *love*, (thus an emphasis on the faithfulness of God rather than the faith of the believer) was the hallmark of primitive Luther, though Luther's successors all too soon also became embroiled in the dead letter of over much propositional defining. Another question that has occupied *scholars* is discussion of the point at which faith becomes operative in a person's spiritual journey, so the distinction between faith by which we believe, and the faith that we believe, which again can be related to the notion of faith as divine gift and faith as human response.

Whilst some have favoured the conviction that faith and reason are not inconsistent with one an other, others argue that faith, whilst not irrational, probes beyond the point at which rational argument operates. This perhaps corresponds to the NT distinction between faith and sight (1Co 13, 2Co 5:7) suggesting the contrast between the hopeful trust of this life, and the certainty that for the Christian must be reserved to be an *eschatological* experience. 1Co 13 not only relates faith to sight but puts it in the overall context of hope and love with the clear indication that it must always remain subordinate to love.

Another classic debate puts faith in contradiction to works, with distortions of NT teaching here being, on the one hand *pelagianism*, and on the other, *antinomianism*. Luther resolved this tension by passionately arguing that good works were not causative of justification, but rather consequent upon it, and that a life which did not issue in good works could only be based upon a questionable faith: 'Faith without works is dead' (Jas 2:26).

The area in which Baptists like other evangelicals are least experienced is that of what might be the implications of living in a world where other 'communities of faith' exist, raising the question of how such faith is to be interpreted, how *dialogue*, without compromise as to the claims of Christ, can be initiated, and the extent to which all persons of faith have common cause against the secular and secularising spirit of the age [see

Secularisation].

JHYB

Faith and Order

Together with the *Life and Work* movement and the *International Missionary Council*, Faith and Order was one of several strands of *ecumenical* activity, founded after the *Edinburgh* Missionary Conference of 1910, enabling the churches to explore their common *mission*. Persuaded by Bishop Charles Brent, the effective father of the movement, the American Episcopal Church campaigned to obtain the support of other churches in the setting up of a commission to prepare for the convoking of a first Faith and Order Conference, which met in *Lausanne* in 1927, bringing together churches of the *Reformation*, the *Orthodox* and those of the *Anglican* Communion. At this, and subsequent, Conferences the wide degree of agreement between the churches was identified, as well as those areas where serious disagreements remained, affirming a *unity* which is both gift and goal. In 1937 at the second Faith and Order world conference, in Edinburgh, Faith and Order agreed to unite with the Life and Work movement to seek to form a council of churches which came into being after wartime delays in 1948.

The Faith and Order movement has a semi-autonomous existence within the *World Council of Churches*. Its staff are employed by the WCC which also funds its activities, but it has its own separate membership which since 1968 has included the *Roman Catholic* Church, together with an increased representation from the Orthodox Churches and from the non-western world. It operates through a standing commission (30 members), and a full commission (120 members), which meets approximately every four years, with world conferences being held more intermittently. It embodies the world's most representative *theological* forum. The third world conference was held at Lund in 1952, the fourth at Montreal in 1963 and the fifth at Santiago de Compostella in 1993.

Its aim, according to its bylaws, is 'to proclaim the oneness of the *church* of *Jesus Christ* and to call the churches to the goal of visible unity in one *faith* and one *eucharistic fellowship*, expressed in *worship* and in common life in Christ, in order that the world may believe.'

British Baptists, Morris West and Keith Clements have been active in the Commission. Some of its more recent work has been a programme entitled, 'Towards the Common Expression of the *Apostolic* Faith Today', the production of its consensus document on *Baptism Eucharist and Ministry* (1982) and the associated Lima Eucharistic text, which have been extensively studied by the churches. Their responses, including those from a number of European Baptist churches have been published; clearly not everything proposed is acceptable to all, for profound differences cannot simply be bridged by ambiguous words. More recently the commission has been exploring the theme of 'The *Unity of the Church* as *Koinonia'* to see how this can help a divided church come together. It has also revisited the subject of *baptism* in which area Professor Paul Fiddes and the General Secretary of the *Baptist World Alliance*, Neville Callum, have been active.

JHYB

FURTHER READING: John H.Y. Briggs, Mercy Amba Oduyoye and Georges Tsetsis (eds), *A History of the Ecumenical Movement Vol III, 1963-2000*, WCC Publications, Geneva, 2004. M. Brinkman, *Progress in Unity: 50 years of Theology within the WCC, 1945-1995*, Peeters, Louvain, 1995. G. Gassmann (ed), *A Documentary History of Faith and Order, 1963-1993*, WCC Publications, Geneva, 1993. L Vischer (ed), *A Documentary History of the Faith and Order Movement, 1927-63*, Bethany, St. Louis, Mi., 1963.

Faith Missions

Faith Missions are organisations which rely on '*faith*' rather than a denomination's budget for their resources. Their distinct feature is a dependence on the free-will giving [see *Free-Will Offerings*] of individuals, churches, and foundations to meet their financial needs. These missions are typically interdenominational although they may be limited to a certain distinctive found in their support constituency. Their activities mirror denominational missions and at times will co-operate closely with existing denominational projects yet remaining outside an exclusive relationship. Their financial philosophy generally does not guarantee the *missionary* a salary. Some faith missions will 'pool' their monies and allow all missionaries and projects equal access to the funds. Other faith missions require that each individual missionary or project raise their own funds and maintain individual accounts. Although the first faith mission is considered to be the China Inland Mission, founded in 1865, many faith missions had their start when many *local churches* left their mainline denominations in the early 20th century. These independent churches were *conservative theologically* and zealous for world mission. Faith missions where established to connect independent churches together to enable them to participate in world missions. Today, there are over 85 faith missions, supporting 20,000 missionaries worldwide. To label some missions as 'faith missions' is not to imply that many denominational missions do not work on similar principles of trusting to God and the *free-will offerings* of his people for the development of their work.

GLN

Fall, The

[See also *Humankind*; *Sin*]
The Biblical [see *Bible*] view of humankind is essentially paradoxical – made in the image of God, but because of his rebellion doomed by sin to *death*, thus Pascal's judgment that humanity is at once 'the glory and scum of the universe'. The classical account of the Fall is found in Ge 3. As a result of human transgression of the commandment of God, of human rebellion against the rule of God, seeking a false autonomy apart from God's intention for his *creation*, relationships are broken, and 'original righteousness' gives way to 'original sin'. As a result, the nature of human subsistence changes, as Adam and Eve are driven out of the garden, away from God, to make a living in a partly hostile environment. Their identity is subsequently formed in relation to the elements of this hostile environment. The ground which they live on is cursed. God's good creation now has a negative signature on it. The former positive creation of man out of the dust (Ge 2:7) is now seen in menacing terms: 'for

dust you are and to dust you will return' (Ge 3:19). The consequences of the Fall soon become apparent with Cain's slaughter of his brother Abel, the corruption of human society prior to the flood and the assault on *heaven* in the building of the tower of Babel – all signs of a fallen creation.

This characterisation of human personality as embracing human depravity is referred to elsewhere especially in the wisdom literature (e.g. Job 4:17-21). Whilst the OT affirms that it is possible for humanity to follow the law and some *men* and *women* are described as righteous, others are designated sinners (Ps 1).

The import of the story of the Fall is that so radical is humankind's separation from God that no number of attempts to keep the Mosaic Law, no matter how dutiful the individual was in offering the prescribed sacrifices, or engaging in good works (as Isa 64:6 says: 'All our righteous acts are like filthy rags'), nothing could atone for the sin committed [see *Atonement*]. As *Luther* constantly affirmed 'What man as man must do, man as sinner cannot do'. Only help from outside can redeem the situation; the Fall is answered by the *grace* of God in *Jesus Christ* doing for humanity what it could not do for itself, by his sacrifice on the cross.

The fallen-ness of humanity also extends to the whole created order, now out of gear with God's original intention for it. But as humankind is offered *redemption*, so provision is also made for the *restoration* of the whole created order, as Paul argues, 'creation itself will be set free from its bondage to decay and obtain the glorious liberty of the children of God'.

KTB & ET

Family Church

The language was coined by the British *Congregationalist*, Revd H.A. [Bert] Hamilton, and publicised in his book *The Family Church in Principle and Practice* (1941). Even during the WWI there was a growing concern that the *Sunday School* had almost a separate existence from the church. It was at this time that a number of churches formed 'Leagues of Young Worshippers' to give children a proper identity within the main *worship* service. As WWII approached, there was an increasing concern as to whether 'school' provided the right associations for the church's work with children Thus the **theological** idea behind 'Family Church' was that children were part of the church rather than part of the **mission** field beyond its boundaries. Indeed whilst some began to talk of children as 'The Church of Tomorrow', others took them to task arguing that they were very much part of 'The Church of Today', with those of every age accorded mutual respect and affection. Hamilton was influenced by secular educational thinking of his time – namely that children learn best through co-operative activity which is best done in the context of community, which came to challenge the churches as to the quality of the community that they embodied – to attempt to find to what extent they could be described as God's family. Thus he argued that Christian **education** should be more concerned with shaping people than passing on a body of knowledge, or rather that such knowledge could not be confined to abstract terms but only came alive in the context of the experience of worship. The problem was how to integrate the children from homes unassociated with church into its family life. The idea was commended to Baptists by Dr. Marjorie Reeves, their most eminent educationalist of those years. The idea took time to permeate a world where **children's work** was still dominated by old Sunday School reports but the Baptist pamphlet, *Growing up in Christ* (1963), commended it. This was followed by a working party which explored the particular Baptist responsibilities to what was now called the **catechumenate** and in previous years would have been referred to as those on the Cradle Roll, placed there at the time of dedication in which service the church would have pledged itself to care for them until such time as they came to **faith** in **Christ** and **baptism** as believers. The working party produced a report entitled *The Child and the Church* (1966) which was still seen as contentious. However by this date social norms were changing and there was much less enthusiasm for afternoon Sunday School and so the practice grew of children sharing in the church's main staple of worship but separating for their own activity for part of that time, and this pattern in fact became the norm for Baptists by the end of the 1960s. These changes were, however, accompanied by another change now seen as vital by those historians who see the 1960s as a decade of crisis for faith in society: when the idea of Family Church was first canvassed 80% of its members came from non-churched families; by the 1960s, 80% of children in church were the offspring of **church members**. In 1963 Hamilton was given the opportunity to canvass his ideas on a wider canvass as he became a Secretary of the World Council of Christian Education.

JHYB

Fascism/Fascist

The word derives from the Italian, from a term meaning a bundle of rods which metaphorically came to describe those **political** groups that assisted Mussolini's rise to power in the 1920s, and hence its use to describe a right-wing authoritarian regime based upon the control of power rather than legitimate consent. It found its inspiration in some romantic, non-rationalist and exaggerated notions of the aggrandisement of the **nation** under a charismatic leader (duce) supported by the power of the fascist party, party and leader recognising no accountability to any constitutional body. This form of government came to be adopted in a large number of European **states** between the wars among others, e.g. **Austria, Bulgaria, Hungary, Romania, Spain, Portugal, Poland** and the **Baltic** Republics, but above all **Germany**. Although in some countries pacts were made with the **Vatican**, and in others nationalistic churches under government patronage created, in the long run because the totalitarian character of these regimes made total claims on the lives of all citizens, and accepted no limits to the authority exercised, conflict with churches of all denominations was inevitable. Such states became cradles for **human rights** abuses. The adjective can be used to describe parties or individuals within democratic states who seek to replace **democracy** with such a pattern of government.

JHYB

Fasting

Fasting or the abstaining, for religious reasons, from some pleasure or resource for life such as nourishment is practised in differing ways by different Christian *traditions*, all noting that *Jesus* and his disciples fasted at times of intense *prayer*. It is seen to be a spiritual discipline related to the ideas of penitence and renewal. It has been common for Christians to fast before important events such as *baptism*, *ordination* or at times when a congregation is seeking to know the will of Christ on a particular issue. There is a common practice of associating fasting with seasons of spiritual discipline and historically the period of *Lent* was often a time to participate in fasting.

For shorter fasts it is typical to abstain from food and drink, other than water to prevent dehydration. For longer fasts lasting several days or weeks it is common for the fast to be broken in the evening with a light meal or collation. Whilst the accent of fasting tends to be on the abstinence from food, it can sometimes include or be replaced by abstinence from *alcohol* or from sexual relations.

Fasting is common in many religious traditions and has deep roots as a purity ritual, but it has been abused in some situations and amongst Baptists it is generally practised with a certain caution and is normally associated with some specific prayer need or liturgical season [see *Liturgy*] and overseen by the congregation or *pastor*.

KGJ

Fat Tuesday

[See also *Lent*]

The preparation for the season of Lent involved both physical and spiritual preparation for believers in the past. As medieval Lenten disciplines involved *fasting* it became common to use up sweet ingredients, fats and items such as eggs, which were not part of the Lenten diet. The language of Shrove Tuesday refers to the need within the *Catholic* tradition to go to confessions (to be shrived) in order to prepare for the coming of Lent.

The Tuesday before the start of the season involving the discipline from the past of giving up rich foods and pastries commences with special preparations in many countries, variously Pancake Tuesday/Fat Tuesday associated with the eating up of such rich foods and fats in preparation for fasting. Examples of special foods eaten include pancakes in the **United Kingdom** and special rich doughnuts in **Poland**.

Some Baptist communities will hold special parties on this day to eat these foods, but combine it with an introduction to the Christian inheritance behind what is now, largely, cultural tradition.

KGJ

Feed the Minds

History. Dating from the *Reformation*, *Protestant* and Radical Reformation churches had always placed an emphasis on literacy, literature and *education* alongside *evangelism* in their *missionary* work, and missionary societies in all the churches recognised its importance. Three major Societies however made it a specialised industry and set both the tone and the pace. They were the Society for the Promotion of Christian Knowledge (SPCK) founded in 1698 and the oldest *Anglican* missionary society, the Religious Tract Society (RTS, re-named the United Society for Christian Literature, or USCL, in 1935), founded in 1799, and the British and Foreign Bible Society (BFBS, now the Bible Society) founded in 1804. Their early work was very largely supporting the missionaries, working with *colporteurs* and exporting Bibles and literature in English. This quickly changed to providing translations [see *Bible Translation*] and encouraging local action but by the middle of the 20th century new developments were required.

If the vision was the needs of the two-thirds world, the internal driving force was the thrust of the *ecumenical movement* in a post-*colonial* world coupled with the need for churches and missionary societies to work more closely together and achieve a greater measure of efficiency.

The *World Council of Churches* set the tone with the Christian Literature Fund (CLF) and the Agency for Christian Literature Development (ACLD) to ensure that funding did not necessarily go to those with the loudest voices, that in the interests of donors, projects were carefully evaluated and monitored, and that multiple agencies were not paying the same bills.

The first British initiative came from Donald Coggan, Archbishop of York, with the Archbishop of York's Fund (AYF) in 1964, followed immediately by the Feed the Minds Campaign which brought together the three historic societies, the AYF and mainstream missionary societies in a three-year Campaign (1964-67) not only to stimulate the churches but also to raise the consciousness of the *nation* in a drive to involve secular organisations and civic authorities to the need for education and the eradication of illiteracy.

At the end of the Campaign the Bible Society withdrew and SPCK, USCL, the missionary societies and the AYF formed Feed the Minds (FTM) as a continuing operation. It was the British arm of ACLD, subsequently the World Association for Christian Communication (WACC), in which FTM played a leading role particularly in Europe. The intention was for all grant applications relating to literature, publishing and distribution received by FTM member bodies would be passed on to FTM which would relate closely to ACLD/WACC and act as a vetting unit and clearing house with major funding coming from member bodies and such other resources as FTM could tap from Trusts, the churches and the general public.

For a quarter of a century the overall objectives of the historic societies and their founding fathers were steadily maintained and resources shared but the road was never smooth. Changes of staff within FTM member bodies led to changes of response and the vision got blurred. Cooperation between SPCK and USCL remained close at the administrative level but their desire to maintain their own separate appeals alongside FTM often left the supporting clientele confused.

Programme. FTM's work and records cover mission in six continents with projects in well over 50 countries. Education was the touchstone in origin and development and a priority for staff, committees and supporters. Three basic principles summarise the FTM commitment:

(1)   A commitment to two-thirds-world Christian publishing and distribution on a professional basis with professionally trained personnel.

(2)   A *holistic* gospel so that 'Christian literature' included literacy primers, books for new readers, with titles on *health*, hygiene, nutrition, local history, legend and tradition every bit as much as prayer books and religious education.

(3)   A conviction that whereas in the early days the need was for tracts and books followed by translations, the urgent need in the latter half of the 20th century and the beginning of the 21st was for local production, by local writers and artists, addressing local issues, with a major investment on training people.

In practice the main grants programme covers four main areas:

(i)   Publishing and Distribution: Grants on a Revolving Fund basis for commercial (or pseudo-commercial) Christian companies with an emphasis on growth, training and professionalism. This focuses mainly on publishing and bookshop capital, paper and raw materials, but also funds small machinery and equipment, book vans and tours, and support for *magazines* and newspapers, religious education (in church or school) and various workshops relating to publishing.

(ii)   Libraries and Colleges: Professional support for librarians, cash or books for non-profitable and non-commercial outlets such as libraries in rural areas, urban reading rooms and theological institutions.

(iii)   Aid and Development: Non-commercial and non-profitable projects with no road to self-sufficiency in themselves but which provide an effective way to enable a community to grow in self-sufficiency. Usually books for new readers, especially for *women* and *children* and the very poor.

(iv)   General and Special: Usually one-off requests or short-term 'seed corn' grants to supplement the other three types.

A programme of tools for theological education includes an annual book grant to theological *students* on *ordination* (*UK* as well as overseas) and grants of specialist English books for library development in theological institutions round the world, always chosen by the institutions and not by FTM. To facilitate FTM runs a free Book Service, receiving selected titles from retired clergy and others and circulating lists to hundreds of colleges round the world inviting them to make a choice. In 1988 FTM launched the *Theological Book Review* which purported to produce brief (around 250-word) reviews of all new titles relevant to religious education within three months of publication mainly to inform librarians and theological specialists as to what was available well before such books appeared in the more long-term theological journals.

In 1979 FTM launched into Eastern Europe with a **EUROLIT** programme which brought significant help to Baptists and other churches in Eastern Europe in the 1980s and 90s.

A new development in the 1990s increased support for literacy programmes associated with **AIDS** in Congo, Kenya and Zimbabwe, working through churches and schools with the encouragement of the local Education Department, to reach children before they become sexually active and to help young people to make the right choices. Most of it was positive, Christian and holistic, sometimes including *marriage* counselling and family life and often in close association with other UK agencies who turned to FTM for help with the literature which was so desperately needed and which was outside their remit.

AG

FURTHER READING: Christian Literature Fund, *Literature and the Gospel, The Work and aims of the Christian Literature Fund, Interim Report, 1965-68*, Lausanne, 1968. G. Hewitt, *Let the People Read*, Lutterworth, London, 1949. J.H. Mair, *Books in Their Hands. A Short History of the USCL*, USCL, Scotland, nd. J.H. Mair, *John Murdoch: Pioneer in Christian Literature*, USCL, Scotland, 1976. Eve Walber, *People Above All: An Introduction to the Work of the Christian Literature Fund and the Agency for Christian Literature Development of the World Council of Churches*, CLD, London, 1972. Eve Walber, *Book Story*, FTM, SPCK, USCL, London, 1972.

Fellowship
See *Koinonia*.

Fellowship groups
See *Bible study meetings*.

Feminism
[See also *Feminist Theology; Women in Baptist life*]
'Feminism' and 'feminist *theology*' are loaded words with elastic meanings, and are thus easily misused. Technically-speaking, one should speak of 'feminisms' rather than using the singular form of the word. The kinds of feminism range from reformist approaches which argue for reasonable changes within existing societal structures, to eco-feminism which sees the connection between the abuse of nature and the abuse of *women* [see *Ecology and the Environment*], to radical feminism which contends that the symbolic world our societies inhabit must be overturned completely. The major, Euro-American, streams of feminism have also been critiqued in their turn by the non-white and two-thirds-world feminists, as represented by womanism (African-American), mujerista (hispanic), and so on.

In broad strokes, feminism is an ideological critique of patriarchy (or sexism/androcentrism) – an outlook which implicitly or explicitly centres on the dominance of the male, and argues for (at least) the equal rights of women and *men* in all aspects of life: social, economic, *political*, etc. One of the significant points of difference between different streams of feminism, especially in its third-wave embodiment and in *dialogue* with post feminists, concerns the issue of gender: whether women and men are *anthropologically* the same, which raises the question whether the way to overcome gender segregation is by fighting against, *or* by blurring, gender categories; or whether there are some essential differences between the sexes and, therefore, expressions of femaleness should be boldly and radically upheld and explored in order to enable equality-based gender cooperation *or* the subversion of the current societal value system. Thus the interplay between sex and gender (typically understood as biological and culturally constructed categories, respectively) alongside the question as to whether gender difference is true in degree or in kind, are continuous objects of discussion.

                                                    LA

Feminist Theology

[See also *Community of Women and Men in the Church*; *Feminism*; *Theology*; *Women in Baptist life*]

In theology, Christian feminist variants range from the total rejection of existing organised religion, arguing the only viable alternative is 'antichurch' or 'sisterhood,' to seeking change in the existing ecclesial structures by trying to find space for female perspectives on God and God's world, highlighting the significance of feminine language, and encouraging feminine expressions of *faith* and faith practice. Yet to a greater or smaller degree, all Christian feminisms present a challenge to the current state of affairs in church doctrine and practice. First of all, feminist theologies point to the importance of understanding and acknowledging the wider context in which theological discourse takes place and the need to assess its influence on the way the *scriptures* are read, language is used, and ideas are shaped. In particular, they criticise the systematic androcentric perspective which sees maleness as representing normative humanity and God being conceived in male terms, both in scripture and church *tradition*. This is seen to have a direct connection with issues of power, which typically receive a great deal of attention in feminist discourse.

Deconstruction of androcentric patterns of theologising receives the prime attention in feminist theologies. As to practices which come under their critique, they would include barriers to *ordination*, the patriarchal subordination of women, sexist linguistic practices, sexual conventions, and so on, both in the *church* and society. On the constructive side, one of the key contributions of feminism is an increased awareness of the need to find space for types of discourse which enable women to speak and reflect authentically without the confines of patriarchal categories, as well as challenging

them. This is an important development in a field still largely dominated by male voices. It also works by challenging the metaphors, images and structures which have unduly come to dominate Christian theology at the expense of other, non-androcentric possibilities for patterns of thinking. In feminist speech, words such as 'embodiment,' 'interdependence,' relationality' and 'experience' feature frequently.

Generally, feminist theology has not come to the fore in the lie and work of European Baptists although it should be noted that *scholars* such as Elizabeth Green have produced writings on feminist (and specifically eco-feminist) theology. Some Baptists also find the writings of *Evangelical* feminist theologians such as Elaine Storkey helpful

One of the central problems with feminism in general and feminist theologies in particular is its confrontational nature which inescapably holds it within the orbit of the problem of patriarchy. Although a number of European Baptists would be committed to women's involvement and equal share in *ministries* and would be concerned about the wrongs experienced by women due to the male-centred system and the need for the change in a number of ecclesial practices, their reluctance to subscribe to feminist thought as such may be an indication that for them it represents too limiting a perspective on God, the church, and the world. In other words, ideologies such as feminism can, and do, bring a needed prophetic challenge to the structures of life, yet the framework of sex/gender binaries or other similar kinds of cultural critique cannot transcend themselves and bring about the envisioned embodiment of the fullness of *Christ*.

                                                    LA

Fertility treatment

See *Childlessness and Fertility treatment*.

Festivals, Religious

Feasts and festivals usually play an important role in every religion. From the OT we are familiar with the initial seven (Lev 23: *Passover*, Unleavened Bread, Firstfruits, Harvest, Blowing Trumpets, Atonement, Tabernacles) and one additional (Est 9: Purim) Hebrew. Later, the Feast of Lights (Hanukkah) was added, which is reported in extra-biblical sources (1Ma 4:52-59), nevertheless it is referred to in Jn 10:22. Throughout the development of the NT some of these gained strong Christian connotation. *Easter* and *Pentecost* along with *Christmas*, the memorial day of the coming of Light into the world, developed later into traditional Christian festivals which enable us to celebrate the pillars of our *faith*. Modern Baptists have also evoked Thanksgiving Day, a feast for the *harvest* blessing. As opposed to biblical Hebrew customs we do not maintain strict *liturgies*. Our culturally and historically varied practices focus on the core meaning and message of the NT. With the movement of peoples around the world Christians need to understand, and make space for, the fact that newer residents will want to celebrate their own festivals: e.g. Dhivali for Hindus, Ramadan for Muslims and occasions such as Divali and Vaisakhi for Sikhs.

EV

Fetter Lane Agreement
See *Meissen, Porvoo and Fetter Lane Agreements: significance for Baptists.*

Finland, Finnish-speaking Baptist history in
[See also *Finland, Swedish-speaking Baptist history in*]
The first Finnish-speaking Baptist groups in Finland were formed in the 1870s: one in Luvia, on the west coast of the country, the other in Parikkala, in Karelia. During the last decades of the 19th century small Baptist congregations emerged in Kuopio, Tampere, Viipuri (Viborg), Oulu and other places. Though Baptists faced marginalisation and even persecution in a predominantly *Lutheran* religious context, the Dissenters Law (1889) improved their situation: the minority denominations were given the right to practise religion freely [see *Religious Liberty*].

In the early stages, the Finnish, and Swedish-speaking, Baptists in Finland worked closely together. However, by the end of the 19th century the language problem became increasingly divisive. In 1896, the Finnish-speaking Baptists founded their own publication, *Totuuden Kaiku* (Echo of Truth), which from 1961 has been retitled *Kodin Ystävä* (Friend of the Home). On 15 Jun 1902 the Finnish-speaking Baptists decided to form a body separate from the Swedish-speaking union, and a board was elected to lead its work. John Gustaf Kokki became the leader of the Finnish-speaking Baptists, in which capacity he worked until 1931. In 1928, they became an official religious denomination with the Finnish Baptist Union (*Suomen Baptistiyhdyskunta*), registered according to the law of religious liberty, which had been effective from 1 Jan 1923. The impact of WWI and its aftermath, as well as the rise of *Pentecostalism*, caused considerable *membership* losses both for Finnish and Swedish-speaking Baptists.

The Finnish-speaking Baptists have made efforts to maintain *theological* training and publishing structures, though with a limited and ageing membership this has become increasingly difficult. The Finnish Baptist Union Bible Institute was founded in 1947. This school was a part of the vision of August Jauhiainen who succeeded Kokki. A small publishing house operates in Tampere. In 1956, the *union* joined the *European Baptist Mission*, and since then six couples and four individuals have engaged in *missionary* work in Africa. In the 1990s, both Finnish and Swedish-speaking Baptists of Finland were involved in several projects in *Estonia*, in order to support youth and *children's work*, publishing activities and other *ministries* of the Estonian Baptists. In their theological positions and in worship style Finnish-speaking Baptists have been comparatively *conservative*, preferring *closed communion* and limited *ecumenical* contacts.

Finnish Baptists, as well as other Finnish Free Churches, have remained a minority in a dominantly Lutheran country. For many years, the membership of the Finnish Baptist Union, a member of the *European Baptist Federation* and the *Baptist World Alliance*, has stayed around 700. The union emphasises the need to find more adequate ways of *evangelising* in present day Finnish society.

AL

FURTHER READING: Anneli Lohikko, 'August Jauhiainen and the Pentecostal Dilemma in the Finnish Baptist Union (1930-1953)', Keith G. Jones and Ian M. Randall (eds), *Counter-Cultural Communities*, Paternoster, Carlisle, 2008.

Finland, Swedish-speaking Baptist history in

[See also *Finland, Finnish-speaking Baptist history in*]

The first Baptists in Finland (until 1917 a part of the Russian Empire) belonged to the Swedish-speaking minority, which 100 years ago constituted c.13% of the whole population (today 6%). Carl Möllerswärd, a sailor who had become a Baptist in New York, introduced the population of Åland, an island in the Finnish archipelago, to the Baptist *faith* in 1854. This young *evangelist* was sent by the Swedish Evangelical Alliance in response to a local request, asking for help to 'awaken the people from their spiritual deadly sleep'. A small Baptist community was formed in 1856, despite resistance from the *Lutheran* church. In the 1870s Swedish-speaking Baptist congregations were formed on the Finnish mainland, in Jakobstad (Pietarsaari), Vaasa, Turku (Åbo) and Helsinki. In the 1880s, Erik Jansson, who did more than anybody to develop Baptist work in Finland, established a dynamic Baptist work in Petolahti (Petalax), which reached out to the surrounding area. Today, the Baptist work among the Swedish-speaking population is concentrated on the coast of Mid-Finland and in the capital city of Helsinki. The Swedish Baptist Union in Finland, officially registered as a religious denomination in 1980, embraces 19 congregations and 1,300 baptised believers [see *Baptism*], not including *children*. *Pastors*, both *men* and *women*, have been trained in Finland as well as abroad. The *magazine*, *Missionsstandaret* (former *Finska Månadsposten* and *Finska Missionsbladet*) was first published in 1892.

Both Swedish and Finnish-speaking Baptists in Finland introduced a new *ecclesiological* model in this Lutheran-*Protestant* country, and emphasised that NT *ethics* must be practiced in everyday life. Pioneers of Christian education in Finland, the Swedish-speaking Baptists organised *Sunday Schools* for children as early as in the 1870s, and a youth organisation was formed in 1907. Since 1913, they have been involved in *mission* work outside the country. Their missionaries, in close cooperation with Baptist *unions* from other Nordic countries, have worked in Congo, Rwanda, Burundi, Brazil and Thailand. Swedish-speaking Baptists have been active in *education* and *politics* as well as in the process of renewal of the legislation on *religious freedom*. They have engaged in *evangelism* in a culturally-sensitive way and have discovered opportunities for deepening *ecumenical* relationships. The union is a member of the Finnish Ecumenical Council (Ekumeniska rådet i Finland). Since 1997 they have been involved in *theological dialogue* with the Evangelical Lutheran Church of Finland [see *National Councils of Churches*]. They work with other *free churches* in Free Church Cooperation (Frikyrklig Samverkan). The Swedish-speaking Baptists are affiliated to the *Baptist World Alliance* and the *European Baptist Federation*.

JE & LEH

Folk High Schools

Folk High Schools (FHSs) are a unique Danish initiative providing boarding schools for adults who want further education. The ideology behind the schools, developed from the 1840s, was that of the Danish *Lutheran theologian*, N.F.S. Grundtvig, whose pedagogy was revolutionary. The *students* did not have to take any examinations. The FHS did not offer degrees or other university-style qualifications. Rather, they concentrated on developing the professional and personal qualities of individual students. The spirit of the FHS is one of openness to new opportunities, readiness to undertake new challenges and a willingness to explore the world and the self in depth. The teachers were to nurture their students' *education* by answering their questions in conversation. The first of more than 350 FHSs were established in 1844. Different FHSs developed their own distinctiveness, depending on the views of their sponsors. All of them are partly financed by the *state*. The Danish Baptist Union had its FHS from 1899 to 1986 when it was closed due to a lack of students. The Baptist FHS served as a splendid frame for training lay people [see *Laity*] for *ministry*. In 1986 the FHS in Tølløse was formed as a private boarding school for teenagers working for their graduation. Danish Baptists have two of these schools today. The other one is located in Jutland.

The concept of FHSs has spread to the other Nordic countries, and both Swedish and Norwegian Baptists have their own FHSs, and in *Finland* there is an *ecumenical* (*free church*) school.

BII

Foot washing

According to Jn 13:1-20, *Jesus* at the Last Supper washed the feet of his disciples and then commanded them to do the same for others. In the Middle East it was a gesture of hospitality to wash the feet of your guests who may have been walking along dusty roads. However, it was the job of the lowest servant to do the actual washing. Jesus' act in the context of the Last Supper is commonly interpreted as an example of true Christian *ministry* of service. In spite of Jesus' command to continue the practice it has never been universally practised among Christians. One reason might be a lack of persistent reports of the first Christians adopting the practice (however, see 1Ti 5:10). Another reason may be unfamiliarity with the custom in cultures outside the Middle East. It was practised by English General Baptists [see *England*] as an *ordinance* instituted by Christ, and is still, practised among parts of the Christian family such as the *Mennonites* and the *Quakers*. It sometimes is also included as part of the *church's* celebration of *Maundy Thursday*, whilst some church *traditions*, including some Baptists, combine its message with their celebration of a *Passover* Meal. Those who have witnessed or participated in it testify to its being a most powerful experience of service and even *reconciliation*.

OL

Forgiveness

Forgiveness is at the very heart of Christian

life. Contrary to popular opinion it is forgiveness not *sin* which is at the heart of the gospel message. The *atonement*, secured through *Christ's* sacrificial *death* upon the cross, calls *women* and *men* to *repentance* and they experience the remission of their sins and the forgiveness of God. They cease to be enemies and become followers of Jesus, praying [see *Prayer*] 'forgive us our sins as we forgive those who sin against us'. There is a mutuality here that shapes the Christian outlook on others. Jesus teaches that Christian forgiveness should be unlimited – 70 times seven if need be. These acts of forgiveness, to resemble God's, must be free, complete, costly and real, not limited to words only. Because forgiveness is God's act and not just a human aspiration, the repentant sinner may be sure that it is complete and all-embracing. In this sense it is more than pardon, for the record still stands against a pardoned sinner even though the punishment may not be imposed. Forgiveness means that the slate has been wiped clean; the offence no longer stands. Because of its centrality, *confession* of sin and the pronouncement of words of forgiveness (not by some special priestly [see *Priesthood*] action) has been at the heart of Christian *worship* from the earliest days

If an offender is unrepentant or insincere in his confession some Christian thinkers would suggest that forgiveness cannot occur. There must be an act of restitution or at least a real apology, giving substance to the proffered words. For others the words of Jesus – 'Father forgive them, they do not know what they are doing' demand a more unconditional view of forgiveness.

In our own experience we discover the need to confess wrongdoing, confront the person wronged and risk the possibility of rejection. Within the Christian community mutual forgiveness is known in our acceptance of one another whatever has happened in the past.

In the *Anabaptist* tradition the shunning of offenders was intended to bring them to repentance and forgiveness by God and the community, not to demonstrate a lack of forgiveness. *Church discipline* must tread warily here.

The Christian doctrine and experience of forgiveness questions ideas of retributive justice yet remains realistic about offences. In no way does it suggest that sins do not matter and can be shrugged off. Therefore forgiveness is costly, both in personal matters and in coming to terms with the actions of persecutors or war criminals. The doctrine raises issues of individual *spirituality*, of legal *ethics* and of justice.

DBM

FURTHER READING: Mary Anne Coate, *Sin Guilt and Forgiveness*, SPCK, London, 1994. Miroslav Volf, *Free of Charge*, Zondervan, Grand Rapids, Mi., 2006.

France, Baptist history in

The story of Baptists in France is complex, with several separate origins, and devoted families providing leadership across successive generations, eventually resolving into a triad of Baptist life, each part majoring on a different Baptist characteristic. France shared in the *Reformation*: in the 16th century a fifth of the population were *Protestants*, but two centuries of persecution greatly reduced these numbers while the French Revolution weakened the *Catholics*. The Napoleonic Concordat, 1801, recognised Catholic, Reformed and *Lutheran* Christians, and *Jews*, and provided *state* salaries for their clergy. Professing churches, 'unrecognised cults', required official permission for more than 20 people to gather, yet the period 1810-32 saw the beginnings of Baptist life.

A peasant farmer, Louis Caulier, gathered a group in Nomain, in the far north, for *Bible study*. They were helped by Henri Pyt, an *evangelist* from Haldane's Continental Society. Coming to Baptist understanding by 1820, they formed a church, built a *chapel*, planted [see *Church Planting*] a second church in Aix, and reached out in *mission* to other northern towns. The new, democratically-minded urban industrial workers were attracted to this way of being church. Most converts [see *Conversion*] were from Catholicism. Caulier baptised [see *Baptism*] Baptist pioneers, Joseph Thieffry and Jean-Baptiste Crétin. They received some help from *Britain* and much from the Triennial Convention, then the missionary body for Baptists across the USA. The Convention sent a Frenchman, M. Rostan, to begin work

in Paris. A church was founded in 1835, but development was slow. *Oncken's* associates were active in Alsace, while Welsh Baptists supported work in Brittany. In spite of restrictions and opposition, pioneers developed the work between 1832 and 70.

By 1850 the American Baptist Foreign Mission Society (ABFMS) employed 14 French evangelists in northern France. Strong leaders emerged, especially Aimé Cadot and François Vincent. Vincent married Aveline Cadot; their three sons and two sons-in-law all became *pastors*. Philémon Vincent, a scholarly evangelist and strong leader, trained at the new Protestant Faculty of *Theology* in Paris. The northern churches developed a pragmatic *evangelism* with some doctrinal *pluralism*, and were willing to work with other Protestants. By 1870 the total Baptist community was about 2,000, with 700 baptised *members*. In Paris the church began to grow under Alexandre Dez and, with American and British help, it built a fine chapel in the rue de Lille (1873). Aimé Cadot worked in Lyons 1868-77. His daughter Jeanne married Ruben, son of Auguste Saillens, an evangelist attracted to the Baptist way of thinking. The new southern churches, facing more Protestant competition, were strict about Baptist doctrinal *orthodoxy*, as were those in the east. In 1890 Ruben Saillens, trained at the East London Bible Institute, founded another church in Paris, in rue St-Denis, subsequently led by his son-in-law, Arthur Blocher. This church was strongly independent and biblically [see *Bible*] *fundamentalist*.

A French Baptist Union was attempted but there were strong tensions. Philémon Vincent and Ruben Saillens clashed publicly in 1893. The ABFMS turned Vincent out of the rue de Lille, where he had been pastor since 1888, but most of the congregation followed him to the Avenue du Maine, proving that a French church could survive without external aid By 1900 the total Baptist community was about 6,000, with over 2,000 baptised members.

Church and State were legally separated in 1905: Baptists now had freedom to function but in a climate of *secularism*. Internal tension continued, centred around Vincent and Saillens. Eventually a federal *union* structure was developed with four regions, clear doctrine and *discipline* and a common budget. Churches of the north and *Belgium* were led by Aimé Cadot. The other regions – Paris and the west, the east and francophone *Switzerland*, and the south (by then six churches led by Robert Dubarry, Saillens' son-in-law) – were grouped in the Franco-Swiss Association under Saillens' presidency. The new *Baptist World Alliance* recognised them all. The north sent several young *men* to train at Rochester seminary in America, where they were influenced by Walter Rauschenbusch. Arthur Blocher and Robert Dubarry trained at *Spurgeon's College*, London. The approach was different but all returned alert to the needs of the *poor*.

Thus a triad of Baptist life developed, with stable structures:

(1) *La Fédération des Églises Évangéliques* (FEEBF) in the north and Belgium cared about *soul freedom*, so had moderately open theology, an *ecumenical* outlook, and lively social concern.

(2) *L'Association Évangélique des Églises Baptistes de Langue Française* (AEEBF), in their deep respect for the gospel, maintained fundamentalism, *inerrancy* and *pietism*, and resisted *liberal* trends.

(3) Blocher's church stressed the independence of the *local church* [see *Autonomy*]. Fundamentalist in theology, vigorous in mission, it had a lively concern for the poor.

This was a period of Baptist consolidation and implantation in French society with little numerical growth. The Association received help from Canada. Blocher's church built the Tabernacle in Montmartre, and founded new churches, and a mission to the Ivory Coast. On Blocher's death in 1929, his widow, Madeleine Blocher-Saillens, effectively succeeded him. The two World Wars hit France hard and survivors faced massive reconstruction, especially in the north. In WWII many Baptists were active in the Resistance. Madeleine Blocher-Saillens and Henri Vincent took great risks to shelter Jews. The Tabernacle was almost destroyed: Association and Fédération both helped the independent church to rebuild.

Between 1945 and 67 many American troops were stationed in France. This led to 12 *Southern Baptist* missionaries working in France. *Billy Graham* and *Youth for Christ*

made considerable impact, especially on Jacques Blocher, who was more open than his parents to work with other Baptists and *Reformed* Christians. French Baptists realised they belonged to an international *evangelical* family, sharing the stress on conversion, religious experience, activism, biblicism, and crucicentrism [see *Atonement*]. Jaques Blocher and, for the Fédération, Henri Vincent and André Thobois, formed links with other evangelicals, founding the European Biblical Institute at Chatou in 1952, the French Evangelical Alliance in 1953, the Association of Believers' Churches in1957 and the Free Faculty of Evangelical Theology in 1965. Charismatic influence was felt, especially within the Fédération.

The period 1950-2000 has seen considerable Baptist *growth*: from 18 churches with 10,000 worshippers and 3,000 baptised members in 1950, to over 100 churches with 40,000 worshippers and 12,000 baptised members in 2000. The Association accounted for 1,500 members, the Fédération 7,000, the Tabernacle and other independent churches 3,500. Nearly all large cities now have a Baptist church. Baptists remain a religious *minority* in France. They still have internal tensions and evangelism is not easy in the Catholic and secular culture, but Baptist Christianity, strong on individual choice, with clear Bible-based values and the welcoming assemblies of *congregationalism* offers 'another way of being Christian in France'.

FWB

FURTHER READING: Sébastien Fath, 'Another Way of Being a Christian in France: One Century of Baptist Implantation *Baptist History and Heritage* Vol. XXXVI, Nos. 1 and 2, (Winter/Spring 2001), pp.153-173.
Sébastien Fath, *Une autre manière d'être Chrétien en France: socio-histoire de l'implantation baptiste (1810-1950)*, Labor et Fides, Geneva, 2001.

Fraternals

A 'Fraternal' is a gathering of local *pastors* for mutual support, encouragement and, in some cases, theological reflection. From the early times of Baptist communities it has been common for those called out to the *ministry* of *Word* and *Sacrament*/pastoral office to meet together for mutual support and encouragement. Such meetings have often transgressed boundaries of denomination and *theology*. So, in Hebden Bridge, Yorkshire, in the early 1800s the *Calvinist*, John Fawcett, met regularly with the *Arminian* Baptist, Dan Taylor, for discussion, encouragement and, in some cases, a concern to 'watch over' the ministry of the other.

The word 'Fraternal' itself is judged by many to have certain male overtones and is not so commonly used amongst Baptist communities today, especially in *unions* and conventions where *women* are called to various offices of ministry.

Such 'fraternal' or ministerial meetings generally do not have a formal place in the structures of a Baptist union or convention. In some denominations they have become quasi trade unions, but this has not generally been a feature of Baptist groupings, though there have been occasions in some countries where the community of ministers have made common cause to seek some change in the general arrangements of the union.

Typically, a 'fraternal' might meet monthly for lunch together or in an afternoon to share news and concern, to read a book of theology together, to engage in *prayer* and in mutual support. Alongside such meetings there might be more infrequent retreats or conferences for ministers. In some unions these are formally organised by the union or regional minister. In others, they are carefully established outside the governance of the union or association. For instance, the English Baptist pastor, D. Tait Patterson, in the early part of the 20th century persuaded *wealthy* members of his congregation in the north of *England* to fund such a retreat experience, or residential fraternal, for a group of ministers in the industrial belt of west and south Yorkshire.

KGJ

Free Churches

Free churches are often *congregational* and always based on voluntary and responsible *membership*. They are communities of *faith* which, respecting the principle of the *separation of church and state*, exist quite separately from government control or patronage, believing that since the Lord *Jesus* is the head of the church, no *political* or ecclesiastical power can intervene between him and his church [see *Lord of the Church*]. Thus in different locations they will differentiate themselves from majority *Roman Catholic* or *Orthodox Churches* closely identified with political rule or social solidarity. But just as significantly they exist independently of *Lutheran* state churches in *Germany* and *Scandinavia*, or of a *reformed* establishment in *Switzerland* or *Scotland*. In this sense they are the opposite of state/established [landeskirchen/volkskirchen] churches [see *National Church*], though they have struggled to secure recognition by the *state* as a significant part of the religious and ethical [see *Ethics*] life of the people as part of a belief in religious toleration. Their history places them in the tradition of the Radical *Reformation*, that is that part of the reformation dependent on the free choice of individual believers, rather than the magisterial reformation which depended so much on a fruitful alliance with the state, and in particular the favour of the godly prince or a reform-inclined city council.

In the *United Kingdom* the description 'Free Church' came to replace the older titles of '*Nonconformity*', the refusal to conform to the teaching, *liturgy* and practices of the Established Church, or 'Dissent', which again signifies a rejection of the church establishment – for both of these terms had negative connotations. By contrast, the title 'Free Church' stresses the positive aspect of churches being formed voluntarily by those who have made a free and unfettered choice to be Christ's disciples. With their origins in *Puritan* separation [see *Separatism*] and the *Evangelical Revival* of the 18th century, the Free Churches shared common beliefs and a common sense of grievance at their exclusion from national life until the reforms of the 19th century. Though they differed over *polity* and *baptism*, they shared a common passion for *evangelism*. In the 1890s a National Free Church Council was formed which brought together delegates from local Free Church Councils and for a short period was remarkably successful in nation-wide evangelism. After WWI, J.H. Shakespeare, then secretary of the British Baptist *Union*, managed to secure a more formal representative body: the Federal Council of the Evangelical Free Churches which he hoped might be a stepping stone towards the creation of a United Free Church, but this was not to be. In 1940 the two Councils amalgamated, and more recently they have thrown their lot in with Churches Together in *England*, the headquarters of which is housed in the buildings of the Free Church Federal Council. It still remains that there is a bond on kinship across all the Free Churches which operates on a deeper level than other *ecumenical* relationships. E.g. there is a mutual recognition of *ministry* and membership (at least in *open communion* churches) which is something more profound than the *Eucharistic* hospitality offered by the *Anglican* Church of England.

In continental Europe the roots of the Free Churches, which have their origins in the 19th century or later, rather than the 17th century, are to be found in the *pietist* movement and in 19th-century revivalism, but there is still that same respect for independence of the state which can call for costly witness when governments and state churches combine to limit their freedom. The title of 'Free Church' makes bold claims to gospel freedom; it is imperative that those who belong to this tradition live up to such a claim

PMIL & JHYB

Free Will

To be able to make decisions about beliefs and behaviour is an essential aspect of being human, of what it means to be created in the image of God [see *Humankind*]. However *theologians* have expressed varied opinions concerning

(1) how this human will relates to the divine will;
(2) the impact of *sin* on human ability to make free choices and
(3) the effects of divine *grace* upon and within sinful human nature.

The most prominent Baptist to address this subject in the *Reformation* era was *Anabaptist* theologian *Balthasar Hubmaier*. Continental Anabaptists were broadly sympathetic to the views expressed by this early German Baptist. English Particular Baptists [see *England*] who emerged in the following century from Independent Reformed circles were more closely aligned with the perspective of *Luther* and *Calvin* on the subject of 'Free Will'.

In his two treatises of 1527 Hubmaier takes a rigorously biblical approach in attempting to prove the freedom of the will. His viewpoint is expressed clearly in the first treatise of Apr 1527 in which Hubmaier declared that there are three wills, that of the flesh, the soul and the spirit. Before the *Fall* humankind was 'wholly free to choose good or evil'; following that event Adam 'lost this freedom for himself and all his descendants...the flesh has irretrievably lost its goodness and freedom'. The 'spirit of the human being, however, has before, during and after the Fall remained upright, whole and good. It had like a prisoner to eat the forbidden fruit...against its will'. The soul, the third part of the human being 'has through the disobedience of Adam become wounded in the will and sick to *death*, so that on its own it can choose nothing good'. After the *restoration* by *Christ*, 'the flesh is still good for nothing', and the spirit willing and ready to do all good'; through the work of the Son and the *Spirit* the soul again knows good and evil and can now freely and willingly be obedient to the spirit . In summary in his first treatise on this subject Hubmaier asserted: 'If I now will, then I will be saved by the grace of God; if I do not will, then I will be damned and that on the basis of my own obstinacy and wilfulness'.

The 1610 General Baptist *Helwys* Confession although using different language held to the same understanding of this subject. 'Man being created good, and continuing in goodness, had the ability...freely to obey, assent, or reject the propounded evil...he through free power (affirmed) to the choice of good...This last power or ability remaineth in all his posterity.' In Article XX 'Of Free Will in Man', The Orthodox Creed of English General Baptists in 1678 stated: 'God hath endued the will of man with that natural liberty and power of acting upon choice, that it's neither forced, nor by any necessity of nature determined, to do good or evil.' However, 'perfection of will is only attainable in the state of glory...after the *resurrection* of our fleshly bodies.' The wording and tone of this *creed* is influenced by the Particular Baptist Confession of 1677. In fact the opening article of Chapter IX 'Of Free Will' in the Calvinistic Baptist document was almost certainly adopted in the Arminian Creed the following year with the remainder of Article XX in the 1678 Creed summarising and quoting the Particular Baptist document extensively. The 1677 discussion of free will is a more extensive contribution and has some distinctive phrases that General Baptists could not have assented to. Article three of chapter IX states: 'Man by his fall into a state of sin hath wholly lost all ability of Will, to any spiritual good accompanying *salvation*; so a natural man...is not able by his own strength, to convert [see *Conversion*] himself; or to prepare himself thereunto.' This is complemented by the declaration in Article four that: 'When God converts a sinner...he freeth him from his natural bondage under sin, and by his grace alone, enables him freely to will and to do that which is spiritually good...yet...by reason of his remaining corruptions he doth not perfectly nor only will that which is good; but doth also will that which is evil...a sinful nature. Man is now free and is thus responsible to God for all his actions, words and thoughts.'

In the second half of the 20th century there was a revival of interest in Reformed *theology* and also in Anabaptist thinking amongst Baptists providing opportunities for further reflection on this topic.

BT

FURTHER READING: W.L. Lumpkin, *Baptist Confessions of Faith*, Judson, Chicago, 1959. G.K. Parker, *Baptists in Europe: History and Confessions of Faith*, Broadman, Nashville, Tn., 1982. H. Wayne Pipkin and John H. Yoder (eds), *Balthasar Hubmaier Theologian of Anabaptism*, Herald, Scottdale, Pa., 1989. S. Wright, *The Early English Baptists*, Boydell, Woodbridge, UK and Rochester, NY, 2006.

Free-Will Offering

See *Offerings/Collection*; *Tithing*.

Freedom of Conscience

[See also *Conscience*; *Religious Liberty*]
The Baptist core conviction of freedom of conscience is rooted in the early struggles of Baptists for religious freedom in the face of civil authorities who wished to impose one form of religion on all their subjects. The 1612 Confession of *John Smyth*'s church in Amsterdam (which influenced subsequent Baptist thinking on the subject) was the first *confession* of modern times to demand individual freedom of conscience and its corollary, *separation of church and State*: 'That the magistrate is not by virtue of his office to meddle with religion or matters of conscience, to force or compel *men* to this or that form of religion, or doctrine; but to leave Christian religion free, to every man's conscience for *Christ* only is the King and lawgiver of the church and conscience.' Rooted in a lofty conception of the Lordship of Christ [see *Lord of the Church*], the appeal to freedom of conscience had continued to inform Baptist identity and action ever since. It is linked to the significance of believers' *baptism* in the understanding that every believer must make his/her own response to the *grace* of God in Jesus Christ.

At its best this principle has enabled Baptists to take a courageous stand against persecution and injustice of all kinds, based on their understanding of *scripture* and the conviction that no-one stand between the individual believer and God. The story of European Baptists is full of believers who exercised freedom of conscience in the face of dire threats from governments and authorities of all kinds, most recently during the *Communist* era in Eastern Europe.

However it must be said that the principle of freedom of conscience can at times lead Baptists towards an excessive individualism which downplays the importance of the believing *community* in discerning and acting upon the will of God. Appeals to individual freedom of conscience have been used to justify conflicts in Baptist life which were later seen to be both damaging and unnecessary. There has also been a link between this kind of understanding of freedom of conscience and the strong Baptist support for *Human Rights* legislation whose basis in *individual* rights is currently in question.

Recent trends in Baptist thinking such as the interest in re-interpreting *Anabaptist theology* for the present time has brought a much-needed corrective in balancing the dictates of the individual conscience with a renewed understanding of the way in which the *Holy Spirit* may speak to the *gathered church* as a whole.

AAP & JHYB

Fruits and Gifts of the Spirit

[See also *Holy Spirit*]
God is understood in Christian *theology* to be at work in the world and in believers by means of the Holy Spirit. The *church* is the community of the Spirit, called into being by the Spirit at *Pentecost* and maintained by that same Spirit ever after. Alive in the Spirit, the fruits are the virtues and moral qualities which are the product of the sanctifying Spirit in the lives of believers; the gifts are specific ways in which God's Spirit equips and enables the church to build itself up in *love* and service. Although never to be separated, the two are to be distinguished in that the fruits involve patient learning of Christian character in the work of *sanctification* which is life-long. The gifts of the Spirit are more immediate and not necessarily in direct correlation with Christian maturity. Paul gives the classic list of the fruits in Gal 5:22-23: love, joy, peace, patience, kindness, generosity, faithfulness, and self-control. Rather than being human achievements, such virtues should be seen as the work of God, and in that sense also as gracious gifts, in the lives of those who submit willingly to God in *Christ*. The NT offers three lists of spiritual gifts: In Eph 4:11-13 the gifts of Christ are listed as *apostles*, prophets [see *Prophecy*], *evangelists*, *pastors*, and teachers. In view here are those gifted persons given by the Head of the church for the sake of its *growth* into *unity*, stability and maturity. In 1Co 12:8-11 the gifts of the Spirit are listed as the utterance of wisdom, the utterance of knowledge, the gift of *faith*, gifts of *healing*, the working of miracles, prophecy, discernment of spirits, various kinds of tongues and the interpretation of tongues. A difficulty here is in understanding what these gifts were in context. The tendency is now to interpret these terms according to the ways in which they have been experienced in *Pentecostalism* and the *charismatic movement*. The context is that of *worship* and of 'the manifestation of the Spirit for the common good'. This suggests a dynamic of heightened and intense spiritual awareness within the context of worship in which the intuition is engaged alongside the intellect. Intuitively worshippers sense wisdom, or knowledge, or a prophetic word from God, or are prompted to speak in tongues or to interpret them, to *pray* with an increase of faith for something specific, or to attempt in faith an act beyond what might normally be considered possible. A third list of gifts is found in Ro 12:6-8 and includes prophesying, ministering, teaching, exhorting, giving and having compassion. From these several lists we might conclude that none of them is intended to be exhaustive: the gifts of the Spirit are broad and diverse and almost certainly go beyond anything listed. Whatever their views about the charismatic movement, Baptists see local congregations as recipients of spiritual gifts and as communities where the fruit of the Spirit is nurtured. Gifts are, therefore, not so much the possessions of those through whom they are manifested as dynamic ways in which God's people are used by God's Spirit to fulfil God's work.

NGW

Fullerism

Fullerism represents a form of *evangelical Calvinism* deriving its name from Andrew Fuller (1754-1815), a Particular Baptist [see *England*] *minister* and *theologian*, who was the founding secretary of the *Baptist Missionary Society*. His reputation as a theologian largely rests on *The Gospel Worthy of All Acceptation* (1785), a seminal book which challenged the high Calvinism prevalent among 18th-century English Particular Baptists. Fuller sought to stress the importance of human responsibility alongside that of divine *sovereignty* and argued, contrary to the high Calvinists, that preachers should openly invite their hearers to respond to the gospel. *The Gospel Worthy* was the classic statement of 18th-century evangelical Calvinism among Particular Baptists; its teaching was referred to as 'Fullerism' even within the author's lifetime. Fuller's tract was certainly influential in helping to bring about a revitalisation in Particular Baptist churches even though 'Fullerism' was bitterly attacked by high Calvinists as a compromising accommodation to *free will* theologies. Arguably as the writings of Thomas Beza had made the teachings of the great reformer [see *Reformation*] more restrictive, so Fuller restored to reformed *theology* its original *missionary* intention.

Fuller's theology confirmed new emphases emerging in Baptist life, and that of the Northamptonshire Association in particular, towards the end of the 18th century. Associated with him here were men like Robert Hall, Sr., and John Sutcliff, both of whom were advocates of the new Calvinism. Perhaps the most important outcome of this revivification of theology was the formation of the BMS in 1792. Fuller was a close friend of **William Carey**, the society's first missionary, serving as the tireless secretary of the BMS from its inception to his **death**.

Fuller wrote a large number of other theological and **apologetic** works, the most significant of which is probably *The Gospel its Own Witness* (1800), a work which sought to combat **deism** and which was widely respected. Fuller also spent the whole of his ministerial career as a **local church** pastor, serving churches in Soham, Cambridgeshire (1775-82) and Kettering, Northamptonshire (1783-1815). Fuller's life, theology and ministry were decisively shaped by forces associated with the evangelical *revival*. He was especially influenced by the writings of Jonathan Edwards and by some of Edwards' disciples in the New Divinity movement. He engaged positively with Evangelical **Arminianism** in the shape of the New Connexion Baptist, Dan Taylor, although he remained a convinced Particular Baptist, not only holding to particular *redemption*, but also defending emphases such as **closed communion**.

PJM & ET

FURTHER READING: P.J. Morden, *Offering Christ to the World: Andrew Fuller (1754-1815) and the Revival of Eighteenth Century Particular Baptist Life*, Paternoster, Carlisle, 2003.

Fundamentalism (Christian)

[See also *Fundamentalism (Non-Christian)*] Fundamentalism came to prominence in North America in the 1920s. There was a growing **theological** polarisation between **liberals** and **conservatives** which had previously been obscured by a common commitment to Christian action. The **evangelist** D.L. Moody was important in bridging divides. Between 1910 and 15 a series of paperback volumes entitled *The Fundamentals* was published and the World's Christian Fundamentals Association was formed in 1919, with a Baptist, W.B. Riley, as its leading figure. It was in 1920 at the Northern Baptist Convention in the USA that the term 'fundamentalist' was coined. W.B. Riley said that Baptists had entered the theological controversy 'knowing that it was not a battle, but a war...and that they will never surrender'. Fundamentalist thinking was shaped by **dispensational premillennialism**, with its apocalyptic outlook. Alongside American leadership there was British influence through the thinking of **Brethren** premillennial figures such as J.N. Darby.

It was the 'Monkey Trial' (so-called) of 1925, at which the well-known William Jennings Bryan sought to prosecute John Scopes, a teacher in Dayton, Tennessee, for teaching **evolution**, which was a watershed in the story of Fundamentalism. As a matter of expediency, the judge who heard the case charged the jury to find Scopes guilty, but for their part Fundamentalists found themselves held up to public derision and caricature. The decline in their standing was seen by many as a rout, although far from Fundamentalism disappearing it focused its attention instead on building up conservative **local church** life, which was precisely where it could most readily succeed. Fundamentalists formed a sub-culture.

The Fundamentalists of present-day America constitute the most conservative wing of **Protestantism**. Jerry Falwell, a Baptist who is also a Fundamentalist leader, has given this definition: 'A Fundamentalist is an **evangelical** who is angry about something'. Fundamentalism in America has seen an upsurge in confidence in recent decades. It has had links with the Moral Majority movement and is characterised by strong opposition to the teaching of evolution and by a commitment to the term 'inerrant' in relation to *scripture* [see **Infallibility and inerrancy of the Bible**]. The influence of Fundamentalism is strong among independent churches and within parts of the **Southern Baptist Convention**. **Billy Graham**, a

Southern Baptist, is an example of a significant world evangelical leader who was nurtured in Fundamentalism but who has distanced himself from the movement. The major difficulty with the fundamentalist positions is that it unchurches all those who do not think as it does and closes the door upon any scrutiny of doctrine by the normal tools of theological scholarship.

In Britain and elsewhere in world-wide evangelicalism Fundamentalism has historically not been as strong as in America. In Britain the *Keswick* Convention, which was predominantly *Anglican*, had a calming influence. Keswick's emphasis was placed on a moderate *piety*, not on controversy. After visiting Keswick in 1928, W.B. Riley criticised the Convention for tolerating error. Within the Baptist denomination in *England* there was a small Fundamentalist party in the 1920s: the Baptist Bible Union, under the leadership of James Mountain, was formed, but made little headway. In 1922, E.J. Poole-Connor, a former Baptist *minister*, launched what became the Fellowship of Independent Evangelical Churches, a grouping of *Free Churches* holding to inerrancy.

A phenomenon which at first sight is very different from early Fundamentalism is the House Church or *Restorationist* ('restoring' the NT church) movement which began in Britain in the 1970s and has spread elsewhere. It is *Pentecostal/charismatic* in its *spirituality*, which has not been common in Fundamentalism. However, there are Fundamentalist tendencies. The teaching in many Restorationist churches is generally characterised by biblical literalism, male leadership, opposition to denominationalism and a lack of a historical understanding. In America and Britain it seems that periods of wider cultural change have produced Fundamentalist-type reactions. This may also be the case in the *growth* of Fundamentalism in other religions. It remains to be seen to what extent Fundamentalism is a long-term phenomenon.

IMR

FURTHER READING: D.W. Bebbington, 'Baptists and Fundamentalism in Inter-War Britain' in *Studies in Church History*, Subsidia 7, Blackwell, Oxford, 1990. K.W. Clements, *Lovers of Discord*, SPCK, London, 1988. G.M. Marsden, *Fundamentalism and American Culture*, OPU, New York, 1980. G.M. Marsden, *Understanding Fundamentalism and Evangelicalism*, Eerdmans, Grand Rapids, Mi., 1991.

Fundamentalism (Non-Christian)

[See also *Fundamentalism (Christian)*]
Some *scholars* argue that the term Fundamentalism should properly be reserved for those *conservative* Christian *Protestant* groups who first adopted the terminology which refers to the four volume *The Fundamentals* published by R.A. Torrey (1856-1928) of the Moody Bible Institute, Chicago in 1909. Many of these conservative Christians themselves object to the use of the term for other religious groups, especially to label *Islamist* Muslims. Nevertheless the term has come to be adopted more widely both in popular and in more scholarly usage to refer to any strongly conservative religious groups who adhere to, or advocate a return to, what are perceived as the defining ideas and practices of a given tradition, the 'fundamentals'. Especially it is used of those who understand their sacred scriptures in an *infallible* or inerrant way. This is often assumed to involve a literalist approach, whereas the key principle is not so much literalism but rather inerrancy; where literal meanings stretch credibility to the limit metaphorical interpretations are sometimes adopted by such groups in order to preserve this more basic principle.

In this wider usage Fundamentalism is used of conservative groups not only in Christianity but also in *Judaism*, Islam and, perhaps more contentiously, of Hindus. What appears to unite these disparate elements is a fierce and sometimes violent rejection of *Modernity* and a strong defence of what they understand to be the ancient *tradition* of their *faith*. The *sociologist* Steve Bruce (b1954) makes the point that those who are labelled 'fundamentalist' in the eyes of liberal modernity are actually the norm within the 'broad sweep of human history' and this approach to religion was commonplace in the West until the last 200 years and it remains commonplace in many parts of the world to the present day. He comments: 'Fundamentalism is a rational response of traditionally religious peoples to social, political and economic changes that downgrade and constrain the role of religion in the public world' (*Fundamentalism*, 2001, p.117).

This is a helpful reminder that often so-called religious 'fundamentalism' is actually less about religion and more about **politics** and social and economic change, especially for people who think of themselves as **minorities**. Its common concern is the preserving of identity in an apparently hostile environment. Bruce also draws attention to the 'rationality' of much fundamentalism, which, in a paradoxical way, often surreptitiously adopts the rationality of modernity, as in the logic of 'empirical proof', e.g., in defence of its pre-modern assumptions.

The significance of the issue of identity is underlined by the strong boundaries which such groups draw between themselves and others, including their co-religionists who hold a 'weaker' or 'compromised' version of the faith. The stronger identity of the conservative groups is reflected in their labels in which the 'born again' and 'bible-believing' language of Protestant Fundamentalists is paralleled by terms such as '*haredi*' Jews [true to the Torah] or *ja'amat* Muslims [the true brotherhood]. It may also be seen in the fierce struggle for the control of sacred sites such as the Dome of the Rock in Jerusalem or the site of the mosque in Ayodyah in northern India which has been a matter of violent dispute between Hindus and Muslims.

Although *The Fundamentalism Project* directed by the American **scholar**, Martin E. Marty (b1928), identifies some Hindu groups as 'fundamentalist' in tendency. Many Hindus would dispute such labelling as inappropriate since the broad Hindu tradition recognises many texts, many traditions, and many understandings of the divine and most would decline to claim final superiority for their own tradition. However, some aspects of the tradition have been recruited for political ends by conservative groups such as the *Bharat Janata Party* (BJP), which is campaigning for the creation of a Hindu **state** to replace the officially secular constitution of India. This is what underlies the dispute over the site at Ayodyah.

During the 1990s the American **political** scientist, Samuel P. Huntington, argued that the rise of religious fundamentalism in what

he identified as eight great cultural traditions of humanity, would lead inevitably to a 'clash of civilisations'. The British Chief Rabbi Jonathan Sacks (b1948) counter-argued that whilst questions of identity, including religious identity, had indeed superseded the great ideological clashes of the first half of the 20th century, it need not necessarily mean violence if people could accord each other the 'dignity of difference'.

NJW

FURTHER READING: G. Almond, R. Appleby and E. Sivan, *Strong Religion: the Rise of Fundamentalism around the World*, University of Chicago Press, Chicago, 2003. K. Armstrong, *The Battle for God: A History of Fundamentalism*, Ballantine Books, New York, 2001. S. Bruce, *Fundamentalism*, Polity, Cambridge and Blackwell, Malden, Ma., 2001. S. Huntington, *The Clash of Civilisations*, Simon and Schuster, London, 1997. M.E. Marty and R.S. Appleby (eds), *Fundamentalisms Observed*, University of Chicago Press, Chicago, 1991. M.E. Marty and R.S. Appleby (eds), *Fundamentalisms Comprehended*, University of Chicago Press, Chicago, 1995. J. Sacks, *The Dignity of Difference*, Continuum, London and New York, 2002.

Funerals

In all civilised societies it is customary to have special procedures for the certification and declaration of a **death** and the disposal of the deceased. Christians from the earliest days have had special **liturgies** and rites for funerals of believers. Baptists generally have tended to use with little adaptation the approaches of the other major Christian **traditions**, though having, for the most part, responsibility only for **members** of their own community , even if those members were not active members at the time of death, unlike **national**, **state**, or **folk** churches who often provide Christian funeral services for the wider society.

In Europe Funeral services are normally held between two and seven days after death, though in the Middle East the time delay can be much shorter because of concerns about the deterioration of the corpse in the heat of summer. Services generally involve some **prayers** for the family of the deceased in the home, then a service of **worship** in the Baptist **chapel** or meeting house, followed either by burial or cremation.

Typically, a funeral service will involve a clear declaration of Christian *faith* and *hope* in the *resurrection* of the dead, readings from *scripture*, often including a Psalm, OT, epistle and gospel passages, with classic selections including Ps 23, Isa 25:8-9, Ro 8, 1Co 15, Rev 21 and Jn 14:1-6.

Most Baptist funerals will include a *sermon* expounding the Christian hope and also, or as part of the sermon, a eulogy about the deceased. In some *post-modern* contexts there has been pressure for a second event which might be a service of thanksgiving for the life of the deceased which will have the accent upon a 'celebration of life' rather than warnings of mortality. At such services of thanksgiving, those attending are as likely to encounter balloons and streamers, bright clothing and mementos of the deceased, rather than sombre garb with *men* in dark suits and black ties and *women* in colours of mourning, black and deep purple.

In some contexts the use of candles and images of the deceased is encouraged. In other contexts the casket containing the deceased is unadorned, though at funerals for those with origins in the Caribbean the coffin is likely to be open with the embalmed body of the deceased person clearly visible. Different cultural aspects reflect the choice of flowers used and increasingly people are requested not to bring or send wreaths of flowers, but to make a donation instead to a Baptist charity or *mission* agency in memory of the one who has died.

In many European contexts as land has become a limited resource, the pattern of burial in large cemeteries whether owned by the municipality or by the church community, has given way to cremation in public crematoria or woodland burial for those interested in *ecology and the environment*. Baptists generally do not seem to have raised *theological* objections to cremation and therefore what happens in particular contexts is more conditioned by local cultural norms and practices.

Whilst many Baptist pastors and ministers do not use service books for the generality of their *ministry*, occasional rites of passage often do have them reaching for some form of published resources. Books offering such resources are published in many languages.

Baptists will not normally answer the question 'What happens at a funeral?' by talking about prayers for the dead. While the story of the dead person is not forgotten, the focus of attention is generally on the bereaved. Those taking funerals will normally see their task as helping the bereaved to come to terms with the death by inviting them to trust in the Lord and to entrust to that same Lord the one who has died. This is, of course, an important part of the Christian rites of death.

At a funeral the life of the one who has died is remembered and thanksgiving offered for all that they have meant to church and family, with the assurance that they are now safe in the *love* and mercy of God, and prayers for the bereaved that in their sorrow and loss they may not lose hope. Above all, however, at a funeral, Baptists come into the presence of God whose self-*revelation* is found supremely at the *cross*: the Father bereaved, the *Son* dying, and the *Spirit* bringing new out of the from the chaos as at the beginning of time.

KGJ

FURTHER READING: Christopher J. Ellis and Myra Blyth (eds), *Gathering for Worship*, The Canterbury Press, Norwich, 2005. Peter C. Jupp and Tony Rogers (eds), *Interpreting Death: Christian Theology and Pastoral Practice*, Cassell, London and Washington, DC, 1997. E.A. Payne and S.F. Winward (eds), *Orders and Prayer for Church Worship* (3rd ed.), Baptist Union of Great Britain and Ireland, London, 1965. P.P.J. Sheppy, *In Sure and Certain Hope: liturgies, prayers and readings for funerals and memorials*, The Canterbury Press, Norwich, 2003. P.P.J. Sheppy, *Death, Liturgy and Ritual: A Pastoral and liturgical Theology*, Aldershot and Burlington, VT: Ashgate Publishing, 2003. P.P.J. Sheppy, *Death, Liturgy and Ritual: A Commentary on Liturgical Texts*, Aldershot and Burlington, VT: Ashgate Publishing, 2004. P.P.J. Sheppy, *Cries of the Heart; a daily companion for your journey through grief*, Norwich, The Canterbury Press, 2005.

Future Life, The
See *Heaven, Hell and the Future Life*.

G

G8 Summits

G8 summits are the meetings held every year between the heads of government of eight countries: the United States, Japan, *Germany*, *UK*, *France*, *Italy*, Canada and *Russia*. The group, which has increased in size over the course of its existence since the 1970s, was originally meant to bring together the most economically powerful countries in the world. The grouping is now anachronistic as it does not contain all of the largest economies in the world. For instance, China has a larger economy than the UK, France, Italy, Canada and Russia.

Historically the G8 existed to reach agreement on issues of international economic management such as exchange rates or international trade negotiations. However, as the G8 grouping has become less economically dominant, such discussions have moved elsewhere. The G8 has instead come to be focused around one or two of the areas the government of the country it is taking place in is concerned with. For instance, the 2005 summit in Gleneagles in the UK featured an agreement to increase the levels of international aid. The 2007 summit in Heiligendamm in Germany tried to reach agreement on tackling *climate change*. However, once G8 summits have finished, governments often fail to implement the commitments they have made.

G8 summits are often met with a counter-G8 summit in the same place, where activists gather to campaign on issues or against the G8. Many of these campaigners argue that the G8 is a self-appointed group which undermines more inclusive processes in institutions such as the *United Nations*. The most infamous protests were in Genoa, Italy, in 2001 when one protestor died and 100s were injured.

Campaigners also make demands of the G8 to do more to tackle world issues such as global poverty or climate change. In 1998, a protest of 80,000 people, many of them from churches including Baptists, gathered outside the G8 summit in Birmingham, UK, to demand the cancellation of debts owed by developing countries to comparatively rich countries. Large protests were repeated outside the G8 summit in 1999 in Cologne, Germany, and at the International Monetary Fund and World Bank meetings in Prague in 2000, again heavily influenced by Christian and Baptist groups.

G8 agreements on debt cancellation in Cologne in 1999 and Gleneagles 2005 have resulted in the cancellation of most of the debts of 22 developing countries, primarily in Africa. As a consequence, countries such as Tanzania, Uganda and Zambia have been able to increase the resources available for *health* and *education*. However, to qualify for such debt cancellation developing countries have to meet a set of criteria set by rich countries, often including contentious economic policies such as trade liberalisation, privatisation of *state*-owned companies, including utilities such as water, and investment deregulation.

TKJ

Gambling

Baptists have had a long standing objection to gambling in all its many forms, considering it unethical [see *Ethics*]. Gambling comes in many forms – all species of betting (dogs, horses, sporting outcomes), the pools, card games, premium bonds (where the interest on the capital invested becomes the element gambled), games machines, casinos and lotteries, all that offers the possibility of a quick gain for little effort. The influence of lotteries becomes the most difficult to avoid when all too many educational, cultural and arts activities, including the conservation of historic buildings have come to depend on this as the only form of funding. The old language describing this activity was 'games of chance' and to benefit from the same was seen to be unethical. Beyond that it is well-known that all forms of gambling are in effect an additional tax on the *poor* who treasure the success of the few without properly calculating that the odds against their success are immense. Moreover there is also gamblers' compulsion where the impulse to gamble overcomes all other calls upon disposable income leading whole families into misery. Some have argued that gambling is no worse than investing in the equity market where the success of the investment cannot be guaranteed, and certainly there are some speculative exercises which are dangerous to the point of being irresponsible. But on the other hand both social and economic development is dependent on the support of the investor.

ET

Gathered/Gathering churches

Terminology. The English word 'church', from the Greek *kuriakon* – 'that which is belonging to the Lord' – 'the place' of *worship*, frequently used with content from the Greek term *ekklesia* and its Hebrew equivalent for *covenant* 'assembly'. The term 'gathered/gathering churches' expresses the *congregational* character of the *church* and the development of a congregational *ecclesiology* and establishment of congregational churches in contrast to that of the **Roman Catholic** Church and established national churches of **Protestantism**, or indeed any church where *authority* derives from the top downwards. Late in the 17th century this idea of church had a chance to develop and survive historically with a lasting impact on Baptist and other congregational *traditions*, gradually also on the understanding of the church within the *ecumenical* community in a world gradually becoming more and more *secularised*.

Ecclesiology. With the Reformation and a new emphasis on the **Word of God** as the living centre of the church, the church as a gathered covenant community emerged as descriptive on one important stream of **Reformed** churchmanship. This led to the demand for more radical reform. This became evident, e.g. within **nonconformity** in **England**, that is those groups, like the Baptists, which in *conscience* could not accept the teaching of the **Church of England** as required by law and which accordingly separated from it [see **Separatism**].

A gathered/gathering church, therefore, stands for:

- a visible body of believers, covenanting with God and each other.
- a spiritual reality, visible in *baptism*, life and work and in participation in the community of *faith*.

- a self-governing and self-supporting local community, *associating* with other congregations to meet a common *call* to *unity* and *mission*.
- a community with an *apostolic* tradition, the **Bible** being their rule for life and thought.
- a *free church* under the *authority* of Jesus Christ as the living **Lord of the church**, demanding *democracy* within the church.
- a church separated from the *state* [see **Separation of Church and State**].

The actual language denotes the coming together of disciples from their daily work for the worship of Almighty God and for mutual *fellowship*, but as the *saints* are gathered so they also need to be dispersed back into the world there to *witness* and engage in mission [see **Priesthood of all Believers**]. The going is just as important as the coming.

PMIL

General Assembly

See *Assembly, General – as governing body of Union/Convention.*

Genetically Modified Foods

See *GM Foods.*

Georgia, Baptist history in

Georgia, one of the earliest Christian countries in the world, adopted Christianity as the *state* religion [see **State Church**] in the first part of the 4th century consequent upon the work of St. Nino, a female *evangelist* who came to Georgia from Cabaducia (Cappadocia). Being surrounded by predominantly **Muslim** nations, Georgia had to fight to protect its Christian identity and in 1801 was forced to unite with **Russia**. The Russians abolished both the Georgian kingdom and the independence of the Georgian **Orthodox Church**. Thus the long *suffering* Georgian people and Church were captured by Tsarist Russia.

The Baptist *mission* in Georgia began in 1862, when a German Baptist, Martin Kalweit from **Lithuania**, settled in Tiflis (Tbilisi) and began *Bible study* and *prayer meetings*. In 1867 Kalweit baptised Nikita Voronin who came from a *Molokan* background. Though dating the origins of any religious movement is always problematic, the *baptism* of Voronin is often considered as the commencement of the Baptist movement among the Russian-speaking population in Tsarist Russia. Tiflis Baptist congregation, which emerged and was strengthened by the evangelistic efforts of Kalweit, Voronin, and Vasilii Pavlov, became one of the earliest centres of Baptist work in Tsarist Russia (besides St. Petersburg and Southern *Ukraine*), though officially the church was established only in 1880. Tiflis church, through its active *members*, participated in Baptist mission both in the Caucasus and in Southern Ukraine, and became the 'mother church' for the emerging Baptist movement in the area. Symbolically, the first Russian Baptist conference took place in Tiflis in 1879.

In 1919 the Baptists in Georgia were actively involved in organising a regional conference. At this conference, the decision was made to establish a Trans-Caucasian Union of Baptists, an important expansion of Baptist vision. In its first decades, the Baptist *faith* addressed mostly Russian-speaking people, but in 1912 Aleksei Khutsishvili and his mother, both from Georgian ethnic backgrounds, were baptised in Tiflis. In 1911 a Georgian soldier named Ilya Kandelaki was baptised in Vilnius, Lithuania and came back to Tbilisi with a desire to serve his own people. With this new focus, during the short period of Georgian independence in 1919 an ethnically Georgian Baptist church was organised in Tbilisi alongside a continuation of services in Russian. The 1920s saw another development. For many decades Baptist work had centred predominantly in Tiflis, but with the evangelistic activity of Ilya Kandelaki and others the gospel message was taken to other parts of the country. Kandelaki had dreams for his fellow Georgians, being very keen to translate the *Bible* into the modern Georgian language [see *Bible Translation*] and to prepare some liturgical materials [see *Liturgy*] for the Georgian Baptist congregations. However, he became the first Georgian Baptist *martyr*, assassinated by Bolshevik agents during one of his *preaching* trips to Eastern Georgia. The task of the

translation of the Bible was continued by a female Baptist leader, Ekaterine Kutateladze, who succeeded in translating the NT and the Psalms from ancient Georgian into Modern Georgian. Under the Soviets, the printing of religious literature was forbidden so the *minister* of the Georgian Baptist congregation, Revd Teodore Kochoradze, who happened to have only one eye, copied out the NT for his disciples at least 5 times.

The Soviet years saw a period of church closures and other persecution, but the Tbilisi church, the central Baptist church in Georgia, continued its *witness*. The church had a 'mosaic' of memberships embracing Russians, Georgians, Armenians and Ossetians; it also united both Baptist and *Evangelical* Christian believers, the latter joining the church after WWII.

Despite persecution and immense pressure from the authorities the Baptist church in Georgia continued to grow. By the early 1960s the Georgian-speaking Baptist community outnumbered other ethnic communities. Georgian Baptist leaders realised that in their traditionally Orthodox country it was necessary to enter into *dialogue* with the Orthodox Church and Revd Teodor Kochoradze became the first Baptist minister to establish formal relations with the head of the Georgian Orthodox Church, Ephrem II. Relations were also cemented by two visits by the British Baptist leader, Dr. Ernest Payne who served as both a Vice-Moderator and later a President of the *WCC* of which the Georgian Orthodox Church became a member 1961.

In the 1970s relations with the Orthodox Church made unprecedented progress; under the leadership of Revd Giorgi Bolgashvili, the Senior Minister of the Georgian Baptist Church, the first formal Baptist-Orthodox dialogue was initiated which resulted in a very impressive *theological* document signed by five Baptist and five Orthodox clergymen and *scholars*. Yet more unprecedented practice was started when under the initiative of the Catholicos Patriarch Ilia II, Giorgi Bolgashvili was asked to preach once a week in the Orthodox Cathedral in Tbilisi. Slightly later the same Patriarch invited a 23-year old Baptist scholar and linguist to serve as a Bible translator for the Orthodox Patriarchal translation of the complete Bible into Modern Georgian. A Baptist *Choir* from the Cathedral Baptist Church was regularly invited to sing in the Orthodox Cathedral. By the end of the Gorbachev era the Georgian Baptists realised that they needed to get organised as an independent Baptist Church. Talks about Georgian Baptist independence started as early as 1988 at the *BWA* Assembly in Seoul, South Korea. Ultimately the Evangelical Baptist Church of Georgia was established in 1990. First of all it was recognised by, and accepted into, the *EBF*, and then the BWA.

After the collapse of the *Soviet Union*, when Georgia regained its independence, Baptist work expanded in three different directions: theological *education*, evangelism and diaconical ministry. A Theological Seminary and other educational programmes trained both *men* and *women* for the ordained ministry [see *Ordination*]. New churches were established all over the country. The Order of St. Nino was organised with a special emphasis on social work among the poorest of the *poor*, and has established 28 social action stations in the country.

Baptists revived their endeavours and took a number of bold initiatives in Christian philanthropy, becoming heavily involved in relief work among Chechen refugees and internally-displaced people. They have made considerable efforts to *contextualise* their ministry in the Georgian culture, at the same time seeking to be a prophetic voice [see *Prophecy*] for the people of Georgia. E.g. the Evangelical Baptist Church of Georgia has its own school of icon painters and has developed a style of *worship* along the lines of Orthodox liturgical traditions. On the other hand they have been boldly working for social justice, *religious liberty* and regional *peace*. Regardless of all the risks involved they have been supportive of fair elections and democratic developments not only in Georgia but in Ukraine and *Belarus* as well.

Due to the rise of religious *nationalism* the Georgian Baptists have been attacked by religious extremists. A lack of vindictiveness to those who have violently abused their buildings, destroyed 1,000s of copies of the Bible and other Christian books, and even threatened the lives of individual leaders in the church, has in itself been a bold testimony to the peaceful spirit of these Baptist Christians. The President of the country, Mr. Shevardnadze went the Cathedral Baptist Church in 2003 to apologise to the church for religious atrocities carried out by the extremists. The Evangelical Baptist Church of Georgia is a driving force for the *ecumenical movement* in Georgia. The Baptists facilitate the building of bridges of peace and cooperation between different churches, denominations and confessions. The opening of Bethel Baptist Centre was celebrated by all representative leaders of all Christian denominations and leaders of Muslim and *Jewish* communities of Georgia. In recognition of the Baptist work and witness in the contemporary society the head of the Baptist church was awarded the Lambeth Cross by the Archbishop of Canterbury [see *Anglicanism*]. The Georgian Baptist leaders keep fraternal relations with a number of Churches and meets regularly with their leaders including the *Pope*, the Ecumenical Patriarch, Oriental Patriarchs and leaders of the churches of the *Reformation* in Europe.

The Georgian Baptists in the country are organised in four regions and each region has its *bishop*, one of whom is female. The leader of the entire Church is the Presiding Archbishop (Malkhaz Songulashvili) who is responsible for the spiritual guidance and teaching in the church. The President of the Church (Merab Gaprindashvili) is in charge of church administration. Between meetings of the Church Councils, the *Synod* of the Church, which maintains a balance of lay [see *Laity*], ordained, male and female members, takes decisions. In 2006 there were 75 churches with a membership of approximately 5,000 and a community of some 18,000. The Georgian Baptist Union is a member of EBF, BWA and the *Conference of European Churches*.

MS & TP

German Baptist Brethren
See *Church of the Brethren*.

German Baptist Theological Seminary Elstal
Since 1880 the Union of Free Evangelical

Churches-Baptists in *Germany* has educated all its *pastors* and *theological* leaders at its own school. For over 100 years the Baptist Seminary was located in Hamburg, where it was founded. Due to the *political* situation and the division of Germany a second seminary (1959-91) was established in Buckow (c.50km east of Berlin) in the former German Democratic Republic. In autumn 1991 the two seminaries were reunited in Hamburg, but because of constraints of space the whole seminary moved to Elstal near Berlin in Oct 1997. In the year 2003 the German Baptist Theological Seminary Elstal was awarded *state* recognition and in 2007 it received college accreditation through the accreditation board of the Federal Republic of Germany.

The *Theologisches Seminar Elstal (Fachhochschule)*, its official title since state accreditation, educates both pastors and *deacons*. The philosophy behind the curriculum seeks to unite three elements – knowledge, personal development and practice. Therefore, the *students* will be

(1) educated in theological *science*;
(2) trained to develop their personality regarding their later *ministry* and
(3) prepared for all the leadership tasks that they will have to face as pastors and deacons in churches or other institutions.

The Theological Seminary Elstal offers a three-year Bachelor degree programme (BA) in *Protestant* Theology, and a two-year Master degree programme (MA) in Protestant Theology, for those who already have the BA degree. Moreover, it offers a four-year part-time Bachelor degree programme (BA) in Diaconics.

The Seminary has connections to various university theological departments in Germany and other theological schools, as well as enjoying a cooperation agreement with the *International Baptist Theological Seminary* in Prague. It is also a member of the *Consortium of European Baptist Theological Schools*. Currently, the seminary has about 90 students and nine full time professors.

VS

FURTHER READING: G. Balders (ed), *Festschrift. Hundert Jahre Theologisches Seminar des Bundes* *Evangelisch-Freikirchlicher Gemeinden. 1880-1980*, Oncken, Wuppertal und Kassel, 1980. G. Balders (ed), *Festschrift 125 Jahre Theologisches Seminar*, Theologisches Gespräch, 2005, Beiheft 6. Adolf Pohl (ed), *Die Ernte ist groß. 25 Jahre Theologisches Seminar des Bundes Evangelisch-Freikirchlicher Gemeinden in der DDR. 1959-1984*, Evangelische Versandbuchhandlung, Berlin, 1983. www.theologisches-seminar-elstal.de.

Germany, Baptist history in

Baptist work in Germany started in 1823, when the young German-born, *missionary*-minded bookseller merchant, *Johann Gerhard Oncken* (1800-84) was sent to Hamburg as an agent of the 'Continental Society for the Diffusion of Religious Knowledge over the Continent of Europe'. Converted [see *Conversion*] in a *Methodist* congregation in London, he devoted himself to spreading the gospel and to founding churches [see *Church Planting*] all over continental Europe. After 11 years of difficult work among the people of the poor harbor-district in Hamburg, Oncken asked the American Baptist *pastor* and professor of *theology*, Barnas Sears, then teaching in Halle, to perform the initial rite of believers' *baptism* on himself and a group of six believers. On 23 Apr 1834, the day after the baptism, Professor Sears organised those who had been baptised into a church and ordained [see *Ordination*] Oncken as *elder* and preacher.

In the following 50 years, Oncken, together with capable and devoted partners (Köbner and Lehmann a.o.) and a host of workman missionaries, founded and organised Baptist churches all over Germany and in more than a dozen European countries. This endeavor was supported by the establishing of a publishing house (1828), a constituted Baptist *union* (1849), and a Theological Seminary (1880) [see *German Baptist Theological Seminary Elstal*]. At the time of Oncken's *death*, the German Baptist family in Europe counted 165 congregations with more than 30,000 *members*.

Among the *Free Churches* in Germany today, Baptists are by far the largest in number. However, the *Bund Evangelisch-Freikirchlicher Gemeinden* (BEFG) [Union of Evangelical Free Churches (Baptists)] in Germany is the only Baptist group with official state recognition as a body of public corporate rights (K.d.ö.R.). In 2008, BEFG churches numbered 836 with 84,098 members. However, total membership of free Baptist congregations is estimated higher than that, because it also comprises churches and groups of international origin, most of them having come to Germany after WWII, the majority coming from the former *Soviet Union*.

BEFG churches, however, are not entirely Baptist. In 1942, the BEFG was formed by *state* intervention, which forcefully joined the then existing Baptist union to the German branch of the **Plymouth Brethren** (Brüdergemeinden) to create an artificial 'church' which still exists today. In 2008, the BEFG counted 132 congregations of Brethren with a total membership of 9,113 (10.8% of the total membership).

BEFG churches are affiliated through the union's office to the **European Baptist Federation**, the **Baptist World Alliance**, the Ecumenical Council of Churches (ACK) in Germany, the German Evangelical Fellowship (DEA), the Alliance of Evangelical Free Churches (VEF) in Germany, and they take part in **bilateral conversations** with other churches in Germany and the Community of **Protestant** Churches in Europe (CPCE). They are signatories of the **Charter Oecumenica** on a German level, but have – together with other Free Churches – refused to sign the agreement on Mutual Acceptance of Baptism (Taufanerkennung) in Magdeburg of 29 Apr 2007. Since 2000, they have commissioned through the VEF a speaker for the free churches at the seat of the German government in Berlin.

Baptist churches of the BEFG generally adhere to these Baptist principles held worldwide:

(1) The *Bible* as authoritative for belief and action [see *Authority*];
(2) The *autonomy of the local church*;
(3) The *priesthood of all believers*;
(4) The baptism of believers only;
(5) The individual freedom of *faith* and *conscience* [see *Freedom of Conscience*];
(6) The upholding of social justice;
(7) The *separation of church and state*.

These theoretical principles, more his-torically than biblically conditioned, constitute the frame for a large diversity in matters of practice. This applies to differing ways of and views on *evangelism*, *worship*, church order, social responsibility, as well as to differences on theological and ethical [see *Ethics*] issues. It is, therefore, not frightening, that German Baptists differ on important issues – e.g. *women* in church leadership, exegesis and *hermeneutics* of the Bible, the appreciation of non-Christian religions, the effective meaning of *salvation*, the theological priority of a union of congregations (BEFG) as compared to the autonomy of a *local church*.

DL

FURTHER READING: Dejan Adam, '"The Practical, Visible Witness of Discipleship": The Life and Convictions of Hans Meier (1902-1992)', Keith G. Jones and Ian M. Randall (eds), *Counter-Cultural Communities*, Paternoster, Carlisle, 2008.

Girl's Brigades/Girl's Life Brigades

See *Boy's Brigades and Girl's Life Brigades*.

Gifts of the Spirit

See *Fruits and Gifts of the Spirit*.

Globalisation and Multinational companies

[See also *Capitalism*]

Globalisation is the process of increased integration and dependence between nation-*states* especially as trade and investments increasingly move across national boundaries. However, globalisation can also describe greater cultural exchange between countries, or global *environmental* threats such as *climate change*.

As an economic process, from the 1980s to the time of writing, the increase in global economic integration has made its impact throughout the world with a lower involvement of the nation-state in economic affairs. For instance, in Eastern Europe and Central Asia following the collapse of the *USSR*, a radical liberalisation of economies has been pursued, often under the tutelage of the International Monetary Fund (IMF). Similar structural adjustment policies recommended by the IMF were also closely followed throughout Latin America and sub-Saharan Africa in the 1980s and 90s.

The main debate concerning greater economic integration between countries is whether it has been driven by technological change, and thus is beyond the control of states, or whether it is the result of conscious governmental actions through reduced government intervention in the economy. For instance, developments in computer technology have lowered the costs of financial transactions, allowing movements of vast amounts of capital rapidly between countries. However, states such as China, Chile and Malaysia have still shown that regulating these financial flows is possible.

The process of globalisation has created large multinational corporations which work across many different countries, and often control more *political* and economic power than the states in which they operate. Multinational companies, often called Transnational Corporations (TNCs), own a large proportion of global investment and technology, and so states compete with each other to offer the best-terms on which a multinational company can operate in a country. Whilst many economists and international institutions have claimed this process extends the opportunities for countries to grow more prosperous, there are fears that there is a consequent decline in the conditions for workers, and the amount of tax governments can collect. Moreover these extremely powerful corporations seem often to stand outside any framework of democratic control, whilst, in their day-to-day operations, demonstrating a measure of tyranny in the lives of 1,000s of people. A Christian conscience against such operations has been persistently articulated by the **World Council of Churches**. Thus its Nairobi Assembly (1975) declared, 'TNCs are a typical example of the ways in which capitalist forces in the international and national sphere join together to oppress the *poor* and keep them under domination'.

Globalisation has created opportunities for countries such as China, India and Vietnam to increase their prosperity at high rates, which has also created the potential to cut poverty in those countries. However, the 'paradox of globalisation' is that those countries which have taken greatest advantage of globalisation are those which have most rejected the dominant paradigm that governments should not interfere with the running of an economy. In contrast, Latin American, sub-Saharan African and former USSR states which have followed drastic liberalisation policies have seen their economies stagnate and poverty increase.

Globalisation adds new dimensions to concerns for justice in a far from just world. Globally, the gap between rich and poor has continued to increase. The process of globalisation appears actually to have caused greater inequality in the world, with the terms of trade between rich and poor needing urgent adjustment.

TKJ

Glossolalia

Glossolalia is the technical term for the phenomenon of 'speaking in/with tongues', sometimes called 'ecstatic speech', that is, the ability to *pray* or praise God in a language that has not been learnt. Generally regarded as distinctive of **Pentecostals** and **charismatics** there is some evidence of its occurrence from time to time in the history of the **church**. The NT records that after the coming of the **Spirit** to the church on the day of **Pentecost** they 'began to speak in other languages, as the Spirit gave them ability' (Ac 2:4). The experience is repeated at other points recorded in Acts and was manifested in the church at Corinth to which Paul gives detailed instruction concerning its use and management in the church's gatherings for **worship** (1Co 14). In contemporary experience glossolalia has been the cause of considerable controversy and disagreement among Baptists. Some believe that all the ecstatic or supranormal gifts of the Spirit ceased with the emergence of the NT canon and so any contemporary claims to exercise them must be illusory, fraudulent or, in the extreme, demonic. Others have insisted that the gift received at Pentecost was literally the ability to speak other known languages whereas contemporary glossolalia is 'preconceptual' or unintelligible speech and so cannot claim to be of the same order. Others have held that tongues are a form of spontaneous utterance at the level of the intuition, similar in nature to spontaneous *music*, and that it is a natural human ability which becomes sanctified by the Spirit to add intensity to prayer and worship. The exercise of such gifts must always be tested against *scripture* and it is generally agreed that such utterances should only occur in public when somebody with the gift of interpretation is also present.

NGW

GM Foods

For 12,000 years farmers have collected, saved and planted seeds that had desirable characteristics, making use of natural genetic variety. New strains were developed by cross-pollination, a relatively random process in which many seedlings would be produced and grown on, but only those few, if any, with increased potential would be retained. So crops with higher yield and drought resistance were developed.

Genetic engineering enables this process to be carried out with greater precision. Genes linked with specific characteristics are identified, then removed or inserted. The novel aspect is that genes can be inserted from widely-separated species, not possible by 'natural' procedures akin to cross-pollination. Some examples of such genetic engineering are:

- Tomatoes with a longer shelf life, produced by removing the gene that triggers a ripening process.
- A human gene transplanted into bacteria to produce human insulin.
- A gene from arctic fish incorporated into cereal crops to allow growth in colder climates.
- Increased vitamin and mineral content in cereals, e.g. 'vitamin A rice' to counter blindness through vitamin A deficiency.
- Increased resistance to viral, fungal and bacterial diseases.
- Increased resistance to *environmental* stress such as drought and salinity.

The range of genetically modified (GM) crops is now considerable.

Christians are divided in their attitude to GM crops. Factors in this concern are:

- Most development is commercially-driven.
- Patents are held by *multinational corporations* which both sell the seed and the herbicide to which it is resistant.
- Greater weed control might affect the food chain of other species and reduce biodiversity.
- Cross-pollination of GM crops with natural plants might generate herbicide-resistant weeds.
- Cross-pollination with 'organic' crops.
- Much turns on whether we regard the production of GM crops as 'playing God' and usurping the *sovereign* rights of the creator, or whether this is *humankind*'s call to be co-creators with God, and to work in this way as one part of the answer to world hunger.

JB

FURTHER READING: Donald and Ann Bruce, *Engineering Genesis: The Ethics of Genetic Engineering in Non-human Species*, Earthscan, London, 1998. Donald Bruce and Don Horrocks (eds), *Modifying Creation? GM Crops and Foods: A Christian Perspective*, An Evangelical Alliance Policy Commission Report. Paternoster, Carlisle, 2001.

Good Friday

See *Great Friday*.

Gospel and Culture

[See also *Contextualisation*]

Gospel and Culture refers generally to the relationship between the Christian *faith* and the cultural contexts in which it takes shape, and more specifically in recent discussions to a movement building on the work of the *missionary bishop* and *ecumenical* statesman, Lesslie Newbigin (1909-98), who after 40 years of *ministry* based largely in India, was shocked by the lethargic condition of the Western churches on his 'retirement' back to *Britain* in 1974. He began a thoroughgoing critique of Western culture in a series of studies *The Other Side of 1984* (1983), *Foolishness to the Greeks* (1986) and *The Gospel in a Pluralist Society* (1989). He argued that Christianity had become so domesticated in European culture and Western civilisation that it had lost its ability to speak into this longstanding context, and was also increasingly dismissed as out of date and too Western by the cultures of Asia and Africa. The German **theologian Ernst Troeltsch** (1865-1923) similarly saw Christianity as intimately entwined with Western culture (e.g. *Die Absolutheit des Christentums*, 1929). Newbigin argued that the gospel existed in a triangular relationship between the delivering culture, the receiving culture, and the gospel itself, which was in transmission and stood over against all cultures.

Many appreciated the pungent critique which Newbigin brought, but critics of his approach have pointed out that the gospel has never existed in an uninculturated form. Others preferred the earlier analysis of the American theologian and ethicist, **H. Richard Niebuhr** (1894-1962), in his influential study *Christ and Culture* (1952) which also wrestled with a triangular dynamic in an ongoing **dialogue**, in this case **Christ**, **Church** and Society (Culture). Niebuhr articulated five possible models for the relationship between gospel and culture:

(1) Christ against Culture;
(2) Christ of Culture;
(3) Christ above Culture;
(4) Christ and Culture in Paradox;
(5) Christ the Transformer of Culture.

At the heart of the discussion is the recognition of an inherent tension: if the gospel is to be communicated at all there needs to be a process of translation into the language and idiom of a given culture which will inescapably relate to ideas and practices already current, to that extent human cultures are affirmed; but the gospel will equally inevitably challenge all cultures into which it is translated, unless through a process of assimilation and syncretism it becomes domesticated and loses its cutting edge; so culture also stands under judgement. The **Methodist missiologist**, Andrew F. Walls (b1928), has characterised this as the tension between the 'indigenising' principle and the 'pilgrim' principle (*The Missionary Movement in Christian History*, 1996).

Recent discussion has focussed particularly on the complex relationship between Christianity and Western culture, especially addressing the historical legacy of **Christendom** on the one hand (as in the work of **sociologists** Grace Davie and Daniele Hervieu-

Léger) and the contemporary relationship with Western **capitalism** on the other (e.g. in the work of Baptist theologian, John Drane). The former aspect has naturally tended to focus on Western Europe and the latter on the influence of American/Global models.

Baptists, drawing on both the continental **Anabaptist** tradition as well as the English **Separatist** tradition have often advocated a counter-cultural approach (e.g. recently Stuart Murray, Nigel Wright), which we might denote as 'Christ against Culture' in Niebuhr's paradigm. But some have tried to suggest the possibilities for a positive, if still critical, engagement (e.g. Paul Fiddes, Nicholas Wood), as in Niebuhr's final model of 'Christ the Transformer of Culture'. The latter approach has been important in a strategic Baptist initiative in the development of the Oxford Centre for Christianity and Culture at **Regent's Park College**, Oxford.

Latest trends have seen various attempts to wrestle with the ambiguity of postmodernity or 'liquid modernity' (Z. Baumann) and its implications for what is often termed 'emerging church' as in Pete Ward's (b1959) creative construction of *Liquid Church* (2002).

NJW

FURTHER READING: G. Davie, *Europe: The Exceptional Case*, Darton, Longman and Todd, London, 2002. J. Drane, *The McDonaldization of the Church*, Smyth and Helwys, Macon, Ga., 2000. P.S. Fiddes (ed), *Faith in the Centre: Christianity and Culture*, Regent's Park College, Oxford and Smyth and Helwys, Macon, Ga., 2001. A. Kreider (ed), *The Origins of Christendom in the West*, T&T Clark, Edinburgh and New York, 2001. S. Murray, *Post-Christendom*, Paternoster, Carlisle, 2004. L. Newbigin, *Foolishness to the Greeks*, Eerdmans, Grand Rapids, Mi., 1986. L. Newbigin, *The Gospel in a Pluralist Society*, WCC Publications, Geneva and Eerdmans, Grand Rapids, Mi., 1989. H.R. Niebuhr, *Christ and Culture*, Faber, London, 1952. A. Walls, *The Missionary Movement in Christian History*, T&T Clark, Edinburgh and Orbis, Maryknoll, NY, 1996. A. Walls, *The Cross-Cultural Process in Christian History*, Orbis, Maryknoll, NY, 2002. P. Ward, *Liquid Church*, Paternoster, Carlisle and Hendrickson, Peabody, Ma., 2002. A. Wessels, *Europe: Was it ever really Christian?*, SCM, London, 1994. N.G. Wright, *Disavowing Constantine*, Paternoster, Carlisle, 2000.

Government/Polity, Church

See *Church Meeting; Ecclesiology (Church Polity); Synods*.

Grace

The 'Amazing Grace' [Greek *charis*], that the *hymn* writer John Newton so rightly affirms, is absolutely central to *evangelical faith*, but though so important, it is too little understood, and its meaning too little explored. Crucial alike to the holding of human society in good order, and to the *salvation* of the individual, grace is not to be conceived of as a substance that can be measured or accumulated. Rather it essentially represents the action of the divine initiative, doing for the world what it could not do for itself. So it is the *love* of God which is the engine force that empowers both that 'common grace' which prevents the physical, social and *political* order from falling apart, and more familiarly, the special grace of God that both takes the initiative to secure sinners' [see *Sin*] redemption, and challenges the individual by faith to accept this gracious provision. Baptist writer, Keith Clements, argues, '*Theology* itself operates *sola gratia*. Unaided human reason cannot uncover the divine majesty; but faith beholds the condescension of God in the humanity of the incarnate [see *Incarnation*] and crucified [see *Atonement*] Christ.... In grace God reaches man in the very depths of his sinfulness, offering the *forgiveness* of sins as the beginning, not the end, of his ways with man.'

Thus in Eph 2, Paul writes, 'For by grace you have been saved though faith and this is not your own doing; it is the gift of God – not the result of works, so that no one may boast. For we are what he has made us, created in Christ Jesus for good works, which God prepared beforehand to be our way of life.' Grace is indeed 'unmerited favour', but in the early years of the church's history this became obscured by ecclesiastical overlays and it was left to St. Augustine to insist, once more, on the priority of grace, etching out starkly the radical and enslaving character of sin, which required resources way beyond the human will to right. Thus Augustine's doctrine of salvation is grounded in the operation of 'prevenient' grace, which alone

makes possible *repentance* and faith, an idea that was keenly developed by the reformers [see *Reformation*] in the 16th century, who came to affirm *sola gratia* as much as *sola fidei*. As **Roman Catholic** author, Johannes Bosseder of Cologne University, expounding **Luther**'s thought, expresses it: 'The gospel of Jesus Christ is grace; it proclaims the gracious God who in Christ has mercy on sinners. In faith human beings 'cling' to the Christ who ascends to the Father. God accepts believers who look in faith on Christ and justifies [see *Justification*] them by faith alone without any merits on their part, vesting them with the righteousness that is God's, since Christ has 'drowned' human sins in his death. Justification of sinners is God's act in Christ. It is actively proclaimed and they partake of it in faith. All this happens in the **Spirit**...Luther's doctrine of grace is a paean to the fact that God is not ours to command and that God alone is efficacious in what he does.'

Calvin, utterly convinced of human helplessness in sin, and inability to do anything to deserve God's favour, distinguished once more between the grace of Christ, which worked in people's lives to secure their salvation, to provide forgiveness, to restore their *fellowship* with the Father, and to nurture their Christian *discipleship*, and 'common grace', which restrained gross sin in society, secured decent behaviour, worked to promote human brother/sisterliness, inspired the artist and directed the scientist's enquiries into the natural universe. All was of grace. In the 20th century, however, Bonhoeffer wisely warned against manipulating grace into a false position which he calls 'cheap grace', in contrast to 'costly grace'. 'Cheap grace', whilst made to look like a highly marketable commodity in the marketplace of *preachers*, is in fact a denial of all that grace stands for, because it distances salvation both from Christ's costly sacrifice and from *The Cost of Discipleship*.

Just how 'prevenient' grace operated provoked considerable speculation, posing the question whether within a theological framework determined by the *sovereignty* of God, grace was 'irresistible? For Baptists this was worked out differently by those whose theology acknowledged General Redemption, and those affirming Particular Redemp-

tion [see *England*], with many subtly nuanced positions developed between the extremes of hyper-*Calvinism* and *Arminianism* in the years following.

ET

FURTHER READING: Dietrich Bonhoeffer, *The
Cost of Discipleship*, SCM, London, 1948. Timo-
thy F. George, *Amazing Grace: God's Initiative,
Our Response*, Lifeway, Nashville, Tn., 2000.
Philip S. Watson, *The Concept of Grace*, Epworth,
London 1959.

Grace before meals

The OT warrant for this is found in Dt 8:10
an emphasis which is fortified by the Talmud where the teaching is that it is 'forbidden to taste of this world without saying a
blessing'. This is the *Jewish berakah* [grace]
referred to in the gospels (e.g. Mt 15:36;
26:27; Jn 6:11, and clearly practiced in the
early church (e.g. Ac 27:35; Ro 14:6; 1Co
10:30). There is, however, a difference between OT and NT practice. In the OT form,
it is the name of God that is blessed not the
food itself; thus the characteristic Jewish
grace: 'Blessed are Thou, O Lord Our God,
King of the world, who has brought forth
this bread form the earth.' By contrast, as in
Lk 9:16, *Jesus* blesses the food itself. The
more our food seems to be the product of
human industry the more important it is to
remember that it is God who provides our
daily bread, and at the same time, because of
the faulty way in which *humankind* share
the produce of his good *creation*, to seek his
blessing on all who are hungry.

ET

Graham, Billy (b1918)

Billy Graham was born in 1918 near Charlotte, North Carolina, USA. He was brought
up a *Presbyterian*, but was baptised as a believer in 1938 [see *Baptism*], while a student
at Florida Bible Institute, and he became a
Southern Baptist. In 1943 he graduated
from Wheaton College, Illinois, a leading
evangelical institution, and in the same year
he married Ruth Bell. Billy Graham spent a
brief but effective period as *pastor* of a Baptist Church (the Village Church) in Western
Springs, a suburb of Chicago. He then
worked with Torrey Johnson, pastor of the

Midwest Bible Church in Chicago, and also
co-founded the interdenominational organisation *Youth for Christ*. In the spring of
1946 Billy Graham, then aged 27, became
part of a small team of Youth for Christ
evangelists who came to *Britain*. During six
months of continuous *evangelism* in Britain
in 1946-47 Graham, accompanied by Cliff
and Billie Barrows as his musical team [see
Church Music], spoke in 27 centres and on
360 occasions, an average of about two
meetings a day. The YFC comment on the
City Hall rallies held in Birmingham in 1947
was typical: Birmingham was 'in the grip of a
revival'. Billy Graham made four further
transatlantic trips up to 1949.

It was Graham's Los Angeles Crusade of
1949, when such celebrities as Stuart Ham-
blen, a popular cowboy singer, Louis Zam-
perini, an Olympic track star, and Jim Vaus,
a wiretapper with underworld connections
were converted [see *Conversion*] which guaranteed Graham's position as America's foremost evangelist. As a result he was invited to
undertake a major 'crusade' in London. This
was held at the Harringay Arena, London,
from Mar-May 1954, and was arranged by
the *Evangelical Alliance*. The scale of the
Harringay Crusade, with an aggregate attendance of over two million at all associated
meetings, including 120,000 at Wembley
Stadium, London, on the closing day – the
largest religious meeting in British history up
to that point – gave Graham the leading
evangelistic place on the world stage. The
London meetings were followed in the subsequent year by meetings in the Kelvin Hall,
Glasgow, *Scotland*. Many individuals were
affected, and Baptist churches, among others
received new impetus. Numbers of baptisms
in Baptist churches increased from around
5,000 per annum in 1954/55 to around
7,000 in 1956/57.

Billy Graham's *ministry* became thoroughly global – he has *preached* to more
people than any other *Protestant* minister –
but in the period of the *Cold War* he had a
particular interest in reaching into the
Communist countries in Europe. Often his
contacts were with Baptists. After delicate
negotiations he was able to speak at large
meetings in *Hungary* in 1977. In the following year he spoke in *Poland*. Here he gave
his first sermon ever in a *Roman Catholic*

Church. Through the efforts of the Russian Baptist leader, Alexei Bychkov, Graham was able to speak in Moscow in 1982, including addressing a *peace conference*. There were a number of further visits to Eastern and Western Europe by Billy Graham and his team, both to speak at large events and to be involved in organising and running major conferences – e.g. the Amsterdam '83 conference and Mission England in 1984. From the 1990s Billy Graham's direct involvement in Europe diminished. The Billy Graham Evangelistic Association sponsored Amsterdam 2000, a world conference for evangelism in 2000 which was attended by 10,000 people, and although Billy Graham himself was not able to attend due to ill *health*, he gave the final address on video via satellite. His influence in Europe has surpassed that of any other Baptist figure.

IMR

FURTHER READING: W. Martin, *The Billy Graham Story*, Hutchinson, London, 1991.

Great Awakening

The term Great Awakening is usually used with reference to a major *revival* among *Protestants* in America in the 18th century. The best-known American *preacher* in this Awakening was Jonathan Edwards (1703-58). During his *ministry* in Northampton, Massachusetts, revival broke out in 1734 and 1735 and awakening spread to cover New England in 1740-42. In 1734 Edwards began to preach a series on 'Justification by *faith* alone'. He said: 'Very suddenly, one after another, five or six persons were to all appearances savingly converted'. Concern about spiritual matters became universal in the town. 'The work of *conversion*...increased more and more, souls did as it were come by flocks to *Jesus Christ*.' By the spring and summer of 1735 the town, Edwards said, 'seemed to be full of the presence of God'. Over 300 were converted in six months, which may have been a quarter of the population. Edwards wrote about the events in his book *A Faithful Narrative of the surprising Work of God in the conversion of Many Hundred Souls in Northampton and the Neighbouring Towns and Villages* (1737). Not only was Edwards at the fore-

front of the revival movement, through his writings he developed a *Calvinist* understanding of the gospel, which was both faithful to the reformer's [see *Reformation*] thought and open to urgent *missionary* enterprise.

The Awakening also owed a great deal to George Whitefield (1714-70), who was ordained [see *Ordination*] a *deacon* in the *Church of England* at the age of 21. There was intense interest in this 'boy preacher'. He was accepted by the Society for the Propagation of Christian Knowledge to assist in ministry to Native Americans and Colonists [see *Colonialism*] in Georgia and as he toured before his departure in 1738 great excitement was generated by his preaching. His initial visit was short and he returned to *England* to be ordained *priest* and raise funds for an *orphanage* in Georgia. It was while touring southern England in 1739 that Whitefield initiated the public revival which was the beginning of the *Evangelical* Revival in England.

Whitefield returned to America on 17 Sep 1739. The dramatic events of the Great Awakening in New England meant that Whitefield's ministry turned in that direction. Indeed the wider awakening did not begin until the arrival of Whitefield in 1740. This proved to be the greatest *evangelising* episode in the history of the area. On one occasion an estimated 20,000 people heard Whitefield preach in Boston. This phase of the revival continued for about 18 months, although Whitefield was there for only six weeks. In New England, out of a population of about 250,000, perhaps as many as 50,000 were added to the churches as a result of the Awakening. Almost half of Whitefield's later ministry was in North America.

There were direct links between the Awakening and the renewal in Particular Baptist life in England in the 18th century. A number of young Baptist ministers were influenced by Whitefield. Also, in the 1780s an English Baptist minister, John Sutcliffe, published a famous book by Edwards, *An Humble Attempt to promote an explicit agreement and visible union of God's people through the world, in extraordinary Prayer, for the Revival of religion, and the advancement of Christ's kingdom on earth, pursuant to scripture promises and prophecies con-*

cerning the last time. Out of this came what Sutcliffe hoped for – many **prayer meetings** focussing on the spread of the Christian message around the world. This vision for world mission was one factor contributing to the formation of the **Baptist Missionary Society** in 1792.

IMR

Great Britain and Ireland, Baptist history in

See *England; Ireland; Scotland; Wales, Baptist history in.*

Great Commission

The command of **Jesus Christ**, reported in two highlighted **Bible** passages (Mt 28:18-20; Ac 1:8), was first given to the 11 **apostles**, but this task is now inherited by the whole **church** as its principal **mission** responsibility which resonates with the whole missionary thrust of scripture It is on this responsibility that Paul focuses in Ro 5:18-19 when he contrasts the activities of the first and the second Adam. Although God's work in **creation** is all too soon spoilt by Adam's **sin**, bringing judgment on the whole human race [see **Fall**; **Humankind**], Adam had initially been charged as God's vice regent with replenishing the earth. In Christ, the second Adam, God has provided the prospect of a new order, created in him and manifested in his church, with the same essential demand of reproduction. This, it will accomplish through **evangelism** – that is literally the proclamation of the good news – with social action as an attesting partner or demonstration of the truth of the proclamation. Baptising in the name of God, according to contemporary **Jewish** custom, meant to certify to the individual and to others that the person baptised belonged to God. Following this concept today, **baptism** represents an individual's public **confession** of a deliberate act of **repentance** of past sin and trust in Christ for all that the future holds. The commission also lays on the church a teaching **ministry** quite crucial for part of the distinctiveness of the instruction is that, in contrast to earlier reticence about a mission to all peoples here it is confirmed that the **salvation** to be found in becoming disciples of the risen Christ is, without qualification, for peoples of 'all nations'. It is after announcing this missionary task that Jesus assures the disciples of his presence, a presence for those who give themselves in mission.

Theologically, it is assumed that the absolute fulfilment of the Great Commission will come about at the Return of Jesus Christ [see **Eschatology**]. Indeed this lead to the early 20th-century imperative in **student** and missionary circles, 'Evangelise to a finish and bring back the king'. Yet, while eagerly anticipating Christ's Second Coming, two queries must be noted in order to avoid misconceptions. Nobody can determine to what extent the gospel has been spread in the world before this can take place, nor are we provided with the criteria by which to determine that the gospel has been effectively heard by an unbeliever. Taking these two issues into consideration, even the slightest attempt to predict the precise circumstances of Christ's return is in vain and may be seen as a misuse of mission.

More than that such speculation can become a distraction from the urgent task as set out at the end of Matthew's gospel. By contrast, Baptists in Europe, from at least the time of **Carey** in **overseas mission**, and **Oncken** in **church planting** across Europe, have been effective implementers of the Great Commission. Oncken's telling phrase 'Every Baptist a missionary' is sure testimony to this, as also are the histories of the **BMS**, **EBM**, and **EBF**'s Indigenous Mission programme amongst many other initiatives.

EV & ET

Great Friday

[See also *Easter liturgies*]
This is the day in **Holy Week**, part of the **Easter** season, or Pascha, when the **death** of **Jesus Christ** is remembered. The practice of remembering the events of the death of Christ did not happen in the first centuries of Christianity as Christians believed they already lived in the age to come by virtue of their **Baptism**. However, the evolution of Holy Week in later centuries gave to this Friday before Easter a special pattern of recalling the death of Christ. Most Baptist

communities will hold a special reflective service on that day, sometimes actually relating to the period of the day when Jesus hung on the *cross*, but in countries where the day is not a national holiday, then often in the evening. The traditional *Reproaches* of God echoing the Prophet Micah and developed in *Spain* in the Gallican services of the 9th century are not commonly used by Baptists, though contemporary variations exist in *worship* resources that some Baptists use. There are some instances of Baptists holding services of Tenebrae (the extinction of all lights and leaving the worship space in darkness).The practice of open-air re-enactment of the journey to the cross and the crucifixion as a form of *witness* still exist in many communities, often acted out in public squares and market places, with some using the forms developed in Jerusalem in the 4th century, as described by the nun Egeria.

In some countries Baptist communities will often take part in a procession of witness, many of which are shared with Christians of other *traditions*. In *Georgia* a six hour service is held in the main Baptist church in Tbilisi. In some other churches in Europe services up to three hours in length might be held. Whilst many churches will have worship in a standard format with a *sermon*, in others, the occasion is used for a more reflective pattern of worship reading the account of the Passion, perhaps with the placing of symbols, such as a cross and crown of thorns, at the front of the worship room as visual aids to reflective remembrance. In other countries especially where this Friday is a bank holiday it is not uncommon for there to be rallies in the afternoon and evening either of an *evangelistic* nature or for the development of the spiritual life, promoted by organisations like *Christian Endeavour*.

It is not normal to have *Eucharistic* services amongst Baptists on Great/Good Friday, as it has traditionally been thought that the celebratory nature of the Eucharist was incompatible with a day of sorrows, though in recent years liturgists [see *Liturgy*] have argued that this is indeed acceptable.

KGJ

Great Thursday
[See also *Easter liturgies*]

The Thursday after *Palm Sunday* and before *Great Friday* is a day when the events of the Upper Room, the Last Supper or institution of the *Eucharist* are recalled in Baptist congregations in line with much of the Christian world. In some congregations the pattern of *foot washing* as part of the *liturgy* is practised with the *pastor*, elders or *deacons* washing the feet of some, or all, of the congregation. In others the occasion is used to link with the older *Jewish* tradition of eating a *Passover* meal of roast lamb, bitter herbs and unleavened bread, together with appropriate *scriptures* linking the OT story with the *Holy Week* narrative.

In many countries the service is very sombre and serious, symbolising the impending darkness of the passion narrative and reaches a proper climax in the Eucharist as the link is made with the events of Holy Week, though, strangely, there are countries, such as *Estonia*, where the Eucharist is not part of the *worship* on this day. The British language of Maundy Thursday derives from the Latin words for the new Commandment [*mandatum novum*] given by *Jesus* to the disciples. In the *state church* foot-washing has been replaced by a ceremony which moves from cathedral to cathedral in which the ruling monarch, in replacement of foot washing, gives purses of Maundy money to worthy citizens of that locality, which from time to time have included local Baptists.

The development of this event and indeed of the whole Holy Week belongs to the 4th century in Jerusalem when the attempt was made to link the culminating events of the *ministry* of Jesus with the days of their occurrence. The focus of the worship on this day rests in a remembrance of the events, or the anamnesis as expressed by the *apostle* Paul. Whilst there is scholarly debate about the relationship of the Last Supper to the Passover, what is undoubtedly true is that the depth of the service on this day lies in our recalling and identifying with the events in the Upper room, but more than that, we are drawn into a profound anticipation of the future and the final *eschatological* meal of the *kingdom of God*. In certain places the occasion has been used, especially among the *Free Churches*, for Christians to cross denominational boundaries and to join together at the Lord's Table.

KGJ

Green Politics

See *Ecology and the Environment*.

Greenbelt

See *Spring Harvest and Greenbelt*.

Growth, Church

See *Church Growth – theory and practice*.

Guides

See *Scouts and Guides*.

Guilt

The word 'guilt' can mean the state of having transgressed the law or the emotional reaction to feeling oneself in the wrong. Breaking human law brings objective guilt. Being at enmity with God's will brings subjective guilt. Guilt is therefore a result of *sin* and sinfulness. If feeling guilty leads to *confession* and *forgiveness* it can be a healthy emotion. On the other hand in the modern world many who are guilty have no sense of guilt, believing 'if I can get away with it, that is fine'. At a more fundamental level there is little sense of *humankind* having rebelled against God and falling far short of his intentions for healthy living (Ro 3:23), past failures which we in our own strength are incapable of undoing. At the heart of the gospel is a message of *salvation* and no-one should read this entry without reading the parallel entry on forgiveness, for the NT always holds the two closely together.

An overemphasis on sin and an underemphasis on *grace*, however, can lead to unreal and unhealthy guilt signified by the idea of possessing a 'guilt complex'. This can occasion an over-active scrupulosity, and can inhibit action or lead to clinical depression. To deal with guilt requires listening and patience, so that true guilt may be distinguished from false guilt and the possibility of forgiveness opened up. Guilt may also lead to a beginning of consideration for the other. E.g. this can be seen when a hitherto neglectful child realises that a parent is dying. Then energetic efforts to make up for lost time may ensue. Many Baptist *conversion* stories suggest that guilt for past actions spurs a person to service when a new life in *Christ* is discovered. So guilt can have both negative and positive results.

Collective guilt is a difficult concept. E.g. how can Western-European *nations* really repent of the actions of their forebears in the Slave Trade? How can *atonement* be made? Can a nation be held accountable for the actions of its leaders in the past? To what extent was the German nation responsible for the actions of the Nazi regime? Whilst establishing present responsibility for events deep in history must remain problematic, it is certainly possible for a group, a class, a nation to be corporately responsible for injustice and oppression, or for a generation to become consumed with a trivialising of moral standards even as in *scripture* Israel was found guilty of departing from God's way and breaking his *covenant*.

DBM

FURTHER READING: Mary Anne Coate, *Sin Guilt and Forgiveness*, SPCK, London, 1994. *New Dictionary of Christian Ethics and Pastoral Theology*, IVP, Leicester, 1995.

Gypsies

See *Roma people*.

H

Haldaneite Tradition

Robert (1764-1842) and James Alexander Haldane (1768-1851), were strongly influenced concerning their Christian *faith* and future *ministries* by David Bogue an Independent *minister* in Gosport, Hampshire, who met the brothers during their naval careers. His itinerant work in Hampshire, *England*, was the model for the Haldanes' own Scottish Society for the Propagation of the Gospel at Home (founded in 1797), a society launched following their failure to gain permission from the British Government in 1796 for *mission* work in Bengal, India. Bogue's small seminary for the training of preachers was the model for the Haldane seminaries in *Scotland* that trained around 300 *men* for *itinerant* work as catechists and *evangelists* between 1799 and 1808, the year in which the Haldane brothers adopted Baptist views. In addition, independent *preaching* centres were erected by them between 1798 and 1808, resulting in the constitution of around 85 new churches, of which more than 20 followed them into Baptist ranks between 1808 and 10.

James, pastor of an Edinburgh church from 1799 until his death in 1851, was a prolific writer of nearly 30 books and pamphlets, mainly on the person and work of *Christ* and on *ecclesiology*, but including also biblical commentaries [see *Bible*]. He was one of the main leaders of the Baptist Home Missionary Society [see *Home Mission*] in Scotland from its formation in 1827 until his death.

Robert, by contrast, after some chastening conflicts with former Independent colleagues, turned his attention to Christian work in Continental Europe between 1816 and 19. His first port of call was Geneva where a largely lay-led [see *Laity*] renewal of *Evangelical* Christianity, under *Moravian* influence, was given greater public prominence and a more rigorous biblical basis by the contribution of this Scottish *theologian*, through his lectures on the Epistle to the Romans. A similar influence was exerted on *Reformed* ministerial students at Montauban in *France*. Robert served as a teacher and mentor to around 25 *theological* students including Frederic Monod, Cesar Malan, Henri Pyt, Louis Gaussen and Merle d'Aubigne. In that list Henri Pyt, whom Haldane had baptised [see *Baptism*], played an important role in the establishing of Baptist work in France. Robert was also one of the founders of the interdenominational Continental Society, under whose auspices *Oncken* started his great work in Hamburg. Oncken kept in touch with Haldane and his circle in Edinburgh, discussing with them the issue of believers' baptism. Advised to baptise himself, as *John Smyth* had done, Oncken refused because of his failure to find such a procedure in the NT.

Robert published less than his brother James, but his literary output was more influential. His *Epistle to the Romans* was his most prominent biblical exposition, though his most influential works concerned the doctrine of scripture: *Evidences and Authority of Divine Revelation*, the first of edition of which was written in 1816 and *On the Inspiration of Scripture* (1828), correcting earlier evaluations of scriptural inspiration which followed Philip Doddridge's understanding that different parts of scripture reflected different degrees of *inspiration*, taught full plenary inspiration and advocated total biblical *inerrancy*. The classic text promoting this opinion, *Theopneustia* was produced in 1841 by Haldane's theological disciple, Louis Gaussen. Haldane's views were much publicised when he opposed the Bible Society's use of versions of scripture which included the (uninspired) books of the Apocrypha alongside the inspired books of the Christian canon.

The influence of the Haldanes was seen in the work carried on by the men they had trained for Christian ministry in activities such as home mission and theological education. James, unlike Robert, was supportive of moves to establish a *union* of Baptist churches in Scotland and was also an active participant at the formation of the *Evangelical Alliance* in 1846. Their influence spread to North America, especially Canada, where some of the men they trained were prominent Baptist leaders and church planters, including John Edwards (1780-1842), William Fraser (1801-83) and John Gilmour (1792-1869).

BT & ET

FURTHER READING: B.R. Talbot, *Search for a Common Identity: The Origins of the Baptist Union of Scotland 1800-1870*, Paternoster, Carlisle, 2003. T.C.F. Stunt, *From Awakening to Secession: Radical Evangelicals in Switzerland and Britain 1815-35*, T&T Clark, Edinburgh, 2000.

Hamburg Agreement

This agreement was made between seven representatives of the *European Baptist Federation* and six officials of the Foreign Mission Board, now International Mission Board, of the *Southern Baptist Convention* (FMB) meeting 11-12 Sep 1992 in Hamburg, *Germany*. The meeting was held as a result of the decision of the Trustees of the FMB to renege on an agreement to provide funding for *IBTS* after the ownership of the seminary was passed from the FMB to the EBF in 1988. The FMB had promised a declining scale of support for a period of years.

This action had led to widespread distrust of the FMB amongst leaders of the EBF and of the member *unions*, so the Hamburg agreement sought to establish a basis for future relationships between European Baptists and the FMB. The agreement called for mutual respect, moral integrity, genuine consultation and reciprocal sharing in which partners learn, work and grow together.

In the intervening years there has been regular consideration of whether the agreement remains operative and respected. Generally, many European Baptist leaders do not feel the Hamburg Agreement is properly respected by the FMB and in consequence several unions in Europe have declined to work with the FMB, believing they do not engage in genuine consultation, nor does it respect some European Baptist unions.

KGJ

FURTHER READING: John W Merritt, *The Betrayal: The hostile takeover of the Southern Baptist Convention and a missionary's fight for Freedom in Christ*, R. Brent and Co., Ashville, NC, 2005.

Harvest Festival

Harvest Thanksgiving as a special moment in the liturgical year [see *Christian Year; Liturgy*] has its roots in the very earliest aspects of the Judaeo-Christian *tradition* where the people of God were encouraged to give thanks for the provision of food and the safe gathering in of the grain and fruits. This tradition continues in baptistic communities and is especially focused upon those churches in agrarian settings, though most Baptist churches in Europe will have a harvest festival Sunday between late Aug and Nov dependant on local seasons and traditions. Whilst food security is not widely seen as a current European challenge, communities are increasingly challenged by the apparent fragility of the harvest as countries experience *climate change*.

Generally, such liturgical celebrations will involve a display of local harvest produce in the *worship* room and traditional songs and *hymns* for the harvest season will feature as part of the Ordo. The *preaching* may also pay particular reference to the theme of thankfulness to God for the bountiful gifts of his *creation*. In coastal areas the accent may well be on the harvest from the sea.

In some settings, especially in cities where local experience is remote from harvest, there might be an emphasis either on the international sources of so much that we eat or on those situations in the world where there is not an abundant harvest and the focus of the offering might be on support for the aid and development work of *Baptist World Aid* or a similar relief and development organisation. Today, given the concerns about *environmental* issues, harvest thanksgiving may also focus on a *theology* of creation care.

Where there is a display of harvested produce for the special festival this might be the focus of a post-liturgical feast, or might be distributed amongst the *poor* and needy of the local community. In some communities this *agape*, or love-feast, is one of the highlights of the church year, especially in more rural parts of Europe with a strong farming tradition such as the *Ukraine*.

KGJ

HBA

See *Hungarian Baptist Aid*.

Health, Sickness and Healing Services

Given the healing miracles recorded in the gospels, and the dominical command to heal the sick (Mt 10:8), Christian *ministries* can hardly ignore ministry in this area. Practically this has been effected through dedicated research and the development of a professional health service available to all, regardless of their ability to pay for such services, in many countries. *State* provision has been supplemented by such movements as *deaconess* care of the *poor*, the more recent ministry of parish nursing, and the establishment of *hospitals* and *hospices*. Talk of 'divine healing' as if this were in some way superior to the healing ministry of dedicated doctors and nurses is to be resisted as imposing a false duality on human nature. Rather, the ministry of the healing profession can in this sense be seen as a sharing in 'the *sacrament* of divine care and *providence*', though this is not to deny the impact of a ministry of *Word* and *Prayer* as well.

The gospel record however also records liturgical action [see *Liturgy*] for the healing of the sick, such as the *confession* and the pronouncement of the *forgiveness* of *sins* (Mk 2:5), the *laying on of hands* (Mk 6:5; 16:18), anointing with oil (Mk 6:13) and the offering of prayer (Mk 9:29). In Jas 5:14-16 a summary of such actions is offered, which is accordingly often cited in texts for such services. The biblical texts [see *Bible*] are careful not to suggest that sin, particularly of the individual, is the source of all sickness, but at the same time to provide for confession and forgiveness as part of a healing ministry, as also the exercise of *faith* both by the community – the people's lack of faith in Nazareth, we are told, prevented *Jesus* from healing there (Mt 13:58) – and by the one who is sick (Mk 5:25-34). Whilst clearly individuals exist who need healing of both sin and *guilt*, care needs to be taken over too easy and uninformed diagnoses of the causes of mental illness and how such illness may be overcome.

At the time of the *reformation* there was a general movement in *protestant* churches away from a sacramental approach to such actions. Indeed some deemed the more deliberate acts such as the laying on of hands and anointing with oil as only appropriate in the *apostolic* age. Protestant use of anointing was only recovered in the 20th century with an increasing realisation of the limitations of medical *science* and the need for wholeness in Christian ministries; the old English *Hal*, from which the word Health derives means 'whole' and is also the source from which 'holy' [see *Holiness*] comes. Healing, increasingly seen as intrinsic to a gospel understanding of *salvation* and the renewal of *humankind*, has led to the renewed availability of forms of *worship* including both anointing and laying on of hands, either within a *Eucharistic* context or standing on their own. Not a large number of Baptist churches have developed specific healing liturgies (using appropriate scripture readings/psalms, prayers, and symbolic actions) for use in church, though sick members of the church would often form a defined object of sustained and specific intercession, and it would be part of good *pastoral* practice to visit the sick in their homes or in hospital and read scripture and pray with them. Baptist convictions on assurance have generally precluded any need for any special service prior to the *death* of a believer. As prayer for the sick can be answered without physical recovery, so death is not an end that can be avoided, but it is properly Christian to maximise efforts that all may die with dignity.

By contrast, the witness of healing as well as the *exorcism* of demons has played a large part in the worship of *Pentecostal*, *charismatic* and *diaspora churches* (as also within particularly the Marian tradition of the *Roman Catholic* Church) as well as playing a large part in their search for authentication of their claims of access to special sources of spiritual power [see *Fruits and Gifts of the Spirit*].

JHYB

Heaven, Hell and the Future Life

[See also *Annihilation and Universalism*; *Kingdom of God/Heaven*]

Whilst in time past Heaven and Hell were seen respectively as on the one hand an encouragement to *faith*, and on the other, a caution on unbelief, they are less frequently the subject of *preaching* in the 21st century to the point where essential Christian teaching is underplayed. The threat of hell in a society in which premature **death** was an ever-present reality was widely welcomed by those responsible for the good order of society, thus the Bristol Baptist bookseller, Joseph Cottle arguing in favour of the disciplinary force of future retribution, pondered 'what an appalling image would society present if all the salutary checks founded on **Satan** and Hell were wholly removed'. This was a view shared by Baptist thinkers and writers such as Robert Hall and Andrew Fuller [see **Fullerism**], who did not hesitate to teach the prospect of Eternal **Judgment**. In the wake of the Downgrade Controversy, the Baptist Union of **Great Britain** in 1888 reaffirmed its belief in the Final Judgment whilst anathematising both the doctrine of Purgatory and Universalism, though noting that not all **ministers** held the common interpretation of **Jesus**' words in Mt 25:46. The Biblical [see **Bible**] concepts of heaven and hell turn around the ideas that whilst heaven or paradise (see Lk 23:43) is defined by the presence of God in the midst, by contrast Hell [Heb. *Sheol*; Gk. *Hades*], indicates a place of total exclusion from God from which there could be no access to him. This is in fact the appalling state rather than the place of physical torment depicted in medieval 'doom' paintings. That said, it should be noted 'it is impossible to soften the severity of Jesus' warning against unrepented **sin** [see **Repentance**], and the sentimentalism that seeks to do so is a distortion of the teaching of Jesus and the NT as a whole' (Alan Richardson).

In the NT teaching about Heaven and Hell is clearly intended to discourage any form of escapism or evasion of responsibility for the welfare of the world in which God has placed his **saints**; rather such teaching was there to invigorate and illuminate life in the present. In just such a way Martin Luther King used his 1963 future 'dream' speech in which he envisioned a world of justice and freedom for all peoples to live in harmony, to strengthen his impatience with the present conditions under which black people in America lived. The writer C.S. Lewis reinforces this view: 'It is', he wrote, 'because Christians have largely ceased to think of the other world, that they have become so inef-

fective in this. Aim at heaven and you get the earth thrown in: aim at earth and you will get neither.'

In the promise of heaven Christian **hope** provides something more than a strategy of depriving death of its prey, or of simply knowing how to survive beyond the grave. It is about moving from a life of limitations, declining capacities, with a body increasingly frail, punished with disease and pain, to a higher and more fulfilled level of experience. Thus the Christian view of heaven enables the Christian to face death boldly without fear or panic. It provides the motivation for doing God's will in this world whilst aiding the transition to the next world, because the assurance is that what lies beyond the grave is **fellowship** with the Risen Lord. It is the **resurrection**, according to the **apostles**' teaching that provides the hope of heaven. Apart from the pictures given to John in the vision he received while in exile on the island of Patmos, the NT is not over full in what it has to say about heaven, though what it does say is full of assurance. Paul speaks to the church at Corinth about God's secret purposes for his saints who are, he says, to experience 'things beyond our seeing, things beyond our hearing, things beyond our imagining, all prepared by God for those who love him' (1Co 2:10). In other words heaven is a very wonderful place but words do not exist to give a trust-worthy account of it; indeed more than that it is even beyond human imagining. That is why attempts to do what cannot properly be done seem so trite and simplistic.

Whilst John talks about a New Jerusalem, it is quite clear that the New Jerusalem and Old Eden have much in common – the themes that are so important in the Genesis story all appear again in Revelation. In the first place, Eden is characterised by God's presence 'walking' in the garden: and the New Jerusalem is distinguished by the presence of the Lamb, a presence responsible for every aspect of life in the heavenly city. This being the very nature of the New Jerusalem, Heaven, in contrast to the old Jerusalem, needs no specially dedicated temple. In Heaven the presence of the Lamb provides all that is required; Heaven needs no moon or sun, for from the Lord God and the Lamb will shine forth all the light that is necessary, poetically captured in the idea that in Heaven there will be no more night. Again, God's throne is in Heaven, which is to say, in picture form, that in heaven his *sovereignty* will be recognised by all. Peter puts this slightly differently, 'We have his promise and we look forward to a new heaven and a new earth, the home of justice' (2Pe 3:13). The Tree of Life is still in the picture, now in duplicate, one tree on either side of the river. So Heaven is not without its garden, indeed we may think of it as a 'garden city'. But now the trees of life are not remote, surrounded by prohibitions, but fully accessible, and very productive, for their leaves are for the healing of the nations, suggesting the end of all wars and enmity between peoples. So note the contrast. In Genesis Adam and Eve are driven out of Eden, which is guarded with cherubim, each bearing a sword, whirling and flashing to guard the way to the tree of life. But in Revelation, John is careful to say, 'The gates of the city shall never be shut...The *wealth* and splendour of the nations shall be bought into it, but anything unclean, false or foul is to be excluded.' The wealth and splendour of the nations will find their proper place in Heaven, indicating that it is not necessary to leave behind all the rich heritage of poetry and art and *music*; rather, in so far as these are good and wholesome, they can be embraced and brought within the gates. And unlike well-guarded Eden, Heaven has open gates. That is to say, it does not exclude, rather the open gates represent the wide embrace of the inclusive *love* of God. Moreover the curse on Adam and his progeny, Cain and the men of Babel, is lifted, so that all those things that came in with Adam's sin are reversed. Following on Adam and Eve's disobedience, sin and *violence* multiplied. Cain killed his own brother, and the men of Babel planned to assault heaven by their own endeavours by building a tower into heaven: the picture is of a world soon grown old with sin and the multiplication of violence and selfishness. This is why John puts such an emphasis on everything being new – a new Heaven and a new earth, and the Lamb upon the throne saying, 'Behold I make all things new.' So work is redeemed. No longer will it be toil, but Heaven will not embrace a soul-

destroying idleness, rather there will be work in which each person finds self-fulfilment. 'The Christian' it has been said, 'dies in hope, not of reclining on some billowy cloud, or playing a harp in timeless eternity, but of entering into the quality of life which God originally made man to enjoy.' No longer will *men* and *women* suffer pain. Human relationships will be mended and all will be in right relationships, one with another. Cain's sin is reversed 1,000 times for in Heaven there will be no more death, no more crying, no more mourning, no more disease, – The Lord himself will wipe away our tears in a world made new for joy. And of course Babel has already been reversed by *Pentecost* – but Heaven itself is, in fact, that city that reaches to the heavens, which human ambition cannot construct, for its builder and architect is God himself. The New Jerusalem is a city full of voices: *men* and *women* and little *children*, deeply engaged in conversation one with another in perfect communication, with everybody fully understanding everybody else. But part of that buzz of voices is the singing of psalms of praise, for Heaven will also be a place of grateful *worship*.

The Church at Corinth asked Paul a number of questions about this – How are the dead raised? In what kind of body? Paul answered them by referring to the metaphor of the farmer or gardener sowing a seed, which has all the appearances of a dried-up husk. It is that dead-looking thing, that worn-out shell that survives when the beauty of the flower has long-time faded, its fragrance gone, no longer dancing in the sun of God's midday sun. But, says St. Paul, it is that poor dried-up thing, which has all the appearance of death, which has within it all the secrets of who you are, and it is from it that God will raise a new plant, 'and clothe it with a body of his own choice' (1Co 15:38). 'What is sown in the earth as a perishable thing is raised imperishable. Sown in humiliation, it is raised in glory; sown in weakness, it is raised in power; sown as an animal body it is raised as a spiritual body.' Paul compares the first Adam, the Adam of Eden, with the second Adam, even Jesus, and says 'as we have worn the likeness of the man made of dust, so we shall, in the New Jerusalem, wear the likeness of Jesus, the man from heaven'. Now even the man made of dust had within him the promise that he was made in the image of God, so what St. Paul is promising in the heavenly existence is a renewal of that image with the presence of the *Spirit* to make it a reality. Even with Jesus there was a difference between his pre-resurrection and his post-resurrection body: his post-resurrection body could do things which his pre-resurrection body could not, – moving from place to place, walking through closed doors, ascending to his Father, but the Risen Christ was more than a ghost or un-embodied spirit; he could eat breakfast. Even as there was enough of the old Jesus about the Risen Christ, for the disciples to recognise him, so in Heaven people will recognise one another. Thus scripture affirms that in Heaven Christians will possess new bodies wherein all the old limitations of their earthly bodies are overcome, but they will not be so different that they do not recognise one another. Personal identity is secure. Jesus spoke to the disciples about preparing a place for them, concluding with the assurance 'Where I am, there will you be also'. So once more his presence is the defining principle of the heavenly experience.

ET

Hell
See *Heaven, Hell and the Future Life.*

Helwys, Thomas (1550-1616?)
Thomas Helwys, a *wealthy* lawyer, was one of a small group of English *Separatists* who left *England* for Amsterdam in 1608 to escape persecution under James I. Together with *John Smyth*, Helwys became a leader in an English-speaking congregation in Amsterdam. In 1609 this group became the first ever Baptist church when Smyth baptised himself and the other *members* [see *Baptism*], and two years later Helwys produced his *Declaration of Faith of English People* (1611), setting out the view that each congregation 'though they be but two or three, have *Christ* given them' and they 'are the body of Christ'. Later 31 members of this group, including Smyth had doubts his se-baptism, applied to join the *Mennonites*. Helwys, however, along with others, uphold-

ing the rightness of the baptism they had received from Smyth, opposed the application, and decided to return to England where in 1612 they established a Baptist church in Spitalfields, outside the city of London – the first Baptist church on English soil. This was the beginning of the General (*Arminian*) stream in Baptist life. Helwys published *A Short Declaration of the Mistery of Iniquity* (1612), a historic document on religious toleration addressed to James I. Helwys argued that while God had given the King 'all worldly power' there was also a *heavenly kingdom* and 'with this kingdom our lord the king hath nothing to do (by his kingly power) but as a subject himself: and that Christ is king alone...' The 'earthly sword' exacted justice, but had no *authority* over *consciences*. In some of the most famous words of the *Short Declaration*, Helwys bravely announced that 'men's religion to God is betwixt God and themselves; the king shall not answer for it, neither may the king be judge between God and man. Let them be heretics [see *Heresy*], Turks, *Jews* or whatsoever, it appertains not to the earthly power to punish them in the least measure'. Helwys was not destined to see the fruit of his call for liberty. He was imprisoned in Newgate prison and died in either 1615 or 1616.

IMR

FURTHER READING: I.M. Randall, 'Early English Baptists and Religious Liberty', *Anabaptism Today*, Issue No. 4, 1993. B.R. White, *The English Baptists of the Seventeenth Century*, Baptist Historical Society, Didcot, 1996.

Heresy
Heresy denotes a religious belief which seriously diverges from or dangerously distorts normative Christian beliefs as determined by *scripture*. Heresy then represents the opposite of *orthodoxy*. In the NT the word denotes that which is *sectarian*, divisive, and *schismatic*, promoted by false teachers. In the early church the emergence of a succession of heresies (e.g. Gnosticism, Arianism, and Nestorianism) provoked the *Church* into a fuller definition of its beliefs in the development both of *apologetic* literature and the writing of *creeds* (the *Apostles'*, Nicean and Athanasian Creeds and the Definitions of Chalcedon) to clarify the proper

range of Christian beliefs Whilst the apostolic *faith* is properly to be defended, this must never be done in such an unloving way that the defence of the faith itself becomes an obstacle to commitment.

JHYB

Hermeneutics

[See also *Bible, Baptist understanding of the*]

Hermeneutics refers to the interpretation of different phenomena and is today interlinked with the philosophy of language/communication. The origins of the Greek term *hermeneuō* probably go back to Greek mythology (Hermes). Early *Jewish* interpretation of the law (Shamai and Hillel School, Qumran, Philo, Josephus and others) as well as Hellenistic texts such as Aristotle's *Peri Hermeneias,* became building blocks for Christian biblical hermeneutics. In its modern form the term emerged in the mid 17th century.

The history of Christian biblical hermeneutics begins in the 2nd century at just that time when the Christian canon was emerging, as early Christians tried to make sense of the Hebrew Bible and of the various writings that were circulating in the early church. Accepted as parts of the Christian Bible, they were organised as the OT and NT. Already the structure of the Christian canon offered a hermeneutical lens as to how the Hebrew Bible was to be viewed in relation to the canonical texts of the early church, and vice versa. Indeed this is seen in the *ministry* of *Jesus* himself when he both speaks of his own *death* as fulfilling OT scripture and interprets the OT in accordance with own ministry and *mission*. This raises the problem for hermeneutics of how both to respect the integrity of the OT writings in their own right but also to recognise their fulfilment in the life of Jesus.

In its search for identity amongst the plurality of different philosophies and vis-à-vis the Jewish community, the early church was inclined to use a Hellenistic rather than rabbinic Jewish hermeneutical methodology. Accordingly patristic hermeneutics became interwoven with neo-Platonic philosophy. This led to different types of interpretation, of which the allegorical was viewed by many

Bible interpreters as the highest form. Origen of Alexandria, e.g., championed allegorical interpretation but John Chrysostom opposed what he thought were his allegorical excesses. The Middle Ages introduced more diversity into hermeneutical methods, but still primarily followed patristic examples, though at this time *Tradition* became as important as scripture for the life of the *church*. The Reformers [see *Reformation*] set a different tone in biblical hermeneutics, prioritising the biblical text; their claim of *sola scriptura* reversed the significance given to Tradition by the late medieval church. For them, far from scripture and Tradition having equal *authority*, the word of scripture was the standard by which Tradition had to be judged, with a consequent reassertion of the importance of hermeneutics as they affirmed the clarity of the meaning of the text without need to resort to hidden meaning. The hermeneutical circle that formed itself around Schleiermacher marked the founding of the modern era of biblical interpretation, moving biblical interpretation on from romanticism and *dogma*-driven interpretation to a modern approach, deploying the historical-critical method (interpretation from behind the text), plying questions not only about the text itself but the experience out of which the text has arisen. Post-modern interpretation focuses more on the text (interpretation in the text itself: narrative, rhetorical, canon criticism, structuralism, etc.) and the reader (interpretation in front of the text: reader-response criticism, ideological interpretation, global perspectives, etc.) and expands the variety of methods, including the deconstruction of a text. Gadamer, Hirsch and Ricoeur with many others stand for alternative hermeneutical approaches.

The present task of biblical hermeneutics is to help the reader to understand the ancient religious writings that the church has used as its formative texts throughout history and which it still uses in the present day. Much of how one approaches and interprets a text depends on one's own personal pre-understanding. The spectrum of presuppositions in the European Baptist family moves from *inspirational, orthodox,* to the anticipation that random texts will provide guidance for making decisions, etc. In all of these different views there is a common understanding that scripture offers communication from God to individuals and to the community in a form which can be easily understood and grasped. The goal of Bible interpretation is to digest and act upon what an ancient text communicates to us. In the language of communication we have a sender, a receiver, and a medium. All of them need to be taken seriously in their·own specific context. Because the biblical text is not directly addressed to the modern recipient, the context, not only of the original recipients, but also that of the modern reader, is of critical importance. Basic aspects of interpretation focus on the words of the text itself. The broader approach looks at the language, structure, rhetoric, style, and genre of the text, all of which belong to the historical-critical/grammatical approach. The goal of this classical approach is to make the text intelligible to the modern recipient and at the same time coherent with the meaning intended by the original author. A majority of Baptist **biblical scholars** would identify with this approach. Some, however, would find text or reader-oriented interpretation of more value or add them to a classical reading.

Anabaptist and pietistic hermeneutics have been influential and formative in baptistic communities in Europe. Stuart Murray's *Biblical Interpretation in the Anabaptist Tradition* offers seven major distinctives of Anabaptist interpretation which Baptists have partly or fully adopted.

(1) Scripture is self-interpreting and
(2) interpretation is guided by Christocentrism which identifies the Christ in the text as both the saviour and a model for life.
(3) In the relationship between the OT and NT, the NT is given priority and the OT is read as fulfilled in the NT. This early Anabaptist view has sometimes been challenged by contemporary Baptist and Anabaptist biblical scholars.
(4) For Anabaptists, the authority of Word/Letter and **Spirit** had to be balanced and
(5) interpretation needs to take place within the community of believers.
(6) Hermeneutics leads to understanding and is incomplete without obedience to the text once interpreted

(7) In hermeneutics there is an enduring tension between the desire to discover coherence and to respect diversity.

Especially continental Baptists, under the influence of Pietism, have been shaped by the way in which group **Bible studies** have been conducted, emphasising the importance of both communal and individual Bible reading, **preaching** by those ordained and **theologically** trained for this ministry [see **Ordination**], but also by lay **church members** [see **Laity**], etc. A specific distinctive of Baptist Bible interpretation is their missional hermeneutics, which finds in scripture an obligation to train 'every Baptist to be a missionary' [see **Missionary congregations**]. One finds among Baptists a diversity of hermeneutical approaches, and a variety of interpretations on the same text as a result of such diversity, which may be considered a Baptist distinctive.

PFP

FURTHER READING: Gerald Lewis Bray, *Biblical Interpretation: Past and Present*, InterVarsity, Downers Grove, Il., 1996. David Ewert, *How to Understand the Bible*, Herald, Scottdale, Pa., 2000. John Goldingay, *Models for Interpretation of Scripture*, Eerdmans, Grand Rapids, Mi., 1995. Stuart Murray, *Biblical Interpretation in the Anabaptist Tradition*, Pandora, Kitchener, Ontario, 2000. Grant Osborne, *The Hermeneutical Spiral: A Comprehensive Introduction to Biblical Interpretation*, IVP, Downers Grove, Il., 1991. Peter Stuhlmacher, *Vom Verstehen des Neuen Testaments – Eine Hermeneutik*, Nandenhoeck and Ruprecht, Göttingen, 1986. Anthony Thiselton, *New Horizons in Hermeneutics*, Zondervan, Grand Rapids, Mi., 1992. Kevin J. Vanhoozer (ed), *Dictionary for Theological Interpretation of the Bible*, Baker Academic, Grand Rapids, Mi., 2005.

Herzegovina
See *Bosnia and Herzegovina*.

Hierarchy
See *Priesthood (hierarchical)*.

Historians, European Baptists in the 20th and 21st centuries
See *Church Historians, European Baptists in the 20th and 21st centuries*.

HIV-AIDS

When European and American scientists identified HIV (Human Immunodeficiency Virus) as the causal agent in AIDS (Acquired Immune Deficiency Syndrome) and indicated that this potentially fatal disease was rapidly spreading among individuals who were engaging in certain kinds of risky sexual practices, not only were national governments alarmed, but the churches were profoundly challenged. AIDS strikes at the very heart of human nature – sexuality – for HIV is mainly a sexually transmitted agent that destroys the body's defences and once embedded, is impossible to eradicate though AIDS can also be spread by intravenous (IV) *drug* users who share injecting equipment, as HIV is a blood-borne disease. Whilst the effects may be mitigated by appropriate and costly treatments, individuals still remain infectious. In Europe the disease is mainly, but not exclusively, found among promiscuous *homosexual* men and IV drug users, while in Sub-Saharan Africa the disease, which spreads as a pandemic, is located equally among the male and female heterosexual population. In some countries as many as 20-30% of the adult population may be suffering from AIDS which thus places another strain on the *nation*'s economy (e.g. training costs can be greatly increased as working lives become stunted). Here too the *sins* of the fathers being visited on their *children* is vividly seen in the cruel fate of AIDS *orphans*.

This disease, however, continues to be a significant *global* health threat. Where HIV originated is still a mystery and a question of debate but its spread is reasonably well documented. The disease is also well understood and its development from infection to *death* (in the absence of antiviral drug therapy) of about 12 years is recognised. The infective non-symptomatic period of about 10 years, poses a real community health problem. Individuals may not realise they are infected and so infect other sexual partners. However, even in the absence of antiviral drugs, much can be done to ease the suffering of persons in the symptomatic stages of AIDS. Professional and non-professional carers run no risk of infection through normal human contact, while maintaining simple hygiene practices.

HIV-AIDS is a profound challenge to lifestyle choices and two main preventive lines have been advocated. Firstly many groups including churches have advocated that persons should stay in faithful relationships and avoid risky sexual practices and IV drug use: abstinence before a committed relationship and then faithfulness within relationships. Secondly, health professionals have promoted the use of condoms during sexual intercourse. Both these approaches have advantages and disadvantages for containing this epidemic, however the number of HIV positive individuals is still rising and the cost of treatment and care is stretching healthcare budgets that have to meet increasing demands from other health issues.

As this is an issue which affects the whole of *humankind*, followers of Christ are called on to respond with great care, e.g. before simply identifying the AIDS pandemic with the *judgment* of God; some victims have been infected by contaminated blood supplies whilst partners and children have been infected through no fault of their own. Christians have always seen epidemics as an opportunity for *witness* and service. Disciples of *Jesus* are taught the biblical principle that sexuality is rightly contained within the bounds of a committed lifelong, loving relationship between a man and a woman. In the case of the HIV-AIDS epidemic many churches have based their response on the teaching and example of Jesus and in particular, looked to texts like the Good Samaritan (Lk 13ff). People affected or infected by HIV-AIDS must be seen as disciples' 'neighbours' and Christian communities have begun, and must continue, to develop policies and practices that promoted care without condoning the risky practices that people with AIDS may have employed. This has proved to be a challenging task, especially in the light of cultural norms and changing attitudes to homosexual behaviour. Issues around the nature of *love* and homosexuality are hotly debated generally but for some, including many Baptist congregations, their understanding of these issues involves an understanding of the transforming power of NT Christianity.

PC & ET

Holiness

[See also *Spirituality*]

A recurring theme in *evangelical* spirituality has been the reality of the power of the *Holy Spirit* to enable the Christian to live a life that is holy. The way in which this reality is understood has been far from uniform. There has been a tendency among Baptists and other evangelicals for the *call* to holiness to be understood as a call to follow a set of rules. By the later 19th century there were three distinct 'holiness' streams within evangelicalism – *Calvinist*, Wesleyan and *Keswick*. Jonathan Edwards grounded his view of holiness in a *theology* of the *Trinity* and the concepts of beauty and harmony. For Edwards the ultimate expression of holiness, which he described as 'the highest beauty', is found in the inner life of the Trinity. In the later 19th century, J.C. Ryle, *bishop* of Liverpool, wrote what became a classic work on living a holy life. Written from a robustly *Reformed* perspective, it was simply entitled *Holiness*. In an extended definition, Ryle suggested that holiness included 'the habit of being of one mind with God, according as we find His mind described in *Scripture*'. For John Wesley there was a definite stage and consequent condition that he called full or entire *sanctification*. This blessing was attainable, but once attained could be lost. At the heart of Wesley's thinking about the fully sanctified life were the concepts of an undivided desire to please and serve God and a 'perfect *love*' for God which excluded *sin*. This was not a doctrine of 'sinlessness'. There was, according to Wesley, no absolute perfection before *heaven*. In the mid-19th-century holiness teaching in North America and Europe was revitalised through such teachers and leaders as Charles Finney, Phoebe Palmer and William and Catherine Booth. Compared with John Wesley himself, holiness teachers of this period made more of instantaneous experience. One new variant of holiness teaching found its focus in the Keswick Convention. This was influenced by Americans such as Hannah Pearsall Smith, with her widely-read book, *The Christian's Secret of a Happy Life* (1875) and Evan Hopkins, Vicar of Holy Trinity, Richmond, through whom the *theology* of Keswick was to a large extent to be fashioned, saw three views of sanctification within late 19th-century evangelicalism. There was the Calvinist tradition that holiness was achieved by earnest effort; there were concepts, popularised within Wesleyan thought, of the 'clean heart', with sin eradicated; and there was the Keswick position that there could be a perpetual 'counteraction' of sin, although never the destruction of the sinful nature. Most Baptists in the 19th century followed the Calvinist view of sanctification. One well-known Baptist who embraced the Wesleyan approach was Oswald Chambers, who in 1901, following a League of *Prayer* event in Perth, *Scotland* (the League of Prayer advocated Wesleyan spirituality) was (as he put it himself) 'baptised with the Holy Ghost'. Keswick teaching on holiness became popular among many Baptists in the early 20th century but has been less influential in recent decades.

IMR

FURTHER READING: D.W. Bebbington, *Holiness in Nineteenth-Century England*, Paternoster, Carlisle, 2000. M.E. Dieter, *The Holiness Revival of the Nineteenth Century*, Scarecrow, Metuchen, NJ, 1980. J.C. Ryle, *Holiness*, Evangelical, Welwyn, reprint 1979.

Holistic Mission

[See also *Mission*]

The term 'holistic mission' has developed in debates about mission within various church councils in the 20th century. It carries the meaning of the Hebrew word *shalom*, which stands for wholeness, fullness, completeness, *salvation* and *peace*. Mission as shalom is frequently used in mission literature. The Greek word behind this understanding of mission refers to *holos* [whole, all, complete and entire] and sets the conceptual understanding of what holistic mission is. It is a clear reminder that the entire (whole) *church* is called to all (whole) mission.

As *conservative evangelicals* and *ecumenical* church representatives debated the issue of what mission is and is not, some polarisation and dichotomy has developed resulting in a separation of social involvement from *evangelism*. One group was over-emphasising social involvement as the primary goal of mission, underlining liberation, justice and peace on earth, whilst the other put the primary focus on *conversion*, salvation of souls and the spiritual aspects of mission that point to eternity. But the biblical [see *Bible*] mandate of God's mission in this world, specifically in *Jesus Christ*, which the church has received seems not to separate or prioritise, but demonstrates a holistic mission *call* and commissioning of the church, with all aspects of the work part of the task whilst recognising that the whole mission is something that is 'greater than the sum of its parts'.

Two NT texts are frequently used to illustrate this polarisation: Mt 28:16-20 and Lk 4:14-30. The so-called *Great Commission* is often said to support evangelism and Jesus' reading of Isaiah in Lk 4 as being fulfilled in his mission is meant to support social involvement of the church. But a close look at each passage demonstrates a holistic mission. Mt 28:16-20, while summarising the whole Gospel of Matthew, calls to a *discipleship* that integrates all the teaching from the five speeches with Jesus' actions, a discipleship that display a holistic mission in the words and deeds of the Master. The same is true for Lk 4:14-30, a text that covers all aspects of human life which the Messiah came to address in *preaching*, liberating and *healing*.

Holistic mission, then, means not to call for some specialised mission activities, to focus on some aspect of mission, to define what are the main and what are the secondary tasks in mission or to prioritise some aspects of mission against others. Holistic mission demonstrates a concern for the whole human being, for humanity [see *Humankind*] as such and for the entire *creation*. As *sin* has affected all areas of human life, society and creation, the church is called to join the mission of God (*missio dei*) who cares not only for some specific aspects of life, but who is creator, sustainer, saviour, healer, reconciler and redeemer [see *Redemption*] of the whole world, reaching out in order to bring healing and salvation, justice, peace and freedom in every aspect of a human, a society, a culture and the whole creation. God sends his church – people whom he called and changed so that they are able to do his mission – to join his mission in this world, following his example. The church is a community of people that should live in the world caring for it as

Christ demonstrated it in his life: serving, restoring, healing, preaching, celebrating, forgiving [see *Forgiveness*], changing, reconciling [see *Reconciliation*], loving [see *Love*], suffering and even dying [see *Death*]. In so doing they continue his work of inviting *women* and *men* into God's *kingdom* and demonstrating signs of God's reign in their life.

On the other hand, while continuing God's mission in this world, God's people should not be of this world. This points to the so-called Great Commandment (Mt 22:37-40), God's call is for men and women to belong to his upside-down kingdom, where the least are the first and where the one who wants to be first must be the servant of all. Holistic mission overcomes all kinds of racial, cultural, national, gender, social and other barriers, inviting all into a different kind of kingdom where all are welcome, wanted and equal in the eyes of God and his people. Holistic mission does not 'target' individuals and communities but non-violently invites and welcomes all who come and at the same time respects positions and decisions different to their own. Holistic mission demonstrates openness and space for *dialogue* but at the same time upholds the uniqueness of Christ as the Sent One of God, as the way, the truth and the life. In Christ, the church in mission is called to imitate and join in with God's calling and mission.

After a century of discussion, disagreement and polarisation on what mission is all about, it seems that an agreement is developing between various *theologians* of mission and missionaries on holistic mission. All sides are attempting to define holistic mission biblically and to focus on individual people, communities, societies, cultures and contexts and on the entire creation, in order to tear down hindrances for those invited to enter the kingdom, as proclaimed by various prophets of the OT, by Jesus, his disciples and the early church and throughout history by his faithful, in words, works and wonders.

PFP

Holland, Baptist history in
See *Netherlands, Baptist history in the.*

Holocaust
See *Anti-Semitism and the Holocaust*.

Holy Communion
See *Communion and Intercommunion; Eucharistic Liturgy; Sacrament Sign and Symbol*.

Holy Ghost, The
See *Pneumatology*.

Holy Kiss
See *Kiss of Peace*.

Holy Land, The
'The Holy Land' is the name generally given to the Land of Israel (so-called by *Jews*) or Palestine (so-called by Arabs). For most Arab Christians, this includes the geographic area west of the Jordan River, west of the Sea of Galilee, and west of the Dead Sea, south to the Gulf of Aquaba. It is considered holy by Jews, Christians, and *Muslims* because so much of God's *revelation* took place within this area, according to the different scriptural texts of each religion. Baptists in the Holy Land cherish biblical names, and the *Bible* calls this geographic area 'holy land' in Ps 78:54 and Zec 2:12. The Bible also refers to particular places in this Land as a 'holy temple', a 'holy habitation', and the 'holy city'; all references to Jerusalem in the OT, or to the *heavenly* Jerusalem in Hebrews and Revelation. 'Holy mountain' in the OT (19 references) also refers to Jerusalem, but in the NT 'holy mountain' (2Pe 1:18) is a reference to the Mount of the Transfiguration. For Baptist Christians, this Land has been blessed and set apart as the location where God chose to reveal his purposes, his *love* for *humankind*, and supremely the revelation of Himself through *Jesus Christ*'s birth, *ministry*, teaching, sacrificial *death* and *resurrection*. Our *salvation* was made possible in this Land. Historically, the Holy Land has often been anything but holy. Tragically, it has been an area where many wars have been fought, where great injustice has also taken place and continues to be inflicted

upon many people who live there. For some it has become an 'unholy land'. However, Baptists believe that they can contribute, in some small but significant way to the Land being justly again called 'Holy' as they *pray* and join in the struggle for *peace* and justice, rejecting the path of *violence* and following the example and teaching of Jesus.

AA

Holy Saturday
See *Easter Eve*.

Holy Spirit
See *Pneumatology*.

Holy Week
See *Easter Day; Easter Eve; Great Friday; Great Thursday; Palm Sunday*.

Home Mission
[See also *Mission*]
The founding of the *Baptist Missionary Society* led to renewed interest in home mission and the undertaking of new initiatives in *itinerancy* and *church planting* by several regional *associations*, and to the formation, in 1797, of The Baptist Society in London for the Encouragement and Support of Itinerant Preaching. In 1817 it became the Baptist Home Missionary Society. Apart from a redirection of its energies in 1835-47 into church *revival* it was chiefly concerned with church extension. Never prosperous, its survival was only guaranteed by uniting with the Baptist Irish Society in 1865. From 1878 it concentrated on rural *evangelism* until amalgamated with the Baptist *Union* of *Great Britain*, in 1882, at which time the concern was also for urban church extension. The work in *Ireland* was separated out in 1890, and in *England* the society's work was absorbed into the Home Mission Fund, which was largely interested in the support of *ministers* while still supporting some itinerant *evangelists* for a time. Home Mission is still the name of the fund to which Baptist Churches in Britain are invited to contribute: supporting the work of the denominational head-

quarters and those churches which cannot fully fund their own local witness plus a number of special projects it reflects the *holistic* nature of Christian mission. Every union in the *EBF* has its own form of home mission, which may involve the favouring of mission undertaken by indigenous *missionaries* as over against the costly presence of ex-patriot missionaries who may spend much time learning both language and culture, and even when these have been conscientiously undertaken still bring 'a foreign accent' to home mission.

DJT

Homeless, Work with the

An example of care for the homeless occurred very early on in the history of the continental Baptist movement. In 1842, the year in which the Hamburg Baptist Church moved to larger premises (a huge granary with three floors), the city was devastated by fire. The fire left 1,000s of Hamburg families homeless. *J.G. Oncken* offered the new meeting place to the authorities for accommodating the homeless and 80 people found food and shelter there for eight months. Such generosity caused the authorities to treat the *church* less severely and the previous persecution came to an end. Moreover, a number of those helped began to attend the services, and rapid *church growth* took place. There was a similar situation in the Memel Baptist Church in 1854, when again a terrible fire struck the city and the church became 'an asylum for the homeless', help that once more was much appreciated by the city authorities, and the attitude of the police changed from hostility to friendliness.

In the contemporary world, homeless/street people have in most cases suffered physical, psychological and emotional losses. One loss often leads to another and a troublesome life becomes even more difficult over time. These losses are connected to the person's relations to other people and to society as a whole. A consequence of other people's choices and actions can make homeless/street people experience a decreasing freedom of choice, meaning that their chances of changing their lives are reduced.

In a *welfare state* many institutions offer help to homeless people. However, to be a client is not sufficient in order to restore life. A Christian congregation can offer a supporting community, without *drugs* and crime – a secure environment in which to change life. For street people to recover, it is important to be supported and believed in. Recovery is a time-consuming process. Experience gained by a Baptist church working with street people in Oslo, *Norway* confirms these observations. In other countries street *pastors* and teams of street workers have begun working with these uncared-for people many of whom resist all forms of institutional support.

As human beings we are responsible for other humans, as all individuals are connected to each other. Helping people in need is also part of bringing the *kingdom* of *Christ* to the world, and it can help us to understand more about the nature of God.

NFS & ET

Homogeneous Unit Principle

The 'homogeneous unit' principle was first articulated by Donald A. McGavran, in developing his foundational ideas about *church growth*. He developed the homogeneous unit principle from the *Great Commission* that stresses the discipling [see *Discipleship*] of *ta ethne* ['all nations', 'all peoples' or, as *missiologists* may say today, 'all people groups']. It was understood that the commandment encouraged disciples to move freely across different borders such as those of culture, language and geography. McGavran pointed out additional boundaries as defined by economics, social class, religious confession, ethnicity, lifestyle, etc.

The homogeneous unit principle argues that, based on experience, people who have much in common are more likely to form and join a cohesive group that shares a common set of values, and that those with many differences face greater difficulties in developing into a group, or unit. Often it is not the gospel that makes it difficult for people to join a church, but rather differences in language, culture, ethnicity, and social status. In order to attract people to become Christians and join a community of believers, the homogeneous unit principle encourages the creation of communities that share as many values and attitudes as possible so that people with similar backgrounds feel comfortable without any need to cross sociological boundaries, but primarily step into Christianity as such without being forced to change their ethnicity, language, etc. In Central and Eastern Europe this would, for instance, mean that, because it is difficult to invite highly educated people into traditional baptistic churches, one would instead start a church that focuses all of church life around this societal group. In the West, where most baptistic churches are middle class, it may be quite difficult to integrate *homeless* people into the community. Instead, a city church may need to be started that would focus on this societal group and arrange all church life according to their needs and experience.

These two examples demonstrate the experience in a European context where the barriers may not necessarily be of nationality only but also of social standing. It is even more true when looking at this phenomenon from the point of view of different ethnic groups. Should *Jewish* people who come to *faith* in *Christ* join a church of Palestinian believers? Is it good to invite native Central Asians (e.g. Kazakhs, Kyrghyz, Uigur, etc.) into Russian-speaking and Russian culturally-orientated baptistic churches? Europe today has many churches which reflect the homogenous unit principle: based on race (e.g. Black-led churches or migrant churches defined by race such as Philippino, Korean or Brazilian congregations) or others defined by language (e.g. Franco-phone churches for Congolese in *England* or English-language churches for American British and Commonwealth personnel in Europe).

The debates about the homogeneous unit principle raise questions about whether it is biblical [see *Bible*], and also about *contextualised*, incarnational *mission* that attempts to adapt the gospel to the context [see *Contextual Missiology*]. Thus, present-day debates on reaching *Muslims* are informed by looking at the ways in which the church spread in the multi-faith context of the first few centuries of its existence. Some present *missiology* that refers to *sociology*, *anthropology* and ethnology seeks to provide arguments for the homogeneous unit principle as well as for other *evangelistic* and mission models. Usually much of the concept derives

from the modern *science* of humanities and interprets biblical texts from this perspective [see *Hermeneutics*].

The main arguments against the homogeneous unit principle come from texts such as Eph 1-2 where it is said that Christ has 'brought near' Jews and Gentiles 'through the blood of Christ' and 'destroyed the barrier, the dividing wall of hostility...to create in himself one new [hu]man[ity] out of the two' (Eph 2:13-15). There are many churches that have sought and do seek to work out this *theological* reality in practice, despite the challenges. Experience shows that differences can be bridged. At the same time, it is argued that a theological construct cannot be applied 'one to one' as in stone, but there is the dimension of being able to be led by the *Holy Spirit* in a particular situation, sometimes holding together and nurturing a multi-ethnic church and sometimes meeting separately.

The early church, as confirmed in the *praxis* of the NT, displayed a great variety of approaches in how to deal with these issues. One finds mono-ethnic, multi-ethnic, international church groups, persons from different social settings, worshipping both jointly and separately and each having good biblical grounding for it. It seems that the so-called *Apostolic* Council in Jerusalem was interpreted somewhat wider to respect the other approach and enjoy the way that God has led a particular church in its distinct context. In a multi-ethnic and multi-cultural world of the 21st century it seems that the homogeneous unit principle can neither be universally accepted nor universally disapproved of, but the church needs to be open to different practices.

PFP & ET

Homosexuality
[See also *Sexual Orientation*]
During the 1990s several Christian denominations in Western Europe considered the issues of homosexual orientation [see *Sexual Orientation*] and homosexual practice or same-sex relationships. There has been much discussion, controversy, disagreement, division and pain in parts of the Christian *Church* about this issue and in recent years it has threatened to split the whole *Anglican*

Communion. In this context there have been attempts by Baptists to engage with the issue. E.g., in 1998 the Baptist Union of Great Britain (BUGB) Council set up a task group to explore the subject in greater depth in order to enable the *Union*'s churches to understand both the *theological* and *pastoral* issues involved. The task group came to the conclusion that homosexuality (both orientation and practice) can only be fully understood in the wider context of the Christian understanding of Human Sexuality.

As Baptists have thought about human sexuality they have gone back to the teaching of *Jesus*, and of the *Bible* as a whole, and have also recognised that there is the need for the guidance of the *Holy Spirit* and for congregations to discern together how they should handle such issues. Sexuality is seen as part of God's good *creation*. This raises issues relating to *singleness, marriage,* cohabitation and *divorce*. Homosexuality (the attraction of one person towards another of the same sex) has always existed and homosexual people are to be found within Baptist churches. Western society has steadily become more tolerant of homosexual people with changes in legislation aimed at ending discrimination in civil rights, employment, etc. From a theological and pastoral point of view, Christians recognise that it is wrong to treat homosexuals as less than human beings made in God's image. There are few Biblical texts referring to the issue but those texts, which need to be read carefully both in terms of content and context, appear unanimous in their condemnation of same-sex genital activity. Although there are some variations in attitudes towards homosexuality among Baptists in Europe, most would, therefore, take the view that homosexual practice is against biblical teaching, although few would argue that homosexual orientation is in itself sinful [see *Sin*]. *Pastors* offering care to congregations which might include homosexual people require great pastoral sensitivity in areas such as the support of parents of adult homosexual people, *ministry* to new converts [see *Conversion*] in homosexual partnerships, and help for those in married relationships who disclose homosexual orientation. No Baptist union in Europe, however, would take the view that it

was appropriate for Baptist pastors to offer anything which could be interpreted as a *wedding liturgy* to two people of the same sex.

In 2001 the BUGB Council commissioned a group to produce an educational tool to enable *local churches*, colleges and *associations* to familiarise themselves with issues surrounding same-sex orientation and relationships. The purpose of this is to equip local churches to better debate issues and come to a considered view on its own policies on same-sex relationships. The material, produced in 2004 and tested with three different groups over 2004/05, is designed to be used over one day or in four evening sessions. It contains contributions from theology, *hermeneutics, pastoral theology, sociology* and those skilled in the study of human sexuality.

SCJ & ET

FURTHER READING: Baptist Union of Great Britain, *Making Moral Choices in Relationships*, BUGB, Didcot, 2000.

Hope

One possible way to describe the *church* is as 'a community of hope'. What then is the nature of this hope? Whereas secular hope represents an optimistic aspiration which may or may not be achieved – 'hope for'; Christian hope is 'hope from' – hope from the *resurrection* of *Jesus* to the complete accomplishment of the work of the *kingdom* (1Pe 1:21). Empowered by this hope the Christian walks by *faith* rather than by sight (2Co 5:7), trusting in God's purposes for the fruitful outcome of his/her earthly pilgrimage, which he/she undertakes in anticipation of entering into God's kingly rule in *heaven*. Christian hope is therefore more certain than secular hope for its fulfilment is rooted in an already accomplished act. That hope, not yet complete, is confirmed to us by the work of the *Spirit*, so Paul speaks of 'Christ in you, the hope of glory' (Col 1:27), whilst the writer to the Hebrews speaks of hope as 'a sure and steadfast anchor of the soul' (Heb 6:19). Peter believes this hope to be such a unique energising force of the Christian's life that he encourages Christians always to be ready 'to give an account of the hope that is within you' (1Pe 3:15). However, hope is not a merely private matter for the scope of God's kingdom is universal out of which arises the broader socio-political dimensions of hope.

Perhaps the **theologian** who has written most meaningfully about hope in recent times is Jurgen Moltmann in his *Theology of Hope* (1967) with its focus on the Resurrection as the ground of **eschatological** hope with its promise of the total transformation of all reality. The promise, then, is for the transformation of present experience with all its shortcomings and failings into a world in which God's rule is perfectly respected, that godly kingdom where justice, **peace**, community and **love** predominate, all this at the end of time. But this also becomes an incentive for world-transforming activity in the present, for if these kingdom values are God's ultimate will for his people, they must surely be what he wants for human societies now. Thus Moltmann uses his **theology** of hope to open the church at one and the same time both to God's future and **humankind's** present. So, says Moltmann, the church, in committing itself both to the proclamation of the gospel and to socio-political struggle for justice and liberation, is 'like an arrow sent into the world to point to the future'. The NT thus sees hope in God's future not as an excuse for inactivity now but as motivation to engage in the struggle for peace and justice. Social action, in such a perspective is grounded in Christian hope: it neither believes that it can of itself create the perfect world, nor does it yield to the many pessimistic predictions of future crises threatening the ultimate cataclysm.

ET

FURTHER READING: R. Bauckham and T. Hart, *Hope against Hope: Christian Eschatology in Contemporary Context*, Eerdmans, Grand Rapids, Mi., 1999. Jurgen Moltmann, *Theology of Hope*, Harper and Row, New York, 1967. S.H. Travis, *I Believe in the Second Coming of Jesus*, Eerdmans, Grand Rapids, Mi., 1982.

Hospices

The word 'hospice', which is currently used to describe residential facilities for those suffering from terminal illnesses, principally cancer, dates from the 4th century AD when various Christian orders welcomed travellers, the sick, and those who came to them in times of need. The word was first applied in terms of a refuge to care principally for the dying in **France** in 1842 and the **Roman Catholic** Irish Sisters of Charity began similar work in Dublin (1879) and London (1905). The next significant development of the movement is associated with Dame Cicely Saunders, in helping those with terminal cancer to die with dignity, in the **United Kingdom** in 1967. The modern hospice movement soon spread in the USA and across Western Europe. There are now over 8,000 hospices world-wide, many of which have a Christian foundation. Although many of the doctors and nurses who work at the hospices may be Christian, the patients can be of any **faith** or of none. It might be declared that hospices, who work with terminally ill people, are concerned to 'glorify God by affirming the sanctity and dignity of life' (from the mission statement of Southwest Christian Hospice in Atlanta, Georgia, USA). The staff not only look after the patients, they help them prepare for their **deaths** and also help the relatives prepare for the loss of their loved ones. The atmosphere at a hospice is principally a loving and caring one, where the patients and their relatives are encouraged to talk about death and dying. Most Christian-based hospices, in which Baptists have played a notable part, are concerned not only with the physical health of their patients but also with their emotional, psychological and spiritual health.

KGJ

Hospitals

[See also **Albertinen-Diakoniewerk Hamburg; Health, Sickness and Healing Services**] Christianity has always had a deep involvement in health and healing. The followers of **Jesus Christ** have taken seriously his **ministry** of healing from NT days until the modern era and the **church** has retained a keen involvement both in liturgical [see **Liturgy**] and prayerful [see **Prayer**] actions, such as the **laying on of hands** and **anointing** with oil for those who were sick and then, with the development of monastic communities, the care of those ill by use of available resources of medicine, nursing skills.

Baptists in Europe have principally been involved in the development of modern hospitals essentially through our **mission** agencies working in Asia, Africa and Latin America. In Europe and the Middle East, Baptists have not been greatly involved in the development of modern hospitals, unlike the **Roman Catholic** Church and Baptists in the USA. However there is a notable exception to this in the Albertinen hospital in Hamburg, which is a modern facility run by the German Baptists and with a good reputation, especially in cardiology and cardiac surgery.

Baptists often serve as **chaplains** in hospitals run by the **State** or by other charities.

KGJ

House Church movement

See **Restorationism/House Church movement**.

Hubmaier, Balthasar (1484?-1528)

Hubmaier might properly be viewed as the leading **Anabaptist theologian** of the Swiss and South German Anabaptists of the first generation. He was a leading figure within the radical **reformation**. Bergsten comments that he 'represented in all essentials the major principles of the English Baptist movement which emerged in the early 17th century'. He was a student at Freiburg in Breisgau and as a diligent **catholic** humanist **scholar** by 1509 at about the age of 24 (his exact date of birth is not known) he was a professor of **theology**. He followed his mentor, Eck, [Is this Johannes Eck, Luther's opponent? If it is I think you should say so] to the University of Ingoldstadt in 1512. After a time in Regensburg, he became a **priest** in Waldshut on the Rhine in 1523. By 1521 he had already been exploring the writings of the reformers and perhaps one of the reasons for him going to Waldshut was its proximity to Zürich, where he joined the Second Disputation in Oct 1523 and was soon regarded as a compatriot of **Zwingli** in the reformation endeavour. Hubmaier inaugurated his own reformation in Waldshut as part of this Swiss movement. He now prepared **Eighteen Theses** which parallel Zwingli's 67 theses. He was forced to abandon Waldshut and moved in exile to Schaffhausen where he started to use the phrase 'Truth is unkillable' (or, as often seen, the less exact translation 'Truth is immortal') which became his motto. He also appealed for **religious liberty**, especially in his document **On Heretics and those who burn them** (1524).

By 1525 Conrad Grebel declared that on the issue of **baptism** Hubmaier stood with them over against Zwingli and others in the **Prophezei School**. Hubmaier certainly developed theologically in this time of intellectual and theological ferment, being influenced not only by Zwingli, but also by Karlstadt and the Grebel circle. He was also a noted and attractive **preacher**. At **Easter**, on 15 Apr, Hubmaier and 60 others were baptised as believers by Reublin, one of the Zürich Anabaptist leaders. By this act, which reputedly took place in the **pulpit** at Waldshut, Hubmaier affirmed the Anabaptist vision. Hubmaier went on to baptise c.300 other citizens over the Easter season. At the same time a new **communion liturgy** [see **Eucharistic liturgies**] was introduced, Hubmaier proving more consistent to the Zürich scriptural reformation principles than his former compatriot, Zwingli. Waldshut capitulated to the Archduke Ferdinand in Dec 1525 and Catholicism was imposed upon the town, but Hubmaier fled to Zürich, where the council demanded he recant his Anabaptist views, then on to Augsburg, and later to Moravia, arriving in Mikulov (then Nikolsburg), in Jul 1526.

Here he received the protection of the Lords of Liechtenstein and the Zwinglian-influenced reformation, already in progress there, took a turn towards an Anabaptist perspective. Soon Anabaptist **worship** and church life were being practised and Hubmaier was writing not only about baptism, but about church life and the eucharist [see **Sign, Sacrament and Symbol**]. For a year he was the leading figure in the creation of an Anabaptist town. However, the Archduke Ferdinand, by now King of Bohemia and Margrave of Moravia wanted him for insurrection and the Lords of Liechtenstein delivered him to the Kreuzenstein fortress north of Vienna in Jun 1527. He was burnt at the stake in Vienna on 10 Mar 1528.

His writings which best expound his Anabaptist views are *On the Christian Baptism of believers*, *A Christian Catechism*, *A Form for water Baptism* and *A Form for Christ's Supper*, all contained in Pipkin and Yoder.

KGJ

FURTHER READING: Torsten Bergsten, *Balthasar Hubmaier: Anabaptist Theologian and Martyr*, Judson, Valley Forge, Pa., 1978. H. Wayne Pipkin and John H. Yoder, *Balthasar Hubmaier: Theologian of Anabaptism*. Herald, Scottdale, Pa., 1989. H. Wayne Walker Pipkin, *Scholar, Pastor, Martyr: The Life and Ministry of Balthasar Hubmaier*, IBTS, Prague, 2008.

Human Depravity
See *Fall, The*; *Sin*.

Human Rights
[See also *Amnesty International*; *Civil Religion*; *Human Rights Advocacy*; *United Nations (UN) – UN Universal Declaration on Human Rights and UN Agencies*]
The concept of human rights is rooted in mainly Western traditions of the dignity of the person and his/her individual, social, cultural and economic rights. It is enshrined in the 1948 Universal Declaration of Human Rights and subsequent legislation based on it, such as the European Charter on Human Rights which has been taken in to the legal framework of most countries in the *European Union*.

Baptists have tended to view human rights through the lens of a concern for *religious freedom* rooted in the Lordship of *Christ*, which has been a fundamental of their identity throughout Baptist history. James E. Wood describes religious freedom as 'the cornerstone of all human rights'. However in a world increasingly scarred by religious *violence* and suppression of human rights which sometimes appear to be as direct result of certain groups exercising their religious freedom, this assertion is becoming a matter of open debate.

Perhaps Baptists have not paid as much attention to the implications of human rights being based on the *imago dei* in terms of universal human rights and justice for all.

Glen H. Stassen claims that the *theological* roots of this wider concern for Baptists can be found in the writings of the 17th English radical, Richard Overton, who was influenced by both Baptist and *Mennonite* convictions. Overton was not only concerned for religious freedom, but a biblically-grounded [see *Bible*] passion for *democracy* for all and economic justice for the *poor*. He declared that all are equally born to natural rights 'delivered of God by the hand of nature'. Though Baptists have continued to make religious freedom their major concern a wider concern for human rights has never been entirely absent. The role of the British Baptist *missionary*, William Knibb, in the ending of slavery in the British Colonies [see *Colonialism*] in the 1830s, and the fearless advocacy of full human rights for blacks in the USA by Martin Luther King in the 1950s and 60s are two outstanding examples, both based on biblically-formed convictions which issued in actions to defend human rights.

More recently European Baptists have turned their attention to human rights concerns, most notably in the *European Baptist Federation* Anti-Trafficking Project established in 2005 to counter the trade in human beings, mainly young women and girls, being 'sold' into *prostitution* in the cities of Western Europe.

In the field of human rights itself recent debates have included the desire to revise the Universal Declaration to put more emphasis on *communal*, as opposed to i*ndividual* rights; and a concern amongst some Christians that to be faithful to the *imago dei* the 'rights' language must be balanced by a concern for the concomitant *responsibilities*. In the much more *secular* setting of contemporary Europe there has also been a debate as to whether human rights are 'foundational' and even replace religious belief in this regard. This has proved problematic when a secular vision of human rights has been used as a yardstick to judge religious questions and in so doing perhaps even to curb religious freedom. Michael Westmoreland-White and others have argued that human rights should rather be seen as a *lingua franca* [trade language] which enables those from the standpoints of different religious *faiths* or none to be able to converse together about the rights and values of contemporary **humankind** whilst preserving their foundational convictions. This seems to provide much more fruitful ground for Baptists to make a positive contribution to current debates on human rights.

AAP

FURTHER READING: John Gladwin, 'Human Rights' in D.F. Wright (ed), *Essays in Evangelical Social Ethics*, Paternoster, Exeter, 1979. C.J.H. Wright, *Human Rights: A Study in Biblical Themes*, Grove Books, Bramcote, 1979.

Human Rights, UN Universal Declaration on

See *United Nations (UN) – UN Universal Declaration on Human Rights and UN Agencies*.

Human Rights Advocacy

[See also *Amnesty International; Civil Religion; Human Rights; United Nations (UN) – UN Universal Declaration on Human Rights and UN Agencies*]

The struggle for human rights in the sense of freedom to think, believe and act has been intrinsic to the Baptist movement right from its beginnings, as the Baptists were confronted with restricting laws and rigid attitudes in the environments where they lived and worked.

The claim for *religious liberty* for themselves led the early Baptists in **England** to call for religious liberty for everybody. Already around 1612, **Thomas Helwys** wrote: 'for men's religion to God is between God and themselves: the King shall not answer for it...Let them be heretics, Turks, **Jews** or whatsoever, it appertains not to the earthly power to punish them in the least measure.'

Two decades later, in 1636, Roger Williams put the principle of full religious liberty into practice in the settlement of Rhode Island, which he founded. He also enlarged the scope of human rights to encompass 'earthly' matters: the land that he as well as 'the Pilgrim Fathers' lived in, belonged to the Indians and nobody else, he maintained.

Towards the end of the 18th century, Baptists in England were awakened, especially by **William Carey**, to the human need for the

gospel in other parts of the world, thereby realising what has recently been termed as the right for 'each person...to hear the good news'. But there were also implications to be drawn from the gospel as to how human society should be organised and this made the Baptist **missionaries** implacable enemies of the practice of 'sati' – the burning of **women** on their husband's **funeral** pyres then enforced in India by the Brahmins – which as a consequence of their campaigning was made illegal in 1829.

Missionary work led to struggle for human rights in general. The most well-known examples may be William Knibb, British Baptist missionary to Jamaica from 1824, who became a passionate opponent to the slavery that still existed in the British colonies [see **Colonialism**], and E.V. Sjöblom, Swedish Baptist missionary to Congo (1892-1903), who denunciated the abuse of the Congo people by the officers and soldiers of the Congo Independent State.

In the middle of the 20th century, the Baptist **minister** Martin Luther King Jr. interpreted human rights as equal rights for every citizen regardless of colour and led a successful campaign for the implementation of human rights for African Americans in the USA. In various situations and countries, Jimmy Carter, former President of the USA and active Baptist, has tried to bring human rights into focus. The **EBF** and the **BWA** have both campaigned for the rights of believers in both **fascist** and **communist** countries and those dominated by other **faith** systems. To achieve these ends Baptists have been content to work with all those of good will, most noticeably seen in joining in coalitions with those of other faiths and no faith to rid the world of such abuses as slavery, racism and trafficking.

The BWA Commission on Freedom, Justice and **Peace** presented a declaration on human rights to the BWA Congress in Toronto (1980), underlining that 'human rights are derived from God' and that they are 'not for a few but for all', listing 20 specific human rights which 'ought to be of concern to persons everywhere'.

DaL

FURTHER READING: H. Wheeler Robinson, *The Life and Faith of the Baptists*, London, 1946. D.

Lagergren, *Mission and State in the Congo 1885-1903*, Uppsala, 1970. C.E. Bryant and R.J. Burke (eds), *Celebrating Christ's Presence through the Spirit. Report from the BWA Congress 1980*, Nashville, Tn., 1981.

Humankind
[See also *Anthropology, Theological*]
The view of humankind (the preferred, modern, inclusive usage for the outdated 'mankind') in the OT and NT is founded upon the central core that humanity is created by God. In the first *creation* story humankind is evaluated as being the climax of creation, presented as being created in the image of God, and thus given a special responsibility as caretaker or steward [see *Stewardship*] of the rest of creation (Ge 1:26). But already from the beginning humankind is distinguished from God through being earth-bound (Ge 2:7, the wordplay with *adam* and *adamah*) implying humankind's perishableness, itself the consequence of its disobedience [see *Fall*; *Sin*]. In this way an ambiguous view of humanity is introduced. Although part of God's creation, humankind enjoys a special place within the created order with an existence somewhere between the rest of creation and the creator. This ontological dilemma is developed into a moral dilemma: Humankind is able to follow the law of God, though recurrently fails to do so.

The Greek thought of dividing the human body into more or less valuable parts finds no justification in the OT. Relevant terminology like *nefesh* [respiration/soul], *neshemah* [respiration/life], *ruach* [wind/might/spirit] and *leb* [heart] all describe aspects of humanity rather than particular body parts. Rather the human body is considered to be a unified whole. It can be argued that the NT view should be seen within the OT framework contrasting with the dominating Greek view of the time.

The NT follows up the moral dilemma of the OT. *Jesus* has a positive view of humankind placing it above the lilies (Mt 6:26-30) and the *Sabbath* (Lk 6:1-5). At the same time humankind is revealed as evil (Mt 7:11) and sinful (Lk 11:29). But the foundation that underpins the *ministry* of Jesus is the belief that humankind can change, and be changed, and therefore the *hope* for a new humankind, freed from sin and *death* with the defaced image of the creator re-imaged, (Eph 2:14-16) because of the *salvation* of Jesus.

KTB

Hungarian Baptist Aid (HBA)
[See also *Emergency and Disaster Relief*]
HBA was registered in Fejer County Court in 1996. HBA was registered in Fejer County Court in 1996 by the Hungarian Baptist *Union*, but its real 'inventor' and current president is Baptist *pastor*, Sandor Szenczy. The goal of HBA from the very beginning has been to help the needy in Hungary and abroad in accordance with *Jesus Christ*'s command of *love*. During the long years since the first donation of 5,000 HUF, Hungarian Baptist Aid has become one of the largest Hungarian aid organisations; with almost 70 full-time workers and several 100 volunteers, being a high public benefit organisation. Over the past decade the basic organisation has grown into a skilled rescue and aid organisation with good professional standing. It is mentioned by the *EU* as one of the four most significant aid organisations of *Hungary*. Its aim is to have a rescue team on site at any major disaster within hours. Specialist staff include a lawyer, a doctor, a social worker, a PR expert, a journalist, a pastor, a translator, an interpreter, an economics or informatics expert, an administrator, a diver and special rescue personnel. In 18 countries Hungarian Baptist Aid provides regular support, food, humanitarian and spiritual help and implements development projects for needy and socially marginalised people, helping them in their difficult situations, presenting a chance for a better life. The goal of the organisation is to fulfil the spiritual and physical needs of disadvantaged people in Hungary and abroad – regardless of their origin, nationality, religion and race. Hungarian Baptist Aid works in providing humanitarian aid; disaster relief; support for disadvantaged *Roma people*, *refugees*, *drug* addicts; a project to rehabilitate people with *disabilities* and several other humanitarian and developmental programmes. HBA co-operates extensively with *Baptist World Aid*.

NC & KGJ

FURTHER READING: www.baptistasegely.hu.

Hungary, Baptist history in

Prior to modern Baptist endeavours, as early as the 1520s, *Anabaptists* were present in Northern Hungary (now *Slovakia*), emphasising 'believers' baptism' as the beginning of *discipleship*. One of them, Andreas Fischer became a *martyr* in 1540. Hutterite (Haban) settlements established in this period had vanished by the end of the 18th century due to severe persecution. In the 19th century a new start was made though the ideological links to the earlier 'baptisers' movements', indirect as these were, continued to inspire Baptists in Hungary. Baptist work began by János (Johann) Rottmayer (d1901) and his colleagues, Karl Scharschmidt and Johann Woyka. Working as migrant carpenters in Hamburg after the Great Fire (1842) they got into contact with Baptists and experienced *conversion*. In 1846, *J.G. Oncken* commissioned them [see *Commisioning of Missionaries*], and some others, to return to Hungary, to *witness* and spread the *scriptures*. Baptist *preaching* took place in Fünfkirchen (Pécs/Pest – today part of Budapest) and other places, with some Baptisms recorded though as yet Baptist witness was very sporadic.

A second period of Baptist movement in Hungary began in the 1870s and by 1894 there were some 4,000 baptised believers in 200 churches. This was due to the *pastoral* and organisational work of a talented young German, Heinrich Meyer (1842-1919) who arrived as a British and Foreign Bible Society *colporteur* to Hungary in 1873. Meyer, founder of the first Baptist church in Budapest (1874), worked among German inhabitants. His co-workers started a Hungarian-speaking mission in Nagyszalonta (Transylvania) in 1875, and Baptist witness spread also to the regions of present day *Serbia* (Vojvodina) and Slovakia. The Nagyszalonta church produced a number of 'peasant-apostles', simple countrymen who travelled through villages witnessing to *Christ* and planting churches [see *Church Planting*]. The most significant of them was Mihály Kornya (d1917) who is said to have baptised over 11,000 people during his period of *ministry*. By 1894 a number of Hungarian-speaking churches claimed non-German leadership and worked as an *autonomous* connexion outside Meyer's supervision. When a Hungarian *union* was formed that year, some earlier tensions came to the surface, and a *schism* occurred between Meyer and the young Hungarian leaders, such as Lajos Balogh and András Udvarnoki. There followed a long period in which Hungarians and Germans worked separately (until 1920). Nevertheless, both groups were successful and the number of Baptists grew to over 24,000 by 1918. After WWI (concluded in the Treaty of Trianon, 1920) large parts of the neighbouring countries that had been under Hungarian rule were given their independence. As a result, the number of Baptists living in Hungary diminished to 8,000, but almost doubled in the following two decades.

In the 1920s Baptist *mission* work in Hungary became more organised: different committees helped the churches, a number of periodicals, literature and tracts were published. The Hungarian Baptist paper *Béke-hirnök* [*Messenger of Peace*] continued to appear. Baptists were also involved in social ministry, caring for *orphans* and the *elderly*. The Theological Seminary [see *Budapest, Baptist Theological Seminary*], founded in 1906, moved to a new building. At that time the most influential leader was probably Imre Somogyi (d1951). WWII and the political changes after 1948 sorely tested Baptist work in Hungary. *Pastors* were controlled by the *State*'s Church Office which issued or withdrew pastor's licences and regularly meddled in church autonomy. The Press was also censored. Yet, there were *revivals* in the 1960s, many new *church buildings* were erected during the Soviet years, and a new *Confession of Faith* was passed in 1967. Dissimilar to some other *socialist* countries, *children's work* in *Sunday Schools* and *youth work* continued comparatively freely.

The *political* changes of 1989 brought new opportunities: out-door *evangelism*, a widened participation in cultural life, and the restoration of the liberty of the press. The beginning of the 1990s saw an increased interest in Christian values in society and Baptist *worship* attendance numbers grew for a while. On the other hand, new cults also appeared in the 'market of souls'. Times were changing faster than Baptists could react. However, recently the work of *Hungarian Baptist Aid* has brought a revival in Baptist *'diakonia'*. The Hungarian Baptist Union has a total **membership** of some 11,000 in more than 300 churches. In addition, almost the same number of Hungarian-speaking Baptists live in *Romania*, Slovakia, *Ukraine* and Serbia. The union runs a seminary, two elderly peoples' homes and several conference centres. The union is a member of both *EBF* and *BWA*, as well as in national and international *ecumenical* bodies.

AS

Hymnody
[See also *Church Music*]
Although absent, or limited to psalm-singing, in early English Baptist life, hymns soon became one of the clearest articulators of the primary *theology* of the congregation, firmly at the very heart of Baptist ecclesial identity. As indicated by the vital role of hymns played in the Arian controversy of the 4th century, hymns instruct and shape the believers in a more powerful way than more explicitly didactic mediums. At the same time they reflect the believers' focal points of commitment and concern. It is not surprising, therefore, that a change of hymns, especially a sudden one, has the potential to cause serious tensions in church life, if not actual splits.

Whereas English can differentiate between 'hymns' (traditional) and 'songs' (modern), this would not be true of some other European languages. Instead, they may have a different word for 'spiritual hymns' to distinguish them from 'secular songs' (e.g. Hungarian or Lithuanian). Another differentiation sometimes is made between songs of 'praise' and 'worship', referring to more energetic and more reverent types of songs, respectively. Below, however, these words are used interchangeably.

The relationship between lyrics and music is a complex and subtle one. The frequency of the use of a song, the pace with which it is sung, the musical accompaniment chosen for it, the melody, the harmony, the rhythm and lyrics all bear on its meaning. Sung with others, a hymn is an embodied expression of our connection with

each other and God and of the formation of something richer and larger than ourselves. We sing with our entire bodies, though the posture may differ. There is a strong *tradition* in some churches to stand while in others the congregation typically sings while seated.

The first English Baptist hymnal appeared in 1691, the work of Benjamin Keach. At this time choral hymn-singing, as over against the singing of psalms, was contentious, and Keach's congregation split over the issue. The first continental hymn book was that produced in German in 1849, edited by the Dane, Julius Köbner, soon followed by those in other languages. Songs have been borrowed from various ecclesial traditions; there have been comparatively few notable Baptist hymn writers to have left a significant trace internationally. Perhaps the most famous hymn, known as 'the Baptist anthem', is John Fawcett's 'Blest be the Tie that Binds' (1782, music by Hans Georg Nägeli), translated into most if not all European languages, a notable illustration of the centrality of *ecclesiology* for Baptists. Beside congregational hymnals, other types of songbooks include those for youth, choirs, *Sunday Schools*, *funerals*, etc.

A significant difficulty was encountered in parts of Europe during *communist* times as authorities restricted or completely prohibited the publishing of religious material, hymnals included, as well as confiscating existing copies. Congregational and choir hymns would be copied by hand and carbon paper and, when possible, secretly by other primitive means. This especially affected the availability of music editions, thus different churches, particularly in the former *USSR*, often sang the same songs to different tunes.

In some countries, such as *Bulgaria*, *Sweden*, or *Lithuania*, several denominations have co-operated to produce a joint hymnal. Hymnals are noticeably less used, however, as a result of the high turnover of new songs and the advancement in technology allowing the projection of the text on a wall.

Baptists share a modest number of songs that have been translated to virtually all European languages and are greatly used in multilingual settings. In terms of music, Anglo-American influence is the strongest both in the case of the old hymns and newer songs, supplemented by some contributions from **Germany**, **Scandinavia**, various classical composers, etc. Fast-growing ethnic congregations within the **EBF** help in introducing songs from other parts of the world. New original, indigenous or folk-based music is barely existent in some regions but fairly strong in others, perhaps most notably among Eastern Slavs and in the Middle East.

Virtually throughout all **unions**, sung canons have been much affected by the explosion of contemporary worship material, in which the dominance of songs translated from English is very evident. Although following scripture texts, quite often verbatim, this tends to have a rather limited range of phrases and topics. Hence the criticism of the poverty of themes and the poetic qualities of much of the contemporary worship scene as failing to reflect the **wealth** of themes addressed in the **Bible**.

Eastern Slavic hymnody is perhaps exceptionally marked by the richness of its biblical motifs intertwined with the believers' current experience, though aspects of social awareness and concern for God's creation are largely absent. These are more prominent in some newer English songs. Much of newer hymnody seems to be uncomfortable with expressions of **suffering**, protest, and doubt. In the equilibrium of songs as idioms of church's corporate journey with God and of personal feeling the latter outweighs the former and strongly reflects **modernity**'s preoccupation with the individual, exemplified in the prevalence of the singular first-person pronoun.

Both in their omissions and inclusions, hymns represent **contextual theology**. The songs turn into life, just as life is reflected in that which the **church** sings.

LA

FURTHER READING: Keith G. Jones and Parush R. Parushev (eds), *Currents in Baptistic Theology of Worship Today*, International Baptist Theological Seminary, Prague, 2007.

I

IBC

See *International Baptist Convention*.

IBTS

See *International Baptist Theological Seminary*.

Iceland, Baptist history in

Iceland is quite different from other Nordic countries in geography, people and Baptist life. There are only 290,000 people living on the small island, 180,000 of whom live in and around the capital, Reykjavik. Baptist work was established 150 years ago in the other four Nordic countries, but it has been difficult founding a Baptist church in Iceland and it has never been possible to establish a Baptist *union*. This is strange because the history and culture is much the same in Iceland as in the other Nordic countries.

The first Baptist church in Iceland was established in 1964 by Wally Rice, a *Southern Baptist* navy serviceman at the Keflavik air base, aimed at American military personnel and their families. But the church dissolved after only a few years. A new Baptist church began in 1982, led by John Opferman, an independent Baptist. It soon took the name of 'First Baptist Church of Iceland' and is located in Njardvik close to the Naval Air Station and the Leif Ericsson International airport outside Reykjavik. The church is independent of any Baptist *mission* agency abroad, but is a part of the 'Baptist Mission to Forgotten People', an independent American Baptist movement which rejects all contact with *Neo-Orthodoxy*, Neo-*Evangelicalism*, the *Ecumenical Movement* and the *Tongues* Movement. From time to time the *Bishop* of the *Lutheran* State Church of Iceland invites leaders of all the churches to meetings, but the Baptists do not participate.

The Baptist church has a *children*'s club, *youth work*, *Bible study* groups, a *Sunday School* and runs a radio station. They built a church in Njardvik in 1998. The church is mission minded and pays part of the salary for 43 missionaries all over the world. It has more than 100 *members* mostly connected to the Keflavik base. They baptised [see *Baptism*] 275 members from 1987-2003. But the personnel at the base changes approximately every second year, which makes it difficult to have continuity in the work of the church. Today John Wright (USA) is their *pastor* and he has been serving for more than 16 years. Once located on the Keflavik military base, Wright felt God's calling to continue working in Iceland after his military service. He took *theological* training in the USA and moved back to Iceland with his family. He has Icelandic citizenship and speaks the language.

It has been difficult to establish a Baptist church among the national people. The first native Icelander was baptised in 1991, and a small church has been established with about 10 members and 20 participants in the Bible School. They co-operate closely with The First Baptist Church of Iceland.

BTar & JS

IFES

See *Student Christian Movement (SCM), Inter-Varsity Fellowship (IVF), World Student Christian Federation (WSCF) and International Fellowship of Evangelical Students (IFES)*.

Images/Icons, Baptist use of

Baptists have been wary of having images in church because of their use in *Catholic/Orthodox* Churches for purposes of veneration with consequent accusations of idolatry, not to mention the apparent condemnation of their construction in the Law of Moses. On the other hand, the word depicts the deepest truths with regard to the doctrine of *creation* in indicating that *humankind* is made in the image or likeness of God, an image defaced by human *sin* but restored in *Christ*. Maybe, because of this most important conception of the word 'image', there has been a proper reluctance to entertain any other form of image in Baptist churches; *worshippers* made in the image of

God should not seek God in any other representational form. These kinds of objections have not been applied to other **church buildings** or to Christian homes – e.g. Baptist Church House in London had a statue of **Bunyan** on the outside and a more than life-size figure of **Spurgeon** in the foyer. Small figures of **preachers** like Moody and Sankey, Spurgeon, and the blind Welsh preacher, Christmas Evans, could be found in many pious homes in the 19th century. More recently as banner making has become common so more and more images have been displayed in Baptist churches.

JHYB

Immaculate Conception

[See also *Mary, Mother of Jesus*]
This language is used exclusively of Mary, the mother of **Jesus**, and is not to be confused with Jesus' conception by the **Holy Spirit**. The doctrine of the Immaculate Conception was first formulated in the Middle Ages, but was only officially endorsed by **Pope** Pius IX in 1854. Since then it has been a constant part of the teaching of the **Roman Catholic** Church. According to this teaching, Mary was conceived through the normal generative human way, however without original *sin* [see *Fall*], that is, she was preserved from humanity's corruption [see *Humankind*], through God's sanctifying *grace* [see *Sanctification*], which was conferred upon her before sin was able to infect her soul. The Vulgate reading of Lk 1:28 (*gratia plena*) is usually understood to be expressing Mary's godlike state of soul, which finds its explanation in this doctrine of her Immaculate Conception. She is also considered as the new Eve who was to be the mother of the new Adam, and as such, immune to inherited sin. Teaching on the Immaculate Conception represents an aspect of the teaching of the Catholic Church, which, because it seems to lack warranty in *scripture* causes obstacles to close relations between **Protestants** and Catholics.

EV

Immanence and Transcendence

Both terms concern God's relationship with his *creation*. God as transcendent is above creation, totally different from humans and other creatures. His knowledge and power, his *holiness* and mercy are high above ours. We cannot even understand him on our own (cf. Isa 55:8-9, Ro 11:33-36). By contrast, the meaning of God's immanence is that he is present and active within the creation, working through natural processes, and accomplishing his plans through humans who may even not believe in him (cf. Acts 17:27-28, Isa 10:1ff, 44:28ff). The immanence of God is, however, made manifest in the *incarnation* with the **Word** becoming flesh and manifesting the character of God in a human life here on earth. In the age of the **Church**, not without reason referred to as 'the Body of Christ', Christians claim the presence of the Risen **Christ** whenever Christians meet together in his name (Mt 18:20).

It is important to keep these two doctrines together. Transcendence without immanence results in a lonely creation, which is perfect in itself (*Deism*), or which finds no *salvation* however much it needs it. Immanence without transcendence means pantheism: God is one with the world not separate from it. Immanence and transcendence are both revealed in perfect harmony in the *Cross* of Christ where God shows himself both Lord and Redeemer [see *Redemption*] of creation, both *sovereign* and *suffering*.

AS & ET

Incarnation

[See also *Christology; Jesus Christ; Logos; Lord of the Church and the Crown Rights of the Redeemer*]
As a christological term, 'incarnation' (Latin *incarnatio* [becoming flesh]) refers to the doctrine that in Jesus, the pre-existent Son of God became human. In the incarnation event, Jesus not only announced a *mission* or proclaimed new teaching from God, but in his person Jesus was God himself coming into this world.

Its most profound biblical basis [see *Bible*] is in the Gospel of John who speaks about the incarnation of the eternal *Logos*: 'the Word became flesh and dwelt among us' (1:14); Jesus is spoken of as the bread of life that 'comes down from *heaven*' (6:32f,41); incarnation and glorification are seen as mirroring events representing coming from the Father and returning to him (16:28). This vocabulary seems to have been provoked by the rise of docetic *heresies* in the late 1ˢᵗ century (1Jn 4:1ff).

Other NT authors express the fact differently: in the synoptic gospels there are birth narratives which speak of conception through the *Holy Spirit* (Mt 1:20, Lk 1:35), whilst Paul, using the term *kenosis* [self-emptying] (Php 2:7), also describes Christ's radical coming into the world in the form of a servant, born in the likeness of *man*, that is, his mission is achieved not by the deployment of God's glorious almightiness but rather by faithful servanthood found in vulnerable human form: Jesus comes among us as a baby, crying in his mother's arms, the condemned criminal *suffering* on the *cross*.

Beyond its significance for Christology, the doctrine of incarnation is also significant for *soteriology* – for only one who wholly shared in the human condition (save for its sinfulness) could secure salvation for sinning humanity. The reality of incarnation also affords new dignity to the whole of human life, now given renewed sanctity [see *Sanctification*] by the fact that Christ shared in it; indeed no part of human experience can be reckoned wholly alien to him, thus emphasising the original goodness of the created order before it was marred by *sin*. Such an insight has sometimes led to the development of so-called 'Incarnation *Theology*' as opposed to '*Redemption* Theology', with the former deployed in favour of a *social gospel* which engages the *Church* in the human struggle against all that oppresses *humankind* in this world and the latter underpinning traditional views of salvation in eternity. This is a false polarisation, for a holistic understanding of the gospel requires an understanding of the importance of this world as the theatre in which God acts, but acts with eternal significance: cross and cradle belong together.

The doctrine of incarnation which implies both the existence of God in Trinity and Christ's dual nature as both God and man, was formulated at several *ecumenical* councils (e.g. Nicea, 325), and Baptists usually embrace it as an integral part of genuine Christian *faith*.

AS & ET

Inclusive language

Behind the language issue lies the belief that the Christian community should be a community that excludes nobody on the basis of gender, age, intelligence, race, colour, physical ability or any other such characteristic. If that is so then the language of *worship* should be so crafted that all are able fully to participate. The plea is therefore not to use masculine nouns – *men*, sons, brothers, *mankind*, etc. – or pronouns where it is not necessary. In practice it has proved easier to revise the language that describes the *worshipper* rather than the One being worshipped, where Baptists alongside other *evangelical* Christians believe that the language and the concepts of the original *revelation* have to be respected, whilst admitting that the searching of the *scriptures* for feminine metaphors describing the behaviour of God remains a worthwhile exercise. They are unlikely to react as negatively as many *Orthodox* to the three persons of the *Trinity* being described in gender-neutral language as Creator, Redeemer and Sustainer, but would balk at the suggestion that *Jesus* cannot be spoken of as 'the Son of God', or God as 'the Father'.

JHYB

Indigenous People Groups

The term 'indigenous' comes from the Latin word *indigena*, which means 'a native.' In its adjectival form together with the noun 'people' it describes the inhabitants of a given territory who have a historical continuity or association with the region. This is most powerfully seen in a largely 'settled' continent like North America where the American Indians are often referred to as 'first nation' people. Indigenous People are furthermore characterised by their language, culture and social organisation which differ from the surrounding population and dominant culture of the *nation* state. According to The Development Gateway Foundation there are about 350 million indigenous people worldwide, also known as 'aborigines', 'native peoples', 'first peoples', or 'Fourth World'. Some examples of European indigenous people are: the Sami people; Bashkirs, Chuvash people, Crimean Tatars; Ingrians;

Karelians; Kashubians; Livonians; Sorbs: Tatars; and others. On other continents some examples of indigenous people groups are: Inuit; Pygmy people; Maasai; Bushmen, Tuareg; Aztecs; Native Americans in USA; Guarani; Tibetans; Buryats; Indigenous Australians; Papuans; Maori; and others.

From the history of church *mission* it is clear that indigenous people have been one of the primary targets of Christian missionary activity for centuries. It is also clear that from the start there were attempts at 'indigenisation' (in *Protestant* missions) and 'accommodation' (in *Catholic* missions), with the goal of establishing 'a native church' understood as 'self-financing, self-governing, and self-propagating'. In the mid 20th century, a fourth adjective was added – 'self-theologising', and this has opened the door for 'indigenous churches' to be recognised as partners and equals by 'mother' churches from the West.

Baptists have been actively involved in missionary endeavours amongst indigenous peoples for centuries, both in mission organisations led by them (e.g. *William Carey*, founder of The Particular Baptist Society for Propagating the Gospel among the Heathen, later named the *Baptist Missionary Society*) and as individuals joining missionary work conducted by other Christian organisations (e.g. Wycliffe *Bible Translators*). One of the most recent initiatives of the *European Baptist Federation* is the 'Indigenous Missionary Project' which aims to support indigenous missionaries in Europe and the Middle East, though there is no special emphasis on first nation people such as the Sami and Tatars. In countries such as *Romania*, *Moldova* and *Bulgaria* attempts are being made to reach out to the *Roma people*. In areas of the former *Soviet Union* such as *Kazakhstan* the national *Unions* are making serious attempts to *evangelise* the original populations as current Baptist communities are essential composed of Russians or Germans moved there by the Soviet authorities in the last century.

KJ & ET

Indulgences

The selling of indulgences by the Dominican monk Tetzel was one of the trigger points of the *Reformation*. The sale of indulgences derived from the idea that in his *death* *Christ* had created what in the Middle Ages was known as 'The Treasury of Christ'. From this treasury resources could be released to mitigate the punishment of those in *purgatory*. This had come about as the transition was made from undertaking acts of penitence to doing penance, which for the rich could be commuted into a money payment, so that Tetzel was selling indulgences to secure funds for the *Pope*'s building plans at St. Peter's in Rome [see *Vatican*]. Such indulgences could benefit not only the purchaser, but the purchaser's dead relations. *Luther* was clear that such fiscal approaches to *salvation* were in direct conflict with his own understanding of *justification* by *faith* through *grace*, and for all the marks that changed hands represented a form of cheap grace.

JHYB

Industrial Mission

[See also *Mission*; *Urban Rural Mission*]
Industrial Mission belongs to that branch of Christian mission known as *sector ministry*. It seeks to speak critically into the world of work from a *theological* perspective. Industrial Mission was inaugurated in 1944 by the *Anglican Bishop* of Sheffield, Leslie Hunter, who appointed Ted Wickham, a *priest* in the diocese of Lichfield, to become chaplain to the steel industry in Sheffield. The aim was to re-establish the *church* among the working classes, focusing on the place of work rather than the home as the location of mission. From this sprang the growth of Industrial Mission teams in areas dominated by *labour*-intensive 'smokestack industries' such as chemical manufacture, iron and steel-making, mining and shipbuilding. A fundamental principle was that chaplaincies were negotiated with management and the trade unions and entry was not permitted nor taken up until both sides had agreed. This measure was designed to show that the chaplain was an objective visitor to the workplace. The early ventures were *evangelistic* and *pastoral*. It has subsequently become a source of tension between chaplains and the churches as to how far industrial mission should be evangelistic and pastoral against a more prophetic role [see *Prophecy*],

speaking the gospel into workplace issues. The strength of Industrial Mission is its **ecumenical** approach to the world of work. Baptist involvement has largely been through the funding of a small number of full-time industrial chaplains and the participation in Industrial Mission activities by interested lay people [see **Laity**]. A significant move was taken by the Baptist **Union** of **Great Britain** in 2000, when it established its sector ministry committee and included within it an Industrial Mission working group.

WJA

Inerrancy

See *Infallibility and Inerrancy of the Bible*.

Infallibility and Inerrancy of the Bible

[See also **Bible, Baptist understanding of the; Inspiration of the Bible**]

The **Reformation confessions of faith** sometimes speak of 'the infallible truth and divine **authority**' of scripture. The context of these statements makes it clear that the 'truth' which is in mind is, to quote both the Westminster Confession of 1647 and the Second London Baptist Confession of 1677, 'The whole counsel of God concerning all things necessary for his own glory, **man**'s **salvation**, **faith** and life'. The meaning of 'infallible' in this context has been defined as that which neither misleads nor is misled. The rise of **enlightenment** rationalism saw increasing attacks on the reliability of the Bible, to which **conservative scholars** responded in two different ways. Some adopted a 'top down approach' (e.g. the 'Princeton School' under A.A. Hodge and B.B. Warfield) and others adopted a 'bottom-up' approach (e.g. the Scottish **theologian** James Orr).

The advocates of the 'top-down' approach argue along the lines: The Bible is the inspired word of God. God does not lie. Therefore the Bible does not lie. This means that it is *inerrant* in all its statements, that it is 'free from all falsehood or mistakes'.

Advocates of the 'bottom-up' approach argue that if we want to know what kind of book the Bible is we have to start from the Bible itself, not from a preconceived position. Otherwise we risk imposing on it a view of what kind of book we think it should be rather than accepting it as God has given it to us. So, they start with the Reformation position that the Bible is an infallible guide for the purposes for which God inspired it, as set out in 2Ti 3:16 e.g.. They point out that the concept of 'truth' is not a simple one. Truth is expressed in different ways in different types of literature and different kinds of language. This makes application of the concept of 'inerrant statements' inappropriate or difficult. Also they argue that the concept of 'error' with which the Princeton approach worked was one derived from the post-enlightenment scientific culture and not appropriate for literature coming from the Ancient Near-East and the Greco-Roman world.

In practice, the assertion that the Bible is inerrant in all its statements has had to be surrounded by all kinds of qualifications. Hodge and Warfield recognised the need for textual criticism, arising from the fact that the surviving manuscripts of the Bible contain numerous, though often quite trivial, differences from one another. This meant that they had to assert that the Bible is only inerrant 'in the original autographs' – that is in the original manuscripts, which no longer exist and which we can only reconstruct (with a high degree of certainty) by means of textual criticism.

Having got a reliable text, what does one do with the fact that there are errors of spelling and grammar? These seem not to worry the inerrantists: 'The truthfulness of scripture is not negated by appearance in it of irregularities of grammar or spelling.'

Then there are statements about the natural world that are somewhat problematic, such as references to the sun moving across the heavens. Again the reply is: 'The truthfulness of scripture is not negated by...phenomenal descriptions of nature', that is statements that describe nature *as it appears to be* rather than *as it really is*.

More difficult for the inerrantist position are cases where parallel passages appear to be at odds. A simple case is the story of the man let down on his bed through the roof of a house. In Mk 2:4 we are told that his friends 'dug through the roof' to let him down. This fits well with the flat roofs that were common in Palestine at the time, made of a mixture of clay and straw and covered with a coating of waterproof plaster. However, in Lk 5:19 the roof is made of tiles. Luke wrote his gospel for a Gentile readership that might not be aware of the flat-roofed houses of Palestine. Instead they were used to the sloping tiled roofs common in places with much higher rainfall. Maybe Luke changed this detail of the story to give a picture that they could visualise more easily. Is the result an 'error'? Some commentators are sufficiently worried about this to try to harmonise the two accounts in some way, though not very convincingly.

Faced with these kinds of problems Howard Marshall concludes, 'It is worth asking whether 'inerrant' is really the most appropriate word to use to describe scripture. It needs so much qualification, even by its defenders, that it is in danger of dying the death of a thousand qualifications. The term 'infallible' in the sense of 'entirely trustworthy' is undoubtedly preferable'.

A point that can get lost in this debate is the importance of the *purpose of scripture*. In practice, acceptance of the entire trustworthiness of scripture for its divinely intended purposes (such as those given in 2Ti 3:16) seems to many Christians to be an adequate basis for taking 'the scriptures of the OT and NT as the primary authority for knowing God's *revelation* in *Christ*'.

A final point worth making is that to try to 'prove' the authority of the Bible by 'proving' its inerrancy is in fact to make human reason a higher authority than the Bible itself. If the authority of scripture is an authority derived from God then it has to be self-authenticating in some way. This is what is asserted in the Reformation creeds, such as the Second London Baptist Confession: 'Our full persuasion, and assurance of the infallible truth, and divine authority of [the Bible], is from the inward work of the *Holy Spirit*, bearing *witness* by and with the Word in our hearts.'

EL

FURTHER READING: P.J. Achtemeier, *Inspiration and Authority*, Hendrickson, Peabody, Ma., 1999. European Baptist Federation. *Who are Baptists?*, EBF, 1992. N.L. Geisler (ed), *Inerrancy*, Zondervan, Grand Rapids, Mi., 1980. J. Goldingay, *Models for Scripture*, Paternoster, Carlisle, 1994. W.L. Lumpkin, *Baptist Confessions of Faith* (rev. ed.), Judson, Valley Forge, Pa., 1969. I.H. Marshall, *Biblical Inspiration*, Hodder and Stoughton, London, 1982.

Infallibility of the Pope

[See also *Papacy*; *Roman Catholicism, Baptists and*]

The infallibility of the Pope (part of the practice of the universal Magisterium) is a *dogma* defined by the First *Vatican* Council in 1870 during the papacy of Pius IX. However, lest the Council were thought to be articulating new doctrine, it made it clear that it was articulating what the church has always believed. A problem that runs parallel and is inseparable from papal infallibility is the question of *authority* in the universal *church*.

The historical affirmation of a 'Roman' supremacy of the church can be traced first to Ireneus (Bishop of Lyon, 248-58) and then to Cyprian (Bishop of Carthage, 248-58). Further definition came with Leo II's spelling out of the claim (449) that the supremacy of his see had divine and *scriptural* authority, which was accepted by the Council of Chalcedon in 451 as standard Christian *orthodoxy*.

Historically the issue of who possessed authority in the church was one which saw the Church of Rome in discord with the Church of Constantinople. This opposition between Latin and Greek *Christendom* lasted for many years with *schisms* that were briefly reconciled up until 1054 when the Eastern Churches finally separated from Western Christendom on the issue of authority in the Church (though a split developed between the Oriental *Orthodox* and both Latin and Greek Christendom at Chalcedon over how to articulate *Christology*). The Eastern churches recognise that the see of Rome has the primacy 'of honour' [*primus inter pares*], but not ecclesiastical jurisdiction or *theological* Magisterium. Today they remain divided.

Papal infallibility came to be seen as the natural corollary of the primacy of the see of Rome. Prior to the adoption of the dogma of the absolute authority of the Pope and his infallibility, the authority of the Magisterium over the universal church was in the hands of 'oecumenical' councils which were attended by all the *bishops* from the different provinces and countries which initially were convened by the Roman emperors. Faced with the see of Rome's intention of establishing itself as the sole authority of the universal church during the 14th and 15th centuries (the Council of Pisa 1409) the doctrine of 'conciliarism' (the authority of the Council also over the Pope) seemed to take root, but was soon thwarted. In time the need arose to re-enforce the doctrine with a figure, who not only had authority, but was infallible.

History tipped the scales in favour of the new dogma: firstly there was the explosion of the *Protestant Reformation*, then the flowering of the *Enlightenment*, followed by the great *liberal* revolutions, and last, but not least, the end of the papal state and its territories. It was during the First Vatican Council (1869-70) that Pope Pius IX's (1849-79) 'policy of infallibility' won the day. The Council ended exactly a month after the fall of Rome (20 Sep 1870) which sanctioned the unity of *Italy*. So both historical and dogmatic reasons contributed to papal infallibility becoming official dogma (decreed with the *Apostolic* Constitution *Pastor aeternus* of 18 Jul 1870). In this case too, there were bishoprics and individual bishops that did not accept the new dogma. They left the Catholic Church and formed the Old Catholic Church. So another dogma brought about a new separation within the Catholic Church which has lasted until the present day.

What does this dogma say? It foresees that some specific definitions by the Pope, as supreme Magisterium of the Roman Catholic Church, are to be considered infallible and cannot be contradicted by anyone wishing to remain in *communion* with the Church of Rome. Not every statement of the Pope is infallible, however; the text of the Apostolic Constitution lays down some clear conditions:

- The first condition deals with the expression *ex cathedra*: that is when the Pope makes a statement as pope of the Universal Church, a statement that must have the value of a norm for all the Catholic Church throughout the world (the practice of Magisterium),

when he acts as *pastor* (for moral issues) and as teacher (for matters of dogma) of the universal church. This is when he wishes to define the meaning and the importance of a doctrine or of ethical behaviour [see *Ethics*]. Before this declaration, if it were possible, the issue could be discussed but afterwards it was no longer possible (*Roma locuta, causa finita*).

- The second condition, stated in the text of the Constitution of Dogmas, deals with the issues which are the object of the declaration of infallibility. They are matters that concern *faith* and morals (*in definienda doctrina de fide vel moribus*). Once the doctrines concerning faith and ethics have been established, one can only obey. Those who do not accept them or wish to contradict them run the risk of excommunication (*anaethma sit*). The Second Vatican Council took a further step: the Constitution of Dogmas *Dei Verbum* (n.9-10) went beyond what was established by the Council of Trent (decree of 8 Apr 1546) on the two sources of *revelation* (scripture and *tradition*). It states that the church takes its authority not only from the scriptures, but also from the living tradition of the Church and that, adopting the tridentine formula, both must be accepted, with the same sentiments of piety and reverence (*pari pietatis affectu ac reverentia suscipienda et veneranda est*). It goes on to state that the duty authentically to interpret the word of God, written or transmitted, is given to the sole Magisterium present in the Church. The conclusion is that tradition, scripture and Magisterium are so closely connected that they cannot exist independently. Magisterium and tradition are placed on the same plane as scripture, but the Magisterium is the authentic interpreter both of the scripture and of tradition.

John XXIII proposed a distinction between the language and the contents of the dogma, and convened the Second Vatican Council for an *aggiornamento* (Renewal of the Church). In recent years John Paul II (23 Mar 1993) clarified the difference between divinely revealed truths, which require a statement of faith (the ordinary power of the Pope) and truths proposed in a definitive way, but not divinely revealed (extraordinary power) that require a definitive assent, which is not, however, an acceptance of faith. In other words, it is a request for obedience.

Another characteristic aspect of papal infallibility is its origin. The apostolic Constitution states that the Pope, on the basis of the divine assistance promised to Peter by *Jesus* (Mt 16:18; Lk 22:32; Jn 21:15-17) and as legitimate successor of Peter and for the unbroken promise of the assistance of the *Holy Spirit*, embodies the characteristic of infallibility. It then states that the definitions of the Pope cannot be reformed (in so far as they have been declared infallible by the Pope) and not because the church has given its consent (*definitiones ex sese, non ex autem consensu ecclesiae, irreformabili esse*).

The final result is that the 'conciliar' view (a form of *congregationalism*) is utterly excluded; the authority of the Pope is absolute. The documents produced by whatsoever Council are valid for dogmas and *discipline* in so far as they are approved and decreed by the authority of the Pope. The authority of one person prevails over the wishes of an entire Council.

DT

Infant Baptism
[See also *Baptism*]

Infant baptism/paedobaptism developed in the early church from the NT practice of *faith*-baptism. The first indisputable evidence of its existence is c.200 AD in the writing of Tertullian in North Africa (*On Baptism* 18) where he is describing a practice which he does not agree with but which clearly antedates him. However, attempts by paedobaptist *scholars* to find infant baptism in the NT (either in the household baptisms of Acts [e.g. 16:15, cf. 1Co 16], in 1Co 7:14 [though this would also legitimate the baptism of the unbelieving partner] or in *Jesus*' blessing of the little *children* in Mk 10:13-16//Mt 19:13-15//Lk 18:15-17 [though it was not so understood until the 6th century]) have strained the evidence and proved unsuccessful. For

an increasing number of paedobaptists what legitimises infant baptism is the practice of the *church*. It appears that the practice itself probably arose as a development of child believers' baptism sometime after the period of the *Apostolic* Fathers at the end of the 1st to the middle of the 2nd century, for their writings show no evidence of the rite. Then, for several centuries, the two forms of baptism co-existed – the norm, which was believers' baptism, and infant baptism, the development of which owed much to the emergence of clinical baptism, the church's response to very high rates of infant mortality, because it was believed that baptism cleansed from original *sin*. However, it was not until after Augustine (from the late 5th to early 6th century) that infant baptism became the norm and faith-baptism the exception. It was around this time that the rite of confirmation emerged to complete the initiatory sequence begun in infant baptism wherein the older child was enabled to express their own faith rather than rely on the faith of sponsors and/or godparents. This situation persisted, with a few exceptions, until it was challenged by the *Anabaptists* in the 16th century and Baptists in the 17th.

With the exception of the Society of Friends (*Quakers*) and The *Salvation Army*, all Christian traditions practice either infant baptism and/or believers' baptism. Indeed all paedobaptist traditions baptise believers on *conversion*, but only if they were not baptised as infants. Technically, therefore, Baptists are antipaedobaptists in that they do not baptise infants at all, only those old enough to have come to faith for themselves. *Theologically* paedobaptists have claimed that their actions stress the priority of *grace* and sacramentally baptismal *regeneration*, though modern scholarship sees paedobaptism as a development, and therefore derivative, from the biblical norm of faith-baptism.

ARC

Initiation
See *Christian Initiation*.

Initiatives of Change
See *Moral Re-Armament*.

Initsiativniki
See *Reform Baptists*.

Inspiration of the Bible

[See also *Bible, Baptist understanding of the; Infallibility and Inerrancy of the Bible*]
To say that the Bible is 'inspired' is to assert that the contents of the Bible, in some special way, owe their origin to God and that the Bible therefore occupies a central and essential place within the Christian *faith*. Our knowledge of God, and contact with God is linked to these records of what God has done and said in the past. However, this assertion does not limit itself to the past, because to say that the Bible is 'inspired' means that God continues to speak to his people through it in the present as the *Holy Spirit* enables them to understand what it says and its application to their situation.

There are only a very few passages in the Bible where scripture speaks about itself. The two most significant are 2Ti 3:16 and 2Pe 1:20-21. Both of these make reference to it as inspired.

The context of 2Ti 3:16 is an encouragement to Timothy to remain firm in the faith which he learned as a child. This faith was grounded in 'the sacred writings'. The phrase used here, *hiera grammata*, is the one that Greek-speaking *Jews* used for the Hebrew Bible, our OT. The beginning of v.16 can be translated as 'All scripture is inspired by God...' or as 'All scripture inspired by God...' In either case, there is no doubt that there is a reference back to 'the sacred writings' of the previous verse and that what is being said is that these are inspired by God. The Greek word used here, *theopnuestos*, means 'god-breathed' and was used in non-biblical Greek of messages or dreams that were believed to have their origin in God. This verse states that the scriptures are inspired by God but says nothing about the process. The main point of the passage is the *purpose* for which the scriptures were given.

The context of 2Pe 1:20-21 is the contrast between certainty about the fulfilment of prophecies about the Lord's return based on the event of the Transfiguration and certainty based on either 'cleverly devised myths' (v.16) or off-beat individualistic interpretations of those prophecies (v.20). The point of v.21 is that the prophetic interpretation of Israel's history was not a matter of the prophet's personal interpretation but was given to the prophet by God. This makes clear why the *prophecies* are 'surer' than 'cleverly devised fables'. This echoes the view of prophecy in 1Pe 1:10-12. Again, while stressing the divine origin of the OT prophecies, the passage says nothing about the process of inspiration.

From quite early on, the dominant way of thinking about the process of the inspiration of the Bible has been in terms of the 'model' of the prophet. However, this model is problematic in a number of ways:

- There is no one model of prophecy in the Bible. In the OT, especially in the earlier period, prophets are sometimes 'possessed' by the Spirit of YHWH and behave in abnormal ways. Although there is an element of this in Ezekiel, on the whole the 'writing' prophets' seem to have functioned differently, but even among them there were different modes of 'inspiration' – hearing God speak in some way (Hos 1:2, 4, 6, 9), having visions (Am 7:1-9), having moments of insight when faced with everyday objects or situations (Jer 18:1-12).

- Often people have understood this model in terms of the biblical authors being passive 'dictating machines', no more than 'divine tools' who contributed nothing to the process. This ignores the evidence of the Bible itself. Much of the biblical material is clearly marked by the personalities and historical situations of the authors, e.g. the 'major' prophets and the four gospels.

- The nature of the material in the Bible is such that it is hard to encompass it by one model. The evidence in the text of Kings, Chronicles and Luke of how the authors worked just does not fit the classic 'prophetic' model. They researched written and oral sources, sifted the material, and organised it to present their narrative in the way that expressed their interpretation of the events they recorded. N.T. Wright argues that if any one model is to be used, that of 'story-telling' is truer to the nature of the Bible as a whole than any other.

- There is convincing evidence that many of the biblical authors used pre-existing material, oral and written, and sometimes did so verbatim. So where is the locus inspiration?

- In at least some cases it seems that a prophetic book in the form we have it does not come directly from the prophet, but from someone else who collected the prophet's oracles, wrote them down in a particular order, and sometimes added narrative material. Jeremiah is a good example, with poetic oracles (no doubt Jeremiah's own words), prose accounts of Jeremiah's words (probably recorded by someone else) and prose narratives about the prophet (no doubt written by someone else). Again, where is the locus of inspiration?

Any understanding of the 'inspiration' of the Bible is deficient if it does not take into account the fact that the Bible is written in thoroughly human thought categories and uses a variety of literary forms, styles and language, and that most of these reflect the cultural situations of the authors. Moreover, the different personalities of the authors often shine through their work. So, when speaking of the 'inspiration' of scripture we are affirming that God so motivated and inspired the authors that their potential for speaking and writing intelligible language was used to produce materials that expressed what God wanted expressed, but did this in a way that did not subvert or destroy the author's human abilities, but rather enhanced them. Where the production of the book was clearly quite a lengthy process, we must surely see this 'inspiration' at work throughout the process until the book reached its final form.

EL

FURTHER READING: P.J. Achtemeier, *Inspiration and Authority*, Hendrickson, Peabody, Ma., 1999. J. Goldingay, *Models for Scripture*, Paternoster, Carlisle, 1994. I.H. Marshall, *Biblical Inspiration*, Hodder and Stoughton, London, 1982. N.T. Wright, *Scripture and the Authority of God*, SPCK, London, 2005.

Intentional Communities

In the late 20th century experiments in intentional community and new monastic communities began to influence European Baptists, especially those seeking to balance traditional Baptist 'activism' with a more contemplative **spirituality**. Whilst such communities have especially influenced European Baptist **worship** through their **music** and **liturgies**, they have also encouraged Baptist experiments in building authentic Christian community. Three of the most significant communities are described below:

Taizé Community, France. This community was founded in 1940 by a Swiss **Reformed pastor**, Roger Schutz (later known as Brother Roger). At Taizé, a small hilltop village in Burgundy, Brother Roger was involved in hiding **Jews** from the Gestapo. After the war he began a small **ecumenical** community of brothers which included both **Protestants** and **Catholics**, committed to the goal of **reconciliation** in the **church** and in the world. During the 1960s, with **student** unrest in Paris and other cities, Taizé became a focus for young people in search of spiritual **renewal** and the community came to welcome them in ever greater numbers. Brother Roger described what was happening as 'a little springtime' in the history of the Church. A style of worship developed based on **prayer**, silence and the repeated singing of simple **scriptural** chants in several languages. Though the main attraction of Taizé has perhaps been for Roman Catholics in search of the renewal of their Church, nevertheless many Protestants, including some European Baptists, have visited Taizé and become part of its search for authentic Christian community and gospel reconciliation. The Community continues to welcome and extend its hospitality to 1,000s of (mainly) young people every week to share its simple lifestyle and contemplative worship. Taizé is perhaps best known among Baptists for its chants which have found their way into the music and worship of many churches as aids to prayer and reflection.

Iona Community, Scotland. The name 'Iona' derives from the tiny island of the same name, lying off the west coast of **Scotland**, and the place to which the Irish Celtic **missionary** Columba first brought Christianity in the 6th century.

The Community was founded in 1938 by George Macleod, a Scottish Presbyterian Minister who ministered in Govan, a ship-building area of Glasgow during the Great Depression. Convinced that the churches were not reaching the needs of ordinary *men* and *women* he conceived the idea of forming a community of *unemployed* craftsmen and church ministers who together would rebuild the ruined cloister buildings of Iona Abbey. Macleod's vision was ecumenical and radical with a strong commitment to justice and *pacifism*. The Iona Community gradually became what it is today; not a 'monastic' community centred on the island of Iona itself, but a group of several 100 men and women engaged in their daily work on the 'front line' of building God's *kingdom* in the world and with the same commitment to justice and *peace*. In Scotland the community is best known for this latter commitment; elsewhere, and among many Baptist churches, the Iona Community is perhaps better known for the thoughtful liturgies and music developed by John Bell and others which, coming from a Presbyterian background, are perhaps more accessible to many Baptists. Iona also expresses a 'modern' Celtic vision of no barrier between sacred and secular and a reverence for the created order which finds its focus in a concern for the *environment*. The Iona Community, whilst based in Glasgow, continues to run two Centres on the Island of Iona where individuals and groups can stay.

Northumbria Community, England. This community began in the 1990s as result of a desire to bring together a concern for Christian mission with a commitment to the contemplative spiritual life, by a group of *evangelical Anglicans* and Baptists who had been influenced by the *charismatic movement*. The founders were inspired to seek God 'through Availability and Vulnerability' and their spiritual vision drew on the Celtic Christian Traditions of Northumbria in North-East England as well as the spirituality of the Desert Fathers and the Franciscans. A Mother House at Hetton Hall opposite Holy Island in Northumbria has been the centre of the Community since 1994 and a place of welcome and hospitality for many. Its best-known Baptist leader has been Roy Searle who was President of the Baptist *Union* of

Great Britain 2003-4. The liturgies, many of which are rooted in the lives of the Celtic *Saints* and Missionaries of North-East England and *Ireland*, and the music of the community, based on folk traditions have become increasingly popular in Baptist churches. The Northumbria community has been an important 'bridge'; first of all for British Baptists wanting to explore a more contemplative spiritual life and latterly for other European Baptists as the community members have visited their churches and introduced to them the life and worship of the Community. In 2005 the Community became an official partner community of the *International Baptist Theological Seminary* in Prague with regular exchange visits arranged and the Community invited to lead Worship Weeks at the Seminary.

AAP

InterAct

[See also *Örebro Theological Seminary, Sweden*]

InterAct has its roots in *revival* movements that swept over *Sweden* in the late 19th century and led to the establishment of the *Holiness* Union Mission, the Örebro Mission and the *Scandinavian* Independent Baptist *Union*. From the beginning, all three were characterised by a strong commitment to international *mission*. Over the years they grew closer to each other and in 1997 they merged into one fellowship, called the *Evangeliska Frikyrkan* in Sweden, and InterAct internationally. The Örebro Mission was the largest of the groups that formed InterAct.

In the later 19th century, the Bethel Baptist church in the city of Örebro became an important centre for renewal, training and mission. The senior *pastor* was the Swedish-American, John Ongman. In 1892, Ongman organised an Inland and Foreign Missions group in the church and also launched a *Bible* Institute in Örebro. In 1897, a new congregation named Filadelfia was formed, with Ongman as its minister. This new church and the wider Örebro Mission, as it came to be known, operated within the Baptist Union of Sweden. In 1908, the Örebro Bible school became a seminary.

As *Pentecostalism* grew within the Swedish Baptist churches in the early 20th century the Filadelfia Church in Örebro became a centre for the growing interest in the Pentecostal message. When some Baptist churches separated from the Union, John Ongman was asked to seek to reconcile the parties, but this effort failed. Following Ongman's *death* in 1931, the Örebro Mission network, which had grown considerably, increasingly moved away from the Swedish Baptist Union and from 1937 began to operate separately, with training taking place at the Örebro Seminary.

Today, InterAct is a church and mission movement with a vision to see 'growing churches [see **Church Growth**] bring the whole gospel to the whole **man** all over the world'. InterAct describes its identity as baptist, **evangelical, charismatic** and mission-oriented. It is a member of the **European Baptist Federation**, being admitted in Sep 2005. It has 330 churches, with a total of 30,000 members, and 150 **missionaries** are engaged in InterAct's international **ministry**, in cooperation with 60 international partners. InterAct is involved in ministry in Africa, Asia, Europe, Latin America and the Middle East. The focus of its international ministry is **evangelism** and **church planting**, leadership training and organisational development, and social involvement.

ET

Intercommunion

See *Communion and Intercommunion*.

Inter-Faith Worship

[See also *Worship*]

During the 1960s and 70s it became increasingly common for groups such as **Scouting** and Guides, the United Nations Association, or Community Relations Councils and their equivalents, to try to hold inclusive ceremonies for the increasingly diverse memberships of such organisations. Since then Interfaith Worship has become for some a controversial issue, especially when linked with the growth of Inter-Faith **Dialogue**. Some enthusiasts for dialogue (e.g. the World Congress of Faiths), as also some critics, have (mistakenly in my view) argued that Inter-Faith Worship is an inevitable concomitant

of a commitment to the process of dialogue. In fact this is rarely the case and the issue of worship has sometimes been used as a 'red herring' to divert attention from the fundamental issue of how *faith* communities engage appropriately with each other in a pluralist society. Some argue that there is a parallel to the *ecumenical* discussion as to how far common worship is the goal or actually the foundation of such an exercise; but the shared understandings within a faith tradition are generally more clear-cut than those between faith traditions. (There is a helpful historical sketch and analysis by Marcus Braybrooke in *All in Good Faith* chs.2-3.)

Pressure for some form of common worship often comes from secular authorities who are trying to find some form of *civic religion* for *pluralist* societies. E.g. in **Britain** the Monarch usually attends an annual Observance for Commonwealth Day for all faiths held in Westminster Abbey (note, however, the careful denotation of this ceremony as 'an observance', rather than as a religious service). Most people with actual experience of encounter and conversation with other religions recognise how sensitive the issue of worship is, with each faith wanting to preserve the integrity of its own *tradition*. Nevertheless, given the religiously plural societies which constitute much of Europe at the beginning of the 21st century, there may well be a need for people to find ways to share, in religious terms, common human experiences of celebration or of solidarity in times of crisis. To exclude any expression of religious faith or worship in such situations is in danger of leading to a barren secularist approach.

Various publications have attempted to delineate more carefully what a term such as Inter-Faith Worship might mean. E.g. a report commissioned for the **Anglican** Archbishops in 1979 described three types of occasion:

(1) Christian services with guest participants from other faiths;

(2) Inter-faith services of a serial type (i.e. representatives from each participating faith offer worship from their own tradition one after the other);

(3) Inter-faith services with an agreed common order,
(*Inter-faith Services and Worship*, 1979).

The British Baptist Joppa Group added two other possibilities, which might possibly come under the label of Inter-Faith Worship:

(4) attending an act of worship as an observer (rather than a participant); this might be for purposes of *education* and mutual understanding, or as an act of solidarity – with a community in mourning e.g.;

(5) sitting in silence with people of other faiths which 'allows us to be ourselves alongside others without imposing anything on one another'; most faiths have some tradition of silent *prayer* or meditation which can be used in such circumstances.

(*A Baptist Perspective on Interfaith Dialogue*, 1992, pp.16f)

Some *theological* principles we may wish to bear in mind in relation to Inter-Faith Worship might include:

(i) both the uniqueness and the universality of *Christ* as seen in the *scriptures*;

(ii) the sense of mystery before the One God, the maker of the whole earth and all its peoples (e.g. Ps 24);

(iii) the apparently universal instinct to worship recognised in the scriptures (e.g. Mal 1:11) in which, according to the Baptist OT *scholar*, H.H. Rowley, 'Malachi claims for Jehovah worship that is not offered to his name but is sincere and validated by a pure heart' (*The Missionary Message of the Old Testament*, 1945, p.73).

(iv) the importance of the avoidance of idolatry, but also due care in understanding of what idolatry truly consists: 'it is easier to denounce idolatry than to define it' (*Multi-Faith Worship?*, 1992, p.29).

(v) the role of the *Spirit* in leading the people of God into all truth (Jn 14).

In 1994 the Baptist *Union* of Great Britain, in a rare statement of policy, published a document on the question of 'Inter-Faith Relations in the Decade of *Evangelism*' which also touched on the question of Inter-Faith Worship. Whilst recognising that meetings specifically for worship were generally inappropriate and potentially offensive to people of several faith traditions, it did recognise that there might well be occasions when people of different faiths might

need to stand alongside one another, sharing their common humanity, especially in the face of a tragedy or disaster that affected more than one faith community. There are also considerable issues for people of mixed faith families; although some work has been done in relation to *marriage* this area will require further work in the plural societies of contemporary Europe.

NJW

FURTHER READING: P. Akehurst and R. Wootton, *Inter-faith Worship?*, Grove Books, Bramcote, 1977. D. Bookless, *Interfaith Worship and Christian Truth*, Grove books, Bramcote, 1991. M. Braybrooke, *Inter Faith Worship*, Stainer and Bell, London, 1974. K. Cragg, *Alive to God*, Oxford University Press, London and New York, 1970. Inter-Faith Consultative Group, *Multi-Faith Worship?*, Church House Publishing, London, 1992. J. Potter and M. Braybrooke, *All in Good Faith: A Resource Book for Multi-faith Prayer*, World Congress of Faiths, Oxford, 1997. N.J. Wood (ed), *A Baptist Perspective on Interfaith Dialogue*, Joppa Publications, Alcester, 1992.

International Baptist Convention (IBC/EBC)

The work of the European Baptist Convention (EBC), as it became from 1964, began in 1957 with the founding of Immanuel Baptist Church, Wiesbaden, *Germany*, as an English-speaking Baptist church. In the following year Bethel Baptist Church in Frankfurt was started. These two churches formed the *Association* of Baptists in Continental Europe. Under the leadership of two brothers, Herman and Herbert Stout, the Association grew to more than 30 churches. The original focus was *ministry* to the needs of US military service personnel and their families stationed in Europe. In 1961, the Foreign Mission Board of the *SBC* sent a *missionary* couple to work with the growing churches [see *Church growth*] and in 1968 the first EBC General Secretary was appointed. In the 1970s several new international churches were begun in the major cities of Europe. After the fall of *Communism* the EBC was able to start churches in Eastern-European countries. In the first half of the 1990s the EBC saw 20 new English-language churches started, including eight in cities in Eastern Europe. By this stage many of the churches in the Convention were becoming international in their *membership*, with up to 30 nationalities represented in some cases. About one-third of the churches are still comprised primarily of US military personnel. In 1996, the EBC called the first General Secretary to be fully supported by the Convention and in 2003 the EBC decided to change its name to the International Baptist Convention (IBC). In 2005 the IBC had 65 churches and missions located in 24 countries, mainly (though not exclusively) in Europe.

IMR

FURTHER READING: H. and H. Stout, *Appointed by Christ Exclusively*, Fort Worth, Tx., 1996.

International Baptist Theological Seminary (IBTS)

[See also *Rüschlikon Baptist Theological Seminary*]

IBTS is a unique institution in the world family of Baptists. It is wholly owned by the *European Baptist Federation*. It was founded in Rüschlikon, *Switzerland*, by the *Southern Baptist* Foreign Mission Board in 1949, was handed over to the European Baptist Federation in 1988 and relocated to Prague, *Czech Republic*, in 1996-97.

No other continental Baptist fellowship has attempted to develop a deliberate multinational, multi-cultural community for the *theological* formation of *women* and *men*. It seeks to provide masters and doctoral level theological *education*, research programmes, conferences, sabbatical and study opportunities for *pastors*, *missionaries* and academics.

The Prague campus is commonly known as the *European Baptist Centre* and houses the offices of the EBF, together with the Hotel Jenerálka, a three star hotel wholly owned by the EBF, the surplus income from which is used to assist in running the seminary.

IBTS offers masters and doctoral degrees validated by the University of *Wales* in the following subject areas – Baptist/*Anabaptist* Studies, *Applied Theology*, *Biblical Studies* and *Contextual Missiology*. IBTS also has a more general Magister in Theology degree which is accredited by the Czech Ministry of Education, making it one of the few confessional theology institutions in Europe to be accredited by the *state*. Both *women* and *men* come as *students* from a range of Christian *traditions*. It has had amongst its teaching staff two people who went on to become General Secretaries of the *Baptist World Alliance* (Dr. Josef Nordenhaug and Dr. Denton Lotz) and two of the current Regional Secretaries of the BWA are alumni of IBTS.

In addition to the higher degree programmes, IBTS also offers a nine month certificate programme in theology. This programme draws up to 20 lay [see *Laity*] students per year aged between 20 and 30 nominated by the EBF member *unions*. They participate in a programme of English and theology. A key emphasis of this programme is to expose the participants to an international and multi-cultural environment and to build friendships across the European Baptist family. IBTS also has a full programme of sabbatical and conference opportunities. The seminary was a founder member of the *Consortium of European Baptist Theological Schools*.

The Academic team support five Research Institutes in Baptist and Anabaptist studies (founded 1982), Biblical Studies (founded 2004), Mission and *Evangelism* (founded 1988), Systematic Studies of *Contextual Theologies* (founded 2004) and the *Thomas Helwys* Centre for *Religious Freedom* (founded 2002 in *Bristol*, transferred to IBTS 2006).

The seminary is governed by a Board of Trustees elected by the Council of the European Baptist Federation. The Council also appoints the Rector (President/Principal). The Board of Trustees appoint an Academic Dean and a Kvestor (Director of Finance and Administration). It is the Rector and these two colleagues who form the Rectorate team and who exercise overall management of IBTS and its ancillary operations.

The Academic Team, of women and men, both full and part time, are drawn principally from Europe, though several adjunct lecturers do come from the USA and Africa. They represent a range of *Christian world communions*, though the majority belong to the *gathering church* traditions.

IBTS has, as part of its mission, the desire to become an *eco-seminary* with a great concern for the *environment*. The seminary has a special module on the environment and an environmental policy addressing all the major areas of energy, waste and recycling, developing the natural outlook of the physical campus and promoting the idea of eco-congregations.

KGJ

FURTHER READING: Petra Veselá, *Fit for a King*, IBTS, Prague, 2004. www.ibts.eu.

International Fellowship of Evangelical Students (IFES)

See *Student Christian Movement (SCM), Inter-Varsity Fellowship (IVF), World Student Christian Federation (WSCF) and International Fellowship of Evangelical Students (IFES)*.

International Missionary Council

An outcome of the *Edinburgh* Conference of 1910, the International Missionary Council was founded in 1921 under the influence of such leaders as John Mott and J.H. Oldham. Its aim was to assist churches, national and international *mission* boards and societies in their essential missionary task of sharing with people everywhere the transforming power of the gospel. It encouraged the growth of national Christian Councils in the several mission fields. Here the principal players were churches newly established as a result of missionary activity. Thus the Council played a vital part in the transfer of decision-making from mission boards in the Global North to newly independent emerging churches in the Global South. The work was in part to encourage cooperation, coordination and where possible united action, in part educational to undertake well-researched study and to disseminate best practice and proficient *missiology* through conferences, consultations and the periodical, *The International Review of Missions*. By contrast with Edinburgh, its first conference held in Jerusalem in 1928 had half the 231 delegates coming from the South – some have in fact called it the first global meeting in human history. There were, however, already tensions over widening definitions of mission to embrace newer social emphases. Later the Council had to face the issue of the relationship of Christianity to non-Christian religions, an issue faced by Hendrik Kraemer in his *The Christian Message in a Non Christian World* which stressed the discontinuity between Christianity and other *faiths*. The Council played a crucial part in the formation of the *World Council of Churches* with which, after considerable reluctance from some of its constituents, it merged in 1961. Many members of the IMC feared the loss of cutting edge in *evangelism* whilst some member churches of the WCC, particularly the *Orthodox* were worried lest the integration of the two bodies be seen to give a license to *proselytism* at their expense. The counter argument was that integration would put mission at the very heart of the work of the WCC. The work of the former IMC was continued within the work of the WCC through the Division (later Commission) of World Mission and Evangelism, but the criticism has subsequently been made that mission within the context of the WCC has received too broad a definition so that it all too easily becomes 'everything the church is called to do'. As a consequence there have had to be periodic reminders within the counsels of the WCC of the need of the specifically evangelistic task for the churches to engage the specific proclamation of the message of *salvation*.

JHYB

Inter-Varsity Fellowship (IVF)

See *Student Christian Movement (SCM), Inter-Varsity Fellowship (IVF), World Student Christian Federation (WSCF) and International Fellowship of Evangelical Students (IFES)*.

Iona Community, Scotland

See *Intentional Communities*.

Ireland, Baptist history in

Baptist history in Ireland really begins with the Cromwellian era (c.1649 onwards). The *members* of the first Baptist churches were almost exclusively from the army, civil government or new settlers, rather than native Irish. Prominent among the *ministers* was Thomas Patient, who founded a church in

Dublin and built the first Baptist meeting-house in Ireland, in Swift's Alley, Dublin, in 1653. There is little information about the latter part of the 17th century.

The earliest information about the 18th century is a letter from Joseph Pettit (pastor in Cork) to Elisha Callender (Boston), dated Nov 1725, which lists 11 churches, nine of which formed the 'Irish Baptist *Association*'. New churches were planted in Ulster in the early 1800s – some as the result of the influence of the Haldanes [see *Haldaneite Tradition*]. The 1859 *revival* led to the birth of a few more churches.

The Irish Baptist Association (re-constituted in 1862) was affiliated to the British *Union*. Growing unease over the 'Down Grade' contributed to the formation of a separate body, the Baptist Union of Ireland, in 1895. In 1999 the Union was re-named the 'Association of Baptist Churches in Ireland'. The Association – not affiliated to the *BWA* – comprises 111 churches, of which 17 are in the Republic of Ireland. Total membership is around 8,000. There are also several independent churches. Irish Baptists are generally *'conservative evangelical'* and practise *open communion*. Many serve in or support a wide range of interdenominational *missions*, as well as the Association's own missionaries in Ireland, Peru and Europe.

MD

Irish Baptist College

The Irish Baptist College was founded in Dublin in 1892. From the beginning it owed much to the vision of the *pastor* of Dublin's Harcourt Street congregation, Hugh D. Brown, who was a close friend of *C.H. Spurgeon*, and Spurgeon's Pastors' College [see *Spurgeon's College*] was the model for the Dublin institution. The College was re-constituted in Belfast in 1963 and for 40 years occupied a site in East Belfast. In May 2003 new College premises were opened near Moira, just outside Belfast.

The College has been a recognised college of Queen's University, Belfast, since 1977 and offers a full range of university studies from the Diploma in *Theology*, Bachelors of Divinity and Theology, through to post-graduate research degrees. In 2003 the col-lege also became a partner institution of the University of Wales and offers undergraduate and postgraduate studies leading to awards from that university. The range of courses on offer has attracted students from as far away as Peru, *Romania*, *Russia*, Korea and the West Indies, many of whom pursue their work in their own country. In addition, the College offers a range of non-university full-time and part-time programmes of study.

Not an independent body, the Irish Baptist College is a department of the *Association* of Baptist Churches in *Ireland* and is overseen by a management committee appointed by the Association. There are six full-time faculty members and around a dozen visiting lecturers (many of them pastors of Irish Baptist churches). The total number of *students* enrolled for the various courses is at present about 180.

MD

Islam, Baptists and
See *Muslims, Baptists and the Common Word*.

Israel, Baptist history in
[See also *Holy Land, The*]
Baptist presence in Israel began in 1911, with the return of Revd Shukri Musa to his hometown of Safed in northern Galilee after his studies in the USA. Musa was supported by Illinois Baptists, and in 1912 he settled in Nazareth. His *evangelistic* efforts led to the establishment of the Nazareth Baptist church, the first Baptist church in the country. During the first 50 years, Baptist work depended on *missionary* efforts sponsored by the *Southern Baptist Convention* (USA). In 1923, the first Southern Baptist missionaries were appointed to Jerusalem; and in 1929, a *mission station* in Haifa was opened, though no organised church was formed

WWII, the conflict in 1947, and the war that followed led to a setback in Baptist work, especially in Jerusalem and Haifa. Missionaries left and many *church members* fled to other countries in the Middle East. The Nazareth Baptist church was less affected, because the *local church* members took over the leadership. In 1949-50, missionaries started to come back and worked with local believers to reorganise the Baptist work. In Nazareth, the first national *pastor*, Fuad Sakhnini, was ordained [see *Ordination*] in 1960. The Jerusalem Baptist Church, with multi-national membership, was reorganised in 1963; today it has congregations which *worship* in Hebrew, Russian, English and Arabic. In 1965, the mission station in Haifa became a church. Its members included Arabs, *Jews* and expatriates in Israel. Baptists used *educational* activities, *Sunday Schools*, book distributing and *music* for outreach and church development. Many of the graduates of the Nazareth Baptist School, founded in 1949-50, became leaders of the Baptist work, particularly in (the) Galilee and Northern Israel. Baptists also began to work in the Tel-Aviv area, on the coastal plain.

The second half of the 20th century saw organisational reform among Baptists in Israel. Several mission stations became organised as churches. In 1963, the *Association* of Baptist Churches in Israel was established, which became an active instrument for promoting different *ministries* in local churches as well as establishing relationships with the wider Baptist family. The Association was granted membership of the *Baptist World Alliance* and the *European Baptist Federation*. It also became a member of the United Christian Council of Israel. Baptists Philip Saad and Fuad Haddad have served on the board of this *evangelical* grouping. Of the 19 churches belonging to the Association, 13 are Arabic-speaking, while others minister to expatriates and hence have services in other languages. There are informal relationships with groups of messianic Jews, who tend to shun denominational labels.

The establishment of the Association provided a channel to organise the relationship with the *International Baptist Convention*, which was composed of expatriate Southern Baptist representatives. Together they composed a *covenant* relationship that included, among other goals, support, expansion and strengthening of the local Baptist work. The relationship between the Association and the Convention developed slowly, having a common vision of leading the churches and Baptist centres to total independence. However, in 1996, the Convention shifted its strategy and began to emphasise work among unreached people groups.

This almost led to a complete termination of the covenant relationship. As a result, the Association became the leader of the local work in the country. Today, the Association focuses on promoting the work of the local churches, aimed at *church planting*. It is also striving to train new leaders for churches, to support present ones, and to become recognised by the authorities.

FH

Israel, Nation of
See *Jews and Judaism, Baptists and*.

Italy, Baptist history in
The history of Baptists in Italy began with a letter from *pastor* J. Berg published in *The Freeman* on 21 May 1862, inviting English Baptists to take seriously the idea of *mission* in Italy. Pastors James Wall and Edward Clarke responded to this *call*, founding the 'Gospel Mission to the Italians'. After an exploratory visit in May, James Wall moved to Bologna in Nov 1863, followed by Edward Clarke who, in 1865 settled in La Spezia. At the beginning Wall worked independently, but on moving to Rome he was employed by the *Baptist Missionary Society*. Clark, however, founded a mission (The Spezia Mission for Italy and the Levant) which was independent until 1966 when the churches of the Spezia Mission joined the Baptist *Union* of Italy. In addition in 1870 Wilfred Nelson Cote arrived in Rome for the Southern Baptist Foreign Mission Board (FMB).

Contemporary to the wars of national liberation, a number of Free *Evangelical* Churches [see *Free Churches*] had been founded by Italian patriots who disagreed with the *Roman Catholic* Church. As exiles in London, Geneva and *Malta* for their political beliefs they had experienced a different way of being Christian and brought it back with them to Italy. The first Baptist missionaries in Italy collaborated with some of the leaders of these free churches and a number of these congregations joined the Baptist Union.

Baptist churches were planted in all areas of Italy despite the great difficulties and persecution by the Roman Catholic Church, often aided by the *state*. To become a Baptist in those early years could mean losing your job, your house and all your possessions. Nonetheless the Baptists grew in number [see *Church Growth*] and the work was divided between the BMS and the FMB until 1922 when the BMS withdrew from Italy (the FMB later withdrew its presence in 1993).

The advent of *fascism* brought renewed persecution for the Baptist Churches, especially after Mussolini signed the *Concordato* [Agreement] with the state in 1929. Baptist Churches resisted and were strengthened to face the terrible time of WWII (1940-45): during the war the American mission could not support the Italian churches, but they were already strong and mature and with the help of God managed to overcome all difficulties.

After the war the Christian Evangelical Baptist Union of Italy with a statute of independence from the mission was founded in 1956. The process of securing independence and taking responsibility for the Italian churches concluded in 1993 with the withdrawal of the FMB. In 1993, according to art. 8 of the Italian Constitution, an agreement [*Intesa*], giving recognition to Baptist churches, was signed with the Italian state. This became law in 1995 and forms the basis of the relationship between the Baptist Union and the Italian state.

Today the Union has about 120 churches (around a quarter of these are ethnic churches) with 5,000 members and c.25,000 sympathisers.

Italian Baptists use the *Waldensian Theological Faculty* and *IBTS* for the training of their ministers.

FS

Itinerancy

The term derives from the Latin word *itineris* [a journey]. The travelling *preacher*, in part modelled on the life of St. Paul, was very much a feature of the 18th-century *Evangelical Revival*: both George Whitefield and John Wesley covered many 1,000s of miles on horseback. Among Baptists in Europe, with the reform of older methods of training and the foundation of new seminaries at the end of the 18th century and in 19th century, itinerancy became part of the practical programme of those training for *ministry*. The Bristol Education Society, e.g., organised a gospel *mission* into Cornwall, in south-west *England*, as early as 1770, and Caleb Evans argued the work of training 'was not only to offer basic *theological education* but to encourage missionaries to preach the gospel wherever *providence* opens a door for it'. Also in England, William Steadman, through the Northern Education Society, with its well-designed itinerant routes into the borders of Yorkshire and Lancashire, not only trained ministers for the churches but provided pioneers to engage in itinerant preaching. This same pattern of itinerant preaching was one of the first functions of the newly established Baptist *associations* of this period, whilst the cumbersomely titled 'London Society for the encouragement and support of Itinerancy and Village Preaching' later became the Home Missionary Society [see *Home Mission*]. Within these enterprises there was an admission of the validity of a call to be a preacher-*evangelist* as much as a settled minister caring for a single congregation. *Oncken* in his work as a *scripture colporteur* also was very much a travelling preacher and encouraged those he saw converted [see *Conversion*] to disseminate the gospel, throughout *Germany*, east to *Poland* and the *Baltic* Republics and south east into the *Balkan* states. Among the most influential travelling preachers in the growth of the Baptist movement across Europe were Gottfreid Alf (Poland), Ivan Kargel (*Russia*) and Heinrich Meyer (*Hungary* and further afield). A number of the most significant preachers with a wider ministry were trained under Oncken in Hamburg. Others, such as the 'Peasant Prophets' in Transylvania – notably Mihály Kornya and Mihály Tóth – emerged through the ministry of local Baptist communities and did not receive formal theological training.

JHYB

IVF

See *Student Christian Movement (SCM), Inter-Varsity Fellowship (IVF), World Student Christian Federation (WSCF) and International Fellowship of Evangelical Students (IFES)*.

J

JEBS
See *Journal of European Baptist Studies.*

Jesus Christ
[See also *Christology; Incarnation; Logos; Lord of the Church and the Crown Rights of the Redeemer*]
The person and work of Jesus lie at the heart of Christian belief. Baptists, with other Christians, have gladly proclaimed the affirmation found at the beginning of John's Gospel that in the beginning the Word who became flesh in the incarnate Christ was with God and was God, that is to say that the uncreated Son of God had a pre-incarnational existence in the *Trinity*, sharing in the work of *creation*. Baptists have also stressed the way in which the gospel records speak of how Jesus Christ would, by his *death* and *resurrection*, secure the *redemption* of *humankind*. Through the centuries these mysteries have often been expressed in simple terms by many ordinary believers (in what has been described as 'primary *theology*'), and in more formal and complex ways by *theologians*, philosophers and guardians of the life of the *church* – whether *Bishops* or *Synods*.

Baptist communities have taken on the challenge, too, of making Christological statements, although in many cases Baptists *confessions* have used wording to be found in other creeds and confessions. Debates about Christology have occurred at different points in the 400 years of baptistic life. An understanding of the work and person of Christ is classically set out in the 17th century Baptist confessions, e.g. The Particular Baptists' *London Confession of 1644*, especially paragraphs IX-XXI where emphasis is placed on the Lord Jesus as the only mediator of the *New Covenant*, or the General Baptists' so-called *Orthodox Creed of 1678*, especially paragraphs IV-VII, XVI-XVIII, XXIV-XXV which are clear about the nature of Christ's person as divine and human and about the significance of his birth, death and resurrec-tion [see *England*].

However, for Baptists confessions do not have the *authority* which they have in some other Christian *traditions*. They are helpful, but for Baptists it is the biblical record [see *Bible*] which is the ultimately authoritative witness to Jesus Christ. The record of the life of Jesus in the gospels is set within a context: Jesus is the Christ, that is the Messiah of OT *prophecy*, God's anointed or chosen one, charged with securing the *salvation* of God's people: so in the synoptic gospels Peter's Confession at Caesarea Philippi makes this crucial connection (Mk 8:29) an identification admitted by Jesus under pressure in the judicial context of his trial before the Sanhedrin (Mk 16:61-62), which also becomes a sarcastic accusatory jibe from the high priests whilst Jesus hung on the *cross*: 'Let this Christ, this King of Israel, come down from the cross that we may see and believe'. But because his way is the way of *suffering* sacrifice that is not a way in which he can proceed. If the messianic statements recorded in the synoptic gospels are measured, even reluctant, perhaps because Jesus' audience had to be educated as to what the true nature of the mission of the Messiah was, in John's gospel the identification is explicit from the very beginning, from Andrew's confession to Peter, 'We have found the Christ' (Jn 1:41) onwards.

The purpose of Jesus here on earth, according to the gospels, was to proclaim the coming of the *kingdom* (Mk 1:15) which is often said to be the central theme in all Jesus' teaching. This kingdom is to be as different from the jurisdiction of 1st-century *Judaism*, where actions were judged by reference to a Pharisaic respect for obeying the Law in every detail, as it was from the coercive rule of the Roman Empire imposed by force of arms. The Kingdom of God which Jesus proclaimed had a much higher purpose, namely to restore God's kingly rule in the world, that is to return to return to what he had intended in the original act of creation. Whilst earthly rulers might claim to exercise *sovereignty*, ultimate authority belongs to God. Because this seemed so often to be frustrated by the activities of evil-doers, the OT prophets looked to a day when God's kingdom would be restored; so Jesus proclaimed that the foretold day had come, and those with eyes to see could see the signs of its coming in the words and works of Jesus, in parable ('The kingdom of God is like...') and miracle, where the power of God as over against that of **Satan** and demonic powers was abundantly demonstrated. In the kingdom of God, earthly values are put into reverse, service rather than the exercise of power becomes the order of the day, the building of community rather than the exploitation of competition, the welfare of people not the accumulation of material **wealth**. This kingdom of God is both already here, but yet fully to be fulfilled, and so, whilst living under the rule of God, his people **pray**, 'Your kingdom come'.

Though the Son is the second person of the Trinity, the gospel record are at pains to spell out the true humanity of Jesus, (Php 2:6-8, Heb 2:10-18, 4:14-16) in his birth in Bethlehem, his life and work in Nazareth, Galilee and Judaea, his entry into Jerusalem, the meal in the upper room, the false arrest, trial, imprisonment and crucifixion, and all this for a purpose. This is enshrined in Jesus' name – Jesus or Joshua – which means 'Jehovah will save'. Thus in Mt 1:21 it is recorded that he is to be called Jesus 'for he will save his people from their sins'; he comes to them not as a military champion, but one who will save humanity from its worst enemy, **sin**.

In his speech at **Pentecost**, recorded in Acts, Peter speaks of the greatest miracle of all, namely God's raising of Jesus from the dead, commenting, 'Let all **Israel** be assured of this: God has made this Jesus, whom you crucified, both Lord and Christ', as if the resurrection were God's signature of affirmation on Jesus' messianic purpose. So the promised Messiah who proclaims God's kingdom and secures the salvation of sinning humanity is also the Risen Lord, thus affirming that other birth name given to Jesus, the fulfilment of Isaiah's prophecy of the coming of 'Emmanuel' – 'God with us' – reflected also in Jesus' promise at the end of Matthew's account of the **Great Commission**, 'And surely I am with you always to the very end of the age (Mt 28:20). Into this story are woven the events of the **Ascension** and of Pentecost, Jesus' return to his Father and the gift of the Spirit, Christ's position in **Heaven** as heavenly advocate and his presence through his **Spirit** here on earth as Comforter and Strength of those who name him as Lord (Mt 26:64). Thus the age of the Church is the age of **mission**, looking forward to the spread of the gospel in all the earth, but the time will come when the age of opportunity will give way to a time of judgment before the return of Christ at the consummation of time, when, in the words of the **Apostle**'s Creed, 'he will come to judge the living and the dead'.

ET

FURTHER READING: Paul Fiddes, *Participating in God*, Darton, Longmann and Todd, London, 2000. Thorwald Lorenzen, *Resurrection and Discipleship*, Orbis, New York, 1995. James Wm. McClendon, Jr., *Systematic Theology* (3 vols), Abingdon, Nashville, Tn., 1986-2000.

Jews and Judaism, Baptists and

Judaism broadly understood is an ethnoreligious phenomenon. The **Bible** bears witness to a people who based their **covenantal** beliefs in the **revelation** of the God of Abraham, Isaac and Jacob. This was confirmed in God's disclosure to Moses at Sinai, which established the religious practices and the moral code which set them apart not only as 'the people of God', but as 'the Jewish people'(a Jew being defined by *halakah* as one who was born of a Jewish mother or who converted to Judaism). In the Post-Emancipation period, and particularly since after the emergence in the last century of the **State** of **Israel**, what constitutes a legal definition of a Jew (in the light of the Law of Return) has been hotly debated, leading to significant tensions between different branches of Judaism today – the **Orthodox**, Conservative and Reformed – particularly with the proliferation of **mixed marriages** and in a situation where Jewish identity is no longer based exclusively on religious practices or beliefs. Significant numbers in world Jewry today define Jewish identity in terms of a common history and sense of destiny, leaving the term Judaism to designate varying religious perspectives on revelation, authority of the received Torah and the tradition of rabbinic interpretations along with different ethical [see **Ethics**] responses to the encounter with the contemporary world.

Christianity developed three distinct perspectives on Jews and Judaism. Traditionally Christianity regarded Judaism as a religion whose essence and existence had been superseded by the gospel: by accepting *Christ*'s message the *church* became the new spiritual Israel, replacing the old Israel in God's economy of *salvation*. Early Christian supersessionism led to an escalating sequence of anti-Jewish confrontations followed by social, *political*, institutionalised and, finally, racial *antisemitism* in Christian *nations*, a view still generally maintained by Christian *fundamentalists* and some *conservative* Christians, though currently under severe theological scrutiny, having been discredited by the *Shoah* (Diprose).

Some have attempted to replace supersessionism with the political philo-semitism of Christian Zionism, which has its roots in 19th-century British premillennial *sectarianism* and early 20th-century American *dispensentialism*, but this has proved equally fruitless in providing grounds for healthy Jewish-Christian relationships (Sizer). While sharing with other philo-Semitic Christian groups some of the constructive aspects of encouraging *dialogue* with Jewish people, standing against antisemitism, educating Christians in the Jewish origins of their *faith*, Christian Zionism, in its literal and futurist *hermeneutics*, is uncritically relying on sectarian *theology*, politics and ideology with dire consequences for political realities in the Middle East. Christian Zionism is essentially paternalistic, deploying the idea of Judaism to Zionism's own ends. By doing that Christian Zionism does not differ in essence from the supersessionist position. Considering two millennia of Christian antisemitism, the task of formulating constructive theologies of Jewish-Christian dialogue demand thorough revisiting, revising centuries-old theological constructs to recover the central Christian purpose of the exercise.

Some *Roman Catholic theologians* (Rosemary Radford Reuter), especially, but also mainline *Protestant* (Karl Barth, Jürgen Moltmann, Paul M. van Buren) and Orthodox theologians have devoted renewed attention to a biblical and theological understanding of Judaism in its special standing in regard to God's revelation. Apart from setting the trend of Holocaust or Post-Holocaust theology, the most pronounced

result of this rethinking is a reinterpretation of the *Apostle* Paul's reflections on God's comprehensive *covenant love* and providential plan for the Jews that argues for a 'two-covenant theology'. This second major Christian perspective on Judaism 'has been recently defined as a "theology of recognition" focussing on Christian recognition of *Israel*'s status as a covenant nation' (Diprose, p.177). According to this reading of Paul, the Sinai covenant is still soteriologically valid for the Jews, while the new covenant in Christ is essentially for Gentiles Two-covenant theology is currently promoted by many academic theologians as an alternative to the supersessionist view, and is often assumed in Jewish-Christian dialogue, but 'hardly does justice to Paul's complex dialectical wrestling in Romans 9-11' (Hays, p.411) and Christian scripture generally.

A third position is now emerging, interchangeably referred to as 'a-people-made-up-of-peoples' (McClendon, p.364), one-covenant-two-peoples (Yoder), or teleological (Edwards, p.222). It follows the lead of baptistic *theologians* such as John Howard Yoder and James Wm. McClendon's *tertium datur* – the third way of restitutionist's theology of 'not-parting-of-the-ways' and reflects a more faithful biblical understanding of the relationship of Christianity to Judaism. It assumes that according to Paul, God's promises to the Jewish people have not been superseded in the sense that they have been discarded. Jewish people-hood continues to play a role in God's eternal purpose. 'Teleological' in this perspective means the direction and arrival of something at its proper destination. From a Christian perspective the proper destination of all *creation*, Jews included, is the reunification of the redeemed with the Messiah, Jesus Christ, who fulfils all things, 'who is and who was and who is to come' (Rev 1:8). For the Jews it is the Messiah yet to come. It has, however, still to be shown to what extent the third perspective of 'one-covenant-two-peoples' theology differs from the 'two-covenant' theology and how claims of soteriological fulfilment in the messianic vision of Christ coincide with soteriological claims of the Sinaitic covenant of the Jews. But this third perspective does invite a hermeneutic of reciprocity and opens the way for a theology of Jewish-Christian mutuality. In line with the argument of Eph 2, the language of the 'new covenant' employed by the Christian scriptures can be seen in the continuation and the renewal of God's covenants with Israel. Thus, the new covenant functions not as a 'replacement or a parallel covenant but as a living covenant that embraces two peoples in a relationship of tense reciprocity' (Bader-Saye, p.100).

For the *Free Church* and Baptist adherents of the Radical *Reformation* in Europe and elsewhere the 'critical revision of Jewish-Christian relationships especially since "the holocaust"' (Yoder, p.37) is an acutely relevant theme too. Historically, this relationship has not differed much from that of the culture at large. Baptists have tried different ways to find a place for the Jews in their theology. One way was to view them as a *mission* field to be *evangelised* as any other group. Another way was the careful millenarian and dispensationalist's schemata of all sorts using the Jewish people as a means in achieving the ends of their own *eschatology*. The third way was to follow the dominant religious culture in its disdain towards the Jews (Strübind, Ross). To the credit of the Baptists and other radical Christian movements in Europe, it must be said that, in addition to Danes, Norwegians, or the French at Le Chambon, Baptists in Eastern Europe have provided examples of individual and collective righteous actions toward Jews in the face of surrounding the unprecedented cultural antisemitism of *the Shoah* (Parushev, Gushee). At the same time, from the very beginning the Baptist movement, through the writings of *Thomas Helwys*, had shown respect for the Jews and their ability to practice their faith without let or hindrance whilst bodies like the *Evangelical Alliance*, with much Baptist support, had from the latter part of the 19th century through the period of the rise of National Socialism expressed their hostility to all forms of persecution of the Jews.

At this critical point of time, two interrelated questions loom large. Considering two millennia of persistent Christian antisemitism, is it possible to redeem the original vision of Jesus' peaceable *Kingdom* and alter Christian attitudes to the closest sibling in the family of monotheistic belief-systems? Is a different way of relating to the Jews and Judaism possible for Christians? With the demise of the old characterisation of Western civilisation as *Christendom*, in either the political or the cultural sense, both Jews and Christians must ask the ancient question, 'How do we sing the Lord's song in a strange land?' (Ps 137:4). For *secularity* has threatened them both quite similarly. A shared threat has created a new commonality. What is at stake is not apologising to the Jews, as important as that may be, but rescuing both Christianity and Judaism from the subverting power of secularism.

Any Christian tradition has to face these questions and contribute to Christian-Jewish conversation from its own perspective. First of all, there is a need of *repentance* for the past misdeeds, as some Christian bodies have been courageous enough to do. Yet this on its own is not sufficient. The necessary prophetic voice of the church [see *Prophecy*], condemning any form of dominance, of ethnic or religious suppression, such as antisemitism, is still largely missing. Yet even this will not be enough. Guided by their best insights into the struggles for *religious freedom*, Baptists should embark on the apostolic mission of educating their communities as well as society at large in another way of Jews and Christians living and witnessing together for the redeeming presence of the God of Abraham and Jesus Christ and, if necessary, both communities to dare to undergo deep surgery to cut off long venerated 'orthodox' beliefs and practices that nurture antisemitism and religious superiority. And finally, there should be readiness for the *pastoral* embrace and caring for those abused because of their gender, race, ethnicity, or faith.

Establishing grounds for a respectful dialogue with Judaism is a work still in progress. For such a dialogue to happen, both the thesis of Christian supersessionism and the antithesis of Jewish counter-supersessionism should be renounced not in the hope of achieving a new Hegelian synthesis but in the interests of advancing mutual understanding and enrichment of two distinct ways of doing theology, the theology of the God of Abraham. Whilst there may be an accidental spill over from Judeo-Christian moral witness arising out of two genuine perspectives on God's salvific working in the world that he has created, improved relations also require a willing and involved participation of Jewish theologians. Happily *Dabru Emet* – the Jewish Statement on Christians and Christianity – provides good evidence for a measure of optimism that such a serious dialogue is already on the way.

PRP

FURTHER READING: Scott Bader-Saye, *Church and Israel after Christendom: The Politics of Election*, Westview, Boulder, 1999. Ronald E. Diprose, *Israel and the Church: The Origins and Effects of Replacement Theology*, Authentic Medium, Waynesboro, 2004. James R. Edwards, *Is Jesus the Only Savior?*, Eerdmans, Grand Rapids, Mi., 2005. David P. Gushee, *The Righteous Gentiles of the Holocaust: Genocide and Moral Obligation*, Paragon House, St Paul, 2003. Richard B. Hays, *The Moral Vision of the New Testament: Community, Cross, New Creation: A Contemporary Introduction to New Testament Ethics*, Harper, San Francisco, 1996. James Wm. McClendon, *Doctrine: Systematic Theology*, Vol 2, Abingdon, Nashville, Tn., 1994. Parush R. Parushev, 'Walking in the Dawn of the Light: On Salvation Ethics of the Ecclesial Communities in Orthodox Tradition from a Radical Reformation Perspective', PhD dissertation, Fuller Theological Seminary, USA, 2007. Robert W. Ross, 'Baptists, Jews, Nazis: 1933-1947', in Alan L. Berger (ed), *Bearing Witness to the Holocaust 1939-1989*, Edwin Mellen, Lewiston, 1991, pp.207-225. Stephen Sizer, *Christian Zionism: Road-map to Armageddon?*, InterVarsity, Leicester, 2004. Andrea Strübind, *Die unfreie Freikirche: der Bund der Baptistengemeinden im "Dritten Reich"*, R. Brockhous Wuppertal/Zürich, and Oncken, Wuppertal/Kassel, 1995. John Howard Yoder, *The Jewish-Christian Schism Revisited*, SCM, London, 2003.

Jordan, Baptist history in

The Hashemite kingdom of Jordan only finally secured full independence in 1946. Most of its Arab population is Muslim, but there is a 5% Christian *minority*. Baptist work in Jordan began with a short-term residence in the country by Finley Graham who ministered in Al-Tayyiba in Northern Jordan, before moving on to work in *Lebanon*.

Secondly, through the visit of Dr. Loren Brown it was possible to acquire a *hospital* that belonged to a small British *mission*. The Baptist hospital began its work in 1952 extensively, powerfully, and effectively until

purchased by the Jordanian Ministry of *Health* in 1987. Among the pioneers at that stage were Drs. Loren Brown, McCray, and August Leifgreen (Lovegren) in Jordan from 1956 until the early 90s. Later came Dr. John Robert, who served in the mission together with his family. They were assisted in the *ministry* on the Arab side by Pastor Jiryes Dallah, of Kefar Yasin (near 'Akko), the first president of a Baptist Convention in Jordan, before he moved on to undertake new work in Lebanon.

The first Baptist church was established in Jordan in 1953, with Jiryis Dallah serving as its first pastor till 1964, Jiryis Al-Ashqar, who had served in the *hospital* and surrounding area since 1993, was secretary of the Jordanian Baptist *Convention* from its foundation.

The mission field was soon enlarged. New churches were established in the 1950s, such as the churches of 'Anajrah, Dabin, and Jarash in 1956, as well as Al-Tayyiba, Irbid, Jerusalem, and Ram Allah, followed in the 1960s by the churches at Al-Zarqa` and Al-Hisn, and in the 1970s by the church in Amman, pastored by Fawwaz Emeish from 1971-2005; the church also runs the Voice of Life Studio. From the church of Amman several churches branched off, such as the church of Al-Fuhayyis, Al-Fuhayyis centre, Al-Rashid suburb, Abyu Nusair, Suwailih, Al-Rabiya, Al-Shamisani, and Western Amman centre. The church of Al-Zarqa` which was established and pastored by Revd Ra'uf Za`mat from 1968 until the mid 90s, planted several churches and *preaching* centres, such as the New Zarqa` church, Amira Rahmah, Al-Hawuz, and Al-Hashimiyya, to mention only a few [see *Church Planting*]. At the end of the 20th century the number of churches had increased to 20, along with a number of preaching centres.

The Baptist Library was founded in 1963, whilst the *Southern Baptists* had established boys and girls schools in `Ajlun in 1953 with feeder elementary schools in several surrounding villages. The Baptist School in Amman dates from 1973, whilst the bookstore in Amman adds another dimension to Baptist *witness* alongside the Conference Centre in `Ajlun (1988).

The Free *Evangelical* Church in Jordan, founded by *Conservative* Baptists from the

USA is also Baptist in church order.

FE

Jordan Evangelical Theological Seminary

Baptist and *evangelical* communities in *Jordan* are *minorities* and have been disadvantaged in the past in terms of official recognition and access to resources. Nevertheless, there has been a strong desire to develop adequate theological *education* for the evangelical communities, including Baptists, in the Kingdom of Jordan. In 1986 Dr. Imad Shehadeh began working towards the goal of establishing a regional evangelical institution for theological studies in Jordan. The mission of the Jordan Evangelical Theological Seminary (JETS) was clearly established early on, and was defined as 'equipping Arab leaders for the planting [see *Church Planting*] and strengthening of churches in the Arab world.'

Classes began in the autumn of 1991. The biggest initial challenges then were to unite the five main evangelical denominations of Jordan to support this effort, and to obtain approval from the Jordanian government for the registration of a Christian seminary. These two challenges were met in Mar 1995 when JETS was officially registered by the Jordanian government with its first elected Board of Trustees. This board grew over the years to encompass members from several Arab and non Arab countries, including JETS graduates.

JETS has an international and interdenominational faculty, including Arabic-speaking Westerners and Arab nationals holding advanced degrees from universities and seminaries around the world. They serve as full-time, part-time or as adjunct faculty. In order to broaden the variety and depth of courses offered at JETS, intensive classes (modules) are taught in Jan and during the summer months by prominent resident and adjunct professors in their fields. The modules are usually taught in English so these classes utilise translators, unless they are at the MTh level. JETS's administrative staff is nearly all Jordanian.

From 1995-2005, the average *student* enrolment was 120-150. Approximately one-third of the students are *women*. JETS graduates serve in several countries throughout the Arab World, as well as among Arab communities in non-Arab countries. Through them many new churches and para-church *ministries* have been established throughout the Arab World.

JETS offers Bachelor's and Master's degree programme culturally and theologically suited to the context of the Arab World. The Bachelor's programme has four major tracks: *Pastoral* Ministries; Women's Ministries; *Music* and *Worship*; Christian Education. The Master's programme offers four core areas: Master of Arts in Christian Education; Master of Arts in Biblical Studies; Master of Divinity; and Master of *Theology*.

Most students gain experience in *practical ministry* where they have the opportunity to develop ministry skills and utilise their *spiritual gifts*. Students are required to engage in supervised internships in *evangelism*, visitation, *discipleship*, church planting, teaching, and pastoring. In 1993 an extension campus was established in Amman, Baghdad, Iraq, whose administration and faculty are graduates of JETS. Instruction in the JETS Iraqi extension campus began in 2004.

IS & ET

Journal of European Baptist Studies (JEBS)

The *Journal of European Baptist Studies* was established by the Directorate of *IBTS*, Prague in 2000. This was in response to requests from young Baptist and *evangelical scholars* in Central and Eastern Europe who sought opportunities to publish in an international English language journal the results of their research and reflection on *theology* with an emphasis in favour of baptistic, *gathering churches*.

From the beginning the criteria for selection of articles has been in favour of the work of new, young scholars from within the *EBF* community. Whilst articles have been commissioned covering biblical, theological, *missiological* and historical studies the accent has been firmly on the application and implementation for search and reflection.

The Journal has developed a high reputation throughout the world in dealing with issues of *ecclesiology*, baptistic history and practice and reflection on authentic *Missiology* in the context of post-modern Europe. Though articles have been published from other continents, the vast majority of contributions are from the area of the EBF. Published three times a year in English, the editorial team is drawn from academics associated with IBTS. It has subscribers in every continent.

KGJ

FURTHER READING: www.ibts.eu/conferences.

Journals
See *Magazines*.

JPIC
See *Justice, Peace and the Integrity of Creation*.

Jubilee and Two-Thirds World Debt

The immediate cause of the international debt crisis can be traced to oil revenues (so-called 'petro-dollars') deposited in western banks in the 1970s and then loaned to poor countries for development purposes. Due to rising interest rates and unfavourable trading conditions the borrowers found it increasingly difficult to service these loans let alone repay them and soon became known as Highly Indebted Poor Countries, faced with hard choices between paying their dues and providing basic services, such as *health* and *education*, for their people. Other factors such as corruption, internal conflicts and economic policies (e.g. Structural Adjustment Policies) imposed on poorer countries by international financial institutions (e.g. the World Bank and the IMF) only made matters worse.

Many Christians, *evangelicals* included, and others came to regard the situation as fundamentally unjust. It looked like yet another example of rich and powerful *nations* oppressing weaker and poorer ones and benefiting from their misfortunes. Above all, impoverished communities, which were

never responsible for the loans and never benefited from them, suffered the dire consequences when things went wrong. E.g. 1,000s of *children* were said to be dying each day for lack of basic medicines.

The international campaign to cancel the debts of over 50 of the poorest countries by 2000 was inspired by the biblical concept [see *Bible*] of Jubilee (cf Lev 25) which, in theory at least, was to act as a corrective to the persistent drift of resources from the *poor* to the rich whereby poor people got into debt, lost their land and even their freedom as they fell into slavery. Every 50th year, at the sound of the trumpet ('Jubilee') slaves were to be freed, land returned and debts cancelled. Many hear echoes of this imaginative social policy in *Jesus*' reference to 'the year of the Lord's favour' in his manifesto-like *sermon* (Lk 4:18) inaugurating a Jubilee not every 50 years but once and for all.

MHT

FURTHER READING: Martin Dent and Bill Peters, *The Crisis of Poverty and Debt in the Third World*, Ashgate, Brookefield, 1999.

Judaism, Baptists and
See *Jews and Judaism, Baptists and*.

Judgment
Towards the end of the OT the idea developed of a coming Day of God, a day of Judgment not only on *Israel* but on her pagan neighbours, a day of universal judgment on both the living and the dead. In the NT this becomes the day which sees the consummation of history and the setting up of the *kingdom of God* with *Christ* himself as both judge and king, indicating that as the biblical record [see *Bible*] begins with God in *creation* so it must conclude with God in consummation. Images of judgment may be less attractive to 21st century Christians than earlier generations with fewer *sermons* being preached on the Great Assize, but the search for respectability should not blind us to failing to see the need for judgment and the need for God to act on what is in many cases self-assessed failure and rebellion. Whilst Christians hold a wide spectrum of beliefs about the last things, but faithfulness to scripture requires caution. E.g. one commen-

tator indicates that whilst there may be legitimate differences of opinion s to the exact literal interpretation of the images of judgment 'there is no justification for categorically denying any such dramatic finale'. The Baptist *Union* of *Great Britain*'s Declaratory Statement of belief after the crisis of the Downgrade Controversy, in its last clause commits itself to belief in 'the Judgment of the Last Day, according to the words of our Lord in Matthew xxv, 46', but then adds a footnote, 'It should be stated as an historical fact, that there have been brethren in the Union, working cordially with it, who whilst reverently bowing to the authority of Holy Scripture, and rejecting doctrines of Purgatory and *Universalism*, have not held the common interpretation of these words of our Lord.' Some certainly had questioned whether it was right to apply eternal torment for temporal *sin*, which led some to uphold views of 'conditional immortality' that is that eternity was reserved for the righteous only. Others argued that the redemptive *love* of God [see *Redemption*], in the end, was so powerful that it took the concept of judgment into itself in saving power. One such was Samuel Cox, *theologian*, editor and Baptist *pastor* in Nottingham, who affirming his belief in 'the sinfulness of *man*' and in the *Atonement*, argued 'but we also believe in an Atonement of wider scope, that Christ will see of the travail of his soul and be satisfied in a larger and diviner way than some of our theologians have supposed.' It is perhaps helpful to record that judgment in the NT is most often to be seen in terms of either enjoying the presence of God, or being separated from him, something that each individual chooses for him/herself.

ET

Just War Theory

[See also *Conscientious Objectors*; *Pacifism and Peace Churches*; *Programme to Combat Racism*]

The just war theory is an *ethical* and critical response to the problem of war or armed conflict between *political* communities. It has a long history, which started with Augustine's attempt to replace the radical Christian *pacifism* of the early church with a theory of war that accepted war as a possible way of securing *peace* and justice – when considered necessary to protect a political community. The theory initially offered direct support to the imperial peace of Rome, even though, it went beyond the old Roman maxim that considered war a lawless activity – by introducing the restraints of a just war theory. The theory, which made it religiously and ethically possible for Christians to serve as soldiers and officers, had a critical edge against armed conflict, especially against wars of conquest, demanding a code as to how the just war might be pursued. The introduction of the theory marks the beginning a new religious accommodation, where war became a means of religious conquest as in the crusades – a Christian version of the Holy War? – in the so-called religious wars that followed the *Reformation*, and in the war-like securing of colonies. The theory has also been bent to justify modern wars by defending them as just answers to one's opponents always defined as evil.

The theory was developed by Thomas Aquinas, Francisco de Vitoria, Hugo Grotius and Samuel Pufendorf and found its place within international law and conventions. Its object was to assert the need for careful evaluation of method and motive, of *human rights* and of justice when armed conflict was proposed. Consequently, rulers have tried to defend their wars as just, even when they are conducted with no other interest, than their own victory over a counterpart, to gain *wealth* and power and enhance an empire. Often the question of legitimacy has appeared in the debate in the midst of or after such wars, as in the Vietnam-war. The brutality of that war contributed decisively to bring it to an end, when the international community and the majority in the US found the war unacceptable – also morally speaking.

It has become a part of modern military strategy to defend the cause of war and the conduct of war by using the language of the just war theory. Thus respect for the criteria of the just war must be exercised as a natural part of *democratic* activity, where political and military leaders are held responsible for their decisions about the 'how' and 'when' of war, and of their actions in war, especially as they effect non-combatants or civil societies. The theory does not renounce war as a possibility. It tries to constrain actions and regulate conduct, which are morally problematic and therefore made subject to constant criticism.

In so far as Baptists, unlike their **Mennonite** cousins, are not a **peace church** it behoves them to be particularly guarded about the way in which just war arguments are deployed. Whilst some might make their protests as conscientious objectors, other will engage in the political challenge presented by the argument in favour of taking up arms. Generally they would wish to see cases argued by first determining that there is a just cause, such as the restraint of an aggressor, protection of the innocent, the restoration of rights wrongly alienated, and the reinstatement of a just order in society. There must also be a just end that is the **restoration** of peace with justice rather than the working through of vengeance or the establishment of an end to conflict without dealing with basic issues of justice thus at best securing only an unstable armistice. For a war to be just the methods deployed must be constrained and appropriate to the cause of the conflict, always seeking to minimise **death** and **suffering** especially amongst the civilian population and non-combatants. By this criterion the saturation of German cities in WWII would be difficult to justify. It also raises important questions such as whether the use of torture should be prohibited as a basic attack on the human rights of the other or whether in an age of **nuclear** weapons any war can be defended as just, or must all war now be considered unjust. Certainly it puts a premium on attempts to further develop nuclear weapons. Just war theory also appeals to the principle of Last Resort, that is to say, all other solutions – diplomatic, economic, etc. – must be exhausted before a resort to arms can be justified.

Allied to such questions is the related question about 'the just revolution' – when is the action of a tyrant – whether individual or corporate – so intolerable that armed resistance is justified? Do rulers have any 'divine right', passé Ro 13, to rule? In this respect those in the **Lutheran** and those in the **Reformed tradition** have often opted for different stances, with the Lutherans more ready to support the prince and Reformed Christians more inclined to name the tyrant

and to oppose him, so that somebody like Oliver Cromwell believed that to remain passive in the face of tyranny was tantamount to becoming complicit with the tyrant. Difficult decisions have to be taken – when does the oppression suffered by a people become so intolerable that action is required? When is a regime seen to be so evil that conspiracy against that regime, the joining of a resistance movement, becomes justified?

PMIL & ET

FURTHER READING: Herbert A. Dean, *The Political and Social Ideas of St. Augustine*, Columbia University Press, New York, 1963. James Turner Johnson, *Ideology, Reason and the Limitation of War: Religious and Secular Concepts, 1200-1740*, Princeton University Press, Princeton, NJ, 1975. Michael Walzer, *Just and Unjust Wars*, Basic Books, New York, 1971.

Justice, Peace and the Integrity of Creation (JPIC)

[See also *Creation; Climate Change; Ecology and the Environment; Peace, Baptists and*]
JPIC emerged as a programme priority within the **World Council of Churches** after the Vancouver Assembly in 1983 replacing an earlier programme which campaigned for a Just, Participatory and Sustainable Society (JPSS) which had been launched seven years earlier following the public debate on sustainability which had begun in the early 1970s. The Nairobi Assembly in 1975 had been clearly alerted to the issue as a matter of Christian **conscience**. At Vancouver there were discrepant interests – the delegates from the two-thirds world, conscious of the pressures of hunger and poverty, were anxious for justice now. Delegates from the Global North increasingly concerned about am escalating arms trade and the possibility of nuclear war were anxious for a peace emphasis. At the same time the **ecological** crisis was becoming more and more obvious with such observable factors as global warming, the pollution of land, sea and air, the exhaustion of such diverse resources as oil and deep sea fish stocks. Indeed it was becoming increasingly clear that the world, the *oikos* itself, was at risk. All this came together in the Vancouver Assemblies invitation to its member churches and other associated bod-

ies to work towards a commitment to a *covenant* to work for the three goals of Justice, Peace and the defending of the Integrity of Creation. Churches were called upon to confess their complicity in the increasing crisis and to pledge to take effective action through a conciliar process of mutual commitment. A preparatory educational process was organised to lead up to a world convocation on these three issues which were seen as three aspects of a single reality. Although the process encountered difficulties with regard to the language of conciliar process and later the language of agreeing a covenant of commitments, the language of Justice, Peace and the Integrity of Creation was taken up in Christian circles well beyond the member churches of the WCC. The World Consultation took place in Seoul in 1990 and in its term made 10 affirmations regarding the exercise of power as accountable to God; God's *preferential option for the poor*; the equal value of all peoples; male and female as made in the image of God; truth as the foundation of free people; the peace of *Jesus Christ*; the *creation* as beloved of God; the earth as the Lord's; the dignity and commitment of the younger generation; and *human rights* as being given by God. The Scoul delegates also identified four concrete issues for specific covenant – the search for a just economic order and liberation from the bondage of *debt*; the true security of all nations and peoples and the nurturing of a culture of *non-violence*; developing a life style that respects the harmony of the created order; preserving the gift of the earth's atmosphere to nurture and sustain life on the world; and finally the eradication of racism and discrimination at all levels.

This agenda was affirmed by both the Canberra (1991) and Harare Assemblies (1998) as the core of *ecumenical* social thinking and showed the Christian Churches to be well ahead of the secular conscience which only really developed a broadcast concern for these issues at the beginning of the 21st century.

JHYB

Justification

[See also *Sanctification*]

The language is essentially that of the court room. Justification means, for sufficient reasons, to deem somebody to be righteous. In gospel terms, the term describes the process whereby a guilty sinner [see *Guilt*; *Sin*] is restored to relationship with God. As such it characteristically describes *Luther*'s essential insight as to how to resolve the human dilemma of not being able, as sinner, to do what, as *man*, he ought to do – justification not by works, not by *sacramental* practice, but by *faith*, or more correctly justification by *grace* appropriated by faith, for it is important not to make 'faith' into some kind of work, but rather to underline that the initiative is always with God, and as far as *humankind* is concerned remains an unmerited favour. Faith can only operate because God has intervened in the sacrifice of his Son, doing for sinful humanity what it could not do for itself [see *Atonement*].

The radical nature of justification is spelt out by *Jesus* in the story of the tax collector and the Pharisee saying their *prayers* in the temple. The Pharisee rehearses before God all his good works as full justification as to why God's favour should rest on him, with not a thought that he might be in need of *forgiveness* or *redemption*, whereas the tax-collector is fully conscious of his shortcomings, which seem so grave that he scarcely dares to hope for any spiritual benefit, but simply prays for mercy, and Jesus tells his hearers that it was this man, not the Pharisee, 'who went home justified before God'.

Justification is the first step in the process of *salvation* which is brought to fruition through sanctification. Justification takes place whilst the sinner is still imprisoned in his sin, but if relationship with a holy God is to be restored and if this change of life orientation is indeed the work of the *Holy Spirit* then there have to be ethical changes [see *Ethics*], *metanoia,* in the spirit's strength a turning round with a new orientation to live the righteous life. Goodness of life is thus not causative of salvation but consequential on a salvation already received. As Luther put it; 'Humankind must be made good in order to do good, not do good in order to become good.' By contrast with Pharisaic codes as to what was clean and what was defiled righteousness is defined in terms of *love* of God and service of neighbour, the

poor and the marginalised, and all those in
special need. Justification and sanctification
belong together – *being* made righteous by
the sacrificial **death** of Christ, and *becoming*
righteous as the Holy Spirit shapes the human will into conformity with the Christ-
like life. But sanctification must always be
seen in the context of justification for it is
justification by faith which provides 'the
assurance that, though Christian obedience
is still imperfect, the believer is already a full
member of God's people'. Thus it establishes
the basis and the motive for love and obedience towards God.

                                              ET

K

Kazakhstan, Baptist history in

[See also *Central Asia, Baptist history in*]
Probably the first Baptist community in Kazakhstan was founded in 1903 in Nikolaevka in the Kustanay region, though some Baptist families may have settled in the country at the end of 19th century. The *evangelical* movement reached the outlying districts of the Russian empire both through Baptists being sent into exile and believers voluntarily seeking good lands for a new life. The movement developed there in three main directions: German *Mennonite Brethren* congregations, Russian-speaking Baptist churches, and German-speaking Baptist groups.

The Baptist *revival* reached many towns and villages in the beginning of the 20th centurty: Aktyubinsk (1906), Pavlodar (1907), Petropavlovsk (1908), Kustanay (1908), Taraz (1909), Verny (Alma-Ata) (1917), and others. In 1917, the year of the Bolshevik revolution in *Russia*, the believers of Turkistan (now called 'Central Asia') established the Central Asian division of the All-Russian Baptist Union. They had local congresses every year (1922-27). Some Mennonite Brethren churches had contacts with the *Union* from the first days of its existence. In the 1920s, many Baptist communities welcomed the Soviet power – sympathising with its social experiments and planting 'Christian co-operative societies' and 'Baptist agricultural communes'. However, difficult years were ahead. In 1932-33, about two million people (about 40% of Kazakhstan's population) starved to *death* because of the forced collectivisation of agriculture. This was also the period of Stalin's repression and destruction of religious communities in the *USSR*. All official Baptist churches in Kazakhstan were closed, but underground (hidden) meetings continued.

A revival of Baptist activity in the country started after WWII with Russian and German-speaking Baptists meeting together. Baptist churches in Kazakhstan grew significantly during the final years of Stalin. How-

ever, those joining the churches were mostly *women*, who still form the majority of *church members*. At the end of the 1950s, the Soviet government, pursuing the course of building a *communist* society in the very near future, tried to eradicate religious communities in the USSR. Kazakhstan became a place of strong resistance to the government's atheistic policy. However, the local Baptists were separated into different camps, of which the two biggest were those belonging to the officially recognised *All-Union Council of Evangelical Christians-Baptists* and those supporting the illegal Council of Churches of Evangelical Christians-*Baptists (Reform Baptists)*. During the Soviet years, while trying to *evangelise* and keep at least some church *ministries* alive, Baptists in Kazakhstan operated both legally and illegally. Many Soviet prisoners of conscience were from Kazakhstan and Central Asia.

Beginning in 1965, Leonid Brezhnev adopted a more pragmatic religious policy, though the discriminative approach towards believers remained intact. Nevertheless, during the 1970s the churches in Kazakhstan grew [see *Church Growth*]. The churches' local characteristics were strict *church discipline* with the possibility of excluding people from the *fellowship* as well as a position of absolute *pacifism*. Undoubtedly, this was due to the Mennonite influence. Discrimination against Baptists gradually stopped in 1985-86 when the new Soviet leader, Michail Gorbachev, initiated the policy of *glasnost* and *perestroika*. In 1988, the celebration of the Millennium of the *Baptism* of Russia, took place with much publicity. This event apparently signified the end of the '70 year captivity' of Christianity in the USSR. However, by the end of the 1980s *emigration* had begun – in the years 1988-2003 more than 30,000 Baptists, mostly Russian and German-speaking, left Kazakhstan for *Germany*, Russia and the USA.

The widespread Central Asian Baptist revival in the 1990s showed again the vitality of the local evangelical movement. The revival reached not only Russians and Germans, but also indigenous peoples. The Baptist *mission* in Kazakhstan has got inspiration also from the historical fact that there were many Nestorian Christians in Central Asia before the *Muslim* expansion in the area in the Middle Ages. Today, approximately 10% of local Baptists are Kazakh or of other indigenous ethnicity. *Worship* services take place in Russian and in Kazakh, but also in Uigur, Tatar and some other Central Asian languages. The total number of Baptists – both those belonging to a union and independents – is approximately 15,000. The biggest official Baptist body, the Baptist Union of Kazakhstan, has 12,000 members. There are around 300 churches and more than 200 groups of Baptist believers in the country.

CP

KEK
See *Conference of European Churches*.

Keswick Spirituality
[See also *Spirituality*]
A huge revival of interest in the life of *holiness* affected North America and Europe in the later 19th century. Older *evangelical* teaching about **sanctification**, suggesting that the holy life was achieved by active effort, had left a large number of the adherents of this teaching with a sense of spiritual failure. There was, therefore, an eager reception of concepts that began to be widely talked about in the 1870s, such as the 'deeper' or 'higher' Christian life, 'victory through *faith*' and 'full surrender'. It was suggested that sanctification, like *justification*, was to be received by faith, and was often an experience subsequent to *conversion* – sometimes called a 'second blessing'. The Keswick Convention, which began in 1875 in the town of Keswick in the English Lake District, presented this theme as an expression of spiritual renewal that appealed to centre-ground evangelicalism. By the early 20th century the annual week of meetings at Keswick was attracting 6,000 people and there were many similar convention meetings across Europe and in other continents. The most famous Baptist speaker was F.B. Meyer. He came to an experience of consecration through the influence of C.T. Studd and Stanley Smith, two of the famous 'Cambridge Seven' *missionaries* who went to China in 1885 with the China Inland Mission. Meyer became the Convention's most

prominent international speaker and introduced Keswick teaching about consecration and the filling of the *Holy Spirit* into the Baptist denomination through a *Prayer* Union for *ministers*. He forged links with holiness movements across Europe, especially in *Germany* and *Sweden*. In the 20th century leading Baptist speakers at Keswick included W.Y. Fullerton, the Home Secretary of the *Baptist Missionary Society*, Graham Scroggie, minister of Charlotte Chapel, Edinburgh, and David Coffey, General Secretary of the Baptist Union of Great Britain. The stress at Keswick on a 'second experience' has gradually faded. Large-scale evangelical events in Britain such as *Spring Harvest*, which began in 1979, have been to some extent modelled on Keswick.

IMR

FURTHER READING: D.W. Bebbington, *Holiness in Nineteenth-Century England*, Paternoster, Carlisle, 2000. C. Price and I.M. Randall, *Transforming Keswick*, Paternoster/OM, Carlisle, 2000. I.M. Randall, '"Capturing Keswick": Baptists and the Changing Spirituality of the Keswick Convention in the 1920s', *The Baptist Quarterly*, Vol.36, No.7, 1996. I.M. Randall, *Evangelical Experiences: A Study in the Spirituality of English Evangelicalism, 1918-1939*, Paternoster, Carlisle, 1999.

Kiev Theological Seminary
Kiev Theological Seminary (KTS) was founded in 1995 through the direction of the All Ukrainian *Union* of Associations of *Evangelical* Christians-Baptists and the vision of Anatoly Prokopchuk, who became KTS president. Their goal, along with other key supporters, was to establish an institution that would provide a strong theological *education* in the region. KTS was started in an old run-down building without doors, windows or heat, but despite these difficulties triple the anticipated number of applicants enrolled. The first classes began in Feb 1996 with a curriculum that was parallel to arrangements of subjects covered in some Masters of *Theology* programmes. Since then the curriculum has been modified to match Western educational standards at Bachelor's level. There is a strong commitment to teaching and learning that is relevant to the local context.

In the years since its founding, KTS has

seen over 300 graduate *students* from its *ministerial formation* programmes. 100s of other Christians have also received training at the seminary. KTS graduates are ministering throughout Ukraine and other parts of the former *Soviet Union* as *pastors*, *elders*, *Sunday School* teachers, youth ministers [see *Youth work*] and *missionaries*. Many are involved in *church planting*.

It has been important to build up the KTS library and there is now a collection of 28,000 volumes of theological literature available to teachers and students.

SVS & ET

Kingdom of God/Heaven

[See also *Heaven, Hell and the Future Life*] *Biblical scholars* all agree that the proclamation of 'the good news of the Kingdom (of God/Heaven)' (Mk 1:14; Lk 4:43; Mt 4:23 [NRSV]) is the central theme of the *ministry* and *mission* of *Jesus* of Nazareth (and by implication of his disciples, Mt 10:7), as seen from the gospel perspective of the synoptic tradition. The concept of the kingdom of God has a rich *Jewish* religious heritage encapsulated in a web of prophetic [see *Prophecy*] and inter-testamental ideas in general circulation at the time of Jesus. Among NT writers, Matthew uses the concept of 'kingdom of...' most prolifically. Indeed, the entire content of the Gospel of Matthew 'can be subsumed under, and unified in, the theme of the Kingdom of God, in connection to the central figure of Jesus' (Viviano, p.157). Outside the NT writings, the concept is rarely used, but in the Aramaic Targum (paraphrase) of Isaiah, which may well have been known to Jesus, 'kingdom of God' spells out God's intervention on the behalf of his people in their restoration from exile.

Much has been made of Matthew's use of the phrase 'kingdom of heaven' (while the other gospel writers seem to prefer the 'kingdom of God') as a pious circumlocution for 'the kingdom of God'. However Matthew does use 'kingdom of God', primarily in the second part of his gospel narrative, in the context of growing hostility towards Jesus' ministry (12:28; 19:24; 21:31, 43; but see also 6:33). However, '"The kingdom of heaven" is favoured because it is a way of referring to God's transcendent work and lordship that is coming down from heaven' (Garland, pp.47 ff.), embracing the immanent as the heavenly meets the earthly in Jesus of Nazareth.

As the first canonical gospel presents it, the proclamation is not good tidings of a *distant* event. Neither is it a forerunner's heralding of royal business such as John's calling for *repentance* in the expectation of the 'one who is to come (11:3)'. By contrast, Jesus' proclamation ushers in a new age with eschatological urgency, 'because the kingdom of heaven is near' (4:17, cf. Mk 1:15).' In fact the kingdom of God is already present (Mt 11:2-19) in Jesus' words and deeds: it 'has come to you' (12:28, Lk 17:21). His words and actions 'are linked as complementary indications of the presence of the kingdom' (Beasley-Murray, p.144). At the centre of Jesus' proclamation is a joyful message that God's reign is coming soon in all its fullness. Meanwhile, Jesus identification with the king of the kingdom and the dawning of the kingdom of heaven in the midst of his hearers (Lk 4:16-21) is enacted in his proclamation, instructions, and *healings*.

In the gospel narratives, the Kingdom of God is both a *present* reality and one yet to be fully disclosed (Mk 9:1) – a mustard seed planted to be nourished into full blossoming. The 'kingdom' is a dynamic not a spatial phenomenon: something that happens rather than something that exists. The kingdom signifies the world's moral order as God longs for it to be, and as evoked in the Lord's *Prayer* (Mt 6:10). It is a '"kingdominion" or a reign' (Carson, p.13) of the sovereign God over his people and the world. It is clear from the gospel story that Jesus' usage of kingdom language means something more precise and focused than the more general biblical [see *Bible*] emphasis on the *sovereignty* of God. The coming of the Kingdom has historic dimensions, for it is organic, not just spiritual, working itself out realistically in the formation of Christian character and in practices of Christian living (Stassen and Gushee pp.32-54; 125-145) with continuity between what happens in this age and in the age to come.

The kingdom theme, therefore, is a key not only to understanding Jesus' identity and the nature of his ministry but also to grasping the way this ministry affects his hearers' perception of the essence of his vision. Jesus' repeated announcement that 'the kingdom of heaven has come near' (Mt 3:2; 4:17 and 10:7), emphasises the thrust of radical **discipleship** in the **eschatological** living in and living out of the righteousness of God: 'But strive for ("seek" in NKJV) first the kingdom of God and his righteousness (6:33, cf. 13:41-42).'

Whilst Jesus' kingdom proclamation is a restatement of the vision of the Hebrew prophets and of John, the forerunner, Jesus transforms the apocalyptic vision of the divine **judgment** by an emphasis on the mercy as well as the judgment of God, and 'on the **love** of God and the neighbour as the criterion for God's moral demands' (Harkness, p.78) with the priority of the reign of God over 'the wrath to come' (3:7). God's reign is a gift: this is why Jesus' proclamation came eventually to be known as 'gospel' or the 'good news (of **salvation**) of Jesus Christ, the Son of God (Mk 1:1). As with the people of Nineveh, Jesus' hearers must see in his **calling** and ministry a sign 'of something greater' than just the fact that he is here (Mt 12:41). Striving for justice and peace, showing mercy, compassion, healing, and restoring the 'harassed and helpless' (9:36) into a community of care and embrace, is the task of the harvesters in that kingdom (5:3-9; 10:8-13). Vengeance and **violence** are not the way of Jesus and should not be the way for his disciples either (10:23). The meaning of 'the good news of God's original revolution' is in the non-violent way of the **cross** (Yoder [2003], p.32). He is 'truly proclaiming a **Jubilee**...a pre-eminent sign of God's justice and salvation on earth. God's Kingdom is here and now...with the good news of divine forgiveness' (Trocmé, p.41). It is a peaceable Kingdom.

There is another distinct characteristic of the kingdom way of Jesus. Unlike the prophets and the teachers of the Law, he chose neither the distance of ascetic separation, nor that of those intellectual exercises which legal experts created *in abstractio* in the comforting tranquillity of the rabbinic thought-world (5:20; 11:25). He discarded these views of the 'Kingdom from above'. Instead he chose to enter into the midst of the messiness of life (11:19) and to argue for the veracity of the kingdom by practices worthy of the kingdom (5:21-7:12). This is the kingdom emerging from below and subverting existing social arrangements at grassroots. Bringing about the kingdom of heaven is a communal concern: as in the dealings of God with the people of **Israel** from Exodus on, the initiative is God's, but participation is human (7:24-27). Only with this human participation can the vision of the kingdom be made effective. The thrust of the gospel narrative is that human reformation is possible and it is on its way as the **Resurrection** of Jesus confirms. As with the **covenant** at Sinai, Jesus' way of the kingdom also requires 'yoking God and **humankind** as co-partners in **redemption** (Goldberg, p.216)'. Only so can the latter be transformed in the character-likeness of the former in genuine reciprocity. Any other vision of the kingdom is deficient, including that of the great prophet, John. In Jesus' vision, the least of the doers of the kingdom is greater than the greatest of the prophets (11:11). But their greatness arises not from their own wisdom and ingenuity but rather because they believed the vision revealed to them (11:27) and welcomed God's reign in their midst.

Jesus' view of the Kingdom is given concrete shape in his teaching, especially in The Sermon on the Mount as recorded in Mt 5-7, the *Magna Charta* of the Kingdom. This Kingdom message, delivered by Jesus in Matthew, and elsewhere, is decisively based in the language and vision of Isaiah, where seven thematic clusters portray God's coming to reign as deliverance/salvation; righteousness/justice; peace; joy; with God's presence as Spirit or light; healing; and securing the return of his people from exile/bondage. These same themes characterise the core message of Jesus as he proclaims that the reign of God is at hand, thus identifying his core message with the prophecies of Isaiah (Stassen and Gushee, pp.19-54; cf. Beasley-Murray, pp.17-25). 'Isaiah is a *theological* source for Matthew, and that *theology* has narrative dimensions.' By interpreting Isaiah 'in light of Jesus' life', (Grams, pp.243, 239) and interpreting Jesus in light of Isaiah's message, Matthew invites his listeners to align themselves with God's salvific mission and together with God's elect [see **Election**] to write the next page in salvation history.

In so teaching, Jesus is not simply passing

on knowledge of what must be done to acquire righteousness exceeding that of the scribes and Pharisees (5:20), for a major characteristic of his teaching is the passionate and compassionate demand for the transformation of the very fabric of human behaviour. Salvation – being right in the sight of God – is inseparably entwined with the transformation of human character, of the disciple becoming an agent of a renewed way of living within the present, by following Christ's way; in other words of being 'united' with him. In the Kingdom Jesus is proclaiming, the conventional social order is changed and a new order has already begun (2Co 5:17). Kingdom realities call for a new convictional framework of how to see the world and how to behave in it. The Teacher does not hide the fact that the transformation of character is difficult (Mt 7:13-14), but this is the specific work of discipleship and there are no short cuts. In fact short cuts are false prophecies (vv.15-20). Knowing the right precepts of God's law and proclaiming them is not sufficient. It is in 'acting upon them (v.24)' that the transformation of human convictions occurs.

Biblical stories of the early Christian communities, testify in a realistic and yet dramatic language that in Jesus' life and ministry a robust and instrumental reality was dawning. He named this reality the Kingdom of God at hand. When acting upon his kingdom vision, the personal and social lives of ordinary **women** and **men** were already acquiring a new quality. Jesus insisted that this Kingdom and new life was 'for everyone' and he urged his disciples to follow him (Mt 19:29; cf. Jn 21:22) even at the expense of daily comfort. Against all the odds they had to 'take up their cross and follow [him]' (Mk 8:34). And they did. Their lives were transformed. As scripture continues telling the story, they in turn witnessed with their lives and deeds and urged others to join them in the re-enactment of the vision so that it could be passed on further. The crucial task of contemporary Christian disciples is to keep the kingdom vision alive without aberrations.

One of the most frequently raised issues here is the relationship of the **Church** to the Kingdom. Following in the steps of Augustine, Christians too often have been tempted to equate the church with the Kingdom of God but history persistently undercuts this presumption. All the evidence suggests that Jesus was more concerned with enactment of the coming of the kingdom, rather than the establishment of the institution of a church. In contra-distinction to the views that the church is the embodiment of the Kingdom held by some institutionalised Christian **communions** especially in the **Catholic** tradition, or that the Kingdom of God represents a parallel or independent realm from the 'kingdoms' of this world, as held by some **Protestant** communions of the magisterial **reformation**, the two are not to be identified the one with the other, but they are not unrelated either. For the church, if it is to be faithful to its Lord [see **Lord of the Church**], must ever be a servant of the Kingdom, and deploy all its energies on kingdom purposes. The communities of the Radical Reformation embraced 'that' vision of Jesus as their calling to be 'conscience and servant' (Yoder [1994], p.155) within 'this' human society (McClendon) where they find themselves. At its best the church, they believe, should be a living 'ikon' of what the coming kingdom, on a larger scale, embracing the whole of a redeemed **creation**, is to be like.

PRP

FURTHER READING: G.R. Beasley-Murray, *Jesus and the Kingdom of God*, Eerdmans, Grand Rapids, Mi. and Paternoster, Exeter, 1986. D.A. Carson, *Sermon on the Mount: An Exposition of Matthew 5-7*, Paternoster, Carlisle, 2001. David Garland, *Reading Matthew: A Literary and Theological Commentary on the First Gospel*, New York, Crossroad, New York, 1995. Michael Goldberg, *Jews and Christians: Getting Our Stories Straight: The Exodus and the Passion-Resurrection*, Abingdon, Nashville, Tn., 1985. Rollin Grams, 'Narrative Dynamics in Isaiah's and Matthew's Mission Theology', *Transformation*, Vol. 21:4, October, 2004, pp.238-55. Georgia Elma Harkness, *Understanding the Kingdom of God*, Abingdon, Nashville, Tn., 1974. James Wm. McClendon, Jr., *Ethics: Systematic Theology, Volume One* (2nd rev. ed.), Abingdon, Nashville, Tn., 2002. Glen Stassen and David Gushee, *Kingdom Ethics: Following Jesus in Contemporary Context*, InterVarsity, Downers Grove, Il., 2003. André Trocmé, *Jesus and the Nonviolent Revolution*, Orbis Books, Maryknoll, NY, 2004. Benedict T. Viviano, *Trinity—Kingdom—Church: Essays in Biblical Theology*, Universitätverlag,

Freiburg and Vandenhoeck and Ruprecht, Göttingen, 2001. John Howard Yoder, *The Politics of Jesus: vicit Agnus noster* (2nd ed.), Eerdmans Grand Rapids, Mi., and Paternoster, Carlisle, 1994. John Howard Yoder, *The Original Revolution: Essays in Christian Pacifism*, Herald, Scottdale, Pa. and Waterloo, 2003.

Kiss of Peace

[See also *Peace, Baptists and*]
The Kiss of Peace, or Pax, is derived from *scripture* references to the kiss of greeting, or holy kiss (Ro 16:16, etc.). The link with the *liturgy* of the *eucharist* is made from such passages as 1Pe 5:14 where the worshippers are exhorted to 'Greet one another with a kiss of *love*'. It seems probable that historically the action of the peace was placed before the offering in *worship* reflecting on the instruction of *Christ* to make peace before bringing a gift 'to the altar' (Mt 5:23). Justin Martyr, in the 2nd century, remarked in his *Apology* [see *Apologetics*] 'at the conclusion of the *prayers* we greet one another with a kiss'.

The church in the East and West divided liturgically over the point at which the peace should take place. Not all the Reformers [see *Reformation*] retained the action. The *Anabaptist*, *Balthasar Hubmaier*, introduced a variant in Mikulov, Moravia, called the 'Pledge of Love', which had the same effect of expressing a recognition of sisters and brothers in Christ and of being a communal way of effecting a sense of peace and *reconciliation* within the believing community before the Great Prayer of Thanksgiving was said [see *Prayers in Worship*].

In many Baptist communities the peace has been restored as part of a return to roots in worship and the influence of the *liturgical* and *charismatic movements*. It is generally placed after the *Word* and before the *offering* and the meal at eucharistic celebrations, though occasionally earlier in the worship. It often involves much congregational movement and the action varies depending on local culture and temperament, from a handshake in northern Europe, to a warm embrace and kiss in more latin and eastern contexts. The Moldovans, among others, share a full kiss on the lips.

KGJ

Koinonia

This is a Greek word meaning 'sharing'/'fellowship'/'*communion*'. Koinonia is used in the NT to signify one of three constitutive aspects of the *church* as a corporate entity (Ac 2:44ff – the two others are *martyria* [witness] and *diakonia* [service]). Koinonia signifies the bond joining the believers together to become the body of Christ. The church is in communion [koinonia] with *Christ* and one another. Koinonia is brought about through the *Holy Spirit* (2Co 13:14), and is a mark of equality among Christians. Entry into church koinonia takes place at *baptism* (Ro 6:3ff), and is expressed in the *Lord's Supper*, the Holy Koinonia (1Co 10:16). Koinonia consists of persons from all classes and races (Gal 3:28; Col 3:11). Individual Christians share the *spiritual gifts* given by the Spirit (2Co 13:14) in the community, and give material support to others (2Co 9:13; Php 1:5). The *local church* needs to be part of a wider community of *faith* to share *stewardship* and *mission*. Part of the mystery of the Christian vocation is that koinonia is both a supreme gift to the church but also needs to be the goal of all its striving.

OAJ

Kyiv Theological Seminary

See *Kiev Theological Seminary*.

Kyrgyzstan, Baptist history in

[See also *Central Asia, Baptist history in*]
According to the volume on Baptist history in the former Soviet areas, published in Moscow in 1989, Baptists reached Kyrgyzstan, a mountainous republic on the borders of China, in 1907 (Albert Wardin suggests 1912, a less probable date), when Rodion Bershadski and his wife moved from Orenburg region to Bishkek (Frunze). The Bershadskis had been baptised by immersion [see *Baptism*] and had joined the Baptists while they lived near Kiev. Together with L. Marudin and his family, who moved to Bishkek in 1908, they began *worship* and *prayer meetings* at Marudin's home. Soon the gatherings which at first brought together a dozen or fewer individuals grew significantly and a larger facility was found

for worship services. In 1916 the congregation consisted of approximately 100 believers, mostly Russian-speaking. In 1919 there was both a Baptist and an *Evangelical* Christian congregation in Bishkek. Stalin's atheistic and *political* repressions in the 1930s caused the Baptist and Evangelical Christian work in Kyrgyzstan to decline.

When in 1945 opportunities were opened to continue legally in a united organisation, the two groups – Baptists and Evangelical Christians – merged. In spite of a difficult and modest new start after WWII, Baptist work began to expand in Kyrgyzstan. Besides Russians, it also involved ethnic Germans from a *Mennonite Brethren* background, many of whom had been deported to Central Asia by Stalin's government at the outbreak of WWII. In addition, believers who had practiced their *faith* secretly because of atheistic and political pressures, now, with a slightly more relaxed religious situation, came out from this 'underground mode of believing' and joined Bishkek Baptist Church or other Baptist groups. By the end of the 1940s the Bishkek church consisted of around 1,000 members, and by the 1980s this membership had grown to 1,900. In addition, Baptist churches in Kant and Tokmak, with a predominantly ethnic German *membership*, had about 1,000 members. Baptist churches operated also in Talas, Kara-Balt, Romanovka, Panfilovka, and other locations. However, Baptist penetration among local ethnic groups, either Kyrgyz or Uzbek, who were nominally *Muslim*, was very modest. This has changed since the collapse of the *Soviet Union*, as Baptists have made an effort to move out of *church buildings*, to *evangelise* in public spaces, and to be involved in a number of serving *ministries* and in Christian literature distribution. Some Baptists have moved to live in Muslim villages, making a serious attempt to be a Christian witness with their presence and lifestyle.

Today, approximately 14-15% of Baptists in Kyrgyzstan represent indigenous ethnic groups, which is an exceptionally high figure, especially when compared to the situation in other Central Asian countries. At the same time, many Russian and German-speaking Baptists have emigrated from the country, thus considerably weakening Baptist work. The Mission, Ray of Hope, supported by the organisation Licht im Osten, was established in 1990 in Bishkek. Ray of Hope has had *mission* projects in other parts of Central Asia, in *Uzbekistan* and in *Turkmenistan*. Baptists in Kyrgyzstan are involved in *theological education*; in 1993 a *Bible* school was opened in Bishkek. The *Union* of Evangelical Christian Baptist Churches of Kyrgyzstan brings together more than 60 churches and 80 groups, with a total membership of about 3,100.

TP

L

Labour
See *Work*.

Laity
[See also *Ordination*]
Laity derives from a Greek word meaning 'people' and has come to represent the corporate identity of those who are not ordained, though in 1Pe 2 it is made clear that it should properly only be used of the whole *church*. The term laity as denoting a separate category in the church does not reflect Baptist beliefs, though it is used out of convenience for ease of conversation with other denominations. It is part of the importance of *Luther*'s teaching that he challenged the idea that only within the monastery could *holiness* be exercised. Accordingly, he restored the gospel to the layperson's world, so that the Christian layperson was now able to fulfil his/her *calling* or vocation in the home, the market place or in his/her place of employment. This he/she did not do by going on pilgrimages or attending special services, but (2Ti 2) by the quality of his/her workmanship. For the positive statement of this idea in the language of 'the *priesthood of all believers*' we are indebted to Luther even though the *Lutheran* Church did not at that time go very far in implementing this. More recently the Dutch *ecumenical* statesman, Hendrick Kraemer, has spoken of 'the laity as the dispersion of the Church'; for many people they are the everyday face of the church as they see it. The voice of the laity has always played an important part in the life of Baptist churches, both in counsel and in active *witness*, with the principle of lay *presidency* at the table observed in many, though not all, places, and perhaps not uniformly through history. To respect the proper dignity of all Christian people and the significance of the calling they receive in *baptism* does not however mean that Baptists have minimised the importance of a separated *ministry*. On the contrary from the time of the earliest *confessions of faith* it

is seen as an essential mark of the church, worthy of proper respect from all the *members*. Part of the problem of the common definition of laity is its negativity as representing 'the unordained' – the objects of *preaching*, teaching and *pastoral care* – as over against the active sharing in those ministries. Thus *Oncken*'s positive challenge for every Baptist to be a missionary is a helpful statement of one important aspect of lay responsibilities, especially if set in the perspective of total Christian witness. 'If the church is to be an effective force in the social and political sphere, our first task is to laicise our thought about it. We stand before a great historic task – the task of restoring the lost unity between worship and *work*' (J.H. Oldham, 1937). The church needs not only to respect the role of the laity but to give dignity to the layman's world as an essential arena of missionary activity, in the belief that God is both Lord in the church and in the world. Another way of expressing this is to say that as Baptists believe in the idea of the *'gathered church'*, so they also have a commitment to the idea of the 'church dispersed'. That is the people of God, after the benediction, return to their homes, their schools, their factories, there to continue the worship of Almighty God, acting as both salt and light.

JHYB

FURTHER READING: M. Gibbs and T.R. Morton, *God's Frozen People*, Collins, London, 1964. H. Kraemer, *A Theology of the Laity*, Westminster, Philadelphia, 1958. S.C. Neill and H.-R. Weber, *The Layman in Christian History*, SCM, London, 1963.

Lambeth Quadrilateral, The
The Lambeth Quadrilateral, or, because it was initiated by the *Protestant* Episcopal Church in America, the Chicago-Lambeth Quadrilateral, identified four fundamentals required by *Anglicans* within a reunited church:
- *The Holy Scriptures* as the Word of God,
- *The primitive creeds* as the rule of *faith*,
- *The two sacraments* ordained by *Christ* himself,
- *The historic episcopate* [see *Episcope*],

adapted to the 'varying needs of the nations and peoples called of God'. Adopted at Lambeth in 1888, the Archbishop of Canterbury thereafter invited other churches to respond in the interest of Christian **unity**. British Baptists, with other **Free Churches**, fully endorsed the first article. They questioned the several meanings that could be attached to the second and third, explaining courteously that they already possessed the historic episcopate of the NT which they did not identify with the Anglican Diocesan Episcopate. Accordingly, whilst grateful for the archbishop's initiative, they did not believe it provided a suitable basis for further conversations.

JHYB

Latvia, Baptist history in

Whilst the first Latvian Baptist, Fricis Jekabsons, was baptised [see **Baptism**] in Memel (Klaipeda) in neighbouring **Lithuania** in 1855, Latvian Baptist history is usually dated back to 1860, when nine Latvians, some of whom had been influenced by **Lutheran pietism**, were baptised in the same Memel church. A year later, Adams Gertners, the first Latvian Baptist **pastor**, baptised 72 persons in the Ziru River in Latvia, but they were soon persecuted by the Tsarist authorities in league with the **Orthodox Church**. Meeting and conducting baptisms secretly, they also encountered Lutheran hostility. Despite this, churches were planted [see **Church Planting**], with both a Latvian (Lettish) and a German church established in Riga in 1867, followed later by Russian language congregations. In the early 1870s **youth work** commenced and **choirs** began to be trained with singing festivals soon a vital aspect of Baptist **witness**. **Bible** Conferences and courses date back to the same period with the first **Sunday School** opened in Riga in 1873. In 1870, the first Baptist day school was established, primarily for Baptist **children**. Many other schools followed, but lack of legal status meant they were staffed by private teachers from Baptist congregations. Only in 1889 was the first Baptist school legalised. In 1874, three Latvian Baptist leaders (J. Hermanis, M. Rīss, J. Rumbergs) enrolled at the Seminary in Hamburg. The next year, a *de facto* **Union** of Latvian Baptist

Churches began, though Latvian Baptists remained formally within the German Baptist Union until 1879, when the Tsar officially recognised the Baptists. In the 1880s, Latvian Baptists started publishing hymnbooks [see **Hymnody**], and a Baptist newspaper *Evangēlists* [The Evangelist]. Whilst the work was growing, there were splits over both administrative and **theological** issues, with the editor of *Evangēlsists* arguing against too much German Baptist influence. Attempts to improve relationships between Latvian and German Baptists saw the establishment of the **Baltic Association** of Latvian Baptist Churches in **Russia** in 1885.

Many Latvian Baptists, for politico-economic reasons, emigrated to Russia (first Latvian church, 1869), to the USA (first church, 1890), and to Brazil (by 1914 there were already nine churches). Moreover, some of the leaders of the work were exiled to Siberia in 1916. Baptists in Latvia continued their witness; new **church buildings** were erected; more newspapers were published, but from 1921-23, following the **prophecies** of some preachers on **Christ**'s second coming in Brazil, around 2,300 Baptists emigrated there. Whilst encountering social and theological problems, these migrants significantly contributed to the development of Baptist work in Brazil, and in 1946 began **mission** work in Bolivia, providing the most thrilling mission story in Latvian Baptist history. There was also missionary activity in India and China. Despite **emigration** Latvian Baptists experienced considerable growth in the 1920s and 30s. In 1927, there were 89 Baptist churches (9,288 **members**), and, 11 years later, 109 churches (12,192 members). In 1922, a seminary was established under the leadership of J.A. Frey (Freijs) [see **Latvian Baptist Theological Seminary**]. By 1940, when the Soviet authorities forced closure, 53 persons had graduated from it. From 1925-29 William Fetler also organised a Mission and Bible School. Unfortunately, Latvian Baptists were not able to avoid divisions; from 1926-34, Latvian Baptists operated in two separate unions.

WWII brought tragedy: besides human losses, many church members and 35 pastors emigrated forming Latvian Baptist churches abroad. Today, there are two Latvian Baptist

Unions outside Latvia – in America and Brazil – with unassociated churches in other countries. In Latvia repression saw some churches compulsorily closed, whilst in 1945 Latvian Baptists were forced by the **State** to join the **All-Union Council of Evangelical Christians-Baptists**. With Christian social work and children's activities prohibited, Baptists declined, so that by 1976 there were only 60 churches with 6,000 members. Despite constraints, illegal or semi-legal attempts were made to evangelise, to organise youth groups, to encourage **Bible study**, and to give Christian instruction to children, all under the leadership of Pēteris Egle and Jānis Tervits. With choirs and music the only legal activity, the Matthew Baptist church in Riga emerged as a major centre for Baptist work, from 1974 organising the youth music group, 'Maranata'. In 1980, permission was given for the organising of lecture courses for preachers and church leaders, which were led by Jānis Tervits.

In 1988 mission and evangelism were renewed, with Baptist pastors actively engaged in open air services and other events. When the Union of Latvian Baptist Churches was re-established in Jan 1990, Sunday School work grew rapidly and publishing recommenced. The Theological Seminary, re-opened in 1991, has from 2002 welcomed Christians of all denominations. Today, one third of Latvian pastors are its graduates, whilst attempts have been made to diversify leadership roles. During the 1990s, new branches of Baptist work have developed, new churches planted with expanding social work, whilst requisitioned church buildings have been returned. In 2005, there were 85 Baptist churches with approximately 6,500 members. The leader of the Latvian Baptists is given the title of '**Bishop**'. The Latvian Baptist Union is a member of **EBF**.

OJ

Latvian Baptist Theological Seminary

The Latvian Baptist Theological Seminary was established in Riga in 1922 by Revd Dr. Janis Freijs (1863-1950) following on from a discussion about the possibility of establishing, seminaries in **Estonia** and **Latvia** at a conference convened by the **BWA** in London in 1920. Financial resources for the establishment of the Seminary came from the USA, Canada and the **UK**. Freijs became the first Principal, serving from 1922-30.The seminary was named the 'Garīgais Seminārs' [Spiritual Seminary], and **students**, who were enrolled every fourth year following the graduation of the preceding class, studied full-time and lived in dormitories. The Seminary remained open until 1940 when the **USSR** occupied Latvia and closed all religious educational institutions. 53 people have graduated from the Seminary, many of them becoming well known Baptist leaders in Latvia. After Soviet occupation **theological education** was severely restricted but did not cease. Graduates of the Baptist Seminary conducted lectures for new **pastors** though this was sometimes regarded as illegal activity. When Revd Dr. Janis Tervits (1936-2003) became the **bishop** of the Baptist **Union** he organised **preaching** lectures (1980-89) as part of a three-year study programme with lectures delivered twice a month at weekends. This activity was not blocked by the KGB despite the existence of the course not being hidden from them. A new Latvian Baptist Theological Seminary, established in 1991, continuing the work of the previous Seminary, became the main theological institution for Latvian Baptists with recruitment taking place every second year. Initially the education offered was full time but since 1999 study has been part-time alongside a **pastoral** placement. In 2005 the seminary was renamed the Christian Leadership College giving a first-level professional qualification for pastoral **ministry**, Christian education and, from 2006, a programme for social workers.

EM

Lausanne Movement/ Committee/Covenant

The Lausanne movement is known primarily for two international congresses which addressed the theme of for world **evangelisation**, the first held in Lausanne, Switzerland in 1974. 'Lausanne II' was held in Manila, Philippines in 1989. There were however other international congresses which were important in the development of the movement, such as the 1966 World Congress on Evangelism in Berlin, the 1980 Conference on World Evangelisation in Pattaya, the 2004 Forum of World Evangelisation also held in Thailand, as well as many regional conferences and committee meetings. The congress in Lausanne was a focal point of the *evangelical* movement defining *conservative evangelical* identity in *mission*. The second defining moment in Manila was less radical and more *holistic* in its achievements. It concentrated more on bridging various different positions. Significantly some 70 Russian leaders were able to be present in Manila in contrast to the Chinese delegation who were represented by empty chairs because a 300 strong Chinese delegation had been denied permission to travel at the last minute.

The Lausanne Covenant and the Manila Manifesto are even today some of the most important documents for most conservative evangelical churches, missions, *theological* institutions and movements in defining their beliefs about the nature of world mission . The Lausanne Covenant was drafted by a group led by John Stott in which Revd Raymond Brown of *Spurgeon's College* played a significant part. Seeking to 'frame a biblical [see *Bible*] declaration on evangelism' the document in 15 chapters carefully spells out those doctrines which impel evangelicals to engage in mission. Hence there is an important chapter on scripture which significantly avoids the language of *inerrancy* preferring to speak of scripture providing 'the only infallible rule of *faith* and practice'. Other chapters affirm the *trinity* and the divinity of *Christ*, here spoken of in terms of his 'uniqueness and universality'. Acknowledging the *unity of the church* and yet its diversity of form, and emphasising the role of the *Holy Spirit* in evangelism, it relates evangelism to Christian social responsibility as both essential parts of the *church*'s mission, indeed expressing penitence for 'sometimes regarding evangelism and social responsibility as mutually exclusive'. The last section admits that a moratorium on sending missionaries 'may sometimes be necessary to facilitate the *national church*'s *growth* in self-reliance and to release resources for unevangelised areas'. Other chap-

ters deal with *religious liberty* and civil rights and the relationship between gospel and culture.

The two conferences resulted in many new evangelical projects, and a number of theological institutions and mission agencies have connections with the events that took place in Lausanne and Manila. Today, whilst the Lausanne Movement has lost something of what the key role that it had in the 1970s and 80s, it is still a major element in defining conservative evangelical faith and mission.

PFP

FURTHER READING: J.D. Douglas, *Let the Earth Hear His Voice*, World Wide Publications, Minneapolis, 1975. C.R. Padilla (ed), *The New Face of Evangelicalism*, Hodder and Stoughton, London, 1976. J.R.W. Stott, *The Lausanne Covenant*, World Wide Publications, Minneapolis, 1975. J.R.W. Stott (ed), *Making Christ Known: Historic Documents from the Lausanne Movement, 1974-1989*, Eerdmans, Grand Rapids, Mi., 1997.

Laying on of Hands

The *ministry* of the laying on of hands accompanied by *prayer* is a feature of most Baptist communities in Europe. It is attested to in many of the early Baptist *Confessions* and in early *association* minutes, such as the west of *England* in 1704. It is used at different times and in differing settings with the multiple significance of blessing, setting apart, *commissioning*, ordaining [see *Ordination*], absolving [see *Absolution*], and *healing*. Underlying this liturgical act [see *Liturgy*] is the understanding from *scripture* that this is an appropriate sign and recognition of the charism of transmitting the spiritual blessing of God from one or more persons, set apart or recognised to do that within a community or wider association of churches, principally for healing or blessing. Hands are normally laid upon the head and upper shoulders, though occasionally in healing, on the affected part of the body.

The gesture signifies the importance of the prayer and it is not generally thought amongst Baptists that the actual act of touching someone is the means by which the *grace* of God is transmitted. Reliance for meaning is placed upon scriptural passages which point to this gesture being used in blessing, healing and ordaining for a specific task (Ge 48; Mk 5:23; 6:5; 10:16; 16:18 Ac 6:1-6; 8:17-19 ; 9:12-17, 13:1-3, 19:6; 1Ti 4:14; 2Ti 1:6, etc.). Baptists follow this NT pattern in that many lay on hands with prayer for healing. Some accompany this with anointing with oil. Most Baptist communities set people apart for *pastoral* ministry (ordination) with prayer and the laying on of hands. Some European Baptists set *Union* officers, Seminary Rectors, *Deacons* and others apart for their tasks with prayer and the laying on of hands. The *European Baptist Federation* sets its General Secretary, the Rector and senior staff of *IBTS* apart with the laying on of hands.

Many Baptist churches practice the laying on of hands with prayer immediately after the *baptism* of a believer, seeking the in-filling of the *Holy Spirit* in the life of the newly baptised, though in the earliest days of the Baptist movement this proved to be a disputed and divisive practice.

Apart from the ministry of healing, it would be normal for the one receiving the blessing of the laying on of hands to kneel and normally, especially at ordination, valediction and commissioning, more than one person would lay on hands, though only one might pray aloud. In some Unions the public laying on of hands for ordination is restricted to *pastors* who are themselves, ordained. In some Unions certain representative figures should be involved at ordination such as Regional Pastors and/or Seminary Rectors. In some Unions representatives of other *evangelical* denominations were deliberately included in this process when the language used was of 'ordination to the Christian (not Baptist) ministry.

KGJ

FURTHER READING: Baptist Union of Great Britain and Ireland, *The Meaning and Practice of Ordination Among Baptists*, Carey Kingsgate, London, 1957.

League of Nations
See *United Nations Universal Declaration on Human Rights and UN Agencies*.

Lebanon
Baptist *witness* in Lebanon started in the late 19th century when Lebanon was still part of the Turkish Ottoman Empire. The earliest impetus was entirely due to the personal initiative of Saeed Juriiedini, a Greek *Orthodox* from Shweifat, near Beirut.

Juriiedini, on a visit to participate in the 1893 World's Fair in Chicago, had a profound religious experience and was baptised [see *Baptism*] at the Third Baptist Church, St. Louis, Missouri in 1894. Returning to Lebanon, he earned his living as a professional photographer, while engaged in *evangelism*. On 29 Sep 1895 *Pastor* W.R. Smith of the Third Baptist Church, St. Louis, on a visit to Lebanon, ordained Juriiedini as Lebanon's first Baptist pastor [see *Ordination*]. The same day Juriiedini baptised eight people, forming the nucleus of the first Baptist Church in Beirut, with his studio doubling as a place of *worship*. Juriiedini played a pivotal role in the establishment of the early Baptist presence in Lebanon and developing the leadership of fledgling new churches. Among the early leaders were Joseph Daoud, Najeeb Khalaf, Ayoub Naeem, Elias Salibi, Butros Khattar, and Saleem Sharouk. Within five decades of the commencement of Baptist *ministry* in Lebanon, churches and congregations were established in Beirut (Ras Beirut, Musaitbe), Rashiyya, Kfar Mishky, and Miyyeh w Miyyeh. This was accomplished by the pioneering efforts of faithful Lebanese believers in the face of strong opposition and at times even persecution.

There has been sporadic interest as well as assistance by individual US Baptist churches right from the beginning. However, it was only after the 1920 London Conference of the *Baptist Missionary Society* that the Baptist ministry in Lebanon attracted any concerted interest from Western *missions*. In response to an appeal, the *Southern Baptist Convention* agreed to send missionaries to *Palestine* and *Syria*, with Lebanon falling under the rubric of the latter. Finlay and Julia Graham, the first Southern Baptist Missionaries took up residence in Lebanon in 1948, and thus began a long and fruitful partnership. Finlay Graham, a gritty Scotsman, was a visionary and indefatigable builder of Baptist institutions. 1955 saw the opening of Beirut Baptist School in the heart of Beirut and in 1960 the *Arab Baptist*

Theological Seminary, in Mansourieh, which draws students from all across Middle East and North Africa. The Publications Department undertook extensive literacy work, preparing **Sunday School** material in Arabic and in translation and the production of other forms of Christian literature; extending the reach of Baptist ministry to many countries in the region. By the middle of the 20th century there were established Baptist churches in Tripoli, Beshmazzine, Bikfayya, Badaro, Hadath, and Ein Dara, in addition to those mentioned previously.

In Oct 1955 the Lebanese Baptist Convention was formed, representing most of the Baptist churches in Lebanon, and later in 1959 the Baptist Women's Union was organised. Some of the published Baptist **magazines** were *Al Mana'er* [*The Candlestands*], discontinued after one issue, *Al Karmah* [*The Vineyard*], and the popular *Al Ghareeb* [*The Stranger*]. The **Evangelical** Baptist Convention of Lebanon now has about 24 member churches all across Lebanon consisting of nearly 1,900 **members**.

In 1998 the ownership and management of the educational and literature ministries of the Southern Baptist Mission were formally handed over to the Lebanese through the formation of the Lebanese Society for Educational and Social Development (LSESD). There have always been a few Independent Baptist Churches in Lebanon; the largest of them is Lebanon Baptist Church, which also runs Lebanon Baptist Seminary.

DDC

FURTHER READING: Jane Carroll McRae, *Photographer in Lebanon: The Story of Said Jureidini*, Broadman, Nashville, Tn., 1969. Julia Graham, *Baptist Beginnings in Lebanon, 1893-1956*, (Unpublished Manuscript), 1986. Lebanese Baptist Convention, *Baptists In Lebanon*, (Prepared for the *Baptist History Committee for the VI Baptist Youth World Conference*), 1963. Salim Sharouk, *Tarikh al-Ma'madaniyyin fi Lubnan*, Lubnan, 1959.

Lectionaries

A Lectionary is a disciplined framework for the reading of **scripture** in public **worship**, probably spread over two or more years with the chosen readings relating to the demands of the different seasons of the **Christian Year**. The practice of using a lectionary in part derives from the worship of the synagogue where set readings of the OT were appointed for different feasts. To what extent these were taken over by the early church is uncertain, but certainly the early church added readings from the gospels and Acts to Revelation, initially for the great festivals, with readings for other Sundays being locally chosen. From the **Reformation** onwards there have been attempts to reform the received forms of lectionary with debate as to how far the three or four selected readings should relate to a common theme, or whether each strand of the lectionary should have its own progression. The object of the exercise has been said to be, 'to immerse the hearers of the word into the entire history of **salvation**...and thereby equip them to become also "doers of the word".' Whilst some Baptists find this an unhelpful external invasion of their freedom to plan worship, others, without following it slavishly, find it a helpful discipline that compels them to consider passages of scripture which they might otherwise neglect. There is also a challenge in so far as the use of a lectionary means that many congregations worshipping in liturgical **traditions** [see **Liturgy**] are exposed to much more scripture-reading, both in range and quantity, than some Baptist congregations that boast the Biblical basis of their **faith**. Whilst there is merit in using one of the well-developed international lectionaries which thereby unite the local congregation to the worship of the wider **church**, a locally developed system of readings also has merit, but this is different from the haphazard ordering of the reading of scripture which seems to lack any order.

JHYB

FURTHER READING: H.T. Allen and J.P. Russell, *On Common Ground: the Story of the Revised Common Lectionary*, Canterbury, Norwich, 1998.

Legal Status in countries for Baptist churches

Baptistic **gathering churches** within Europe and the Middle East have suffered from the time of the very first **Anabaptist** community in Zollikon, **Switzerland** (1525), with securing legal status to exist as communities of believers independent of the controlling authority of the **nation** state. Whilst seeking independency from State control, they have wished to obtain some validity and security to meet safely for public **worship**, to own **property** and to engage in **mission**. For 500 years this has been a problematic area as baptistic gathering communities have disowned the notion of **Luther** that the *'faith* of the prince should be the faith of the people' and, as **Balthasar Hubmaier** argued (1524) in *On Heretics and Those who Burn Them*, and **Thomas Helwys** in the *Mystery of Iniquity* (1612), the worship of the believers and faith of citizens and subjects is not a matter that should be subject to detailed control by the government.

However, even in enlightened regimes where baptistic gathering communities are permitted to exist and given a legal status, there is a concern for a measure of control in the registration of places of worship, the ability to establish religious **associations** (vereins) and to guard against spurious or dangerous practices. In many instances Baptists have benefited from laws which confer a legal reality upon such communities with the nations concerned providing for certain rights and privileges including exemption from certain forms of taxation, or the ability of **members** of the communities to make gifts for the purpose of the church which are tax-free, or attract a payment by the government to the church effectively giving to the church tax paid by the members on their earnings. The **Council of Europe**, the **United Nations** and others are careful to try to ensure that countries have in place laws which permit non national and non **state churches** to exist, but the legal status created often fails to give members of such communities the same legal standing as the state, or national religious organisation. Even such apparently enlightened and modern states such as the **United Kingdom**, **Denmark** and **Belgium** have areas of law and civic life which disadvantage those belonging to baptistic churches over against state and national churches in higher **education**, **marriage** law and similar areas.

However, in most of Europe nations are signatories to the European Convention of **Human Rights** (drafted 1949) which in Article 9 provides for freedom of religious belief, practice and teaching, subject only to such limitations as are in conformity with the general principles of law recognised by civilised nations to protect the rights of others and in meeting the just requirements of morality [see **Religious Liberty**]. To achieve this standard most nations look to have places of worship registered and generally have laws with regard to the designation of particular religious groupings such as Baptists.

In some situations Baptist groups themselves believe on grounds of **conscience** they should not accept registration of their buildings or organisations by the State. During the post WWII **communist** era this was a point of contention amongst believers in **Russia** and the **Ukraine** with some groups registering and recognising the measure of control this might bring, whilst other groups refused to register and became, in effect, 'underground assemblies'. Today, most baptistic churches will seek to register where the framework of the law conforms to international norms and provides for rights of assembly, freedom to worship, the ability to own property and freedom from State control in the matters of who can be members, who can be called to serve as **Pastor**, decisions as to the basic life of the church community and the ability to engage in **Bible study**, social activity and some forms of mission.

PV & KGJ

Leisure

A Christian attitude to the **stewardship** of time will involve a right appreciation of time devoted both to work and leisure. Leisure represents freedom from work that gives space for 're-creation'. It makes space for hobbies, entertainment, and cultural pursuits. At the highest level leisure can be seen to have a transcendent character enhancing the quality of life. It should be distinguished from idleness, which carries a pejorative meaning, but often in **evangelical** thought leisure too has been seen as a danger, an invitation to worldly pursuits, or something unworthy of a truly spiritual person.

In the account of **creation** God rested on the seventh day, and enshrined in the **Sabbath** commandment is the concept of a balance between work and leisure. In the gospel story we are soon aware that *Jesus* did not work incessantly. He took time to share meals with friends, to admire the flowers, to be apart in solitude. He commanded his disciples to stop ministering to the crowds and to spend time refreshing themselves. A biblical ethic [see *Bible*; *Ethics*] of leisure takes note of the fact that God created trees that were good for food, and also 'pleasing to the eye' (Ge 2:9). Paul comments that 'God richly furnishes us with everything to enjoy' (1Ti 6:17).

In Christian *tradition* there have been different attitudes to leisure. Augustine wrote, 'the life of leisure ought to consist not in idle activity, but in the opportunity to seek and find the truth, so that everyone may make progress in this regard, and not jealously withhold his discoveries from others'. This is a very practical description of leisure, and may reflect Augustine's preference for the life of a monk over that of a *bishop*, but it reminds us that leisure is no empty or wasted time, but a means to our growth in *grace* and to the glory of God. A link has often been made between *worship* and leisure, to the extent that Sabbath observance for some Christians in Europe has ruled out many forms of re-creation. While there is much common ground shared by worship and leisure, there is a legitimate Christian place for recollection, relaxation, both bodily and mental, the cultivation of the imagination by involvement in the arts, and sharing friendship. In more recent years Baptists, like other Christians, have given more attention to the doctrine of creation, seeing that beyond work and obligation, Christians should affirm that God has given *humankind* a marvellously rich creation to enjoy.

DBM & ET

FURTHER READING: D. Atkinson and D. Field (eds), *New Dictionary of Christian Ethics and Pastoral Theology*, InterVarsity, Leicester, 1995, pp.547-48. J. Pieper, *Leisure: The Basis of Culture*, Faber and Faber, London, 1998.

Lent

The word 'Lent' means 'spring', but within the context of Christianity it has come to refer to the 40 days [Latin: *quadragesima*] of spiritual discipline before the Easter season

and is linked with the testing of *Jesus* in the wilderness.

The season commences with special preparations in many countries, variously Fat/Pancake Tuesday associated with the eating up of rich foods and fats in preparation for *fasting*, Mardi gras or carnival prior to abstinence, almost universally opposed by Baptists because of its descent into ludeness and debauchery in certain Latin countries and *Ash Wednesday,* with the accent on *repentance* and spiritual preparation for a season of intensified *discipleship*.

By the 2nd century Irenaus was recording the habit of believers to fast before participating in the Pasha, or Christian *Passover*. By the 4th century Athanasius was making a distinction between the 40-day season and the final week between *Palm Sunday* and *Holy Saturday*, often called *Holy Week*. It is associated in earlier centuries with a time of preparation for the *catechumenate* before their *baptism* as believers on *Easter Eve* or *Easter Day*.

In many Baptist communities the season of Lent is marked by special extra services, or midweek study groups. There is often encouragement for people to read a book of spiritual devotion, taking on some extra activity as a way of enhancing discipleship. This is in contrast to an older practice amongst society in general to give up various pleasurable activities or enjoyable foods for the season of Lent. In *Georgia* Baptists have a special theme of activity for each week of Lent in this attitude of taking things on rather than giving things up. These activities include work with prisoners, *children*, victims of human trafficking, and the sick as well as *environmental* issues.

KGJ

Leuenberg Church Fellowship
See *Community of Protestant Churches in Europe*.

Leuenberg Confession Conversations on Baptism
[See also *Baptism; Bilateral Conversations; Community of Protestant Churches in Europe; Infant Baptism*]
Conversations on the nature of baptism took

place from 2002-04 between the *European Baptist Federation* and the Churches of the Leuenberg Confession (*Lutheran, Reformed, United, Methodist* as well as *Waldensians, Czech Brethren* and Hussite), more recently known as the Community of *Protestant* Churches in Europe (CPCE). These churches are bound together by the Leuenberg Agreement of 1973 which resolved the major doctrinal differences between the Lutheran and Reformed Churches in Europe, especially on the meaning of the *Eucharist*; the Methodists being admitted to 'church fellowship' sometime later by means of a separate agreement.

The overall aim of the Conversations with the EBF was to 'consider under what conditions mutual recognition of baptism is possible', with the wider objective of seeing whether European Baptists could enter into a 'church fellowship' with CPCE as defined by the Leuenberg Agreement, strengthening CPCE's desire to be a 'Protestant voice for Europe'. This was the first time the EBF as a body had entered into *theological* conversations with other Christian *traditions*. Preparatory conversations, mainly with German and Austrian Baptists took place before the EBF Council agreed that the EBF itself could be the conversation partner.

The talks were constructive and much agreement was reached on the nature of *salvation* and of the gospel. As expected the difficult area was the question of baptism. It was acknowledged that in many churches belonging to CPCE parents are increasingly leaving baptism until their child can decide for him/herself to be baptised. However many CPCE churches are *national/state churches* which still practise what looks to Baptists like 'indiscriminate baptism' where in some cases there is not subsequent nurture of the child in the Christian *faith*.

From the standpoint of CPCE it was not possible to accept anything which looked like re-baptism' i.e. where a person baptised as an infant came to a living faith for themselves and wished to be baptised as a believer.

The Conversations carefully examined the work of Baptist *theologian*, Paul Fiddes, and his advocacy of the recognition of a 'common process of initiation', where the outcome of the process, i.e. a believing Christian disciple, can be commonly affirmed, despite baptism appearing at different moments in the process itself. It was recognised that in practical terms, such recognition was more possible where Baptist churches are 'open' in *membership* [see *Open Membership*], i.e. willing to receive into membership individuals baptised and confirmed in their faith in a paedobaptist tradition. Most European Baptist Churches, however have 'closed' membership, only admitting as members those baptised as believers.

An important question underlying the Conversations was whether doctrinal agreement on '*Word* and *Sacrament*' was the only basis for a *unity* of 'church fellowship' as defined by CPCE. Baptists might prefer to say that they find can find *koinonia* with any Christian tradition in which they discern the marks of the true *church* of *Jesus Christ*, and with any believers in whom is evidenced the *fruit of the Spirit*.

Not surprisingly, as a result of these Conversations, CPCE did not find sufficient agreement for a 'church fellowship' with European Baptists to be possible. The 2004 EBF Council which received the Report of the Conversations recognised their importance and urged that nevertheless some kind of 'associate status' might be found for European Baptists in CPCE. At the time of writing (2008) this has not proved possible for CPCE to agree, though discussions are ongoing.

AAP

FURTHER READING: W. Hüffmaier and A.A. Peck (eds), *Dialogue between the Community of Protestant Churches in Europe (CPCE) and the European Baptist Federation (EBF) on the Doctrine and Practice of Baptism* (Leuenberg Documents Vol. 9), Lembeck, Frankfurt am Main, 2005.

Liberalism and Modernism

These terms cannot be separated from their usage in secular history as seen, e.g., in the rise of the liberal democracies, the modern movement in literature and in art, and more recently the widespread usage of the language of post-modernism,. In the post-modern the rationality of modern understanding gives way to the personal where each person's 'what the test means to me' is as valid as another's.

All such intellectual movements have to be related to the historical context in which they emerge: when in 1737 the *Congregational minister*, Mathias Maurice, enquired in opposition to a pervasive hyper-*Calvinism* whether it was 'the duty of poor unconverted sinners [see *Sin*], who hear the Gospel preached or published, to believe in *Jesus Christ*', a question he answered in the affirmative, he entitled his pamphlet, *A Modern Question Modestly Answered,* and so the controversy that prepared the way for Andrew Fuller's [see *Fullerism*] enunciation of a new *evangelical* Calvinism was seen as an answer to 'The Modern Question'.

The terms Liberalism and Modernism in the 19th century took on denominational connotations as *scholars* described Liberal *Protestantism* and *Catholic* Modernism. Liberalism initially indicated a rejection of all bigotry and a readiness to entertain new ideas. In 19th-century *Germany* in particular, greatly influenced by changes in philosophical thinking and presuppositions, three *theologians* came to dominate protestant theology: Schleiermacher, who with his strong emphasis on feelings, politely described religion as 'a sense and taste for the infinite', Ritschl, who placed a strong emphasis on the Christian community and on the ethical dimension [see *Ethics*] of life in the *kingdom of God*, and von Harnack with his emphasis on the fatherhood of God, the infinite worth of the human soul, and the commandment of *love*; all three contributed to a Liberal Protestantism that came to stand for an 'anti-*dogmatic* and humanitarian reconstruction of the Christian *faith*'. It was unfortunate that early Biblical criticism [see *Bible*] was often associated with such advanced views which consequently drew to these methods of study an unnecessary amount of hostility, though it was also true that philosophical presuppositions skewed some criticism in a corrosive direction not justified by the study of the texts themselves. A similar movement in the Roman Catholic Church was particularly associated with the names of Loisy and Tyrrell, both of whom in due course suffered excommunication, and the layman [see *Laity*], Baron von Hugel, who avoided ecclesiastical censure. This Catholic movement has normally denominated modernism.

Within English-speaking Christian scholarship, modernism came to describe more radical attempts to amend Christian doctrine, and liberalism rather more moderate efforts to restate *traditional* teaching in the light of insights derived from the development of knowledge in the modern world. Modernism in its most extreme forms dismantled the *authority* of scripture and seriously questioned *apostolic* doctrine, focusing on the human and the ethical, coupled with an exaggerated confidence in human goodness, emphases which were undermined by two World Wars and the totalitarianism of the 20th century. In some senses such teaching fulfilled *Spurgeon*'s worst fears as to what he perceived to be the dangerous theological trends which he condemned in the Downgrade Controversy. However some of what the modernists condemned was the superstition of the sacerdotalism and sacramentalism [see *Sacrament, Sign and Symbol*] fostered in the catholic tradition, which efforts paralleled similar condemnations by Baptists.

Within the Baptist tradition the struggle has always been to balance freedom and fidelity, tolerance with truth, *creed* with encounter, that is to say the statements of the mind with the experience of the heart, for they well remembered that it was conscientious objection to subscription to religious articles that was a large element in the birth of the denomination. But early Baptists were also quick to produce confessions of faith to demonstrate that they shared in the faith of the apostolic church. At the heart of the issue is the belief that there is an apostolic faith that must not be watered down but rather *preached* afresh in every generation.

Part of the problem is that it is easy to believe that the inherited *theology* is truly biblical, though in fact all theologies tend to represent an accommodation to the prevailing culture, and so the need constantly to interrogate doctrine to discern what really is the faith handed down by the *apostles*, and what the legacy of particular cultural contexts. There has also been a proper reluctance to impute to language more meaning than it could legitimately bear. Whilst it might be right to be reluctant to invest religious language with too much significance, it is also true that language remains a principal, and sometimes the only available, means of communication and, therefore, the verbal exploration of Christian truth has been necessary for the health of the **Church**. Granted this, such a task needs to be undertaken with all the precision that a God-given intelligence can harness. However, it is also possible to perfect a formulaic representation of Christian truth, whilst altogether failing to experience the reality of the power it expresses, that is to say the ultimate test of religious truth is that it is to be experienced, not only to be certified in *credal* statement.

Whilst there have been Baptist theologians who would be happy with the description Liberal Evangelicals, the emphasis on a regenerate **church membership** symbolised in believers' **baptism** as the rite of initiation into the life of the living Body of Christ, has protected the denomination from the worst excesses of liberal theology. Believers' baptism means that Baptists have always believed in the necessity of **conversion** and identification of the believer with the saving work of Christ. Indeed the denomination, with its dissenting background, can be characterised as conservative in its theological views but radical (liberal) in working them out in daily **discipleship**. However both individuals and local congregations have been jealous of anything like a standard being imposed upon them because each, under Christ, is its own **sovereign** authority.

ET

FURTHER READING: R.J. Coleman, *Issues of Theological Conflict: Evangelicals and Liberals*, Eerdmans, Grand Rapids, Mi., 1980. J.I. Packer, *'Fundamentalism' and the Word of God*, InterVarsity, Leicester, 1958. B. Reardon, *Liberal Protestantism*, Adam and Black, London, 1968. A.M.G. Stephenson, *The Rise and Decline of English Modernism*, SPCK, London, 1984.

Liberation Theology

[See also *Theology*]

Liberation Theology is the generic name given to a late 20th-century **Catholic** and increasingly **ecumenical** theological movement which originated in Latin America. It is not a theology that can be set down in a series of propositions. Rather as Gustavo Guttierez says: 'This is a theology which does not stop with reflecting on the world but rather tries to be part of the process through which the world is transformed' (Gutierrez, 1971).

Two pan Latin America Conferences in Medellin, Colombia (1968) and Puebla, Mexico (1979) helped give international prominence to this new way of 'doing' theology. Common themes include:

-   *Conscientisation* – the process of consciousness-raising often drawing on the insights of social scientists.
-   **Orthopraxy** – 'right actions' which are as important as **orthodoxy** ('right beliefs').
-   *The Base Communities* – **faith** communities rooted in **Bible Study**, Christian **worship** and and social and community action.
-   **Evangelisation** – spreading a **holistic** gospel concerned for the bodies of the world's majority as well as their souls.
-   A vision for the coming of *God's* **Kingdom** and not just the good of the **Church**.
-   **Violence and non-violence** – with a range of approaches from the **Marxism** of the Colombian guerilla priest Camillo Torres to the **pacifism** of the Brazilian **Bishop** Dom Helder Camara.
-   *Contradicting reality* – drawing on the insights of Jürgen Moltmann's especially his *The Crucified God* (1974).
-   *The* **preferential option for the poor** – liberation theology's best known tenet: '...anyone who wants to elaborate relevant liberation theology must be prepared to go into the examination hall of the poor' (Leonardo and Clodovis Boff, 1987).

In Europe the 1985 confrontation between the Brazilian Leonardo Boff and then Cardinal Joseph Ratzinger led to Boff's 'silencing' and to two significant Vatican reports: *Instruction on Certain Aspects of the Theology of Liberation* (1984) and the more eirenic *Instruction on Christian Freedom and Liberation* (1986). Those associated with liberation theology in Latin America have known significant persecution and harassment. Its most prominent **martyr** was Archbishop Oscar Romero of El Salvador whose increased involvement in the **human rights** struggle of his people led directly to his murder on 24 Mar 1980. Also murdered were 6 Jesuits and two of their domestics in the University of Central America, San Salvador on 16 Nov 1989. Others died as 'liberationists' simply for possessing 'subversive' materials or for living near guerrilla controlled territory, or for giving humanitarian assistance such as food or medical care to rebels or soldiers.

The movement rapidly influenced theology on the continent of Latin America and internationally. Whilst emerging from radical Catholicism, several Latin American **Protestants** were also heavily influenced by the movement notably people like Jose Miguez Bonino, Jorge Pixley and Emilio Castro. It also played an important part in the beginnings of the Latin American Theological Fraternity in which Baptists like Renee Padilla, Samuel Escobar and Orlando Costas have played key roles. The theme of liberation was a recurring one in the Church's significant role in the melting of the Iron Curtain in the late 1980s, including **Poland**'s *Solidarnosc,* and also in Black American and African theology [see **Black Theology**] with their reflections on **racism**, slavery, **apartheid** and the end of **colonialism** in Africa; Caribbean, especially Rastafari, spirituality; **feminist** and womanist theology; and some Asian theology including Korean *minjung* theology.

When asked once whether liberation theology had now had its day Jon Sobrino replied: 'One day liberation theology may be obsolete when oppression, demeaning and unjust poverty, cruel and massive repression cease to exist. On that day liberation theology will be obsolete, and this is the day that liberation **theologians** are working for, even though on that day they will be out of a job.'

MIB

FURTHER READING: Leonardo and Clodovis Boff, *Introducing Liberation Theology*, Burns and Oates, Tunbridge Wells, 1987. Michael I. Bochenski, *Theology from Three Worlds*, Regent's Park College, Oxford and Smith and Helwys, Macon, Ga., 1997. Harvey Cox, *The silencing of Leonardo Boff: the Vatican and the future of World Christianity*, Meyer-Stone Books, Oak Park, Il., 1988. Gustavo Guttierez, *A Theology of Liberation*, SCM, London, 1974. Peter Hebblethwaite, 'Liberation Theology and the Roman Catholic Church' in Christopher Rowland (ed), *The Cambridge Companion to Liberation Theology*, Cambridge University Press, Cambridge, 1999. Jürgen Moltmann, *The Crucified God*, SCM, London, 1974. Jon Sobrino, Ignacio Ellacuria and others, *Companions of Jesus: the Jesuit martyrs of El Salvador*, Orbis, New York, 1990. Theo Witvliet, *A Place in the Sun*, SCM, London, 1985.

Liberty of Conscience

See *Freedom of Conscience.*

Life and Work

Three strands of work link the **Edinburgh** Missionary Conference of 1910 with the founding of the **World Council of Churches** – the **International Missionary Council**, the Life and Work Movement and **Faith and Order**. Whilst international concern for **peace** and justice had existed before WWI, that catastrophe made the task so much more urgent. Accordingly some 90 representative **protestant** leaders met in Geneva in Aug 1920 to plan such a world conference under the leadership of the Swedish Archbishop Söderblom of Uppsala. Invitations were sent to all churches for a meeting in Stockholm in 1925 with the hope that those that gathered there would 'formulate programmes and devise means...whereby the fatherhood of God and the brotherhood of all peoples will become more completely realised through the **church** of **Christ**.' The organisers gave insufficient weight to the problems faced by post-war society and they had realistically to confess 'the world is too strong for a divided church'. The motto 'doctrine divides while service unites' led them too easily to put **theological** issues to one side.

This mistake was remedied at the second Life and Work Conference held in Oxford in 1937, for which valuable work was done in seeking to relate the ideal of the **kingdom of God** to the sinful world of human experience [see **Fall**; **Sin**]. It was at this conference that the German Baptist General Secretary, Paul Schmidt, found himself, with his German **Methodist** colleague, peculiarly isolated. Representatives of the **Lutheran** Church had been denied visas to attend and **Pastor** Niemöller was already in prison. Because of this the Conference was intent on sending a message of solidarity to the **Evangelical**

Church in *Germany*, making specific reference to the afflictions and the steadfast *witness* of the Confessing Church in Germany. Schmidt and his Methodist colleague spoke against this, arguing that to support such a message was to vote against their legitimate government who had guaranteed them freedom for their church activities, including 'full liberty of proclaiming the gospel of Jesus Christ'. Oxford 1937 revealed just how difficult it was for the churches in the context of militant *Marxism* and a strident *fascism* to engage with the *secular* agenda.

Life and Work, in emphasising the contribution of the Christian layman [see *Laity*] and his daily experience, broadened the *ecumenical* agenda and rooted it in the problematic life of human society. It is because of its pioneering work that the World Council of Churches, when founded in 1948, took on to its agenda issues such as international relations, racism, economic justice, *human rights* and *religious liberty*.

JHYB

FURTHER READING: *A History of the Ecumenical Movement*, Vol I, R. Rouse and S.C. Neill (eds); Vol II, H.E. Fey (ed); Vol III, John Briggs, Mercy Amba Oduyoye and Georges Tsetsis (eds), World Council of Churches, Geneva, 1954, 1970 and 2004.

Lithuania, Baptist history in

Lithuania, a *Catholic* country, was the last region in Europe to adopt Christianity (1387). In the 16th century, the expansion of *Reformation* ideas was suspended by the counter-Reformation which gained momentum after 1579. *Lutherans* and the *Reformed Church*, though still represented today in some regions of the country, survived only as religious *minorities*. In 1841, the first Baptist congregation was formed in Klaipeda (Memel) in western Lithuania, then controlled by Prussia. This came to be the mother church not only for Lithuanian, but initially also for Latvian Baptists, as in 1875 it seems to have had more than two dozen *mission stations* in Latvian areas. The Klaipeda (Memel) Baptist *mission* reached even further. Martin Kalweit of Memel was instrumental in starting the Russian Baptist movement in Tiflis (Tbilisi) in 1867.

The founder and early leader of Klaipeda church, Eduard Grimm, had experienced spiritual rebirth among the *Mennonites* in *Switzerland*, where he was baptised by affusion [see *Baptism*]. Upon returning to his native town, Grimm began to share his *faith* with others and so a group of mostly German-speaking believers emerged. One attender was an Englishman whose father was a Baptist *pastor* in *England*. He raised the question of baptism and, after discussion, a decision was made to seek baptism by immersion. This was conducted by *Johann Gerhard Oncken* from Hamburg, who came to Memel and in Oct 1841 and baptised 25 persons: 16 *women* and 9 *men*. Baptist work grew predominantly among ethnic Germans, but soon the Baptist message also reached ethnic Lithuanians, mostly those of a Lutheran background. This led to the baptism of the first Lithuanian in 1851. Six congregations, three of which were purely Lithuanian, were soon established in the region.

Another area of Baptist activity was North West Lithuania, as in the second half of the 19th century a considerable group of Latvians had moved there, some of whom were already Baptist. At the turn of the century three Latvian-speaking congregations were formed, but unfortunately, they did not make a significant impact on the Lithuanian-speaking population.

Several Baptist congregations were founded during the first decades of the 20th century. Whilst a German-speaking Baptist church in Kaunas dates back to 1889, it was only later that *worship* services in this church began to be held in Russian and Lithuanian. A Baptist church in Vilnius, initially only Russian-speaking, was established in 1912. After WWI, Teodoras Gerikas (1891-1946) began to organise and coordinate Baptist missionary work among Lithuanians, and as a result, some five small Lithuanian Baptist churches were founded. Christian literature in Lithuanian, for which there was a great demand, began to be published.

In 1933 the Baptist Union of Lithuania was established in Klaipeda, but its activity was terminated by the Soviet occupation in 1940. During the war, many Baptists with German roots migrated to *Germany*. During the Soviet time, two or three registered congregations were functioning as well as some unregistered groups. All of these maintained ties with the *AUCECB*, an umbrella organisation for *Evangelical* Christians-Baptists in the Soviet Union. Towards the end of the Soviet era, there were about 550 ECB *church members* (including some *Pentecostals*) in Lithuania. In 1980, these congregations formed a more formal association, with Jonas Inkenas, and later Ivan Panko, serving as Senior Presbyters. In 1989, the Pentecostals left to form their own *union*. The Union of Evangelical Baptist Churches in Lithuania was re-established in 1991, with Albertas Latuzis serving as the Chairperson until 2005. He has been succeeded by Henrikas Zukauskas, a graduate of *IBTS*. Currently, seven congregations participate in the renewed work of the Union. Several churches have been formed by independent missionaries from the United States, with one of these later joining the Union. In 2004, three Free Christian Churches [see *Free Churches*] left the Union to join other Free Christian churches in their own *association*. In 2005, there were approximately 400 members within the Baptist Union and nearly the same number of independent Baptists outside the Union.

ALa

Lithuanian Baptist Bible School, Klaipeda
See *Non-residential Bible School, Lithuania*.

Liturgical Movement
[See also *Liturgists, European Baptists of the 20th and 21st centuries*; *Liturgy*]
The Liturgical Movement describes that movement which in the last half century has seen the different church *traditions* taking *worship* more seriously, often giving a new centrality to *Holy Communion* (or Lord's Supper or Eucharist) as at the heart of the church's worship, as well as thinking of different ways in which worship can become more participatory for all *members* of the congregation. Thus a weekly celebration of the Eucharist has become the norm in many traditions: other traditions respect the communion less frequently but with more obvious preparation for its celebration. At its best the liturgical movement encourages the de-

velopment of local liturgy always looking for ways in which a congregation can own its worship as of its own culture, e.g. by the use of local language, art and music, rather than that borrowed from elsewhere, whilst at the same time being part of the worship of the universal *church*.

Baptists have been among those denominations least affected by the movement except in those places where there has been hard thinking about how an *Anabaptist* and a *Puritan-Evangelical* tradition might combine. In doing this, appropriate focus would need to be given to *word* and *sacrament*, to order and spontaneity, congregational *prayer* and congregational service, the realisation of the local congregation as corporately the manifestation of the Body of Christ, the inter-relationship of the local and the universal, that is in the local engaging in the worship of the world-wide company of God's people. Of itself the liturgical movement should not be seen as in competition with the *charismatic movement*: rather liturgical change needs to develop a capacity to embrace charismatic passion and joy, whilst the charismatic movement might learn from the importance of shape and continuity secured by liturgy.

One of the major influences in liturgical renewal has been the recovery of community life, and the impact of that life on the wider church through materials produced by such communities as *Iona*, *Taizé* and *Northumbria*, with their enrichment of local congregational experience. Focus on their activity also saves the *student* from thinking of liturgical renewal as exclusively about rites and liturgical texts. Its concern is so much wider, embracing all that renews the human soul in worship.

JHYB

Liturgists, European Baptists of the 20th and 21st centuries
[See also *Liturgical Movement*; *Liturgy*]
The study of liturgy and its use in public *worship* is not a common practice for Baptists who claim to have 'free and open worship' unimpeded by forms prescribed by *unions* and *associations*. Nevertheless there have been individuals who have reflected

and written on the worship life of Baptists, including their *hymnody* and worship structures. The books of worship and *prayers* they have produced have been used in many parts of Europe and, in fact, most Baptist communities do at least have common ordos of worship for the main Sunday service, *Lord's Supper*, *baptism*, *funerals* and *weddings*.

Pre-eminent amongst such *scholars* who have helped Baptists with liturgical issues must be Stephen F. Winward, who with Ernest A. Payne produced the widely used *Orders and Prayers for Christian Worship* in the 1960s. An earlier generation benefited from the work of David Tait Patterson in the north of *England* and his book *The Call to Worship* (1930). The *theology* of Baptist worship has been most fully explored by Christopher J. Ellis, *Gathering: A Theology and Spirituality of Worship in the Free Church Tradition*, now widely used as the course book on Baptist worship in seminaries in Western and Central Europe. Other writers and reflectors on Baptist worship include Paul Beasley-Murray, *Faith and Festivity*, Michael H. Taylor, *Variations on a Theme*, Parush R. Parushev and Keith G. Jones (eds), *Currents in Baptistic Theology of Worship Today* and Leonid Mikhovich on Baptist worship practice in *Belarus*. Neville Clark, Maurice Williams, Michael J. Walker and Paul P.J. Sheppy have all been involved in *ecumenical* study groups on worship producing material for Baptism, *Lent*, *Holy Week* and *Easter*, which many Baptists use. Myra Blyth has, with Christopher J. Ellis, produced a contemporary book of worship orders and materials for worship on special occasions, *Gathering for Worship: Patterns and Prayers for Communities of Disciples*. Additionally Paul P.P.J. Sheppy has served on the international commission responsible for the *lectionary*. Internationally **BWA** General Secretary, Neville Callam, has done much work on liturgical and *sacramental* theology and is engaged in seeking to enhance the worship life of the BWA.

In the field of hymnody writers of hymns and songs have included Keith W. Clements, Christopher J. Ellis, Lina Andronoviene, David R. Goodbourn and research on hymnody has been a specialism of Gunter Balders and Meego Remmel, whilst David Peacock assisted the BWA by producing *World Praise*

which encouraged Baptists and others to sing the best of modern Christian *music* produced throughout the world. Roy Searle and the *Northumbria Community* have also added much original contemporary music for use in morning and evening prayer.

KGJ

Liturgy

[See also *Liturgical Movement; Liturgists, European Baptists of the 20ᵗʰ and 21ˢᵗ centuries*]

The word liturgy derives from two Greek words literally meaning the **work** [*ergon*] of the people of God [*laos*]. It emerges from what we know of the biblical [see *Bible*] pattern in which there is a contrast between the more ceremonial practice of sacrifices and offerings associated with the temple and the more didactic patterns associated with the synagogue where the **Word** was all important. These traditions receive different weight in *Catholic*, *Orthodox* and *Protestant Evangelical* practice. Within the Catholic and Orthodox *traditions* the *sacrament* of the *eucharist* tends to be normative and all else derives from this. In Orthodoxy the expression 'The Liturgy' is the most common description of the main focus of Christian *worship*, describing the sacramental worship of the *sanctuary*. In more recent years orthodox *missiologists* have realised that this is incomplete so that they have begun to talk about 'the liturgy after the liturgy', namely the service of the church in the world. Both the worship of the congregation of the people of God, called out of the world, and the ongoing worship of those same people, dispersed back into the world there to make God known, are essential. Liturgical *scholars* have identified the essential elements of the Christian Liturgy which influence the shaping of even what might be called 'non-liturgical worship'. Thus the liturgy begins with a call to worship and develops with the celebration first of God's initiative, through the reading and expositions of the scriptures. The divine initiative is also celebrated in the sacraments of *Baptism* and the Lord's Supper. Worship always ends with the commissioning of the church for service as it disperses to the world in a *prayer* of dismissal. The second element in the liturgy is the worshippers' response seen in adoration and thanksgiving, offered to God in both *hymns* and prayers. Prayers of confession lead to an assurance of forgiveness, and intercessions ensure that the needs of church and world are brought before God [see *Prayers in Worship*]. The offering of the people's *gifts* is not simply an administrative convenience but symbolises the setting apart of ordinary things, not least the lives of the *members*, for the work of God's *kingdom*. On some occasions these two elements of the liturgy – the divine initiative and the human response – may be celebrated in the renewal of *covenant* vows in which the ongoing *love* of God and the dedication of his people are clearly articulated.

JHYB

FURTHER READING: I. Bria, *The Liturgy after the Liturgy*, WCC Publications, Geneva, 1996. Neville Clark, *Call to Worship*, SCM, London, 1960. Tony Cupit, *Baptists in Worship, Report of International Baptist Conference in Berlin*, Baptist World Alliance, McLean, Va., 1998. Christopher Ellis, *Gathering: A Theology and Spirituality of Worship in Free Church Tradition*, SCM, London, 2004. J.R.K. Fenwick and B.D. Spinks, *Worship in Transition: the Liturgical Movement in the Twentieth Century*, Continuum, New York, 1995. R.P. Martin, *The Worship of God*, Eerdmans, Grand Rapids, Mi., 1982. N. Micklem, *Christian Worship*, Clarendon, Oxford, 1936. A. Schmemann, *Introduction to Liturgical Theology*, Faith P., London, 1966. J.F White, *Protestant Worship, Traditions in Transition*, Westminster/John Knox, Louisville, Ky., 1989.

Local Church

[See also *Church, The; Church: Universal, Triumphant, Invisible*]

The Christian church is understood both as a whole and as a body or an organisation, which is concrete and local. The local character of the church is of primary significance in the NT. The usage of the word *ekklesia* shows this multiple meaning of the term church, where the local significance of a visible body of baptised believers [see *Baptism*] linked together in a common *faith* in *Jesus Christ* is inevitable. The historical development included a development of leadership, which tried to strengthen a *unity of the church* and its ability to include a human and spiritual multiplicity, that reflected

the wealth of the gospel.

The local character of the church is reflected in *credal* statements, such as the Nicene Creed, where the church is defined as one, holy, *catholic* or universal – and *apostolic*. Here the local character of the church is implied in all of the four characteristics. Unity and *holiness* does not suggest some perfect quality of the believers, but states the spiritual and personal nature of Christian life, which is at the heart of the church. Nominal Christians became a real problem later, when the church was recognised and became privileged by the *state*. Augustine even teaches that the real church is invisible and known only to God. This idea has had an impact on historical *ecclesiology*, which challenges the need to let the apostolic features of the NT church be of lasting significance. The credibility of the church depends on a presence of these four features, as suggested by the *prayer* of Jesus in Jn 17. The *ecumenical movement* aims at a visible unity within human history, and not just on an international level, but locally in the daily life of the church. The church cannot be a universal and spiritual reality without this local foundation.

Within a *free-church tradition* the church is an assembly of believers, brought together by God's *grace* through baptism and voluntary *association*. This personal character of the local church distinguishes their ecclesiology from the ecclesiology of the established churches, where the geographical character of the parochial church depends on a *hierarchical* system of government and the decision by the state to include the whole population in the established church. *Secularism* has forced the established churches to try to recapture the original character of the local church.

The church is not understood as an accidental *gathering* of people, and it is not primarily an institution – even though it needs a system of government – but a living community, the people of God. The church is gathered in the name of Jesus Christ. Here God is *worshipped*, and the *members* are ministering to each other, and reaching out to the community and the world with the gospel. A church that is independent of what serves the universal and ecumenical aspects of the Christian church may soon develop sectarian tendencies. A local church is never just local, but expresses the commonalities of local churches everywhere.

PMIL

FURTHER READING: BUGBI, *The Baptist Doctrine of the Church*, Carey Kingsgate, London, 1948. Paul Fiddes, *Tracks and Traces: Baptist Identity in Church and Theology*, Paternoster, Carlisle, 2003. A. Gilmore (ed), *The Pattern of the Church: a Baptist View*, Lutterworth, London, 1963. John Knox, *The Church and the Reality of Christ*, Harper and Row, New York, 1962. Hans Kueng, *The Church*, London, 1967. Bill J. Leonard, *Baptist Ways: A History*, Judson, Valley Forge, Pa., 2003.E.A. Payne, *The Fellowship of Believers, Baptist Thought and Practice Yesterday and Today*, Kingsgate, London, 1959. N.G. Wright, *Free Church, Free State: the Positive Baptist Vision*, Paternoster, Milton Keynes, 2005.

Local Ecumenical covenants and partnerships

See *Ecumenical covenants and partnerships/Union Churches/Dual Alignments.*

Logos

[See also *Christology*; *Incarnation*; *Jesus Christ*; *Lord of the Church and the Crown Rights of the Redeemer*]

Logos, a Greek term, usually rendered in English as 'Word', is a key word in the NT, describing the relationship of Jesus Christ to God ('the Word became flesh', Jn 1:14), and also used to denote 'message', 'teaching' or 'speech' (e.g. Lk 4:32: 'His word was with *authority*'). There has been some confusion over the term Logos, partly due to translation from Hebrew into Greek but principally because of the influence of Platonic thought, in which the Logos can be a bridge between the perfect, unknowable Creator, and the material world.

In early Christian *theology*, developing as it was in a largely Greek-dominated world of thought, this confusion and debate led to conflict and misunderstanding between different perspectives and schools of Christian thought. Today there is considerable interest in understanding the Johannine literature, which is central to any understanding of the Logos from a biblical point of view [see *Bible*], on its own terms. An appreciation of the Logos in the person and life of Jesus

Christ has a powerful bearing not only on the Christian doctrine of Christ, but also on the doctrine of the *Trinity* – 'the Word was with God, and the Word was God' (Jn 1:1) – and the doctrine of *creation* ('All things were made through him [Jn 1:2]). There are implications for how we perceive the Holy Spirit active in and through Christ's humanity (*Pneumatology*) and our own (theological *anthropology*).

In *Anabaptist* and Baptist *tradition* there has generally been a proper emphasis on Jesus Christ as Logos incarnate, although there have also been disputes about issues such as whether Christ received his human flesh from Mary (Melchior Hoffman, an early Anabaptist, denied this, and others followed him) and about the Eternal Sonship of Christ (which was denied by some 19th-century Strict Baptists in *England*). There is a constant challenge to develop an informed appreciation of Jesus as uniquely the Word of God, the Word made flesh and dwelling among us.

JGMP & ET

Lord of the Church and the Crown Rights of the Redeemer

[See also *Christology*; *Incarnation*; *Jesus Christ*; *Logos*]

The term 'Lord' refers to the Greek *kurios*, a title of *authority* in the NT, especially used about the risen Lord Jesus Christ. It represents the discovery which made the disciples Christians in the sense of becoming witnesses to the *resurrection*, confessing, 'Jesus is Lord'. The term 'crown rights' refers to another messianic title 'King', traditionally the third of three great offices used in *theological* reflection, describing Jesus as 'Prophet, Priest and King'. Jesus is represented as the anointed king, expected by the *Jews*. Christ is the Greek equivalent [*Xristos*] to the Hebraic *Messiah*, but the title carries the full theological significance of who Jesus is. The term 'redeemer' refers particularly to Jesus as the one who brought about *redemption* through his *incarnation*, life and *death*, but the emphasis is on the redemptive significance of his death.

This terminology links the *church* to the rule and the resources afforded her by her Lord. In him the church is a unique entity, independent of all other authorities. Talk of the Crown Rights of the Redeemer thus became the banner under which reformed churches [see *Reformation*] claimed their independence of *state* interference. State supremacy over the church is known as Erastianism; but if Christ is *sovereign*, then no earthly monarch can unseat his *authority* in his church. When the Huguenots were besieged in St. Quentin in the French Wars of Religion, the Habsburg forces shot an arrow into the city requiring surrender, but the Huguenot leader ordered the arrow to be shot back again with the message, *Regem habemus*, 'We have a King'. In similar fashion the Covenanters Memorial at the Greyfriars Church in Edinburgh makes reference to 'the Prerogatives of Christ the King.' But let it be noticed that there is little point in campaigning for Christ's rule in the Church unless we do all in our powers to obey his rule in our personal lives.

Note that there is a distinction between the Lord of the universe, or of *creation*, and the Lord of the church. The emphasis here is not on the powerful work of creating and sustaining the universe, but on the redeeming work, which brought the church into being and makes the church the necessary vehicle for Christ in the work of communicating *salvation* to all *humankind*. With Jesus Christ as Lord, the church is not on its own. Dependant on his *grace* and presence, the church must always be in a process of reform and *renewal* in order to serve him effectively, as he also served the *Kingdom of God*, so Christ, sovereign in his Church, makes that Church a vehicle for advancing his rule of justice and *peace* in the world.

PMIL & KGJ

Lord's Day
See *Sabbath*.

Lord's Supper/Table
See *Communion and Intercommunion*; *Eucharistic Liturgy*; *Sacrament, Sign and Symbol*.

Losungen
Losungen is a devotional booklet containing a collection of *Bible* verses for each day of the year. Following on a simple *prayer*, a verse from the OT is chosen which is supplemented by an exhortary NT verse on the same theme. There are also suggestions for continuous Bible reading while Sunday listings include gospel and epistle readings, a *sermon* passage and a song.

Losungen [Pl. 'motto'] originated in May 1727 in Herrnhut, Moravia. Since then, for almost a quarter of a millennium, this aid to devotion has been used by many *pietistic* and *evangelical* Christians, who take these texts as their motto for the day and hope to be influenced in their decision-making by the message of the text.

From the beginning of Moravian *mission* activities in 1732, this devotional tool has spread around the world and is today used in more than 50 languages. In Europe alone, *Losungen* is available in at least 25 languages such as Bulgarian, Croatian, Czech, Danish, Dutch, English, Estonian, Finish, French, German, Hungarian, Italian, Latvian, Polish, Rumanian, Russian, Slovakian, Spanish, Swedish and Turkish. This clearly demonstrates how through this little devotional tool most Baptist *unions* on the mainland of Europe have been, and continue to be, influenced by pietistic *spirituality*.

PFP

FURTHER READING: www.ebu.de.

Love
A large part of the rhythm of the OT is taken up with its exploration of the relationship between the Love of God to *humankind* and humankind's responding love to God, as intrinsic to the idea of *Covenant*. Thus God's choice of *Israel* as the object of his covenant love is clearly set out in Dt 7:6-11, and in the Shema, Dt 6:4-7, which *Jews* still reverence as the essence of the OT *revelation*, the required covenant response from Israel is defined. The writers of the NT have, in describing God's love, a number of words in classical Greek to choose from, including *agape, philia* and *eros*. *Eros* is commonly used of sexual love but it also denotes human aspiration after ideal virtue and indeed the divine, whilst *philia* is used of affection between friends. By contrast, *agape* is a rather pas-

sion-less word little used in classical Greek, but it is this word that the NT writers distinctively use to describe the self-giving love of God revealed in the life of *Jesus*.

By using this little-used term they underline the uniqueness of what it is that is at the heart of the Christian gospel. Whilst human imagery is used to describe the love of God, e.g. as father, marriage partner, gracious provider, care needs to be used in understanding such images since even the best in human experience is marred by *sin*. By contrast God's love is *sovereign* and free, eternal but focused on the individual in need. It is conferred on individuals not on the basis of their goodness or attractiveness but is extended to rebels and sinners who have no claim upon his compassion. This love is manifest in the life of Jesus, in his teaching and example even to the point at which he lays down his life for others. Thus it has been written: 'The self-emptying of the creator to take human nature at Bethlehem; the *ministry* and care of Jesus towards the despised, the outcast and the neglected; his parables of the Father's love and care; his deliberate humbling himself to endure the ignominy, shame and agony of his sin-bearing *death* and passion on behalf of those who rejected him; all these declare with one voice the amazing love of God.' But that is not all: 'His *resurrection* showed the invincibility of such holy love, and the promised gift of the *Holy Spirit* transforms it from an outward demonstration into an inner reality of deep assurance and life-changing power, by which he renews *men* and *women* progressively into his own image.'

Receiving this love of God should liberate the forces of love in the believer's life – prompting an imitation process in which believers learn to love others as Christ has loved them, forgiving one another as Christ had forgiven them [see *Forgiveness*]. Such a process should not only be domestic within the *church* but should extend to the unlovely and the unloved, the despised and the rejected, by such action making real the love of God in ever increasing circles of compassion. Such love extends well beyond the demands of the law for legalism, as seen in the behaviour of the scribes and the Pharisees, is a sure enemy of the spontaneity

of *agape* love. The other part of the covenant of love is to return love and obedience to God, always acknowledging that this is a response to his prior love; indeed it is he who gives the power to love, to live within covenant *grace*.

ET

FURTHER READING: C.S. Lewis, *The Four Loves*, Geoffrey Bles, London, 1960. L. Morris, *Testaments of Love*, Eerdmans, Grand Rapids, Mi., 1981.

Love Feast
See *Agape Meal*.

Lund Principle
The Lund Principle, stated in its own language, was that the churches should commit themselves 'to act together in all matters except those in which deep differences of conviction compel them to act separately'. Originally posed as a question it became accepted as a working aspiration of *ecumenical* cooperation. It is extracted from 'A Word to the Churches' formulated at the third world conference on *Faith and Order* meeting in Lund in 1952 in the aftermath of the optimism created by the launching of the Church of South India. Some churches took it as a text with which to justify their occasional united activity, such as in the Week of Prayer for Christian *Unity*, but the Lund drafters' intention was rather more purposeful, seeking a permanent change in relationships and the way in which *mission* strategies were developed by the churches.

JHYB

Luther, Martin (1483-1546)
Martin Luther was born in Saxony, the son of a successful miner who hoped that his son would have a career in law. Luther had a good secondary *education* in a school run by a lay [see *Laity*] reformist group called the Brethren of the Common Life. Luther spoke of how much he learned more from one of their major texts 'of God, *Christ*, and *man* than from any book outside the *Bible*, and the works of St. Augustine'. Martin Luther's abandonment of the law, after a significant religious experience, and his decision to be-

come an Augustinian canon, certainly did not please his father. His choice of Order was important, since the Augustinians were part of the *Catholic* reform movement within *Germany*, with Von Staupitz, Luther's superior, an influential figure in that movement. Luther, situated in Saxony towards Germany's eastern margins, was more influenced by late medieval ideas rather than by the latest Renaissance thinking, especially the so-called *Via Moderna*. Luther engaged with fundamental questions regarding *salvation* and how it might be achieved. Was it the case that humankind's obligation to love God implied a capacity to fulfil the obligation? 'I must love God therefore I can love God.' Luther searched for a *theology* in which he could believe, for his personal experience seemed to deny what the *church* was teaching about human ability to contribute to salvation.

The young man experienced an increasing sense of despair as to how he could please God – 'What man as man must do, man as sinner cannot do'. The old remedies, the *discipline* of the monastery, the services of the church, salvation through the *sacraments*, seemed not to work. In his deepest self he seemed to encounter evil in its most desperate and persistent form. However much he saw that his duty was to love God, he was increasingly aware of his moral incapacity to do this. Seconded by his order to the University of Wittenberg – newly established by the Elector of Saxony – he became successively Professor of Philosophy and Professor of Theology, which brought with it the special duty of defending the *faith* in the world beyond the university. This led him to read the Bible with a new seriousness and he began to discover new things: 'I did not learn my theology all at once but I had to search deeper for it where my temptations took me'. At the same time he began to answer questions about how *authority* was exercised in the life of the church. In his diary in May 1517 he writes: 'Our theology and St. Augustine's are going ahead and reign in our university, and it is God's work. Aristotle is gradually going down hill, perhaps into eternal ruin. It is wonderful how the lectures on the *Sentences* (commentaries on Aristotle) are out of favour.' The rediscovery of Augustine led thinkers back to the

doctrines of *grace* and *justification* by *faith*: what humanity, because of *sin*, could not do, God had done. God's initiative in giving his Son to die for the sins of the world upon the *cross* achieved salvation.

Just at this critical moment, a Dominican monk named Tetzel, sought permission to sell indulgences in Saxony. The Indulgence Issue heightened Luther's sensitivity, for it seemed to him to be the offer of cheap salvation, demonstrating the *papacy*'s insensitivity to the spiritual crisis emerging in Germany. This lead to him to publishing his *95 Theses* in Oct 1517 as a challenge to the Church's *hierarchy* to put matters right. There were further stages in Luther's spiritual experience and theological development which led to a break with Rome in 1521, when the emperor put his authority behind the Pope's excommunication.

As this narrative worked itself out, Luther began to lay down the framework of *Protestant* faith, stressing the authority of scripture, justification by grace through faith, the *vocation* of the Christian and the *priesthood of all believers*. These latter two emphases restored the place of lay people in the life of the church, now called to live out the holy life not in the confines of the monastery but in the workaday world of family, employment and market place and within the congregation. All of Luther's emphases that were to have considerable impact on Baptist life, although the *Reformed* rather than the *Lutheran* strand of the *Reformation* had more influence in shaping Baptist soteriology and *ecclesiology*. Luther was not a *systematic theologian* and aspects of his theology were open to criticism by other Reformers, e.g. his thinking about the *Lord's Supper*. Also, through placing much confidence in the role of the godly prince, Luther failed – from a Baptist perspective – to work out a way in which the Lutheran Church could function as a genuinely '*free church*'.

ET

Lutherans/Lutheranism, Baptists and

[See also *Bilateral Conversations*; *Leuenberg Confession Conversations on Baptism*]
Historically, both Baptists and Lutherans have their spiritual origins in the soil of the

Reformation, though some recent Baptist scholarship has linked Baptist beginnings to the 16th-century Radical Reformation rather than the work of *Luther*, *Calvin* and *Zwingli*. More directly, however, the first Baptist churches grew out of English 17th-century *separatism*.

Despite the ongoing discussion as to the extent to which mainstream Reformation or *Anabaptist tradition* have shaped the Baptist movement, there is no doubt that Baptists are characterised by an emphasis on the *conversion* experience, commitment to a life of *discipleship*, as well as to *evangelism* and *mission*. Baptist rejection of *infant baptism*, a critical element in the teaching of the early Baptist leader, *John Smyth*, which they share with Anabaptists, has caused grave misunderstandings, even to the extent of penal action by Lutherans, as well as by other mainline Protestant churches. Though Lutherans teach that the central truth of Christianity is *justification* by *grace* through *faith* – a doctrinal statement with which Baptists agree – the difference between these two Christian traditions is focused on the fact that Baptists believe a personal and clearly observable witness to faith in the life of the baptismal candidate should be a preliminary to *baptism*, which is administered in the form of immersion.

For centuries there was little contact between Baptists and Lutherans. In 19th-century Europe, when the Baptist movement spread in traditional Lutheran regions, Lutherans often saw Baptists as a disturbing element, though it should be admitted that Baptist *spirituality* often had its roots in Lutheran *pietism*. *Dialogue* and closer relations grew in the second half of the 20th century, when Baptists became involved in the work of the *World Council of Churches* and other national and regional *ecumenical* agencies. Conversations between the *Baptist World Alliance* and the Lutheran World Federation took place in 1986-89, focusing on issues, such as agreements and differences in the area of faith, discipleship, the nature of the *church*, and finally the nature of the *authority* required for teaching and *preaching*, on which an agreed paper was prepared in 1989. A large part of the discussions was devoted to the *theology* of baptism, especially since Baptists were concerned at the

Lutheran condemnation of their positions and practices in several historic Lutheran *confessions*. Similar topics – mainly in the area of *ecclesiology* where the structures of folk/*state churches* encountering the *gathered church* of *covenanting* believers – have also been discussed in conversations on a national level, such as in *Germany* in the 1980s. The difference between the two *communions* has sometimes led to Lutheran opposition to the appointment of Baptists to university theological posts as in a famous case in recent times at the University of Bochum.

The *European Baptist Federation* has had a series of conversations with the *Community of Protestant Churches in Europe* (formerly Leuenberg Church Fellowship or Churches of the Leuenberg Confession), which includes both Lutherans and *Reformed* Churches. The conversations on the topic of the nature of baptism took place from 2002-04, though the Community of Protestant Churches did not find it possible to establish 'church *fellowship*' with European Baptists. The materials and documents of these conversations have inspired further dialogues at a local level. Whilst Lutheran Churches in *Scandinavia* have long been thought of as archetypal state churches, from 1 Jan 2000 the church of *Sweden* was disestablished choosing instead to relate to the state as a faith community. However it still likes to see itself as a folk church, which it argues denotes a church which embraces the whole country, 'not a gathered church, ministering only to those who actively belong'.

During the last half century, Lutherans and Baptists in Europe and worldwide have taken a long step towards mutual understanding, though different views on baptism and aspects of ecclesiology continue to challenge the scholarship and church leaders in both traditions. However the authoritative article in the *Dictionary of the Ecumenical Movement* written by a leading Lutheran with long ecumenical experience, significantly concludes, 'The participants have been able to recognise each other's churches as true churches that live from the gospel.'

TP

M

Macedonia, Baptist history in

Early information about Baptist presence in Macedonia, a predominantly *orthodox* country with a significant *Muslim minority*, dates back to 1924 when the publication *Evangeliumsbote* mentioned that there were some Baptist believers in Macedonia, which was then the southern province of the *Yugoslavian* Kingdom. In 1928, a group of eight believers was baptised [see *Baptism*] in Skopje by Vinko Vacek, general secretary of the Yugoslav Baptist *Union*. In 1930, Vacek and Ivan Rusjakov, the latter being a *member* of a Baptist group in Skopje, baptised seven members of the local *Evangelical* church in the city of Radovis. Radovis Evangelical church had been founded in 1884 by *Congregational missionaries* from the United States, and in 1901 it was turned over to the *Methodists* to administer it. After the baptisms it became a Baptist church. In Skopje, it was not until 1960 that the Baptist church, 'Good Tidings', was formally founded. The church survived three decades of severe police persecution under the *Communist* regime. Skopje and Radovis Baptist churches were in the Yugoslav Baptist Union until 1991, when the former Yugoslavia dissolved into five new countries, one being Macedonia. As a consequence a separate Macedonian Baptist Union was established in 1991. In 1998, a group of 20 members separated from 'Good Tidings' and founded a new church named 'Voice of God', also in Skopje. Today in Macedonia, there are three Baptist fellowships with about 100 baptised believers, while Sunday attendance is close to 200. A small Baptist publishing house *Bozilak* [*Rainbow*] was founded in 1999.

BB

Magazines

For most European Baptists, with their emphasis on *education* and freedom of expression, magazines (including journals and periodicals) form one of the most important means of literary communication, second only to the *Bible* and, in the more open and prosperous western countries, only a whisker in front of more substantial books which magazines do much to promote.

Some have long lives, some have short lives. In *Britain*, monthly periodicals date back to the 1790s and the early years of the 19th century. The *Baptist Times,* an independent weekly, is an amalgamation of the privately owned *Freeman* (which began in 1855), purchased by the Baptist *Union* in 1891 (to become *The Baptist Times and Freeman)* which in 1910 absorbed *The Baptist,* a journal dating from 1872. The current readership approaches 25,000, and extends beyond the UK. The German Baptists began very early to publish periodicals: *Wahrheitszeuge* (Witness to the Truth) began publication in 1879. The present-day Baptist publication in *Germany*, is the monthly *Gemeinde* (Congregation). which serves as a means of information exchange and supports denominational *unity*, and *theological* cohesiveness.

Most European Baptist unions have something similar, their age, size and frequency depending very much on time and circumstance. Content varies but usually includes news of the union and the churches, biblical and devotional contributions, developments taking place in the wider church and in other parts of the world, and in some cases comment on national political issues. Larger denominations, and even smaller ones able to tap sufficient resources, would expect to have one or more magazines, some with specialist features (e.g. Bible teaching, church history, resources for *worship*), some aimed at specialist groups (e.g. *ministers*, *women*, *children*, young people) and some addressing specific issues. Most are a product of the 20th century and in Western Europe have varied little. Thus Baptist periodicals can be found in almost every country in Europe, in Latin Europe, the Nordic countries, as well as Central Europe.

In Eastern Europe, and particularly in the second half of the 20th century, the story is different due to *State* control, smaller unions, limited resources and a different culture, in which printing often had to be done by State printers, distribution was confined to the faithful and in some cases (notably the DDR) only available by post.

In these countries publishing of all kinds (poetry, *politics*, philosophy, etc.) has long been largely *samizdat* [self-published], often hand-written but more usually typed, duplicated, photocopied or printed, and since for most of the latter half of the 20th century photocopiers and printing were closely guarded and monitored, many such publications had to be done in secret and with great danger. A good example of *samizdat* is the *Chronicle of the Catholic Church* in *Ukraine* which reported on Christian education programmes for young people in Transcarpathia, the number of *priests* being ordained [see *Ordination*] and the activities of *missionaries* in Eastern Ukraine and *Belarus*. Another is the *Chronicle of the Lithuanian Catholic Church,* dating from 1972, and the best-known piece of *samizdat* from **Lithuania**. Despite the obstacles, however, most countries managed to produce a number of open periodicals and magazines but their production was often sparse and spasmodic.

Czechoslovakia had a monthly periodical (*Messenger of Peace*), from the beginning of the 20th century. Suspended during the war years it was re-started in 1920 with a new title (*Chelcicky*) together with an annual *Kalendar Chelcicky*. In 1914 the Baptist Union started a monthly magazine, *Rozsievac* [*Sower*], containing Baptist news and information from the wider religious world, education articles and resources for **Sunday Schools**. Banned in the 1950s it was revived in the late 60s though subject to censorship and is still the main diet for Czechs and Slovaks. Though very active in the production of Christian literature between the two world wars, life became more difficult under **Communist** rule but even so most **Protestant** churches, including the Baptists, had the benefit of a regular news publication though printing restrictions often meant that demand exceeded supply.

The DDR recognised three major publishing houses, a **Roman Catholic**, a Protestant and one belonging to the Christian Democratic Union. Churches were fairly free to produce duplicated or photocopied material and at one point there were over 30 church magazines, the best known being *Die Kirche* (Protestant), *St Hedwigsblatt* (RC), and ENA

(*Evangelischer Nachtrichtendienst*), a Protestant weekly news service, with 600 duplicated copies.

At the other extreme, under Communist rule in **Bulgaria** no new publications were allowed. Bibles were unobtainable and such publications as did exist, such as the **Congregationalist** Magazine, *Zornitsa* [*Morning Star*], were discontinued. At the same time the **Methodists** maintained a modest Calendar, other churches managed a few innocuous publications and much literature was distributed in secret. After 1989 **Evangelical** Christian Churches came together and, since over the years 1,000s of Bibles and much Christian literature had been seized, argued that they be allowed to import literature and be given permission to print a new edition of *Zornitsa*.

Since Communist rule required all **faiths** and religions to be treated equally opportunities for journals and other literature were marginally greater in countries where one church was dominant and therefore able to push out the frontiers. Sometimes this provided a spin-off for minority churches.

In **Yugoslavia,** one of the first countries to achieve normalised relations with the socialist authorities in the post-war period and dominated by **Islam**, the **Orthodox** and the Roman Catholics, churches were less affected by restrictions than elsewhere and Protestant minority churches found themselves at something of an advantage. Restrictions on magazines were few. Almost all religious communities had at least one, the Baptists having a fortnightly *Glas Evandjelja* and the monthly *Glasnik*, each with a circulation of about 3,000.

In **Romania**, the Orthodox Church had a substantial publishing programme with full permission to publish Bibles (in conjunction with the United Bible Societies), a remarkable range of books, various theological journals and nine periodicals plus *Romanian Orthodox Church News* (in English and intended for a foreign readership). Baptists, in common with most other religious bodies, had a regular journal or magazine and enjoyed good relationships at the highest level with the Orthodox Publishing House, nurtured and cherished by Ioan Bunaciu, Rector of the Baptist Seminary in **Bucharest**. On occasions this meant that the Orthodox

Church was printing material for Baptists because the State had given permission, authorised the Baptists to import paper from the West (usually from the **European Baptist Federation** or **EUROLIT**) and required the Orthodox Church to oblige.

Poland, where the Roman Catholic Church held sway, had several Catholic publishing houses and 31 recognised periodicals including two from Catholic dissident groups: *Spotkania* [*Encounters*] and *Krzyz Nowohucki* [*The Cross of Nowa Huta*]. Many unofficial publications sprang up after 1977 and Polish Baptists and most other denominations were able to maintain a regular periodical and publish a few books a year. Censorship of magazines was always tight and the number of church publications overall fell from 151 in 1948 to 27 in 1998.

In *Hungary*, where the dominant **Reformed Church** also had a large publishing house, Baptists in common with other churches managed to retain their weekly newspaper, *Békehírnök* [*Herald of Peace*], plus a modest output of other literature based on self-censorship and State fixed limits on print runs.

In Tsarist *Russia*, at the beginning of the 20th century, several Evangelical Christian and Baptist periodicals were published: *Vera* [*Faith*], *Gost'* [*Guest*], *Baptist*, and others. Religious printing in the **Soviet Union**, always on State presses, was mainly Bibles, *hymn* books, calendars and journals, aimed primarily at particular communities (mostly the Baptists and the Orthodox) with very little in any language but Russian. In 1945, the government gave permission to publish *Bratskii Vestnik* [*Brotherly Herald*], though under restrictive conditions. Some concessions, under relaxed rules between 1975 and 85, permitted an increase in the print run from 3,000-5,000, to 8,000 and (with the arrival of *perestroika*) to 10,000, as well as a modest literature plan allowing Baptists to publish some Bibles and a licence to import others. As the political scene changed so too did the productions especially after 1992.

1990 saw the appearance in Ukraine, of *Slova Verbi* [*Word of Faith*], a simple black and white newspaper with a circulation figure of 10,000, offering serious home reading for Christians, including *sermons*, church history and biography. The same year the

All-Union Council of Evangelical Christians-Baptists launched two magazines, *Christian Word* and *Brotherly Love*, prepared on computer and printed by State printers, with a circulation of 25,000. Early in 1991, *Christian Times*, a monthly paper, eight pages of A3 and the only Christian newspaper in colour, with a circulation of 50,000 copies a month and an estimated readership of 200,000, planned as a weekly in the early days of *perestroika*, became a monthly for economic reasons. *Christianity and Time*, a glossy colourful magazine consisting of basic Christian teaching and articles with several pages for children was published six times a year with a circulation of 20,000.

In general terms, after political and *religious freedom* dawned in Eastern Europe, new Baptist journals and periodicals were initiated. Whilst some have not survived the test of time, others continue to be important vehicles for communicating the Baptist message, for *evangelism* and in support of mission. E.g. since 1989 the Russian Evangelical Christian-Baptist publication, *Protestant*, has been published with considerable effectivenss.

With the advance of technology, Baptist journalism is increasingly using new possibilities opened up by the availability of internet communications.

AG & TP

FURTHER READING: Sabrina Petra Ramet (ed), *Protestantism and Politics in Eastern Europe and Russia, The Communist and Post-Communist Eras,* Christianity Under Stress, Vol III, Duke University Press, Durham and London, 1992. Philip Walters (ed), *World Christianity: Eastern Europe,* MARC, Eastbourne, 1988.

Magisterial Reformation
See *Reformation*.

Malta, Baptist history in
The population of the island of Malta in the Mediterranean is mostly **Roman Catholic.** Baptist work in this small country commenced only recently, as in 1985 Joe and Jenny Mifsud, *missionaries* of the Baptist **Bible** Fellowship International, initiated a small Baptist group which today focuses on

the Bible Baptist Church of Sliema. With the initiative of another missionary couple, Ray and Wanda Hoover, and a local believer, Edwin Caruana, an Independent (later *Evangelical*) Baptist Church of Malta was organised. The third *church plant* was established in Zejtun, in 1991. The Evangelical Baptist Church of Malta, with approximately 80 *members*, is an affiliated church of *EBF*.

TP

Mammon
[See also *Property*; *Wealth*]
This Aramaic word for Wealth or Property or Money comes from NT usage (Mt 6:24 and Lk 16:13) to mean all those things when conceived of as objects of *worship* or an exclusive goal in life. In the gospels *Jesus* quite bluntly says that the believer cannot serve God and Mammon because if Mammon takes that degree of importance in a person's life it will be at the expense of serving God. The NT is not simply ascetic in its teaching on material wealth for clearly the good things of *creation* were made to be enjoyed; rather, the emphasis of *scripture* is upon wealth as a gift held in *stewardship* for God's work and especially meeting the needs of the *poor*. Whilst Jesus certainly had followers like Joseph of Arimathea who were people of substance, he is well aware that the relentless search for wealth, or the over consumption of the benefits wealth secures, can corrupt, so Jesus flags it up as an area for concern. Its pursuit can shackle an individual into absolute servitude, as is seen in the case of the would-be follower of Jesus who has a good record of keeping the law, but when challenged with selling his possessions and giving to the poor, declines to follow Jesus (Mk 10:17-22) Putting one's trust in one's bank balance is not only economically problematic but spiritually debilitating, diverting trust and dependence from where it should properly be located, namely in God's fatherly care alone. Paul has the emphasis right, '*The love of* money is the root of all evil' (1Ti 6:10). The teaching of the NT sometimes seems a million miles away from the emphases of *prosperity theology*.

JHYB

Man/Mankind
See *Humankind*.

Manchester Baptist College
See *Northern Baptist College, Manchester*.

Manse
Manse is the traditional word used in Britain to describe a *minister*'s residence, in *Scotland* for the clergy of the Church of Scotland [see *Reformed Churches, Baptists and*], elsewhere for the residence of *nonconformist* ministers. Traditionally this has been owned by the *local church*, which obviously causes a problem for ministers and their dependents when they retire especially if this has to happen prematurely. Accordingly ministers increasingly own, or part-own, their own homes. The word is also used adjectivally to describe the ministers' *children*, sometimes colloquially called 'manse kids', or with greater dignity the children of the manse, as if that placed them in some special position within the life of the community.

JHYB

Marriage/Matrimony
[See also *Singleness*]
Generally, Baptist Christians are entirely *orthodox* in their understanding of marriage as being a Christian *vocation* which is entered into between one man and one woman, for life for mutual benefit, comfort and the procreation of *children*. Most Baptist communities in Europe have services for the Christian marriage of believers, sometimes which include the official civic or *state* recognition of the marriage or, in some countries, as a proper event for believers, entered into alongside the requirements of the state for the registering of marriages.

In the OT there is a developmental notion of marriage and by the time of *Christ* a general assumption of monogamy. For the *Jew* marriage was considered a duty for *men*, in order to perpetuate the family name. The NT largely followed this understanding and it seems that Jesus Christ regarded *divorce and remarriage* as a failure and essentially to be deplored. The *Apostle* Paul used the imagery of the mystical union between Christ and His **Church** as applying to marriage and generally this has led to a very high view of marriage and the important place and dignity of **women** within marriage by Christian communities.

The promotion of stable families centred around marriage would be a common theme for most Baptist communities, with young people being brought up to understand this was appropriate and that within Christian marriage was the place for the full expression of active sexual life and the procreation of the next generation.

Throughout Europe Baptists have had to face a series of challenges and anxieties beyond this norm which has been the standard to Baptist communities for 400 years. The first has been the growth of freedom in sexual relations and the challenge to young people of cultural realities around them in society which have accepted sexual intercourse outside of marriage. Though resisted in most Baptist communities and with special campaigns to encourage chastity before marriage, there is general recognition that this situation is not widely accepted by a growing generation, even if they disguise the fact from their own church communities. The second challenge is that of the break up of marriages, even where there are children, and the reality of the churches having to come to terms with single parent families within their midst or those in the congregation with second partners. Many churches have sought to exercise **discipline** in this area, but this has not made churches throughout Europe immune to the growth of patterns of divorce in society in general. Then, more recently, the advocacy of same sex relations [see **Homosexuality**] within the wider community has provoked severe debate and discomfort within our churches. The development of civil same-sex partnerships in several countries within Europe has presented a challenge to the churches and some more **conservative** Baptist communities have perceived latent support for same-sex relationships within certain European Baptist contexts. However, much of the criticism has been ill-informed and inaccurate.

The response of many churches to the development of new norms within wider society and the fear they might invade the church, has been to engage in programmes of marriage enrichment, to seek to recover a sense of the wider communal family and to emphasise within **worship** and **discipleship** the importance of marriage, believing that pressures within the nuclear family often contribute to the feeling that the **ordinance** of marriage is under threat. This, in turn, has had a negative effect on how single people within the life of the church experience their place and their worth as **members** of a Christian community.

KGJ

Martin Luther
See **Luther, Martin (1483-1546)**.

Martyrdom
[See also **Martyrology**]
Having an experience of being persecuted at different stages in their history, European Baptists have interpreted martyrdom as a test of ultimate faithfulness to God and as an extreme form of **witness** of their **faith** in **Jesus Christ**. In this conviction they have shared the general understanding of martyrdom with the wider **Church**, however, avoiding any tendency to elevate martyrs to the special status of **saints**. Baptists have seen their martyr-models both in the early centuries of Christianity when martyrdom was a reality during periods of Roman persecution, as well as in **Anabaptist** history. An Anabaptist leader and **theologian, Balthasar Hubmaier**, who was burned at the stake in Vienna in 1528, has often been referred to as a model of witness to the faith for Baptists. The early Anabaptists in fact suffered so much loss of life that they reflected deeply on the **call** to **discipleship** as a call to suffer with Christ in a **baptism** in blood. In the late 19th as well as in the 20th century, **Russia** and later the **Soviet Union** was the country of a number of Baptist martyrs. Probably the first Baptist martyrs in Tsarist Russia were Yakim Belyi and Iosif Tyshkevich who suffered **death** in 1874 in a prison in Kiev. During Stalin's purges in the 1930s up to 25,000 Baptists and other **evangelicals** were tortured and/or killed, many of them in Stalinist prison camps. Among them were the presi-

dent of the Baptist *Union* Nikolai Odintsov, the Union's secretary Pavel Ivanov-Klyshnikov and treasurer Pavel Datsko. Georgy Vins, during the Soviet years, was a widely known persecuted Baptist, but not a martyr. Martyrdom, or at least severe persecution, was idealised by 'underground Baptists' in the Soviet Union, while registered groups tried to avoid the topic. The Romanian evangelical *minister*, Richard Wurmbrand, himself tortured in *Communist* prisons, has, in some European countries, influenced Baptist thinking about martyrdom and persecution. Wurmbrand, who was not a Baptist himself, was known as 'a voice of the underground church' in former socialist block countries. His interdenominational organisation *The Voice of the Martyrs* reached – through illegal literature and personal contacts – the underground Baptist groups in the Soviet Union. However no balanced *theology* of martyrdom has developed among Eastern European Baptists. Indeed they have not even composed a detailed history of Baptist or Evangelical martyrs in Russia. In the 20th and 21st century, Western Baptists have also paid comparatively little attention to theology of martyrdom, though many of them have been aware of persecutions that their fellow believers have suffered in other regions, and they have tried to help, not least by collecting and publicising the stories and data of persecutions. A major agency in this respect has been the Keston Institute. Although its archive and book collection has now been deposited at the Baptist-associated Baylor University in Texas, the trustees in *England* have limited funds to help Eastern European students access the collection.

TP & JD

Martyrology
[See also *Martyrdom*]
The word martyr initially meant a *witness*, but in the life of the *church* it came to mean somebody whose witness was born even to the point of *death* for what they believed. The Church has from the death of Stephen in Ac 7, the first Christian martyr, throughout its history been strengthened by the testimony of its martyrs – e.g. in the witness of the early church under an oppressive Em-

pire, focussed in Tertullian's famous observation that the 'blood of the Christians is seed'. Baptists will call to mind the high cost paid by many *Anabaptists* in the 16th century in their courageous testimony to the truth as they saw it. Nor was the modern *missionary* movement established without the willing sacrifice of many lives. Modern history has its own record of Christian martyrs to *political* movements of both the extreme left and the extreme right, especially in Central and Eastern Europe. Whilst Baptists do not have any official list of martyrs or accord them any special spiritual rewards, (though the *BWA* did attempt to produce a roll of modern martyrs at the end of the 20th century) they do respect the lives of those who gave their all in the cause of *Christ*. Martyrdom in the modern world, too easily anonymous in form, is a very model of gospel living as it so clearly represents nonviolent resistance to social and political evil. A church which fails to celebrate the memory of the martyrs sacrifices a crucial part of its own integrity, for there can be treachery in forgetfulness.

JHYB

Marxism
See *Communism/Marxism/Socialism*.

Mary, mother of Jesus
[See also *Immaculate Conception*]
The NT reports only those glimpses of Mary's life which are of relevance to Jesus. This fact determines decisively how *Protestants* think of her. Mary's first appearance in the *Bible* is found in *Jesus'* infancy narratives (Mt 1-2; Lk 1-2). In her home town, Nazareth in Galilee, an angel, named Gabriel, declares to her the forthcoming birth of Jesus. While pregnant, Mary visits Elizabeth, her relative who is expecting John the Baptist at the same time. During this visit, Mary sings a song of *praise* known as the *Magnificat*. Eventually, she gives birth to Jesus in Bethlehem in Judea, since her fiancé, Joseph has had to report to his home town with his family for a census. Mary is present in the stories of Jesus' childhood: the flight to and the return from Egypt; his circumci-

sion at the Temple in Jerusalem; the 12 year-old Jesus lost and found during the *Passover* feast. As for the few later occurrences, John notes (Jn 2) her presence at Jesus' first miraculous sign in Cana, Galilee. The Synoptic Gospels report an event when the presumably widowed Mary with Jesus' brothers and sisters attempted to direct his *ministry* (cf. Mk 2:31ff). At the *cross* Mary and the beloved disciple are entrusted to each other (Jn 19). Finally, we find her praying with the disciples after Jesus' ascension (Ac 1).

Whilst Baptists are happy to speak of Mary as the mother of Jesus they would not use the language of 'Mother of God', and would reject ideas of either Mary's Immaculate Conception, Dormition or Bodily Assumption. Whilst they see no Biblical warrant for attributing to her any special intercessory ministry, they do recognise in her devoted service to her Son worthy of being copied.

EV & ET

Mass Evangelism
See *Crusade Evangelism*.

Massy Pastoral School
See *École Pastorale, Massy, France*.

Matrimony
See *Marriage/Matrimony*.

Maundy Thursday
See *Great Thursday*.

Meeting
See *Church Meeting*.

Meeting Houses
See *Chapels*.

Meissen, Porvoo and Fetter Lane Agreements: significance for Baptists
The Meissen, Porvoo and Fetter Lane agree-

ments (and the earlier, but not so significant Reuilly Common Statement between the *Church of England* and the *Reformed Church* in *France*) represent attempts by the Church of *England*, the Church of *Ireland*, the Episcopal Church in *Scotland* and the Church in *Wales* (all Anglican) to engage in *dialogue* and move towards agreement on matters of doctrine, *liturgy*, *eucharist* and *ministry* with the Reformed, *Lutheran* and *Moravian* churches in Europe. Outside these international agreements Baptists have worked closely with the Moravians: e.g. a Baptist *minister* served a circuit of churches in Wales of both Baptist and Moravian commitment.

The concern has been principally focused on national, or *state churches*, but inevitably, relationships amongst 'families' of churches in Europe has continually widened the boundaries. For instance the Porvoo Common Statement has been signed by British and Irish Anglican Churches and the Nordic and *Baltic* Lutheran Churches, though excluding the Lutheran churches in *Denmark* and *Latvia*, the Meissen Agreement only by the Church of England and the Evangelical Lutheran Church in *Germany* (EKD).

These discussions between an episcopal family of churches which declares itself to be firmly in the *catholic* and *evangelical traditions* and various magisterial *reformation* churches opens up the possibility of dialogue between Anglicanism and Baptist communities in Europe, not least because of the developed understanding of how *apostolic* succession is carried within the churches as well as through an episcopal succession.

The European Baptist family, by engaging in conversations with the Community of *Protestant* Churches in Europe (CPCE) has opened up the possibility of engagement, at least indirectly, with Anglicanism in the European context. In a more localised setting the Baptist *Union* of Great Britain has had over 12 years of informal conversations with the Church of England resulting in the report *Pushing at the boundaries of unity*. Additionally, the *Baptist World Alliance* has had five years of dialogue with the Anglican *Communion Conversations Around the World 2000-2005*.

The significance of these conversations

lies in the development of historical and contemporary understanding of the other traditions involved, to a recognition of much that we hold in common, especially out of the reformation era and the possibility of committed and realistic cooperation in *mission* and ministry as we seek to present the Christian *faith* in a *post-modern* Europe.

· KGJ

Membership
See *Church Membership*.

Men's Work
Notwithstanding the Baptist emphasis on the *Priesthood of All Believers* the denomination's history has too often been clericalised. From time to time special endeavours have been made to attract laymen [see *Laity*] into the life of the *church* – *women* often predominating in *church membership* lists in recent years. In the 19th century special efforts were made to attract working men to what were called 'Pleasant Sunday Afternoon' (PSA) services, held in churches where all seats were free. These were advertised as being 'Brief, Bright and Brotherly', which incorporated elements like special solos and short addresses from celebrities. Later under the influence of F.B. Meyer and others these were remoulded into the Brotherhood Movement with international *associations*. Denominationally, British Baptists established the Baptist Laymen's Missionary Movement in 1817 in support of the missionary society which took on a wider role in 1944 when it changed its name to the Baptist Men's Movement, promoting two periodicals: *The Layman* and *World Outlook*. The objectives were to 'give united and effective *witness* in every department of life, to 'win men outside the churches for he service of *Christ* and His *Kingdom*, and to 'support Baptist endeavours'. Locally the movement sought to set up 'contact clubs' where in a friendly social context friendships could be developed with non-churched men and nationally inspiration was derived from the Annual Conference normally held at the Swanwick Conference Centre in Derbyshire. For a number of years the movement sent a delegation to the European Conference of Churchmen where they met with delegates mainly from the *Lutheran* and *Anglican traditions*. In more recent years the Movement has been particularly active in supporting *Operation Agri* providing practical assistance by ways of seeds, livestock tools, etc. for agricultural *missionaries* in developing countries and 'Tools for mission' renovating machinery for missionary use. In the 21st century, church networks based on gender distinction have found their work increasingly difficult, with, rather surprisingly, men's organisations outliving the once stronger work focused on women.

JHYB

Mennonite Brethren
[See also *Mennonites*; *Mennonites, Baptists and*]
The Mennonite Brethren Church came into being in South *Russia* in 1860 as a product of a *Pietistic revival* among Mennonites who had emigrated to Russia after 1789. In 1845 a *Lutheran pastor*, Eduard Wüst, who had been influenced by the *Moravian movement*, was the instrument in bringing this revival to the Mennonite community. On 6 Jan1860, some 18 brethren established a new Church with an accent on personal *salvation* and upright conduct in the Molotschna Mennonite colony in South Russia. The formal organisation of the Church was completed by 30 May1860 when ministers were chosen. On 23 Sep1860, the first *baptism* there took place, which, due to Baptist influence, was by immersion. In Mar 1862, a second Mennonite Brethren Church in the colony of Chortitza was set up.

The first Brethren were jealous *missionaries* and even had the courage to baptise several ethnic Russians from 1863-65, but due to harsh punishment, the brethren ceased these activities. Baptism by *faith* as practised by the Mennonite Brethren became an example for other pietistic groups, and in this way, the first German Baptist Church in Alt-Danzig in South Russia came into being in 1864. The first baptisms here were conducted by Jakob Kowalsky from the Mennonite Brethren Church. In 1869, Abram Unger, an *elder* from the Mennonite Brethren Church, baptised Efim Tsÿmbal in Alt-

Danzig who became the first Ukrainian to baptise others, laying the foundation for an independent Russian and Ukrainian Baptist movement.

After 1869, the relations between the Mennonite Brethren Church and other revival groups weakened, but several members of the Mennonite Brethren Church continued their work with the Russian and Ukrainian Baptists on a personal basis. Johann Wieler was instrumental in establishing the structure of the new Churches making them very Mennonite-like and co-authored their first Confession of Faith in 1870. In 1884, he became the founding president of the Russian Baptist *Union* and laid the basis for its own mission work. In 1887, Peter M. Friesen became actively involved in the work between Russians and Ukrainians. After 1905, and especially after 1917, their work was continued by several Mennonite Brethren *evangelists*. Among them was the founder of the first tent mission [see *Crusade Evangelism*] in Russia, Jakob Dyck, who was murdered by bandits in 1919.

From 1929-38, the Mennonite Brethren Church in *USSR* was dissolved by the *communist* regime. After 1955, some of the remaining *members* of the Mennonite Brethren Church joined Baptist churches, whilst others managed to organise churches under their own name, but a third group migrated to the West, forming their own separate churches there.

JD

FURTHER READING: Peter M. Friesen, *Die Alt - Evangelische Mennonitische Brüderschaft in Rußland (1789-1910) im Rahmen der mennonitischen Gesamtgeschichte*, Raduga, Halbstadt, 1911, reprint: Verein zur Erforschung und Pflege des Kulturerbes des rußlanddeutschen Mennonitentums, Göttingen, 1991.

Mennonites

[See also *Mennonite Brethren*; *Mennonites, Baptists and*]
The Mennonites, the largest group in the modern *church* stemming directly from the *Anabaptists* of the Radical *Reformation*, derive their name from the Dutch reformer, Menno Simons, a *Roman Catholic priest* who renounced his orders in 1536. He played a key role in gathering together the persecuted Anabaptists following on from the fall of the Anabaptist city of Munster after its long siege in 1534. The name originated from outsiders who called his followers 'Mennonites'. Stressing believers' *baptism*, they developed a *congregational* form of *church polity*, rejected Christian participation in the magistracy and declined to take up arms. With the *Quakers* and the *Church of the Brethren* they constitute one of a group of *Peace Churches* These German-speaking Anabaptists, described by one historian as 'eternal Abrahams', were throughout their history frequently on the move trying to escape persecution, leaving their homes as *state* authorities drove them further and further east. Thus many of them moved from *Holland*, to Prussia, then to *Ukraine* and, then further east within the Russian Empire. *Political* turmoil in the late 19th and throughout the 20th century drove many of them to a new life in the Americas, North and South, whilst others returned from Siberia to *Germany* after the end of the *Cold War*. Mennonites, who emphasise the *autonomy of the local church*, relate to other churches by way of conferences or *associations* and feel uneasy about *unions* with centralised hierarchical structures. However since 1925 the Mennonite World Conference has provided a mechanism for international *fellowship* and mutual encouragement. The Anabaptist *believers' church* concept has been maintained in the different contemporary Mennonite groups as well as a strong emphasis on community building, the *priesthood of all believers* and simplicity of church structures. They refer to themselves as children of the Radical Reformation or the movement of the Third Way, clearly separating *church and state*, but at the same time accepting a prophetic voice [see *Prophecy*] in society when calling for *peace* and justice, getting involved in *reconciliation*, relief work, and other *mission* activities. Having their roots in the European Reformation, Mennonites have changed ethnically from a predominantly white Caucasian group to a majority of non-white members who live on all continents. Nevertheless, they remain one of the smaller denominations counting worldwide about a million *members*. Notwithstanding their small numbers, their contributions on issues of

church and state, mission, *ethics* and peace witness are recognisable on the international arena, with authors such as John Howard Yoder, Alan and Eleanor Kreider, and Ron Sider being very influential among Baptists.

PFP

Mennonites, Baptists and

[See also *Bilateral Conversations*; *Mennonite Brethren*; *Mennonites*]
Baptists and Mennonites originate from the same roots in the *witness* of the early *Anabaptists*. While in many parts of the contemporary world Mennonites and Baptist seem not to engage in many overlapping activities, they have in common. With the *Pentecostals* and other *Evangelical* Groups both denominations belong to the *Believers Church tradition* that emphasises the biblical model [see *Bible*] of the *priesthood of all believers*. This results in a simple *worship* style where *Baptism* and *Eucharist* belong within the community of believers with only believers participating in them, a conviction that dates back to the Schleitheim Confession (1527). Another key area of common ground is the emphasis on the *holistic mission* of the whole *church*. While Mennonites belong to the historic *peace churches*, exercising a critical view of governments and toward Christian involvement in *politics*, the majority of Baptists strongly identify with their *nation*, with involvement in politics, accepting the '*just war*' view of war and *peace*. More similarity and mutuality, in fact, almost identical views, can be found between Mennonites and Baptists on the territory of the former *Soviet Union*, where these groups look back to a common history and for some time even belonged to the same *union*. At an earlier period Dutch Mennonites funded some Baptist work in *England*, and their support was sought for the early *Baptist Missionary Society* and their churches are listed by John Rippon as Baptist Churches in his *Baptist Annual Register* whom he hoped would soon send representatives to a meeting of all baptised believers in London. Baptists and Mennonites belong to the same church tradition and have happily cooperated together in several projects.

PFP

FURTHER READING: Baptist-Mennonite Theological Conversation final Report: 1989-1992.

Messiah

See *Christology*; *Incarnation*; *Jesus Christ*; *Logos*; *Lord of the Church and the Crown Rights of the Redeemer*.

Methodism, Baptists and

[See also *Bilateral Conversations*; *Leuenberg Confession Conversations on Baptism*]
John Wesley (1703-91) grew up in the high church *tradition*, was converted [see *Conversion*] as a *student* at Oxford to religious seriousness in 1725. 10 years later, with his brother, Charles, the *hymn-writer*, he went as a *missionary* to America where he encountered the *Moravians* and became aware that he did not share the assurance of *salvation* that they possessed. It was during the reading of the Preface to *Luther*'s commentary on Romans at a small meeting in Aldersgate Street in London on 24 May 1738 that Wesley had a second conversion experience often described in Wesley's own language that he felt his 'heart strangely warmed'. That was the beginning of the *Evangelical revival* in *England* also promoted by George Whitfield who had an experience similar to Wesley's. Whereas Wesley's work was underpinned by an Evangelical *Arminian theology*, Whitfield remained a committed *Calvinist*. Neither leader intended to found new denominations but the success of their *preaching*, and the antagonism of the leadership of the *Church of England*, led Wesley's followers to withdraw from the Church and to establish their own separate denomination. Methodism was born and on Wesley's own confession 'born in song' for one of the new denomination's richest contributions to the whole church, Baptists included were Charles Wesley's hymns.

The influence of the Wesleys and of Whitfield spread even further because their activities led to new life coming to both Independents and Baptists. E.g. the number of those who became Baptist *pastors* and leaders in the denomination who had been converted by Whitfield was considerable, whilst the General Baptists in England regained evangelical *orthodoxy* through the founding of the New Connexion in 1770 largely under Methodist influence.

At the beginning of the 19th century, Baptists and Methodists stood together as leading promoters of the Evangelical Revival. Together with other Evangelicals they joined together in a number of crucial enterprises such as the *Bible Society* and the Religious Tract Society. The inheritance of this common Evangelical history is what makes Methodists and Baptists natural allies in the task of mission. In many parts of Europe they share the experience of being Evangelical minority churches in countries where the dominant or established church is *Orthodox*, *Roman Catholic* or *Lutheran*. They have also joined with one another in giving leadership within the *Free Church* movement.

JHYB

FURTHER READING: W. Morgan Patterson, 'The Evangelical Revival and the Baptists' in W.H. Brackney, P.S. Fiddes and J.H.Y. Briggs (eds), *Pilgrim Pathways: Essays in Baptist History in Honour of B.R. White*, Mercer, Macon, Ga., 1999. Patrick Philipp Streiff, *Methodism in Europe: 19th and 20th century*, Baltic Methodist Theological Seminary, Tallinn, 2003.

Migration

[See also *Diaspora churches in Europe*; *Emigration Societies*]

The history of *humankind* is a history of unrest and flight (Ge 4:11). Even the people of God share this destiny (Ex 1; 1Pe 1:1). Again and again God reminds his people of this as he asks them to respect the strangers around them (Ex 23:9), to love them (Lev 19:33s), but to keep their own *faith* identity firmly not adopting the strangers' worldview (Ezr 9s). *Jesus Christ* finally put down all religious and cultural walls between *men* and *women* (Eph 4:14s). As all people are created by God in the image of God and, as Jesus died for all people in all cultures, Christians, whatever their culture, must respect people of other cultures. The vision of the *Kingdom of God* is the New Jerusalem where people of all races and nations move on as pilgrims (Mic 4) to live together in *peace* and *love* (Rev 21).

The 20th century has been a century of migration, from the influx of *Jews* at the beginning of the century into Western Europe fleeing the pogroms in *Russia* and the East. After WWII many countries in Western Europe experienced the arrival not only of displaced persons from the East but the immigration of people from former colonies in Africa, Asia and Latin America. But there has also been a migration movement within Europe. E.g. in the 1960s many Italian, Spanish and Turkish *Gastarbeiter* [guest workers] settled in *Germany* to help in its growing economy. In the last decades of the 20th century, since the fall of the Berlin Wall, the number of immigrants has drastically increased. Millions of *Aussiedler* Germans who had lived in the former *Soviet Union* for many generations migrated back to Germany, amongst them many Baptists (e.g. in 2005 in Germany 20% of the population is of 'not-german' origin). Such a development to a multicultural society has occurred in many Western European countries. Whilst this may at one time have been motivated by a search for freedom, later migrants have been motivated by a search for better and more secure economic circumstances in Western Europe and America. Only certain countries, e.g. *Poland*, *Czech Republic*, *Hungary*, now belonging to the *EU* with newly growing economies see a mounting number of immigrants in their midst.

Christian immigrants have formed many and sometimes very large ethnic Christian congregations in their new home countries. many of which have a *charismatic*, or *pentecostal* character. Initially independently organised under strong leadership, they have subsequently sought to establish relationships, including sometimes integration, into existing *protestant* churches or *unions*. All Baptist *unions* in Western Europe have developed structures to integrate these ethnic and international congregations. Sometimes this is done by establishing an ethnic group within a *local church*; sometimes an independent ethnic church seeks associate or full membership of a national union. In some Baptist unions the ethnic congregations (e.g. in *France* and *Belgium*, African (Congolese) congregations) might be as numerous as the previously existing churches. In *nations* with a longer history of immigration, the process has advanced so far that immigrants are now in responsible positions in the Baptist unions (e.g. **United Kingdom**, Belgium).

Hesitations about such integration both on the part of indigenous congregations and on the part of new ethnic congregations should not be condemned too quickly as **racism**, for the process requires patience and openness on all sides. There is no supracultural Christian or Church denying all cultural or contextual character. Human existence is a cultural existence (Ge 5; 11), with external and much more internal implications. The first generation of immigrants must establish their ethnic congregations as fortresses preserving their ancestral identity in a strange land, but the second generation often begins to move away from their parent's culture to the culture of their home country. The third generation has to decide whether they will remain culturally isolated or become integrated. In such a situation an ethnic church often becomes an international, multicultural church, also attracting members of the indigenous population. In this process people frequently move from the condemnation to the acceptance of other cultures and to an attitude which integrates their own cultural inheritance into that of their neighbours.

MKi & ET

FURTHER READING: Milton J. Bennett, 'Towards ethnorelativism: a development model of intercultural sensitivity' in R. Michael Paige (ed), *Education for the intercultural experience*, Intercultural, Yarmouth, Me., 1993. Peter Penner (ed), *Ethnic Churches in Europe – a Baptist Response*, Neufeld, Schwarzenfeld, 2006.

Millennialism

[See also *Premillennialism*]

Baptist thinking about the millennium future has shown considerable variety. In the 17th century there was a strong postmillennial strain within Baptist life. This theological **tradition**, which drew from the thinking of the English **Puritans**, held that the gospel would triumph and that **Christ**'s return would follow a golden age (perhaps 1,000 years as in Rev 20; certainly a lengthy period of time) in the history of the **church**. Some Baptists believed that the 'rule of the **saints**' should be inaugurated. This was associated with the 'Fifth Monarchy' movement in **England** which, with the suspension of the monarchy, attracted support from both General and Particular Baptists, its followers believing that immediate **political** actions should be taken to establish such a godly regime. In the 18th century the most influential postmillennial **theologian** was the American, Jonathan Edwards. The views of Edwards inspired **William Carey** and other English-speaking **Protestant missionaries**. Carey and his **Baptist Missionary Society** colleagues, in their *Form of Agreement* at Serampore, India, spoke of the certainty in their minds that the **conversion** to Christ of the people of India would happen in the 'not very distant period'. Samuel Pearce, another English Baptist **minister**, felt 'a passion for missions' when he heard Thomas Coke, an 18th-century **Methodist** missionary statesman, **preaching** on 'Ethiopia shall soon stretch out her hands unto God'. (Ps 68:31). But in the 19th century the premillennial understanding of the Last Things, which taught that Christ would return to overthrow the Antichrist and to inaugurate a reign of 1,000 years, grew in popularity among **evangelicals** and began to affect Baptists. From the time of WWI, F.B. Meyer became a leading premillennial advocate, becoming a founder of the Advent Testimony and Preparation Movement which made a considerable appeal to Baptists. A sub-set of premillennialism is **Dispensationalism**. A third view to be found among Baptists, amillennialism, takes biblical references [see **Bible**] to the millennium as being figurative and as applying to the whole period between Christ's first and second advents. This view became increasingly accepted by Baptists in Europe from the second half of the 20th century. The danger in such speculative **theology** was certain endeavours to impose on God a precise timetable of fulfilment which when not accomplished could lead to considerable disillusion, but many have found the expectation of Christ's return a powerful imperative to **evangelise**.

IMR

FURTHER READING: D.W. Bebbington, 'The Advent Hope in British Evangelicalism since 1800'in *Scottish Journal of Religious Studies*, Vol. 9, No. 2 (1988), pp.103-14. R.G. Clouse (ed), *The Meaning of the Millenium: Four Views*, Inter-Varsity, Downers Grove, Il.,1977. I.H. Murray, *The Puritan*

Hope, Banner of truth Trust, Edinburgh, 1975.

Ministerial Associations

See *Fraternals*.

Ministerial Formation

[See also *Call/Calling; Ministry*]

The office of *pastor* or minister has been common in most Baptist communities from the 1600s onwards. Whilst Baptist *polity* clearly asserts that the local *gathering* community of believers discerns and calls out those it wishes to exercise ministry amongst it, by the 1700s there was an acceptance that there was a need for those in whom *gifts* were discerned to be prepared for the office to which they were called. There was, however, fierce debate as to whether it was exclusively the *Spirit*'s task to prepare *men* for ministry rather than any educational institution, only some perceiving that the Spirit might prepare such ministers through a disciplined programme of theological *education*. The gift of Edward Terrill to Broadmead Baptist Church, Bristol, *England* in 1679 setting aside money for a minister to prepare 'young men for *ordination*' marks the beginning of a move amongst Baptists to ensure there was an appropriate process of preparation by education and formation, for those in whom gifts of ministry were seen and who had been marked out for preparation to be called to local congregations as ministers.

From the 1700s onwards the most appropriate way of engaging in this work of formation was seen to be through the establishment of Colleges and seminaries and this gradually replaced what might be thought of as an older pattern of apprenticeship with a form of in-service training with a senior minister, often living as a member of his extended family.

Today, in almost every Baptist *union* in Europe there is a college or seminary owned, or licensed, by the union to prepare men, and in many instances, *women*, for ministry. A classic curriculum of general arts education, mastering the biblical languages, study of the *Bible*, church history, *theology, ethics,* philosophy, denominational identity, *pastoral* and practical studies might be almost universally seen as appropriate. Sometimes the 'seminary' is devoted exclusively to training for church service; in other places the training deliberately takes place in a 'college' set within the wider context of a secular university.

However, it is recognised that the acquiring of academic knowledge, including formal qualifications, and even experience in practical application may not be sufficient for the task. Formation accepts the need for all of these things, but asserts more is necessary. Through the modelling of tutors, through a communal life of *prayer* and *spirituality* those called out to enabling ministry in baptistic communities are understood to be shaped and formed for the task in a holistic way. Thus the work of ministerial formation rises above training which is about skills and education, which is about knowledge, to embrace a deepening *discipleship* and a way of being to enable those called to continue if an appropriate and Christ-like service to the churches. As such, it is a high ideal not always achieved in practice, because it requires more than the two to seven years (the length of preparation varies across Europe – the average is no doubt four years) devoted to preparation in a college or seminary.

KGJ

Ministers

See *Ministry*.

Ministries, Diversity of

[See also *Ministry*]

The relatively high priority that Baptists give to *freedom of conscience* and local *autonomy*, together with the rich variety of historical and *theological* influences impinging upon Baptist *ecclesiology*, has given rise to a considerable diversity of expressions of ministry. There is equal diversity in the understanding of the nature and purpose of ministry. A Biblical [see *Bible*] remit for this diversity is argued from the writings of St. Paul in Ro 12:4-8; 1Co 12:4-11 and especially Eph 4:11-13.

In the early recognition of 'Messengers', with their ministry beyond the local congregation, this diversity was given structural expression, to be later developed in the early 20th century into the General Superintendency in **Britain** and, elsewhere in Europe, the development of Baptist **bishops**. Here, an **evangelistic** or **apostolic** ministry was recognised alongside the presbyteral ministry of the **pastor**-teacher with oversight of a **local church** familiar from the very beginnings. While the typical Baptist minister remains a local **pastoral** leader, responsible for a single congregation, or small group of linked congregations, other varieties of ministry include **evangelists**, youth specialists (both recently recognised as separate categories in the Baptist Union of Great Britain,) theological educators, **health** care, **educational**, military and industrial **chaplains** and those who offer service to national **unions** or local **associations**.

However, diversity of ministry is not confined to those who are ordained [see **Ordination**], and Baptists also welcome and recognise the ministry of every **member** of the church, with mature and gifted lay **women** and **men** [see **Laity**] offering pastoral, **preaching**, **missionary** and administrative gifts to the local church and beyond. While Baptists do not endorse any formal hierarchy – and in that regard all Baptist ministers are 'equal' to every other church member – there is nonetheless a recognition that some are called to specific ministries especially to that of the ministry of **Word** and **Sacrament**.

The tensions that give rise to this diversity arise from differing approaches to ordination and the creative relationship between ordained ministers, lay leaders and every member's ministry. A similar diversity arises from the focus of ministry, whether it be directed primarily at the Christian **church** or at the community in which it is set. Influences as diverse as **charismatic** renewal and **ecumenism** continue to foster diversity of ministry.

                                                              PG

Ministry

[See also **Baptism, Eucharist and Ministry**; **Ministries, Diversity of**]

Baptist gathering communities affirm very strongly that everyone called by God through **Jesus Christ** to repent and to be baptised and be incorporated into a particular assembly, or ecclesia of believers is so called [see **Call/Calling**] and gifted to participate in every activity of the community of **discipleship**. The **priesthood of all believers** is a common assertion which declares that no other **priest**, or specially prepared person, stands in the way of each believer exercising God-given ministries or fulfilling their discipleship.

Nevertheless these assertions have two qualifications. Whilst we come individually to **faith** and trust in Christ, by **baptism** we are incorporated into a community which has responsibilities for enabling the disciples together in such a **gathering** community, to walk in the journey of faith. In such churches gifting is not uniform. Every individual has specific **gifts** which are to be discerned by the community and encouraged and developed for the edification of the whole body [see **Church**] as it seeks to **worship** God and participate in His **mission**.

From the earliest days of Baptists, an examination of the NT has suggested that some might be called out and gifted in proclamation of the **Word**, teaching the Word, presiding at the **Eucharistic** table, **pastoral care** of the community and enabling the disciples to grow and to flourish, often spoken of as 'the ministry of Word and **Sacrament**'.

Baptists have, for the most part, rejected the **traditional** three-fold ministry of some other Christian world communions – **Bishop**, Presbyter, **Deacon**. However some form of two-fold enabling ministry, with, in places, a modified third pattern of the ministry of regional oversight, certainly exists within most parts of the European Baptist family.

In most places an **episcopal** figure has a role in a local gathering community [see **Local Church**] –not with **authority** and power as used within **Orthodox**, **Roman Catholic**, **Anglican** and **Lutheran** traditions, but rather a servant ministry affirmed by the church offered to the minister by the church for the better enabling of the life of discipleship. Such an episcopal person is often called 'minister' or 'pastor'. Both terms are used these days without too fine a distinction. This person will generally exercise a preaching and teaching ministry and preside at the eucharistic table. She, or he, might have other colleagues in a gathering church who assist in every way and we might consider them as having a presbyteral office. The word 'preacher' is used in different ways throughout the Baptist community. Sometimes designating a person called to the office of presbyter, sometimes in a more limited way indicating a person who has a ministry of *preaching* without any other gifting related to ministry or the pastoral office.

Again, most gathering churches involve others in diaconal forms of ministry (see *Diakonia*). The offices of pastor, minister, preacher, deacon varies from Baptist community to community. Historically pastor [literally 'shepherd of the flock'] was the title of the highest esteem, with clergy sometimes serving for a year or so as minister [literally 'one who serves'] before being inducted to the pastoral office. Whilst in some countries the whole process of *ordination* is rejected, in other countries there is a tradition of ordaining people to the office of deacon as well as minister after due preparation and training and following a decision of the *church meeting*. In other places the office of deacon is by periodic election and does not involve ordination, as with the minister. Generally, the particular diaconal ministry only loosely relates to the NT usage and in some countries the board, or assembly of deacons functions much more as an executive of the church meeting and the historic diaconal tasks of serving at the eucharist or *agape* table and taking care of the widows and *orphans* are marginal to the core activity.

KGJ

Minorities

As a handy working definition says, minorities – either marked by ethnic, linguistic or religious characteristics – are groups of people numerically smaller than the rest of the population in a *state*, usually occupying a non-dominant position in society, and having a sense of solidarity between their members. The European Baptist approach to minorities has ideally been guided both by the biblical message [see *Bible*], which exhorts to respect a 'stranger in your land' (Lev 19:33-34), as well as by historical Baptist experience of themselves being a religious minor-

ity, often having been persecuted for their religious convictions in the past. *Thomas Helwys*, the 17th-century Baptist, argued for freedom of religion for 'minorities' [see *Religious Liberty*]: 'For *men*'s religion to God is between God and themselves. The king shall not answer for it. Neither may the king be judge between God and *man*. Let them be heretics [see *Heresy*], Turks, *Jews*, or whatsoever, it appertains not to the earthly power to punish them in the least measure.' However, Baptists recognise that in some occasions minority rights, when pushed toward an extreme, may also cause a frustration of a majority by a minority. This happened during Soviet years in some regions of the *Soviet Union*, such as in the *Baltics*, where the Russian-speaking minority, with the support of the *political* powers, often neglected the local culture and language. In cases like this the Baptist conviction concerning the importance of *human rights* should offer a framework for both minority and majority rights. Political changes and *migration* in a rapidly unifying Europe at the turn of the millennium have added another aspect to this issue of minorities. The number of ethnic churches – both Baptist and other – in Europe has increased. E.g. there are *Roma* churches in *Romania*, Russian and Ukrainian-speaking churches in *Czech Republic* and in *Portugal*, there are English and French-speaking African churches in *Germany*. Also, the expanding *Muslim* minority in Europe poses a challenge for many churches, including Baptists, to be facilitators of mutual understanding and *unity* in a shared civil society. Baptist *sociologist* Paul Weller has argued that responses to a *believer's church witness* to *Jesus* in multicultural Europe are likely to be pluriform. 'This is perhaps especially the case where people need to find ways of responding to Jesus that do not seem to imply an inevitable betrayal of their cultural and religious heritages'.

TP

FURTHER READING: Peter F. Penner (ed), *Ethnic Churches in Europe: A Baptist Response*, Neufeld and IBTS, Prague, 2006.

Minsk Theological Seminary

This is an institution of the Union of Evangelical Christians-Baptists in **Belarus**, offering higher **theological education** at bachelor's and diploma level. Established in Sep 1997, it continues the work of **Bible** courses which had started in Minsk in 1989. To provide well-trained **local church** workers, graduates are expected to have a good knowledge of the Bible and to apply **Christ**-centred **discipleship** in their life and **ministry**. The Seminary focuses on training in practical ministry: **pastoral** and **missionary** work, **church music**, as well as Christian work with **children** and young people [see **Youth Work**].

LM

Missio Dei

[See also **Mission**]

Missio dei, as we understand it today, carries a variety of definitions acquired over the last 50 years. Most **theologians** of mission agree that the term speaks about the triune God [see **Trinity**] in his mission. God is missionary by nature. The term had already been used by Augustine, but found its way into **missiology** only at the **International Missionary Council** conference in Willingen, **Germany** in 1952. Key **scholars** who explored the term are Karl Hartenstein and Karl Barth who introduced the term at this conference. Whereas Georg Vicedom widens the term by setting it within the **theology** of the trinity, the reinterpretation of Johannes Hoekendijk gives it a more social orientation and a more balanced perspective. It has been used in recent times by **missiologists** of different orientations to correct previous faulty understandings of mission which make the **church** rather than the triune God the starting point of mission. The dimension of *missio dei* presents this triune God, who is a missionary God by nature. In his intention [*actio dei*] the Father sends the Son. The **Holy Spirit** is the spirit of mission to be sent by God to enable the sending church to partake in his mission. The church has no mission of her own but is taken into God's mission, a **holistic mission** modelled by **Christ**. But God's mission is wider than the mission in which he has involved his church. Still, the church must be by divine intention and by her very nature a missional church [*missio ecclesiae*], being sent by God to continue, as his partner in this mission, until the fulfilment of time.

PFP

Missiologists, European Baptists in the 20th and 21st centuries

[See also *Missiology*; *Mission*]

Missiology, as a distinctive discipline within **theological** thought, is relatively new. Clearly, we can argue that individual Baptists of earlier generations, such as **William Carey** and **Johann Gerhard Oncken**, as well as Andrew Fuller [see **Fullerism**] who served the churches well by rewriting a traditional **Calvinism** in a way that brought out the **missionary** imperative, have been missiologists of distinction. At the beginning of the 20th century, the Welsh missionary to China, Timothy Richard, caused a stir within the whole missionary movement by giving a wider definition to mission by his activities as the General Secretary of the China Literature Society His plea at the founding congress of the **BWA** in 1905 was for a **holistic** form of mission, pursued **ecumenically** which met the needs of 'the whole man, body and soul' saving him 'from **hell** in this world as well as in the next'. Richard's voice was also heard at the famous **Edinburgh** Conference of 1910. Two Baptist missionaries to India sought to make sense of other **faiths** by their writings: George Howells' *The Soul of India: an Introduction to the study of Hinduism in its...Internal and Historical Relations to Christianity* (1913) argued that the task of the missionary in India was to show how **Jesus** fulfilled the aspirations of Hindu devotion; and Bevan Jones' *The People of the Mosque* (1932) fulfilled a similar task for **Islam**. All three missionaries made pioneering contributions to the Christian understanding of other faiths and thereby to early thinking about **dialogue**, though their labours were not well received by all Baptists.

The development of a specific discipline with an identity remains an activity of the second part of the 20th century and might be associated with such seminal writers as Lesslie Newbigin, **David Bosch** and Andrew F. Wall. Within the European Baptist community key developments in seminaries include the establishment of specialist post-graduate degrees in Missiology in Prague, Manchester and London.

It is difficult to be continent-restricted in this field. In the wider missionary debate distinguished contributions have been made by Latin American Baptists – Orlando Costas (Puerto Rico), René Padilla (Argentina) and Samuel Escobar (Peru) who were major forces in founding the Latin American Theological Fraternity which sought to interpret *Liberation Theology* in language which made sense to *Evangelicals*, again bringing a wider perspective to European ideas about mission, not least by leading the revolt against a monopolistic Western leadership in the *Lausanne* movement for world *evangelisation*. An Asian Baptist whose missiological thinking has had considerable impact is Raymond Fung of Hong Kong who was much involved in the Melbourne CWME conference in 1980 (where he gave a paper on the importance for missionary strategy of identifying with the marginalised as 'the sinned against' before telling them they were 'sinners' [see *Sin*]) and the publication of the *consensus* document *Mission and Evangelism: an Ecumenical Affirmation* (1982) in the writing of which he played a large part. European Baptists such as Brian Stanley, now Andrew Walls' successor in Edinburgh, and David Langeren (*Sweden*) have made significant contributions to mission history and to the need for new mission policies in the context of changed *political* realities, especially in terms of decolonisation [see *Colonialism*], and therefore to aid the processes of change as 'mission to' has given way to 'partnership with'.

Noted European Baptists who have done work at doctoral level in missiology include Peter F. Penner, working firstly in St. Petersburg, then Prague, who also did work with David Bosch at the University of South Africa, Soren Ostergaard , of Copenhagen, whose specialist work has been in alternative *church planting*, Rene Erwich in the *Netherlands*, who has focused on church development and Darrell C. Jackson, whose activities have included an examination of mission methods across Europe under the auspices of the *Conference of European Churches*.

KGJ

Missiology

[See also *Contextual Missiology*; *Mission*]
Missiology is a relatively young area of study among theological disciplines. Prior to its establishment as a separate discipline, studies in mission played a minor role in higher *education*, usually only as part of practical *theology* and mainly at places where universities were required to train *missionaries* for *overseas*.

There were limited attempts before 1900 to develop missiology in theological education. Pioneering work in missiology had already been done in the late 13th century by Raimondus Lullus and other Catholic *scholars*. The *Roman Catholic* Church as well as the *Orthodox Churches* continued to be intensively involved in mission even after the *Reformation* – while *Protestants* at first were not – and had to reflect on mission (or, *propaganda fidei*, as it was called then) theologically. *Colonial* developments and the involvement of Protestant *nations* in mission introduced the issue of mission studies into Protestant and *Pietist* educational institutions. Philip Jacob Spener, August Herman Francke and Nicolaus Ludwig von Zinzendorf represent Moravian and German pietistic mission thinkers and strategists of the 17th and 18th centuries. The Baptist missionary, *William Carey*, sometimes called the father of modern missions, stands for pioneering activities of British mission at the end of the 18th and the beginning of the 19th century.

Friedrich Schleiermacher played a key role for modern missiology when he subdivided theological studies into 4 major areas: biblical, systematic, historical and practical theology. Mission studies became part of practical theology, thus defining missiology as a practical discipline, where it continues to feature in various academic curricula, a response to the needs of missionaries in the colonies. *Bible* schools, colleges and seminaries in various ways picked up the training of missionaries starting with less academic aspects with a healthy focus on mission *praxis*. During the second half of the 20th century the first specialised missiology programmes appeared primarily in the Anglo-American seminary system and developed from bachelor onto Master and doctoral levels. At the centre of such programmes were also, alongside theology, areas such as *soci-*

ology, communication, **anthropology**, and contextual studies. Later they also orientated themselves toward **church planting** and **church growth**, witness amongst ethnic **minorities**, and many other areas of studies. Today most programmes in missiology are well established, even though there is a regrettable tendency to over specialise in mission, **evangelism** and church growth, which all too often become detached from other theological studies. Since the late 1980s, missiology has lost some of its popularity and needs reshaping in a way that complies with W. Dyrness' statement that 'mission lies at the core of theology'. Some more recent research studies call **missiologists** to curb the trend of excessive specialisation, rather including mission studies as an indispensable ingredient of all theological reflection. Current missiological research is exploring new areas, whilst also evaluating the past and present mission activities of the **church**, of mission agencies and of individual missionaries. During the last decades much academic and pragmatic work has been published, offering both missiologists and practitioners regional and international help to focus understanding both globally and locally. Thereby, they are providing the essential tools for education whilst developing studies that help to enhance mission work done by both indigenous and expatriate churches and parachurch agencies.

PFP

Mission

[See also **Commissioning of Missionaries**; **Missions (church related and evangelistic events)**]

Mission is the subject area of **missiology** studies. The term originates from Latin and picks up on the Greek verb *apostello* [to be sent – *missio*]. Only during the late second millennium did it come to refer to the mission of the **church**; before that it described the activity of the missionary God. Before the use of 'mission' the Latin term *propaganda fide* was used to describe the outreach of the church or its missionaries. The 20th century witnessed a debate as to what activity the term 'mission' could properly describe. In this search for meaning two streams disagreed for much of the 20th cen-

tury: while the **International Missionary Council** which became part of the **World Council of Churches** in 1961, speaking for both the historic and young churches, was in danger of giving mission an over-wide definition which legitimised those who so wanted to concentrate on the social engagement of the churches, the **Lausanne movement** strongly underlined **evangelistic** activities and the specific proclamation of the gospel. Baptist churches, **missiologists** and missionaries have found themselves on both sides understanding mission as including both aspects.

After a century of discussion Christians are still called to continue God's mission [see **Missio Dei**] that embraces *martyria* [witness], *diakonia* [social service], *kerygma* [proclaiming the whole gospel], *koinonia* [the **unity** of the faithful community of God] and *leiturgia* [celebration and **worship**]. Baptists strongly underline the need for **discipleship**, referring to Mt 28:16-20 [see **Great Commission**], and that mission is the responsibility of the whole church and of each **church member** [see **Missionary Congregations**] (**Oncken**: 'Every believer a missionary'). Mission is, then, the church's continuation of **Christ**'s mission, namely that of being sent [*apostello*] by God into this world to be salt and light and in this way to do the will of God, proclaiming and living out his reign and his **kingdom** until Christ comes.

When the term mission is used today, it refers to the one mission and the whole mission mandate that the church derives from the **scriptures**. To differentiate this understanding from the practical realisation of the church's mission, mission is often distinguished from missions. This differentiation caused some debate in the 1970s between groups representing IMC and Lausanne. The **conservative evangelicals** argued, in view of mission and *missio dei*, that by dropping the 's' the practical commitment and active mission work of the church and individuals was in danger of becoming lost. Baptists were again found on both sides of the argument emphasising both the unity and wholeness of mission and the specific evangelistic endeavours undertaken by Baptist churches.

In recent decades, the term 'mission' has encountered difficulties as it is seen to represent not only aggressive mission toward non-Christians, but, influenced by secular and military usage especially in the context of the perceived conflict between the Christian West and the *Islamic* world, it is seen to convey the idea of a *crusade*, a word often used to describe sustained evangelistic endeavour [see *Crusade Evangelism*]. A sensitive use of the word is important as, on the one hand, it, more than any other term, such as *'evangelism'*, or 'witness', best expresses the understanding of the whole church as sent to engage in the comprehensive task of both proclaiming and incarnating the gospel, but, on the other hand, due to current use, it also carries some negative and aggressive connotations which need to be carefully avoided.

PFP

Mission in Europe

[See also *Mission*; *Missions (church related and evangelistic events)*]
In the Book of Acts, Paul and Barnabas' *missionary* journeys included Cyprus, Asia Minor, Greece and Macedonia. By 200AD, converts [see *Conversion*] from these churches together with others in *France*, *Spain*, *Italy* and *Germany* boosted the Roman Empire's Christian population to 15%. Consequently, in 313AD, Constantine felt sufficiently confident to establish Christianity as the Empire's official religion. By 290AD *Armenia* had proclaimed itself a Christian *nation*.

With Imperial patronage the *church* became susceptible to the use of coercive missionary methods. Following the collapse of the Roman Empire, rulers elsewhere were equally ruthless, offering *baptism* or *death* to conquered subjects. Outstanding exceptions were monks like St. Patrick (c.430AD) and Martin of Tours (316-97AD), who *evangelised Ireland* and Gaul respectively.

The British Isles and most of Europe south of the Danube and Rhine had been evangelised by 400AD. Monastic centres of learning, *prayer*, hospitality and mission were founded but Germany proved more resistant, only comprehensively evangelised by the mid 8th century. *Scandinavia* was later still, with *Norway* as late as 1030AD.

Eastwards, the Slavic Lands of *Slovakia*, *Slovenia*, and *Croatia* were evangelised from 780AD onwards by missionaries from Rome.

By 1000AD the Slavic lands of Central and Eastern Europe had been evangelised by missionaries from Constantinople, inspired by Ss. Cyril and Methodius.

With the onset of *Christendom*, distracted by encroaching *Muslim* and barbarian armies, the Church lost her missionary motivation. The *Reformation* failed to overturn Christendom assumptions and mission from the 15th-17th centuries was left to the *Roman Catholic* Orders, with only a few *Protestant* exceptions, including the *Moravians*.

Carey's 1792 *Enquiry into the obligations of Christians to use means for the conversion of the heathen* includes seven pages of European demographics. The first continental Baptist church was founded in Germany by *Johann Oncken* in 1834, yet by 1929 there were 5,129 Baptist churches in Europe. Bernard Green observed, 'No other denomination had such a comprehensive European presence.'

In 1948 the *BWA* Evangelism Committee challenged the European Leaders' meeting to win people for *Christ*, plant new churches [see *Church Planting*], and strengthen Baptist work through evangelism. The *EBF* was founded in 1949 to stimulate *fellowship*, evangelism, and mission within and outside Europe. Its 1952 Congress theme was, Baptists and the Evangelisation of Europe.

The EBF commitment to mission saw it establish an Evangelism Committee in 1960, later the Evangelism and Education Committee. An Institute for Mission and Evangelism was directed by the International Mission Board (IMB) of the *SBC* personnel (later the *CBF*) on its behalf from 1988-98. EBF restructuring incorporated a Division for Mission and Evangelism in 1990. To strengthen *missiological* reflection, an *IBTS* Director assumed responsibility for an MTh. programme in *contextual missiology* from 1999. In 2003, Daniel Trusiewicz was appointed to the post of indigenous church planting coordinator; the EBF's first full-time mission appointment and a practical expression of the 2003 'EBF Resolution on Mission'.

In the aftermath following WWII, North American Mission Boards helped renew mission activity in Europe and a joint Cooperative Committee had EBF and Mission Board representatives. The IMB remains committed to mission in Europe though its relationship with the EBF became increasingly strained throughout the 1980s and 90s. In 1996 the IMB adopted a new strategy for 'Mobilising Church Planting Movements', later allied with a 'Gateway City' strategy in 2001.

EBF work among migrants reaches back to 1962 but the presence of displaced·peoples from the *Balkans*, Iran and Iraq, Asia and Africa, many of them Muslim, has seen an increased emphasis on work among such peoples.

From post-*Soviet* countries, agencies such as *Hungarian Baptist Aid* have emerged alongside existing mission societies, becoming an exemplary relief and development agency, hosting, e.g., the EBF Conference on Human Trafficking in 2005 [see *Prostitution*].

With the re-engagement of mission societies in Europe, the existence of three-way *union* mission partnerships into Central Europe and Eastern Europe, the presence of vibrant migrant churches, declining union memberships across Europe, and the challenge of *secularisation*, the reality that Europe is a mission field no longer escapes the EBF and its member unions. Oncken's catchphrase, 'Every Baptist a missionary' has never been more apposite.

DJ

Mission stations

See *Missions (church related and evangelistic events)*.

Mission strategy in a post-modern age

[See also *Liberalism and Modernism; Mission; Missions (church related and evangelistic events)*]

Much has been written during the second half of the 20th century on mission strategy. Various outreach models have been proposed and tested to improve effectiveness in mission. To list only a few of the buzz concepts: sending individuals and/or teams, training nationals, developing *church planting* and *church growth* strategies, studying social dynamics, better understanding ethnic and cultural issues, testing and learning by experiencing, developing cross-cultural patterns of working, etc. Different methods are needed for urban and rural contexts; everywhere there are new *evangelistic* methods to be exploited, using e.g. the witness model by serving the needy and by modelling a community under God's reign, together with many other approaches.

Strategies have had and continue to have a high value. One can, as some biblical theologies of mission try to prove, see *Jesus* the Messiah God acting strategically in choosing and sending disciples. One may agree that Paul pursued a strategy of reaching the known world of the Roman Empire through going to urban centres and starting Christian communities on the grounds of the presence of an existing *Jewish witness* to the nations. Strategies have differed from century to century, seeking to respond creatively to changes in culture, context and purpose. In some periods of church history there are missionary monks who carry God's *salvation* to the Gentiles and spread the gospel in Europe, South East Asia, Siberia, Alaska and other regions. There are the *Anabaptists* strategically sending teams of three: one who invites people to listen while selling goods to support the team, one who *preaches* and baptises [see *Baptism*], and one who watches out for potential dangers that might confront the team. There is Zinzendorf and the *Moravian* Brethren with their strategy to send missionaries into the new world. *William Carey*, the bright Baptist star, leads the whole *protestant* world into the modern mission age. The 20th century then is marked by both, continuing mission endeavours and, during conciliar debates, a redefinition of what mission is.

The world has tremendously changed from the time of the mission century to the present day. So-called mission fields, such as Africa and Latin America, have a higher percentage of Christians than Europe that hastens into a post-Christian and neo-pagan direction. Individualism, secularism, postmodernism, post-*Christendom*, post-*communism* and many other terms describe European and North American societies. While at the beginning of the mission century most Christians were white, in the 21st century the 1st century's multicoloured face of Christianity has returned. The young so-called **national churches** have developed into strong partners. Any mission strategy in the post-modern age needs to be formulated in true partnership, leaving behind Western **colonial** and neo-colonial approaches in an age of economic dominance Another indispensable element is a strong emphasis on indigenous missionaries supported by expatriates, where, in the wake of **globalisation**, any **nation** and church sends and receives missionaries in strategic partnerships. A third key aspect in strategy development is an emphasis on a missional church, that is, the mission of the **church** is entrusted not to a few specialised individuals but to the whole community of God. Various movements such as the emerging churches, post-church communities and youth churches, disappointed by traditional approaches, attempt to be missional in the 21ˢᵗ century. They may lack some of the background, **traditions** and mission strategies, that traditional churches have, but they have been most successful in connecting with the present post-modern culture and context. And as in any strategic mission planning in any time, the church in mission needs to witness to the 'already and not yet' **kingdom of God** through words and deeds, being salt and light.

However, the development of new strategies is not, of itself, enough. Success will only come when the missional **Spirit** of God takes control of his missional communities and individuals and fulfils God's purpose in them. Without the Spirit of mission any strategy fails, as it failed in the past, when people attempt to do their mission by their own power instead of entrusting the mission of God to the God of mission. Spirit and strategic planning are not 'either or' issues but 'both and'. The Spirit inspires and leads Christians from different denominations to respond together and with creative strategies that are most needed and best suited to the challenging realities of the post- modern world.

PFP

Missionary Congregations

[See also **Mission**; **Missions (church related and evangelistic events)**]

The language rather surprisingly derives from the Third Assembly of the **World Council of Churches** meeting in New Delhi in 1961 though nine years earlier the World Missionary Conference meeting in Willingen in **Germany** in 1952 was already considering 'The Missionary Obligation of the **Church**' in a world recovering from WWII. The question posed was, 'What changes in the external structure and self-understanding of the local congregation are needed for it to be able to **witness** credibly to the message of the **kingdom of God** in a secular world of rapid change?' A study group was established which brought a statement to the WCC's Central Committee in 1965, and a longer report published in 1967 entitled, *The Church for Others and the Church for the World: a Quest for Structures for Missionary Congregations*. At around the same time Johannes Blauw published *The Missionary Nature of the Church*, 1962. It was now clearly seen that mission originated in the nature of God [see **Missio Dei**] not in the church. Obedience to him involved a realisation that the church exists not for itself but for others. Thus mission, originated by God, is of the essence of the church's **calling**: 'A church exists by mission as a fire exists by burning.'

In the past, too often 'missions' were seen as separate from the church, and had become the specialised prerogative of agencies in the Global North and West (the 'sending' bodies) charged with the task of converting the pagan world [see **Conversion**] in the Global South and East (the 'receiving' societies). The World Missionary Conference which met in Mexico City in 1963 abandoned this geographical distinction in favour (under the title of 'Witness in all Six Continents') of a more universal understanding of the presence of the mission field. Thus it affirmed: 'The missionary frontier runs around the world: it is the line that separates belief from unbelief; the unseen frontier which cuts across all other frontiers and presents the universal church with its primary missionary challenge.' Lesslie Newbigin put it even more succinctly by arguing that as 'the home base of the world mission is world-wide' so 'the mission field is also world-wide'; the neo-paganism of the West was as much a mission field as the countries to which missionaries had been sent in the past. Europe and North America now needed the enthusiasm of the growing church in the Global South, now well capable of sending missionaries to Europe and North America.

Much of this chimes with historic Baptist emphases on the *priesthood of all believers* and its resistance to the clericalisation of the church. The *Great Commission* was not addressed to a small group of professional *evangelists* but is an obligation laid upon all Christians. Mission is the work of the whole church and all believers are required to be active partners in the missionary task of both proclaiming the good news of the gospel and in living it out in loving care of neighbour in purposeful *diakonia*, and as the church seeks to be, in *Jesus*' words, 'the salt of the earth', that is, it is under obligation to cooperate with the living Christ as he seeks to transform the secular world. Such an issue was addressed by the *Conference of European Churches* in its concern to foster 'Missionary Congregations in a Secularised Europe'. These issues were also addressed by a number of leading *Evangelicals* who, meeting at Wheaton, Illinois in 1966, drafted a statement on Evangelical perceptions as to the nature of mission. In the context of a reaffirmation of Biblical *authority* [see *Bible*], they reaffirmed the central place assigned to evangelism within mission, but also condemned racism, war and armaments production, the population explosion, poverty and the disintegration of the family. Also in 1966, another group of Evangelicals met in Berlin, and out of this emerged the *Lausanne movement*, concerned to give priority to 'the unfinished task of evangelisation'. Seeking to overcome uncertainties about the relationship of evangelism to social responsibility, it devised the motto 'the whole church taking the whole gospel to the whole world', expressing 'penitence...for having sometimes regarded evangelism and social concern as mutually exclusive'. These are issues that a missionary congregation has to resolve as it seeks to incarnate Christ for the people amongst whom God has set it as his witness.

JHYB

Missionaries, Commissioning of
See *Commissioning of Missionaries*.

Missions (church related and evangelistic events)
[See also *Evangelism*; *Mission*]
The word mission has been used not only to describe the total outreach of the *Church* or, in the plural, its *overseas* witness, but also particular evangelistic programmes undertaken by a local congregation. The issue has sometimes been the extent to which the *local church*'s strategy should be focused in special mission activities rather than the regular, week by week witness of the local congregation in *worship* and service as Baptists have always understood that church and mission are inseparable. Mission is the raison d'être of the church. The term 'missional church', increasingly used in recent decades, attempts to break away from the term 'missionary church'. The missional church is one where everyone is a missionary and where each member and the whole church are involved in the mission of God [see *Missionary Congregations*]. This attitude results in specific involvements and different activities conducted by the whole church. Ever since McGavran initiated the *church growth* movement, churches have re-evaluated some of their evangelistic events, such as mass *crusades*, distribution of tracts, open-air services, etc. Increasingly other creative ways are found to reach out into the society and to invite others into the community of believers. Strategic planning, seeker-oriented services, small groups emphasising personal relations and *fellowship* have been more common in Baptist churches. Personal evangelism was preferred to many other methods of reaching out. While in the 1970s and 80s evangelistic coffee bars created space for open conversation about *faith* instead of aggressive evangelism, today different recreational activities and invitations to study the *Bible* or to experience Christian faith are the popular ways in mission as evangelistic outreach.

In the 19th century 'mission' (sometimes 'mission station') also had another meaning, signifying a building sponsored by a well-established church, often in a poorer downtown area. Whereas a church was a self-governing fellowship with the *church meeting* shaping its *mission strategy*, missions were normally run on a more paternalistic principle under the direction of a few powerful individuals, either self-appointed or appointed by the mother church. In programme and outlook they differed very little from the missions run by the great evangelical societies (e.g. the London *City Mission*). The theological question is whether the promotion of such missions represented a loss of confidence in the *congregational* principle.

PFP

Mixed marriages
[See also *Marriage/Matrimony*]
The term has been used with different connotations, meaning marriages across ethnic, racial or religious lines, or crossing the line between believer and non-believer. In former times, marriages across all these lines were problematic and sometimes even forbidden or impossible. People who broke the marriage rules of their *tradition* were in many cases regarded as outcasts in their communities.

As people from different cultures now increasingly live together, work together and socialise across such dividing lines, it has become more accepted that *men* and *women* make their own choices when it comes to marriage. However mixed marriages can still represent problems. In some *Muslim* countries marriages between a Muslim and a Christian or a *Jew* ('people of the book') may be accepted under certain conditions. In other countries it is not allowed and will have very serious implications. Even within the Christian Church when a *Catholic* marries a non-Catholic he/she needs special permission and must, by the requirements of the church, promise that the children be brought up in the Catholic *faith*.

PMi

Modernism
See *Liberalism and Modernism*.

Moldavian College of Theology and Education
In an atmosphere of new *political* and *religious freedom*, in 1992, programmes of *Theological Education by Extension* were offered in *Moldova*. However, there was a need for Moldavian Baptists to establish their own Baptist theological school. In 1993, Feodor Mocan helped to start a one-year programme at a *Bible* school in Kishinev (Chisinau). The school, offering education for Russian-speaking *students*, was soon renamed Grace Bible College and the curriculum was expanded with courses on *mission* and leadership, thus meeting the *congregational* need for *worship* leaders, *Sunday School* teachers and *evangelists*. In 1994 another school, Trinity Bible Institute was founded, with Valeriu Ghiletchi as its first director. The two schools merged in 1995 and formed the Moldavian College of Theology and Education, located in Kishinev. The College, founded with an aim to equip missionaries, teachers of theology and *pastors*, today offers bachelor level *education*. The students can specialise in *pastoral theology*, *missiology*, social work or Christian education. The languages of instruction are both Russian and Romanian (Moldavian). There are approximately 230 students, one-third of them part-time and two-thirds of them full-time. Besides Moldova, the students come from *Ukraine, Russia, Uzbekistan, Kazakhstan, Tajikistan, Turkmenistan, Kyrgyzstan, Azerbaijan* and *Georgia*.

TP

FURTHER READING: Oleg Turlac, *Short History of the College of Theology and Education in Moldova, 1993-2003*, TFM, Homewood, Al., 2004.

Moldova, Baptist history in
The Baptist message reached the Moldovan areas (until 1940 Bessarabia) in 1876, when German Baptist *missionaries* baptised as believers [see *Baptism*] nine ethnic Germans in Turtino (today in the *Ukraine*), and three years later a Baptist church was established. Ethnic Germans, influenced by *Pietism*, formed more churches, and at the outbreak of WWII there were some 30 congregations with more than 1,000 *members* in the German Baptist association in Bessarabia. However, WWII brought German Baptist work practically to an end, with many Germans repatriating to *Germany*, losing their lives or becoming scattered.

Another branch of Moldovan Baptist work was Russian-speaking. As Moldova was until 1917 a part of Tsarist **Russia**, it was only natural that close links were developed with believers in the neighbouring Ukrainian region, where both **Stundist** and Baptist groups had emerged. In the first decade of the 20th century in Kishinev there were some groups of **Molokan** and **Orthodox** believers who gathered for **prayer** and **Bible study**. In 1908, Andrei Ivanov, from a Molokan background, was baptised by immersion by Baptists when visiting Odessa. Also Tihhon Hizhniakov, a former Orthodox, became convinced about believers' baptism, due to his own individual Bible study and influences from the Odessa Baptist Church. Some Odessa Baptists, including Vasilii Pavlov, visited Kishinev and assisted the Russian Baptist congregation which had been formed there in 1908 with Ivanov as its leader. Though Russian-speaking work was not widespread, some other Russian (Ukrainian) congregations and **mission stations** emerged, and in 1918, when Moldova became a part of the Kingdom of **Romania**, there were approximately 250 Russian-speaking Baptists, including about 100 members in Kishinev church. Gradually, especially under the leadership of Boris Bushilo, from 1921 onwards the Kishinev church became an important Baptist centre in the country. In the 1920s, Baptist mission activity reached the northern parts of Moldova, with the town of Balti (Beltzy) becoming a centre of Baptist work in this region. The Russian-speaking branch of Moldovan Baptists formed the Bessarabian Evangelical Christian Union in 1920 with Vassilii Asiev as chairman. In 1927, after the Evangelical Christians and Baptists merged into one structure, the word 'Baptist' was added to the name of the **Union**. The Union published periodicals, such as *Svet Zhizni* [The Light of Life], and other literature both in Russian and in Romanian. The Romanian influence on Moldovan Baptists should not be underestimated. Several outstanding Moldovan Baptist **preachers**, such as Ivan Slobodchikov and others, secured their **theological education** at the **Bucharest Baptist Theological Seminary**.

The Baptist work also penetrated the Moldovan (Romanian) speaking local population. Phenomenal growth among both Russian (Ukrainian)-speaking and Moldovan (Romanian)-speaking populations took place in the 1920s and 30s, in spite of restrictions and even persecution from both the Orthodox church and the Romanian authorities. Also, in 1926, in Kishinev a second Baptist **church building** ('Bethel') was opened, with converted **Jews** providing the majority of the membership. This church was led by Lev Averbuch, who preached in Hebrew with a translation into Yiddish . This Jewish Baptist community, however, was destroyed in the turmoils of WWII. According to A. Wardin, there were 18,000 Baptists in 347 churches in Bessarabia in 1942, though other numbers can be found in other sources (10,000 members in 1939 or 14,000 in 1940). Baptist missionary efforts in pre-war Moldova and Romania were supported by **Southern Baptists** from the USA. Moldovan Baptists had well organised **ministries**: **evangelism**, youth work, theological courses for preachers.

In 1940 the northern part of Moldova (Bessarabia) was annexed by the Soviet army and hastily the Republic of Moldavia, a part of the **Soviet Union**, was set up. The **political** circumstances, changes of borders, starvation, **migration** and atheistic and political repressions drastically diminished the number of churches and believers in Moldova (in Soviet years it retained the name of Moldavia). The Baptists, in approximately 80 churches with a total membership of less than 4,800 in 1949, in order to operate legally, joined the **All-Union Council of Evangelical Christians-Baptists** which had its headquarters in Moscow. Some Baptist groups in Moldavia resisted this solution and operated secretly without official registration. **Unity** among Moldavian Baptists was shattered. The first Senior Presbyters in the region often acted as representatives of the **State** rather than spiritual leaders. Only in 1965 did the Moldavian Baptists get a Senior Presbyter with a local background, Sergei Malanchuk, who had trust among the believers. However, by that time the split of the 1960s among Soviet Baptists had taken place, having its repercussions also in Moldavia. The tensions between registered and unregistered churches have not been fully solved even today, and there are several independent **evangelical** churches in today's

Moldova. During the Soviet years some *Pentecostal* churches also joined the Moldavian ECB Union. In the *preaching* ministry, one of the main ministries during Soviet years, *women*, such as Lidia Caldararu and Evangelina Goroholinskaja, took their place alongside the *men*.

After a politically independent Moldova was established in 1991 and in the atmosphere of *religious freedom*, Baptists were soon engaged in *church planting* and active evangelism in public institutions, such as in *hospitals*, stadiums, cultural palaces and schools. They revived their *children's work*, and the *Moldavian College of Theology and Education* in Kishinev was established in 1995. Some Moldovan Baptists have been involved in the country's political life; from 1998-2000 Valeriu Ghiletchi, later *bishop* of the Moldovan Baptists, was a member of the Moldovan Parliament. In 1991 an independent Union of Evangelical Christians-Baptists in Moldova was established, today consisting of approximately 400 churches and *mission stations* with a total of 21,100 members. When compared with Soviet years, the growth has been phenomenal, especially if taken into account that approximately 10,000 believers from Baptist churches have emigrated abroad since 1990. The Union is a member of *EBF*. The Moldovan Union continues to be multi-national: there are Moldavians, Ukrainians, Gagauz, Bulgarians and others who are represented in the *local churches*.

TP

FURTHER READING: Irina Bondareva, 'Baptist Origins and Early Development in Moldova' in *Journal of European Baptist Studies,* vol. 2, no. 3 (May 2002), pp.31-44. Irina Bondareva-Zuehlke, 'Separation or Co-operation? Moldavian Baptists (1940-1965)', Keith G. Jones and Ian M. Randall (eds), *Counter-Cultural Communities*, Paternoster, Carlisle, 2008.

Molokans

The Molokans [literally 'milk drinkers'] were an indigenous Russian *sect* who reacted against the pomp of the *Orthodox* Church forming Quaker-like *prayer* groups in the late 18th century, *pacifist* in outlook, with a simple trust in Biblical [see *Bible*] *authority*. Whilst initially rejecting all sacramental practice and ritual, by the late 1860s a number of them began to question whether their rejection of the *sacraments* in favour of an exclusively spiritual religion – they called themselves 'Spiritual Christians' – was too radical. Perceiving now the need for water *baptism* and *communion*, many were attracted to Baptist forms of churchmanship, though bringing with them some particular Molokan ways, e.g. of psalm singing. From their ranks came a number of early Baptist leaders, in particular Dei Mazsev, a rich sheep farmer who was long-time head of the Russian Baptist *Union*, Vasilii Pavlov. the son of a Tiflis merchant who was president of the Baptist Union from 1909. His father was *wealthy* enough to finance his study for a year under *Oncken* in Hamburg. The third was Ivan Prokhanov also a merchant's son who himself became a mechanical engineer. That many of the early Baptists in Russia had prior experience in either the Molokan or *Stundist* movements is important in understanding the indigenous roots of the Russian Baptist movement.

JHYB

Monastic Communities
See *Intentional Communities*.

Montenegro, Baptist history in
See *Serbia and Montenegro, Baptist history in*.

Moral Re-Armament
The Oxford Group (later Moral Re-Armament – MRA), an interdenominational network which flourished from the 1920s, was started by an American *Lutheran minister*, Frank Buchman. In 1912 a leading English Baptist, F.B. Meyer, met Buchman in Pennsylvania and encouraged him to spend time listening to God and to make personal relationships the focus of his *evangelism*. Buchman was also influenced by D.L. Moody's Northfield Conferences, Jessie Penn-Lewis, a Welsh *holiness* teacher, and Oswald Chambers, particularly his *My Utmost for His Highest*. In 1921 Buchman began evangelistic work in *Britain*, largely cen-

tred in Oxford (hence the popular name of the Oxford Group, not to be confused with the Anglo-*Catholic* 'Oxford Movement' of the 19th century). He drew together a team of what he called 'life-changers', committed to the standards of absolute honesty, purity, unselfishness and *love*, and a vision to 're-make the world'. Group *spirituality* stressed on relationships, mutual sharing of weaknesses and failures, and the seeking of direct guidance from God. Over the next decade the movement particularly drew *students* and young professional people. A Group 'house-party' in Oxford in 1933 attracted around 5,000 people. A number of Baptist ministers, ministerial students and lay people [see *Laity*] became involved, although others were critical. In the 1930s Group campaigns were held in many parts of Europe. The Group espoused a contemporary approach to evangelism, avoiding religious terminology and featuring many testimonies. By 1938, in the face of the challenges of *Fascism* and *Communism*, Buchman became committed to a more general message – Moral Re-armament. Some Baptists continued to be involved. E.g. Eric Worstead, Principal of *Spurgeon's College*, received spiritual help from MRA in the 1950s, but this was controversial and he had to resign as Principal. In 2001 MRA changed its name once again to Initiatives of Change.

IMR

FURTHER READING: D.W. Bebbington, *Evangelicalism in Modern Britain: A History from the 1730s to the 1980s*, Routledge, London, 1995. G. Lean, *Frank Buchman: A Life*, Constable, London, 1985. I.M. Randall, '"Arresting People for Christ": Baptists and the Oxford Group in the 1930s' in *The Baptist Quarterly*, Vol. 38, No. 1 (1999).

Moratorium

John Gatu, an East African *Presbyterian*, boldly argued in 1971 'that the time has come for the withdrawal of foreign *missionaries* from many parts of the third world' so that the churches in those countries 'be allowed to find their own identity'. This call for a 'moratorium on missionaries' was presented to the Commission on World *Mission* and Evangelism conference in Bangkok, Thailand in Jan 1973. The conference did not endorse the call though recognising it as

one of the 'more radical solutions' that would enable the receiving church 'to find its identity, set its own priorities and discover within its own fellowship the resources to carry out its authentic mission'. However the All Africa Conference of Churches (AACC)'s assembly in Lusaka, Zambia in May 1974 did unequivocally call for a moratorium. The AACC working group in Lusaka linked the moratorium to liberation and called for 'a moratorium on the receiving of money and personnel' as 'the most viable means of giving the African church...power'. At least some wanted the moratorium limited to personnel. E.g. Burgess Carr, AACC General Secretary, described the moratorium as 'a demand to transfer the massive expenditure on expatriate personnel...to programme activities manned by Africans'. Such a stance cost the AACC a substantial part of its membership. The 1975 Assembly in Nairobi again gave a cautious welcome to the idea of moratorium as an option: 'there may be occasions of dependence between churches where, for the sake of the integrity of a church's *witness* in its own culture, there should be a temporary moratorium'. Others advocated that the call for a moratorium should be totally rejected. E.g. *Billy Graham* did so at the International Congress on World *Evangelisation* in *Lausanne*, Switzerland in Jul 1974. Also, the *Baptist Missionary Society* in fact recruited more new missionaries in the latter half of the 1970s than in the first half.

PH

Moravian Movement

The Moravian movement dates from 1457 when followers of Jan Hus established the Unitas Fratrum (Unity of the Brethren) in eastern Bohemia. By 1517 the Unity of Brethren numbered at least 200,000 people. By 1557 the churches were spread through Bohemia, Moravia and *Poland*. The main leader of the church in the 17th century was Jan Amos Comenius, who became famous for his progressive views of *education*. The 18th century saw the renewal of the Moravian movement through the patronage of Nicholas Ludwig von Zinzendorf, a Saxon Count who had been educated in a German *Pietist* environment. In 1722 Zinzendorf, opened his estate in south-east Saxony to a group of Moravian *refugees*. Zinzendorf's estate, Herrnhut (the Lord's Protection), became the scene in 1727 of a profound spiritual *renewal*. Four girls in the Moravian community came to powerful spiritual assurance and this intense experience spread to the whole community at a subsequent *communion* service. One result was that in 1732 the Moravians committed themselves to what proved to be a remarkable *missionary* work, reaching places such as Greenland and Lapland. The community also became a place of continuous *prayer*. Moravians were distinctive for the stress they placed on the wounds of *Christ*. It was at a Moravian-led meeting in Aldersgate Street in 1738 that John Wesley had his experience of assurance. Charles Wesley was influenced by the Moravians and this contributed to his own *conversion*. *William Carey* was similarly indebted to the Moravians. The Moravian Church grew especially in North America, through *emigration* from Europe, and became a world-wide denomination, with significant work in Nicaragua, the Caribbean, South Africa, and especially Tanzania. In the 19th and 20th centuries the Moravian emphasis on prayer and *mission* had an influence within Europe on Baptists and other *evangelicals*.

IMR

FURTHER READING: K.G. Jones, 'The Labyrinth of the World and the Paradise of the Heart' in *Baptist Quarterly*, Vol. 40 (2003). A.J. Lewis, *Zinzendorf: The Ecumenical Pioneer*, SCM, London, 1962.

Moscow Theological Seminary of the Evangelical Christians-Baptists

The idea of establishing an *evangelical* seminary on the territory of *Russia* was first discussed at the first Baptist World Congress in London in 1905. In the same year, under the influence of the First Russian Revolution, Russian Evangelicals obtained an opportunity to run *educational* projects. The first training of church *ministers* was organised by the leader of the Evangelical Christians, Ivan Prokhanov. It was a short-term programme that took place at the end of 1905 in St. Petersburg and was repeated several times in the following years. The education of ministers of the Russian Baptist *Union* (which was separate from the Union of the Evangelical Christians) was provided at the Lodz Theological Seminary of Russian German Baptists in *Poland* (a part of the Russian Empire at that time). At the All-Russian Congress of Baptists in 1909 the leaders of the Union raised a question about the possible foundation of a theological seminary in Moscow. But in 1909 the Russian Baptists did not have money to start the seminary. The money was collected during the second Baptist World Congress in 1911. Nevertheless the seminary was not opened because of sudden changes in Russian laws on the threshold of WWI.

After the *Communist* Revolution both Evangelical Christians and Baptists ran many local schools but they all existed only for a short time. In Moscow there were two projects. V. Pavlov and M. Timoshenko conducted Christian training courses in 1923. In 1927 the Baptist Union started a programme for training church ministers designed as a three-year course of study. P. Ivanov-Klishnikov was appointed director of the programme. But this school was closed by the authorities in 1929. After 1930 Evangelical Christian education was forbidden in the *Soviet Union* for almost 40 years.

Educational activity was resumed only in 1968 by the *All-Union Council of Evangelical Christians-Baptists*. That year the AUCECB received permission to open the *Bible* Correspondence Course. A. Mitskevich became the leader of the Course. A. Bichkov, M. Zhidkov, A. Karev, V. Mitskevich and S. Timchenko were some of its first teachers. The teachers wrote special course notes which were distributed, with assignments, along with each lecture, among *students* of the school. The students had to visit Moscow for several days to take examinations, listen to lectures, and receive an allocation of training aids. The programme was designed to be completed in two years and it included such subjects as *theology* (*dogmatics*), introduction to the Bible, the history of Christianity, the history of Baptists in Russia, comparative religions, *pastoral care*, and religious law in the USSR. Every year up to 100 people entered the Course.

In 1973 the programme was expanded

and the training period increased to three years. In 1979 the Course added a new department of training for *choir* directors. In 1994 this department was reorganised to become the Institute of Spiritual Music. The period, after the end of Communism, brought several significant changes. In 1991 the Bible Correspondence Course was renamed the Moscow Bible Institute. P. Savchenko became its new rector. In 1995 the programme was altered substantially to fit the standards of European Christian education. The Institute began five-year programmes in Christian *ministry* and Christian education. V. Ryaguzov became the head of the Institute.

Also at the beginning of the 1990s the Union of Evangelical Christians-Baptists opened the long-awaited seminary which was able to provide residential education for Baptist ministers. Initially the Union received permission to open a seminary in 1991. But because of the lack of a location for the seminary in Moscow the project was moved to Odessa (*Ukraine*). In 1993 the Union got new facilities and this allowed the seminary to open in Moscow. The inauguration took place on 3 Oct 1993. A. Kozynko, who had previously worked at the Moscow Bible Institute, became rector of the new seminary.

Initially both the Seminary and the Institute were placed in the Union building. In 2000, however, the seminary acquired its own building and in 2003 it moved to the new location. In 2007 the Moscow Bible Institute was integrated into the seminary in order to combine full-time and part-time education at one institution. The united school is headed by P. Mitskevich, the grandson of A. Mitskievich, the first director of the Bible Correspondence Course.

Since 2004 the seminary has been run in collaboration with Russian Leadership Ministries (RLM) in the United States, which provides 90% of the financial support it receives. Ian Chapman, a *Baptist World Alliance* vice president and chairman of the BWA Promotion and Development Committee, is chairman and president of RLM.

AP

Multinational companies
See *Globalisation and Multinational companies*.

Music
See *Church Music*; *Hymnody*; *Musical instruments in worship*.

Musical instruments in worship
[See also *Church Music*; *Worship*]

As recently as a century ago, some Baptists were still arguing against any use of musical instruments during worship, maintaining, along the line of some *Reformed churches*, that their use should have ceased with the end of worship in the Jerusalem temple. In particular it was sometimes argued that organs were too *Catholic*, though from the middle of the 19th century they came to dominate the musical offerings of most churches which possessed their own *buildings*. Today they are becoming as little respected as once they were highly esteemed.

Nevertheless today, wherever an instrument and a musician are available, little would be sung *a cappella* among European Baptists. The role of instruments, however, is often pragmatically limited to that of supporting the human voices that communicate *words*. Instrumental support is then only an auxiliary means of communicating a text that is understood to be the principal aspect of worship.

In contrast, some other Baptist churches (especially those touched by the *charismatic* renewal movements) would see instrumental music as an expression of the creative energy that is an appropriate response in the human worship of the Creator. Such churches tend to track the cultural moves in their societies and are eager to experiment with new ways of using instrumental music in worship.

The choice of instruments (varying from strings, organ, brass, or mandolins to piano, electronic keyboards, guitars and drums) reflects the *theological* stance of the churches towards their cultural environment. This may affirm the use of popular or indigenous instruments, or reject them as 'worldly'. In the case of congregations planted by foreign *missionaries*, the adoption of the missionary's choice of instruments, either unconsciously or by making a link between those particular instruments and 'proper' worship, can prevent the *contextualisation* of the church's *witness*.

LA

Muslims, Baptists and the *Common Word*

The relationship between Christianity and Islam, at times a very difficult relationship, has a long history. The place of Islam was recognised by *Thomas Helwys* in his book the *Mystery of Iniquity* (1612) when he spoke of the need for all people, including Turks – Muslims – to be free to hold to their own beliefs. Although Baptists are to be found in countries in the Middle East where Islam is the majority *faith*, it has not been common to have *dialogue* between representatives of the Baptist communities and the Muslim communities. In Oct 2007, however, 138 Muslim *scholars*, clerics and intellectuals came together to declare the common ground between Christianity and Islam in *A Common Word Between Us and You*. This event has been seen as the first of its kind since the days of the Prophet Mohammed. Every major Islamic country or region in the world was represented in this message, which was addressed to the leaders of all the world's churches, and to all Christians everywhere.

Many Christian bodies and individuals responded, including Baptists. In Oct 2007 David R. Coffey, President of the *Baptist World Alliance* and former General Secretary of the Baptist *Union* of *Great Britain*, welcomed the letter and commended it as a groundbreaking initiative which could make a major contribution to a better understanding in Christian-Muslim relations, the cause of *religious liberty* and global *peace*. David Coffey is one of the European Baptists who has taken a considerable interest in communication with Muslim leaders, in the Middle East and elsewhere, and he reflected on this and on the need to affirm the call of the Muslims scholars to 'Respect each other, be fair, just and kind to each other and live in peace harmony and mutual good will.'

David Coffey expressed his concern about situation in which Christians or those of any faith were denied full religious liberty, which included the right for all persons to freely *worship* and live their faith without fear and prejudice.

This letter was followed by an extended response from the BWA which came out of its Annual Meeting in Prague in Jul 2008 when leaders from Baptist unions and conventions in 66 countries discussed the *Common Word* letter in an open forum. The Baptist response out of the meeting noted that many of those gathered in Prague came from areas of the world in which they had experienced distressing religious conflicts, but there was a common desire to respond positively to the invitation to dialogue, and a recognition of the friendly and hospitable intentions that lie behind it.

The response affirmed areas that were indeed common ground, such as the two Greatest Commandments. In the light of the human response of *love* for God, however, the Baptist statement emphasised that the question which arises is the way in which Baptists understand the love of God himself as a free gift: the very nature of God is love, and this is always prior to *our* love for God. The response also contained reflections on the Christian doctrine of the *Trinity* and on religious liberty.

In the section on religious liberty, the Baptist response commended the case advanced by the Muslim scholars for religious freedom. It continued: 'As Baptist Christians, we have always defended the right of religious freedom for all people, regardless of their religion, grounding this *theologically* in the *sovereignty* of God. All people are responsible to God alone for their faith or lack of faith, and not to human powers...It seems to us that you are directing your argument in the first place to a defence of the right of Christians, Muslims and *Jews* to practice freely the religion in which they have been born, or which they already hold – "to follow what God has commanded them". This is obviously of critical importance, and we can think of many local situations where tensions would be eased if this were more widely understood. It is not altogether clear to us whether you think that this principle can also cover the freedom of people to change their religion, or to move from a community of one faith to another of a different faith. As Baptist Christians, we believe that the same principle of accountability to the sovereign God gives freedom to make such a change, from Christianity to Islam or from Islam to Christianity. Of course, we are concerned here with a person's *own* conviction that God is calling them into a different community of faith ("to follow what God has commanded them"), not with unjust human means of persuasion, inducement or compulsion.'

The Baptist response recognised that both Islam and Christianity are 'missionary faiths' and affirmed that there is a legitimate kind of *mission* in which people can, in appropriate ways, share their beliefs with others, and in which people seeking God should have the freedom to explore the way that God is calling them into faith. As part of the 'way forward' the Baptist response suggested that Baptist Christians might avoid words to describe *evangelism* (or telling the gospel story) which appear threatening to others, such as 'evangelistic *crusades*' and emphasised that it is not necessary to be critical of another faith in order to commend what we believe to be true in ours; the story of *Jesus* has power to persuade in its own right.

This response to the *Common Word* had four signatories – Neville Callam (BWA General Secretary), David Coffey (BWA President), Prof. Paul S. Fiddes, from Oxford, who was Chair of the Commission on Doctrine and Inter-Church Cooperation of the BWA, and Regina Claas, who is the General Secretary of the German Baptist Union and Chair of the Commission on Freedom and Justice of the BWA. This indicates the involvement of European Baptists in this historic dialogue.

The response was well received by the Muslim scholars, particularly HRH Prince Ghazi bin Mohammed, cousin to King Abdullah of Jordan, who met with Baptist leaders at the dedication of a BWA baptismal site at Bethany beyond the Jordan in early 2009 and expressed his thanks for the quality and seriousness of the Baptist response.

ET

FURTHER READING: http://acommonword.com. www.bwanet.org.

Mysticism

Like *spirituality*, mysticism is not language that springs readily to Baptist lips, though it seeks to identify a depth of religious experience with which many would empathise. Modern *scholars* have identified mysticism as a source of influence on the origins of both the *Reformation* and the *Evangelical* Movement, medieval mysticism often representing the search of individuals for authentic religious experience unaided, even discouraged by the official church. In the Eastern Church hesychasm, a pattern of piety focussed in the repeated invocation of the name of *Christ*, finds its most popular expression in the recitation of the Jesus *prayer*: 'Lord Jesus Christ, Son of God have mercy upon me.' The word 'mysticism' was coined by the French in the 17th century, but the experience it describes in much older going back to the NT itself and indeed back beyond that to *Jewish* piety. Linguistically the word has the same root as the word 'mystery' and thus refers to a deeply experienced reality that remains secret (unrevealed) to superficial observers. For St. Paul, mystery described the hidden wisdom and depths of God, the things not seen by human eyes or heard by human ears, but graciously made known in the gospel through the activity of the *Holy Spirit*. This is most perfectly revealed in the *incarnation*, which is the most profound aspect of *revelation*, the revealing of the secret of God's purposes for *humankind*. It has properly been said that mysticism defies definition, for to try to define the word is to place it within an analytical or syllogistic context to which it is hostile; it has to be experienced, not reduced to some linguistic formula, that it is to say, its very existence poses a question about the adequacy of all *theological* formulations, indicating that there must always be a depth of spiritual experience that goes beyond the form of words. The path to mystic experience is secured by a life of concentrated prayer moving into a life in which the *fruits of the Spirit* are displayed.

JHYB

Myth/Mythology

Myth is a term that is difficult to define. It

has been used with a variety of meanings in scholarly contexts, past and present. In the field of biblical interpretation [see *Bible*] it often occurs in describing a world remote in time and space and involving superhuman beings. Foundational stories about the origins of humanity, gods and the universe are commonly viewed as myths. In dealing with the problems of human existence they reflect people's perceptions of transcendent reality. The field of cultural and social *anthropology* likewise addresses the phenomenon of myth. Myth is seen as a story explaining the origin of social organisation, practices and customs. French anthropologist, Claude Lévi-Strauss, developed an influential structural approach to the interpretation of myth. Using structural linguistics he proposed that myths attempt to overcome what appear to be contradictions that pertain to reality. Besides the anthropological study of mythology, the approaches of Sigmund Freud and Carl Jung have contributed to psychological interpretations of myth. The work of philosopher, Paul Ricoeur, has seen myth, through emphasis on symbolic language, as playing a significant role in the appraisal of human thought.

Theology too has its own special use of the word 'myth', which can be applied to parts of the Biblical record. This usage needs to be carefully appraised and distanced from the identification of myth with fictional stories that are patently mental constructions, less than historically true. Myth is a well-established literary form and there is, therefore, no reason why the writers of scripture, like other writers, should not employ it to communicate important truths about the nature of God's relationship with humanity, even as for a similar purpose *Jesus* employed parables, some of which may have embraced historical narratives, whereas others were constructed for just this purpose. Such use of the mythical form, mainly to be found in the OT, may however be more limited than some *scholars* have suggested. The criterion for judging a 'myth' is not so much historical happening as to whether the point made by the myth is true or false. Under such criterion 'myth' functions as history-like narrative. Moreover a 'myth' has to make its point both for people schooled in the methods of historical criticism, as well as for those who

lived in an age prior to the emergence of such *hermeneutical* tools. Thus the story of the fall can be seen to be a valid 'myth', whereas a story which taught *humankind*'s moral infallibility could not be so considered. 'Myths' often deploy poetic and symbolic forms which are not amenable to critical analysis: they thus convey not so much that which is less than the truth, but themes of eternal significance which represent more of truth than can be contained within the description of any past event or movement. Beyond this examination of technical literary forms, it is particularly unhelpful when some radical *theologians* move from such a usage as characterising in a technical sense some forms of ancient writing to a usage which suggests the unreliability of certain central affirmations of the Christian *faith* such as suggested by 'The Myth of God Incarnate' slogan. Such reductionist usage of the term is far distant from the usage discussed in this entry and is not common among Baptists.

LK

N

Nation/Nationalism

[See also *National Churches*; *State, Baptist approaches to the*]

The rise of the Nation State, making obsolete the older reality of the Holy Roman Empire, around the time of the Renaissance, was a precursor to the challenge of the emergence of a number of national churches as over against the previously existing unity of *Catholic* Europe. The nation was now a discrete *political* reality owning no superior authority beyond its own boundaries. Behind and within the new reality lay the forces of nationalism based upon a variety of phenomena that drew people together: race, language, culture. Some nations, however, had to face diversity in these areas, with adjacent nations sometimes embracing cognate peoples. This automatically introduced a certain instability to the life of many nations, if the uniting cultural ties proved insufficiently strong, or if challenged by strong external forces. This can be seen in the re-writing of political boundaries in many parts of Eastern Europe and especially in the *Balkans* throughout the 20th century; an experience much less felt in Western Europe, where political boundaries in recent history, whilst·not absolute, have proved more enduring.

The word 'nation' as over against its synonyms, 'country', 'land' and 'state', underlines the relationship between nation and nationalism. It was the emergence of Balkan nationalism in the context of the crumbling empires of Austro-Hungary and the Ottoman Turks, and then the acceleration of nationalist forces in *Germany* in the early years of the 20th century, which destabilised the continent, leading to the outbreak of WWI. The Versailles peace treaty sought to put in place a supra-national body in the form of the League of Nations (1920) to act as a restraint on future nationalistic challenges to the integrity of surrounding nations and thus of international *peace*, but it proved impotent to control either *fascist Italy* or Nazi Germany, with their imperial ambitions which once more challenged the peace and stability of the whole continent. Nor has the *United Nations* since 1945 proved very much more successful, largely because article 2 in its charter declares, 'The organisation is based on the principle of the sovereign equality of all its members'. This article also upholds what it terms, 'the domestic jurisdiction provision'. Together these principles disallow any UN intervention in the internal affairs of any member state, however much *human rights* in that state may seem to be abused.

The rise of nationalism amongst subject *colonial* peoples was the major force which brought to an end the world-wide empires of several Western European nations, creating a quite new context for European Christian *missions*, indeed challenging them to recognise as partners the emerging national churches of the countries of the two-thirds world. At the end of the 20th century, the same forces of nationalism came to destroy *Soviet* hegemony in Central and Eastern Europe, and in Central Asia, again creating a new context for the mission of the Christian churches.

If nationalism too easily suggests a pathological, selfish, exaggerated and exclusive concern with one's own nation, which seeks either to dominate others, or, in isolationist withdrawal, to take no responsibility for the needs of those living beyond their nation's borders, patriotism may be seen as representing a healthy concern for the welfare of the nation, which, when absent, creates a dangerous void. By contrast healthy nation-building, under God, securing the freedom of once dependent peoples, is a process in which the churches ought to play their part. Such a patriotism necessarily concerns itself with the welfare of all citizens, as over against the ambitions of emerging elites to exploit the nation for their own class benefits. Fighting against the false values of national security politics, proper patriotism places high priority on the *democratic* participation of all citizens, with a new emphasis on 'peoples' rights'. In this respect part of the tragedy of the contemporary world is that some *Trans-national Corporations*, sometimes seen as the harbingers of a new imperialism, can become more powerful than the nations in which they do their business, indicating that in the long run 'economics' can prove to be more powerful than 'politics'.

JHYB

National Churches

[See also *Nation/Nationalism*; *Separation of Church and State*; *State, Baptist attitudes to the*]

Since the time of Emperor Constantine (c.275-337), the Christian *Church* in Europe has enjoyed a privileged relationship with the Roman State and its successors either in the Holy Roman Empire or the independent nations which emerged after the *Reformation*. In the era of *Christendom* Christianity functioned as the official religion of the Empire. It both legitimated its rulers and benefited from its support in the suppression of dissenters and heretics [see *Heresy*].

With the emergence of the nation state a variety of relationships developed with individual nations or provinces with the aim of continuing a privileged status. In the case of the *Protestant* and *Reformed* (*Lutheran*, Presbyterian, *Moravian*, *Waldensian*, *Anglican*) Churches the civil authority, sometimes in the form of the monarch, assumed the governmental role of the *Catholic Pope* over the national church. For reasons of history and *theology* alike a variety of church-state relations emerged which, although often referred to by Baptists as 'state church', involve a more complex set of relationships. The term 'state church' is most accurate when the church is seen as an aspect of national life under the direct government of the state and financed by it as, for instance, in *Denmark*.

By contrast the *Volkskirche*, or People's Church, found in varying forms in post WWII *Germany*, is internally self-governing but supported by means of a government church-tax. The 'established church' model, as found in *England* is formally (if nominally) governed by the monarch acting on the advice of the Prime Minister in regard to the appointment of its senior clergy. However the Presbyterian Church of *Scotland*, drawing upon the Reformed distinction between church and state, denies that it is either a state church or an established church. As an entirely self-governing and self-

financing body it sees itself as a national church in that it carries a sense of *pastoral* responsibility for all the nation's people and all its affairs.

The concept of the national church therefore is justified by its advocates as part of the *mission* of the church. At the same time it risks compromising the nature of the church as an international community with obligations to all the nations and a duty to avoid idolatrous nationalisms.

The Roman Catholic Church, named in some European constitutions as the significant religious institution within the nation, concludes where possible a concordat with individual states to regulate arrangements concerning church-owned institutions such as schools and *hospitals*.

Baptists have consistently opposed state sponsored religion or attempts on the part of the state to govern or control church life. At times this has meant opting out of church-tax arrangements and refusing state finance. It may be claimed that once any church assumes a legal form and submits to the formal regulations and recognition of a nation's legal and charitable systems, it becomes in some sense established. Baptist concern is that on the one hand the freedom of the church before God should never be compromised, and on the other that the freedom of the state from any one controlling religious interest, giving rise to the possibility of the persecution of others, should be maintained. However, in more recent times Baptists have drawn a distinction between their opposition to state support for religious institutions, though even here they often claim charitable status and the tax benefits that accrue from this, and their willingness to enter into partnership with the state in projects and institutions serving the wider community, especially where that community is marginalised and has special needs.

In Eastern Europe the legacy of caesaropapism, the church as the handmaid of the state, died hard, for in the Byzantium Empire no distinction was made between the things belonging to Caesar and those belonging to *Christ*. That is why in 1917 the Russian *Orthodox Church* collapsed with the rule of the tsars. In post-*cold-war* Eastern Europe the different national Orthodox churches looked to the emerging regimes to re-establish them as state churches on the old model, at the cost of the freedom of *evangelical* and *pentecostal* groups, claiming that there was a natural bond between their *spirituality* and the spirit of the nation, seen in such claims as 'To be a true Russian you need to be Orthodox'. All this is embraced by the Orthodox reluctance to admit to anything like there being a free market in religious commitments determined by an individual's conscientious choices.

By contrast a dominant *orthodoxy* in many parts of Central and Eastern Europe has developed the concept of 'canonical territory' with its reluctance to allow either protestant or catholic *communions* an entry to nations they consider rightly theirs. In post *communist* Europe the Orthodox churches in *Russia*, Greece, *Serbia*, *Bulgaria*, *Belarus* and the *Ukraine*, as well as the Apostolic Armenian Church have sought to place themselves firmly as national churches with close governmental ties, even if not formally the state church.

NGW

National Council of Churches

A National Council of Churches (NCC) is a voluntary organisation of churches within a *nation*, which without compromising the distinctive identity and authority of its members, enables their sharing in common reflection and action on matters of Christian *unity*, *faith* and *ethics*, and in programmes of common Christian *witness* and service ('Council of Churches', *Dictionary of the Ecumenical Movement* [2nd ed.], Geneva, 2002).

The forming of NCCs was brought about at the beginning of the 20th century as a result of a deepening understanding of the need for Christian unity. This was made possible when at the same time the notion of *religious freedom* and *separation of church and state* allowed the co-existence of a number of churches in a given nation.

The basis for membership of a council is rooted in the belief in a triune God, Father, Son and *Holy Spirit* [see *Trinity*], *Jesus Christ* as God and Saviour and the *Bible* as the *revelation* of God's *salvation*. All Christian denominations in a given country can thus be members of a council. NCCs often include churches who are not members of regional or global *ecumenical* bodies, such as the *Roman Catholic* Church and many *Pentecostal* churches.

Councils are seen as instruments of Christian unity or even as preliminary expressions of unity. Churches continue to explore new models for NCCs trying to avoid councils from becoming a structure alongside the churches. Therefore *consensus* decision making and 'churches together' models, where churches themselves use their specialised resources to help one another, or to advance the common good, without creating a large and separate ecumenical bureaucracy, are gaining ground. The number of NCC's world wide has grown from two in 1910 to more than 100 in 2001.

Councils of Churches exist in many European countries; in some Baptists are full members, indeed in a number of them the effective leadership has come from Baptists. In other councils they are present as observers, in others not present at all, not necessarily because of a lack of desire to cooperate, and in others they are only represented by intermediary bodies. In some countries *associations* of *free churches*, the *Bible Society*, or national *Evangelical Alliances* offer Baptists the best platform for cooperation.

Below is a table of membership of National Councils:

- Ecumenical Council of Churches in Austria: Observer
- Consultation of Christian Churches in Belgium: Not represented
- Ecumenical Coordinating Committee of Churches in Croatia: Member*
- Ecumenical Council of Churches in the Czech Republic: Member*
- National Council of Churches in Denmark: Member*
- Estonian Council of Churches: Member
- Finnish Ecumenical Council: Swedish-speaking Churches: Member; Finnish-speaking Churches: Observer
- French Protestant Federation: Fed of Ev Baptist Churches: Member*
- Council of Christian Churches in Germany: Member*
- Ecumenical Council of Churches in Hungary: Member*
- Irish Council of Churches: Not represented

- Federation of Protestant Churches in Italy: Member*
- Ecumenical Council of Churches in Lithuania: Member
- Council of Churches in the Netherlands: Not directly represented
- Christian Council of Norway: Member
- Polish Ecumenical Council: Member*
- Portuguese Council of Christian Churches: Not represented
- Ecumenical Association of Churches in Romania [AIDROM]: Not represented
- Ecumenical Council of Churches in Serbia and Montenegro: Council inactive
- Ecumenical Council of Churches in Slovakia: Member
- Spanish Committee of Cooperation between the Churches: Not represented
- Christian Council of Sweden: Member*
- Council of Christian Churches in Switzerland: Member
- Churches Together in England/Britain and Ireland: Member (BUGB only)*

* = Also a member of the *Conference of European Churches*, of which the *European Baptist Federation* is an associated organisation and in which the following Baptist churches which have no national council of churches hold membership:

- Baptist Union of Bulgaria
- Union of Evangelical Christians-Baptists of Georgia
- Euro-Asiatic Federation of the Unions of Evangelical Christians-Baptists

GAW & ET

National Young Life Campaign (NYLC)
See *Youth for Christ*.

Nationalism
See *Nation/Nationalism*.

Natural Law
The concept of natural law for Christian thinkers is derived from the *theology* of *creation* as presented in the first two chapters in the letter to the Romans where Paul asserts that there is a reasonable foundation in creation for everybody to believe in God (Ro 1:20) and live righteous lives. Similar thoughts are also found in the OT (Job 11:7-10 and Ps 19:2-5). More than this Paul says that the requirements of the law are written in the hearts of *women* and *men* (Ro 2:14-15). When, however, they refused to acknowledge God in creation, he gave them over to unrighteous behaviour (Ro 1:28-32) which raises profound questions, if not about the nature of natural law, about human capacity to live by it. The concept of natural law also owes much to the philosophy of Aristotle, who in the 4th century BC thought that every object and every action had a final purpose [*telos*] which determined its 'good'. In the Middle Ages *theologians* derived from this principle the argument that nature manifests the purposes of the Creator who establishes an order in all things. The most famous exponent of natural law was Thomas Aquinas, who 'baptised' Aristotle's ideas to argue that the natural 'purpose' [*telos*] of the world is to be found in God.

The concept of natural law implies that the fingerprint of God in creation indicates how men and women ought to live their lives and indeed provides a standard by which even those unfamiliar with the Christian *scriptures* can be judged. Because of human intelligence and *free will*, *humankind* is able to distinguish the right from the wrong and can freely choose the ways of God, found in creation. This implies that we through natural law, by reason, can discern the will of God to a certain degree. The rule, then, which God has prescribed for our conduct, is, according to Natural Law, found in nature itself. Those actions which conform with its tendencies are constituted right and morally good, while those at variance with our nature are wrong and immoral. But here also a corporate perspective must be added. That which constitutes the best action for all nature is good while the action that only benefits a part of creation is not good. Here the command to rule over nature in a responsible way found in Ge 1:26 [see *Stewardship*] functions as a backcloth.

Natural Law, most developed by *Roman Catholic* thinkers, thus assumes an optimistic *anthropology* with all people able to distinguish good from evil by use of reason.

Protestant theologians have by contrast been much less hopeful about the moral capacity of humankind rather seeing **sin** as compromising reason so that it can no longer be relied upon as a moral steer, for which humanity is dependent on God's gracious **revelation** of requirement and obligation. Thus the dominance of Natural Law in the life of the undivided church was seriously challenged at the time of the **Reformation** by the reformers, who did not altogether dismiss the value of human reason, recognising the usefulness of reason in discerning the good in everyday human experience, but argued that human defection consequent upon human sin, meant that reason needed revelation to arrive at a true perception of the nature of human reality, thereby undermining the whole edifice of natural law as existing at the end of the Middle Ages. More recently secular thinkers influenced by either positivist or existential philosophy have denied the idea of an immutable human nature, thereby undercutting the existence of a universal natural law entailed therein, a judgement confirmed by **sociologists** and **anthropologists** who deny the existence of such universals. But there is a danger in all this which can be focused in the question: Is there then no common ground between Christians and non-Christians on which there can be agreement as to what constitutes the human good and what forces and conditions challenge the foundations of human society – e.g. on such issues as the deployment of **violence** within and between **nations**, the freedom of all peoples regardless of ethnicity, colour, **education**, the eradication of poverty, the abuse of women and **children**, and tackling the causes and consequences of the **ecological** crisis? Thus the search for what J.H. Oldham called 'middle axioms' on which Christians and non-Christians could agree as representing some agreement as to what are desirable goods and what avoidable evils, even though no longer claiming that these derive from some universal and unchangeable natural law. Maybe such conversations should be seen more in terms of a **dialogue** between the **church** and the world in which both sides mutually give and receive, the church interrogating and being interrogated by scientific achievement, human culture, and other living **faiths**, the church offering but not imposing its vision of what is meant by true humanity, measured by the exemplar provided by the incarnate **Christ** [see **Incarnation**], and informed by revealed truth as much as reason.

KTB

FURTHER READING: J.N.D. Anderson, *Morality, Law and Grace*, InterVarsity, Leicester, 1972. M. Cromartie, *A Preserving Grace: Protestants, Catholics and Natural Law*, Eerdmans, Grand Rapids, Mi., 1998. B. Mitchell, *Law, Morality and Religion in a Secular Society*, Oxford University Press, London, 1967. O. O'Donovan, *Resurrection and Moral Order: An Outline for Evangelical Ethics*, InterVarsity, Leicester, 1986. H. Thielicke, *Theological Ethics*, Eerdmans, Grand Rapids, Mi., 1979. T.F. Torrance, *Theological Science*, Oxford University Press, Oxford, 1969. D.F. Wright (ed), *Essays in Evangelical Social Ethics*, Paternoster, Exeter, 1978.

Natural Theology

[See also **Theology**]

Natural theology (as distinct from a theology of nature) is the belief that it is possible to construct theology from God's general **revelation** in nature and humanity without appealing to God's revelation in **Christ** or to the **scriptures**. General revelation and natural theology have always been used in Christian theology but the degree to which the knowledge of God through natural theology is accepted varies. In general the accepted role for natural theology is seen as being an introductory stage which comes prior to the work of a more developed theology.

Natural theology is based on the understanding that humanity is endowed with qualities that enable **humankind** to know God and therefore that arguments for the existence of God can be developed with the help of reason. Such arguments have been developed throughout the history of the **church**. E.g. the ontological argument attempts to prove the logical necessity of God's existence by reason (Anselm developed it in his *Proslogion*). Another argument is the cosmological one which argues for the existence of God as the first cause of the world as we know it. (Thomas Aquinas used this Aristotelian argument in his *Summa Theologica*). The teleological (from Greek telos – 'end') argument (also used by Aquinas) points to the existence of purpose in nature as a demonstration of God's existence. Lastly, the moral argument takes note of the shared beliefs and recognised moral values that people have in various cultures and considers these as evidence of the existence of a transcendent dimension of reality ultimately grounded in God. Natural theology is used more in *Catholic* than *Protestant* theology. Whilst general revelation is not denied by Protestants they emphasise that the knowledge of God that is certain is only possible through revelation.

In the 20th century Karl Barth launched a radical attack on natural theology which he saw as challenging the exclusive role of Christ as God's revelation. The well known disagreement between Barth and Brunner on the issue of natural theology determined the split between them. Brunner was arguing for the necessity of a 'point of contact' for humankind to be able to understand God but Barth defended his rejection in a vigorous if somewhat unfair manner (as far as Brunner's position was concerned). In his later theology Barth was willing to acknowledge the possibility of a role for general revelation although he was always suspicious of natural theology.

In modern Protestant theology a new form of natural theology is process theology which is inspired mainly by the ideas of A.N. Whitehead. Although process theology finds it challenging to express the transcendence of God in a manner entirely consistent with traditional theological approaches, it does attempt to explain how God is intrinsically involved in transforming the world.

Although it is difficult to harmonise the claims of natural theology with those of revelation, an adequate understanding of general revelation is useful as a bridge building tool between theology and *science*. This *apologetic* use of general revelation does not have to be expressed as a theology in which God's revelation in Christ and through the scriptures is replaced.

OB

NCA
See *Norwegian Church Aid*.

Neo-Orthodoxy
[See also *Orthodoxy, Orthopraxy, Orthohexy, Orthopyre*]
The title is used to describe the 20th century theological developments associated with European *theologians* such as Karl Barth and Emil Brunner who reacted strongly against the *liberal protestantism* of the 19th century and especially against the fact that it made the human experience of God the starting point of theological reflection. Instead, they proposed that *theology* starts with God's *transcendence* and his self-*revelation* in *Jesus Christ*, the *incarnate* Word of God. Influenced by Kierkegaard and Dostoyevsky, Karl Barth, was not persuaded by liberal confidence in human progress. Rather, seeing Europe after WWI caught in a deep sense of crisis, he was convinced that humanity's only *hope* had to be a source of power and *authority* outside human culture and experience. Accordingly, he argued for the otherness of God who reveals himself to humanity in Jesus Christ. This understanding led him both to a new approach to theology and to a new way of engaging with contemporary social issues.

Neo-orthodoxy developed along several different lines and the theological positions held by those associated with this approach remained diverse. Its various contributors disagreed on many issues. Neo-orthodoxy is orthodox in the sense that it attempts to recover the main themes of *Reformed* theology but it does this by taking into account modern theological developments.

Barth's radical emphasis on God's self-revelation in Christ led to his rejection of *natural theology*. He saw natural theology at work in the traditional approach in theology (mainly *Catholic*) but he also identified it as being embodied in other forms, such as liberal theology, German National Socialism and Western *capitalism*. Barth's well known disagreement with Brunner on the possibility of general revelation and natural theology led to an eventual parting of the ways between them. In his later theological contributions Barth was willing to allow a place for general revelation as long as this was not in any way made a substitute for God's revelation in Christ.

Barth understood the Christian life in terms of obedience to Christ and this determined him to be a champion against the abuses of the Nazis. He was among the few German theologians who had the courage to take a stand as part of the Confessing Church, playing a major part in drafting the Barmen Declaration of 1934 which proclaimed Jesus Christ as the ultimate authority over and against the existing *political* authorities in Nazi Germany.

The central point given to the revelation of God in his incarnate Word was combined by neo-orthodox *theologians* with an understanding of the scriptures as a *witness* to this Word. Although this represents a high view of the scriptures, some *Evangelicals* criticised this understanding because they felt that it did not emphasise strongly enough the 'intrinsic' authority of the *Bible*. The focus of the criticism was against the expression that scripture 'became' the Word of God. However, Barth considered that the authority of Jesus Christ as the incarnate Word of God is that which gives strength and authority to the written Word of God, which points to Christ. *Preaching*, as it bears witness to Christ, can also be the Word of God. The 'becoming' is to be understood in a Kierkegaardian sense that the Bible receives authority in a person's life when that person hears it and obeys it as the Word of God bearing witness to Jesus Christ. It was thus typical of Barth's neo-orthodoxy that he valued his endeavours in the *pulpit* as more significantly 'doing' theology than all his work in the study. In like vein he saw *prayer*, 'talking to God' rather than 'talking about God', as another essential aspect of doing theology.

One of the issues relevant to a Baptist perspective of the Christian *faith* but of lesser importance in neo-orthodoxy itself is Karl Barth's rejection of *infant baptism*, a position which challenged the theology behind the practice of the *sacrament* in most Churches. Emil Brunner also conceded that it was difficult to know what the *apostles* would have made of the practice of infant baptism.

OB

Neo-Pentecostal Movement
See *Charismatic Movement*.

Netherlands, Baptist history in

On 15 May 1845, seven people were baptised by immersion [see *Baptism*] in the Gasselternijveen Canal, in the northern part of the Netherlands, leading to the formation of the first 'Church of Baptised Christians', with Johannes Feisser as its *pastor*. Feisser, a *reformed* minister, had been dismissed on 1 Jan 1844, because, having come to the conviction that a church should be a gathering of *visible saints*, he stopped those who were not able to offer personal testimony to being born again from taking *communion* whilst also refusing to baptise *children* [see *Infant Baptism*]. *Johan Gerhard Oncken* from Hamburg heard about Feisser, and sent Köbner to talk with him, and it was Köbner who baptised these seven Christians in 1845.

Feisser was and remained a *Calvinist* who concentrated totally on the formation of 'a true church of true believers' without overt commitment to *evangelism*. When he died in 1865, Baptists were still a small and isolated group. This changed through the work of *evangelists* from the Evangelists School of Jan de Liefde, a former *Mennonite* minister, who had been in contact with Feisser and Köbner, but considered their 'Strict Baptist principle' of closed *membership* and closed communion, *sectarian*. For De Liefde, evangelism and the *salvation* of souls was of more importance than the formation of true churches. Many of the evangelists he trained worked in or around Baptist churches, or their converts [see *Conversion*] formed Baptist churches later, whilst some of the Free Evangelical Churches which they founded, later became Baptist Churches. The combination of their *revivalist preaching* and the formation of Baptist churches by others, gave the Baptist movement in the Netherlands an impulse that led to its *growth* in numbers, but with a more *Arminian* emphasis in *theology*. In 1881 a *union* of seven churches was formed at Foxhol which by the time of its 25th anniversary, in 1906, had 15 member churches. By 2008 the Union was composed of 85 member churches, with 12,000 members, two of which are Ghanese-English-speaking churches in Amsterdam.

Professor Olof H. de Vries divides the Union's 127 year history into four periods. The period 1881-1910 was that of 'one united front against the enemy of the *state churches* which only made rather nominal demands of its members. Baptists found their identity in what they were *not*. For them the established church was dead *tradition*, *dogmatism* and non-freedom; it was a threat to living *faith* and to the preaching of the gospel. Infant baptism represented this dead tradition at its worst.

The period 1910-63 was one of emancipation. A growing self-awareness manifested itself in the Union producing its own *hymnal*, sponsoring radio broadcasts, distributing a monthly evangelisation *magazine* and the inauguration of organisations like the Fellowship of Baptist Ministers (1923), the Dutch Baptist Youth Movement (1925) and the Dutch Baptist Women Movement (1929), all within the wider fellowship of the Union. After WWII, in which Dutch Baptists suffered considerably, they sought *ecumenical* relations, which had previously been denied them. In 1948 they became a member of the newly-founded *World Council of Churches*. In 1958 the Union started its own Seminary [see *Netherlands Baptist Seminary*]. In 1963 the Union, after much discussion, withdrew from the WCC, because its theology was thought too *liberal* and some of its programmes too *political*, whilst it was thought not right for the Union to commit *autonomous* individual congregations to such an organisation: how could anybody represent them all in an ecumenical body?

The third period, 1963-90, was a time of growing theological self-awareness but accompanying polarisation. In 1976 the Baptist Seminary started working more closely with the University of Utrecht, with more and more Baptist *students* studying at both the Seminary and the University. In the 80s a group of *evangelical-fundamentalist* ministers took objection to what they saw as – the liberal theology taught at the University and at the Seminary. In 1986-87 two of the three teachers left the Seminary.

The last period, 1990-2008, can be called a period of dominant evangelicalism. In a short time most of the Baptist Churches changed their *worship* style from the 'sandwich-model' into 'Global Praise and Worship', became engaged in Church Development programmes from *Willow Creek* and *Purpose Driven*, started *Alpha*-courses, whilst more and more young people felt attracted

to evangelical activities. In 2002 the Union started a pilot scheme with paid staff workers to implement the Natural Church Development programme from Christian Schwarz in different churches. Later they also used the *Purpose Driven* programme. Since 2007 the Church Development workers as well as the Seminary have followed the *Healthy Churches Programme* of Robert Warren.

In 2002 after years of discussion a far reaching reorganisation of the Union was implemented. Five task forces were formed: Church Development and Evangelism, Theological Formation, Mission and Social Work, *Youth Work* and *Women's Work*. In 2005 the staff and board proposed three spearheads with regard to the forthcoming 5-10 years concerning the whole Union, which the *Assembly* of that year agreed to: Church Development, Mutual Solidarity and *Church Planting*. Utrecht and Amersfoort were the first cities identified for a church plant. In the summer of 2008 'De Vinkenhof', an old building bought in 1958, in which the Seminary and the Union Office were located, was sold; a new building in Barneveld in the middle of the country, is now being rented.

TvdL

Netherlands Baptist Seminary

From its beginning in 1881, what was then called the 'Union of Baptised Christians' was anxious to have its own school to educate *men* for the *ministry*. Many plans were made and several leaders talked about their visions, but lack of money meant that these remained unfulfilled. An activist for the establishment of a seminary combining both theoretical study and practical work was J. Louw (1889-1969) who motivated the *Union* to think about the *education* of its *ministers*, underlining that 'ministers should know more than their *church members* with a good academic profile in order to take their place in society' (1915). Louw was very conscious of how few the Dutch Baptists were, but believed that good *pastoral* education would force other people to take them more seriously. Hitherto, most candidates for ministry studied either at the Hamburg Seminary or at *Spurgeon's College* in London. Whilst the Dutch Union was grateful for this, they remained hopeful that they could start their own seminary as had happened in *Sweden* (Stockholm) and *Denmark* (Töllöse). The ideal was for every local Baptist Church to have an academically-educated minister.

After WWII an experiment in 'seminary' work was begun: seven *students* living together in a house in Utrecht, each being educated by an experienced minister such as K. Reiling, J. Louw, D. Slort and G. Tijman. However, lack of money and skilled teachers brought this experiment to a halt in 1950. From that time on, students were able to study at the international seminary in *Rüschlikon, Switzerland*, which started in 1949. Nevertheless, founders of Rüschlikon, like Dr. E.A. Bell and Dr. J. Nordenhaug, pushed ahead with plans to establish a seminary in the Netherlands as well, and even raised a gift of $25,000 from the *Southern Baptist Convention* for this purpose.

On 23 Feb 1957 the Union bought a large residence at Bosch en Duin (near Utrecht), called 'De Vinkenhof', where students could study and live together. The 6,000 Dutch Baptists were excited by this. They now had their own position among the *Protestant* and *Pentecostal* churches in the *Netherlands*. The acquisition of their own seminary was seen as a moment of emancipation for the Netherlands Baptists. They felt that now they should be taken seriously! At the same time the Dutch Union built churches and developed activities with regard to *mission* and *evangelism*. It was a time of expansion.

Jan J. Kiwiet (1925-2006) and Jannes Reiling (1923-2005) were the first teachers. In his opening speech in Sep 1958, Reiling, who became the first rector, dreamed of a 'scientific *Bible* school'. From the beginning theoretical study and practice were combined. Five students started in 1958 (G. van 't Wout, A. H. Agtereek, Th. Pothof, C. de Jong and H. Dekker), with seven more added the following year. They all lived in 'The Vinkenhof' and formed a community *worshipping* together morning and evening. The first two students graduated in 1962, the year in which Jan J. Kiwiet left to go to Bethel College in St. Paul, Minnesota, USA, as a teacher of philosophy. Later he would teach church history and *systematic theology* at the Northern Seminary in Chicago, Illinois and at Southwestern Seminary in Forth Worth, Texas.

All lectures were given at 'De Vinkenhof', until 1970, mostly by Jannes Reiling, assisted by G. Vegter, J. Louw, K. Reiling and D. Slort. Jannes Reiling became lecturer in NT at Utrecht University in 1967 and stimulated cooperation between the University and the Seminary. Students could now study *theology* at the University and specific Baptist subjects such as systematic and practical theology, and the theology and history of the Baptists at the Seminary. The relationship with the University developed very positively and in 1973 a Special Professorship in 'Baptist History and Doctrine' was inaugurated with Reiling the first holder. Baptist and other students at the University could apply to take the specially-identified Baptist courses. The emancipation of the Baptists was finally a reality!

In *ministerial formation* at the seminary, more attention was given to practical theology and in 1977 Theo van der Laan (1935-2007) was appointed to direct this, placing the emphasis on Pastoral Education. In 1981 a third teacher started, Olof H. de Vries (b1941), a graduate of the Seminary who had done his Ph.D. at the University on 'Teaching and Institutions of the Early *Anabaptists*, Interpreted as a Theology of History'. In 1994, he succeeded Reiling as Special Professor at the University.

But not everything was successful. At a time of polarisation in Dutch Society – over matters concerning *peace* and war and secularisation – in 1993 a critical group of ministers initiated discussions about the theology of the Seminary, which they deemed too *liberal* in *hermeneutics* and *ethics*. They also disagreed with *women* studying at the Seminary, the first of whom was Hetty Lalleman-de Winkel in 1976 who now teaches OT at Spurgeon's College. These discussions led to the departure of Theo van der Laan in 1986 and Jannes Reiling in 1987, with Olof H. de Vries becoming the new rector.

In 1988 Yme Horjus (b1950), who had served as a minister in several Baptist churches became lecturer in practical theology. He introduced Church Development into the curriculum, and increased the link with *local churches*. Horjus succeeded De Vries as rector in 1993, though De Vries continued teaching. In 2000 Horjus ended his career at the Seminary, returning to the local pastorate. He was succeeded in 2002 by René Erwich (b1964), then teaching at the International Baptist Theological Seminary in Prague, but he only stayed for three years, leaving to become director of the Evangelical Theological College in Ede. Under the leadership of interim rector, Joop Brongers, a new vision was devised, which emphasised more networking with other colleges and universities. Brongers was one of the initiators of the Centre for Evangelical and *Reformation* Theology (CERT) at the Free University of Amsterdam, which began to offer masters studies in evangelical theology in 2004. In 2006 a new team of teachers was appointed: Henk Bakker (b1960), Eduard Groen (b1959), Wout Huizing (b1957) and Teun van der Leer (b1959), and in 2007 the Union appointed Teun Van der Leer the new rector. Olof H.deVries retired in 2008, after 27 years of teaching. Since 2006 the number of students has doubled from 20 to 40. The Seminary offers three levels of training: masters level (from 1976-2008 in cooperation with Utrecht University and, beginning in 2009, in cooperation with the Free University in Amsterdam), bachelors level (mainly in cooperation with the Evangelical Theological College in Ede) and a part-time course for 'later *callings*'. Networks are increasing with among others: the Church of the Nazarene, the independent Baptist Churches and the Pentecostal Azusa College.

WH

New Age Movement

Often, and best, described as a network, the New Age Movement (NAM) developed in its current form out of the counter-cultural movements of the 1960s. Its adherents, however, trace the movement's history back much further. Various Eastern religious and *mystical traditions*, such as forms of Hinduism and Buddhism, are frequently drawn on, and key figures in the past few centuries include the Swedish writer, Emanuel Swedenborg (1688-1772), the Austrian psychologist, Franz Anton Mesmer (1734-1815), and the founder of Theosophy, Helena Petrovna Blavatsky (1831-91). Because of its structure, it is impossible to say how many people belong to the NAM, but it has a notable presence in the US and many European countries. Several features are common to most of those aligned to the NAM. They tend to be *universalist* in a variety of ways, positing one religion (although expressed in different forms), and some sort of overriding and unifying power or energy, which can be equivalent to a concept of God, though commonly a pantheist one. Typically there is a belief in some form of reincarnation, rewarding or punishing current behaviour by progress or regress. Often gurus or spiritual guides, however styled, are important, though in general these are to help in personal rather than communal growth. The unifying tendencies are found at work also in the emphasis on holistic medicine, with a preference for homeopathic remedies and more 'natural' diets. The centrality of the unifying force leads many NAM participants to have an interest in astrology and other forms of reading the present and future, and in types of occultism. Of considerable importance for many in the NAM are various stones, especially crystals, which are related both to prediction and to *healing*. Some sites are also held to be of special significance, either because of communities which are established there (e.g. Findhorn in *Scotland*) or because of historical associations (e.g. Glastonbury in the southwest of *England*). *Fundamentalist* Christian groups have seen the NAM as expressive of demonic possession, but other Christians have recognised in the NAM a spiritual longing which can serve as a starting place for *mission*.

TFTN

FURTHER READING: John P. Newport, *The New Age movement and the biblical worldview: conflict and dialogue*, Eerdmans, Grand Rapids, Mi., 1998. Michael York, *Historical Dictionary of New Age Movements*, The Scarecrow Press, Lanham, Maryland and Oxford, 2004.

New Birth

[See also *Conversion; Regeneration*]

For the *theology* of 'New Birth', or 'being Born Again'/'Born from Above', which all bespeak a radical new beginning when somebody becomes a Christian, reference should be made to the entry on *regeneration*. The language, which derives from Jn 3 and the conversation between Jesus and Nicodemus, is instructive because just as an individual is not involved in his/her own physical birth, so neither do they command the process of their spiritual birth, which is all of the work of God's **Spirit**. The moment of new birth is powerfully set forth in **baptism** by immersion, since water is an element in which people cannot naturally live. Accordingly, whilst putting the old life to **death** in a watery Jordan, candidates emerge from the baptismal **pool**, born into new life of **Christ**'s **resurrection**. Thus Tit 3:5 speaks of **salvation** 'through the water of rebirth and the renewing power of the new birth', whilst elsewhere in 1Jn and 1Pe (1:3) the language of becoming 'the children of God' or indeed 'being begotten of God' implies the same process of new birth, replete with the ethical obligations of living a godly and Christ-like life as befits those born by God's spirit to a new life [see **Ethics**]. Birth also implies healthy development towards maturity, for stunted or unbalanced growth is not part of God's intention for his new creation.

ET

New Covenant, The

[See also **Covenant, Theology of; Creeds, Covenants and Confessions of Faith**]

The same word which is translated 'Covenant' is also translated as 'Testament' as in the OT and NT, indicating the two different phases in God's dealing with **humankind**. The concept of Covenant [Hebrew *Berith*] is of fundamental importance in Christian **theology**. It must not be confused with a 'contract', the terms of which can be negotiated by each of the contracting parties. By contrast, a Covenant is all of God's **grace**: it is he who chooses his people and offers them a special relationship. The terms of its several parts cannot be negotiated rather the human response must be simply to accept, to live within both its grace and its demands, for whilst the covenant is unilateral in establishment it involves mutual commitment. Whilst God offers faithfulness, he seeks of his people obedience and loyalty. Thus the OT records a series of failed divine initiatives – that is God reaches out to a succession of Hebrew patriarchs – Adam, Noah, Abram, and Moses, and later David, but successive generations of the **Jewish** people fail to live up to the demands placed upon them by

these covenants. Pledges of loyalty and faithfulness are made, the pattern of righteous living is spelt out, but the human side of the agreement is all too soon broken, so that the need for a more radical initiative becomes all too obvious.

Thus the need for the new covenant, a covenant which **Jesus** seals with his own blood as signified by Christ himself when he describes the cup at the Last Supper as 'the new covenant sealed by my blood', that is to say he affirms the **cross** as an all-sufficient sacrifice for **sin**, though clearly the cross must here be seen in the context of the **resurrection** and the gift of the **Spirit**, all of which distinguishes the New Covenant from the Old. In the new Covenant instituted by Christ's sacrifice 'made once for all upon the cross', the believer is assured of the forgiveness of sins, and full and total **restoration** of relationships with our **heavenly** Father. It is significant that it is the same word which is translated as 'Testament' in the OT and NT, for it is the **incarnation**, **death** and resurrection of Jesus that ushers in the New Covenant with both its requirements to follow Jesus, and the power, provided by the sacrifice of Jesus and the gift of the Spirit, to fulfil them.

In this way the new covenant, no longer ethnically defined but open to those of any race who repent and believe, displaces the old. Because it is argued that the new covenant cannot provide less than the old, and because the old covenant embraced all members of a Jewish family, the **children** of believers also belong within covenant grace, and hence the development in the 16th and 17th centuries of what is often called federal theology. This would be agreed by Baptists but they deny the next stage of the argument, as taught by **Zwingli** against the **Anabaptists**, that this meant that **baptism**, as a sign of the new covenant, as circumcision was a sign of the old, should be administered to infants [see **Infant Baptism**].

The rediscovery of Covenant at the time of the **Reformation** was largely the work of **Calvin** and those in the **reformed tradition**, though Anabaptists in many traditions also placed emphasis upon it. Calvin clearly saw the need for a covenant of grace to replace the violated covenant of works as witnessed by the record of the OT, so that covenant became a principal emphasis of those English **puritans** out of whose life the Baptist movement was most immediately born [see **England**].

JHYB

New Monastic Communities
See **Intentional Communities**.

New Religious Movements
'New Religious Movement' (NRM) has become the most common term for discussing groups who cannot easily be classified under existing religious divisions. However, the phrase NRM is itself disputed. In seeking to avoid the use of words such as 'cult' or **'sect'**, because of their perceived negative connotations, NRM has been accused of inaccuracy on three counts: many of the groups thus called deny they are new, some deny they are religions, and others that they are movements. Nevertheless, it has offered the greatest objectivity for social scientists and remains the preferred term. It is hard to determine the number of NRMs and their membership. There are undoubtedly many (estimates of up to 1,000 in the USA alone), but most are small. By contrast others such as the Unification church (Moonies) and the Church of Scientology can have an extensive following. Whilst some may embrace a distorted form of the Christian **tradition** others find their origins in the various religions of Asia, or aspects of popular 'psychology' as e.g. Hare Krishna and Transcendental Meditation.

The sheer number of NRMs makes attempts at typology or classification difficult. Perhaps it is better to ask how a given NRM relates to society, how a social setting aids or hinders its establishment, and what factors will provide for its growth or decline. The increase in NRMs since the 1960s has been variously understood as a response to or a consequence of **secularisation**. Although the reasons for people joining them undoubtedly differ, important features are their stress on experience, on the inner spiritual dimension of life, and on knowing over believing. Many display marked millenarian tendencies, and offer strong communal experiences.

Charismatic leaders are common in NRMs. This can in extreme cases have tragic consequences (e.g. the mass **deaths** in Jonestown, USA). Other groups manage to survive the death or disgrace of their founder and continue to flourish. Belief systems frequently draw on existing sources, though often eclectically. Many claim to offer some form of elite or secret knowledge to adherents. There is no empirical evidence of widespread 'brainwashing', though some NRMs have used deception to gain members. The very high drop-out rate among NRM members is evidence that most NRMs do not hold a strong pull on those who join them. Nevertheless, a very small number have also been responsible for **violence**, usually self-inflicted. This, though, is the exception. Christian responses have ranged from outright blanket condemnation to attempts to understand and engage with members of NRMs in a **contextual** manner. However, although the study of NRMs has grown exponentially since the 1970s, church responses have taken longer and only recently have they become more nuanced, providing more understanding, making it easier to offer both pastoral responses and tools for **mission** and **evangelism**.

NRMs should be sharply distinguished from what have sometimes been called 'New Church Movements' which do not diverge from orthodox Christian doctrine [see **Restorationism/House Church movement**].

TFTN

FURTHER READING: Peter B. Clarke (ed), *Encyclopedia of new religious movements*, Routledge Curzon, New York, 2006. Irving Hexham, Stephen Rost and John W. Morehead II (eds), *Encountering New Religious Movements: A Holistic Evangelical Approach*, Kregel, Grand Rapids, Mi., 2004.

New Years Eve
See **Watchnight**.

Next Step Ministries
See **One Step Forward**.

NGOs
See **Non-Governmental Organisations**.

Niebuhr, Helmut Richard (1894-1962) – Sociology of the Church

See *Sociology of the Church – Troeltsch and Niebuhr*.

Non-Governmental Organisations (NGOs)

NGOs are associations, or *vereins* of individuals who cooperate together to engage society on particular issues. The World Bank defines NGOs as 'private organisations that pursue activities to relieve *suffering*, promote the interests of the *poor*, protect the *environment*, provide basic social services, or undertake community development' (Operational Directive 14.70). In wider usage, the term NGO can be applied to any non-profit organisation which is independent from government. NGOs.are typically value-based organisations which depend, in whole or in part, on charitable donations and voluntary service. Although the NGO sector has become increasingly professionalised over the last two decades, principles of altruism and voluntarism remain key defining characteristics. There are many such organisations in most countries in Europe. Governments establish principles by which such not-for-profit generally beneficial organisations can be created and operate within civil society. NGOs often have certain tax privileges – an the ability to receive tax advantageous donations from their supporters.

Baptists have formed many such organisations or are active participants in them. They quite often relate to the diaconal *ministries* of the church or to campaigning and direct action on behalf of the two-thirds world or environmental issues.

The legal status of such NGOs varies from country to country. Despite calls from many people the **European Union** has not established a common policy or created the legal infrastructure by which an NGO can exist as a legal entity across Europe. It is generally considered the most liberal legal regime for NGOs exists in the Swiss law on vereins. The **EBF**, **EBM** and **IBTS** have their legal bases in **Switzerland** for this very reason. Other countries have more restrictive laws. For instance, the status of NGOs in **Great Britain** involves strict rules about the avoidance of *political* campaigning for a category of NGO known as charities which also have to demonstrate that they offer a public good not restricted to any class or group of peoples. This can lead to conflict with the Government. E.g. the aid and development agency of the British churches, **Christian Aid**, has at times been subject to investigation by the UK Government Charity Commission as a result of campaigning on behalf of the poor of Africa.

PV & KGJ

Nonconformist Conscience

The nonconformist conscience describes the attitude adopted by nonconformists, in the **United Kingdom**, that is those who belonged to the **Free Churches**, in whose life Baptists played a major part, to moral issues. Its origins lie in joining the great *Evangelical* campaigns e.g. against the slave trade, slavery both in the British Empire and the southern states of the USA, as also in their campaign to rid themselves of a number of civil disabilities. As they grew both in numbers and in *wealth* they aspired to playing a larger part in the government of the *nation*, and to this end allied themselves with the Liberal Party which embraced Laissez-Faire and Self-Help principles of a minimum of *state* intervention in social affairs, which easily allied with their ideas of the *separation of church and state*. This determined their early *political* strategies: thus early concerns for *temperance* led to educational rather than legislative programmes. Partly, but not exclusively, because of the impact of the *missionary* movement the Conscience engaged with a series of issues relating to imperial affairs, but missionary bureaucracies were often reluctant to get involved with 'political issues', though very often missionaries saw such issues as matters of simple justice for their congregations.

A crisis of conscience rose when their ambitions seemed to require an extension rather than a retraction of state activity. This was clearly seen when temperance enthusiasts in the UK Alliance turned from educational to interventionist devices – to make the nation sober by legislation. Closely related to temperance was the issue of *gambling* and horse-racing which tended to lead to Nonconformists being cast in the role of 'kill-joys'. But other problems threw up similar challenges some earlier, some later. So factory reform came early – and not always initially with nonconformist support – and housing reform late. But it was the sexual debasement of the people living beside the Thames that gave *The Bitter Cry of Outcast London* special piquancy, and put the issue of urban dwellings on the church's agenda. Accordingly many saw the need to move beyond the ambulance work of philanthropy into the political world of trying to prevent destitution and deprivation, seeking a radical structural change within society. A slightly different axis is the movement from a *conscience* which was *against* certain situations to a conscience which positively promoted working-class welfare.

A major issue was the passing of the Contagious Diseases Acts (1864-69) which raised issues of gender inequality as well as appearing to provide legal support for military men's need for 'clean' prostitutes. The argument ran that if the government could legislate to support depravity legislation might also be the instrument of moral reform The social purity issue was also pursued by W.T. Stead with his articles on 'The Maiden Tribute of Modern Babylon' on juvenile *prostitution*, the data for which was collected by Stead in liaison with a *Salvation Army* officer.

This led on more particularly to the issue of the sexual morality of politicians, as in the case of the divorce of Sir Charles Dilke, who was ostracised by the Nonconformist Conscience for some 20 years: 'There is no political object, however much desired that can compare with the maintenance of family life and NT morality' (Robertson Nicholl). More famously this issue was to arise when Parnell the leader of the Irish Party was cited in Nov 1890 in a divorce case. This provoked both renewed nonconformist commitment to *Ireland*, with its proper aspirations to Home Rule, but affirming Hugh Price Hughes' defining words, 'we stand immovably on this eternal rock; what is morally wrong can never be politically right'. It was in this context that the phrase 'the nonconformist conscience' was coined by *The Times*. In fact the language of 'the Nonconformist Conscience' was developed at a time when the phenomenon, already several generations old, was nearing the end of the period of its greatest effectiveness.

After 1900 a Liberal Party in office found itself either unwilling or unable to reward its nonconformist allies, whose policies did not appeal to the wider franchise of the period. On the other side of the equation, the Liberal Party was no longer the automatic choice of its nonconformist partners. And a nonconformity which spread its patronage across all three main parties made it difficult for political issues to be championed in dissenting fora, whilst its voting strength so spread was no longer a bidder for effective power. The hope of nonconformists exercising a decisive influence in British politics had proved elusive.

Similar concerns occupied the commitment of Baptists in other European countries though to be effective in political action required concentrated numbers and a democratic system [see *Democracy*] within which to work.

JHYB

Non-residential Bible School, Lithuania

The Non-residential Bible School (NEBIM – in Lithuanian) was officially started in 2003 and offers two tracks: the Diploma Programme and the Seminar Track. The Diploma Programme requires a three-year commitment of active engagement in seminars, individual tutoring, practical assignments, written assignments, independent study and writing, all of which are assessed. The programme consists of four modules: Biblical Studies, Church History, *Theology*, and Church Ministries. Some of the Diploma Programme courses are offered as open seminars that are available to all interested. These seminars, called the Seminar Track, complement the vision of a pattern of the continuing theological *education*, which is also embodied through extended weekend visits of the core faculty to *local churches* to follow up the themes covered in the seminars. The *students* are not required to have any prior theological education but are expected to be actively involved in the *ministry* in their church. NEBIM partners with

IBTS and *Northern Baptist College, Manchester* in delivering a quality theological education accessible to all Baptists in *Lithuania*.

LA

Non-Violence
See *Violence/Non-Violence*.

North Wales Baptist College
See *Bangor Baptist College*.

Northern Baptist College, Manchester
Northern Baptist College was established in 1964 as a result of the amalgamation of Rawdon College (founded in 1804) and Manchester College (1866). Rawdon was founded in 1804 near Bradford, Yorkshire as the Northern Education Society, one of the many societies arising out of the *Evangelical Revival*, seeking to train *men* for effective evangelical *ministry* by both class work and practical training whilst itinerating in the neighbourhood. Manchester College was founded in 1866 to serve the *closed communion* churches in North-West *England*, with the *students* initially living in the community to avoid 'the disadvantages of the Monkish system' of residence , moving to Manchester in 1873, when it became a fully residential college. Northern Baptist College is part of the Northern Federation for Training in *Ministry*, based at Luther King House in Manchester, and works closely with its *ecumenical* partners to provide training for ministers and lay people [see *Laity*] within the Baptist denomination. Ministerial training, leading to accreditation by the Baptist *Union* of *Great Britain*, is provided on a full-time and part-time basis. Some receive training as 'student-ministers' and are based in *local churches* throughout their course. This pattern of training was pioneered by the college in the 1970s. The Federation has developed its own 'Faith in Living' courses in *contextual theology* to degree level, and also provides opportunities to pursue research degrees. These are validated by the University of Manchester. Through its Community Learning Network, the college acts as a regional training resource for churches throughout the north of England.

PS

Northern Ireland, Baptist history in
See *Ireland, Baptist history in*.

Northumbria Community, England
See *Intentional Communities*.

Norway, Baptist history in
In 1837 a young Norwegian, Enoch Richerd Haftorsen Svee, went to Copenhagen, *Denmark* to prepare for foreign *mission* work. There he became a Baptist and founding member of the first Baptist church in Denmark. In 1842 he returned to Norway supported by American Baptists but he died the following year before establishing any Baptist work.

The founder of Baptist work in Norway was a former Danish sailor, Frederick Ludvig Rymker, who between 1857 and 62 established several Baptist churches. The first was the Baptist Church of Porsgrund and Solum (now Skien) established on 22 April 1860. During the following years, Baptist work spread to most parts of Norway with the help of the *BMS*. In 1872 Norwegian Baptists formed their first district *association*, and a Baptist *union* in 1879. In the beginning Norwegian Baptist were recruited from the working class: farmers, fishermen, tenants, industrial workers and the like. Today the majority of Baptists belong to the middle class. The Baptists of Norway have always had the benefit of a closely knit fellowship, without major divisions, although a few churches have left the Union to become *Pentecostal* or independent *charismatic* congregations.

After having had their *pastors* trained abroad, the Norwegian Baptists began a *theological* seminary in 1910 [see *Norway, Baptist Theological Seminary of*]. This has been the most important instrument not only for the professional training of ministers and *missionaries*, but also for building and promoting Baptist identity in the Union. The seminary is now an accredited institution for higher learning and offering degrees which are recognised by the *state*. It also cooperates with Swedish and Danish Baptists in *Scandinavian Academy for Leadership and Theology*.

In 1915 the Baptist Union formed its own foreign *mission* work, after having cooperated with the American Baptist Missionary Union since 1892. In 1918 Bernhard Aalbu went to Africa and in 1920 he opened a field in the Belgian Congo, now the Republic of Congo. Since around 1980 they also have undertaken mission work in Nepal, Thailand, Cameroon and most recently in Sierra Leone, the last two of which were as a partner in *EBM*.

In 1916 the Norwegian Baptist Women's Association was formed and in 1922 came the Norwegian Baptist Youth Association. The *women's* organisation has been active in collecting funds for mission work at home and abroad. The youth organisation has a strong emphasis on *evangelism* and youth training.

The first 25 years after the formation of the Union in 1879 Baptists enjoyed remarkable *growth* in a country which had a strong confessional *Lutheran state church*. During this period they cooperated closely first with BMS and later with ABMU. A peak in membership came in 1948, with 7,436 baptised [see *Baptism*] *members* in Union churches, but since then the Baptist Union has declined by some 2,500 members. This negative trend seems to have stopped in recent years, mainly due to groups of *refugees* joining some churches, or establishing ethnic churches that have applied for membership of the Union. In 2007 there were Vietnamese, Burmese, Tamil, African and English-speaking member churches.

Norwegian Baptists have, both on a local and a national level, participated in *ecumenical* projects and organisations, often pioneering such initiatives. This applies to the *Free Church* Council, the Norwegian *Faith and Order* Forum and the *National Council of Churches*. Internationally they have been active in such Baptist organisations as *BWA*, *EBF* and EBM.

PAE

Norway, Baptist Theological Seminary of

Baptists in *Norway* secured their own theological seminary in 1910. Prior to that Norwegian Baptist *pastors* were trained in *Sweden* or the USA. For the first 50 years the seminary was located in the First Baptist Church, Oslo, and, from 1958, in its own buildings at Stabekk, 10km west of Oslo. Nearly all the pastors, *missionaries* and leaders in the Baptist *Union* of Norway have been trained at the Seminary, which has been of great importance for *unity* and cooperation among Norwegian Baptists. The school has from its beginning offered a four-year course with a good mix of practical training and theoretical studies.

In 2001 the Seminary received *state* accreditation for one year of basic theological training, and, in 2004, college accreditation. It can award a Bachelor's degree in *theology* after three years of study with three different options (*youth*, *pastoral* and theological ministry). Practical training is integrated with academic study during the whole period, with *students* working in a *local church*, having a mentor to supervise that part of the course. The Bachelor's degree is recognised by the Norwegian Department of *Education*, and the Seminary gets financial support from the Norwegian Government, which is helpful for the students. The Seminary is a member of the *Scandinavian Academy of Leadership and Theology*.

In 2008 the Seminary opened a new school for higher education in cooperation with the *Pentecostals* in Norway. In many ways it can be seen as a continuation of the afore-mentioned Bachelor's programme with the inclusion of new owners. The name of the school is the Norwegian School of Leadership and Theology and is also a member of SALT.

In the spring of 2009 there were 56 students (both full-time and part-time) enrolled in the school. Its main focus is to train pastors and leaders for ministry. The programme is open to all denominations, and we experience that both professionals as well as lay people [see *Laity*] find it useful for ministry. At the moment there is no programme specifically for missionaries, but many of the leadership courses, as well as the basic theological training, are also relevant to such people.

BTar & KTB

Norwegian Church Aid (NCA)

[See also *Emergency and Disaster Relief*]
The biggest church related relief development and emergency organisation in Norway, Norwegian Church Aid started as a response to the desperate needs in Central Europe following WWII. The National Association for Assistance from **Lutheran** Churches [*Menighetspleienes Landsforbund*] was formed in 1945. In 1947 the Association initiated a special program for aid to **Germany** and **Austria** in cooperation with The **World Council of Churches** and the Lutheran World Federation. This program was named '*Kirkens Nødhjelp*' [Norwegian Church Aid] which became the name of the organisation that was officially formed in 1953.

During the first years NCA concentrated on emergency assistance to areas struck by disasters. A major increase in the activities of NCA occurred in 1966 during the Biafra hunger catastrophe. An appeal for help was sent to the Norwegian population who responded promptly. Millions of Norwegian kroner were collected and 100s of planeloads of food and other commodities were dropped in this part of Nigeria. A few years after this, NCA initiated the most comprehensive development project ever implemented by a Norwegian organisation, in Southern Sudan. In 1971 assistance was given to the **suffering** people in Bangladesh in connection with the war that led to independence. Five years later NCA started work in Latin America in the wake of the earthquake in Guatemala.

The emergency operations made it clear for NCA that it was not enough to give assistance in a crisis situation, but that the people needed help to rebuild their life and to improve their living conditions. This insight has led to an increase in the number of development programmes wherever the organisation has operated.

During this process, NCA also became an *ecumenical* organisation, being the aid organisation for all Norwegian denominations, except for the **Catholic** Church that operates through Caritas. It has enjoyed distinguished service from Baptist personnel. Once a year a collection is made during **Lent** in all churches, and also a country-wide door-to-door collection , to raise money for the NCA activities all over the world. The annual budget of the NCA in 2000 was about $60 million. More than a quarter comes from churches and the Norwegian public; the rest is support from the Norwegian Government.

In recent years, NCA has also found it increasingly important to lobby in the international arena for the **poor** of the world, also campaigning for **human rights** and **peace**. The information activities, spreading knowledge and awareness about the living conditions of the many poor in this world, have also been a focal point for the organisation.

There has also been a shift in the mode of operation – moving away from being an implementing agency towards being a partner-oriented organisation. This means that the aim now is to strengthen local partners to do whatever is required.

NCA works in close cooperation with other aid agencies, both the main ecumenical organisations and others, like **Baptist World Aid**.

PMi

Novi Sad Baptist Theological School

Formal Baptist theological education in **Serbia** (formerly **Yugoslavia**) commenced in 1940 when the **SBC** Foreign **Mission** Board started a seminary in Belgrade with six **students**, but only six months later, in April 1941, it had to be closed because of the Axis invasion. A fresh attempt began in 1954, in Zagreb, **Croatia**, where the Baptist **Union** of Yugoslavia opened a two-year programme housed in a **church building**. In 1955 this school moved to Daruvar, Croatia, and in 1957 finally settled in Novi Sad, Serbia, where the school began a four-year programme, including **pastoral** and **missions** training as well as general subjects as would be taught in a secular secondary school. 81 students graduated from this programme, of which 27 were **women**. The first president of the school was Dr. Josip Horak (1954-55) followed by Adolf Lehotsky (1955-71),

Franjo Klem (1971-74), and Stjepan Orčic (1975-86).

In 1975, the programme was redeveloped, now focusing on *theology* but with a two-year junior college level programme, in addition to the programme previously offered. By 1987, 28 students had graduated, of whom 17 were at secondary-school level and 11 at a junior college level theological programme. During this period, the school also offered a *Theological Education by Extension* programme, which, after promising initial results, withered. Evidence for the period 1978-85, is provided by a student-body mimeographed bulletin *BTŠ*. In 1987, the secondary-level programme was closed. The school came to offer two-and-a-half-year long theological *education* programme, under the auspices of the biblical [see *Bible*] theological centre 'Logos', led by Želimir Srnec. During the 11 years of work before Logos' closure in 1997, 32 students studied and 8 graduated but more than half of those enrolled came from churches other than Baptist. Logos stopped further enrolments in 1997. At least 54 of the alumni from the period 1954-97 were involved in full-time local *mission* work, 46 as church workers, whilst at least 14 continued further theological studies elsewhere. In the same period, the school printed 114 titles, of which more than 35 were written by the local Baptists.

In 2000, the school reopened as Novi Sad Theological College, a Baptist school welcoming students from other denominations, under the leadership of Dr. Dimitrije Popadić (president) and Dr. Aleksandar Birviš (academic dean). In 2004, the enrolment was 212 students (25 full-time students, the remainder studying by extension) from 18 different Christian denominations. Approximately, half of the students were from Baptist churches. The College offers six BA programme tracks: Biblical Studies, *Pastoral* Studies, *Contextualisation* of the Gospel (*Evangelism* and Missions), Social Work (Church Based), Christian Counselling, and Communications. The College has a library with about 7,000 books. NSTC publishes annually the *Journal of Theology* [*Teološki časopis*] in Serbian.

BB

Nuclear Threat

The first atomic bomb was dropped by the USA on Hiroshima, Japan, on 6 Aug 1945. Three days later a further bomb was dropped on Nagasaki and Japan surrendered, ending WWII and heralding the beginning of the Nuclear Age.

During the 1940s and 50s, the US, *Russia* and *Britain* continued to develop and test atomic weapons which led to growing fears of nuclear war breaking out, especially against the backdrop of the *Cold War*, and also concern at the *environmental* damage caused by these tests. A mass movement for non-violent direct action, advocating unilateral nuclear *disarmament* developed across Europe. Building on the work of earlier anti-war movements, the Campaign for Nuclear Disarmament (CND) was launched in London in Feb 1958, followed at *Easter* that year by the first of many marches and vigils at the Atomic Weapons Establishment in Aldermaston. Initially, CND had a huge following from all sections of society, with many scientists along with religious leaders such as Canon John Collins of St. Paul's Cathedral. The Society of Friends (*Quakers*) had strong representation and most other Christian denominations, including Baptists, were involved. CND advocated a policy of unilateral nuclear disarmament. In 1981, the Christian Campaign for Nuclear Disarmament (CCND), supported by many British Baptists, was established as a distinct but affiliated part of CND to provide a Christian perspective on disarmament. Anti-nuclear groups, such as the Dutch Interchurch *Peace* Council (IKV), and similar groups in East and West *Germany*, also flourished across mainland Europe.

During the 1950s and 60s, the quest to halt the spread of nuclear weapons was the subject of national and international negotiations. In 1968 the nuclear Non-Proliferation Treaty was agreed and signed. Although, designed to stop the spread of nuclear weapons, it also called for those countries in possession of nuclear weapons to begin talks that would lead to total disarmament.

The initiatives of Mikhail Gorbachev, *USSR* president from 1985-91, of *glasnost* [openness] and *perestroika* [restructuring] in the late 80s led to the end of the Cold War and the signing of the treaty banning land-based Intermediate Nuclear Force missiles. At the Eighth Convention of the European Peace movement in *Spain* in Jul 1989, there was recognition of the potential reversal of the arms race. By this time, tension between East and West eased considerably and already the 'bloc' system was loosening.

After years of further negotiations, the Comprehensive Test Ban Treaty (CTBT), which outlaws nuclear testing of any kind, was ready for signing in 1996. The CTBT needed to be signed and ratified by the 44 countries identified as having nuclear power plants or research reactors. All relevant European countries have now signed but other leading world countries have yet to do so. Many countries still retain and continue to develop nuclear weapons, such as Trident in UK.

MEW

NYLC
See *Youth for Christ*.

O

Odessa Theological Seminary, Ukraine

In all the history of the Russian-speaking world *Protestant educational* institutions have seldom existed. Even before the 1917 Bolshevik Revolution, the *state*-sanctioned Russian *Orthodox Church* blocked measures to create a Protestant system of education. After the revolution, *Bible* courses were offered for a short time in Moscow and St. Petersburg, but eventually militant atheism quashed these first bursts of *growth*. The next attempt occurred in 1969 when a Bible Correspondence School was offered from Moscow with a restricted enrolment of only 50 *pastors*.

The freedom of 1989 allowed various Bible schools to open in the *Soviet Union*. One of the first, the Odessa Bible School, opened in Aug of that year. Sergei Sannikov, a teacher in the Moscow programme, a local pastor in Odessa, *Ukraine*, and a professor at the Odessa State University, became the first director. More than 180 members of Evangelical Christian Baptist churches of *Moldova* and Ukraine began their studies on the four-year non-residential diploma programme. They were appointed as pastors and *deacons* in various key cities such as Kiev, Kishinev, Odessa, and Yalta. In these cities they began the first *preaching ministries* and the first *Sunday School* programmes of the post-*communist* era.

In Jan 1991 the Odessa Bible School was transformed into the first Baptist Seminary in the Soviet Union. The opening ceremony of the Seminary was held in Moscow, at the Evangelical Christians-Baptists *Union*'s headquarters, and Sergiy Sannikov was appointed as the principal of the Seminary. Because of the political situation in Moscow and lack of resources, the Seminary was relocated to Odessa and began its daily ministry on the campus of Odessa Bible School. By the end of the year the Soviet Union was collapsing and the two schools were merged and renamed 'Odessa Theological Seminary' (OTS). At that time, the school launched a four-year residential Bachelor of *Theology* programme. 19 *men* were selected from over 50 applicants from all over the Russian-speaking world to begin this first residential Protestant *ministerial formation* programme.

When Ukraine separated from the Soviet Union, OTS came under the control of the Ukrainian Baptist Union (All Ukrainian Union of Evangelical Christians-Baptists Churches). In the 15 years since its founding, more then 800 *students* have graduated from OTS programmes.

Today, the Odessa Theological Seminary has grown into a school with more then 150 students, 28 teachers and 20,000 volumes of books in its library. OTS now offers seven different academic programmes and still attracts students from all Russian-speaking countries. It also operates extension campuses in *Kazakhstan* and *Uzbekistan*.

SVS

Oecumenical Movement

See *Ecumenical/Ecumenical (Oecumenical) Movement*.

Offerings/Collection

[See also *Tithing*]

Christian giving makes two acknowledgments. Firstly, everything in this world belongs to the Creator God, and when we give we are only giving back to him what is already his. Secondly, it demonstrates recognition that God, in giving us his only Son, is the greatest giver of all. In these respects giving properly belongs to the nature of God rather than the scale of human need, and this is recognised in the pattern of offerings that emerges in OT and NT, which have been taken over into Christian *worship*. Deliberately eschewing resource from *state* funds, Baptists have always been clear that the *ministry* and *mission* of the *church* properly place financial responsibilities on the *members* of local congregation. Baptists have also been wary of endowing ministry to any great extent, applying to their own churches the principle of the *faith mission*. In the past the gifts of the members were collected by way of subscription and even here there was sometimes concern at non-members becoming subscribers especially if subscribers tried to intrude on such vital issues as the calling of a *pastor*. A later generation developed the system of pew rents as a major means of generating congregational income. *Theological* reflection suggested that a system to secure the *free will* gifts of members, most often based on a principle of *tithing*, contributed on a regular basis was a better way of proceeding. Churches also moved to greater discipline in their giving, working to an annual budget both for the congregation's own use, mission in the community and for its giving to world mission. Today, in many *unions* this includes a mechanism for larger and more affluent churches to give to the union so that ministry can be provided in poorer and often more challenging areas. It is such gifts, freely given by the people of God, which are collected within the Sunday service and then offered to God for the work of his *kingdom*. In this action, the congregation not only offers its monetary gifts, it *prays* for *grace* to use what is retained in personal *stewardship* responsibly; it offers all the gifts of time and talent which it possesses; and brings before God the daily work of the people in home, school, *hospital*, factory and wherever the members are to be found. All this is offered to God that it may become part of the work of his kingdom.

.   JHYB

Oikoumene

[See also *Ecumenical/Ecumenical (Oecumenical) Movement*; *Unity of the Church*; *World Council of Churches*]

This Greek word, which means 'the whole inhabited world', lies behind the adjective 'ecumenical' which describes the movement seeking the unity of the Christian churches. In the Roman period it came to be synonymous with the civilised world of the Greco-Roman realm, and by the 4th century had come to mean the Christian world, thus an ecumenical council was a council whose decisions were universally accepted in the period of the undivided church. The secular origins of the word 'oikoumene' have encouraged some commentators in recent years to emphasise that the ecumenical goal must

be not just the unity of the churches, but the unity of all *humankind* of whatever creed. In so doing they relate to Paul's emphasis in Eph 1 on God's intention in the fullness of time 'to gather everything together in a unity in *Christ*, things in *heaven* and things on earth', rather than Jesus' *prayer* in John 17 that his disciples 'might be one...so that the world may believe'.

JHYB

Oncken, Johan Gerhard (1800-84)

Oncken was born on 26 Jan 1800 in Varel in Lower Saxony. After being confirmed in 1814 he left his hometown to work for a Scottish tradesman. The five years he spent among *Presbyterians* in *Scotland* and Independents in *England* had a profound influence on his life. He was converted [see *Conversion*] in a London *Methodist* church in 1820 and had contact with the *Congregationalist revival* movement in Scotland [see *Haldaneite tradition*]. From 1823 Oncken, by then a member of an English-Reformed church, worked as an agent of the British 'Continental Society for the Diffusion of Religious Knowledge over the Continent of Europe'. The main emphasis was on the distribution of Bibles and other Christian literature (from 1828 it had its own publishing house and was an agency of the Edinburgh *Bible Society*), besides *mission* work among seamen and Oncken's own initiative in establishing the first German *Sunday School* in 1825. The search for a spiritual home for the believers gathered in his revival movement led Oncken to the question of *baptism* and regenerate *church membership*. The solution was to establish the first German Baptist church and for Oncken to secure *ordination* as its *elder* on 23 Apr 1834. This took place after Oncken and six others had been baptised the previous day by Barnas Sears, a professor of *theology* who was in *Germany* to study. From then on Oncken maintained close contact with North American Baptists through Sears. Together with Oncken's British friends they supported his work financially and encouraged him wherever possible. Because Oncken sought to follow the biblical pattern [see *Bible*] he established churches for those who had come to *faith* on his many mission journeys.

Through Oncken's own activities and the work of his most important co-workers, Gottfried Wilhelm Lehmann (1799-1882) and Julius Köbner (1806-84) and numerous other mission workers, often travelling craftsmen, Baptist churches spread within Germany and into the neighbouring countries and especially into Eastern and South Eastern Europe. As elder of the mother church in Hamburg he enjoyed a high reputation all his life. The next generation saw the gaining of independence for *local churches* after a conflict with him that hindered the work for a time, but this was not detrimental to the close cooperation with the *Union* of Baptist Churches, which had been founded in 1849. When Oncken died, the Union comprised 165 churches with over 30,000 members in more than a dozen European countries. Oncken's theological position is set out in the Baptist *Confession of Faith* of 1847; besides articles on baptism and on the *church* which have a clear Baptist profile, the text is thoroughly reformed and *Calvinistic*. Devotion to *Jesus* and zeal to convert souls clearly demonstrate the influence of the Anglo-Saxon revival on Oncken and on the Baptist churches he established in continental Europe. It was not by chance that at the meeting in London that led to the founding of the *Evangelical Alliance* in 1846, Oncken was the only German participant who did not belong to a German national church. Oncken's special contribution was the mode of baptism he insisted upon and the stress he laid on the importance of the local congregation (congregations are the 'true mission agencies, appointed by God's *Word*'), for whom he provided a pattern of church administration which he integrated into the structures of the Baptist Union. Gottfried Wilhelm Lehman, influenced by the Herrnhut congregations, contributed the *pietistic* emphasis on personal consecration and practical church life. Oncken died on 1 Jan 1884 in Zürich.

GB

FURTHER READING: G. Balders, *Theurer Bruder Oncken* (2. Aufl.), Oncken, Wuppertal and Kassel, 1984. G. Balders, 'Die deutschen Baptisten und der Herrnhuter Pietismus', *Freikirchenforschung* 3 (1993), pp.26-39. G. Balders, 'Zur Frömmigkeitsgeschichte des deutschen Baptismus', *Theologisches Gespräch* 2 (1994), pp.16-28. R. Bohl, 'Die Sonntagsschule in der Hamburger Vorstadt St. Georg', *Zeitschrift des Vereins für Hamburgische Geschichte* 67 (1981), pp.133-175. W.A. Detzler, 'British and American Contributions to the »Erweckung« in Germany, 1815-1848', Ph.D. diss. Manchester, 1974: ch.XI. W. Gundert, *Geschichte der deutschen Bibelgesellschaften im 19. Jahrhundert*, Luther-Verlag, Bielefeld, 1987. H. Luckey, *J.G. Oncken und die Anfänge des deutschen Baptismus* (3. Auf.), J.G. Oncken Verlag, Kassel, 1958 (first published 1934).

One Step Forward

The story of 'One Step Forward', as a *ministry* of spiritual renewal and growth, is the story of the vision of Bryan Gilbert. While a *student* at *Spurgeon's College*, London, in the 1950s, Gilbert, whose background was in *music*, started a music group, the Venturers. His experience in this period of café *evangelism* and other innovative forms of outreach focused his attention on the need for churches and individuals to take steps forward in *mission* and *discipleship*. After two pastorates he became full-time director of a movement called 'One Step Forward' (1969-86), and later 'Next Step Ministries' (1992ff). The emphasis of 'One Step Forward', as over against the 'Forward' movement earlier in the century, with its general concern for renewed *missionary* endeavour, was to invite churches to respond to the grand vision of mission by undertaking immediate, finite, and manageable steps; 'one step forward' successfully undertaken encouraged churches to keep on taking steps forward in what for some led to a major advance. By the end of the 1960s a considerable number of churches had taken up his challenge and were holding 'One Step Forward' missions and seeing people taking steps forward in their Christian lives, and churches in their outreach. Some were brought to *Christ*, some baptised [see *Baptism*], and some entered full-time Christian ministry. These events might be led by Bryan Gilbert or might be 'do-it-yourself', using Gilbert's ideas. During the 1970s 'One Step Forward' spread more widely and has been used by many 100s of churches across Europe and beyond.

IMR

FURTHER READING: Edward Parker, *Give a Man a*

Vision: The Story of Bryan Gilbert and the Growth of One Step Forward, Lutterworth: One Step Forward, Walcote, Leicester, 1974.

Open Communion
[See also *Communion and Intercommunion; Eucharistic Liturgy; Strict Communion*]
In *England* early *Calvinistic* or Particular Baptists often came to their distinctive understanding via Independent, *paedobaptist*, *gathered* congregations. Some Baptist groups separated completely, but others were reluctant to break *fellowship* with those who shared their beliefs except on *baptism*, so they practised an open table. In the early period *John Bunyan*, author of *The Pilgrim's Progress,* was the best known advocate that differences over baptism should not be a bar to communion. Later Robert Hall (1728-1831) argued that 'no man, or set of *men*, are entitled to prescribe as an indispensable condition of communion, what the NT has not enjoined as a condition of *salvation*'. Joint activities with other *Evangelicals* in the early 19th century led more churches, especially new foundations, to have an open table. There were, however, limits to such openness: in 1851, with large numbers of American visitors expected in London for the Great Exhibition, the Bloomsbury church let it be known that only those Americans who actively opposed slavery would be welcome at that church's table. In some churches there had to be, for some time, parallel communions, one limited to those baptised as believers, the other open to all sincere disciples. *C.H. Spurgeon* practised an open table, although he only admitted to *membership* those baptised as believers [see *Open Membership*]. During the 20th century more churches opened the table: the majority of English Baptist churches now practise open communion, which in recent times has secured some support in parts of continental Europe.

FWB

Open Membership
[See also *Baptism; Church Membership; Infant Baptism*]
A few early churches in *England* combined within one fellowship Christians of *Calvin-istic* Baptist and Independent (*Congregational*) persuasion, either as notionally separate churches *worshipping* together as at Broadmead, Bristol, or as one church respecting individual *conscience* on baptism as at the Bunyan Meeting in Bedford. At New Road, Oxford, *Presbyterians* and Baptists shared *fellowship* in spite of *ecclesiological* differences. Following the *Evangelical Revival* of the later 18th century, evangelical Christians across the denominations worked increasingly together, recognising one another as fellow-believers in spite of differences in practice. This led to a number of Baptist churches being formed which would only baptise believers by immersion but opened membership to believers coming from other *traditions*. The Bloomsbury church in central London was founded on this principle in 1849.

By the late 20th century, with a more mobile population and many Christians more influenced in seeking a church based on the style of worship and warmth of fellowship than by *theological* nuance or ecclesiological understanding, many English Baptist churches have opened their membership. Sometimes, however, this is not legally possible, where Trust Deeds specify the requirement of believers' baptism.

With good *ecumenical* relations in England, 'open' Baptists are aware of the offence caused to those who see a 'repeated baptism' when someone baptised as an infant is later baptised as a believer; nevertheless, although willing to open membership to believers whose Christian initiation and formation was in another tradition, they defend the right to baptise as a believer anyone seeking this with an 'informed conscience'. For open Baptists there is a continual struggle between a consistent ecclesiology and generosity in Christian fellowship.

FWB

Operation Agri
See *Agricultural Mission*.

Ordinances and Sacraments
[See also *Sacrament, Sign and Symbol; Sign and Symbol*]
Baptists have used both the word 'Ordi-

nance' (where the emphasis is on obedience to specific dominical commands), and 'Sacrament' (which in origin refers to a soldier's sacred oath but normally conveys the concept of mystery suggesting divine initiative of a quite special order) to describe two liturgical acts [see *Liturgy*] with *scriptural* foundation – the *baptism* of believers and the *Eucharist*/Lord's Supper/Communion. Baptists, like other *Protestants*, confine the concept to these two and do not extend it to such serious moments of solemn pledging as focused in e.g. *marriage* or *ordination*. Whilst Baptist authors and *theologians* over the centuries have discussed the difference of view about what is implied and what happens in baptism and at the meal, nevertheless, whatever word is used there is a general common affirmation that in these events, which are seen as required of *gathering churches*, there is outward demonstration by sign and symbol of an inward and spiritual experience. Some Baptists much prefer to use the word 'ordinance' (especially in North America and some parts of Europe), but the use of the word does not necessarily imply that the event itself is not taken with the utmost seriousness and there is not some clear understanding that this is a special moment and event in which there is an expectation that God will be present and act in some significant way. The Baptists of the 18th century appeared to use 'ordinance' and 'sacrament' interchangeably (c.f. Fowler) often, when using 'ordinance' quoting an understanding based on the Westminster *Confession*, which used the word 'sacrament'. There is a suggestion that 'ordnance' appears to have denoted a wider event including *Word* and *prayer*, whereas sacrament was confined to the actual baptism or the immediate actions of the Lord's Supper.

Though many Baptists in Eastern Europe would not use the word 'sacrament', the special preparations and careful and serious celebration of the events indicate these are pivotal moments of divine-human encounter in the life of the believers in community. Indeed, the approach to the ordinances or sacraments amongst European Baptists implies they are held in very high regard.

Current practice across Europe suggests that both events – the baptism of believers and the celebration of the meal – are high points in the divine-human encounter of gathering churches and are treated with the utmost care and attention with appropriate preparation and joyful anticipation of the presence of the *Holy Spirit* amongst the community. It is rare to find in this century casualness to the events and a minimalising of their significance as might be attributed to *John Clifford* and others in the early 1900s.

Therefore, whatever word is used, the actions of the communities and the *pastors* demonstrate an understanding that baptism and the meal are outward signs and symbols of important *theological* and spiritual realities.

KGJ

FURTHER READING: Stanley K. Fowler, *More than a Symbol*, Paternoster, Carlisle, 2002. Keith G. Jones, *A Shared Meal and a Common Table*, Whitley Publications, Oxford, 1999. Michael Walker, *Baptists at the Table*, Baptist Historical Society, Didcot, 1992.

Ordination

In common with the large majority of churches throughout the world, Baptists have seen ordination as a significant sign of the admission of *men*, and in recent years, *women*, to the *ministry* of the *church*. However, there are important emphases that Baptists afford to the rite and the understanding that undergirds it, that gives a distinctively Baptist flavour to ordination.

Ordination to ministry is an ancient act of the church, dating from the patristic period. Presbyters were ordained by the presiding local *bishop* accompanied by all the existing presbyters. The core act was the *laying on of hands* and *prayer*, emphasising the invitation to the *Holy Spirit* to fill the candidate and endue him with *grace*. This itself is derived from the practice of the church in the NT, where the laying on of hands for particular ministry seems commonplace, (see Ac 13:1-3; 2Ti 1:6). While the mediaeval period saw considerable elaboration of the rite, including the presenting of chalice and paten, symbols of the *eucharist*; the anointing of the hands and the giving of vestments, in the *Reformation* churches there was a return to the core elements of laying on of hands and prayer. It is within this context that the early Baptists continued the practice of ordination, and today the core elements of an ordination remain: an enquiry into the suitability of the candidate for admission to ministry, promises made by the ordinand to serve with faithfulness and godliness, a prayer of ordination that in particular seeks the anointing of the Holy Spirit upon the *minister* for effective service, and the laying on of hands. A final word of blessing is included, often using the Aaronic blessing: '*May the Lord bless you and keep you; The Lord make his face to shine upon you and be gracious to you; The Lord lift up the light of his countenance upon you and give you peace.*'

There are problems however with the *theology* of ordination for Baptists. One issue that gives rise to problems is the question of ordination as a *sacramental* act, particularly one that passes on *apostolic authority* through a supposed tactile succession of ordained persons or as an act of authorisation. The historic *Catholic* and *Orthodox churches* see ordination as an act that confers upon the ordinand a change in status, in other words, there is an ontological transformation. Grace is conveyed to the ordinand that empowers him or her to preside at the eucharist, absolve the sinner [see *Sin*] and bless a congregation. This view has been rare amongst Baptists, who generally see ordination as an act which authorises a person, but does not change their status. This is expressed in the belief that the Lord's Supper can be presided over by someone other than an ordained minister, and in the doctrine of the *priesthood of all believers*, (understood as the corporate ministry of the whole church to fulfil the ministry of *Christ* in the power of the Spirit. This is opposed to the more recent 'every *member* ministry' which is individualistic in its conception, and essentially a way of saying there are no bystanders in the church, only active participants).

Baptists' non-hierarchical view of the church prevents an unwonted clericalism, and honours the service of all believers in the church, and not the minister only. That is why a number of leading pastors have in the past rejected both *clerical dress* and clerical title. This notion, derived in part from the doctrine of the *gathered church*, where the whole congregation discerns the

mind of Christ, not the minister only, nor even the minister and lay leaders [see *Laity*] only, sometimes gives rise to an unhealthy diminishing of the significance of the ministry, considering it as merely a category to describe those who are stipendiary, or who fulfil a particular function. Another aspect of this very low view of the work of the ministry is the statement sometimes made that 'every member is a minister in this church'. While this has a healthy emphasis upon the role of Christian service that every believer is called to make (and in this sense everyone is a minister, and shares in the ministry of the risen Christ) it can lead to an unhealthy usurping of the proper authority and task of leadership that the minister who is the *pastoral* leader of a church is called to exercise by virtue of being a minister of the *Word*, set apart by the church to teach the *faith* in accordance with the *scriptures*, administer the sacraments or ordinances of *baptism* and Lord's Supper, and to pastor the flock. While Baptists have always valued the gift of the Spirit to every believer through faith in Christ and marked by baptism, there has sometimes been a reluctance to also see the gifts of the risen Christ to the whole church as those who minister, as Paul relates in Eph 4:11, as *apostles*, prophets [see *Prophecy*], *evangelists*, pastors and teachers. The rediscovery of this understanding of ministry through the advocates of *charismatic* renewal has done much to renew the theology of the ordained ministry, and its practice within Baptist churches (although, conversely, the same renewal has also at times emphasised precisely the rediscovery of every member ministry that has collapsed ordained ministry into a form of paid *chaplaincy* to the *local church* which diminishes the office unhelpfully).

A second set of problems arises from the Baptist *ecclesiology* that places the local church in its position of primacy, even if inter-dependence and *associating* makes independence untenable theologically. Is the ordained leader, a minister of word and sacrament, authorised only for that local church that he or she serves, or is there some form of *character indelebilis* about ordination that makes it a transferable or translocal act? The fact that this is actually so is indicated by the way in which ministers retain their ordained status after retirement from pastoral charge of a congregation (although the functionalists sometimes renounce their ordained status when not in a pastorate) or when exercising a role beyond the local church, such as involvement in a para-church organisation.

Currently in some *unions* accreditation is removed when a person ceases to fulfil the functions of pastoral charge, but the fact that upon resumption of ministry such a one is not re-ordained points to something about the 'being' of the minister that precedes their 'doing' of ministry. Authorisation to exercise leadership in the church through prayer and the gift of the Spirit, symbolised in the laying on of hands, may be regularly renewed in a change of location (induction into a new office) but is not repeated at each fresh induction. The recognition of the gift of the Spirit for ministry and to the church is continual.

A third question concerns the tasks that are appropriate to the ministry, and in this regard Baptists follow their fellow historic *Protestant* churches in emphasising that the ordained minister is called to pastoral leadership of the flock, teaching and proclaiming the Word and administering the sacraments. As we have seen, this is not restricted to ministers, but a congregation with a minister will generally expect that these responsibilities are the minister's, even if they are delegated to others on occasions. These tasks are those appropriate to the ministry and ministers undergo training to equip them to fulfil these tasks and seek the daily renewing of the Spirit to enable them to do so faithfully and effectively.

PG

Örebro Group
See *InterAct*.

Örebro Theological Seminary, Sweden
[See also *Interact*]
The seminary [Swedish *Örebro Missionsskola*] in Örebro, *Sweden*, was founded in 1908 by the Baptist *pastor*, John Ongman, and owned by the Örebro Mission.

Ongman was convinced that there were enough candidates for two schools within the *Union* and a place for a second school with an emphasis on *spiritual gifts, holiness* and *mission*. The focus was on biblical teaching [see *Bible*] and *spiritual formation* from a quite *fundamentalist* and *pentecostal* perspective.

From the 1970s the seminary developed, under the leadership of Sigfrid Deminger and later Göran Janzon, an *evangelical* theological identity and a diversified programme: The School of *Theology*, The Youth Leader Institute, The Bible Institute, The Mission Institute, a Church-based ministerial training programme [see *Ministerial Formation*] (The Scandinavian Academy for Leadership and Theology) and, in collaboration with the nearby *state* university, an institution for training teachers of religion in public schools. Several cooperative agreements with other schools have been signed.

The seminary has grown considerably with *students* from different denominations and is accredited by the Ministry of Education (BA, BD) and by the European Evangelical Accrediting Association (M Div). The present principal is Pekka Mellergard, appointed in 2001.

GJ

Orgkomitet
See *Reform Baptists*.

Orphanages and Orphans
Baptist gathering churches have, from *C.H. Spurgeon* onwards, had a concern for issues of *Child Protection*. One particular area in which Baptists in many European countries have been proactive is the care of orphans (children who have lost their parents) by the establishment of adoption ages to find children new parents and orphanages, to provide secure homes in a Christian community setting for *children* who cannot be placed in a new family.

Baptists clearly recognise that orphanages are generally a second-best option to adoption of children within loving Christian families, but where this is not a possibility, many Baptist communities in various parts of Europe have raised funds and sought assistance to erect premises in which children can be raised in a loving and Christian way in community looked after by committed people.

Today governments in Europe are not generally disposed to children being raised in what are now often called 'institutions' and in Western Europe the move away from orphanages has led to the closure of some of the best known institutions. E.g. Spurgeon's own orphanage no longer engages in residential work but now deploys its resources much more diffusely in a series of community-based initiatives in support of children at risk. However, in Central and Eastern Europe the demand for residential care remains very high and, since the collapse of soviet-style *communism*, Baptist communities in countries such as *Bulgaria*, *Romania*, *Moldova* and the *Ukraine*, have sought to rescue orphans from poor quality care provided in some facilities, and to provide institutional support for their upbringing.

ET

Orthodox Churches, Baptists and the

[See also *Bilateral Conversations*]

The relationship between Baptists and the Orthodox churches in countries in Eastern Europe where Orthodoxy is the majority *faith* has generally not been an easy one. In many cases when Baptists first emerged in these countries, typically in the 19th century, they were persecuted by the *state* and by the leaders of the Orthodox community. During the *Communist* decades Baptists and Orthodox believers all suffered under communist pressure, and this created some sense of commonality. However, since the 1990s there have been fresh tensions.

Against this background, it has been important to seek *dialogue*. After preliminary meetings in 1994, a major dialogue was held in Istanbul in May 1996, 'Conversations between Baptists and the *Ecumenical* Patriarchate', or 'Pre-conversations'. These were held with a view to later full conversations between the *BWA* and representatives from the autocephalous Orthodox churches. At Istanbul, Denton Lotz, then the General Sec-

retary of the BWA, spoke on Baptist identity. Other speakers included Tony Cupit from the BWA, the *biblical scholar* Wiard Popkes from *Germany*, James Leo Garrett from the USA and Bruce Milne from Canada. Other Baptist *theologians/historians* participating included Gerald Borchert, William Brackney, Russ Bush and Paul Fiddes.

The last 'pre-conversation' meeting took place in Oxford in May 1997. Paul Fiddes, the Principal of *Regents Park College*, Oxford, addressed the topic, 'Mission: Essence or Responsibility of the *Church*'. Further contact took place in Dec 1997, with Denton Lotz and Wiard Popkes meeting with the Patriarch of the Romanian Orthodox Church in Bucharest, *Romania*. Relations between Baptists and Orthodox in some countries had by that stage become quite difficult, with Baptists often being accused of being a foreign (usually American) *sect*.

In 2001 a report on *Evangelicalism* and Eastern Orthodoxy was published: *Evangelicalism and the Orthodox Church*. This was the result of a study by a working group of ACUTE – the Alliance Commission on Unity and Truth among Evangelicals. ACUTE was established by the British *Evangelical Alliance* in 1995 to work for consensus on *theological* issues that test evangelical *unity*. Ian Randall, a British Baptist, was at that time chair of ACUTE and many Baptists across Europe have participated in the wider evangelical movement.

In Aug 2002 a Conference on Baptists and Eastern Orthodoxy was convened, sponsored by and held at *IBTS*. A number of factors suggested this was an important topic including the significant number of Baptist *students* at IBTS who were from countries where the Orthodox Church was the main Christian *tradition*. By this time scholarly work was being done by Baptists in Europe on aspects of Orthodox thinking. A good example of theological reflection from a Western European context is the essay by Paul Fiddes 'Church and *Salvation*: A Comparative Study of *Free Church* and Orthodox Thinking'. From an Eastern European Baptist there is the important *Deification in Eastern Orthodox theology: an evaluation and critique of the theology of Dumitru Staniloae* by Emil Bartos from Romania. In the same year Ken Manley, Principal of Whitley College, University of Melbourne, at a joint meeting of the BWA Baptist Heritage and Identity and Doctrine and Interchurch Co-operation Commissions (meeting at Seville, **Spain**, Jul 2002), rehearsed the conversations that had taken place up to that point.

People from 11 countries, primarily from Eastern Europe but also from Western Europe and America, participated in the 2002 Prague conference. Tim Grass, associate lecturer at **Spurgeon's College**, London, and the editor of *Evangelicalism and the Ortho-dox Church*, gave two papers. The subject of Orthodox relationships with evangelicals was dealt with by a leading Orthodox theo-logian involved in ecumenical affairs, Fr. Vladimir Federov, from St. Petersburg, Con-sultant in Theological Education in Eastern and Central Europe for the **World Council of Churches**. Papers were also given by Emil Bartos, Octavian Baban and Oti Bunaciu, all **scholars** from Romania, and by David Hil-born, the Theological Adviser to the Evan-gelical Alliance in Britain. The papers were published in a volume produced by IBTS, *Baptists and the Orthodox Church: On the way to understanding* (2003). The search for greater understanding continues.

IMR

FURTHER READING: Emil Bartos, *Deification in Eastern Orthodox theology: an evaluation and critique of the theology of Dumitru Staniloae*, Paternoster, Carlisle, 1999. P. Fiddes, 'Church and Salvation: A Comparative Study of Free Church and Orthodox Thinking' in A.R. Cross (ed), *Ecu-menism and History: Studies in Honour of John H. Y. Briggs*, Paternoster, Carlisle, 2002. Tim Grass (ed), *Evangelicalism and the Orthodox Church*, Acute/Paternoster, Carlisle, 2001. Ian Randall (ed), *Baptists and the Orthodox Church: On the way to understanding*, IBTS, Prague, 2003.

Orthodoxy, Orthopraxy, Orthohexy, Orthopyre

'Orthodoxy' derives from two Greek words meaning 'right' [*ortho*] 'belief' [*doxy*]. With the word 'catholic' it has been used to de-scribe those Christians of the whole church who uphold right belief. In the course of church history **Orthodox** has come to be associated with a descriptor of those churches, principally in Eastern and South Eastern Europe and the Middle East, who

take their descent from the one early **catho-lic**, **apostolic** and orthodox church and exist as national or regional churches in **commun-ion** with the **Ecumenical** Patriarch in Con-stantinople.

In wider usage, orthodoxy properly means those churches or communities of believers holding fast to the historic Chris-tian **faith** based on the Biblical **revelation** [see **Bible**], with those who depart from this standard described as heterodox, that is holding 'other beliefs', synonymous with infidelity or **heresy**. For Baptists, the concern is not simply about right belief, but also or-thopraxy, that is to say believers acting in a right way consistent with the revealed truth of Christianity in their **discipleship** and **mis-sion** and orthohexy or right attitudes be-tween believers in their interaction in the life and work of the **church**. More recently some **scholars** have also added to this con-cern for authentic Christianity orthopyre or the 'right fire'. By which is meant believers and churches exhibiting a style of being in tune with the primitive church of **Pentecost** who, endowed with the **Holy Spirit**, were empowered in their **witness** and mission.

Whilst orthodoxy in terms of basic Chris-tian belief has generally been the norm amongst Baptists, the history of **schism** and division within Baptist communities across the world suggests that many do not have a proper orthohexy within their **ecclesiology** and in the 1700s until the impetus of **Wil-liam Carey** it might be argued that the Par-ticular Baptists [see **England**] lacked a proper orthopyre in their way of being church.

KGJ

Osijek Evangelical Theological Faculty, Croatia

The Evangelical Theological Faculty (ETF; often called 'Seminary' in English transla-tions, thus ETS) started in 1972 in Zagreb, **Croatia**, under the name Biblical Theologi-cal Institute (BTI). The founding institution was the **Pentecostal** Church in **Yugoslavia** and Peter Kuzmič has served as the President from the beginning. The purpose of BTI was to provide residential training for church **ministry** and para-church ministries as well as instruction in Biblical studies and **theol-**

ogy. In 1973 a building was purchased in Zagreb with the support of the Assemblies of God from the USA. The residential program was suspended in 1978, but the work continued in several extension centres in Croatia.

In 1984 BTI reopened its residential program in Osijek, Croatia. In the late 1980s BTI was renamed the Evangelical Theological Faculty, and became explicitly interdenominational in theology and international in nature as the Overseas Council International, an interdenominational *evangelical* foundation, replaced the Assemblies of God as the main financial supporter of ETF. Marking this shift, the ETF Board of Directors invited representatives of various evangelical and *Protestant* denominations from the former Yugoslavia to join them. During the war in the former Yugoslavia (1991-95) ETF continued to operate in Osijek except in the academic year of 1991/92 when it temporarily relocated to *Slovenia*. Over the years ETF has run extension programmes in Timișoara, *Romania*, in Mostar, *Bosnia and Herzegovina*, and in Ljubljana, Slovenia.

The original undergraduate three-year BTh program was replaced by a four-year BTh course in 1989 only to revert back to a three-year course in 2005 in order to adjust to the Bologna convention. In the early 1990s ETF started a post-graduate program to meet the needs of evangelical churches in Eastern Europe and the former *Soviet Union* under the direction of Emmanuel Gitlin, followed by Davorin Peterlin and then Corneliu Constantineanu. The course was initially validated by the University of Leeds, *UK*. Up to 20 ETF graduates have gone on to doctoral studies in the USA and the UK. Instruction for both courses was provided in Croatian and English. Teaching staff have come from different denominations and countries and prominent visiting lecturers have been able to teach at ETF due to the modular system of instruction.

From 1993 ETF has offered a two-year professional programme, comprising of religion and *educational* subjects, which equips students for teaching Religious Education [see *Comparative Religion*] in elementary schools and *Ethics* in secondary schools in Croatia. ETF also offers one-year and two-year certificate courses as well as a correspondence course which was originally based on the International Correspondence Institute (ICI) materials translated into Croatian. The total number of *students*, including resident, non-resident and correspondence students in the last five years has been around 200. Students have come from more than 20 countries of Central and Eastern Europe, the former Soviet Union, Africa and elsewhere and represent more than 20 denominations.

The physical extension of ETF, directed by Business Manager, Antal Balog, includes the newly erected multi-purpose building which houses the library (with more than 40,000 books), a lecture hall, accommodation for visiting lecturers and post-graduate students.

Since the fall of *Communism* in Central and Eastern Europe, ETF has remained one of the leading evangelical theological seminaries in the region and is the place where Baptists of the area are most likely to go for *ministerial formation* and theological training.

DP

Overseas missionary activity

[See also *Commissioning of Missionaries*; *Mission*]

Just over 200 years ago the modern missionary movement was begun. The missionary society was concerned with raising funds and supporting by *prayer* the sending of missionaries from established churches to countries with largely pagan populations, with a view to their *conversion*, thinking that in so doing the *Great Commission* of Matthew's gospel was being fulfilled. This pattern of sending churches and receiving mission fields still predominates in many people's minds. Europe had been the centre of Christianity, the well established *Corpus Christianum*, and therefore it played a major part in the missionary movement. However, with European missionaries came not only the gospel but also Western culture, *education*, values and economic interests. In such a model, missionaries are seen as working *for* the Africans, the Asians, the Latin Americans. Moreover the idea of 'Commerce and Christianity', championed by many like the iconic Scottish missionary, David Livingstone, advocated the idea that well-ordered trade prepared the way for the gospel by bringing stability to a region, as well as dealing with the problem of the illegitimate, that is the slave, trade.

But since WWII this pattern has changed completely. European countries have, more or less, given up their overseas colonies [see *Colonialism*]. New independent countries have developed in Africa and Asia. At the same time European churches no longer have a position of supremacy in World Christianity. Large new independent churches have developed everywhere in the Global South. Very many of them have grown significantly and today have become much larger than their 'mother churches' in Europe.

These changes in *political* and church life have led to changes also in the life of mission agencies. Among the large variety of mission organisations three major understandings have been developed during recent years:

(1) *the ecumenical and development-aid oriented understanding*: many of the **state church** related mission organisations have turned their interest towards the support of the sending out of development-aid workers in general and towards the support for so-called 'ecumenical co-workers' working in partnership with the **local church** providing church-to-church aid;

(2) *the independent evangelical understanding*: most of the 'free mission-agencies', the independent mission organisations without any formal link to churches, conventions, **unions**, focus more and more on mission to the so-called *'unevangelised people groups'* often times ignoring the existing churches in the respected areas of work;

(3) *the partnership-oriented holistic mission understanding*: mission agencies rooted and linked towards *Free Churches* (Baptists, **Methodists**, **Congregationalists**, **Pentecostals**, etc.) try to implement a holistic partnership-oriented understanding of mission including *evangelistic* and social work and developing mission strategies together with the partners in Africa, Asia and Latin America.

In this latter way most Baptist mission

agencies in Europe have tried to respond to the changes in the political and church life

- by sending out European missionaries to overseas countries only on request and only in full cooperation with the partner churches in Africa, Asia and Latin America,

- by supporting indigenous mission co-workers and thus bringing together the often times stronger financial resources from the European countries with the spiritual strength and personal commitment of co-workers in the Global South,

- by receiving so-called 'reverse-missionaries' from Africa, Asia and Latin America to work in the *secularised* societies in the post-Christian European communities.

Today a new understanding of the work of mission and how it is best to be supported, is being worked out, a new pattern which will open up the churches in Europe to receiving as well as sending. In that new understanding Europe is no longer the centre of *Christendom*, for nowhere are there truly Christian countries: the need for evangelism and mission is urgent everywhere.

No longer should missionaries promote their culture, economic interests and Western values, rather they will work under the partnership and leadership of national churches and unions with these partners involved fully at all levels. Missionaries now will work *with* the Africans, the Asians and the Latin Americans.

HG

Oxford Group
See *Moral Re-Armament*.

P

Pacifism and Peace Churches

[See also *Church of the Brethren, Baptists and the*; *Mennonites*; *Mennonites, Baptists and*; *Peace, Baptists and*; *Quakers, Baptists and*]

Whilst Baptists share with their *Anabaptist* cousins a concern for peace, they have not like the historic peace churches – Mennonites, Church of the Brethren and Quakers – made commitment to pacifism a condition for *membership*, though they have always respected those of their number who believed that Christian *discipleship* required a commitment to pacifism, and more generally have been critical of encouragement of the arms trade as part of the national economy, and have encouraged diplomatic rather than military action.

Pacifism is the belief that *violence* and war, even in self-defence, are unjustified. It refers to the sanctity of human life and the teaching of *Jesus* to love one's enemy. It refers to a *love* which is prepared to suffer. War cannot be justified as a tragic necessity; rather it calls for war-prevention, working for peace and justice by non-violent means. If love towards an enemy would expose innocents to violence, it represents a moral dilemma. Hence the criticism, that pacifism is absolutist. Historically pacifism seeks to solve human conflicts in non-violent ways, confronting human reality, where violence takes place on a personal level, and where *political* militarism and war threatens even the future of *humankind*. Indeed the potential dimensions of *nuclear* war are such that many have questioned whether the old arguments of the '*just war*' school continue to work, creating what have been called 'nuclear pacifists', and here it is not only the deployment of nuclear weapons that has changed the situation, the existence of nuclear power plants mean that even conventional war could have nuclear consequences.

Pacifism in a modern sense emerged in the 19th century and became a term in English in the early 20th century, derived from a contemporary French term and the Latin term *pax* (peace between *states*, or within an empire). Christian pacifism professes a call to peacemaking, where *prayer* leads to protest and contemplation to non-violent resistance. Obstacles to peaceful co-existence call for resolution before conflict erupts into violence. Peacemakers seek a common future for all, with full respect for the individual, and an end to racism or ideologies that do not respect human rights. With an escalating militarism, and nuclear weapons of mass destruction, the just war theory from the post-Constantinian period has lost credibility as a Christian answer to human conflict. Pacifists see war and terrorism as evils, no matter how good a cause they may profess to serve in a violent world.

Civil rights should include the *human right* to *freedom of conscience*, affirming the right to obtain and practice a pacifist conviction. In Europe a law of exemption normally follows a law of general conscription, where an individual conviction_of pacifism should qualify for exemption from military service as *conscientious objectors* and lead to a peace-relevant service.

PMIL

FURTHER READING: Martin Ceadel, *The Origins of War Prevention*, Clarendon, Oxford, 1996. Martin Luther King, Jr., *A testament of hope*, Harper and Row, San Francisco, 1986. Norman Kember, *Hostage in Iraq*, Darton, Longman and Todd, London, 2007. Thomas Merton, *Peace in the Post-Christian Era*, Orbis, Maryknoll, NY, 2004. Leo Tolstoy, *Christianity and Pacifism*, 1893.

Paedobaptism

See *Infant Baptism*.

Palestine

See *Holy Land*.

Palm Sunday

This day marks the beginning of Great Week or *Holy Week*. The Sunday before *Easter Day* is a commemoration of the entry of *Jesus* into Jerusalem riding on an ass and recalls the gospel account of how the people cried 'Hosanna to the Son of David' and strew Palm branches in his way.

The celebration of the day in this way

began in Jerusalem towards the end of the 4th century when Christians would ascend the Mount of Olives and towards the end of the afternoon the gospel passage telling of the triumphal entry into the city was read. Then the people would process into the city – young and old – carrying Palm branches. It was some time before the practice spread elsewhere, but now in many traditions Palm branches, olive branches or willow branches are used as part of the *liturgy* on Palm Sunday. In *Armenia* congregations carry branches into the churches taken from the local area. In *England* children sometimes distribute North African Palm crosses to the congregation. In some churches a procession is held and an attraction can be to include a live donkey or ass, though this is not without its challenges in the confined space of a *worship* room. Various themes are naturally associated with Palm Sunday celebrations, especially humility and the search for the way of *peace*, and with Jesus showing especial concern for Jerusalem, the claiming of urban life for the *kingdom of God*.

KGJ

Pancake Tuesday

See *Fat Tuesday*.

Papacy

[See also *Infallibility of the Pope*; *Roman Catholicism*; *Vatican, The*]

The language of Papacy signifies the claims of the *Bishop* of Rome (thereby termed the Roman Pontiff or Pope) to an exclusive prerogative in the life of the Universal *Church*. Thus the pope determines all *dogma*, exercises a supreme Magisterium in all matters of *ethics*, and in jurisdiction the primacy of the Roman See over all other *episcopal* sees.

The first mention of the recognition of the supremacy of the See of Rome is to be found in a reference by Ireneus, the Bishop of Lyon (178-200AD), to the Bishop of Rome as *potentiorem principalitatem*. Rather later the Bishop of Carthage, Cyprianus (d.258), appealed to Rome over questions of *church discipline* and made the comment *Rome locuta, causa finita* [when Rome speaks, the problem is resolved].

Provincial churches resisted the supremacy of one see; in fact, five of the most important patriarchal sees were recognised: Jerusalem, Alexandria, Antioch, Constantinople and Rome. Each of these 'patriarchs', elected by their respective presbyters, had authority over the churches in the 'Roman province' where they were to be found. They nominated local bishops and settled questions of discipline. For *theological* matters, which involved the *faith* of all the churches, a *council* was convened, usually by the Emperor, to put an end to the relevant controversy and thus bring *peace* to the Empire. Each patriarchal see jealously claimed its own jurisdiction. At the end of the 5th century, a legal expression was coined, which later was to become part of the Code of Canon Law which recognised a certain degree of supremacy on the part of the See of Rome over church discipline: *Prima sedes (romana) a nemine iudicatur* [the see of Rome can not be judged by anyone]. Though a negative assertion, it was very important.

The system of patriarchal sees and *oecumenical* councils worked for some centuries, until conflict arose between the various patriarchal sees, and councils, which only met occasionally, were not always able to solve the issues. Reiterating continuity and a legitimate *apostolic* succession with the *Apostle* Peter (because he sat on the *cathedra Petri*) and supported by the promise made by *Jesus*, the Bishop of the See of Rome claimed supremacy (*plenitudo potestatis*) over the whole Christian Church. Although there was much and lasting resistance, in the end this 'primacy' of the jurisdiction and the universal Magisterium of the Bishop of Rome was established with its *hierarchical* structure. The dogma *Infallibility* was placed alongside the Magisterium in 1870. The primacy of jurisdiction brought about the *schism* with the Eastern Churches which became fixed in 1054.

The authority deposited in the see of Rome raised questions as to how this pontiff was to be elected. The old procedure was once more adopted, with the pope being elected by the heads of the old churches of Rome and its suburban area. With a *fictio juris* [a juridical invention] all the cardinals were nominated as holders of these positions and thus they, meeting in conclave, became the papal electors. In the beginning the Bishop of Rome became Pope, now the Pope becomes Bishop of Rome.

Papal primacy acquired added attributes, first the office acquired the title *vicarius christi* and shortly afterwards with a rather more **vocational** attribute: *servus servorum Dei*. These two titles, an official acknowledgement of the pope's attributes, beg the critical question of whether the papacy is a vehicle for service, or for power, and in these two cases do they exclusively refer to the Roman Catholic Church or can they be extended to include all other Christian churches? This is a question for debate with some Christian churches which have an episcopal **tradition**.

DT

Participation

There is something distinctly Christian in insisting on the importance of participation, whether in the life of church or **state**. Theologically, Baptists come to this through their championing of 'the **priesthood of all believers**' and their commitment in church order to the development of church policies and strategies by the whole **church meeting**. The whole **church membership** is required to be involved in the **mission** of the **church** to the utmost of the gifts given to them. For Baptist, belonging entails participating, and structures which make it difficult for any group – whether it be **women**, youth, the **disabled** or a particular ethnic or social group – fully to play a part, need to be challenged. It may be easier for all to participate in a small church than a large church but the large church then needs to look at how its membership can be broken down into smaller clusters to achieve the desired end. Difference of gift will affect the nature of any individual's participation and it is important to esteem the service of all as equally important in the service of the **kingdom**. In national **unions** small churches need to be confident that their voice and contribution is as much valued as that of larger fellowships.

Between 1975 and 83 the **WCC** ran a programme concerned with the search for a Just, Participatory and Sustainable Society as a means of linking together its several concerns about social developments. The con-

cern for a just society had obvious historic support, and increasingly the churches were coming to think about nurturing a life-style that could sustain a fragile planet confronted with **environmental** challenges like pollution, global warming [see **Climate Change**] and the using up of non-renewable resources. The middle adjective did not always get the support it deserved. Development workers quickly identified participation as vital to the healthy advance of their work: without it project success was very doubtful. Maybe it was so obvious to those with long **democratic traditions** that people had a right to participate in all decisions affecting their lives that they did not always give sufficient support to movements for racial equality, decolonisation [see **Colonialism**], and the championing of **human rights** especially of those who had no voice and who continued to live on the margins in a big-business **globalised** society. Even within so-called democratic societies' styles of government, including rule by so-called experts, called for renewed alertness. The call for proper participation was none other than an affirmation that the Christian understanding of **koinonia** had **political** implications.

ET

Passive Resistance

[See also **Conscientious Objectors**]

Passive Resistance represents the conscientious objection of **nonconformists** to obey what they considered unjust laws. When it was proposed in **Britain** in 1902 that government would impose a rate, that is a tax, to fund denominational schools, the Baptist MP George White gave notice that Free Churchmen might bind themselves not to pay the rate, and in the autumn of that year the Baptist **Union** Council passed a resolution with little dissent to recommend such a course of action. The ensuing campaign of civil disobedience was headed by *John Clifford*. So began a campaign in which rate refusers had their possessions seized and then auctioned (often to the bid of a friend of the resister), to raise sufficient funds to pay the rate. Clifford himself appeared in court some 41 times before the outbreak of WWI. If a resister refused to allow his goods to be distrained, then imprisonment followed. By Mar 1906 there had been almost 71,000 summons, 2,550 auctions and 176 persons jailed.

At the inaugural Congress of the **Baptist World Alliance** in London in 1905, Clifford expressed gratitude for the support he had received in the Passive Resistance Movement, but instead of 1,000 in prison he thought that, if free-churchmen were true to their principles, there should be 2,000, in protest at the anomaly of the school situation which was a pernicious medieval legacy. F.B. McGowan of Godstone, a village south of London, a participant in the debate, had been three times to prison for non compliance with the 1902 Education Act, for he saw no reason to pay for an **Anglican priest** to contradict on Monday the teaching he had given in **Sunday School** the previous day. Others who had been imprisoned were invited to stand in their seats, which they did, with a rather larger number indicating that they had had goods distrained for non payment of rate, thus demonstrating at the congress that persecution was neither an historic experience, nor something only experienced in Eastern Europe. Here was demonstrated in a relatively minor way how Baptists, with dignity, could resist the unfair demands of the state.

JHYB

Passover Celebration

This festival, observed on the 14th day of the month of Nisan (Mar-Apr) within **Judaism** commemorates the Exodus of the Hebrews from **Egypt** (Dt 16:1-8). It is associated in the OT narrative with a celebration lasting seven days in which only unleavened bread is eaten. The narrative in Ex 12:1-36 sets out an explanation of the origin of the Passover as well as some of the features involved in its celebration, including typically a lamb cooked in herbs, with a dip made of nuts, fruits and vinegar. The meal typically had four **wine** cups of blessing. The festival recalls how the angel of **death** 'passed over' the Hebrew homes in Egypt because of the mark of the blood of the lamb on the door posts and lintel of their homes. The Passover, as described in Ex 12, was a climactic moment for the Hebrews in their **redemption** from slavery in Egypt and was to be

recalled thereafter in families with the annual celebration of the event when the **children** would question their parents about the significance of the meal.

The meal marks a movement from sorrow to gladness, from a time of mourning to a festal reality. The style of the meal is taken by some Christians as setting the context for the Christian **Eucharist**, given the attestation from the gospels that **Jesus** went up to Jerusalem at the time of the Passover. Others suggest that the NT does not make clear the meal in the Upper Room was a strict Passover meal. Gregory Dix in *The Shape of the Liturgy* argues for another festal meal as the base event of the Eucharist, the *Chabûrah* meal.

Today, some Baptist communities hold a Passover-type celebration in **Holy Week**, often combining it with **foot washing** or similar modern equivalent, and the reading of appropriate **scriptures** in answer to the ancient question, 'What is the meaning of this meal?' Other communities insist on eating Eucharistic bread in the pattern of the Passover, where the bread was unleavened as a sign of the haste of departure from Egypt. Other Baptists reject this link and claim that the Christian Eucharist is complete only with the vision of the exalted and Risen **Christ** [see **Resurrection**], therefore the proper bread of the Eucharist has benefited from a raising agent such as yeast.

KGJ

FURTHER READING: Gregory Dix, *The Shape of the Liturgy*, Dacre, London, 1945.

Pastoral Call

[See also *Call/Calling; Vocation*]
Every Christian has been called to serve **Christ** and his world, and upon every believer is placed the call to **love** and care for their brothers and sisters in Christ and to be faithful witnesses to Christ, but the call to be a **minister**, or pastor, does not come to everybody. Over the centuries Baptists have recognised those **men** and **women** who receive such a call as pastors, and they have generally exercised a **ministry** of leadership and service to a local congregation, leading the church in its **worship**, **preaching** the **Word** and administering the **ordinances** of **bap**-

tism and the *Lord's Supper*, offering *pastoral care* and leading the church in its *mission* and *evangelism*.

How is such a call received and recognised? Certainly there must be an element of personal conviction without which any individual would be foolish to embark upon a demanding life of sacrificial service. However, that is not the heart of the matter, nor is a personal sense of call necessarily the start of a person's call to ministry. In our individualised culture, it is easy to see a call to ministry as simply an individual's personal conviction, as if that is the end of the matter, but Baptist *ecclesiology* emphasises the corporate decision of the church to call a man or woman into ministry. It is God who calls through the church, for it is the ministry of Christ's *church* into which pastors are called.

So for some the first stage of a call might be the ability of others to discern in a man or woman the potential to be a pastor, to act upon that discernment in encouragement and opportunity to develop gifts and skills needed in ministry, such as preaching or pastoral visiting. With a growing personal conviction that God might be calling them into ministry, this needs to be tested by the church. Differing ecclesial structures enable that testing to be varied in its stages (thus in a large *union* like the Baptist Union of *Great Britain*, testing of a call has four stages: *local church*, regional *association* and then the national Union, followed by the final confirmation that upon completion of training, a church calls the person to be their pastor). Whether in a large union or small, the testing of call will involve the following elements: a confirmation of call by the church of which the individual is a member, by the wider church through the structures enabled by its associating and *fellowship*, and finally by the call to serve in a particular local church.

Without such wider confirmation, the conviction held by an individual that God is calling them to be a pastor lacks the necessary breadth of affirmation by the church. Many pastors would testify that when times are tough and perhaps they question their calling, it is the reminder that it is the church that has discerned the call of Christ, not them alone, which gives fresh courage and renewed commitment to the demands of that calling. Here the rite of ordination plays its part as a sign that others have recognised the call of God, and until God, through his people, removes that call, the pastor is to be faithful in exercising all the duties of his or her office.

PG

Pastoral Care

[See also *Pastoral Theology*]

This essential element of the *church*'s life is not defined by denominational allegiance. All branches of the church have contributed insights and writings to its considerable literature, and certain common features are evident. The *Anabaptist*/Baptist *tradition* has its own contribution to make, particularly to the concept of *discipleship*.

That our idea of pastoral care must be based on *scripture* and church life may seem obvious but needs to be stressed in the light of recent emphasis on psychotherapy and specialised counselling *ministries*. It has been defined by A.V. Campbell as 'Those activities of the Church which are directed towards maintaining or restoring the *health* and wholeness of individuals and communities in the context of God's redemptive purpose for all creation' (*New Dictionary of Pastoral Studies*, p.252).

Pastoral care may be taught within the discipline of *Practical · Theology*, and its practitioners may be trained in some form of psychotherapy, but the giving of care is not limited to specialists. It is the task of the whole people of God, and in the context of a congregation it should be shared between the *ministers* and the *laity*.

Pastoral care is, however more than a series of 'hints and tips'. It has sometimes seemed to consist in instructions on the conduct of *weddings*, *funerals*, and other pastoral events. Important as it is to know 'how to do it well,' that is not the essence of pastoral care. It should rather be seen as the outworking of a *theological* understanding of the work of God in His world, healing, guiding, sustaining and reconciling [see *Reconciliation*] his people. It is the provision of care to troubled people, and as such is central in the life of the church, and requires both theory and practice.

As a central part of Christian responsibility, pastoral carers require some form of accreditation, whether that is formal qualification in counselling, or the endorsement of the Christian community and the recognition of *gifts*. Carers must be accountable, whether to a pastoral care group, or to a church leader. This does not denigrate the casual and informal caring contact that occurs between persons, which may take place at work or at home, but does affirm the seriousness with which caring is to be treated. For some this will mean formal qualifications such as Clinical Pastoral Education (CPE), which involves clergy, laity and *students* in supervised encounter with persons in crisis. This is intended to lead the carers to personal insights and new understandings of the needs of others, and it is widely used in many parts of the world. For others attachments at *Hospitals*, *prisons*, schools and *hospices* provide supervised learning and experience. For yet others more or less formal arrangements in the local congregation can give a base for learning and accountability.

Michael Taylor, an English Baptist writer, in his *Learning to Care* stresses the importance of personal stories, the stories in the *Bible* and the Christian beliefs of the carer. There is much to learn from counselling techniques and *secular* psychology, but in order to be Christian care, pastoral action must be rooted in the tradition. Paul Ballard and Stephen Holmes, two other British Baptist *theologians* have recently edited *The Bible in Pastoral Practice*, a comprehensive series of essays on the place of scripture and *exegesis* in the pastoral life of the Church. It would seem to be evident that a typical Anabaptist/Baptist stress on the centrality of the *Word*, *incarnate* and written, is occupying an important position in writing on pastoral care.

Certain areas of care have attracted more attention. *Marriage* guidance was traditionally given in family settings, and reinforced from the *pulpit*. Because of the rapidly changing mores of contemporary society there is confusion amongst many Christian people, and pre-marital counselling, marriage preparation, and the confrontation of marital difficulties had become part of the pastoral work of the church. There are of course specialised agencies in most countries, but the caring congregation has an important part to play, as has the pastor. New situations arise, and the line between teaching and caring needs to be carefully drawn. E.g. a *dogmatic* rejection of a *divorced* person's request for remarriage is not now appropriate if it ever was. Sensitive application of *Jesus*' teaching has led to happy outcomes.

No carer can escape experience at some level of the care of the dying and of the bereaved. *Death* occurs at any age and under many different circumstances. Knowledge acquired by personal experience may be more valuable than that learned from textbooks, but as the expectancy of life increases, such knowledge is acquired later in life. There has been a great deal of work done on the pastoral care of the dying, some of it influenced by the Hospice Movement which in many countries has had Christian roots. Medical and psychological advances in understanding of dying have been accompanied by the rediscovery of the Christian *calling* to enable a 'good death.' Elisabeth Kübler-Ross, Cecily Saunders and others have examined the dying process and this body of knowledge has spread to doctors, nurses and pastoral carers through widespread educational programmes.

There are many ways in which Christians are involved in the care of the bereaved. There are specialist counselling and caring agencies. Many congregations have bereavement care teams, and in others widows are put in touch with widowed neighbours. Bereavement care can last a long time, and the informal befriending can continue long after formal care has ceased. Carers can be taught to distinguish normal from abnormal grieving, and to be alert for danger signs, anniversaries, and church occasions such as *Christmas* when the bereaved are especially vulnerable. We soon learn that grief never entirely ends.

Support for those with psychiatric illness calls for patient listening, an understanding of the conditions, and probably for cooperation with the Psychiatric Hospital care staff. Here and elsewhere sensitivity to the need for referral to the experts has to be learned. Christian carers must address the stigma that is attached to mental illness in many cultures.

Physical *disability* presents the Christian church with many practical issues, from accessibility of *worship* areas to the need for good acoustic provision and provision of *hymn* words for the visually impaired. These technical matters are of the essence of pastoral care, as is education in the acceptance of people who are 'different' whether in appearance or behaviour, or indeed ethnic origin.

Pastoral care can take place in the context of Christian worship. The words of hymns sensitive *prayers* and *sermons* which apply the word of scripture to concrete situations have an affect on worshippers, and may lead to pastoral conversations, or more extensive counselling. The worshipping community is alerted to its responsibility to its *members*, and while confidentiality must be maintained, burdens can be shared.

A small group may provide a more intimate setting for confidential conversation and mutual support. Various forms of Christian education have replaced a more formal catechesis [see *Catechumenate*] and there too opportunities for questioning, learning and possibly rebuking arise.

The Anabaptist/Baptist emphasis on discipleship and on finding a meaning for *suffering* through following the suffering Christ has an important contribution to make to pastoral care. The biblical image of the shepherd, who leads his sheep to good pastures and fresh waters, was contrasted by the Swiss Brethren with the image of the *priest* or *scholar* who leads his people astray. The pastor's responsibilities are set out in the Schleitheim Confession: 'his office should be to read, to exhort, to teach, to admonish, to reprimand, and to exercise the ban in the congregation. He should pray for the improvement of all the brothers and sisters, be the first to break bread and in all things to do with the body of Christ, take care that it is raised and improved, and that the slanderer is silenced.' Goertz comments: 'anti-authoritarian and solicitous: this was the anticlerical model behind the Schleitheim catalogue of responsibilities' (Goertz, p.43).

Since the 1970s pastoral care and Counselling Conferences have taken place, firstly in Europe, and then since 1979 on a world wide basis, so that insights from different cultures can be shared. One of the earliest of these was held at *Rüschlikon*, and Keith Parker, a *Southern Baptist* teacher, played a large part in the movement, in which many other Baptists from every continent have since played their part.

DBM

FURTHER READING: P. Ballard and S. Holmes (eds), *The Bible in Pastoral Practice*, Darton, Longman and Todd, London, 2005. Wesley Carr (ed), *The New Dictionary of Pastoral Studies*, SPCK, London, 2002. H.-J. Goertz, *The Anabaptists*, Routledge, London, 1996.Michael Taylor, *Learning to Care*, SPCK, London, 1983.

Pastoral Theology

[See also *Pastoral Care*; *Theology*]
Clearly the adjective derives from the caring work of a shepherd, so, in the broadest sense, pastoral theology is a theology of caring. Whilst it has an ancient pedigree going back to the writings of the Fathers, it early came to be used as a description of those aspects of theology which related to the day-to-day work of the ordained *ministry* [see *Ordination*], which has increasingly become focused on that part of the task that has to do with the pastoral care and counselling of individuals, where its agenda may include issues as diverse as *ethical* discernment and therapeutic need, but today the individual is increasingly seen as located in the community. Historically the concern of *Reformed Churches* with new high standards for its *pastors* (see Baxter, 1656) focussed attention in this area in the later *Puritan* period, though the pastoral, as over against the theological, preparation of ordinands is a very recent revision in the syllabus, partly influenced by Latin American experience in *Theological Education by Extension* and by the needs of the increasing numbers of mature candidates for ministry who train in local pastoral situations. Pastoral theology has also moved on to the consideration of mainline theological themes from a pastoral perspective, and thus, released from its focus on the ordained ministry, it has come to embrace the ministry of the whole church, both lay [see *Laity*] and ordained, a much healthier emphasis than the earlier 'hints and helps for the clergy' approach. Pastoral theology, has, moreover, adopted a *praxis*

approach, that is to say, it raises questions from, and seeks solutions to, actual pastoral problems found in real-life situations, constantly travelling between *scripture* and situation, situation and scripture. *Othopraxis* becomes as critical a test as **orthodoxy**. The relationship between pastoral theology and pastoral psychology presents certain hazards, and the message here seems to be to be wary of any theory or practice that endorses the outlook of any particular psychological theory. E.g. Frank Lake, who had a large following in the *UK*, was criticised from just this point of view. Changing situations in a post-Christian society make ever increasing demands of the pastoral **theologian**, now required to address issues relating to **women** and people of colour amongst many others. Elaine Graham describing how the discipline is developing writes: 'the discipline no longer regards itself as "applied" theology concerned with promoting clerical competence, but is gradually being reconstructed as a primary theological discipline relating to the self-understanding of the community of **faith** in the world. Within this wider undertaking pastoral theology is commissioned to enable the community of faith to practice what it preaches, exploring how action corresponds to belief, how the historical **witness** of faith relates to contemporary dilemmas, and examining the diversity of practice by which communities of faith embody and enact their theological values.'

DBM

FURTHER READING: P.H. Ballard (ed), *The Foundations of Pastoral Studies and Pastoral theology*, University College, Cardiff, 1986. R. Baxter, *The Reformed Pastor*, Robert White for Nevil Simmons, London, 1656. D. Tidball, *Skilful Shepherds*, InterVarsity, Leicester, 1986.

Pastors

See *Ministry*; *Pastoral Call*; *Pastoral Care*; *Pastoral Theology*.

Peace, Baptists and

[See also *Conscientious Objectors*; *Disarmament*; *Pacifism and Peace Churches*; *Peace Camps*; *Peace Conferences*]
Although Baptists have roots in the *Anabaptist tradition* and share those roots with the

Mennonites – a peace church – Baptists collectively have not been inclined towards pacifism although there have been individual pacifists throughout the centuries.

Baptists fought in Cromwell's armies and have been active in the military forces of most countries where there are Baptist churches. The early mind among English Baptists was for Patriotism, thus following the teaching of Paul (Ro 13:1ff) and Peter (1Pe 2:13ff) that we should obey the powers that are ordained by God. This argument was put forward by both British and German Baptists on the opposite sides of the 1914-18 conflict. It continues to be the majority position. In their outlook on peacemaking Baptists may be influenced as much by nationality as *theology* so that the Scandinavians will incline more towards non-*violent* solutions to conflict.

Following the Napoleonic wars there was a growth of anti-militaristic opinion and a number of Baptists took leading roles in the Peace Societies of the 19th century. We find *William Carey* and *C.H. Spurgeon* making statements against militarism and resolutions were passed at assemblies in 1878, 1886 and 1900 against the waste of war and the fostering of the war spirit. A number of Baptist **ministers** played an important part in the work of the Peace Society (founded at the end of the Napoleonic Wars), several serving as its secretary for long periods. As such they helped to organise International *Peace Conferences* and secured the inclusion of a paragraph on arbitration in the terms of the Peace of Paris which ended the Crimean War in 1856. *John Clifford* was outspoken in his opposition to the Boer War in 1899-1902 – but supported the war effort in 1914.

It was the introduction in 1916 of conscription into the armed forces that brought the pacifist argument to the fore in *Britain*. Christians, whose understanding of the example and teaching of *Jesus* led them to maintain that they could not love their enemies and kill them, refused to take up weapons. They took Peter and John's position (Ac 4:19) that they should obey God rather than *man*. These first conscientious objectors (COs) suffered greatly at the hands of the authorities until the right to objection was established and accepted. However, Baptist leaders who supported the war also upheld the right of individual Baptists to be COs.

The revulsion to the slaughter of WWI brought many peace movements into being. In Britain the Baptist Pacifist Fellowship was founded in 1932, initially as a fellowship for ministers but shortly opened its membership to all Baptists. 'We, members of and adherents of Baptist churches, *covenant* together to renounce war in all its works and ways, and to do all in our power, God helping us, to make the teaching of Jesus Christ effective in all human relations.'

During the 1939-45 war many Baptist COs pleaded their case before tribunals and agreed to accept alternative work in agriculture, rescue or medical services. Other European *nations* have been slower to accept the right to conscientious objection but now offer alternative civic service to military conscription. E.g. in *Switzerland* religious objection is recognised but the objector has to serve a longer period in civil than in military service. The European Parliament has recommended that all its member *states* should recognise this right.

While the Baptist Peace Fellowship (BPF) has had a particular responsibility to keep the issue of Christian peacemaking before the Baptist denomination its members have always been active in the wider Christian and *secular* peace movement through the inter-denominational Fellowship of *Reconciliation*, Campaign against the Arms Trade, Campaign for *Nuclear* Disarmament, World Disarmament Campaign, etc. Because justice and peace are always linked, BPF members, like other Baptists, have campaigned for economic justice and world development.

Baptists have not contributed to recent debates about the doctrine of the *Just War* and its extension to 'pre-emptive wars'. Pacifists argue that one of the 'Just War' conditions, that of protecting civilians during fighting, cannot be met in modern war. The 'Just War' direction to seek all methods to end a dispute before resorting to arms entails a serious consideration of and attempt to apply non-violent approaches to conflict resolution. The example of Martin Luther King has not opened up a debate on the role of active *non-violence*. The 1996 Baptist *Union* of Great Britain document, '5 Core Values', suggested that Baptists should explore the possibility and *missionary* impact of becoming a 'Peace Church'. That exploration has not taken place widely in the churches. Some individuals have taken part in non-violent demonstrations against nuclear weapons or joined the *Ecumenical* Accompaniment Programme in *Palestine* and *Israel* or the Christian Peacemaker Teams in Hebron and Iraq.

In a series of resolutions at the annual assembly, the Baptist Denomination in the UK has opposed nuclear weapons, antipersonnel land mines and the unregulated trade in arms. The leadership initially took a strong stance against the Iraq war in 2003 but were quiet on the outbreak having a loyalty to Baptists serving in the armed forces and to Baptist *chaplains*. Since chaplains wear military uniform and take an oath of loyalty to the Queen some Baptist ministers have done *pastoral* work to the armed forces as padres with the *YMCA*.

At an International World Peace gathering of Baptists at Sjoviks, *Sweden* in 1988 there were representatives of many European nations. Apart from the BPF the only formal Baptist peace organisation was in *Germany* – the Initiative Shalom. The Baptists in *Italy* have been prominent in taking a stance against militarism. Individual Baptists in all countries have worked with other peace groups (e.g. MIR in France) and national Campaigns against Nuclear Weapons. Baptists have generally been quiet supporters of the *United Nations*.

The Iraq war has made many Christians re-think their attitude to armed conflict as an instrument of peacemaking. In this instance the deception was obvious and the effects catastrophic. Armed intervention can no longer be seen as a general solution to injustice or conflict. A *Christ*-like understanding of the path to peace between communities and nations remains an unresolved debate between Baptists.

NK

FURTHER READING: Paul R. Dekar, *For the healing of the nations*, Smyth and Helwys, Macon, Ga., 1993. H.F. Lorkin, *Baptist views on war and peace*, Baptist Union of Great Britain and Ireland, London, 1969. N.G. Wright, *Disavowing Constantine*, Paternoster, London, 2000.

Peace Camps

[See also *Peace, Baptists and*]

There are and have been two kinds of peace camps. Firstly, Youth camps, organised by major peace campaigners, such as the Danish War Resister's International and the Religious Society of Friends (*Quakers*), have brought young people together from different countries for shared recreation and a programme of seminars and activities on issues relating to war and peace.

Secondly, Peace camps may involve non-violent protest about particular wars or conflicts. The establishment of peace camps has been largely the prerogative of *women*. The Greek playwright Aristophanes introduced the character of Lysistrata [she who disbands armies] in a play in the 5th century BC and the historical relationship between *feminism* and anti-militarism is recorded from before the 1915 Women's International Congress for Peace at The Hague, *Netherlands* [see *Disarmament*].

Part of the global 'peace movement', peace camps grew in number with increasing *nuclear threat*. A women-only peace camp was set up in 1981 at the Greenham Common US Air Base, Berkshire, *England* to protest at the nuclear installation of Cruise missiles and their potential deployment across Europe. Despite British government opposition to the camp and many arrests, 1,000s of women and many *men* continued to hold peaceful protests at the camp until 1991 when, following agreement between *USSR* and USA, Cruise missiles were deactivated. The peace camp continued until 1995 and since 2000 a permanent memorial has been established at the site. Other peace camps grew in the *UK*, such as those at Faslane, *Scotland* in 1982 in protest at the nuclear naval base in Gareloch; and later in 1993, at Menwith Hill in North Yorkshire where the protest focused on the US military telecommunications base. Many women and men of *faith*, particularly from the Quaker and *Mennonite traditions* and also including British Baptists, were involved in these camps.

Across Europe, further peace camps were established, inspired by the Greenham Common camp. In 1982, a women's peace camp was established at the US airbase in Valkenburg, Netherlands and in *Germany*, the *Friedensdorf* [*Peace Village*] at Mutlangen. In *Denmark*, the Women's Peace Camp at Ravnstrup ran from 1984-86. In Comiso, Sicily a women's camp, *La Ragnitella* [*Spider's Web*] was established in 1983 in protest at the setting up of Europe's largest arsenal of Cruise atomic missiles at this site in southern *Italy*, strategically placed to link Europe with the Middle East and North Africa. In the early 1990s, women in *Georgia* used the traditional 'white scarf' strategy (waving their white headdresses to signal peace) as the basis for intervention in the *Armenia/Azerbaijan* conflict. In 1993 women, many of them Christian, met in several European cities, including Tbilisi, Warsaw, Moscow, Paris and London, as a symbol of peace.

The 2003 invasion of Iraq by Britain, the United States, Australia, *Poland* and Denmark (with other countries involved since) was prefaced by a resurgence of peaceful protest across the world, including a strong Christian voice with many Baptists involved. In Europe today, many peace protests are held still, although few of these have become camps like those of the 1980s.

MEW

Peace Churches

See *Church of the Brethren, Baptists and the*; *Mennonites*; *Mennonites, Baptists and*; *Pacifism and Peace Churches*; *Quakers, Baptists and*.

Peace Conferences

[See also *Peace, Baptists and*]

The problem of war and peace became a central concern for the churches in Europe during the 20th century, especially after WWII. An international community of *faith*, such as the churches which came together in the *European Baptist Federation* in 1949, had been critically affected by the war, for it represented minorities of believers living in most of the European countries, but divided by the 'Iron Curtain' and affected by the *political* and military conflict of the *Cold War* Era. A major part of the EBF lived within the borders of the *Soviet Union*, and its satellites in Eastern Europe, that were brought under Soviet control shortly after the war. There were various initiatives to hold conferences on the theme of peace as this was acceptable to the *communist* authorities and often people from the West would be allowed to participate under controlled conditions. The Russian Baptists with leaders like Jakub Zhidkov became involved in one such initiative involving most of the Christian *traditions* in the Soviet Union. This was held at the Troitse-Sergiyeva Monastery of Zagorsk in May 1952, which gathered representatives from all the major churches in the USSR. Ernest A. Payne of *Great Britain* discovered on a visit to *Russia* two years later, that churches within the *AUCECB* used the peace-question even in regular *worship*-services, as a way of safeguarding their fragile *religious freedom* under Joseph Stalin. The next conference in this series was held at Helsinki, and political pressure from the USSR was put on the EBF and the *BWA* officials in order to have them participate, and arrangements were actually made to have the general secretary of the EBF, W.O. Lewis, attend, but only as an observer. This took place despite protests from Finnish Baptists, who saw the conference as a communist tool of propaganda. Despite the risk of being misunderstood as soft on communism, the EBF sought opportunities to have real contact and *dialogue* between Christians, seeking a common future of a more stable and lasting peace.

Another initiative came from Central Europe, where Hungarians called for a Peace conference in 1958, which was followed by the development of a series of conferences in Prague. These became a major diplomatic challenge to the EBF and the BWA. For many Baptists the Christian Peace Conferences (CPC) were controversial in a number of ways. Given the principle of the division between *church and state*, there was concern about an organisation which it was suspected was majorly funded by the communist government whose views on international peace were often mirrored in conference statements. Nevertheless without renouncing this position it was seen that the CPC opened up a larger arena, where a concern for *human rights* and protest against the growing threat of *nuclear* war could be expressed. Participation gave opportunities

for contact beyond the official programme, not least on the human level. The threat overshadowing the European generation that grew up in the aftermath of WWII, with parents that had survived two world wars, had resulted in a strong awareness of the evils of war and militarism, and the need to surpass the climate of suspicion. Here Baptists found a common ground with other Christians in a protest against the Cold-War trauma that had reduced Europe to an arena of political combat between the two superpowers, the US and the USSR.

The European Baptist involvement in the CPC was in part a function of a deep concern for religious toleration in the East. The Christian Peace Conference movement met in Prague spasmodically between 1959 and 78. Henry Cook, as President of the EBF, attended the first and made a full report to the EBF executive, as Baungaard Thomsen of Denmark, President 1962-64, was to do four years later. In this he indicated that Eastern European Baptist leaders needed the support of their colleagues in the West, but the US put pressure on the BWA to prevent an official participation in the conferences. The Conferences continued in 1968 which turned out to be a disaster for the movement with the overthrow of Alexander Dubcek who had sought to establish '*socialism* with a human face' in the so called 'Prague Spring', and the invasion of *Czechslovakia* in Aug of that year. The Secretary of the movement was dismissed, and its president, the *Protestant theologian*, Josef Hraodmádka, resigned and died broken-hearted a few weeks later. During this period a number of Baptists served on the CPC-Working Committees.

In 1988, five years after the *ecumenical* Life and Peace Conference in Uppsala at the crucial time when Mikhail Gorbachev called for major reductions of nuclear weapons, a new international conference for Baptists committed to the peace cause was arranged in Sjoevik, *Sweden*. The official report edited by H.W.W. Pipkin of *IBTS* does not give an official attendance list and numbers of those attending are reported as 170-200 people from 30-35 countries. This conference was enabled by the Baptist Peace Fellowship of North America (BPFNA), which later sponsored further conferences in Nicaragua

(1992) and more recently *Italy* (2009).

The afore-mentioned report – *Seek Peace and Pursue It* – has a foreword by the EBF secretary Knud Wümpelmann. Ken Sehested, then director of the BPFNA, expressed the hope that a new moment in Baptist history had arrived. With this conference, 50 years after WWII, Baptists had finally gathered from both sides of the Iron Curtain and made their position clear. The threatening split between East and West seemed to come to an end, and many Baptists had a new awareness of the Christian *call* to peacemaking, with or without a principle position on *pacifism*.

PMIL & ET

FURTHER READING: Paul R. Dekar, *For the healing of the nations*, Smyth and Helwys, Macon, Ga., 1993. Keith G. Jones, *The European Baptist Federation 1950-2006: a case study in interdependency*, Paternoster, Milton Keynes, 2009. H. Wayne Pipkin (ed), *Seek Peace and Pursue It: Proceedings form the International Baptist Peace Conference*, Institute for Baptist and Anabaptist Studies, Rüschlikon and Baptist Peace Fellowship of North America, Memphis, Tn., 1989.

Pelagianism

This term refers to the *heresy* articulated by the British monk, Pelagius, in the 5th century, which asserted that *man* could save himself by his own efforts through the doing of good works. Pelagius claimed that to argue otherwise would be to take away all motivation for the moral life and resisting *sin*. The doctrine was fiercely attacked by St. Augustine and condemned at the Council of Ephesus in 431. Notwithstanding this, Pelagianism or semi-Pelagianism continued to have a following at a popular level, the term coming to mean any *theological* emphasis which unduly emphasised *humankind*'s ability to secure its own *salvation*. The reformers [see *Reformation*] re-enforced Augustine's insistence on the priority of *grace*, appropriated by *faith* as the basis of assurance. The believers' only hope of salvation was grounded on what *Christ* had secured by his sacrifice on the *cross*, which did for sinners what they could not do for themselves. To teach otherwise was an offence against the cross.

JHYB

Pentecost

[See also *Pentecost Sunday, Pentecostalism, Baptists and*]

This refers to the *Jewish harvest festival* at which the *Holy Spirit* descended upon the *church* and gave rise to its dramatic expansion into the Mediterranean world. Pentecost is the Septuagint reading for the 50 days which were to be counted after the offering of the barley harvest at Passover (Lev 23:16). In the *Christian calendar* Pentecost is 10 days after the celebration of the *Ascension* of the Risen Lord into *heaven* at which time *Jesus* told his disciples that they would 'receive power when the Holy Spirit has come upon you; and you will be my witnesses in Jerusalem, in all Judea and in Samaria, and to the ends of the earth (Ac 1:6-8). At Pentecost itself some 120 believers were gathering when the Spirit came like 'the rush of a violent wind', resting on them like tongues of fire and causing them to be filled with the Holy Spirit and to speak in other languages (Ac 1: 15; 2:1-4). The *Apostle* Peter interpreted this as the fulfilment of the *prophecy* in Joel 2:28-32 concerning the new age of messianic fulfilment. Pentecost therefore represents not only the birth of the Christian *church* but the dawning of the messianic age in which, on the basis of the saving life, work and *resurrection* of Christ, the open offer of *salvation* is proclaimed and the Spirit of God's age of fulfilment, the Spirit of the last days, is bestowed. The nature of Pentecost as a harvest festival is meaningful at this point as the first-fruits of a new humanity are offered up to God.

NGW

Pentecost Sunday

[See also *Pentecost; Pentecostalism, Baptists and*]

This day celebrates the gift of the *Holy Spirit* to the first followers of *Jesus* gathered in the Upper Room. Originally it was a unitive festival commemorating both the *Ascension* of Jesus and the infilling of the Holy Spirit in the *apostles* and disciples. However, during the 4th century it evolved into two commemorations corresponding to the distinct aspects of the biblical record [see *Bible*].

The Greek word 'Pentecost' refers to the

50th day after the paschal season. Recalling the tongues of fire signifying the gift of the Holy Spirit to those gathered in Jerusalem, it came to be celebrated as the birthday of the *church* as the new ecclesia of God. Certainly, many Baptist churches have celebratory services on this day. In some places there are open-air *evangelistic* events or processions and marches of witness. There might often be special music and some churches take the opportunity to link the birthday of the church universal with a remembrance of the establishment of their *local church*. The Monday following Pentecost used to be a public holiday and this was often the occasion for the 'Whit Walks' in which all local *Sunday Schools* participated.

In *Georgia* it is an occasion for the all the ordained *pastors* [see *Ordination*] to gather together and they include the consecration of oil for the *anointing of the sick* on this *festival*.

KGJ

Pentecostalism, Baptists and

[See also *Pentecost*; *Pentecost Sunday*]
European Pentecostalism has its roots in the 19th-century *Holiness* movement, the revitalisation of European *Pietism*, and the impact of Transatlantic *Revivalism*, with the *Welsh Revival* of 1904 serving as a powerful catalyst. The pioneer of the movement is often regarded as T.B. Barratt, a *Methodist minister* who was a naturalised Norwegian of English birth. From his base in *Norway* the message and experience spread widely through literature, conferences and personal *witness*, across Northern Europe in 1907. In *Britain* some of the earliest to be influenced were *Anglicans* but subsequently several denominations of a *free-church* persuasion came into being, notably Elim and the Assemblies of God, to which some Baptists were attracted. Whilst some Baptist leaders were encouraging towards the new movement, others – seeing it as potentially divisive – were cool, if not hostile, in their response. When immigrants from the Caribbean arrived in Britain in the 1950s, many of whom had been Baptist in their homelands, they established black-led Pentecostal churches such as the New Testament Church of God and the Church of God of Prophecy.

European Pentecostalism was strongest in *Scandinavia* where a number of former Baptists became part of the new movement. The most notable of these was Lewi Pethrus whose Baptist church in Stockholm became Pentecostal in 1913. He exercised a remarkable leadership over *Sweden*'s many Pentecostal churches, though their structure was highly *congregational* with little room for outside influence. Many other Baptist congregations and pastors – over 100 it was claimed in 1923 – including Carl Hedeen of Stockholm, K.G. Hellström of Gothenberg and the editor of the Baptist paper, J.A. Borgström, followed Pethrus into Pentecostalism, giving the new denomination sufficient numerical strength to make a public impact seen in Pethrus's forming of the Christian Democrat Party. In Norway, where the first Pentecostal Church was founded by Baptist pastor Carl Seehaus, in Sweden and in *Finland*, Pentecostals soon became the largest church group outside the *Lutheran state churches*. Often this *growth* occurred at the expense of the Baptists.

In *France*, former Baptist Piers Nicholl became pastor of the Rouen congregation, the leading church of the French Assemblies of God. All in all 'the Baptist family felt itself threatened by the rising tide of Pentecostalism.'

In *Russia*, the establishment of Pentecostalism is often attributed to Ivan Voronaev, a Baptist pastor, who, forced to emigrate, was baptised in the *Spirit* in New York in 1919. He left his Baptist pastorate to become pastor of the Russian Pentecostal Church in that city. Under a sense of divine compulsion he returned to Europe and established churches in *Bulgaria* which soon had more *members* than all the other free churches combined. He then undertook work in Odessa and Leningrad, establishing some 350 congregations especially in *Ukraine*, often drawing strength from former Baptists, including such leaders as D.L. Ponomarchuk and D.S. Ponurko, before his imprisonment in 1920. This caused considerable conflict between the two groups with Baptists calling the Pentecostals 'deceivers' who insisted that all Christians had to work miracles and speak in tongues. In Finland the *Evangelical* Christian leaders, N.P. Smorodin and N.I. Ivanov also converted to Pentecostalism, before moving to undertake *mission* work in Russia, whilst the notable Estonian lay leader [see *Laity*], Baron Uexküll, who had played a notable part in early *BWA* congresses, was by the 1930s declaring himself a Pentecostal.

In 1945 Stalin coerced Russian Pentecostal churches to join the *All-Union Council of Evangelical Christians-Baptists*, but since Baptist congregations were opposed to the exercise of *glossolalia*, this was not a happy union, and many Pentecostals refused to join and were persecuted as unregistered congregations, which helped to spread the movement throughout the federation. Similar *unions* were required in other Eastern European countries, with a withdrawal and the establishment of separate Pentecostal witness after the end of the *Cold War*.

Pentecostalism is strong in *Romania*, in Bulgaria and in some other parts of the *Balkans*. The Pentecostal movements in this region have produced *theologians* of international significance in Peter Kuzmič and Miroslav Volf. In Southern Europe Pentecostal Churches have been growing rapidly and like their counterparts in Latin America, with whom there are close associations, essentially represent a church of the *poor*.

In 1966 the European Pentecostal Fellowship came into being with the more congregational churches holding Pentecostal European Conferences from 1969, the two bodies amalgamating in 1987 to form the Pentecostal European Fellowship.

JHYB

Periodicals
See *Magazines*.

Perseverance of the Saints
[See also *Saints*]

This is the final point in five point *Calvinism*: total *depravity*, unmerited favour, limited *atonement*, irresistible *grace*, and the perseverance of the saints. The idea is that if one belongs to the number of the elect [see *Election*], *predestined* thereto, then one's final destiny is secure, whatever the tests and temptations encountered on the way (Jn 6:39-40; 10:28-29). Differently expressed it is the conviction that a *sovereign* God cannot accomplish other than a perfect work and thus if God begins a work of *regeneration*, to be true to himself, he cannot but complete it. Those NT passages which seem to suggest the possibility of a falling away (e.g. 2Pe 2:20) are then argued as warnings against superficial commitment, or as hypothetical argument or as persuasion to be better established in *holiness*. The importance of the doctrine is not so much to emphasise the need for Christian determination as much as the enduring grasp of God's *grace* There is however no grounds here for *antinomian* complacency.

ET

Phenomenon of Religion
Religion as a phenomenon of human history, society and culture has received special attention in Europe since the late 19th century. The pioneers of the new field of study such as Friedrich Max Müller or Cornelius P. Tiele wanted to distance themselves from a confessional *theological* approach and expected that modern philosophy, *anthropology*, *sociology* or psychology would grant them the objectivity of approach of an independent and a truly *scientific* observer.

In 1890 a Scottish anthropologist, Sir James George Frazer, published the first edition of his *Golden Bough: A Study in Magic and Religion*, comparing the rites and beliefs of ancient religions with each other and with modern religions such as Christianity. He was convinced that in the history of religions we can trace the linear progress of *humankind* from primitive magic religions to more superior positions, a belief which has come in for strong criticism. However, his emphasis on the importance of *symbols*, myths and rituals for understanding various human cultures has been accepted. At the beginning of the 20th century other significant studies of religion emerged. William James wrote *The Varieties of Religious Experience* (1902) which approached religion from a philosophical and psychological point of view, and demonstrated that especially at the limit experiences we can trace phenomena that cannot be explained from within a conscious subject, although they significantly influence human feeling and acting. James was criticised for too sharp a distinction between the subjective and the objective factors of religion, for praising religious feeling, and ignoring the **traditional**, doctrinal, ritual and institutional aspects. On the other hand, Émile Durkheim in his *Elementary Forms of Religious Life* (1912) showed that religion cannot be viewed separately from the society in which it is practiced, and opted for the sociological study of religion. Rudolf Otto's book *The Idea of the Holy* (1917) claimed that religion could not be reduced either to reason or to morality; through an investigation of non-rational factors in religion, he came to a non-reducible experience of the numinous that both creates a distance and attracts, that is *mysterium tremendum et fascinans*.

By the second half of the 20th century '**religious studies**' emerged as a prominent academic discipline devoted both to the comparative accounts of world religions and to the analysis of the phenomenon of religion as such. Including the earlier insights, religion was studied through its sacred narratives, rituals, doctrines and ethical codes, religious experiences and institutions. Influenced by new developments in epistemology, phenomenology and **hermeneutics**, new studies devoted to the phenomenon of religion dropped the conviction of pure independent scientificity, as well as the narrowly progressivist approach, judging between the higher and the lower forms of religion. Mircea Eliade (1907-86), a Romanian writer, historian of religion and philosopher, who taught at the University of Chicago, became the leading figure in the field. He turned his attention to 'hierophanies' and to their mythical and ritual expressions that gave religious people a sense of belonging and participation, as well as patterns for behaviour in the world which as they perceived it from within this sacred order. His insights are widely used not only for the traditional religions, but also for new forms of religiosity we encounter in the formerly **secular** cultures.

IN

FURTHER READING: J.D. Bettis (ed), *Phenomenology of Religion: Eight Modern Descriptions of the Essence of Religion*, SCM, London, 1969. É. Durkheim, *The Elementary Forms of the Religious Life*, Allen and Unwin, London, 1964. M. Eliade, *Patterns in Comparative Religion*, University of Nebraska Press, London, 1997. M. Eliade, *The Sacred and the Profane: The Nature of Religion*, Harcourt Brace Jovanovich, San Diego, 1987. M. Eliade, *The Quest: History and Meaning in Religion*, Chicago University Press, Chicago, 1969. W. James, *The Varieties of Religious Experience: A Study in Human Nature*, Fontana, London, 1960. R. Otto, *The Idea of the Holy*, Oxford University Press, London, 1958. P. Ricoeur, *Figuring the Sacred: Religion, Narrative and Imagination*, Fortress, Minneapolis, 1995.

Philanthropy

The term derives from the Greek words for '**love**' and '**humankind**' and means the desire to promote the welfare of others, particularly through establishing and funding charitable bodies devoted to the care of the **poor**. The growth of such societies in Britain in the 19th century was a fruit of both the **pietist** movement and the **evangelical revival** both of which believed that the **Word** had not only to be **preached** but demonstrated in daily life. Indeed, it has been calculated by Kathleen Heasman in *Evangelicals in Action* that a good three quarters of the charitable and voluntary societies seeking to ameliorate the less desirable outcomes of the industrial revolution in 19th-century **Britain** were evangelical in origin: the same authority affirms, 'there was scarcely a human contingency that was not met and publicised...Many of the functions of the **Welfare State** were recognised and met, not by social; economists and **Socialists**, but by these practical and practicing Christians, whose action was characterised by an intensely personal concern for the individual and his family, for **prostitutes**, cripples, drunkards [see **Alcoholism**], and even navvies and cabmen.'

Leading British Baptist **ministers**, such as **Spurgeon**, **Clifford**, Archibald Brown and F.B. Meyer, amongst many others, played their part. Individual lay people [see **Laity**] achieved distinction in this area such as the Scot, William Quarrier. Philanthropy was the arena for what has been called the 'Epiphany of **women**' occurred as they founded and ran successful **orphanages**, led the work in **Sunday Schools** and played a major part in **overseas missions**. Philanthropy had never to be advanced at the expense of justice in the **work** place; indeed a proper reward for labour represented a prior commitment to all philanthropic activity? Widespread poverty in one of the richest **nations** of the world was nothing less than an offence to the gospel. Baptists were accordingly amongst those who pioneered new initiatives in such areas as paid holidays, **health** insurance, pension provision, and profit-sharing amongst employees.

Philanthropy within the evangelical and Baptist community in Europe in the 19th century was by no means confined to Britain. The story of evangelicals in **Russia** also shows this philanthropic spirit. In 1868 a prominent British evangelical, Granville A. W. Waldegrave (Lord Radstock) spoke about the evangelical **faith** to several members of the Russian aristocracy who were in Paris. These contacts led to Radstock visiting St. Petersburg several times in the 1870s. The effect was extraordinary. Through his preaching several **wealthy** and influential figures became evangelicals, notably Count Aleksey Bobrinskiy, at one time Russian Minister of Transportation, Count Modest M. Korff and his wife, Princess Vera Gagarin, her sister Princess Natalia Lieven and other members of her family, and Colonel Vasiliy A. Pashkov, a former soldier of the Royal Guard, and his wife.

A mansion owned by Pashkov on the Neva in St. Petersburg – he was an aristocrat who had several large estates and owned a number of mines – became an important meeting place. It was Pashkov who became the main leader of the group – the name 'Pashkovite' began to be used – and he and others began to pass on the evangelical message to their work people and the peasants on their estates in the provinces of Northern and Central Russia, to print and distribute tracts, and to organise Christian philanthropic efforts. Their efforts on behalf of the **poor** included **hospital** and **prison** visiting, helping **unemployed** people to find work, and setting up a shelter for **homeless children**.

Alongside Pashkov, Korff was an important figure, and by the end of the 1870s, through a visit to **Switzerland**, he had met Baptists and embraced Baptist beliefs. Korff also founded the Society for the Encouragement of Spiritual and Ethical Reading and published a popular weekly, *Russkiy rabo-*

chiy [*Russian Worker*]. The Society distributed religious literature, especially the **Bible**, across Russia. Through such literature, contacts began to be made between the Pashkovite evangelicals and the Baptist movement in Southern Russia.

In other parts of Europe the merging Baptist communities were often to be found among working-class people and so opportunities for wider philanthropic work by Baptists was limited. However, a great deal of mutual aid was practised. Social ministries became more prominent in many parts of European Baptist life in the 20th century but the language of 'philanthropy' gradually fell out of use.

ET

Pietism

[See also *Piety, Baptist*]

Pietism as a label was first applied to that movement within **Lutheranism** at the end of the 17th and the beginning of the 18th centuries associated with the names of P.J. Spener (1635-1703) and A.H. Franke (1663-1727) and their circle at the University of Halle in Saxony. Much of the life of the church was in the cold grip of an over-formal scholasticism and in need of renewal. Those associated with the movement sought a new sense of vital relationship with God on a day by day basis, cultivated by coming together for meetings for **prayer** and **Bible study** and the deepening of the individual's spiritual life, so that the movement put a new emphasis on an active **laity**. The movement was fruitful in reforming clerical training, in the establishment of schools, engagement in **philanthropy** (in the form of an **orphanage**, a home for widows and the founding of a **Bible Society**), and the development of **overseas missions**. They believed their work continued the work of **Luther** that as he had reformed doctrine they were seeking a reformation of life, but their championship of lay involvement and extra ecclesial societies has sometimes been seen to undermine the **authority** of the **church**. The movement has also been criticised for being over subjective with an undue emphasis upon the emotions and too much focus on the self. The accusation is that it too easily gave up on the task of christianising society or nurturing Christian culture in the **state**, turning attention to the individual, and thereby privatising religion. In the Rhineland, with an impact in neighbouring **Holland**, was a similar movement associated with the name of Gerhard Tersteegen (1697-1769) amongst the **Reformed Churches.**

One of the principal offshoots of the movement was the establishment of the **Moravian** Church under Count Zinzendorf (1700-60), a godson of Spener and a student of Francke, who created a new community of Hussite Brethren, otherwise known as the *Unitas Fratrum*, on his estate at Herrnhut. The Moravians, like the **Methodists** originally a grouping within the Lutheran church, established extensive missions in North America and were instrumental in the religious conversion of the Wesley brothers and so played their part in the foundation of Methodism which may be considered the English variant of Pietism. Another group to have its roots in early 18th century pietism is the church currently known as the **Church of the Brethren** but previously known as the German Baptist Brethren.

Pietism continued to be an influence within Lutheran **State churches** in Europe. In the 19th century, a new wave of pietism gave rise to the Inner Mission Movement often associated with the name of J.H. Wichern in Hamburg in the mid 19th century, soon spreading into Scandinavia where it was particularly important where e.g. the Mission Covenant Church was born out of the awakening associated with the name of C.O. Rosenius. German pietists also took the movement into southern **Russia** where their teachings and practices played a significant part in the birth of the **Stundist** movement. Questions may be raised as to whether pietism has served as a safety valve enabling spiritual 'enthusiasts' to remain within state churches, or whether to the contrary it has served as a staging post for those on the way to founding and joining one or other of the **free churches**. In this way, pietism has played an important part in the pre-history of a number of Baptist groups in Northern Europe.

JHYB

FURTHER READING: Ian Randall, '"Pious Wishes": Baptists and wider renewal movements in 19th century Europe', *Baptist Quarterly*, Jul 2000, vol. 38, no. 7, p.316-31.

Piety, Baptist

[See also *Pietism*; *Spirituality/Devotional Life*]]

Piety can signify both a person's inner life and how they choose to live in society. Whilst belonging to the **believers' church tradition**, Baptists have inherited much from the wider **Protestant** world, including elements of **Puritanism**, 19th-century pietism and **revivalism**. Their piety is seen in their focus on **scripture**, their emphasis on a personal **conversion** experience, their discipline in **prayer**, the engagement in Christian **witness** through words and service which will most immediately be expressed through the **fellowship** of the **local church**. Baptists experience God's presence both through corporate **worship**, and in developing their own individual spiritual lives. In the church there will be **Bible study** and prayer groups, with encouragement of their **members** to set aside a time for devotional **Bible** reading and prayer, often called 'The Quiet Time' by an earlier generation, every day. This could also be expressed in the gathering of the household for corporate prayer or more simply Baptist parents teaching their **children** to say their prayers at the end of the day. Baptist piety would also be expressed in the saying of **grace** before meals. **Preaching** the **Word** is still a central element in Baptist worship, traditionally symbolised by a **pulpit** which used to be (and still is) a conspicuous element in Baptist church architecture. Congregational singing as well as prayer, usually extemporaneous, constitute the occasions when the **Holy Spirit** may make himself known. Baptists often build close relationships with one another within the local church, worshipping and sharing together in its life and witness.

Part of a wider **evangelical spirituality** is the centrality of individual conversion, often described as '**new birth**', though in the contemporary situation this may be seen more in terms of gradual process than sudden crisis. **Baptism** by immersion is restricted to believers. Here Baptists find their **initiation** into the life of the **church** which includes the **commissioning** of all to **missionary** service since this is seen as the responsibility of every member. The Baptist search for freedom in cultivating the spiritual life finds expression in various ways: exercising *freedom of conscience* and indeed pursuing the goals of **religious liberty**. European Baptists, following the **apostolic** injunction, are forever seeking ways to become more **Christ**-like in their individual spiritual journeys, thereby seeking to replicate the life of the apostolic church.

Baptist piety in different parts of Europe has been shaped by local religious and historic circumstances. In some places such as **Sweden** or **Britain** this has sometimes led to the embracing of modest liturgical forms [see **Liturgy**] or the discipline of the **Christian Year** in corporate worship. In Eastern Europe, Baptist understanding of piety has been very much oriented towards preaching and verbally expressed prayer. In other regions, especially in the West, silence and retreats have been increasingly found helpful in order to deepen a believer's relationship with God, though the traditional word-oriented spirituality has not disappeared. Baptists in **Russia**, **Ukraine** or **Romania**, in part due to their historical experiences of living under an oppressive **state**, have traditionally emphasised piety in exemplary living and upholding high moral standards as a **'fruit of the Spirit'** and a sign of a life devoted to following Christ. Baptists in **Germany** or **Scandinavia** have made attempts to express their piety in becoming more sensitive to social issues through greater involvement in the life of the community where they live, not only as individuals but also as churches, thus understanding piety as a way of life which includes social, and even **political**, activity and **ecological** responsibility as well as a robust prayer life and dutiful participation in the life of the sanctuary.

TP

Pluralism

Pluralism refers most commonly to Religious Pluralism, and is an ambiguous term that recognises both the religious and ideological diversity found within contemporary societies, but also imputes a **theological** or philosophical significance to that diversity. For that reason some would distinguish between the fact of *plurality* and the notion of *pluralism* as a philosophical position in relation to such diversity, which often, implicitly or explicitly, embraces *Relativism*. So, e.g., Lesslie Newbigin (1909-98) argued that the **Church** 'can never accept...pluralism as a **creed** even if it must – as of course it must – acknowledge plurality as a fact' (*Foolishness to the Greeks*, p.115).

In a model commonly used in theological discourse since the last quarter of the 20th century, *Pluralism* is often contrasted with *Exclusivism* and *Inclusivism* and is particularly associated with the approach of the British **reformed** philosopher and **theologian**, John Hick (b.1922), who has raised significant ethical [see **Ethics**] and philosophical questions in numerous publications since his *God and the Universe of Faiths* (1973), especially in his Gifford Lectures, *An Interpretation of Religion* (1989). Hick characterised his approach as a 'Copernican Revolution', which reoriented the 'universe of **faiths**' from a Christocentric to a Theocentric (and subsequently a Soteriocentric) perspective [see **Christology; Salvation and Soteriology**]. Hick's approach is based on a *Realist* philosophy of God, but uses the Kantian distinction between *phenomena* (outward experienced reality) and *noumena* (inner **transcendent** reality). This understands the various phenomena of religion as cultural and historical responses to the noumenal Real; such phenomena may be characterised as *personae* or *impersonae* of the Divine. This analysis recognises that in different religious **traditions** Ultimate Reality is variously characterised in both personal and impersonal terms. Hick's criteria for assessment of religious traditions are profoundly ethical and turn on whether the tradition transforms a person from self-centredness to Reality-centredness.

Criticisms of this approach have included questions about its philosophical coherence, its adequacy to the reality of religious phenomena, and, from a Christian theological perspective, its marginalising of the person and work of **Christ**.

Alternatives such as *Exclusivism* argue that the **mission** of God is centred on the **Incarnation** and that only through some clear relationship to God in Christ is there any hope of salvation. However, the terminology of *exclusivism* is ambiguous in that it applies both to language about the uniqueness or 'exclusivity' of Jesus Christ, and to the 'exclusion' or otherwise of people from God's ultimate purpose of salvation. Some so-called *exclusivists* are clear about the importance of the former usage, but remain ambivalent as to the latter (e.g. Lesslie Newbigin). *Inclusivist* critics point out that *explicit* knowledge of the person and work of Christ would inevitably exclude the vast majority of humanity from any **hope** of salvation simply by the accidents of birth, history, geography or culture. From this point of view this is a travesty of the gospel as a message of hope for all peoples at all times, and raises serious theological and ethical questions about the justice and righteousness of God. The *Inclusivist* alternative is to argue that the salvific purposes of God are fulfilled and achieved in Christ alone (contra to the pluralist hypothesis), but that it is possible to be related to this saving work in some *implicit* way, perhaps even through the channel of other religious traditions. Unsurprisingly **Roman Catholic** theologians (famously Karl Rahner (1904-84) with his theory of 'anonymous Christians') have generally been more sympathetic to such an understanding of religious systems, whilst **Protestants** have by and large been more sceptical of seeing religion in such a way, but retain the possibility that divine **grace** may be communicated in other ways, such as through creation, family life, the creative arts and so on.

Baptists, with their emphasis on the centrality of Christ and their caution about organised religion have tended to take a *conservative* view of such matters and many would identify themselves as 'exclusivist' in approach. However, the emphasis on **religious liberty** has also meant that Baptists have embraced and argued for religious plurality within society as far back as **Thomas Helwys**' (1550-1616?) famous plea for toleration to include the '**Jew**, Turk (i.e. **Muslim**) and **heretic**'. The logic of religious liberty requires acceptance of religious diversity or plurality but not necessarily of a philosophy or theology of pluralism.

British Baptists such as Paul Weller (b.1956), professor of inter-religious relations at Derby University and Nicholas Wood (b.1954), tutor at **Regent's Park College, Oxford** have been working at appropriate contemporary responses which affirm both the centrality of Christ but also aim to take seriously the significance of other experiences and traditions in a religiously plural society.

NJW

FURTHER READING: G. D'Costa (ed), *Christian Uniqueness Reconsidered*, Orbis, Maryknoll, NY, 1990. G. D'Costa, *Theology and Religious Pluralism*, Blackwell, Oxford and New York, 1986. J. Hick, *God and the Universe of Faiths*, Macmillan, London, 1973. John Hick, *An Interpretation of Religion*, Macmillan, Basingstoke, 1989. J. Hick and P. Knitter (eds), *The Myth of Christian Uniqueness*, Orbis, Maryknoll, NY, 1987. H. Netland, *Encountering Religious Pluralism*, InterVarsity, Downer's Grove, Il., 2001. L. Newbigin, *The Gospel in a Pluralist Society*, Eerdmans, Grand Rapids, Mi., 1989. P.G. Weller, *Time for a Change*, T&T Clark International, London and New York, 2005. N.J. Wood, *Confessing Christ in a Plural World*, Whitley, Oxford, 2002.

Plymouth Brethren

See *Brethren*.

PNBC-E

See *Progressive National Baptist Convention of Europe (inc.)*.

Pneumatology

Pneumatology is the study of the doctrine of the Holy Spirit. Both in the early church and in modern *theology*, including Baptist theology, the doctrine of the Spirit has lagged behind *Christology* partly because clarifying the person of *Christ* is logically prior to clarifying the person of the Spirit of Christ. The Spirit is 'another Advocate' (Jn 14:16). Some European Baptists have, however, addressed issues of pneumatology, most notably H. Wheeler Robinson of **Britain**. In more recent years a great deal more attention has been given to pneumatology, not least in the wake of the birth of **Pentecostalism** and the coming of the **charismatic movement** and through renewed interest in **Orthodox** theology. The Nicene-Constantinopolitan **creed** clearly identified the Spirit as 'Lord and giver of Life. With the Father and the Son he is worshipped and glorified.' This lays down fundamental *orthodoxy* in relation to the Spirit: the Spirit is truly divine, sharing with the Son and the Father essential deity and so worthy of *worship* and honour as God. The Spirit is also distinctively personal, the agent of the Father and the Son but possessing the full attributes of divine personhood in the life of the Triune God [see *Trinity*]. More recent reflection, in which a discipline of Trinitarian thinking has become more intentional, has enlarged upon the Spirit's work in *creation*, in the *incarnation* and *ministry* of Jesus, in the life of the *church* and its *members* and in the drawing of creation towards its *eschatological* goal in the new *heaven* and new earth. So the Spirit is seen to be active in creation itself as the breath of God through which the creative *Word* is spoken. The Spirit who spoke through the prophets is to be discerned in the incarnation of the eternal Word as Jesus of Nazareth, preparing the way for his coming in the prophetic [see *Prophecy*] expectations of the devout circle of *Jewish* believers into which Jesus was born, bringing God's Son to conception and then to birth in the womb of the Virgin *Mary*, endowing Jesus with wisdom and insight as he grew to manhood, anointing him for the ministry into which he entered after his *baptism*, empowering him for the mighty works he accomplished, enabling him to offer himself in atoning sacrifice upon the *cross*, retrieving him from *death* so that he would not see corruption and then raising him from death as the triumphant victor and Lord. If it is right to see the Spirit as God's gift through the Son to the church then it is equally right and *scriptural* to understand the Son as the Father's gift through the Spirit. The effect of these broader perspectives on the Spirit is to develop a more complete Trinitarian theology and to move away from a common *evangelical* perspective which tended to reduce the Spirit's role to that of expounding or applying the saving work of the Son in the experience of the believer, an approach derived from the conviction that the Spirit's role was only to glorify the Son (Jn 16:14).

NGW

Poland, Baptist history in

The Baptist movement in the territory of present-day Poland started among German colonists [see *Colonialism*]. In 1844, *Johann Gerhard Oncken* founded in Elblag (then in Prussia, today's North-East Poland) the first German Baptist church. However, Baptist convictions spread also in the Russian part of Poland. Gottfried F. Alf, after his *conversion*, under the influence of the German Baptist *mission*, established a Polish-speaking Baptist church in Adamow, near Warsaw, in 1861, the origin of the Polish Baptist movement. In the second half of the 19th century Baptist churches were started in Kurówko (1870), Warsaw (1875), Łódź (1878), and in other places. Though some Poles joined the churches, the Baptist *faith* spread mostly among Russian and German-speaking people, experiencing persecution from both the *Roman Catholic* Church and the *state* authorities. Before WWI, the major centre of the Baptist movement was Lodz, which had both a German and a Polish-speaking Baptist church. In the years of independence (1918-39) Baptists were denied the rights given to the Roman Catholic Church. A *union* of Slavic Baptists in Poland, including Polish, Russian, Ukrainian, Belorussian and Czech congregations, was formed in 1921. A publishing house, *Słowo Prawdy* [Word of Truth], was established in 1925, and social activities expanded: an *orphanage* and a house for the *elderly* were started as well as a *hospital*, *Betlehem,* and a house for *deaconesses*. A Baptist theological seminary was established in Łódź (1924). For historical and ethnic reasons, Baptists were, before WWII, organised in two unions: the Union of German Baptist Churches (about 8,000 *members*) and the Union of Slavic Baptist Churches (about 7,000 members). Plans to unite as the Evangelical Baptist Church in Poland, were thwarted by the war. By 1945, as a result of the war and the changing of borders, the number of the Baptists in Poland had fallen to about 1,000.

Based on the decision made by the government authorities in May 1946, the Polish Evangelical Christian-Baptist Church received the right to exist as a fully recognised church. However *communist political* systems affected Baptists critically with the forced closure of the reopened seminary and publishing house a few years after war ended. Even some of the leaders of the churches were arrested for a short time and interrogated. Just after WWII (May 1945) Baptists, the Christian *Free Church* and the Evangelical Christian Church formed a united denomination known as the Union of Evangelical Christians and Baptists of Poland. This united evangelical Church did not last long, collapsing a couple of years later. In the communist period almost all church activities were limited to a congregation's spiritual needs with major decisions concerning Baptist churches made in Warsaw by the Executive Board of the Baptist Church. For Polish Baptists, the decades following WWII were a time of slow recovery from the scars of war; only after 1956 did modest *growth* begin. Contacts with foreign countries were gradually renewed. Relationships with the Theological Seminary in *Rüschlikon* were established and *ecumenical dialogue* on the national scene begun, with involvement in the *Billy Graham Crusade* in Poland in 1978.

After the collapse of communism, Baptists exploited many new opportunities; in 1992 241 people were baptised [see *Baptism*]. A Seminary which had many difficulties during the communist time was provided with a permanent building for the first time. Today the *students* can secure a degree in *theology* in the new Seminary located in *Radosc*, Warsaw built in 1994 alongside a conference centre. Most of the mission of the church is undertaken by local congregations without prompting from the Union Executive. Whilst during the time of communism, Baptists were discouraged and denied promotion to managerial positions, this has changed, and many Baptists are at present involved in working in the wider society and some in the political sphere. Nevertheless, the legacy of the previous political regime, discouraging believers' social and political activity, can still be found in Baptist churches. Currently the Baptist churches in Poland have 4,100 members in 70 *local churches*.

ZW

Politics, Baptists and

Perhaps more than the entry on any other topic, the preface here should say that what follows represents *a* Baptist approach not an obligatory schema requiring endorsement or consent from his fellow believers. Politics has been defined as 'the organised conduct of relationships in any form of human community, e.g. 'ecclesiastical politics' or 'sexual politics', which means that politics covers everything relating to the government of human affairs within the life of the *State*. Two NT texts have been seen as particularly relevant. In Mk 12: 13-17 *Jesus* makes the point that God's rule over his people does not exclude Caesar's legitimate rights. In Ro 13 Paul teaches that government has a God-given rôle and is entitled to cooperation from Christians. Political life is part of the process of ensuring a secure and just society and therefore Christians must take a positive attitude to government. However, if governments act against God's laws, then Christians have a duty to be disobedient (Ac 5:29).

Church and State, often closely allied, severely persecuted the *Anabaptists* making them a *suffering* people, and in *England* after 1660, when the brief experiment of the republic and the reign of the *saints* was over, *Nonconformists* were with rare exception barred from local and national political power. Until 1828 in *Great Britain*, and even later in other countries, Baptists were deprived of the vote, and therefore excluded from political life, and even then many Baptists remained disenfranchised, not so much because of religious discrimination, but because of class restrictions. The strength of *pietism* amongst Baptists, has often led them to regard politics with some suspicion as a realm hopelessly compromised by human *sin,* and therefore best avoided. Nevertheless, once enfranchised, most Baptists saw the need to use their vote and in different countries a number became elected representatives and indeed members of government. Baptists unlike some of their Anabaptist predecessors never denied the authority of the magistrate, or disallowed a believer taking on such an office. By contrast, e.g., the English confessions of the 17th century both required respect for the office of the magistrate and legitimised serving in that office.

Their concern for the *separation of church and state* has meant that Baptists have not generally favoured the development of separate Christian parties, which have often been linked to the interests of members of **State Churches**, or the internationalism of the **Roman Catholic** Church. Working through mixed confession **secular** parties, by contrast, necessarily requires the compromise of working with those of different **faith** commitment and none. This is little more than a recognition of politics, in its classic definition, as 'the art of the possible', or to recognise that in a fallen world [see **Fall**] pursuit of' 'the lesser evil' (which, of course, is also 'the greater good') is **theologically** respectable; the luxury of working with uncontexted and unqualified ideals is never practical in politics [see **Contextualisation**] However, in such situations, Christians will be wary of parties which represent only a sectional interest, and fail to give priority to work for justice for all citizens, especially the most marginalised and disadvantaged. In the last century, totalitarian regimes of both the left and the right have excluded Baptists from political power, more occasionally persuading them to collude with them either because e.g. National Socialism in Central Europe was seen as a bulwark against **Communism**, or from fear and under persecution. The rift amongst Soviet Baptists concerning obedience to restrictive laws has left its scars, which are still a cause of division even in the 'Free' world. For many Baptists during the **Cold War** period political involvement had perforce to be minimal

The place of power in human society, the relationship between churches and the state, and the right of the state to coerce people into action against their **consciences** (such, e.g., as serving in the armed forces) remain. Moral issues, such as legislation allowing **abortion**, or for the sanctioning of same-sex partnerships [see **homosexuality**], are also flashpoints for political and religious concern. Some Baptists retain an apolitical stance, unwilling to see that believers can influence political decisions or that political decisions must impinge on Christian life. More believe that Christians should take their responsibilities as citizens seriously, and participate in the political process by using their vote responsibly, and, if opportunity should arise, being willing to represent their fellow citizens as elected representatives. In this they reject the false separation of sacred and secular, recognising the claim of God's rule to be honoured and respected in all spheres of life. Put differently they cannot allow God to be 'privatised', and to be excluded from the public sphere. As the NT makes clear, **redemption** is not just for individuals, though that is ever their **hope**, but for the whole of the created order and the Christian **calling** is to participate in this. Saying this is not to adopt a secularised **eschatology**, but rather to be obedient to a God who is concerned for all he has created.

Christians may give expression to their political consciences by constitutional action or by participating in protest movements which question the very existence of unjust laws and practices, which burden the **poor** and oppress the marginalised. Whilst political activity can seek to anticipate the coming of the **Kingdom of God**; of itself it cannot inaugurate the eschaton [see **Eschatology**]. So, like all human endeavours, whilst politics has a vibrant appeal to many, it must always be subordinate to the divine rule. Yet it will only be suffused with Christian values if Christians participate at local and national level.

As the world seems to be moving towards an **ecological** crisis, many see the need to work in the political sphere against programmes which over-exploit the natural world, and contrariwise to support proposals taking the need for conservation of the environment seriously, whilst exercising some concern for 'one issue' parties. Given their history, Baptists will always be apprehensive of any system which makes for the dominance of politics by one party, always fighting for respect for the right to dissent. This concern for domination extends also to the media, and its ability to bring undue pressure to bear on the political process, especially since the public can so easily be manipulated through control and distortion of the information source. By contrast good education in independent critical thought and discernment is the natural ally of **democracy** for it has been well-said that a 'democracy cannot be ignorant and free'. Again in exercising their political power, wise Christians will realise that a church which, whilst respecting each individual's free choice, is not working for change, is de facto legitimising the status quo, whether it intends to or not. However at the end of the day, it has to be recognised that in their pursuit of power, political parties can become idolatrous, that is to claim for themselves a devotion and loyalty that belongs to God alone.

                                                 DBM & JHYB

FURTHER READING: 'Politics' in *The New Dictionary of Christian Ethics and Pastoral Theology*, InterVarsity, Leicester, 1995. Orlando Costas, *Christ Outside the Gate*, Orbis, Maryknoll, NY, 1982. C. Elliott (ed), *Christian Faith and Political Hopes*, Epworth, London, 1979. Richard Mouw, *Politics and the Biblical Drama*, Eerdmans, Grand Rapids, Mi., 1976. J.H. Yoder, *The Politics of Jesus*, Eerdmans, Grand Rapids, Mi.,1972.

Polity
See *Assembly, General – as governing body of Union*; *Ecclesiology (Church Polity)*; *Unions/Conventions*.

Pollution
See *Climate Change*; *Ecology and the Environment*.

Pool, Baptismal
See *Baptistry*.

Poor, The
See *Preferential Option for the Poor*.

Pope, The
See *Infallibility of the Pope*; *Papacy*; *Roman Catholicism*; *Vatican, The*.

Population Explosion
See *Ecology and the Environment*.

Portugal, Baptist history in
Portugal, situated on the western seaboard of the Iberian Peninsula, has had a Baptist *witness* since the 1880s. Baptists in Portugal face all the problems of living in a dominant *Roman Catholic* culture. The intrinsic difficulties of the task have not been helped by

the way in which Baptists from other parts of the world have at times promoted their own independent outreach in the country. The origins of Baptist work in Portugal date back to 1888 when Joseph Charles Jones formed the first Baptist congregation, in Oporto. Joseph Jones, who was of Welsh descent, had been born in Oporto, where his father was active in several businesses and became very *wealthy*. The younger members of the family were deeply involved in the Oporto *Methodist* Church. However, their Baptist convictions led to Joseph Jones being baptised in Spurgeon's Metropolitan Tabernacle in London, by James Spurgeon (the brother of *C.H. Spurgeon*), and to the founding of a Baptist group in Oporto. This congregation, like the Tabernacle, practised *open communion*.

In 1906 Robert Young, from Canada, who had been a *missionary* in Brazil, started an independent Baptist congregation in Oporto. This group proved somewhat unstable. In this period Brazilian Baptists became involved in *mission* in Portugal, with Jeronomio de Sousa, from Brazil, taking *pastoral* responsibility for *members* of the group started by Robert Young. In 1908 the Brazilian Baptist *Convention* sent Zachary C. Taylor to Portugal to investigate the longer-term potential for mission work. Their vision was to make Portugal one of their fields of outreach. Taylor visited Oporto and established the group led by de Sousa as a Baptist church connected to wider Baptist life, and this became known as the First Baptist Church of Oporto.

A colourful character in the Portuguese scene was João de Oliveira (1883-1958), a graduate of Southwestern Baptist Seminary in Texas and formerly a missionary in Texas, an energetic but restless personality who ministered both in Portugal (1911-30 and 1945-58) and to the Portuguese *diaspora* in the USA. He came to Oporto under the auspices of the Foreign Mission Board of the *SBC* and became *pastor* of the First Baptist Church. In 1912 the church led by Joseph Jones joined the First Baptist Church. A spacious building for *worship* was completed in 1916, the land for the *building* being bought by Joseph Jones. The building was modelled on Spurgeon's Tabernacle in London and was called the Baptist Tabernacle.

Progress in Oporto led to the emergence of mission congregations and the publication of an *evangelistic* newspaper. In 1920 the Convenção Baptista Portuguesa was formed, with Joseph Jones as the first President. The impact of the depression years in the USA on funding and instances of poor personal relations between missionaries hindered advance. Baptist work in Portugal has been supported by missionaries both from Brazil and the USA, who helped establish the seminary [see *Portuguese Baptist Theological Seminary*], and run a radio ministry and a bookstore. The Portuguese Baptist Convention is a member of both the *EBF* and the *BWA*. It is currently concerned to aid ministry amongst the Portuguese diaspora in Northern Europe.

ET

Portuguese Baptist Theological Seminary

The very first Baptist seminary in *Portugal* was opened in 1915 in Viseu, in the centre of Portugal. It moved the following year to Porto where it remained until the middle of the 20th century. Meanwhile, in 1948 the Baptist Theological Seminary of Leiria was opened. This closed in 1965, and it was in 1969 that the current Baptist Theological Seminary, owned by the *Convention* of Baptists in Portugal, opened in a suburb of Queluz, a city just to the northwest of Lisbon. The first director was *Pastor* Lester Bell, an American *missionary*. Eight *students* entered that year. Since then the seminary has served Baptists but also other *evangelicals* in Portugal, as well as Baptists from other countries in Africa, Europe and South America.

The current director is Pastor Paulo Pascoal. The teaching staff consists of both missionaries from the United States and *Great Britain* and of Portuguese teachers. The school has an average of 50 students per year on its various courses. It offers a variety of levels of courses, from a one year basic theological course to a three-year Bachelor's and four-year Licentiate programme. The seminary focuses on five main areas of study, which are Biblical Studies, *Theology* and *Ethics*, *Pastoral* and *Practical Theology*, History of Christianity and Christian Education. It

has a library with some 10,000 volumes.

Apart from the courses in Queluz the Seminary also has centres in other parts of Portugal where theological courses are offered. It has pioneered work in theological E-learning for Portuguese speakers. Over 50 of the Baptist pastors in Portugal are graduates of the school, whilst other graduates are heavily involved in churches in the field of *education*, *worship*, *mission* and other leadership roles.

TFTN

Porvoo Agreement
See *Meissen, Porvoo and Fetter Lane agreements: significance for Baptists.*

Post-Christendom
See *Christendom.*

Post-Modernism
See *Liberalism and Modernism.*

Poverty
See *Preferential Option for the Poor.*

Practical Theology
[See also *Theology*]
Practical theology is now an accepted discipline within theological *education*. It is seen as complimentary to *systematic theology* in that it takes the work of theology and encourages theological reflection in practice. Some prefer the term Applied Theology. Certain schools of 'high' theology have disparaged anything other than the philosophical and reflective nature of systematic theology, and made this the preserve of academia. However, this view is generally criticised by Baptist communities who see primary theology being developed in the life of the *local church* and not in the gleaming towers of the universities and who believe that such primary theology, understood as '*faith* seeking understanding', has to be applied in practice within the lives and works of the believing communities. Therefore, it might be strongly contended that the root of all

theology is the *witness* of the believing community 'in *worship*, proclamation, service and daily living' (Ballard). Within the European Baptist community we have produced several outstanding applied and practical *theologians* in recent decades and it is to be noted that our seminaries are at the cutting edge of such work.

CJMG

FURTHER READING: Paul H. Ballard (ed) *The Foundations of Pastoral Studies and Practical Theology*, University College, Cardiff, 1986. Paul Ballard and John Pritchard, *Practical Theology in Action*, SPCK, London, 1996.

Praise
See *Worship*.

Praxis

The concept of *praxis* lies near the heart of *liberation theology*. It is best understood as an insistence that right action and lifestyles (*orthopraxy*) are as important to God as right beliefs (*orthodoxy*). Brazilian educationalist Paulo Freire's definition proved influential: 'It is only when the oppressed find the oppressor out and become involved in the organised struggle for their liberation that they begin to believe in themselves. This discovery cannot be purely intellectual but must involve action; nor can it be limited to 'mere activism, but must include serious reflection: only then will it be a praxis.' The concept, however, has its roots in classical European philosophy. For Aristotle, *praxis* was a moral disposition to act truly and rightly allied to a concern to further human well being and the good life. In *praxis* there can be no prior knowledge of the right means by which we realise the end in a particular situation. For the end itself is discerned in the process of deliberating about the means found to be appropriate in any given particular situation. Eastern European *Marxists* were fond of the concept in the post war years: e.g. in neo-Marxist academic circles of the late 1950s in *Yugoslavia*, *praxis* was understood as a concept of focussed action which, among other things, resulted in social change and the advancement of *socialism*. The re-working of the concept

by liberation *theologians* helped to focus on the difference between traditional North American and Eurocentric academic approaches to *theology* and their own. Liberation theologians' understandings of the concept have, however, drawn on the *eschatology* of Jürgen Moltmann's *Theology of Hope*.

The function of theology, from this point on, is to reflect critically on the misery and *suffering* of the majority poor of the world and, through acts of solidarity with them, to work out how best to serve the cause of their liberation. Theological reflection, integrated with practical action, must be the new norm. In theological education praxis has helped *students* to work out of their own situations and by reflecting on these in the light of *scripture*, to develop a theological and educational agenda the outcome of which must always be tested in practice. Praxis is then a superior way of knowing. Within a liberation theology context, it means learning by reflecting on experiences of working with God's poor. Praxis, nonetheless, remains a somewhat imprecise term within literature. Sometimes it can refer to the liberating conduct of the individual believer within a given social and *political* context. It is also seen to be a new distinctive of *evangelisation* in the contemporary world: 'Religions divide, but liberating action unites...The hope is that a liberating praxis will show the superiority of *Christ* and Christianity over other world religious figureheads and teachings' (Jose Comblin). Sometimes it refers to the activities of liberation theologians, *priests*, and other church professionals. It also defines all of those actions of the *Church* which are in conformity with the message of the gospel: *orthopraxy*. 'It is not presumptuous to say that no other theology has done better at touching the world where it hurts – and it really does hurt – at defending the *poor* and the victims; at generating *hope*; at eliciting a praxis and expressing a meaning that are not found anywhere else' (Jon Sobrino).

MIB

FURTHER READING: Aristotle, *The Nicomachean Ethics* (trans. J.A.K. Thomson), Penguin, London, 1976. Michael I. Bochenski, *Theology from Three Worlds*, Regent's Park College, Oxford, 1997. Jose Comblin, *The Holy Spirit and Liberation*, Burns and Oates, London, 1989. Paulo Freire, *Pedagogy of the Oppressed*, Seabury, New York, 1970. Jürgen Moltmann, *Theology of Hope - on the Ground and the Implications of a Christian Eschatology*, SCM, London, 1967. Routledge Encyclopaedia of Philosophy article on South Slavs: www.rep.routledge.com/article/N003. Jon Sobrino, *Witnesses to the Kingdom – the martyrs of El Salvador and the crucified peoples*, Orbis, Maryknoll, NY, 2003.

Prayer

[See also *Prayer Meetings*; *Prayers in Worship*]
Christian prayer represents both the basic aspects of human prayer, and the Christian understanding of prayer, especially as it is expressed in the Lord's Prayer, with its praise, petitions and longing for the *Kingdom of God*. Prayer must be the language of intention not the expression of pious sentiment, so the *hymn*, 'Prayer is the soul's sincere desire, Uttered or unexpressed'. Basically, prayer reflects the human need for meaning in life and a conscious relationship to the mystery of human existence. *Theologically*, prayer is a reflection of how God is perceived. Christian prayer is a necessary and vital function of *faith*, a central part of *worship* and communal life – anywhere and at any time – in the privacy of the human heart as well as in the community of faith. Prayer is only possible because of belief in a personal God who is accessible to *humankind*. Prayer assumes that God is present, listens, and answers according to his *love* and wisdom. Prayer is not a magical technique by which the believer may produce the answers that he/she wants. Nor is prayer essentially about communicating information about ourselves; our needs are already known to God. In the prayer of *Jesus* in Gethsemane, prayer is the precursor to the greatest act of sacrificial *love*. Prayer is not simply a human activity through liturgical [see *Liturgy*] or non-formal prayers, but depends on the spiritual presence of God in human life. Prayer certainly is not an attempt to change the mind and intention of a reluctant God to grant our wishes. Rather because it is part of his purpose that we should seek him in prayer our prayers are to be conceived as frail humankind seeking to be conformed to his holy will and purposes

'on earth as in *heaven*'.

PMIL

Prayer Houses
See *Chapels*.

Prayer Meetings
[See also *Prayer*]
In an earlier generation mid-week *worship* often took the form of a prayer meeting to which was attached systematic *Bible study*. There was often also a prayer meeting on Sunday mornings prior to the main service, and there would nearly always be vestry prayers by the *deacons* before *worship*. Events like the Annual *Assembly* would have been prepared for by an opening prayer meeting. The form of prayer at such meetings was nearly always free prayer articulated by *members* of the congregation often with very little guidance from the leader of the service. Attendance at prayer meetings was often taken as a sign of a church's vitality, but there seem to have been constant concern that at too many churches these were ill-attended, with censure on those churches which did not have a prayer meeting. This may have been because the services were not well structured with insufficient information about the areas for which prayer was being sought. More recently central prayer meetings have been discontinued in most churches in favour of house groups encouraging more intimacy and sharing of *fellowship* as the context for more participatory Bible Study and sharing in prayer. The underwriting of a local congregation's *ministry* and *mission* in prayer remains an ongoing concern of Baptist leadership.

ET

Prayers in Worship
[See also *Prayer*; *Worship*]
In church worship prayer is a necessary part of the God-persons dialogical encounter, where *humankind* expresses different aspects of its relationship to God. Traditionally there are seven types of prayers recognised in a worship service:
  (1) Invocation (or invitation) – a call upon

God to be present and assist those assembled in their worship;

(2) Adoration and praise – extolling the worth of the triune God;

(3) Thanksgiving – expressing an emotion of gratitude;

(4) *Confession* and penitence – the people recognise their unworthiness and sinful acts in the encounter with the Holy One. This may well lead on to words from *scripture* which assure those who have made confession of the *forgiveness* of their *sins* and their acceptance once more for service;

(5) In intercessory prayer the church brings all the needs of the world before God, that His purposes be realised on earth, involving reading the daily newspapers through the eyes of scripture;

(6) Prayer of *petition* is closely related to intercessory prayer – asking God's *grace* for the needs of individual *church members* so that the church fulfils its purpose;

(7) The prayer of oblation (or dedication), often at the end of the service, where the congregation rededicate themselves to serve God and practice his *love* in their daily lives. As the congregation have been gathered from the world at the commencement of worship so they are now sent back into that world to *witness* for *Christ*.

OAJ

FURTHER READING: Paul Beasley-Murray, *Faith and Festivity: A Guide for Today's Worship Leaders*, Marc, Eastbourne, 1991. Merrill M. Hawkins, Jr. (ed), 'Baptists and Spirituality' in *Baptist History and Heritage*, Vol 37, (2002). Graham Kendrick, *Ten Worshipping Churches*, Marc, Eastbourne 1987. Rob Warner, *Walking with God: Discovering a deeper spirituality in prayer*, Hodder and Stoughton, London, 1998. R.E.O. White, *A Guide to Pastoral Care*, Pickering/Inglis, London, 1976.

Preachers

See *Ministry*; *Preaching, Baptist*; *Pulpit*; *Sermon*.

Preaching, Baptist

[See also *Pulpit*; *Sermon*]

From the great Baptist *confessions* of the 17th century onwards preaching has been regarded as fundamental to Baptist *worship*. Sermons – both in oral and written form – play a central part in Baptist *piety*. The very language of '*Minister* of *Word* and *Sacrament*' underlines the solemnity of what is happening when preaching takes place for it must be a handling of the Word of God in and through which God speaks to his people. Biblical commentators [see *Bible*] make it clear that in the NT preaching is always concerned with the announcement of good news to the unconverted and 'has nothing to do with the delivery of sermons to the converted' [see *Conversion*] or the teaching and nurture of the faithful. Two Greek words indicate these separate functions: *kerygma* [proclamation] and *didache* [teaching]. Later in the history of the *church* these two elements came to be combined in the church's preaching *ministry*. The Word, however, remains of critical importance in the life of the church. The centrality of the sermon in *protestant* worship here contrasts with the catholic pattern where the drama of the mass is everything and the sermon has been replaced by a brief homily.

Traditionally, preaching has served three goals for Baptists: to offer a better understanding of the setting and original intentions of the Biblical texts, to give help in interpreting these texts for present-day believers, and to provide guidance on how to apply the message of the Bible to Christian *discipleship* in the contemporary world. This *hermeneutical* task has not changed over the years, even if methods of preaching and understanding of how a sermon functions have altered. Historically, *Charles Haddon Spurgeon*, a famous Baptist preacher of Victorian *England*, set a model for Baptist preaching for almost a century. His sermon style, full of biblical and everyday imagery, his *Christ*-centred approach to preaching, and his unswerving trust of the biblical message, inspired several generations of preachers not only in *Britain* but also in Continental Europe. His sermons combine two important elements of Baptist preaching: *evangelistic* fervour and Biblical teaching. It is hard to understand, living after the great Victorian preachers, that there was a time when the high *Calvinism* of some Baptists deemed it tantamount to infringing the work of the *Holy Spirit* for the preacher to invite sinners [see *Sin*] to *repentance*: Joseph Ivimey spoke with contempt of those who followed the 'non-invitation, non application system'. But as the *Evangelical Revival*, and especially the work of George Whitfield impacted more and more on Baptist life, it became customary 'to preach for a verdict', and to give those who felt touched by God's spirit opportunity to make a visible response within the framework of Christian worship.

German Baptist preachers, perhaps less colourful in their language but nevertheless rooted in the scriptural text in a similar way, also offered a preaching style to be emulated Europe-wide. This tradition of preaching based on logical arguments, ideally well structured and offering an exposition of Baptist and Evangelical doctrine but illustrated either with incidents or practices from everyday life or from the Bible, is continuously widespread in many Baptist churches in Europe. There were, however, other styles: many Welsh preachers excelled in telling Bible stories with such emotional force that those present had such a vivid perception of the event that they almost imagined they were present, participating, in the event (e.g. as David effects the timely end of Goliath). More recently, Baptist preaching has redeveloped some of these styles, such as placing emphasis on narrative and dramatic-experience. Instead of focusing on rational argumentation, a considerable trend in Baptist preaching is to offer the hearers or readers an experience of identifying with the characters of the Biblical text. More and more Baptist preaching is aiming at the spiritual transformation of hearers, not only at providing Biblical information.

Other preachers have challenged their audiences with standing for justice in an unjust world. Thus *John Clifford*, embracing the best aspects of modern thought challenged Baptists to be active in the *political* and social realm. Although lost to the *Germany* of his fathers, Walther Raushenbusch's influence, as a herald of the *social gospel*, echoed all round the world but like Clifford he still upheld the importance of evangelism and conversion.

The *pulpit* ministry in Baptist churches has embraced great variety. Some pastors have taken their congregations systematically through the books of the Bible in sermons which have been essentially exegetical and expository, others have sought to woo those outside the church by announcing a series of topical sermons dealing with the great issues of the day, whilst others have used the discipline of the *Christian Year*, and a Lectionary reflecting that, to ensure balanced and biblical teaching. Whatever the detailed methodology, it is clear that it is an essential task of the church to witness to the Word of God, both written and *incarnate*, within the world today.

TP

FURTHER READING: David M. Brown, *Transformational Preacing*, Virtualbookworm, College Station, Tx., 2003. Alec Gilmore, *Preaching as Theatre*, SCM, London, 1996.

Predestination
[See also *Calvinism*; *Election*]

Numerous passages in the *Bible* either explicitly or implicitly teach a doctrine of predestination. However, there have been fierce controversies amongst Baptists, as in other Christian denominations, regarding a biblical understanding of this subject. Some Baptists have in effect defined predestination as identical to God's foreknowledge. This view would have found favour e.g. with the mainstream *Anabaptists* in the 16th century, the General Baptists in *England* in the 17th century and later in the 19th and 20th centuries the majority of Eastern European Baptists. On this view God in his omniscience has foreseen how individuals will respond to the offer of the gospel and as a result has predestined to eternal life those whom he has foreseen responding in *faith* and obedience.

A different understanding of this subject can be traced back to the 4th-century Christian leader Augustine. In light of his own experiences Augustine believed that each individual is so damaged by *sin* that his fallen will [see *Fall*] cannot seek *salvation*. Therefore out of necessity God must take the initiative. His *grace* seeks out sinners and opens their eyes to their need of salvation and the *Holy Spirit* efficaciously draws people to receive the gospel and the free gift of salvation. On this view it is according to God's eternal and **sovereign** purpose that some sinners are rescued and others perish in their sin. The foundation of this understanding of predestination is simply the good pleasure of God. It has the merit of taking seriously the biblical teaching on sin and the glorious nature of the grace of God in salvation. The difficulty for many Christians concerns the negative side of predestination – reprobation. The standard **Reformed** view of reprobation states that God according to his sovereign will passes over some sinners, leaving them in their sins and ultimately will condemn them justly for remaining in them. The leading **Protestant** Reformers [see **Reformation**], **Luther**, **Zwingli** and **Calvin** all accepted the Augustinian understanding of this subject.

The majority of Baptists in England in the 17th-19th centuries, identified themselves with the standard Reformed position in line with **Anglicans**, Presbyterians and **Congregationalists** and expressed it in the 1644, and later 1677 (promoted more widely in 1689) Particular Baptist **Confessions of Faith**. In Section 3.5 on God's Decrees in the 1689 edition it states: 'Those of **mankind** who are predestinated to life, God chose before the foundation of the world was laid, in accordance with His eternal and immutable purpose and the secret counsel and good pleasure of His will. God chose them in **Christ** for everlasting glory, solely out of His free grace and **love**, without anything in the creature as a condition to cause moving Him to choose.' Some English Baptists such as Hanserd Knollys (1599-1691) and John Gill (1697-1771) held to a high form of Calvinism that led some of their followers to take an over cautious approach to **evangelical preaching** and outreach activities, but others including those trained at the **Bristol Academy** between 1690 and 1791 held to an Evangelical Calvinism that retained the zeal of the earlier Particular Baptists. The most famous European Baptist, **Charles Spurgeon** (1834-92), who was **pastor** of the largest Baptist congregation in the world in his day and who currently has more works in print than any other English-speaking Baptist minister, reprinted the 1689 Confession in an attempt to promote the older Particular Baptist **the-**

ology in London in the second half of the 19th century.

A minority of Baptists in England known as the General Baptists held to **Arminian** sentiments. This viewpoint gradually gained the ascendancy in the 19th century over the Calvinistic understanding of this subject. **John Smyth** and **Thomas Helwys** in 1609-10 issued confessions of faith upholding what became known as the Arminian position. The 1612 Confession issued by followers of John Smyth declared that: 'God before the foundation of the world hath determined the way of life and salvation to consist in Christ and that He hath forseen who would follow it...that as God created all **men** according to His image so hath He redeemed all that fall by actual sin, to the same end...that the efficacy of Christ's **death** is only derived to them, which do mortify their sins...' One of the most influential English General Baptist leaders was Dan Taylor (1738-1813), the leader of the New Connexion of General Baptists, a body characterised by evangelical zeal and connexionalism. Taylor's leadership and revivalistic techniques led to the establishment of many churches, **Sunday Schools** and a **missionary** society. The churches under his leadership issued Articles of Religion in 1770 that included the following statement: 'We believe that the Lord Jesus Christ...suffered to make a full **atonement** for all the sins of all men – and that hereby he has wrought out for us a complete salvation; which is received by, and as a free gift communicated to, all that believe in him.'

Gerhard Johann Oncken (1800-84), the leading German Baptist pioneer, was influenced by both Robert Haldane [see **Haldaneite tradition**] and Charles Spurgeon; in his Confession of Faith of 1847, article 5, Oncken writes unequivocally of election unto salvation along classic Reformed lines. He wrote: 'it is no 'free-will' which could objectively choose two possibilities, rather a will set free by the Holy Spirit to give a salutary answer. A man's yes! to Christ is nothing other than an echo to the call of the Gospel and has its ultimate foundation in God's election.' However, the Baptist movement on the continent of Europe, much of which traces its origins back to Oncken, has not espoused a Calvinistic position. Thus the clause in the Polish Baptist **Union**'s confession of faith, 'Election to Salvation', reads: 'We believe that God desires that every man should be saved. Therefore the duty of every man is to accept the gift of salvation by sincere and obedient faith in Jesus Christ. Only a stubborn persistence in sin and a refusal to amend and to submit oneself to God may block a sinner's way to salvation. In this matter every man is responsible for himself before God.'

BT

FURTHER READING: G. Balders, *Theurer Bruder Oncken*, Oncken, Kassel, 1978. R. Hayden, *Continuity and Change*, Baptist Historical Society, Didcot, 2006. W.L. Lumpkin, *Baptist Confessions of Faith*, Judson, Chicago, Il., 1959. G.K. Parker, *Baptists in Europe: History and Confessions of Faith*, Broadman, Nashville, Tn., 1982. B. Stanley, *History of the Baptist Missionary Society 1792-1992*, T&T Clark, Edinburgh, 1992.

Preferential Option for the Poor

The phrase has its origins in **Liberation Theology** which understands the gospel from the perspective of disadvantaged groups, in this case the poor, who need to be set free from oppressive social and economic structures. It finds support in a reading of the **Bible** as the story of a downtrodden people to whom God shows especial favour and who pin their hopes on the coming of one who, in the words of the Magnificat (Lk 1:52f), 'has torn imperial powers from their thrones, but the humble have been lifted high. The hungry he has satisfied with good things, the rich sent empty away'. This **love** of God for the poor is also found to be reflected in the life of **Jesus**, who had 'nowhere to lay his head' (Lk 9:58), and his concern for the poor and the outcast. In practice it means that Christians, in their efforts to transform the world according to God's will, should prioritise the needs of the poor and the structural changes in both the economy and society which are most likely to benefit them. The last must be first.

If it is argued that this is a distortion of the gospel since God loves everyone equally and seeks the **salvation** of all, rich and poor alike, two comments may be made in reply. First, a good deal of traditional, Western **theology** has been biased in favour of the powerful. By concentrating on spiritual aspects of salvation it has often side-stepped issues of justice and social change and in so doing has upheld the status quo and the interests of those who benefit from it.

Second, the poor are not to be prioritised because they are more virtuous or deserving than the rich (though they may be more 'godly', as in the Psalms, in that they have nothing and no-one but God to turn to) but because their needs are greater and dealing with their poverty is the most strategic starting point for understanding and dealing with the poverty (material, social and spiritual) of all – a strategy somewhat reminiscent of the gospel saying (Mt 6:33): 'Set your mind on God's **kingdom** and his justice before everything else, and all the rest will come to you as well.'

MHT

FURTHER READING: Ronald J. Sider, *Rich Christians in an Age of Hunger*, Hodder and Stoughton, London, 1990.

Premillennialism
[See also **Millennialism**]
In the 19th century two key figures in the upsurge of interest among British **evangelicals** in the Second Advent were Edward Irving, a flamboyant Scottish **Presbyterian minister** in London, and John Nelson Darby, a young **Anglican** curate from County Wicklow, **Ireland**. Darby became the most formative thinker within the developing **Brethren** movement of the 1830s and 40s. Premillennial views gained ground, with significant factors being the **growth** of the Brethren movement across Europe and the espousal of these views by evangelical Anglicans. Baptists were drawn towards premillennial thinking through their involvement in the **Keswick** Convention movement, where evangelical Anglicans predominated. In 1917 an important premillennial manifesto was widely published in **Britain**. It affirmed that **Jesus** might return 'at any moment', that **Israel** would be territorially restored and converted by Christ's appearing [see **Conversion**], and that under the subsequent millennial reign of Christ there would be a 'great effusion of the **Holy Spirit**'. A number of Baptist ministers, notably F.B. Meyer, were

involved, and Meyer became chairman of the Advent Testimony and Preparation Movement. During the early 20ᵗʰ century premillennial beliefs became quite widespread among Baptists in Europe, and although the later decades of the century saw the spread of the amillennial position, premillennial views continue to be common among Baptists.

IMR

FURTHER READING: D.W. Bebbington, 'The Advent Hope in British Evangelicalism since 1800' in *Scottish Journal of Religious Studies*, Vol. 9, No. 2 (1988), pp. 103-114. I.M. Randall, *Spirituality and Social Change: The Contribution of F.B. Meyer (1847-1929)*, Paternoster, Carlisle, 2003.

Presbyterianism, Baptists and
See *Reformed Churches, Baptists and*.

Presidency
See *Communion and Intercommunion; Eucharistic Liturgy; Sacrament, Sign and Symbol*.

Priesthood (hierarchical)
[See also *Priesthood of all Believers*]
The concept of a hierarchical priesthood is part of the *ecclesiology* in confessional families such as the *Anglican* Communion, the *Roman Catholic* Church, the *Orthodox* Churches, and some *Lutheran* Churches. The hierarchical priesthood is regarded as constitutive of the *church*. The Baptist teaching on the universal priesthood of all believers stands in opposition to the prevailing *tradition* of those churches with a hierarchical understanding of the priesthood derived from their emphasis on the *apostolic* succession, traced back to the *Apostle* Peter.

Baptist *pastors*, though assigned a specialist function, are not perceived as having a different level of *authority* from any other believer. In continental Europe, especially in the countries under Roman Catholic dominance the *Anabaptists* opposed the hierarchical understanding of the priesthood, a position reinforced at the Council of Trent (1545-63) that vindicated the medieval doctrine of priesthood, teaching that not all in

the church have the same authority [*spiritualis potestas*], and that hierarchical church government was by divine appointment [*divina ordinatione*]. They were also more radical than other churches of the *reformation* in affirming the *vocation* of all believers. Early Baptist groups in *England* reacted against the three-fold order of *bishops*, priests, and *deacons*, though still assigning to the pastor a place of high esteem, as minister of *word* and *sacrament*, enabling the whole people of God to exercise their priestly *ministry*.

The First *Vatican* Council (1869-70) also maintained a hierarchical view of priesthood that found its maximum expression in the *dogma* of the *infallible* authority of the *Pope* who holds primacy within the church. The Roman Catholic emphasis after Vatican II on the Church as the people of God has not, in many countries, apparently influenced the church's ecclesiology either in theory or in practice.

FMM

Priesthood of all Believers
[See also *Priesthood (hierarchical)*]
The reformers [see *Reformation*] encountered a clericalised church in which everything was dependent on priestly activity. It was *Martin Luther* who rescued the church for the *laity* from priestly control; 'he put the layman on his theological feet' (J.H. Atkinson). He could thus find the true *apostolic* succession 'where one disciple of *Christ*, apprehended by *grace*, declares to another the word of grace' (J. H. Whale). Whilst this is a critical understanding, the doctrine of the priesthood of all believers must never be reduced to a negative anticlericalism denying esteem to *ministers* of *word* and *sacrament*.

The doctrine is all-important, first, in asserting that Christ was the only mediator with God. Because of Jesus' high-priestly sacrifice, everyone had access to the Father, without the need of priest or *saint* or the virgin [see *Mary, mother of Jesus*] to intercede on their behalf. But, secondly, with the privilege came the responsibility of representing the world to Christ in a *ministry* of intercession. As a priest, the believer is required to offer him/herself to God as a living sacrifice, making personal desire wholly subsidiary to doing God's will, offering him the *worship* of heart and mind (Ro 12). Part of this priesthood is to fulfil the missionary task of confessing the true nature of God and his *love* for sinful humanity. This, as Luther underlined, might be through specific Christian *vocation* but equally it could be through undertaking the ordinary roles of parent, spouse, citizen, teacher, worker in sacramental fashion as workers who have no cause for shame (1Ti 2), discovering the service of Christ in the earthy and the mundane as much as in more churchly and 'spiritual activities' what A.G. Dickens refers to as 'the secular utility' of Luther's thinking on this point. But there is also a responsibility to undertake specific proclamation, as required in 1Pe 2:9, 'you are a royal priesthood...that you may declare the wonderful deeds of him who called you out of darkness into his marvellous light.' Hans Küng, in a rich exposition of the priesthood of all believers, argues that the *missionary* success of the early church was found here in that the Christian message 'was proclaimed by all...And not just by a few with a special commission...Every believer can and must, having been taught by God, teach others; can and must, having received the word of God be its herald...' (H. Küng, p.376).

Luther had the theological insights but the part of the reformation that bears his name did not fully implement the doctrine. What Luther was emphasising was the priesthood of *all* believers, rather than the priesthood of *each* believer. That is to say, this doctrine does not dissolve the corporate life of the *church* as the body of Christ under him as head into a series of atomistic private actions undertaken by unrelated individuals. Indeed the doctrine is derived from Luther's insistence on the church as the community of believers, thus fulfilling God's promise to Moses that the whole people of *Israel* was to be priesthood, dedicated to the service of God (Ex 19). *Baptism* can in this sense be regarded as an *ordination* to this universal priesthood of all believers: in carrying out such a priestly task the believer is fulfilling his baptismal obligations. Accordingly the royal priesthood of all believers will be manifest in the sharing of decisions about the church's ministry and *mis-*

sion as decided in *church meeting*.

In all this there is spelt out the *theology* of believer responsibility that justified *Oncken* in coining his famous slogan 'Every Baptist a missionary'.

ET

FURTHER READING: H. Küng, *The Church*, Image, Garden City, NY, 1978.

Prison ministry

[See also *Ministries, Diversity of; Ministry*]
The best-known Baptist pioneer of ministry to prisoners was F.B. Meyer (1847-1929), who was a Baptist *minister*, a leading speaker at conventions associated with the *Keswick* Convention, and a social activist. What became known as Meyer's 'prison-gate' ministry began when he was a minister in the 1880s in Leicester, in the English Midlands, and he discovered that *men* coming out of the Leicester prison tended to gravitate to the nearest public house, where they joined their old companions who often drew them straight back into crime. Meyer decided to do something. With the cooperation of the governor, he visited the prison each morning, taking discharged prisoners to a coffee house for a plate of ham. He estimated that he had provided breakfasts for between 4,500-5,000 men and *women* by the time he left Leicester in 1888. Having contacted the ex-prisoners, Meyer's next objective was to find them employment, and when he found manufacturers reluctant to help, he started his own businesses and also arranged accommodation for former prisoners. Others in *England* in this period were involved in visiting prisoners and helping ex-prisoners through the Discharged Prisoners' Aid Society. In this respect *Evangelical* agencies anticipated functions later developed by the *state*. In the 20th century prison ministry became a more widespread part of the general ministry of Baptist churches. The international Prison Christian Fellowship became influential. *Alpha* courses were run in prisons by people from a number of churches, including Baptists.

Evangelicals in Eastern Europe were influenced by the way in which the wider evangelical movement identified and emphasised certain areas of social ministry. In

406   **Programme to Combat Racism**

the later 19th century F.W. Baedeker from England, who was a *member* of the *Brethren* but whose instincts were pan-denominational, travelled over the vast expanses of *Russia*, engaging in *preaching* the gospel. In 1889 he was accompanied by J.G. Kargel, a German-Russian Baptist leader, and they preached in the prisons of Siberia. During his 18 years of ministry in Russia Baedeker made two long trips from St. Petersburg as far as to Sakhalin, using every opportunity to preach and often preaching in prisons. Adam Podin, an Estonian Baptist of Latvian descent, a well-known figure on the international Baptist scene in the first decades of the 20th century, invested much of this time in prison ministry in Tsarist Russia. In 1905, due to relationships he had in the Tsarist court, he obtained permission to have access even to the most dangerous criminals in all the prisons in Russia. He preached and delivered NTs and other Christian literature in prisons in Moscow, Irkutsk, Samara and other places. Later in the 20th century, during the *Communist* period, the 'underground' or unregistered Baptists were active in visiting imprisoned believers in the *Soviet Union*.

IMR & TP

Programme to Combat Racism

From at least the time of movements to abolish the slave trade and later the institution of slavery itself, Christians in general, and Baptists in particular, have been concerned with the issue of race. From the 1780s onwards many fine *sermons* were *preached* against such abuses of the biblical understanding [see *Bible*] of the nature of humanity which could easily have served as arguments for the basic concerns of those who founded the Programme to Combat Racism. In the 1960s the leadership given by Martin Luther King to the Civil Rights movement in America and his assassination in 1968 revived Baptist concern with the issue of race.

In the following year the *World Council of Churches* established its Programme to Combat Racism which placed major emphasis on white racism and the way that was institutionalised in the deployment of social and economic power. Such power needed to be transferred from the powerful to the powerless and generally to develop a strategy to combat racism including analysis of the extent that the churches were beneficiaries of racism with the urgent need to change that. A sub-unit was developed to promote the work which undertook research and began to publicise material on the struggles of the oppressed, and to convoke a number of high-level consultations. From 1972 onwards the programme developed a special focus on South Africa opposing the government's *apartheid* policies. Accordingly the PCR campaigned for the withdrawal of church funds and a boycotting of banks trading in South Africa and for the development of an effective sanctions policy against the South African government.

Separate from the sub-unit, the WCC also established a Special Fund to Combat Racism which in the 30 years following 1970 distributed more than US$12 million. This was entirely funded by special gifts and derived no benefit from the general income of the WCC. The fact that some of its funds were given to liberation movements in Southern Africa, albeit in support of their *educational* and relief work, provoked much criticism that the programmes of the WCC had become over-*politicised*, and calls were made for churches, to withdraw from the Council, especially since the gifts made by the Special Fund were not monitored as this was argued to represent a paternalistic form of control. The critical churches were in a weak position in so far as most of them had not contributed to the Special Fund, and part of the argument was that the authorities in South Africa supported by the white churches defended apartheid with *theological* arguments. The Council refused to change its policy and after the end of apartheid the programme was seen to have been one of its most successful in a world of injustice. The beneficiaries were the ordinary people of South Africa who saw in this act of solidarity The Christian *Church* taking its moral responsibilities seriously in effective action.

JHYB

Progressive National Baptist Convention of Europe (inc.) (PNBC-E)

The Progressive National Baptist Convention

(inc) is a relatively large African-American Baptist Convention in the **Baptist World Alliance** with over 2.5 million **members**. It arose out of a division in the National Baptist Convention and was the convention to which young civil rights leaders such as Martin Luther King, Jr., Jesse Jackson, Andrew Young and Ralph Abernathy belonged.

In the late 1980s several small baptistic groups of Afro-Caribbean Christians in the English West Midlands came into contact with the leadership of the PNBC, who offered them support and encouragement in the development of their life and **mission**. The PNBC leadership encouraged these churches to join PNBC as an association in Europe and also put them in touch with the leadership of the Baptist **Union** of **Great Britain** (BUGB). The PNBC then developed an official European organisation (PNBC-E) and encouraged Afro-Caribbean and African majority churches in **England** to join both the PNBC and BUGB. A handful of churches with Afro-Caribbean majorities already in membership with BUGB also joined PNBC-E and some of the small communities in the PNBC-E joined the Heart of England Baptist **Association** of BUGB. PNBC leaders from the USA often attend the PNBC-E annual assembly held each year in either Greater London or the West Midlands, generally with representatives of BUGB in attendance. Efforts of the PNBC (inc) to develop a world-wide network of black-majority Baptist churches have not, as yet, borne fruit, as many African Baptist churches do not appear to share the same concerns and issues as African-American churches and Afro-Caribbean churches in Europe. However, the European network remains a useful additional way for Afro-Caribbean majority churches in Europe to work together on issues of lifestyle and mission.

KGJ

Property

[See also **Wealth**]

Christianity has not generally denounced the ownership of property though many calls have been issued to the followers of **Jesus** to give up their possessions for the sake of the **Kingdom** and the **poor**. People need some things to call their own if they are to express themselves and have dignity. The right to property can therefore be seen as a natural right. More difficult questions have to do with how it is used, who should own what, and what should not be regarded as property or owned by anyone at all.

With ownership comes the idea of **stewardship**. What we have are gifts from God. They are certainly not purely the result of our own hard work or a just distribution of resources and opportunities. We are accountable to others and need to use what we have with care and respect and a concern for the common good. Our possessions are held in trust. Such ideas are especially relevant to the treatment of the **environment** where texts (cf. Ge 1) have been misused to justify exploitative attitudes to natural resources., rather than to hold them in respect as God given and part of a legacy to be passed on to successive generations Similar ideas have inspired experiments in **communal living** (cf. Ac 4 and 5).

Capitalism saw the means of production, including factories, raw materials and the **labour** of working people, fall into the ownership of a few powerful industrialists able to decide the fate of many workers. Later the interests of shareholders as risk-takers had to be balanced against the needs of consumers and the welfare of employees. Trade unions, employment laws and workers' collectives represent attempts to moderate the power of ownership and ensure equity, whilst leaving room for enterprise and flair.

Discussions about **usury**, first opposed but later embraced by Christians, were an early example of the debate about what should ever be regarded as property however well it is cared for and used. Is money a means of exchange or something which, as in the modern world, can be bought and sold in its own right at both profit and loss? The anti-slavery movement remains emphatic that human beings should never be regarded as 'property'. Landownership, the enclosure and distribution of land, common land and a people's identity with land all raise similar questions. In the late 20th and early 21st centuries the discussion took on fresh dimensions. One example has to do with the co-modification of genetic strains, modified to produce say higher-yielding seeds. Another has to do with the privatisation of water and to what extent such a basic, natural resource, can be put into private hands in the name of efficiency and then used to make profits, rather than be publicly managed for the benefit of all.

MHT

Prophecy

Christianity is undeniably a prophetic *faith*, much of its *scriptures* consisting in the major and minor prophetic writings contained in the Hebrew scriptures. In the life of the NT prophets and prophetic utterances are also to be found as an aspect of life in the *Spirit* (Ac 2:17). Yet it is widely accepted that these prophetic dimensions belong to and are regulated by the canonical scriptures; reticence prevails about any continuing prophetic *ministry* in the life of the churches. It should be acknowledged that self-styled prophets have been the cause of considerable problems and at times tragedy as the cases of Thomas Müntzer, the prophets of Zwickau and the leaders in Münster illustrate from *Anabaptist* history. In this regard it might be asserted that any supposed prophet who claims to bring new *revelation* or who denies the canonical *witness* of scripture is certainly speaking falsely. On the other hand, the biblical witness needs to be applied in new contexts and at new times and to do this effectively requires a degree of *inspiration* bordering on the prophetic. In essence, this is a task which can largely, but not exclusively, be identified with the *preaching* ministry in which through the Spirit the canonical revelation is made to come alive and the *Word* of God applied to changing contexts. Yet no claim to prophecy, however shaped and delivered, can presume to be self-authenticating and go without testing. The *church* is exhorted to do just this, to test all things and to hold fast to what is good (1Th 5:19-22). The Baptist emphasis on the *authority* and the responsibility of the congregation is an indispensable ingredient in this process of discernment. Two contrasting usages of the language of prophecy are that deployed within the *pentecostal* movement to claim a supernatural authority for certain church decisions, and that by Christians, concerned to engage with the *politics* of a fallen world [see *Fall*] who believe that the church, out of scripture, should speak 'prophetically' to the deficiencies of party political programmes.

NGW

Proselytism

The word proselyte in the NT signifies somebody not of *Jewish* ethnicity who has decided to follow the Jewish *faith*. In modern usage proselytism is distinguished from *evangelism* as a mode of securing a person's *conversion* to a given religious system using improper methods. This might include external coercion even though the coercive element may be concealed, the offering of secular inducements, the manipulation or exploitation of the would-be convert, all forms of 'sheep-stealing' of people of existing religious commitment. The *Orthodox Church* has often accused the *Roman Catholic* Church of doing this, and more recently has extended the accusation to *protestant sects* operating in an Eastern Europe newly opened to external influences. A 1970 definition of the boundaries between proselytism and normal Christian witness affirms, 'Proselytism embraces whatever violates the rights of the human person [see *Human Rights*], Christian or non-Christian, to be free from external coercion in religious matters or whatever in the proclamation of the gospel does not conform to the ways God draws free *men* [and *women*] to respond to God's *call* in spirit and in truth.'. Thus the emphasis in recent years in some churches on 'Doing *Christ's mission* in Christ's own way', that is even in a task as important as evangelism there are illegitimate unethical ways of behaving [see *Ethics*]. That some resort to this does not lift the obligation placed on all believers to share their faith with others, only that they take care to do it in proper gospel fashion.

ET

Prosperity Theology

[See also *Property*; *Theology*; *Wealth*]
A form of theology often associated with *charismatic* churches and teachers, which emphasises God's will that God's people should prosper in terms of their worldly pos-

sessions. All too easily this becomes a methodology for material and personal success. Typically, prosperity theology might promise that those who in **faith** donate to **Spirit**-filled **ministries** can expect to receive back a greatly multiplied blessing. It has a particular attraction in the United States of America where it chimes in with high expectations of personal wealth and happiness, and in African **nations** where it is felt to address the context of entrapment and **poverty** in which many live. Critics believe that on the one hand it baptises a materialist culture and on the other awakens unrealistic expectations. Yet, it could never be claimed that God's will is for people to be impoverished and there are abundant examples in the Hebrew **scriptures** of faithfulness to God leading to divine provision and blessing. Equally, there are widespread examples throughout Christian **missions** of 'redemption and lift', of the fact that embracing Christian faith and living leads to material improvement in people's circumstances. But it is dangerous to interpret an absence of these things as a **judgment** on a lack of **piety**. Perhaps the weakness of prosperity theology is not that it stresses the goodness and favour of God but that it attempts to transform these into a technique which can be manipulated by human beings for reasons of self-interest. It also overlooks the voluntary embracing of poverty by the Son of God [see **Jesus Christ**] for the sake of others.

NGW

Prostitution, Work with people in

Prostitution is legal in most European countries. This represents an attempt to control the massive illegal activities associated with it (**drugs**, trafficking, **violence**), control the age of those working (over 18) and thus protect **children**, and also provide social benefits (**health** care, retirement, etc.) to the 'workers'. However, in many situations, those in prostitution do not register because they want to avoid paying taxes or because they are illegal immigrants, some victims of trafficking. The attempt to control the illegality of prostitution has only encouraged it to flourish, giving the 'pimps', traffickers, own-ers of the brothels, bars, nightclubs, the opportunity to make massive amounts of money, some of which is shared with the prostitutes.

There is a spectrum of reasons why **women** and **men** begin working in prostitution. On one end of the spectrum are those who come from countries where economies are difficult and **unemployment** is high. They feel desperate to support their children, their parents, their siblings, and so are vulnerable to the promises of traffickers who promise them 'good' jobs in Western countries. They may know that they will be required to work in prostitution, but they usually have no idea that it will be as violent or coercive as it is. They are so motivated to send money home that they will usually continue working. Much prostitution in Europe results from trafficking from Eastern Europe, Africa and Asia to Western countries.

On the other end of the spectrum are the many women and men who come from more prosperous countries, where employment and social services are available but who, nevertheless, find themselves involved in prostitution. As many as 85-95% of these people have been victims of childhood sexual abuse and most often, drug use is also involved. They are extremely wounded individuals, who seek to dull the pain of their past through fast money, drugs and sexual control.

The easiest church response is simply to say that the problem is too overwhelming, has been with us since the beginning of time, and cannot be solved. But we have to examine **Jesus**' response to prostitution and know that he was and will continue to be our guide, as he calls us to minister to this large 'unreached people' group. And what was Jesus' 'method' of ministering to people in prostitution and victims of sexual abuse? He befriended them, he cared for them, he loved them, he let them know that he knew everything about them, he forgave them [see **Forgiveness**] and sent them on to discover a New Life. Effective **ministries** with people who are in prostitution begin with simple acts of care and kindness, unconditional **love** and support, meeting them where they are, and above all, surrounding everything that is done with **prayer**.

There are many individual members of

the **EBF** who are working with people in prostitution, sometimes in cooperation with their church and in other situations, with para-church organisations and **non-governmental organisations**. The EBF sponsored an 'Anti-Trafficking Conference' in Apr 2005 in Budapest, **Hungary**, and from that, an 'Anti-Trafficking Working Group' was formed. The working group encourages churches to become involved in anti-trafficking work, and provides resources and networking links among the member bodies.

LB

Protestant/Protestantism

This is the common language to describe churches and Christian believers who stand in the **tradition** of the **Reformation** taking their guidance from the teachings of the great reformers especially **Luther**, **Zwingli** and **Calvin**. The actual language derives from a minority who, at the Second Diet of Speyer (1526), drew up a solemn *Protestation* declaring that the signatories would not carry out the coercive imperial edicts against the new religious teaching then emerging. As over against the **authority** of **Pope** and Emperor the protestant princes and city councils protested their commitment to 'fidelity to the Gospel, the **Word of God** contained in Holy **Scripture**, as the final court of appeal for the **Church**.' Scripture, interpreted under the guidance of the **Holy Spirit**, became the fundamental touchstone for both belief and practice. Some have claimed that the language of Protestantism is essentially reactive, that is to say it is defined by the abuses, which may not be eternal, against which it reacts. To this it is objected, 'The life of Protestantism does not depend on any protest. It depends on the **grace** of our Lord **Jesus Christ**, and the **love** of God and the **fellowship** of the Holy Spirit.' The word protest has as its prime meaning a solemn declaration, from which the idea of 'protest against error' is a later derivation.

In Europe, the word **evangelical** is often used as a synonym for protestant, especially when applied to the **Lutheran** tradition. It is therefore right to start a theological definition of Protestantism by emphasising again the importance of Luther's insistence on **justification** by grace through **faith**. In *The*

Freedom of a Christian Man Luther sought to free the idea of Christian **vocation** from the cloister and set it fairly in the market place. Vocation was not for the few but for the many, and was not to be worked out in undertaking 'religious tasks' like attending special services and going on pilgrimages, but in working to the glory of God in the secular world. Congruent with such thinking was the emphasis on the **priesthood of all believers**, though this was not fully worked through for there was an essential erastianism (that is to say deference to the secular magistrate in the ordering of the affairs of the church) in Luther's thinking arising out of his dependency on the patronage of the princes. This meant that the new Evangelical and Protestant Churches were formed as **state churches** relating to the newly emerging **nation** states in much the same way as the medieval **catholic** church related to the Empire.

Because of this Baptists, like others in the **Believers' Church** and **Free Church** traditions, only belong within the family in a qualified way in so far as they argue that one is not born into the church but rather admission to the church reflects a second birth, and that the church under the Lordship of Christ [see **Lord of the Church**] must be free of all state authority [see **Separation of Church and State**].

JHYB

Protestant Work Ethic

[See also **Protestant/Protestantism**]

At the beginning of the 20th century the sociologist, Max Weber, wrote his classic study on *The Protestant Ethic and the Spirit of Capitalism*. The hypothesis was that protestant religion, particularly in its **Calvinist** form, was the most powerful agent in stimulating a new attitude to economic enterprise. His thesis was carefully expressed; it was the 'Protestant Work Ethic' and 'The Spirit of **Capitalism**' that were the terms of the argument. That is to say, the *Spirit* of capitalism has to be distinguished from capitalism *per se*, for the late medieval world, in, e.g., the urban culture of the North Italian cities, was well acquainted with capitalism, but the spirit of capitalism was something new. The protestant work ethic was a fruit of the reformers [see **Reformation**] reclaiming the everyday life of the layman [see **Laity**] as having religious significance, for it was in the market place, on the farm, and in the workshop that the Christian was called to fulfil his **vocation** to serve God. Here attitudes of thrift, diligence, sobriety, the **stewardship** of time (increasingly measured by the clock and not the seasons) [see **Leisure**] and moral responsibility were all carefully cultivated. The generation of **wealth** was not something ignoble; indeed economic success was to be seen as the blessing of God, a sign of God's favour. Calvinist **faith** was not only concerned with a **work** ethic but also a **spending/saving** ethic, that is to say Calvinists were generally puritanical in lifestyle, not given to frivolity or excess. Accordingly those of such religious commitments, whilst they put a premium on hard work and consequent earnings, severely limited the amount of personal spending with the natural consequence of capital accumulation. In the subsequent arguments questions have been raised as to whether Calvinism sponsored new economic enterprise, or whether those who were economically mobile found the new religion particularly attractive, with the suggestion that there was a natural alliance between the **catholic** faith, with the dual headship of **Pope** and Emperor, and the feudal organisation of medieval Europe. Thus **Marxists** argued that the new religion **reflected** changing secular priorities whilst Weber argued that it **played its part** in bringing about the change. Others have argued that the connexion was essentially accidental rather than causative – urban dwellers were the first to hear the new teaching and were those, within the social order, most free to respond to it.

Weber's thinking was further refined by the English historian, R.H. Tawney, a dedicated **Christian socialist**, who wrote *Religion and the Rise of Capitalism* in 1926. Tawney noted that the protestant countries of the Atlantic seaboard were those where the new economic enterprise began to raise the standard of life of all citizens, who were schooled to their new tasks by the discipline and order of their religion. Popular axioms, such as 'the devil finds work for idle hands to do', characteristic of this new protestant seriousness, became an essential part of child

education. Even **predestination** and the doctrine of the invisible church [see **Church: Universal, Triumphant, Invisible**] played their part. Whilst good works as securing **salvation** could be censured as part of a regrettable **pelagianism**, popular theology could speak about 'proving your **election**'. That is to say that whilst certainty as to being one of the elect might be denied, it was prudent to act as if you were so denominated, and to live the life the elect might be expected to live. Other issues were involved. E.g. the exclusion of **nonconformists** from the instruments of government and the institutions of education by penal legislation after the restoration of the monarchy in **England** in 1660 meant that their leading **men**, and also **women**, were compelled to find satisfaction in their lives in business, trade and production.

JHYB

Providence

Baptists have no specific or divergent positions on the **theology** of providence from those generally held amongst **evangelicals** and **orthodox** Christians. God himself foresees the future not as a passive spectator but as ruler of all things and in taking an especial care of His **creation**. Providence therefore rightly belongs in the larger doctrine of creation and, as such, has recently been the subject of much theological debate. Do Baptists truly believe, in an active sense, in the doctrine of providence? Have they a real concern to act with, or against, God in his intentions for his created order? For surely Christian theology asserts that God, having created the world, acts towards it in the same spirit and with the same intention with which He works for its **redemption** and acts to hold all things in being. This action is universal in scope: as the **hymn**-writer, characterising the comprehensive breadth of God's care, expresses it, 'wings an angel, guides a sparrow'. There is much theological debate about the intentions of God and the ability of **humankind** to interact with God through an apparent **free will**. The discussion on **election**, as most powerfully expressed in five point **Calvinism** and free will, the accent of the **Arminian tradition**, both belong to the heart of the theological *dia-*

logue amongst baptistic communities.

Providence might be summed up, in the simple phraseology of Baptist *theologian* James Wm. McClendon, Jr. as God knows and cares; God rules and overrules; God purposes and disposes. Providence, surely, finds its clearest expression in the *covenant* made between God and Noah and 'all that lives on earth' (Ge 8:20-9:17) which demonstrates the providential purpose of God for the good and *love* of all He has created. It is we who fail God in our miserable and deviant response to His divine providence.

KGJ

Pulpit

[See also *Architecture*; *Chapels*; *Church Building (Sanctuary)*; *Preaching*; *Sermon*]
The pulpit is a raised reading desk from which the sermon is normally delivered which began to appear in churches towards the end of the middle ages, normally located on the north side of the nave. In *Puritan worship* this rather than the altar was the focus of worship: often there was a deep read cushion on which the *Bible* was placed and overhead there was a great sounding board to make the message more audible to the congregation.

In Baptist Churches the pulpit is usually to be found towards the front of the church either in the centre, or to one side if the centre is occupied by a *communion* table and open *baptistry*. The position of the pulpit has been the subject of some pride in *Protestant* Churches, the central position being seen to underline the centrality of the sermon within the *liturgy*. This could sometimes even distort the whole shape of the liturgy thus the 18th-century criticism of dissenting preaching by the wag who commented 'your *prayers* are too short and your sermons too long'. However, for an example of its importance in Baptist life, notice that until recently when *pastoral* subjects have come to play a properly significant part in *ministerial formation*, the sermon class was the only pastoral preparation that many training for *ministry* had.

'Pulpit' sometimes becomes an analogy for sermon or for preaching, thus the '19th-century Pulpit' would refer to the accumulated preaching over the whole century. At the present time when distinctive focuses are less in favour within chapel buildings, and when *preachers* wish to use power-point presentations, and perhaps even include clips of film in their preaching, and to adopt a more conversational style of preaching, pulpits are often unused except on very special occasions.

ET

Purgatory

This is the title of the intermediate state that *Roman Catholics* believe to exist after *death* and before a person receives their final *judgment*. It came to be seen as a place of punishment, maybe temporary but punishment nevertheless, where a person suffered for their misdemeanours on earth until sufficiently cleansed to qualify for *heaven*. In the causes of the *Reformation* it was linked to the issue of the sale and purchase of *indulgences*, papal dispensations [see *Papacy*] that could shorten the period of time spent in Purgatory by either the purchaser or any person they chose to nominate. *Martin Luther* found this to be in conflict with the doctrine of *justification* by *grace* through *faith* which he took to be the cardinal *evangelical* understanding about *salvation*. The idea of Purgatory belongs to a legalistic understanding and perpetuates the idea of *Pelagianism*, salvation by works, beyond the grave, and is offensive to *Evangelicals* as compromising the sufficiency of the grace secured by *Christ*'s death on Calvary, and represents the accumulation of the uncertainty about the future which accompanies any system that makes salvation depend on human endeavour, and hence the need to *pray* for the dead to secure their release from purgatory.

ET

Puritanism

'Puritanism' is a word that began its life as a term of abuse for somebody who engaged in over-zealous criticism of the *Church of England* in the 16th and 17th centuries. More accurately it represented those who thought that the established church represented an imperfect or incomplete *reformation* and were anxious for the process to be pursued to its completion. This, the puritans sought in terms of deepening personal *piety* so that the church visible more nearly corresponded to the church invisible. They also sought the reform of the government of the church though they were divided as to whether this should have an Episcopalian, *Presbyterian* or *Congregational* order. They sought the ending of all corruption and the establishment of a better educated and more disciplined clergy, and most obviously the reform of the church's *worship*. Because the church was an established one the Puritans necessarily were cast in the role of *political* agitators, and indeed in the 1640s, after the beheading of the king the puritans acceded to power in *England*. But the very notion of an Established Church was unsatisfactory to many who took the argument one step further in becoming *Separatists*: such were, e.g. Robert Browne, Francis Johnson and John Robinson. It is among such men that the first Baptists found their roots. In general terms Puritan *theologians*, aided by the publication of the Authorised (King James) version of the *Bible* [see *Bible Translation*] in 1611, expounded an English version of *Calvinist* doctrine, such as would be enshrined in the Westminster Confession (1646) under the leadership of men such as William Perkins (1558-1602), William Ames (1573-1633), John Owen (1616-83), Thomas Goodwin (1600-80) and Richard Baxter (1615-91). The puritan imagination is best seen in the allegorical writings of *John Bunyan*, (1628-88) the author of *The Pilgrim's Progress*. Early Baptists were both a part of the Puritan movement and an off-shoot from it. *Charles Haddon Spurgeon* revelled in the Puritan *tradition* which provided him with his staple reading much of which he put on to the reading lists of *students* at Pastor's College: it was the Puritan standard from which he was anxious that his students should not stray.

JHYB

Q

Quakers, Baptists and

The Quakers, later called the Religious Society of Friends, date their foundation back to 1652 in North West *England* with their founder an itinerant *preacher* named George Fox, who, dissatisfied with formal religion, had been seeking a deeper spiritual experience from the mid 1640s onwards. They are the most radical of the surviving *sects* of English *Puritanism*. *Ernst Troeltsch* even argues 'the Society of Friends represents the final expression in its purest form of the *Anabaptist* Movement,' and along with the *Mennonites* and the *Church of the Brethren* they have become one of the historic *Peace Churches*. Originally known as 'Friends of the Truth', under Fox they came to respect the 'Inner Light' or 'that of God in every *man*' speaking directly to the soul as their ultimate standard of truth. Such insight was to be informed by the *scriptures* and to operate within a distinctly Christian framework, but was not bound by either written word or *creed*. In such a context they have developed a distinctive spiritual discipline, and govern their common life by decisions made through a patient process of group discernment. But even so unstructured a group needed some rules of procedure and these Fox provided in the 'Rule for the Management of Meetings' adopted in 1668.

Despite cruel persecution in *Britain*, the Quakers grew rapidly in the early years of their existence and their *missionaries* won over, amongst others, whole congregations of General Baptists, especially in Midland England, so not surprisingly a pamphlet war between Baptists, both Particular and General, and Quakers developed. From England they spread to *Ireland*, Northern Europe, and North America, the latter group led by William Penn under whom they settled in Pennsylvania. In the 19th century there was a renewal of the *Evangelical* strand within Quakerism which became caught up in that century's great missionary enterprises especially in Africa and Latin America. Today there are four strands in Quakerism: evangelical, pastored, conservative and liberal unprogrammed, those who worship in silent waiting upon God. Each of these strands has its own organisation such as Evangelical Friends International, Friends United Meeting (the pastored tradition) and Friends General Conference (liberal unprogrammed tradition). Friends of all four *traditions* come together in the Friends World Committee for Consultation, founded 1927, which represents rather less than 400,000 Quakers worldwide.

Quakers reject the celebration of the *sacraments* in favour of a sacramental evaluation of common life. All *members* may participate in the Sunday meeting held in a plain building without ecclesiastical *decoration*. As pacifists they reject all forms of military service; their campaigning against war has received recognition by the award of Nobel Prizes both to individuals and to Quaker organisations. 'More concerned with the here and now than with the hereafter', they believe they are called to incarnate 'the authentic counter culture of a better way, the only way that holds true hope and the promise of life for mankind.' Accordingly they have secured for themselves a deserved reputation for compassionate service as e.g. in the part they played in opposing the Slave Trade and Slavery, in which there was much Baptist-Quaker cooperation, in prison reform, in the securing of female suffrage, and more recently in international relief. In Europe today Quakers are to be found in *Scandinavia*, the *Baltic* republics, *France* and the Benelux countries, *Germany*, *Austria*, the *Czech Republic*, *Hungary*, Greece, *Spain* and *Italy*. With the exception of *Russia*, where the Moscow Monthly Meeting is listed, and the *Lebanon* (the Middle East Yearly Meeting), they are not organised in the eastern part of *EBF* territory.

ET

R

Racism
See *Programme to Combat Racism*.

Radical Reformation
See *Reformation*.

Radosc, Warsaw, The Baptist Seminary

Baptists moved to Radosc [meaning 'joy'], a suburb to the southeast of Warsaw, to establish a Baptist Seminary in the early 1920s. Its programme complemented *theological* courses then existing in different cities of *Poland* such as Lodz, Malbork and Warsaw itself over the course of the century. One of the pioneers in Radosc was Moses Gitlin, a Christian of *Jewish* origin. He was born in a Russian Jewish family. Soon after his *conversion* at the age of 16, he left for America and studied there at the Moody Bible Institute. Gitlin desired to come back to *Russia* as an *evangelist*, but Russia, then already under the rule of Bolsheviks, was closed to *missionaries*. So, he went as a missionary to Eastern Poland, where Russian and Ukrainian were widely spoken. Married with five *children*, he engaged in *preaching* and teaching in the Volhynia and Polesie districts, and began to use a villa, a wooden house in the middle of the woods, bought from a former *Catholic priest*. *Bible* courses were available in Radosc from as early as Nov 1923. The opening celebration took place in the old wooden villa now re-named 'Bethel'. From that time Radosc, became the centre for different forms of Bible education among Polish *evangelicals*. Among them the International Bible School was very popular. This work grew in the period of Poland's independence between the two world wars.

During the Warsaw Uprising, when the capital of Poland was being destroyed house by house by Nazi troops, many evangelical leaders fled to the safety of Bethel. After WWII, Swedish Baptists organised charitable work there for undernourished Polish chil-

dren from several denominations. The Bethel complex continued to host church-wide annual conferences of the Polish Baptist *Union*, *pastoral* training conferences, workshops for *Sunday School* workers, as well as camps for children and young people. It was Krzysztof Bednarczyk (one of the then Polish Baptist leaders) who had the vision to build some bungalows around the Bethel. Accordingly, holidays could be hosted every year as well as camps for young people and children.

During the 1980s, in the Solidarity era, there emerged a new vision of constructing in Radosc a complex of modern buildings for the purpose of theological *education* and a variety of other Christian activities. The *Communist* authorities, at first, refused permission to remodel or enlarge the existing buildings. They also denied permission to build a new centre adjacent to the large house. Many attempts were made to reverse this decision and to secure building permission but each application was refused by the authorities. When, in 1984, the area was reclassified to allow the suburb to develop and expand, the Union received official permission to erect a new Polish Baptist Centre in Radosc. In 1987, the authorities agreed to sign a 99 year lease with the Polish Baptist Union allowing them to continue their *ministry* on the property, and two years later the cornerstone was laid, though the building process only began in earnest in 1990 with the invaluable help of Baptist workers from Kiszyniow, *Moldova*. A three-year partnership also began with the North Carolina Baptist Convention which concluded in the autumn of 1992. This Convention sent 23 groups of workers during this time and also supported the work in various other ways.

The opening ceremony of the campus in Radosc took place on 17-18 Sep 1994. Among the official guests were Dr. John David Hopper – then President of the *International Baptist Theological Seminary* then in *Rüschlikon*, (*Switzerland*), Tony Cupit – chairman of the Education Department of *Baptist World Alliance*, John Floyd – European representative of the *Southern Baptist Convention* and Perry Green – coordinator of the partnership between North Carolina Baptist Convention and the Baptist Union of Poland, which helped to make the construction of a new campus possible.

The first rector, Gustaw Cieslar, began work in 1993 when he moved with his family into the wooden structure of Bethel. On 30 Jun 1995, the Parliament of Poland passed a law on the relationship between the *State* and the Polish Baptist Union (Official Gazette No. 97 item 480) which in article 14.2 stipulates that Warsaw Baptist Theological Seminary (WBST) has the right to confer on its graduates a Bachelor of Divinity degree which is equivalent to BA degrees conferred in the public educational system. In 2003 a Seminary *Chapel* was added to the complex. Gustaw Cieslar's sterling work as rector ended in 2005 by which time the Seminary complex had been completed and WBST established as a major training institution for evangelicals across Poland and elsewhere. In Oct 2005 the Seminary's second rector, Michael I. Bochenski – a British Baptist whose father had escaped to the *UK* during WWII – was inducted.

MIB

Ragged Schools

Ragged schools were a product of Christian compassion responding to the problems brought into being by the industrial revolution and were mainly a British phenomenon. Dating from around 1810 they sought, generally under *evangelical* leadership, though some related to unitarian churches, to provide basic *education* for *children* so dirty, wild and uncared for that no other school would take them. The classes were initially on Sundays and provided by middle and upper class volunteers. Local initiatives came together in 1844 in establishing the Ragged Schools Union of which two years later Lord Shaftesbury became a very active president. Another member of the society's committee was Revd Baptist Noel, President of the Baptist *Union* in 1855, who for a long time led London Evangelicals in the *Church of England* until he resigned his orders in 1849 on seeking *baptism* as a believer. By 1849 there were 11,000 and 8,000 day/evening *scholars*, with the latter category rising to c.40,000 by the late 60s when there were some 400 paid teachers. Their work was justified not only on compassionate grounds but also on those of social expediency, as the movement rep-

resented an attempt to integrate into society those who otherwise might turn to crime or *violence*.

Large urban Baptist churches either ran their own Ragged Schools or contributed, by manpower and finance, to interdenominational schools. E.g. Bloomsbury put more finance into Ragged Schools than its *Sunday Schools*. The Ragged Schools were related to the *chapel*'s Domestic *Mission* under the expert leadership of George M'Cree (1822-92), sometimes lovingly called the '*Bishop* of St Giles' a slum area immediately adjacent to Bloomsbury Chapel. At the time of *Spurgeon*'s death, the Metropolitan Tabernacle ran 27 Ragged and Sunday Schools, and Ragged School teachers were amongst those first coming to Pastors' College for training.

The RSU quickly learned that it could not confine its activities to education – accordingly it became involved with providing meals, clothing clubs, penny banks, infant nurseries, and hostels for the family-less young. Excursions were organised and facilities for holidays for the *poor* initiated. An *emigration* scheme offered new opportunities in Australia for children whose healthy development seemed blighted by drunken homes, and for this Shaftesbury secured a parliamentary grant. One of its more imaginative experiments was to establish a Shoe Black Brigade created especially to exploit the opportunities offered by the 1851 Exhibition in London. This offered Ragged School graduates their first sheltered and disciplined employment.

Environmental improvement in the 1870s coupled with the development of *state* education after the 1870 Education Act caused the RSU to rethink its role. In 1893, three years after compulsory education had become free, the RSU re-launched itself as the Shaftesbury Society with the more specialised task of providing education for the disabled [see *Disabilities*], practical instruction for destitute boys and *missions* catering for the whole family in urban slums.

JHYB

Rawdon Baptist College, Leeds
See *Northern Baptist College, Manchester*.

Rebirth

See *Conversion*; *New Birth*; *Regeneration*.

Reconciliation

Reconciliation describes the process whereby broken relationships are restored, conflict overcome, quarrels settled, embracing a term derived from a Latin word which literally means 'to bring back together'. The expression, which is not found in the OT, is not used to depict the resolution of problems between individuals, where, as e.g. in Mt 5:24, a different word is employed. In the NT it is used to describe the changed relationship between *humankind* and God brought about by the *death* and *resurrection* of *Jesus Christ*, and because of this it is not found in the gospels but only in the Pauline epistles. Thus it describes a radical new relationship in which previous hostility or estrangement is overcome by God's initiative in the sacrifice of his Son (Ro 5:10-11; 2Co 5:18-20).

Although primarily concerned with the way God's estranged people are brought back into relationship with him, the *restoration* of that Edenic *fellowship* marred by the intervention of human sinfulness [see *Sin*], there are also consequences for interpersonal relations, because those reconciled to God are committed to the *ministry* and message of reconciliation, to indicate to others the good news that a way of return to God has been established, whilst in Eph 2:14-18 Paul draws the conclusion that if *Jew* and Gentile are alike reconciled to God, then the barriers between them are also removed. Thus the *church* is properly to be seen as the fellowship of the reconciled, and, therefore, the building up of a community in the *Spirit* is of the very essence of its being. Consequently, a divided or un-reconciled church represents a *heresy* of the first order, as essentially denying God's central act of *grace*.

In Col 1:19-22 Paul engages in the even more daring deduction that the death and resurrection of Jesus reconciles a created order at odds with its Maker back into harmony with him, for if the notion of reconciliation is not found in the OT, the *alienation* of *creation* from Creator, inherent in the *Fall*, is central to the message of Genesis; indeed this is the great OT problem requiring a NT answer.

ET

Reconciling histories and memories

In the complex story of Europe there are countless historical accounts of invasion, ethnic cleansing, tension within communities, disagreements and persecutions of different *minority* communities by larger national groupings. History and memory is passed on from generation to generation as accounts of how 'the other' has perpetrated some great act of pain and terror against 'us'. As Christians the claim is made that we are agents of a gospel of *reconciliation* and, as such, believing communities should have those strategies based in *Christ* which enable them to address painful memories, to bring those with accounts of repression together with those often seen as oppressors, those who are seen as the 'powerful ones', in an attempt to offer a pathway to healing and reconciliation. The work necessarily begins in local congregations, where there can be disputes between families going back in time. The same activity needs also to take place in *unions*, where perhaps churches were formed by antagonistic splits from another church and the reasons for the split remain unaddressed, or between unions who follow the narrative of their *nation*, or people in recalling acts of a neighbouring country and the believers within it as aggressors. Strategies for addressing such painful memories have been worked out in the past from the *ministry* of Jesus and refined amongst baptistic communities. It is easily acknowledged that bad memories are kept in a retributive way. To transcend such memories is only possible when human beings come to deeply value 'the others' and recognise the 'Christlikeness' that exists in others. Then, truth telling has to occur when the history or memory is 'named' and the story is retold from both perspectives. Certain techniques will be useful here: to agree that criticism is wherever possible balanced by positive assessment, always to check that a criticism of other groups is also impartially applied to one's own group, never to claim certainty when there is an ambiguity in the evidence.

In the *dialogue* which ensues the journey towards truth and justice has the possibility of taking place. The work of reconciliation may not remove the memory, but may remove the power of the history and memory to poison, to destroy both present realities and future possibilities. European Baptists have been very concerned to do this, and *IBTS* has had such a ministry at the core of its purpose.

KGJ

Redemption

[See also *Salvation and Soteriology*]
The word finds its origin in business transactions where it signified the buying back of something which had formerly been owned, but which for some reason had become somebody else's possession. Thus something which has been pawned might be redeemed as might a slave in the year of *jubilee*. Redemption is the motif at the heart of the OT story of Ruth, in which Boaz as her second nearest of kin takes over from her nearest of kin both the duty of redeeming her dead husband's land and also the obligation to marry Ruth [see *Marriage/Matrimony*]. God was *Israel*'s redeemer by delivering the people from Egyptian slavery. Deutero-Isaiah is particularly rich in references to God as Redeemer; 'Fear not, for I have redeemed thee; I have called them by name and thou art mine' (Isa 43:1).

In NT times, redemption was commonplace in the Graeco-Roman Empire describing the process whereby the freedom of a slave was secured often on the payment of a ransom to the slave's owner. Supremely, however, redemption describes *Jesus*' purpose in becoming incarnate [see *Incarnation*]: 'The Son of Man did not come to be served but to serve, and to give his life a ransom for many' (Mk 10:45), that is Jesus gives his life in exchange for lives that are forfeit and thereby sets them free. Redemption then secures, through *forgiveness*, freedom from the tyranny of *sin*, not simply from the 'wages of sin', but from the power of sin that holds *men* and *women* in direst thraldom. Redemption is thus a synonym for salvation. 1Pe 1:18-19 provides a classic statement of NT teaching on redemption: 'you know that it was not with perishable things such as

silver and gold that you were redeemed from the empty way of life handed down to you from your fathers, but with the precious blood of Christ...', where some translations paraphrase the language of redemption by referring to the purchasing of freedom. Emphatically and unambiguously slaves become sons. The emphasis is on the action of Christ as voluntary, costly, and effective, doing for the redeemed something they could not do for themselves, thus underlining the sheer unmerited *love* of God manifest in the *suffering* and *death* of Christ.

Peter and Paul make the cost of redemption the motivation for the dynamic of service and *holiness* (1Pe 2:21-23; 1Co 6:20; 7:23). There is also an *eschatological* dimension to the language of redemption as described by Paul in Ro 8:18-25: for the experience of redemption now experienced is but a foretaste of that full redemption which will come at the end of history.

ET

Reformation

As those whose origins were formulated within the European crisis known as the Reformation, Baptists have a natural interest in its history. Three elements are distinguishable with hindsight but in the turmoil of the 16th century such divisions were not always so clear. The first is *Catholic* Reform, better language rather than 'Counter Reformation', for a number of Catholic movements had their own dynamic and were not responses to events in *Germany* or *Switzerland*. Some of these movements were prereformation posing the question whether the reformation was caused as much by a revived *piety* in the late middle ages rather than by widespread corruption. However, whilst there were earlier reform movements, those who have tried to trace a continuity of *evangelical* life outside the catholic church have undertaken a fruitless exercise: only the reformation in the 16th century caused a lasting rupture in the *unity* of *Christendom*. Much within the late medieval church called for reform; alongside much genuine piety there existed both superstition and corruption as well as an over optimistic *theology* of the will which put too much emphasis on the potential of human endeavour.

The Reformation is irrevocably associated with **Martin Luther**'s posting of his 95 theses on the Castle Church door in Wittenberg. Crucial to Luther's success was the protection he received from the Elector Frederick the Wise of Saxony, and the support that his movement received from other German princes, often hard pressed with debt. In the Lutheran world the principle established by the Peace of Augsburg in 1555 was *cuius region, eius religio*, that is to say it was for the rulers to determine the religion in their respective *states*. Later the movement was to spread through *Scandinavia* by way of royal advocacy. In Switzerland the reformers received the support of the City Councils of a newly prosperous urban society. Whether by the actions of hard-pressed princes or prosperous city oligarchies, this was a reformation from above, so it is often called the 'magisterial reformation'.

By contrast the Radical Reformation was a reformation from below with, for the most part, princely opposition rather than support, for the state was not lightly going to abandon its control of religion, so often conceived of as the glue which held society together; certainly the princes saw potential threat in allowing people free choice in religion with the emergence of self-authenticating local congregations. The magisterial reformation under the leadership of Luther, *Zwingli* and *Calvin* saw the main contours of the reformed *faith* established in the lives of individuals. *Scripture* rather than the *Papacy* or *Church Tradition* was to be the authority for all matters of faith and practice. There was new stress on the divine initiative in *incarnation*, *atonement* and *resurrection*, to be appropriated in the life of the believer by trusting commitment rather than by any programme of either good works or *sacramental* actions; good works could never save, but were a natural and thankful responses to the divine initiative. In other words in reformed theology they were not causative of salvation but consequential upon it. Whilst the reformation in Saxony was conservative with change kept to the minimum necessary. Zwingli in Zürich was more complete, retaining in the life of the new reformed church only that which had specific Biblical sanction, but he drew back from anything really radical. In Geneva,

Calvin developed a more systematic presentation of reformed theology, with the articulation of what has been called five-point **Calvinism** starting with the human dilemma entailed in Total **Depravity**, As with Luther, he stressed the importance of God's gracious initiative as **humankind** became the subject of Unmerited Favour. Distinctive emphases began with an emphasis on Limited Atonement, Irresistible **Grace** and the **Perseverance of the Saints**. Whilst in Switzerland there was more thought given to how reformed churches should govern themselves, those churches remained **state churches** without final freedom to determine their own ecclesiastical life.

The emergence of **Protestantism** shattered the unity of Western Christendom in the 1520s, but because protestants did not agree among themselves, and because of what may now be properly called the Counter Reformation, the fracturing of Christendom was in many directions, aided by the emerging existence of the **nation** state. Only with the Radical Reformation is there a search for the freedom to choose confession within a state, and the admission of voluntary belief.

The Schleitheim Articles (1527), a confession of agreed faith [see **Creeds, Covenants and Confessions of Faith**] and practice which helped to unite early **Anabaptism**, emphasised believers' baptism, committed **discipleship**, **church discipline**, the **ethics** of **love** and separation from earthly government structures. Perhaps the most important Anabaptist distinctive was their *ecclesiology* – the church (brotherhood) consists only of spiritually renewed persons who voluntarily join the fellowship. As over against the *volkskirchen* or *landeskirchen* of the **Lutherans**, Anabaptists were committed to the idea of the **Believers' Church**, a church made up of those who of their own free will had committed themselves to a covenant relationship with God and with their fellow **church members**, whose direction, under God, was in the hands of the church members without any state, **Episcopal** or **synodical** interference. Their concern for **sanctification** as well as **justification** meant that more than others they strove to make the visible church here on earth reflect the glory of the invisible church [see **Church: Universal, Trium-**

phant, Invisible]. Thus the Anabaptists had a high view of the Christian community but a non-sacramental view of the ordinances regarding them as signs devoid of the power to communicate grace. In underlining the **authority** of scripture they insisted on the interpreting power of the **Holy Spirit**. They were suspicious of 'Justification by Faith Alone' language as being too formulaic or forensic and preferred to talk of 'faith that obeys' for a faith that comes by the gift of the Holy Spirit has to lead to the visibility of a holy life [see **Holiness**]: there was no room for **antinomianism** here. Nor were the Anabaptists enamoured of **predestinarian** emphases, rather arguing that humankind had the freedom to respond to or reject God's **call** [see **Freedom of Conscience**]. Responding to grace was not simply empowered by God but required a measure of human cooperation. It was from this source mediated through the **Mennonite** churches in **Holland** rather than from **Arminius** that early General Baptists [see **England**] derived their ideas of *free will*. The Anabaptists worried about the danger of over-intellectualising theology which they believed had to be lived rather than analysed. It was out of this matrix of ideas that Anabaptists in the 1540s developed their unwillingness to take up arms, to underline their testimony by oath, and to decline to serve as magistrates. Though themselves major advocates of religious toleration since true faith could never be coerced, ere long the experience of extreme persecution was to led them to develop a special theology of **martyrdom**.

JHYB

Reform Baptists

The Reform Baptist movement, which refused cooperation with the **communist state**, came into being as a reaction to the revised church statutes and an accompanying letter of instruction to the senior presbyters issued by the **All-Union Council of the Evangelical Christians-Baptists** in Dec 1959 under the pressure of the government in the **Soviet Union**. The revised statutes and the so-called Letter of Instruction limited the work of churches even more, in addition to the restrictions that were already in place. The Reform Baptist movement started under

the leadership of Gennadii Kryuchkov and Aleksei Prokofyev as an Initiative group that protested against the compromises that official AUCECB was yielded under the state pressures (hence they are also known as the *Initsiativniki*). In Aug 1961 a delegation of the *Initsiativniki* delivered their first petition to the AUCECB. A great number of letters to believers followed. A number of persons and churches followed the appeal of the *Initsiativniki* that now claimed to represent the non-registered churches. In Feb 1962, they reorganised themselves into an Organisational Committee for calling a congress (hence *Orgkomitet*) as opposed to the AUCECB. In Jun 1962, all AUCECB members were declared as excommunicated from office and **church membership** by the *Orgkomitet*, thereby splitting the Baptist brotherhood in the USSR. Nevertheless in 1963, the AUCECB managed to convene a conference that was declared a congress.

With the disempowerment of N. Khrushchev in Oct 1964, the religious policy of the state changed, with less insistence on the registration of churches, at least *de facto*, and the release of some believers from prison. In Sep 1965, leaders of the *Orgkomitet* met with A. Mikoyan, the President of the Soviet Union. The *Orgkomitet* was not prepared to change its original position but in Sep 1965 changed its name to Council of Churches of the Evangelical Christians-Baptists (CCECB), challenging the leadership of AUCECB. G. Kryuchkov became president of CCECB, and Georgii Vins its secretary. In 1966, the AUCECB formed a Unity Commission that consisted of highly respected Soviet Baptist leaders, but the effectiveness of this commission's work was limited. Two basic views regarding church-state relations – that of 'discretion' and 'valour' – became more and more evident, and hindered mutual understanding of registered and non-registered groups. These different perspectives had long term effects on the identity of these groups.

CCECB persisted in its policy of strict denial of official registration of **local churches**, and continued its work 'underground'. For this they paid the price of a high number of arrests with consequent prison sentences. The interests of these prisoners came to be represented by the Council of Prisoners' Relatives. The persecutions continued until the end of the 1980s. Until 1975, the total number of prisoners related to CCECB at any one time remained around 180, though over the whole period as many as 700 were imprisoned. All leaders of CCECB were imprisoned at different times, and in 1979 G. Vins was expelled from the country. From 1971 the underground *Khristianin* publishing house was printing Christian literature. This initiative was supported not only by the CCECB, but also by different groups and persons from other church bodies.

In spite of the clearly defined goals of the CCECB, its high centralisation did not satisfy all its members. From 1975, a significant number of Reform Baptists churches decided to register with the government office remaining independent of both CCECB and AUCECB. Reform Baptists were strongest in *Ukraine*, *Kazakhstan* and *Russia*, but were also found in other regions of the Soviet Union. European Baptists through both the *EBF* and *BWA* sought to remain in conversation with both the AUCECB and CCECB, exploiting such diplomatic channels as were open to them to seek mitigation for those in prison. In particular Dutch Baptists in the spring of 1973 tried to get in touch with the relatives of some of those in prison shortly before Klaus Meister of *Germany* made a visit to Russia as President of the EBF. Others chose to work outside denominational organisations such as those Baptists who associated with the organisation called 'Prayer for the Persecuted'. The *Anglican priest*, Michael Bourdeaux, set up a research institute called Keston College in 1969 with the task of undertaking research and collecting documentation on religion in Russia and associated communist lands. Accordingly its archives contain much material on the Reform Baptists.

JD & ET

FURTHER READING: *Podrashaïte vere ikh, 1961-2001: 40 let probushdennomu bratstvu*, Sovet Tserkveï EKHB, Moscow, 2001. Michael Bourdeaux, *Religious Ferment in Russia. Protestant Opposition to Soviet Religious Policy*, Macmillan and St Martin's, London and New York, 1968. Michael Bourdeaux, *Gorbachev, Glasnost and the Gospel*, Hodder and Stoughton, London, 1990. E.A. Payne, *Out of Great Tribulation: Baptists in the USSR*, BUGBI, London, 1974. Walter Sawatsky, *Soviet Evangelicals since World War II*, Herald, Kitchener, 1981.

Reformed Churches, Baptists and

[See also *Bilateral Conversations*; *Leuenberg Confession Conversations on Baptism*; *Reformation*]

Reformed (or Presbyterian) Churches are children of the Reformation especially the part associated with *Jean Calvin*. In this respect they share a common heritage with Baptists.

In many European countries Baptists suffered persecution from the *state* for representing forces beyond state control, while Reformed Churches as heirs of the Magisterial Reformation and functioning as a *state church* enjoyed more *political* support. Yet Baptist *witness* often appealed to *members* of *pietist* renewal movements within the Reformed community. On the one hand, people desiring spiritual growth or recognising a scriptural truth not taught in Reformed communities (e.g. believers' *baptism*) became Baptists, while remaining loyal to certain aspects of their former beliefs (e.g. *Calvinist* teaching on double-*predestination* or the verbal *inspiration* of *scripture*). On the other hand, some Reformed leaders successfully created *prayer*-groups that functioned as centres of *renewal* whilst retaining their existing church allegiance. The part of the reformed church family which adopted a *congregational* form of *church government* has come to closely resemble the Baptist model. Indeed it is sometimes difficult to determine at what point a Congregational Church becomes a Baptist Church, and certainly in *England* no less than *John Bunyan* was anxious that water baptism should not be a cause of division. Accordingly there have existed a number of 'Union churches' which identify with both *traditions* as well as *associations* containing churches of both allegiances.

Sharing the Reformation principles of *solus Christus, sola Scriptura, sola gratia* and *sola fide*, Baptist and Reformed *theology* have much in common. Traditionally Baptists side with Calvin on issues of doctrine where Calvinist teaching and *Lutheran* teaching differ (e.g. the *Lord's Supper*). However, doctrinal debates concerning *election*, the nature of *grace* and *perseverance* have found their way into Baptist churches causing controversy and division (e.g. the General and Particular Baptists in 17-18th century England). Baptist *theologians* have often turned to Reformed theologians, especially Calvin and Barth, for guidance. It has been claimed that Baptist and Reformed doctrine differ only on the question of baptism. However, believers' baptism also entails other doctrines and practices, and cannot be tied into a Reformed system of doctrine in itself. In addition, certain issues of debate in *Evangelical* theology (e.g. the nature of scripture or *eschatological* questions) are present in both and distinctions cannot be drawn along denominational lines. Indeed Baptists have often remained even more faithful to the Calvinist tradition than the Reformed Churches.

The name Presbyterian (from the Greek *presbúteros* [elder]) refers to the order of Reformed churches, namely that they are governed by an elected council of *ministers* and *elders*, which is authoritative rather than advisory. Though having elders, deacons and presbyters, Baptist churches are organised and governed along congregational principles (from the Latin *congregatio* [community]). It means that the mind of *Christ* is discerned in the *church meeting* wherein all *members* of the *local church* have the right to speak and to vote: the *authority* of the whole congregation is superior to that of the leaders. This difference can be interpreted as a more profound application of the *priesthood of all believers* than that usually observed amongst the Presbyterians.

In general Reformed and Baptist churches mutually recognise each other as part of Christ's people on earth. Yet Baptists sometimes see Presbyterians as not wholly obedient to scripture in certain doctrines and ethical demands [see *Ethics*], while Presbyterians may see Baptists as too pietistic, in particular denying the validity of *infant baptism*. Both denominations are involved in ecumenical processes. Officially, many Baptist and Reformed churches are members of *WCC* and *CEC* as well as national *ecumenical* bodies. Additionally, local churches all over Europe join forces with each other in common witness and *ministry* to the world in prayer, *evangelism* and *diakonia*. Formally, *dialogue* took place between members

of *BWA* and of the World Alliance of Reformed Churches (WARC) in the years 1973-77. This was seen as an important development in inter-church relations, representing a deliberate attempt to talk across the boundaries that separated the Magisterial from the Radical Reformations. It boldly recommended developing churches which offered alternative patterns of *initiation* – either infant baptism followed by confirmation after a personal decision to follow Christ has been made or a service of *thanksgiving* at birth followed by believers' baptism once the person in question has chosen to follow Christ. An evaluation of the responses to this in 1982 did not indicate widespread support for this as a way forward. Recently, a dialogue between *EBF* and *CPCE* (Leuenberg Fellowship) on 'The Beginning of Christian Life and the Nature of the Church' has been summarised in a document, which could bring new insights to the old doctrinal questions that divide the Reformed and Baptist churches.

AS

Refugee work

Refugees are those forced to leave their home countries in order to escape war, persecution or natural disaster, including the victims of social, *political* and economic injustice, or ethnic or religious prejudice.

In 1943 the *Baptist World Alliance* established a Committee on World *Emergency Relief*, reinstituting an initiative first started in 1920. Through this Baptists played an important part in the resettlement of refugees after WWII. By 15 Jun 1950, Baptists had settled 5,692 displaced persons from European refugee camps to the USA. The worldwide total was over 9,000. The BWA was also one of the founders of the Cooperative for American Remittances to Europe (CARE). So considerable was the plight of displaced persons in considerable measure caused by changing political boundaries that there was a Slavic Baptist Union established in *Germany* in the post-war years as later churches were founded by ethnic Germans migrating from Siberia and other parts of the *USSR*. In Germany many Baptists moved west in front of the Soviet armies. These movements, by *migration*, also reinforced the *witness* of ethnic European churches, with their distinctive linguistic *liturgies*, in the Americas.

In 2005, the BWA celebrated 85 years of relief, development and refugee work. Through *Baptist World Aid* it has continued to support refugees and displaced persons not only in Europe but throughout the world. In recent years emphasis has been given to refugees from the ethnic cleansing in Rwanda and the *Balkan* countries. Sadly, few Baptist conventions/*unions* still have specific staff to handle refugee case work.

In addition to Refugees, those who have fled their countries, Internally Displaced Persons (IDPs) still reside in their own countries, even though displaced from their homes. Many Baptists are now involved in standing with and supporting 'Asylum Seekers', who are seeking to escape from political and religious persecution. Indeed there have been a number of occasions on which Baptist churches have acted as places of *sanctuary*, providing a place of safety from arrest by the authorities for refugees and asylum seekers.

The *United Nations*' High Commission for Refugees (UNHCR) is charged with providing protection for refugees, IDPs and Asylum seekers. In 2003 UNHCR was responsible for 20.6 million people; among these, 10.4 million were refugees, 1 million are Asylum seekers and 5.7 million were IDPs. As the *wealthier* parts of the world find it more difficult to absorb all those who seek a higher standard of life within its borders, so a distinction is frequently made between refugees and asylum seekers and those now termed economic migrants. Much of the economic *migration* in Europe has been from east to west and south to north thus churches in *Britain* have been looking at the employment of, e.g., Portuguese and Polish *pastors* to minister to their co-patriots in the west. In like fashion there are many separately established churches, some very large, ministering to the African *diaspora* in Europe.

PM

Regeneration

[See also *Conversion*; *New Birth*]
Regeneration reflects the gospel emphasis on 'New Birth'. It describes the divine action which is the mirror image of the human commitment to a radical change of life represented by conversion. Conversion is the act of turning from *sin* and self towards God through *Jesus Christ*, perhaps in response to an *evangelistic sermon* or perhaps through witnessing a service of believers' *baptism*. Regeneration describes what God's *Spirit* does in the life of the new believer, bringing to birth within them a new life of Christ-like living. Conversion describes *humankind*'s part and regeneration God's part in the creating of a new Christian, which are normatively represented in believers' baptism. The fact that regeneration is God's doing not just an individual's aspiration, provides one important ground for the *evangelical* understanding of Christian assurance.

Regeneration, being 'born again', then, describes the inner *renewal* of life which takes place when a person becomes a Christian. On the basis of Christ's *death* and *resurrection* and the gift of the Spirit, sin is forgiven [see *Forgiveness*] and a new spiritual life created which is to be shaped by *faith*, *love* and *hope*. Such a new creation can only be the work of God. Just as a human experiences birth, but has no part in engineering it, even more so regeneration stands outside and beyond all human endeavour. Like birth, rebirth is a once-and-for-all event, but if regeneration is to achieve its goal the baby must grow into the child and the child into mature adulthood 'measured by nothing less than the full stature of Christ' Eph 4:13).

Just as the family is the essential environment for physical growth so the *church* is the only proper milieu for the development of the spiritual life of the new Christian. Baptist *ecclesiology* on this basis distinctively insists on the need for a regenerate *church membership*. Indeed the church is defined by the living faith of its members.

JHYB

Regent's Park College, Oxford

Regent's Park College has its origins in an *education* society established in the middle of the 18th century, the London Baptist Education Society of 1752, which trained *men* for *ministry* under its own tutor. At the beginning of the 19th century the *evangelical* movement looked to consolidate its influence by establishing colleges for *ministerial formation* in the belief that 'the light of *Revelation*' and the 'light of Reason' were complementary manifestations of the truth of God. Under such motivation the older education society was transformed into 'The Baptist Academical Institution at Stepney' in 1810. The syllabus embraced both the humanities and theology and from an early date the College enrolled lay [see *Laity*] as well as ministerial *students*. In 1840 the College was affiliated to London University in whose foundation Baptists, and especially those associated with the College, had played an important part. Joseph Angus, long-serving principal, believed it was both advantageous for ministerial students to share their education with non-theologians and good for a number of lay students to read for their degrees in a Christian community. In 1856 the College moved to Regent's Park which was near enough to University College for students to attend classes there. When the University was reconstituted at the beginning of the 20th century Regent's Park became a Divinity School of the University with its tutors becoming recognised teachers of the new Theology Faculty.

The distinguished OT *scholar*, H. Wheeler Robinson, saw the advantage of moving the College to one of the ancient universities and in 1927 bought a site in Oxford for that purpose. For a while the College existed both in London and Oxford until in 1939 the College was consolidated once more on a single site and in 1958 achieved the status of a 'Permanent Private Hall' of the University which gave its students equality of status with those of other colleges with its fellows and lecturers able to become members of the various faculties of the university, and indeed to take a leading part in the life of the university by their scholarship and by holding office in these. In 2005 the university's prestigious Bampton Lectures were given by the Principal of Regent's. This means that whilst the College offers residence to students, and is the focus for tutorial teaching, which is still the chief focus for student progress in Oxford, all the rich facilities of the University in lectures, communal life and library provision are open to Regent's' students who work for University of

Oxford degrees (BA, BTh, a range of Masters' degrees, both taught and secured by research, and the DPhil), which enables Regent's to serve the whole Baptist community worldwide in providing access to the most highly regarded higher degrees in the world. The College works in close cooperation with colleges of other Christian denominations in Oxford which offer ministerial training, whilst its own non-ministerial intake embraces students from all Christian churches. The policy of Joseph Angus in integrating students being formed for ministry with lay students reading for degrees in the humanities, law and the social sciences still characterises the College, with rather more graduate students reading for higher degrees these days as the University itself weights its student body in that direction.

The College, whilst receiving no direct funding from the Baptist *Union* of *Great Britain*, is a member of the Union and recognised by it as an institution for the training of *women* and men for ministry. Indeed the first college-trained female minister serving with the Baptist Union, Revd Violet Hedger, was admitted to the College in 1920. Since those days the age of those training for the ministry has gone up so that it now averages about 35 with a number of these older students undertaking their ministerial preparation by church-based training, working from a student pastorate which enables the student to reflect on actual *pastoral* situations as they study for a University qualification in theology. A marked feature of Regent's life is the location in the College of The Oxford Centre for the Study of Christianity and Culture which focuses the College's intention to give all students, both ministerial and non-ministerial, opportunities to develop a Christian mind about contemporary society, and to see the theological significance of all scholarship, whether that be history or law or philosophy or literature.

Whilst the University's Bodleian Library is of international quality, Regent's own Angus Library is the world's primary collection of both archives and printed material relating to the Baptist denomination incorporating as it does both the archives of the *Baptist Missionary Society* and the Library of the Baptist Union. The Angus Library's collection ranges from the 17th century to the present day and offers a rich range of resources for those undertaking doctoral studies. It provides strong support to the Centre for Baptist History and Heritage which is also part of the College.

JHYB

Religion(s), Study of

See *Comparative Religion*.

Religious Festivals

See *Festivals, Religious*.

Religious Freedom

See *Religious Liberty*.

Religious Language

Reflection on religious language should quickly reveal the major problem with its usage, namely the recognition that finite words, even many of them, can never fully describe the infinity that is God. Christian *theologians* therefore need to be aware that whilst they have to express themselves in words – for they are the only tools known to *humankind* for the purposes of theological analysis – these words and the statements that they make, must always be treated with a measure of caution, given that the reality described is always larger and more wonderful than the words used to describe them. Wordy definitions or theological formulae must therefore never be allowed to confine spiritual experience to these descriptions, which are always less than the experience they seek to describe or explain. This is one of the reasons that many in the *Free Church tradition* have been wary of *creeds*, because of their conviction that wordy formulae, of themselves, be they never so sound, cannot guarantee the presence of the *Spirit*. The reverse truth is that common language, deployed in a religious context, will often express or convey a deeper meaning than when the same words are used in common parlance. Thus to say that '*Jesus Christ* was crucified on a hill outside the city of Jerusalem' must always be more than an historical or *political* statement because of who Jesus

was.

The problem of how to grasp in our human language religious phenomena that break into our experience, but reveal themselves as transcendent, is then as old as religion. In Christian *theology* there are two classic approaches to this problem, one presented by the Greek Fathers, the other by Latin scholastic theology. The first emphasised the symbolic nature of language that spoke about God without defining God, and thus led both the speaker and the hearer into participation in the divine mystery. The second preferred to speak about God through analogies with the created world.

Modern logical positivism attacked religious language as meaningless – as it could not clearly define the subject it wanted to disclose. This provoked further development. Some theologians, particularly in the Anglo-Saxon world, adapted Wittgenstein's theory of 'language games' for religious language: if you know the rules, you understand the meaning of the game of religion, if you stand outside, it does not make sense to you. Western continental theology was more influenced by *hermeneutics*, and with the help of Heidegger, Gadamer and Ricoeur, recovered the symbolic roots of language. *Orthodox* theologians opposed logical positivism (if they reacted to it at all) by exposing the reductionist view of language on which it was based, and offered in contrast to it a neo-Patristic concept of *symbol* and mystery.

IN & ET

FURTHER READING: C.S. Evans, *Philosophy of Religion: Thinking about Faith*, InterVarsity, Downers Grove, Il., 1985. J. Genova, *Wittgenstein: A Way of Seeing*, Routledge, New York and London, 1995. F. Kerr, *Theology after Wittgenstein*, SPCK, London, 1997. P. Ricoeur, *Symbolism of Evil*, Beacon, Boston, 1967. P. Ricoeur, *The Conflict of Interpretations: Essays in Hermeneutics*, Northwestern University Press, Evaston, 1974. P. Ricoeur, *Figuring the Sacred: Religion, Narrative and Imagination*, Fortress, Minneapolis, 1995. A. Schmemann, *For the Life of the World: Sacraments and Orthodoxy*, St. Vladimir's Theological Press, New York, 1998. D. Tracy, *The Analogical Imagination*, SCM, London, 1981.

Religious Liberty

Religious Liberty, a fairly modern reality,

liberty of conscience, e.g., being still condemned by the **Vatican** in the Syllabus of
Errors in 1864, and only put right some 100
years later. Such freedom, had however, begun to be a possibility with the rise of **nation**
states after the **Reformation**: this did not
create religious liberty as such but at least
provided the opportunity for people to move
from one regime to another, where a different religious preference existed. However
amongst the **Anabaptists** the idea was born
that since **faith** was a matter of free personal
choice, nobody should be coerced by army
or magistrate into espousing any particular
religious commitment. Rulers, for their part,
still preferred conformity to one set of beliefs
as making for national unity, with religious
dissent seen as all too easily providing a pre-
text for **political** opposition. However in the
New World, Roger Williams, (c1603-83) who
was a Baptist for part of his life, founded at
Rhode Island, a state which secured a royal
charter in 1663 and which had from the
1630s provided religious freedom for all.
Rhode Island secured. Whilst the philosopher, John Locke in his *Letters on Toleration*
[c1690] made out a very convincing case for
toleration, this was slow to be incarnated in
practical legislation, the Toleration Act of
1689 providing a very restricted freedom to
British dissenters – proper freedom waiting
for the abolition of the penal legislation
against Protestant Dissenters and **Roman
Catholics** in 1828-29. With the increasing
secularisation of society and the reduction
of ecclesiastical power, incidents of religious
persecution greatly decreased. In the 20th
century the threat to religious liberty was to
come from both the right and the left, that is
to say from National Socialism, with the
Holocaust against the **Jews** often seen as the
worst example of religious persecution
within a supposedly Christian society, and
Marxist **Communism**, which impacted very
severely on Baptist **witness** in Eastern
Europe. At the present time the acute issues
are the rejection of liberty by **fundamentalist Islamic** and Hindu regimes in Asia and
the terms on which adherents of such faiths
in a **pluralist** Europe can be guaranteed their
religious rights without putting civil society
at risk from **preachers** who advocate or support the use of **violence** to secure their ends.
A Christian **theology** of religious liberty

would derive from all people being created
in God's image and that image, however
marred, redeemed [see **Redemption**] by the
death of his **Son**.

ET

Religious Society of Friends, Baptists and
See **Quakers, Baptists and**.

Religious Studies
See **Comparative Religion**.

Remarriage
See **Divorce and Remarriage**.

Remembrance Sunday
In the UK Remembrance Sunday initially
celebrated the armistice which brought to an
end fighting in WWI at the 11th hour on the
11th day of the 11th month, 1918. As a mark
of respect, those in participating nations
observe two minutes silence at this time,
with a similar act of remembrance taking
place within the **worship** of the **church** on
the nearest Sunday. On this day there would
also be outdoor services at the local war
memorials, where wreaths of poppies would
be laid. Such poppies symbolise the sacrifice
made by those who laid down their lives in
the conflict, and members of the public
would also wear these on the days leading
up to 'Armistice Day'. Today, those who
have lost their lives in subsequent conflicts
are also remembered and the retrospective
respect for past sacrifice is balanced by a
commitment to work for **peace** with justice
in the world today, for which some have
argued that white lilies are more appropriate
than the traditional poppies. Similar acts of
remembrance occur in different countries on
appropriate national days of remembering.
The over-riding theme for celebration is that
freedom is not secured without cost, that the
community needs to give practical support
to those who still suffer from wounds received in battle or from the aftermath of war
(e.g. though landmine explosions), and a
renewal of a commitment not to tolerate war

any more. In other counties it is occasions such as Independence Days that give the church opportunity to identify with, and *pray* for, the life of the nation.

JHYB

Renewal/Revival/Revivalism

There is considerable overlap in the use of these terms: e.g. some Christians are happier speaking about renewal rather than revival but in so far as there are distinctions they may be seen in the following terms. The cycle of decline and renewal is a common one in *scripture* (cf. Jdg), in church history, in individual churches and in personal biographies. Spiritual life is apparently hard to maintain on a continual basis and 'times of refreshing' (Ac 3:19) become necessary.

In this context, *renewal* denotes a work of God's *Spirit* in which following a period of lethargy or decline, the work of God is once more enlivened, either through a new faithfulness in *theology*, a renewed depth in *worship*, or a fresh sense of the presence of God within the *church*.

Revival refers to more dramatic and intense seasons when, usually in a culture which has previously been Christianised and often in connection with disasters that bring a renewed sense of mortality, people experience conviction of *sin* and call upon God in *repentance* resulting in a large influx into the churches. Baptists in *Britain* were affected by the 18th-century *Evangelical* Revival, itself part of the *Great Awakening* which was associated with Jonathan Edwards' restatement of *Calvinism* in a positive Evangelical fashion. Revival movements in other parts of Europe – e.g. in the *Baltic* region – contributed to Baptist *growth* in the 19th century.

Revivalism, more negatively, refers to methodologies which seek to induce revival by human effort or imitation, thus the unfortunate language of people trying 'to organise a revival'. The attempt is made to prolong or produce the effects of revival through the emotionally-charged use of *music*, altar calls, camp meetings or *crusades*. Out of revivalism arose the specific work of the revivalist, who often exercised an itinerant *ministry*, which sometimes came into conflict with the regular ministry of the settled pastorate. Revivalism, which owes much to the *Arminian*, Charles G. Finney's brilliant *Lectures on Revivals* (1835), has been a particular hallmark of American evangelical religion and *Pentecostalism*. The evangelistic crusades of the Baptist *evangelist, Billy Graham*, may be seen to be in this *tradition* (in the United States evangelistic campaigns are commonly called 'revivals'), although in a more sober form which has rendered them acceptable to European Baptists.

NGW

Repentance

There are frequent calls to repentance in the prophetic writings of the OT. The people are called to return to creaturely dependence on God, and to turn away from *sin* to a new life. In the gospels John preaches *baptism* for the repentance of sins and *Jesus* comes into Galilee *preaching* the gospel of the *kingdom* and calling his hearers to a change of mind and direction of life, to repent. The Greek word is *metanoia* [literally 'a radical turning around']. In the NT as a whole repentance is both the gift of God and the duty of every person who hears the gospel. At *Pentecost* repentance is linked with baptism.

In the pre-*Reformation* church repentance became part of an elaborate penitential system, and the *Anabaptists*, according to G.W. Williams, replaced the *sacrament* of penance with believers' baptism. 'The initial *call* to believers' baptism stressed, over against *paedobaptism* , not the adult's capacity to believe but rather to repent' (Williams, p.218).

Grebel, Manz and others were powerful *preachers* of repentance. As Anabaptism developed, the desire for pure *communion* led to the concept and occasional imposition of the ban (exclusion from communion), which Menno Simons saw as an instrument of *reconciliation*, hopefully leading to a declaration of repentance for post-baptismal sin.

The call to repentance has becomes a keynote of *evangelical* preaching and the need for repentance remains a constant in Christian life and growth. '[Jesus] demanded more than a radical alteration. To repent means to make a turnabout of a profound moral and religious import. Repentance implies not merely a recognition that one has made a bad mistake, but that one has *sinned* (Volf, p.113 [original italics]).

In the *pastoral ministry*, the call to repentance is part of 'soul-healing' and becomes a necessary part of the journey to wholeness. In the NT repentance is inseparable from *faith*, and should not be regarded as a necessary precondition for the exercise of faith, rather repentance and faith are two aspects of the same movement of an estranged sinner into a reconciled relationship with Almighty God.

As in the OT, so with Christians today there is a social element to Repentance. It may be debatable whether a *nation* can repent for e.g. the atrocities of the Slave Trade or whether a church as a whole can meaningfully repent for collusion with an unjust *political* system, but the question, once raised, will not disappear. Repentance is a personal move towards God, an amendment of life and a spur to examine the wider areas of Christian *witness*.

DBM

FURTHER READING: Miroslav Volf, *Exclusion and Embrace*, Abingdon, Nashville, Tn., 1996. G.H. Williams, *The Radical Reformation* (3rd ed.), Sixteenth Century Essays and Studies, Kirksville, Mo., 1992.

Resource sharing

Inter-church aid used to be seen in terms of giving churches and receiving churches, with the power of donation being exercised by the former, and the latter coming to the table as supplicants, rather as in the *missionary* society world, there were churches that sent personnel *overseas*, and those that received such missionaries. In such a series of relationships there was little of equality of respect or decision-making, with the *secular* notion of power of possession clearly dominating. A *two-thirds-world* church might, after *prayerful* discussion, attribute high priority to a particular *mission* programme, but unless the Northern paying agent agreed the priority, it would not happen because it would remain unfunded. The notion of resource sharing seeks to break that correlation between supremacy and subordination, with the new picture of a round table at which all have seats with equal status, and all have

something both to contribute and receive, all under an overall understanding of partnership in mission, of *koinonia* in *faith* and practice, with none coming to the table under the constraint of the need to meet donor church requirements. When, therefore, 'Round Table Conference' is referred to, it is to a gathering of Christian churches, *Councils* of churches, and mission and development agencies in a particular locality, meeting under this mandate of mutuality. In this new world, the definition of resource has been expanded from the old focus on personnel and finance to include, among other gifts, *spirituality* and faith experiences. Thus, e.g., whilst an African church might receive finance, it contributes to a rather tired church in the Global North, stories of faith and *growth* and a deepening of spirituality. A church in Latin America might receive equipment and medicines, but contribute to mission in Europe *reverse mission* workers. The Church in China might need Bibles, but it brings to the table stories of the increased number of believers even whilst Christians in the West were fearfully praying for its survival. This rather than the old pattern of manifestly unequal relationships reflects the worldwide *church* as so many different parts of the Body of Christ joyously sharing together all the good things that God has given.

JHYB

Responsible Society/Third Way

In the first half of the 20th century, it became increasingly apparent that neither *capitalism* nor *communism* was capable of meeting the needs of human society, and so a number of Christian thinkers and practitioners became convinced of the need to search for a 'Third Way'. The search picked up on work that had been done on the idea of the 'Responsible Society' as a social/economic criterion for judging politico-economic systems. The first Assembly of the *World Council of Churches* gave this definition to the idea: 'A responsible society is one where freedom is the freedom of *men* who acknowledge responsibility to justice and public order, and where those who hold *political* authority or economic power are responsible for its exercise to God and the people whose welfare is affected by it.' Behind that statement were two **traditions**, first that of **theologians** and thinkers influenced by Karl Barth, such as J.H. Oldham, who insisted that the criteria for right political action derived specifically from Christian **revelation**. The other tradition, which argued that they were matters of natural law and did not need to invoke **theological** criteria, was championed by J.C. Bennett and William Temple. Oldham, the author of the language of the 'Responsible Society', argued that human beings needed to respond to what they discerned to be the will of God as they encountered new situations, and political structures should be such that they enabled this to happen. Thus a responsible society will be a free and participatory society which respects a concern for justice for all. To this end, Oldham created the idea of 'middle axioms' which converted absolute theological principles into practical programmes enabling action to be taken, recognising that such programmes were always provisional. In such a way Oldham sought to relate the Lordship of **Christ** in the created order to the messiness of actual political situations. Bennett and Temple more easily accommodated coalitions between Christian and non-Christian in ordering a society intent on implementing justice, freedom, **participation** and welfare. Others such as the Swiss-born plastics manufacturer, Ernest Bader, made a contribution through converting his company into a commonwealth, implementing **democracy** within the workplace, with all workers sharing in the venture's profits. Though in later life a Quaker, Bader, when he first came to **England**, was associated with Ferme Park Baptist Chapel in North London where he met his wife.

After a period of lesser urgency, the fall of soviet communism has brought the issue back on to the human agenda. With only states like North Korea and Cuba holding to the old Marxist analysis of human history, commentators now resort to the language of 'post-communism', for it is not yet clear what systems are to prevail as successor **states** try to work out a way forward embracing elements of both democratic **socialism** and capitalism. Guided by a prevailing pragmatism this cannot be identified with the principled search for a 'third way' that

Christian thinkers campaigned for earlier. Nor should the eclipse of socialism be interpreted as a vote of confidence in capitalism and the all-powerful influence of the market. Their capacity to reinforce injustice, allowing the rich to become richer whilst the **poor** become poorer, and to impede human development, clearly remains to the detriment of many states and economies especially in the **two-thirds world**. The unfettered determination of world trade by market forces alone without a determined effort to secure the welfare of all peoples is as un-christian as it ever was, for the God of **Mammon** seen in its inherent materialism and associated consumerism is very clear. In capitalist societies, profit and success at work can all too easily distort other criteria of human worth. An additional concern is the relentless exploitation of non-renewable resources, with consequential **ecological** crisis. All these concerns reinforce the call for a new people-friendly international economic order which changes the terms of trade so that producers are as fairly treated as consumers. Economic systems are not neutral but need to be disciplined by effective value criteria.

JHYB

Restorationism/House Church movement

The Restoration or House Church movement in Europe emerged out of the **charismatic** renewal of the 1960s. It became clear over time that there were two distinct directions within charismatic renewal. In some charismatic Baptists churches there was a trend away from **fellowship** with other Baptists. The opposite tendency was that those involved in **renewal** reached out both **ecumenically** and towards their fellow Baptists. The first stream, designated the House Church movement or Restorationism (expressing the belief that a NT model of the **church** could be restored), drew **members** away from many existing churches, but perhaps more from Baptist churches than any other denomination.

Restoration magazine began in 1975, edited by Bryn Jones, in Bradford, and Arthur Wallis, whose background (as with a number of Restorationist leaders) was in the **Breth-**

ren. Wallis wrote: 'I see no future for denominations, but a glorious future for the body of **Christ**.' In 1976 Jones launched the Dales Bible Week, in the north of **England**, which was soon attracting 9,000 people. New fellowships began, as people left Baptist and other denominations. E.g. Saltersgill a church in the Yorkshire Baptist **Association**, welcomed a house church group, and later the church left the Association. A network of churches led by Terry Virgo, a former Baptist, was to grow significantly, and attract a number of Baptist ministers. Another example of movement into Restorationism was Basingstoke Baptist, in the south of England. Restorationists tended to reject **congregational church government** in favour of a system of '**apostles**' – leaders who exercised **authority** over a number of **ministers** who put themselves under the authority of these men without reference to the local membership – and **elders** – appointed by the local ministry team rather than elected by the **church meeting**.

There were many examples of Baptist ministers and members affected by charismatic renewal who were committed to the Baptist denomination and did not espouse the more **sectarian** and often triumphalistic outlook of Restorationism. It was this broader view of charismatic experience that Douglas McBain, who became London Baptist Superintendent, expounded with great vigour. McBain argued against Restorationist thinking and urged positive attitudes within the denomination to charismatic renewal.

By the 1980s there were at least 10 distinct Restorationist networks in England alone, led by various apostles. These included a group which developed out of Basingstoke Baptist Church; Harvestime churches under Bryn Jones; Coastlands, later New Frontiers, led by Terry Virgo; Pioneer, with Gerald Coates as leader; and Roger Foster's Ichthus Fellowship in London. Nigel Wright, tutor and later Principal at **Spurgeon's College**, London, became the foremost Baptist analyst of Restorationism. He was critical of the 'rigid and slavish attempt' by some Restorationists 'to decode the NT and to bring life into a sterile conformity with it', and he argued for a view of renewal that embraced the whole church. It was such inclusive renewal that most Bap-

tists welcomed.

IMR

FURTHER READING: P. Hocken, *Streams of Renewal: The Origins and Early Development of the Charismatic Movement in Britain*, Paternoster, Carlisle, 1997. William K. Kay, *Apostolic Networks in Britain*, Paternoster, Milton Keynes, 2007. A. Walker, *Restoring the Kingdom* (rev. ed.), Eagle, Guilford, 1998.

Resurrection

A central tenet of the Christian **faith** is that God the Father, on the third day after his crucifixion, raised our Lord and Saviour **Jesus Christ** from the dead. The first witnesses to the empty tomb of the Resurrected Jesus were the **women**, a fact commemorated in Baptist Churches in Eastern Europe by a **tradition** of women breaking open the Word [see **Sermon**] on **Easter Day**.

Thorwald Lorenzen argues this is *THE* question of Christian faith. He goes on to comment 'the resurrection is not merely an object of faith, and it is not merely a creedal statement to accept; it is the origin and ground of faith.' Lorenzen served for many years as the **theologian** at **IBTS** and might be said to represent European Baptist views on the subject. Some have wondered about the nature of the resurrected Christ but by and large European Baptists decline to be reductive in this sense confirming the non-reductive physicalism of Baptist philosophers such as Nancey Murphy. That is to say that Jesus the Crucified Messiah was raised from the dead by God and is now the Risen and Ascended Lord of history [see **Ascensiontide**]. Here is no false dichotomy of body and spirit beloved of Greek philosophy, but a full orbed understanding of the centrality of the resurrection grounded in faith though recognising from the Biblical accounts [see **Bible**] that the resurrected Christ might not immediately be identified as the crucified Messiah though could certainly be known to believers 'in the breaking of the bread' (Lk 24:35). The Biblical record makes it quite clear that there is both continuity and difference between the pre-resurrection Christ and the risen Christ: he is recognised by his disciples but is not limited by physical distances or barriers, whilst the **Apostle** Paul lists his encounter with the risen Christ on the Damascus Road as of the same order as the appearances in Galilee and Judaea.

Understanding and applying **resurrection theology** in the life of the believing community has always been complex, for here we are dealing with an act of God at the heart of our faith and life. The limitation of human intellect and understanding has often been a barrier to full comprehension of this event where God signals the new redemptive order [see **Redemption**] He has inaugurated in His only Son. In the end, true resurrection is indescribable because as well as infinitely **transcending** us, it also encompasses us, as H.A. Williams wrote 'informing everything we are as the water informs and fills the sea'.

KGJ

FURTHER READING: Thorwald Lorenzen, *Resurrection and Discipleship*, Orbis, New York, 1995. H.A. Williams, *True Resurrection*, Mitchell Beazley, London, 1972.

Retreats

The formation in 1887 of the Baptist **Ministers'** and **Missionaries' Prayer** Union, under the leadership of F.B. Meyer, introduced Quiet Days or Retreats (a word at that time not normally used outside **Roman Catholic** or Anglo-Catholic circles) into British Baptist life. Membership of the Prayer Union reached 770 by 1896. In the early 20th century the importance of silent retreats was underlined by another British Baptist minister, Newton Marshall, who had links across Europe – he gained his doctorate in Halle, **Germany**, fostered German-English contacts, and was the 'father' of the first European Baptist Congress, in Berlin in 1908. Paying tribute in 1914 to Marshall, whose early **death** in that year deprived European Baptists of a fine thinker, J.H. Shakespeare, the General Secretary of the British Baptist **Union**, noted that Marshall had recently spoken of the need for a 'Retreat movement' concentrating on prayer and penitence. 'Alas!', observed Shakespeare, 'We have no room in our bustling life for Retreats.'

The retreat movement had a period of vigour in the 1920s and 30s. F.C. Spurr, who had an international ministry among Baptists, advocated congregational retreats for spiritual **renewal**. This was linked to a wider **Free Church** retreat movement. Tait Patterson, a minister in Yorkshire, who had a strong sense of **spirituality** and **liturgy**, produced a manual of prayers for **worship** [see **Prayers in Worship**], entitled *Call to Worship*, and organised annual retreats. H. Wheeler Robinson, a fine OT **scholar**, was another Baptist minister who encouraged retreats in this period. His book, *The Christian Experience of the Holy Spirit* (1928), owed a great deal to his experiences in prayer. He became increasingly interested in John Henry Newman, the 19th-century Anglo-Catholic and then Roman Catholic, and Robinson led Baptist ministerial retreats in which time was given to quiet worship introduced by simple litanies.

Half a century later, Margaret Jarman, the first female minister to be President of the British Baptist Union, contributed to what would be an increasing interest among Baptists in contemplative prayer. She led many prayer retreats and was the first person to chair the Baptist Union Retreat Group, which was formed in 1988. From the 1990s retreats became a much more common feature of Baptist life in a number of parts of Europe. This reflected a more open spirit and a desire to learn from the spiritual **traditions** found in other denominations, particularly in the area of contemplative spirituality.

IMR

Revelation

The starting point for an **Evangelical** understanding of Revelation must be that God's revealing of himself is all of his **grace**, and not essentially the product of human intellectual deduction, bound as this must be, both by its inability to probe authoritatively beyond the finite, and also because of its warping by **sin**.

However, it is not right to narrow down the ways in which God is able to reveal himself, for God, in fact reveals himself in many ways. Surely there must be evidence of the Creator in the world he has created – 'the heavens', the Psalmist reminds us, 'are telling the glory of God' (Ps 19:1), and the **apostle** confirms such **witness** as he writes, 'Ever since the **creation** of the world his eternal power and divine nature, invisible though they are have been understood and seen through the things he has made' (Ro 1:20). The argument is that there is something in the texture of the world as we experience it which bears witness to the work of God, and that the world as we encounter it cannot be understood without reference to Him. That revelation continues in the moral texture of human society, however much challenged by particular perverse behaviour, and this continues in the processes of human history where all too many **preachers** have perceived the hand of the **judgment** of God. All this provides common ground where believer and unbeliever are able to begin **dialogue** the one with the other. More personally God reveals himself in human experience, and through the activities of a God-prompted **conscience**. Therein is seen a movement from the general revelation of God in the created order to the particular way in which his reality impinges upon the lives of individuals.

The interpretative key for all such revelations must nevertheless be the revelation found in the life, **death** and **resurrection** of **Jesus** as testified to in the Christian **scriptures**. The scriptures also themselves bear witness to the different ways in which God makes himself known – in e.g. the history of his dealings with his people, **Israel**, where the moral demands of a Holy God are clearly revealed, as also in the NT in the history of the new Israel, the **Church**, with its witness to the empowering of the **Holy Spirit**. But even within scripture there is a hierarchy of significance, for the Incarnate **Word** [see **Incarnation**] must ever be the critical reference point for the reading of the written word. Moreover, here is to be found a revelation not merely about the existence of God, but concerning the fulfilling of his purposes for the **salvation** of **humankind** in the sacrifice of His Son to redeem humankind [see **Redemption**] and make possible our salvation. But as Clark Pinnock, perhaps in part contentiously affirms, 'God not only raises the crucified Christ from the dead, but also explains to us the redemptive significance of that action...The divinely given interpretation of the **cross** is practically as important to us as the cross itself, at least as far as our being able to appropriate its benefits intelligibly is concerned. In the biblical account, the divine speech is every bit as central to revelation as the divine action. Revelation is to be found both in God's deeds and in God's words.'

But there is a further stage to revelation: James Packer writes, the 'present and continuing reality of revelation through each believer's life occurs under the enlightening **ministry** of the Holy Spirit, who interprets to us the contents of scripture, however these are met. The Reformers [see **Reformation**] rightly insisted that as only scripture, unaugmented from any philosophical or religious source, can bring us to know God, so it is only as the Spirit opens scripture to us and writes its teachings on our hearts that this knowledge becomes reality for us.' Word and Spirit belong together in the revelation of God's purposes.

ET

Reverse Mission

This term is often used to describe the cross-cultural **globalisation** of **missionary** activity. The great era of missionary expansion amongst baptistic communities began in the 1790s with the formation of the **Baptist Missionary Society** (now BMS World Mission) in the **United Kingdom**. For the best part of two centuries Christian communities in Europe and North America (sometimes termed the first world or developed world) sent out **women** and **men** to engage in **mission** and **evangelism** in Africa, Asia, South America and Oceania (the **two-thirds world**, or developing world). The sending countries were deemed to be the repository of Christian **faith** and resources. Less extensively, missionary activity was also undertaken in Europe and the Middle East. By the second half of the 20th century Christian communities in Africa, Asia and South America had gained strength and purpose, whereas in Western Europe, especially, the churches were experiencing a plateauing of development, if not an actual decline. With the collapse of communism churches in Eastern Europe also grew extensively from 1990 onwards. So, in the 21st century we have seen a growing trend for missionaries to come to Europe from Africa, Asia and South America to 're-evangelise' the place where Christianity gained its place in society and its resources for mission. Today baptistic Christians from South Korea, **Russia**, **Ukraine** and West Africa are to be found engaged in **church planting** and mission activities in many of the countries of Western Europe in a reverse of the missionary flow of the previous 200 years.

KGJ

Revival/Revivalism
See *Renewal/Revival/Revivalism*.

Roma People
The Roma people, often commonly called Gypsies (though this term has become increasingly unacceptable due to its frequent derogatory usage), can be considered as a 'nation' without a land, who can be found in almost every country in Europe. It is assumed that they left their native land, India, in the 10th century and in time they spread across the whole of Europe. Their nomadic life-style, their traditional involvement in fortune-telling and a non-orthodox attitude toward private ownership by *gadje* [non-Romani men] have created the stereotypical picture of a Roma as someone who roams the countryside, and is engaged in questionable or illegal activities. This negative image became one of the chief reasons for their extermination by the Nazis during WWII. In Europe they usually accept the dominant religion of their 'host' country, but their religiosity is highly influenced by their own laws and traditions. They are able to preserve their distinctiveness mainly due to the strength of their family life and group cohesiveness. In several Eastern European countries (e.g. **Romania**, **Bulgaria**) Roma people have responded very positively to **Evangelical missions** with the subsequent founding of lively Roma Baptist churches.

KJ

Roman Catholic
This term is used to specify that there can be, as in fact there are, other Catholic churches which are not Roman! First of all it should be pointed out that the adjective *'catholic'* is part of the **Apostolic** Creed ('I believe...the holy catholic church'), an adjective that

originally meant 'universal', a term that all Christian churches claim for themselves. In time the expression 'catholic' has increasingly been applied (from an historical point of view but not from a **theological** or **dogmatic** one) to the Church of Rome, and other Christian churches have preferred to speak of universality rather than catholicity [see **Church: Universal, Triumphant, Invisible**]. However, from a theological point of view all Christian churches are 'catholic', in so far as they accept for themselves and confess the four *notae ecclesiae*, the basic and distinctive features of church of the Lord: *una, sancta, catholica, apostolica*. Even Baptist churches when referring to the declaration of **faith** of the Universal Church legitimately claim the title 'catholic'. If there is no affirmation of the universal, **ecclesiological** dimension, catholicity is simply a contradiction. The **local church** cannot, by itself, attribute to itself catholicity; it would be nonsensical. This is the theological crux where a type of *landmarkist* view of the church is to be found.

Within non-**Protestant** Christianity all those Christian churches that profess adherence to the *depositum fidei* of the primitive church have the right to be catholic churches, but, as they do not recognise the **authority** of the Church of Rome, they are non-Roman Catholic churches. We can cite the Old Catholic Church, which separated from Rome after 1870 repudiating the doctrine of papal **infallibility** [see **Papacy**] and was joined also by churches of the Union of Utrecht which separated from Rome in 1723, which retains the adjective 'catholic'. We can also mention the Eastern **Orthodox churches** or the pre-Calcedonian oriental orthodox churches (the Coptic, Syrian, Armenian, Ethiopian and the Malankarese Church of India) whose **hierarchical** structure is separate from that of Rome. There are also the various Orthodox churches, now divided by nationality, which are to be found in many countries throughout the world because of **emigration**. The Uniate (Eastern Catholic churches) however, for local historical reasons, whilst orthodox in life and **liturgy**, accept the jurisdiction of Rome. This is a cause for ongoing controversy between Roman Catholic and Orthodox churches, especially the Oecumenical

Patriarchate of Constantinople and the Patriarchate of Moscow.

DT

Roman Catholicism, Baptist relations with

[See also *Bilateral Conversations*; *Dialogue*; *Roman Catholic*; *Roman Catholicism, Baptists and*]

Conversations between Baptists and Roman Catholics began with two North American conversations in the 1960s and 70s. Between 1967 and 70 there was dialogue between the USA *Bishops* Conference and the American Baptists, from 1978 onwards there was a set of talks between *Southern Baptist scholars* and American Catholic scholars.

In 1980 the retiring chair of the *BWA* Commission on Doctrine and Inter-Church Cooperation recommended that approaches be made to open a *theological* dialogue with the Roman Catholic Church, and such a possibility was welcomed by the RC Secretariat for Promoting Christian *Unity*. However at the BWA General Council in 1981 concerns about the process were raised as to what the implications for Baptist identity might be and the matter was referred back to the Executive to clarify the purpose of such talks, and a planned visit to the *Vatican* in Dec 1981 was cancelled. A small group from the Doctrine and Inter-Church Commission was appointed to explore the conditions for such talks and a preliminary meeting took place in Frankfurt, even though objections continued to be raised particularly by Baptists from Latin America. However, the consensus was that a minority should not be allowed to prevent such conversations taking place. Accordingly the BWA General Council in 1983 agreed to initiate conversations 'in order to come to a mutual understanding of convergences and divergences [in the] ecclesial [see *Ecclesiology*], pastoral and *mission* concerns between the Baptist and the Roman Catholic world confessional bodies.' It was argued that such conversations would mean that the Vatican recognised the BWA as a world confessional body, would provide opportunity to raise the issue of persecuted churches in Catholic-dominated *nations*, and would give opportunity for representa-

tives to underline the centrality of the doctrine of the church for Baptists. It would also provide opportunity to draw attention to helpful statements by Vatican II on liberty of conscience and the primacy of *scripture*.

Five meetings were to take place over five years (1984-8) and the first took place in West Berlin when the theme was '*Evangelism*/Evangelisation: the Mission of the Church'. Meetings in Los Angles and New York focussed on *Christology*, *conversion*, *discipleship* and the *church*. A second meeting in Europe took place in Rome in 1987 when the agenda was *religious freedom* and evangelism versus *proselytism*. The final meeting in Atlanta in 1988 agreed the report which was published under the title *Summons to Witness* (RC version) and *Christian Witness in Today's World*, (Baptist version). At the 1989 General Council in Zagreb, a city where Roman Catholics were in the majority, the report was commended but was bitterly opposed by the Brazilian delegation. In the end the Council both received the report and the Brazilian response. BWA President, Noel Vose, a participant in the conversations noted that there were notes of positive appreciation on both sides, without any attempt to conceal the doctrines that divide our world *communions*.

The report was glad to report that the participants 'discovered a remarkable amount of consensus'. The church's witness is based on the centrality of Christ as God's most authentic *revelation* and the sole mediator between God and *humankind* which therefore becomes the touchstone for other matters of doctrine. Discipleship beginning with conversion is to be nurtured in *faith* and love. The idea of the church as representing the koinonia of the *Spirit* was found to be a helpful point of departure, though for Baptists this was found primarily in the local congregation, Roman Catholics were always concerned to relate the local to the universal which thus for them took on a necessary institutional shape. The relationship between spirit and structures was noted as a topic for further discussion. Both churches saw the importance of the *Great Commission* but further work was needed on how the language of evangelism and evangelisation was to be worked out in practice. The report contains a confession that both parties have been guilty of proselytism in its negative sense, and lament that division and strife between Christians 'can be such a scandal that non-believers may not be attracted to the gospel'. There was also a stress on vigilance in respecting religious liberty.

Since 1989 there have been further meetings. In 1996 the Secretary and the President of the BWA met with officers of the secretariat for the Promotion of Christian Unity in Rome and at the end of 2000 a delegation of twelve Baptists met in Rome with leaders of the same body, now upgraded to a Pontifical Council to express their opposition to certain emphases in the encyclical 'Dominus Jesus', which led on to a more positive discussion in Buenos Aires in 2001. Moreover in recent years fraternal delegates have been exchanged between BWA World Congresses and the *synod* of Bishops in Rome. In addition to these international contacts, meetings are held at a local level to promote dialogue and to solve even the minor problems of living together (e.g. *marriages* and similar issues) where Baptist are a *minority* in a predominantly Catholic culture.

JHYB

Roman Catholicism, Baptists and

Even though their origins go back to the mainstream of the **Protestant Reformation** at the beginning of the 17th century, Baptists also claim continuity in both history and theological thought with the life of the Western Church in preceding centuries. At their outset they strongly underlined a *restitutio in integrum*, a return to the fidelity to the gospel of a church which had historically 'degenerated' with respect to its biblical roots [see **Bible**]. But as Baptists their intention was to distinguish themselves from other Churches, by restating some specific theological and *ecclesiological* features on which their confessional identity is based: namely the nature of the church as comprising believers only who have identified themselves by deliberate action with **Jesus Christ** in the waters of **baptism**.

The designation 'Roman' does not sit too easily with 'Catholic' for the one is particular and the other lays stress on universality. **Catholicity**, or rather universality, is one of the four *notae ecclesiae* [distinctive features

of being church]. But Baptists can also claim to be 'catholic'. As self-determination, and not recognition by any human authority, is crucial to being **church**, so Baptist churches define themselves as churches of Jesus Christ, fully aware of the historical and theological responsibility that this entails. The Catholic Church claims the title of 'church' exclusively for itself, with some recognition of a number of **Orthodox churches**. For all others it uses the expression *comunità ecclesiali* [**worshipping** churches] or *fratelli separati* [estranged brethren]. It believes that the *plenitudo ecclesiae* is only to be found in the Catholic Church, in others only *vestigia ecclesiae* [traces of church] are to be found. This is on the grounds of the principle of **apostolic** succession, or ministerial continuity down the centuries. The churches of the Reformation, including Baptists, reject this interpretation of apostolic succession, maintaining that there is a continuity of a theological nature: churches are founded on **preaching** and on apostolic **witness** and at the same time propose again the same message in the present, that is there is faithfulness to the teaching of the **apostles** in witness and doctrine. **Theology** determines history, not vice versa.

The theology which the Catholic Church professes is contained in its **dogmas**, in the fundamental statements of **faith**, initially defined by the various councils of the ancient church, and which now, to be valid, must be issued by the Magisterium (doctrinal body) of the Roman pontiff [see **Papacy**]. Any Catholic who finds any of the established dogmas unacceptable is excluded from the **communion** of the Church. At the same time, considerable weight is given to the Code of Canon Law, the fundamental law of the Church which is valid throughout the world. By and large it is possible to say that the Bible supports the statements relating to dogma and that Canon Law, valid for all Catholic churches which wish to be in communion with Rome, is the 'juridical translation' of the various doctrinal statements and views.

Baptist churches reason differently: the statements of the faith of the past are important and carry weight: various Baptist churches have their own **Confessions of Faith** and juridical means of regulating their own internal affairs. Their theological and juridical assertions are based on the study of the bible text. The *Sola Scriptura* of the Reformation is of key importance to Baptist churches. This means that the two churches are on different levels even when they meet for discussion, as their fundamental terms of reference are different. Even though in recent years the study of the Bible has considerably increased within the Catholic Church, the system outlined here has not yet been substantially modified. The balance is not yet in favour of the scriptures.

Another fundamental feature of Roman Catholic **orthodoxy** which cannot be ignored is the **hierarchical** conception of the Magisterium. The Roman pontiff is invested with absolute authority, guaranteed by his **infallibility** when he speaks *ex cathedra* on matters concerning faith and custom, an authority that he possesses as the successor of the Apostle Peter. This dogma was defined by the First **Vatican** Council in 1870 and led to the **schism** with the Old Catholic Church. The pope has absolute power in every field of life within the Church; the Church is like an elected but absolute monarchy. In his doctrinal capacity, the pope has the power to interpret in a binding way both Scripture and **Tradition** (the study of faith) and to indicate acceptable ethical behaviour [see **Ethics**]. The need for obedience, which is imposed on every believer, derives from this, with little room at present for *freedom of conscience* [*forum internum*]. On this point they differ greatly from Baptists, who believe in the principle of personal responsibility and freedom of conscience.

                                                    DT

Romania, Baptist history in

At the beginning of the 19th century the Turkish or Ottoman Empire included two adjoining provinces – Moldova, or Moldavia, and Valahia, or Wallachia – which in 1859 were brought together under the name Romania. Independence for Romania was gained later, in 1877-78, after the Russian war against the Ottoman Empire. Baptist life was established in Romania in the 1850s during a period of agricultural and industrial development. Economic opportunities attracted many workers and craftsmen, the majority of whom were Germans. Among those who took up employment in Bucharest was Karl Johann Scharschmidt, together with his wife, Augusta. Scharschmidt had been baptised [see **Baptism**] in Hamburg by **Johan Gerhard Oncken**. The Scharschmidts who had originally moved from Hamburg to **Hungary**, where they had been deeply involved in Baptist **witness**, arrived in Bucharest in Apr 1856, the first Baptists to settle in the city.

Scharschmidt sought to gather a circle of friends, especially among the German-speaking community, for **Bible study** and **prayer**, and Baptist ideas began to be discussed. After three years of meetings, Scharschmidt wrote to the Hamburg church: 'Here there is freedom of religion [see **Religious Liberty**]. We have used this freedom and [have] founded an **association** in order to spread religious tracts. Eight families help with money. We have printed and distributed until now 3,000 tracts. There are 20,000 Germans here and nobody to guide them to **Christ**.' The concern was with the German community, most of whom had either **Lutheran** or **Catholic** connections.

Other Baptists found themselves in Bucharest and began to consider forming a Baptist church. There were requests for baptism, but Scharschmidt was not ordained [see **Ordination**]. Feeling frustrated at the inability to make progress, he wrote to Oncken, asking for help: 'Could not a brother be ordained and sent here to found a congregation according to God's command?' The result was that Heinrich Koch arrived in 1861 and a year later the first baptisms took place. Franz and Maria Tabory were baptised and then engaged in **mission** work in Sarajevo. In 1863 August Liebig from Hamburg moved to Bucharest. Apart from a short period of study at the Hamburg **theological** school in 1865, Bucharest became his base. In 1864, there were 11 **members** in the recently-formed Bucharest Baptist church. In 1867 Liebig moved to Calalui in Dobrudja, then part of **Turkey**.

Friedrich Weigel, who like Liebig was a locksmith, supported the church in significant ways. It was largely through his help – as a businessman – that the Bucharest church obtained a **building**, in Popa Rusa Street. A degree of legal recognition was granted in 1865 when the church was given permission by the city magistrate to keep its own *marriage* register. August Liebig's travels took him to *Serbia, Croatia* and *Bosnia-Herzegovina*, and also to *Ukraine*.

Evangelical migrants [see *Migration*] from Ukraine, who had been threatened with exile and had come down from Southern Ukraine into Romania in the early 1860s, provided another source of Baptist witness in the region. 37 families of German origin from Neu Danzig, Ukraine, were allowed to settle in the mid 1860s in a German colony near the village of Cataloi (or Kataloi), Dobrudja, between the Black Sea and the Danube, an area in Turkish territory which was then North-East Bulgaria but in 1878 became part of Romania. With help from Oncken, and more directly from Liebig, a German-speaking Baptist church was formed.

With the help of Edward Millard in Vienna, who led the work of the British and Foreign *Bible Society* in the region, Daniel Schwegler took up the *pastoral* leadership of the Bucharest church in 1878. Another *preacher* involved in pastoral *ministry* in the Bucharest church was Johann Hammerschmidt, a *colporteur* with the German Bible Society. Romanian Baptist *growth* was slow, partly due to *emigration* to the USA and to other parts of Europe. During this period the Baptist community in Bucharest numbered about 90 people.

Johann Hammerschmidt baptised the first ethnic Romanians in the Bucharest church. On 27 Sep 1896 Stefan Pirvu was baptised, followed two days later by Nicolae Manole. Gradually the Baptist witness spread among Romanians. This aroused concern among the authorities, who saw the position of the Romanian *Orthodox Church* being challenged, and in 1900 the city authorities told the church that they must serve Germans only, not Romanians. It was difficult to make the transition from German Baptist life, but in the early 20th century a young Romanian, Constantin Adorian, who had studied in the Hamburg Baptist seminary, gave leadership to the growing Romanian-speaking Baptist community. In 1912 Adorian became minister of a Romanian-speaking Baptist church in Bucharest. In 1919, when Transylvania became part of the Romanian Kingdom, there were about 21,000 Baptist believers in Romania. By then Germans were a small proportion of the total Baptist community. A Romanian *Union* was formed. Despite persecution, from 1920-30 the number of Baptists grew to 44,828 members, and a Seminary was established in Bucharest [see *Bucharest Baptist Theological Institute*].

The dictatorial *political* regime that ruled Romania during WWII meant further persecution for Baptists. On the wider European front, Romania lost some of its territories. On 9 Sep 1940 a decision was taken by the Minister of Cults (religion) according to which eight Christian denominations and the *Jewish faith* were recognised and other denominations or religious organisations, including Baptists, were banned. The Baptist Seminary was closed in Mar 1942 and in the following year the Seminary buildings were confiscated. After the end of the war, however, they were returned to the Baptists. Unfortunately, the ministry of a Training School for *Women* was not started again.

After the war a new Congress was organised, but the year 1948 saw the start of a new time of repression and persecution. The *communist* government began to develop legal ways in which it could control the life of the churches. The formation of new churches was virtually stopped. New Baptist Union leaders had to be confirmed by the government. Several ministries had to be closed: the Baptist *Youth* Union, the *Sunday School* Organisation and the Women's Organisation. In 1961 the government told the Baptist Union to reduce the number of churches by 25%.

Towards the mid 1970s an increased concern about *human rights* in the international political arena was evident. This was to affect Romania's relationship with the USA, which, under President Jimmy Carter, made respect for human rights a part of the discussions when Romania applied for 'Most Favored Nation' status. A group of Romanian pastors who felt that the Romanian government was not living up to its declared commitments engaged in some acts of protest by writing letters which they sent to the government and also to the West. Their efforts, and especially a protest signed by 40 pastors that was presented to the authorities, raised awareness about the situation of Baptists and led to some relaxation of the ways in which the laws were applied. However, the communist authorities persuaded or forced most of the protesters to leave the country and only a few have remained.

There was also opposition to the government from the *Apararea libertatii religioase si de constiinta* (ALRC – Romanian Christian Committee for the Defense of Religious Freedom and of Conscience [see *Freedom of Conscience*]). This organised group of nine Baptists requested membership of the Swiss organisation Christian Solidarity International and wrote a number of documents which they addressed to government institutions and to leaders of denominations. Although the organisation was started by Baptists it acted on behalf of any persecuted believers. In the end the group was silenced. To be a believer was difficult, but life in the Baptist churches during this period was vibrant.

After *Christmas* 1989, when the communist dictator of Romania, Nicolae Ceaușescu, was executed together with his wife, a new period of challenges and opportunities began. At the 1991 Baptist Union Congress, the first in the post-communist era, a new generation of leaders was elected, mainly from among those who were considered to have protested against the abuses of communism. In spite of previous differences and tensions between the old and new leaders, some *reconciliation* was achieved, maintaining the *unity* of the denomination and focusing the attention of the churches on *evangelism*, *church planting* and *education*.

A dramatic deterioration in the economic situation, massive emigration from the country, and growing *secularisation* dashed many of the early hopes and became new challenges for the Baptist community. However, if in 1990 there were about 1,200 churches (including smaller mission points and daughter churches), at the end of the century there were about 1,800 churches. The Baptist Seminary in Bucharest expanded its work and applied for accreditation to become a degree-offering institution. Baptists were among others able to start theological colleges in the University of Bucharest. The *Facultatea de Teologie Baptistă* was founded in the University in 1991 and became the first Baptist theological college to receive

accreditation in 1995.

For some years the Romanian Baptist Union did not participate very often in the *EBF*'s meetings. New Union leadership from 2007, however, has meant that Romanian Baptists are re-engaging with the EBF and the *BWA*.

IMR & OB

Rüschlikon Baptist Theological Seminary

[See also *International Baptist Theological Seminary*]

The Baptist Theological Seminary (BTS), founded in 1949 in Rüschlikon, *Switzerland*, by the Foreign Mission Board (FMB) of the *Southern Baptist Convention*, was one of the initiatives arising out of the *BWA* sponsored London Conference of 1948 to consider reconstruction of Baptist life and work on the mainland of Europe after WWII. Although the FMB produced advertising literature featuring sites from *Italy* and *Croatia* as the background images, the site eventually selected was an estate beside the Zürichsee in Switzerland.

The FMB asked their Director for Europe, Dr. George Sadler, to commence the work and with a small team of FMB career *missionaries* a Bachelor of Divinity programme, intended to be comparable to the US Master of Divinity programme, was commenced. *Students* were enrolled from throughout Western and Central Europe and the FMB provided all the funds. After the first year Dr. Sadler returned to his duties and Dr. Josef Nordenhaug was appointed President. He served for 10 years (1950-60) and was the longest serving President of the institution during its 55 years in Switzerland. During his time a free-standing un-accredited Master of *Theology* (ThM) course was commenced and the seminary developed with additional accommodation for families and faculty. Dr. Nordenhaug left BTS in 1960 to become General Secretary of the BWA.

From 1970 American Baptist Churches USA committed missionary personnel to the faculty and Dr. Denton Lotz was appointed Professor of *Missions*. He commenced the Summer Institute of Theological Education, which proved very helpful in providing theological *education* for *pastors* who had not had opportunity to attend seminary over a longer term. Dr. Lotz went on to serve on the staff of the BWA, latterly as General Secretary (1988-2007).

In the 1980s operations in Rüschlikon became more difficult as it proved impossible to appoint a President who would serve more than a few years and as costs in Switzerland became oppressive with a changing exchange rate between the Swiss franc and the US dollar. Eventually, FMB Missionary, Dr. John David Hopper, was appointed and he served with distinction during a time of turbulence (1988-97). Following his appointment the FMB Vice President, Dr. Isam Ballenger, based in Richmond, Virginia, and the FMB Area Director, Dr. Keith Parker, began to see that the way forward was to hand the institution over to the *European Baptist Federation* which was done in 1988. This was also important as Europeans were becoming concerned that the theological direction towards *fundamentalism* amongst the leadership of the Southern Baptist Convention was not compatible with the more diverse theological patterns and emphases of European Baptists. The FMB Trustees promised a 15 year financial support package for BTS, but the Trustees reneged on this agreement, leading to serious relational difficulties between the European Baptist community and the FMB for many years.

Lacking essential financial support and facing the challenge of the new post-*communist* Europe, the EBF leadership proposed to the member *unions* that the seminary be relocated from high cost, limited access Switzerland where it was not possible to seek accreditation for the seminaries own degrees of BD and ThM. Various European venues were canvassed, but ultimately the unions voted to move the seminary to Prague in central Europe. The institution was re-titled 'The International Baptist Theological Seminary of the European Baptist Federation' and has gone from strength to strength following the move.

KGJ

Russia, Baptist history in

The Russian Baptist movement began in the middle of the 19th century but with roots going back to the late 18th century, when the *Molokans* found themselves unsatisfied by with the religious ceremonies of the *Orthodox Church*. Though refusing all *traditional* rites, even water *baptism* and the *Lord's Supper*, the Molokans' high view of the *scriptures* and their emphasis on Biblical *ethics* suggest attitudes empathetic to later *evangelical* movements. By the end of the 19th century the majority of Molokans had merged with the Baptists so that many Russian Baptist pioneers, e.g. Nikita Voronin and Vassilii Pavlov, reveal Molokan backgrounds. In addition, the birth of the Baptist movement has to be set within the context of the general spread of evangelical ideas in Russia and the publication of the second edition of the gospels in Russian (1862) as well as of the publishing of a new Russian Bible (1876) which was soon sold and distributed by *colporteurs*. A crucial element in Baptist beginnings in Imperial Russia was German Baptist *missionary* work as well as 'stundism' and the activities of the German *Mennonites*. German Baptists contributed to Slavic Baptists in *church polity*, *mission* models and *hymnody*, an influence which spread via the *Baltics*, St. Petersburg and *Poland*, where German-speaking Baptist churches had emerged in the mid 19th century.

The 'cradle' of the Russian Baptist movement is often considered to be Tiflis (Tbilisi) in *Georgia* where Nikita Voronin (1840-1905) was baptised in Aug 1867 in the Kura river by a German Baptist, Martin Kalweit who came from Memel (today Klaipeda in *Lithuania*). Voronin was probably the first Russian convert [see *Conversion*] to receive believers' baptism, and the year 1867 is usually considered the formal date denoting the beginning of the Russian Baptist movement. From Transcaucasia Baptist ideas spread northward into Russia up the Volga River; Russian Baptists in the Caucasus Region also maintained contacts with believers of similar views in *Ukraine* (both Ukrainians and Germans in *diaspora*). Gradually this Baptist development joined with the so-called Stundo-Baptist movement which had begun in the 1860s in the Ukraine.

The Southern Ukrainian Baptist movement was deeply influenced by the *spirituality* of Stundism, a *pietist* strand among

Ukrainian peasants, as well as by *Mennonite Brethren*. In 1869 Efim Tsymbal was baptised by Mennonite Brethren, and from that date on it is possible to speak about a Stundo-Baptist movement in Southern Ukraine, though only some of the Stundists accepted believers' baptism.

In addition to Transcaucasian and Ukrainian beginnings, an important Baptist centre developed in St. Petersburg, then the capital of the Russian Empire. Already in 1855 C. Plonus, a German Baptist, had conducted missionary work here, and gathered a small group of followers. However, only in 1880 was a German Baptist church formed in St Petersburg. Other non-Slavic Baptists such as the Swedes, Estonians and Latvians also formed congregations in the city.

An influential evangelical, who made a long-term contribution to the Baptist cause, was Lord Radstock, a British nobleman influenced by the *Plymouth Brethren* who visited St. Petersburg in 1874. His *preaching* began to attract Russian nobility and led to the conversion of Colonel Vasiliy Pashkov and Count Modest Korff. They, as well as other aristocrats, influenced by evangelical convictions, began to organise *evangelistic* meetings. In addition, Pashkov was involved in publishing tracts and undertook *prison ministry* from St. Petersburg to as far as the Sahhalin. This source of the Russian Baptist movement was inspired by the wider evangelical ideas spread in Europe in the 19th century with their focus on *repentance*, *justification* by *faith* alone, Christocentrism, evangelism and social ministries. Many adherents of 'Radstockism' or 'Pashkovism', at first a renewal strand within Orthodoxy, joined Russian Evangelical Christians, a 'baptistic' movement which in the 20th century came to be shaped by the *theology* of Ivan Kargel and the organisational skills of Ivan Prokhanov. It was not long before the Movement spread beyond its aristocratic origins and secured an artisan following. The Evangelical Christians, in turn, were to merge with the Baptists, under Stalinist pressures. As for the beginning of the 20th century, Baptist and Evangelical Christian ideas spread also to Moscow where William Fetler established a Baptist church before WWI.

The different evangelical – more specifically Baptist – movements began to seek ways to unite and cooperate. In 1884, due to Pashkov's initiative, Russian Baptists and other evangelical believers held a united conference in St. Petersburg until the police intervened. That same year, another conference, bringing together both Russian and Ukrainian Baptists, took place in Novovasilevka in Ukraine. At this historical meeting the Baptist *Union* of Southern Russia and the Caucasus (usually referred to as the Russian Baptist Union) was established, with Johann Wieler, a member of the Mennonite Brethren church, as its chairman. However, formal *unity* was not achieved in these early years. Though having close ties with Baptists, Ivan Prokhanov, as a strong leader, founded a separate union in Sep 1909 – the Union of Evangelical Christians. This Russian evangelical movement was Baptist in both practice and doctrine though Prokhanov considered *ordination* unnecessary and supported *open communion*. Whereas the Baptist Union's *confession of faith* was *Calvinistic* in *soteriology*, the Union of Evangelical Christians had *Arminian* leanings. In practice, especially at a *local church* level, these theological differences were not of major importance, though they could be used to justify a breach between the leaders. Russian Baptists developed relationships with the wider Baptist family: the Russian Baptist Union was represented at the first World Baptist Congress in London in 1905 by Vasilii Pavlov, Dei Mazaev and Vassili Ivanov, who helped to give 'face' to Russian Baptists in the international arena. The Union of Evangelical Christians became a member of the *Baptist World Alliance* in 1911, and Prokhanov was elected as a vice-president.

In spite of some exceptional freedom that evangelical aristocrats could make use of, at least temporarily, Russian Baptists from their early years, were persecuted by both the Russian government and by Orthodox clergy. In the Baltic region of Imperial Russia Baptists faced rejection and criticism also from the Lutheran Church. Despite ridicule, restrictions, even imprisonment and banishment, the number of Russian Baptists grew steadily [see *Church Growth*]. After the Toleration Manifesto of 1905 Baptists received greater freedom to carry out mission work; for the first time in their history it was not a crime to share their views with Orthodox people.

By the first decade of the 20th century Baptists had reached Siberia, with Novosibirsk and Omsk becoming important centres of Baptist witness. In addition, the Far East Baptist Union was formed in 1913. William Fetler, from a Baltic-German background, established a Russian Baptist church in St. Petersburg in 1908 which soon took possession of a building, named *Dom Evangeliya* [House of the Gospel], festively opened in 1911. At this time Russian Baptists began publishing the **periodical**, *Baptist.* In general, the years 1905-12 were characterised by active evangelism, though new difficulties arose, especially during WWI. In 1912, there were approximately 115,000 Baptists and 31,000 Evangelical Christians in the Russian Empire, though these statistics vary from one source to the next.

The first 10 years of the Soviet period, after the **Socialist** revolution in 1917, were comparatively favourable for Russian Baptists and Evangelical Christians, though devastating for the Russian Orthodox Church. Baptist and Evangelical Christians exploited the opportunities for evangelisation that arose in a civil war-ridden country, and by the end of the 1920s, according to some (never fully proved) estimations, the number of evangelicals had grown to 500,000. Attempts to unite both unions in the 1920s unfortunately failed. Both unions, under government pressure, made statements which supported military service, though **pacifism** was inherent amongst most evangelicals in the **Soviet Union**. Soviet evangelicals tended to remain silent about the atrocities that were directed by the **state** towards the Orthodox Church. They may have hoped that 'this cup' would pass them by. It did not. Hard times lay ahead. Stalin's repressions of the 1930s, almost wiped out all organised religious life in the Soviet Union. Evangelical leaders and active **church members** became subject to severe repression, **church buildings** were closed or destroyed, whilst many believers were falsely accused on **political** grounds. In this the authorities exploited the historic connection with German Baptists and membership of the BWA, and conceived of an international organisation rooted in America and the UK. By 1935, the work of the Russian Baptist Union and the Union of Evangelical Christians centrally

had practically stopped, though local churches and groups continued to operate outside the law. Many German-speaking Baptists, who at the end of the 1920s numbered well over 10,000, were deported to Siberia at the outbreak of the war.

For political reasons, during WWII, churches were given some limited freedom, which at least allowed them to function legally. In 1944, the representatives of Baptists and Evangelical Christians held a meeting in Moscow. Under strict government control, the **All-Union Council of Evangelical Christians-Baptists** was established, with Yakov Zhidkov (1885–1966) as its chairman. In 1949, under government pressure, **Pentecostals** joined the Union, and later on a number of Mennonites. As a condition for joining, the Pentecostals agreed to keep 'order' in their **worship** services, which meant avoiding **speaking in tongues** and giving up their practice of **foot washing**. During the Soviet years, the Moscow Central Church of Evangelical Christians-Baptists became the centre of Baptist life in the Soviet Union.

'Unity' became a buzz word for Soviet evangelicals for many decades. However, this unity was fragile. In the midst of Khrushchev's atheistic campaign, in 1961 a split occurred. Protesting against the government's restrictive policies, and accusing the official leadership of compromising with an atheistic state, a number of evangelical believers, known as *initsiativniki*, left the Union. In 1965, an illegal organisation, the Council of Churches of Evangelical Christians-Baptists, was formed, led by Gennadii Kryuchkov, later Georgii Vins and others. Though these 'underground' churches had a tendency to stick to the identity of a persecuted **suffering minority**, even later, when the political situation had changed, their prophetic voice [see **Prophecy**], reminding both believers and the atheistic government of the value of **religious freedom**, was crucially important for Baptists in the Soviet Union.

Meanwhile, the registered churches did their best in a difficult situation, mainly within the framework of worship services, without publicly confronting the state imposed restrictions. The AUCECB published *Bratskii Vestnik* [*Brotherly Herald*], and from 1968 distance-learning **ministerial** training courses were organised in Moscow. The All-Union Council had a highly centralised structure, with Senior Presbyters in every Soviet republic or larger region. Limited contact with the wider world, carefully observed and guided by the state, was allowed but only through the official Union. Aleksander Karev's role as a Baptist leader during these Soviet years cannot be over emphasised.

In the second half of the 1980s, under Gorbachov, new religious freedom was granted. With the collapse of the Soviet Union into a range of separate independent states, the AUCECB was also dissolved. Instead, in 1992, the Euro-Asiatic Federation of Unions of Evangelical Christians-Baptists was formed, an 'umbrella' organisation for 10 independent (Evangelical Christian-) Baptist unions in the former Soviet Union. In Russia, the Union of Evangelical Christians-Baptists of Russia, a member of the **European Baptist Federation**, has 1,400 churches and about 100,000 members in total. However, the former 'underground' or **Reform Baptist** churches as well as a number of independent Russian Baptist churches also continue to witness both in Russia, and in the other former soviet territories. Russian Baptists, whatever their affiliation, face many challenges: to cooperate with other churches and partner organisations, to develop Baptist educational structures, to redefine their relationships with society, in general, and political structures in particular, to engage in **contextually** relevant theological reflection and to revive worship and mission in the midst of profound social and cultural change.

MI, MK & ET

FURTHER READING: All-Union Council of European Christians-Baptists, *History of the Evangelical Christians-Baptists of the USSR*, AUCECB, Moscow, 1989. M. Bourdeaux, *Faith on Trial in Russia*, Harper and Row, New York, 1971. Heather Coleman, *Russian Baptists and Spiritual Revolution, 1905-1929*, Indiana University Press, Bloomington, 2005. E. Heier, *Religious Schism in the Russian Aristocracy, 1860-1900*, Nijhoff, The Hague, 1970. W Kolarz, *Religion in the Soviet Union*, St. Martin's, New York, 1961. E.A. Payne, *Out of Great Tribulation: Baptists in the USSR*, Baptist Union of Great Britain and Ireland, London, 1974. Constantine Prokhorov, 'The State and Baptist Churches in the USSR (1960-1980)', Keith G. Jones and Ian M. Randall (eds), *Counter-Cultural Communities*, Paternoster, Carlisle, 2008. W. Sawatsky, *Soviet Evangelicals since World War II*, Herald, Scottdale, Pa., 1981. A.W. Wardin, *Evangelical Sectarianism in the Russian Empire and the USSR: a Bibliographic Guide*, Scarecrow, Lanham, Md., 1995.

Russian Missionary Society

[See also *Mission*]
The Russian Missionary Society was founded by William Fetler (known also as Basil Malof), a Latvian, born in 1883, who studied at **Spurgeon's College** from 1903-07. During his studies, he was deeply affected by the **Welsh Revival** and in particular by Evans Roberts. Fetler was supported from 1907 by the Pioneer Mission, which was associated with Spurgeon's College, and he saw remarkable results in St. Petersburg, Moscow and Riga, the capital of **Latvia**. As a result of his work in St. Petersburg a **church building** was opened in 1911 seating 2,000 people. The Principal of Spurgeon's, Archibald McCaig attended the opening and continued to take a keen interest in Fetler and the Russian Missionary Society, which Fetler launched. Fetler was banished from **Russia** in 1912, but he continued to direct the front-line work of the Russian Missionary Society, which organisationally was London-based (at Spurgeon's Tabernacle). The Society sought to employ indigenous **missionaries** and developed a special work among Russian prisoners of war during WWI. With the help of local friends and British supporters, Fetler bought an empty Russian barracks church in Latvia which became the centre of his work. Fetler raised money through travels in the USA in 1923-24 and returned to Latvia in 1924 with strong financial support. As well as the Mission he founded a Bible Institute. The Mission and Bible Institute had three sections. Two were located in Riga, with Russian and Latvian divisions. The Russian **students** came from **Poland**, the Latvians from local Baptist churches. The third section was the English department, located in London. The Institute lasted approximately 10 years and approximately 100 **ministers** were trained. Fetler founded the 'Salvation Temple' in Riga, a huge church building which was opened in 1927. By this stage the Russian Missionary Society had grown to 200

staff. In the 1930s, Fetler and his family moved around Europe a great deal, and then in 1939 they settled in the United States from where he continued to lead the Society.

IMR

S

Sabbath/Sabbatarianism

The Sabbath, a word signifying Jehovah's day of rest after his six days of creative activity [see *Creation*], became enshrined in the decalogue as a day of rest to be observed by all *Jews*. Thus, Sabbath-observance, a hallmark of Jewish religion, by the time of Jeremiah at least had become part of the law of righteousness. It was to be observed by a pious Jew as an occasion for *worship*, as a weekly reminder that all time was given by God and needed to be lived out in that understanding.

By the time of *Jesus*, the Sabbath had become the focus of much Pharisaic regulation which seemed to focus more on what could not be done on the sabbath rather than the joyous celebration of earlier years. Jesus sought to correct such defects by his claim to be the Lord of the Sabbath, which Paul sees as bringing to the infant *church* new freedoms, which were not to be countermanded by the attempts of the Judaisers to re-impose rule and regulation. In Jesus' teaching on the sabbath, he powerfully spells out the gospel requirement that places relationship with the Christ above the observance of legal regulation, because it is the Messiah and not the Law that gives true sabbath rest. Nevertheless, for some time it seems as if the early Christians respected both the seventh and the first day. Celebration of the first day, Sunday, derives from this being the day on which Jesus rose from the dead [see *Resurrection*], completing his work of *salvation*. Christians have always held the first day to be a day for worship and Christian nurture, though the NT has few references to it (however see Rev 1:10).

Not all Christians in the reformed *tradition* [see *Reformation*] were convinced that the Christian observance of the first day of the week had replaced the Jewish sabbath. Respect for the Mosaic Law led some Silesian *Anabaptists*, notably Oswald Gait and Andreas Fischer, to become sabbatarians. Similarly in *England* in the first half of the 17th century there emerged a group of Seventh Day Baptists who established a presence in America in 1671.

Sunday observance has come under threat in modern society as modern commerce argues that every day should be a working day leading to campaigns 'to keep Sunday special'. Some, however, offer caution about legalistic endeavours to secure this, arguing that this can all too easily create 'a day of tyranny and gloom', a total contradiction of the spirit and intention of Jesus. Nevertheless, properly observed the Lord's Day is a reminder to all that work and rest need to exist in balanced relationship. The modern terms 'Sabbatarian' and 'Sabbatrianism' are not necessarily applied to the seventh day and are used to describe special respect for the observance of 'the Lord's Day'.

JHYB

Sacrament, Sign and Symbol

[See also *Ordinances and Sacraments*; *Sign and Symbol*]

In Baptist churches the *theology* of sacrament varies from place to place. At heart a sacrament is an outward and visible sign (as Augustine and Aquinas agreed) of something spiritually deep and significant in the life and experience of the believer which is God-given by *grace*. Baptists always insist that sacramental language belongs to only two Biblical events [see *Bible*] – the *baptism* of a believer and the celebration of the *Eucharist,* the so-called dominical sacraments. The word derives from the Latin *sacramentum* referring to the oath of allegiance made by a soldier, but in Christian usage it is related more closely to the Greek word *musterion* [mystery].

In both these events we engage with deep spiritual experiences as we seek to fulfil the command of *Christ*. Some Baptists have been unhappy at the use of sacramental language, preferring generally the use of the language of ordinance, symbol or sign.

However, recent scholarship has reminded Baptists that there is a strong historic use of sacramental language, especially in relationship to the eucharist and much of the writing around the word ordinance, sign and symbol could equally well be applied to a discussion of sacramental theology. *John*

Smyth in his confession of 1609 referred to the task of the **church** in 'administering the sacraments' of baptism and the Lord's Supper (article 13). The words 'ordinance' and 'sacrament' appear to have been used synonymously by European Baptists in the 17th century.

Baptists would not accept that the sacraments of baptism and eucharist, are only valid if presided over by someone performing priestly functions. The theology of the **priesthood of all believers** puts the emphasis on the church being duly assembled and participating in the sacrament and whilst some may be set apart by the church community to exercise particular functions such as the act of baptism or presiding at the eucharist, they are not thereby endowed with special spiritual powers, but are appointed to roles of **prayer** and presidency by the community and it is Christ himself who is the true celebrant.

The **incarnation** demonstrates that matter is capable of being a vehicle or expression of the deep truth of God. So water in baptism and bread and **wine** in the eucharist, together with the lives of God's faithful people provide that outward and visible sign of the life of **faith** focused in these two particular moments when God approaches us and is at work in us. The efficacy and value of baptism and the eucharist is not impeded in any way by any inadequacy of the **covenantal** response of the participants. Those who receive in faith and trust God's promise are assured of his grace as they participate in these community experiences. Baptists are reluctant to overload the sacrament with meaning and significance that properly belong to the faith and grace that the sacraments symbolise.

Though the language of 'sacrament' is avoided in certain parts of Central and Eastern Europe, it is nevertheless clear that Baptist communities in these regions have a very high sacramental value placed upon these actions in the context of worship – even higher than in Western Europe where the language of 'sacrament' has been more common since the liturgical renewal movement [see **Liturgy**] impacted on Baptists in the 1960s.

Baptists reject, without further attention, the other so-called sacraments enumerated by Peter Lombard in the 12th century – confirmation, penance, unction, **ordination** and **matrimony**, though ordination and matrimony are treated as important events in the life of the believing community.

KGJ

FURTHER READING: J.E. Colwell, *Promise and Presence: An Exploration of Sacramental Theology*, Paternoster, Milton Keynes, 2005. A.R. Cross and P.E. Thompson (eds), *Baptist Sacramentalism*, Paternoster, Carlisle, 2003. A.R. Cross and P.E. Thompson (eds), *Baptist Sacramentalism 2*, Paternoster, Milton Keynes, 2008. Stanley K. Fowler, *More than a Symbol*, Paternoster, Carlisle, 2002.

Saints

[See also **Perseverance of the Saints**; **Priesthood of all Believers**]

In the OT the language of saintlines is closely associated with that of **holiness**, or that which is separated from profane use and consecrated to divine purposes. The equivalent term in the NT is *hagioi*. Most often translated as 'Saints' it is always descriptive of all Christians, never of some limited elite, for all believers have been made holy by means of the sacrificial blood of **Christ**, and thus stand in a **New Covenant** relationship with God (Acs 9:13, 32; Ro 1:7; 15:25, 31; 16:2; 1Co 1:2; 6:2; 2Co 13:12; Php 4:22; Col 3:12; Heb 3:1, etc.). Their holiness must express itself in a life of **love** and obedience to Christ: as He is holy so they must be holy.

In the **Orthodox tradition**, as also amongst **Roman Catholics**, the word 'saint' has come to refer to a specific limited category of people. The word is applied, usually posthumously, to those Christians who have achieved significant progress on what is seen as the route to deification, the process that starts here in the present life and is accomplished after **death**. This is achieved by taking part in the **sacramental** life of the **Church** and by performing 'holy deeds' in which the practice of asceticism and pursuit of the contemplative life play a specially important part.

Accordingly, the saints are thought of as those persons who, by participating in the divine life, share in God's **grace**, understood here in terms of qualities of immortality, holiness and incorruptibility. Thus 'saints' in the orthodox (and catholic) traditions, having reached the point of deification, can come to the assistance of the faithful still on earth. They are also enabled to perform miraculous signs, *healings*, and receive special *revelations* directly from God. The faithful have accordingly come to perceive of saints as some kind of intercessors, standing between those who are still alive and God himself, and thus may be the recipients of *prayers* for healing and protection. Conceiving of them as semi-divine beings is unacceptable to Baptists and other *Evangelicals*, for they find no scriptural justification [see *Authority*; *Bible*] for attributing this special status to them. Rather the teaching is that God alone can hear and answer prayer, he and no other. As the Epistle to the Hebrews so clearly shows, Jesus Christ, who is wholly accessible to his people, by his death on the *cross*, alone is the intermediary between God and *humankind*. The reformers at the time of the *reformation* were anxious to assert the significance of that word 'alone' [*sola*] – by *faith* alone, on the authority of the scriptures alone, with the believers' confidence in Christ alone.

Both OT and NT clearly teach that 'saint' is not a specific *elite* but anyone who is in partnership, that is *covenant* relationship, with God. In the NT the believer is by grace and faith *made* a saint by adoption as a son of God. There can be no accumulation of merit through 'holy deeds' that persuades either God or his church to confer 'saintly' status. This emphasis constitutes a major difference between Baptists and both Orthodox and Catholic Christians.

AK

FURTHER READING: Sergey Bulgakov, *The Orthodox Church*, St. Vladimir's Seminary, Crestwood, NY, 1988. Donald Fairbarn, *The Eastern Orthodoxy Through Western Eyes*, John Knox, London, 2002.

SALT
See *Scandinavian Academy of Leadership and Theology*.

Salvation and Soteriology
The word 'salvation' and its cognate forms, '*saviour*', 'save' are not exclusively used in a religious sense. In *secular* usage they denote any form of deliverance – from illness, from enemies, from disaster, from *death*, from ignorance, from the elemental forces of 'the powers', or indeed from self. Salvation does not even always carry the negative idea of escaping tragedy, but can be used to describe a consequential state of well-being, or *shalom*, very often not just for individuals but the whole *nation*. This can be seen especially in the main paradigm for deliverance/liberation in the OT: the Exodus, which has in recent years been looked to with *hope* by many oppressed peoples. Whilst such general usage can be found in the OT, increasingly in NT writings, the focus of salvation is on deliverance from *sin*, and sinners being spared the forthcoming wrath of God. Indeed Matthew explains that the very name '*Jesus*' means 'one who will save his people from their sins' (Mt 1:21).

The tenses associated with salvation in the NT are various: Christians are described as those '*who will be saved*' (e.g. 1Co 5:5; Heb 9:28 and Paul's encouragement in Ro 13 that 'salvation is nearer us now than when we became believers' v.11). But they are also described as those '*that have been saved*' (Eph 2:5, 8; Tit 3:5). And yet again as those '*who are being saved*' (Ac 2:47; 1Co 1:18). The emphasis, however, is consistently on the fact that salvation comes from outside of human experience; it is the action of God, Father, *Son* and *Holy Spirit* [see *Trinity*] – human beings cannot save themselves by their own efforts.

To secure our salvation, the Son comes from the Father and becomes incarnate; 'the *Word* became flesh and dwelt among us, and we have seen his glory, the glory of a Father's only son, full of *grace* and truth' (Jn 1:14). The Nicene Creed then is right to affirm that Christ became *incarnate* 'for us men and for our salvation'. Thus the Father, who nobody has seen, finds a human face in the face of Jesus Christ, the Christ who did not take his place in the godhead as a protected position 'but emptied himself, taking the form of a slave, being born in human likeness. And being found in human form he humbled himself and became obedient to the point of death – even death on a cross' (Php 2:7-8). This sacrificial death makes *atonement* for sinful *humankind*, but for them to benefit from this, the good news of 'the message about the cross', foretold in OT *scripture*, has to be proclaimed (1Co 1:18-25). Given an explicit response in *faith*, prompted by the Spirit, in believing that God raised Christ from the dead [see *Resurrection*], and by confessing the Lordship of Christ, the assurance of salvation is guaranteed (Ro 10:8-13).

Some of the benefits of the salvation will be experienced immediately, others will only be realised or consummated at the end of time (Php 3:20-21); thus Ro 5:9 where Paul contrasts *justification* now with salvation from God's wrath at the time of *judgment*, the same idea expressed in 1Th 5:8 where Paul speaks of the *hope* of salvation. This *eschatological* hope has wider scope than merely the salvation of individuals. For Paul, it involves the liberation of the whole *creation* from its present bondage to decay, as also the freeing of our bodies from their present limitations and imperfections, through resurrection, that is to say the whole created order is released to join in the glory of God. The salvation envisaged here does not represent an avoidance of *suffering*, but rather that, beyond defeat and destruction, lies God's new future. Thus in the context of contemporary crisis, J.C. Fenton wisely says that 'The faith that God will save the world does not exclude the possibility that humanity will first destroy it.'

Soteriology, derived from the Greek, *soteria*, is the study of how the doctrine of salvation has been expounded within the life of the *church*, necessarily impinging on other doctrines such e.g. as *Christology* for to secure salvation for humankind it is necessary that Jesus be both genuinely human and divine. Surveying then the different approaches to salvation in the history of the Church, the most common fallacy concerning salvation is that it can be earned or merited by undertaking actions such as going on pilgrimages, engaging in philanthropy, submitting to ascetic disciplines, etc. This was very much the warped *theological* teaching that *Luther* sought to correct. Other distortions that have occurred through the ages have been to separate salvation form the person of Christ, or to underplay the seriousness of humankind's rebellion against God and the sin that followed. Whilst salva-

tion cannot be confined to the spiritual health of the individual, and whilst it embraces a correction of all that limits the enjoyment of life for all too many of God's children, struggling with manifold deprivations in the world today, salvation from sin must remain a central feature in the Christian understanding of salvation, which must never be obscured. It is the selfishness born of this sin that causes such an unfair distribution of *wealth* in the world today, that put its *peace* at risk, and that threatens the earth's survival. All of these things are the fruit of sin. However, the spiritual task, which is inseparable from the compassionate concern to meet material needs, remains fundamental.

ET

Salvation Army

The Salvation Army was formed in 1878 out of what was formally William Booth's East London Christian *Mission* established in 1865. In a sense the Salvation Army was one of the last groups to break away from *Methodism*, Booth having been a New Connexion Methodist *preacher/evangelist* for the best part of 10 years. The new society was formed 'to bring under the Gospel those who were not in the habit of attending any place of *worship*.' Booth had deep insight into what would make his new movement popular – the military image with its associated chain of command and use of uniforms, the *sanctification* of band music for *evangelistic* purposes, –Booth was reputedly the author of the quip 'Why should the *Devil* have all the best tunes?' – its offering of leadership positions to *women*, the much respected 'Salvation Army Lassies', its particular blend of social work and *evangelism*, and the broadcasting of its concern for the 'submerged tenth' of the inner cities in Booth's very influential *In Darkest England and the Way Out*, 1890. The Army exposed such abuses as the white slave trade, founded hostels for the *homeless*, ran numerous soup kitchens, worked to create employment for the *unemployed*, and ran a missing persons bureaux amongst other social tasks. The work of the Army rapidly spread around the world being introduced to *France* in 1881 and *Sweden* in 1882. The Salvation Army sees itself as an 'integral part and element of the Great **Church**, a living fruit-bearing branch of the True Vine.' Other churches have often seen the Army as a specialised agency undertaking work on behalf of all the churches so that, e.g., they have been invited to take up a retiring collection in Baptist Churches from time to time.

JHYB

Sanctification

'Sanctification' [literally 'being made holy'] is the complement to *justification*. Paul Fiddes expresses the relationship thus: 'justification [being put right] and sanctification [being made right] are inseparable dimensions of one process'. The late Stanley Grenz argued that 'in the strict theological sense sanctification is the *Holy Spirit* accomplishing God's purpose in us as Christian life proceeds.'

In *scripture* sanctification is closely related to words meaning 'holy' and 'sacred or set apart.' Places, animals, points of time and human beings are sanctified in the OT. Rituals, such as sacrifice, anointing or *laying on of hands* may be the agents of sanctification but the prophets were keen to argue that ritual sacrifice, symbolic of sanctification, without real moral change was worse than useless. In the NT sanctification represents the process by which people or things are cleansed and *dedicated* to God, both ritually and morally; it is the process of becoming what justification declares the believer already is.

Baptists have generally rejected the *Catholic* view of sainthood whereby certain individuals among the holy dead are given special status as *Saints*, and have held that sanctification is the possibility and goal of all believers: all Christians are called to be God's special, set-apart people [see *Priesthood of all Believers*]. Sometimes, however, in *protestant* theology the two processes have been artificially separated with sanctification seen as a kind of developing add-on to a justification already complete. In so doing the moral dimension of the *atonement* becomes separated from its legal significance with disastrous consequences. The balance in 2Co 5:20-21, by contrast, holds the moral and the forensic together: 'We beseech on behalf of *Christ*, be reconciled to God. For our sake he made him to be *sin* who knew no sin, so that in him we might become the righteousness of God.' The righteousness of God' as part of the new life of the believer in union with Christ is then at the centre of what Christ in his self-giving sacrifice achieves for sinful humanity. The Cross actually creates a new relationship which transforms the quality of the Christian's life in the here and now, as much as dealing with his eternal destiny. For Christ 'the righteousness of God' meant an active obedience to the Father in every aspect of life. Consequently in restored relationship with God, the Christian is given the power, or rather the *grace*, to nurture a like obedience to the will of the Father, and this is the nature of sanctification.

Sanctification was especially important in the teaching of John Wesley who, basing his thought largely on 1Jn 3:6-9, taught a doctrine of 'entire sanctification' which said that a believer could be saved from all forms of wilful sin, though he did suggest that this state was rare and only usually given shortly before *death*. *Spurgeon*, on the other hand, was scathing about those who claimed that their struggle with sin was over. In the *Keswick* movement an early emphasis on a 'second blessing', received after *conversion*, was influential in many British and American Baptist Churches amongst those seeking a deeper spiritual experience. Thus the *holiness* movement spoke of the filling and the baptism of the *Spirit* as an instrument of sanctification under the complete Lordship of Christ by many who had already accepted Him as Saviour.

In conversion/sanctification. Christians are sanctified at the beginning of their new lives but at the same time the search for holiness is a life-time's activity. This is not undertaken in isolation but rather within the fellowship of the *church*. Thus Paul Fiddes argues, 'whilst Baptists have understood justification to be an individual matter in which a person stands alone before Christ, sanctification, or growth in grace is a corporate experience in the fellowship of the *local church* which is serving the wider society.' That reference to a wider society underlines the fact that part of the genius of the *Reformation* was to insist that the holy life was not confined to the cloister but could be found in the market place, in the secular world rather than just in church. Thus sanctification is about holy lives representing holiness in a far-from-holy world.

DBM & JHYB

FURTHER READING: Paul S. Fiddes, *Past Event and Present Salvation: The Christian Idea of Atonement*, Longman and Todd, Darton, 1989. Paul S. Fiddes, *Tracks and Traces: Baptist Identity in Church and Theology*, Paternoster, Carlisle, 2003. Stanley J. Grenz, *Theology for the Community of God*, Eerdmans. Grand Rapids, Mi., 1994.

Sanctuary
[See also *Church Building (Sanctuary)*]
'Sanctuary' [literally 'a holy place'] is a word descriptive of the *worship* area of a church: other parts of the building may fulfil social purposes but this area is set apart for the worship of God. In the middle ages it was associated also with the idea of a church as a place of refuge or asylum where those in difficulties could seek protection and claim immunity from the officers of the law. To pursue them in such a shelter could incur the charge of sacrilege for it was not simply the individual but the building that was being violated. That **tradition** has been claimed by some Baptist churches that have provided shelter to some asylum seekers being pursued by the officers of the law with a view to deportation. Hence there is sometimes talk of the 'sanctuary movement'. This has involved in some extreme cases the care in church of persons under threat for some considerable period of time. The *ministry* of sanctuary needs to be distinguished from the more general involvement of churches in the care of *refugees* and asylum seekers which is much more broadly based.

JHYB

Satan
See *Devil, The*.

Saviour
See *Christology*; *Incarnation*; *Jesus Christ*; *Logos*.

SBC
See *Southern Baptist Convention*.

Scandinavia, Baptist history in
See *Denmark*; *Norway*; *Sweden, Baptist history in*.

Scandinavian Academy of Leadership and Theology (SALT)
SALT started as a joint venture of four schools situated in Örebro and Malmö (*Sweden*), Oslo (*Norway*) and Copenhagen (*Denmark*). In Denmark four denominations were partners, i.e. Baptists, The Covenant Church, *Pentecostals* and *Lutherans*. Roland Spjuth (Malmö) was the pioneer of the project that began in 2000. The basis for the work of SALT is the classical *confessions* of the Christian *faith* and a life of *discipleship* developed in the *fellowship* of the Christian congregation. SALT belongs within theological *traditions* formed by international *evangelical theology*, *charismatic* renewal, and the quest for Christian *unity* as professed by the *ecumenical movement*. The purpose is to provide a church-based theological *education* for leaders of contemporary churches to focus on the identity of the Christian *Church* and its *mission*, and to contribute to the *renewal* of theology from a mission-oriented perspective. The objective is to create a flexible educational program that exists in a consistent *dialogue* with church and society. *Students* of SALT are able to focus their work on a specific profile within Christian leadership: accordingly there are specific concentrations on the work of *missionaries*, *pastors*, youth ministers [see *Youth work*], *church planters* and Christian social workers. SALT offers a three-year Bachelor of Theology degree with different profiles. Today SALT has about 100 students. Recently Pentecostals in Norway have begun closer cooperation with the Baptist institution in Oslo and the programme offered is focusing more on lay education [see *Laity*]. There are now three regional centres for SALT in Sweden .In Denmark it is difficult to continue the work of the school in Copenhagen and students may be more attached to the programmes in Sweden or Norway. The design of SALT is

still developing.

BH

Schism

'Schism' derives from a Greek word meaning 'division'. The ancient churches, both *orthodox* and *catholic*, tend to think of all other churches as schismatic in existing outside their *authority* structures. However, these two great churches themselves do not have fellowship one with the other since The Great Schism of 1054.

Schismatic developments have unfortunately not been rare within the Baptist fellowship. That is not very strange if we recognise that *freedom of conscience* and freedom of private judgement are two of the fundamental Baptist principles. Various leaders and various congregations have differed in thinking and beliefs, in interpreting the *Bible* and in attitudes towards contemporary culture and society.

Among the major schisms may be mentioned those between

- General and Particular Baptists in *England*, caused by differing views on the *Calvinistic* doctrine on *election*, although this was more a case of parallel development since these groups had never been united.
- *Southern* and *Northern* (later *American*) Baptists in the USA, originating in the question of slavery and developing into different views on various aspects of *theology*.
- Baptists with or without *Pentecostal* convictions, an issue that has caused major splits among the Baptists of *Sweden* and evoked tension in several Baptist communities.
- Regular and dissident Baptist in the *Soviet Union*, caused by different attitudes towards *State* regulations of religious life.

Other issues over which Baptists have been divided are open and closed *communion* [see *Open Communion*], differences of belief with regard to *free will*, Biblical Criticism, the nature of *humankind* as conceived by biologists, Biblical criticism, the *ordination* of *women*. The identification of schism with *sin* over the last century has led the churches to seek mutual reconciliation within the context of the *ecumenical movement*.

DaL

FURTHER READING: David Lagergren, *Förändringstid: Kris och förnyelse: Svenska Baptitsamfundet 1933-1948*. Bokförlager Libris, Örebro, 1994. E.A. Payne, *The Fellowship of Believers*, Kingsgate, London 1954. R.G. Torbet, *A History of the Baptists*, Judson, Valley Forge, Pa., 1963. Gunnar Westin, *Protestantismens historia i Amerikas Förenta Stater*, Svenska Kyrkans Diakonistyrelse, Stockholm, 1931.

Scholars, European Baptists in the 20th and 21st centuries

See *Biblical Scholars; Historians; Liturgists; Missiologists; Theologians, European Baptists in the 20th and 21st centuries; Ecumenical Movement, European Baptist contributors in the 20th and 21st centuries*.

Science

[See also *Creation and Science; Evolution; Science and Faith*]

Modern science grew out of a belief in the orderliness of the physical world, which could be relied upon because the Creator made it. By contrast, the later *Enlightenment* of the 18th century considered it the very nature of science to be independent of any form of religious *dogma*: it investigates facts about the physical world without any preconceptions, being both detached and objective. A scientific hypothesis arises by gathering, ordering and systematising, is tested by observations, and when widely recognised as reflecting a rational explanation is deemed to be a 'law'. That is not a permanent expression of truth: it remains a law until a deeper, often more subtle, understanding challenges and displaces it.

This empirical approach is questioned by *post-modernism* which challenges the idea of reason and an objective world, for the conclusions of an observer are coloured by the nature and limitation of the observer himself. This dilemma is not unknown to scientific theory, especially when treating matter at the sub-atomic level: the intrusion of observation limits what may be observed, as in the Heisenberg Uncertainty Principle (either the position or the energy of an electron can be determined, but not both). The empirical approach can be underpinned if we believe that reason itself has its source in God.

Science and religion are not in conflict because they are essentially concerned with different levels of meaning, engage in different spheres of discourse, each having its own proper sphere of inquiry. Science may be interested in the chemical make-up of my body, its biological relationship to other species, even the intricacies of human psychology, but religion's focus is in spiritual significance, in how I am to face my ultimate destiny. Science is interested in 'how' questions, religion in 'why' questions.

Science is trusted because it appears to 'work': the development of its discoveries through technology (q.v.) has transformed society. Future significant areas of exploration lie in the biological sciences (especially in cytogenetics, the study of chromosome structure), in the extremes of nanoscience and astrophysics, where many laws relating to intermediate dimensions do not hold, and in the pursuit of a unified theory, 'the theory of everything'.

JB

Science and Creation

See *Creation and Science*.

Science and Faith

[See also *Creation and Science*; *Evolution*; *Faith*; *Science*]

Science and faith are best seen as complementary disciplines which seek to understand and explain the nature of the physical world. Many passages in the *Bible* affirm that God's majesty and faithfulness are seen in *creation* (Ps 8, 104; Job 38-39; Mt 6:28, 16:1-3; Ac 14:15-17, 17:24-26; Ro 1:20), while Ge 1 and 2 affirm God's ordering of creation, God's design, crafting, and God's purpose.

Modern science helps us to recognise the immense size of the universe, its origin, age and complexity. Cosmology reveals a universe that is 10-20 billion years old, 10-15 billion light years across, and composed of over a billion galaxies the size of the Milky

Way, each containing some 100 billion stars the size of our Sun. We have discovered an intricately designed and inter-related universe, which is the unique location for human life.

Although there have been times of conflict between science and Christianity, notably after Charles Darwin published *The Origin of the Species* in 1859 and *The Descent of Man* in 1871 [see *Evolution*], most *theologians* today have found that there can be a healthy *dialogue* between the two disciplines.

Scientists have not in general set out to oppose the Bible, in fact both Galileo and Darwin considered that their research was discovering and explaining more about God's creation. Above the entrance to the Cavendish Science Laboratory in Cambridge is an inscription that sums up what many 17th, 18th and 19th-century scientists felt about their research, it says: 'To the Glory of God'. Today eminent scientists such as Arthur Peacocke, John Polkinghorne, Sam Berry and British Baptist, former director of the British Meteorology Office, Sir John Houghton, would say the same.

Jesus noted that people saw the signs of order that were provided by creation: Mt 16:1-4. God is faithful. Science does not disprove the Bible, in some senses science supports the Bible and indeed points us toward God. Modern cosmologists pose *theological* questions concerning the origin of the universe. The conditions of the explosive Big Bang beginning of our universe had to be so precise that some cosmologists, such as Paul Davies, suggest that the universe was created with human beings in mind, that our existence was woven into the fabric of the universe from the beginning.

The Bible presents us with a picture of creation which has its source in the purposes of God. The climax of that purpose is seen in human beings who live in a relationship of *love* with their creator. God reveals both his transcendence and his immanence in his creation. Cosmology is helping us to understand the magnitude, majesty, and careful purpose that is to be found in the universe, and so helps us to understand more about the power and care of God.

The transcendent God is before and beyond this universe; its source, origin, and its consummation and eternal purpose. This is the Creator.

The immanent God is present in the evolving universe, within the sub-atomic uncertainties and genetic mutations, and in the large scale terrestrial tectonics and galactic processes. This is the *Covenant* God, who accompanied his people in the wilderness as a pillar of cloud and a pillar of fire, who encountered them through his prophets, who was *incarnate* as Jesus of Nazareth, and who is present with his *Church* as *Holy Spirit*.

Geology and Biology are helping us to see the evolutionary path that has culminated in the presence of conscious human beings, and help us to recognise the God who has journeyed with his creation. In the 'disasters' of exploding stars, earthquakes, volcanoes, storms, and mutated plants and animals we see the *suffering* that is involved. This suffering is a demonstration of God's self-giving love that takes risks in giving freedom to creation.

We are created in the image of God; we have been called into a relationship with the creator, with a task to be undertaken and a destiny within his purpose. There are important implications for Christian *discipleship* here. In considering science and faith we enter an enormous field of dialogue which involves: care of creation; genetics and genetic engineering; natural disasters; suffering and theodicy. While it is correct to speak of Jesus Christ as the true Human Being, we can describe ourselves as 'Human Becomings'.

JDW

FURTHER READING: Paul Davies, *The Mind of God*, Penguin, London, 1992. Malcolm Jeeves and R.J. Berry, *Science, Life and Christian Belief*, Apollos, Leicester, 1998. Alister E. McGrath, *The Foundations of Science and Religion*, Blackwell, Oxford, 1998. Alister E. McGrath, *Science and Religion: An Introduction*, Blackwell, Oxford, 1999. Nancey Murphy, *Reconciling Theology and Science*, Pandora, Kitchener, 1997. John Polkinghorne, *Science and Christian Belief*, SPCK, London, 1994. John Polkinghorne, *Science and Theology: An Introduction*, SPCK, London, 1998. John Polkinghorne, *The Work of Love: Creation as Kenosis*, SPCK, London, 2001. John Weaver, *In the Beginning God*, Regent's Park College, Oxford, Smith and Helwys, Macon, Ga., 1994. John Weaver, *Earthshaping, Earthkeeping: A Doctrine of Creation*, SPCK, London, 1999.

SCM

See *Student Christian Movement (SCM), Inter-Varsity Fellowship (IVF), World Student Christian Federation (WSCF) and International Fellowship of Evangelical Students (IFES)*.

Scotch Baptists

These churches have their origins in those who seceded from the activities of John Glas (1695-1773), himself dismissed from the *Presbyterian ministry* in 1730 because of his upholding of the *priesthood of all believers*, and the *crown rights of the redeemer*. Archibald McLean, the founder of the 'Scotch Baptists', separated from the Glasites in 1763 over a *disciplinary* issue and in the process became convinced that *baptism* should be of believers only and should be by immersion. His fellow seceder, Robert Carmichael secured baptism as a believer from John Gill in London; returning to Edinburgh, he baptised McLean and some others and formed the first Scotch Baptist congregation. *Calvinist* in *theology*, the Scotch Baptists were *congregational* in *polity*, celebrated *strict communion* weekly, with each church led by a plurality of *elders* rather than a single *minister*. They soon established churches in *England* and *Wales* as well as *Scotland*; indeed after McLean's *death* in 1812 the leader of the movement was the Welshman, William Jones, who having established Scotch Baptist Churches in Chester and Liverpool, brought the denomination to London with a *church plant* in 1812. These Scotch Baptist Churches generously supported the *BMS*. Over the years their *chapels* have gradually come into membership both with the local *association* and BUGB.

JHYB

Scotland, Baptist history in

The earliest records of a Baptist presence date from the 1650s. Soldiers and *chaplains* in Cromwell's army promoted their principles in the towns in which they were based, establishing causes in Bonnington Mill, near Leith, Cupar, Perth, Ayr and Aberdeen. Persecution from 1658 led to the disappearance of these churches and it was not until 1750 that the oldest continuing Baptist Church at Keiss in Caithness was constituted by the local laird, Sir William Sinclair. In the 1760s *Scotch Baptist* churches were planted in Glasgow and Edinburgh, with congregations emerging in other major urban centres later in the 18th century. This branch of the Baptist family promoted the plurality of *elders*, weekly *communion* and the use of (male) lay-preachers [see *Laity*] and uniformity of views in its connexion. The other main network of congregations in Scotland, the 'English' Baptists, identified with English Particular Baptists [see *England*] and adopted a *pastor*-deacons leadership model. Baptist ranks were significantly strengthened after 1808 by the addition of former Independent pastors, including Robert and James Haldane, together with their congregations [see *Haldaneite tradition*].

At the heart of Baptist identity in Scotland was *mission*; three home mission agencies merged to form one Baptist society in 1827, a body that achieved an extraordinary degree of success in the 19th century, principally in more remote Highland and Island communities. In 1889 conscious of the rapidly expanding urban areas of central Scotland the Baptist *Union* launched an *Evangelism* Committee to carry out short-term mission initiatives in these locations. This body was renamed the Church Extension and Evangelism Committee in 1901. The work was extremely successful. Between 1898 and 1935 the total *church membership* rose by 35% to 23,310 and from 108 to 152 churches, a rise of 29%. Its success was attributable to many dedicated workers engaged in innovative and creative forms of outreach in urban communities. However, the *Home Mission* working in rural locations experiencing significant depopulation saw declining number of adults and *children* at their services. Despite regular and sustained initiatives in evangelism there has been a slow overall decline in membership from 1935 to the present day. Exceptions to this came in 1955 with the *Billy Graham* Glasgow *Crusade* from which Baptist congregations saw many new members following *conversions*, and the 1980s Simultaneous Evangelism programme which resulted in conversions followed by the highest baptis-

mal figures [see *Baptism*] amongst Scottish Baptists since the 1920s.

Support for *overseas* evangelism and medical work, especially through the *Baptist Missionary Society*, has been consistently strong. A large number of its members served overseas. In 1926, e.g., 197 members of its 143 congregations were listed as serving in the mission field. The largest proportion (55) worked with BMS mainly in India, China or the Congo in Africa, but locations of listed workers included Algeria, Argentina, *Egypt*, *Italy*, *Israel*, Jamaica, Morocco, Peru, *Spain*, St Helena, The Gold Coast (Ghana) and *Turkey*. Although not as prominent as its evangelistic activities social action was also a significant part of Scottish Baptist life. The most prominent individual in this regard was William Quarrier who pioneered the provision of welfare and *educational* provision for street children at Bridge of Weir. 1,000s of poor children were aided by Quarrier's Homes. A proportion of them were assisted to build new lives in Canada. He was also responsible for the erection of the first tuberculosis sanatorium in Scotland (1896) and the first medical facility for epileptics (1903). The *temperance movement* was also a significant feature of Baptist witness and by the early 20th century expectations of abstinence were strong in its ranks. By 1923 all ministers were teetotal, all churches used unfermented *wine* at *communion* and no licence holder held membership in a local congregation. Rest Homes for the elderly, centres for the *homeless* (Elpis in Glasgow and Bethany in Edinburgh), together with the Ark Housing Association in Edinburgh providing community homes for the mentally-handicapped, were some of the *ministries* carried out under Scottish Baptist auspices. Scottish Baptists have contributed to the public debate on a wide variety of social issues including *gambling*, broadcasting standards, *abortion* and *euthanasia*, world *poverty*, immigration and atomic weapons [see *Nuclear Threat*].

Baptists in Scotland were enthusiastic supporters of inter-church ventures such as the 1910 Missionary Conference in *Edinburgh* and were represented by two members of the BMS delegation. In a similar way 75 Scottish Baptists were appointed as delegates for the Missionary Congress of Scottish

Churches in Glasgow in 1922. They were one of six founder members of the Scottish Churches' Council in 1924, though they had reservations about some of the doctrinal teaching of the **Episcopal** and **Roman Catholic** Churches. Close ties with the **Congregational** Church were nurtured through the resolution of common grievances, e.g. over the under-representation of their ministers as Armed Forces chaplains during WWI. Although the Baptist Union of Scotland joined the **World Council of Churches** after a tied vote was passed on the casting vote of the chairman in 1948, it had been an unwise decision to proceed on such a slim majority. Increasing criticism led to a withdrawal from the WCC in 1955, a decision that was confirmed in 1963, although, between 1965 and 85 there were Scottish Baptists taking prominent positions in the Scottish Churches' Council. At different times Donald McCallum, Derek Murray and Andrew Mac-Rae as individuals chaired its' Evangelism, **Christian Aid** and Mission committees respectively. In 1989 Scottish Baptists decided not to join ACTS, the new **ecumenical** body established for Scottish Churches. However, an overwhelming majority of the churches voted to join the **Evangelical Alliance** in 1997. Scottish Baptists were very clear about their support for the **EBF** and the **BWA**, but struggled to find a **consensus** in their ranks on involvement in inter-church relationships at a national level on the threshold of the 21ˢᵗ century.

BT

FURTHER READING: D.W. Bebbington (ed), *The Baptists in Scotland*, Baptist Union of Scotland, Glasgow, 1988. B.R. Talbot, *Search for a Common Identity: The Origins of the Baptist Union of Scotland 1800-1870*, Paternoster, Carlisle, 2003. B.R. Talbot (ed), *A Distinctive People: A Thematic Study of Scottish Baptist life in the Twentieth Century* (forthcoming in 2010).

Scottish Baptist College

The Scottish Baptist College was founded in 1894, although from as early as 1806-37 Scottish Baptist churches of the 'English' **Calvinistic tradition** had been sending **men** to Horton Baptist College, Bradford, **England** to train for Baptist **pastoral ministry**. The big concern at that time was that the vast majority of men sent to England for their theological **education** did not return to serve in Scottish Baptist congregations. For the next half-century a large proportion of candidates for future pastoral ministry were trained by a small number of serving **ministers** who were employed by the Baptist **Union of Scotland** as part-time tutors in biblical [see **Bible**] and theological studies.

During its first 30 years the Baptist College was housed in Adelaide Place Baptist Church, Glasgow, prior to the move to West Regent Street, Glasgow, in 1925 where premises were shared with the Baptist Union. This institution obtained its own accommodation near Glasgow University in 1969 at a time when there were unrealised hopes of closer ties with that body. A more substantial **property** was bought jointly with the Baptist Union in Pollockshields in 1981 which allowed more space for their activities until 2001, at which time the college moved to rented accommodation on the Campus of Paisley University, now known as the University of the West of Scotland. The long-term aspiration to offer its own BD degree course, validated by the University of Paisley, was achieved during Dr. Kenneth Roxburgh's time as Principal (1994-2002).

Student numbers have always been low. The highest number of full-time students attending, 29, was recorded in the1991-92 session during the Principalship of Dr. Ivor Oakley (1988-94). In the 2007-08 academic year this total was reduced to 16 men and **women**, though the number of part-time students engaged in a range of **vocational** studies has increased in recent years. The College's understanding of its **mission** is clear. It is committed to 'holding together academic excellence, practical training and formative spiritual development [see **Spiritual Formation**]'.

BT

FURTHER READING: D.B. Murray, *Scottish Baptist College Centenary History 1894-1994*, Scottish Baptist College, Glasgow, 1994.

Scouts and Guides

The Scout and Guide movements were the brainchild of Robert Baden-Powell, an English army officer, who returning from the

Boer War in South Africa wrote a book called 'Scouting for Boys'. This was published in 1907. Soon boys were writing to Baden-Powell asking how they could follow through his outdoor activities and after an experimental Scout Camp on Brownsea Island in Pool Habour, *England*, Baden-Powell soon found himself leading a movement with a religious, though not specifically Christian, ethos. His wife, Olive, became leader of a sister organisation for girls and today Scouts and Guides are to be found in 216 countries with approximately 28 million members catering for young people aged from about six upwards. The basic promise made by all uniformed members of the movement includes some reference to a higher being. The movement seeks to develop the mental, spiritual, physical and emotional aspects of young people. Many churches became involved in founding Scout Groups or Guide Companies, though Baptists generally preferred youth movements with a more overtly Christian basis, with a requirement that groups be church-based. Baptist Scout and Guide Groups exist in several European countries, but especially in *Denmark* and England. There is a Baptist Scout and Guide Fellowship in *Great Britain*.

KGJ

FURTHER READING: www.scout.org.

Scripture(s)
See *Bible, Baptist understanding of*.

Scripture Union
In 1867, Josiah Spiers, having already conducted some special services for *children*, gathered 65 children together in Islington. London, for the start of the Children's Special Service Mission (CSSM). A year later he began to conduct services on the beach at Llandudno. From this a variety of *evangelistic* initiatives among children developed on an interdenominational basis, Boys' Camps were introduced in 1879, a Caravan Mission to Village Children in 1893, and much later an Inter-Schools Christian Fellowship (1947) supporting Christian Unions in schools. A daily *Bible* Reading scheme, under the name

of Children's Scripture Union, was started in 1879. The diverse activities were brought under the name of Scripture Union in the 1960s. By then the SU had introduced popular choruses which were widely influential for many years and widened its *ministry* to include publications for adults. Its Bible Reading notes, graded for different reading constituencies, are now very widely used by thoughtful evangelicals and its *Sunday School* materials have been widely used in Baptist Sunday Schools, encouraging good teaching practice. Today it is engaged in all forms of children's *mission* working both in churches and schools and with families.

Though never making a great impression in the US, SU rapidly grew to be an international movement with a widespread ministry across Europe, working through 25 national movements. A visit to the Scripture Union Europe website, e.g., gives reports of work in *Scandinavia*, Latin Europe, *Germany*, *Switzerland*, and in many countries in Eastern Europe from the *Baltic* through *Poland*, *Hungary*, and the *Czech Republic*, to the *Balkan* countries and different parts of the former *Yugoslavia*. Many Baptists have participated in its activities and read its Bible Reading notes.

DJT

FURTHER READING: www.su-europe.org.

Sectarianism/Sects
The sectarian is the opposite of the *Catholic*, in the best sense of that word. Whilst 'Catholic' represents the worldwide community of those who in all times and all places have upheld the teaching of the *apostles*, as attested to in the *orthodox creeds* of the *church*, the 'sectarians', by belief and behaviour, detach themselves from that mainstream of Christian *witness*. It was to counter such imputations against the Baptists that Alexander McLaren suggested the wisdom of those assembled for the first Congress of the *Baptist World Alliance* joining together in affirming the Apostles' Creed, even though Baptists have sometimes claimed to be a non-*credal* people. There is also an academic and *sociological* use of the term which intends a neutral usage. *Ernst Troeltsch* developed a categorisation of reli-

gious institutions which distinguished the 'inclusive' Church with its parish structures, from the 'exclusive' sect. Thus most often whilst one is 'born' into a church, entry into a sect, in this sense is, by being 'born again'. **H.R. Niebuhr** has developed from this basic nomenclature a later stage of development suggesting that as sects become less exclusive in admitting others as validly part of the whole church of God and as **state churches** do the same, so a new kind of religious organisation emerges which he calls the 'denomination'. State churches which fail to see any aspect of Christian presence in other churches are themselves, by such action, acting in a sectarian, excluding, fashion. Baptists admit with no sense of guilt that they have their origins in **separatism**, but would distinguish this from an exhibition of the sectarian spirit, in so far as they are not exclusivist in their claims to truth, whilst it can be shown from their earliest confessions of faith that they have never wanted to be other than part of the whole church of God. The Particular Baptist Confession of 1677 lays obligation on Baptist churches 'to **pray** continually for the good and prosperity of all the churches of **Christ** in all places' whilst the so-called General Baptist Orthodox Creed of 1679 makes a similar affirmation with regard to the church both invisible [see **Church: Universal, Triumphant, Invisible**] and visible [see **England**]. Driven to separation by the context of the times, the early Baptists were not sectarian, and in more recent times Baptists have made a conspicuous contribution to the development of the **ecumenical movement** at its several levels and in its different forms of **association**, through groupings of **free churches** and **evangelical alliances** to participation in local, national, regional and international ecumenical bodies. The contemporary scene is burdened with those who operate out of sectarian motivation and are properly called either sects or cults, those, e.g., who in sending **missionaries** to a given area make no attempt to contact the already existing churches. It is also possible, it must be admitted, for a 'sectarian' spirit to exist within a mainstream church which is not itself sectarian. Such an accusation could be raised against those who over-emphasise some particular doctrine or over-rigorously insist on

some particular pattern of behaviour, or begin to narrow the horizon of God's gracious concern for the whole of **creation**. In some countries the historic presence of the Baptist church is properly understood and respected but in others some leaders of state churches too easily cast the slur of sectarianism on the Baptists, ignoring their commitment to the trinitarian **faith** [see **Trinity**], their long history, their working with others, their membership of the same ecumenical bodies to which these state churches belong, as also their world-wide organisation. The accusation of sectarianism in those countries where one church is very closely associated with national identity is that those involved put at risk the unity of the **nation**.

JHYB

Sector Ministry
See *Chaplaincy*.

Secularisation/Secularism
Secularisation is generally understood as a process and as a theory of emancipation from religion, a shift from the feudalistic societies of medieval **Christendom** to modern **capitalist** societies, in which, it was believed, the churches as well as religion as such would cease to play any important role.

The word comes from Latin *saeculum* ['human age'/'century' but also 'temporality'/'terrestiality']. Besides these meanings in the background, the word 'secular' translates also as 'non-ecclesial'/'non-religious'/'non-spiritual'/'profane'. Then, although there is a wide spectrum of definitions of secularisation, they usually rely on the separation of the profane from the sacred. Or historically more accurately, they are reactions to the separation of the sacred from the profane. *Profanum* originally meant the place before the *fanum*, the holy place, like walking through the market to the temple. But when separated, the *fanum* was interpreted against the *profanum*, the 'world inside' against the 'world outside' of divine presence, as if they were not but 'one world' approached from different sides. Different theories of secularisation then, speak of a *volte-face* effect, when the 'world outside' of the dominance of the *church*, of religion, of *spirituality*, turns its back to the 'world inside' as illusory and as dangerous for the development of human autonomy and civic *democratic* society.

Social and cultural changes associated with the process of secularisation include the *Reformation*, with the ending of a single church *authority* in the West, the Renaissance, the *Enlightenment*, but also the religious wars of the 17th century and subsequently also the French Revolution. The new *political* and legal settlements of Europe arising from these phenomena, as well as the rise of modern *science* and technology, with their emphases on rationality, human experience and human potential contributed to what was seen as the 'modern world'. In that world, religion became a suspect. As we can see in the philosophy of Friedrich Nietzsche, it belonged to the old dark ages, while acceptance of the *death* of God and radical human freedom was what was needed now. According to Karl Marx's social analysis, religion was 'the opium of the people', which needed to be given up, so that the people could deal with the real problems of their lives rather than being silenced by illusory comforts. Sigmund Freud's psychoanalysis classified religion as a 'wishful illusion' based on a father complex and as an 'obsessional neurosis'. These forefathers of secularisation theories, and others, such as Max Weber or Emile Durkheim, believed that an eruption of human knowledge together with the modernisation of society would lead to a decline in levels of religiosity, and that this process would be beneficial for the individual as well as for the whole of the society.

Modern wars and modern secular dictatorships, however, proved that separation from religion did not bring brighter ages, freer of *violence* and manipulation. The earlier dualist models of secularisation were complemented by new non-dualist approaches, such as Jürgen Habermas's adaptation in his theory of communicative action. The relationship of religion and society or religion and science, and culture is seen here as the relationship of equals, where opposition is replaced by the need of communication, and thus also by the need of translation, of mediation from one realm to the other. The process of secularisation, then, can be seen as making this equality possible, as rehabilitating the *profanum* without losing the need of the *fanum*. Further discussions continue as to whether this shift means moving beyond the secular and moving beyond the modern society, and if so, in which sense, whether as breaking with the past or as finding a better appropriation of the past.

In all this the ideology of secularism needs to be distinguished from the process of secularisation. Whilst secularism is clearly hostile to all forms of religion, it has been argued that radical *Protestant* Christianity is part responsible for a healthy secularisation, e.g. in the marginalisation of resort to all forms of magic and its insistence on a God of order, with its emphasis on the *separation of church and state*, and with nature desacralised by the English *puritans* leading to the scientific revolution of the 17th century.

The imminent death of religion is proving a false prediction with the resurgence of a variety of world *faiths* – Christianity in the Global South, and the ancient religions of the East both in their homelands and in their *diaspora*. Theorists of secularisation now have to learn how to spell 'Ayotollah'.

IN

FURTHER READING: S. Bruce, *God is Dead: Secularization in the West*, Blackwell, Oxford, 2002. H. Cox, *The Secular City: Secularization and Urbanization in the Theological Perspective*, SCM, London, 1965. O. Chadwick, *The Secularization of the European Mind in the Nineteenth Century*, Cambridge University Press, Cambridge, 1975. J. Habermas, *The Theory of Communicative Action I-II*, Beacon, Boston, Ma., 1984, 1987. D. Martin, *A General Theory of Secularization*, Harper and Row, New York, 1978.

Seminario Teologico UEBE
See *Spain, Baptist Theological Seminary of, Madrid*.

Separation of Church and State
[See also *National Churches*; *State, Baptist approaches to the*]
Baptists have often prided themselves on their commitment to a total separation of

church and state. Certainly Baptists rightly have **theological** objection to monarchs as heads of churches and to state appointed **bishops** or other church officers, a clear affront to the Lordship of Christ within his **church**, often spoken of as '**The Crown Rights of the Redeemer**'. In 1639 the English Particular Baptist [see **England**], William Kiffin wrote in 1639, '**Christ**'s kingly power in his church was not committed to a Hierarchy, neither to a National Presbytery, but to a Company of **Saints** in a **Congregational** Way'. Within its own area legal authority was to be respected on the principle of 'rendering unto Caesar what is Caesar's' and the Pauline argument in Ro 13 that secular power is divinely instituted. With Constantine what had been a persecuted church became a favoured **faith** within the Empire, and under Theodosius in 380AD 'the official religion of the empire.' At the time of the **Reformation**, and the ensuing religious wars, the **nation** state was **sanctified** in place of a fragmented and fragmenting Latin Empire.

The position is not, however, without its difficulties, though clearly, **suffering** as they have done from over-privileged state churches in both Eastern and Western Europe, the identification of the need for such a separation has good reason. However, does this 'privatise' religion and suggest that the church has no **witness** to make to the state, and is the state to be valueless and does not this too easily slide into a partnership between the state and **secularism**? Can there be no justifiable partnerships between faith organisations and state authorities in meeting social need? Is the registration of a congregation with the state authorities a breach of the separation principle, especially if the church is deemed to be a charity and secures tax benefits because of such a status.

Giving the state church supremacy in **education** has characteristically been a prime way of promoting the influence of folk or state churches, occasioning fierce hostility from **free-church** people, but today **evangelicals**, worried about the quality of the education given in some state-run schools, themselves have turned to setting up faith schools. Such has been the increase of child abuse [see **Child Protection**] that even those historically suspicious of state bureaucracies have had to yield to all youth workers having to be vetted by the police to ensure that they do not have a past record which might endanger the children with whom they seek to work. There are also issues of moral scandal – e.g. the international trafficking of **women** for sexual purposes [see **Prostitution**] – in which the churches know that they can only hope to be effective if they work with government to work out their Christian **conscience**. Accordingly with good conscience traditional **nonconformists** have been forced to see increasing occasions in which the church should properly ally with the state for the service of a cause such as the confronting of the increasing deterioration of the **ecological** stability of the universe, or to allow the state limited intervention within its domestic territory to avoid any charge of scandal in matters of finance and personnel management.

Certainly the classic North American stance on the separation of church and state might need to be amended within the very different culture obtaining in Europe.

JHYB

Separatism

'Separatism' is the technical term for the **ecclesiology** of those advanced **Puritans** in **England** who, impatient for a thoroughgoing reform on proper Biblical principles [see **Bible**], separated themselves from the Established Church [see **National Churches**] of which the monarch was head and which was **episcopally** organised. Part of the objection was doctrinal, part to liturgical practices [see **Liturgy**]. More moderate '**presbyterian**' puritans were content to bide their time and wait within the established church. The movement does not have a definite beginning for some moved from the established church via semi-separatist congregations into full-blown separatism (and some later to Baptist beliefs), but basically the movement can be dated back as far as the 1550s and the implementation of the Elizabethan Settlement of the **Church**. The first person to be identified as a separatist is Robert Browne (c1550-c1633) who formed one such separated congregation migrating with it to **Holland** in 1582, but Browne soon returned to England and was reconciled to the Established Church. Other early separatists, most of whom were associated with the University of Cambridge, include Henry Barrow (c1550-93), John Greenwood (d1593), John Penry (1559-93), Francis Johnson (c1562-c1617) and John Robinson (1575-1625). Many of these became *martyrs* and others were forced into exile, including the Pilgrim Fathers who in 1620 set sail in *The Mayflower* for America. It was out of this *tradition* that the earliest English Baptists were to emerge. From Separatism, therefore, Baptists derive their commitment to *scripture*, a *gathered church* confined to the regenerate, non-episcopal church government and the practice of simplicity in *worship*, without resort to ceremony and ritual. Baptists went beyond the separatists in confining *baptism* to believers and insisting on full *religious liberty*.

JHYB

FURTHER READING: T. George, *John Robinson and the English Separatist Tradition*, Mercer University Press, Macon, Ga., 1982. B.R White, *The English Separatist Tradition*, Oxford University Press, London, 1971.

Serbia and Montenegro, Baptist history in

Baptist *witness* began in Serbia (Vojvodina), then still under Austro-Hungarian rule, among ethnic Germans. In 1875, six people were baptised [see *Baptism*] in Novi Sad by Heinrich Meyer, also instrumental in spreading Baptist witness in Hungary. Amongst these converts, who had a Nazarene background (a group founded by S.H. Froehlich), with an emphasis on personal *holiness*, was Adolf Hempt who as a Bible *colporteur* spread Baptist convictions in the region. However, Baptist work in Novi Sad only developed into a formal church in 1891, and was led for three decades by Julius Peter, a successful organiser and *evangelist*.

By the beginning of the 20th century Baptist *evangelistic* efforts had reached ethnic Hungarians, Slovaks, Serbs, and Romanians. The first ethnic Romanian Baptist church was established in Straža in 1924. Slovak work, initiated in 1898-99 in Bački Petrovac by Josip Turoci, grew to such an extent that a Slovak conference was founded in 1918. In Belgrade, there were German-speaking Baptists as early as in the 1880s, gathering for *prayer* and *Bible study*. However, a Baptist church bringing together all local ethnic groups was only established in the late 1920s.

In 1924, the Baptist Union of *Yugoslavia*, which existed until just after the break up of the Yugoslav Federation in 1991, was founded. *Southern Baptists* from the USA provided help; in 1938, a *missionary* couple, John and Pauline Moore, arrived and made the first short-lived attempt to establish a seminary in Belgrade (1940). This was reconstituted in 1954 in Zagreb, then moved to Daruvar, and since 1957 has operated from Novi Sad. After WWII, Adolf Lehotsky provided strategic leadership enabling the Baptist Church in Novi Sad to regain its strength, though without German *members* who had been forced to emigrate in 1944-45.

Since 1992, two Baptist *unions* have existed in Serbia: The Union of Baptist Churches in Serbia, a multinational union with 51 congregations and 2,100 members (within which the largest conference is Slovak with more than 1,100 members in 19 churches and 12 *mission stations*), and the Union of the Evangelical Christians–Baptists with 13 congregations and approximately 600 members, who are predominantly Serbian. There are no registered Baptist churches in Montenegro, although a group of believers meet regularly in Nikšić. *Novi Sad Baptist Theological School* serves as a *theological* training centre for Serbian Baptist and other evangelical church workers. Baptists in Serbia publish several *periodicals*: *Misijne pohlady* [*Mission Views*] and *Novy rod* [*New Birth*] in Slovak; *Kapcsolat* [*Contacts*] in Hungarian and *Sestrinski list* [*The Sister's Magazine*] in Serbian.

BB

FURTHER READING: Branko Bjelajac, *Protestants and Evangelicals in Serbia until 1945*, Branko Bjelajac, Belgrade, 2001.

Sermon
[See also *Preaching*; *Pulpit*]
Baptist *liturgies* normally climax in the sermon, or sermons – the proclamation of the gospel for the people of God today. Sermons do not have primarily to do with instruction or argument though they may contain both.

They should not take the form of a Biblical or ethical lecture [see **Bible**; **Ethics**], but should seek to make contemporary the message of **Jesus** for the contemporary world. Dodd on *Apostolic Preaching* is instructive when he underlines the NT writers' distinction between preaching [*kerygma*] and teaching [*didache*]. Teaching was important for the instruction of new Christians in·the **faith** and the moral responsibilities which **discipleship** embraced. Preaching by contrast meant public proclamation of Christian truth to a non-Christian world. 'It was by *kerygma*, says St. Paul, not by *didache*, that it pleased God to save men'.

Preaching then is a **sacramental** act, for to be true to itself, beyond the **preacher** there needs to be a sense that in this action God himself is speaking; it represents the breaking of the **Word** alongside the breaking of the Bread [see **Communion and Intercommunion**; **Eucharistic liturgy**]. For this to happen the preacher needs to be open in a special way to receiving the **grace** of 'God-possession'. Another way of expressing the same truth is to speak of the **incarnational** character of preaching, that it is to say, it so brings the Word of God and what is being said in the newspapers together, that, by a modern miracle, the Word again becomes flesh once more in our own time. Bernard Manning has defined a sermon as 'a manifestation of the Incarnate Word, from the Written Word, by the Spoken Word.'

Preaching which may be doctrinal, expository, **pastoral**, ethical, exhortatory, topical, or even **prophetic**, is served by a vivid command of language, the capacity to analyze and develop a topic cogently, engagement with the Biblical text and **theological** reflection thereon, the ability to illustrate the sermon's theme with fresh and empathetic illustrations, and the imaginative ability to arouse and hold a congregation's interest – and never to bore them with what they already know. A sermon, as it applies the gospel to a particular situation, should always seek a response from those hear it – indeed the act of preaching is incomplete without that response. Such a response could be a first commitment to Christ [see **Conversion**], or a resolve to follow him further in some new adventure of discipleship in the world.

In Western and Central Europe there is normally one sermon in worship lasting between 20 minutes and an hour. In **Russia**, **Belarus**, **Ukraine** and **Central Asia** there are generally up to three sermons, with the senior pastor preaching the final sermon and in total time these can last between one and three hours.

ET

FURTHER READING: David M. Brown, *Transformational Preaching: Theory and Practice*, Virtual Bookworm, College Station, Tx., 2003 [This book is also published in Russian for the Brjansk Baptist Institute of Preachers]. Michael J. Quicke, *360 Degree Preaching: Hearing, Speaking, and Living the Word*, Paternoster, Carlisle, 2003.

Seventh Day Baptists
See **Sabbath**.

Sexism
[See also **Feminism**; **Inclusive Language**]
The language comes from the 1970s and reflects a growing impatience amongst **women** with the patriarchal systems which have placed a glass ceiling on their full development as persons. The argument was that all social institutions, including the **church**, had developed within frameworks of patriarchy with the highest social value always given to the father, with women always **suffering** from a culture of discrimination. In particular, it was argued that the oppression of current systems was buttressed by **theological** arguments based on the **Bible**. It is at this point that well-founded criticisms of contemporary society move into areas where fundamental elements of Christian **revelation** come under challenge – the personhood of the **Trinity**, the male Sonship of **Jesus Christ**, etc., leading to arguments that the church is 'the ideological backbone and stronghold of sexist practices.' It is not an argument about appropriate actions in the life of the church, its liturgical language [see **Liturgy**], the role of women in **ministry**, etc. but about the foundation documents themselves, and here some, who may be sympathetic to the idea of quite radical practical changes, find that they cannot support the arguments used to advance such changes, and that accordingly some of the rhetoric

becomes self-defeating. The need to find a more worthy place for women in the life of the church, to remove all unnecessary sexist language and practice, to use female perspectives to interpret scripture are all tasks that need urgent attention, but to engage with these tasks does not require the rewriting of the revelation.

JHYB

Sexual Orientation

[See also *Homosexuality*]

Sexual orientation can be heterosexual, homosexual or bisexual. The majority of people feel attraction to members of the opposite sex (heterosexual) whilst a small minority are attracted to the same sex (homosexual). Of the latter a tiny proportion are attracted to both sexes (bisexual). In Western society for many centuries up to the middle of the 20ᵗʰ century homosexual orientation was seen as a sickness or a pathological deviance, and in the case of the Christian *church*, as *sin*. *Scientific*, *sociological* and sexological research in the second half of the 20ᵗʰ century has contributed a body of knowledge which indicates that a minority of people are born with an attraction to their own sex. Biblical material [see *Bible*] does not refer to the concept of homosexual orientation. Today a distinction is often drawn between homosexual orientation (given) and homosexual practice (chosen).

During the latter part of the last century a number of Christian denominations in Europe gave attention to the questions raised by same-sex orientation. In 1988 the Baptist *Union* of *Great Britain Council*, following the work of a specially convened task group, agreed guidelines which were subsequently reaffirmed in 1991, concerning 'Conduct unbecoming to *ministry*', which include the statement that 'Homosexual orientation (whether male or female) is not of itself a reason for exclusion from ministry, but homosexual genital practice is to be regarded as unacceptable in the *pastoral* office, and is to be treated as falling within these guidelines. Ministers are expected not to advocate homosexual or lesbian genital relationships as acceptable alternatives to male/female partnership in marriage.' While there is some variation in viewpoint among Baptists in

Europe, this statement probably represents the most commonly held position.

One European Baptist *theologian*, Nigel Wright, in his chapter 'Baptists and the sexuality debate' in *New Baptists New Agenda* quotes the American theologian James Nelson who identified four responses to same-sex attraction and relationships:

(1) The *rejecting-punitive* position: homosexual orientation and practice are unconditionally rejected and this is accompanied by a punitive attitude towards lesbians and gay men.

(2) The *rejecting-nonpunitive* position: homosexual acts are rejected as violating divine intent but a distinction is drawn between orientation and acts. Homosexual acts are rejected as irregular and unnatural but orientation is seen as a flaw rather than a sin. Homosexual persons are to be treated compassionately.

(3) The position of *qualified acceptance*: God's intention in *creation* is heterosexual in nature. However those who find themselves homosexual in constitution (for whatever reason) need to be supported in their struggle to live holy lives. If re-orientation or celibacy prove to be counsels of perfection, then faithful same-sex relationships may be the least worst option open to people in an imperfect and unredeemed world. These relationships are informed by the Christian *tradition*'s understanding of *marriage* but would not be regarded as equivalent to marriage.

(4) The position of *full acceptance*: Sexual relationships should be evaluated according to their 'unitive' rather than 'procreative' purpose. All sexual acts are tested ethically [see *Ethics*] according to their relational qualities. The same criteria apply therefore to hetero- and homosexual behaviour. This should lead to equal treatment expressed in the blessing of same-sex unions and the *ordination* of practising gays and lesbians as well as full civil equality.

It is likely that the majority of Baptist church members in Europe would affirm response (2), although a minority might support (1), (3) or perhaps (4).

SCJ & ET

FURTHER READING: BUGB Ministerial Guidelines concerning 'Conduct unbecoming to Ministry' 1991. Sue Clements-Jewery: Paper on Sexual Diversity 2004, part of the BUGB educational tool. Nigel Wright, 'Baptists and the Sexuality debate' in *New Baptists New Agendas*, Paternoster, Carlisle, 2002.

Sheltered Housing

[See also *Elderly, Care for the*]
With increased mobility of Europeans during the second half of the 20th century, many Baptist families became dispersed with *children* and grandchildren often living significant distances away from the senior generation. Thus the pattern of families living in close proximity so that the younger generation could provide support for the more elderly family members began to break up. This process has been accelerated within the *European Union* with its accent on the free movement of people and a 'borderless' Europe, to disperse families at greater distances across the continent.

In these circumstances the pattern of alms houses developed by the medieval churches moved into a new phase with communities of *faith* showing an interest in developing forms of communal housing with support from a warden and from a neighbouring church suitable for more senior members in society. In *Germany* this diaconal *ministry* grew out of the work of the order of *Deaconesses* and the work associated with the *Albertinen* in Hamburg. The German Baptists also deliberately included a large complex of sheltered housing for senior people in the Baptist complex at *Elstal* in the western suburbs of Berlin. In *Britain* the Baptist *Men*'s Movement began a Housing Association to develop surplus church land for sheltered housing in the 1960s and some smaller Baptist and *ecumenical* housing associations followed suit.

Sheltered housing is often in the form of a series of apartments in a complex with a common room in which weekly services of *worship* and social events are held. There might also be a guest suite for relatives to use and special features such as emergency cords in bathrooms and bedrooms to summon help from a warden or on-call carer. Normally in larger complexes there is the provision of a warden on site to help develop a sense of community and to be available to provide practical support for residents.

In Germany and in the United Kingdom, Governments have been supportive of churches taking this type of action as important for social cohesion and have often made loans available for the developments at advantageous rates of interest, normally on condition that they are able to nominate people to a certain number of vacancies.

The operation of these diaconal ministries have been possible by the willingness of church people with commercial and business skills to join vereins or associations engaged in such developments and to provide the necessary legal, development and financial expertise.

In more recent years with changes in the *political* and economic climate there has been a move towards larger economic associations with the ability to draw upon more professional expertise and this has disadvantaged some Baptist initiatives and in some instances reduced the involvement of *local churches* in this caring ministry.

KGJ

Shrove Tuesday

See *Fat Tuesday*.

Sickness

See *Health, Sickness and Healing services*.

Sign and Symbol

[See also *Sacrament, Sign and Symbol*]
The representation of something of deep significance by actions and elements representative of this deeper truth is nowhere better seen than in the breaking of bread and the pouring out of *wine* in the *communion* service which bring to mind the body and blood of *Christ* and his sacrifice upon the *cross*. Paul in Ro 6 spells out the symbolism of the watery grave in the baptismal service [see *Baptism*] as rehearsing the *death* and *resurrection* of Jesus with which the new believer is to be identified. The empty cross, rather than a crucifix, in a Baptist Church not only reminds the *worshipper* of Jesus'

sacrificial death but also indicates that he is now their risen Lord. Symbolism such as Paul's portrayal of the armour of God in Eph 6 has had a long usage in the church. In the early church the sign or symbol of the fish was used to represent Jesus as the Son of God. Or again John's Gospel makes constant references to Jesus' messianic presence as seen in the signs or miracles that he performed. In non-Biblical [see *Bible*] representation one of the most pervasive works of sign and representation is *Bunyan*'s great allegory of *Pilgrim's Progress*, a classic of Christian *spirituality*. A number of national *unions* have their own symbols – the Swedish Union uses a cross and a blazing fire over the waters of baptism, the British Union an emblem encompassing the cross over the waters of baptism joined together with the sign of the fish, whilst the *EBF* has deployed various signs which embrace the cross and the world. Baptists always insist that signs and symbols be not divorced from that which they signify – so communion can never stand alone apart from the dying and rising again of Jesus, providing a sign to the disciples, as in the Emmaus Road story, that he is alive in the world today.

JHYB

Signs and Wonders

[See also *Charismatic movement*; *Pentecost*; *Pentecostalism*]

The NT records that signs and wonders were performed after Pentecost through the *apostles* (Ac 5:12). The Signs and Wonders movement is associated with the name of Californian *evangelist*, John Wimber (1934-98), and the Vineyard movement of churches which gained ground from the early 1980s, first of all in the US, and then internationally. Wimber's argument was that in the NT the church's *evangelistic* impact was directly proportional to its ability to perform signs and wonders. For this reason, the most effective *church growth* would be brought about not through organised programmes but through *power evangelism*, that is, proclamation, accompanied by and validated with, signs such as miraculous *healings* and deliverance from evil spirits. Wimber's *ministry* came to be identified as the 'Third Wave', following on from the first

wave of Pentecostalism and the second of charismatic renewal. It was accompanied by unusual spiritual phenomena sometimes seen in times of *revival*: trembling, falling in the *Spirit* (sometimes called 'being slain in the Spirit'), groaning, ecstatic prophesying and laughter. This was denounced by some Baptists but made a considerable impact on many others in Western Europe and *Scandinavia*, as it did in the United States and Australasia. Wimber's thesis has been criticised for failing to deliver the healings envisaged, especially in the form of the '*Bible*-type' miracles to be seen in the ministry of *Jesus*, thus calling the thesis into question. Although replete with 'wonders', in that many unusual things took place through the movement, 'signs' were fewer and farther between.

NGW

Sin

A variety of terms is used for concepts related to 'sin' in the OT. The three major terms are *hattah* [to be mistaken/to be deficient/to miss a goal], *pasah* [wilful violation of a norm] and *awon* [error/iniquity]. In the NT the major term is *hamartia* [to miss the mark], as classically set out by Paul in Ro 3:23, with its consequences uncompromisingly set out in Ro 6:23.

In the OT, sin is fundamentally the transgression of the will of God, a breach in *covenant* relationship with Him. It can be seen in the transgression of the commandment of God in the Garden of Eden. Later on in Isaiah's *prophecy* the exile is seen as the result of the constant violation of the covenant. At the beginning of Genesis, sin, here portrayed as a clutching after a moral autonomy which is rooted in Adam's rebellion and denial of God's *authority*, leads to *alienation* from God (the deportation from the garden, Ge 3:22-24), from other peoples (the sewing together of fig leaves as coverings, Ge 3:7), and from nature (the curses in Ge 3:14-19). It provokes the wrath of God, the estrangement of *humankind* and the conflict with nature. Sin is universal in both the OT (1Ki 8:46) and the NT (Ro 3:23), always involving a radical separation from God: even sin against other people is ultimately sin against God, and that is the measure of its seriousness.

In the gospels frequent use is made of words implying a state of universal sin, e.g. the repeated call to *repentance* (Mk 1:15) and the pronouncement of *forgiveness* (Mk 2:5) which became central to *apostolic preaching* as recorded in Ac 2:38. In the NT, the sacrificial system is no longer effective, instead *Jesus* by his *death* on the cross makes full and complete *atonement* for sin (Heb 10:11-12).Thus Paul's message is focused on the simple truth that 'Christ died for our sins' (Ro 5:8; 1Co 15:3), However, taking the example of the life of Christ seriously along with the injunction to be Christ-like, the Christian is required to live blamelessly (Php 2:15), though all too often the church exhibits a sad and sorry failure in this respect (1Co 5-6).

The reformers [see *Reformation*] saw sin not as an external constraint but as an inner reality rooted in that perversity of human nature, indicated by the language of 'original sin', that deeply imbedded bias towards sin inherent in all humanity. The reformers also speak of humanity's 'total *depravity*', indicating that there is no aspect of human nature not spoilt by sin – reason, emotions, affections, ambitions, all have been corrupted. It does not mean that fallen humanity is incapable of good works but that there is no aspect of human being unaffected by sin. There is certainly not an inner core of the spirit uncontaminated by bodily corruption as the 16th century *mystics* believed. By contrast *Luther* found his innermost being the place where the conflict with sin was most fiercely to be fought. Sin, operating though human pride, produces a false evaluation of reality. Because the fall is so total, humanity is wholly incapable of saving itself; only the initiative of divine *grace* can do that. As John Colwell writes, 'The totality and inclusiveness of Adam's sin and the consequent depravity of all is an issue that is only truly made known in the cross.'

For Baptists a key text is Ro 6 because of the way in which Paul shows how in the action of *baptism* believers are completely freed from the domination of sin when they identify with Christ's dying and rising again [see *Resurrection*]. Because identified with the risen Christ and dead to their sinful past it behoves those baptised into Christ to live

the new life that he provides. But this does not mean that the Christian is immune from temptation as is made abundantly clear in 1Jn 1:5-2:2., which relates the liability to sin to the remedy that is provided by Christ, whose *love* for sinners must always take priority over their love for him (1Jn 4:10).

Sin cannot be confined to the lives of individuals: its infection has upset the whole created order, hence Paul's vision of Christ's work being finally achieved in a restored *creation*, once more reconciled to its maker (Eph 1:3-12). Meanwhile sin not only infects individual lives by way of personal sin, it also spoils social relationships in terms of deeply imbedded structural or institutional sins, which also must be overcome both in terms of obedience to Christ in our everyday *callings* as in the *eschatological* vision of the *heavenly* realm where the new order is fully installed, the old order is passed away and sin is finally no more (Rev 21 and 22).

KTB & ET

Singleness

[See also *Marriage/Matrimony*]

A significant and accelerating issue in European societies, singleness is a personal reality for a number of European Baptists, especially *women*. It is often an involuntary reality resulting from a significant unevenness in the male-female proportions in many congregations, as well as the disapproval of many churches of *members* marrying outside the Baptist/Christian community.

The churches largely opt to avoid discussions of the issue and instead point to the need of accentuating the *theology* of marriage. As worries are raised about the crumbling institution of family in the society, the nuclear family model is often idealised and presented as literally biblical [see *Bible*]. In such context, single believers are theoretically encouraged to accept their singleness, yet practically that is coupled with the idea of proper waiting for a marriage partner.

In church life, singleness that is consciously chosen is, in reality, frequently discouraged, especially for those in *pastoral* positions. It is often held, whether implicitly or explicitly, that a single person will lack certain experience and therefore will provide inferior leadership for the church. This seems to be an over-reaction to the *catholic tradition* where singleness via celibacy is a requirement of those entering the *ministry*. Churches have also ignored the way in which singleness on the *mission* field has been used to the benefit of the *kingdom*. In addition to the intimate *suffering* that accompanies singleness, and especially involuntary singleness, single believers often experience further pressure coming from the sex-driven and/or still marriage-status-sensitive culture that characterises much of Europe. One of the ways of seeking a healthier attitude towards singleness is the practice of *intentional communities*. It is a fitting way of sustaining a Christian life and, although not concentrating on single women, it is able both to offer support for single Christians as well as to provide opportunities for supporting others.

LA

SITE

See *Summer Institute of Theological Education*.

Slavic Gospel Association

The Slavic Gospel Association grew out of the *ministry* of Peter Deyneka, Sr., born in Storlolemya, *Russia*, in 1898. His parents sent him to the USA in 1914 to earn money for the family. He was converted [see *Conversion*] at Moody Memorial Church, Chicago, under the ministry of Paul Rader and after Bible School training felt a *call* in 1925 to be a *missionary* in Russia. He *preached* among Slavic communities in *Czechoslovakia*, *Estonia*, *Latvia*, *Poland* and *Yugoslavia*. Through meeting Ivan Prokhanov, leader of the All-Russian Evangelical Christian Union, Deyneka became the Union's representative in the USA and Canada for five years. In early 1934 he and others formed the Russian Gospel Association. In 1949 the name was changed to Slavic Gospel Association (SGA). Initially Deyneka preached in Europe and the USA, but outreach spread to Slavic communities in South America, Australia, New Zealand, South Africa, and Asia. The SGA headquarters moved from Chicago to Wheaton, Illinois, in 1975,

with offices in other countries becoming independent national boards. In 1975, an Institute of Slavic Studies was opened in Wheaton at SGA headquarters, to offer courses in Slavic culture, together with aspects of training in SGA's areas of ministry – *evangelism*, radio, literature preparation, and Christian *education*. From the early 1980s, this programme was offered by the Wheaton College graduate school. By 1980, the number of SGA workers was 210, including indigenous workers partially or completely supported by SGA. Leadership passed to Peter Denyka Jr. and his wife Anita. Tensions led to the setting up of Peter Deyneka Russian Ministries in 1991, with the SGA operating under new leadership. SGA began to sponsor seminaries and Bible institutes, *church planting* and TV broadcasts, as well as continuing with literature and humanitarian work.

IMR

Slovakia, Baptist history in

When Baptists entered Slovakia in the late 19th century, it was part of the kingdom of *Hungary*, a constituent member of the dual monarchy of *Austria*-Hungary. While the work in Bohemia and Moravia (today part of the *Czech Republic*) was orientated toward *Germany*, Slovak Baptists were influenced largely by Baptists in Hungary. The pioneer of the work was August Meereis, a former *colporteur* of the British and Foreign *Bible Society*, who had served in Bohemia but, from 1888-1902, served as a Baptist *missionary* in Slovakia. As early as 1878 Meereis began to minister in Kežmarok, where he formed a German Baptist congregation on 15 Jul 1888, the first in Slovakia. Another centre for Baptist work developed at Liptovsky Sväty Mikuláš, where Vacla Brož, who was of Czech descent, settled around 1880. Meetings in his home soon spread to neighbouring villages. In 1882 Heinrich Meyer, the Baptist leader in Budapest, baptised 18 believers in the Vah River in Brož's home village. Meereis also visited Bratislava, where he baptised converts [see *Conversion*] as early as 1889. In 1897 Baptists formed an independent church at Vavrišovo, followed soon by two others. In 1900 the four churches which by then had been established had about 200 *members*. With the establishment of an independent Czechoslovakia, Czech and Slovak Baptists formed a Baptist *union* in Vavršovo.

After the *Communists* took control of the government in 1948, many believers faced open persecution. Some Baptist properties like the recently completed camp in the Tatra Mountains or the *orphanage* in the town of Bernolákovo were confiscated by the *state*, whilst a small *magazine* of the Baptist Union called *Rozsievac* [*The Sower*] could no longer be published. The state's atheistic propaganda was powerful and the overall pressure upon the church unrelenting. Some significant Baptist leaders were arrested and imprisoned and the Baptist Union was under constant control of the police. In the 1960s Czech and Slovak Baptists established regional conferences within the Union and the 'Prague Spring' of 1968 promised reforms including the rehabilitation of persons unjustly convicted in the period of 1949-54. But they were scrapped by the Soviet-led invasion and Soviet troops occupied Czechoslovakia until the fall of the regime in 1989. At that time, Baptists had nine churches in Slovakia.

In 1992 the work began to expand when two dozen members left the Bratislava church to begin a separate work. The new congregation has directed much of its *ministry* towards helping drug addicts. With the division of Czechoslovakia in 1993, Slovak Baptists formed their own Baptist Union (Bratská jednota baptistov v Slovenskej republike). The Union cooperates with international Baptist agencies and after it signed a three-year partnership with the *Southern Baptists* of Virginia in 1995, some 400 Virginia Baptist volunteers came to Slovakia to help repair buildings and train young people for various ministries and for *mission* [see *Youth Work*].

Baptists continue to be a small *minority* in this predominantly *Roman Catholic* country, but their *evangelistic* outreach and other activities have become increasingly significant. They have a *Bible* school in Banská Bystrica. Teenagers are trained for the mission field which now includes the homelands of ethnic Slovaks in *Serbia* and *Slovenia*. The activities of the Slovakian Baptist churches include evangelistic *crusades*, English as a Second Language summer camps, occasional *sports* evangelism, and regular youth conferences. There are now over 20 Baptist churches in the Union.

PeM

Slovenia, Baptist history in

Baptist beginnings in Slovenia are linked with the work of Martin Hlastan, Sr., a Bible *colporteur* and *member* of the Free *Brethren*. As a result of Hlastan's *witness* Jurij Čater was converted [see *Conversion*] before WWI. After the war he gathered together a small group of believers in Hrastnik. They may formally be considered as Baptists from 1923 when they invited Ivan Zrinščak from Zagreb Baptist church to baptise them [see *Baptism*]. This first Slovenian Baptist church, established in Hrastnik, later moved to nearby Trbovlje. In 1922, Anton Starc from Rosalnica returned from Russian imprisonment as a converted Baptist, and also initiated a small Baptist group. Another group started in Maribor (Franc Južina). Since 1927, the work in the Trbovlje area was under the auspices of the Zagreb church. The first Slovenian Baptist conference was held in 1938.

Another impetus to the Baptist movement came in 1939 when a Slovenian, Andrew Derchar, returned from the USA and together with Franjo Klem from *Croatia* founded a *mission station* in Kranj. Derchar started publishing the *magazine Glas Evangelija* [*Voice of the Gospel*] and a number of Christian booklets. Because of *Catholic* reaction this work did not last long. Derchar came in contact with Andrej Thaler and a group of believers who were part of the *Novi človek* [*New Man*] *evangelical* movement in the Jesenice area, and in 1942 the Jesenice Baptist church was founded. During the latter part of WWII, when the Italians occupied Slovenia, all Baptist churches were closed. Derchar was arrested and disappeared in 1942. Čater was sent to the Dachau concentration camp, but survived. In 1945, another evangelical movement, *Cesta evangelija* [*Gospel Road*], led by Vekoslav Korošec in Ljubljana, joined the Baptists. Korošec, a gifted writer and lecturer with formal *theological* training, was promptly ordained as a *preacher* [see *Ordination*]. In 1947, a Baptist

Church was started in Celje.

At this time there were about 100 Baptists in Slovenia, linked with other Yugoslavian Baptists in a common **union**. After WWII there was little progress. Larger congregations existed in Ljubljana, Celje, and Trbovlje, smaller ones in Javornik, Kranj, and some other places. With the collapse of **Yugoslavia**, Slovenian Baptists formed their own union, but there also exist several independent congregations. The union has about 200 **church members** in four **local churches**. Both the Conservative Mission International and the Foreign Mission Board of the **Southern Baptist Convention** have sent **missionaries** to work in Slovenia.

RK

Smoking and Tobacco

Until quite recently it was perfectly acceptable for both **pastors** and **church members** in Western Europe to smoke, with a number of well-known preachers such as **C.H. Spurgeon**, known to enjoy the habit. It is still to be found amongst Baptists in German-speaking countries, **Denmark** and **Italy**. However, elsewhere it became increasingly unacceptable in the second part of the 20th century, in large measure due to the causal link established between smoking and a number of life-threatening diseases, including a number of cancers as well as damage to the heart, on the argument that this was to abuse the human body otherwise called the temple of the **Holy Spirit**. More recently such illnesses have also been associated with passive smoking so that the practice has become a threat to other people, to such an extent that a number of governments have banned smoking in public places. Thus the issue has moved beyond a concern of **conscience** to a matter of legality. Within the wider Baptist family the growing of tobacco was the staple crop in some areas of Baptist strength in the USA, with Baptist **witness** and outreach in those areas sustained by its successful trading.

ET

Smyth, John (1570?-1612)

John Smyth was an early British Baptist pioneer. He was ordained into the **Anglican** Church in 1594 and was a **Puritan**, but by 1606 he had become convinced of **congregational church polity** and adopted **separatist** views. He joined a group of separatists in Gainsborough which included William Bradford, one of the Pilgrim Fathers. In 1608, Smyth and an associate, **Thomas Helwys**, led a small group of separatists into exile in Amsterdam. Smyth and Helwys were committed to the idea of a pure church, organised as a **gathered covenant** community, and wanted to model **church** on what they believed to be the **apostolic** ideal. By 1609 they had also become convinced that Christian **baptism** should be for believers only. Smyth first baptised himself, then Helwys and the rest of the group, by effusion or pouring from a basin rather than immersion. Soon after this Smyth came into closer contact with **Mennonites** meeting in Amsterdam who also practiced believers' baptism. Smyth began to regret his decision to baptise himself, and called on **members** of his church to join him in renouncing their baptism, something which Helwys and a number of others refused to do, thus splitting the congregation. In 1611 Helwys led a small group back to **England**, where they established the first British Baptist church. By the time of his **death** from tuberculosis in 1612, Smyth had also rejected **Calvinism** in favour of **Arminianism**. Formal union between most of his followers and the Mennonites was completed in 1615.

Smyth's role in the genesis of British Baptist life has been exaggerated by some, probably because of the ready availability of his works which were republished in 1915. But he was a significant figure. Smyth's belief in general **atonement** and congregational church government, as set out in his writings, helped provide a foundation for the life and thought of future General Baptists.

PJM

FURTHER READING: B.R. White, *The English Separatist Tradition: From the Marian Martyrs to the Pilgrim Fathers*, Oxford Theological Monographs, Oxford, 1971.

Social Class

Social class is the same as social rank; the system of social caste; it refers to the hierarchical distinctions between individuals or groups in societies or cultures; people having the same social or economic status. *Anthropologists*, *historians* and *sociologists* identify class as universal, although what determines class will vary widely from one society to another. Even within a society, different people or groups may have very different ideas about what makes one 'high' or 'low' in the hierarchy. Social stratification is a sociological term for the hierarchical arrangement of social classes, castes, and strata within a society.

The economic changes brought about by the industrial Revolution of the 18th and 19th centuries in the West saw the feudalism of an agrarian society develop into the class structure of the industrialised society. Sociologists recognise a number of changes that take place in the development of modern society:

(1) Democratisation [see *Democracy*]: a move from hierarchy and rank to equalisation of conditions among people. Differences in *wealth* and intellect remain but status becomes the main focus. Alexis de Tocqueville (1805-59) saw status based on money and other visible symbols of personal identity including ethnicity, race, gender, and possessions.

(2) *Secularisation*: intellectual rather than social change. Scientific rational thought taking over from religious and metaphysical ways of thinking. Auguste Comte (1798-1857) saw a time of transition from the *theological* feudal order to a new morality – a progress to a peaceful, prosperous, scientific-industrial society.

(3) The Bourgeois Revolution: Karl Marx (1818-83) [see *Communism/Marxism/Socialism*] saw the move from the theological feudal to the new urban, property owning city dwellers (the bourgeoisie). Modern social problems find their origin in the struggle over wealth and *property* created by a *capitalist*, market dominated society. Marx taught that democracy was the way in which the bourgeoisie cemented their hold on power, and only revolution would see an end to *poverty* and injustice.

(4) The rise of a diverse, secular, organic society: Emile Durkheim (1858-1917) saw modernisation as a shift to moral and social diversity, and to a solidarity based on the division of occupational *labour.*

(5) Increasing rationalisation of all spheres of life. Reason and not feelings determine what people do. The feudal society was based on community where those with social prestige also had the power and the wealth. The modern world has produced different groups based on intellect and entrepreneurial gifts.

(6) The achievement of *women*'s legal and *political* equality began with the suffrage movement led by Emmeline Pankhurst (1858-1928). They were also concerned with child welfare, and Adela and Sylvia Pankhurst devoted themselves to a socialist transformation of the capitalist economy. In recent years the *feminist* movement and *feminist theology* have continued to seek for gender and social equality.

Many Christians have sought to address the exploitative and oppressive aspects of the capitalist system, identified by Marx. *Christian Socialists* such as F.D. Maurice (1805-72), J.M.F. Ludlow (1821-1911), Charles Kingsley (1819-75), and Thomas Hughes (1822-96) brought together socialism and Christianity. Maurice and Ludlow both formed cooperative movements and sought to develop a corporate and communal understanding of human life. These and later Christian Socialists such as William Temple (1881-1944) sought to address the problems of poverty and social division in British society.

Earlier in the European *Reformation* some *Anabaptist* groups sought to develop classless church communities, e.g. the Hutterites under Jacob Hutter (d.1536) established a community in Moravia, who had common ownership of property. Other groups such as the *Mennonites* were *congregational* churches with no *hierarchical* leadership. Outside the *church* there were other attempts at developing a classless society, e.g. Robert Owen, the founder of Socialism and Cooperation in *Britain*. Owen was anti-clerical, if not anti-Christian, as well as extremely utopian.

In the 20th century Latin American **Liberation Theology** has sought to enable the **poor** to transform the social, political and economic situations in which they find themselves. One of the aims of this approach is to break through the classist society in which the poor find themselves to be the oppressed. They take their lead from **Jesus'** identification with the poor, the declaration of the gospel for the poor (Lk 4:18), and therefore the conclusion that the transformation of the poor was the **mission** of Jesus. There tends to be a Marxist division of society into two classes: the proletariat (the poor) and the bourgeoisie (the owners and leaders).

In the OT we find a variety of social groupings, from the early tribal/clan system to the cities and the royal court with their own social structure. While in social relationships, as far as God is concerned, no group in society is more important than another and all **men** and women are equal, nevertheless the **priests** interpreted the Law (Torah); the wise men gave advice on everyday affairs; and the prophets brought the direct word from God [see **Prophecy**].

However Liberation **Theologians** often see the story of God's people in the Exodus as a picture of their own condition. The poor peasants identified with the children of **Israel** and the right wing governments and multi-national corporations in general being identified with Pharaoh. A critique of this has been made in recent years by Jon Levenson. He takes the commentary of liberation theologian George Pixley, as a warning of building on one's own situation at the expense of engaging the text. For Pixley the exodus is seen as a socio-political revolution by and for the poor and oppressed; a class struggle, an underclass breaking free from slavery in Egypt. He believes that succeeding redactors, for whom the monarchy and **nation** state or priestly ruling class were seen as positive, have sought to disguise the original story.

The picture of the people of Israel in Egypt as a classless society (primitive communism) is a case of historical projection, as we see in the Book of the **Covenant** (Ex 20:22-23:33), which assumes property rights and the presence of tribal chiefs, freemen and slaves. The Book of the Covenant does, however, call for a special concern for the poor, the widow and the stranger and takes great pain in making provision for them. But it is an anachronism to identify justice with equality in Israelite society.

Similarly the NT presents us with the view that all people are equal before God (Gal 3:28), but Levenson is right to point to the stratification of society in Phm 11-16 and Eph 6:5 and show that there is no charter for a new revolutionary society here either.

Wayne Meeks notes that society was stratified and that the church congregations reflected that stratification. E.g. the leading figures in the Corinthian church belonged to a relatively high economic and social level, and Malherbe notes that the Greek of the NT documents indicates a literary culture. The extreme top and bottom of Greco-Roman society is missing from the churches, while the intermediate levels of household slaves, free artisans and small traders are well represented. Some of the more wealthy were able to travel and provide housing and meeting places for the church.

Bruce Malina notes that the NT represents a 'peasant society' where the majority of people lived in villages or in the artisan districts of preindustrialised cities. The main focus for all groups in society was human existence and the need of security. The patron-client system of landowner and workers was also reflected in the church.

We can conclude that society has always been stratified into different social groupings, but that every man and woman is equal before God. Clearly people are differently gifted, but as Jesus says: 'From everyone who has been given much, much will be demanded; and from the one who has been entrusted with much, much more will be asked' (Lk 12:48).

JDW

FURTHER READING: Bonnie S. Anderson and Judith P. Zinsser, *A History of Their Own: Women in Europe from Prehistory to the Present*, Vol II, Harper and Row, New York, 1988. John Drane, *Introducing the Old Testament*, Lynx/Lion, Oxford 1987. David A. Fraser and Tony Campolo, *Sociology through the eyes of faith*, Apollos/IVP, Leicester, 1992. Robin Gill, *Theology and Social Structure*, Mowbrays, London, 1977. Jon D. Levenson, *The Hebrew Bible, the Old Testament, and Historical Criticism: Jews and Christians in Biblical Studies*, Westminster/John Knox, Louisville 1993. Abraham J. Malherbe, *Social Aspects of Early Christianity*, Fortress, Philadelphia, 1983. Bruce J. Malina, *The New Testament World. Insights from Cultural Anthropology*, Westminster John Knox, Louisville, 2001. Wayne A. Meeks, *The First Urban Christians. The Social World of the Apostle Paul*, Yale University Press, New Haven, 2003. George V. Pixley, *On Exodus: A Liberation Perspective*, Orbis, New York, 1987. Gerd Theissen, *Studien zur Soziologie des Urchristentums*, Mohr (Siebeck), Tübingen, 1979. Ernst Troeltsch, *The Social Teaching of the Christian Churches*, 2 vols (Translated by Olive Wyon), Macmillan, London, 1931.

Social Ethics

[See also *Ethics*; *Natural Law*; *Responsible Society/Third Way*]

The best way to understand the term 'social ethics' is by analyzing the meaning of both words: the word 'ethics' comes from a Greek term meaning 'custom' and is used in philosophy to signify an attempt to understand the nature of morality; to distinguish what is right from what is wrong. The adjective 'social' (a word relating to society or its organisation) narrows down this broad category to issues concerned with human relationships within the local, national or wider community.

Social ethics, which are of particular importance for the Christian *conscience* because *women* and *men* are designed by God to live in society, attempt to find answers to a wide range of questions – ranging from the protection of the family, *educational* opportunities and proper *health* services for all, decent shelter for all citizens, concern for the *poor*, the advocacy of *human rights*, the controlling or corporate greed and corruption, to global issues such as those of war and *peace*, the economic oppression sometimes exercised by over mighty *transnational companies*, *globalisation*, the misuse of the earth's resources to the point where its very survival is questioned [see *Ecology and the Environment*], etc. Such questions may seem formidable – and the *theological* insight that *humankind* lives in a good *creation* fatally marred by human *sin* [see *Fall*] does little to simplify the situation, but belief in the saving and restorative power of the Crucified and Risen Christ commits the believer to dare to *hope* of a transformed world reconciled to its Creator through *Jesus Christ*. Different thinkers and different social groups will develop different strategies for understanding this and working it out in practice.

For their part, European Baptists have a long history of involvement with such issues from the standpoint of their beliefs formed by their understanding of the Holy *Scriptures*. They have sought to be faithful to their original firm stand in support of *religious liberty*, as exemplified in the life and teaching of the founder of the first Baptist church on English soil, *Thomas Helwys*, who died in captivity for his own testimony to the same freedom and belief in the equality of all human beings before the Creator. Baptists became actively involved in combating such social evils as slavery and *racism*. Baptists first played a distinguished part in striving for the abolition of the Slave Trade, and, a generation later, of the institution of slavery itself, first in the islands of the Caribbean, where the Baptist *missionary*, William Knibb, played a notable part, and then in the southern states of the USA. In this region much injustice continued to exist even after emancipation and this led to the campaign of Baptist *pastor*, Martin Luther King, against all the evils of segregation, prior to his assassination for the cause.

Recently, the *European Baptist Federation* has become involved in a very similar fight against the modern-day slave trade of the sex-industry – the main topic of a consultation on 'human trafficking' which took place in Budapest in Apr 2005 [see *Prostitution*].

KJ

Social Gospel

If the gospel is interpreted *holistically* it must always embrace corporate and social dimensions, and to deprive it of these elements is to court *heresy*. On the other hand the danger of the language of the social gospel is to suggest that its only sphere of influence is social, depriving it of its essential eternal significance for the individual soul, and that too represents heresy.

Although it is suggested that the language is essentially North American, where it has been identified as arising, in part at least, out of the *revivalist tradition* where personal *holiness* and social reform were seen to be closely related. It was not, however, unknown in the *United Kingdom* in the last two decades of the 19th century. E.g. in 1889, T.W. Bushill, director of a box-making company in Coventry, and *deacon* of the Queen's Road Church, an advocate of profit-sharing and industrial partnership who was to give evidence to a Royal Commission on Labour in 1892, addressed the Baptist *Union Assembly* on 'The relationship between employer and employed in the light of the Social Gospel'.

Its most notable North American exponent was the Baptist Walter Rauschenbusch who came from a German family where some other members continued to play an important part in Baptist life, and where some of his *education* took place. Before becoming a Professor of Church History (like his father before him) he carried out a remarkable *ministry* in the slums of New York in the 'Hell's Kitchen' area which persuaded him that the church had to find in the *scriptures* a message which spoke to the exploitation and destitution that the processes of industrialisation had produced. In the *Bible* he found much relevant material in the denunciation by the prophets of the corruption of their day and in *Jesus*' own warnings about letting service of *Mammon* (which could be interpreted as living by the profit motive) motivate the way one lived one's life in the world, and in his teachings about the coming of the kingdom. Rauschenbusch wrote a number of significant books such as *Christianity and the Social Crisis*, 1907, *Prayers of the Social Awakening*, 1910, *Christianizing the Social Order*, 1912 and *A Theology for the Social Gospel*, 1917. His passionate address to the second *BWA* Congress in Philadelphia in 1911 was entitled 'The Church and Social Crises' in which he argued that the *church* was 'a chief sufferer in every social crisis' especially when she appeared 'impotent and perplexed', not knowing how to handle such issues. Historic churches had all too often allied themselves with conservative forces as at the times of Revolution in both *France* and *Russia*, as also in *Germany* and *Italy*. By contrast

Rauschenbusch argued 'We Baptists are called of God to reverse this attitude of the older churches...We are the heirs of the glorious *Anabaptist* movement of the *Reformation*, which embodied the religious and social hopes of the common people...We are the predestined friends of the young democracy in all *nations*...I covet for our great denomination a place second to none in this holy cause of God and the people. There is more religion, more of the spirit of Jesus and the prophets, in the little finger of that cause than in the thigh-bone of most of the theological controversies of the past...'

JHYB

Socialism

See *Christian Socialism; Communism/Marxism/Socialism*.

Society of Friends, Baptists and

See *Quakers, Baptists and*.

Sociology of the Church – Troeltsch and Niebuhr

Ernst Troeltsch (1865-1923). The German *theologian* and philosopher, Troeltsch was concerned with different types of religious life and created in Cupertino with Max Weber an understanding of the differences between 'church' and '*sect*'. The church, claiming to possess the truth, is open to all in the parish, without a clearly defined committed *membership*. Members are usually born into the church and are free not to take part in specific activities. By contrast, the sect is exclusive, and is more demanding in time, service and money, for it is maintained by the free-will gifts of its members, who join of their own *free will*, and who provide the human resource for its activities. Whilst the church has historically been supportive of the *state*, the sect tends to be more critical of government and society.

Helmut Richard Niebuhr (1894-1962). The American theologian and religious sociologist, Niebuhr found Troeltsch's church-sect understanding too simple and coined the mediating concept of the *denomination*. He perceived a process in history in which both churches and sects modified their historic standpoint. On the one hand established churches were persuaded by the presence of other Christian groups that they could no longer claim to represent the totality of the Christian population in a given country and therefore had to give some recognition to dissenting bodies. *Anglican* churches have been quicker to recognise this than *Lutherans*, though striking changes took place in the Church of *Sweden* at the end of the 20th century. The *Orthodox*, by contrast, are still generally reluctant to admit this analysis especially in their 'canonical territories'. *Roman Catholics* have been more willing to agree to this when they represent one of the minority churches and less ready to do so when they are in the majority. Niebuhr also sees a change in the development of sects from an exclusivism that un-churches all other christians to a similar standpoint which places the validity of their own position within a wider *ecumenical* framework whether or not this is structured or not. Another part of the story is the way in which sects over the year become encumbered with institutional responsibilities such as seminaries, a range of societies necessary to the fulfilment of their *mission*, denominational headquarters, national and international networks, newspapers and other publications. Very often they too have to find a way of relating to the state. Moving to a denominational position they begin to see themselves as one among many. According to Niebuhr church and sect are two opposite poles on a scale with many variations in between which themselves are constantly changing.

Troeltsch's and Niebuhr's work has been criticised because factors other than the type of membership and nature of the demands made of the members can be used to distinguish between church and sect. Niebuhr's idea of development from sect to denomination has been criticised for being too mechanical and deterministic. The criticism has brought about many perspectives in church-sect theory, which should be seen as mutually complimentary.

NFS

Solidarity

Solidarity most immediately calls to mind the activities of the trades unions in *Poland* in the years following 1980 and the part they played in overthrowing the corrupt *communist* regime in that country, but long before that in *Catholic* Social thinking, as in the papal bill [see *Papacy*], *Rerum Novarum*, of 1891, it stood for the responsibility of all for the individual and of the individual for all.

In the contemporary world the word has been more widely used to suggest the need for a *universal solidarity* amongst all people of good will as they confront such problems as *nuclear threat* and *ecological* crisis, problems which cannot be faced by individual *nations* on their own, whilst *solidarity with the poor* expresses the challenge that comes to the *church* from a world of contrasting riches and *poverty* that God's people stand with and alongside, 'be solid with', those in greatest need, both to relieve that need, and to work for a world where the fruits of God's *creation* are more equally shared amongst all peoples.

JHYB

Son of God
See *Jesus Christ*.

Soteriology
See *Salvation and Soteriology*.

Soul Freedom and the Soul's Freedom

Soul Freedom is, today; a term used much in North America, but not in Europe, where much more emphasis is placed on the '*priesthood of all believers*'. The last notable European-based reference was when Dr. *John Clifford* used the phrase in addressing the founding Congress of the *Baptist World Alliance* in 1905. In his 1908 book *Axioms of Freedom,* USA Baptist *scholar* E.Y. Mullins said soul freedom is 'the sinner's [see *Sin*] response to the gospel message as an act of moral freedom'. It is summarised as determining the individual has the 'inalienable right and responsibility to deal with God without the imposition of *creed*, the interference of clergy or the intervention of civil government' (Walter Shurden). British Baptist scholar H. Wheeler Robinson held the view that the soul's freedom was a Baptist insight that drew together the right to personal interpretation and obedience to *scripture*, encounter with God directly and in *politics* the *separation of church and state*.

Today, this personal responsibility has been challenged in some Baptist communities where affirmation of a statement of *faith* or creed has taken on a regulatory form and where the role of separated leadership to direct and control other believers has become pronounced, but these should be seen as aberrations of true Baptist identity.

KGJ

South Wales Baptist College, Cardiff

The South Wales Baptist College, Cardiff traces its beginnings to the formation of the 'Welsh and English Baptist Education Society' in 1807. Micah Thomas, a *minister* of an English-language church in Abergavenny, became the first Principal of an Academy formed in that town to teach young Welsh-speaking *men* to communicate the gospel in English. In 1836, Micah Thomas was succeeded by Thomas Thomas who returned to *Wales* from London in order to assume responsibility for the Academy. He became the minister of an English-language church, Crane Street, Pontypool and the College was moved there and housed in a new building erected on a hill overlooking the town. In 1877, W. Mortimer Lewis became the third principal, but due to poor *health*, served only until 1880. He was succeeded by William Edwards who would remain the principal of the College until 1925. In addition to his contribution to scholarship, Edwards and his wife, Sarah Ann (Evans) were influential leaders among Baptists in *Britain* and outspoken in their concern for social reform and the cause of world *mission* and *evangelism*.

As the work of the Academy developed, some *students* were prepared for degrees from the University of London, since Wales was without a University at the time. However, when the University of Wales was established, and the University College of

South Wales and Monmouthshire founded in Cardiff, it was decided to move the Baptist Academy from Pontypool to Cardiff so that it could have closer links with the University of Wales. Since 1893, when it moved to Cardiff, the South Wales Baptist College, as it came to be known, has been affiliated with the University. Students in the Baptist College are registered students of Cardiff University and the tutors are recognised lecturers in the University and take a full part in the Department of Religious and *Theological* Studies. From the time it moved to Cardiff, the College has been ably served by the following Principals: J.M. Davies (1925-28), Thomas Phillips (1928-36), T.W. Chance (1936-43), John Griffiths (1943-47), Edward Roberts (1947-59), Ithel Jones (1959-69), Dafydd Davies (1969-85), Neville Clark (1985-91), Hugh Matthews (1991-2001), John Weaver (2001-).

Today, South Wales Baptist College is recognised by both the Baptist *Union* of Great Britain and the Baptist Union of Wales as a College for training Baptist ministers. The College is recognised as a community of learning in *ministry* and an international centre for the study of *practical theology*. In addition to providing training for applicants from Baptist churches, especially those belonging to mainstream *associations* or unions of churches in Great Britain, the College has a number of post-graduate students who come to Cardiff from the wider global Baptist family.

The core role of the College is the training of potential Baptist ministers, but in addition it is a centre for research and is a resource centre concerned with the equipping of the churches to enable them to be engaged in the mission of *Christ* in the world.

KES

Southern Baptist Convention (SBC)

The SBC is arguably the largest Baptist grouping in the world. Its roots are found in the southern states of the USA, but there are now Southern Baptist churches throughout the USA and Canada and churches which retain close affiliation to the SBC in many parts of the world. It was a founding member of the *Baptist World Alliance* in 1905, but resigned from membership in 2004.

As Baptist congregations were established in the USA in the 1700s their first cooperative venture, in Europe, was in *mission*, through what was called the Triennial Convention founded in 1814. This General Missionary Convention of the Baptist Denomination in the United States of America for Foreign Missions, to give the full title, was a mission-focused agency, initially supporting *overseas mission*, but by 1817 including home mission and *education*. This focus brought diverse Baptist congregations together. However, the issue of slavery and whether a slave-owner could be a missionary gradually divided Baptists north and south of the Mason-Dixon Line. In 1845 most Baptists in the southern states united to form a Southern Baptist Convention working in home and overseas mission where slave-owning would not debar appointment.

The Convention grew through *church planting* and church splits and its Foreign Mission Board (FMB) grew to be the largest *Protestant* international mission organisation in the world.

The SBC, acting through its FMB, has supported work in Europe using their own missionaries and with national Baptist *unions* from 1845-c.2000. Taking part in the BWA meetings to aid reconstruction in Europe in 1920 and 1948, the SBC assisted in work in many parts of Europe, developing the seminaries in *Rüschlikon* (*IBTS*) and Beirut (*Arab Baptist Theological Seminary*) amongst others. From 2000 onwards in most parts of Europe SBC have engaged in parallel mission or working with other '*great commission* Christians', a phrase popular amongst their *missiologists*.

Generally a *conservative* Baptist grouping, issues of *theological* alignment have caused conflict within the Convention at various times in its history. The issue of Landmarkism from the 1850s; Biblical commentaries – especially on the book of Genesis in the 1960s and more recently, what has been called the *Fundamentalist* resurgence from 1979 onwards, have all had repercussions in Europe arising out of the debates in the USA. Now, many Baptist unions in Europe experience the SBC as a group concerned with parallel mission, though some

unions have continued in a satisfactory working relationship with the various Boards and seminaries of the SBC family. Today, the theological climate of the SBC is set largely by the *Calvinist* Albert Mohler (President of Southern Baptist Seminary, Louisville, Kentucky) and Paige Patterson (the *inerrantist* President of South Western Baptist Theological Seminary, Fort Worth, Texas).

KGJ

FURTHER READING: Bill J. Leonard, *Baptist Ways: A History*, Judson, Valley Forge, Pa., 2003. H. Leon McBeth, *The Baptist Heritage*, Broadman and Holman, Nashville, Tn., 1987. Paul Pressler, *A Hill on Which to Die*, Broadman and Holman, Nashville, Tn., 1999. Albert Wardin (ed), *Baptists Around the World*, Broadman and Holman, Nashville, Tn., 1995.

Sovereignty

By definition God must be sovereign in his universe, that is, the one who possesses supreme or ultimate power, for if there were a higher power than his, he would not be God: the word would have lost its meaning. Indeed, to speak of Almighty God is redundant, for 'almightiness' is part of the very nature of God. So to the Hebrew, as later the Christian, mind, all things derive their existence from God and the behaviour of the natural world, the history of the nations, and the lives of all his people are all determined by him just as the potter shapes the clay and determines what it will become. Nothing falls outside his control, and therefore all that happens in the birth, life, *death*, *resurrection* and *ascension* of *Jesus* occurs because he determines that it should be so. But the God who determines the shape of *Christ*'s sacrificial self-giving for the *salvation* of a lost world, also determines the way in which people will respond to his gospel of *grace*, set out in three classic passages of Pauline *theology*: Ro 8:26ff; Ro 9-11 and Eph 1:1-12. But within *orthodox* teaching God's sovereignty must always stop short of, first, making God the author of *sin*, and, secondly, of violating the *free will* of *humankind*, over-riding that ability to make moral choices which is at the heart of its identity. Human choice is real choice. God works through it, rather than over-riding it. To say that God foreordains all things does not mean that he, as in some other *faith* systems, is the cause of all things – as it has been said, 'Our unbelief, e.g., is *our* unbelief; and our coming to Christ, is *our* coming to Christ...Human choices are real choices.' Contrary to the emphases of some *scholars*, you do not make God bigger by making humans smaller, rather the miracle of humanity, with all its complexities of intelligence and emotion, is the peak of his creating skills. Likewise a sovereign God must be free to exercise his grace as he chooses and not be coerced within the constraints of any particular theological system. But a sovereign God cannot be relativised by some modern intellectual fad. Rather this essential affirmation of his sovereignty is an essential guard against all that and a defence of God's authentic character.

ET

Soviet Union, Baptist history in

See *Armenia*; *Azerbaijan*; *Belarus*; *Estonia*; *Georgia*; *Kazakhstan*; *Kyrgyzstan*; *Latvia*; *Lithuania*; *Moldova*; *Russia*; *Tajikistan*; *Turkmenistan*; *Ukraine*; *Uzbekistan*, *Baptist history in*.

Spain, Baptist history in

In the second half of the 19th century, the first modest attempts toward *evangelical* work in *Roman Catholic* Spain was prepared for by the introduction of the liberal Constitution of 1869, which was called *La Gloriosa* and which introduced a brief period of religious tolerance. The way was paved for *Protestant missions* by the liberal Constitution of 1869, which was called *La Gloriosa* and which introduced a brief period of religious tolerance. In the 1870s, the Baptist *evangelist* and *missionary* William Knapp began work in Madrid, Alicante, Valladolid, and Linares. He established the first distinctly Baptist Church in Spain in Madrid in 1870, with a *membership* of 33. By the end of 1876, there were approximately 250 Baptists in Spain. However, after Knapp left Spain in 1876, the churches in Alicante and Linares were closed. The Baptist mission might have been lost altogether had it not been for Eric Lund, a Swede sponsored by the American Baptist Mission [see *American Baptist Churches*], who gave it new fresh impetus. Lund was not alone, however, as Charles A. Haglund came from *Sweden* in 1882, and John Uhr in 1886. Haglund established the first Baptist church in Valencia and Uhr in Bautista de Sabadell.

Baptist missionaries sponsored by the ABM worked specifically in Catalonia, the Swedish Baptists focused their work in the province of Valencia while independent Baptists without denominational links worked in Madrid and central Spain. By the turn of the 20th century, local leadership had grown among Spanish Baptists: Manuel of Canencia in Madrid; Ricardo Cifré, who was working in Barcelona, Hospitalet, Cornellà and Figueres. G.S. Benoliel, pastoring in Alicante, was a founder figure of Alcoy and Lorca's churches. Figueres Baptist Church produced an outstanding evangelist, Gabriel Anglada, who distributed Bibles throughout the Girona province. Francisco Bardonet established the church of *La Escala*, and Manuel Marín became a *pastor* in Barcelona.

When Lund left Spain (1900), Manuel Marín was nominated as the representative of the ABM in Spain. Marín took responsibility for the pastorate in the Sabadell Baptist Church (1905) and devised the publication of a *magazine* El Eco de la Verdad [*The Echo of the Truth*] which continues to be the official publication of the Spanish Baptist *Union*. At the beginning of the 20th century, the Catalonia Baptist churches became independent from the Valencia churches, but the relationships were friendly. Other Baptistic groups had also established work in Spain. E.g. Percy Buffard who had trained at *Regent's Park College* in London established the Spanish Gospel Mission in 1913 with Principal Gould on its Council of Reference. Its headquarters was at Valdepeñas, 200 km south of Madrid. On Percy Buffard's retirement his son Frank, trained at *Spurgeon's College*, took over his father's work.

In 1920, the Executive Committee of the *Baptist World Alliance* restructured the missionary work in Europe. Spain remained under the supervision of the *Southern Baptist Convention*. In 1922 the Spanish Baptist Union was officially established, consisting of 22 churches with 667 members, as well as a *Theological* Institute with 14 *students*. Four years later, in 1926, there were 921

Spanish Baptists. In 1928 at a convention held in Barcelona, Julio Nogal was elected as president and Francisco País as vice president. This convention also dealt with the need to organise the work better by defining areas of Baptist work, and forming area committees. The Spanish Baptists saw a need to promote cooperation between *local churches* and to improve the process of *pastoral* training, which led to the founding of the *Spanish Baptist Theological Seminary*. Mission, *evangelism*, and youth *education* were given priority, and the concern for publishing activities brought about the establishment of a department of publications.

The Spanish Civil War (1936-39) marked a change in the development for all Spanish Protestant groups. A new wave of intolerance towards evangelicals followed, *religious freedom* was seriously hindered in Spain and public opportunities for evangelical work were severely restricted. It would not be until the Constitution of 1978 that Protestant groups could gain new opportunities for work.

However, even during 13 'silent years' (1935-48), in which no conventions could be held, Baptists continued to witness. In 1948 the Baptist Seminary opened its doors, though without any external or public signs. The same year John David Hughey, representing the Foreign Mission Board of the Southern Baptist Convention, arrived in Spain and a *pastoral* conference was held to determine what strategy might be implemented in this situation. In the same year, a convention was held under the motto 'Each Baptist a Missionary'. Also, the first Baptist *Women*'s Conference was organised, with the aim to support Christian homes and to promote missions. Elvira Peradejordi de Vallmitjana became the first President of the Spanish Baptist Women's Missionary Union.

Reorganisation began in 1949 when Samuel Vila, the pastor from Terrassa Baptist Church, left the Spanish Evangelical Baptist Union, because he and those who supported him were unwilling to confine the receipt of financial support exclusively to the Southern Baptist Convention, taking with him 400 members. At that time, Samuel Vila was president of the Spanish Baptist Convention, and director of the Spanish Christian Mission. Vila resigned his position in the Span-

ish Baptist Convention, and continued with the Spanish Christian Mission. Churches related to this mission followed Vila and left the Spanish Baptist Convention. Because of this break off, a new organisation – the Spanish Independent Evangelical Churches Federation – was established.

From its beginning until present, the *Union Evangélica Bautista Española* (UEBE) has undergone a long process of development. In 1959 it had 42 churches and 2,270 members, with 32 Spanish pastors. In 2001 it had 75 churches, 50 domestic missions, and around 8,500 members. The UEBE was one of the founders of the Commission for the Defence of Spanish Evangelical Churches, which at present is known as the Spanish Evangelical Religious Entities Federation. During the last 20 years the UEBE has developed projects focusing on mission work, theological education and social work. Spanish Baptists have also contributed to the field of religious freedom in their country. In 1992 an agreement was reached with the Spanish *state* in which egalitarian treatment was extended to all religious confessions, opening up the possibilities for the action and interaction of the churches with Spanish society. Since WWII, *fundamentalist* Baptists from North America and Strict Baptists from *Britain* have established small-scale mission work in Spain, but outside the fellowship of the *EBF* and the BWA.

AAD

Spain, Baptist Theological Seminary of, Madrid

One of the oldest and most representative institutions of the *Protestant* church in *Spain*, the institution was founded in Barcelona in 1922 as a biblical institute, under the auspices of the Foreign Mission Board of the *Southern Baptist Convention*. The financial crisis of 1929 brought about the closing of the institute, fully dependent as it was on foreign contributions. In 1948, the institution opened again this time as a seminary. In the 70s the seminary moved its location to Alcobendas (Madrid). Although over the years its primary focus has been the training of candidates for the Baptist *ministry*, the Spanish seminary is now an open institution with *students* from different denominations and nationalities. The academic programme has grown to a four-year residential degree, together with an open curriculum programme offering training in different areas of ministry at different levels and a growing non-residential programme geared towards the training of lay leadership who serve in local congregations [see *Laity*].

FMM

Speaking in/with tongues
See *Glossolalia*.

Spirit
See *Pneumatology*.

Spiritual Formation
In recent decades there has been much discussion of spiritual formation, particularly in the area of *theological education*. The increased attention given to spiritual formation has been a marked feature of seminary education, among Baptists and others. E. Glenn Hinson and Molly T. Marshall have been among leading Baptist educators who have given attention to this issue. Glenn Hinson wrote on 'The Spiritual Formation of the *Minister* as a Person' in 1973, and in the following year his important book, *A Serious Call to a Contemplative Life-Style*, appeared. In 1998 Molly Marshall described how Baptists, like other *Protestants*, were going to *retreat* centres, using spiritual directors, and incorporating silence and the *lectio divina* into their private prayer.

However, Baptist seminaries have always given attention to the spiritual life. E.g. *Spurgeon's College*, which for most of the times since its establishment in 1856 has been the largest Baptist seminary in Europe, was started by *C.H. Spurgeon* because he believed that 'the maintenance of a truly spiritual College is probably the readiest way in which to bless the churches'. In the 20th century, however, the priority in many Baptist Colleges seemed to be academic excellence. A British Baptist *Union* report in 1928 suggested that 'the spirit of consecration and Christian zeal is in danger of evaporating in an atmosphere dominated by intellectual and technical studies'.

From the 1980s in particular, European Baptist seminaries began to introduce courses that had spiritual and *missional* formation as their focus. Many new seminaries have opened in Eastern Europe since the early 1990s and across Europe there is a Consortium of Baptist Schools. The *International Baptist Theological Seminary*, Prague, is at the heart of this network and Parush Parushev, the Academic Dean of IBTS, has contrasted *theological* education within and for the 'thick community of *faith*', an education that develops and shapes the identity of those who belong to it, with the 'thin community' of academic and public discourse, which is concerned only with academic pursuits according to the rules of the academic game. A desire for training which offers *holistic* development has become central to the European Baptist vision.

IMR

FURTHER READING: M.T. Marshall, 'The Changing Face of Discipleship' in *Review and Expositor*, Vol. 95, No. 1 (1998). P.R. Parushev, 'Towards Convictional Theological Education: Facing challenges of contextualisation, credibility and relevance' in P.F. Penner (ed), *Theological Education as Mission*, IBTS, Prague, 2005, pp.198-99. P.R. Parushev, '"To give the first place to spiritual fervour": Priorities for seminary education' in *Journal of European Baptist Studies*, Vol. 7, No. 2 (2007), pp.6-20.

Spiritual Gifts
See *Fruits and Gifts of the Spirit*.

Spirituality/Devotional Life
[See also *Piety, Baptist*]
The language of Spirituality, replacing the more familiar language of the Devotional Life, has to do with our relationship with God and also with others. There are theological and practical dimensions to spirituality, which in recent years has received renewed attention from Baptists and *Anabaptists*. Using a framework proposed by Philip Sheldrake in an essay in *Exploring Christian Spirituality* (2000), spirituality may be seen as concerned with the conjunction of *theology*, *communion* with God and practical Christianity. In *believers' church traditions* Christian commitment begins with *conver-*

sion, which is almost always regarded as an intensely personal experience, and is followed by **baptism**. Although some Baptists have seen baptism as primarily a human act of **witness**, in which the believer expresses obedience to **Christ**, others have understood it as a spiritual experience and a means of **grace** as believers identify themselves with the **death**, burial and **resurrection** of Jesus, thereby underlining what he has done for us. For Baptists the Christian life is nourished primarily by the **Bible**, by **prayer** and through participating in the **fellowship** of believers within the life of the **local church** which historically, in Baptist congregations has been strong. In the Baptist context, prayer, whether corporate or individual, has usually been spontaneous, with only the rare use of printed aids. **John Smyth**, following the **Separatist** tradition, saw **church members** as bound together in a mutual **covenant**. The church members committed themselves both to obey God and to carry out the 'duties of **love**' to each other. In the 19th century, as Baptist congregations in **Britain** and America grew larger, there was much less sense of sharing: the **preacher** was seen as the person with the inspired message and the people were present to receive it. A final characteristic of Baptist spirituality has been a strong commitment to **mission**. The 18th-century **revival** movements had a powerful impact on Baptists and since then there has been a great deal of commonality between **evangelical** and Baptist spirituality In the contemporary situation some Baptists have found their spiritual quest enhanced by participating in retreats or visiting centres such as **Iona** or **Taizé**.

IMR

FURTHER READING: G.A. Furr and C.W. Freeman (eds), *Ties that Bind: Life Together in the Baptist Vision*, Smyth and Helwys, Macon, Ga., 1994. I.M. Randall, *What a Friend we have in Jesus*, Darton, Longman and Todd, London, 2005. Philip Sheldrake, 'What is Spirituality?', in K.J. Collins, (ed), *Exploring Christian Spirituality*, Baker Books, Grand Rapids, Mi., 2000.

Sport, Baptists and

In the 19th century Christians made a significant contribution to the development of sport in **Britain**. This was an important as-

pect of what was sometimes called 'the institutional church' which sought to provide a total cultural experience for its **members** not one confined to the **worship** of the **sanctuary**. Many churches formed sports teams and encouraged the playing of sport to promote 'a healthy mind in a healthy body', so that, e.g., a number of famous football teams have church or **Sunday School** origins. There was, however, opposition to sport, often because of its association with drinking [see **Alcohol**; **Alcoholism**] and **gambling** and with Sunday play [see **Sabbath**], though equally sporting activity, detached from the public house, was seen as a powerful antidote to an alcohol controlled **leisure** environment.

Baptists were to be found in both camps. There were Baptist church teams in Mansfield in the East Midland region of **England** in the late 19th century. Sunday School and **Boy's Brigade** teams were very common. By contrast, in 1896 the **deacons** of Linanus Baptist Chapel, Treherbert, in **Wales**, threatened excommunication to 'anyone connected with rugby'.

In 1911 one of the best known Baptist **ministers** of that period, F.B. Meyer, led a successful campaign to stop a world heavyweight boxing match from taking place in London. His main concern appeared to be the brutality of it. In the end the fight was halted when the owners of Earls Court (the venue for the fight), obtained a court injunction stopping the fight from taking place. The judge who granted the injunction was a Baptist. For many people this was an example of an encounter between sport and Christianity where Christians showed a negative attitude to sport.

In the late 20th century Baptists played a prominent part in the re-engagement of sport and Christianity. Two British Baptist ministers, Peter Swaffield and John Boyers, served as **Chaplains** at the Olympics and the Commonwealth Games. John Boyers also founded a Sports Chaplaincy organisation, SCORE, with Baptist **Union** of Great Britain **Home Mission** support, and has promoted sports chaplaincy in Britain and other countries. From the 1960s onwards many Baptist churches became involved in running football teams and organised sports events as a bridge to the community.

IMR

FURTHER READING: S. Mews, 'Puritanicalism, Sport and Race: A Symbolic Crusade of 1911' in *Popular Belief and Practice*, Studies in Church History, Vol. 8, G.J. Cuming and D. Baker (eds), Cambridge University Press, Cambridge, 1972.

Spring Harvest and Greenbelt

Spring Harvest (SH) and Greenbelt emerged from the *UK* Christian *music* sub-culture of the 1970s. 2,000 people attended the first Greenbelt festival (Suffolk, 1974), 3,000 the first SH holiday (North Wales, 1979). Both events have subsequently been held annually, with considerable growth during the 1980s followed by decline during the 1990s; from a high for SH of 80,000 and of 30,000 for Greenbelt. In 2005 SH catered for 55,000 at two sites during its annual *Easter* event, whilst Greenbelt drew 17,500.

Despite a similar heritage, each has their distinct ethos. SH's *evangelical* leadership welcomed *charismatic* renewal and declared itself to exist, 'to equip the *church* for action'. Greenbelt developed a keen interest in the relationship of Christian *faith* to culture, particularly the arts. It has tended to see the concern for global justice as a higher priority than charismatic renewal. Initially, Greenbelt had the more global vision, though SH has not been slow to engage at notable moments. It wrote to the UK Government about the Falklands crisis (1982) and, through its Charitable Trust, has supported agencies working with *HIV-AIDS* (1988), the *Balkans* conflict (1994), and the Kosovo crisis (1999).

Similarities remain, however. Each supports a considerable musical Christian sub-culture and their respective markets. Throughout the 1980s a series of new *worship* resources began to displace unused copies of the Baptist *Hymn* Book. Baptist Praise and Worship (1991) struggled to survive in an over-supplied worship marketplace. Mildly charismatic worship styles became commonplace in Baptist churches as a consequence of SH's influence. Greenbelt offered a safe space for experimenting with forms of alternative worship; 'Celtic', *Taizé*, *Iona*, and *Northumbrian*, that would similarly reappear in Baptist Sunday worship. Each has enabled new life and energy to flow into existing mainline denominations.

By 2005 both events had developed extensive partnerships. Greenbelt's 'open' evangelicalism strengthened its ties with agencies including *Christian Aid*, CMS, and SPCK, that enabled it to maintain its identity as a festival, located within the mainstream that exists for those unimpressed by overly charismatic worship. Simultaneously, Baptists represented on the Leadership of SH (including former BUGB General Secretary David Coffey, Ian Coffey, Steve Chalke, and Steve Gaukroger) have helped to ensure that the SH emphasis on teaching and worship, whilst maintaining an evangelical focus, has broadened its appeal to the mainstream of denominational life in the UK.

Though each continues to attract its own distinctive enthusiasts, Baptists in the UK would be the poorer in their common worship and *witness* if it were not for these two events; each creating, in their own way, a space, 'where the church can be re-imagined'.

DJ

Spurgeon, Charles Haddon (1834-92)

Charles Haddon Spurgeon was regarded as the greatest *preacher* in the Victorian era in *Britain*. His *conversion* took place at 15, in a *Methodist chapel* in Colchester. Following this, Spurgeon was baptised [see *Baptism*] in 1851. He began to preach and at the age of 17 became *pastor* of the Baptist chapel in the village of Waterbeach, near Cambridge. Two years later he was called to the historic New Park Street Chapel, Southwark, London – once the congregation of John Gill and later of John Rippon – but was in decline. The crowds coming to hear Spurgeon's powerful *preaching* were so great that the largest available building in London – the Royal Surrey Gardens Music Hall – was hired. A new place of *worship*, the Metropolitan Tabernacle, at the Elephant and Castle, London, was opened in 1861. The Tabernacle, which held over 5,000 people, was filled twice every Sunday throughout Spurgeon's life. During his *ministry* 14,460 people were baptised and added to the *membership*. The *theology* espoused by Spurgeon was *evangelical Calvinism*. He engaged in two major controversies. In 1864 he challenged evangelical clergyman in the *Church of England* to show that it was possible in good *faith* to service a church that officially taught baptismal regeneration. During this controversy he resigned from the *Evangelical Alliance*, although he later re-joined. In the 1880s Spurgeon became concerned about *liberal* trends in theology and he resigned from the Baptist *Union* in the Downgrade Controversy. In 1856 Spurgeon started the Pastor's College (later *Spurgeon's College*) to train those converted under his ministry who were developing as preachers. Other significant developments included the founding of a *colportage* society and of a successful *orphanage*. Land was secured at Stockwell, London, for the orphanage, and orphan houses were opened in 1867. Spurgeon's *sermons* were published each week and were read widely across the world. He also published a range of books such as *Lectures to my Students*, which has had a great influence on Baptist preaching, and a six-volume commentary on the Psalms, *The Treasury of David*. Spurgeon's health was not robust: he often went to the south of *France* to recuperate, and it was there that he died.

IMR

FURTHER READING: J.C. Carlile, *C.H. Spurgeon: An Interpretative Biography*, The Kingsgate Press, London, 1933. L.A. Drummond, *Spurgeon: Prince of Preachers*, Kregel, Grand Rapids, Mi., 1992. P.S. Kruppa, *Charles Haddon Spurgeon: A Preacher's Progress*, Garland, New York, 1982.

Spurgeon's College, London

Spurgeon's College (originally the Pastor's College), was founded by *C.H. Spurgeon* in 1856. Of all Spurgeon's endeavours, he saw the College as his 'first-born and best beloved'. George Rogers, a *Congregational minister*, was the first Principal. Within 10 years the College grew to 80-90 *students*, many of whom planted new Baptist churches. Spurgeon was College President. It was reported in 1872 that 20,000 people had been added to the *membership* of churches where former students were pastors. In 1923 the College moved from near the Metropolitan Tabernacle to South Norwood, London. In 1881 David Gracey, an Irishman, became Principal, followed in 1898, by Archibald McCaig, a Scot. When Spurgeon died in 1892 the number of students trained at the

College was 863, with 627 serving as pastors, *evangelists* and *missionaries*. A considerable number of Spurgeon's students have gone *overseas*. In the early decades of the College there was little emphasis on academic achievement and many students had very limited *education*. The focus was on preparing effective preachers and spiritual leaders. Percy Evans, Principal from 1925-50, enhanced the College's academic reputation, developing University links. George Beasley-Murray, who joined the staff in 1950, was an outstanding academic. He had a period teaching at the Baptist *Theological* Seminary, *Rüschlikon*, and became Spurgeon's Principal in 1957. His combination of exacting scholarship and *evangelistic* commitment set the direction the College would take under the principalships of Raymond Brown, Paul Beasley-Murray (the son of George), Michael Quicke and Nigel Wright. Spurgeon's, now a multi-cultural community, is the largest Baptist college in *Britain*, offering full-time and part-time training for ordained [see *Ordination*] and lay [see *Laity*] *ministries* as well as Open Learning and postgraduate courses.

IMR

FURTHER READING: D.W. Bebbington, 'Spurgeon and British Evangelical Theological Education' in D.G. Hart and R.A. Mohler, Jr. (eds), *Theological Education in the Evangelical Tradition*, Baker Books, Grand Rapids, Mi., 1996. M. Nicholls, *Lights to the World: A History of Spurgeon's College, 1856-1992*, Nuprint, Harpenden, 1994. I.M. Randall, *A School of the Prophets: 150 years of Spurgeon's College*, Spurgeon's College, London, 2005.

St. Petersburg Christian University, Russia

St. Petersburg Christian University (SPCU) had its origins in the Krasnodar region of Southern *Russia*. It dates back to autumn 1990, when the Russian Bible Institute was founded as an initiative of the Russian-German *mission* Logos Int. and the Russian Baptist *Union*, then under the leadership of Victor E. Logvinenko. In 1992 the school moved to the northern capital of Russia, to St. Petersburg, and changed its name in Nov 1993 to St. Petersburg Christian University.

Today the institution is governed by an

international Board and offers Bachelor degrees in *Theology*, Christian *Education* and Youth Ministries [see *Youth Work*] as well as a validated Master of Theology degree in Biblical Studies. *Students* come primarily from Baptist churches of countries of the former *Soviet Union* and are trained to go back to their region to continue in their various Christian *ministries*. From 1990 until today the institution has developed from having purely Western leadership and faculty and supported by Western resources to a position where it is able to include more national faculty, appoint full national leadership and raise some national resources. SPCU has its own facilities. Its educational programmes are supported by a theological library of about 18,000 volumes.

PFP

State, Baptist approaches to the

[See also *Nation/Nationalism*; *National Churches*; *Secularisation*; *Separation of Church and State*]
The word state can be used in a number of ways. Sometimes it means a *politically* defined geographical territory, sometimes a nation, sometimes the administration and government. At the time of the *Reformation*, the Magisterial Reformers allied themselves with secular rulers whom they construed in the role of the godly magistrate whether a German prince or the corporate magistracy of a Swiss town council, who became active partners in implementing the reformation. By contrast the radicals eschewed all alliances with state authorities, living in their own separated, and, as far as possible, self supporting communities, refusing the swearing of oaths and office as magistrates. Persecuted for this, their response to state authority was often the acceptance of *martyrdom*.

Baptists do not follow the *Anabaptists* in rejecting the State. Rather they are committed to being good citizens and to offering lawfully appointed governments their support. In the 1644 Particular Baptist confession [see *England*], which sought in part to distinguish English Baptists from continental Anabaptism, there are paragraphs about the magistrate (that is the ruler) exercising *authority* as 'an ordinance of God...for the

punishment of evil doers and for the praise of them that do good' and two years later they added a new paragraph making it quite clear that it was perfectly legitimate for a Christian to undertake the office of magistrate. The magistrate was there to maintain order and punish *sin* in a fallen world [see *Fall*]: the state is not part of the *creation* order but for the control of a world in rebellion against its Creator. This in no way lightens Christian responsibility to be critically involved in the work of the state in active citizenship, with the corresponding requirement that forms of government enable *democratic* participation in all that affects the citizen's lives. Indeed Christians as citizens of God's *kingdom* have an obligation to challenge secular authority to do justice, to seek *peace*, to exercise mercy and act compassionately towards those in need.

The extent of the state's agenda is fiercely debated. Whilst some would argue that it has a responsibility to promote the welfare of all, and especially the improvement of the lot of the *poor* and the marginalised, others argue that the state's functions should be minimalist, leaving to individual and voluntary initiative such matters as *educational* improvement. Complicating the issue is the undeniable fact that in the process of *globalisation* the sovereignty of the state is challenged by powerful international organisations whose budgets, and therefore power to intervene and to control, dwarfs that of some nation states.

Jesus teaches the obligation to give to God that which is God's and to Caesar that which is Caesar's but does not define where the line of demarcation is to be drawn. Thus, if the secular power were to require actions which violated an individual's *conscience*, then refusal to comply, argued the early Baptists, was appropriate though the individual should not resist the punishment consequent upon this, and over the ages, including the present time, many Baptists have been fined and imprisoned for reasons of conscience. Baptists generally believe in the separation of church and state, rather than granting to the state, powers within the church as found, e.g., within those 'established' or state churches which enjoy a number of privileges from the state but also are overall subject to its intervention, e.g. in the appointment of **bishops**. The principle is easy to state, more difficult to implement, e.g. when registration with the state is the price of **pastoral** survival. Even in the western democracies churches have come to accept certain privileges from the state, e.g. in tax matters, for which they then become accountable.

How citizens should react to a state behaving unjustly raises many questions. At what point does a government forfeit the allegiance of its citizens? How are opposition politics to be organised, what is legitimate and what is not? How do the powerless respond to unjust state systems that have a monopoly of power? The **Lutheran tradition**, working from the instructions in Ro 13, has tended to be more accepting of government action, whereas the **Reformed** tradition, influenced by Rev 13 has been more suspicious of state authority abusing its supremacy. In the modern world some states have so exaggerated their powers that they put themselves, by way of supreme **heresy**, in the place of God as the sole arbiter of affairs.

JHYB

State Churches

See **National Churches**; **Separation of Church and State**.

Stewardship

The concept of stewardship is inherent to Christian **theology** and is expounded in the **creation** accounts where humanity is given the responsibility by God to take care of creation – to be the steward of that which God has created.

This concept of stewardship has had a varied career within the Christian **church**. At some times in church history it has been assumed that this provided a *carte blanche* for the people of God and the Church to take and, use and abuse all the created order. At other times it has provoked within the Church a deep ethical concern for the care and preservation of creation so that Christians have been in the forefront of calls not to exploit the earth and to find ways of ameliorating the worst effects of industrialisa-

tion. In contemporary times this has come to lead to concerns about **ecology**, **climate change**, the proliferate use of non-renewable resources such as coal, oil and gas, the despoiling of water courses with human made chemicals and pollutants.

A secondary understanding of stewardship amongst Baptists has been the concern that all within a particular community of **faith** should commit portions of their time, talents and treasure to the work of the church. Some Baptists in Western Europe had special 'Stewardship campaigns' in the second half of the 20th century when those involved in gathering churches were encouraged to **tithe** and then make specific commitments to give so much of their time each week to the diaconal and **missional** programmes of their churches and to identify and use their talents in the service of the **local church**. Such campaigns were intended to place a proper reminder within the communities of the ongoing demands of **discipleship**. This form of stewardship campaign is not now so common in Baptist churches, but the concern for disciples to commit themselves in a regular and sustained way to the total **ministry** of the church and to participate in funding the ministry and mission of the local church and its world-wide concerns continues to be an important feature of Baptist churches across Europe.

KGJ

Stockholm School of Theology, Sweden

The Stockholm School of Theology/*Teologiska högskolan Stockholm* (THS) was founded in 1996 as an amalgamation of institutions from the Baptist **Union** of **Sweden**, the United **Methodist** Church of Sweden and the Swedish Mission Covenant Church. Previously Swedish Baptists had their own Bethel Seminary (founded 1866). It is the school where Swedish Baptist **pastors** are trained and is a member of **CEBTS**.

THS provides under-graduate education (Bachelor's degrees) in both **theology** and a **human rights** programme. The theology programme lasts for four years. Through cooperation agreements with other universities in the Nordic countries, THS also provides post-graduate education (MA, PhD/ThD) through courses as well as supervision of theses. It is the major provider of religious and human rights education in the Stockholm region.

In full-time as well as part-time courses THS gives training to some 500 **students** annually. The School receives students with a variety of denominational and non-denominational backgrounds, in a climate of academic rigour, international exposure and intellectual challenge. Most programmes are in Swedish, but occasionally courses or seminars are offered in English, according to need and interest. A wide network of international academic and other institutional contacts gives a resource-base for international exchange for the School's students and professors, as well as for a flow of international guests, students, and visiting **scholars**. It is located in Bromma, a few kilometres from Stockholm, and close to the Castle of Åkeshof.

KGJ

Street People, Work with

See *Homeless, Work with the*

Strict Communion

[See also *Communion and Intercommunion; Eucharistic Liturgy; Open Communion*]
For many Baptists strict (or closed) communion is the norm. Admission to the table is restricted to **members** of the **local church**, baptised as believers by immersion [see *Baptism*], and extended only to visitors commended as similarly qualified. In 19th-century *England* many churches moved to a more open stance, sharing table fellowship with other *evangelical* Christians, but other Baptists reacted against this, stressing their strict practice. Joseph Kinghorn (1766-1832) of Norwich was a leading advocate of the strict position. This was shared by *J.G. Oncken* of Hamburg and the European Baptists of the 19th century connected with the German Baptist movement. In England some strict *Calvinistic* churches formed bodies of Strict (and Particular) Baptists, separate from the churches of the Baptist *Union*, that is to say they upheld the doctrine of Particular

Redemption and practiced Strict Communion. But *C.H. Spurgeon* held together Calvinistic *soteriology* and an open communionist *ecclesiology*, and his stance on communion had considerable influence. During the 20th century other ecclesial issues came to the fore and fewer Baptist churches were inclined to make an issue of strict communion. Practice varies significantly in the unions and conventions within the *EBF*, however, and the restriction of communion to those baptised as believers would be the normal procedure in a considerable number of communities.

FWB & ET

Student Christian Movement (SCM), Inter-Varsity Fellowship (IVF), World Student Christian Federation (WSCF) and International Fellowship of Evangelical Students (IFES)

[See also *Students, Baptist*]
The Student Christian Movement has its origins in three developments: the establishment of *YMCA* branches on University and College campuses in the late 1850s; the consuming interest of university students in *missionary* endeavour which developed at the same time and which would later be called the 'volunteer' movement with the Student Volunteer Movement for Foreign *Missions* formed in 1887; and the work of the D.L. Moody on university campuses also in the 1880s. The primary aim of the movement was 'missionary and *evangelistic*', a motivation which overcame initially differences of *nation*, denomination and *theology* in pursuit of the great aim succinctly expressed in the watchword: 'the evangelisation of the world in this generation'. In 1877 the Cambridge Inter Collegiate Christian Union was founded and its Oxford counterpart followed a year later. In 1893 an Inter-University Christian Union was founded with the aim of deepening the spiritual life of students and winning others for *Christ*.

Similar developments were taking place in North America, and in *Scandinavia* Karl Fries of the Stockholm YMCA, Count Moltke of the Danish student missionary union, and Pastor Martin Eckhoff who exercised a simi-

lar role in **Norway** began to organise international conferences at one of which convened
at Vadstena Castle in Sweden the World Student Christian Federation was founded in
1895. Increasingly seen as an impediment to
mission, the divisions of the churches became a central concern of the movement
and it is not surprising that out of its counsels would emerge so many leaders of the
emerging **ecumenical movement**, such as
J.H. Oldham from the **United Kingdom**,
John Mott of the USA, and Nathan Söderblom, later to become Archbishop of **Sweden**. By 2000 it was active in some 60 countries. Not only so but the SCM formed a
training ground for church leadership in the
first half of the 20th century, providing opportunity for future church leaders to forge
deep friendships.

In 1910 the Cambridge Inter-Collegiate
Christian Union withdrew from the SCM
partly over divergent views on the **inspiration** of **scripture** and partly because it did
not agree with an increasing emphasis on
social and **political** problems in the SCM's
study programmes. This division was later
compounded by SCM's desire to open its
membership to all Christians, including both
Roman Catholics and **Orthodox**. From this
decision of the CICCU has grown the Inter-
Varsity Fellowship (later renamed the Universities and Colleges Christian Fellowship
[UCCF]) which joined together with other
national bodies in 1947 to form the International Fellowship of Evangelical Students
which by 2000 was active in 140 countries
with a **ministry** which is both evangelistic
and concerned to deepen **discipleship**
through disciplined **Bible study**. Both the
conservative IFES/IVF and the increasingly
radical WSCF have brought into being major
publishing houses – the SCM Press and the
Inter-Varsity Press (IVP).

JHYB

Students, Baptist

In Europe, societies for Baptist students at
University have existed since the beginning
of the 20th century. The Robert Hall Society
was formed in Cambridge in 1902 and the
John Bunyan Society in Oxford soon followed. The Baptist Students' Federation (BSF)
was established in 1947, to 'increase among

Baptist students a sense of responsibility and
opportunities of service in the Denomination'. The 1950s saw considerable advance
within the BSF. The number of societies grew
to 24, and some attracted more than 100
students. An annual conference was held.
Total BSF membership reached 882 in 1967.
Many Baptist leaders were nurtured through
the BSF. Among the BSF Presidents was John
Briggs, later one of the leading lay figures
[see **Laity**] in Baptist life in Europe and beyond. He was Pro-Vice-Chancellor of Birmingham University. Another BSF President
was Keith Clements, who became Secretary
of the **Conference of European Churches**.
David Goodbourn, BSF Secretary in the
1970s, became the first lay person to hold
the post of General Secretary of Churches
Together in **Britain** and **Ireland**. Another
problem was that the language of student
was broadened to include all in post secondary **education**, many of whom remained in
their home churches, whilst university and
college students were increasingly reluctant
to separate themselves from other young
people.

From its beginning the BSF sought to
avoid aligning itself with either the **Student
Christian Movement** or the more theologically **conservative** Inter-Varsity Fellowship. It
tried to promote closer cooperation between
all Christian students. For a time the BSF was
active in encouraging Baptists to think about
overseas mission and also involved students
in **local church** missions during vacation
periods. But by the 1960s Baptist young
people starting university were increasingly
attracted to the growing interdenominational Christian Unions associated
with the IVF. The weakening of a sense of
denominational identity meant that fewer
Baptist students were interested in joining a
denominational society. Also, as David Bebbington, notes, the collapse of the SCM in
the 1970s gave the IVF (which changed its
name to the Universities and College Christian Fellowship) a clear field.

Through the fellowship that they experienced in the BSF, students were introduced
to Baptist life beyond Britain. In 1952 the
first post-war **Baptist World Alliance** student conference was held at the Baptist
Seminary in **Rüschlikon, Switzerland**. BSF
representatives attended. Other **European**

Baptist Federation student conferences were held later, e.g. in Hamburg. But across Europe the growth of the International Fellowship of Evangelical Students (IFES) meant that many Baptists at continental European universities were drawn into wider *evangelical fellowship*, rather than specifically Baptist student groups. In Britain uncertainty about the role of the BSF led to the decision in 1977 to wind it up, a move regretted by some Baptist leaders such as Ernest Payne. What the BSF did achieve was the encouragement of many Baptist students to take seriously church-based Christian commitment, the result being that many went on to make a significant contribution to Baptist life.

IMR

FURTHER READING: D.W. Bebbington, *Evangelicalism in Modern Britain: A History from the 1730s to the 1980s*, Routledge, London, 1995.

Stundism

The Russian word *Stundist* is etymologically related to the German *stunde* [hour] and designates the German and Russian participants of *worship* and *fellowship* gatherings which were held in addition to the main Church service. German **Pietism** became known in **Russia** in the early 19th century through writings of J.A. Bengel and J.H. Jung, who is normally known as Jung-Stilling, and others, as well as through the *preaching* of Ignaz Lindl and Johann Gossner in St. Petersburg, Johann and Karl Bonekemper in the Black Sea area, Eduard Wüst in South Russia among others. Through their work, Pietist groups among German colonists mainly in the southern part of Russia came into being. The colonists did not hide their convictions before their Ukrainian and Russian neighbours, and in the late 1850s, the first Ukrainian, Fedor Onishchenko from the village of Osnova near Odessa, experienced *conversion*. The spread of Stundism in Russian **Orthodox** parishes went hand in hand with the growing self-determination of the Russian peasants following their release from serfdom in 1861. Additional impulses came from the newly available Russian NT that was published in 1862 with the blessing of the Holy **Synod**.

Stundism, as a Russian form of Pietism, unfolded its real power through fellowship. In a short time, half of Osnova participated in Stundist meetings. The mode of those meetings was very different from the Orthodox **Liturgy**. The Russian Orthodox Church strictly rejected such new forms of piety and made the Stundists its enemies. The tensions culminated in a complete split caused by the *baptism* of believers and the establishing of new separate Churches especially by those Stundist who had been influenced by German Baptists and **Mennonite Brethren**. This split occurred in 1869 (after the baptism of the Ukrainian Efim Tsÿmbal) and 1870 (the establishing of the first Russian Baptist Churches). In this way, the Stundist movement became a preparation for the emergence of Baptist Churches. In this sense, the Stundist phase lasted only a decade ending in 1870.

Not all Stundists became Baptists. Some of them experienced a new feeling of freedom and did not want to follow the strict order of a Baptist Church. So, the Stundist community in the village of Chaplinka near Kiev had more than 1,000 *members*. Stundists were also sometimes considered the *Novomolokane* (New *Molokans*) who *preached* conversion but did not reject *infant baptism* as the Pietists usually did. These communities were led by Zinovii Zakharov and numbered about 20 congregations.

The Russian government deliberately did not distinguish between Baptists and Stundists and harshly persecuted both groups until the end of the 19th century.

JD

FURTHER READING: *Istoriya evangel'skikh khristian-baptistov v SSSR*, VSEKHB, Moscow, 1989.

SU

See *Scripture Union*.

Suffering

The question of suffering has led to profound *theological* reflection and at the same time has called for a *pastoral* response rather than an academic one. For Baptists theological reflection takes place in relation to *scrip-*

ture. In the OT *sin* is presented as the dominant reason for the suffering in the world. The story of the *Fall* (Ge 3) presents human disobedience as the root cause of suffering. As a result of sin there is a reversal of the arranged world of the first story of *creation*, to some extent a reversion back to a state of chaos. Suffering as retribution for sin, often as a collective punishment as well as a response to individual sin, is dominant in the Deuteronomic writings. The exilic experience of suffering is explained by the sins of the fathers, and especially the sins of the Kings. Other insights are to be found in some of the Proverbs (e.g. Pr 2:21-22).

The experience of the exile in the story of *Israel* is taken up by the Prophets. Both Ezekiel and Jeremiah (Eze 18, Jer 31:29-30) question the common view which simply stated that all suffering could be explained as a punishment for the sins of the fathers. Ezekiel insisted that everyone must answer for their own sin (Eze 18:4).

Job, as the most sustained work on suffering in the OT, answers the question about unjust suffering in two ways. Firstly the book stresses the participation of an evil force [see *Devil*]. Secondly, the book allows life to have a certain mystery, which is especially clear in the response of God when he refuses to answer directly the accusations of Job.

In the NT the gospels take some of these themes further. In Jn 9 the question is asked of *Jesus* about a blind man – who sinned, this man or his parents, that he was born blind? The answer of Jesus is clear: neither this man sinned nor his parents. Similarly, in Lk 13 Jesus denied that 18 people in Siloam who were killed when the tower fell on them were worse sinners than others in Jerusalem.

It is evident in the gospel records that part of the agenda of Jesus was to diminish suffering (Lk 4:18-19). This was seen in his *healing ministry*. Also, the passion narratives in the gospels emphasise Christ entering into the depths of human suffering on the *cross*. The way in which God in Christ took suffering on himself has, most famously, been explored by Moltmann in *The Crucified God* and by the European Baptist *theologian* Paul Fiddes in *The Creative Suffering of God*. The way in which the NT focuses on the cross does not solve all the problems of human suffering, and the engagement with issues of theodicy remains a theological challenge. Alongside this, Baptists have been very much aware that the NT does not teach that Christians will be exempt from suffering. Paul words have often been quoted: 'through many tribulations we must enter the *kingdom of God*' (Ac 14:22). Such suffering has been the experience of many Baptist communities.

There is an important *eschatological* element to the biblical understanding of suffering. The vision of the Book of Revelation is that there will be the final retribution for sin at the end of time, and that in the new *heaven* and the new earth God will 'wipe away every tear from their eyes, and death shall be no more, neither shall there be mourning, nor crying, nor pain any more, for the former things have passed away' (Rev 21:4).

KTB & ET

FURTHER READING: James L. Crenshaw (ed), *Theodicy in the Old Testament*, SPCK, London and Fortress, Philadelphia, 1983. Paul Fiddes, *The Creative Suffering of God*, Clarendon, Oxford, 1992. John McDermott, *The Bible on human suffering*, St. Paul, Slough, 1990. Jürgen Moltmann, *The Crucified God*, Harper and Row, New York, 1974.

Summer Institute of Theological Education (SITE)

SITE was the brain child of Denton Lotz when serving as Professor of *Missions* at *IBTS, Rüschlikon*, in the early 1970s. It was agreed that during the months of Jul and Aug when the regular *students* of the seminary were on summer vacation, *pastors* and leaders from throughout Europe would be gathered for an education programme to give them skills in English and lectures in *theology*, *Bible* studies and mission and *church* development topics. Largely funded by *American Baptist Churches* International Ministries, the SITE event became an important feature of the life of the institution and acquired a good name amongst pastors in Central and Eastern Europe who had not had many opportunities for formal education. Successive ABC missionaries attached to IBTS ran the SITE programme including Harry L. Moore and, latterly, David M.

Brown. With the change in style and work of the seminary in 1998, the SITE programme was re-named as 'Director's Conferences' and held in shorter periods at different points during the year as many pastors found it increasingly difficult to be away from their responsibilities for several weeks at a time. SITE, which lasted in that particular format for about 25 years, was an important way of bringing Baptist pastors together from all over Europe in a situation encouraging mutual learning, common *prayer* and development of *koinonia*.

KGJ

Sunday Observance
See *Sabbath*.

Sunday Schools

The founding of Sunday Schools from the 1780s onwards was one of the many outcomes of the *Evangelical Revival*. They had overlapping objectives. Many were concerned with basic literacy and inculcating decent standards of disciplined behaviour. Next to *overseas missions* they represented the major mission investment – in terms of finance, *labour* and skills – of Baptist churches, and so they had a clear *evangelistic* intention. In the 1851 government census Baptist churches in *England* had more than 155,000 enrolled *scholars* with a peak figure of some 570,000 in 1906. Not easily fulfilled alongside that task was the Christian nurture of *church members' children*, fulfilling that crucial catechetical task of bridging the gap between infant *dedication*, and the parental promises there made, and believers' *baptism*. There were two ways of considering Sunday School statistics. From the point of view of the membership of the church many would claim life in the Sunday School as a formative experience in their coming to Christian *faith*. Viewed, however, from the perspective of those initially recruited the wastage was enormous with barely a tithe becoming church members. They were, however, effective in diffusing a basic Christian culture widely across society.

In the early years there were disputes over a number of things, whether writing could be taught on Sundays, as unlike reading not essential to the communication of gospel truths, the legitimacy of corporate punishment, the use of paid or exclusively volunteer teachers. The major lay [see *Laity*] initiative of the century, offering situations of useful involvement for almost the first time to armies of evangelical *women*, it was 'the only religious institution which the 19th century public in the mass had any intention of using' In the manufacturing communities in *Britain* about half those who received any elementary *education* in the first part of the century received it from Sunday Schools indicating that the churches were thereby making a major contribution to mass literacy. Across Europe *J.G. Oncken* was a great believer in the Sunday School movement and so a similar pattern of classes and graded teaching began to flourish wherever Oncken's *missionaries* established causes. A clear evangelistic intention amongst children was at the core of his concern.

In many towns in England Sunday Schools originally enjoyed *ecumenical* sponsorship but soon became functions of emerging denominationalism, indeed a source of rivalry between competing *chapels*. The building of a school behind or next to the sanctuary became characteristic of English *nonconformist* churches, distinguishing them from the English parish church which had no ancillary buildings. However, in mainland Europe the space for the Sunday School was normally within the curtilage of the main building, which might have several halls for events, smaller classrooms and guest accommodation for visitors. In England and *Wales* it was the Sunday School building which enabled chapels to develop an institutional life with a whole range of social activities. With buildings and capital of their own, Sunday Schools sometimes existed separately from the chapels with which they were associated and there needed to be forthright action to bring them under the control of the *church meeting*. In all of this profound changes about the nature of the *church* were being worked out. 'The Sunday School open to all rather than the *covenanted* meeting of baptised *saints* was the sign of the times. Evangelism rather than *sanctification* was the church's business and the more the slogan of "the missionary church" caught on, the more the *kingdom of God* seemed delivered over to associational principles.'

To see Sunday Schools as a *capitalist* device to subdue the working classes [see *Social Class*] and school them to the virtues that the new industrial means of production needed – sobriety, diligence, regularity, punctuality and honesty – as radical historians have sometimes characterised them is not true, for the altruism was sincere and in many places working class *men* shared in the promotion of the movement. However Sunday Schools were in the business of encouraging rational recreation as an antidote to that dangerous sensuous entertainment that focused on the public house and the music hall, and were proud to encourage wide reading, reasoned argument though best of all was knowledge of the *scriptures*. Indeed as the English Baptist, Robert Hall encouraged the Sunday School teachers of Leicester, England, 'Lead them [the scholars in their classes] to the footstall of the *Saviour*; teach them to rely, as guilty creatures, on his merit alone, and to commit their eternal interests entirely into his hands. Let the *salvation* of these children be the object, to which every word of your instructions, every exertion of your authority is directed.' Thus there was a widespread expectation that as the Sunday School worked effectively with the church's *catechumens*, there would be a steady natural flow from the senior classes of the Sunday School to the baptismal pool: were that not to be so the church 'ought to betake itself to the most earnest examination and *prayer*'.

The Sunday School movement was one of the agencies that early pioneered ecumenical relationships among *protestant* Christians in certain countries across Europe. The first World Sunday School Convention was held in 1862 and many schools adopted the disciplined reading of scripture/class topics worked out by the International Lessons Committee in 1874, producing what were called 'graded lessons' and the idea that Sunday School scholars would progress from class to class dependent on their age and understanding. For private devotions the International Bible Reading Association (1882) produced noted for different age groups, working both in the developed and developing world.

Sunday Schools were pretty successful with younger children in Europe, flourishing in the *Baltic states*, for instance, but as the century progressed and indeed into the late 20th century maintaining the interest of maturing teenagers proved increasingly difficult, notwithstanding the development in some countries of organisations like *Boys/Girls Brigades*, *Scouting*, *Christian Endeavour* societies, juvenile *temperance* societies, *YMCA/YWCAs*, mutual improvement societies and a variety of *sporting* activities which was where some major football clubs had their origins.

The social upheaval of two world wars and changing patterns of weekend *leisure* made their impress, it became harder to maintain large Sunday Schools. In *communist* Eastern Europe Sunday Schools were banned being seen as a way of 'indoctrination' of children and church members forbidden to involve their children in the life of the church. Clandestine ways of doing this developed, though, of course, children never featured in 'official' photographs of the church and Sunday Schools ceased to exist. For many, the family had to be the focus of sharing *faith* and the role of the mother in imparting Christian truth was especially important, as sometimes the father was imprisoned for his beliefs. With teenagers, more organised work often took place, usually in separate rooms and at different times to the Sunday *worship*. *Choirs* and youth meetings featured prominently in the *soviet* bloc countries, though much depended on the attitude of the local communist authorities.

As the century progressed in the West, a variety of ways developed to reshape the Sunday School and generally, they became more clearly related to the main Sunday act of worship. In some countries, especially in Central Europe, the Sunday School for children meets before worship whilst the adults have a prayer and testimony meeting, in others children became engaged in 'Family Worship', then leaving for their own activity at the point of the *sermon*, in still others experiments in All-Age Worship with children present throughout and perhaps people breaking up into activity and discussion groups in place of a sermon. With the ability of the churches in the post-communist countries to have activities for children, a variety of patterns have emerged or been reformed from earlier models.

One thing became clear that although the church's work with children would be ongoing, it was unlikely in the future to be focused in 'Sunday Schools', both of which words had become problematic by the beginning of the 21st century in many countries.

It should be noted, however, that in Europe, there was no widespread move to the all-age pre-worship Sunday School Class system beloved of many Baptists in the USA. The norm remained of the Sunday School being for children and increasingly sessions were for part of the worship time during the sermon, rather as fully separate meetings in an afternoon.

JHYB, KGJ, NC & ALa

Sweden, Baptist history in

Baptist influence in Sweden started when the Baptist G.W. Schröder, a sea captain, met the *Methodist preacher*, F.O. Nilsson, in 1845 in Gothenburg. Two years later, Nilsson went to Hamburg to be baptised [see *Baptism*], and in the following year, 1848, five more were baptised in Vallersvik on the west coast and formed a Baptist church. Nilsson continued his work, and had a congregation of 52 persons when he was banished from Sweden in 1850. Two years later at *Lutheran* clergyman, Anders Wiberg, wrote an influential book in which Baptist convictions were presented. Wiberg emigrated to the USA. On his way he stopped in Copenhagen, where he met F.O. Nilsson and was baptised by him. In 1854 two men from Stockholm went to Hamburg to be baptised. One of them, P.F. Hejdenberg, was ordained [see *Ordination*] and went back to Sweden, where he baptised 100s of believers. The following year Wiberg came back to Sweden and became the leader of early Baptist work, became pastor of the first Baptist church in Stockholm and drew up the first Swedish Baptist *confession of faith* which was widely used by other churches. He founded the *periodical Evangelisten* in 1856 and began sending out *colporteurs* with American support. In 1851 Baptists formed the first *Sunday School* in Sweden.

Baptists in Sweden, as in other places, faced serious opposition from authorities of both *church* and *state*. A royal edict dating from 1726 forbade devotional meetings that were not authorised by the Lutheran Church. The penalties were a severe fine for a first offence, imprisonment for a second and banishment on the third occasion. As an example, in a period of two years in the early 1850s over 600 people were fined or put in prison for breaking the law on religious practice. Baptists were part of this wider movement of dissent. In securing *religious freedom* external intervention also played its part. At the second general *assembly* of Swedish Baptists two leading English Baptists were present, John Howard Hinton and Edward Steane. They travelled in Sweden and wrote a book, *Notes of a Tour in Sweden*.

Nilsson also travelled to London to attend a meeting of the *Evangelical Alliance*. He was asked to speak about his experiences, since the Alliance was committed to taking up the cause of those persecuted for their *evangelical* convictions. A letter was read from the Lutheran Archbishop of Sweden, Carl Fredrik Wingård, who spoke of his sympathy for the work of the Alliance. *Prayer* was offered by the Alliance for Sweden. In view of the fact that Baptists were suffering the forced baptism of their *children* in the Lutheran Church, and also fines and *violence*, it was decided at a meeting of Swedish Baptists that all who wished to emigrate to the USA should do so. Nilsson was asked to be the leader of the group that left. In 1853 Nilsson, his wife, and 21 *church members* settled in Illinois. However, in 1860 his banishment order was annulled, and he returned to Sweden. Both Schroeder and Nilsson helped with Baptist work in Göteborg. Although in the 1860s persecution began to abate, Baptists did not obtain significant relief until 1873 when an act providing for civil *marriages* was passed, although it was not until 1952 that Swedish Baptist pastors could legally preside at a marriage and Baptists could leave the *state church* without loss of civil rights.

In 1866 a *theological* seminary (*Betel-seminariat*) was started, led by K.O. Broady, a Swedish emigrant who had become an army colonel in the civil war in the USA where he received theological training. He was the man behind the organising of the Swedish Baptist Mission Society in 1889, and became the dominating leader for 40 years. The Baptist advance had been conspicuous during this period, and continued to be so for the next 30 years, when Jakob Byström was the leading person. *Mission* work was started in China in 1891, and the following year in Congo, with a number of additional initiatives instituted thereafter.

At home Baptists grew in numbers· rapidly [see *Church Growth*]: in 1914 there were 635 churches with some 54,000 members. Baptist institutions included a Young People's Association (1905), a Publication Society (1919), a *Folk High School* (1921), a Nurses and *Deaconesses'* Association, (1922) a Boy's *Orphanage* (1932) and a Young *Men*'s Hostel (1951) besides Homes for the Aged. The Swedish *Union* has been very supportive of other European unions, encouraging the work in *Norway*, supporting mission work in the former Russian Empire in *Finland*, *Estonia* and St. Petersburg. Because Sweden as a *nation* was a neutral power in WWII it was able to make a large contribution to the restarting of Baptist work in countries which had suffered grievously in the war and to provide invaluable assistance to the many Baptists who became displaced persons as a result of the war.

The Swedish Union has suffered a number of withdrawals, e.g. with the founding of the small Free Baptist Union in 1872, but more significantly with the rise of *Pentecostalism* at the beginning of the 20th century, e.g. Lewi Pethrus and the Filadelfia Church in Stockholm, were excluded from the local Baptist *association* in 1913, and became the flagship of Swedish Pentecostalism A special branch of Baptist work was founded in *Örebro* by the Baptist minister, John Ongman, who had returned from the USA where he had been influenced by the *holiness* movement. A new centre was established in Örebro, but it developed different emphases and in the 1930s it broke .away from the Baptist Union with a consequent loss to the Union of 68,000 or one-third of its membership. This separate group of churches is now called *InterAct*. Both the Baptist Union of Sweden and InterAct are members of the *EBF*.

From the 1950s Swedish Baptists began to accept *women* pastors. As in most of the *Free Churches* of Sweden, the Baptist membership has shrunk since 1940. Influenced by the *ecumenical movement*, the Baptist Union has accepted *open communion*, *open membership* and united churches. Initiatives exploring unification with other Free Church denominations have been taken several times, but have not led to any results. However, the theological seminary has merged with the Covenant Church seminary to form the *Stockholm School of Theology*. In 1932 the Baptist Union elected its first mission director (general secretary), Hjalmar Danielson. He was succeeded first by Erik Rudén followed by Simon Öberg and then David Lagergren until 1984, when Birgit Karlson was elected, the first Baptist woman in the world to serve in that capacity. When her successor, Sven Lindström, retired, another woman, Karin Wiborn, was elected in 2002. The Baptist Union of Sweden currently has 220 churches and 17,545 members while InterAct has 330 churches and 31,000.

DaL & ET

Switzerland, Baptist history in

Switzerland [*Confoederatio Helvetica*] is a country with four officially recognised languages: German, French, Italian and Rhaeto-Romanic. These different languages and cultures play an important role and are highly valued. Accordingly, Baptist churches trace their origins to different roots:

- Baptist churches in German-speaking Switzerland (North and East) have originated under influences from *Germany*;
- Baptist churches in French-speaking Switzerland (West) have developed under influences from *France*.

Even today Swiss Baptist churches belong to different *unions* or are completely independent.

Baptist churches of the Swiss Baptist Union [Bund Schweizer Baptistengemeinden]: Whilst Switzerland was the location for some of the earliest *anabaptist* initiatives, there is no continuity between them and present-day Baptist *witness* in the federation, which dates to the 19th century. In fact, the origins of the work can be found in the endeavours of Samuel Heinrich Fröhlich (1803-57) and *pietistic* Christians from *state churches* within the *Reformed tradition* who had accomplished much of the spiritual preparation in Switzerland. Spiritual renewal also came in the wake of the *Genfer Réveil* [Geneva Revival]. Many Christians in the newly founded Baptist churches came from these circles.

Johann Gerhard Oncken (1800-84) visited Switzerland in 1847. In Basel he baptised a man in the Rhine in the baptistic way of immersion [see *Baptism*]. During a further trip to Eastern Switzerland he visited an independent *Bible study* group of some 12 persons, baptised upon their *faith*, and integrated them as the church of Toggenburg into his first German Baptist church in Hamburg (founded in 1834). In 1849 the oldest Baptist church of Zürich still existing was founded and this soon became a major centre of Baptist *mission*.

After a long period of stagnation, when the churches seemed to be occupied with little more than survival, they have recently developed a greater sense of *unity* and urgency of mission which bodes well for the future development of Baptist witness in Switzerland.

Baptist churches in AEEB [*Association Évangélique d'Églises Baptistes de Langue Française*]: The Baptist church Montbéliard, France, founded in 1870, two years later established a *preaching* station in Tramelan in the Swiss Jura.

After several other Christians joined the Baptists in Tramelan, the community was accepted in 1893 as an independent church by the *Union des Eglises Baptistes en France*.

Various baptistic *missionary* efforts were undertaken from Tramelan.

Today the AEEB comprises six Baptist churches in Biel-Bienne, Court, Genf, Malleray, Moutier and Tramelan. The AEEB belongs neither to the *EBF* nor to the *BWA*, but to the *Association Baptiste Européenne*.

Independent Baptist churches: Such churches exist in Genf (English-speaking *Evangelical* Baptist Church), Lausanne, Neuchâtel and Payerne. The latter three churches belong together and maintain loose relations with AEEB, without being members of this *association*.

Since 2003 *preachers* from the various Swiss Baptist churches mentioned above have met together annually on an informal basis.

LN

FURTHER READING: Lothar Nittnaus, *Baptisten in der Schweiz: ihre Wurzeln und ihre Geschichte*, WDL-Verlag, Berlin, 2004.

Sylvester

See *Watchnight*.

Symbolism

See *Sacrament, Sign and Symbol; Sign and Symbol*.

Syncretism

Syncretism signifies a religious position which results from the amalgamation of elements from a number of different religious *traditions*. Thus Sikhism can be said to be syncretic because it amalgamates elements of Hinduism and *Islam*. Within the Christian tradition syncretism refers to the incorporation of non-biblical [see *Bible*] cultural elements in the celebration of the *faith*. This is delicate territory which calls for considerable discernment. There is a sense in which all attempts to make the Christian message relevant to different peoples – *contextualisation* – can be accused of syncretism, but unless the attempt is made to express the gospel in terms of a local culture, effective communication will not take place. Thus some aspects of syncretism may be desirable, whilst others are harmless, e.g. the widespread purchase of *Christmas* trees in Northern Europe as part of Christmas celebrations. Thus it ill-behoves Western *missionaries*, whose mind set is heavily influenced by post-*enlightenment* thinking, to condemn certain accommodations to innocent local practices in the *mission* field. The problem arises acutely when accommodation is at the expense of essential Christian truths, that is, where the accommodation to local custom or patterns of thought compromises the unique *reconciling* work of *Jesus Christ*. Questions arise then as to the extent to which Christians in Asia can contemplate any spiritual function assigned to the ancestors, or whether *discipleship* in Africa can be combined in any way with the practice of polygamy. It is always easier to condemn syncretism in another's position than to recognise it in one's own tradition.

Western missionaries sometimes condemned practices in two-thirds world societies whilst presenting a gospel which carried with it a large measure of Western *secular* culture. Only belatedly did they become aware of their own syncretism, and begin to face the question as to the essence of the gospel, a task which a discussion of syncretism demands of all Christian *scholars*.

ET

Synod/Church Council

[See also *Episcope*]

In the traditional ecclesiastical sense 'synod' [Greek οδοσ = 'way' and συνοδοσ = 'fellow traveller'] and 'council' are assemblies of representatives of churches in order to discuss and make decisions about *faith*, church order, points of *discipline* and moral issues. The decisions made are binding on the local congregations and upon each *member*.

The earliest synods seem to have been held in Asia Minor when groups of *local churches* met under the leadership of their *bishops* to discuss the Montanist movement. It has been maintained that these synods came about during the second half of the 2nd century, at the time when the monarchical episcopate was also established. Thus there was at this time no conflict between the episcopal and synodical modes of government. Others hold that the roots of synods are found already in the NT churches, when representatives of the churches met in order to discuss questions of doctrine or church order (e.g. Ac 15), or when they visited each other at the installation of church officers.

The first synods were *ad hoc* gatherings. Later came Provincial Synods meeting once or twice a year, constituted primarily by the bishops, who made the decisions, even though also presbyters and lay people [see *Laity*] attended the meetings. The provincial synod became the most important instrument for the episcopal government of the ancient *church*. The metropolitan called it and presided over it, and it was invested with the competence to discuss and decide upon any question in the churches brought before it.

The first *ecumenical* council of the ancient church was that of Nicaea in 325AD. This has been followed by numerous others,

the first seven, that is up to the second Council of Nicea (787AD) recognised by both Eastern *Orthodox churches* and the *Roman Catholic* Church. Thereafter, recognition was restricted to one *tradition* only, convoked by emperors or kings, or by *popes*.

The *Reformation* broke with the ideas on synods and councils held by the ancient and medieval church. The Reformed Church in its different expressions became the home of the new synodical system, which was adopted by several denominations in the *Reformed* (*Calvinist*) tradition.

Baptists, with their *congregational ecclesiology*, have not adopted or established synodical systems. The term 'synod' is not common in Baptist teaching on the church. The term has, however, occurred. In 1976 and 1984 the Baptist *Union* of *Denmark* convoked 'synods'. Actually it was their Annual Conference, but with a focus on *theology* and *ethics* rather than the usual Union business. These were *ad hoc* gatherings and a synodical system was not implemented. What is important in these discussions is the direction in which *authority* flows: in Baptist ecclesiology regional *associations* or national conventions may elect councils which can advise local churches but they cannot instruct or control them. Such authority as regional and national bodies possess come from the local church; it does not mean the right to determine local church policy.

Baptist church councils may also be called at the *ordination* of *ministers*, at which occasion not only representatives of neighbouring churches but also officers of associations and the union are invited to participate. But again, the council is an institution of the local church, not of the superstructure.

PAE

Syria, Baptist history in

The Baptist presence in Syria, whose population is 90% *Muslim* and 10% Christian (*Orthodox* or *Roman Catholic*), had a relatively slow start. The work was begun by Ibrahim Brake, who encountered Baptist beliefs while in Canada. With help from US Christians, he founded the American *Evangelical Mission* to Syria in 1948, re-named the Syrian Baptist Mission in 1955, and joined Evangelical Baptist Missions in 1957. In 1948 and after, Brake established **preaching** stations in the south-western part of the country, and in 1951 the first Baptist church, in As Suwyada, was established, followed by a couple of small churches in the neighbourhood. In 1963, Brake founded a Baptist church in Damascus and also began an **orphanage**. However, the weakness of Syrian Baptist work was its focusing on one able leader, and the lack of team-work experience. Conflict between Brake, now the **pastor** of the Evangelical Baptist Church in Damascus and Boutros Narrouz, the pastor of the Homs church, divided the small Baptist presence into two groups. Today, the Baptist Convention in Syria, founded by Narrouz in 1983, is a member of the **European Baptist Federation** and consists of some half a dozen churches and **mission stations**. Recognised by the government, it has also received support from **Southern Baptists**. The Evangelical Baptist Church in Damascus continues independently from the Syrian convention.

TP

Systematic Theology

[See also *Theology*]

European Baptists' diverse approach to the challenge of laying out a structured approach to theology reflects diversity in theological and cultural traditions. Many approach the subject from the traditional Western European route, revising or restructuring the method laid out by the mediaeval **theologian**, Thomas Aquinas, whose *Summa Theologica* set the structure and methodology adopted in subsequent works on Systematic Theology. Theological thought of the early reformers [see **Reformation**] such as Jan Hus, **Huldrych Zwingli**, **Martin Luther**, **Jean Calvin** in the 15th and16th centuries and their followers in the subsequent centuries led to a radical break with Thomist grand synthesis of natural and divine **revelation**. The reformers emphasised God's **grace** and **sovereignty** as revealed in **scriptures** in theological reflections on matters of **faith** and **church** life. The work of the Calvin, in his *Institute of the Christian Religion*, provided the template for many **protestant** systematic theologies, especially those influenced by British and North American Reformed schol-

arship. This method drafts out a scheme of theology as an integrated matrix of truths deduced from scripture, as they apply the revelation of God in **Christ** to the human condition. In the 19th and 20th centuries, **Lutheran** and **Reformed** systematic theologians such as Friedrich Schleiermacher, Paul Tillich, Karl Barth, Jurgen Moltmann and Wolfhart Pannenberg had a massive influence across Europe, engaging Baptists amongst many others in mapping out systematic schemas of wider appeal.

An example of this style of Systematic Theology would be found in the influential work of **Southern Baptist** Theologian, Millard J. Erickson. In *Introducing Christian Doctrine*, Erickson follows 12 partitions, beginning with prolegomena of a methodology and progressing through doctrines of General and Specific Revelation, the Nature of God, the Work of God, **Anthropology**, the doctrine of **Sin**, the Person and Work of Christ, the Doctrine of the **Holy Spirit**, the doctrine of **Salvation**, the Church and then The Last Things [see **Eschatology**].

In contrast to the rigid propositional epistemology of the **Enlightenment** and **Marxist**-Leninist humanism, combined with **nonconformist** influences such as **Orthodox** dissent (e.g. Russian **Molokans**) and radical communitarianism (e.g. Ukrainian **Mennonites**), has led to a growing interest in constructing European baptistic theologies that embrace the convictions and practices expressed in the continuing life of the **gathering** faith community. Recent emphases on Narrative theology, such as in the work of J.Wm. McClendon, Jr., and on the confessional nature of the theological task, as in the works of Dietrich Bonhoeffer and John H. Yoder, have led to the understanding that theology is properly born out of the convictions of the confessing community. Such understanding exemplifies an alternative methodology emphasising a continuing process of rediscovery and reforming scriptural perspectives within the relational, Christian community and under the leading and interpretation of the Holy Spirit, over against timeless principles birthed and codified within the cultures, contexts and power structures of historic **Christendom**.

JGMP & PRP

FURTHER READING: Millard J. Erickson, *Introducing Christian Doctrine*, Baker Academic, Grand Rapids, Mi., 2001.

T

Tabernacles
See *Chapels*.

Taizé Community, France
See *Intentional Communities*.

Tajikistan, Baptist history in
[See also *Central Asia, Baptist history in*]
The beginning of Baptist presence in Tajikistan, a *Muslim* country, dates back to the end of the 1920s, when some Baptist families were deported by the *Soviet* authorities to this Central Asian region. These families, living in Dushanbe, the capital, and in its immediate neighbourhood, began to gather for *prayer* and sharing of the *Word*. Some Baptist influences and encouragement came also via Samarkand through travelling Baptist *preachers*. The Baptist church in Dushanbe was formed in 1929 and, in the next year, I. Danilenko was elected as its pastor. In 1936, Dushanbe Baptists and the *Evangelical* Christians, who had started their *ministry* in the same city, decided to join. Unfortunately, the Soviet authorities closed the church in 1937. The Baptist work had had a very short time to develop – both organisationally and spiritually. In spite of the closure of the Dushanbe church, some small groups continued to meet in homes. When in 1944 the Dushanbe church was again allowed to be re-registered officially, the *membership* had shrunk to 35. With the new possibility to operate legally, and receive new members from the believers who migrated to the area, Dushanbe church began to grow again [see *Church Growth*]. Church members, in the mid 80s numbering around 800, were mostly Russians and Germans, though Ossetians and other ethnic groups were also represented. There were also some other Baptist congregations which emerged in the country, however, these were considerably smaller. In 2006, there were 350 Baptists in 14 congregations in Tajikistan. The *Union* of Evangelical Christian Baptist Churches of

Tajikistan is a member of the *EBF*.

TP

Tashkent Theological Seminary
Tashkent *Theological* Seminary was founded in 1992 by the *Evangelical* Christians-Baptists *Union* of *Uzbekistan*, with the founding rector being Renat Askhatovitch Khaibullin. It is located in the Central Baptist Church of Tashkent. The seminary was created to offer practical training at a Bachelor and Certificate level. It has been a full member of the *Euro-Asian Accreditation Association* since 1997. The seminary primarily services the Russian-speaking churches of *Central Asia* which includes both Russian and non-Russian ethnic groups. Since its beginning the majority of the seminary's faculty, administrators, and students have been Russian. In 2005, the school offered a three-year full-time degree in *Pastoral* Studies, as well as various full-time one year programmes for the preparation of *preachers*, *Sunday School* teachers, *choir* directors, or *ministers* to the deaf. In the first 15 years of existence, it produced approximately 250 graduates from these programmes. Enrolment has, however, steadily decreased as a result of the *emigration* of Russian-speakers from Central Asia.

GLN

Team Ministry
See *Ministry*.
From an early stage in Baptist history there have been Baptist churches, or in rural areas groups of churches, that have had more than one *minister*. With the growth of the *deaconess* movement in large cities ministers were assisted in their community and *pastoral* ministries by the devoted service of salaried deaconesses. Baptists have also always had teams of lay preachers [see *Laity*] and *deacons*. However, the language of 'team ministry' became common only in the second half of the 20th century. In the 1970s a number of Baptist churches began to experiment with forms of team ministry that involved a group of Baptist congregations working together. There was particular interest in this in the north of *England*, and in

Bradford two new 'Fellowships' (or groups) with Team Ministries were set up in the 1970s. One of these represented a pioneering effort in inner-city **ministry**. Four ministers formed a team with five churches. Another Bradford group had four churches and two ministers.

In the same period, team ministries of an **ecumenical** nature became more common. Again the north of England was a significant area of experimentation, although ecumenical initiatives were to be found in various parts of Europe. In Skelmersdale new town, Lancashire, an Ecumenical Centre took shape with **members** of **Anglican**, Baptist, **Methodist** and United **Reformed Churches** sharing a team ministry. Another example was in Sheffield. St Thomas's Anglican Church and Mulehouse Road Baptist Church in Crookes began joint **worship** in 1977 and a Local Ecumenical Project was inaugurated in 1982. This became one of the largest congregations in England, at once ecumenical and **charismatic**. In many new towns ecumenical teams were seen as normal by Baptists.

Other large Baptist congregations (over 1,000 members) in different parts of Europe, such as Oliveste Church, Tallinn, **Estonia**, operated with teams of ministers for one congregation. Especially from the 1980s, churches began to look for teams which included a team leader and other ministers with specific functions – youth ministry [see **Youth Work**], community ministry or pastoral ministry, e.g. Such teams were already common in the mega-churches of the USA, but among European Baptists this was a fresh development. In the 1990s many more large churches with team ministries emerged in the former **communist** countries of Eastern Europe, notably in **Ukraine**.

In addition to teams serving **local churches**, those involved in wider Baptist oversight – in **union** leadership and regional ministry – began from the 1980s in particular to use the language of 'team ministry'. In many areas of Baptist life in Europe the maintenance of the older idea of 'one man ministry' has been abandoned.

IMR

Tearfund

A significant development for British **evangelicals** in the 1960s was the establishment of an **Evangelical Alliance** (EA) department which became known as TEAR Fund. It was originally E.A.R. – the Evangelical Alliance Relief Fund. The launch of TEAR Fund (later Tearfund) took place in 1968 in part because Mary Jean Duffield, a 21-year-old who was concerned about the famine in the Bihar region of India, joined the EA and was given the task of examining the potential for a relief fund. Evangelicals in **Britain** and elsewhere were re-awakening to a world of immense material need. George Hoffman, who became TEAR Fund's first director, had been profoundly affected by the 1967 Anglican evangelical Keele Congress. The section on social responsibility in the Keele report acknowledged the past failures of evangelicals in the area of social responsibility. Younger evangelicals in particular began to articulate a more comprehensive view of evangelicalism's **mission** in the world. John Stott, the foremost **Anglican** evangelical leader, was crucial to the acceptance of this broadening view of mission. The EA was one of the agencies seeking to show that the dichotomy between the social and the spiritual dimensions of the gospel was a false one. With their own relief agency there was no longer any excuse for evangelicals opting out of social action on the basis of disagreeing with the **theological** stance of the existing relief agencies. Initially, TEAR Fund sent money to a limited number of countries – India, the Congo and Vietnam – but it grew at a remarkable rate under George Hoffman's leadership. By the 1980s it was supporting relief and development in many countries and was the largest and best-known interdenominational evangelical agency in Britain engaged in global social action. Many Baptist churches in Britain began to support Tearfund and a number of Baptists have work for the organisation including Doug Balfour, who was appointed General Director in 1995 and Dewi Hughes, Tearfund's theological adviser. Born out of Tearfund's activities, Tearcraft seeks to market in the developed world goods which have been created by ethically [see **Ethics**] responsible **two-thirds-world** producers, the argument being that fair trade is a better approach to the problems of emerging economies rather than charitable aid.

IMR

Technology

Technology is the practical application of *scientific* discoveries. In the last two centuries it has transformed the standard of living in Western *nations* and has had a profound impact even on *two-thirds-world* countries, and all of this at an increasing rate. Simply to list the areas of advance is a reminder of the effect technology has had, and is having, on the quality of human life:

Vehicular and air transport; the development of electric power generation and its use industrially and in domestic utensils; radio and television; rocket science and the use of satellites; nuclear power; chemically-derived drugs, man-made fabrics, plastics, pigments, detergents, fungicides and herbicides, liquid crystal displays (LCDs); transistors, electronic computers and information technology; antibiotics, immunosuppressants and transplant surgery; genetic engineering; stem-cell and molecular biology; nanotechnology (the technology of the infinitely small).

Currently the uptake of new technology is unprecedented, because it is seen to work extremely effectively. Sometimes things have gone wrong when an unknown property emerges: chlorinated hydrocarbons (such as DDT), used as insecticides, enter the food-chain of birds and animals and affect their reproductive capacity; chlorofluoro (hydro)carbons (CFCs) used as refrigerants and aerosols destroy the ozone layer in the stratosphere [see *Climate Change*; *Ecology and the Environment*].

There are, however, marked geographical variations in the uptake in new technology, and an increasing awareness that the application of technology should be appropriate to a local situation: the work of E.F. Schumacher was seminal in establishing 'intermediate technology', that is technology appropriate to developing economies, which did not seek to reduce the work force to a minimum, but rather sought to protect employment.

There are also marked differences in the acceptance of some new developments such as those within genetic engineering [see *GM Foods*] and stem cell biology which pose considerable ethical challenges.

JB & GA

FURTHER READING: E.F. Schumacher, *Small is Beautiful*, Harper and Row, New York, 1973.

Temperance work

[See also *Alcohol*; *Alcoholism*]

The temperance *conscience* was late to develop. It was a function of the urban culture born of the industrial revolution and was dependent on such things as the universal availability of clean water, and the popular access to hot water beverages as they became more affordable. Until that date alcoholic drinks were often the only safe liquids to drink. The conscience was always stronger in Northern Europe than in the *wine*-drinking countries of the South, and has survived longer amongst Baptists in Eastern Europe. As the cause developed so the language changed with teetotalism and total abstinence refining the nature of the commitment being sought. In the first couple of decades of the 19th century, temperance enthusiasts were essentially opposed to spirit-drinking, and beer was canvassed as a temperance drink promoted to curb the viciousness of addiction to gin and other spirits. Indeed in *Scandinavia* the concept of 'Baptist Beer' as a moderate alcoholic drink had an even longer life.

By the 1840s, however, there was enthusiastic canvassing for total abstinence. Temperance was essentially a social conscience rather than a moralistic peccadillo for the concern was more with the drunkard's family, deprived by the husband's excesses of all means of physical support, rather than the drunkard himself. In an increasingly drink-sodden society, the movement represented a genuine attempt to help the *poor*, not a conspiratorial attempt to impose middle-class values on a reluctant working class. To this end the more aristocratic anti-spirits campaign was inadequate; only the radicalism of total abstention could change lives spoilt by excessive drinking.

The Biblical basis [see *Bible*] for abstaining from strong drink derives not so much from texts condemning drunkenness and commending temperance as a *fruit of the spirit* (e.g.. Gal 5:19-22), about which there would be widespread consent, but rather Paul's teaching in 1Co 8 about not offending the weaker brother by eating food offered to idols, which applied to drink represents at best a rather indirect application of Biblical counsel.

The first temperance tract was the work of Baptist *pastor*, ('Boatswain') George Smith of Penzance, whilst Benjamin Godwin pastor in Bradford was reckoned one of the principal supporters of that city's Anti-Spirits Society whose energetic paid agent was James Jackson, formerly Baptist pastor in Hebden Bridge. He was responsible for starting a society in Preston out of which emerged the more radical teetotal pledge. Championed by 'the seven men of Preston' whose leader was Joseph Livesey, a Baptist who was anxious never to be *sectarian*. In this group temperance concerns were already overlapping with the emergence of more general working-class *politics*. Francis Beardsall, a New Connexion minister, the son of an inn keeper who drank to excess, editor of the first temperance *hymn* book as also of the *Temperance Star*, campaigned to replace the wine in the *communion* service with unfermented grape juice which he had a part in manufacturing. By the end of the 19th century, 2007 out of 2,900 churches had abandoned true wine in the communion service. Jabez Tunnicliffe, another New Connexion minister, was one of the founders of the *children*'s organisation, The Band of Hope which by the end of the 19th century had some three million members with over 2,000 branches in Baptist Churches. It was also the temperance movement that launched Baptist layman [see *Laity*], Thomas Cook, on his internationally famous career in travel agency: the first railway excursion he arranged was for a temperance outing. There were also temperance provident and friendly societies such as the Sons of Temperance and the Rechabites, linking temperance with working-class savings movements.

In 1853 yet another New Connexion minister, Dawson Burns, later the historian of the temperance movement, was one of those who helped to found the *United King-*

dom Alliance. This marked a turn in temperance history. Hitherto its promoters were content to rest on the strength of educational work persuading a drunken world into sobriety. The Alliance by contrast believed that only by legislative intervention limiting the sale of alcohol could further advances be made. This was a wholly new departure for Baptists who had up to this time thrown their weight behind a political liberalism which had little confidence in the *state*, rather upholding the principles of *laissez-faire* and a maximum of individual initiative. In 1873 the Baptist Total Abstinence Society was founded with **John Clifford** one of its secretaries. There was however a danger in all this. Dr., later Sir, Benjamin Richardson, FRS, a major pioneer in promoting sanitary and public health reform, wrote in the *General Baptist Magazine* for 1877 advocating 'A Total Abstinence Church'. Were the churches over focusing on the issue of temperance to the exclusion of other issues of citizenship, and was there an element of *pelagian 'salvation* by works' in such exaggerated emphases?

Since WWII British Baptists have reverted to a more relaxed approach to drink, at the same time as its attitudes to *smoking* became much more hostile (in line it should be said with the legislation of a number of states). Changes came about partly because of increased foreign travel, partly because the *welfare state* made better provision for the drunkard's family. There have indeed been occasions in European life when American and Northern consciences have tried to impose their own consciences on our churches in Latin Europe and have been politely advised that they should not trespass upon other believers' consciences. Indeed at the beginning of the 21st century no longer were *chapel* and pub the foci of alternative social networks, but *church planters* were to be found experimenting with 'new ways of being church' through the 'café church' and the 'pub church'. That is not to say that the undisciplined use of alcohol was not still a social problem, especially the 'binge drinking' of young *women*, but the inculcation of total abstinence amongst *church members* was no longer seen as an effective way of tackling this abuse.

JHYB

Temples
See *Chapels*.

Tent Evangelism
See *Crusade Evangelism*.

Tent-Maker Ministries
See *Bivocational Ministries*.

Teologiska högskolan Stockholm
See *Stockholm School of Theology*.

Thanksgiving for Children
See *Children, Blessing of*.

Theism and Deism
Although 'Theism' and 'Deism' have parallel derivations from the Greek and Latin words for God, respectively *theos* and *deus*, by usage they have developed contrasting meanings. The Deists were those rationalists who in the late 17th century and after, denying both *dogma* and *revelation*, came to postulate the existence of a supreme being but one who by definition did not intervene in human affairs. Their most famous adherent in Europe was by usage Voltaire. By contrast, 'Theism' described belief in a Creator who did not desert his *creation* but rather intervened as necessary. The concept is refined in the concept of monotheism or belief in one God, who, as over against the principle of pantheism, is not embraced by, but exists over against the created order. The God of Theism is personal, intelligent and powerful. Theistic *faiths* include Christianity, *Islam* and *Judaism*. Within the broad philosophical category of Theism, much needs to be refined before the seeker discovers the Christian God made known to his people in the life and work of *Jesus Christ* as revealed in the Christian *scriptures*.

ET

Theocracy
The word 'theocracy' conveys different meanings. Most often it refers to a system of government in which *priests* rule in the name of God, most clearly seen in ancient *Israel* prior to David becoming king. More loosely it has been used to describe a society where there exists a union of *church and state* – thus it has been said that *Calvin*'s Geneva and Cromwell's *England* were, or aspired to be, theocracies. In Baptist circles the term is sometimes used of a *local church* and the way it governs itself when the remark is made that the local congregation is not a *democracy* but a theocracy. Such a remark corrects the notion that every *member* possessing the vote makes the church some kind of democratic community. Whilst all members do have the vote they are not free to use that vote for personal purposes, for the fuller truth is that the people of God meet in *church meeting* around the open *word* and are prompted by the *Spirit* to seek the mind of *Christ* to know and fulfil his holy will.

ET

Theologians, European Baptists in the 20th and 21st centuries
[See also *Theology*]
Baptist and baptistic communities in Europe have produced only a handful of significant theologians during the 20th century. European Baptists appear to have been much more productive in terms of nurturing *Biblical scholars* and Church *historians*, than in producing classic theologians in the European sense.

However, Henry Wheeler Robinson, one time Principal of *Regent's Park College, Oxford*, surely counts as one such. Though principally an OT scholar, he sought in a number of major publications to restate Christian doctrine in a world of changed philosophical and psychological understanding. Four major works may be cited in particular: *The Christian Doctrine of Man* (1911), *The Christian Experience of the Holy Spirit* (1928), *Suffering, Human and Divine* (1939) and *Redemption and Revelation in the Actuality of History* (1942). He also wrote insightfully on Baptist principles, history and identity.

Some of Wheeler Robinson's work had been anticipated by T. Vincent Tymms, principal of Rawdon College, who published *The Christian Idea of the Atonement* (1904) in which he emphasises that it was human *sin* not the punishment for that sin that *Christ* bore on the *cross*, that is to say the cross is the consequence of human iniquity rather than divine anger.

Miroslav Volf is not strictly a Baptist, but belongs to the baptistic and free *evangelical* communities in *Croatia* and retains close connections with the whole baptistic community in Europe. Though now a Professor at Yale, his theological work reflects his European origins. His principal works, *Exclusion and Embrace* and *After His Likeness*, are highly regarded within the theological world.

Paul S. Fiddes has devoted himself to the work of the Faculty of Theology in the University of Oxford, which has honoured him with a Personal Professorship. Though his first discipline was OT, over the years he has written more general theological works such as *Participating in God – a Pastoral Doctrine of the Trinity, Past Event and Present Salvation – The Christian Idea of Atonement* and *Freedom and Limit: A Dialogue Between Christian Literature and Christian Doctrine*. He was the moving force in the creation of the *European Baptist Federation* identity statement 'Who are Baptists?', writing on Baptist identity in such books as *Tracks and Traces* and has played a key role internationally in the *Baptist World Alliance* discussions with the *Anglicans*, *Catholics* and *Orthodox*, and in *WCC* discussions on the meaning of *baptism*.

Nigel G. Wright, Principal of *Spurgeon's College, London* from the mid 1990s onwards, with experience within the *charismatic movement* has become noted for his work on the theology of *church and state* and reflection on the nature of evil. His *Free Church: Free State* and *New Baptists: New Agenda* are constantly used as course books in Baptist seminaries. He has been very active and is highly regarded within the European Baptist family and has exercised key leadership within the BWA.

Uwe Swarat, systematic theologian working in the *German Baptist Seminary at Elstal*, has written and spoken at conferences in the field of *systematic theology* and he has been important for the German-speaking communities of Europe. He played a key part in initial theological conversations between European Baptists and the *Community of Protestant Churches in Europe*, the former Leuenberg Fellowship. Eric Geldbach, a prolific author, was for many years on the staff of the Ecumenical Research and Study Centre at Bensheim, *Germany*, until appointed as a Baptist, notwithstanding considerable state church opposition, to be Professor of Ecumenical Studies at the Ruhr-University in Bochum, North Rhine Westphalia.

Thorwald Lorenzen, for a long time lecturer in systematic theology at *Rüschlikon* was much involved in theological reflection on *human rights* and *religious liberty*. His most significant theological book is *Resurrection and Discipleship*.

Parush R. Parushev, a Bulgarian convert [see *Conversion*] from *communism*, is one of the most influential Baptist theologians in contemporary European life. Studying under the North American Baptist scholars, Jim McClendon, Nancey Murphy and Glen Stassen, he holds doctorates in both *science* and theology and serves at *IBTS* as academic dean. He has taken a particular interest in the relationships between Christians and *Jews* and in the reaction of the baptistic communities in Europe to *post-modernity*.

Otniel Bunaciu holds degrees from *Bucharest* and Oxford and is Dean of the Baptist Theological Faculty in the State University in Bucharest, *Romania*. He is an influential figure amongst the Slavic baptistic communities of Central and South-East Europe. Henk Bakker from the *Netherlands* has a defined post in 'Baptist theology' at the Vrije University in Amsterdam.

Others to be noted as having worked at an advanced level in theological reflection include Elizabeth Green (*Italy*), Haddon Willmer, for a number of years head of the influential Theology Department in Leeds (*England*), Brian Haymes (England) noted for his *The Concept of the Knowledge of God*, Stephen R. Holmes of St. Andrews *Scotland* – his book *Listening to the Past: The Place of Tradition in Theology* and his collaboration with Colin Gunton and Murray A. Rae in *The Practice of Theology* has established his reputation as a theologian of some consequence. John E. Colwell of Spurgeon's College has explored *liturgy* as a shaper of theology in his *The Rhythm of Doctrine*; he has also written on other topics in *sacramental* and systematic theology.

Keith W. Clements (*Switzerland* and England), who has written extensively on Bonhoeffer, more generally on modern theologians and written a fine biography of J.H. Oldham, and Michael Taylor, latterly concerned with Christian understanding of the experience of the *poor* are considered under the heading of those making particular service to the *Ecumenical movement*.

KGJ

Theological Anthropology

See *Anthropology, Theological*.

Theological Education by Extension

Theological Education by Extension (TEE), at the level of structures, is a comparatively simple idea. Instead of confining theological *education* to a central, often residential college or seminary, it is 'extended' to the *student*'s local situation by means of information technology, correspondence courses, local centres and tutors, making it more accessible, less expensive and available on a part-time as well as a full-time basis. It is also referred to as 'distance learning'.

TEE has however often been associated with an underlying agenda which challenges the idea that '*theology*' and biblical interpretation [see *Bible*] are matters for experts and intellectual elites alone. It is not only theological education which is extended but the concept of theology to include as decisive ingredients the insights and perspectives of all the people of God, not least the *poor* and disadvantaged. *Scholars* and professional *theologians* represent important resources for doing theology but they are not the sole or even the main actors in the enterprise.

Theology is 'done' where people reflect on their struggles and attempts to be obedient to God in their own communities and contexts, by learning from one another, reading the scriptures through their own eyes, and encountering the wider *faith* (theological) *traditions* of the *church* in an ongoing cycle of action (or *praxis*) and reflection. In this way the agenda for theological education is not established by a classical curriculum of necessary elements but by the participants reflecting on their own local situation and experience.

Theological education is closely related to training for *ministry* and leadership in the church, and TEE has well expressed the conviction that they too, like theology, should not be the preserve of an elite. By making it much easier for everyone to participate in training, the central role of all God's people (the '*laity*') in *mission* is strongly upheld not just in theory but in practice.

In the end, theological education by extension becomes a matter of principle rather than convenience if theology is to be generated and the work of God's church pursued not in ivory towers but by faithful people in their everyday worlds.

MHT

FURTHER READING: Samuel Amirtham and John S. Pobee (eds), *Theology by the People: Reflections on doing theology in community*, WCC, Geneva, 1986.

Theology

[See *Theologians, European Baptists in the 20th and 21st centuries*]

There are many who have sought to argue Baptists have no distinctive baptistic theology outside the general *systematic theology* of the standard Reformed [see *Reformation*] *Protestant* theology or a more eclectic pick-and-mix theology, based, possibly, on the *Arminian* theology of *Smyth* and *Helwys*, a theology linked, in a later generation with Charles Wesley and the *Methodist revival*. However, in our current generation there has been the development of reflection of a primary baptistic theology formed in the *gathering*, intentional churches of Europe. Increasingly, there is the drive for an authentic and rooted theology of the people of God which is not so absolutely reliant on the academy. Despite those believers who think theological reflection in any reasoned intellectual way is a waste of time, many others are concerned to give a coherent account of the hope that is in us. This can be assisted, shaped, informed by the more academic pursuits and writings that go on amongst *schol-*

ars. Others Baptists believe that theology is integral to the life of the church. Without it, the church can stagnate, become atrophied, or decisions about life and purpose become arbitrary, or opportunist, or worst of all, desperate. Indeed, desperation might be a sort of theology in some parts of the *church* in Europe.

Theology – derived from the Greek – means an account of, or study of God, or more particularly, the nature of God. In English it derives from THEOLOGIST (noun). The root of the word goes back to Latin *theologia* and the Greek *Theo* [God] and *logia* [Latin for the 'study of']. Here we are principally working with notions of Christian theology, which the patristic age affirmed as the biblical account [see *Bible*] of God's dealing with *humankind*, with particular reference to *Christ*. So Christians would argue a definition such as 'talk about God' is certainly inadequate. At least it must be talk about the activity of God since we do not know Him in himself, but only as He has acted and revealed himself. To this we Christians have added His most revealing activity is in Jesus. Baptistic theology has a conviction that God is active everywhere, all the time and although He does not always do the same things, what he does is always, 'Christlike'. That is, consistent with the nature and purposes of his paradigmatic activity in Christ. So theology is engaged in talking about God's activity now, and as such it has not only a backward (to Jesus) but contemporary (here and now) look. For Bonhoeffer, theology begins in silence. Some Baptists have sought to model their theology on the lines of Karl Barth and his systematic and *dogmatic* approach in the Reformed *tradition*, especially in *Hungary* and *Germany*, whilst others have been interested in *liberation theology*, especially in *Poland*, *Italy* and *England*.

Some Baptists have a very wide definition of theology, so whoever has any beliefs, or any religious beliefs, may be said to have a 'theology'. In that case 'Everybody has won and all must have prizes'. However, we perhaps have some intuitive idea of what a theology must be, regardless of formal definitions. We know that a theology represents something deeply self-involving and consistent for the individual. For Baptists the pri-

mary beginning of theology is in the gathering community in *worship* and breaking open the *Word*. In theologising our convictions in community become very important for the shaping of our theology. Most Baptists readily distinguish our convictions from our opinions. Opinions are the stuff of debate and discussion. We acquire opinions quickly. We shed them just as quickly. They may require thought, even intellectual rigour, but they require no commitment. Convictions, on the other hand, are less readily expressed but more tenaciously held and this is at the heart of our theological exploration. Such an approach is not so inclined to the systematising beloved of some, though the convictions held to should have coherence – a theological map for the community, which may have segments, but ought to fit together like a jigsaw.

For Baptists there are several key reference points in our theological enterprise. Overall, the Magisterial *Reformation* and the three great figures who spearheaded the ideas – *Zwingli*, *Calvin* and *Luther* (in order of their effect upon Baptists) have been very influential. However, just as important is the Radical Reformation linked, in some aspects to the Magisterial Reformers – Zwingli and Carlstadt in particular, but grouped much more around the Swiss *Anabaptists*, the south German Anabaptists and *Balthasar Hubmaier*, Thomas Müntzer, Melchior Hoffmann, Menno Simons- who founded the Mennonites/Waterlanders, who played hosts to Smyth and Helwys, the first General Baptists of England and the USA.

Others point to the influence of the English *Separatist* Tradition, based on a *pietism* which drew insights from the Continental Reformers Zwingli and Calvin, but which was also heir to the pre-radical reformation in England of John Wycliffe, who influenced Jan Hus. Whatever the rootage, it is the case that baptistic communities have not been at the forefront of profound systematic theological reflection in the way the Reformed or *Lutheran* communities have been. They have not even produced a John Owen who did so much for their *Congregational* cousins; indeed he was the favoured systematic theologian of many early Baptists, too.

Today this lack of home-made theologians is argued as a positive point. From our identity, the case is made that primary theology is the work of the local gathering, convictional community meeting around the Word and the Table [see *Communion and Intercommunion; Eucharistic liturgy; Sacrament, Sign and Symbol*]. Secondary theology is reflecting upon that primary theology by scholars in the academy.

Whilst we cannot list one European Baptist who has produced a major work of comprehensive (systematic) theology in the past century, we can make creditable claims for those who have engaged in theological reflection which has had an influence beyond the 'narrower' Baptist world. For classical systematic theology we have to look back to the 1700s to find a European, such as John Gill, engaged in such an exercise.

                                            KGJ

FURTHER READING: Millard J. Erickson, *Christian Theology*, Baker Books, Grand Rapids, Mi., 1983. James Leo Garrett, Jr., *Systematic Theology* (2 Vols), Eerdmans, Grand Rapids, Mi., 1990. James Wm. McClendon, Jr., *Systematic Theology* (3 Vols.), Abingdon, Nashville, Tn., 1986, 1994, 2000.

Third Way
See *Responsible Society/Third Way*.

Third World
See *Jubilee and Two-Thirds-World Debt; Two-Thirds World*.

Tithing
[See also *Offerings/Collection*]
Tithe is a voluntary contribution, tax or levy introduced in the OT. References can be found in Ge 14:20, Lev 27:30 and Dt 14:22. Tithing was paid as a tenth of the harvest for the support of the *priesthood*. Tithing in the NT is not much mentioned. There is a reference in Heb 7:2, but 2Co 9:7 refers to another form of giving. Tithing was unknown in the *church* of antiquity, but was introduced later by ecclesiastical decree and formally recognised under *Pope* Adrian I in 787AD. In the Middle Ages, farmers had to offer a tenth of their *harvest*, while craftsmen had to offer a tenth of their production. Special barns were built in villages to store

the tithe. By the time that tithes were commuted into a money payment in the 19th century they had very often been *secularised*.

Views of, and the practice of, tithing has changed over the years. Today tithing is in most churches a voluntary contribution the church expects from its *members*. The most common method of calculation is 10% of income after tax. Statistics over church incomes indicates the collected amount is considerably lower than 10% of the member's net income. Traditionally the Sunday service has been the collecting place of the tithe. In more and more churches the traditional offering at the Sunday service has been replaced for many givers by direct transfers from personal bank accounts to the church account. Some churches have even introduced terminals to facilitate this in church. Whatever the method of receiving payment, it is the strength of the *free-church tradition*, including the Baptists, that their members have a long tradition of disciplined and generous giving in what has often been called the Free-Will Offering.

Some independent churches controversially require members to sign a contract in which they agree a certain lifestyle, including a commitment to tithing. Some countries in Western Europe have a mandatory church tax collected by the *state* which is repaid to churches according to the size and *wealth* of their members. This can be seen as a way to carry through something like tithing in countries with strong majority churches.

                                            JS

Tobacco
See *Smoking and Tobacco*.

Tongues
See *Glossolalia*.

Toronto Blessing
[See also *Charismatic movement; Charismatics*]
The phrase 'Toronto Blessing' first appeared in 1994. It referred to the Toronto Airport

Vineyard (TAV) – a church then overseen by the influential charismatic *evangelist* and teacher, John Wimber. In Jan 1994, at the TAV, as people came forward for *prayer*, large numbers manifested a range of dramatic physical phenomena, from falling and then 'resting' in the *Spirit*, to laughing, shaking, and prostration. Within weeks, word of what was happening had spread, visitors to TAV were increasing, and some had begun to fly in from overseas to investigate. Among those in Europe who were interested were Terry Virgo, leader of New Frontiers International, Queen's Road Baptist Church, Wimbledon, London, the Ichthus Fellowship in South London, the Vineyard congregations in Britain, and the high-profile *Anglican* charismatic church Holy Trinity, Brompton, London.

Within a few weeks, the 'Blessing' had spread to 100s of churches. Views among Baptists and others about the phenomena were sharply polarised. Some rejected it, some were enthusiastic and others were not sure. The *Evangelical Alliance* brought together representatives of different positions for discussions. A series of essays from prominent *evangelical* thinkers on the impact of the 'Blessing' was compiled. The debate died down relatively quickly and those churches that had been most committed to the Toronto Blessing appeared to revert to the kind of *spirituality* – usually of a more moderate charismatic style – that had previously characterised their *worship*.

IMR

Totalitarianism

Totalitarianism represents the ultimate in *state* power, that is to say a totalitarian state is one which wholly subordinates personal freedom to the demands of central government, whether that be of the right as in Hitler's *Germany* [see *Fascism*] or of the left as in Stalin's *Russia* [see *Communism/Marxism/Socialism*]. The totalitarian state in its relentless determination to achieve its ends legitimises and deploys unrestrained organised *violence*; all opposition must be eliminated at whatever cost. Totalitarianism in Mussolini's *Italy* was expressed in the formula: 'All within the state, none outside the state, none against the state.'

Thus the totalitarian state controls all aspects of the citizens' lives but is itself subject to no external control. The *theological* rejection of the totalitarian state is to be found in the affirmation that the only true *sovereignty* in human affairs is that of God himself and in respect for what is properly human. Understood in these terms the totalitarian state becomes a species of idolatry dethroning God and defacing his image in humanity.

ET

Tradition/Traditions
[See also *Authority*]
Baptists are inclined, alongside other *Protestants*, to oppose *Scripture* and Tradition even though in the *apostolic* period they were each intimately connected with the other; it was within the *church* that the traditions of the *apostles* were collected and eventually written down to become the canon of the NT. Thus the word tradition(s) will be found in the epistles, as in 1Co 11:23 where Paul talks about receiving the tradition about the celebration of the *Lord's Supper* from the Lord himself. In 2Th 2:15 he tells the church to stand firm 'in the traditions you have learned from us by word or by letter', whilst in 3:6 he speaks of the contrary situation with the instruction to his readers to hold aloof from those who 'disregard the traditions you have received from us.' Similarly in Php 4:9 Paul exhorted his readers to 'put into practice the lessons I taught you, the tradition that I passed on, all that you heard me say or saw me do'. Critically Paul asks the church in Corinth, 'Did the word of God originate with you? Or are you the only people to whom it came?' (1Co 14:36). Thus scripture bears witness to how tradition and the traditions of the apostles, nurtured in the life of the church under the guidance of the *Spirit*, became scripture. Indeed there are practically no other sources which describe the traditions of the apostles. So for the early church the primary tradition is scripture and scripture is the primary tradition.

With the rise of Gnosticism and other *heresies*, and more particularly their appeal to a superior form of knowledge, the fathers appealed to scripture as offering a standard by which to judge such teaching. Later the patristic tradition, the teaching of the Church Fathers, secured honoured respect alongside the apostolic tradition contained in scripture, not as an addition to scripture, but as true interpretations of it. Later such interpretations in summary form were promulgated as *creeds* with the authority of successive *church councils* as representing the common understanding amongst the churches of Christian truth. One of the reasons that some Baptists have developed heterodox views on the *Trinity* was their reduced regard for such formalised teaching of the church. The tradition of the church in these centuries was increasing rapidly, with tradition now having a definition separate from scripture. Of itself its existence represented a critical process of passing on from one generation to another the things most firmly believed within the community of the Church. Within the *Catholic* tradition it came to possess a weight separate from that of scripture itself until the Council of Trent in the 16ᵗʰ century, distinguished the written books of scripture [*libri scripti*] from the unwritten traditions of the Church [*sine scripto traditiones*], ascribing to each equal authority.

Not surprisingly, Protestants, affirming *Sola Scriptura*, have, ever since the *Reformation*, been suspicious of tradition as potentially representing an alternative source of authority to that of scripture. The benefits of tradition were not denied, but tradition had always to be tested by scripture, for as the *Anglican* Book of Common Prayer puts it: 'Holy scripture containeth all things necessary to *salvation*.' In that sense tradition can add nothing. On the other hand as representing 'the dynamic movement of God in history', it is not lightly to be laid on one side, for it represents 'not so much a long line stretched out in time, as the gathering of time itself into God's eternity.' Tradition represents the Church's memory, a recalling to mind of all the way that God has led his people and all the guidance and empowering provided by the Spirit not only in times of progress and *revival* but also when the forces of evil have seemed to be poised to destroy the Church.

Baptists are clearly not without their own 'traditions' or indeed what are sometimes referred to as 'sacred cows', that is special doctrinal emphases which are particularly emphasised and revered. The notion that Baptists do not follow 'Tradition' seems spurious when the denomination reveres so many baptistic and local 'traditions'. Moreover most *local churches* have traditions within their life, but these need to be examined and tested by each new generation in the light of reading scripture and reflecting upon them in communion with those with whom they are *associated*.

JHYB

Translation, Bible
See *Bible Translation*.

Trans-national corporations
See *Globalisation and Multinational companies*.

Transcendence
See *Immanence and Transcendence*.

Trinity
The doctrine of the Trinity of God as Father, Son and *Holy Spirit*, or Creator, Redeemer and Sustainer is a *theological* construct belonging to the early centuries of the Christian *church* designed to guard the *orthodox* communities of *faith* against various forms of deviant belief that the mainstream church came to see as *heresies*, or serious challenges to orthodoxy. These concerns included Arianism, Unitarianism, Montanism and Gnosticism, and especially addressed concerns at any attempt to break apart a *holistic* view of God's world and the place of the creator in the *redemption* and sustaining of the total cosmos.

Christianity is one of the great monotheistic religions of the world with *Judaism* and *Islam*, but unlike these two religions which have common roots in the Hebrew or First Testament, Christianity asserts that the God whom we *worship* is known to us in three persons – the Father, the Son (*Jesus Christ*) and the Holy Spirit. If God is seen as asexual and the Son is seen as male, some parts of the Christian *tradition* see the Holy Spirit as female, noting that the Hebrew word for spirit, *ruach*, is feminine.

As Rowan Williams comments, the history of doctrinal development could be described as a record of discarded solutions. In terms of the Trinity the difficulty is to hold together the importance of seeing Jesus as fully God and yet fully human and so entering into the pain, *suffering* and turmoil of humanity.

The doctrine of the Trinity has been much debated and is the subject of marvelous icons and works of art. The churches of the East and of the West have struggled over the third person of the Trinity and whether the Holy Spirit proceeds from the Father/Creator or from the Father/Creator and the Son/Redeemer.

Baptists have generally been absolutely orthodox in their adherence to the mainstream Christian doctrine of the Trinity. Churches in Western Europe have held to the Latin form of the Nicean *creed*, but those in Eastern Europe have been content with the Slavic and Orthodox form of the creed up to this point, without the so-called filioque clause. When some of the English Baptist Churches in the 1700s became attracted to theological Unitarianism as part of the prevailing theological climate of the day, others within the General Baptist tradition [see *England*] led by the Yorkshire leader Dan Taylor, rejected this move towards Unitarianism and re-formed the *evangelical* and orthodox General Baptists into a New Connexion holding true to the doctrine of the Trinity.

KGJ

Troeltsch, Ernst (1865-1923) – Sociology of the Church
See *Sociology of the Church – Troeltsch and Niebuhr*.

Trusteeship
The *gathering* communities of intentional believers drawn together by the Triune God [see *Trinity*] are essentially *theocratic* and *missional* communities composed of those the *Holy Spirit* has drawn into *koinonia*. Such groups are therefore groups of disciples

who will vary in shape and task from time to time. However, it is recognised that such groups, over the years, acquire a way of being – forms of **worship**, **buildings** in which to gather, funds acquired by gift or other means for carrying forward the mission of the church [see **Offerings/Collection**; **Tithing**] which can be spent over several generations.

In such communities issues have existed in law as to how these more tangible assets might be used and protected for the purpose for which they were original given 'in trust'.

Here the notion of appointing some to act in a legal sense as trustee of the specific beliefs and practices of a community. In this way, protecting the possessions and funds of the community often stand in tension with the dynamic of the on-going life of an individual believing community. Sometimes the protections of the past are helpful, in other instances they can be irksome as when the wording of a trust fails to anticipate a changed world situation, e.g. the dedication of funds to training medical **missionaries** for service in China, when such a thing became **politically** impossible.

For Baptists, the question has been about ensuring the dynamic life of **discipleship** of a particular gathering community, whilst keeping in trust what has been passed on from earlier generations and ought to be passed on in a usable form to those who follow.

There have been notable situations in many parts of Europe where property and funds used by Baptists have been lost to the overall mission and purpose of the baptistic family through theological development or change, by misappropriation or mismanagement. To safeguard against this, the idea of trusteeship assumes there will be some individuals or body corporate appointed to safeguard these more permanent features. In some countries the **union** or convention has this trusteeship role with **property** and assets being held centrally. In other situations individuals are appointed and have standing in law as the trustees of the assets of a particular community. In other situations variants and mixes of these two extremes hold sway. Inevitably, to balance the situation properly between the legitimate desires for a community, acting under the guidance of the Holy

Spirit to use resources in a specific way, over against the proper respect to hold certain assets 'in trust' from the past and of use in the future is far from simple. *Theology*, law and financial regulations often come into conflict.

KGJ

FURTHER READING: K.G. Jones, 'The Theology of the Trust Deed: A Yorkshire Perspective' in *The Baptist Quarterly* Vol. 33, No. 3, 1989.

Turkey, Baptist history in

The first, and until now the only, Baptist church in the history of Turkey was established officially in 2001 in the outskirts of Izmir. Today it brings together approximately 35-40 adult *worshippers* every Sunday. The services take place in an historical *Anglican church building*. However, the beginning of Baptist work dates back to the 1990s when Ertan Cevik, having been converted [see *Conversion*] to Baptist beliefs in *Germany*, began to gather a home group for *fellowship*, *Bible* reading and *prayer* in his home town of Izmir. The present *ministries* of the church include *Sunday School* for *children*, a *women*'s group and regular *Bible study meetings*. Given the fact that although Turkey is a *secular state* the dominant population is *Muslim*, in *witness* much emphasis is put on *Christ*-like *discipleship*, being 'the salt and the light' in the local community. The Baptists in Izmir are committed to remain culturally Turkish, whilst being confessionally Christian – a combination that seems unbelievable for many of their fellow citizens.

AD

Turkistan, Baptist history in

See *Central Asia, Baptist history in*.

Turkmenistan, Baptist history in

[See also *Central Asia, Baptist history in*]
The Baptist Church, like Christianity in general, has very little presence in Turkmenistan, a Central Asian country which has seen a revival of *Islam* during recent decades. In its history, Baptist work, limited as it was and is, has reached mostly the Russian-speaking population. In general, the Turkmens, Uzbeks and Kazakhs, who constitute the majority of the population, have not been receptive to Baptist beliefs. Baptist work in Turkmenistan dates back to 1890 when I. Saveliev moved to Ashkhabad from Vladikavkaz. Saveliev was supported by F. Ovsyannikov, a former *Mennonite Brethren* believer, who arrived in Ashkhabad from the Samarkand area. Saveliev and Ovsyannikov had contacts with the local *Molokans* some of whom converted [see *Conversion*] to the Baptist *faith*. In the beginning this group *worshipped* together with the Molokans, and later with some *Protestant* Armenians, who lived in this region. In 1892 they formed a settlement and a small Baptist church in Keltitshivar (later Kuropatkinsky), some 20km from Ashkhabad. In addition, Baptist as well as *Evangelical* Christian work commenced among the Russian-speaking population in Ashkhabad. Before WWI the Ashkhabad Baptist church had approximately 100 *members*, some of whom had been *Orthodox*, others Molokans, and was led by F. Kabaev, from the North Caucasus, and later by Y. Morozov. According to A. Wardin, in 1913, there were 410 Baptists and 220 Evangelical Christians in Turkmenistan. *Soviet political* and atheistic persecutions in the later 1930s struck a serious, almost a deadly, blow to Baptist work in Turkmenistan. After WWII, and the earthquake in 1948, Baptists gathered in one another's homes. The Ashkhabad church was officially registered by Soviet authorities only in 1977, and in the mid 1980s it had some three dozen members. During recent decades, there has not been any significant *revival* among Turkmenistan Baptists. In 1995 there were little more than 100 Baptists in three churches, in Ashkhabad, Nebitdag and Krasnovodsk. Baptist work continues to be restricted in Turkmenistan, at present mostly due to Islamic religious and political preferences. Some help, both in *evangelism*, literature distribution and humanitarian aid, has been directed to Turkmenistan through the Central Asian Christian *Mission* and through *Licht im Osten*. The small number of Baptists cannot worship publicly. They affiliate to the *Union* of ECB in Central Asia but are not members of the *EBF*.

TP

Two-Thirds World

[See also *Jubilee and Two-Thirds-World Debt*]

Sociologists, economists, *politicians* and international developers have sought over the years to establish broad terms to describe stages of economic development and to use these in relationship to economic growth, civil society and political organisation. At best they are rough and ready tools and are constantly subject to qualification and re-categorisation in the light of events. So, for instance some oil rich countries in the Middle East now have highly developed cities and economic structures, in what have been categorised in the past as 'third-world' zones, but now in many ways have outstripped the so-called industrially developed countries of the 'first world'. 'Third world' was originally principally used to describe most of the countries of Africa (with the possible exception of South Africa), as well as poorer countries in Asia, South America, Polynesia and the Caribbean. This, in contrast to the 'First world' of industrial Europe, North America, Japan and Oceania (formerly Australasia) and the 'Second world' of the command economies of the *Soviet* sphere of influence. The first and second worlds have, since 1990, begun to merge, with *Russia* admitted to the *G8* group of industrialised *nations*. The admission of a number of former Warsaw Pact counties into the *European Union* and their rapid economic development also challenge the older language. Again, as India and China industrialise, the categorisation will become even more meaningless. The term 'Third world' has almost universally ceased to be used in these discussions, with the preference now to use 'Two-Thirds' World' as a reminder that the great bulk of the population of the world live in Africa, Asia and Latin America. For Christians the use of the title has normally accompanied the concern of believers to assist in responsible and sustainable development of the two-thirds world through *education* and investment and to respond to the needs of the two-thirds world when famine, disease and natural disaster have threatened the lives of ordinary people.

KGJ

Two-Thirds-World Debt

See *Jubilee and Two-Thirds-World Debt*.

U

UCCF

See *Student Christian Movement (SCM), Inter-Varsity Fellowship (IVF), World Student Christian Federation (WSCF) and International Fellowship of Evangelical Students (IFES)*.

UK, Baptist history in the

See *England; Ireland; Scotland; Wales, Baptist history in*.

Ukraine, Baptist history in

Baptist history in Ukraine dates back to the second half of the 19th century when the first instance of believers' baptism took place in a rural area in the southern part of the country. Shortly thereafter churches were started and the First Baptist Congress took place in the village of Novovasilivka in the Tavriysky region in 1884, the year normally recognised as the beginning of the organised *evangelical* movement. The Russian Baptist *Union* was organised at this congress.

Different sources give different information about the number of Baptists at the end of the 19th century, varying from 100,000-300,000. Even the lower figure is a testimony to rapid *growth* when the severity of the mass persecutions of evangelicals for their *faith* is taken into consideration. The cruelest years were 1880-1905, the so-called 'Pobedonostsev era'.

After the proclamation of the Ukrainian People's Republic at the beginning of 1918, the First Ukrainian Baptist Congress took place in Kiev (1-8 Oct 1918). There the Ukrainian Baptist Union was organised and it was decided to publish the *Ukrainian Baptist magazine*. However, at the Second Ukrainian Congress (1922) the Ukrainian Baptist Union was united with the Russian Baptist Union with its centre in Moscow. The Third Ukrainian Congress unanimously renewed the Ukrainian Baptist Union and the first issue of *Ukrainian Baptist* was eventually published the year after.

The well known 'Law about Cults' of 1929 began a new tragic period in the history of Ukrainian Baptists. A brotherhood numbering hundreds of thousands was under a threat of *death*. In the middle of the 1930s all Baptist churches were closed and *church buildings* confiscated. By 1944 1,000s of leaders and *members* had been imprisoned many of whom were never seen again leaving no knowledge of when and where they died. The Ukrainian Baptist Union started its work again at the Forth Ukrainian Congress in 1943 but the next year it was liquidated and *ministers* were subjected to oppression. In the same year the Party decided to organise the *Soviet Union* Association of Evangelical Christian Baptists in which all other *protestant* denominations were included.

Only in 1990 was the Ukrainian Baptist Union renewed and a new era begun. After the independence of Ukraine was proclaimed on 24 Aug 1991, and, in the context of *religious freedom*, some kind of spiritual life was revived. New regulations were adopted at the 22nd Congress (8-11 Feb) and the name 'The Ukrainian Union of Evangelical Christian Baptists' was changed to the 'Ukrainian Union of Evangelical Christian Baptist Churches' by the decision taken at the 25th Congress (10-13 May 2006). In the early 21st century Baptists in Ukraine are once again experiencing rapid growth, and it is estimated that there are currently around 200,000 Baptists in Ukraine, mostly in the Union of Evangelical Christians Baptists, with smaller numbers of *Reform Baptists* and of those belonging to *autonomous* non-affiliated churches.

SVS

UN Universal Declaration on Human Rights

See *United Nations Universal Declaration on Human Rights and UN Agencies*.

Unemployed, Work with the

[See also *Unemployment*]

The response of Christian bodies to unemployed people tends to operate in three ways.

The general response of churches is one

which provides *pastoral* help for unemployed people. This is offered through drop-in centres where facilities are available to alleviate the impact of unemployment upon the person.

The reformist approach seeks to re-integrate unemployed people into employment through providing church-based projects offering skills training (such as basic IT training which is offered by Baptist churches in *Britain* and *Scandinavia*) to jobless people to help equip them to return to work. This can lead the *Church* to challenge government to change employment structures to enable more people to find employment. The 1997 the Churches' report entitled *Unemployment and the Future of Work* was a critique of such structures which called for measures such as the reform of taxation and the benefit system to ease people back into work. At a different level as churches engage with the community through initiatives like homework clubs or senior citizen luncheon clubs so they create employment.

A third approach aims at radical transformation of societal structures which traditionally equate personal worth with employment thus devaluing unemployed people. Although this has been on the *Industrial Mission* agenda it is not an approach the churches are comfortable with and little has been achieved in this area.

WJA

Unemployment

[See also *Unemployed, Work with the*]
One outcome of changes in working practices during the last quarter of the 20th century was severe unemployment, particularly, but not exclusively, in the traditional smokestack industries. For some people, job loss provides the opportunity to pursue new challenges in life. For others, to lose their job is also to lose self-worth, status and financial security. This is reinforced in a society which estimates human worth against the type of job one has.

Unemployment can be defined in several ways:

- *Seasonal Unemployment* is generated by changing demands for *labour* during the year. Workers are hired for *harvest* or summer vacation work and when the job has been completed then the workforce is laid off. This type of unemployment is common in many societies.
- *Cyclical Unemployment* is part of the boom/bust economics. As the economic cycle moves from boom to bust so workers are dismissed to reduce costs, hoping to be recruited again in the upturn. Cyclical unemployment is common among companies who recruit a workforce to complete a manufacturing order and then dismiss workers until the next order arrives.
- *Structural Unemployment* is the most far reaching and most severe type and is chiefly the result of change in working practices. Factors which bring about structural unemployment include new *technology*, social change and the impact of *women* in the workplace. A contemporary factor is 'out-sourcing' – the movement of menial jobs to countries where the rates of pay are significantly lower than in developed *nations*. These, and other shifts in the way work is structured and carried out, have left a legacy of fewer jobs for increasing numbers of people.

WJA

Unevangelised People Groups

See *Unreached and Unevangelised People Groups*.

Union Churches

See *Ecumenical covenants and partnerships*.

Unions/Conventions

[See also *Assembly, General – as governing body of Union; Ecclesiology (Church Polity)*]
Unions or conventions are terms used by Baptists and others to describe a cooperative community of *faith* beyond the level of the *local church* within a country or a region.

This development reflects an ecclesiology, which is present in the NT, even though it is still at an early stage of development. Both *Catholic* and *Orthodox Churches* are *episcopally* organised and this form of government was continued in the churches of the magisterial *reformation* that is where reform was initiated by the magistrate whether prince or city council, though in the reformed *tradition* a church *synod* often took the place of the *bishop*. Churches which developed a *congregational* polity, whilst they may have separated from the *state church*, were wary of becoming a series of totally isolated units. Initially they began to organise among themselves for purposes of *fellowship* and cooperative action. This became even more necessary as such churches faced the needs of the new urban society created by the industrial revolution as well as the need to promote *overseas missions*. Such factors gave rise to the emergence of national organisations, which have taken the name of either unions or conventions, governed by a representative assembly and/or council. But the essential ecclesiological unit remained the local church. Such larger bodies, able to discuss issues of doctrine and to represent Baptist opinion in national debates, came to secure great respect but their conclusions could never be imposed on local churches or their officers against their will. The acceptance of their decisions has always been voluntary. That does not mean that such organisations are 'to be regarded as optional and secondary'. 'They are the necessary expression of Christian fellowship, a necessary manifestation of the *church* visible. The local church is not truly a church if it lives an entirely separate life' (E.A. Payne) There is accordingly little *theological* justification for an independency which has no regard for the wider church, nor for multiple unions/conventions existing within a single country, especially if they are seem to be competing with one another. Indeed the need to manifest the *unity* of the Body of Christ as a *witness* to a *reconciling* gospel argues that Baptist unions and conventions should seek to work as far as they are able with fellow believers of other Christian *traditions*, especially those with whom they share a common *evangelical* faith.

PMIL

Unitarianism
[See also *Trinity*]
Unitarianism signifies belief in the Oneness

of God, and thus the denial of a separate divinity for *Jesus* and the *Holy Spirit*. Though later influenced by the rationalism of the *Enlightenment*, in the beginning early Unitarians like Michael Servetus came to this position because they could not find sufficient basis for specifically Trinitarian beliefs in *scripture*.

Some early *Anabaptists* had similar difficulties with the doctrine of the Trinity, and soon came to follow the teaching of Faustus Socinius (hence Socinianism) who spent the latter part of his life in modern *Poland* where his views came to dominate the anabaptist movement. In Poland in 1569 John Sigismund of Transylvania issued an act of toleration recognising the Unitarians. When later proscribed in Poland the movement spread to *Holland*, where it also became forbidden teaching from 1639.

A number of English General Baptists [see *England*] in the later 17th century and early 18th century moved in this direction, it is suggested because of their *association* with Dutch *Mennonites* who adopted the *Christology* of Melchior Hoffman, with its minimalist views of the *incarnation*. Whilst many General Baptists following the teaching of Thomas Grantham remained *orthodox*, others moved via the adoption of Arian views (a denial of the true divinity and pre-existence of Christ, affirming him rather as the Father's special creation) in a Unitarian direction, as did a smaller number of Particular Baptists, especially from Bristol, at the end of the 18th century. The name 'Unitarian' only gained currency after 1774 when Theophilus Lindsey seceded from the *Church of England* and founded Essex Chapel, the first congregation to bear this title. Other non-trinitarian congregations still called themselves *Presbyterian* or General Baptist. It was because the 'old' connexion of General Baptists seemed seriously compromised in this direction that Dan Taylor, who had a *Methodist* background, founded the New Connexion of General Baptists in 1770, espousing a lively *evangelical* and *evangelistic Arminian theology* of a Wesleyan variety.

This history has made Baptist groups particularly concerned to ensure Christological orthodoxy within their fellowship. In the 19th century Unitarianism became closely associated with *Universalism*, the belief that a loving God could never condemn any creature to *hell*, and more generally came to stand for a non-*dogmatic* approach to Christian theology now much influenced by the thought of the enlightenment in a way which differed markedly from the wrestling with scripture which characterised the searches of an earlier generation. Although in the 19th century, especially in America, Unitarianism seemed to be at the cutting edge of theological exploration, in the 20th century Unitarianism had reduced attraction and became a minority interest amongst a small number of intellectuals. Historically, however, Unitarians have played an important part in *nonconformity*'s search for full religious toleration.

JHYB & TP

United Churches in Sweden

Since the 1950s Swedish church life has been strongly influenced by the *ecumenical movement*. One result is the emergence of so-called united congregations. The first one was organised in Höör in Southern *Sweden*. There, for the first time in Sweden, a Baptist congregation practicing only believers' *baptism* and a congregation which was a member of The Swedish Covenant Church, practicing both *infant baptism* and believers' baptism, were united. Of the Swedish Baptist *Union*'s 18,000 *members* by the end of 2002, a little more than 9,700 or rather more than half belonged to united churches. The majority of these churches have dual membership in The Baptist Union and The Covenant Church. In addition a majority of the other Swedish *free churches* are part of this local ecumenical movement: The *Evangelical* Free Church and the *Pentecostal* movement, which practiced believers' baptism, the *Methodist* Church practicing infant baptism, and the Swedish Alliance *Mission* which adheres to both infant and believers' baptism. The number of united churches in Sweden was, in 2004, approximately 200.

A significant driving force in this free-church ecumenical movement has been the question of *fellowship* at the *Lord's Table*. Until the middle of the 1950s most Swedish Baptist churches exclusively practiced closed communion. However, with reference to early Baptist *tradition* in *England*, Swedish Baptist congregations began to practice *open communion*. The next step in this development the Baptist Union of Sweden took in 1969, when the Annual Conference voted to accept *open membership* in the churches. Accordingly membership in a Baptist church would be granted a person upon profession of *faith* in *Christ*, without any baptism at all. A similar manner of gaining membership is transferred membership, by which a person baptised as an infant and holding membership in a paedobaptist church, upon request may be granted membership in recognition of the baptism and membership she or he already has.

Through these changes the way was opened for local Baptist churches to unite with paedobaptist congregations and establish united churches, in some cases holding membership in several denominations. Parallel to these changes in *church polity* a more *sacramental* view of baptism has developed among Swedish Baptists. Baptism is now generally understood as an expression of an objective act of God, as well as the believing person's response to the divine act, and not only as a human confession of faith in Christ, and an act of obedience to him.

TB

United Kingdom, Baptist history in

See *England*; *Ireland*; *Scotland*; *Wales, Baptist history in*.

United Nations Universal Declaration on Human Rights and UN Agencies

[See also *Human Rights*; *Human Rights Advocacy*]

In the context of the loss of life and physical damage caused by WWI, US President Wilson developed a vision for the establishment of an international organisation which would make future war impossible. Accordingly a *covenant* for the establishing of a League of Nations was signed by those attending the Versailles Peace Conference and became an integral part of the subsequent *Peace* Treaty. The League, which had its headquarters in Geneva, began its work at the beginning of 1920, but was fatally disadvantaged by the failure of the USA to join. However, by 1929, 54 other *nations* had joined. Whilst the League accomplished some useful work in technical cooperation it failed in its main peace-keeping function: it did not stop Japan invading Manchuria in 1931, nor *Italy* invading Abyssinia in 1935, whilst *Russia* was expelled for attacking *Finland* in 1939. By 1939, 13 other nations had left the League, which took no action against the expansionist policies of the National Socialist government in *Germany*. It was dissolved in 1946.

This failure must have been in the minds of those who began to think about a successor organisation to try and secure peace after WWII. The language of 'United Nations' had first been used by the allies in 1942 at a conference in Washington which was fleshed out with organisational detail at the Dunbarton Oaks Conference in Oct 1944. The United Nations was founded in 1945 when some 50 nations signed the UN Charter. By 2000 this number had become 189. Its purpose is 'to maintain international peace and security', 'to develop friendly relations among nations', to achieve international cooperation in solving international problems' and for 'promoting and encouraging respect for human rights and fundamental freedoms'. The United Nations works through an Assembly where all nations are represented, a Security Council which is made up of permanent and elected members and a secretariat (led by the secretary-general elected by the Assembly for a five-year term) as well as other specialised committees, dealing with legal, social and economic affairs. The 1945 Charter, drawn up in a pre-nuclear age, remains unchanged and does not accordingly adequately meet 21st century needs but amendment would be a laborious and possibly unfruitful process. One of the greatest impediments to a wider usefulness is its commitment to the doctrine of national sovereignty which deliberately disallows any intervention in the internal affairs of member states, notwithstanding the abuse of human rights that might be occurring. As the League of Nations suffered from the absence of the USA, the UN has suffered from an over-dominant partner and dependence

in much of its work on US funding. More successful than its predecessor it has achieved more in peace-keeping than peace making.

It has also done well in the humanitarian, development and cultural field especially through its associated agencies such as the High Commission for Refugees (UNHCR taking over the function of the older body UNRRA), the UN Children's Fund (UNICEF), the UN Development Programme, the UN Educational, Scientific and Cultural Organisation (UNESCO) and the World Health Organisation (WHO) bodies with which the churches have readily cooperated, the *Baptist World Alliance* being accorded *non-governmental organisation* status.

In Dec 1948 the UN issued its Universal Declaration on Human Rights, though this was not of itself binding on member states without further conventions and declarations. Basic human rights are normally considered to focus around four basic considerations:

(1) the *inviolability* of the person in terms of both physical and psychological well-being, privacy of the family and the home, and of correspondence;

(2) *freedom* from all illegal restrictions especially on the part of *state* power including freedom of thought, *conscience*, religion, association and assembly [see *Freedom of Conscience*],

(3) the *equality* of all persons precluding discrimination of every kind,

(4) the upholding of the right of *participation* in both *political* decision-making as well as in decisions relating to the economic processes in which the individual is engaged.

These are issues with which Baptists have engaged from the time of *John Smyth* onwards. Whilst concern for *religious liberty* has been a major part of this concern, Baptists have, in working out the doctrine of *creation*, developed a *theological* basis for wider human rights concerns. E.g. *William Carey* early became concerned about the Indian cultural practice of *sati,* the burning of a widow on her husband's funeral pyre which was abolished in 1829. Even before the establishment of modern *missions* Baptists were concerned about the iniquity of the Slave Trade and campaigned for its abolition. Missionary endeavour in the West Indies brought them into contact with slavery as an institution and again they became eager campaigners for abolition and for the securing of a stable post-slave society. In the Civil Rights Movement in the USA in the 1960s and 70s Baptists took a leading part under such black Baptist leaders as Martin Luther King, Jr. Similarly they played their part in opposing Human Rights violations in South Africa during *Apartheid*, though in both situations Baptists could be found who *pietistically* opted out of what they deemed over political programmes.

JHYB

Unity of the Brethren
See *Czech Brethren and the Czech Reformation*.

Unity of the Church
[See also *Ecumenical/Ecumenical (Oecumenical) Movement*; *Ecumenical covenants and partnerships/Union Churches/Dual Alignments*; *Ecumenical Movement, European Baptist contributors in the 20th and 21st centuries*; *Oikoumene*; *World Council of Churches*]
The Unity of the Church is both gift and goal. The *church* possesses spiritual unity given to it by its *Lord* but it still has to struggle to demonstrate that unity in its life and *witness*. Above all spiritual unity must not be made an excuse for staying with visible fragmentation and isolation. *Bishop* Leslie Newbigin of the united Church of South India argued that the first stepping stone in this process was 'the unity of all in each place'. This is where unity counts and where it needs to become visible. But the local is only a starting point for also involved is the unity of all believers in every age, and the unity of the whole people of God throughout the world. Local unity can take the form of a fully integrated united congregation sharing one *church meeting*, though not yet one in table fellowship [see *Communion and Intercommunion*] if the *Roman Catholics* are involved. Other models will stress cooperation and as much joint activity as *conscience* allows. At the national level the

stress may be on participation in conciliar bodies, where much work in a given situation can be done on behalf of all the churches. Here, there is increasing stress on the *missionary* responsibilities of the church, that is, the union of the people of God is for a purpose, that 'the world may believe' (Jn 17). Internationally, *bilateral conversations* and even agreements (such as *Meissen* and *Porvoo* between *Anglicans* and *Lutherans* and Reuilly between Anglicans, Lutherans and *Reformed Churches*) have helped to move the agenda onwards. Baptists have not been involved in this kind of conversation beyond the mutual recognition between the *Free Churches* established in many countries at the beginning of the 20th century. More recently, a number of *unions* have expressed interest in being part of the ongoing *Leuenberg* process of discussion between Lutherans, Reformed and Free Churches in Europe. Internationally, too, the *Faith and Order* movement has sought to identify points of convergence and clarify differences between the churches. This is to be seen in documents such as the Lima statement on *Baptism, Eucharist and Ministry* whilst the Commission on World *Mission* and Evangelism has sought to challenge all churches with their missionary responsibilities in *Mission and Evangelism: An Ecumenical Affirmation*. Both documents published in 1982 had significant Baptist inputs through the pens of Morris West and Raymund Fung respectively, the latter in particular being widely welcomed by *Evangelicals*.

Clearly any proposal for expressing the unity of the church must embrace the concept of 'unity in diversity' for brigading different *traditions* together is both unachievable and unattractive. On the other hand there need to be boundaries to what is acceptable diversity, determined by the parameters of the *apostolic faith*. This is especially true if that diversity is to become what has been called a 'reconciled diversity', which gives meaning to the affirmation that the churches do share a mutual *fellowship* even if it is an imperfect fellowship. All churches are encouraged to affirm that the Church of God is larger than their particular communion and are encouraged to recognise something of the true church of God in one another. The largest problems concern the **Orthodox** and the Roman Catholic Church. Those of other traditions are able to come to a common table with **eucharistic** hospitality frequently practiced between them, even when full recognition of **episcopal** and non-episcopal orders has yet to be achieved. Confidence between churches has to be worked at and it is disappointing when churches separate from one another even claiming not to be able to **pray** together, and catholic, orthodox and **protestant** all bare a measure of responsibility for not being able to kneel together before the one **Lord of the Church**. Sometimes it seems that there is need for a holy revolution by people at the grass roots level to overcome such difficulties.

JHYB

Universal Declaration on Human Rights
See **United Nations Universal Declaration on Human Rights and UN Agencies**.

Universal Week of Prayer
See **Week of Prayer for Christian Unity/Universal Week of Prayer/Women's World Day of Prayer**.

Universalism
See **Annihilation and Universalism**.

Universities and Colleges Christian Fellowship
See **Student Christian Movement (SCM), Inter-Varsity Fellowship (IVF), World Student Christian Federation (WSCF) and International Fellowship of Evangelical Students (IFES)**.

Unreached and Unevangelised People Groups
About 100 years ago at the first World Mission Conference in **Edinburgh 1910** John R. Mott had the vision that it might be possible to **evangelise** the world within that generation. This great vision broke down due to two disastrous world wars, the development

of anti-Christian ideologies (**Fascism** and **Communism**) and the crisis of **traditional church** life in the Western world.

According to statistics from the **United Nations**, from the **theologian** David Barrett and from the International Mission Board (IMB) of the **Southern Baptist Convention** out of a world population of 6.4 billion people the major religions today are represented as follows:

Christians:	2.1 billion
Muslims:	1.3 billion
Hindus:	850 million
Buddhists:	370 million
New Religionists:	105 million
Non-religious/Atheists:	774 million

Many churches and mission agencies especially from the **evangelical** part of Christianity have discovered over recent years that they had put their resources primarily into **mission** work in areas that had been 'reached' already, more or less, by the gospel. Initiated by individuals like **Billy Graham** and by movements like '**Lausanne**' and 'AD 2000' the focus in the 1990s, therefore, was driven more and more towards the so-called 'unreached' people-groups. **Missiologists** discovered that about 3.5 billion people worldwide especially in the area of the so-called '10/40-window' (living between the 10th and the 40th global lines of longitude) belong to those groups that have no or very little access to any witness of the gospel.

The terms '**unreached**' and 'unevangelised' are used in the literature in different ways of understanding. A helpful guideline may be the definition given by the IMB of the SBC. They define an unreached people group as 'a people group in which less than 2 % of the population are Evangelical Christians'. In this way out of the more than 11,000 different people groups (with their own language and culture) 6,400 people groups including a population of 3.5 billion persons have been identified as 'unreached'.

Most of these people live in the Middle East, in the Arabic world, in India and in the Far East. They predominantly belong to one of the other great world religions, to Islam, Hinduism or Buddhism. People in these countries and cultures now receive the Good News of **Jesus Christ** in a much stronger way than before. The strategy of focusing on the 'unreached people groups' therefore on the one hand has led to evangelism and *church planting* in many of these formerly closed countries, on the other hand has contributed also to the already existing conflicts and clashes between cultures and religions.

In the discussion about the strategy of focusing on the 'unreached people groups' critical questions have been put on the table. E.g.:

- What do we mean by 'reached by the gospel' with regard to maturity and sustainability?
- How can we develop a wider understanding of 'unreached people groups' not only in geographical but also in *sociological* terms (regarding sub-cultures in large cities for instance)?
- How can we develop a wider understanding of world mission including the challenging movement of *secularism* in the *post-modern* world?

The focus on the 'unreached people groups' nevertheless has developed an important emphasis towards the fulfilment of the *Great Commission*. We therefore should broaden our horizon in the view of this strategy and in the understanding that the implementation of this world mission movement should not be done primarily by 'Westerners' (Europeans and Americans), but predominantly by missionaries from the area of the 'New *Christendom*' (Philip Jenkins) [see *Mission strategy in a post-modern age*; *Reverse Mission*].

In this way it certainly may be an encouragement to look at the statistics for world Christianity in another very positive way. When in 1900 about 85 % of the Christians worldwide were in Europe and America, today 55 % of Christians are in the so-called *Two-Thirds World* of Africa, Asia and Latin America. Whereas in 1990 only 5.4 million Baptist believers were living in the Global South, in 2004 that number had increased to 12.7 million. Thus these first-generation Christians in Africa, Asia and Latin America can be the ones to fulfil the Great Commission.

                                                                                HG

FURTHER READING: Philip Jenkins: *Next Christendom: The Coming of Global Christianity*, Oxford University Press, Oxford, 2003. www.imb.org. www.religiontoday.com. www.un.org/popin.

Urban Rural Mission

[See also *Industrial Mission*; *Mission*]

Processes such as industrialisation and urbanisation which date back to the 18th- century *England* made more and more impact on the economies of very many countries in the 20th century causing great distress to large sectors of the world's population caught up in them. When the *International Missionary Council* merged with the World Council at the New Delhi Assembly of the *WCC* in 1961 these were the challenges that the new Division of World Mission and *Evangelism* churches had to face. Following the new Division's World Conference in Mexico City, a working group on Urban Industrial Mission was set up, which produced a valuable report for the Uppsala Assembly in 1968. This led to a call to the churches to become engaged with the new poor in both city and country, and to become the servant church amongst emerging and struggling groups of the powerless.

At first, urban and rural concerns were addressed by different offices, but in 1978 the two concerns were amalgamated as Urban Rural Mission (URM) which undertook its work by supporting local initiatives. In the 80s the task intensified with the need to grapple with militarisation, the escalation of *violence* in all too many societies, and the suppression of democratic processes in others. A People's Movement began to emerge, campaigning for *human rights* as national elites and *trans-national corporations* worked together in unholy alliance to increase profits at the expense of those who worked in both factory and in field.

In many places URM played a significant part, listening to and recording peoples' stories, under-girding the many campaigns with basic Biblical and *theological* reflection, reading the *scriptures* in the actual contexts where these marginalised people lived. In their campaigning for *political* and socio-economic enfranchisement, these people groups were helped to find a place at the tables where vital decisions, which had such profound effects on their lives, were being made.

Out of this experience, URM wrote the following sentences in self-description: 'Urban rural mission is primarily a movement of *men* and *women* rooted in the Christian *faith* who are called, along with others, to the mission of God to participate in the struggle of the exploited, marginalised, and oppressed for justice and liberation URM is involved in concrete situations of human *suffering* where people are victimised in the process of rapid social change caused by modernisation and industrialisation, and exploitative economic and political systems...URM has been committed to work with slum dwellers, the *unemployed*, industrial and women workers, *indigenous people*, fisherworkers, rural *poor* and landless labourers, migrant workers, etc.' But URM not only sought to offer solidarity to peoples' movements, it also sought to influence the churches' *missiological* thinking by encouraging church agencies to engage in sociocultural analysis as they sought to think biblically and theologically about how they could support community action for social transformation.

JHYB

USSR, Baptist history in

See *Armenia*; *Azerbaijan*; *Belarus*; *Estonia*; *Georgia*; *Kazakhstan*; *Kyrgyzstan*; *Latvia*; *Lithuania*; *Moldova*; *Russia*; *Tajikistan*; *Turkmenistan*; *Ukraine*; *Uzbekistan, Baptist history in*.

Usury

Usury, or the business of living by levying interest on loans of money, is condemned in the OT, though the NT makes no judgment on the issue. The Church Fathers also argued against the practice and the *Roman Catholic* Church remained opposed to it until the 19th century. *Luther* and *Zwingli* also opposed the practice but *Calvin* allowed modest charges on loans. This is one of the reasons why he has been seen as friendly to the emergence of *capitalism*. This was one of the most important issues in the relationship between 'gospel', that is Christian teaching and 'culture' in the great changes of the 16th century, with *Protestantism* identifying itself with the modernising forces that were challenging the accepted practices of traditional society. The modern *church*, unlike the medieval church no longer thinks of

money as a barren means of exchange but as productive of *wealth* like any other form of *property*, though clearly the levying of excessive rates of interest must still be condemned as one of the unacceptable faces of capitalism. *Islam* also has difficulties with the practice of the levying of interest but has, with some difficulty, found ways of sponsoring Islamic banking/mortgages and other financial enterprises.

ET

Uzbekistan, Baptist history in

[See also *Central Asia, Baptist history in*]
The Baptist movement in Uzbekistan, a predominantly *Muslim* country, began as Russian Baptist immigrants moved into the area in 1896. Early Baptist fellowships are reported in the smaller villages around the capital, Tashkent. These early fellowships were strengthened by Christians serving with the Russian army in the area as well as by Bible *colporteurs*, but it was the establishment of the Tashkent Baptist congregation that united Baptist efforts in Uzbekistan. In 1905, Ivan Sevastianovich Turuhin was ordained [see *Ordination*] as the first *elder* of the Tashkent Baptist congregation which rented a house of *prayer* [see *Chapels*] near the Salar River. In 1926, they built a building on Kafanova Street. From 1925-28, the annual congresses of the Central Asian *Union* of Baptists met in the Tashkent House of Prayer. The Baptist fellowship of ethnic Germans and Russians living in Uzbekistan grew to 15 communities and 10 *preaching* points. On 13 Feb 1932, the Tashkent community was forced to close and it remained officially closed until Oct 1944. With its reopening came a renewed effort to open the former preaching points and rebuild the Baptist *association*. The Tashkent church grew [see *Church Growth*] up to 1,300 members in the 1950s, but a decline in *membership* numbers followed. In 2002 there were approximately 30 officially established Baptist churches in Uzbekistan. The majority population of each of these churches is Russian but Uzbeks, Tajiks, and Armenians are also included in their membership. Also some Korean groups that adhere to the Baptist *faith* have emerged. The Baptist population is currently in decline due

to the exodus of ethnic Russians from the former *Soviet* Republic. Few native Uzbeks have joined the Baptist faith which has been dominated by Russian culture. There are fewer than 10 Baptist fellowships with a majority of native Uzbeks. Their size and exact location are currently unavailable due to the sensitive nature of their existence within an Islamic nation.

GLN

V

Validity of Orders

The notion of validity as a *theological* and *sacramental* concept exists principally within the *Catholic, Orthodox* and *Anglican* Christian *traditions* though it can be found to greater or lesser extent in some others of the magisterial *reformation* traditions, such as the *Lutheran* and *Reformed communions*.

On the whole the concept occurs in relation to the three orders of *ministry* which some Christian communions perceive – *bishop, priest* and *deacon*. As such, it is immediately, in its normal usage, outside the range of reference of most Baptist communities which do not readily work with the model of three orders of ministry in the classical form. So the Roman Catholic Church determines from scripture and tradition the three orders and that to be valid, those ordained [see *Ordination*] to Christian ministry as a deacon, priest or bishop should have this performed according to the teaching and *liturgy* of the *Church* and by a regular bishop in the *apostolic* succession as defined and regulated by the Roman Catholic Church. There are disputes amongst the churches for whom this is important about the validity of the orders of those in the other traditions who make the same claim for authenticity and succession from Peter. Negatively such churches would not regard those ordained in one of the *free churches* as having proper orders and therefore not able, e.g., to preside at the *eucharist*. Or if they were to do so in a building of that denomination, then such a service would be regarded as an '*ecumenical*' service or a celebration according to the order of the church of the visiting clergyman, not of the *episcopal* church concerned.

Whilst many Baptist *unions* and churches in Europe and the Middle East guard very carefully those recognised and ordained to the *pastoral* ministry or to regional ministry and though this might be seen as a form of the concept of validity, where the *associating* churches choose to protect and regulate with care those called to certain ministries amongst them, the language of the Validity of Orders is not used. These unions at ordination ensure the liturgy and *prayer* are performed with representation from the wider church and in accordance with regulations laid down by the union, nevertheless, the form and purpose would be different to that of the episcopal and some of the magisterial reformation churches. This does not mean that there is any difference of concern for ministry to be recognised decently and in good order, but it does stand outside of the classic debate in Christianity about the validity of orders. It is also true to say that some Baptist communities take no notice of order and decency as theological concepts, but work on the approach of pragmatism – this person seems to have a *gift*, so they should exercise it without formation, testing and ordination within a prescribed framework.

This issue cannot be avoided where Christians of different traditions operate together in ecumenical partnership. In such situations the discipline of the participating churches is respected: thus a Baptist layperson [see *Laity*] could preside at communion but not a *Methodist* or Anglican layperson. Much ecumenical debate turns around the recognition of one another's orders. Thus in Europe free churches normally recognise one another's orders but in the European agreements between confessional families, such as *Meissen, Porvoo*, Reuilly, the Anglican-Methodist *Covenant*, and *Leuenberg*, there are different levels of recognition, but none of these involve Baptists.

KGJ

Vatican, The

[See also *Infallibility of the Pope*; *Papacy*; *Roman Catholicism*]

The Vatican, or rather, the Vatican City is a *state* with all a state's characteristics: territory, money, jurisdiction. It replaces the more extensive Pontifical State which was lost to the Papacy in 1870 in the struggles leading up to the unification of *Italy*. Its *political* position was further clarified in 1929 when the Lateran Treaty named after the Roman Basilica where the documents were signed, clarified the status of the new

Vatican state. At the same time, a Concordat was reached between the Roman Catholic Church and the Italian State, spelling out the privileged position of the Catholic Church within the Italian state. The Treaty and the Concordat were signed by the Vatican Secretary of State, Cardinal Pietro Gasparri, and the Head of the Italian Government, Benito Mussolini. This was the very same pope who called Mussolini 'the man of Providence', because of the exceptional benefits that were accorded to the Pope with the Lateran Treaty. A revised Concordat was signed on 18 Feb 1984 by the Vatican Secretary of State, Cardinal Agostino Casaroli, and by the Italian Prime Minister, Bettino Craxi.

The Vatican has diplomatic representatives in all the accredited countries (these are known as 'nunciatures' and 'papal nuncios' rather than embassies and ambassadors) and, with the principle of reciprocity, the accredited countries nominate their ambassadors to the Holy See (usually they are different from those accredited to the Italian government, and some *protestant* countries have been reluctant to make such appointments). In the same way, like other states, there are papal nuncios to other international organisations, e.g. the *United Nations*.

The Vatican incorporates in one body two quite different aspects, which should always be kept distinct, yet cannot be wholly separated. On the one hand it is a state on a par with all other states with its relative rights and duties, on the other it is the centre of world Catholicism, two sides of the same coin. Pope Pius XI, when the Treaty and Concordat were signed, to underline the close relationship between them, commented *simul stabunt, simul cadunt*, [the two aspects of the Vatican stand and fall together].

Arising from these two aspects of the Vatican's existence, the Vatican in common speech also stands for the central ecclesiastical bureaucracy (sometimes also known as the Roman Curia) which aids the Pope in governing the Roman Catholic Church. There are more than 30 departments making up the Vatican bureaucracy which in 2000 cost just under $200 million to run. The most important departments are called congregations with the Congregation for the Doctrine of the *Faith* the most important.

The Present pope, the former Cardinal Ratzinger, was known as a conservative defender of *traditional* Catholic values as President of this congregation. The next level operates under the *authority* of Pontifical Councils, such as that responsible for Promoting Christian *Unity*, or that responsible for issues of Justice and Peace. The third group relate to Commissions such as those concerned with *theology* and the *Bible*. All are headed by a Cardinal President. Sometimes observers note different attitudes coming from these different departments with some adopting a more conservative and others a more *liberal* approach. Sometimes, also, the policies emerging from the Vatican are seen to be at variance with the positions developed by different national *bishop* conferences, or the different religious orders.

DT

Violence/Non-Violence

Violence is all too much an unwanted part of the context of modern life, from the violence of *political* rhetoric from which it is difficult to disengage to violence in the home to the gun/knife crime that causes carnage amongst the youth of our inner cities which clearly demonstrate that violence does not need high *technology* tools to wreak its havoc.

Domestic violence, despite the forces of family solidarity which all too easily coalesce in a pattern of denial, remains the most pervasive yet hidden form of violence, taking both physical and psychological forms, extending to assault, rape and even killings, calling for safe places to be established for its victims, mainly *women* and *children*. Closely related is the violence associated with the trafficking of women and their exploitation for sexual purposes [see *Prostitution*]. Worst of all is sexual abuse within the life of the *church*: that it can happen has to be regretfully acknowledged whilst church officers need to be ever vigilant against this possibility.

International conflict has been discussed in terms of the competing *creeds* of *pacifism* and the *just war theory*, though the question now arises whether *nuclear* weapons does not make nuclear pacifists of all peoples of *conscience*? In 1966 a World Conference on Church and Society posed the question, 'whether the violence which sheds blood in planned revolutions may not be a lesser evil than the violence which, though bloodless condemns whole populations to perennial despair?' Questions may be raised as to whether in modern politics there has been a loss of confidence in argument and reasonable persuasion, and too easy resort to violent intervention. But as a last resort is the deployment of armed force to secure justice ethically justifiable? It is one of the ironies of modern history that one of the most eloquent advocates of the way of non-violence, Baptist *pastor*, Martin Luther King, should himself have been killed by an assassin's bullet.

More recently the rise of the suicide bomber raises questions as to what legal constraints the *state* needs to invoke in protection of its citizens. Within all conflicts there are undoubtedly elements that cannot be countenanced by the Christian conscience, such as all forms of torture, the holding or maltreatment of innocent hostages, the deliberate or indiscriminate slaughter of non-combatants, the use of biological or chemical weapons against *humankind*. Other elements to be guarded against include the deliberate *pollution* of the atmosphere and damage to the environment affecting not only the present but the inheritance of future generations.

Even good causes have to be pursued in the right way: when the *WCC* began thinking about a programme to deal with the pervasive violence of the modern world, its first thoughts were to create a 'Programme to Combat Violence' modelled on its older initiative, the *'Programme to Combat Racism'*. Then it realised that the language itself was a poor *witness* and so it sponsored 'The Decade to Overcome Violence: Churches seeking *Reconciliation* and *Peace*, 2001-10'. The question that has to be answered is, what does it mean to be the Church in a world of violence? How can churches help create a culture of non-violence?

Religion as a cause of violence between communities has done great disservice to the witness of the church. The *Catholic-Protestant* struggle in *Northern Ireland* whilst fuelled by deep *secular* community divisions was fought under the banners of

appeal to religious loyalties, whilst in the former *Yugoslavia*, Catholic-Orthodox-Muslim divisions have been used to justify the most appalling massacres. In South Africa the ugly violence of *apartheid* was justified by *theological* arguments. More recently the politics of terror has taken a new turn with the violence of the 9/11 events in New York and Washington and the London bombings. All too easily the conflict has been made into a Holy War with religion appealed to, to justify sanctions on both sides. The demonisation of religious opponents and the deployment of theological anathemas has to be avoided, and in such situations patiently developed *dialogue*, without theological compromise, working from a common humanity and respect for each others beliefs, though not their endorsement, must be allowed to develop mutual understanding and sympathy.

JHYB

Vocation
See *Call/Calling; Pastoral Call.*

Volkskirche
See *Believers' Church and Volkskirche.*

Voluntary church
The term voluntary religion reflects a situation, where *religious freedom* is legally recognised by the *state*. Religious freedom permits the formation of voluntary religious organisations. If there is a religious establishment of the state [see *National Churches*], this freedom is often conditioned by *traditional* privileges of the majority. The core of the matter is the freedom to establish communities of faith that are self-governing and self-supporting without any interference by the state. In that sense it is a *free church* in contrast to an establishment of religion that is supported and run by the state. Majority churches clearly differ from the churches where *membership* is a matter of voluntary and free choice. This is not to say that voluntary religion has no place in human society at large, as if it were a purely private matter. Also free churches have an awareness and involvement in public mat-

ters, but religion and *politics* are in principle and practice kept apart [see *Separation of Church and State*].

The distinction between voluntary and established religion has been of special significance in Europe. In the aftermath of the *Reformation*, religion became an integral part of the establishment of the states in Europe. Free churches are in this setting a variety of religious *minorities*, which the authorities often defined in negative terms as *sects*, dissenters or *separatists*, since they differed from the majority. This could lead to discrimination in a variety of ways, a burden that often was a part of becoming a member of a minority. In other settings with no state religion, the term voluntary religion or free church could describe any independent church or denomination, whether they represented a small or large segment of the population. That is particularly the case in the USA, were religious freedom or *freedom of conscience* became a part of the constitution. In Europe a similar freedom was established in *France* since 1906 with the separation of church and state. With the *pluralism* of modern society this process of dissolving the old ties between church and state, has accelerated. Historically there is a marked difference between *Lutheran* and *Reformed* states of Europe with respect to the variety and number of free-church developments. The modern free churches came about during the last 350 years, where some degree of religious freedom existed. They grew in numbers through religious awakenings, *evangelisation* and *mission*, and developed great national and international networks. Some of them have spread to most parts of the world over the last 200 years. Throughout history, voluntary commitment has been crucial to the life of the Christian *church*.

A voluntary membership depends both on the decision of the individual and the acceptance of the individual by the community on the basis of some norm. This may seem exclusive in contrast to the majority churches 'of the people' with a membership that is nominal or due to *infant baptism*. Still, free churches may in practice often seem closer to the needs of the ordinary people and less exclusive than nominal religion.

PMIL

FURTHER READING: G.R. Cragg, *Freedom and Authority*, Westminster, Philadelphia, 1975. A.S. Moreau (ed), *Evangelical Dictionary of World Mission*, Paternoster, Carlisle and Baker, Grand Rapids, Mi., 2000. G. Westin, *Den kristna friförsamlingen genom tiderna*, Westerberg, Stockholm, 1954.

Voluntaryism (The Voluntary Church)

[See also *Free Churches*]

It is difficult to read very far in 19th-century Baptist history without encountering this concept of the *church* being a voluntary association of believing people. Its classic statement is to be found in Joseph Angus' *The Voluntary Principle* (1839). A quarter of a century later Angus, by then Principal of *Regent's Park College*, found it necessary to clarify his meaning: 'Christian voluntaryism, it cannot be too often repeated, is not the authority of the self-will. It is the willing submission of the heart and of the life to Christ and the after-devotion of will to his cause' (*The Christian Churches*, 1862). The language emerged as a protest against the privileges that *state churches* enjoyed in terms of patronage and power. The danger was that in a period when inherited *Calvinist* affirmations were being questioned, a voluntaryist *ecclesiology* was a disguise for the acceptance within the church of what were essentially the *secularist* values of non-interference of a feared pretence to increasing *state* power often denominated by the phrase '*laissez faire*'. That is not to deny that at the heart of voluntaryism was the principle that American authors were to term 'soul liberty' [see *Soul Freedom*]. Thus Charles Stovel of believers' *baptism* in 1843: 'its prerequisites were *conversion* and peace in *Christ*. The act was a voluntary, open and *sacramental* self-consecration to God.' Free Churches believed that the establishment of any religion breached the important principle of the *separation of church and state*. This was often coupled with a doughty *congregationalism*. Thus John Fawcett, having described the *local church* as 'a free and voluntary society' which derives from its head full power for its own government argues that on its independence no *synod* or external *minister*, not to mention any dictate of the state, dare not trespass. Of course that freedom from state interference had not always existed. Baptist communities from **Britain** to **Russia**, and from **Norway** to **Italy** had, at different times suffered discrimination and outright persecution from the state often acting in alliance with powerful state churches. Some of the attitudes rooted in the notion that only the religion of the majority has true legitimacy still survive even in an age of public ecumenism [see **Ecumenical Movement**], seen, e.g., in the German **Evangelical** Churches attempt to prevent a Baptist filling a **theological** chair in the University of Bochum. European free churchmen oppressed by dominating state churches often referred to the paradigm of the USA, where without the establishment of any particular creed, religion seemed greatly to prosper. Instead of state finance the voluntary church depended on the voluntary – often called **free-will** – gifts of its members who were also responsible for funding its agencies including schools and **Sunday Schools**. These agencies also depended on another aspect of voluntaryism, namely the massive energies of so many people who were happy to be unpaid volunteers in the work of the **kingdom**. That Baptist churches adhere to the principle of voluntaryism, based on the separation of church and state, does not mean that they should be wholly **pietistic** with nothing to say on important social and **political** issues. Rather because they speak from an unfettered position, what they have to say carries the greater weight.

JHYB

W

Waldensian Faculty of Theology, Rome

[See also *Waldensians*]

The Waldensian Faculty of Theology is the main *protestant* theological and cultural reference point in *Italy*. The Baptist *Union* of Italy now uses the Faculty as the main place to form *pastors* to serve in Italian Baptist churches and a Baptist representative serves on the governing body.

From the time when the Waldensians joined the protestant *Reformation* (*Synod* of Chanforan, 1532) until their emancipation (Patent Letters, 1848), the training of Waldensian pastors had to be done outside of Italy, mainly in Geneva, Lausanne and Basel. Once civil rights were obtained, the Waldensians expanded their *mission* activity to the rest of Italy, then in the process of unification. It was this missionary prospect which created the need for an Italian institution for the training of pastors.

The Waldensian School of Theology began offering courses in 1855 near Turin with two professors and two *students* and stayed there until 1861. In the rest of Italy, the Waldensian presence was still scarce and caution suggested it was better for the Faculty to develop in a supportive environment. In 1861 it was transferred to Florence, the new capital of Italy, where it remained until 1922. Under the influence of the *Revival* in protestant life between the two world wars, the professors thought that their task should be more towards *evangelisation* rather than towards research and writing. The training objective, however, remained preparation for supporting '...a serious, cultivated, spiritual and conscientious pastorate'. Giovanni Luzzi (1856-1948) taught in Florence and was the translator of the edition of the *Bible* in use in the *evangelical* churches for most of the 20th century [see *Bible Translation*].

In 1922 the Waldensian Faculty of Theology was transferred to Rome which had become the capital of Italy in 1870, to a purpose-built facility, which it still occupies today. In Rome, at that time, there was already a Baptist Faculty of Theology, which was closed and later reopened in Rivoli (Turin) in 1949, until it closed at the beginning of the 1970s. Unfortunately, the new spirit of *unity* did not lead to the fusion of the Faculties of Theology or to the unifying of the theological training of the pastors.

Under the influence of the *theology* of Barth, introduced in Italy after WWII the Waldensian Faculty discovered again the original link of the Waldensian church with the theology of the 16th century Reformation. The Faculty abandoned references to the Revival and focussed decisively on theological research without giving up its original missionary *vocation*.

Internationally-known professors like Jan Alberto Soggin, OT *scholar*, and Paolo Ricca, church *historian* and well-known ecumenist, has brought distinction to the Waldensian Faculty of Theology. Today, the Waldensian Faculty of Theology has greatly diversified its educational offerings. Besides the traditional five-year master's course, designed for the training of pastors, the three-year bachelors course is attended by the *laity* and evangelical pastors from other denominations who want to reinforce their theological preparation. From 2004, courses at PhD level have also been offered. It is the only Italian protestant academic institution. The Faculty continues to trains pastors for ministry. It draws insights from various protestant and evangelical influences and scholars in Europe. It also carries out an *ecumenical* task in *dialogue* with the *Roman Catholic* Church as well as in inter-religious dialogue. The library has more than 100,000 books and 300 periodicals. Since 1952, the Faculty has published a *magazine*, *Protestantesimo*, which contributes to protestant dialogue with Italian culture.

IB

Waldensians

The Waldensian Movement has its origins in the 12th century in the self-denying *piety* of Peter Waldo, a rich merchant from Lyons who in 1173 was persuaded by *Jesus'* words in Mt 19:21 to sell all his possessions and to give the proceeds to the *poor*. Waldo had the Vulgate translated [see *Bible*; *Bible Translation*] into the vernacular and himself became an itinerant *mission preacher* teaching simple biblical *faith* and practice, in the process condemning the worldliness of the clergy, thus provoking institutional opposition which led to their being banned at the Council of Verona in 1184. As a consequence they organised themselves as an alternative movement with their own clergy and rule of life. They spread rapidly in Southern *France* and North Western *Italy* and further afield from *Spain* to Bohemia. In 1209 the *Pope* instituted a crusade against them, in 1211 some 80 *men* and *women* were burnt alive in Strasbourg, and in 1237 some 15 of their number in Spain. By the 15th century they had shed what loyalty they had to *Catholic* doctrine with their main area of strength lying in Savoy where they were much persecuted. In 1532 their leaders met with representative reformers including Guillaume Farel (the reformer [see *Reformation*] responsible for calling *Calvin* to his life's work in Geneva) at Chamforans where a new *Confession of Faith* was agreed which included a paragraph on *predestination*.

Protestant historiography has played romantic games with their origins, e.g., some have argued, with little evidence, that they were founded by St. Paul on his way to Spain, an idea supported by no less than Thomas Beza, Calvin's successor in Geneva. Others dated Waldensian origins to the time of Constantine and the pact made by the church and the Roman *state* at that time. Such ideas were readily taken up by those Baptists looking for a succession of 'pure' churches providing an unbroken link of *theological* truth and practice from *apostolic* times through to the early years of the founding of the denomination outside the institutional church.

In the 17th century measures of toleration alternated with fierce persecution, including the infamous massacre of 1655, which provoked the English poet, John Milton, to pen his celebrated sonnet on their behalf, whilst, in the international sphere, Oliver Cromwell also came to their defence. The Revocation of the Edict of Nantes in 1685 caused many to traverse the Alps to find freedom in *Switzerland*, and some as far away as Latin and North America. In the 19th century the *liturgy* changed from French to Italian with freedom finally assured after 1848.

In 1975 Waldensians and *Methodists* in Italy united to become one church, with a single national *synod*, though individual congregations retain their separate identity. At the beginning of the new century they numbered some 25,000 in 130 congregations, and offered significant diaconal services both in their heartland and in the needy south with centres both in Naples and Sicily, as well as running an important publishing house. Italian Baptists have close relations with the Waldensians. Since 1990 there has been a mutual recognition of *membership* and *ministry*, and together the denominations combine to produce the weekly journal, *Riforma*. Baptists also use the *Waldensian Faculty of Theology* for initial ministerial training and because of this are represented on its governing body.

ET

Wales, Baptist history in

The first Baptists in Wales were the followers of Hugh Evans, a Radnorshire weaver, who had been won to the cause by Jeremiah Ives, the Worcestershire Baptist leader, in the early 1630s. Evans returned to his native land and established a few congregations of *open-communion Arminian* Baptists in mid-Wales in 1633. During the upheavals of the English Civil War, John Miles established a more ecclesiastically structured and doctrinally strict body of closed-communion *Calvinistic* Baptists at Ilston near Swansea. Between 1649, when the Ilston church was formed, and the restoration of the monarchy in 1660, this movement struck deep roots within Brecknockshire, east Carmarthenshire, Glamorgan and Monmouthshire, all in South Wales.

During the post-restoration persecution the group persisted, though the mid-Wales Arminians were supplanted by the closed-communion Calvinist body, with John Miles having emigrated to New England in 1663 leaving Lewis Thomas as the movement's principal guide. The period of the Older Dissent, c.1689-1760, saw slow consolidation rather than dramatic *growth*. It was not until the *Evangelical Revival* that Baptists became numerous and their *witness* widespread. Some of their main leaders such as Enoch Francis, Miles Harry, Joshua Thomas spanned the period between the Older Dissent and the new revivalism, while it was their *missionary* zeal which spread the movement from beyond its heartlands to other parts of Wales including the North. Following the North Wales *mission* of 1776, which was followed by a surge of exceptionally dramatic revivalist energy, Baptist presence became a feature within each of the 13 Welsh counties.

If the Evangelical Revival served to energise the movement, not all Welsh Baptists approved. A *liberal* Arminian *schism* occurred in South-West Wales and a high Calvinist secession, led by the Sandemanian, J.R. Jones of Ramoth, took place in 1798-99, both as reactions against the popularistic scheme. Most of the church leaders and the bulk of the people wholly affirmed the new ways, and by 1820 the Welsh Baptists, along with the Independents, the Calvinistic *Methodists* and latterly the Wesleyans had turned Wales into 'a *nation* of *Nonconformists*'. Their greatest *preacher* was Christmas Evans though others such as Titus Lewis, Joseph Harris 'Gomer', John Jenkins gained renown. A monthly *magazine* entitled *Seren Gomer* served the movement, while the colleges at Abergavenny (1807), Haverforwest (1840) and Llangollen (1862) trained ministers. By 1866, when the Baptist *Union* of Wales was established, there were nine *associations*, 600 churches and a baptised membership [see *Baptism*] of 70,000.

Although there were over 100,000 Welsh Baptists in 1914, the 20th century witnessed serious decline. Anglicisation, the impact of war, a *secular* mindset and an inability to retain the adherence of working-class *men*, adversely effected Baptist witness. If the movement still produced powerful preachers such as R.B. Jones, *biblical scholars* like J. Gwili Jenkins and national leaders of the calibre of Lewis Valentine during the first half of the century, by the later decades its strength and influence had seriously waned. Worshipping in both the Welsh language and in English, the movement still retains a presence throughout the country.

DDM

Watchnight

The turn of the year on 31 Dec-1 Jan, is often marked in Baptist communities with a special late night service on the 31 Dec, often accompanied by a social event as the congregation awaits the coming of the New Year. The accent of this service will be on recalling the events of the past year, spiritual preparation in prayer for the New Year and often the renewal of a church *covenant* or *membership* or *baptismal* vows as the New Year begins.

In Central Europe the last day of the year is called Sylvester, after the *death* of the Christian *saint* Sylvester on 31 Dec 335AD. Sylvester was *Bishop* in Rome at the time of the Edict of Milan and so the first to lead the church in the West without persecution.

The development of such services in Baptist communities is no doubt associated with the *evangelical revival* in *England* in the 1700s when groups would gather during the night, especially in *Methodist* communities, for spontaneous services of *prayer* and *praise*. In this respect, it needs to be remembered that until 1752, the Julian calendar was generally followed with the year ending on 25 Mar. In 1752 with the adoption of the Gregorian calendar in countries like *Britain* the start of the year was restored to 1 Jan. A further complication is that in some, but not all *orthodox* countries, the calendar, with liturgical consequences [see *Liturgy*], lags 13 days behind the Western calendar.

By the 20th century the general occurrence of such events had become focused on the turn of the calendar year. The themes and pattern of the worship focuses on spiritual renewal, *repentance* and anticipation of the final *judgement*.

KGJ

Wealth

[See also *Property*]

Material wealth is generally treated with more suspicion in the NT than in the OT. OT prophets such as Amos certainly condemned ill-gotten gains made at the expense of the *poor* but very often OT writers rejoiced in the abundance provided by the creator God and regarded riches as God's reward for faithfulness. Even Job, who had good reason to question such a view, lived to see it vindicated when he emerged from his *sufferings* a far richer man.

The NT warns that riches are by no means everything. We do not live on bread alone (Mt 4:4). Earthly treasures, eroded by moth and rust, do not last (Mt 6:19f). More seriously however, riches can come between *humankind* and God. It is all too easy to put our trust in the one rather than the other, and you cannot serve both (Mt 6:24) [see *Mammon*]. Riches make it hard for a man to enter the *Kingdom* and, enjoyed without thought for the poor in this world, they can separate him eternally from God in the next (Lk 16:19). Far safer to give everything away and follow *Christ* on the road of voluntary poverty (Mt 19:21-24).

Although a strong strain of asceticism runs through the history of Christianity, there is a discernable change in attitude towards wealth as trade, commerce and *capitalism* began to flourish in the 16th and 17th centuries. Some Christians, *Puritans* among them, saw getting rich almost as a *calling* as long as it was achieved honestly and by hard work and the profits were not spent in an ostentatious way or without regard for the needy. John Wesley advised his followers to earn, save and give all they could. It became increasingly hard for Christians to go against a culture which assumed that economic growth and wealth creation was the answer to most problems, and we can understand why 'blessed are the poor in spirit', rather than simply 'blessed are the poor', became the preferred reading of Mt 5:3. What mattered to God was not your wealth but your attitude.

Until recently, Christians, especially in the West, have not been over critical of wealth creation but have questioned an economic order which allows a minority to prosper at the expense of poorer countries and communities and seems better at creating wealth than distributing it fairly. Nowadays however even wealth creation comes under scrutiny because of a growing concern for the *environment* and *stewardship* of the earth's resources.

The Prosperity Gospel, however, has no doubts about the godliness of wealth. It has been *preached* in both rich and poor countries and believes that the key to prosperity is *faith* in the saving power of Jesus Christ.

MHT

Weddings
See *Marriage/Matrimony*.

Week of Prayer for Christian Unity/Universal Week of Prayer/Women's World Day of Prayer
[See also *Baptist Women's Day of Prayer*; *Prayer*; *Unity of the Church*]

There are three special set times for prayer which are widely observed in the Christian *Church*. The modern *missionary* movement was born out of certain 18th century prayer calls that were issued to *evangelical* Christians, most famously Jonathan Edwards call for simultaneous prayer for *revival* issued in 1740 and John Sutcliff's reissuing of the same to the Northamptonshire Baptists in 1784, which has been seen as the immediate precursor to the founding of the *Baptist Missionary Society* some eight years later. The *Evangelical Alliance*'s annual week of prayer early in its history, following in this *tradition*, became, at the request of Indian missionaries, a Universal Week of Prayer normally celebrated during the first week of a New Year.

The Women's World Day of Prayer is celebrated on the first Friday in Mar. It derives from the emergence of *women*'s auxiliaries in the 1860s when the main *mission* boards were male dominated. In the 1880s and 90s women's groups in different denominations began to celebrate days of prayer for Christian mission which formed a joint committee in 1897 which in 1912 called for one united day of intercession. After WWI *peace* concerns were added to older mission interests and in 1928 it was reported that this network of prayer had spread all round the world. In 1969 *Catholic* Women gave up their separate celebration to join in the Women's World Day of Prayer which today also secures *Orthodox* support. Since 1968 an international committee has met every four years to choose themes and national groups to prepare these for worldwide use. All this helps to develop *ecumenical* solidarity amongst women's groups around the world.

The week of Prayer for Christian Unity has more Catholic origins, begun by an *An-*

glican convert [see *Conversion*] (Paul Watson) who in 1908 argued for a church unity octave between the feasts of the Confession of St Peter (18 Jan) and the Conversion of St Paul (25 Jan). Its Catholic origins were broadened by the Abbé Paul Coutourier's desire to universalise the programme, praying for a unity to be achieved 'as *Christ* wishes and by means which he desires'. From 1926, *Faith and Order* began to publish 'Suggestions for an Octave of Christian Unity 'to be celebrated around *Pentecost*. From c.1957, a common WPCU text was prepared by informal cooperation between Faith and Order and the Roman Catholic ecumenical agency Unité Chrétienne and from 1966 the Pontifical Council for Christian Unity acting for the Roman Catholic Church. An international/interdenominational team of experts now develop readings, prayers and commentaries in English and French on the chosen theme which have been prepared by different national teams every year. The material is translated into many other languages, with local *contextualisation* encouraged, and distributed through both Catholic and ecumenical agencies.

ET

Welfare state

The term 'Welfare state' describes a governmental system in which the state undertakes collective responsibility to act for the *health* and well-being of all its citizens, providing a guarantee of their welfare from cradle to the grave, with a special concern for the less well-off, deploying taxation and benefit systems to provide for their basic human needs. William Temple, Archbishop of York, in 1941, a year before he moved from York to become Archbishop of Canterbury, affirmed, 'In place of the conception of the power state we are led to that of the welfare state.' Such a concept reversed the 19th century idea of the Laissez Faire state which limited the power of the state in favour of the discipline of the market and the exercise of individual effort. Prophetic Christians [see *Prophecy*] saw such a system as making the *poor* poorer whilst the rich became richer, and came to the conclusion, often reluctantly, that even massive philanthropy could not do enough

to remedy the plight of the poor and therefore the *state* had to be trusted to do more to improve the lot of society's weakest members. Thus the state began to intervene to ensure basic standards in such areas as *education* for all with associated services for *children* such as school meals, national health provision, *unemployment* benefit, old-age pensions and the availability of decent housing. In the *United Kingdom* the Atlee government (1945-50) did much to give legislative shape to the idea which also became an important force in other western *democracies* and especially in *Scandinavia*. This concern for a state dedicated to the welfare of its people can be related to the *theological* search for the '*Responsible Society*'. With the rise of forces such as *globalisation* the 'welfare state' became an insufficient goal as people began to call for a 'welfare world'.

JHYB

Welsh Revival

[See also *Renewal/Revival/Revivalism*; *Wales, Baptist history in*]

The Welsh Revival, which was at its height in the years 1904-05, was a massive movement which brought at least 100,000 new *members* into Welsh churches. The most famous revivalist was Evan Roberts, who was aged 26, had been a miner for 12 years, and was a candidate for *Calvinistic Methodist ministry*. The effects of his ministry were phenomenal. It became increasingly clear in 1905, however, that he could not sustain his punishing *preaching* schedule and he had to withdraw from public ministry.

Several Baptists were deeply involved in the Revival. In 1903 some young Welsh ministers seeking spiritual help asked a Baptist, Owen Owen, who had trained at *Spurgeon's College*, to ask advice from F.B. Meyer, a leading London Baptist figure. Meyer commended a Welsh '*Keswick*' convention being organised by Jessie Penn-Lewis, to be held in Aug 1903. R.B. Jones was one of several Baptist ministers who left this convention sensing new spiritual power, and he and others became leaders in revival *missions*.

Meyer spoke of the 'manifestation of the Divine power' that he later witnessed in meetings led by Evan Roberts. These soon attracted crowds of over 1,000 people and would go on for hours. *Chapel* and open air meetings took place. Many people were dramatically converted [see *Conversion*] and chapel members spoke of being baptised [see *Baptism*] with the *Holy Spirit*. There was a great deal of singing, led by young *women* in Roberts' team, and visions, *healings* and *prophecy*.

The impact was felt beyond Wales. E.g. six *students* from Wales were at Spurgeon's College training for Baptist ministry in 1904-05 and the events that they reported led to the College Principal, Archibald McCaig, visiting Wales and writing about God's 'wonderful working'. He highlighted 'the sense of the reality of spiritual things', the intensity of *prayer*, singing and joy, and the many testimonies of changed lives. It has been claimed that preaching was somewhat marginalised in the Revival, but McCaig spoke of hearing Roberts preach for nearly an hour at a time, with 'a few slight interruptions of prayer or *praise*', and argued that Roberts had 'powers of speech of no mean order'. A further consequence was the holding of a mission in the neighbourhood surrounding the Metropolitan Tabernacle, the Spurgeon founded church in South London conducted by College staff and students, led particularly by the Welsh students. There were open-air meetings, *evangelistic* services in the Tabernacle, and 'midnight meetings'. In all, 745 professed *faith* and joined the church.

Baptists were among those who took the message of the Revival beyond the British Isles. It was well reported at the first congress of the *Baptist World Alliance* in London, 1905 to the delight of the delegates. Revival meetings in Algeria, conducted by the French Baptist leader, Reuben Saillens, attracted 1,200 people. In Apr 1905 F.B. Meyer spoke to large audiences in Los Angeles about the Revival. Joseph Smale, a Baptist minister in Los Angeles who had been a member of the Metropolitan Tabernacle, visited Wales and brought glowing reports. Smale later founded the First New Testament Church, and *speaking in tongues* broke out there on *Easter* Sunday 1906. The Welsh Revival had a widespread impact, moving into the emergence of *Pentecostalism*.

IMR

Whit Sunday
See *Pentecost Sunday*.

Wine
See *Alcohol*; *Eucharistic liturgy*.

Witness
See *Evangelism*; *Mission*.

Women in Baptist life
[See also *Women's work*]
Constituting a majority in most Baptist churches, women take up a variety of responsibilities in church life. Some of the more '*traditional*' roles have included those of *Sunday School* teachers, *hymn* writers, *missionaries* and slum visitors. They decorate the space for *worship*, they clean the *sanctuary*, they provide administrative and catering services. They sing, they offer intercessions, read *scripture* and recite poetry. Such customary tasks have often been assigned to women.

Another set of ministries has been more contentious and has been part of some serious disagreements in and among churches or *unions* of the *European Baptist Federation*. These would involve women in counselling, *chaplaincy*, teaching, *pastoring*, and other *eldership* roles. In some of the EBF unions (e.g. *Austria, Denmark, Georgia, Germany, Great Britain, Italy, Norway, Sweden, Wales*) women are ordained for such tasks [see *Ordination*]. In some other unions these ministries are carried forward by women in a variety of ways but under different names (they might be called '*deaconesses*', 'Bible workers', 'missionaries'). Still in some other unions, principally in Central and Eastern Europe and the Middle East, women's involvement is strictly prescribed and their eldership in the church is seen as compromising the teaching of the *Bible*.

Although women's involvement in church life in the course of European Baptist history has generally been from lesser to greater involvement, there are some interesting aspects to the story. Women often played a vital role in the initial stages of establishing a *ministry* or planting a church [see **Church Planting**] (e.g. the 'Radstock-ists', Duchess Natalia Lieven, Mme. Elisaveta Chertkova and Duchess Veronika Gagarina were at the centre of St. Petersburg **Revival** of the end of 19th century, and thus the beginnings of the Russian **Evangelical** movement, leading **worship** services, **preaching**, engaging in **evangelistic** journeys, etc.). Missionary ministries have also often been a way of employing women whose talents could not be accepted and much used by their **local church** community.

In **England**, General Baptists were more open to women in preaching and similar ministries than the Particular Baptists, though even in the 17th century women in the right category were appointed to the 'widow's' office to undertake pastoral duties. Only at the end of the 19th century following **pietist** experiments in Germany was the modern order of deaconess created, initially combining both medical and pastoral service. Those appointed to this office had to resign on **marriage**, wore a distinctive uniform which included a flowing veil covering their hair, and were normally addressed as 'Sister' followed by their Christian name The ordination of women to the pastoral ministry in any number only really began after WWII, though there had been a small number of women pastors in the inter-war years In both Great Britain and Germany, earlier diaconal orders placed women in leadership roles, leading later into women being fully accepted to serve as pastors on the same conditions as **men**. Several ordained women within the EBF have been called to leadership of their union as Presidents or General Secretaries.

In Eastern Europe, the service of sisters in leadership roles has been rarely recognised officially, apart from an occasional title of deaconess, although their actual ministry at times was crucial in the face of the shortage of brothers. The issue of women in ministry became a new point of controversy with the fall of **communism** and the influx of missionaries, financial support and **education** possibilities from the West, particularly from **conservative** or **fundamentalist** pockets of the United States. Thus defining the role of women in church ministry has become part of the agenda for some bodies who were not much concerned with the subject previously.

But exclusion is not universal e.g. Georgia, have women pastors, and women **bishops**, whilst teaching in some Eastern European seminaries seems an acceptable activity.

The use of the Bible in this matter is an enlightening example of the application of **hermeneutics**. Passages highlighting the gifting of the **Body of Christ** and the newness brought into the relationships of the community of disciples of **Christ**, such as 'there is no longer male and female; for all of you are one in Christ Jesus' (Gal 3:28) are seen to be the key in properly interpreting the issue for a contemporary context by those in favour of women's equal participation in church ministries as co-workers. Those who first cite Paul's instruction that 'the women should keep silence in the churches' (1Co 14:34) would contend that women have to be subordinate to men, either because of Eve's leading of Adam into **sin**, or in an analogy of Christ's subordination to the Father. As usual, there are historical and cultural reasons and influences for the development of the current views. Some would see a difficulty in the way the meaning of ordination has evolved, and instead of arguing for ordination for both women and men, suggest rethinking the role of ordained members within the community of disciples.

In most cases within the EBF, it has been agreed to respect the discernment of each particular community or union when it comes to women's leadership roles. This is perhaps best exemplified when the Council elected as President an ordained woman from Sweden, though the majority of unions at present do not ordain women. The issue of the role and the ordination of women remains a challenge, however, especially when differing views arise in the midst of a single community or union, which is a growing reality in Europe with the increase of possibilities for free movement between countries. The way the churches continue to address the issue will be an important test of how they exercise wisdom in Christ and will require much mutual listening, sensitivity, and discernment.

The European Baptist Women's Union (EBWU), established in 1948, has played an important role in building bridges and supporting women's work in post-war Europe. **Political** realities excluded the participation of sisters from Eastern Europe for a long time, but since the fall of the iron curtain, the EBWU's activity in the East is greater than in Western or Southern Europe. Some other informal networks of women in ministries are being developed as an attempt to help find creative ways especially for women exercising various forms of ministry in a wider context to the whole church or to segments of society.

LA & KGJ

Women's (World) Day of Prayer

See *Baptist Women's Day of Prayer; Week of Prayer for Christian Unity/Universal Week of Prayer/Women's World Day of Prayer*.

Women's work

[See also *Baptist Women's Day of Prayer; Women in Baptist life*]

In each member *union* of *EBF* there are many different forms of work among, by and for women. The European Baptist Women's Union (EBWU) is the only organisation which has links to a woman leader in every union; although it cannot interact with individual meetings, it does have a role of encouragement and training, of education and challenge to leaders, which benefits the local work. EBWU was formed in 1948 in London during a *BWA* conference. During succeeding years similar organisations were formed in all the other continents. All work closely with the relevant BWA member bodies. The ongoing purpose of EBWU remains constant, re-defined in readiness for a new millennium as:

- Equipping new leaders for national and international leadership;
- Building a Europe-wide fellowship of women through their leaders;
- Working with individual and community needs
- Uniting women in *mission* and *ministry*.

Within this general purpose EBWU has always sought to give practical help in various ways: different national projects have been assisted in most member unions; special offerings were made for Chernobyl suf-

ferers and war-torn *Georgia*; most recently work is being done in the area of human trafficking [see *Prostitution*]. A *magazine* is published three times a year; a pan-European conference is held every five years, and mini-conferences for specific groups are arranged as appropriate. The annual celebration of the Day of Prayer in Nov is the glue which holds women together, as well as the springboard from which mission and ministry take off.

Women's work in the different unions of the EBF has various characteristics, dependent on a country's needs and possibilities. Generally there are two goals, such as:

(1) Encouragement of women in: spiritual growth; discovering *gifts* and serving with them; greater involvement in *prayer* ministry; mission action; recognising women's needs and problems and fulfilling them; cooperation and exchanging ministry's experiences with women from different countries.

(2) Providing help for: leaders in equipping to the ministry for women and among women; women in realising their *call* to be wives and mothers in the best possible way; women who are in difficult life situations (single mothers, widows, women who have unbelieving husbands, victims of *violence* in the family, women who have been trafficked); *children* in need (those from dysfunctional and pathological families, *orphans*, *homeless*, victims of violence, disasters and military conflicts).

These goals are achieved through: national and regional conferences; training conferences; women's and *Bible study* groups in *local churches*; mother's prayer groups; the participation in work to help people in need; mission work; the editing of the women's magazine and materials helpful in women's ministry; the translating and editing of Christian books; the participation in the Women's World Day of Prayer.

YP

Word (of God)

See *Bible; Christology; Incarnation; Jesus Christ; Logos*.

Work

Theologically there has been an ambiguity about the nature of work. On the one hand it may be conceived of as sharing in the divine creativity, yet on the other hand work (as hard labour) is seen as a consequence of the *fall* and as a punishment for *sin*. Such a *judgment* may well reflect the experience of those agricultural workers who strive against the odds to produce crops in a barren land, and on the other hand on the urban worker who has, since the industrial revolution, become *alienated* from the production process in situations where the division of labour coupled with mechanisation denies to the modern worker the creative satisfaction of the craftsman of old. Even more in the 21st century the place of work needs redefining. In the past, work had been equated to paid work and a full-time job. The dominant relationship was a transactional one in which an employee traded knowledge or skills to an employer for income. This type of work has greatly influenced communications, *education*, geography, legislation, the road systems and many other aspects of European life.

Not all jobs operate on this transactional basis. Many people carry out work as self-employed consultants or artisans and employment legislation recognises the two, imposing different constraints on them. Charles Handy develops the concept of the portfolio worker. This is the person who undertakes a 'mixed bag' of work to obtain a living wage.

In the voluntary sector people often work for nothing, or for the payment of expenses. Many who have retired from paid work find an outlet for their energy and their *gifts* by serving on committees or performing social services such as voluntarily driving out-patients to *hospital* appointments.

The Christian *church* relies heavily upon such gift work to sustain the many types of activity being offered in the name of *Christ*. By such work, Christians transcend themselves and give service to others.

Part of the confusion over what is work arises from the fact that *men* and *women* can undertake the same tasks at work, in *leisure* time, as a hobby and in the home. It is not all paid work. A person can be a paid gardener, a hobby gardener and help others by doing gardening for them for nothing and do it all as service for Christ.

WJA

FURTHER READING: Charles B. Handy, *The Furture of Work*, W.H. Smith, London, 1992.

World Confessional Families
See *Christian World Communions*.

World Council of Churches
The WCC planned before WWII had its first meeting in 1948. Representatives from 44 countries and all the main Christian *traditions* except the *Roman Catholic* Church met in Amsterdam and agreed that the new body should be 'a fellowship of churches which accept the Lord *Jesus Christ* as God and *Saviour*.' This was expanded at New Delhi in 1961 to incorporate scriptural *authority* [see *Bible*] and a trinitarian *faith* [see *Trinity*] by adding the words 'according to the scriptures, and therefore seek together to fulfill their common *calling* to the glory of the one God, Father, Son and *Holy Spirit*'. Current European Baptist members include the Baptist *Union* of *Great Britain*, and Baptists in *Denmark*, *Hungary* and *Italy*. In earlier years the Scottish and Dutch Baptists and the *All-Union Council of Evangelical Christians-Baptists* in the *Soviet Union* had been members. A number of Baptists have played a crucial role in the work of the Council especially in its early foundation. Perhaps the most distinguished service was provided by Dr. E.A. Payne who was both a long-serving Vice-Moderator of the Central Committee (1954-68) and a President (1968-75).

Four streams feed into the work of the World Council: *Life and Work* (1925), *Faith and Order* (1927) combined in its foundation. The *International Missionary Council* (1921), integrated into the Council in 1961, and the work of the World Council of Christian Education, which arose out of the World *Sunday School* Association of 1889, fed into the WCC in 1971. These emphases still spell out the major thrusts of the council's work, and whilst ideally they represent complementary programmes, they have sometimes been seen to offer conflicting priorities: the search for **unity**, which has led to a series of meetings between PaedoBaptists [see **Infant Baptism**] and those in the Believers' **Baptism** tradition, inspiring **mission** and **evangelism**, looking for convergences in faith and order, not to mention encouraging the churches to act prophetically in solidarity with the marginalised and oppressed, to address issues of justice and **peace**, and to take seriously the Christian calling to take care of God's good **creation** in the midst of a culture of exploitation that is putting its future in jeopardy [see **Climate Change**; **Ecology and the Environment**]. All these are part of WCC's current concerns as well as operating a large **diakonia** programme of service and aid, undertaking **educational** work especially in aid of the two-thirds world and those who have been denied these facilities in Eastern Europe. With greater consciousness of other faith traditions the WCC has had to give considerable attention to **dialogue** between and among people of living faith. That dialogue does not call for the dumbing down of dearly held beliefs. Indeed genuine dialogue puts a premium on each side being faithful to the fullness of **revelation** it has received and only from that basis to explore a common humanity and search for true community in a divided and violent world.

Very early on it became necessary to be very clear about the status of the World Council and in particular to make it abundantly clear that the Council did not aspire to any churchly status and certainly not to operate as a super-church. Nor would it challenge the church claims of any of its member bodies, or demand that they recognise other members as fully churches, thereby affording confidence to its **orthodox** members. Only churches were to be allowed membership and the Council was to have no power to legislate on their behalf. Such actions as it took and statements that it issued depended on their intrinsic truth and value for acceptance. This was spelt out in 1950 in what came to be known as the Toronto Statement.

The council brings together, not without difficulty, a wide diversity of Christian traditions, the principal being Orthodox (both Eastern and Oriental), **Anglican**, **Protestant**, **Pentecostal** and African Instituted. That said a number of major traditions do not belong.

The Roman Catholic Church, which is often to be found in National and Regional Councils of Churches, argues that its **catholicity** claims would be compromised if it were to join a worldwide fellowship of churches as just another member. Because of this the Council relates to the **Vatican** through a joint committee which discusses matters of mutual concern. Many in the **evangelical** tradition, including many Baptists, find it difficult to relate to a body that does not comprehensively share all their doctrinal affirmations and is perceived by some to be over-concerned with **political** actions, placing too little emphasis on evangelism. That said Evangelicals are divided on their evaluation of the WCC. Whilst some are very critical, there have always been Evangelicals/Baptists both on the staff and in the governing bodies of the WCC. In like manner the number of Pentecostal churches in membership of the World Council does not represent the movement's global strength. To develop relationships, the WCC has in recent years initiated a series of meetings with both these traditions.

The weight of council membership, now c.350 churches, has significantly moved towards the churches of the Southern Hemisphere and away from Europe and North America. Because the WCC is a council of churches, para church bodies, though clearly crucial to worldwide Christian witness, are denied membership. Accordingly, since 1998 work began on establishing a Global Christian Forum capable of overcoming all these deficiencies. Bringing together a broader spectrum of Christian organisations/denominations but without any commitment in membership, its first meeting was held in Kenya in 2007.

JHYB

World Evangelical Alliance/Fellowship

[See also **European Evangelical Alliance**; **Evangelical Alliance**]

Those who attempted to establish a world Evangelical Alliance in 1846 found little difficulty initially in agreeing a basis of belief (**Inspiration** and **authority** of **scripture**, the unity and triune nature of the godhead [see

Trinity], the fallenness of human nature [see Fall; Sin], the incarnation and atonement of Jesus Christ, justification by faith alone, resurrection and final judgment) though some argued that this would exclude non-credal denominations but the Alliance as it occurred was a union of individuals not of institutions. However, it foundered on the issue of slave-holding, which British delegates held inimical to the gospel whereas American delegates, with vested interests in the Global South, could not so agree. As a consequence a number of national alliances were established with only loose federal relationships between them. In Europe alliances were immediately established in England (which included some continental members such as Oncken), Sweden and strangely Turkey, though in 1846 the Sultan still controlled much of the Balkans. Spain and Portugal were established later. The Alliance encouraged cooperation in missionary activity including 'comity' arrangements, that is, a division of labour between different fields by mutual consent. The Alliance also promoted the Universal Week of Prayer spurred on my Indian missionaries, and sponsored several missionaries conferences which were precursors to Edinburgh, 1910. The British produced the periodical, Evangelical Christendom, kept the constituency prayerfully concerned about persecuted Evangelical minorities. Stephen Neill saw the Alliance as 'the first society formed with a definite view to Christian unity'. Baptists such as E.J. Steane, J.H. Hinton, F.A. Cox and Baptist Noel, were all influential in establishing the Alliance, but Spurgeon early decided to resign following his attack on Anglican Evangelicals for using words in the Anglican liturgy, which appeared to support baptismal regeneration, which many deemed to be unduly sectarian. He later rejoined and became an active member.

The USA Alliance movement, facing tensions over theological liberalism, ceased to function after 1900. Accordingly there was need for a more formal international body which was established in 1951 as the World Evangelical Fellowship (WEF) with representation from 21 countries. The basis of belief mirrored that of 1846 though there was division between the International and the European body, separately founded in 1952,

over the use of the language of infallibility in the article on scripture. Only in 1968 did the European body join the WEF. For about 40 years the secretariat of the Fellowship both in personnel was either British or North American but in 1987 the headquarters was moved to Singapore and in 1992 the first non-Western international director was appointed when Augustin Vencer of the Philippines took office. By 2000 the WEF had 108 national and regional members some 70% from the two-thirds world: its ambition is for every country to be represented in its fellowship. It works through a General Assembly, which meets every four to six years, an international council and a number of specialised study commissions.

Gilbert Kirby of England sought to hold the new body to the slogan 'Spiritual Unity in Action': it was averse to seeing the Lausanne Committee on World Evangelisation emerge as a separate organisation, as splitting evangelical energies. But when it did take on a separate existence the WEF sought to cooperate as much as possible with it. At the very beginning of the whole movement in 1846, the WEF has focused on the spread of theological liberalism and the dominance of a traditional Catholic Church in many areas. More recently members of the Fellowship have come to see the Catholic Church as an ally rather than an opponent especially in maintaining theological orthodoxy as over against relating to foot-loose liberal Protestantism, and in upholding traditional Christian ethical stances. However, not all members were immediately ready for such changes in relationships. For some their Protestantism seemed more important than their evangelicalism, but from 1977-84 a series of talks called ERCOM (Evangelical Roman Catholic Dialogue on Mission) took place, with the Evangelical side informally convened by John Stott, who was much involved with the Lausanne process. Since 1993 there has been a further series of conversations, now with delegates named by the WEF. Their meetings have become more regular and have begun to issue statements on converging theological emphases.

From Jan 2002 the Fellowship adopted the title of World Evangelical Alliance.

ET

World Missionary Conference, Edinburgh 1910
See *Edinburgh 1910 – World Missionary Conference*.

World Student Christian Federation
See *Student Christian Movement (SCM), Inter-Varsity Fellowship (IVF), World Student Christian Federation (WSCF) and International Fellowship of Evangelical Students (IFES)*.

World Trade Organisation
The World Trade Organisation (WTO) is an international institution created in 1995 with a primary purpose of liberalising trade between its member countries, and making such liberalisation binding in international law. The WTO's origins lie in the General Agreement on Tariffs and Trade (GATT), an international treaty signed by 23 countries in 1948 agreeing to lower taxes on trade in goods between the member signatories. Through a succession of eight 'rounds' of negotiations, between 1948 and 94, tariffs were steadily lowered and more members added.

In 1986, the Uruguay Round of the GATT began, which, as well as seeking further decreases in trade tariffs, sought to extend its work into new areas. In 1994, the Uruguay Round was concluded with the signing of the Marrakech agreement. The signatory countries agreed to create the WTO as a formal international institution with its headquarters in Geneva. As well as trade in goods, the WTO now covers trade in services, investment and intellectual property rights. Since 1995, the WTO's membership has increased from 123 to 150.

Under the WTO agreements, if one member *state* believes another member to be in violation of a particular rule, it can lodge a case with the WTO secretariat. The case is judged by three international trade lawyers. If the lawyers find in favour of the claimant, the claimant can impose sanctions on the accused until the accused changes its policy. In 2003, the *European Union* won a case against the US concerning tariffs the US had imposed on steel. The EU consequently threatened a range of tariff increases on US exports to the EU, and the US responded by lowering its steel tariffs.

As well as implementing the current agreements, the WTO has a built-in agenda to negotiate further liberalisation of trade in agriculture, goods and services. The focus of these negotiations has been the biennial ministerial meetings of the WTO. A new round of negotiations was launched at the Doha Ministerial Meeting in Nov 2001.

The WTO has faced a range of criticism and public protest for a variety of different reasons since its inception. One of the most widespread criticisms is that the WTO's structure as it currently exists primarily reflects the interests of the richest countries and their *multinational companies*. The one WTO agreement which seeks to create trade barriers rather than reduce them is the TRIPs agreement, which allows companies to patent products internationally, and thus prevent their manufacture by other companies. In the pharmaceutical sector this has led to artificially high prices for life-saving goods. In contrast, the *poorest* countries have continually called for international agreements on agricultural commodity prices, but such issues have not been included within WTO negotiations. The WTO is part of the governmental structures of the international community which all too often operate in the interests of the rich *nations* of the world and to the disadvantage of the underprivileged. It is part of the context in which Christians constantly have to strive to secure justice for the world's poorest nations.

MHT

Worldwide Church (insights from)
The shrunken dimensions of the world brought about by rapid electronic communications, fast air travel and the associated movements of people, often provoked by *political* and economic distress, makes its impact on every aspect of modern life. Images, whether they be of flood waters in Bangladesh or shanty town living in Haiti or refugee camps in the Sudan, flash across our television screens whilst our trolleys in the supermarkets carry exotic fruit and vegeta-

bles flown in from the four corners of the earth. Many cities in Europe have their Black-led churches, many of a baptistic nature, with the **membership** coming from a Baptist background. **Diaspora** congregations relating to one of the large African-instituted churches are also to be found. A number of Baptist churches will host Baptist groups of different languages or cultures, whilst some of the liveliest growing churches are those which appeal to a particular ethnic group. Different regions have made their own special impact. Clearly the old pattern of a 'sending' north and a 'receiving' south no longer reflects reality, when e.g. **mission** workers come from the Global South to work in our great cities and a tired Europe is encouraged by Christian advance in the Global South. From Africa come heartening stories of **church growth** and the **music** of lively **worship**, but set against a background of much political instability and market oppression, not to mention the challenge that comes from a continent so tragically under the burden of the **HIV-AIDS** pandemic. The republic of South Africa, whilst still facing many problems, offers something of how political divisions may be responsibly handled through the work of the Truth and Reconciliation Commission. Latin America has led the whole world in **Theological Education by Extension**, which has now become commonplace in Europe, both East and West. Latin American **Evangelicals** have done most to ensure that **evangelism** and concern for social need are held together as part of Christian outreach. This is the continent of **Liberation Theology**, the most powerful of all the **contextual theologies** of the modern world, which the Latin American Theological Fraternity has interpreted in ways that speak powerfully to Evangelicals. At the same time the base community movement has, at its best, emphasised the importance of reading **scripture** in community with the newspaper open in front of you. Asia has raised questions about the need for **dialogue** with those of other living **faiths**, at the very least representing other faith communities by the best they have to offer rather than by some mean caricature. Questions then need to be faced about the way in which dialogue relates to straightforward evangelism, and does not supersede it.

From Asia also comes the story, not just of the survival of the church in China, but its amazing expansion. A senior civil servant visiting Europe recently made the comment that he was not sure whether the **communist** party would last out his life time but he was quite sure the Christian **Church** would! All churches in the Southern Hemisphere raise questions which have become focused in what has been called 'God's **preferential option for the poor**'. The witness of the church around the world reminds us that the story of Christian **martyrdom** is not yet a matter of history, whilst forms of religious **fundamentalism** allied to a rising **nationalism** can put small Christian churches in the Global South under very great threat.

ET

Worship

Worship (sometimes also referred to as 'The Liturgy', or 'Sunday Services', or even in some languages the 'Cult') finds its origin in the gatherings of the Jewish synagogues at the time of Jesus, the rituals of the temple cult in Jerusalem, and the spiritual experiences in the early church. It takes place when the people of God come together before God, waiting on him to reveal himself. This he does as the people listen to **scripture** readings, hear them expounded in the **sermon**, and share the experience of what God is doing today in testimonies. In response, they offer their praise to God in **prayers** and **hymns**, bring the needs of the world to him in intercessory prayer, and make an **offering** thereby symbolising presenting to God their time and talents. Thus, the worship of the **church** takes the form of a dialogue between God and his people, as believers respond to all that God has done and is doing for them. This same pattern of dialogue is present in the celebration of the **baptism** of believers, the **sacrament** of beginning on the Christian life, and the observation of the **Lord's Supper**, the repetition of the mystery of the paschal meal between Jesus and his disciples, for both rehearse what God has done for his people and also offer special opportunities of responding to God's **grace**. All this is done within the context of the **mission** of the church which embraces the several elements of worship [*leitourgia*], teaching [*didache*], fellowship [*koinonia*], witness [*martyria*], and the service of the community [*diakonia*].There is no common ritual or order of service universally used by Baptist congregations. Influences from *pietism*, *nonconformity* and *puritanism* have all played their part. The order of service is uncomplicated. There are at least five different approaches:

(1) Traditional thematic where scriptures, lessons, prayers and hymns are arranged around a common theme;

(2) Liturgical/reflective [see *Liturgy*], following the patterns of liturgical *renewal* or the spirituality of *Taizé, Iona* or *Northumbria*;

(3) *Charismatic*/celebratory, employing active forms with individual spontaneous exclamations;

(4) Modern/Contemporary – using modern expressions such as dance, film, media, and musical bands;

(5) Seeker-sensitive forms, often embracing stage performances, with everything aimed at allowing modern persons not acquainted with church culture to participate meaningfully.

However from scripture it becomes clear that what is important is not precise forms of ceremony but the attitude of the worshippers' hearts, for only this secures worship 'in Spirit and in truth'. Whilst traditionally worship takes place in specially dedicated *buildings* on a Sunday, there is increasing flexibility today as to both place and time, for scripture teaches that *Jesus* is present wherever his people gather in his name. Moreover the presence of Jesus is retained as the people disperse into the world where their worship is continued as they faithfully do their daily work, make their witness as Christians and serve the community in the name of Christ. This too is *leitourgia*, a word which literally means the work of the people of God, that is the service of both God and neighbour. Every Baptist congregation is free to celebrate according to their cultural, historical, *theological* and social contexts.

OAJ & ET

FURTHER READING: Paul Beasley-Murray, *Radical Believers*, Baptist Union of Great Britain, Didicot, 1992. BWA Study and Research Division, *We Baptists*, Providence House, Franklin, Tn., 1999. Christopher J. Ellis, *Gathering: A Theology and Spirituality of Worship in the Free Church Tradition*, SCM, London, 2004. Sune Fahlgren and Rune Klingert (eds), *I enhetens tecken*, Libris, Örebro, 1994. Keith G. Jones and Parush R. Parushev, *Currents in Baptistic Theology of Worship Today*, IBTS, Prague, 2007. Odd Arne Joø, *Menigheten – et feirende fellesskap*, Baptistenes Teologiske Seminar, Stabekk, 1997. I. Judson Levy, *Come, let us worship*, Print'N Press, St. Stephen, 1979. S.F. Winward, *The Reformation of Our Worship*, Carey Kingsgate, London, 1964. James F. White, *Introduction to Christian Worship*, Abingdon, Nashville, Tn., 1980.

Wroclaw Evangelical School of Theology, Poland

In the mid 1980s, Polish Baptist pastor, Dr. Zygmunt Karel, worked with others to design and develop an interdenominational *evangelical* school of *theology* (EST) to serve Baptists and other evangelical Christians in *Poland*. It was the first of its kind in this country – a school that would minister among Poles in Polish to serve and strengthen the evangelical movement in Poland. The first group of *students* began studies in Oct 1990 using the Baptist church. In Sep 2001 the seminary moved to a newly renovated historical building near the centre of the city. EST is located in the immediate vicinity of the main campus of the University of Wroclaw. In Apr 2005 EST submitted its application for national accreditation with the Polish Ministry of Education. In Oct 2006 final documents were signed by the Polish Minister of Education allowing EST to be officially recognised as an accredited school of higher *education*. EST is the first private, non-denominational school in Poland and this part of Europe to receive national accreditation. EST offers a B.A. programme and School for Leaders and also offers E-learning, Open University type courses, a *Bible* Languages School, courses in *Spirituality* and Art, Christian Counselling, and promotes events for evangelical pastors.

ET

WSCF

See *Student Christian Movement (SCM), Inter-Varsity Fellowship (IVF), World Student Christian Federation (WSCF) and International Fellowship of Evangelical Students (IFES)*.

Y

YFC

See *Youth for Christ*.

Young Men/Women's Christian Association (YMCA/YWCA)

The YMCA 'the oldest *ecumenical* organisation next to the *Evangelical Alliance*', was founded in 1844 by (Sir) George Williams with its original target clientele young apprentices coming to London who in those days lived in house with no provision being made for their *leisure* time. George Williams was himself an apprentice with the London drapery firm of Hitchcock and Rogers of Ludgate Hill. Early meetings were principally concerned with *prayer* and *Bible Studies* but as the movement grew it developed other activities with a very deliberate policy of nurturing a rounded development of body, mind and spirit. Its leadership was from the first lay [see *Laity*] and interdenominational. Williams is reputed to have said of an early meeting of the organisation, 'Here we are, an *Episcopalian*, a *Methodist*, a Baptist and a *Congregationalist* – four believers but a single *faith* in *Christ*. Forward together.'

In 1854 the YWCA was founded and the two organisations came to be known as the 'Ys'. These powerful lay movements, a fruit of mid-Victorian *Revivalism* and the early ecumenical movement, not only provided for the nurture of late 19th and 20th-century youth but those trained in the YMCA/YWCA became some of the foremost statesmen of the Ecumenical Movement; this was true e.g. of both John R. Mott and Visser't Hooft, first secretary of the *WCC*. Though not initially interested in *ecclesiological* questions, the experience of working across denominational boundaries, created an interest in the *unity of the churches*. Thoroughly *evangelical* and *evangelistic*, the 1855 basis of the international based YMCA contained language that was later to become part of the basis of the WCC: 'The YMCA seeks to unite those young *men* who, regarding Jesus Christ as their God and Saviour, according to the Holy *Scriptures*, desire to be his true disciples in their *faith* and in their life, and to associate their efforts for the extension of His *Kingdom* amongst young men.'

In an age increasingly concerned with the manly virtues, the YMCA was not slow to see the need to embrace a *holistic* approach to *mission* if it was to effectively engage with young men and their interests. Their concern was not to be some abstracted spirit but 'The Whole Man – Body, Mind and Spirit'. Southend, Essex, UK, YMCA in 1899, whilst emphasising its concern for its members to come to know Christ as a Personal Saviour put this in the context of objects which aimed at the 'Spiritual, Social, Intellectual and Physical Welfare of Young Men'. Thus local branch headquarters came to provide something like club facilities for members together with associated cycle, cricket, debating and mutual improvement clubs within a comprehensive educational and recreational programme. In large towns and cities the YMCA/YWCA operated large hostels. During two world wars they developed a considerable *ministry* both to soldiers and prisoners of war and displaced persons.

JHYB

Youth for Christ (YFC)

In 1944, under the leadership of Torrey Johnson, the successful *pastor* of Midwest Bible Church in the Chicago area of the USA, 'Chicagoland' Youth for Christ rallies commenced, attracting up to 30,000 young people. The following year saw over 600 North American youth leaders gathering to form Youth for Christ. *Billy Graham*, a young *Southern Baptist*, was recruited to the movement, and from 1945 Graham was YFC's first field representative. In the spring of 1946 Billy Graham, then aged 27, became part of a small YFC team which came to *Britain*. There were existing youth networks in Britain such as the National Young Life Campaign (NYLC), founded in 1911 by the brothers Frederick and Arthur Wood, which claimed 13,000 members in 1947. One of the NYLC *evangelists* was Alan Redpath, later a leading *Keswick* Convention figure and Baptist *minister*. But Youth for Christ became the leading youth organisation in Britain. In the later 1940s Billy Graham made several visits to Britain, addressing large youth rallies. In 1968 representatives from 16 **nations** formed Youth for Christ International. By the early 1970s British Youth for Christ (BYFC) had lost its early momentum, but under Clive Calver as director (1975-83) significant growth took place, and many Baptists were involved. Rob White, a subsequent BYFC director, later became a Baptist minister. Today YFC operates in over 20 countries across Europe and in at least another 60 countries worldwide.

IMR

FURTHER READING: I.M. Randall, 'Conservative Constructionist: The Early Influence of Billy Graham in Britain', *The Evangelical Quarterly*, Vol. 67, No. 4 (1995).

Youth work

The term 'youth work' came into popular usage in the 1940/50s, although work with young people had been a feature of society since the middle of the 19th century when people like George Williams, a draper in London, started the **YMCA** (1844), followed by other organisations including The **Boys' Brigade** (1883), the first of the uniformed youth work organisations. These organisations were started by Christians who wanted to make a difference in the lives of young men. In 1888 the **Christian Endeavour** was imported into **England** seven years after it had been founded in the USA. An international organisation for older young people too old for **Sunday School**, it was a means of encouraging those who had been touched by the **missions** of **evangelists** such as D.L. Moody. It was around this time that many of the denominational churches, challenged by the developments that were taking place among young people, established their own youth departments.

In **Britain**, the interdenominational Crusaders movement began in 1900 and was formally instituted in 1906. In 1935 Pathfinders was formed for young people in the **Church of England**, closely followed by the organisation which became the Church Youth Fellowships Association. In America, **Youth for Christ** came into being officially in 1944 following rallies in Chicago organised by Torrey Johnson. Around this time the phrase 'teenager' came into vogue and advertisers especially were quick to target a group with increasing spending power. As they had few financial commitments at this age, it was a key market. Here was a group able to react and/or think through the implications of moving from dependence through independence to inter-dependence.

During the 1960s various organisations were formed, including Frontier Youth Trust in Britain, which was committed to the **poor** and marginalised young people in society. At the same time there was growth in organisations being formed outside of, or alongside, the official church and denominations. In the 1970s, as a reaction to a general retreat from Christianity and partly through the work of YFC, Christian youth workers began going into schools and taking part in the formal **education** lessons and assemblies, re-introducing the **faith** to young people within the school system. This was not possible in some countries, but in Britain many secondary schools were open to visiting Christian input, e.g. within the Religious Education syllabus. In the 1970s and 80s there was the development of street work and detached youth work.

In the 1990s there was a rise in many parts of Europe of alternative **worship**, youth cells, youth congregations and youth churches. Such projects have attempted to create a relevant expression of the Christian faith for the young people of today.

IH & DH

FURTHER READING: Pete Ward, *Growing Up Evangelical*, SPCK, London, 1996.

Yugoslavia, Baptist history in

See *Bosnia and Herzegovina*; *Croatia*; *Macedonia*; *Serbia and Montenegro*; *Slovenia, Baptist history in*.

Yugoslavia, Baptist Union of

[See also *Bosnia and Herzegovina*; *Croatia*; *Macedonia*; *Serbia and Montenegro*; *Slovenia, Baptist history in*]

The Baptist Union of Yugoslavia, which existed from 1922-92, was formed when the new Kingdom of Yugoslavia was created, and was dissolved in 1992 when Yugoslavia broke into five countries: Slovenia, Croatia, Bosnia and Herzegovina, Macedonia, and Serbia/Montenegro. In 1924, the *Union* embraced four churches, 709 *members*, 426 *Sunday School* attenders and six *ministers*, with Vinko Vacek the first President. The church members were mostly ethnic Germans, Slovaks, Hungarians and Romanians, with a small number of Croats and Serbs. Up to 1940, they experienced steady *growth* despite disputes between their foreign partners, the *Southern Baptist Convention* and the German Baptists (*Donaulandermission*). In 1941, when WWII reached Yugoslavia, there were approximately 2,500 members. The Union published three periodicals: *Glas Evandjelja* [*The Voice of the Gospel*] in Serbo-Croatian, *Novy Rod* [*A New Birth*] in Slovak, and *Der Evangeliumsbote* [*The Gospel Messenger*] in German. In 1940, the SBC founded a Baptist seminary in Belgrade, but closed it six months later due to the war. The Union was reactivated in 1945, but wartime losses and the *emigration* of most ethnic Germans diminished numbers. *Missionary* work in Vojvodina was curtailed. The seminary was reopened in 1954 in Zagreb, but moved to Novi Sad in 1957 as *Novi Sad Baptist Theological School*. In 1959, the Union started a new monthly *magazine Glasnik* [*Herald*], and in 1965 *Sestrinski list* [*The Sister's Magazine*]. When in 1967, the Union in Novi Sad played host to the *EBF* Executive Committee, it was the first time during the *socialist* period that many Baptist leaders from Eastern Europe were able to attend. During the socialist years, the Baptists in Yugoslavia enjoyed better relations with the *state* than Baptists in other Eastern European countries, allowing the churches to grow. In the early 1990s, the Union had 3,500 members.

                                        BB

Z

Zwingli, Huldrych/Ulrich (1484-1531)

Often referred to as the 'Third Man of the *Reformation*' (Jean Rilliet, 1964) chronologically Zwingli was the second of the Magisterial Reformers and influential in his reforming work for both *Anabaptists* and Baptists. Born at Wildhaus in the Toggenburg region of *Switzerland*, he imbibed the humanist spirit of Erasmus of Rotterdam in various Swiss universities and in Vienna, before settling to *pastoral* work in Glaurus, then Einsiedeln. Called to be town *preacher* in Zürich in 1519, he began a reforming programme supported by the town council. He developed the Prophezei School, where the preachers gathered to explore the *Bible* together comparing scripture with scripture. This group included those like Grebel and Manz, who were to part with Zwingli and driven on by his approach to Biblical study become the first Swiss Anabaptists.

Zwingli laid the groundwork for the Reformed *Protestant tradition*, developed in a more systematic way by *Calvin* and others. Zwingli was essentially a preacher working his theories out in the reality of *local church* life in Zürich. He died on the battlefield fighting against the *Catholic* Cantons and left no thought-through *systematic theology* because of the constant demands of the reformation movement. However, many aspects of the Zürich reformation helped form Anabaptist and later Baptist approaches to the Bible, *ecclesiology*, *theology* and *liturgy*.

Zwingli had a keen sense of the Christian community celebrating the *eucharist* together and his theological understanding of this has been described by Baptist *scholar* H. Wayne Pipkin as 'trans-signification'. Those who claim to be 'mere memorialists' (Dom Gregory Dix on the Zwinglian tradition) in their eucharistic theology have not read or understood Zwingli himself who had a developed understanding of the theology and of the importance of the meal. This he sees as the point at which the Christian congregation truly becomes the *body of Christ*, for it is in a celebrating people that the real presence of *Christ* is to be found.

KGJ

FURTHER READING: E.J. Furcha and H. Wayne Pipkin (eds), *Prophet, Pastor, Protestant*, Pickwick, Allison Park, Pa., 1984. H. Wayne Pipkin, *Zwingli – the positive value of his eucharistic writings*, Yorkshire Baptist Association, Leeds, 1985. G.R. Potter, *Zwingli*, Cambridge University Press, Cambridge, 1976. W.P. Stephens, *The Theology of Huldrych Zwingli*, Clarendon, Oxford, 1986.

Studies in Baptist History and Thought

(All titles uniform with this volume)
Dates in bold are of projected publication
Volumes in this series are not always published in sequence

David Bebbington and Anthony R. Cross (eds)
Global Baptist History
(SBHT vol. 14)

This book brings together studies from the Second International Conference on Baptist Studies which explore different facets of Baptist life and work especially during the twentieth century.

2006 / 1-84227-214-4 / approx. 350pp

David Bebbington (ed.)
The Gospel in the World
International Baptist Studies
(SBHT vol. 1)

This volume of essays from the First International Conference on Baptist Studies deals with a range of subjects spanning Britain, North America, Europe, Asia and the Antipodes. Topics include studies on religious tolerance, the communion controversy and the development of the international Baptist community, and concludes with two important essays on the future of Baptist life that pay special attention to the United States.

2002 / 1-84227-118-0 / xiv + 362pp

John H.Y. Briggs (ed.)
Pulpit and People
Studies in Eighteenth-Century English Baptist Life and Thought
(SBHT vol. 28)

The eighteenth century was a crucial time in Baptist history. The denomination had its roots in seventeenth-century English Puritanism and Separatism and the persecution of the Stuart kings with only a limited measure of freedom after 1689. Worse, however, was to follow for with toleration came doctrinal conflict, a move away from central Christian understandings and a loss of evangelistic urgency. Both spiritual and numerical decline ensued, to the extent that the denomination was virtually reborn as rather belatedly it came to benefit from the Evangelical Revival which brought new life to both Arminian and Calvinistic Baptists. The papers in this volume study a denomination in transition, and relate to theology, their views of the church and its mission, Baptist spirituality, and engagements with radical politics.

2007 / 1-84227-403-1 / approx. 350pp

Damian Brot
Church of the Baptized or Church of Believers?
A Contribution to the Dialogue between the Catholic Church and the Free Churches with Special Reference to Baptists
(SBHT vol. 26)

The dialogue between the Catholic Church and the Free Churches in Europe has hardly taken place. This book pleads for a commencement of such a conversation. It offers, among other things, an introduction to the American and the international dialogues between Baptists and the Catholic Church and strives to allow these conversations to become fruitful in the European context as well.

2006 / 1-84227-334-5 / approx. 364pp

Dennis Bustin
Paradox and Perseverence
Hanserd Knollys, Particular Baptist Pioneer in Seventeenth-Century England
(SBHT vol. 23)

The seventeenth century was a significant period in English history during which the people of England experienced unprecedented change and tumult in all spheres of life. At the same time, the importance of order and the traditional institutions of society were being reinforced. Hanserd Knollys, born during this pivotal period, personified in his life the ambiguity, tension and paradox of it, openly seeking change while at the same time cautiously embracing order. As a founder and leader of the Particular Baptists in London and despite persecution and personal hardship, he played a pivotal role in helping shape their identity externally in society and, internally, as they moved toward becoming more formalised by the end of the century.

2006 / 1-84227-259-4 / approx. 324pp

Anthony R. Cross
Baptism and the Baptists
Theology and Practice in Twentieth-Century Britain
(SBHT vol. 3)

At a time of renewed interest in baptism, *Baptism and the Baptists* is a detailed study of twentieth-century baptismal theology and practice and the factors which have influenced its development.

2000 / 0-85364-959-6 / xx + 530pp

Anthony R. Cross and Philip E. Thompson (eds)
Baptist Sacramentalism
(SBHT vol. 5)

This collection of essays includes biblical, historical and theological studies in the theology of the sacraments from a Baptist perspective. Subjects explored include the physical side of being spiritual, baptism, the Lord's supper, the church, ordination, preaching, worship, religious liberty and the issue of disestablishment.

2003 / 1-84227-119-9 / xvi + 278pp

Anthony R. Cross and Philip E. Thompson (eds)
Baptist Sacramentalism 2
(SBHT vol. 25)

This second collection of essays exploring various dimensions of sacramental theology from a Baptist perspective includes biblical, historical and theological studies from scholars from around the world.

2006 / 1-84227-325-6 / approx. 350pp

Paul S. Fiddes
Tracks and Traces
Baptist Identity in Church and Theology
(SBHT vol. 13)

This is a comprehensive, yet unusual, book on the faith and life of Baptist Christians. It explores the understanding of the church, ministry, sacraments and mission from a thoroughly theological perspective. In a series of interlinked essays, the author relates Baptist identity consistently to a theology of covenant and to participation in the triune communion of God.

2003 / 1-84227-120-2 / xvi + 304pp

Stanley K. Fowler
More Than a Symbol
The British Baptist Recovery of Baptismal Sacramentalism
(SBHT vol. 2)

Fowler surveys the entire scope of British Baptist literature from the seventeenth-century pioneers onwards. He shows that in the twentieth century leading British Baptist pastors and theologians recovered an understanding of baptism that connected experience with soteriology and that in doing so they were recovering what many of their forebears had taught.

2002 / 1-84227-052-4 / xvi + 276pp

Steven R. Harmon
Towards Baptist Catholicity
Essays on Tradition and the Baptist Vision
(SBHT vol. 27)

This series of essays contends that the reconstruction of the Baptist vision in the wake of modernity's dissolution requires a retrieval of the ancient ecumenical tradition that forms Christian identity through rehearsal and practice. Themes explored include catholic identity as an emerging trend in Baptist theology, tradition as a theological category in Baptist perspective, Baptist confessions and the patristic tradition, worship as a principal bearer of tradition, and the role of Baptist higher education in shaping the Christian vision.

2006 / 1-84227-362-0 / approx. 210pp

Michael A.G. Haykin (ed.)
'At the Pure Fountain of Thy Word'
Andrew Fuller as an Apologist
(SBHT vol. 6)

One of the greatest Baptist theologians of the eighteenth and early nineteenth centuries, Andrew Fuller has not had justice done to him. There is little doubt that Fuller's theology lay behind the revitalization of the Baptists in the late eighteenth century and the first few decades of the nineteenth. This collection of essays fills a much needed gap by examining a major area of Fuller's thought, his work as an apologist.

2004 / 1-84227-171-7 / xxii + 276pp

Michael A.G. Haykin
Studies in Calvinistic Baptist Spirituality
(SBHT vol. 15)

In a day when spirituality is in vogue and Christian communities are looking for guidance in this whole area, there is wisdom in looking to the past to find untapped wells. The Calvinistic Baptists, heirs of the rich ecclesial experience in the Puritan era of the seventeenth century, but, by the end of the eighteenth century, also passionately engaged in the catholicity of the Evangelical Revivals, are such a well. This collection of essays, covering such things as the Lord's Supper, friendship and hymnody, seeks to draw out the spiritual riches of this community for reflection and imitation in the present day.

2006 / 1-84227-149-0 / approx. 350pp

Brian Haymes, Anthony R. Cross and Ruth Gouldbourne
On Being the Church
Revisioning Baptist Identity
(SBHT vol. 21)

The aim of the book is to re-examine Baptist theology and practice in the light of the contemporary biblical, theological, ecumenical and missiological context drawing on historical and contemporary writings and issues. It is not a study in denominationalism but rather seeks to revision historical insights from the believers' church tradition for the sake of Baptists and other Christians in the context of the modern–postmodern context.

2006 / 1-84227-121-0 / approx. 350pp

Ken R. Manley
From Woolloomooloo to 'Eternity': A History of Australian Baptists
Volume 1: Growing an Australian Church (1831–1914)
Volume 2: A National Church in a Global Community (1914–2005)
(SBHT vols 16.1 and 16.2)

From their beginnings in Australia in 1831 with the first baptisms in Woolloomoolloo Bay in 1832, this pioneering study describes the quest of Baptists in the different colonies (states) to discover their identity as Australians and Baptists. Although institutional developments are analyzed and the roles of significant individuals traced, the major focus is on the social and theological dimensions of the Baptist movement.

2 vol. set 2006 / 1-84227-405-8 / approx. 900pp

Ken R. Manley
'Redeeming Love Proclaim'
John Rippon and the Baptists
(SBHT vol. 12)

A leading exponent of the new moderate Calvinism which brought new life to many Baptists, John Rippon (1751–1836) helped unite the Baptists at this significant time. His many writings expressed the denomination's growing maturity and mutual awareness of Baptists in Britain and America, and exerted a long-lasting influence on Baptist worship and devotion. In his various activities, Rippon helped conserve the heritage of Old Dissent and promoted the evangelicalism of the New Dissent

2004 / 1-84227-193-8 / xviii + 340pp

Peter J. Morden
Offering Christ to the World
Andrew Fuller and the Revival of English Particular Baptist Life
(SBHT vol. 8)

Andrew Fuller (1754–1815) was one of the foremost English Baptist ministers of his day. His career as an Evangelical Baptist pastor, theologian, apologist and missionary statesman coincided with the profound revitalization of the Particular Baptist denomination to which he belonged. This study examines the key aspects of the life and thought of this hugely significant figure, and gives insights into the revival in which he played such a central part.

2003 / 1-84227-141-5 / xx + 202pp

Peter Naylor
Calvinism, Communion and the Baptists
A Study of English Calvinistic Baptists from the Late 1600s to the Early 1800s
(SBHT vol. 7)

Dr Naylor argues that the traditional link between 'high-Calvinism' and 'restricted communion' is in need of revision. He examines Baptist communion controversies from the late 1600s to the early 1800s and also the theologies of John Gill and Andrew Fuller.

2003 / 1-84227-142-3 / xx + 266pp

Ian M. Randall, Toivo Pilli and Anthony R. Cross (eds)
Baptist Identities
International Studies from the Seventeenth to the Twentieth Centuries
(SBHT vol. 19)

These papers represent the contributions of scholars from various parts of the world as they consider the factors that have contributed to Baptist distinctiveness in different countries and at different times. The volume includes specific case studies as well as broader examinations of Baptist life in a particular country or region. Together they represent an outstanding resource for understanding Baptist identities.

2005 / 1-84227-215-2 / approx. 350pp

James M. Renihan
Edification and Beauty
The Practical Ecclesiology of the English Particular Baptists, 1675–1705
(SBHT vol. 17)

Edification and Beauty describes the practices of the Particular Baptist churches at the end of the seventeenth century in terms of three concentric circles: at the centre is the ecclesiological material in the Second London Confession, which is then fleshed out in the various published writings of the men associated with these churches, and, finally, expressed in the church books of the era.

2005 / 1-84227-251-9 / approx. 230pp

Frank Rinaldi
'The Tribe of Dan'
A Study of the New Connexion of General Baptists 1770–1891
(SBHT vol. 10)

'The Tribe of Dan' is a thematic study which explores the theology, organizational structure, evangelistic strategy, ministry and leadership of the New Connexion of General Baptists as it experienced the process of institutionalization in the transition from a revival movement to an established denomination.

2006 / 1-84227-143-1 / approx. 350pp

Peter Shepherd
The Making of a Modern Denomination
John Howard Shakespeare and the English Baptists 1898–1924
(SBHT vol. 4)

John Howard Shakespeare introduced revolutionary change to the Baptist denomination. The Baptist Union was transformed into a strong central institution and Baptist ministers were brought under its control. Further, Shakespeare's pursuit of church unity reveals him as one of the pioneering ecumenists of the twentieth century.

2001 / 1-84227-046-X / xviii + 220pp

Karen Smith
The Community and the Believers
A Study of Calvinistic Baptist Spirituality in Some Towns and Villages of
Hampshire and the Borders of Wiltshire, c.1730–1830
(SBHT vol. 22)

The period from 1730 to 1830 was one of transition for Calvinistic Baptists. Confronted by the enthusiasm of the Evangelical Revival, congregations within the denomination as a whole were challenged to find a way to take account of the revival experience. This study examines the life and devotion of Calvinistic Baptists in Hampshire and Wiltshire during this period. Among this group of Baptists was the hymn writer, Anne Steele.

2005 / 1-84227-326-4 / approx. 280pp

Martin Sutherland
Dissenters in a 'Free Land'
Baptist Thought in New Zealand 1850–2000
(SBHT vol. 24)

Baptists in New Zealand were forced to recast their identity. Conventions of communication and association, state and ecumenical relations, even historical divisions and controversies had to be revised in the face of new topographies and constraints. As Baptists formed themselves in a fluid society they drew heavily on both international movements and local dynamics. This book traces the development of ideas which shaped institutions and styles in sometimes surprising ways.

2006 / 1-84227-327-2 / approx. 230pp

Brian Talbot
The Search for a Common Identity
The Origins of the Baptist Union of Scotland 1800–1870
(SBHT vol. 9)

In the period 1800 to 1827 there were three streams of Baptists in Scotland: Scotch, Haldaneite and 'English' Baptist. A strong commitment to home evangelization brought these three bodies closer together, leading to a merger of their home missionary societies in 1827. However, the first three attempts to form a union of churches failed, but by the 1860s a common understanding of their corporate identity was attained leading to the establishment of the Baptist Union of Scotland.

2003 / 1-84227-123-7 / xviii + 402pp

Philip E. Thompson
The Freedom of God
Towards Baptist Theology in Pneumatological Perspective
(SBHT vol. 10)

This study contends that the range of theological commitments of the early Baptists are best understood in relation to their distinctive emphasis on the freedom of God. Thompson traces how this was recast anthropocentrically, leading to an emphasis upon human freedom from the nineteenth century onwards. He seeks to recover the dynamism of the early vision via a pneumatologically-oriented ecclesiology defining the church in terms of the memory of God.

2006 / 1-84227-125-3 / approx. 350pp

Philip E. Thompson and Anthony R. Cross (eds)
Recycling the Past or Researching History?
Studies in Baptist Historiography and Myths
(SBHT vol. 11)

In this volume an international group of Baptist scholars examine and re-examine areas of Baptist life and thought about which little is known or the received wisdom is in need of revision. Historiographical studies include the date Oxford Baptists joined the Abingdon Association, the death of the Fifth Monarchist John Pendarves, eighteenth-century Calvinistic Baptists and the political realm, confessional identity and denominational institutions, Baptist community, ecclesiology, the priesthood of all believers, soteriology, Baptist spirituality, Strict and Reformed Baptists, the role of women among British Baptists, while various 'myths' challenged include the nature of high-Calvinism in eighteenth-century England, baptismal anti-sacramentalism, episcopacy, and Baptists and change.

2005 / 1-84227-122-9 / approx. 330pp

Linda Wilson
Marianne Farningham
A Plain Working Woman
(SBHT vol. 18)

Marianne Farningham, of College Street Baptist Chapel, Northampton, was a household name in evangelical circles in the later nineteenth century. For over fifty years she produced comment, poetry, biography and fiction for the popular Christian press. This investigation uses her writings to explore the beliefs and behaviour of evangelical Nonconformists, including Baptists, during these years.

2006 / 1-84227-124-5 / approx. 250pp

July 2005

Other Paternoster titles
relating to Baptist history and thought

George R. Beasley-Murray
Baptism in the New Testament
(Paternoster Digital Library)

This is a welcome reprint of a classic text on baptism originally published in 1962 by one of the leading Baptist New Testament scholars of the twentieth century. Dr Beasley-Murray's comprehensive study begins by investigating the antecedents of Christian baptism. It then surveys the foundation of Christian baptism in the Gospels, its emergence in the Acts of the Apostles and development in the apostolic writings. Following a section relating baptism to New Testament doctrine, a substantial discussion of the origin and significance of infant baptism leads to a briefer consideration of baptismal reform and ecumenism.

2005 / 1-84227-300-0 / x + 422pp

Paul Beasley-Murray
Fearless for Truth
A Personal Portrait of the Life of George Beasley-Murray

Without a doubt George Beasley-Murray was one of the greatest Baptists of the twentieth century. A long-standing Principal of Spurgeon's College, he wrote more than twenty books and made significant contributions in the study of areas as diverse as baptism and eschatology, as well as writing highly respected commentaries on the Book of Revelation and John's Gospel.

2002 / 1-84227-134-2 / xii + 244pp

David Bebbington
Holiness in Nineteenth-Century England
(Studies in Christian History and Thought)

David Bebbington stresses the relationship of movements of spirituality to changes in their cultural setting, especially the legacies of the Enlightenment and Romanticism. He shows that these broad shifts in ideological mood had a profound effect on the ways in which piety was conceptualized and practised. Holiness was intimately bound up with the spirit of the age.

2000 / 0-85364-981-2 / viii + 98pp

July 2005

Clyde Binfield
Victorian Nonconformity in Eastern England 1840–1885
(Studies in Evangelical History and Thought)
Studies of Victorian religion and society often concentrate on cities, suburbs, and industrialisation. This study provides a contrast. Victorian Eastern England—Essex, Suffolk, Norfolk, Cambridgeshire, and Huntingdonshire—was rural, traditional, relatively unchanging. That is nonetheless a caricature which discounts the industry in Norwich and Ipswich (as well as in Haverhill, Stowmarket and Leiston) and ignores the impact of London on Essex, of railways throughout the region, and of an ancient but changing university (Cambridge) on the county town which housed it. It also entirely ignores the political implications of such changes in a region noted for the variety of its religious Dissent since the seventeenth century. This book explores Victorian Eastern England and its Nonconformity. It brings to a wider readership a pioneering thesis which has made a major contribution to a fresh evolution of English religion and society.
2006 / 1-84227-216-0 / approx. 274pp

Edward W. Burrows
'To Me To Live Is Christ'
A Biography of Peter H. Barber
This book is about a remarkably gifted and energetic man of God. Peter H. Barber was born into a Brethren family in Edinburgh in 1930. In his youth he joined Charlotte Baptist Chapel and followed the call into Baptist ministry. For eighteen years he was the pioneer minister of the new congregation in the New Town of East Kilbride, which planted two further congregations. At the age of thirty-nine he served as Centenary President of the Baptist Union of Scotland and then exercised an influential ministry for over seven years in the well-known Upton Vale Baptist Church, Torquay. From 1980 until his death in 1994 he was General Secretary of the Baptist Union of Scotland. Through his work for the European Baptist Federation and the Baptist World Alliance he became a world Baptist statesman. He was President of the EBF during the upheaval that followed the collapse of Communism.
2005 / 1-84227-324-8 / xxii + 236pp

Christopher J. Clement
Religious Radicalism in England 1535–1565
(Rutherford Studies in Historical Theology)
In this valuable study Christopher Clement draws our attention to a varied assemblage of people who sought Christian faithfulness in the underworld of mid-Tudor England. Sympathetically and yet critically he assess their place in the history of English Protestantism, and by attentive listening he gives them a voice.
1997 / 0-946068-44-5 / xxii + 426pp

Anthony R. Cross (ed.)
Ecumenism and History
Studies in Honour of John H.Y. Briggs
(Studies in Christian History and Thought)

This collection of essays examines the inter-relationships between the two fields in which Professor Briggs has contributed so much: history—particularly Baptist and Nonconformist—and the ecumenical movement. With contributions from colleagues and former research students from Britain, Europe and North America, *Ecumenism and History* provides wide-ranging studies in important aspects of Christian history, theology and ecumenical studies.

2002 / 1-84227-135-0 / xx + 362pp

Keith E. Eitel
Paradigm Wars
The Southern Baptist International Mission Board
Faces the Third Millennium
(Regnum Studies in Mission)

The International Mission Board of the Southern Baptist Convention is the largest denominational mission agency in North America. This volume chronicles the historic and contemporary forces that led to the IMB's recent extensive reorganization, providing the most comprehensive case study to date of a historic mission agency restructuring to continue its mission purpose into the twenty-first century more effectively.

2000 / 1-870345-12-6 / x + 140pp

Ruth Gouldbourne
The Flesh and the Feminine
Gender and Theology in the Writings of Caspar Schwenckfeld
(Studies in Christian History and Thought) ·

Caspar Schwenckfeld and his movement exemplify one of the radical communities of the sixteenth century. Challenging theological and liturgical norms, they also found themselves challenging social and particularly gender assumptions. In this book, the issues of the relationship between radical theology and the understanding of gender are considered.

***2005** / 1-84227-048-6 / approx. 304pp*

David Hilborn
The Words of our Lips
Language-Use in Free Church Worship
(Paternoster Theological Monographs)

Studies of liturgical language have tended to focus on the written canons of Roman Catholic and Anglican communities. By contrast, David Hilborn analyses the more extemporary approach of English Nonconformity. Drawing on recent developments in linguistic pragmatics, he explores similarities and differences between 'fixed' and 'free' worship, and argues for the interdependence of each.

2006 / 0-85364-977-4

Stephen R. Holmes
Listening to the Past
The Place of Tradition in Theology

Beginning with the question 'Why can't we just read the Bible?' Stephen Holmes considers the place of tradition in theology, showing how the doctrine of creation leads to an account of historical location and creaturely limitations as essential aspects of our existence. For we cannot claim unmediated access to the Scriptures without acknowledging the place of tradition: theology is an irreducibly communal task. *Listening to the Past* is a sustained attempt to show what listening to tradition involves, and how it can be used to aid theological work today.

2002 / 1-84227-155-5 / xiv + 168pp

Mark Hopkins
Nonconformity's Romantic Generation
Evangelical and Liberal Theologies in Victorian England
(Studies in Evangelical History and Thought)

A study of the theological development of key leaders of the Baptist and Congregational denominations at their period of greatest influence, including C.H. Spurgeon and R.W. Dale, and of the controversies in which those among them who embraced and rejected the liberal transformation of their evangelical heritage opposed each other.

2004 / 1-84227-150-4 / xvi + 284pp

Galen K. Johnson
Prisoner of Conscience
John Bunyan on Self, Community and Christian Faith
(Studies in Christian History and Thought)
This is an interdisciplinary study of John Bunyan's understanding of conscience across his autobiographical, theological and fictional writings, investigating whether conscience always deserves fidelity, and how Bunyan's view of conscience affects his relationship both to modern Western individualism and historic Christianity.
2003 / 1-84227- 151-2 / xvi + 236pp

R.T. Kendall
Calvin and English Calvinism to 1649
(Studies in Christian History and Thought)
The author's thesis is that those who formed the Westminster Confession of Faith, which is regarded as Calvinism, in fact departed from John Calvin on two points: (1) the extent of the atonement and (2) the ground of assurance of salvation.
1997 / 0-85364-827-1 / xii + 264pp

Timothy Larsen
Friends of Religious Equality
Nonconformist Politics in Mid-Victorian England
During the middle decades of the nineteenth century the English Nonconformist community developed a coherent political philosophy of its own, of which a central tenet was the principle of religious equality (in contrast to the stereotype of Evangelical Dissenters). The Dissenting community fought for the civil rights of Roman Catholics, non-Christians and even atheists, on an issue of principle which had its flowering in the enthusiastic and undivided support which Nonconformity gave to the campaign for Jewish emancipation. This reissued study examines the political efforts and ideas of English Nonconformists during the period, covering the whole range of national issues raised, from state education to the Crimean War. It offers a case study of a theologically conservative group defending religious pluralism in the civic sphere, showing that the concept of religious equality was a grand vision at the centre of the political philosophy of the Dissenters.
2007 / 1-84227-402-3 / x + 300pp

Donald M. Lewis
Lighten Their Darkness
The Evangelical Mission to Working-Class London, 1828–1860
(Studies in Evangelical History and Thought)
This is a comprehensive and compelling study of the Church and the complexities of nineteenth-century London. Challenging our understanding of the culture in working London at this time, Lewis presents a well-structured and illustrated work that contributes substantially to the study of evangelicalism and mission in nineteenth-century Britain.
2001 / 1-84227-074-5 / xviii + 372pp

Stanley E. Porter and Anthony R. Cross (eds)
Semper Reformandum
Studies in Honour of Clark H. Pinnock
Clark Pinnock has clearly been one of the most important evangelical theologians of the last forty years in North America. Always provocative, especially in the wide range of opinions he has held and considered, Pinnock, himself a Baptist, has recently retired after twenty-five years of teaching at McMaster Divinity College. His colleagues and associates honour him in this volume by responding to his important theological work which has dealt with the essential topics of evangelical theology. These include Christian apologetics, biblical inspiration, the Holy Spirit and, perhaps most importantly in recent years, openness theology.
2003 / 1-84227-206-3 / xiv + 414pp

Meic Pearse
The Great Restoration
The Religious Radicals of the 16th and 17th Centuries
Pearse charts the rise and progress of continental Anabaptism – both evangelical and heretical – through the sixteenth century. He then follows the story of those English people who became impatient with Puritanism and separated – first from the Church of England and then from one another – to form the antecedents of later Congregationalists, Baptists and Quakers.
1998 / 0-85364-800-X / xii + 320pp

Charles Price and Ian M. Randall
Transforming Keswick
Transforming Keswick is a thorough, readable and detailed history of the convention. It will be of interest to those who know and love Keswick, those who are only just discovering it, and serious scholars eager to learn more about the history of God's dealings with his people.
2000 / 1-85078-350-0 / 288pp

Jim Purves
The Triune God and the Charismatic Movement
A Critical Appraisal from a Scottish Perspective
(Paternoster Theological Monographs)
All emotion and no theology? Or a fundamental challenge to reappraise and
realign our trinitarian theology in the light of Christian experience? This study
of charismatic renewal as it found expression within Scotland at the end of the
twentieth century evaluates the use of Patristic, Reformed and contemporary
models (including those of the Baptist Union of Scotland) of the Trinity in
explaining the workings of the Holy Spirit.
2004 / 1-84227-321-3 / xxiv + 246pp

Ian M. Randall
Evangelical Experiences
A Study in the Spirituality of English Evangelicalism 1918–1939
(Studies in Evangelical History and Thought)
This book makes a detailed historical examination of evangelical spirituality
between the First and Second World Wars. It shows how patterns of devotion
led to tensions and divisions. In a wide-ranging study, Anglican, Wesleyan,
Reformed and Pentecostal-charismatic spiritualities are analysed.
1999 / 0-85364-919-7 / xii + 310pp

Ian M. Randall
One Body in Christ
The History and Significance of the Evangelical Alliance
In 1846 the Evangelical Alliance was founded with the aim of bringing together
evangelicals for common action. This book uses material not previously utilized
to examine the history and significance of the Evangelical Alliance, a movement
which has remained a powerful force for unity. At a time when evangelicals are
growing world-wide, this book offers insights into the past which are relevant to
contemporary issues.
2001 / 1-84227-089-3 / xii + 394pp

Ian M. Randall
Spirituality and Social Change
The Contribution of F.B. Meyer (1847–1929)
(Studies in Evangelical History and Thought)
This is a fresh appraisal of F.B. Meyer (1847–1929), a leading Free Church
minister. Having been deeply affected by holiness spirituality, Meyer became
the Keswick Convention's foremost international speaker. He combined
spirituality with effective evangelism and socio-political activity. This study
shows Meyer's significant contribution to spiritual renewal and social change.
2003 / 1-84227-195-4 / xx + 184pp

Geoffrey Robson
Dark Satanic Mills?
Religion and Irreligion in Birmingham and the Black Country
(Studies in Evangelical History and Thought)
This book analyses and interprets the nature and extent of popular Christian belief and practice in Birmingham and the Black Country during the first half of the nineteenth century, with particular reference to the impact of cholera epidemics and evangelism on church extension programmes.
2002 / 1-84227-102-4 / xiv + 294pp

Alan P.F. Sell
Enlightenment, Ecumenism, Evangel
Theological Themes and Thinkers 1550–2000
(Studies in Christian History and Thought)
This book consists of papers in which such interlocking topics as the Enlightenment, the problem of authority, the development of doctrine, spirituality, ecumenism, theological method and the heart of the gospel are discussed. Issues of significance to the church at large are explored with special reference to writers from the Reformed and Dissenting traditions.
2005 / 1-84227330-2 / xviii + 422pp

Alan P.F. Sell
Hinterland Theology
Some Reformed and Dissenting Adjustments
(Studies in Christian History and Thought)
Many books have been written on theology's 'giants' and significant trends, but what of those lesser-known writers who adjusted to them? In this book some hinterland theologians of the British Reformed and Dissenting traditions, who followed in the wake of toleration, the Evangelical Revival, the rise of modern biblical criticism and Karl Barth, are allowed to have their say. They include Thomas Ridgley, Ralph Wardlaw, T.V. Tymms and N.H.G. Robinson.
2006 / 1-84227-331-0

Alan P.F. Sell and Anthony R. Cross (eds)
Protestant Nonconformity in the Twentieth Century
(Studies in Christian History and Thought)
In this collection of essays scholars representative of a number of Nonconformist traditions reflect thematically on Nonconformists' life and witness during the twentieth century. Among the subjects reviewed are biblical studies, theology, worship, evangelism and spirituality, and ecumenism. Over and above its immediate interest, this collection provides a marker to future scholars and others wishing to know how some of their forebears assessed Nonconformity's contribution to a variety of fields during the century leading up to Christianity's third millennium.
2003 / 1-84227-221-7 / x + 398pp

Mark Smith
Religion in Industrial Society
Oldham and Saddleworth 1740–1865
(Studies in Christian History and Thought)
This book analyses the way British churches sought to meet the challenge of industrialization and urbanization during the period 1740–1865. Working from a case-study of Oldham and Saddleworth, Mark Smith challenges the received view that the Anglican Church in the eighteenth century was characterized by complacency and inertia, and reveals Anglicanism's vigorous and creative response to the new conditions. He reassesses the significance of the centrally directed church reforms of the mid-nineteenth century, and emphasizes the importance of local energy and enthusiasm. Charting the growth of denominational pluralism in Oldham and Saddleworth, Dr Smith compares the strengths and weaknesses of the various Anglican and Nonconformist approaches to promoting church growth. He also demonstrates the extent to which all the churches participated in a common culture shaped by the influence of evangelicalism, and shows that active co-operation between the churches rather than denominational conflict dominated. This revised and updated edition of Dr Smith's challenging and original study makes an important contribution both to the social history of religion and to urban studies.
***2006** / 1-84227-335-3 / approx. 300pp*

David M. Thompson
Baptism, Church and Society in Britain from the Evangelical Revival to
Baptism, Eucharist and Ministry
The theology and practice of baptism have not received the attention they
deserve. How important is faith? What does baptismal regeneration mean? Is
baptism a bond of unity between Christians? This book discusses the theology of
baptism and popular belief and practice in England and Wales from the
Evangelical Revival to the publication of the World Council of Churches'
consensus statement on *Baptism, Eucharist and Ministry* (1982).
2005 / 1-84227-393-0 / approx. 224pp

Martin Sutherland
Peace, Toleration and Decay
The Ecclesiology of Later Stuart Dissent
(Studies in Christian History and Thought)
This fresh analysis brings to light the complexity and fragility of the later Stuart
Nonconformist consensus. Recent findings on wider seventeenth-century
thought are incorporated into a new picture of the dynamics of Dissent and the
roots of evangelicalism.
2003 / 1-84227-152-0 / xxii + 216pp

Haddon Willmer
Evangelicalism 1785–1835: An Essay (1962) and Reflections (2004)
(Studies in Evangelical History and Thought)
Awarded the Hulsean Prize in the University of Cambridge in 1962, this
interpretation of a classic period of English Evangelicalism, by a young church
historian, is now supplemented by reflections on Evangelicalism from the
vantage point of a retired Professor of Theology.
2006 / 1-84227-219-5

Linda Wilson
Constrained by Zeal
Female Spirituality amongst Nonconformists 1825–1875
(Studies in Evangelical History and Thought)
Constrained by Zeal investigates the neglected area of Nonconformist female
spirituality. Against the background of separate spheres, it analyses the
experience of women from four denominations, and argues that the churches
provided a 'third sphere' in which they could find opportunities for
participation.
2000 / 0-85364-972-3 / xvi + 294pp

Nigel G. Wright
Disavowing Constantine
Mission, Church and the Social Order in the Theologies of
John Howard Yoder and Jürgen Moltmann
(Paternoster Theological Monographs)
This book is a timely restatement of a radical theology of church and state in the
Anabaptist and Baptist tradition. Dr Wright constructs his argument in dialogue
and debate with Yoder and Moltmann, major contributors to a free church
perspective.
2000 / 0-85364-978-2 / xvi + 252pp

Nigel G. Wright
Free Church, Free State
The Positive Baptist Vision
Free Church, Free State is a textbook on baptist ways of being church and a
proposal for the future of baptist churches in an ecumenical context. Nigel
Wright argues that both baptist (small 'b') and catholic (small 'c') church
traditions should seek to enrich and support each other as valid expressions of
the body of Christ without sacrificing what they hold dear. Written for pastors,
church planters, evangelists and preachers, Nigel Wright offers frameworks of
thought for baptists and non-baptists in their journey together following Christ.
2005 / 1-84227-353-1 / xxviii + 292

Nigel G. Wright
New Baptists, New Agenda
New Baptists, New Agenda is a timely contribution to the growing debate about
the health, shape and future of the Baptists. It considers the steady changes that
have taken place among Baptists in the last decade – changes of mood, style,
practice and structure – and encourages us to align these current movements and
questions with God's upward and future call. He contends that the true church
has yet to come: the church that currently exists is an anticipation of the joyful
gathering of all who have been called by the Spirit through Christ to the Father.
2002 / 1-84227-157-1 / x + 162pp

Paternoster
9 Holdom Avenue,
Bletchley,
Milton Keynes MK1 1QR,
United Kingdom
Web: www.authenticmedia.co.uk/paternoster

July 2005